General Editors: Peter Garside, James Raven, and
Rainer Schöwerling

The English Novel 1770–1829:
A Bibliographical Survey of Prose Fiction
Published in the British Isles

Volume I: 1770–1799

JAMES RAVEN

ANTONIA FORSTER

with the assistance of
STEPHEN BENDING

OXFORD
UNIVERSITY PRESS

OXFORD

UNIVERSITY PRESS

Great Clarendon Street, Oxford ox2 6DP

Oxford University Press is a department of the University of Oxford.
It furthers the University's objective of excellence in research, scholarship,
and education by publishing worldwide in

Oxford New York

Athens Auckland Bangkok Bogotá Buenos Aires Calcutta
Cape Town Chennai Dar es Salaam Delhi Florence Hong Kong Istanbul
Karachi Kuala Lumpur Madrid Melbourne Mexico City Mumbai
Nairobi Paris São Paulo Singapore Taipei Tokyo Toronto Warsaw

and associated companies in Berlin Ibadan

Oxford is a registered trade mark of Oxford University Press
in the UK and certain other countries

Published in the United States
by Oxford University Press Inc., New York

© Peter Garside, James Raven and Rainer Schöwerling 2000

The moral rights of the author have been asserted
Database right Oxford University Press (maker)

First published 2000

British Library Cataloguing in Publication Data

Data available

Library of Congress Cataloging in Publication Data

Data available

ISBN 0–19–818317–8

1 3 5 7 9 10 8 6 4 2

Typeset in Minion by
Jayvee, Trivandrum, India
Printed in Great Britain
on acid-free paper by
Biddles Ltd.,
Guildford and King's Lynn

The English Novel 1770–1829: A Bibliographical Survey
of Prose Fiction Published in the British Isles

Volume I: 1770–1799

Acknowledgments

The greatest single debt in the compilation of this volume is to the Leverhulme Trust for its funding of two major awards for research assistance. The first of these enabled the initial bibliographical trawls by Margaret Jones to expand the existing files and collected materials, and then the additional computing and editorial assistance of Stephen Bending. The second award enabled full-time library and computing work by Antonia Forster, Neil Hitchin, and Nigel Hall. Without this generous support this project could not have been completed. Other grants were provided by the Deutscher Akademischer Austauschdienst, the British Council in Germany, and the British Academy, for visits to the Projekt Corvey at Paderborn University, and by the Cambridge Project for the Book Trust and the Faculty of Modern History, Oxford University, for the final indexing work by Antonia Forster, Alexander Lindsey, and Susie Day. Alexander Lindsey also undertook careful reading of earlier drafts. At Paderborn Verena Ebbes checked references to German translations, and Karin Wünsche maintained the style-sheet adopted by the general editors, and supplied advice and much general assistance. The success of the project also rests with Antonia Forster's tireless additional research, providing indispensable on-line investigative skills and transforming the structure of this bibliography by reworking the entries and adding, amongst many revisions, review extracts and newspaper references. The Trustees of the Cambridge Project for the Book Trust sponsored the grant applications for this volume and provided constant support and encouragement in this seven-year undertaking.

Many dozens of scholars have assisted the compilation of this bibliography, most obviously by facilitating access to special collections, but also by sending in suggestions, alerting us to new discoveries, and answering follow-up inquiries. Many curators and staff of rare book and research libraries, great and small, offered indispensable advice and support. The editors are particularly indebted to the expert assistance of Clarissa Campbell Orr, Mike Crump, John Dowson, Ian Gadd, Vincent Giroud, Moira Goff, John Goldfinch, Richard Goulden, Jeannine Green, Susan Halpert, Graham Hogg, Carol A. Johnson, Warren McDougall, Cindy Ann May, Simon May, Martin Moonie, John Pollack, Mary Pollard, Paul Berthold Rupp, William St Clair, Margaret M. Sherry, Greg Smith, Elinor Shaffer, Christopher Skelton-Foord, Roger Stoddard, Bruce W. Swann, Marvin J. Taylor, Dan Traister, and William Zachs. Marie-Luise Spieckermann and her assistants at the University of Münster corrected and supplied further references. Generous communication and advice were also received from Emily Bartels, Charles Benson, Sheppard Black, Anthony Bliss, John Bloomberg-Rissman, Maria Brynda, Lorna Clymer, Julia Cooper, Roberta Copp, Nicholas Daly, Elizabeth Durkee, Jan Fergus, Amanda Hall, Mam Harlow, Steven Johns, Thomas V. Lange, Gráinne Mac

Lochlainn, Rolf Loeber, Jan Martin, Barbara D. Miles, Heather Moore, Janie C. Morris, Michael Perkin, Robert Petre, Amy K. Presser, Jean Rainwater, Katherine Reagan, David Riley, Elizabeth Rumics, John Sherlock, Robert R. Shields, Ellis Shookman, Helen Small, Carl Spadoni, Patrick Spedding, Magda Stouthamer-Loeber, Michael Suarez, W. M. Verhoeven, Kermit Westerberg, Rutherford W. Witthus, George H. Yetter, and Georgianna Ziegler.

Without the assistance of these and numerous other researchers and book custodians, professional and private, many of these novels could not have been located and studied. The general editors of this bibliography are hugely indebted to this world-wide community of librarians and scholars.

Contents

List of Tables and Figures   ix

List of Abbreviations   x

General Introduction   1
  Peter Garside, James Raven, and Rainer Schöwerling

Historical Introduction: The Novel Comes of Age   15
  James Raven

AN HISTORICAL BIBLIOGRAPHY OF PROSE NOVELS IN
ENGLISH FIRST PUBLISHED IN THE BRITISH ISLES 1770–1799   123
  Antonia Forster and James Raven with Stephen Bending

APPENDICES

Index of Authors and Translators   822
Index of Titles   830
Index of Booksellers and Printers   848
Notes Index   860

Tables and Figures

TABLES

1. Publication of New Novels in Britain and Ireland, 1770–1799   26
2. Publication of Epistolary Fiction, 1770–1799   32
3. Republication Rates before 1801 of Novels First Published 1770–1799   36
4. Place and Frequency of Publication before 1801 of Further Editions of Novels First Published 1770–1799   37
5. Novels First Published 1770–1799 with Five or more Further Editions (British and American) before 1829   40
6. Authorship of New Novels, 1770–1799   46
7. Surviving Receipts to Novelists for Surrender of Copyright, 1770–1799   52
8. First Editions of English Translations of French and German Novels, 1770–1799   58
9. First Translations before 1850 into German of English Novels First Published in Britain and Ireland, 1770–1799   68
10. First Translations before 1850 into French of English Novels First Published in Britain and Ireland, 1770–1799   69
11. Production of Novels in Britain and Ireland, 1770–1799: Place of Publication of the First Edition   72
12. Leading London Novel Publishers, 1770–1799, by Publication of New Prose Fiction Titles   73

FIGURE

1. Publication of New Novels in Britain and Ireland, 1770–1799: Five-Year Moving Average   27

Abbreviations

*	No copy of first edition located
&c.	[following details of holding libraries] ESTC gives additional verified holdings
ABu	Aberdeen University Library
AC	Alexandre Cioranescu, *Bibliographie de la littérature Française du dix-huitième siècle*. 3 vols. (Paris: Éditions du Centre National de la Recherche Scientifique, 1969)
acc.	according
adv.	advertisement/advertised
AF I	Antonia Forster, *Index to Book Reviews in England 1749–1774* (Carbondale: Southern Illinois University Press, 1990)
AF II	Antonia Forster, *Index to Book Reviews in England 1775–1800* (London: The British Library, 1997)
AJM	Archives of John Murray Ltd., Albemarle Street, London
AJR	*The Anti-Jacobin Review* C&K 20
AMu	Amsterdam Universiteitsbibliothek
App	Appendix
AR	*The Analytical Review* C&K 10
ArU	University of Arkansas
AUG	Universitätsbibliothek, Augsburg
AWn	National Library of Wales, Aberystwyth
AWu	Hugh Owen Library, University College of Wales, Aberystwyth
AzU	University of Arizona
BB	Robert Watt, *Bibliotheca Britannica or A General Index to British and Foreign Literature*. 4 vols. (Edinburgh, 1824)
BC	*The British Critic* C&K 61
Bentley	G. E. Bentley, Jun., 'Copyright Documents in the George Robinson Archive: William Godwin and Others 1713–1820', *Studies in Bibliography* 35 (1982), 67–110
BGR	Angus Martin, Vivienne G. Mylne, and Richard Frautschi, *Bibliographie du genre romanesque français 1751–1800* (London and Paris: Mansell Information and France Expansion, 1977)
BI	Britain and Ireland
BL	British Library
Blakey	Dorothy Blakey, *The Minerva Press 1790–1820* (London: The Bibliographical Society, 1939 [for 1935])
BLC	British Library Catalogue
BMp	Central Library, Birmingham

BMu	Birmingham University Library
BN	Catalogue of the Bibliothèque Nationale, Paris
Boaden	James Boaden, *Memoirs of Mrs. Inchbald: including her Familiar Correspondence with the Most Distinguished Persons of her Time*. 2 vols. (London, 1833)
Bodl.	Bodleian Library, *Pre-1920 Catalogue*
BRG	Central Library, Brighton
Bristol	Roger P. Bristol, *Supplement to Charles Evans' American Bibliography* (Charlottesville: University Press of Virginia, 1970)
BRu ENC	Bristol University Library, Early Novels Collection
BRw	Wesley College, Bristol
Burney	Burney, Frances *The Journals and Letters of Fanny Burney (Madame d'Arblay)*. Vol. III (1793–1797) ed. Joyce Hemlow et al. (Oxford: Clarendon Press, 1973)
BUYs	Bury St Edmunds, Suffolk Record Office
c.	circa
C	Cambridge University Library
CaAEU	University of Alberta
CaBVaU	University of British Columbia
CaNfSM	Memorial University of Newfoundland
CaOGU	University of Guelph
CaOHM	Mills Memorial Library, McMaster University
CaOLU	University of Western Ontario
CaOONL	National Library of Canada
CaOTP	Toronto Public Library
CaOTU	University of Toronto
CaOTV	Victoria University
CaQMBN	Bibliothèque Nationale de Québec
CaQMM	McGill University
CaQQLa	Université Laval Bibliothèque
CaSRU	University of Regina
CaSSU	University of Saskatchewan
CCC	California, Honnold Library, Claremont Colleges
cf.	compare with
CFu	Cardiff University Library
CG	The card index of Chester Noyes Greenough, Houghton Library, Harvard
CHIr	West Sussex Record Office, Chichester
C&K	R. S. Crane and F. B. Kaye, *A Census of British Newspapers and Periodicals 1620–1800* [1927] (London: Holland Press, 1966)
CLU-C	William Andrews Clark Memorial Library, University of California, Los Angeles

CLU-S/C	Special Collections, University of California, Los Angeles
CME	Corvey Microfiche Edition
COCu	Albert Sloman Library, University of Essex, Colchester
CoFS	Colorado State University
COR/Corvey	Corvey, Fürstliche Bibliothek zu Corvey
CR	*The Critical Review* C&K 156
C-S	California State University, Sutro Branch, San Francisco
CSdS	San Diego State University
CSmH	Henry E. Huntington Library, San Marino, California
CSt	Stanford University
Ct	Trinity College, Cambridge
CtHT	Trinity College, Connecticut
CtHT-W	Watkinson Collection, Trinity College, Connecticut
CtU	University of Connecticut
CtY	Sterling Library, Yale University
CtY-BA	Yale Centre for British Art
CtY-BR	Beinecke Library, Yale University
CtY-Med	Medical Library, Yale University
CtY-Mudd	Mudd Library, Yale University
CtY-Walpole	Lewis Walpole Library [Yale University], Farmington, Connecticut
CU-BANC	Bancroft Library, University of California, Berkeley
CU-Riv	Rivera Library, University of California, Riverside
CU-SB	University of California, Santa Barbara
CWhC	Whittier College
D	National Library of Ireland, Dublin
Darnton	Robert Darnton, *The Forbidden Best-Sellers of Pre-Revolutionary France* (London: Harper Collins, 1996)
Darton	*The Life and Times of Mrs. Sherwood* ed. F. J. Harvey Darton (London: Wells, Gardner, Darton, n.d. [1910])
DBI	Deutsches Bibliotheksinstitut, Berlin
DBL	Cathedral Library, Dunblane
DeGE	Hagley Museum and Library, Delaware
DFo	Folger Shakespeare Library, Washington DC
Di	Dublin, Royal Irish Academy
DLC	Library of Congress, Washington DC
DNLM	National Library of Medicine, Bethesda, Maryland
Dt	Trinity College Library, Dublin
DWR	*The Diary; or, Woodfall's Register* C&K 174
E	National Library of Scotland, Edinburgh
EA	Continental Europe, Australasia, Asia, and Africa

EAG	'The Publication of English Authors in Germany, 1680–1810: A Bibliographical Catalogue'—project in progress at the University of Münster, directors Prof. Bernhard Fabian and Prof. Marie-Luise Spieckermann
ECB	*English Catalogue of Books 1801–1836*
ed.	edited
edn.	edition
EM	Eighteenth-Century Microfilm Series, Primary Source Media (formerly RPI or Research Publications International)
EMf	Forthcoming in EM series; microfilmed but not yet published as of April 1998
EngR	*The English Review* C&K 213
ESTC	*English Short-Title Catalogue* (formerly *Eighteenth-Century Short-Title Catalogue*) on-line via BLAISE and RLIN
Eu	Edinburgh University Library
EurM	*The European Magazine* C&K 218
Facs: BWN	Facsimile (London: Routledge/Thoemmes, 1992) *British Women Novelists 1750–1850*
Facs: FCy	Facsimile (New York: Garland, 1974) *The Feminist Controversy in England, 1788–1810*
Facs: GNI	Facsimile (New York, Arno, 1972) *Gothic Novels I*
Facs: GNII	Facsimile (New York: Arno, 1974) *Gothic Novels II*
Facs: GNIII	Facsimile (New York: Arno, 1977) *Gothic Novels III*
Facs: N	Facsimile (New York: Garland, 1979) *The Novel: 1720–1805*
Facs: RWN	Facsimile (London: Routledge/Thoemmes, 1995) *The Romantics: Women Novelists*
Facs: SO	Facsimile (New York: Arno, 1976) Supernatural and Occult Fiction
FB	Frank Gees Black, *The Epistolary Novel in the Late Eighteenth Century* (Eugene, Oregon: University of Oregon Press, 1940)
FC	Virginia Blain, Isobel Grundy, and Patricia Clements, eds., *The Feminist Companion to Literature in English* (London: Batsford, 1990)
FU	University of Florida
GDAs	Library of the Polish Academy of Sciences, Gdansk
GEP	*The General Evening Post* C&K 262
GEU	Woodruff Library, Emory University
GlM	*The General Magazine and Impartial Review* C&K 265
GM	*The Gentleman's Magazine* C&K 277
GND	*The Gazetteer and New Daily Advertiser* C&K 261
GOT	Niedersächsische Staats- und Universitätsbibliothek, Göttingen
Grieder	Josephine Grieder, *Translations of French Sentimental Prose Fiction in late Eighteenth-Century England: the History of a Literary Vogue* (Durham, NC: Duke University Press, 1975)

Gu	Glasgow University Library
Hamilton	Harlan W. Hamilton, *Doctor Syntax: A Silhouette of William Combe, Esq.* (Kent, OH: Kent State University Press, 1969)
Hayley	William Hayley, *Memoirs of the Life and Writings of William Hayley, Esq. The Friend and Biographer of Cowper, Written by Himself* ed. John Johnson. 2 vols. (London, 1823)
H&C	PRO C104/75/1–3 Records of Hookham and Carpenter, 1798
HWS	Harold Wade Streeter, *The Eighteenth-Century English Novel in French Translation: a Bibliographical Study* [1936] (New York: Benjamin Blom, 1970)
IaU	University of Iowa
ICN	Newberry Library, Chicago
ICU	Regenstein Library, University of Chicago
IEN	Northwestern University
IlfC	Lake Forest College, Illinois
imperf.	imperfect
InU-Li	Lilly Library, Indiana University
INV	Inverness Public Library
IPSr	Suffolk Record Office, Ipswich
IU	University of Illinois, Urbana-Champaign
JR	James Raven, *British Fiction, 1750–1770: A Chronological Check-List of Prose Fiction Printed in Britain and Ireland* (Newark, London and Toronto: University of Delaware Press, 1987)
KEmU	Forsyth Library, Emporia State University, Kansas
KIK	The Baikie Collection, Tankerners House, Kirkwall, Orkney
KM	Keith Maslen and John Lancaster, *The Bowyer Ledgers: The Printing Accounts of William Bowyer, father and son, reproduced on microfiche, with a checklist of Bowyer printing, 1699–1777*, 1 vol. and 70 microfiche (London and New York: The Bibliographical Society and Bibliographical Society of America, 1991)
KU-S	Spencer Research Library, University of Kansas
KyU	University of Kentucky
LA	Longmans Archive, Reading University: Impression Book H4 (1794–1801), reproduced in *The House of Longman 1794–1814* microfilm edn. (Chadwyck-Healey, 1978) reel 37.
LC	*The London Chronicle* C&K 389
LEP	*The London Evening-Post* C&K 394
LEu	Brotherton Library, University of Leeds
Lévy	Maurice Lévy, 'English Gothic and the French Imagination: A Calendar of Translations, 1767–1828' in *The Gothic Imagination: Essays in Dark Romanticism* ed. G. R. Thompson ([Pullman]: Washington State University Press, 1974)

Lg	London, Guildhall Library
Lics	University of London Institute of Commonwealth Studies
LM	*The London Magazine* C&K 398
LMM	*The Lady's Monthly Museum* C&K 359
Lnt	London, National Trust
Loeber	Rolf Loeber and Magda Stouthamer-Loeber, 'Literary Fiction as a Mirror of the Times: a Guide to Irish Fiction Published in Europe and North America', project in progress
LP	*The London Packet; Or, New Lloyd's Evening Post* C&K 408
LR	*The London Review* C&K 410
Lu	University of London Library, Senate House
Luk	King's College Library, University of London
LVp	Liverpool Central Libraries
LVu	University Library, Liverpool
MA	Amherst College, Massachusetts
Marshall	Peter H. Marshall, *William Godwin* (New York & London: Yale University Press, 1984)
Martin	John Martin, *A Bibliographical Catalogue of Books Privately Printed; including those of the Bannatyne, Maitland and Roxburghe Clubs, and of The Private Presses at Darlington, Auchinleck, Lee Priory, Newcastle, Middle Hill, and Strawberry Hill* (London, 1834)
MB	Boston Public Library
MBAt	Boston Athenaeum
MBNEH	New England Historic Genealogical Society
MC	*The Morning Chronicle, and London Advertiser* C&K 584
MChB	Boston College
MdBJ	Johns Hopkins University
MdE	Phillips Library, Mount St Mary's College
ME	*The Monthly Epitome* C&K 571
MeB	Bowdoin College
MHer	*Morning Herald* C&K 585
MH-H	Houghton Library, Harvard University
MiDW	Wayne State University
MiEM	Michigan State University
Min	Prospectus of the Minerva Library (1798) reproduced as Appendix IV in Blakey
MiU	University of Michigan
MM	*The Monthly Mirror* C&K 577
MnU	Meredith Wilson and James Ford Bell Libraries, University of Minnesota
MoSW	Washington University, Missouri
MoU	Ellis Library, University of Missouri-Columbia

MP	*The Morning Post* C&K 586
MR	*The Monthly Review* C&K 580
MRu	John Rylands Library, Manchester
MV	*The Monthly Visitor* C&K 581
MWA	American Antiquarian Society
NA	North America
NCBEL	*New Cambridge Bibliography of English Literature.* 5 vols. (Cambridge, 1974)
NcD	William R. Perkins Library, Duke University
NCp	Central Library, Newcastle upon Tyne
NcU	Wilson Library, University of North Carolina, Chapel Hill
NCu	Newcastle upon Tyne University Library
n.d.	no date
NIC	Cornell University
NjP	Princeton University
NjR	Rutgers University
NLR	*The New London Review* C&K 610
NN	New York Public Library
NNC	Columbia University
NNPM	Pierpont Morgan Library
NNS	New York Society Library
NNU	New York University
NOu	Nottingham University Library
n.p.	no place of publication
n.s.	new series
NSbSU	State University of New York at Stony Brook
NSTC	*Nineteenth-Century Short-Title Catalogue* (1984–)
NSyU	Syracuse University
NUC	*National Union Catalog*
NUN	University of New South Wales Libraries, Sydney
O	Bodleian Library, Oxford
Oa	Codrington Library, All Souls College, Oxford
OAU	Ohio University, Athens
Oc	Christ Church Library, Oxford
OClW	Case Western Reserve University
OOxm	Miami University, Oxford, Ohio
OPA	*The Oracle, and Public Advertiser* (formerly *The Public Advertiser*) C&K 393
Ot	Trinity College Library, Oxford
Ota	Taylor Institution Library, Oxford
OU	Ohio State University
Owo	Worcester College Library, Oxford

P	Bibliothèque Nationale, Paris
PA	*The Public Advertiser* C&K 393
PBm	Bryn Mawr College
PC-S	Privately-owned copy, South Australia
PL	*The Public Ledger* C&K 764
Pm	Bibliothèque Mazarine, Paris
PPL	Library Company of Philadelphia
PPRF	Rosenbach Museum and Library
Price	Mary Bell Price and Lawrence Marsden Price, *The Publication of English Literature in Germany in the Eighteenth Century* (Berkeley: University of California Press, 1934)
PRTup	University of Pretoria Libraries, Pretoria
Ps	Bibliothèque de la Sorbonne (Réserve), Paris
pseud.	pseudonym
PSt	Pattee Library, Pennsylvania State University
PU	University of Pennsylvania
QR	*Quarterly Review.* 305 vols. (1809–1962)
QSL	State Library of Queensland, Brisbane
QU	University of Queensland Central Library
RA	Robinson archive: Collection of Literary Assignments, Manchester Central Library MS F 091.A2
REu	Reading University Library
rev.	review/reviewed
RG	annotation by Ralph Griffiths, editor of the *Monthly Review*, in his marked set of the MR now in the Bodleian Library, Oxford
Rink	Evald Rink, *Printing in Delaware 1761–1800* (Wilmington, DE: Eleutherian Mills Historical Library, 1969)
RLF	Archives of the Royal Literary Fund 1790–1918, on loan to the British Library (MS M[icrofilm] 1077). References are to the reel and entry number.
RM	Robert D. Mayo, *The English Novel in the Magazines 1740–1815* (Evanston: Northwestern University Press, 1962)
Rogers	Deborah D. Rogers, *Ann Radcliffe: a Bio-Bibliography* (Westport, CT and London: Greenwood, 1996)
RPB	Brown University
RPB-JH	John Hay Library, Brown University
RS	Rainer Schöwerling and Verena Ebbes, 'Die Rezeption englischer Romane in Deutschland 1790–1834, eine Bibliographie' (project in progress at the University of Paderborn)
RT	*The Register of the Times* C&K 779
SAN	St Andrews University Library
Scott	Sir Walter Scott, 'Prefatory Memoir to Mrs. Ann Radcliffe' *The Novels of Mrs.*

	Ann Radcliffe. Ballantyne's Novelists Library (London and Edinburgh, 1824), pp. i–xxxix
ScU	University of South Carolina
SDA	*The Star and Daily Evening Advertiser* C&K 843
ser.	series
sig.	signature
SRGS	Royal Geographical Society of Australasia, South Australian Branch, Adelaide
SS	*Stuart's Star and Evening Advertiser* C&K 843
SSL	State Library of South Australia
Strahan	BL Add. Mss 48815–17, Printing Ledgers 1777–99 [cited as 15, 16, 17]
SU	Barr Smith Library, University of Adelaide
Summers	Montagu Summers, *A Gothic Bibliography* (London: Fortune, n.d. [1948]; reprinted New York: Russell and Russell, 1964)
TALa/ TALn	Estonian Academy of Sciences, Tallin
TAU	Taunton Library, Somerset
TCM	*The Town and Country Magazine* C&K 874
TNJ	Joint University Libraries, Nashville, TN
Todd	Janet Todd, ed., *A Dictionary of British and American Women Writers 1660–1800* (London: Methuen, 1987)
Tompkins	J. M. S. Tompkins, *The Popular Novel in England 1770–1800* [1932] London: Methuen, 1969)
t.p.	title-page
trans.	translation
trans.	translator
Troide	*The Early Journals and Letters of Fanny Burney*, vol. II (1774–1777) ed. Lars E. Troide (Montreal & Kingston: McGill-Queen's University Press, 1990); vol. III (1778–1779) ed. Lars E. Troide and Stewart J. Cooke (Montreal & Kingston: McGill-Queen's University Press, 1994)
TxHR	Fondren Library, Rice University
TxU	Humanities Research Centre, University of Texas Austin
unn.	unnumbered; no page numbers marked
ViU	University of Virginia
ViWc	Colonial Williamsburg Foundation
vol.	volume
WA	Biblioteka Narodowa, Warsaw
WAu	Biblioteka Uniwersytecka, Warsaw
WC	*OCLC WorldCat* on-line data base
WEP	*The Whitehall Evening-Post* C&K 958
WFA	*The World, and Fashionable Advertiser* C&K 967
WIS	Wisbech and Fenland Museum

WIW	University of Witwatersrand Library
xESTC	not entered in the *English Short-Title Catalogue* (at February 1998)
xNSTC	not entered in the *Nineteenth-Century Short-Title Catalogue*
ZABH	Pompallier Diocesan Centre, Auckland
Zachs	William Zachs, 'Checklist of the Publications of John Murray', appendix to *The First John Murray* (Oxford: The British Academy and Oxford University Press, 1998)
ZAP	Auckland Public Library
ZAU	Auckland University Library
ZCMU	Museum, Canterbury, New Zealand
ZDP	Dunedin Public Library
ZDUHO	Hocken Library, University of Otago, Dunedin
ZWTU	Alexander Turnbull Library, Wellington
ZWU	Victoria University of Wellington

GENERAL INTRODUCTION

Peter Garside, James Raven, and Rainer Schöwerling

What was a novel in the late eighteenth and early nineteenth centuries? Did popular novels address a broad range of topics and plots and characterizations or were they generally confined to domestic, sedentary themes? Were there as many historical as contemporary settings, as many novels in letters as in continuous narrative? How many were based on real events? Who wrote them? Who published and sold them? How expensive were they? What was their appeal and popularity? How were they reviewed? These and other questions are the starting point for this bibliography.

The period is the first great age of the popular English novel. Post-Richardson and pre-Dickens, these are the years of Burney, Austen, Edgeworth, and Scott, of Beckford, Godwin, Hogg, Inchbald, M. G. Lewis, and Mary Shelley. It is also the age of hundreds of other writers of novels. But what does the full cast of British novelists of the late eighteenth century and Romantic period look like? Who were the most popular writers in their own day? We know that the young Jane Austen cantered through scores of novels, that Leigh Hunt devoured them like crumpets before the fire, that critics complained of a plague of the things. We also know that Austen was far from the most popular writer of her generation, and that the literary fame of most of her rivals was transitory. The authors of one-hit wonders have been forgotten—however influential or notorious they were in their own day. Some writers, indeed, guarded their identity at the time. Many novelists, including Ann Radcliffe and William Godwin, published their first work anonymously; many others were unable or unwilling to acknowledge their authorship throughout their lives. Burney, Austen, and Scott were not named in the original title-pages to any of their novels.

The questions are not trivial: they are essential for anyone examining the literary history of the period and the background to the success—or failure—of particular authors, the representativeness of particular literary genres, the allusions made to other writers and fiction of the day, the exact timing of publication and reprinting, the potential audience, and the contemporary critical reception of the early novel. The absence of such study is apparent in recent republications. Prefaces to dozens of reissued 'lost' novels of the period have lamented current ignorance about the fuller publishing profile of those years and the occurrence of particular literary tropes and styles.

This historical bibliography of fiction therefore addresses the void faced by generations of literary scholars and historians concerned with the development of the English novel. It attempts, for the first time, to provide a basis for an assessment of the work of all novelists of the period. It seeks to list all novels of the period whether or not surviving in extant copies, their publication and pricing details, and contemporary review information. In the case of surviving novels it supplies full references to allow their consultation either on microform or in modern library and research collections all over the world. A copy of every identified surviving novel has been examined for the bibliography. By providing a transcription of the title and title-page, which often includes a contemporary proposal of genre, and further bibliographical and historical information (sometimes including evidence of imitation and plagiarism), the bibliography allows users to make their own comparisons between novels.

Despite the long-acknowledged need for such a bibliography, until now it has been impossible to identify the full range of fiction published in Britain in the late eighteenth century or during the Romantic period. The standard existing guide is Andrew Block's *The English Novel, 1740–1850*, first published in 1939, but it is often unreliable, while offering very little detail on author and title (and none on other issues).[1] Check-lists of specific genres such as those for the gothic novel and the epistolary novel vary greatly in range and detail. Without considering the broader context of all fiction production, these check-lists can give an inflated sense of the importance in the period of the genre under survey.[2] Dorothy Blakey's cataloguing of the publications of William Lane has been a model for other check-lists of leading publishers of fiction of the period, but her survey is incomplete and, in respect of research in recent years, dated.[3] Listings in the *Cambridge Bibliography of English Literature* are very selective, and although a new edition is now underway, it does not intend to include details of all popular fiction of the period. Check-lists based on particular collections are naturally bounded by the range of the particular holdings used, and some do not extend their otherwise very important coverage beyond a certain date or theme.[4] In recent years, women writers have been better served than their male counterparts, but even the fullest existing guides remain limited in their coverage of publication and reception details and, by their nature, do not offer information about the location of consultable copies of novels.[5]

---

[1] An attempt to replace Block (new and revised edn. 1961; reprinted 1963, 1967, 1968), Leonard Orr, *Catalogue Checklist of English Prose Fiction, 1750–1800* (Troy, NY, 1979) falls far short of doing so.

[2] Frederick S. Frank, *The First Gothics: A Critical Guide to the English Gothic Novel* (New York, 1987); Maurice Lévy, 'Bibliographie chronologique du roman "gothique" 1764–1824,' in his *Le Roman 'gothique' anglais 1764–1824* (Toulouse, 1968); Dan J. McNutt, *The Eighteenth-Century Gothic Novel: An Annotated Bibliography of Criticism and Selected Texts* (London, 1975); R. D. Spector, *The English Gothic: A Bibliographic Guide to Writers from Horace Walpole to Mary Shelley* (Westport, CT, and London, 1984); Montague Summers, *A Gothic Bibliography* (London, [1940]; reprinted 1969); Frank Gees Black, *The Epistolary Novel in the Late Eighteenth Century* (Eugene, OR, 1940).

[3] Dorothy Blakey, *The Minerva Press 1790–1820* (London, 1939). Cf. James Raven, 'The Noble Brothers and Popular Publishing', *The Library*, 6th ser., 12 (1990): 293–345; Peter Garside, 'J. F. Hughes and the Publication of Popular Fiction, 1803–1810', *The Library*, 6th ser., 9 (1987): 240–58; and Deborah McLeod, 'The Minerva Press', unpublished PhD dissertation University of Alberta, 1997.

[4] For example, William H. McBurney's *English Prose Fiction 1700–1800 in the University of Illinois Library* (Urbana, 1965) excludes the rich nineteenth-century fiction holdings.

[5] Janet Todd, ed., *A Dictionary of British and American Women Writers 1660–1800* (Totowa, NJ, 1985); J. R. de J. Jackson, *Romantic Poetry by Women: A Bibliography 1770–1835* (Oxford, 1993); Virginia

The continuing *English Short-Title Catalogue* (now subsuming the *Eighteenth-Century Short-Title Catalogue*) has transformed our understanding of the range of eighteenth-century publications and of the libraries that currently hold them. ESTC allows on-line computer and CD-ROM searches for specific words in the title and short form of publication line (amongst other information in each entry), but it has no genre field. The best alternative, a title-word search on 'novel',[6] produces listings of under ten per cent of those works clearly identifiable as novels. Bibliographical assistance for early nineteenth-century English literature is even more problematic for those attempting to identify novels. The *Nineteenth-Century Short-Title Catalogue* now offers a rich resource for locating nineteenth-century literature, but its restricted library coverage and its retention of the Dewey Decimal classification frequently leads to limited or inappropriate subject guidance for the early nineteenth-century novel.

This bibliography will complement existing check-lists for the period before 1770, and together they will provide a full research guide to prose fiction from 1700 to 1830. A series of fiction check-lists spanning the period 1700–1770 has been compiled over many years, starting with W. H. McBurney's *Check List of English Prose Fiction 1700–1739* (1960), followed by J. C. Beasley's *Check List of English Prose Fiction 1740–1749* (1972), and James Raven's *British Fiction, 1750–1770* (1987). The following work continues this series, but is also much more extensive than its predecessors in the bibliographical, literary, and holding-library information that it offers.

It has to be restated that no bibliography of this kind can escape difficult editorial decisions over inclusion and exclusion. 'Novel' was by no means an agreed term in the eighteenth century, and books which do not now appear to us to be novels were then reviewed under that category. But the instability of the term also points to the new opportunities provided by this survey in chronicling contemporary notions of fiction and in understanding the broader cultural and historical significance of the 'rise of the novel'. The bibliography aims to add to our understanding of the character of fiction in this period, while seeking to avoid rigid categories of sub-genres. From the evidence of reprinting and patronage to that of the mediating response of critical reviewers, the bibliography aims to identify authorship, communities of writing, the themes embraced and repeated by writers, the circumstances of novel production, and the nature of literary circulation and reception. Existing literary canons might be challenged, refined, or better understood by revisiting this history of the novel, by the contextualizing of the fuller output of imaginative prose of the period, by the recovery of rare books now scattered across the world, and by the very basic reconstruction of books now lost.

Blain et al. eds., *The Feminist Companion to Literature in English* (London, 1990); Dale Spender, *Mothers of the Novel: 100 Good Women Writers before Jane Austen* (London and New York, 1986).

6 It is also possible to search for the term 'novel' using the ESTC '500 note field', but that field has been applied patchily and cannot be used in all cases.

Scope

The bibliography records the first editions of all known novels in English published in the British Isles between 1770 and 1829 inclusive, and gives details of subsequent editions to 1850. Also included are the first English translations in this period of novels originally published elsewhere in Europe.[7] Novels in English first published in North America in this period and subsequently published in the British Isles before 1830 are described in an entry for the first British edition. The bibliography does not include subsequent editions of novels first published before 1770. It also includes brief references to subsequent editions up to 1850, including the first American editions and German and French first translations.

The listings adopt a more rigorous definition of the 'novel' than in earlier volumes by McBurney, Beasley, and Raven. This is partly because of the huge upturn in the number of publications over this period (especially from the 1790s), but also because the forms of the prose novel became more readily identifiable. The bibliography includes what contemporaries thought of as novels, incorporating works categorized as 'novels' in contemporary periodical reviews and under 'novels' headings in circulating library catalogues, but excludes religious tracts, chapbooks, literature written only for children and juveniles, and very short separately issued tales. Collections of tales (including some mixed genre compilations) are included; separate verse novels are not.

The bibliography gives a full description (together with catalogue number) of the copy of the novel examined (more complete details are given below of the arrangement within each entry). To assist detailed recovery of the publication history of each novel, detailed imprint information and a variety of contemporary source references are also given. The imprint line is exactly reproduced (save for the exceptions detailed below under 'Components of each entry'). Other printing or publishing information is also given in a further notes section within each entry. The full publishing information is given in detail unavailable in other bibliographies.

Each entry also provides information concerning other copies of the novels held at libraries and research institutions world-wide. These holding details are taken from current short-title catalogues and other on-line resources, but the compilers of this bibliography have also undertaken extensive further research in individual libraries and special collections.

---

[7] Sources used to verify translations into English include Alexandre Cioranescu, *Bibliographie de la littérature Française du dix-huitième siècle*, 3 vols. (Paris, 1969); Angus Martin, Vivienne G. Mylne, and Richard Frautschi, eds., *Bibliographie du genre romanesque français 1751–1800* (London and Paris, 1977). Sources used to identify translations from English into German include Mary Bell Price and Lawrence Marsden Price, *The Publication of English Literature in Germany in the Eighteenth Century* (Berkeley, Ca, 1934); Norbert Otto Eke and Dagmar Olasz-Eke, *Bibliographie: Der deutsche Roman, 1815–1830* (Munich, 1994); Rainer Schöwerling and Verena Ebbes, *Rezeption englischer Romane in Deutschland 1790–1834, eine Bibliographie* (forthcoming); and the 'English authors in Germany, 1680–1810' project, University of Münster (forthcoming).

A further significant feature within the entries are the references to reviews and listings in *The Monthly Review, The Critical Review, The Quarterly Review, The Edinburgh Review,* and other contemporary reviews and notices.[8] The periodicals provide evidence that the title was considered to be fiction by contemporaries, and also supply corroborative information about pricing, format, and general date of issue. Appropriate extracts from review notices are also given in the pre-1800 entries, with the name of the reviewer where identified.[9] *The Monthly Review* and *The Critical Review* are listed in volume I wherever they supply a review either in the main or the subsidiary section of the periodical. References to periodicals other than the *Monthly* and *Critical* are cited when these offer the only review of the novel before 1800, together with other review references in existing bibliographies. In many cases newspaper advertisement references are listed to pin-point publication dates. In addition, booksellers' advertisements found within novels examined are cited where they supply useful further evidence for the dating and verification of other novels. For the post-1800 period, when contemporary reviewing policy was changing, the references given correspond mainly to simple lists of new publications given in *The Edinburgh* and *The Quarterly,* although full reviews of novels in these two journals are also noted.

Procedure

The guiding principle has been to work from a range of eighteenth- and nineteenth-century bibliographical records and to examine actual copies of all known surviving novels entered in the bibliography. In identifying the existence of rare copies and their location, ESTC and NSTC have been complemented by other catalogues and extended by use of on-line resources such as the *OCLC WorldCat* database. Copies of novels identified from contemporary sources, OCLC, the STCs, the *National Union Catalog* (NUC), and other catalogues were all examined afresh and further searches undertaken in libraries and collections. Library stack-work has ensured in particular that the bibliography corrects and amplifies existing bibliographical aids to novels of the period. The importance of this hands-on work is underlined by the number of titles located during the course of research but not listed by the eighteenth- and nineteenth-century short-title catalogues. The bibliography is not, therefore, merely a derivative or synthesis of catalogues and bibliographical databases. It includes rare editions not identified by the STCs, as well as titles which have not survived in extant copies and whose existence and further details have been ascertained by printing and publishing records[10] or contemporary

---

    [8] See also below under Contemporary Review References, pp. 10–11.
    [9] Using the copy of the MR marked up by its editor, Ralph Griffiths, and held in the Bodleian Library, Oxford; also, Benjamin Christie Nangle, *The Monthly Review First Series 1749–1789: Indexes of Contributors and Articles* (Oxford: Clarendon Press, 1934) and Benjamin Christie Nangle, *The Monthly Review Second Series 1790–1815: Indexes of Contributors and Articles* (Oxford: Clarendon Press, 1955).
    [10] These include the archives of John Murray, Albermarle St., London; the archives of Longmans

reviews, or by a combination of corroborative sources such as advertisements and circulating library catalogues.[11] These last two sources must usually be taken together, as some advertising puffs are not by themselves proof of certain publication (some seem to have been wishful thinking or attempts at relaunches) and at least some of the entries in early library catalogues are loose descriptions that can mislead.

Similarly, review references have been identified from contemporary periodical reviews and magazines, and not merely from existing published guides to the reviews. As a result, the bibliography both locates reliable references for novels no longer surviving in extant copies and excludes the many ghost entries which litter earlier attempts at such a bibliography.[12] For the 1790s in particular, a trawl of newspaper advertisements has revealed much new detail about publication dates and confirmation of authorship, pricing, and (for lost works) title. Where later editions of non-surviving first editions do exist, further details of these are included in the entry.

Where, as in the great majority of entries, copies of novels do survive, recording practice for the examined copy is uniform, with reproduction of title-page information and a basic formula for the description of each volume (full details are given below in the explanation of the constituent parts to each entry). Measurements of title-pages (as often included in the NUC for example) are not included. Novels were often cut back drastically when bound or otherwise presented, and dimensions vary considerably between different copies. Instead each entry provides basic format information by collation of leaves. In the past, many catalogues and checklists have included erroneous multiplication of editions as a consequence of one library listing a book as 8vo and another listing it as 12mo. One of the benefits of the hands-on research for these volumes is the elimination of such ghost entries. Format information is also followed by the price of the novel, according to its condition cited in given contemporary sources. The usual distinction was between sewed (that is, sewed with paper covers), bound, or in boards.

As will be clear from the entries, a very large number of libraries have been visited world-wide. Often relatively small collections preserve unique copies of novels, but

---

held at Reading University; the records of the Bowyers (Keith Maslen and John Lancaster, *The Bowyer Ledgers: The Printing Accounts of William Bowyer, father and son* . . . (London and New York, 1991); and copyright documents belonging to George Robinson held at Manchester Central Library.

[11] In entries before 1800 many newspapers—such as the *St James's Chronicle* and the *Public Advertiser*—were consulted where appropriate. The introduction to volume 1 provides a full list and discussion. In the same volume, various booksellers' catalogues and advertisements are cited, including for example, those of the Noble brothers (but all usually only as corroboration to other sources, given the often unreliable titles and details provided). In volume II *The English Catalogue of Books 1801–1836* and catalogues by William Bent are used. Full details are given in the volume introduction.

[12] Ghosts are plentiful in Block, *The English Novel*; and even more so in the repository of file cards collected from libraries and scholars worldwide by Chester Noyes Greenough and on deposit at the Houghton Library, Harvard University. The Greenough file (with its broad, miscellaneous coverage) was nevertheless a valuable early guide, particularly for volume II, and its suggestions were followed up. The editors are grateful to the Trustees of the Houghton Library.

most of the major libraries have also contributed significantly to the following work. This does not mean, however, that all their novels were listed in their own catalogues. Recent moves at the British Library, for example, uncovered many eighteenth-century editions not surviving elsewhere but also believed to have been lost by the Library. Our research at the Bodleian Library similarly included copies of numerous novels listed in the library's pre-1920 catalogue but not listed in ESTC. Amongst many other examples, full checks were made of the novels in the closed stacks at Aberdeen University, the Early Novels Collection at Bristol University Library, the post-1800 titles in the stacks at the University of Illinois, Urbana-Champaign, card index files for the Sadleir-Black collection at the University of Virginia, Charlottesville, and card index files recording fiction at Trinity College, Dublin. One recently rediscovered library has also been a major contributor to the project. For the years between 1795 and 1830, the collection of novels at Schloss Corvey, near Höxter, Germany, assembled by two Romantic *belles-lettres* enthusiasts, has been a vital resource. It is listed in its own right in the library location-line of each entry.[13]

Arrangement

Entries are arranged chronologically by year of imprint. Within each year, anonymous works are ordered alphabetically by title and precede entries for novels by known authors and/or translators, ordered alphabetically by author's name or by the given pseudonymous name where no real author's name has been found. Evidence of authorship has been scrutinized afresh. Where some doubt remains about an attribution a question mark is placed before the author's name; where major doubt exists the novel is entered as anonymous (with further possible attribution details in the notes to the entry). *All's Right at Last* (1774), for example, remains an anonymous work given that the *Critical Review*'s allusion to the style of Frances Brooke is ambiguous. All author references (as here to Mrs Brooke) are entered in the author index. Pseudonyms of identified authors do not appear in the author line but are given appropriate cross-references within each year and index entries. Remaining pseudonyms treated as authors' names for the sake of the alphabetical listing include the false appropriation of real names. Examples include the use, again in 1774, of 'Mr Helvetius' when the novel (*The Child of Nature*) is clearly not by Claude-Adrien Helvétius. Entries for authors with several works in one year are ordered alphabetically by title. Where necessary, further details of the precise chronology are given in the final notes to each entry.

---

[13] A provisional account of the fiction holdings is given in Peter Garside, 'Collections of English Fiction in the Romantic Period: The Significance of Corvey', in Rainer Schöwerling and Hartmut Steinecke, eds., *Die Fürstliche Bibliothek Corvey* (Munich, 1992), pp. 70–81. A further description is also given in Rainer Schöwerling, Hartmut Steinecke, and Günter Tiggesbäumker, eds., *Literatur und Erfahrungswandel 1789–1830* (Munich, 1995).

Novels are entered under the year of their title-page imprint date, irrespective of evidence of earlier and (very rarely) later issue. Post-dating on imprints—to make a fashionable work seem more up to date—was common. Evidence for an earlier publication is often apparent from periodical reviews, newspaper advertisements, or, later in the period, from the dates of publication given in *The English Catalogue of Books, 1801–1836* (ECB).

Occasionally, it is highly problematic—or even impossible—to determine which of two editions (or translations) of a novel was issued first in a particular year. In such cases separate 'a' and 'b' entries are given. Only one entry is given for editions published in the same year but where the order of publication is clear and uncontroversial. In all cases, the final notes section provides further information on the alternative edition.

7   Novels with volumes published in different years are not normally separately entered under the respective years of publication, unless, for example, a significant break occurred in their publication. The bibliography attempts a distinction between those volumes of a novel issued in successive seasons as a single entity, and those volumes of a novel often published with the same title and as a deliberate continuation, but conceived as a separate publication (and often separated from the earlier volumes by several years). This point is of particular importance for the pre-1800 volume where the separate listing of successively issued volumes would misleadingly inflate the number of entries. A publishing season (from September to May) also, of course, crossed two calendar years, and certain novels have volumes bearing different imprint dates but were actually issued in the same season. The notes section to novels whose constituent parts are entered separately provide full cross-referencing to the subsequent or previous volumes. Where titles are entered according to the imprint date of the first volume, cross-references back to this entry are given from the years in which the subsequent volume(s) were published.

Cross-referencing is provided by the indexes, and, where necessary, within the main body of entries. This is especially important for women writers changing to married names during the period covered by each volume, but also to locate novels which a reader might associate with one of the many mistaken former attributions. Cross-references are also given to works whose authorship and (very occasionally) publication date is in doubt. Many attributions are made for the first time in this bibliography and in the case of well-known works the cross-reference is intended as an additional aid. Volume indexes are provided to authors (including pseudonyms) and translators; to titles; and to booksellers, publishers, printers, and place of publication.

Where no copy of a novel survives, and its title and publication details are reconstituted from outside evidence, the reconstituted entry is marked with an asterisk * before the title and the absence of any located copy is noted in the line reserved for shelf-marks and catalogues. Where not already explicit, sources are given for the various elements of the reconstitution.

Components of each entry

A standard entry consists of the following:

Entry number (within each year)
Author's name
Full title
Place of publication and imprint publication details
Pagination, format, and price
Contemporary review references
Location and shelf-mark of copy examined and references to other copies and catalogues
Notes

ENTRY NUMBER
Numbering starts afresh each year. Cross-references and indexes cite the number prefixed by the year—e.g. 1770: 26, 1829: 43.

AUTHOR'S NAME
Each entry opens with the name of the author(s) and translator(s) where known (or where attribution can be made with some certainty, as further described in the entry). Unless bracketed, names are given as they appear on the title-page. Square brackets are used around names supplied wholly by outside evidence. Additions which complete names, and which are, again, derived from outside sources rather than the novel itself, are also given in square brackets—as, for example, JONES, A[nne]. Occasionally, although no author's name appears on the title-page or it appears in shortened or altered form, the novel itself supplies valuable additional details, for instance at the end of a preface or dedication. Where the author's name is derived from this internal evidence, either wholly or substantially, it is enclosed by curly brackets. 'Mr', 'Mrs', and 'Miss' are omitted unless these are the only quali-fication to the surname or the only indication of gender. Where no author has been identified 'ANON.' is given. Entries for anonymous works, listed in alphabetical order by title, precede entries with known authors or remaining pseudonymous names. Doubtful attribution is indicated by a question mark. Where a novel is listed as anonymous evidence about possible attributions may also be given in the notes section.

Translators are treated similarly to authors, but with the addition of '(*trans.*)' immediately after the name. Square brackets indicate the attribution of a translator. Further information about the translation may also be given in the notes to each entry.

FULL TITLE
The title is taken in full from the title-page. Because it has been impossible to repli-cate exactly the original—and sometimes eccentric—mixture of uppercase, lower-case, small capitals, italic, black letter and other fonts, titles are reproduced in

simple uppercase throughout, but with original punctuation retained. This offers a
much fuller reproduction than the short titles of ESTC and NSTC. Mottoes are
excluded. Other points of interest may be recorded in the notes section. Use of
'[*sic*]' to indicate the given spelling or typography is sparing but included where
necessary. Where there is significant variation in the titles of the different volumes
of a novel, each title is reproduced in full, or in the case of minor variation, the differences are recorded in the notes section.

PLACE OF PUBLICATION AND IMPRINT PUBLICATION DETAILS
The first-named town of publication is given first, followed (after a colon) by the
full details of booksellers and publishers as they appear on the title-page up to the
imprint date. A comma separates this information from the date, which is always
given in arabic numerals even when in roman in the original. Where a town of publication is not named but inferred from other imprint details this is given in square
brackets. Where no date is given on the title-page this is recorded as 'n.d.' followed
by an attributed date in square brackets, with source reference where necessary.
Where title-page publication details vary between volumes of the novel, this is fully
indicated. Where such details are identical in each volume except for the dates,
these are combined—e.g. '1770/71'. Where further significant publication or printing details are given in the novels (usually in the colophon or prefatory material),
these are recorded under the notes section.

PAGINATION, FORMAT, AND PRICE
The last roman and arabic page number of each volume is given. These are preceded, in the case of multi-volume novels, by the volume number in upper-case
roman. Where volumes were published in different years this is indicated in parentheses after the volume numbers. Where pagination information is unavailable
because no copy has survived, the number of volumes only is indicated.
     The format of each volume—usually 8vo or 12mo—has been individually checked
by collation of leaves (existing secondary references have not been trusted).
     Price is given in shillings (s) and pence (d) as on the title-page and/or in review
and newspaper notices, with given form ('sewed', 'boards', &c). The source for the
price is also given, including title-page (t.p.), spine label (s.l.), CR, MR, ER, and QR.
Where reviews are absent or insufficient to provide publication date and pricing
information, use is made of other contemporary sources. Conflicts between
sources are frequent; all variants are provided. For the post-1800 period, *The English Catalogue of Books 1801–1836* (ECB) is used extensively for information relating to retail price and date of publication.

CONTEMPORARY REVIEW REFERENCES
References are given to the appearance of the novel in the major eighteenth-
century periodical reviews, *The Monthly Review* and *The Critical Review,* and in
The Edinburgh Review and *The Quarterly Review* in the early nineteenth century.

The abbreviations (CR, MR, for example) are followed by volume, page, and date references. *The Monthly* is cited consistently to 1803 when *The Edinburgh* (founded 1802) began extensive listings. Similarly, *The Critical* is cited up to 1809 when *The Quarterly* was founded. References are also given to any further reviews of the novel, as already indexed to 1800 by Antonia Forster, and to 1826 by William S. Ward.[14] The absence of a reference to a review in any of the leading periodicals (or to Forster and Ward) is therefore significant. For novels listed in volume I (1770–1799) and *not* reviewed by *The Monthly* and *The Critical*, a direct reference (to short-cut Forster) is given to a review found in another periodical (*The Analytical Review*, *The British Critic*, *The European Magazine*, and *The Gentleman's Magazine*, for example).

LOCATION AND SHELF-MARK OF COPY EXAMINED AND REFERENCES TO OTHER
COPIES AND CATALOGUES

This line always begins with an abbreviation for the location of the copy of the novel examined (or statement of apparent non-survival), followed by the holding library's own shelf-mark. In the case of novels held at the Corvey Library, where no current catalogue numbers exist, the ISBN of the Corvey Microfiche (CME) is given as the most useful and accessible identifying call number.

The examined copy's shelf-mark or Corvey ISBN is followed (as applicable) by the ECB page number, the novel's reference number in the Primary Source Media Eighteenth-Century Microfilm series (EM), and the verified ESTC record control number or the NSTC entry number. EM numbers, identifying novels available in microfilm (although often not the copies examined for this bibliography) are given for the filming completed and published by December 1997. Where the novel has been microfilmed by the Primary Source Media project but is not yet published, this is indicated by the abbreviation 'EMf' [Eighteenth-Century Microfilms forthcoming].

In volume I (1770–1799), up to nine further holding libraries are cited in addition to that of the copy examined (although in practice many novels are extremely rare and survive at very few locations). All ESTC numbers are followed in parenthesis by an indication of the verified location in other libraries (given in standard abbreviation) of copies of this edition of the novel. Unverified locations, including those listed in ESTC but marked as unverified, are excluded. In a surprisingly large number of cases, holding libraries (including the location of the examined copy) are not amongst the major libraries of the world. Where a novel is held by many libraries, priority is given to the five main holding libraries in the British Isles (including Ireland, denoted as 'BI'), to eleven main libraries in North America (denoted as 'NA'), and up to three libraries elsewhere (Continental Europe,

---

[14] Antonia Forster, *Index to Book Reviews in England 1749–1774* (Carbondale, IL, 1990), and *Index to Book Reviews in England 1775–1800* (London, 1997); and William S. Ward, *Literary Reviews in British Periodicals 1798–1820*, 2 vols. (New York, 1972); William S. Ward, *Literary Reviews in British Periodicals 1821–1826* (New York, 1977).

Australasia, and other, denoted as 'EA'), in addition to the location of the copy examined.[15] In all cases, however, where further locations are listed in ESTC (used by the pre-1800 volume as the basis for further holding-library references) an indication ('&c') is given. It is important to note, however, that the volume offers corrections to previously published editions of ESTC. Details of some new findings were supplied to the ESTC on-line project team.

The libraries given priority listing for novels published before 1801 are as follows:

BI
> British Library, London; University Library, Cambridge; National Library of Ireland, Dublin; National Library of Scotland, Edinburgh; Bodleian Library, Oxford.

NA
> Henry E. Huntington Library, California; Sterling Library and Beinecke Rare Books Library, Yale University; Library of Congress, Washington; Newberry Library, Chicago; Library of the University of Illinois, Urbana-Champaign; Houghton Library, Harvard University; Princeton University Library; New York Public Library; Library of the University of Pennsylvania; Harry Ransom Humanities Research Center, University of Texas at Austin; Library of the University of Virginia.

Very occasional examples have been found of a library listed by ESTC in which the apparently verified copy cannot be found. In these cases references to the libraries are omitted. Similarly, research for these volumes has often identified further copies, not listed in ESTC, but these are included in the main holding library lists.

In the case of the second volume, 1800–1829, NSTC has served as the main source for libraries holding copies of the titles listed. NSTC has been compiled from a more limited library consultation than ESTC, but its citations are presented in a manner similar to that of volume I, with the NSTC reference number given first, followed by holding libraries in parenthesis. In cases where NSTC includes more than one number for the same title (under both author and title, for example), the number cited is normally the one based on author, or (in the case of works without identified authors) the most substantial. In each instance, cited holding libraries are taken from all the NSTC entries for this title. Because NSTC begins with the year 1801, and contains relatively few original works actually published in 1800, the first year in volume II of this bibliography is supplemented by material from ESTC entered under the same guide-lines as used in volume I. Because entries in NSTC are based on printed catalogues of the libraries rather than fresh examination of their holdings, it naturally carries over mistakes from earlier cataloguers, and a number of errors concerning matters such as title description and author attribution have been corrected and recorded. NSTC Series 1 (1801–1815) records holdings at six major libraries:

---

[15] This policy is adopted to provide references to leading research libraries holding copies of the novel, avoiding, in the case of widely held novels, a short-list restricted to abbreviations from the start of the alphabet (and usually, therefore, because of the codes used, exclusively Canadian libraries).

British Library; University Library, Cambridge; Trinity College, Dublin; National Library of Scotland, Edinburgh; University of Newcastle Library; Bodleian Library, Oxford.

NSTC Series 2 (1816–1870) supplements these libraries by two others:

Library of Congress, Washington; Harvard University.

When one of the libraries listed in ESTC or NSTC provides the actual copy consulted for the entry (and given therefore with shelf-mark at the beginning of the line), the library is omitted from the holding libraries abbreviated later in parenthesis. In cases where the specific edition of the novel forming the entry is absent from ESTC (pre-1801) or NSTC (post-1800), this is indicated by xESTC and xNSTC.

NOTES

These notes are not intended to be comprehensive but to record additional information thought to be of particular interest to readers, including, for example, dedications, subscription lists, and advertisements within the novels. In the case of translations from another language, basic details are provided of the original title and date and place of publication. These are followed by any additional information about authors and translators, as well as past mis-attributions of authorship. Further notes are given in much the same order as the other parts of the full entry. In the first (eighteenth-century) volume, epistolary novels are noted because this form was then both distinctive and significant. For the years to 1777, information from Keith Maslen's *Bowyer Ledgers* is also included to give an indication of the size of the edition.

Also listed are further editions of the novel published up to and including 1850. In the case of reissues first published before 1801, ESTC and the *OCLC WorldCat* online database have provided rich sources of information. NSTC is used as a source of reference for further editions in both volumes: in the case of the first volume it is supplemented by *OCLC* and in the case of the second volume by other catalogues, notably NUC, and by reliable sources such as the published records of the nineteenth-century fiction collections of Michael Sadleir and Robert Lee Wolff.[16] In volume I up to five further editions are listed in chronological order with place and date of publication and ESTC entry number. If more than five editions were published before 1850, the number of these is also given in the form of the number of further entries in ESTC (an important distinction because separate ESTC entries sometimes record variant rather than separate editions). Such references also allow readers to pursue further detail in ESTC entries. Where the further editions include the first Irish edition, booksellers and basic format details of this edition are given. In such a case we include all the information on booksellers of these subsequent

---

[16] Michael Sadleir, *XIX Fiction: A Bibliographical Record based on his own Collection*, 2 vols. (Cambridge, 1951); Robert Lee Wolff, *Nineteenth-Century Fiction: A Bibliographical Catalogue*, 5 vols. (New York, 1981–6).

Irish editions given by ESTC, but it should be noted that ESTC practice is variable in this instance, sometimes listing all the names of booksellers in what were often large publishing associations, but sometimes listing only a few, followed by the number of others omitted.[17]

In the second volume slightly different editorial procedures are followed with regard to subsequent editions. Up to five further editions published in Britain and Ireland are listed, with supporting references given in parenthesis. Places of publication for these further editions are recorded when they differ from that of the main entry. Where more than five further editions have been identified, the number of additional editions, as evident from NSTC when viewed in conjunction with other catalogues, is given in square brackets (e.g. as 'at least 8 more edns. to 1850'). Because the practice of producing pirate or parallel Dublin editions virtually disappears after the Act of Union of 1800 (when English copyright laws were extended to Ireland), Irish editions are placed in the same chronological sequence as British editions, without additional details being supplied. The sequence of British and Irish editions is then followed by citation of the first known North American edition before 1850, except in cases where the American edition preceded the British (in which case the latter supplies the full entry). In cases where editions were published in different places in North America during the first known year of publication there, the first of these alphabetically by place of publication is given, followed by the others in square brackets.

Both volumes also list the first known translations into German and French.

In the first volume (with fewer entries overall), space has allowed the inclusion of extracts from the reviews. These are reproduced with original spelling and punctuation except in cases of ambiguity (round brackets replace square brackets, for example).

---

[17] This means that while the imprint index, including booksellers, printers and others listed in the imprint line, can be used to identify Irish booksellers involved in the publication of all novels *first* published in this period, the index is no guide to determine *all* the Irish booksellers involved in the novel reprint trade.

HISTORICAL INTRODUCTION:
THE NOVEL COMES OF AGE

James Raven

The modern novel is a product of the eighteenth century. With roots extending to the sixteenth- and seventeenth-century romance and to the influence of French, Italian, and Spanish writers, what has for long been called the 'rise of the novel' is very largely an eighteenth-century development.[1] In 1785 Clara Reeve, an accomplished fiction writer herself, set about chronicling the history of the novel in her *Progress of Romance*. 'We had early translations of the best Novels of all other Countries', she concluded, 'but for a long time produced very few of our own.' In recent times—and she brought her account down to 1770—the situation had been transformed, even though she confessed to fright in trying to review the subject and admitted that any conclusion to her story 'is yet a great way off'.[2] As Reeve's account suggested, a new critical maturity in English novel writing was reached in the three decades before 1770 and this furnished the climax to her 'investigation of novels'.[3] During the next three decades of the century, however, the achievement of Richardson, Fielding, Hayward, Smollett, and Sterne, was hugely extended in quantity and range, if not always in quality. As already evident to Reeve, writing in the mid-1780s, these were years in which 'the press groaned under the weight of Novels, which sprung up like Mushrooms every year'.[4]

We still await a reliable historical account of this rage for the novel. This is not only because of the past bibliographical weaknesses discussed in the general introduction above, but also because of the extraordinary variety of narrative forms contributing to the formative phase of the novel: fables, romances, biographical and autobiographical memoirs and histories, satirical tales and narratives in letters. Boundaries between these types of fiction are very problematic and many publications do not easily fit under any one label. For many writers the fluidity was

[1] See Michael McKeon, *The Origins of the English Novel, 1600–1740* (Baltimore and London, 1987). An ambitious rebuttal of this literary historical view is given by Margaret Anne Doody, *The True Story of the Novel* (New Brunswick, NJ, 1996), but see also the objections of John Richetti, *American Historical Review* 103: 1 (Feb. 1998), pp. 137–8. The following essay seeks to extend the discussion first offered for the 1750s and 1760s in James Raven, *British Fiction 1750–1770: A Chronological Checklist of Prose Fiction Printed in Britain and Ireland* (Newark, London and Toronto: Associated University Press, 1987), pp. 7–42; it could not have been completed without the generous assistance of all those already listed in the acknowledgements to this volume.

[2] Clara Reeve, *The Progress of Romance*, 2 vols. (Dublin, 1785): 1, 108, 117. Her observations on her undertaking are given in the form of a fictional dialogue.

[3] Reeve, *Progress of Romance*, 1: 108, 2: 52.   [4] Ibid. 2: 7.

intentional. Some played merrily with the conceit, in the style of Charlotte Palmer who entitled her 1792 contribution *It Is and It Is Not a Novel*.[5] Novelists, then as now, challenged the reader to engage with questions of probability, realism, the supernatural, and pseudo-history. Imitation of other literary forms was essential to the art of many writers. Satire, for example, depended upon the recognition of different originals, 'secret lives' assumed familiarity with genuine autobiography, and mock travels fed upon accounts of real journeys. 'The word novel', wrote the Revd Edward Mangin in 1808, 'is a generical term; of which romances, histories, memoirs, letters, tales, lives, and adventures, are the species.'[6]

At the same time, this remarkable literary diversity encouraged rather than undermined the development of a new cultural form. During the final thirty years of the eighteenth century the 'novel' was secured as an acknowledged category of fiction. It was a label used to convey increasingly precise ideas of content and ambition. Plots were often spectacularly implausible, yet also designed to persuade of the authenticity of a 'Life', 'Memoir', 'History', or 'Series of Letters'.[7] Some boasted complex plots, even if many were inadequately resolved or riddled by inconsistencies. In most, hasty writing is obvious. Lasting literary fame was not the aim, however. Writers, purveyors, and customers were looking to amusement, diversion, and fashion. All contributed to the development and contemporary interest in the formation of this new and sometimes shocking thing called a novel. It was clearly a dynamic form, not simply reliant upon existing models but also inventive in developing new types of prose fiction ranging from the novel in letters and the sentimental novel, to the Gothic romance and the historical epic. In the opening words to the preface of his 1780 fiction, *Alwyn: or the Gentleman Comedian*, Thomas Holcroft declared that 'Works of imagination have ever been the ornament of civilized nations. The progress from barbarism to politeness is always accompanied by a similar gradation in the perfection of literary amusements.' According to Holcroft, the origins of the novel were to be found in the fable, which developed stage by stage. The history of literary forms paralleled society's growth from primitive pasturage and hunting to a new age of commerce, civility, and luxury. As a result, 'the legitimate Novel is a work much more difficult than the Romance', even though, Holcroft added, it had already fallen into disrepute and only the shining model of Tom Jones now saved it.[8]

It is this 'progress', its history and breadth, that is reconstructed by the following bibliography. The recovery of authorship, publication and reception details of all novels of the period—both those surviving and those now lost—offers a chronicle of literary variety. It reveals a sociology of the novel that is extraordinarily wide

    [5] It also brought one of the more patronizing critical verdicts (1792: 47).
    [6] Edward Mangin, *An Essay on Light Reading, as it may be Supposed to Influence Moral Conduct on Literary Taste* (London, 1808), p. 5.
    [7] This engagement with 'reality' is discussed in J. C. Beasley, *Novels of the 1740s* (Athens, Ga, 1982), ch. 3, Michael Crump, 'Stranger than Fiction: the Eighteenth-Century True Story', in *Searching the Eighteenth Century*, edited by M. Crump and M. Harris (London, 1983), pp. 59–73.
    [8] *Alwyn: or the Gentleman Comedian* (1780: 18), pp. [i], vii.

ranging. Novelists comprised men and women in roughly equal numbers. Most, not unexpectedly, were from the propertied classes. Beyond this, numerous identifications can be suggested, including novelists who were leisured gentlewomen, high-profile aristocrats, obscure vicars, and curates, sea captains, destitute merchants' wives, reformed and some unreformed prostitutes, over-achieving adolescents, and pious autodidacts. The majority of writers imitated specific models; all too many to the extent of constructing identikit fiction. Several novels, indeed, seem to have been put together above the print-room—a few chapters from a hack writer, other parts culled from an old romance, something more translated from a foreign pot-boiler.[9] A reason for writing was sometimes spelled out in a preface or (not necessarily more succinctly) in a title-page. There were many different commitments or causes, but a notable invocation was to the impecunious author. The diversity of writers and circumstances matched the range of success and failure. A few novels were quickly reprinted; others were revived after a few seasons or achieved a limited success in the writer's own circle or locality. Many novels were destined for either a very dusty or a very brief shelf-life following a few polite readings by friendly subscribers or meagre outings from a fashionable circulating library.

The publishing history of these novels also confirms the advance of specialist booksellers and commercial circulating librarians, as well as their advertising techniques and promotional ploys. These included identifiable house-designs, continuation series, and end-page catalogues issued in particular typographical and packaging styles. Novels, like other leisure and fashion goods, were promoted by a variety of entrepreneurs, many modestly financed but eager to exploit new markets. As with many other manufactures, the success of the product was determined by customer identification, new ways of attracting and retaining custom, metropolitan trend-setting, and the exploitation of a country market. Contemporary recognition of this novel industry was swift and not always complimentary. Even one of the more sympathetic reviewers, declaring an approved work to be harmless, added that this was 'more than can be said of half the novels that make their monthly appearance for the entertainment of masters and misses in this reading age'.[10] For good or ill, the novel was recognized as a new cultural force, as distinctive as the theatre or newspaper. Reviewers might find a tale that 'affords many lessons to the youth of both sexes' but also—and far more usually—a novel deemed to be 'one of those pernicious incentives to vice that are a scandal to decency'.[11]

Such commentary contributed to increasingly self-referencing novel-writing and novel-reading. Standards were suggested by the achievements of other novelists; the values and possible effects of their productions were discussed by a range of published intermediaries. From this a tradition of the novel was developed. Formal

---

[9] See, for example, the reviews of 1771: 30, 1773: 17; 1793: 44; 1794: 37; 1796: 14.

[10] CR 54 (1782): 152, of *Blandford Races* (1782: 3).

[11] CR 33 (1772): 180, and CR 55 (1783): 234, of *The Cautious Lover* (1772: 3) and *Frailties of Fashion* (1782: 6).

critical interest added to notions of the ambit and proper concerns and characteristics of the novel, of what was successful and of what was not. As the following entries demonstrate, reviews (and where known, specific reviewers) proposed particular—and changing—assertions of what made a novel and made it work.[12] Occasionally a reviewer also confessed to confusion about the proper classification for a novel.[13] More often, however, the critics regarded the novel as a separate and distinguishable class of books.[14] In an age when Linnaeus and others categorized natural phenomena, many observers described novels according to their 'order', 'species', 'kind', 'race', or 'tribe'.[15] In more military fashion, novels were assigned a 'rank' or placed within a 'list'.[16] In turn, some novels offered self-commentary about their design—notably Clara Reeve's preface to her reissued *Old English Baron* (to be extended by her *Progress of Romance* eight years later). As the preface to the 1787 *Orlando and Seraphina* observed: 'It hath often been made a question, whether novels and romances (for upon this occasion they are not distinguished) have been productive of greater good or harm in the world.' In answer, almost all commentators agreed that literature must offer either truth or utility and that the danger of the novel was that it might offer neither. Entertainment alone was no proper manifesto for the novelist; only when this was combined with useful instruction might the novel escape charges of insignificance or depravity. This concern about the effects of novel-mania was a serious one, and should not be unthinkingly dismissed with retrospective levity, however enjoyable the reviewers' wit and scorn.

In order to offer a broad perspective on this history, the following entries provide a range of references enabling verification of author and publication details and, where possible, assisting the reader to examine the history of the novel's production and dissemination. For the 90 per cent of novel titles of the period that survive, details are based upon a fresh examination of an existing copy.[17] This gives the entries new authority and often offers corrections to current catalogues. Where no

[12] All extracts from the reviews retain original spelling and punctuation, although some square brackets are replaced by round brackets to avoid ambiguity. 'Sic' is used sparingly.

[13] Examples include CR 67 (1789), pp. 77–8, of *The Amicable Quixote* (1788: 6); MR 80 (1789): 552, of Henry James Pye, *The Spectre* (1789: 61); and MR n.s., 12 (1793), pp. 338–9, of Charles Henry Wilson, *The Wandering Islander* (1792: 57).

[14] Of many examples, MR 44 (1771): 173 excluded *Louisa* (1771: 24) from 'the first rank in this order of books'. CR 63 (1787): 308, considered Elizabeth Helme's *Louisa* (1787: 37) in terms of 'the numerous productions of this class'. Thomas Holcroft and Ralph Griffiths regarded Thomson's *Major Piper* (1793: 40) as in the 'meanest of the class of novels', MR n.s. 14 (1794): 465.

[15] Including (amongst many) 1770: 21 (CR); 1771: 2 (MR); 1778: 14 (MR); 1788: 36 (CR, MR); 1789: 54 (CR). Samuel Badcock reviewing Catherine Parry's *Eden Vale* (1784: 21) includes a reference to the botanical lower orders. Degree is also associated with the rank and class of readers—see for example MR on 1770: 29, and MR on 1793: 39.

[16] Including CR on 1772: 31; CR on 1777: 16; CR and MR on 1788: 56; and CR on 1789: 10; CR on 1793: 43, CR on 194: 35 (a 'decent rank in the circulating libraries'), CR on 1795: 45 (amongst many others—in one year alone, CR on 1791: 21, 31, 68, 69).

[17] Novels issued in different volumes over successive seasons are given one entry (e.g. Harriet and Sophia Lee, *Canterbury Tales*, 1797: 51); on rare occasions, novels with longer intervals between an original and a continuation (able to stand alone in its own right) are separated (e.g. Sophia Lee, *The Recess*, 1783: 15 and 1785: 37).

copy of a novel title is known to survive—even after exhaustive research—literary records have been trawled to reconstruct as far as possible details of the missing book. Resources range from newspaper advertisements,[18] periodical reviews,[19] and references in other surviving works by the same author or bookseller.[20] Where no copy of an edition survives, any bookseller's advertisement has to be supported by other firm evidence of publication (most notably by periodical review verification) before the edition is included in this bibliography. Past attempts at a listing of this sort have often been deceived by the puffs of eighteenth-century booksellers, by generic titles in circulating library catalogues, and by attempts of writers of the period to persuade of the existence of an unwritten or unpublished book.

Identification of surviving eighteenth-century literature has been greatly assisted in recent years by the progress of the ESTC. As explained above, the ESTC is unable to offer guidance on categories of literature, and notably not on the novel; but it remains, together with *OCLC WorldCat*, an invaluable source for the location of surviving copies. Research for this volume (particularly that derived from newspaper advertisements) has, however, offered new corrections, many of which were sent on to update the continuing ESTC.[21] Further revisions are offered below, particularly where the copy examined is not listed in ESTC. As explained in the general introduction, a precise formula is followed for listing holding libraries also listed in ESTC. Where, in the case of novels with few existing copies, further copies of works not listed in ESTC have been discovered, these are added to our list of holding libraries. Revisions are also often made to format and page number information as given by ESTC. The NSTC is a very different resource to ESTC and although a useful guide to the location of particular titles, it is not a reliable or comprehensive indicator of the number or further details of subsequent editions. NSTC is restricted to particular library collections and entries repeat information in a way which does not allow clear identification of different editions.

---

[18] In each case, verification or new details have been taken from amongst the following: *The Diary; or, Woodfall's Register, The Gazetteer and New Daily Advertiser, The General Evening Post, The London Evening Post, The London Packet; or, New Lloyd's Evening Post, The Morning Chronicle and London Advertiser, The Morning Post, The Oracle, and Public Advertiser, Public Advertiser, Public Ledger, Register of the Times, Star and Daily Evening Advertiser, Stuart's Star and Evening Advertiser, The Whitehall Evening Post,* and *The World, and Fashionable Advertiser.*

[19] Where they carry a review, MR and CR page references are cited in each entry, with any further reviews indicated by a reference to the entry no. in Antonia Forster, *Index to Book Reviews 1749–1774* (Carbondale and Edwardsville, 1990) and *Index to Book Reviews 1775–1799* (London, 1996) (hereafter AF). For convenience, this reference is also given in cases where neither MR nor CR reviewed the novel, but another reviewing journal did notice the novel.

[20] Throughout this essay the term 'bookseller' is used as it was in the eighteenth century, to refer to publisher–booksellers (i.e. those contributing in whole or part to the financing of publication and distribution of the books—also often printed on site) as well as to retailing booksellers. Where confusion might otherwise occur, the terms bookseller–publisher and retailing bookseller are used.

[21] Research for this volume uncovered many dozen surviving titles which have since been sent on to ESTC, many more corrections and additions (including for example, redating Anna Maria Mackenzie's *Monmouth* to 1790). Some 60 of the novels with surviving copies remain to be recorded by ESTC at the time of going to press (Aug. 1998).

We must, however, stress the rarity of many of the novels recorded below. Many of the titles listed survive world-wide in only one known copy. For the 1780s alone, unique responsibilities attend the libraries holding (amongst many other such titles) Miss Edwards's *Otho and Rutha* (1780: 15), Miss Elliott's *History of the Hon. Mrs Rosemont and Sir Henry Cardigan* (1781: 17), John Robinson's *Love Fragments* (1782: 19), Anna Maria Mackenzie's *Burton-Wood* (1783: 16), William Godwin's *Imogen* (1784: 16), John Dent's *Force of Love* (1785: 28), Mrs Cartwright's *Platonic Marriage* (1786: 20), Susanna Rowson's *Victoria* (1786: 39), Elizabeth Tomlins's *Victim of Fancy* (1787: 51), George Wright's *Unfortunate Lovers* (1788: 80), Ann Howell's *Mount Pelham* (1789: 47), and Jean-Claude Gorjy's *Louis and Nina* (1789: 45). Of other notable examples, the only remaining copy of *Norman and Bertha* of 1790 resides in private hands in southern Australia where it was imported by the present owner's great grandmother, having once, according to its book-label, been the prized possession of a captain in the 28th Light Dragoons.[22] From 1790 neither of the two novels translated from the French novels of Jean-Claude Gorjy survives in more than one copy world-wide. As the following entries record, dozens of single or very rare copies of English novels of the period are now preserved in the guardianship of diverse institutions stretching from Wisbech to Warsaw and from San Diego, California, to Auckland, New Zealand.

Less fortunately, not a single copy appears to survive of 133 or almost a tenth of the total novels published between 1770 and 1799 (although of these a dozen or so have surviving later editions). Forty-one of the lost novels were published in the 1770s, 43 in the 1780s, and 49 in the 1790s. No pattern to the loss and survival rate seems obvious. All novels published[23] in three years—1776, 1783, and 1784—survive in at least one copy. By contrast, 13 of the novels published in 1771 have vanished, as have 13 from 1788, 12 from 1789, 10 from 1790 and 10 from 1792. Fifty-three, or more than one in ten of the total novel titles definitely known to have been published between 1788 and 1792 inclusively, can no longer be read. Most of the lost novels remain unassociated with any particular author, but a substantial number (41 of the 133 ones that have disappeared) are by known authors.

In certain cases titles and reviews suggest that the artistic loss is bearable,[24] but there are also some distinguished casualties. Amongst the more unfortunate writers in this respect is Martha Hugill, whose *Countess of Hennebon* (1789: 49) and

---

[22] The editors are greatly indebted to Miss Mollie C. Depledge, its present custodian.

[23] That is, according to the practice adopted in the following entries, with an imprint of that year. In numerous cases novels were actually published in the previous calendar year but post-dated to retain freshness. This does mean, of course that such novels were 'published' in the year of their imprint, in the eighteenth-century sense of available and circulating, but it also means that post-dated novels might also be included in tallies for the earlier year (see discussion below).

[24] Of the lost novels, *Coquetilla; or, Envy its own Scourge* (1771: 10), *The Prudent Orphan* (1774: 20), *The Penitent Prostitute* (1788: 27), *The Recluse of the Appenines* (1792: 53), and *An Olio of Good Breeding* (1797: 79) do not sound promising; while the *Monthly* found *The Frailties of Fashion* (1782: 6) 'equally remarkable for its stupidity and obscenity', *The History of Philario and Clementina* (1777: 4) 'too stupid, and vulgar, for particular criticism', and in the lost *Perplexities of Riches* (1770: 31) 'no circumstances that render it in the smallest degree interesting or valuable'.

Juliana Ormeston (1793: 22), are both lost, as are novels by Phebe Gibbes (1777: 11), Susannah Minifie Gunning (1796: 48), Mary Pilkington (1799: 74), Regina Maria Roche (1793: 38), Jane Timbury (1789: 70), and Elizabeth Sophia Tomlins (1785: 45). The quality of Anna Maria Mackenzie's well-reviewed *Calista* of 1789 can now only be suggested by a surviving 1798 French translation. Also commended by the critics and also lost is the original 1780 London edition of Elizabeth Blower's *Parsonage House*, although a Dublin reprint does survive. Another missing novel, *Lord Winworth; or, the Memoirs of a Heir* (1787: 16), was puffed at the time of publication in a series of advertisements claiming that an initial impression of 1,500 copies had sold in a month—'a Circumstance scarcely to be equalled in the Memory of Man'. The productions of Treyssac de Vergy, usually styled 'Councillor of the Parlement, Paris', regularly infuriated the periodical reviewers, but we are now unable to validate the criticism for many of his most infamous productions (1770: 39; 1771: 55; and 1772: 41; with 1771: 54 unavailable in the first edition). Lost novels whose critical reception suggests that their rediscovery would be welcome include the Sternian *Extract from the Life of Lieutenant Henry Foley* (1782: 4), *The History of Henrietta Mortimer* (1787: 14), *Frederic and Louisa* (1792: 16), the Gothic *Cavern of Death* (1794: 6), and the curiosity piece (see below) *The Indiscreet Marriage* (1779: 14).

Defining the Novel

What, however, was a novel in this period? While, manifestly, its definition determines what is included in this bibliography, the range of publications that contemporaries originally regarded as 'novels' is extremely diverse. As already noted in the general introduction, because this is a first edition bibliography, reworkings of older publications, including translations, are excluded. These omissions include the 1771 *Pupil of Nature* and 1786 *Sincere Huron*, both versions of Voltaire's *l'Ingenu*, first translated into English in 1768.[25] *The History of Mademoiselle de Beleau or the New Roxana* of 1775 shadowed a translation of *Roxana* of 1724 and is therefore omitted, as are extracts from much older collections such as those packaged in the 1799 *Story of Al Raoui, A Tale from the Arabic* and other versions of the *Arabian Nights*. Included, however, are antique derivatives where at least part of the story was translated for the first time. These include the retelling of a section of Ovid's *Metamorphoses* as *The Samians* (1771: 32), the English translation of the thirteenth-century Persian classic of Sadi, published as *Select Fables from Gulistan* (1773: 37), and the English translation from the French version of *Eustathius* (1788: 52).

Amongst apparently new titles were many fraudulent attempts to persuade the public that an old work was in fact freshly minted. Where identified, these retreads are also omitted from the bibliography, although a note of explanation is usually provided. One such exclusion is the 1774 offering of Charles Pinot-Duclos, *The Pleasures of Retirement*. Its title declared it to be 'now first translated from the

[25] Raven, *British Fiction* entry no. 1239 (hereafter JR no.).

original French' but it had in fact appeared under a different title (*The Confession of Count de Harcourt*) in the 1740s. Francis Noble's *Amoranda* of 1785 was said to be by a clergyman's widow but was actually a blatant reissue of Mary Davys's *Reform'd Coquet* of 1724. Although William Enfield, reviewing for the *Monthly*, failed to spot it, the *Critical* did identify John Murray's 1786 publication, the anonymous *Adventures of George Maitland, Esq.*, as Edward Kimber's *James Ramble* of 1754: 'The names are changed; the story, with the minutest incidents, is the same ... This literary imposture deserves the severest reprehension; and the harshest term in our language may be aptly applied to it. We have done our duty in detecting the plagiarist.'[26] Three years later the *Critical* accused *Fanny Vernon* of being 'republications from *Magazines*, or *vamped* up from *older volumes*', further declaring that 'long experience has made us suspicious'.[27]

Novelists were not unaware of the caution required in crossing the line between imitation and direct borrowing. An advertisement opposite the opening page of *The Interesting Story of Edwin and Julia* (1788: 19) warned that 'the sentences which the Author has been obliged to borrow from other Productions are printed without a Mark of Quotation'. So far unproven review allegations of plagiarism included those levelled at *The Lady's Tale* (1786: 7) and *Fatality* (1796: 8), but sharp practice was not always the cause of borrowings. Derivative plots and episodes abound in these works, with many writers not consciously intending to deceive. This contemporary uncertainty about how much reuse of material was acceptable causes further difficulties in deciding which novels to include as first editions in this bibliography. No satisfactory line can ever be drawn, but an attempt has to be made to exclude the more obvious deceits and to include those with inadvertent or only modest borrowing ('echoes of echoes, and shadows of shades', as the *Monthly* described a novel by Mrs Fogerty[28]). Examples of exclusions from this bibliography include *The Story of David Doubtful* published by Vernor and Hood in 1798, but comprising little more than an extract from Henry Brooke's *Fool of Quality*. Where new material is added to old stock we have erred on the side of generosity. Amongst the listings, for example, is *The Oxonian* (1771: 30), said by a critical reviewer to have deceived its bookseller because it was partly taken from an earlier work. Inclusions stretch to the anonymous 1786 *Appearance is Against Them* (itself a title later borrowed for a play by Elizabeth Inchbald), despite its shadowing of Voltaire's *L'Ecossaise*, and to Francis Noble's extremely posthumous issue of *The History of Leonora Meadowson* (1788: 55), partly, at least, by Eliza Haywood (d. 1756), if based by her on past work. Also included is Henry Pye's *Spectre* with its copying of at least two earlier ghost-sighting episodes from *The Sylph* (1779: 8) and (apparently) *The*

[26] CR 60 (1785): 394.
[27] *Fanny Vernon, or the Forlorn Hope* 1789: 8. The AR also thought that it was the same work as *The American Hunter* (1788: 5), but this cannot now be verified as no copy of the 1788 novels appears to survive. We have decided to include both titles in our listings. This is amongst the most problematic of such decisions, with no evidence available about the exact extent of the borrowing. A similar doubt concerns 1785: 18.
[28] MR 49 (1773): 150 on *The Fatal Connexion* (1773: 32).

Apparition (1788: 7).[29] Rather than extensive and deliberate plagiarism, the *Spectre* is more guilty of a weak borrowing of narrative incidents. Like George Walker's hotch-potch, *The Romance of the Cavern* (1793: 44), the models were too exposed. The translated *Man of Nature* by Lafontaine (1799: 62) was based on *Rasselas* and a thirty-year old French novel. Parts of Henry Summersett's *Probable Incidents* (1797: 77) bore close resemblance to *Roderick Random*.

More positively, many variant genres were still regarded during this period as members of the extended 'novel' family, even if the boundaries were difficult ones. Although chapbooks and very short chapbook-like romances are very different in quality to the new novel (and are therefore excluded from this bibliography), booksellers were not averse to the occasional borrowing of forms. *Perjured Lover* (1790: 25), for example, with its multiple lines of title summarizing the entire contents, resembles a very old-fashioned petty romance. The style and contents of small books like the *History of Miss Harriot Fairfax* (1780: 4), *Louisa Wharton* (1780: 9), and Theophilus James Bacon's *Maid of the Farm* (1784: 10), bridge older romance forms and the developing novel. Many tales so apparently different from fashionable domestic and sentimental fiction such as the English version of Raspe's *Baron Munchausen's Narrative of his Marvellous Travels* (1786: 38), imitated the design of the new novel, especially in expanded later editions. Some novels published in parts in the magazines also started life as separate editions; others remained serial publications (and hence are excluded from this bibliography).[30]

The exclusion of factually based memoirs, biographies, and political satires from lists of semi-fictionalized 'novels' depends on subtle interpretation, then and now. Much writing about real life is obvious but there are many productions requiring careful consideration. Captain Richard Muller's *Memoirs of the Right Honourable Lord Viscount Cherington*, for example (1782: 18), appears to be about a real person, but the named landed family is untraceable, and the plot soon incorporates an increasingly improbable series of miraculous discoveries including that of a long-lost brother—'you will easily know him, he has the mark of ripe guava on his left breast'.[31] Several novels, such as the *Memoirs of an Unfortunate Lady of Quality* (1774: 16) and the controversial *Letters to and from the Countess du Barry* (1779: 16), embroidered liberally upon real-life romances. Sir Herbert Croft's *Love and Madness* (1780: 14) was based on a recent murder committed by a clergyman; *Belle Widows* (1789: 66) partly retold the colourful past of its author, Margaret Rudd, recent mistress of Boswell, former society prostitute, former lover of a financial speculator, and then partner to his forger brother, before she was tried with them in a forgery case ending in their hanging and her acquittal. Historical fiction must also be divided as

[29] *The Apparition* is lost; the accusation is made by CR 68 (1789): 76.

[30] Amongst notable examples, Joseph Trapp's translation of *Alexis* in 31 parts in the *Lady's Magazine* 1791–1793. For novels published separately but also in magazine parts, references are given within the entries to Robert D. Mayo, *The English Novel in the Magazines 1740–1815* (Evanston: Northwestern University Press, 1962).

[31] Richard Muller, *Memoirs of the Right Honourable Lord Viscount Cherington* (1782: 18), 2: 377. A ripe guava is of strawberry-coloured hue.

best as possible from straightforward histories wrapped in the covers of novels. Omitted from this bibliography is Bicknell's 1776 *History of Edward Prince of Wales*, noted by the *Critical* as 'written in manner of a novel' but firmly categorized by the review as a miscellany. Bicknell's *History of Lady Anne Neville* of the same year (1776: 7) is more of a fiction, as is his *Prince Arthur*, published three years later. Even if somewhat derivative (a novelizing of Spenser), *Prince Arthur* (1779: 6) was judged by the reviewers to profit the sort of readers unlikely to be familiar with the original.

Political satire also operates in different gradations. *The Characters of the Present Most Celebrated Courtezans*, published in 1780, is not included in this bibliography, along with many similar barely disguised guides to political and sexual scandals of the day. Sometimes however these incidents are embedded within a more subtle novel form. Among the more transparent satirical novels were those contributing to the gossip of town and country, including *The Divorce* (1771: 12) and *Harriet: or, the Innocent Adultress* (1771: 18), both jests on the infamous Grosvenor divorce case of 1770. Readers of *The Expedition of Little Pickle* (1792: 13) would not have missed the nickname allusion to the actress Dora Jordan, recently notorious for the beginning of her affair with the Duke of Clarence, the future William IV. Other examples of topical scandal novels include the 1771 *Vicar of Bray*, the 1782 *Genuine Anecdotes and Amorous Adventures of Sir Richard Easy, and Lady Wagtail*, and the 1784 *Modern Atalantis*, as well as various offerings—such as the anonymous 1792 *Excursions of Osman*—whose jokes were so recondite that they baffled even the reviewers. The 1775 *Correspondents*, purportedly concerning Lord Lyttleton and the widow of the Governor of Bombay, was believed to be genuine by both Horace Walpole and the *Monthly* reviewer, although the *Critical* was clear that it was fiction and a novel. The *Letters between an Illustrious Personage and a Lady of Honour at B******** (1785: 10) targets the Prince of Wales and Mrs Fitzherbert, but was apparently regarded as more tedious than offensive.[32]

Amongst other inclusion difficulties confronted by this bibliography, two categories stand out. The first is the novel or tale for children, the second the travel memoirs and multifarious publications spawned by the popularity of Sterne's *Sentimental Journey* of 1768. There is no satisfactory solution to these boundary disputes, given that the term 'novel', however well-used in the late eighteenth century, can never be defined with absolute precision. The decision taken in this volume is to include novels for juveniles and young persons, but to exclude publications more clearly intended to be read to very young children. In cases where ambiguity remains publications are listed in an appendix, the first part of which is devoted to children's works. Where the novel for children is apparently designed for adolescents and young people, the work is entered in the main section of the bibliography. Humble tales of improvement for youth are close kin to the adult novel proper, especially given the tender years of many of the novelists themselves. Main listings therefore include novels such as Joachim Heinrich Campe's *New Robinson Crusoe*

----

[32] CR 60 (1785): 399; MR 73 (1785): 73.

(1788: 47), Elizabeth Pinchard's *The Two Cousins* (1794: 45), and Mary Pilkington's *Tales of the Cottage; or Stories, Moral and Amusing for Young Persons* (1798: 56). The full title of *The Contrast* (1787: 4) assured the public that it was written for the benefit not only of Sunday school pupils but of intelligent servants. In similar vein, reviewers emphasized that many young persons' novels might be read by older readers. Elizabeth Moody in the *Monthly* commented of de Genlis's *Young Exiles* (1799: 41) that 'The letters before us, though addressed to young persons and written principally for their amusement and instruction, are by no means so frivolous as to preclude those of maturer years from a participation of the repast.'[33] Although many tales designed for young children (and most published by the Newberys and by John Marshall and Co. of Aldermary Churchyard) are excluded altogether, perhaps the most famous early children's tale, *Sandford and Merton*, is fully listed in the appendix, as are works by Mary Ann Kilner, Charlotte Sanders, and Elizabeth Griffin.

Also excluded from the main listings are imitations and sequels not reviewed as novels or otherwise not generally regarded as novels, including miscellaneous direct derivatives from Scripture and classical mythology. This is not, however, to marginalize novels inspired by other literary works but standing independent of them. Many Sterne imitations and derivatives, such as Samuel Jackson Pratt's *Travels for the Heart* (1777: 15), William Combe's *Letters Between Two Lovers* (1781: 15), and the translation of Diderot's *Jacques le fataliste*, a work commonly regarded at the time as a Shandeian fantasy (1797: 35), are all given main entries. Included in the appendix are Combe's *Letters Supposed to have been Written by Yorick and Eliza*, the spurious continuation of Sterne's *Letters from Yorick to Eliza*, and the 1788 *Continuation of Yorick's Sentimental Journey*. The appendices also allow listings for Anna Maria Mackenzie's *Joseph* of 1783, a simple reworking of the biblical tale, but one that followed her successful novel, *Burton-Wood* and was given prominence in the title-page of her next, *The Gamesters* (1786: 33). A similar work, also in the appendix, is Hall's *Death of Cain* of 1789. Excluded even from the appendix, however, are romance miscellanies, such as Francesco Algarotti's *The Congress of Cythera* published by Kearsley in 1783 and derived from a 1744 Italian allegorical fable.

In a number of particularly difficult cases the review notice is used as final arbiter. The 1777 *History of the Curate of Cramen*, for example, appears to be a personal memoir with a careerist agenda—and one published by subscription. It was reviewed as a novel by the *Critical* and placed under 'novels and memoirs' by the *Monthly*. Similarly, the *Authentic and Interesting Memoirs of Miss Ann Sheldon* of 1787 might suggest autobiography, but the work was reviewed as a novel. Where a publication has not survived in its first edition (or not at all), the initial review category is even more significant, as, for example, in the case of the *Genuine and Entertaining Memoirs of a Well-Known Woman of Intrigue* (1787: 9).[34]

Even at the time, it was often impossible to agree on a general classification for

---

[33] MR n.s., 33 (1800), pp. 101–2.
[34] MR 77 (1787): 327. In one case (1797: 15), a surviving novel styled 'the second edition' is included where no first edition can be traced (and no review appeared of either) on the grounds that this topical

many of these variegated publications. As the *Critical* lamented of *Melwin Dale* (1786: 9): 'Is it new? Is it old? We confess we do not know.'[35] It is one of the challenges taken up by this bibliography, and—always allowing for the warnings about inclusion criteria given above—this introduction can provide some simple tallies of categories and author and publishing profiles. The basic summary of the production of new novels in this period, as listed in detail in the entries below, is given by Table 1, together with Figure 1 (charting a five-year moving average).

Table 1. **Publication of New Novels in Britain and Ireland, 1770–1799**

Year	Total	Year	Total	Year	Total
1770	40	1780	24	1790	74
1771	60	1781	22	1791	74
1772	41	1782	22	1792	58
1773	39	1783	24	1793	45
1774	35	1784	24	1794	56
1775	31	1785	47	1795	50
1776	17	1786	40	1796	91
1777	18	1787	51	1797	79
1778	16	1788	80	1798	75
1779	18	1789	71	1799	99
	315		405		701
					1,421

7

Table 1 suggests a sharply fluctuating annual publication rate, somewhat tempered by allowance for certain differences between the year cited in the imprint (and the year under which the novel is listed in this bibliography) and the actual time of publication. It certainly cautions against an over-literal interpretation of this table. The practice of post-dating was common, designed to extend the currency of the novel. In some cases, novels printed and published in August, or, in one case, as early as April, gave the date of the following year.[36] In addition, a publishing season extended from November to May, spanning the division of the calendar year. Even so, bumper 'imprint years' like 1771 stand out, before a steep decline in novel production in the late 1770s followed by a strong rally from the late 1780s. A slight dip in the mid 1790s precedes a late-century surge in novel output. The moving average

novel is clearly recent and that it should be recorded. It might even be the case that the style 'second edition' was a promotional ploy by the bookselling partners, one in London and one in the country.

[35] CR 61 (1786): 235.

[36] See, for example, *The Happy Release* (1787: 11) and *The Minor* (1788: 23). There are also some troublesome cases—notably 1770: 21 where a title-page imprint of 1770 might well be an error given other evidence suggesting a 1772 publication, and 1790: 33 where the only evidence for a 1790 release is the date given by the MR reviewer which again (in the face of all other evidence suggesting 1791) might be erroneous.

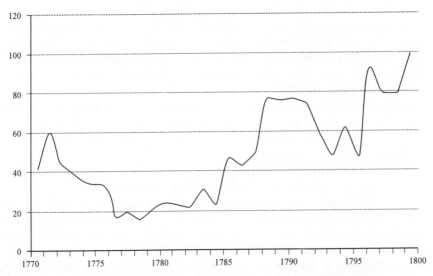

Fig. 1. Publication of New Novels in Britain and Ireland, 1770–1799: Five-Year Moving Average

charted by Figure 1 shows more clearly the general trends. These are marked. The malaise in new novel production seems to have lasted from about 1775 to 1783, co-terminous, perhaps incidentally, with the American war. General publication rates, at least as determined by the annual number of titles of printed items given by ESTC,[37] suggest no such downturn; but what it was that so depressed novel production in these years currently remains unexplained. Perhaps a reaction had set in to a decade or more of numerous poorly produced novels; perhaps reprints (or the issue of large editions of fewer new novels) compensated for temporary artistic exhaustion; perhaps other fictional forms—notably poetry and drama—achieved greater relative popularity in these years. More certainly, the recovery from the late 1780s can be explained by the energies of a new generation of novelists, by more translations into English of French and German novels, by new emphasis on the female novelist and reader, by the increased number and activities of circulating libraries, and by the marketing panache of a new generation of booksellers.

These novels certainly did not comprise an homogeneous group. The 1,421 novels detailed in this bibliography encompass a striking variety of plots, settings, characters, and styles of narrative. Some novels are set in an ageless land of nowhere in particular; others are located in a very specific time and place; some (probably because of borrowed models) reek of the manners and interests of past generations; many others are packed with fashionable referents, a few deliberate spin-offs from

---

[37] James Raven, *The Commercialization of the Book*, ch. 1.

the latest craze. *The Adventures of Alonso* attempts to debate contemporary Portuguese politics in 1775 (as, in part, does Muller's novel of 1782); the recent war is the backdrop to *The American Hunter* (1788: 5); and Calcutta, much in the news in the years of the Hastings trial, pervades Phebe Gibbes's *Hartly House* (1789: 41). In 1785 *The Aerostatic Spy: or, Excursions with a Air Balloon* trailed the first manned air balloon flight by the Montgolfier brothers in 1783. Far less exhausting are the contemplative characters of *Sempronia* (1790: 26), whose plot, indeed, has claims to be the most slender of any of the period. In others, however, adventures and digressions are so rapid that the skip of a few pages will obliterate whole series of confessions, reunions, and deaths.

Many novels are domestic dramas where heroines blush, swoon, or face unbearable social ostracism because of minor breaches of decorum; in others, exotic narratives relate daring and near-pornographic activity. The hero is separated from his Testament in *The Rambles of Mr Frankly* and from his testicles in *The Methodist Lady*; the knaves of *Euphemia* are condemned for refusing to drink tea without the extravagance of cream, but the crime of the villain of *Louisa* is so shocking that it can be described only by her final agonies: 'her face swelled, and all her features distended; a white froth bubbling out of her parched and livid mouth; and her large eyes, red and glassy, were rolling from side to side'.[38] No such reticence attends the cavortings in the *Adventures of Christopher Curious* (1788: 2). Many review verdicts anticipating national moral catastrophe might be dismissed as po-faced over-reaction, but some of the novels do contain episodes approaching more modern definitions of the obscene—some marvellously so. Just as we should not be too condescending in laughing away the more strident protestations against inelegant writing and the unguided representation of indelicate conduct, so we should not overlook the earthy voyeurism of novels like *The Nun* (1771: 28), *The Adventures of a Speculist* (1788: 74) or the alleged pornography of lost novels like *Frailties of Fashion* (1782: 6), *The Victim of Deception* (1788: 39), and *The Adventures of Christopher Curious* (1788: 2). The latter, according to the *English Review* 'would disgrace the police of any civilised country upon earth. The mind who could rake together from brothels such a nauseous collection of filth, must be yet more depraved than even the miscreant he would describe'.[39] Other volumes, from the *Adventures . . . of Timothy Ginnadrake* (1770: 29) to *The Laughable Adventures of Charles and Lisette* (1796: 10), continue the tradition of tavern humour and juvenile bawdiness. As worldly in a different sense are the astonishing expeditions offered by the *Travels of Hildebrand Bowman* (1778: 7), *Baron Munchausen's . . . Marvellous Travels* (1786: 38), and William Thomson's *Mammuth* (1787: 69), the latter greatly enlivened by monsters and giants. Several novels resist all categorization. Satires, but also a variety of polemical novels, featured idealized and imaginary worlds, from the translation of Guillaume-Hyacinthe Bougeant's Arcadian *Travels of Prince Fan-Feredin* (1789: 35) to *Modern Gulliver's Travels* (1796: 46). It is difficult to define *The Modern*

---

[38] *Louisa* (1790: 16), 2: 146.   [39] EngR 14 (1789): 470.

Hero in the Kingdom of Cathai: In the Year 90000 published pseudonymously in 1791. *The Pleasing Companion* of 1788 is a curious hotchpotch of styles. *The School Candidates* (1788: 48), by one Henry Clarke of Salford, mystified its critic in the *Monthly Review* and is still a reading challenge.

Within this diverse pageant certain broad characteristics were identified by commentators and reviewers seeking to define a novel. One key component, despite the more fantastic of the creations, was credibility. The violation of this, much though it continued, was deemed proof of artistic failure. Reviewers warmly applauded Clara Reeve's intention, in the *Champion of Virtue* (1777: 16) of 'going into the marvellous without transgressing the bounds of credibility'.[40] Reeve herself believed that 'the Novel is a picture of real life and manners, and of the times in which it is written'.[41] The *Critical* approved Indiana Brooks's 1789 *Eliza Beaumont and Harriet Osborne* because 'nothing is greatly exaggerated, or raised beyond credibility'.[42] In a number of cases, as highlighted by the notes section of the entries below, the acceptance of realism was not agreed. Amongst many such examples, the authenticity of the 1790 *Memoirs of Maria, A Persian Slave* divided its critics. The *Monthly* dismissed the novel as the product of an overwrought mind, but the *Critical* believed that 'the little improbabilities which appear may arise from our ignorance of Eastern customs, or be owing to the European additions, retouchings which may have been supposed necessary to adapt them for the "English market".[43] As the critics also observed, novelists regularly over-stretched claims of authenticity, especially in constructing historical fiction. The most popular vehicle was the miraculously recovered manuscript. Typical of these bravely titled efforts, all apparently appealing to antiquarian chic, were the 1792 *The Rock of Modrec, or, the Legend of Sir Eltram: An Ethical Romance. Translated from an Ancient British Manuscript, lately discovered among the ruins of an Abbey in North Wales* and the 1799 *Azalais and Aimar; A Provencal History of the Thirteenth Century; From an Ancient Manuscript.* Less obviously artful but in many ways just as contrived were the increasing number of historical tales, notably James White's *Earl Strongbow* (1789: 71), his *Adventures of John of Gaunt* (1790: 72), and his *Adventures of King Richard Coeur-de-Lion* (1791: 72), or the more modest and anonymous *Lady Jane Grey* (1791: 17). As will be discussed further below, however, it was the new popularity of the Gothic novel that was to put realism to its greatest trial. In the hands of its most assured exponents it was an examination to be enjoyed for its own sake.

Besides credibility, the other acknowledged virtue was the ability to communicate knowledge and wisdom. Aspiring novelists took severe note. As Mary Julia Young reflected, 'I have invariably, to the extent of my abilities, endeavoured to render the strictest observance of the relative duties indispensable [*sic*] to amiable and sensible characters, and to inculcate virtue, fortitude, and benevolence by the most engaging examples.' Phebe Gibbes claimed that she wrote 'to convey some

---

[40] CR 44 (1777): 154.   [41] Reeve, *Progress of Romance*, 1: 111.
[42] CR 67 (1789), pp. 397–8.   [43] CR n.s., 1 (1791), pp. 349–50.

moral values for amusing Literature, Novels, to young and inexperienced minds as an antidote, to the best of my skills, for the Poison in general Instances believed to be imbibed therefrom'.[44] Where the marriage of instruction and entertainment seemed unequal and to favour diversion, critics of the novel reserved their remaining plaudits for its being innocent entertainment.[45] Originality in such writing was especially praised. Even if this required deft distinction from the 'tonnish' whimsy so decried by the reviewers, critical acclaim for novelty reinforced condemnation of plagiarism and dullness. It might also ward off another common charge against these novels—that they were not only 'hackneyed' and 'insipid', but 'trifling' and 'worthless'.[46] Delicacy was the cardinal quality.[47] The *Adventures of a Cork-Screw* (1775: 1) was 'coarse', the *Indian Adventurer* (1780: 6), was rejected as 'vulgar and indelicate' and 'insufferably coarse', the love scenes in *Agitation* (1788: 3) were dismissed as 'so coarsely, so very inelegantly delineated . . . they can only awaken disgust'.[48] Critics frequently related such entreaties for politeness to standards of grammar and expression. Characteristically, the *Critical* dismissed the anonymous *William and Charles* (1789: 30) as 'deformed by inelegant provincialisms'.[49] Elizabeth Blower was accused of including 'ladyisms' in *Features from Life* (1788: 44).[50] A large proportion of the review notices condemned stylistic vulgarities and an ignorance and neglect of grammar.[51] The *Critical* advised readers of *The Launch* (1796: 11) that 'they must have recourse to Johnson's Dictionary, to discover the sense of nineteen out of twenty of the words'.[52]

In terms of structure, the most distinctive type of novel was that written in letters. The epistolary novel in English enjoyed a distinguished history from the early models of Richardson to the translations of Grafigny, Le Prince de Beaumont, and Riccoboni.[53] Its renown was in part a consequence of these eminent archetypes, although it has also been suggested that first-person prose writing within the apparently verifiable document was the product of moral doubt.[54] More certainly, the novel-in-letters was an easy form to adopt for the inexperienced or unimaginative writer. Potentially, it was the most serviceable for domestic and credible settings. As a result, its popularity was assured. In the words of the *Monthly*, endorsing the 1771

---

[44] M. J. Young to the Royal Literary Fund, 20 Mar. 1808 (RLF 6: 216); Phebe Gibbes to the Royal Literary Fund, 17 Oct. 1804 (RLF 2: 74).

[45] Of many examples, MR 62 (1780), pp. 323–34, of *Letters Between Clara and Antonia* (1780: 8).

[46] See, for example, the positive reviews to 1775: 7, 1779: 2, 1779: 7 and 1787: 46 (and by contrast, 1777: 1).

[47] Note, for example, the critical unanimity about 1783: 24.

[48] MR 52 (1775): 557; CR 51 (1780): 319; MR 63 (1780): 233; MR 81 (1789): 460.

[49] CR 68 (1789): 494.

[50] MR 78 (1788): 531; these expressions excepted the novel was deemed 'pleasing and correct'.

[51] In just one year, for example, the critical reviews of 1789: 6, 9, 14, 31, 32, 46, and 58.

[52] CR n.s., 16 (1796): 472.

[53] Robert A. Day, *Told in Letters: Epistolary Fiction before Richardson* (Ann Arbor, 1966); Frank Gees Black, *The Epistolary Novel in the late Eighteenth Century* (Eugene, 1940); and for the early decades of the century, Ruth Perry, *Women, Letters, and the Novel* (New York, 1980).

[54] Perry, *Women, Letters, and the Novel*, p. xi.

Fatal Compliance, 'the epistolary form is become the high mode of modern romance'. The following estimates, based on the entries in this volume, will, if anything, understate the extent of epistolary fiction given the number of novels with no surviving copy and where reviews or advertisements give no comment upon narrative form. Where titles to lost novels indicate 'in letters' these works are included in the epistolary tally, but the absence of this description is no certain indication that a novel was not written in letters. With this minor warning in mind, we can say that between 1750 and 1760 new novels in letters averaged no more than a tenth of the annual total of new fiction, but by 1766 and 1768 nearly one quarter annually and in 1769 more than one third of all new novel titles were epistolary.[55] As shown by Table 2, at least 30 per cent of all novels published between 1770 and 1790 were in letters. Epistolary novels with imprint dates of 1776, 1777, 1779, 1780, 1781, 1783 and 1784 comprised at least half the annual novel output, and often far more (in 1776 a year of relatively few publications, more than two-thirds of the titles were epistolary novels). The average for both the 1770s and 1780s was remarkably consistent. Just over 40 per cent of all novels from those decades were published in letter form. The turning-point seems to have been in 1791 when only 15 (or about a fifth) of the 74 novels published that year were in letters, and this proportion remained about the same until a further decline to some 10 per cent of the total for each of the three years 1797–1799. By the final years of the century, the epistolary form had lost its popularity, swamped, it seems by the diversity and directness of new historical and Gothic narratives that were not well-suited to relation by imaginary letters.

The other continuing novel genre at the beginning of this period, even though it was to maintain only token representation, was the 'Adventures of' tale. These spy novels had flourished at least since the popularity of Coventry's *Pompey the Little* of 1751 and Haywood's *Invisible Spy* of 1755. The run-away success of Charles Johnston's *Chrysal or The Adventures of a Guinea* had ensured a further generation of Adventure novels, most of which met with critical contempt.[56] The later Adventures included those of a corkscrew (1775: 1), of a hackney coach (1781: 1), and of a rupee (1782: 20). It was said by the *Critical* to be a mode 'almost exhausted' by the time of the 1783 *Phantoms: or, the Adventures of a Gold-Headed Cane*, but the occasional title continued to appear. *The Memoirs and Adventures of a Flea* was published in 1785, *Adventures of a Watch* in 1788, and *Adventures of a Pin* in 1796. Novels such as *The Adventures of Lucifer in London* (1786: 1) extended what were by now rather weary satires of Le Sage and the *Devil Upon Two Sticks*.

In contrast to this declining novel form, the clear fashion-leader of the period was the sentimental novel. Sentiment claimed Richardsonian credentials, but sentimentalism was also reprocessed by Sterne's *Sentimental Journey* and refined by Henry Mackenzie's immensely popular *Man of Feeling* in 1771. William Russell's *Sentimental Tales* of 1771, still associated with Sterne in the reviews, launched a

---

[55] Raven, *British Fiction*, p. 12.   [56] See Raven, *British Fiction*, pp. 11–12.

Table 2.　Publication of Epistolary Fiction, 1770–1799

Imprint Year	Total Novel Titles	Epistolary Titles	Epistolary Titles as % of Total Year
1770	40	14	35
1771	60	21	35
1772	41	20	49
1773	39	17	43.6
1774	35	17	48.6
1775	31	12	38.7
1776	17	12	70.6
1777	18	9	50
1778	16	7	43.8
1779	18	9	50
	315	*138*	*43.8*
1780	24	13	54.2
1781	22	12	54.5
1782	22	8	36.4
1783	24	12	50
1784	24	14	58.3
1785	47	20	42.5
1786	40	15	37.5
1787	51	22	43
1788	80	26	32.5
1789	71	27	38
	405	*169*	*41.7*
1790	74	27	36.5
1791	74	15	20.3
1792	58	14	24.1
1793	45	11	24.4
1794	56	12	21.4
1795	50	8	16
1796	91	14	15.4
1797	79	8	10.1
1798	75	8	10.6
1799	99	11	11.1
	701	*128*	*18.3*

prodigious post-Mackenzie melancholia and sensitivity. Only a year later a reviewer was already complaining that the epithet sentimental was used too frequently.[57] As

[57]　CR 33 (1772): 325, of *The Birmingham Counterfeit* (1772: 2).

John Mullan reflects, by the end of the century the description of a novel as 'senti-mental' was as likely to be pejorative as laudatory, but the advertisement of prose fic-tion as Sentimental did not greatly diminish.[58] Sensibility in such novels was embodied by the reactions of heroes and heroines to circumstances designed to evoke fine feelings. The parade of these occasions, as constructed by the novelists, presented opportunities for humanitarian responses, from alleviation of the distress of weeping slaves who hug the knees of the hero in Sarah Scott's 1766 *History of Sir George Ellison* (JR 1038) to assistance for the one-legged (but pertly hopping) pau-per in *Caroline, The Heroine of the Camp* (1790: 6). In the darker (or sometimes more absurd) pages of these novels, excessive sensibility brings on the English dis-ease, although it was the translation of Goethe and the suicide of Werther (1779: 10) that established this as the ultimate expression of the sentimental.

The other most distinctive novel genre, the Gothic, also offered an outlet for the sentimental imagination, as well as for some of the most preposterous plots and his-torical recreations. The compass of the Gothic novel is much expanded by the list-ings of this bibliography.[59] Claims of Horace Walpole's *Castle of Otranto* (JR 868) to the origination of the Gothic novel were reinvoked by his own preface to the 1765 second edition, describing it as 'a new species of romance'. It was also an admission of the puzzled reception this startling work received. Imitations were slow, but boosted by the popularity of Clara Reeve's *Old English Baron* of 1778, first published as *The Champion of Virtue* a year earlier (1777: 16), and setting out, as Reeve herself was to explain, to soften the impact of *Otranto* by introducing a more naturalistic, credible Gothicism. The influence of the original model remained strong, however, and was obvious, amongst others, in *The Apparition* (1788: 7), Joseph Fox's *Tancred* (1791: 37), Ann Radcliffe's *Romance of the Forest* (1791: 58), and *The Castle of St Vallery* (1792: 5). More mock Walpolery came in the mid 1790s with Isabella Kelly's *Abbey of Saint Asaph* (1795: 27), Francis Lathom's *Castle of Ollada* (1795: 28), and Elizabeth Hervey's *Church of St Siffrid* (1797: 44). The Gothic novel now flourished. In a decade of popular translations of horror and 'horrid' tales from the German, home-grown medievalism achieved both new subtlety and extravagance with Lewis's *The Monk* (1796: 63), Godwin's *St Leon* (1799: 42), and novels by Anne Rad-cliffe, including the *Sicilian Romance* (1790: 61) and *The Italian* (1797: 70). Anony-mous mystery novels like *Saint Julian's Abbey* (1788: 32), Radcliffe's *Mysteries of Udolpho* (1794: 47), and John Bird's *Castle of Hardayne* (1795: 12), also contributed to the popularity of 'suspense' and novels full of what the reviewers mocked as 'hair-breadth 'scapes'.[60] Such fiction was, of course, a direct confrontation to cherished notions of the credible, and Gothic transgressions against probability (and often

[58] John Mullan, 'Sentimental Novels,' in John Richetti, ed., *The Cambridge Companion to the Eighteenth-Century Novel* (Cambridge: Cambridge University Press, 1996): 236–54.

[59] Existing and extensive Gothic novel bibliography begins with Montague Summers, *A Gothic Bibliography* (London: Fortune [1948]). See also Maggie Kilgour, *The Rise of the Gothic Novel* (London: Routledge, 1995).

[60] Including Joseph Lavallée, *Maria Cecilia* (1788: 61), *Albertina* (1789: 1), and Eliza Kirkham Mathews, *Arnold Zulig* (1790: 56).

against indecorum) caused problems for the reviewers.[61] The way out, when critics wished to indicate at least some pleasure from reading these novels, was to deem the wonderful 'partly allowable'[62] and even, as wrote the *Critical* about George Moore's *Grasville Abbey* (1797: 58), that 'allowance being made for a foundation of the mysterious sort, probability will not appear to be very grossly violated'.[63]

In the age of the Sentimental and the Gothic the lionizing of several writers led to a succession of imitations and mock sequels. Amongst publications listed in the appendix, Peregrine Phillips's *Sentimental Diary* (1778) was written in imitation of Sterne, as was *Reveries of the Heart* (1781) and *Sentimental Excursions to Windsor* by Leonard Macnally (1781). More broadly influenced by Shandy and Sterne were the *Extract from the Life of Lieutenant Henry Foley* (1782: 4), *Unfortunate Sensibility* (1784: 9), *Memoirs and Opinions of Mr Blenfield* (1790: 20), and the derivative *Letters of Maria* by Miss Street (1790: 68). The anonymous *Man of Failing* (1789: 18) managed reference to three masters. It opened in Sternian style, with pseudo-Shandeian memoirs of early life, but then caught the spirit of Fielding and *Tom Jones*—something increasingly uncommon in this age of sensibility, as the reviewer pointed out.[64] The mock-Mackenzie title echoed more extended satires like James Thistlethwaite's *The Man of Experience* (1778: 15).

Questions of authorship will be discussed in more detail below, but the creation of particular schools of writing in imitation of one or more particular novelists was marked in these years. The contemporary caricature of the novel as a faddish, super-ficial make of literature is validated by many entries in this bibliography. It parades a succession of rushed attempts to mimic the fêted few. Imitations of Richardson, so marked in the 1750s and 1760s, continued to spawn during this period. Most were not distinguished. *Jessy* and *The Undutiful Daughter*, both of 1771, were followed by the pitiable 'farmer's daughter of Gloucestershire''s *Virtue in Distress* in 1772, the *History of Mr Stanly and Miss Temple* in 1773, and, later, the *History of Lord Belford* in 1784 and *The Liberal American* in 1785. The *History of Sir William Harrington* (1771: 20) even claimed to have been revised and corrected by Richardson. A still more remarkable feature of the following listings is the rediscovery of a flock of imi-tators of Frances Burney. *Harcourt: A Sentimental Novel* (1780: 3) was falsely claimed to be 'by the authoress of Evelina'. The *Critical*'s reviewer identified *Oswald Castle* (1788: 25) as 'a production of the Cecilia school'. Other Burneyana of the season included Anne Hughes's *Henry and Isabella* (1788: 59) and Anna Maria Mackenzie's *Retribution* (1788: 63). A year later, the anonymous *Self-Tormentor* (1789: 26) was marked out as of the Burney-school and in *Darnley Vale* (1789: 34) even Mrs Bonhote, according to her *Critical* reviewer, 'steps too nearly in the steps of Cecilia'.[65]

---

[61] See for example, review comments on Mary Anne Radcliffe's *Fate of Velina de Guidova* (1790: 62) and *Radizivil* (1790: 63).

[62] Arthur Aikin in the MR on Bird's *Castle of Hardayne* (1795: 12); cf. CR on Ann Howell's *Rosenberg* (1789: 48), and MR on Anne Radcliffe, *Castles of Athlin and Dunbayne* (1789: 62).

[63] CR n.s. 21 (1797), pp. 115–16.   [64] CR 67 (1789): 237 (on 1789: 19).

[65] CR 68 (1789): 407.

The wanderings of Anna Maria Mackenzie's *Calista* (1789: 53) were compared to *Cecilia*, and the anonymous *Matilda Fitz-Aubin* (1792: 20) was said to resemble both Burney and Charlotte Smith.[66] By contrast, admitted imitation of Fielding and Smollett (despite Holcroft's eulogy) was slender. A rare exception, John Raithby's *Delineations of the Heart* (1792: 49), was, in the words of the title, 'attempted in the manner of Fielding'.

Other novels took their inspiration from other and often much older literature. Thomas Skinner Surr's *George Barnwell* (1798: 70), for example, was based on Lillo's *The London Merchant*, the popular and influential play first performed in 1731. Nor are sequels composed by other writers a twentieth-century weakness. Ellis Cornelia Knight was complimented in many quarters for her continuation of Johnson's *Rasselas* by her *Dinarbas* (1790: 50). *The New Monk* by R.S. (1798: 62) far less successfully satirized Lewis's notorious *Monk* of 1796. A few writers drew attention to influences closer to home. Elizabeth Pinchard, in her *Two Cousins* (1794: 45), allowed a character to read from one of her earlier works, its title—*Dramatic Dialogues*—usefully footnoted for further reference.[67]

One other characteristic marks many of these novels—their transience. Most were produced in editions of no more than 500 (and even the most successful in editions of some 800 at a time—to be discussed further, below). Moreover, as table 3 shows, the majority of titles were never reprinted. A remarkably consistent 58–59 per cent of the total novel titles first published in the 1770s and 1780s did not achieve a second edition, even in Ireland where many novels were reprinted in Dublin (and occasionally elsewhere). Ireland was outside the Union of England and Scotland until 1801 with no copyright law in force. Dublin booksellers published cheap, undercutting reprints apparently for illegal import to England and Scotland, but many also supplied an Irish home market.[68] Because the NSTC does not continue the coverage of edition reprintings offered by the ESTC, and because the undigested entries of *OCLC* do not enable safe distinctions to be made between different editions, table 3 offers only limited information about republication of novels in the 1790s. Over 34 per cent of novel titles first published in that decade were reprinted before 1800, however, suggesting that republication rates in the longer term were similar to, or might even have been greater than, those of the previous two decades. Both more certain and significant are the lowly multiple reprinting totals of the earlier years. Although many new novel titles achieved one reprinting—even though this was often in Dublin—very few went on to enjoy greater popularity by further editions. None of the 24 new novels with 1784 imprints was republished more than once. With a few exceptions (1779 appears to have been a productive year with 8 of the 18 new titles going on to at least two further editions), the table confirms the ephemeral condition of the novel. As might be expected, anonymous novels (totals shown in parentheses in Table 3) faced particular obscurity.

---

[66] CR 68 (1789): 327; and CR n.s. 9 (1793): 117–18.   [67] Pinchard, *Two Cousins*, p. 112.
[68] The importance of the Irish home market, supplementing any 'piratical' import trade to England, has been convincingly restated by Mary Pollard, *Dublin's Trade in Books 1550–1800* (Oxford: Clarendon Press, 1989).

Table 3. Republication Rates before 1801 of Novels First Published 1770–1799

Imprint Year	Total no. Titles	Titles Reprinted once only	Titles Reprinted more than once	Titles not Reprinted
1770	40	11 (6)	8 (1)	21 (13)
1771	60	14 (5)	3 (2)	43 (28)
1772	41	8 (3)	6 (3)	27 (22)
1773	39	9 (6)	3 (—)	27 (17)
1774	35	3 (3)	4 (1)	28 (17)
1775	31	17 (7)	3 (1)	11 (8)
1776	17	5 (1)	5 (2)	7 (3)
1777	18	5 (2)	3 (—)	10 (6)
1778	16	6 (4)	3 (1)	7 (4)
1779	18	3 (2)	8 (2)	7 (2)
	315	81 (39)	46 (13)	188 (120)
		25.7%	14.6%	59.7%
1780	24	7 (1)	4 (1)	13 (9)
1781	22	7 (4)	3 (1)	12 (10)
1782	22	7 (4)	3 (—)	12 (7)
1783	24	7 (—)	3 (—)	14 (6)
1784	24	9 (2)	—	15 (7)
1785	47	15 (3)	7 (1)	25 (18)
1786	40	13 (4)	6 (—)	21 (8)
1787	51	11 (6)	10 (2)	30 (18)
1788	80	22 (10)	11 (2)	47 (28)
1789	71	12 (3)	13 (5)	46 (25)
	405	110 (37)	60 (12)	235 (136)
		27.2%	14.8%	58.%
1790	74	14 (4)	6 (—)	54 (31)
1791	74	19 (5)	11 (1)	44 (22)
1792	58	15 (5)	11 (1)	32 (22)
1793	45	16 (2)	6 (2)	23 (10)
1794	56	8 (—)	13 (3)	35 (12)
1795	50	12 (2)	13 (—)	25 (8)
1796	91	14 (2)	13 (1)	64 (16)
1797	79	8 (—)	11 (1)	60 (22)
1798	75	20 (3)	6 (1)	49 (10)
1799	99	16 (2)	9 (1)	74 (17)
	701	142 (25)	99 (11)	460 (170)
		20.3%	14.1%	65.6%

(titles remaining anonymous shown in parenthesis)

Table 4. Place and Frequency of Publication before 1801 of Further Editions of Novels First Published 1770–1799

Imprint Years of 1ˢᵗ edn.	Within 2 yrs	3–5yrs	6–10yrs	11–20yrs	21+yrs	++[69]
1770–74 (total titles—215)						
Titles reptd	L D	L D	L D	L	US	
once only	3 25	3 3	2 7	2	1	
No. edns. of titles	L D US	L D	L	L D US O	US O	
reptd 2x & more	13 21 1	7 3	1	6 4 1 1	4 1	54
1775–79 (total titles—100)						↳
Titles reptd	L D	L D	L D	L		
once only	1 20	4 2	1 6	1		
No. edns. of titles	L D	L D US O	L D US O	L		
reptd 2x & more	17 18	7 6 2 1	8 9 1 1	5		56
1780–84 (total titles—116)						
Titles reptd	L D	L D	L D	O		
once only	1 30	1 2	1 1	1		
No. edns. of titles	L D US O	L D US	L D	L	US	
reptd 2x & more	15 14 1 1	3 3 1	4 3	1	1	20
1785–89 (total titles—289)						
Titles reptd	L D O	L D O L		L		
once only	7 50 1	6 2 1 4		2		
No. edns. of titles	L D US O	L D US O	L D US O	L D	US O	
reptd 2x & more	48 40 1 1	10 5 6 1	9 6 5 1	5 1	6 1	41
1790–94 (total titles—307)						
Titles reptd	L D	O L	L			
once only	7 51	2 7	3			
No. edns. of titles	L D US O	L D US	L D US O			
reptd 2x & more	28 43 9 5	19 2 14	9 2 8 4			12
1795–99 (total titles—394)						
Titles reptd	L D US O	L D US O	US			
once only	20 38 4 2	4 1 5 1	1			
No. edns. of titles	L D US O	L D US O	US			
reptd 2x & more	32 40 22 6	15 1 10 5	1			11

1770–99	L	D	US	O
Total reprinted edns. *within 2 years*	192	390	29	18
3–5 years (before 1801)	86	30	38	9
6–10 years (before 1801)	42	34	16	7
11–20 years (before 1801)	22	5	8	2
more than 21 years but before 1801			5	1
	342	459	96	37

Other edns. (ESTC entries for titles reprinted more than 5 times) 194

L = London   D = Dublin   US = British North America / United States   O = Other

[69] This ++ column records further editions of the most popular novels (as listed in table 5) where place and date of publication are not given in the entries for the sixth or more reprintings before 1850 (but because space constraints are entered only as the number of further entries in the STCs).

The dominance of Dublin in the novel reprint trade is confirmed by Table 4, showing the place of publication of further editions of novels first issued in this period. Again, the value of the table in charting long-term republication diminishes in years leading up to 1800, but the date limitation does at least give some sense of the number of further editions of the novels listed in this bibliography printed and in circulation during the last three decades of the century. The table does not record the place of publication of the sixth or later editions of the most popular novels as these (separately listed in Table 5) are given in terms of the number of further entries recorded in ESTC and OCLC in the main listings below. As a summary of all but the most popular titles, however, just over 49 per cent (or 459 of 930) of these further editions (including, of course, many multiple editions of individual titles) were Dublin imprints, and the great majority of these (85 per cent) were published within two years of the first (almost always) London edition.

The 342 London further editions remain significant. Even though the otherwise very intriguing reappearance of novels in further editions after a gap of many years is bounded by the 1801 cut-off date (and is therefore significant only for novels of the 1770s), Table 4 does firmly support what might have been expected—the greater like-lihood of London reprints (like Dublin reprints) appearing during the first two years after publication of the original. In fact, the strength of republication some three or more years after first publication is relatively pronounced, especially from the mid 1780s. London reprintings of works published three or more years previously eclipse those from Dublin throughout the period, but by the last five years of the century London reprinting challenges that from Dublin even including the one-edition-only Irish republications (71 editions compared to 81). Even more marked in the late 1790s is the great increase in American editions of British novels. Until the early 1790s the dominant export book trade to the American colonies and early republic, and the handicapped state of their publishing industry, ensured that both private and institu-tional customer was supplied by London and other British booksellers.[70] As Table 4 records, almost all the American reprints of British novels were published in the 1790s, and especially the late 1790s, and included five editions of titles first published in the early 1770s. Thirty-five novels first printed in Britain during the 1790s appeared in an American edition in the same season as their London publication. By contrast, between 1770 and 1790 only three novels were reprinted on the other side of the Atlantic even within two years of the imprint date of the British original (1774: 24, 1782: 20, 1789: 55, together with the apparent transatlantic reissue, 1785: 18).

Amongst the reprinted titles were 56 novels that went through more than five editions before 1801. All contribute to the catch-all 'other' category of Table 4, of

[70] See James Raven, 'The Export of Books to Colonial North America', *Publishing History* 42 (1997): 21–49; James Raven, *London Booksellers and American Customers: Transatlantic Literary Community and the Charleston Library Society, 1748–1811* (Columbia, SC: University of South Carolina Press, 1999); and Robert B. Winans, 'Bibliography and the Cultural Historian: Notes on the Eighteenth-Century Novel', in William L. Joyce, et al., eds., *Printing and Society in Early America* (Worcester, MA: American Antiquarian Society, 1983): 174–85.

multiple further editions recorded in ESTC. Table 5 lists the most popular novels in alphabetical order for ease of recognition. It is hardly a surprise that all three Burney novels and three Mackenzie novels of this period appear in the lists, and the final novel by Smollett, but numerous surprises include novels by Croft, Helme, Hughes, Pinchard, and Roche.

The Authors

As already noted, a handful of novelists dominated the terrain both as popular writers enjoying frequent republication and as critically acclaimed models for dozens of aspiring, if talentless, authors. The listings below, contributing to the history of the development of the novel, include the last novel by Smollett, the first three (and most significant) by Burney, no less than eleven by Charlotte Smith, and the remarkable work of Wollstonecraft, Godwin, and Lewis. Another, lesser but still very significant raft of novelists included Robert Bage (six novels), William Beckford (three novels), Elizabeth Bonhote (seven novels), Henry Brooke (the conclusion to *The Fool of Quality* and one other novel), Richard Graves (four novels), Thomas Holcroft (five novels before 1800), Samuel Jackson Pratt (nine novels), Ann Radcliffe (five novels), Clara Reeve (six novels), Mary Robinson (seven novels), and Susanna Rowson (seven novels). For every virtuoso or prolific favourite of the libraries, however, there were a dozen more tone-deaf scribblers. The cumulative entries of this bibliography will reveal networks of novel-writing relationships, of influences and imitations, of new developments and responses, but the entries also offer a cultural history that is as much about the changing nature of production, consumption, and assessment as it is about the identification of singular artistic achievement. The obscurity of authors of such novels as *Persiana, the Nymph of the Sea* (1791: 22) and *The Animated Skeleton* (1798: 1)—whoever they were—is well deserved, but the listings also throw up some extraordinary figures, including the prolific Treyssac de Vergy (1770: 37, 38, 39; 1771: 54, 55, 56; 1772: 40, 41), styled 'Chevalier' and 'Counsellor in the Parliament of Paris', and a benchmark of awfulness for the reviewers. The anonymous *Irishman* (1772: 14) was said to be in the manner of one of Treyssac de Vergy's worst performances.[71] By contrast, Mrs H. Cartwright (even though her first name remains elusive), won critical praise for all but the last of her six novels published between 1779 and 1787. More productive in the long term even than Charlotte Smith were Anna Maria Mackenzie Johnson (eleven novels and miscellanies before 1800, and four more before 1809) and Mary Meeke (seven novels before 1800 and nineteen more to come before 1823, the last published posthumously). Almost as tireless with the pen—and eventually earning modest critical praise—were Anna Maria Bennett,[72] Martha Hugill, Isabella Kelly Hedgeland (five novels before 1800 and a further five before 1813), Eliza Kirkham Mathews, the intriguing Henry Summersett, and the master pot-boiler, George Walker—who also publicly declared his ambition to write for profit.

---

[71] MR 47 (1772): 487.
[72] Not Agnes, as has sometimes been given in guides to novels of the period.

Table 5. Novels First Published 1770–1799 with Five or more Further Editions
(British and American) before 1829

anon., *Adventures of a Hackney
    Coach*, 1781: 1

anon., *Cavern of Death*, 1794: 6

anon., *The Correspondents*, 1775: 3

Bage, *Hermsprong*, 1796: 21

Bennett, *The Beggar Girl*, 1797: 26

Brooke, *Fool of Quality* (vol. 5), 1770: 24

Burke, *Ela*, 1787: 32

Burney, *Camilla*, 1796: 26

Burney, *Cecilia*, 1782: 15

Burney, *Evelina*, 1778: 10

Campe, *New Robinson Crusoe*, 1788: 47

Combe, *Letters of an Italian Nun*, 1781: 16

Croft, *Love and Madness*, 1780: 14

Cullen, *Haunted Priory*, 1794: 20

Cumberland, *Henry* 1795: 17

D'Israeli, *Romances* 1799: 31

Ducray-Duminil, *Ambrose and Eleanor*,
    1796: 38

de Genlis, *Tales of the Castle*, 1785: 29

Godwin, *Caleb Williams*, 1794: 23

Godwin, *St Leon*, 1799: 42

Godwin, *Things As They Are*, 1794: 23

Goethe, *Sorrows of Werter*, 1779: 10

Helme, *Farmer of Inglewood Forest*, 1796: 51

Helme, *Louisa*, 1787: 38

Hughes, *Caroline*, 1787: 41

Inchbald, *Nature and Art*, 1796: 57

Inchbald, *Simple Story*, 1791: 41

Jacson, *Plain Sense*, 1795: 26

Keate, *Sketches of Nature*, 1779: 12

Knight, *Dinarbas*, 1790: 50

Kotzebue, *Sufferings of the Family of Ortenberg*
    1799: 60

Lee, *The Recess*, 1785: 37

Lee and Lee, *Canterbury Tales*, 1797: 51

Lewis, *The Monk*, 1796: 63

Mackenzie, *Julia de Roubigné*, 1777: 13

Mackenzie, *Man of Feeling*, 1771: 46

Mackenzie, *Man of the World*, 1773: 36

Marmontel, *Tales*, 1792: 44

Montolieu, *Caroline of Lichtfield*, 1786: 34

Moore, *Edward*, 1796: 67

Moore, *Zeluco*, 1789: 54

Peacock, *Adventures of the Six
    Princesses*, 1785: 40

Peacock, *Visit for a Week*, 1794: 43

Pinchard, *Blind Child*, 1791: 56

Pratt, *Emma Corbett*, 1780: 23

Radcliffe, *Castles of Athlin and Dunbayne*, 1789: 62

Radcliffe, *Mysteries of Udolpho*, 1794: 47

Radcliffe, *Romance of the Forest*, 1791: 58

Radcliffe, *Sicilian Romance*, 1790: 61

Radcliffe, *The Italian*, 1797: 70

Raspe, *Baron Munchausen*, 1786: 38

Reeve, *Champion of Virtue*, 1777: 16

Robinson, *Vancenza*, 1792: 50

Roche, *Children of the Abbey*, 1796: 78

Rowson, *Charlotte*, 1791: 60

Saint Pierre, *Indian Cottage*, 1791: 64

Saint Pierre, *Paul and Virginie*, 1788: 71

Smith, *Emmeline*, 1788: 72

Smith, *Old Manor House*, 1793: 39

Smollett, *Humphry Clinker*, 1771: 53

Surr, *George Barnwell*, 1798: 70

Trusler, *Modern Times*, 1785: 46

Walker, *The Vagabond*, 1799: 94

West, *Gossip's Story*, 1796: 89

[Williams], *Village Curate / Curate of Elmwood*
    1795: 49

Wollstonecraft, *Original Stories*, 1788: 79

Yearsley, *Royal Captives*, 1795: 50

In all, 506 different authors and translators are identified in the entries of this bibliography, although half a dozen or so of these names might yet be shown to be pseudonyms. Of these 506 writers 377 were British and 117 foreign-born (with 12 unidentified).[73] Male writers (292) hugely outnumbered female writers (189), with 25 identified authors of unknown sex (usually where a surname is preceded only by an initial and where no biographical information survives). Authorship—in terms of the relative *number of novels* written by men and women—will be discussed further below, but one of the most striking features of these novels is that the overwhelming majority of them were published without attribution of authorship either on the title-page or within the preface or elsewhere in the text. Over 80 per cent of all novel titles published in the 1770s and 1780s were published anonymously. During the 1790s more novels were published with admitted authorship. Over the decade more than a third (38 per cent) of all novels carried some sort of specific attribution, but the majority of writers hid behind an anodyne title-page mask, with many of the anonymous novels bearing a very general and unverifiable ascription. For reasons ranging from genuine modesty to fear of public ridicule and the wrath of their families, authors hid their identities. Phebe Gibbes, one of the most prolific of novelists in this period, later declared that 'being a domestic woman, and of withdrawing turn of Temper I never would be prevailed upon to put my name to any of my Productions.'[74] We can only guess at the full output of such writers. Elizabeth Helme, for example, asserted that she was acknowledged as the author of ten novels and three translations, but had also 'translated sixteen volumes for different booksellers without my name'.[75]

Many novels did carry references to earlier work by the same writer, declaring themselves to be 'By the author of . . .'—and this has been a critical aid in unravelling relationships between entries in this bibliography. Some of these couplings (1773: 23/1777: 8 and 1790: 9/1792:6, for example) are still unattributable to a specific individual, but groups of up to six novels can now be associated with a particular (unknown, unnamed, writer).[76] A complication to this (if a rare one) is the subsequent claim of an author to have written a work attributable to another author by some other source. Phebe Gibbes, for example, laid written claim to *Zoriada* (1786: 24), usually attributed to Anne Hughes, and stated that she was the real, unacknowledged author of *Heaven's Best Gift* (1798: 54), 'wrote for the credit and emolument of another hand dec[ease]d' (one Mrs Lucius Phillips). In total, Gibbes claimed to have written 'twenty-two sets' of novels[77] and, if true and not merely the hallucinations of an ailing hack, then several other novels ascribed at the time to

---

[73] Amongst those counted as 'British' are several writers bearing British surnames, but for whom no biographical information survives.

[74] Phebe Gibbes to the Royal Literary Fund, 17 Oct. 1804 (RLF 2: 74).

[75] Elizabeth Helme to the Royal Literary Fund, 20 Oct. 1803 (RLF 3: 97).

[76] These include the 7 novels, 1787: 6, 1788: 14, 1788: 30, 1789: 23, 1791: 3, 1792: 2, and 1793: 8, all by the same, still anonymous writer; and 6 novels, 1787: 16, 1788: 22, 1788: 28, 1789: 29, 1790: 17 and 1791: 12, all by another anonymous writer.

[77] Phebe Gibbes to the Royal Literary Fund, 18 Oct. 1804 (RLF 2: 74).

Anne Hughes and other shadowy figures might have been by Gibbes. In another case, *The Young Philosopher* (1782: 11), the source of much bibliographical confusion,[78] can now at least be associated with the mysterious author of two other novels of the previous season (1781: 2 and 3). In a few instances the original anonymity of this 'By the author of . . .' device was unlikely to have been a secret to enthusiastic novel-readers. *Camilla . . . By the Author of Evelina and Cecilia* (1796: 26) was hardly an 'anonymous' publication for anyone with current literary interests.

Amongst the 72 per cent of all novels published throughout this period without attribution, the vague and often highly dubious tag of 'By a Lady' or 'By a Young Lady' gained special popularity. It carried the further implication about social station of the author; something that towards the end of this period became too much for at least one critic. As the *Critical*'s reviewer observed of one such claim, 'as every woman is now "a lady", we need not examine our author's pretensions to this title; but, from the occasional vulgarity of her language and descriptions, they cannot be very high'.[79] The general declaration 'By a Lady' and its variant forms ('young', 'genteel', etc.) fronted some 160 (or just over 11 per cent) of all novels of the period. For reasons not entirely clear, authors resorted to this style with particular enthusiasm in the late 1780s, when the overall publication of fiction began a marked growth. In 1785 nearly a third and in 1787 nearly a quarter of all novel titles were said to be 'by a Lady'.[80] These and other general descriptors cannot, however, be simply transferred to gender classification. Several male writers assumed 'young lady' title-page identity, and a few young women pretended to be male. Amidst this parade of literary transvestites, William Henry Hall published his tedious *Death of Cain*, an imitation of Gesner's death of Abel (1789 appendix), as 'By a Lady', and was forced to repeat this (with the addition of 'young') three years later for his *Pathetic History of Egbert and Leonora* (1792: 37). Arthur Gifford's *Omen* (1785: 30) was puffed by its publisher in the newspapers as 'by a Lady', and Henry Whitfield similarly accredited his *Villeroy; or, The Fatal Moment* (1790: 73). Many novels, like Elizabeth Mathews's *Constance* (1785: 38), and the still anonymous *Lumley-House* (1787: 18), *The History of Georgina Neville* (1791: 15), and *Fanny; or, The Deserted Daughter* (1792: 15), were also entitled 'The First Literary Attempt of a Young Lady'. Martha Hugill more confidently offered a 'First Literary Production of a Young Lady' (1786: 25), but 'attempt' remained the more common subtitle, especially where an introduction acknowledged the inspiration of a particular model like Burney or Richardson. Prefaces, such as that of George Hutton's *Amantus and Elmira* (1794: 32), frequently confessed to youth and inexperience; in the case of Eliza Bromley, to 'a virgin pen' (1784: 13). Novels published without any indication of authorship on the title-page or in the preface or other preliminary matter, might

---

[78] One contemporary review (*European Magazine*) gives Mr Seally as the author; the ESTC suggests, for one edition, that it is possibly by Charlotte Smith, but for another edition that it is 'apparently not' by Charlotte Smith.

[79] CR n.s. 22 (1798): 478.

[80] For those wishing to pursue this, the author index to this volume includes entries under 'Lady.'

also be announced in the bookseller's newspaper advertisement as by a juvenile or female hand.[81]

Contemporary critics were not unaware of these ploys and approached the question of authorship with great caution. 'We are not without suspicion', wrote the *Critical*, 'that in anonymous publications, the words *written by a lady* are sometimes made use of to preclude the severity of criticism; but as Reviewers are generally churls and greybeards, this piece of *finesse* very seldom answers'.[82] The dedication in the *History of Eliza Warwick* (1778: 3) 'To the Reviewers' was signed by 'a female, and a very young one', but the *Critical* reserved judgment, observing that in this matter 'there is no such thing as distinguishing men from women' and surmising that this particular author might be of 'the masculine gender'.[83] Writing in the *Monthly*, Samuel Badcock observed that although *The Ring* (1784: 6) was 'said to be the production of a *very* young Lady. She appears, however, to be so well acquainted with the tricks of the profession, that one would be led to imagine that she had been an old practitioner.'[84] The public evaluation of almost all new novels by the period-   ✓ ical reviewers was itself a leading cause of title-page disguise and the publication of works anonymously. As the *Critical* reviewer said of the 1774 *School for Husbands*, the artifice of 'by a lady' (or, even better, 'by a young lady') was used to ward off criticism.[85] The *Monthly*, indeed, thought this novel to be 'hammered out of the brainless head of a Grubstreet hireling'.[86] Typical of critical scorn was Samuel Badcock's view of *Distrest Virtue* (1781: 5): '"I am aware (says the Author), that many, on reading this little Work, will throw it aside with much disdain." We are very much of the Author's opinion.'[87] For a few—and it was a minority—timidity did keep the critics at bay. The novelist who signed herself 'Sabina' (1790: 65) seems to have won her appeal to 'the Gentlemen Reviewers' to 'in pity spare a simple maid'. William Hall later recalled falsifying his identity: 'it afforded me some consolation that my name was not announced; but it came to the public eye, as the production of "A Lady"'.[88] The Revd Charles Lucas allowed a coy 'C. L.' to appear at the foot of his introduction to *The Castle of St Donats* (1798: 44). In characteristic style, the bookseller, James Lackington, made much of the anonymity of his new novel *Louisa Mathews* (1793: 7), reporting that the author was a 'very respectable Lady' but, most regrettably, too timid for her name to appear on the title-page.[89]

Perhaps because of the availability of these general identifiers, pseudonyms were not as prevalent as might be expected, even though it is possible that a small number remain hidden from view. In a few instances the authenticity of a named author

[81] Including for example 1771: 23; 1777: 17 (adding 'young').

[82] CR 37 (1774): 317 of *The School for Husbands. Written by a Lady* (1774: 21). At the same time, critics did also contribute to the belief that female identity might be helpful. Take, for example, William Enfield on 1779: 13, 'A novel which appears before the Public under the sanction of two female names, seems entitled, if not to favour, at least to lenity.'

[83] CR 44 (1777), pp. 477–8. The reviewer's guess still remains as good as anyone's.

[84] MR 71 (1784): 150.   [85] CR 37 (1774), pp. 317–18.   [86] MR 50 (1774): 327.

[87] MR 65 (1781): 75.   [88] *Death of Cain* 4th edn. (London, 1800), p. vii.

[89] SJC 2–5 Feb. 1793.

cannot be confirmed. Harriet Squirrel (1790: 67) is believed to be the author's real name; more suspect are Pollingrove Robinson (1789: 63) and Benjamin Frère de Chérensi (1791: 33). Other pseudonyms include both predictable historicisms and flowery pretension. Matilda Fitz-John, registered in the records of her publisher, Hookham, but possibly hiding behind a mock-historical pen-name, was not well received (1796: 40). Sylvania Pastorella, announced author of *The Cottage of Friendship*, was no more successful (1788: 66). The *Child of Nature* (1774: 29) offered the suggestive 'Mr. Helvetius' as its author. More subtle was Courtney Melmoth, the established pen-name of Samuel Jackson Pratt, one-time cleric, and adopted by him during his time as an actor.[90]

Those prepared to admit to authorship comprised a motley society. It certainly included members of the aristocracy, military, and clergy. Cassandra, Baroness Hawke of Towton published *Julia de Gramont* (1788: 54) as 'The Right Honourable Lady H***', to be saluted by supine reviews. *Greenwood Farm* (1778: 2) was proclaimed to be by a 'Warrant Officer belonging to the Navy' and the announced author of *Monk-Wood Priory* (1799: 92), Francis Tracy Thomas, was described as 'Cornet in the East and West Lothian Light Dragoons'. James Penn additionally identified himself as 'Vicar of Clavering Cum Langley, Essex; Chaplain to The Right Hon. Earl of Gower, And Lecturer of St. Ann's, Aldersgate' on the title-page of his *Surry Cottage* (1779: 15). Later clerical novelists included William Cole (*Contradiction*, 1796: 29), James Douglas of Chiddingford (*The History of Julia d'Haumont*, 1797: 38), and Henry Evans Holder (*The Secluded Man* 1798: 29). Of the last, the *Critical* remarked that it was 'sorry to see the name of a clergyman, and, we believe, a philologist, in the title-page of so dull a novel'.[91] Numerous gentlemen also declared themselves, but in general, research into the occupation of even acknowledged male novelists of the period is not yet well advanced. Title-page ascription also offered other ways of presenting authorship. Regional loyalties were occasionally stressed, presumably to encourage the local market, but also to give provincial authenticity to the novel and its author. Mrs Skinn (Miss Masterman) 'of York', Mrs Gomersall 'of Leeds', and Mrs Bonhote 'of Bungay', all traded on their local residence. For her ninth novel, *The Neapolitan* (1796: 64), Anna Maria Mackenzie disguised herself as 'Ellen of Exeter'. Elizabeth Bonhote, adjudged 'not a writer of the vulgar caste', actually bought the eponymous ruin of her most famous Gothic novel, *Bungay Castle* (1797: 27).

The age range of the novelists was also extensive, largely because of the tender years of many of the writers. Numerous women novelists in particular were not of age. Amongst the most youthful writers were Anna Maria Porter, thirteen when the first volume of *Artless Tales* (1793: 36) was written, and Miss Nugent and Miss Taylor of Twickenham, authors of the *Indiscreet Marriage* (1779: 14) whose combined

    [90] See Josephine Grieder, '"Amiable Writer" or "Wretch"? The Elusive Samuel Jackson Pratt', *Bulletin of Research in the Humanities* 81 (1978): 464–84.
    [91] CR n.s. 25 (1799): 473.

ages were said not to exceed thirty.[92] If *Emma: or The Unfortunate Attachment* was indeed by the Duchess of Devonshire (1773: 28) then it was published when she was sixteen. Only a year older was Elizabeth Todd when her *History of Lady Caroline Rivers* was published in 1788, and also Margaret Holford (if indeed it is Margaret *junior* and the preface is to be believed) when her *Calaf: A Persian Tale* was published in 1798. In this case the reviewers were indulgent, if not patronizing. Amongst the more credible title-page claims of extreme youth was that for the 1791 *History of Georgina Neville*, whose author—if we are to believe the reviews—was also from the aristocracy. Sarah Lansdell, at eighteen, was by comparison a senior when her *Manfredi* (1796: 60) was published, even though it was written in twelve days and she later wrote an apology for it in one surviving copy.[93] The non-surviving *Revolution* (1781: 11) apparently opened with a preface declaring it to have been written by a deceased teenage labourer of no formal education. Thomas Rickman proudly advertised his seventeen years in the title to his *Evening Walk* (1795: 37), partly printed at the author's expense. Hall was eighteen when he wrote *The Death of Cain* 'to oblige a lady who was then young and pious'.[94] Countering these youngsters were novelists like Robert Bage, whose first novel (of six), *Mount Henneth* (1782: 12) was written when he was fifty-six, following a setback in his business.

As shown by Table 6 the balance between the number of novels written by male and by female novelists changed significantly over this period, both amongst the writers openly named in the novels and amongst the total of writers identified by our research. It must be stressed at the outset that no one should over-interpret figures derived from problematic materials,[95] but the table does give the best available indication of the gender of the writers of published novels of the period. In addition to the authors acknowledged in title-pages and prefaces, the table includes only clearly identified genders of other attributed authors (and most of these will be named authors with a plain 'Mr' or 'Miss' in very few cases). It excludes assumptions made by reviewers where no other supporting evidence for the gender of an author has been found,[96] and it obviously excludes unsubstantiated title-page claims as being 'by a Lady' etc. From the total number of novels first published in the 1770s nearly 10 per cent provided title-page or preface attribution to named men, compared to nearly 6 per cent to named women. In only one year of the decade (1775) were more novels published with the names of women as authors than with the names of men. During the 1780s, however, this relationship was reversed, with 5 per cent of all new novel titles announcing a named male author, but some 10 per cent of the total naming a female author. The female lead

---

[92] CR 49 (1780): 76.

[93] Bodleian copy, 256.f.2337–8, MS note on fly-leaf of vol. 2, dated 6 Oct. 1809.

[94] *Death of Cain* 4th edn. (London, 1800), preface, pp. [i], [vii].

[95] Where, for example, general labels such as 'lady' or 'young gentleman' have not been matched to a specific individual, the novels remain classified as anonymous.

[96] Even where firmly stated—e.g. 1796: 6. More reliable (and very rare) exceptions include advertisement sources affirming that *The Self-Tormentor* (1789: 25) was 'written by a lady'.

Table 6. Authorship of New Novels, 1770–1799

Publ. Date	Total no. Novels	Proper Names from Title-pages and Prefaces only				Total of Identified Proper Names		
		Male	Female	Anon.	Other[97]	Male	Female	Anon.
1770	40	5	1	33	1	15*	3*	21
1771	60	7	4	49		18	7	35
1772	41	3	1	37		7	6	28
1773	39	4	2	33		12	4	23
1774	35	4	2	28	1	9	2	23
1775	31		3	28		10	5	16
1776	17	2	1	14		7	4	6
1777	18	2	1	15		5	5	8
1778	16	1	1	14		2	5	9
1779	18	2	2	14		9	4	5
	315	30	18	265	2	94	45	174
%		(9.5)	(5.7)	(84.1)		(29.8)	(14.3)	(55.2)
1780	24	1	5	18	2	4	7*	11
1781	22			22		5	2	15
1782	22	3		19		8	3	11
1783	24	4	2	18		9	9	6
1784	24	2	2	20		10	5	9
1785	47	3	5	38	1	8	17	21
1786	40	2	4	33	1	12	15	12
1787	51	1	4	46		11	14	26
1788	80	3	9	65	2	18	20	40

	71	2	10	57	2	14	26	29
1789	405	21	41	336	8	99	118	180
%		(5.2)	(10.1)	(83)		(24.4)	(29)	(44.4)
1790	74	3	13	57	1	13	25	35
1791	74	15	8	48	3	24	20	27
1792	58	7	7	44		16	14	28
1793	45	6	10	25	4	12	15	14
1794	56	11	13	30	2	15	24	15
1795	50	8	7	34	1	21	18	10
1796	91	16	25	45	5	31	36	19
1797	79	14	18	45	2	23	31	23
1798	75	16	18	38	3	22	36	14
1799	99	25	27	45	2	37	40	20
	701	121	146	412	23	215	260	205
%		(17.2)	(20.9)	(59)		(30.7)	(36.9)	(29.6)
1770–99	1,421			1,013	408	423	560	
%				(71.3)	(28.7)	(29.8)	(39.4)	

Authors take precedence over translators who are not included in this table except where the original author is unknown and the translator was announced

* includes a novel with multiple authors; only one is included in the table, and where authors include both genders, the first given author is recorded

[97] Includes title-page pseudonyms, initials, and names where gender is unclear. Also includes instances where a translator is declared but the original author is not; translators are not counted as authors in this table.

continued—if not so strongly—during the less reticent 1790s, when many more writers put their names on title-pages or in prefaces. A total of 17 per cent of novels in the 1790s were published with named male writers but more than a fifth (21 per cent) gave named female writers. In particular years a striking number of women authors were acknowledged. Between 1788 and 1790 thirty-three women authors were named on novel title-pages and prefaces. Why this change came about is unclear, but the comparison to eight named male writers in novels of the same years, might suggest that female authorship was being deliberately promoted, and it was exactly at this time, as already noted, that an unprecedented number of otherwise anonymous title-pages also bore the attribution to 'a Lady'. It certainly seems to have been some sort of turning-point, although 1791 provided a striking if brief riposte to the trend, with fifteen acknowledged male novelists outnumbering the women by nearly two to one.

Far more significant are gender comparisons amongst the total of writers now identified by research for this bibliography. This has uncovered the actual author-ship of many anonymous (or mistakenly ascribed) novels, and the summaries in Table 6 suggest that of the authors now identified (1770–1799), the number of indi-vidual novels written by men was only slightly less than that by women (407 titles compared to 419), but also that far more novels were written by men than by women in the early years of this period. Novels by identified male writers outnum-ber those by women writers by more than two to one in the 1770s. These profiles, of course, include novels *by the same men and women*, and must be compared to the gender division of the total number of individual writers of the period identified by the bibliography (506) where 292 (58 per cent) were men and 189 (37 per cent) were women. In total, individual women writers were more prolific than their more numerous male counterparts. Other recent research has revealed the surprisingly poor showing of known women writers in earlier decades. Only 14 per cent of all new novel titles published between 1750 and 1769 can be identified as by women writers. Moreover, even if all the titles that remain anonymous are assumed to be by women (hardly likely), and this total is added to the known number of titles by female writers, the combined total (58 per cent) far from overwhelms the remaining number of novels (42 per cent) known for certain to be by male writers.[98] The results of the new research for 1770–1779 suggest affinity to the preceding decade, with the number of novel titles with identified female authors remaining at 14 per cent of the total (compared to the near third of all titles that can now be given an identifiable male author). Thereafter, the balance shifts, with slightly more novels by women than by men identified for the 1780s and 1790s. In this the tallies of novels remaining anonymous are important, particularly in the 1770s where the authorship of over half of all novels is still unidentified, but also in the 1780s where

[98] See Raven, *British Fiction*, esp. p. 18 (this combined total for 1750–1759 and 1760–1769 (57.7 per cent) corrects the error in the calculation for the 1750s given in footnote 46); and Catherine Gallagher, *Nobody's Story: The Vanishing Acts of Women Writers in the Marketplace, 1670–1820* (Berkeley and Los Angeles, 1994), pp. 153–5.

more than 40 per cent of all titles are without a known author. By comparison, well under a third (29 per cent) of all novel titles published in the 1790s remain anonymous, boosting the significance of the continuing closeness of the male–female contest (31 per cent compared to 37 per cent). From the late 1780s, then, the march of the woman novelist (and of the more prolific individual woman novelist) is clearly visible, but through the 1790s and to the end of the century it is not at all certain that women greatly outpaced the male writers of novels.

Bridging the gender divide are associations of family and kinship. Several of the writers were related to each other. Mary Wollstonecraft was the mother of Mary Shelley and of Fanny Imlay, daughter of the American writer Gilbert Imlay (1793: 23), and later married William Godwin in 1797. Wollstonecraft and Godwin were, in retrospect, the most prominent partnership represented in this bibliography, but as widely notorious at the time, perhaps, were magazine *bêtes noires*, the Gunning trio, Susannah (née Minifie), her sister, Margaret Minifie, and Susannah's daughter, Elizabeth. The Minifie sisters wrote novels together (JR 785/856, 1028), and then Margaret wrote four more in letters (JR 1121, 1322; 1780: 20; 1783: 17). After her first solo novel in 1764 (JR 854) Susannah published four novels between 1792 and 1797, and Elizabeth five between 1794 and 1799.[99] In 1791, when John Gunning threw his wife and daughter on to the street for refusing the suitor proposed for Elizabeth, the Gunning scandal filled the popular periodicals as well as their own subsequent novels. Like Mrs Rudd, Elizabeth Gunning, later Mrs Plunkett, was accused of forgery, and she also, like most of her fictional heroines, pursued aristocratic brawn with dramatic intensity. Amongst other related novelists, Elizabeth Hervey (four novels between 1788 and 1797) was elder half-sister to William Beckford, and apparently much upset by his parody of her work in his *Modern Novel Writing* (1796: 22).[100] Maria Elizabeth Robinson, author of *Shrine of Bertha* (1794: 51), was daughter of Mary Robinson (or 'Perdita', mistress of the Prince of Wales, recipient of extravagant praise from Coleridge, and author of seven novels in this bibliography). Anne and Annabella Plumptre (like the Gunnings, often confused), were sisters and close friends of Eliza Fenwick. The Margaret Holfords (with novels divided between both volumes of this bibliography) were mother and daughter. It is possible that the obscure Streets—Miss Street and Thomas George—novelists and German translators apiece, were also related. Joint authorship was also usually familial. However the work was apportioned, novels were produced in this period by the husband and wife, Richard and Elizabeth Griffith (1770: 31), and the sisters, Harriet and Sophia Lee (1797: 51). Elizabeth and Jane Purbeck wrote six novels together before 1800 (one not published until 1802).

---

[99] Four of these, 1796: 48 and 1797: 42 (by Susannah), and 1794: 25 and 1796: 47 (by Elizabeth) are not in the revisonist account of the Minifie-Gunnings, sorting out the different writings, in Virginia Blain, Patricia Clements, and Isobel Grundy, eds., *The Feminist Companion to Literature in English: Women Writers from the Middle Ages to the Present* (London, 1990). After 1800 Susannah also wrote three novels and Elizabeth, five, together with various translations and drama—see vol. 2 of this bibliography.

[100] Blain et al., eds., *Feminist Companion*, p. 517.

In another sense, novelists and booksellers also invited recognition of kinship between writers and readers, emphasizing links between one title and another, their own networks of authors, and back-lists of publications, as though novel publication was part of a continuing and involving project. The social aspect of this continuing body of work was ever present—as critics of the novel phenomenon constantly reminded its producers. Novel writing, indeed, was increasingly regarded as an occupation during this period. Samuel Badcock in his review for the *Monthly* described *The Fortunate Sisters* (1782: 5) as 'the hacknied cant of a novel-writer by profession!'[101] Notwithstanding the additional and obvious allusion to the oldest profession, the idea of novel writing being a trade underpinned even complimentary verdicts such as that on Maria Regina Roche (*Vicar of Landsdowne*, 1789: 64) as 'an author unhackneyed in the tricks of the profession'. The *Critical*, indeed, straightforwardly reported that the author of *The Maid of Kent* (1790: 19) is 'a man unhackneyed in the profession of novel-writing'.[102] As a career, however, it was rarely self-supporting, despite its apparent attraction to indigent and desperate gentry.

Most famously, Charlotte Smith took up her pen to alleviate her family's distress following the bankruptcies of her merchant husband (including her own imprisonment with him for debt in 1784, and her flight from him in 1788), but it was a course pursued by a large number of the novelists in this bibliography. Ann Masterman Skinn, like Mrs Smith, had to support herself after leaving her brutish husband. Anna Maria Mackenzie and Eliza Parsons took up their pens as impoverished widows with four and eight small children respectively. Eliza Kirkham Mathews tried to stave off debts and find funds to alleviate her consumption while her actor husband toured the country. Ann Gomersall, Elizabeth Hervey, and Charlotte Lennox all wrote to re-establish family fortunes, as did Elizabeth Griffith until a nabob son brought home his Indian wealth. For almost all, an assured income from novel-writing was an unrealizable dream, and many, including Skinn, the Lee sisters, Charlotte Palmer, Mary Pilkington, Jane Timbury, and the far more distinguished Lennox, took to teaching to eke out a living. Not all could, like Frances Burney and Ellis Cornelia Knight, attain positions in the royal household, and even Eliza Parsons's brief post in the Wardrobe was soon succeeded by more novel writing. Poverty featured frequently in title-page and prefatory pleas, and Gomersall, Mathews, and Eliza Ryves all died utterly destitute. Those soliciting indulgence from the public and the reviewers included the allegedly widowed author of *Disinterested Love* (1788: 11), although the reviewers were unmerciful.

At the time, payments to authors for the customary outright surrender of copyright were usually pitiful. A bookseller's purchase of copyright, moreover, was often the most enviable of the possibilities for authors attempting to have a book published (as will be discussed in more detail below). Even by mid-eighteenth-century standards, the *Critical* was able to charge that the bookseller-publishers and circulating librarians, the Noble brothers 'never paid to any author for his labour a sum

---

[101] MR 66 (1782): 474.   [102] CR 69 (1790): 592.

equal to the wages of a journeyman taylor'.[103] In reply, the Nobles could only insist that they did not keep a stable of hireling writers 'but, on the contrary, that all we have hitherto published have been sent to us unsolicited from their authors, without any stipulated pay, promise of reward, or previous agreement whatsoever, either by ourselves or any other person for us. And, moreover, that many of them are written by persons of rank, property, and fortune, above accepting any other return for their labours than a few printed copies for themselves and friends, but a gentleman and a scholar'.[104] Many writers, however, continued to excoriate the booksellers. Alexander Thomson, author of *Memoirs of a Pythagorean* (1785: 44) for which he was paid 25 guineas by bookseller, George Robinson, complained that 'the great source of my calamity is the illiberal and rapacious disposition of Booksellers, at all times vigilant to over-reach in negociations with an Author . . . and particularly successful in their policy, when urgent necessity compels him to accede to their proposals, however inadequate the recompense to his time and labor, and however repugnant to equity'.[105]

It is difficult to be sure about the range of payments to authors (and the question will be pursued further below in examining the financing of production). Where surviving evidence of copyright payment and the still rarer commission agreements has been uncovered in the course of constructing this bibliography, details are given in the notes section to each entry. Most notable survivals are the records of many of the payments to authors by Robinson and by Murray. A few payments by Lowndes and several by Hookham and Carpenter and, at the very end of the period, by Longman and Rees, have also been found, but the vast majority of the agreements has been lost.[106]

The 51 survivals listed in Table 7 (and an average payment of about £80) are unlikely to be fully representative of the payments to all the authors and translators of the 1,421 novels recorded below. The spectacular rewards to Radcliffe for her *Italian* (1797: 70) and the earlier *Mysteries of Udolpho* (1794: 97), came towards the end of the period, heavily skew the total average, and the table also relies heavily on the surviving contracts of Longman in the late 1790s, and the Robinsons, known for their relative generosity. In his contract with Henry Brooke for *Juliet Grenville* (1774: 24), George Robinson agreed, instead of outright purchase of the manuscript, to pay the author profits after printing and publication costs not just on the

[103] CR 4 (1757): 384. For the Nobles see James Raven, 'The Noble Brothers and Popular Publishing', *The Library*, 6th ser., 12 (1990): 293–345; and 'From Promotion to Proscription: Arrangements for Reading and Eighteenth-Century Libraries', in James Raven, Helen Small and Naomi Tadmor, eds., *The Practice and Representation of Reading in England* (Cambridge: Cambridge University Press, 1996): 175–201.

[104] 'Advertisement to the Public', appended to the 2nd vol. of *Rational Lovers* (London, 1769).

[105] Thomson to the Royal Literary Fund, 4 July 1799 (RLF 2: 44).

[106] Collection of Literary Assignments of George Robinson, Manchester Central Library MS F 091.A2; John Murray I, Account Ledger, Daybook, Booksellers' Book and other records, John Murray Archive, 50 Albermarle St., London; PRO Chancery Masters' List, Ledgers of Hookham and Carpenter, 1791–1798; Reading University Library, Longman Impression Book H4 (1794–1801), reproduced in *The House of Longman 1794–1914* microfilm edn. (Chadwyck Healey, 1978), reel 37.

Table 7. **Surviving Receipts to Novelists for Surrender of Copyright, 1770–1799**

Bookseller	Author	Novel Entry	Payment (gns. Unless Stated)
Cadell, Davies	Ann Radcliffe	1797: 70	£800
Robinson	Ann Radcliffe	1794: 47	£500
Payne, Cadell	Frances Burney	1782: 15	£250
Longman	Samuel Jackson Pratt	1797: 68	£225[107]
Robinson	William Hayley	1789: 44	£200[108]
Robinson	Elizabeth Inchbald	1791: 41	£200
Robinson	Ann Yearsley	1795: 50	£200
Robinson	Elizabeth Inchbald	1796: 57	£150
Longman	Mary Robinson	1797: 71	£150
Longman	Mary Robinson	1799: 78	£150
Robinson	Charlotte Smith	1792: 52	£135.5s.
Longman	Jane West	1799: 95	£90
Hookham	Matilda Fitz-John	1796: 40	60
Longman	Eliza Parsons	1797: 62	60
Longman	Clara Reeve	1799: 77	60
Longman	Mary Robinson	1799: 79	60
Robinson	Anna Thomson	1788: 75	55
Robinson	James White	1790: 72	55
Robinson	Anna Thomson	1791: 70	£40
Robinson	Peter Will (trans.)	1795: 44	£40
Lane	Mary Sherwood	1799: 83	£40
Robinson	John Poulin (trans.)	1789: 56	36
Murray	Beddoes (trans.)	1791: 53	30
Lowndes	Robert Bage	1782: 12	£30
Robinson	Susanna Rowson	1788: 70	£30
Robinson	William Hooper (trans.)	1772: 36	£28.17s.6d.
Robinson	Alexander Thomson	1785: 44	25
Robinson	Sarah Pearson	1794: 44	25
Robinson	E. & J. Purbeck	1791: 57	21
Lowndes	Anne Dawe	1770: 26	20
Lowndes	Sophia Briscoe	1772: 31	20
Lowndes	Frances Burney	1778: 10	20
Robinson	William Godwin	1784: 17	20
Robinson	Charles Dodd	1787: 34	20
Robinson	A. M. McKenzie	1788: 63	20

[107] Payment described in Longman impression book H4, f. 18, as 'copyright of first edition', implying agreement to further author entitlement for subsequent edns. (one further London edn., 1798).
[108] This, however, is according to Hayley's own memoirs which might well exaggerate.

Robinson	Edward Davies	1795: 18	20
Robinson	anon (?Boldero)	1788: 33	15
Lowndes	Cavendish (?Briscoe)	1779: 8	12
Robinson	Elizabeth Tomlins	1792: 56	11
Lowndes	Miss Ferguss	1777: 10	10
Lowndes	Arthur Gifford	1785: 30	10
Robinson	Anna Eden	1790: 42	10
Lane	William Godwin	1784: 16	£10
Murray	John Heriot	1787: 39	£10
Lowndes	anon. (?Wlm Warren)	1773: 18	8
Robinson	Thomas Street (trans.)	1792: 42	8
Murray	Helenus Scott	1782: 20	5
Robinson	Anne Burke (?Ustick)	1787: 32	5
Robinson	Lewis Lyons (trans.)	1787: 35	5
Murray	Jane Timbury	1788: 76	5
Hookham	William Godwin	1784: 15	3

first edition but also on subsequent editions, although no separate London second edition was in fact issued, the novel later appearing in magazines and in Dublin. More typical payments might have been those by Murray, such as the five guineas paid to Helenus Scott for his *Adventures of a Rupee* (1782: 20), or even those by Hookham. The latter's agreement to buy *Joan!!!* by 'Matilda Fitz-John' (1796: 40) for an over-the-top 60 guineas has been seen as evidence of his poor business judgment.[109] Many surviving agreements also highlight the role of intermediaries. Authors did not always conduct arrangements directly with booksellers, causing further problems in author identification for this and past bibliographies.[110] In some of the records from the end of the period, authors also seem to have extracted a few modest concessions or additional payments in kind. Longman gave Eliza Parsons 20 sets of her *Old Friend with a New Face* (1797: 62) in addition to her copyright payment of £60, just as he agreed to giving Mary Robinson 13 sets of *False Friend* (1799: 78) in addition to her £150. In the same season, Pratt's sale of copy to Longman for his *Family Secrets* (1797: 68) was pointedly 'copyright of first edition', although there followed only one further London edition (from which he might then have benefited).[111]

[109] Jan Fergus and Janice Farrar Thaddeus, 'Women, Publishers, and Money, 1790–1820', *Studies in Eighteenth-Century Culture* 17 (1988): 191–207 (p. 193). Matilda Fitz-John is quite possibly a pseudonym.
[110] Notably, that Sophia Briscoe collected the money for *The Sylph*, traditionally ascribed to the Duchess of Devonshire (1779: 8); that Boldero was possibly the author for 1788: 33; that one Anne Ustick or Urtick was the author of 1787: 32, not Anne Burke; and that one William Warren, collecting the money for 'The Adventures of a Footman' in 1773 might have been the author of *The Sentimental Spy* (1773: 18). 'Mr Ratcliff; is recorded in LA as collecting £40 for the 1792 2nd edn. of *Romance of the Forest* (1791: 58).
[111] Longman archives, impression book H4, ff. 18, 42, 44.

Despite these cautions, Table 7 does suggest both the extraordinary differences in the financial rewards of novel writing in this period, and the meagreness of many returns. The range is also hugely extended if the later earnings of Frances Burney are considered: from her contracts securing a share in the returns from later editions of Camilla (1796: 26) and *The Wanderer* of 1814, Burney gained more than £4,000, having earned a total of £280 from her first two novels (1778: 10 and 1782: 15).[112] Lane issued advertisements offering from between 5 and 100 guineas for 'manuscripts of merit',[113] and although very few Lane authors (if any) could have claimed his top reward, the range was perhaps more credible than has formerly been recognized. Even so, Lane's ominous starting price of 5 guineas was accepted even by Robinson authors, and the poverty of many writers of the time is probably not exaggerated.[114] Translators seem to have fared no better, although even fewer records of agreements have survived. Longman paid the sometime reader and corrector, Woodbridge, 20 guineas and one free copy for translating Lafontaine's *Klara du Plessis und Klairant* (1797: 50) Two years later Longman paid Matthew O'Hinkley 38 guineas for his translation of de Genlis's *Les Voeux téméraires* (1799: 40).[115]

It was certainly for good reasons that in 1790 a band of philanthropic gentlemen established the Royal Literary Fund to dispense modest grants to authors fallen on hard times. Many of the authors in this bibliography petitioned the committee. The first recipient of a grant (25 guineas between 1790 and 1793), The Revd Edward Harwood, Nonconformist minister of Bristol, had translated La Roche's *Sophy Sternheim* (1776: 13B). In 1790 (and by then with 24 works and translations to his name) he pleaded 'great distress', being 'oppressed with age, indigence and the palsy'.[116] Amongst other recipients of relief were Alexander Bicknell, Ann Gomersall, Elizabeth Helme, Martha Hugill, Charlotte Lennox, Charlotte Palmer, Mary Pilkington, Jane Timbury, and eighteen other writers of novels between 1770 and 1800. Despite their relatively healthy showing in Table 7, with payments for novels of £225 and £60 respectively, both Samuel Jackson Pratt and Eliza Parsons had been suppliants. In 1792 Mrs Parsons wrote *Woman As She Should Be* (1793: 33) in penniless agony, having crushed her left leg, leaving her, for six months, 'confined to my Room, my leg on a Pillow, Splinters of bone continually working thro' which keep me in extreme Tortures'.[117] In 1791 Bicknell declared that without relief from the Fund he would 'be obliged to exchange a comfortable and respectable situation for a Prison'. Five years later, the Fund paid for his pauper's funeral.[118]

Subscription schemes supported many of the novels published in this period, often acting as a broader form of the vanity press. Collection methods varied, but

---

[112] Jan Fergus, *Jane Austen: A Literary Life* (London: Macmillan, 1991), pp. 13–15.

[113] One version of this adv., in *Adelina* (1790: 1).

[114] Five guineas might also have been a basic standard for some time—Lowndes gave Phebe Gibbes 5 gns. for her *Francis Clive* of 1764 (JR 839), GM n.s. 94 (1824): 136.

[115] Longman archives, impression book H4, f. 42.

[116] Harwood to the Royal Literary Fund, 1790 (RLF 1: 2).

[117] Parsons to the Royal Literary Fund, 17 Dec. 1792 (RLF 1: 21).

[118] Bicknell to the Royal Literary Fund, 22 Mar. 1791, and note, 1796 (RLF 1: 6).

the anonymous impoverished clerical author of *History of the Curate of Cramen* (1777: 5) began advertising for subscribers two years before the novel was finally published by Johnson, naming Dodsley and George Keith as collectors. In this case, payment by signatories was not required until the work was published, although subscribers were warned that available copies were likely to be limited to the number of subscribers and the failure to locate any surviving copy of the novel does not suggest a large edition. For her *Ianthé* (1798: 23), Emily Clark received £43.1s in subscriptions and a further net profit of £1 from 229 copies sold by Hookham in an arrangement of part subscription and part publishing on commission.[119] By contrast, Jane Gosling's later *Ashdale Village: a Moral Work of Fancy* (1794: 24) boasted a total of 397 subscribers, with some buying up to four copies each. Based in Sheffield, the author's scheme was co-ordinated by the Robinsons in Paternoster Row. In 'The Author's Address to her Subscribers', Gosling wrote

That I have been enabled to procure a Subscription *equal to the expence of printing*, is (at the present crisis) the effect of an intelligent sensibility, and confirms, beyond dispute, the conspicuous principle of this age to be that of urbanity and liberal consideration.[120]

An army of subscribers frequently lined up, often in order of rank. Eliza Parsons's *History of Miss Meredith* (1790: 58) claims one of the longest lists and also boasts quality names. Mary Martha Sherwood's *Traditions* (1795: 40) parades 640 subscribers' names. Jane Gosling's list in *Ashdale Village* (1794: 24) reaches 357 names, including 162 women and 31 clergymen. The gender division of these public supporters was often extreme. *Emma; or, the Unfortunate Attachment* (1773: 28) listed 16 men and 100 women; John Palmer's *Mystery of the Black Tower* (1796: 70), 82 men and 31 women. Many other subscription lists were small but delicately formed. Amongst the smallest subscription list was that prefacing George Brewer's *History of Tom Weston* (1791: 31) comprising 19 men and 22 women. Anne Ker's *Heiress Di Montalde* (1799: 55), dedicated to HRH Princess Augusta Sophia featured 8 male and 43 female subscribers, including a royal duchess, another duke and duchess, 3 countesses, and a dowager countess. Isabella Kelly's *Eva* (1799: 54) flourished 69 subscribers only, of whom 33 were women and 36 were men. Margaret Lee's *Clara Lennox* (1797: 52) managed only 68 names, none of them men, but including two members of the royal family, the Princess of Wales and the Duchess of York, 9 non-royal duchesses, 3 marchionesses, 9 countesses, 23 Ladies, 6 Hon. Mrs and only 16 completely untitled women.

The often elevated patronage extended to the novel has been much remarked upon, but this becomes all the more apparent when the full range of novels is recovered. As the examples given above make clear, a particular attraction for novelists seeking subscribers was association with an illustrious dedicatee, a device used,

---

[119] H&C G/137, 126; calculations discussed in Fergus and Thaddeus, 'Women, Publishers, and Money', p. 193, esp. n. 10.
[120] Gosling, *Ashdale Village* (1794: 24), 1: iv.

indeed, to promote many other commercial publications. All dedications to novels in this period are given in the entries below (dates in the dedications are normalized, days preceding months). Dedications did include those to 'the generous and candid public' or 'the reviewers' or 'the Inhabitants of Bristol', but the great majority of dedications cited named individuals. Some of these had not been asked in advance for their permission. Of the surviving novels published during the 1770s, 42 carried dedications of some sort (or 13 per cent of the total of 315 novel titles). This compares to 23 surviving novels with dedications in 1796 alone (or 25 per cent of the total of 91 titles); to 15 of new novel titles with a 1797 imprint (19 per cent of 78 titles); and to 13 of those with a 1798 imprint (17 per cent of 75 titles). More significant are the quality of the dedicatees, headed by the Queen (6 novels), the Prince of Wales (5), and the Princess of Wales (4). Most popular were the Duchess of Devonshire (9 novels, and herself an alleged novel writer[121]), the Duchess of York (6), and the Duchess of Cumberland (4). Other prominent dedicatees included the Earl of Chesterfield, Horace Walpole, Richard Sheridan, John Wilkes, William Pitt, and Mrs Hastings, wife of Warren Hastings.

Many such dedications support the accepted assessment of the minor novel of this period as the predictable, drab writing of gentlewomen, and some gentlemen, living in modest seclusion. Although many of the products described in this bibliography might indeed be so categorized, the fuller account is much bolder and an extraordinary number of these novels reflect the astonishing lives of their writers. The reviewers' comparisons between novelists and the 'oldest profession' were not always misplaced. Margaret Rudd and Elizabeth Gunning Plunkett were hardly proto-Victorian 'angels of the house'. Elizabeth Griffith and Elizabeth Blower were actresses. Anna Maria Bennett was high-profile mistress to an admiral (with her first novel in the year of his death—1785: 22—apparently selling out in a day). More notoriously, Mary 'Perdita' Robinson wrote from a debtors' prison before appearing at the Drury Lane theatre and then in the bed, amongst others, of the Prince of Wales and Charles James Fox.

Translations and Translators

More than a tenth of all novel titles first published in Britain in this period were translations from Continental novels. Some of these originals were elderly and obscure; almost all until the mid-1790s were from the French. This continued the pattern of the previous two decades. At least 95 (or 18 per cent) of the 531 novels first published in Britain 1750–1769 were translations. Of these, 84 were from the French, 2 from the Spanish and only 9 from other languages including German.[122] In the 1770s and 1780s a few more novels were translated from the German,

[121] *Emma: or the Unfortunate Attachment* (1773: 28); and *The Sylph* (1779: 7).
[122] Raven, *British Fiction*, p. 21.

but it was a popular source only during the final decade of the century. From 1795 translations from German exceeded those from other languages for the first time. Other translated novels, 1770–1799, were taken from the Italian (3), Spanish (1), and Persian/Sanskrit (3). Table 8 provides a summary of these borrowings, although its notes reveal some of the difficulties in identifying translations. It has not always been possible to find the date of the French or German original, and some translations came through intermediate translations (a German novel via a French translation for example) with conflicting evidence about the text used for the translation (whatever the title-page or puffing advertisement said).

Even more fundamental is the difficulty in verifying the claims—either by a title-page and preface or by a reviewer—that a novel was derived from a foreign original. Where a novel does not survive and its advertised title does not admit to being a translation, it is impossible to prove a foreign origination save (and even then by no means certainly) where a contemporary reviewer or other commentator so alleges.[123] When a novelist or bookseller took the easy route to producing a new novel by simply translating an obscure French or German romance, proper names were often changed and narratives rearranged. Not all were as candid as Elizabeth Tomlins who acknowledged in the preface to her *Memoirs of a Baroness* (1792: 56) that her tale was founded on a French original. This did not prevent suspicions being voiced. The *Monthly*, for example, lingered over the many Gallicisms of *Letters from Henrietta to Morvina* (1777: 6), and the *Critical* believed Mrs Fell's *Peasant; or, Female Philosopher* (1792: 33) to be an unacknowledged translation from the French. The *Critical* suggested German origins for the two tales that made up *Statira: or the Mother* (1798: 64) by Mrs Showes, already established as a Germanist with her *Interesting Tales* of 1797.

Increasingly, however, the reverse confusion arose. As the fashion for French, and then German, novels increased, along with an interest in ancient British or exotic Eastern tales, novels were falsely inscribed as translations, much in the way that so many mysterious old manuscripts were also uncovered. According to one critic, the title words of *The Siege of Belgrade: An Historical Novel. Translated from a German Manuscript* (1791: 24) 'insinuate *secret history*; and under these specious outlines, we apprehend that we have been reading as mere a circulating-library-story as ever was fabricated'.[124] These bogus translations are excluded from Table 8, but they are at least as numerous as the genuine translations from languages other than French and German. Among the more outlandish of the 'foreign' novels of the 1790s are Mary Anne Radcliffe's *Radzivil . . . Translated from the Russ* (1790: 63), John Thelwall's *The Rock of Modrec . . . Translated from an Ancient British Manuscript, lately Discovered Among the Ruins of an Abbey in North Wales* (1792: 55), *The*

---

[123] As, for example, in the case of *The Orphan Marion* (1790: 23).
[124] John Noorthouck in MR n.s. 5 (1791), pp. 338–9.

Table 8. First Editions of English Translations of French and German Novels, 1770–1799

Imprint Year	Total no. of novel titles	Trans. from French	Trans. from German	Trans. from other languages
1770	40	4 (5)		
1771	60	1 (3)	1	2
1772	41	6 (7)		
1773	39	4	2	1
1774	35	4 (5)		
1775	31	4		
1776	17	1	1	
1777	18		(1)	
1778	16	2		
1779	18	2	1	
	315	28 (34)	5	3
		9%	2%	
				11%
1780	24	1		
1781	22	1 (2)		
1782	22	2 (3)		
1783	24	3		
1784	24	2		
1785	47	2		1 (language unknown)
1786	40	7 (8)	2	
1787	51	4		1
1788	80	8[125]		
1789	71	5 (6)	2	
	405	35 (39)	4	2
		9%	1%	
				10%
1790	74	5 (6)	1	1 (2)
1791	74	12	1	
1792	58	6 (7)		1
1793	45	3 (4)	1	1
1794	56	2 (3)	3 (4)	
1795	50	2 (3)	4	1
1796	91	6[126] (8)	9	2
1797	79	7	5 (6)	
1798	75	2 (3)	5[127] (6)	1 (1)
1799	99	13 (14)	10	2 (3)
	701	58 (67)	39 (42)	9 (11)
		8%	6%	1%
				15%

Obvious deceits are excluded, as are translations from a foreign text into another language before the English translation—which is, of course, included. Totals in parenthesis include alleged translations.

Siamese Tales . . . Translated from the Siamese (1796: 18), and the dubiously exotic *Adventures of the Pyrenean Hermits. Translated from the Spanish* (1799: 1).

The interest in French fiction was long-standing, but gained new popularity in the mid-eighteenth century.[128] Some 15 per cent of all new prose fiction titles published in Britain 1750–1769 were translations from the French.[129] A catalogue for John Noble's St Martin's Court circulating library, almost certainly issued in 1767, listed 1,027 French titles from a total of 5,535 entries.[130] Samuel Noble's library catalogue (*c*.1773), listing 4,484 titles, boasted a similar proportion of French literature. In fact, as Table 8 suggests, the proportion of translated French novels fell to some 9 per cent of total new novel titles during the1770s and 1780s, and some 8 per cent in the 1790s, but as Table 8 also shows, annual totals of translated fiction fluctuated markedly. At the peak, some 15 per cent of the total novels (41) with the imprint date of 1772 were translations from French originals, as were 18 per cent of the 40 dated 1786, and 16 per cent of the 74 dated 1791. Some of these translations followed very swiftly upon the publication of the original in Paris, especially where an author enjoyed an established reputation. At least seventeen separate editions of English translations of novels by Marie Jeanne Riccoboni were published between 1750 and 1769.[131] Her *Lettres d'Elisabeth-Sophie de Vallière* was translated into English in the same season as its appearance in Paris (1772: 37), and her *Letters from Lord Rivers* (1778: 14) and *History of Christina, Princess of Swabia* (1784: 23) were both published in London only one year after the first French edition. Most, like these three, seem to have been fashionable curiosities, reprinted in Dublin, but never again.

France was an enduring source of anxiety. In the easy opinion of critics, unwilling to contemplate domestic origins for worthless or dangerous novels, Paris supplied insipidity and indecent imagination. Moral pollution began abroad. This verdict was simple when translated frivolities like *The Danger of the Passions* (1770: 36), *The Captive* (1771: 7), *Coquetilla* (1771: 10), and dozens more in the

---

[125] One French novel was itself a translation from the German.

[126] Includes one doubtful translation.

[127] Includes one title with conflicting evidence about the source of the translation—the original German or a French intermediary.

[128] See in particular Harold Wade Streeter, *The Eighteenth-Century English Novel in French Translation: a Bibliographical Study* [1936] (New York: Benjamin Blom, 1970); and Josephine Grieder, *Translations of French Sentimental Prose Fiction in Late Eighteenth-Century England: The History of a Literary Vogue* (Durham NC: Duke University Press, 1975).

[129] Raven, *British Fiction*, p. 22.

[130] *A New Catalogue of the Large and Valuable Collection of Books (Both English and French) in John Noble's Circulating Library* (London, n.d. [1767]), Bodleian library.

[131] Raven, *British Fiction*, p. 14. For Riccoboni's career, see Emily A. Crosby, *Une Romancière oubliée, Mme Riccoboni: sa vie, ses oeuvres, sa place dans la littérature anglaise et française, du XVIIIe siècle* (Paris, 1924); Joan Hinde Stewart, *The Novels of Mme Riccoboni* (Chapel Hill, NC: University of North Carolina Press, 1976); and Andrée Demay, *Marie-Jeanne Riccoboni: ou de la pensée féministe chez une romancière du XVIIIe siècle* (Paris, 1977).

next decades arrived in the circulating libraries. When Crébillon's *La Nuit et le moment* was translated into English (1770: 25), it was thought to be 'too well executed', giving all too accurate an account 'of the manners of the French people of quality . . . such as, we hope, never will be imitated, like their other fashions and follies, by those of the same class in this country'.[132] Eventually, even this cliché palled. John Noorthouck, reviewing the Chevalier Rutlidge's *Memoirs of Julia de M******, A Reclaimed Courtezan* (1791: 62), declared it to be 'full of business and intrigue; and like many other novels of French manufacture, represents depravity of manners in that country, as being reduced to system'.[133] Still more problematic were connoisseur pieces. When, in 1797 both Diderot's *Jacques le fataliste* and *La Religieuse* were translated (within a year of their original, posthumous publication), respect for the novels was upheld by insistence, for the first, upon British, Sternian influence, and for the second, that indelicacy was justified in the crusade against fanaticism.[134]

Nevertheless, the allure of French novels was also sustained. Although the non-sense pieces continued throughout the thirty years, with repeated calls for the importations to cease,[135] a surprising number of translations earned appreciative notices. Mercier's *Memoirs of the Year Two Thousand Five Hundred* (1772: 36) achieved encouraging reviews and several further editions before the early nineteenth century, and a translation of Riccoboni's latest novel of the same season was greeted by critical rapture.[136] Rival translations from Voltaire brought critical praise and further editions (1774: 33A, 33B). Remarkable acclaim also sustained the popularity of Marie Le Prince de Beaumont, well established since the mid 1750s, and the Comtesse de Genlis.[137] The unknown translator of *Pauline, or the Victim of the Heart* (1794: 19) was congratulated for modifying Contant d'Orville's original, and *Amasis* translated from Saint-Pierre's *L'Arcadie* (1799: 81) was well received and reprinted in both Ireland and New England. More sensational, and roundly denounced by the periodicals, was the translation of Laclos's *Liaisons dangereuses* (1784: 18). The popularity of the French novel was also confirmed by its many imitations, however bogus the alleged source. Impersonations included *Les delices du Sentiment; or the Passionate Lovers in a series of Letters which have recently passed between two celebrated characters* (1781: 3), and *Letters from a French Nobleman to Mademoiselle de P—* (1793: 6), which drew scathing observations from the critics: the letters 'have never spoken any language but our own'.[138]

Interest in German literature developed gradually. Of the 1,421 novels listed in this bibliography as known to have been first published in Britain between 1770 and

---

[132] CR 29 (1770): 396.   [133] MR n.s. 5 (1791): 339.

[134] 1797: 35, 36; CR n.s. 20 (1797), pp. 433–45; CR n.s. 19 (1797), pp. 420–24.

[135] MR on 1793: 27, for example.   [136] CR and MR on 1772: 37.

[137] Both CR and MR reviews for 1775: 26, 1775: 27, and 1783: 9; for the earlier success of Le Prince de Beaumont, see entries in Raven, *British Fiction*.

[138] BC 1 (1793): 453.

1799, 46 were definitely translated from the German (and possibly as many as 51, including several translated via the French, and two versions of the same work). Most notably, these included novels by (or constructed out of the writings of) Wieland, Naubert, Schiller, Lafontaine ('the German Fielding') and Kotzebue. In his *Account of the German Theatre*, first read at a meeting of the Royal Society of Edinburgh in 1788, Henry Mackenzie repaid the compliment of his own popularity in Germany, lauding German romantic drama, especially Schiller's *Die Räuber*. His lecture stimulated, according to Mackenzie's editor Brian Vickers, a great new interest in German literature in England. Walter Scott certainly credited this with his early literary interest in German literature and his translations of ballads by Bürger and of Goethe's *Götz von Berlichingen*.

The translations of lesser German works in the early years of this period brought frequent critical unrest. Lack of cheer or downright indecency was the common charge. William Woodfall in the *Monthly* complained of coldness in Albrecht von Haller's *Usong: An Eastern Narrative* (1772: 33), and Wieland's *History of Agathon* (1773: 38) produced charges of indelicacy.[139] Of a further translation of Wieland that season, Woodfall complained that 'no man should write a novel, or any book of entertainment, which a gentleman cannot read aloud in a company of ladies'.[140] By the mid 1770s, however, new German writers were the subject of literary enthusiasms. In 1776 Joseph Collyer and Edward Harwood competed to get out the fastest translation of Marie Sophie von la Roche's *Geschichte des Fräuleins von Sternheim*, which had been edited by Wieland. The novel, greatly influenced by Richardson, from its letter form to details of plot and characterization, is preoccupied with promoting exemplary womanhood, and by a mode of instructional and extreme sensibility that predated (just) both Mackenzie and Goethe. Goethe, in fact, was not an immediate import—*The Sorrows of Werter* (1779: 10) appeared five years after the original and the English version came via the French. Thereafter, however, spin-offs proliferated, many even attracting their own translation into German and republication in Germany.

By 1790 German novels were seen as a solid counter-weight to the frivolity and indecency of the French product.[141] Even so, a 1792 review of Musäus's *Tales of the Germans* (1791: 53), declared that 'so little are we still acquainted with the German literature, that these Tales, which have been read with much avidity in Germany, have been considered by many here as an English fabrication'.[142] At least the *Tales* contributed to the advancing familiarity with things German. Mounting interest in 'vivid' and 'terrific' German novels was fuelled, amongst others, by Kahlert's ghost and sorcerer novel (1794: 35), Naubert's historical fiction (1794: 40 and 41), Schiller's *The Ghost-Seer* (1795: 39), to be copied by many including Tschink (1795: 44), *The Dagger* (1795: 23) and two further related supernatural tales from Grosse

---

[139] MR 48 (1773), pp. 160–61; CR 37 (1774): 199.
[140] MR 48 (1773): 129, reviewing *Reason Triumphant Over Fancy* (1773: 39).
[141] AR on *Charles Altman* (1790: 7).   [142] EngR 19 (1792): 248–9.

(1796: 44 and 45), together with Wächter's *Sorcerer* (1795: 45) and *Black Valley* (1796: 87). Many of these had been very quickly translated into English within a month or so of their first appearance in Berlin or Leipzig. This extension of the Gothic received, for the most part, critical admiration, but it hardly changed the continuing charge of cheerlessness.[143]

End-of-the-century enthusiasm for things German—if with a peculiarly Gothic and sensationalist hue—was further confirmed by the appearance of novels entitled 'from the German' but in fact penned at desks in London and the home counties. Nine novels, all published after 1790, were manifestly invented 'German tales'. Eliza Parsons joined in relatively early with her *Castle of Wolfenbach; A German Story* published by William Lane in 1793. In the next season Lane produced 'C. R.''s *Castle Zittaw. A German Tale*, and Mrs Parsons returned in 1796 with another Lane novel, *The Mysterious Warning, A German Tale. In Four Volumes.* Lane's by now annual pseudo-German contribution continued in 1797 with Mrs Showes's somewhat weakly titled, *Interesting Tales. Selected and Translated from the German.* The *Critical* was unimpressed: 'We have some doubts whether these tales were translated from the German; but we are clearly of opinion that they were not worth the trouble of translation.' Francis Lathom's 1798 *The Midnight Bell, A German Story, Founded on Incidents in Real Life* was even translated a year later into German (*Die Mitternachtsglocke*, Erfurt 1800), and in 1799 Longman and Rees entered the lists, publishing the anonymous *Spirit of the Elbe: A Romance.* This novel appalled the critics, although one was glad that only a single ghost was introduced.

Novels taken from other languages were rare. Those translated—often very loosely indeed—from Middle Eastern and Indian stories reflect increasing interest in the East during this period. *Select Fables from Gulistan* (1773: 37) were based on a thirteenth-century Persian collection. Also from the Persian, via a Hindustani text, was William Franklin's translation, *The Loves of Camarupa and Camalata* (1793: 18). Oriental and Indian interest increased, even with, for example, Jonathan Scott's translation of some of the tales of the *Bāhar Dānish* (1799: 51), but the cause did not always enhance the art of the novel. It was painfully clear that Phebe Gibbes, author of the Calcutta-based novel, *Hartly House* (1789: 41), had never been to India. Western fascination with the East extended beyond Britain, and French novels about the Orient entered the English lists of fiction via translation.[144] Amongst other language translations were a couple of novels from the Dutch, the disastrous *Magnanimous Amazon* (1796: 14), and the earlier, and more successful *Young Grandison* (1790: 40). This last was a further example of pervasive

---

[143] See for example, the enthusiastic reviews in MR n.s. 18 (1795), pp. 346–7 (on 1795: 39), AR 28 (1798): 518 (on 1798: 68), and CR n.s. 26 (1799), p. 117 (on 1799: 58). A fuller discussion of these translations, is given in James Raven, 'Cheap and Cheerless: English Novels in German Translation and German Novels in English Translation, 1770–1799,' in Werner Huber, ed., *The Corvey Library and Anglo-German Cultural Exchanges 1770–1837* (Munich: Wilhelm Fink, 2000): 1–35.

[144] Notably, *The Vizirs* (1774: 26).

international exchange—a derivative from Richardson's novel, now turned back into the language of its progenitor. Still more evident cross-border creations included French tales badly disguised as Oriental (1773: 26), a translation of a French work said to be from the Greek (1775: 17), and later, a German novel claiming to be from the Arabic (1796: 59). It was unsurprising that when the seventeen-year old Margaret Holford the younger sought a subject for her first novel she turned to Eastern manners.[145] Of *The Tales of Elam* (1794: 14) William Enfield asked 'whether the pleasure, which is taken in the extravagance and impossibility of Eastern fictions, be not the effect of childish taste, of the same kind with that which has given popularity to the stories of George and the Dragon, and Jack the Giant-killer'.[146]

Just as translations hid attempts by authors to disguise plagiarism (and lack of imagination), their attraction to bookseller-publishers was also evident. Second-rate novels could be translated by ill-paid hacks with relative ease and cheapness. The Longman ledger account for *Clara Duplessis and Clairant* (1797: 50), with total publication costs of nearly £136, strikingly includes, in addition to the 20 guineas paid to the translator, a charge of nine shillings for 'copy to print from', that is a set of Lafontaine's original from the open market (either the 1794 German edition or the recent 1797 French translation). As noted, already, most novel writers were paid a pittance for their original manuscript (after which they had no rights to any further profit) but even this expense was avoided if the text was borrowed from abroad. Much translation was the resort of indigent writers and scholars huddled in Grub Street garrets or moonlighting from poorly paid clerkly or clerical positions. As a result, the identity of the translators has been the source of mystery and confusion. A recent discovery reveals Thomas Beddoes as translator of *Popular Tales of the Germans* (1791: 53), an edition of Musäus's *Volksmärchen der Deutschen* (first published at Gotha in 1787–1788). Traditionally, the translation has been attributed to William Beckford, but the Murray archives show that John Murray paid Beddoes thirty guineas for the work, together with a promise of a further ten guineas if a second edition was printed.[147] Other translators, like Mr Porney, a teacher of French at Richmond, who translated a collection of novels in 1780, are known only by name. The Revd James Beresford, translator of de Genlis (1796: 41), and Fellow of Merton College, Oxford, was at least named. Many remain translations 'By a Lady.' They must include those sixteen novels translated by Elizabeth Helme without attribution (with only one, 1791: 39, tentatively identified today).

Booksellers often seemed undecided about giving priority to a translator or an original author. Of two translations in the same season of different novels by Marie Le Prince de Beaumont, one was promoted with her name on the title-page (1775: 26), but the other as 'By' the named translator (1775: 27). Less of a problem

---

[145] *Calaf: A Persian Tale* (1798: 30).

[146] MR n.s. 15 (1794): 354. Earlier that season, the same critic congratulated Joseph Moser for not including the familiar extravagances of the genre in his *Turkish Tales* (1794: 39), MR n.s. 15 (1794): 226.

[147] William Zachs, *The First John Murray and the Late Eighteenth-Century Book Trade* (Oxford: British Academy and Oxford University Press, 1999), pp. 253–409, check-list of Murray publications.

for booksellers were the few notable contributors who joined the ranks of translators. Frances Brooke had already popularized Madame Riccoboni with a translation of her *Lettres de Milady Catesby* in 1759 (JR 502). She now undertook the translation of Framéry's *Mémoires de M. le Marquis de S. Forlaix* (1770: 30) in the same season that it appeared in Paris. Elizabeth Griffith translated Dorat's *Malheurs de l'inconstance* (1774: 25); and twenty years later Elizabeth Gunning translated the *Mémoires de Madame de Barneveldt* (1795: 19). In the next season Gunning exploited this work to produce a novel whose subtitle 'Altered from the French' was apparently quite spurious.[148] By contrast, some translations seem never to have left the bookshop. Joseph Trapp complained that his translation in four volumes of 'The Perverted Clergyman; or the Dangers of the Town' remained in the possession of the notorious bookseller, John Trusler.[149] No trace of the work or its original can be found.

The reception of translations was mixed. Many were written off as impostures, and many more condemned as illiterate and unconvincing.[150] Critics frequently appealed for greater intervention by translators in order to offer more positive mediation between poor foreign texts and new English versions. As one such notice declared of one of the two versions of *Zélie dans le désert* (1789: 39B) 'In the delineation of English manners, the author is very faulty, and the translator has not corrected the errors'.[151] Occasionally a translation or a translator was singled out for special praise. Frances Brooke was widely congratulated; Grafigny's *Peruvian Letters* was said to be translated with particular accuracy; and the translation of both Restif de la Brétonne and the anonymous *Oriental Fables* was held to be 'elegant'.[152] Catherine Lara, translator of *Louis de Boncoeur* (1796: 62), was congratulated by Arthur Akin in the *Monthly*. A *Critical* reviewer approved of the bowdlerization of *Emily de Varmont* (1798: 43), while William Taylor praised the editing in Karl Grosse's *The Dagger* (1795: 23): 'The completeness of the fable, and its well-timed catastrophe, in the English impression, are merits of the translator; who has judiciously omitted some hacknied episodical adventures.'[153]

Even in this case, however, the translator's identity remains hidden. A further example, where anonymous translation led to lasting confusion, was William Lane's publication in 1798 of a translation of Christian Heinrich Spiess's 1792 *Mausefallen und Heckelkramer* (*The Mountain Cottager*). As our new bibliography reveals, the *Analytical* reported that the translator was Anne Plumptre, Annabella Plumptre's sister, and an advertisement for the novel placed in two other contemporary novels quotes the passage containing this point. However, the title-page of

---

[148] *The Foresters* (1796: 47); not derivative but an original work according to ESTC.

[149] Trapp to the Royal Literary Fund, 2 Jan. 1792 (RLF 1: 11).

[150] Notably, reviews of 1789: 52; 1792: 33; 1796: 44; 1796, 61; 1797: 23; 1799: 86.

[151] CR 67 (1789): 67. Similar comments include those on the probable sham-translation *Gomez and Eleonora* (1798: 5) and on Kotzebue's *History of my Father* (1798: 35).

[152] MR on 1774: 28; TCM on 1790: 64; MR on 1797: 17.

[153] CR n.s. 22 (1798): 235; MR n.s. 19 (1796): 207.

Annabella's 1799 translation of August Wilhelm Iffland's play *The Foresters* declares the translation to be 'by Bell Plumptre, translator of the Mountain Cottager'. By the end of the period, however, largely as a result of popular, critically praised French translations and the new interest in the German novel, anonymous translation declined. In the 1790s Peter Will, 'Minister of the Reformed Congregation in the Savoy' was regularly announced on title-pages as the translator of Kotzebue, Tschink, Grosse, and Lafontaine. Booksellers were also keen to add distinction to a new translation by announcing a celebrity involvement—hence John Bell's boast of reliance in these matters on the counsel of Charlotte Smith (1798: 37).

The English Novel Abroad

Translation of the novel was not simply a textual import trade. Many English novels were quickly translated into German, French, and other languages, and the novel industry involved both literary and commercial exchanges back and forth between Britain and Europe. Indeed, in reviewing one of the borrowings—*Innocent Rivals* (1786: 6)—the *Critical* referred to a cross-Channel battle, each side capturing each other's voguish texts. Of the 1,421 titles of new novels listed in the entries below, 500 are known to have been translated into French or German before 1850. A dozen or more titles were also translated into Spanish and Italian by the same date.

Basic details of the first translations in a foreign language are given in the entries to this bibliography. They reveal both the extensiveness of this export and surprising time differences in the reappearance of an English novel abroad. Notable amongst the slow-movers is Smollett's *Humphry Clinker* (1771: 53), not published in French until 1826, probably as a result of his unpopularity in France in the wake of his *Travels through France and Italy* (1768). By contrast, *Humphry Clinker* was published in German in the next season. Few notable authors were not translated into German. Another novel of 1771, Henry Mackenzie's *Man of Feeling*, delineating sensibility or, in the author's words, 'the sweet emotion of pity' and 'the luxury of grief', was translated into German three years later and into French the year after that. His *Man of the World* of 1773 was translated into German in the same season and into French within two years.

Tables 9 and 10 offer summaries of the relative speed of translation of English novels of the period, although it is important to stress, first, that the tables do not include *subsequent* translations of the same titles (a few of which were issued in further translated editions during this period), and, second, that these must be preliminary findings, given the continuing research in both France and Germany to identify English translations. Novels of the 1770s were translated into German more frequently and with greater speed than into French. Amongst titles reappearing in German in the same season are Richard Graves's *Spiritual Quixote* of 1773, Henry Brooke's *Juliet Grenville* of 1774, Charles Johnstone's *The Pilgrim* and Henry Man's *Mr Bentley* of 1775, and Elizabeth Bonhote's *Rambles of Mr Frankly* of 1776.

Perhaps only Graves was translated because of the immediate critical and public response in London; the others are more likely to have been translated in response to earlier success by these authors or because of assumed interest in the topic or a publishing inducement. More broadly, however, the rage for the English novel in Germany induced translations of a range of writers from the famous to the obscure. Novels first published in Britain in the 1770s also maintained greater long-term popularity in Germany than in France—well over a third of all titles from this decade were translated into German before 1850 but only 10 per cent of these titles were translated into French during the same period. After some renewed interest in translating English novels in France in the late 1780s (with some retrospective translating of novels issued in London two to five years previously during the first years of the Revolution), a marked turnaround came at the very end of the century. Nearly a quarter of all novels first published in London 1796–1799 were translated into French within five years of their appearance.

No full modern study yet exists of the influence of the English novel in France or Germany in this period. Existing analyses are either partial or inaccurate. In particular, the various works by Lawrence Marsden Price and Mary Bell Price, the fullest listings to date of English novels in translation in eighteenth-century Germany, are flawed by misleading attribution and incorrect dating.[154] Since Price, numerous scholars have explored the history of the popular novel in Germany in this period in an attempt to understand its broader literary and social context. Eva Becker, Michael Hadley, and Manfred Heiderich each offered profiles of novels published in a single year, studying 1780, 1790, and 1800 respectively. Given the foreign origins and influences of so much of the material, they have been let down by English bibliographical failings. Translation of English novels of the period into French has been better served by scholarship, but even here existing guides are incomplete and currently undergoing revision.[155] The notes sections to the following entries do not pretend to be comprehensive, but, as far as the editorial resources of this volume made possible, they do attempt to notice the first translations of the English novels published during this period.[156]

---

[154] Lawrence Marsden Price, *English German Literary Influences: Bibliography and Survey*, *University of California Publications in Modern Philology* 9: 1 (Jan. 1919); Lawrence Marsden Price, *English Literature in Germany*, *University of California Publications in Modern Philology* 37 (1953) [a revised edn. of Lawrence Marsden Price, *The Reception of English Literature in Germany* (University of California Press: Berkeley CA, 1932)]; and Mary Bell Price and Lawrence Marsden Price, *The Publication of English Literature in Germany in the Eighteenth Century* (University of California Press: Berkeley CA, 1934). Most uncomfortably, Price includes some dates for German translations of English novels which predated by some four or five years their first publication in London.

[155] Angus Martin, Vivienne G. Mylne and Richard Frautschi, eds., *Bibliographie du genre romanesque français 1751–1800* (London and Paris: Mansell, 1977); and (more problematically) Alexandre Cioranescu, ed., *Bibliographie de la littérature Française du dix-huitième siècle* (Paris: Editions du Centre National de la Recherche Scientifique, 1969).

[156] Works in progress include the 'Bibliographie englischer Romane in Deutschland 1790–1834', compiled by Rainer Schöwerling, Karin Wünsche and Verena Ebbe at the University of Paderborn; and the 'Publication of English Authors in Germany' project, directed by Bernhard Fabian and Marie-Luise Spiekermann at the University of Munster.

At least 282 titles were translated into German within ten years of their appearance and a further fourteen more than ten years after first publication in English (and before 1850). By comparison, no fewer than 184 titles were translated into French within ten years of their appearance in English, with a further twenty-one titles translated more than ten years later. Translations into German were, generally, much swifter—many, within the same season or the next. There is also considerable variation in the proportion of titles translated into both languages over the full period. Tables 9 and 10 offer a preliminary summary of both features. At the very least it confirms Price's fears that his claim that German translation had been undertaken for no less than three-quarters of all the titles identified by J. M. S. Tompkins's *Popular Novel in England 1770–1800* (then recently published) would be qualified when fuller listings were available of the range of English novel production.

It is important to stress that both tables record the advance of the English novel in Germany and France from the perspective of annual publication of *new* English novels. The total translations of these into German (296 titles to 1850) varied from four of the annual English new titles to seventeen (the class of 1796). A particularly high proportion of the total output of new English novels was also translated into German in a nine-year period from the mid-1770s (see the final column of Table 9). Of all English novels first published between 1773 and 1781, never fewer than one quarter of all annual titles were translated into German. In the peak years of 1776, 1777 and 1779 three-quarters and then two-thirds of all annual titles were translated into German. We also know from other sources that total translations of all English novels, including much older titles, was markedly high in these years. The late nineteenth-century work of Carl Heine—itself probably an underestimate—suggests that at least 87 novels were translated from the English and published in Germany between 1773 and 1778 (more than twice as many as were translated from the French in the same years).

By comparison, indeed, French translations of new English novels never reached even a third of the total number of English titles available in any one year of these decades. The highest total of 40 or 30 per cent of the publications with an imprint date of 1786, was also achieved slowly, over subsequent seasons. There was certainly no rush to translate English novels into French. In English terms, the most auspicious years for producing novels later to be translated into French were 1786–1789 and 1796–1799, but such trends are hardly explicable without a much more searching questioning of translation patterns across a broad range of literature and without more precise investigation into the actual years and circumstances of translation in Paris.

Table 9 further suggests that the proportion of new English novels translated into German declined from the 35 per cent of all fiction titles published in 1781 to something like an average of 10 per cent in the 1790s. Certain health warnings should be observed—fine distinctions between two successive years are less meaningful when one considers that a publishing season, as already noted, might extend from the

Table 9. First Translations before 1850 into German of English Novels First Published in Britain and Ireland 1770–1799

Imprint Year	Trans. in the Same Year	Next Year	2–5 Years	6–10 Years	10+ Years	Total Trans.	Total Novels	%* of Trans. into German
1770	3	2	1	2	2	10	40	25
1771	2	4	2		1	9	60	15
1772	1	1	2	2		6	41	15
1773	2	3	6	3		14	39	36
1774	2	8	3			13	35	37
1775	4	8	3		1	16	31	52
1776	6	4	2		1	13	17	76
1777		10	1	1		12	18	66
1778		7	2			9	16	56
1779	2	6	4			12	18	66
1780	2	4	2			8	24	33
1781	1	7	2			10	22	45
1782	1	2	1	1	1	5	22	23
1783		2	2			4	24	17
1784		2	2			4	24	17
1785	1	2	4	1		8	47	17
1786		3	6	1		10	40	25
1787	1	1	5	1	3	11	51	22
1788	1	2	3	1	3	10	80	13
1789	1	5	9			15	71	21
1790	(1 n.d.)	8	4			13	74	18
1791	1	4	6			11	74	15
1792	1	5		1		7	58	12
1793		1	3	1		5	45	11
1794	1	7	2			10	56	18
1795		4	1		1	6	50	12
1796		6	9	2		17	91	19
1797	1	2	5	1		9	79	11
1798		5	3		1	9	75	12
1799	2	4	4			10	99	10
Total	36	129	99	18	14	296	1,421	21

n.d. (no date) similarly indicates the absence of exact dating for the translation

    * rounded up to the nearest percentage point

October of one calendar year to the May (at least) of the next. Some novels apparently published a year later than their first appearance in English might have appeared only a month or so after the original novel despite its imprint date of an

Table 10. **First Translations before 1850 into French of English Novels First Published in Britain and Ireland 1770–1799**

Imprint Year	Trans. in the Same Year	Next Year	2–5 Years	6–10 Years	10+ Years	Total Trans.	Total Novels	%* of Trans. into French
1770	4				1	5	40	13
1771		2	2	1	2	7	60	12
1772	1	2	1	1		5	41	12
1773			3			3	39	8
1774			2		1	3	35	9
1775			1			1	31	3
1776		2			2	3	17	18
1777		1	1			2	18	11
1778		1	1			2	16	13
1779			1			1	18	6
1780	(2 n.d.)		1			3	24	13
1781				1		1	22	5
1782		1			1	2	22	9
1783		1				1	24	4
1784			4		1	5	24	21
1785			4	1		5	47	11
1786	1	2	7	1	1	12	40	30
1787	1	6	4	2		13	51	25
1788	7	5	1	1		14	80	18
1789	6			4	2	12	71	17
1790				1		1	74	1
1791	1	1	2	(1 n.d.)	1	6	74	8
1792		2	1		1	4	58	7
1793	(1 n.d.)			1		2	45	4
1794	(1 n.d.)	1	3		3	8	56	14
1795			2	2		4	50	8
1796	(2 n.d.)	8	7		2	19	91	21
1797	4	8	9		2	23	79	29
1798	7	7	4	(1 n.d.)		19	75	25
1799	2	6	8		2	18	99	18
Total	*40*	*56*	*69*	*18*	*22*	*204*	*1,421*	*15*

n.d. no date given for the foreign translation
 * rounded up to the nearest percentage point

earlier year. As pertinent, for titles published in both countries, is the usual warning about imprint post-dating by booksellers anxious to appear à la mode.

Even so, the frequency of translation into German of English novels of the 1770s does seem marked. Various considerations might apply. There was probably a need to supply a German market for novels that was growing but where relatively few native novels were available. Supportive evidence includes the constant base-line demand for translations from the English. Notably, in 1776 and 1777 the proportion of novels taken from the English is especially high given the exceptional drop in overall output of the novel in Britain and Ireland in these years. Richardsoniana continued to attract German readers throughout this period. Novels that dwindled into deserved obscurity in Britain were often quickly translated when styled as having been written in the manner of Richardson. *The New Clarissa* (1771: 37) was translated into German a few seasons later, while *The History of Sir William Harrington* also of 1771, was published in English and in German in the same year.

This last possibility has perhaps been the most overlooked. In years when French and particularly German booksellers sought foreign novels to translate to satisfy new demand, the output of particular London booksellers might have appealed. Most noticeable (and surprising) about the novels from Table 9 that were swiftly translated into German is the number of titles first published by the Noble brothers of the newly fashionable West End of London. Four Nobles' titles from 1773, a further four from 1774, and two from 1775, were translated and published in Germany, most within two years of their original publication in London. In Paris Thomas Hookham advertised his *livres vendu* from his New Bond Street shop in extensive lists of French and English titles. For all the surviving notices (such as those appended to 1781: 17 and 1784: 1) the business arrangement here is still unclear, but the cross-Channel activities of Hookham and his later partner, James Carpenter, contributed significantly to English–French novel exchange in the period. Other connections seem to include those between Longman and L. L'Homme, French bookseller of New Bond Street, who, possibly in return for the supply of French texts to Longman, contributed very modestly to the financing of the translation and publication of de Genlis's *Rash Vows* (1799: 40).

The later translation of very obscure English titles might also suggest one other agency: the mediating role of the major periodical reviews. Here was a readily available, exported dictionary of past publishing and critical assessment from London. Given the profuse publication by the Nobles and Lane it might be asked how certain titles (many marked by queasy frivolity) were selected for translation. Noticeable amongst *translated* Noble novels from the mid-1770s was an above average verdict from the London critics (not that that is saying much in the context of the reviewers' magnificently dismissive notices of most novels). 'Merit enough' sniffed the *Monthly* of *The Mercenary Marriage* (1773: 13; *Die eigennützige Heurath*, 1776). 'Calculated to be of service to the unmarried fair ones,' noted the *Critical*, and 'of very useful tendency' echoed the *Monthly* of *The Way to Lose Him*, also of (1773: 21; *Der Weg ihn zu verlieren*, 1774). 'Not very ill written,' admitted the *Monthly* of *The Journey to London* (1774: 12; *Geschichte der Familie Selby*, 1775). English originals seem to have been attractive to a wide spread of German publishing booksellers as well as those in the predominant—and then (in novel publishing terms) sharply declining—centre of Leipzig. What, apart from flimsy review reputation might explain the translation and publication within one year of the London printing of the Nobles' *Capricious Father* (1775: 2; *Der eigensinnige Vater*, 1776), a novel so inconsequential that no copy appears to survive anywhere in the world today? Whatever it was, it seems not to have been operative in France where apparently none of these grudgingly approved titles found a translator.

Bookseller–Publishers and Printers

Almost all these novels were first published in London. Of the 315 titles with imprints of the 1770s only nine (3 per cent) were published outside London. In the 1780s some twenty-six (6.5 per cent) of the 403 titles were not published in London. Eleven of these were published in Dublin, and seven of these in the two years 1780–1781. The contribution of Dublin booksellers in combining to bring out rapid reprints of novels just published in London has already been discussed. Table 11 demonstrates graphically both the relatively minor role of Dublin booksellers in publishing original fiction titles in the period, and the sudden demise of new Dublin novels in the 1790s. Apparently, no new novel title was published first in Dublin between 1791 and 1799. By comparison, a marked increase in titles first published in English towns other than London in the 1790s brought the total of novels first printed in the provinces to 44 (or 6.3 per cent of the total of 697 novels). English provincial novel publishing in the 1790s was led by Bath, but also included the work of bookseller–publishers in Brentford, Birmingham, Bristol, Chelsea, Newcastle, Norwich, Shrewsbury, Southampton, Wakefield and York, amongst others. In some cases, booksellers in these towns published local authors—Clara Reeve in Colchester (1777: 16), Henry Clarke in Manchester (styled 'Utopia', 1788: 48), Alethea Lewis (of Penkridge, Staffordshire) in Stafford (1794: 36), Ann Thomas (of Millbrook, Cornwall) in Plymouth (1794: 55), and Ann Gomersall (following her move from Leeds) in Exeter (1796: 42). Printing of first editions in Scotland was negligible, as was the Irish publication of novels outside Dublin. During the 1790s these provincial initiatives did, however, include Cork, where three new novels were published by the press of John Connor.[157]

More than 250 firms were involved in the publication of the listed novels in this bibliography, and just over 200 of them were London booksellers and printers. Although many bookseller–publishers each produced only one or two of these titles, novel production generally was more concentrated than in previous decades, headed by the presses of a dozen or more firms. In the twenty years between 1750 and 1770, for example, some 260 different booksellers contributed to the publication of new novels. By the 1770s the contribution from country towns had increased, but London remained predominant, sustained by major novel-publishing

---

[157] See Rolf Loeber and Magda Stouthamer-Loeber, 'John Connor: A Maverick Cork Publisher of Literature', *18ᵗʰ–19ᵗʰ Century Irish Fiction Newsletter* 5 (May 1998).

Table 11. **Production of Novels in Britain and Ireland, 1770–1799:**
Place of Publication of the First Edition

Year	London	Dublin	Other Engl.	Scotland	Other Ire.	Total
1770	38	1	1			40
1771	59		1			60
1772	39	1	1			41
1773	39					39
1774	34	1				35
1775	30		1			31
1776	16			1		17
1777	17		1			18
1778	16					16
1779	18					18
	306	*3*	*5*	*1*		*315*
1780	17	4	2	1		24
1781	18	4				22
1782	21		1			22
1783	24					24
1784	24					24
1785	44		1	2		47
1786	36	2	2			40
1787	48	1	2			51
1788	77	1	1		1	80
1789	69		2			71
	378	*12*	*11*	*3*	*1*	*405*
1790	71	1	1		1	74
1791	68	3	3			74
1792	53		3	2		58
1793	44				1	45
1794	54		2			56
1795	46		3		1	50
1796	87		2	1	1	91
1797	70		5	2	2	79
1798	71		4			75
1799	91		8			99
	655	*4*	*31*	*5*	*6*	*701*
	1,339	*19*	*47*	*9*	*7*	*1,421*

firms such as John and Francis Noble, Thomas Becket and Peter Abraham de Hondt, John Bew, John Roson, and Thomas Lowndes. During the next three decades, four particular firms boosted publication totals: Thomas Hookham, the Robinsons, the Nobles (until 1789), and, from 1775, the newcomer and greatest novel manufacturer of all, William Lane. At the same time, the country market, as exploited by London publishers, continued to expand and prompt further critical anxiety about the influence of new fiction.

Table 12. Leading London Novel Publishers,[158] 1770–1799, by Publication of New Prose Fiction Titles

	No. New Titles		
	1770s	1780s	1790s
Becket / de Hondt	17	3(Becket)	
Bell	9		30
Bew	21	24	10(1792)
Cadell	16	14	4(1793)
			14(Cadell & Davies)
Dodsley	11	8	1
Hookham	5	41	19
			35(& Carpenter)
Lane	(1775)3	80	217
Lowndes	22	8(& William)	6(William & family)
Nobles	38	21(1788)	
Robinsons	14	34	54
Roson	18(1774)		
Symonds		6	23
Vernor	9	4	5
			27(& Hood)
All London booksellers	306	378	655

Table 12 lists those primarily responsible for the publication of the novels. That all are London booksellers is evident, but their geographical spread across London is also significant. Some, like the Robinsons and Bew, operated from Paternoster Row,

---

[158] That is, the bookseller–publisher identified from an imprint as apparently having a role in financing the publication (usually as 'Printed for') and excluding the appearance of these booksellers' names in the 'sold by' advertisements to novels when not also cited in the actual imprint. Some of the novels, jointly financed, appear more than once in this table. There is one other important caution to this table: where no copy of a novel survives, entries often depend on the original review or advertisement, and in these the names of bookseller–publishers are often given very generally and without the sort of filter provided by an imprint.

by then the main publishing street in London, close to the traditional stationery and bookselling centre of St Paul's Churchyard.[159] Other booksellers, like Hookham and the Nobles, set up shop in the newly-built and fashionable squares and lanes of the West End. Still others, like Lane and his Minerva Press in Leadenhall Street, made an address famous despite an unusual site. The distribution is telling. Some of the leading publishers of novels worked within the established network and as part, indeed, of the Stationers' Company; others seemed to relish the challenge to the book-trade establishment and made the popular novel a weapon in their battle for commercial and public success. Self-publicists like the Nobles, Lane, and Hookham and Carpenter can be credited with pioneering efforts in the establishment of commercial circulating libraries and in the publication of fashionable, almost production-line novels.

Like so many of the novelists, however, most of those responsible for the financing and marketing of novels, have left little trace. Many publisher–booksellers were very small operators and most feature hardly or not at all in the remaining book trades records of the period. Of those listed in the index to this bibliography as involved in the printing, publishing, and selling of the novels, more than half were outside the Stationers' Company, and many remain frustratingly mysterious figures. Metropolitan addresses certainly did not guarantee recognition. London connections with regional publishing, in the sense of some shared financing rather than the more usual 'sold by' distribution arrangements, are similarly shadowy. One such case is the apparent cooperation between Skelton of Southampton and Charles Law to publish Richard Warner's *Netley Abbey* (1795: 47). This was shamelessly reissued with cancel title-pages by William Lane who then issued a brazen advertisement warning of a poorer copy in circulation 'with a Country Printer's Name in the Title'.[160]

The Noble brothers, in many ways the founders of formula novel publication, are all too typical in furnishing a couple of letters as the sole remnants of their business and personal papers.[161] Only scant civic taxation records, newspaper advertisements and some of their own publications remain to chronicle and explain their career. By 1770 the Nobles were notorious operators, having established themselves in the 1750s as the most prolific single publishers of new fiction.[162] Francis Noble set up shop in St Martin's Court, Leicester Fields, in 1737, his brother John beginning his own publishing career seven years later. Francis died in June 1792, fourteen years after his brother, and famously retired from the novel business after his

---

[159] See Peter W. M. Blayney, *The Bookshops in Paul's Cross Churchyard* Occasional Papers of the Bibliographical Society 5 (1990); and James Raven, 'Memorializing a London Bookscape: The Mapping and Reading of Paternoster Row and St Paul's Churchyard, 1695–1814', in R. C. Alston, ed., *Order and Connexion: Studies in Bibliography and Book History* (Woodbridge: D. S. Brewer, 1997): 177–200.

[160] OPA 26 May 1795.

[161] Francis Noble to J. S. Charlton, 1750, 1751, BL Add Mss 32720 f. 113, 32725 f. 321. Nothing of John Noble seems to have survived.

[162] Raven, *British Fiction*, fig. 2.

daughter won a prize in the state lottery. Beginning in the mid-1740s, the brothers established what was for twenty years the leading circulating library for modish London and French literature, and supplied dozens of London and provincial libraries with their wares. At least 176 novels and miscellanies (and further editions) were issued jointly for F. and J. Noble between 1745 and 1778, with another thirty or more by Francis Noble between 1777 and 1789. The peak years in the first period were 1756 and 1757, but in the long second period of activity, at least fifty-two novels were published between 1766 and 1770 and a further forty-one novels by 1775.[163] For nearly half a century the imprints of John and Francis, and then Francis on his own, were synonymous with a particular type of fashionable popular novel, Frances Burney, for example, offering casual reference to their endeavours in popular literature.[164] Vilified as 'novel manufacturers' and hawkers of immoral and licentious literature, the Nobles were the literary equivalents of the managers of Ranelagh gardens or the masters of ceremonies at tonnish spa resorts.

From 1760, the Nobles' chief competitor in the novel market was probably Thomas Becket, trading in the Strand with his Dutch partner, Peter Abraham de Hondt. Where the Nobles were novel specialists, the Becket firm published a broader range of fashionable literature. Becket, the former apprentice of Andrew Millar, was both an importer of new French literature and a publisher of modern tracts and *belles lettres*. His Tully's Head shop sign directly imitated the Dodsleys of Pall Mall, whose publication of the early volumes of Sterne's *Tristram Shandy* had been extended to continuation volumes by Becket in 1762, 1765, and 1767. The history of the firm spans triumph and disaster. The thirteen-year partnership produced at least 477 publications, and de Hondt claimed that the firm had enjoyed an annual profit of £6,000 when he left the country in 1766. From 1772 the Becket shop was incorporated in the north-east corner of the Adam brothers' new Adelphi in the Strand.[165] It is not known whether this rearrangement played any part in the dissolution of the partnership in 1772, for which de Hondt was paid what he regarded as a paltry recompense of £1,300, but following Becket's bankruptcy in 1778, de Hondt publicly voiced his sense of grievance. De Hondt seems to have been principally active in the importing and exporting side of the business, and his role as a partner become a contentious issue after his departure from the Strand in 1766. De Hondt later insisted that he had retained no involvement with Becket for seven years before the bankruptcy and hence was in no way liable for the firm's debts. Certainly, his last joint imprint with Becket recorded in this bibliography is from 1772/3. Becket was re-established by 1783, but surviving letters from de Hondt, now based in Nimwegen, repeat numerous allegations of bad practice against

[163] Raven, 'Noble Brothers,' pp. 315–45. Three more editions have been discovered since publication; undoubtedly, more will be found (although the Nobles' puffing advertisements alone are insufficient evidence without further support).

[164] *Diary and Letters of Madame D'Arblay*, edited by Charlotte Barrett, 4 vols. (London, 1904), 2: 81.

[165] Demolished 1937. Views are given in John Summerson, *Georgian London* rev. edn 1978 (London, 1945), plates 19a, 19b.

Becket and 'the injustice which was proposed against me' during the bankruptcy proceedings.[166]

Thomas Lowndes traded from Exeter Court before moving to Fleet Street proper in 1756. He was in business there for thirty years until his death in 1784. The publisher of *Evelina* (1778: 10), Thomas Lowndes is thought to be the basis for the miserly and rough-speaking Briggs in Burney's next novel, *Cecilia* (1786: 15). Uneducated but immensely rich, Briggs is presented as

a short, thick, sturdy man, with very small keen black eyes, a square face, a dark complexion, and a snub nose. His constant dress, both in winter and summer, was a snuff-colour suit of clothes, blue and white speckled worsted stockings, a plain shirt, and a bob wig.[167]

A notable publisher of plays, music, and directories, as well as founding one of the earliest and most extensive commercial circulating libraries, Lowndes fathered a successful booktrading family many of whom were also novel printers and publishers. Thomas was succeeded by his eldest son and partner, William, who moved the shop to Bedford Street, Covent Garden, in 1806, having left his brother Henry at the Fleet Street premises in 1797.

Despite its lowly origins, the successful Lowndes family resembles the other two respected firms featuring prominently in Table 12: John Bew and the Robinsons. John Bew of Paternoster Row was best known for publishing the *General Evening Post* for twenty years after 1774 and the *Political Magazine* from 1780 until its publication by John Murray in 1785. His firm at no. 28 Paternoster Row, in a small block backing on to Newgate Market, was successor to Bladon's famous Paper Mill, reconstructed after a disastrous fire at the eastern end of the Row in 1770. Dealing mainly in tracts and periodicals, but also selling prints, Bew's name appears on at least 737 different imprints, including the fifty-five novels listed in this bibliography. Even so, Bew did not escape the bankruptcies so prevalent in this high risk enterprise, his failure in 1790 coming three years before his death.

Perhaps the most remarkable establishment in the Row, however, was that of George Robinson (1737–1801), trading under Addison's Head at no. 25, two doors down from Bew. The firm's output of novels steadily advanced during the final third of the century. If a distant second behind the brash dominance of William Lane in the novel market of the 1790s, Robinson still published more novels than any other bookseller in the decade and sold titles generally recognized to be of greater interest and distinction than Lane's potboilers. On his arrival in London in 1755 George Robinson worked first under John Rivington, and then, from about 1759, for William Johnston, the great copyholding bookseller of Ludgate Street. Five years later, Robinson set up in Paternoster Row with John Roberts who died in 1776. This partnership published five of the novels listed in this bibliography between 1770 and 1772. In 1784 Robinson took into partnership his brother John,

---

[166] Bod. MS Add.c.89, Correspondence of Ralph Griffiths, f. 32, de Hondt to Griffiths, 18 Oct. 1780.
[167] Burney, *Cecilia*, bk II ch. 1. The original attribution is by John Nichols, *Literary Anecdotes of the Eighteenth Century* 9 vols. (London, 1812–1815), 3: 646.

trading since 1781, and his son George, both of whom succeeded him in 1801. The inscriptions G. G. and J. [George, George and John] and G. G. J. and J. [George, George, John and James] Robinson appear both familiar and seemingly inter-changeable in novel imprints between the late 1780s and the end of the century.[168]

Contributing further to this market profile, the Robinson family published some of the most popular and influential periodicals of the century. In 1774 George Robinson bought a share in the *Critical Review*, and from 1772 he partnered Archibald Hamilton, the main publisher of the *Town and Country Magazine*. The *Lady's Magazine*, founded in July 1770, was transferred to Robinson in 1771 for the sum of £500, but not without protest, litigation, and the publication of a rival maga-zine with the same title by the original promoter, John Wheble, who traded next door. The magazine, which with the spicier *Town and Country*, made very obvious appeal to novel-reading young women, was continued by the Robinsons until 1819, when ownership was finally transferred again. In his later years, Robinson was increasingly drawn to reform and radical causes, and contributed to the political metamorphosis of the *Critical Review* in the 1790s. In 1793 he was fined for selling *The Rights of Man*. Robinson's place amongst the great booksellers of the century was never questioned. The *Gentleman's Magazine* obituary in 1801 remarked upon his 'warm and sincere, affectionate and tender' virtues, and William West, book-seller neighbour of George Robinson from 1800, wrote of him as 'the Prince, nay, the King of Booksellers; for added to his fine, manly, prepossessing appearance, and dignified manners, his walk was as majestic as that of his friends Drs Glover and Buchan; never shall I forget these outstanding personages each standing 6 feet in height, at their great climacterick'.[169] Like that of the bookselling Dilly brothers, and the nearby radical publisher, Joseph Johnson, the Robinson house was the scene of renowned entertainment. Mrs Radcliffe, Mrs Thrale, and Mrs Inchbald were fre-quent visitors.[170]

The social and political activities of booksellers like the Robinsons, the Dillys, and others including Cadell, Longman and Robson, lifted them to a respectability not always at ease with the sponsorship of fiction, even though much was increas-ingly dressed up as the charitable patronage of the indigent and deserving.[171] The meagre representation of certain important publishing houses in the index of booksellers to this volume suggests how fiction manuscripts were avoided in par-ticular quarters for politic as well as economic reasons. With the exception of Charles Moser's *Moral Tales* (1797: 59), said by the *Monthly* to 'uniformly tend to promote the cause of good morality',[172] no novels were issued by the piously

---

[168] See the listings in the index to booksellers and printers.

[169] *Gentleman's Magazine* n.s. 71 (1801): 578–80; William West, *Fifty Years' Recollections of an Old Bookseller* (London, 1837), p. 92.

[170] Leslie F. Chard, 'Bookseller to Publisher: Joseph Johnson and the English Book Trade, 1760 to 1810', *The Library*, 5th ser., 32 (1977), 138–54 (138).

[171] The Robinson obituary ranked him as the most respectable bookseller after Cadell and Strahan, themselves said to be the heirs in reputation to Tonson and Millar, GM n.s. 71 (1801): 578.

[172] MR n.s. 25 (1798): 346–7.

Anglican Rivington family, publishers of more than 6,000 different titles between 1711 and 1800.[173] Thomas Longman II, nephew to the founder of the house, published only one work in this period that can count as a novel, and that, in combination with Cadell and the Robinsons, a highly moralistic tale 'for the benefit of intelligent servants' (1787: 4). This was followed by some twenty-four Longman novel titles between 1794 and 1799, but all, following the withdrawal of Thomas II from business in about 1792, under the direction of his son, Thomas Norton Longman, and his partner Owen Rees (the latter only acknowledged on the novel imprints from 1799). The otherwise fulsome obituary of George Robinson concluded that if criticism were to be offered 'it would be that Mr R, rather gave too much than too little, and that he sometimes gave a consequence to works, which neither their own merit, not the opinion of the publick, would ever sanction'.[174] Thomas Cadell was involved in the production of various prestigious and profitable works, but also in the publication of some thirty-four of the novels listed in this bibliography. Cadell had succeeded to the business of the greatly respected Andrew Millar of the Strand in 1767, was a liveryman of the Stationers' Company for thirty-seven years, and accepted election as a City Alderman five years after his retirement in 1793. The novels published by Cadell and by his successors, his son Thomas and his partner, William Davies, are a select group, including the novels of Henry Mackenzie, Charles Johnstone, and Charlotte Smith, translations of Wieland and Grafigny, Burney's *Cecilia* and *Camilla*, and almost no completely anonymous or poorly reviewed volumes. Cadell also sustained a spirited list of authors thought worthy of encouragement including Bicknell, Blower, Frances Brooke, Sophia Lee, Lennox, Moore, and Helen Maria Williams. Burney's *Cecilia* supposedly 'cleared 1,500 pounds the first Year' according to the author's own journals.[175]

While the great majority of booksellers was not averse to publishing new novels, even by unproven authors, when the purchase of rights was so cheap and the market apparently so good, it was the activities of a few notorious operators that continued to cause a certain lofty concern, even if it also boosted public interest in the novel. In terms of dedicated novel publishing, the real rivals and successors to the Nobles were Hookham and Lane. Thomas Hookham traded in Hanover Square from the mid 1750s until 1767, changed his address (although not necessarily his premises) to Hanover Street from 1775, and then moved to New Bond Street sometime before 1787. Shortly thereafter he opened a further shop in Old Bond Street, although the relationship between the two shops continued to be somewhat confusing. By 1793 the business operated mainly from Old Bond Street, but an advertisement in 1795 announced the retention of the circulating library in Old Bond

[173] The black sheep of the family, James Rivington, exiled to America after bankruptcy in 1758–1759, was, however, a major dealer, though not publisher, of fiction.

[174] GM n.s. 71 (1801): 579. The example given above (p. 55) of Mrs Gosling's subscription scheme might well be an example.

[175] Joyce Hemlow, et al., eds., *The Journals and Letters of Fanny Burney (Madame d'Arblay)* 12 vols. (Oxford: Clarendon Press, 1972–1984), 3: 140.

Street with the return of the bookselling and stationary business to New Bond Street.[176] On his own or in combination with David Hookham, publishing from 1756, and Jordan Hookham, his nephew and successor, Hookham issued over 500 books until the litigious dissolution of his partnership with his son-in-law, James Carpenter, and his retirement in the late 1790s. As already noted, his bookshop and circulating library keyed in to both London demand for French literature and literary demand from France, particularly during his business association with Carpenter. The Hookhams' *Agatha; or, A Narrative of Recent Events* (1796: 2), published for its author in combination with other booksellers, was advertised as having been translated in Paris 'notwithstanding its counter-revolutionary Principles'.[177] The survival of two rare Hookham novels in Paris is probably a result of the original French custom.[178]

By the 1780s William Lane had established himself as the leading novel publisher in Britain. By the 1790s his dominance was overwhelming. During that decade Lane published one third of all new novel titles in London, even if few were reprinted.[179] The son of a London poulterer and a member of the Poulters' Company in his early years, Lane began bookselling from his father's shop. By 1773 he graduated to his own premises in Aldgate High Street and in 1775 he moved to 33 Leadenhall Street. Lane's activities in the late 1770s are still unclear. He published relatively few titles but also seems to have pursued business interests in the West Country.[180] By at least 1784, however, he had established a press at his London shop, took apprentices within the year, and in 1788 became proprietor of the new afternoon newspaper, *The Star and Evening Advertiser*. In 1790–1791 his Leadenhall Street premises was expanded to incorporate two neighbouring houses. Styled the 'Minerva Press' from at least 1790, the Leadenhall building housed not only the celebrated circulating library, carefully developed since the early 1770s, but a large workforce, numbered as 'upwards of 30' and at least four printing presses by 1791.[181] Anthony King Newman, who joined the firm in about 1801, was made partner by 1803 and Lane retired sometime between 1803 and 1808. He died in 1814. Newman, who retired in 1848, continued the 'Minerva' name until 1820.[182]

William Lane fought for honourable recognition all his life, even after admission

---

[176] *Morning Post* 29 May 1795.   [177] GEP 27–30 Jan. 1798.

[178] Notably (1781: 18), held only at the Sorbonne, and (1784: 1), where the Bibliothèque Nationale copy is one of only two known copies.

[179] Notable exceptions include the very popular *Children of the Abbey* by Regina Maria Roche (1796: 78) and the reprinted *Anna* (1785: 22) and *The Beggar Girl* (1797: 26), both by Anna Maria Bennett. Some 60 Lane novel titles published during the 1790s were themselves reprints (either of Lane originals or of titles first published by others).

[180] I owe this point to E. D. Pitcher, who identifies Lane's involvement with Samuel Jackson Pratt and the *Bristol and Bath Magazine*.

[181] *The Star* 9 May 1791.

[182] The standard account, Dorothy Blakey, *The Minerva Press 1790–1820* (London and Oxford: Bibliographical Society, 1939), has recently been supplemented by Deborah Anne McLeod, 'The Minerva Press' unpublished Ph.D. dissertation, University of Alberta, 1997. McLeod's listings are themselves substantially revised by the entries in this bibliography.

to the Stationers' Company in 1777. Cartoons and satirical odes lampooned Lane as the 'chicken-butcher' and 'scribbling poulterer' who paraded in gold carriages and brandished gold-headed canes.[183] His renowned shortness of temper did not assist his efforts to be accepted as a respectable member of the book-trade. The greatest obstacle of all, however, remained the pretentions of the classically styled Minerva press and library, supremely self-confident, yet characterized by all too many pitiable products. As noted, Lane had no compunction about buying up stock and reissuing it as his own with new title-pages, just as the Nobles and their rivals had done in earlier days.[184] Lane also reprinted recent pot-boilers under new titles, including a Nobles novel, *Sketches from Nature* (1778: 6), reprinted as *Female Sensibility* in 1783. During the 1790s non-fiction comprised more than a quarter of all Lane titles, but the writing was rarely distinguished and continuing attacks on circulating libraries and popular novels ensured that the Minerva remained an easy target.[185] In Austen's *Northanger Abbey* the nine 'horrid' novels enthused over by the foolish Isabella Thorpe were all authentic titles and six of them were published by Lane.[186]

However ridiculed, Lane's dominance in novel manufacture translated into enviable material success. It was a notable achievement given that most novels were hardly valuable property and that (as will be discussed further below) the ownership of rights to reprint them was an irrelevance in the case of all but a handful of important novels. William Lane's profits derived primarily not from copy-holding, but from the returns of his newspaper, circulating library and novel printing business (although other business ventures remain at present unclear). By comparison, great wealth gained in other successful bookselling careers was based on copyright-owning and wholesale dealing. Obviously, wills alone cannot assess booktrade profitability, but they are a measure of individual wealth. Lane left at his death in 1814 a fortune of about £17,500.[187] Amongst others involved (to whatever extent) in the publication and sale of novels in this period, Joseph Johnson left about £60,000 net and a country house at Fulham at his death in 1809. James Dodsley left over £70,000 and a landed estate near Chislehurst. Charles Dilly bequeathed over £80,000 to his heirs. At his death in 1802, Cadell was estimated to have been worth at least £150,000. He gave his daughter £20,000, left her £30,000 more, and settled £10,000 on his daughter-in-law. Thomas Longman II left over £60,000 at his death in 1797. These last examples in particular reinforce the belief that novel publishing contributed only modestly to the most successful wholesale bookselling businesses and their literary investments.

---

[183] Briefly recollected in the *Reminiscences and Table Talk of Samuel Rogers*, ed. G. H. Powell (London: R. Brimley Johnson, 1903), p. 108.

[184] Raven, 'Noble Brothers,' pp. 301–3.

[185] McCleod, 'Minerva Press' listings of all Minerva publications total 1,636. Her tables 3.4 and 3.5 provide estimates of Minerva non-fiction publication, 1790–1830.

[186] These are 1793: 31; 1794: 34; 1796: 45, 71; 1798: 61, 66.

[187] Marginal note in the will of Lane, cited Blakey, *Minerva Press*, p. 23.

A further, even more obvious distinction must be made between the publication and the printing of these novels. The majority of bookseller–publishers issuing new novels did operate a printing press, although more than one bookseller often combined to produce many of the novels and printing was then naturally confined to one shop. Other notable publishers of novels, from the Nobles to Longman, did not undertake their own printing, but rather contracted out the presswork. In such cases, the obscurity of the printers is often far greater than even that of the booksellers. We cannot now identify the majority of the contract printers who were employed on these novels. Even in the few instances where newspaper advertisements (or rare surviving business accounts) added names of such printers, almost nothing is known of the firm mentioned. This is certainly the case with Richie and Sammells, listed in the *Morning Chronicle* as printers of William Renwick's *Solicitudes of Absence* (1788: 69). It is also an example which illustrates the dangers of assuming that the bookseller named on the title-page was the printer as well as the publisher (in this case 'printed for the Author and sold by C[hristopher] Forster' but who was not, therefore, the printer).

The commissioned printers that we can identify included some of the most enterprising of the period and popular novel printing clearly had to be accommodated between weightier literary endeavours in the commercial print-shops. The printer to the House of Commons, Luke Hansard—'our name is not unknown among the Literati'—was employed at the height of his fame to print novels for the esteemed Cadell.[188] George Bigg, first of Chelsea and later of the Strand, and successor to Dryden Leach (scion of a well-established printing dynasty), was employed by many publishers of novels, notably Johnson, Payne, and the unesteemed Nobles, although his known work on popular novels after 1770 is slight.[189] With fourteen or more novels released in their peak seasons, the Nobles relied on several printers at any one time, but their names are rarely given in the imprints. It is not known how many printers were employed in total, and only by comparison of type and decorations is it possible to ascribe work to the few printers for whom we do have names. In addition to Bigg and Leach, printers commissioned by the Nobles included William Hoggard, former apprentice of William Bowyer, and Caesar Ward and William Adlard, both of Fleet Street. Several of these pressmen had been apprenticed to distinguished printers and commanded large print-shops. William Adlard boasted an apparently prosperous establishment, binding twenty-seven apprentices after his own release from apprenticeship in 1759. In 1768 he moved to Wine Office Court, from where much of the work for the Nobles was undertaken. Adlard's sons, James and Thomas, are also identified printers of novels in the 1790s.[190] Leach bound seven apprentices in the ten years after his move to Fleet

---

[188] John Gustavus Lemaistre, *Frederic Latimer* (1799: 65); Robin Myers, ed., *The Auto-Biography of Luke Hansard, Printer to the House, 1752–1828* (London: Printing Historical Society, 1991), p. 63.

[189] He is known to have printed 1771:1, 1771: 25 and a version of 1795: 48.

[190] 1794: 37, 1797: 52, 1799: 63.

Street. Bigg, also bound eight apprentices in the 1770s.[191] Thomas Wilkins of Snow Hill, involved in the printing of at least ten novels detailed in this bibliography, bound thirteen apprentices between 1782 and 1797.[192]

When, from 1794, Thomas Norton Longman began occasional publication of novels (perhaps as a result of the retirement of his father and his recent partnership with Owen Rees), he employed many of the leading printers of London, notably Andrew Strahan and George Woodfall. Strahan and Woodfall headed perhaps the most distinguished and long-standing printing firms in London and their rapid turn-round as well as the quality of their work made them obvious choices. Of those Longman novels of the 1790s with surviving accounts, nine titles were printed entirely by Strahan and a further two by Woodfall. In the case of Pratt's *Family Secrets* (1797: 68) Longman divided the manuscript between four different printers who produced the five different volumes in an edition of more than 1,000 copies. William Chapman, stationer of Cheapside, supplied all the paper, with Longman acting as distributor. On the more modest scale, Thomas Sabine, father and son, of Shoe Lane, printed and probably financed (in whole or part) the publication of several novels. Sabine volumes recorded in the entries below are distinguished by three things: inordinately long title-pages, silence from the reviewers, and undated work, all resulting in their productions being amongst the most problematically ordered novels in the bibliography.[193]

Very few of those publishing novels in this period owned a large number of presses, but an obvious exception was William Lane. By 1792 his printshop claimed a superintendent, twelve compositors, ten pressmen and a warehouseman.[194] In advertising for manuscripts Lane also promised authors that his pressmen would execute the work to the very highest standards. Unfortunately, in the absence of business records, the boasts of advertisements do not add much to our understanding of printshop practice or of the financial relationships between booksellers and authors. In some cases, attempts at faster publishing are evident. George Kearsley rapidly put Elizabeth Helme's *Louisa or the Cottage on the Moor* (1787: 37) into a second edition, with an advertisement proclaiming that 'in order to expedite the New Edition, [the 'publisher'] distributed it to four different Printing Houses, who have engaged to complete it by Monday next, when a large impression will be ready to supply the increasing demand for this favourite Production', and listing the four printers, Henry Sampson Woodfall, Thomas Spilsbury, Thomas Bensley, and the firm of William Thorne and Mary Harrison.[195]

The notes section of each entry in this bibliography records identified reprintings and advertisements announcing publication dates. These offer further profiles of the

[191] D. F. McKenzie, *Stationers' Company Apprentices 1700–1800* (Oxford, 1978), pp. 3–4, 36, 43–4, 175, 211.
[192] McKenzie, *Apprentices*, pp. 378–9.   [193] 1780: 4, 9; 1790: 25.
[194] In an advertisement for Susannah Gunning's *Anecdotes of the Delborough Family* (1792: 36), SDA 20 Mar. 1792.
[195] LEP 26–28 Apr. 1787.

publishing season of the original editions, even though great caution is required in interpreting both imprint dates and the significance of newspaper announcements. Post-dating on title-pages was common practice. As the *Critical*, rather late in the day, remarked of Francis Noble's *Happy Release* (1786: 6) in November 1786, 'by an ingenious contrivance this novel will continue to be a new one till the end of next year for it is dated 1787'.[196] In fact, the novel had first been advertised five months prematurely in the *London Evening Post* in late August 1786. This particular example is unusual because, with no extant copy, the novel is listed in the bibliography under the date of the surviving evidence of publication, that is, 1786. Amongst similar examples, the now lost *Prudent Orphan* (1774: 20) is assigned to 1774 on the strength of a November newspaper advertisement, even though the timing of the reviews suggests a 1775 imprint date. In the case of all surviving novels, however, imprint dates are used for cataloguing in this bibliography, irrespective of the evidence also often supplied of an earlier publication date. The further point is that calendar years should not be taken as sharp breaks, not only because of false dating, but because, as already noted, a publishing season ran from autumn until late Spring. Of the more extreme examples, *The Minor* (1788: 23), with a 1788 imprint date, was first advertised in the newspapers in October 1786. The *Critical* commented that 'in the middle of the year 1786 we reprehended a publisher for dating his work in 1787. On this day, the first of April, 1787, we peruse a book of 1788'.[197] The Nobles had practised false dating since the mid 1750s, but they sometimes preferred not to date at all, leaving them free to claim a work to be new whenever it pleased them—as can be seen in innumerable newspaper and end-page advertisements for 'lately printed' books. When advertised, many such works were at least a decade old. The brothers' founding novel, *Harry Herald* of 1754, was still promoted in the catalogue of books appended to one of the last novels published by Francis Noble thirty-four years later.[198]

In fact, what evidence there is of the exact month of publication, as given in many of the following entries, suggests a gradual elongation of the publishing season by the end of the century. Evidence for the actual date of publication is weakest in entries for the earlier years in this period, but what does remain indicates a novel publication season much more confined than in the final decade of the century. The key source here is the advertisement (often repeated over several issues of a newspaper) for a novel 'this day published'. This phrasing, however, was almost always to be taken in a continuous present tense. It did not preclude the possibility that the novel was also published yesterday and that it would continue to be published tomorrow and days after. Only on rare occasions did newspaper advertisements, with self-conscious precision, identify a more exact time of publication in the sense of the first day of issue—as for example, 'on Monday at Noon' for Fauque de la Cépede's *Vizirs* (1774: 26) and 'this Morning at Eleven' for the *Adventures of a Hackney Coach* (1781: 1).[199]

[196] CR 62 (1786): 391.   [197] LEP 10–12 Oct. 1786; CR (1787): 307–8.
[198] Phebe Gibbes, *The Niece* (1788: 53).   [199] SJC 26–28 Apr. 1774; PA 26 July 1781.

Any attempt to gauge the length of the publishing season is constrained by these problems of evidence and interpretation. One calculation might be made on the basis that in the majority of cases with known publication dates a review appeared about a month later. Where no newspaper advertisement has been found it could be assumed, in the absence of other evidence, that publication occurred in the month before the earliest periodical review. On this assumption, publication months can be given to twenty-six of the forty novels with 1770 imprint dates. Seventeen of these date from between January and May. No novels bearing a 1770 imprint are known to have been published in July, August, September, or December. December more certainly invited imprints of 1771, just as four of the twenty-six dateable 1770 imprints were actually published in November and December 1769. A similar exercise for 1780, where thirteen of the twenty-four novels with imprints of that year can be given a rough date of publication, reveals that all but three were published between February and May. With the exception of one novel dateable to August, no 1780 imprint is known to have been published after May. A more reliable survey of 1790 imprints, where only ten of the seventy-four novels cannot be generally dated, suggests a more extended season. Some thirteen novels were probably published between January and March, six in April, eight in May, eight in June and six in July, but a further twelve were apparently issued in August and September—the original dog days of publishing—and a further seven in October and November. Of course, the use of advertisements and reviews to suggest publication dates, even if more reliable than title-page evidence—is extremely hazardous. How, for example, are we to explain, other than in terms of a bookseller's re-promotion, the August newspaper advertisement for the *Memoirs and Opinions of Mr. Blenfield* (1790: 20), boldly proclaiming it to be 'in the Press, and shortly will be published' when in fact it had already been reviewed by the *Critical* in May?[200]

The further and crucial feature of the businesses of Lowndes, the Nobles, Hookham, and Lane was the extent to which their publishing and retail operations turned on the success of their own circulating libraries and the supply of ready-made fiction and belles lettres libraries to other booksellers and new proprietors. More than twenty metropolitan circulating libraries operated by 1770, and many copies of the majority of the novels listed in this bibliography were probably sent directly to libraries.[201] In effect, novels were published to rent out. It was not only Hookham, the Nobles and Lane who used imprints to register that the novel was printed at their circulating library and to give its address. Benjamin and Thomas

[200] SJC 7–10 Aug. 1790; CR 69 (1790): 592.

[201] Hilda Hamlyn, 'Eighteenth-Century Circulating Libraries in England', *The Library*, 5th ser. 1 (1947): 197–218; Hilda M. Hamlyn, 'The Circulating Libraries of the Eighteenth Century', unpublished MA dissertation, London University, 1948; Paul Kaufman, 'The Community Library: A Chapter in English Social History', *Transactions of the American Philosophical Society*, n.s., 57, pt. 7 (1967); both updated by Robin Alston, *Library History Database* (1998), a website which includes listings of 3,071 libraries (of all types) founded 1700–1799.

Jones so advertised their various novels and libraries in the Strand and Westminster,[202] as did Lowndes and, with more need, the less prominent establishments of Riley and Cooke in Berkeley Square, Roson off Newgate St., Hall in the Strand, Boosey in Cheapside, Bowen in New Bond St., and, amongst others, Geary in Oxford St.[203] Regularly printed library catalogues provide extensive stock records, even though the titles cited are often general and it is not always possible to match a library catalogue title with a surviving published work.[204] The original core of John Bell's circulating library were 'Romances, Novels and Other Books of Entertainment'[205] and his library catalogue of 1778 lists some 8,000 titles of which 11 per cent were fiction. In 1790 Lane claimed 10,000 volumes in an advertisement for his 'General and Encreasing Circulating Library', increasing a year later to 600,000 volumes after his purchase of the stock of John Walter's Logographic Press. Lane's *Minerva Catalogue* of 1802 lists 17,000 separate titles. Hookham's 1794 *Catalogue* lists 8,866 titles, 14 per cent of which are fiction. The libraries of Lowndes, the Nobles, Hookham, and Lane, and their lending activities, explain much of their managers' publishing efforts. Benefiting from the experiments of other bookseller–book-lenders of the early 1740s, the Nobles and their later rivals depended upon strict rules, stringent borrowing records, fixed subscription rates, and published catalogues with accompanying postal services.

Both the Nobles and Lane advertised wholesale supply to other booksellers to establish libraries of their own, but the production of novels by all the London booksellers from Hogg to Longman reflected built-in assumptions about library demand. Commercial libraries outside London numbered at least 250 by 1790, and very many of the novel titles published by the Nobles, Hookham, and Lane resided in them. These booksellers' novels were to be found, for example, in Heavisides's circulating library at Darlington and Ann Ireland's library at Leicester, or were offered in country sale-rooms such as Drewry's at Derby.[206] In Leeds John Binns was offering both sets and odd volumes of Noble novels.[207] More generally, the 1796 catalogue of John Lowe's commercial circulating library at Birmingham listed 3,500 volumes of which 40 per cent were fiction. This compares to James Sanders's smaller Derby library where 85 per cent of the stock had been fiction in 1770, and to James Corkhill's library at Whitehaven, Cumberland, where 75 per cent of the titles were fiction in 1793. At Darlington, 90 per cent of Heavisides's 466 titles in his 1790

[202] 1771: 5, 14; 1772: 13, 20, 28; 1773: 4, 11, 20; 1786: 3, 5.

[203] 1771: 1, 48; 1774: 20; 1771: 27; 1778: 15; 1782: 11; 1787: 17.

[204] Particularly the case, for example, with *A Catalogue of Hookham and Co.'s Circulating Library . . . Consisting of Several Thousand Volumes . . .* [1766]; *Nouveau Catalogue François de la Bibliothèque Circulaire de Messrs Hookham* [Bond Street, 1791]; *A New Catalogue of Hookham's Circulating Library. On a New and More Extensive Plan* [Bond Street, 1794] Bodleian.

[205] *A New Catalogue of Bell's Circulating Library* [*c*.1766], pp. 69–90.

[206] *A Catalogue of Books, Instructive and Entertaining, which are lent out by M. Heavisides* (Darlington, 1790), Bodleian library; *A Catalogue of Books . . . which will begin to be Sold . . . on Friday, July 17th, 1789 at the shop of Ann Ireland*; and *Drewry's Sale Catalogue for 1790* (Derby, 1790), Cambridge University.

[207] *A Catalogue of Books Containing Several Valuable Libraries lately purchased . . . By John Binns . . . Bookseller . . . in Leeds* (Oct. 1789).

library catalogue were novels. George Allen, running a circulating library in St Martin's Lane by the late 1780s, boasted in the imprint of one of his novels that it 'may be had at every Circulating Library in the Kingdom'.[208] Further afield, circulating libraries in the North American colonies and in India were taking the products of the London bookseller-librarians.

The publication of many novels simply to stock circulating library shelves was quickly appreciated by both authors and critics. Gregory Lewis Way's *Learning at a Loss* (1778: 16) was dedicated 'to all the Circulating Librarians in the Kingdom of Great-Britain'. With more plaintive reflection, reviewers commonly regarded a novel as fit, or fit only, for a circulating library. A *Critical* reviewer regarded *The Favourite* (1771: 15) as deserving 'some preference to the great majority of those which are published every day for the emolument of circulating libraries'.[209] Miss Palmer had produced her novel *Female Stability* merely for a library's 'eager visitors' according to Samuel Badcock in the *Monthly*, and a year later he was describing another effort as destined to be part of 'the furniture of a circulating library'.[210] Badcock had, in fact, written to the editor of the *Monthly*, Ralph Griffiths, complaining that 'Female Stability is all I can get from my Librarian'.[211]

Production and Marketing

Greatest profits in eighteenth-century book publication derived from the ownership of copyrights to successful works. The right to reproduce a book was almost always bought outright by the bookseller–publisher or consortium of booksellers. The author surrendered all claims to subsequent entitlement. Most copyrights were then divided into shares between several combining booksellers. Such division was made according to the booksellers' stake in the original financing of the publication, although the intricacies of this are now often irrecoverable. Part-shares formed the staple investments to be bought at the London trade auctions, and commerce was brisk. One contemporary commentator, Thomas Mortimer, despaired of calculating ownership of shares because they were so greatly divided and exchanged hands so rapidly.[212] Although the history of the associations of booksellers is well known,[213] the surviving series of marked-up trade sale catalogues, covering both copy and stock transactions, continue to provide valuable information about the course of transactions by different booksellers, about prices and share divisions, and about the comparative worth and long-term investment potential of different types of publication or even of individual titles.[214] The greatest accumulator

[208] *Edward and Harriet* 1788: 13.   [209] CR 31 (1771): 159.

[210] MR 66 (1782): 394 on 1780: 21; MR 68 (1783): 456 on Maria Smyth's *Woman of Letters* (1783: 21).

[211] Bod MS Add.c.90, f. 70, Badcock to Ralph Griffiths, 4 Jan. 1782.

[212] *The Universal Director* (London, 1763).

[213] Marjorie Plant, *The English Book Trade*, 3rd edn. (London, 1974), pp. 222–4; C. Blagden, 'Booksellers' Trade Sales 1718–1768', *The Library*, 5th ser., 5 (1951): 243–57; Terry Belanger, 'Booksellers' Trade Sales 1718–1768', *The Library*, 5th ser., 30 (1975): 281–302.

[214] Terry Belanger, 'Booksellers' Sales of Copyright: Aspects of the London Book Trades, 1718–1768',

of the second half of the eighteenth century was probably George Robinson who was a keen rival to the established literary investors by the early 1770s, and before 1780 'had the largest wholesale trade that was ever carried on by an individual'.[215] By 1800 the businesses of Cadell and of Longman and Rees surpassed all others in the extent of their literary holdings.

The production history of the novels in this bibliography was obviously determined by this broader background, although two critical features stand out. First, novels had little intrinsic value. Copyrights to most of these publications, had most of these ever been traded, would have fetched very little at sale, and authors, as already noted, were paid paltry sums for their surrender of rights to works which booksellers knew were very unlikely to be reprinted or to return much profit in their own right. The second critical issue is that because this bibliography is most concerned with establishing the full range of new novels published, that is with first editions and their subsequent publishing history, it does not include reprints of novel titles first published before this period, and it was exactly this type of popular publication of elderly texts that was to feature so significantly in new market development.

Nevertheless, the broader consequences of the transformation of the market and the encouragement to new booksellers (as well as the temptation to over-reach), did boost efforts to write, produce, and promote novels. Most conspicuously, the book-trade was transformed by the successful assault on the publishing monopoly maintained by the booksellers' associations for most of the century until 1774. The value of all copyright shares clearly depended on their remaining exclusive rights to publish. Under the Copyright Act of 1710 copyright to existing publications had been limited to twenty-one years for books already in print and fourteen years for new books. After expiration of the fourteen-year term, copyright was to remain with the author, if living, for a second fourteen-year term, even though the author's rights were more technical than actual, and ones, apparently, not previously greatly considered by those passing the legislation. In invoking authorial rights, in fact, the Act introduced uncertainty about the validity of Common-Law claims by the booksellers, who, far more than authors, submitted testing injunctions in subsequent decades. Immediately following the mid-century technical expiration of rights to older works and works first protected under this statute, the booksellers' associations seemed successful in arguing that its spirit sanctioned perpetual copyright under Common Law. A 1768–1769 King's Bench decision and then injunction by the Court of Chancery prohibiting Alexander Donaldson from continuing his cut-price reissues of the works of Thomson and others, marked the high-water mark of the efforts by closed associations of booksellers to control copyright. In 1774 a

unpublished Ph.D. dissertation, Columbia University, 1970. He also warns of the dangers of 'promiscuous isolation of individual literary copyrights' when the sale price of individual shares was tied to the fluctuating value of the total share market. Further evidence is considered in Belanger, 'Trade Sales', and Blagden, 'Trade Sales'.

[215] Nichols, *Literary Anecdotes*, 3: 445–6.

ruling of the House of Lords, overturning the 1768 restraining injunction and con-
firming the limitations of the 1710 Act, ended the booksellers' invocation of
Common Law to sanction perpetual copyright. A Bill to quash the Lords' verdict
failed in the following year.[216] It opened the way for those without ownership of
share-copies and outside the charmed circle of leading booksellers to publish cheap
reprint editions of classic works. Dozens of new, modestly resourced publishers
were the clear beneficiaries of the syndicates' loss of control over copyright. From
the mid-1770s, the reprint of popular texts rejuvenated the market, and most
notably the advancing provincial market. At first, these ventures were led by
London booksellers taking advantage of the loss of control by the booksellers' associations, but by the end of the century a regrouping of copyowners re-established
familiar methods of sharing the financing of publication.

Although the basic structure continued, the battle over copyright transformed
the market in popular publishing. This was clear in terms both of the literary investments by bookseller–publishers and of the availability of well-known texts, but the
consequences for first-time novel publication were more indirect. Few of the new
fiction titles were to enjoy commercial benefit from new opportunities to reprint
old favourites nearly three decades after their first appearance. Rather, the efforts of
many booksellers, based on new promotional techniques, advertising, and more
adventurous retail and distribution, continued to erode the power of closed booksellers' associations, and many of the new novels published by the new booksellers
benefited from the changed market and marketing activities. As will be shown, by
the 1780s novels headed the publications financed by booksellers acting on their
own and not in association with others. This is especially true of John Bell and
William Lane. Although Donaldson and his brother John are rightly credited with
the initial actions which baited and finally defeated the bookseller consortiums, it
was John Bell who seized the initiative in cheaper, part-issued, and reprinted popular literature. Early Bell editions proved highly competitive and sent shock-waves
through the trade. He published thirty-nine of the novels listed in this bibliography,
from 1770 through to 1799, with a peak year of 1794 when his ten novels comprised
nearly a fifth of all that year's new prose fiction titles. Notably, however, his name
appears on no novels known to have been first published between 1777 and 1792.
He was then preoccupied with more lucrative and enduring publishing concerns.
Between 1776 and 1778 Bell issued twenty-one volumes of *The British Theatre* in 6d
weekly parts. *The Poets of Great Britain Complete from Chaucer to Churchill*, published by Bell in partnership with the Martins of Edinburgh, and begun in 1777,
comprised some 109 1s 6d volumes by 1792. Both series were re-issued in 1791.[217]

Many booksellers—and many publishers of novels—deliberately imitated Bell.
'Robin Hood' Donaldson, as Dr Johnson called him, continued to issue cheap

[216] See Mark Rose, *Authors and Owners: The Invention of Copyright* (Cambridge MA and London:
Harvard University Press, 1993); and Gwyn Walters, 'The Booksellers in 1759 and 1774: The Battle for
Literary Property', *The Library*, 5th ser., 29 (1974), 287–311.
[217] See Stanley Morison, *John Bell 1745–1831* (Cambridge: Cambridge University Press, 1930).

editions until 1789 but he was not involved in publishing new fiction titles. Others who also revived or continued collaborative reprints and part-issues also sponsored new work. George Kearsley, who from 1777 published on his own or in collaboration popular series of *The Beauties* of Shakespeare, Sterne, Fielding, Richardson, Goldsmith, and others, also issued eighteen new novels between 1770 and his death in December 1790, with his wife and son publishing a further twelve new novels before 1800. In cheap reprints and weekly numbers, however, the clear rivals to Bell were firstly James Harrison and then John Cooke and Alexander Hogg. None of these were significant publishers of new novel titles, despite their prolific publishing of other fiction. In November 1779, for example, Harrison commenced his weekly *Novelists Magazine*. At their peak, twelve thousand copies were sold each week, with twenty-three volumes extant by the date of completion.[218] In 1781 Harrison launched his *New Novelists Magazine*, followed by *British Classicks* and *Sacred Classicks*, and a periodical *British Magazine*. Novels featuring in Kearsley's *Beauties*, as well as *The Tatler*, re-issued by the large London combinations, were prominent in these Harrison series. Cooke's editions of classic fiction were issued in the 1790s in 6d weekly numbers, and followed by various other series of poets and classics. As Richard Altick noted, these were amongst the most popular and accessible genteel primers of their day, avidly read by such students as Hone, Clare, Leigh Hunt, and Hazlitt.[219] While they are quite distinct from the new fiction listed in this bibliography, their popularity and even design cannot be understood without appreciating the boost to fiction reading and circulating library developments given by Bell, Harrison, and their rivals.

By the end of the century popular reprint series were issued by all types of bookseller, from the confident newcomer acting on his own, to the more established Stationers' Company or other livery company member, in all likelihood sharing publication with others and shadowing earlier, more exclusive collaborative practice. At the same time, interest in these developments was rivalled by the attention given to Irish piracies and Scottish reprints, not least by the London booksellers themselves. Cheap imported piracies from Dublin but also reprints from Edinburgh (many of which might well have been legally published within the limits of the 1710 Act) had long been condemned by the London trade. Many Irish reprints were half the price of the London originals. Cheaper paper was used and closer printing and sometimes hidden abridgement enabled two- or three-volume works to be issued in a single volume. Despite vociferous protests made at mid-century, however, the threat from Ireland was either largely illusory or a trumped-up promotional gambit. As now seems clear, Dublin reprints were never imported in sufficient numbers nor aimed at the right targets to pose an effective direct challenge to the London booksellers, even if the effects on the Scottish trade, and Scots incursions in England, are more debatable. At least until the problems of the 1790s,

---

[218] Rees and Britton, *Reminiscences*, p. 22.
[219] Richard D. Altick, *The English Common Reader: A Social History of the Mass Reading Public, 1880–1900* (Cambridge, 1957), p. 54.

Dublin publishers appear to have concentrated on an expanding and potentially valuable Irish market. They had more to fear from London booksellers than London booksellers had to fear from them. Scottish competition was more complicated, with the costs and likely ineffectiveness of prosecution deterring actions against the efforts of the Edinburgh and Glasgow presses. In the early 1780s Scots booksellers were themselves under threat by Irish piracies smuggled in and bearing false imprints. In all of this, title-page assertions of being printed in London cannot always be taken at face value.[220]

Another material feature of the system for publishing and marketing these novels, as for most other books, was the involved relationship between booksellers, both financing bookseller–publishers and their retailing, usually bookseller, agents. Co-operation in some form was essential to most operations. The weakening of the share book system also increased the risk for all and rewards resulted from many gambles in the late-eighteenth-century book trades expansion. The increased number of bankruptcies after 1774 is testimony to the new adventuring. Unprecedented turnover in books was matched by unprecedented turnover in booksellers, many quickly returning to the battle to secure a cut of the new literary market place. Although some London traders continued joint-ventures and ad hoc partnerships, a new vulnerability and rivalry was introduced into the trade. Hundreds of small firms, many of them engaged in additional trades, attempted to make their fortunes from publishing or selling books. For every ostentatious success-story, from the eminence of Cadell to the audacity of Lane's Minerva Press and Lackington's Temple of the Muses, there were dozens with miserable or wildly fluctuating returns.

Recovering these trading relationships is not at all easy, with many distribution agents unspecified, and, in the absence of most business records, very little idea of the relative financial participation in the publication of a new novel. As in all books of the period, the information offered about the connections between booksellers in the imprint line on the title-page is difficult to interpret. Some booksellers (and some authors, wholly or partly) acted as the publisher, that is, as the entrepreneur accepting the risk of financing publication; others remained as manufacturers of the product, already assured of payment even if the book sold badly; still others (including many general traders) served in various distribution and retailing capacities, also identified at the time as 'publishers' of books in the sense of making them public. Single names of booksellers might appear the simplest indicators to publication but it cannot be taken for granted that a novel 'printed for' was entirely paid for by that bookseller. Moreover, where a novel was sold by a consortium of booksellers, some or all might contribute to the financing of its publication (in proportions usually unknown), and it was not always the case that all those listed

---

[220] See the discussion by Warren MacDougall, 'Smugglers, Reprinters and Hot Pursuers: The Irish-Scottish Book Trade and Copyright Prosecutions in the Late Eighteenth Century', in Robin Myers and Michael Harris, eds., *The Stationers' Company and the Book Trade 1550–1990* (Winchester and Delaware: St Paul's Bibliographies and Oak Knoll, 1997): 151–83.

contributed directly to publication costs. Arrangements between booksellers listed as the principal financing publishers ('printed for' etc.) and first-level associates ('also sold by' etc.) usually, but not always, implied an agreement to share costs roughly in proportion to the number of copies to be taken by the participating shops. Newspaper advertisements for these titles extend the problem further, often including additional names of 'sold by' booksellers to those listed on the title-page or advertisements at the end of the novel. Where found, advertisements naming non-imprint booksellers and agents are included in the following entries to give some indication of the broader business and retailing networks.

Despite these reservations, we can at least be certain that in most cases inclusion of a name in an imprint line indicates some sort of financial involvement. This is particularly the case where the author is mentioned—almost always as 'printed for the author'. Where a bookseller was unwilling to take the risk of publishing a novel, he might nevertheless print or enable the printing of the work on the understanding that the author advanced the costs. In some cases the provision of the actual paper, not merely its costs, was expected. Here, with the author as publisher, the bookseller often acted as little more than a vanity press, although in some cases authorial risk-taking did pay off. To most booksellers, the acceptance of such a commission must have seemed like simple jobbing printing. Of the total number of first editions of novels published in the 1770s, 5 per cent were described as 'printed for the author', a proportion rising very slightly to 7 per cent of the total in both the 1780s and 1790s.[221] These must also be minimum figures, when many title-pages, such as Mary Robinson's *Widow* (1794: 51), hide known commission agreements 'on account of the author' where the publisher–writer assumed responsibility for any loss.

For some authors then, the only option was to fund the costs of publication from their own resources, although subscription schemes, as discussed in detail above,[222] might also be launched. Booksellers often acted as collecting agents for such support, but where a project looked particularly uncertain the authors, their friends, or patrons organized subscription themselves. Contributions to publish a novel by the young Misses Nugent and Taylor were solicited by Miss Taylor's local circulating library at Twickenham.[223] Nevertheless—and circumstantial evidence is scarce—it seems that a bookseller rarely turned down a novel if financing were available. It is simply not known how many manuscripts of authors looking for booksellers' support were refused. Negotiations over publication where the bookseller acted wholly or even in part as financing publisher are obscure. Few letters survive between first-time or even popular novelists and booksellers, and refusals (such as that of Trapp's 'Perverted Clergyman', declined and confiscated by Dr Trusler) are rarely glimpsed. In one still anonymous Lane novel, a character describes at length

---

[221] 16 titles between 1770 and 1779; 29 between 1780 and 1789; 50 between 1790 and 1799 (totals include the less usual alternative 'printed for the proprietor').

[222] See above pp. 54–56.   [223] PA 30 Nov. 1778, for *The Indiscreet Marriage* (1779: 14).

her efforts to have her own novel published. She is rejected by all the booksellers she tries until she enters Leadenhall Street and meets Lane, 'liberal in his ideas, and equally polite in his manner, who, not only with spirit receives those kind of light airy readings, but, in a manner that does honour to his publications, introduces them to the whole'.[224] This view of marketing from Leadenhall Street was delightfully disingenuous. The library-shelf filler, bought cheaply as a manuscript, and printed in small numbers, did not imperil the finances of a successful but artistically indiscriminate operator like Lane. In his own novel, Trusler even suggested that more underhanded booksellers might agree to print a novel at the author's expense and then print half as many again, selling, moreover, the booksellers' portion first and then claiming unsold copies as entirely from the number paid for by the author.[225]

What this did, particularly in the case of novels, was to put heavy responsibility upon authors to choose, in what was largely a buyer's not a seller's manuscript market, the best option for having their work published. They usually risked heavily if they wished to avoid the easy but disappointing option of a meagre outright copyright sale. As has been shown, before the early nineteenth century, very few novelists—and certainly very few first-time novelists—could avoid outright copy sale, full self-financing (and thus acting as publisher themselves), or deals in which the author bore liability for all losses.[226] Commission agreements whereby the bookseller put up the capital for printing an edition on the understanding that the author would bear any loss, seem to have been very rare, although Hookham and Carpenter favoured several authors with such deals in the 1790s including Mary Barker (1798: 15) and Margaret Holford (1798: 30). Booksellers appear to have interpreted commissions as between 7½ and 10 per cent of the wholesale price, although few agreements have survived. Profit-sharing arrangements, as favoured by Longmans in the early nineteenth century, seem to have been even rarer. Better than having to find all the capital or walking away from the shop with a few guineas for outright sale of copy, a commission agreement could nevertheless bring financial loss as well as reward. Mary Robinson's *Sicilian Lover* lost £22, and, having left Bell for Hookham with whom she made commission agreements on three novels (1794: 51, 1796: 76, and 1796: 77), she seems in total to have earned less than £10. After further publications by commission agreement, Robinson owed Hookham and Carpenter over £133 in 1797, a debt that was never repaid.[227]

The basis of any analysis of the economics of producing these novels is therefore that copyright was cheap, that the author had almost no bargaining position, and that where financed, the novel was published either in the slim hope of future

---

[224] *Follies of St James's Street* (1789: 10), 2: 16–18; also discussed in Blakey, *Minerva Press*, pp. 70–71.

[225] John Trusler, *Modern Times* (1785: 46), 3: 39.

[226] Fergus and Thaddeus, 'Women, Publishers, and Money', based in part on the Hookham and Carpenter ledgers 1791–98, PRO Chancery Masters' Lists.

[227] Fergus, *Jane Austen*, pp. 16–17; Fergus and Thaddeus, 'Women, Publishers, and Money', pp. 193, 196–7.

returns if it proved popular and worthy of a subsequent edition, or, more likely, to supply a relatively closed system based, for some, on the stocking of circulating libraries and, for most others, on high mark-ups in direct sales to the public. Where booksellers acted as real publishers, taking on the full financial risk, key factors were the costs of paper, labour, and wear on type or new type requirements. These, however, were not the sole determinants of profits, given that the choice of a particular price structure seems to have been based on more than the factor costs of manufacture, encompassing considerations of design and market profile. The idea that a title might yet prove a surprise success must have encouraged some booksellers, and was certainly a spur to new marketing and promotional enterprise. More realistically, a commercial strategy based on maximum variety and novelty in the library, but supporting wholesale back-lists for a decade or more, required a particular balance between printing sufficient copies of an edition to maximize the unit costs of the press work, but limited enough to avoid tying up capital in unsold stock and the burden of long-term storage space. For the main publisher-librarians, it must also be stressed, printing calculations for a new novel were effectively decisions about the supply to other circulating libraries, a limited but at least relatively knowable market. By 1770 one author's contemporary estimate (taking an optimistic line on total edition size) suggested that 400 of every 1,000 copies of novels were sold to circulating libraries.[228]

The main result of these considerations was the printing of a relatively small number of copies to each edition and the encouragement of favoured formats and styles of presentation to maximize pricing advantage, most notably the publication of novels in two or more volumes. In most cases, the labour costs of composition and presswork made it unviable to print very small editions, while the risks of high capital expenditure and storage made it unwise to print large editions. Most novel editions therefore ranged between 500 and 750 copies. William Bowyer printed the *Fatal Friendship* (1770: 3) for Lowndes in 750 copies, the same number ordered by Dodsley for his edition of Frances Brooke's translation of Faméry's *Memoirs of the Marquis de St Forlaix* (1770: 30). Where possible, the size of print runs is given in the entries, but records for these are disappointingly few. The very informative Bowyer ledgers end in 1771; the equally valuable ledgers of Longman survive only from 1794. Although missing the transactions with Reeve and Radcliffe, the surviving Hookham and Carpenter records from the 1790s suggest editions of 500 or 750, except where those authors prepared to risk loss on a commission basis demand more.[229] Bookseller Allen's claim to have sold all 1,500 copies of *Lord Winworth; or, the Memoirs of a Heir* (1787: 16) cannot be verified.[230] Larger editions, even as boasts, were highly unusual, booksellers always wanting to assess the popularity of a novel and even then only printing a relatively modest second edition. All

---

[228] Elizabeth and Richard Griffith, *A Series of Genuine Letters Between Henry and Frances* 6 vols. (London, 1767–70), 5 (1770: 31): 15.
[229] PRO C104/75/1-3, records of Hookham and Carpenter.
[230] Adv. SJC 27 Feb.–1 Mar. 1787.

remembered the sorry history of Andrew Millar's first 1751–1752 edition of Fielding's *Amelia* of 8,000 copies in two impressions. Millar had hoped to emulate the runaway success of *Tom Jones* (10,000 copies printed between 1749 and 1750), but was left embarrassed, with copies still for sale ten years later. Robinson printed the first edition of *Juliet Grenville* (1774: 24) in 2,000 copies, also agreeing to allow its author, Henry Brooke, profits on later editions, but perhaps its unusually large size helps explain why no further London edition was in fact published. It was Mary Robinson's own decision to order Hookham to print 1,500 copies of her *Widow* (1794: 51) that apparently, despite initial good sales, contributed to eventual disaster.[231]

The fullest profile of novel edition sizes at the very end of this period is offered by the 'impression book' of Longman and Rees 1794–1801. Eleven accounts for new novels published by the firm before 1800 supply details of print runs. These editions ranged from 1,000 copies (three titles) to 750 (six titles) and 500 (two titles), an average print run of 773. This compares to editions of 2,000 copies or more for many Longman plays of the period, but palls before the huge printings commissioned by the firm for staple titles such as Watts' hymns, Johnson's *Dictionary* and numerous school books, including an 18,000-copy edition of Fenning's spelling manual. Novels did not occupy much space in the Longman stockroom at 39 Paternoster Row. The same size restraint applied to most second and later editions of novels issued by Longman. Risks were taken with an 1801 edition of Pratt's *Pity's Gift* (1798: 60) of 2,000, and with an 1802 edition of *Village Orphan* (1799: 17) of 1,500 copies.[232] Even so, many later editions remained very cautious. The Longman 1804 fifth edition of Jane West's *Gossip's Story* (1796: 89) was limited to only 500 copies.[233]

The high return expected on the publication of these novels is illustrated by further analysis of production costs from the scant surviving evidence. The Bristol printer George Routh charged William Combe £28 8s 6d to manufacture 700 copies of his two-volume *Philosopher in Bristol* (1775: 19). At eight shillings a ream, the required nineteen reams of paper cost a total of £7 12s and the folding and stitching in blue paper of the finished sheets a further £6 7s 6d. The greatest expense, however, was the composition and presswork, charged at 17s per sheet, or £14 9s in total. This ratio of paper to printing costs is reversed in the Longman accounts of novel publication in the late 1790s, where paper costs are always greater than printing costs. The proportion of both to total production costs varied greatly, however, and depended upon the additional contribution of advertising, copyright, and incidental costs. The ledger entries for the eleven pre-1800 novels in the surviving Longman accounts, suggest that paper costs ranged between 29 per cent and 41 per cent of total production costs. Printing expenses, always less than those of paper, ranged between

---

[231] Fergus and Thaddeus, 'Women, Publishers, and Money', p. 196.
[232] Longman Archives, impression book H5, ff. 8, 27.
[233] Longman Archives, impression book H5, ff. 104, 117.

22 per cent and 34 per cent of total costs. Bills for printing sent to Longman were calculated at rates per sheet, with additional labour charges for the corrections made to the presswork before the sheets left the printing house. In the case of Pratt's *Family Secrets* (1797: 68), where Longman employed four printing firms to produce the different volumes as quickly as possible, comparison is possible between operators. Baldwin, who printed volumes one and five, was significantly more expensive than the others (who included Strahan but not Woodfall), but his correction costs were cheaper.

From these records calculations can be made about cost price compared to retail price. Everything points to high potential returns. If all 1,400 volumes of Combe's *Philosopher in Bristol* had been sold at the advertised price of 2s 6d the receipts would have totalled £175. Based on the bill of costs already described, this represents a net profit, excepting advertising and any other (unrecorded) marketing charges, of over £145. From the bill, with no hint of shared costs, it seems that Combe paid the printer to produce and advertise his work, and then secured all returns on sale (although it is unclear whether Routh took a further cut for any retail services). On this basis, a full sale would have placed Combe at the upper end of the equivalent authors' copyright league table. In another example, but from a manuscript already sold to the publishers, James Thistlethwaite's *Child of Misfortune* (1777: 18) cost John Murray and William Richardson £33 17s 6d to produce an edition of 800. Advertised at 6s bound (and 5s sewed), the cost price per novel set was therefore a fraction under 10d, or just under 5d per volume. If the original, remarkably modest, costings from Murray's account ledger are reliable,[234] then the mark-up appears to have been 5s 2d or eight times the production cost. Excluding whatever was paid to Thistlethwaite for the copy (very unlikely to have been more than £30), the total potential profit to the publishers amounted to just over £206. The cost price to Longman and Rees of producing *Clara Duplessis and Clairant* (1797: 50) was 3s 8d per three-volume set, retailing at 10s 6d, with a potential profit on the sale of the 750 sets printed of £256 5s. Eliza Parsons's *Old Friend with a New Face* (1797: 62) also sold at 10s 6d for the three volumes. Its cost price to Longman was 4s 4d, or a profit per set of 6s 2d and a total potential return on all 750 sets of £231 5s. The three volumes of Jane West's *A Tale of the Times* (1799: 95) were produced for a fraction under 5s a set. The advertised retail price of 12s. therefore represented a mark-up of 7s per set, or a total potential profit on the edition of 1,000 of exactly £350.[235]

Such high potential returns were presumably justified on the grounds of extreme risk in a market where even an edition of 500 might prove a slow earner. In almost all cases of publication by the London firms, however, potential profit calculations must be reduced for whatever allowance was made for discount to the retailing booksellers buying within the trade. The trade discount offered to other booksellers,

---

[234] Murray archives, account ledger of John Murray I, f. 248; Zachs, *The First John Murray*, entry 168.
[235] It is not clear from the Longman accounts whether cutting and sewing were included in the printers' bills or whether the operation was undertaken at the Longman shop. If the latter was the case then allowance for further, if modest, labour costs must be made to the financial calculations.

some of whom were library managers, was especially important for provincial retailers developing local markets for new literature. Most of the later trade offers were advertised as bound; earlier discounts often specified sheets. Hookham allowed his trade customers a free copy for every twenty-five bought. From their earliest years, the Nobles offered a trade discount of 14 per cent on twenty-five volumes of the same title. When in business on his own after 1778, Francis Noble continued the offer, explaining that dealers might buy assorted titles at 40 shillings for twenty-five volumes in quires, with a further discount of one shilling in the pound for buyers of more than 100 volumes.[236] Based on the Nobles' usual retail price per bound volume (3s), the trade buyers' forty-shillings' worth of books could be sold for 75s once bound. If 100 volumes were bought, the £7 12s paid to the Nobles could be converted to a sale of £15 or a profit of £7 8s minus binding costs. If country booksellers were able to sell their volumes for the metropolitan price of three shillings, the potential for profit appears large. In practice, the largest profits were almost certainly taken by the London wholesalers.

Where high risk was moderated by high retail pricing, other production decisions followed. The most conspicuous of these was the distribution of the text over more than one volume, attempting to ensure, at standard pricing per volume, greater returns from retail and, for many, from library lending charges. Such packaging contributed to decisions about price structure and served to force sales of more volumes—sometimes, by the end of the period, of five or more volumes in a set—but at great critical cost. Complaints about bloated novels pepper the reviews, although the practice became so established that one critic, when complaining about the quality of production in the late 1780s, acknowledged what was by then an anticipated form:

Whatever may be the contents of a *two-volume novel* we at least expect two neat pocket volumes, printed on fine paper, price 5s. The one before us is two volumes stitched in one, and vilely printed on vile paper. Perhaps this was all that could be afforded for three shillings; and we will venture to pronounce it as much as the work deserves.[237]

The emphasis upon 'neat pocket volumes' was also significant. Duodecimo was the favoured format for novel production throughout the period, although the alternative octavo was adopted in particular cases. Library shelving arrangements and the order of sales and library catalogues were dictated by the size of a book, recognizably described according to its physical composition. The association of the novel with the 'twelve' was reinforced by the listings of collections, sale descriptions and advertising and review notices. Because of it, the adoption of an octavo format was the more distinctive. Of the forty new novels in this bibliography with 1770 imprints, thirty-three were duodecimos, and seven octavos (all but two of these, single volume publications). Proportionally more octavos are found in the 1780 imprints where fourteen of the twenty-four titles were in duodecimo and ten in

---

[236] Advertisement, *The Niece* (1788: 53), final page insertion to vol. 3.
[237] EngR 15 (1790): 232, on *The Young Lady of Fortune* (1789: 30).

octavo. All but one of these octavos were single volume novels, ranging from the small imitations of novels of sixty-four pages to large 328- and 392-page books. The exception was Pratt's three-volume *Emma Corbett* (1780: 23), financed both by Baldwin in London and by Pratt himself, bookselling with Clinch at Bath. It was an instance, perhaps, where the author himself preferred the more distinguished octavo.[238] Of the forty-seven 1785 imprints thirty-nine were duodecimos, the remainder in octavo. Of the seventy-four 1790 imprints fifty-eight were duodecimo. The great majority of the octavo new novel titles of 1790 (ten of thirteen) were two- or three-volume sets, the octavo no longer serving as an alternative form for single volume new novel publication but as an alternative format for standard multi-volume sets. It was usually adopted by booksellers including Lane and Robinson to give publications a certain distinction. In some cases it promoted more efficient as well as more elegant composition when, in difficult times, the amount of text per page was being increased. Nevertheless, for both these publishers, as for their competitors, the duodecimo remained the favoured option, with well over three-quarters of the new novels of the 1790s published in duodecimo, a proportion rising to 85 per cent amongst the 1799 imprints.

Trends in publication format and price are charted by the entries in this bibliography, but of the two, format details are the more reliable, confirmed by the consultation of surviving copies of the novels. Price is a more elusive feature. Advertised price was at least related to the finish of the novel: sewed, unbound in paper wrapping or in boards, or bound (usually in calf rather than bottom-of-the-range sheep). With few exceptions, the difference between sewed price and bound price remained 6d per volume throughout the period, with an additional 3d per volume charge for gilt. Typically, a three-volume novel advertised as 9s sewed in blue paper wrapping or in boards cost 10s 6d bound in calf and lettered (and, if available, 11s 3d with gilt edges). Many were described as 'neatly bound' but the description 'unbound' seems to have been very rare. Towards the end of the period more novels seem to have been sold already bound (and the Nobles' catalogues, for example, advertised each title 'marked as it sold, bound, unless otherwise stated'[239]), but by far the most common advertised price remained that of the novel sewed in paper or boards. This left the buyer with the option of having the novel bound according to his or her choice, and the binding either undertaken by the retailing bookseller or independently. It is now exceptionally rare to find a novel in its original blue papers.[240] Although boasts of being printed on good quality paper (usually 'on fine writing paper'),[241] appear frequently in advertisements, very rarely

---

[238] Minifie's *Count de Poland* (1780: 20), also published in part by Pratt and Clinch at Bath in the same season, was issued in duodecimo.

[239] In the Catalogue, for example, appended to *The Niece* (1788: 53).

[240] One example examined for this bibliography is the University of Pennsylvania copy of *Illicit Love* by Mrs Morris (1791: 52).

[241] Of the novels published by Bew, for example SJC 22–25 Nov. 1777 on 1778: 4, and MC 24 Aug. 1784 on 1784: 14. 'Superfine Writing Paper' was claimed for 1780: 23.

did this result in a much higher price, except where two variant quality editions were offered from the same press.

Information about the advertised price of a novel, however, often has to be derived from its formulaic appearance in the periodical review notices rather than from patchy and lost booksellers' advertisements. Where given in the entries in this bibliography (and reviews are often the only information on price) the advertised state of the novel ('sewed' etc.) is also included as well as the source of the information. When the binding state was not given by the review it is usually safe to assume that this was the price 'sewed'. But cautions about using the reviews as a source must be heeded. In 1780 the *Monthly Review* responded to an inquiry from a female correspondent 'relating to the prices of books, as commonly inserted at the head of each Article in the Review' and which

complains that she does not understand, precisely, what is meant by the distinctions of *unbound,*—in *sheets,*—in *boards,* &c.—These are matters with which the Reviewers have little concern. They are left to the *Collector,* who (it is understood) generally takes them from the news-paper advertisements, and in the very terms there used; and where those vehicles of information are silent with regard to the price of any publication, the deficiency is always supplied by inquiry of the publisher.[242]

Despite these reservations, certain matters are clear. For twenty years after 1770 pricing remained relatively consistent, but in the final decade the range of different prices for the novel was extended and the average price per volume increased markedly. The general inflation at the end of the century and thus the change in the value of money does offset this increase in the nominal retail price of novels, but price inflation alone cannot account for what seems to have been a marked rise in the real price of new novels at the close of the century. The contrast with the falling real price of reprinted favourite fiction was also sharp. Claims that the price of the novel tripled between about 1780 and 1810 fail, however, to distinguish between gradual increases of the late 1780s, and then a widening of the nominal price range in the 1790s, from the far steeper acceleration in nominal prices after 1800.[243] At the beginning of this period the vast majority of novels were priced at 2s 6d sewed and 3s bound per volume. A few two-volume sets were advertised at 4s sewed, and some smaller volumes at 1s 6d. During the 1780s several of these humbler works emulating and reviewed as novels remained at 1s 6d or cheaper, with two sixty-four-page tales published by Sabine priced at 6d (1780: 4 and 9). The 2s 6d norm for sewed volumes continued through most of the 1780s, but during 1787 a handful of volumes, in sets or separately, were advertised at 3s and even 3s 6d sewed. In the next season the number of 3s volumes increased, especially when sold in 6s two-volume sets. It is not clear why

[242] MR 63 (1780): 480.

[243] Claims summarized in Hugh Amory, *New Books by Fielding: An Exhibition of the Hyde Collection* (Houghton Library, Harvard, Cambridge, 1987), p. 44, and that seem to originate from remarks by J.M.S. Tompkins, *The Popular Novel in England 1770–1800* (London: Constable and Co., 1932), Blakey, *The Minerva Press,* pp. 95–6, although their original estimates were in fact modest. Cf. CR Jan. 1800 insisting the price of labour and materials had doubled between 1752 and 1800.

this price was given to these particular novels, however. Hookham, Kearsley, and Lane all advertised novels at 3s sewed per volume (1788: 35, 44, 56, 58, 65), but all also sold their other novel titles of that season for 2s 6d sewed, none with notably fewer pages (and some with more). A few, but not the majority, of these 3s volumes were advertised in notices late in the year, tracking, perhaps, a price rise over the 1788/89 season. In at least one case (1788: 54) reviews published with some interval between them clearly revised the pricing, suggesting also that the reviewing journals applied estimated prices where not supplied by the originating bookseller.

From all the indications offered by the review listings, a price rise was unmistakable at the very end of the 1780s. What was to be a long-running increase in the price of novels resulted from the increase by about a third in the labour costs of composition and press work between about 1785 and 1810, but, more importantly (as demonstrated by the comparison between the Combe-Routh 1775 and Longman's 1790s production costs), from the doubling in the price of quality paper between about 1793 and 1801.[244] Pricing at 3s per volume sewed increased markedly amongst the 1789 imprints, even though most remained at 2s 6d sewed. By 1792 twice as many novels were advertised at 3s per sewed volume than were advertised at 2s 6d (thirty-two of the total fifty-eight titles), and, if the notices are accurate, two novels were markedly more expensive.[245] Several 3s 6d sewed volumes appeared in 1793, and, although in several cases sources offer conflicting prices, by 1795 a 3s 6d tag was given to nine of the fifty titles compared to thirty-three advertised at 3s per volume sewed. The continuing differences in advertised price for the same novel in these years extend even to the advertisements placed in the newspapers by the booksellers, which, one might expect, would be more consistent than the prices noted in the critical reviews.[246] By 1797 more novels (twenty-nine) were advertised at 3s 6d per volume sewed than those (twenty-four) advertised at 3s per volume sewed, but the range of prices also increased, with one title priced at 1s, two others at 2s, and six at 2s 6d per volume sewed. At the other extreme, six 1797 titles were priced at 4s, three at 4s 6d, and two at 5s and over per volume sewed. This same expanded price range continued to the end of the century. Novels with 1799 imprints (a total of ninety-nine) ranged from 1s to 5s per volume sewed, with most priced between 3s and 4s (seventy-eight) and the majority of these (forty-nine) priced at 3s 6d per volume sewed (or, increasingly, as 'sewed in boards' or just 'boards'). Again, variation between advertisements for the same novel points to contemporary confusion about pricing, not just because of the different state of packaging offered, discount rates within the trade, and the varying number of novels in a set, but because of different decisions by different publishers about the costing and pricing of the products.

Further analysis of pricing trends does not suggest much. The distribution of

[244] Amory, *New Books by Fielding*, p. 44.
[245] 1792: 31 was advertised by the SJC as 4s 6d the two-volume 1792: 42 was advertised in both major reviews as 10s 6d boards (5s 3d per volume).
[246] See, for example, 1795: 18 and 24.

different prices seems not to have been affected by the number of volumes in each set, with two volume sets priced at 5s or 6s sewed and three volume sets priced at 7s 6d or 9s sewed. The differences remained in larger sets, and the number of volumes per set continued to have no direct relationship to relative pricing as the average price of the novel increased later in the decade. The question of whether particular booksellers marked up more than others is more complex, and again subject to cautions about the review-based source for most of the cited prices. In 1794 and 1795, for example, the novels published by Sampson Low were more expensive than those by other booksellers, one priced at 3s 6d per sewed volume, another at 4s and another, if the *Critical* and the *Monthly* notices are to be believed, at 6s per volume in boards.[247] Low's 1796 imprints, however, were all priced at 3s per volume sewed, with the exception of Mrs Smith's *Marchmont* (1796: 82), advertised at 16s sewed in four volumes or, for fifty special hot-pressed copies, '£1 extra large and fine paper'.[248] Lane consistently priced his volumes at 2s 6d or 3s during the 1780s and early 1790s, increasing the range to between 2s 6d and 3s 6d between 1792 and 1796. In 1797 the top price for a single Lane volume increased to 4s 6d, but he also offered volumes at 2s 6d. During the last two years of the century, however, Lane's volumes were priced between 3s and 4s 6d.

The final and no less important explanation of success in the novel business was the development of marketing. This in turn influenced specialization by booksellers and the particular style in which they promoted themselves and their wares. Identifying new opportunities but also new dangers in the less-regulated but expansive market, many new literary entrepreneurs concentrated on particular, fashionable, and distinctive types of publication, these increasing disproportionately to the output of the traditional staples. Producers of novels made obvious appeals to a modish and leisured audience and allowed their readers to identify–possibly quite fictitiously–with that implied readership. Domestic heroines and heroes were set amidst the very latest metropolitan fashion toys, even if most steadfastly lectured on the dangers of the ton. If there is any conclusion to be drawn from the turbulence in the late eighteenth-century London book trades, it is that both investor–publishers, petitioning and counter-petitioning over de facto copyright and their new and usually much smaller and short-lived rivals, realized that increased competition and insecurity were a result of unprecedented market potential. Most followed Lowndes, the Nobles, and then Lane to tailor their products to interest provincial audiences, while attempting to maintain high-profile, fashionable London establishments. This itself could appeal to the fascinated country audience—feeding on the myth of the new literary establishment, the fashionable metropolitan bookseller and circulating library, never visited but ever-present in the newspapers and periodicals.

The axiom that all publicity, good or bad, could only be helpful to business seems to have been followed by the more notorious booksellers. The Noble brothers deliberately provoked what was to be a long-running confrontation with Robert

---

[247] 1794: 38; 1795: 4, 19, 41.   [248] OPA 24 Oct. 1796.

Baldwin. His *London Magazine* was the most important reviewing organ after the *Critical* and *Monthly*, but in an 'Advertisement to the Public' of January 1769 the Nobles accused the *London*'s 'Impartial Review' of damning 'every novel we publish, and, as we have reason to believe, frequently without reading them'.[249] The Nobles further challenged Baldwin to withdraw accusations that they underpaid their authors. In response, the *London* simply repeated the charge, instantly prompting a further 'Rejoinder' from the Nobles. Further rounds with the *London* followed two years later. In January 1773, after disappointing notices of two novels issued in November 1772 (1773: 21 and 22), the brothers published a fifteen-page *Appeal to the Public*, appended, it seems, to all the Nobles' novels published that season.[250] The Nobles brothers condemned the critic's 'servile profession' and cited two approving reviews to contrast with the *London*'s verdicts on *The Way to Lose Him* and *The Way to Please Him* ('Written solely for the use of the circulating library, and very proper to debauch all young women who are still undebauched' and 'See the last article. The same character will do for both').[251]

Such controversy, propelled by both parties, created publicity as likely to be helpful as harmful. When Baldwin countered the Nobles' *Appeal* with another of his Advertisements,[252] this was again immediately reprinted in full by the Nobles in a twenty-two-page *Second Appeal*. They note that Baldwin has read their *Appeal*, adding, by reprinting his contemptuous declaration that he 'like all men of sense, laughs at it . . . But where is the wonder? Ignorance and Folly (like J. and F. Noble) are relations, appear always together, and live in a Circulating Library . . . their Novels are the worst of all Novels'.[253] Yet further correspondence was also produced and distributed by the Nobles, and in June the author of the novels which initiated the argument introduced a preface (or one written for him) in his new novel, addressed to the Nobles and congratulating them on their achievement and public behaviour.[254] Finally, the Nobles printed a long, sarcastic defence of the Editor of the *London Magazine*, and issued an 'Advertisement to the Country Booksellers', warning them that they would be unable to buy Noble novels from Mr Baldwin as his supplies had been cut off.[255] This technique of drawing explicitly on bad publicity to then mount a heavily advertised defence was adopted by the Nobles' natural successor, William Lane. He was even willing in the cause of self-promotion to accept critical remarks about his operations included in one of the novels he published—Mrs Bennet's distinctly sarcastic references to the Leadenhall empire in *The Beggar Girl* (1797: 26).

---

[249] 'Advertisement' appended to the 1769 novels, *Rational Lovers* (JR 1289), vol. 2, and Rogers, *Reclaimed Libertine* (JR 1329).

[250] *An Appeal to the Public (By F. and J. Noble, Booksellers) From the aspersions cast on them by the anonymous Editor of the London Magazine.* Surviving examples in *The Self-Deceived* (1773: 17), vol. 2 (NjP copy; BL copy is damaged), *'Twas Wrong to Marry Him* (1773: 19), vol. 2 (MH–H copy), and *The Way to Please Him* (1773: 22), vol. 2 (BL copy).

[251] *Appeal*, p. 2; LM 41 (Nov. 1772): 543.   [252] LM 42 (1773): 52.

[253] *Second Appeal to the Public, from F. and J. Noble* (London, Feb. 1773), p. 8.

[254] *'Twas Right to Marry Him* (1774: 23): 1, pp. [i]–[ii].   [255] *Second Appeal*, p. [24].

More orthodox advertising proved increasingly important to the success of all novel businesses, even though it was not cheap and accounted for a remarkably high proportion of production costs. The total advertising charge to Combe for his *Philosopher in Bristol* (1775: 19) came to £5 4s or more than 18 per cent of the total printing and publication expenses. His payment secured twenty-seven advertisements, nineteen in four local and regional newspapers and a further eight in four London newspapers.[256] The seven advertising charges for new novels surviving from amongst the Longman accounts in the late 1790s are never less than 3 per cent of total production costs, and comprise 9 per cent in one case (1797: 50) and 12 per cent in another (1799: 16). Reasons for this variation are not clear and seem unrelated to the relative size and price of the editions or to the fame or otherwise of the author. The exceptional advertising costs of a Longman 500-copy 1799 edition of the *Natural Son* which amounted to 22 per cent of total production costs, might have been required given its shadowing of the earlier *Julius* by Ridgway (1789: 51). In most cases, however, the decisions about advertising outlay were probably based on an assessment of immediate competition and marketing opportunity.

Many newspaper advertisements were simple but effective formulaic notices; others attempted eye-catching descriptions of contents and, occasionally, complimentary extracts from the reviews. Hookham advertised Mathews's *Constance* in the *St James's Chronicle* (1785: 38) with three columns of single words to convey its appeal.[257] Lane extended the title of Anna Bennett's *Juvenile Indiscretions* (1786: 16) to fill a dozen or more lines in the *London Evening Post*.[258] Presumably it was for more than the simple advertisement in the *St James's Chronicle* that Longman made the exceptional payment of a shilling for 'writing [the] advertisement' to *Love's Pilgrimage* (1796: 13).[259] Bell, and then Lane, took over from the Nobles in shameless self-advertisement. Without undertaking the large and expensive full-column newspaper advertising that so occupied Longmans, Dodsley, and Newbery, the names of the new operators were rarely absent from the journals and newspapers. Lane and rivals even employed positive puffs from the critical reviews for inclusion in end-volume advertisements, and occasionally in the newspapers.[260] Advertising by Dublin booksellers was often even more desperate and audacious. In 1780 C. Jackson published one novel claiming in its title to be 'by the authoress of Evelina' (1780: 3) and another 'by the author of the Man of Feeling' (1780: 7). Neither was by Burney or Mackenzie.

It was both the regularity and the large and often distant circulation that made a London newspaper an obvious vehicle for announcing new publications (and

---

[256] The bill is reproduced in Harlan W. Hamilton, *Doctor Syntax: A Silhouette of William Combe, Esq* (Kent, OH: Kent State University Press, 1969), pp. 35–6.

[257] SJC 29 Sept.–1 Oct. 1785; the full list is given in the entry (1785: 38).

[258] LEP 25–7 May 1786.

[259] Longman archives, impression book H4, f. 9.

[260] Of many examples, CR extracts concerning *The Platonic Guardian* (1787: 42) and *Blenheim Lodge* (1787: 2), and an MR puff for *Warbeck* (1786: 14), all used in advertisements at the end of *The Man of Failing* (1789: 17).

especially so if, like Robinson, Bell, and Lane, a bookseller partly or wholly owned and published such a newspaper). Notices also advertised novels as being in the press and about to be published. Typically, Thomas Davies declared that the anonymous *Edward* (1774: 6) 'speedily will be published' in the March newspapers and then issued another alert a week before the actual publication in May.[261] Many, and notably Lowndes and Baldwin, favoured pre-publication publicity in the two weeks or so leading up the release of a new novel. Dozens of the entries in this bibliography include references to these warning advertisements, but inevitably these amount only to a small selection of all those published. Less honourably, imprint dating, already noted as an inexact science, was stretched to blatant deceit. John Bell announced the publication of the anonymous *History of Sir William Harrington* (1771: 20) in the *St James's Chronicle* in January 1771, but the same newspaper carried advertisements for it as 'just published' six years later.[262] Given such manoeuvres, both well-disposed and devious, it is remarkable that on occasion publishing booksellers advertised new titles under incorrect or provisional titles. Amongst various examples, Thomas Davies seemed uncertain about the final title for one of his later novels (1774: 6), as did Archibald Hamilton, apparently in search of the main title when making up his puff for the newspaper (1792: 8). On at least one occasion John Bell preferred to drop the entire first part of his advertised title in its final publication (1799: 33).[263]

Design

Both the commercial and the cultural success of the novel in England in the second half of the eighteenth century was very particularly constructed. For its supporters, the novel industry combined entertainment with valuable instruction, and also with fast and publicly responsive manufacture. For its detractors, the novel industry made up the froth leading a deluge of print that overwhelmed imaginations and threatened social stability. It combined dubious instruction with all too fast and slipshod manufacture.

Reeve's *Progress of Romance* rehearsed both these arguments. The novel was bringing benefits to the ill-informed, yet circulating libraries and the quickly written and quickly published drivel that filled their shelves were damaging young minds and devaluing literature. All this has been much chronicled, even though there is still room for more detailed study of changing reactions to the early novel. What has hardly been noticed at all is that the popular novel was judged in terms of the quality of its material existence—the clarity of its printing, the size and style of type and ornaments, their composition and arrangement on the page, and other design issues, including wrapping and binding.

The entries in the bibliography that follows make us aware not only of the varying

---

[261] SJC 29–31 Mar., 3–5 May 1774.   [262] SJC 3 Jan.–2 Feb. 1771; 11–13 Mar. 1777.
[263] Advs. SJC 29–31 Mar. 1774, SJC 24–6 May 1792, *Morning Post* 29 Jan., 13 Feb. 1799.

quality of production, but also of a critical reception that included analysis of typography and materials. It is hoped that this presentation of the full array of novel production will encourage further study of the varying quality of manufacture of the English novel in this period, the contemporary discussion of this, and the consequences of the debate about the appearance and presentation of the texts. By detailed study of the surviving work of these authors, several issues attracting much late-eighteenth-century criticism are reassessed—the use of space in the composition of the page, the size of margins, the spinning out of the text to fill several volumes, and the quality of composition. All these design matters raise questions about the original work of the authors, including the use of dialect, the methods of presenting dialogue, and the differences between errors of composition and misreadings of the manuscript.

The leading novel publishers of the second half of the eighteenth century gave new attention to the visual appearance of their works. Experiment was almost entirely in textual presentation. Frontispiece illustration did increase over the period but remained rare. Separate illustrations were even scarcer. Lane used them in only a handful of novels, notably *Orlando and Seraphina* (1787: 45), *Solitary Castle* (1789: 57), and *Ruins of Avondale Castle* (1796: 58), including, most strikingly, a two-compartment monument akin to Sterne's tombstone of Yorick. This also echoed a tombstone printed mid-page in an earlier Lane novel.[264] Engravings inserted by other booksellers were often crude, or even 'contemptible', as the *Critical* complained in the case of Vernor and Hood's edition Meltzer's *Laura; or the Influence of a Kiss* (1796: 66).[265]

Much more noticeably, printer–booksellers developed distinctive ornamentation and display, and those using different printers, like the Nobles, seem to have demanded particular house styles. Longman, also commissioning outhouse printers at the end of the century, chose distinguished firms to undertake the presswork. A certain independence of judgment seems to have been allowed, but Longman novels also share design traits that suggest the publisher's influence. Most booksellers' newspaper notices certainly puffed the quality of their work, often advertising a novel as handsomely printed. An advertisement for the *Amourous Tale of the Chaste Loves of Peter the Long* (1786: 18), typically announces that it will be beautifully printed upon a fine writing paper.[266] Assurance was also given to writers. In a 1791 advertisement for more manuscripts William Lane insisted that 'Authors may depend their Literary Productions will appear with Correctness, Beauty, Taste, and Style, at the Shrine of Public Approbation'.[267]

For consumers of these novels, possession of a beautiful thing had its own importance, and well executed typographical design, from the representation of dialogue, to distinctive chapter breaks and familiar house-layouts, added to the reading experience. To read was to be involved in a tactile experience of handling the text, of

---

[264] *Follies of St James's Street* (1789: 10): 1, 15.   [265] CR n.s. 22 (1798): 357.
[266] LEP 12–14 Oct. 1786.   [267] *The Star* 26 Oct. 1791.

appreciating and actually feeling a good binding, good paper, and good type impression. Many of the otherwise abject examples from this bibliography survive in finely executed state and elegant original bindings.[268] Sardonic praise by the reviewers confirms the point: 'The only thing worth of admiration in this novel', wrote the *English* about *Alvarez* (1791: 32) 'is the beauty of the type, and the fineness of the paper. The publisher, no doubt, was sensible that the work required those adventitious aids.'[269]

A less happy consequence appears in the many printing disasters and frequent unintentional effects, most the result of rushed work. The Bowyer records log the despatch of printing but turn-rounds seem to have increased over the period, with, for example, the multiple presses of Lane responding to his advertisements imploring fresh supplies of material, from whoever, from wherever. 'Wanted, Novels against the next Season, apply as above.'[270] Although Lane's standards were in fact, relatively high, rushed work by rivals was often problematic. Careless, uncorrected composition, including the hurried use of inappropriate type and ornament, and poor imposition, resulted from the increased speed demanded from the print room and its manual printing press. Authors of these quickly produced novels enjoyed little apparent influence over even intentional design and were more completely the victim of unintentional outcomes. Most blamed the booksellers. Booksellers' financial control, and, to many, their tyranny, was the constant complaint of both authors and reviewers.

The response to the design of the novels was led by the critics in the *Monthly* and *Critical*. Two concerns predominated—first, ridicule of poor slipshod composition and negligent or non-existent proof reading and correction; and, second, condemnation of thin plots stretched over many volumes. As the *British Critic* said of the *Shrine of Bertha* (written by the daughter of the late mistress of the Prince of Wales), 'the incidents in this novel—like the letter-press—are but thinly sprinkled'.[271] Critics were well aware of booksellers' ploys to create two- or three-volume sets from one manuscript novel. Not only was each volume priced at about 2s 6d bound, but each might carry a separate borrowing charge when taken out from a circulating library. Critics lambasted poor work by many inexperienced or inexpert printers and booksellers, but the two leading publishers of novels, the Nobles and Lane, were the most frequent targets. The first jointly published novel by the Nobles in 1754 had established a design house-style, and the critical response was immediate. As the *Monthly* declared, 'the press has not acquitted itself so well as the author. The number of sheets in each volume is so small, the printing so diffuse, the words so disjoined, the lines at so wide a distance, the margin so large, and the blank spaces at the end of the chapters so long and numerous, that it has all the appearance of a jobb.'[272] John Cleland in the *Monthly* regarded the liberal use of blank space in

---

[268] Of many, the 1783 Noble's *Lesson for Lovers* is a splendid example of the elegant manufactured novel. The CUL copy with its marble paper half calf, encases very elegant printing.
[269] EngR 19 (1792): 71.   [270] SJC 7–10 Aug. 1790.   [271] *British Critic* 4 (1794): 314.
[272] MR 11 (1754): 467, on *Harry Herald* (JR 221).

The Assignation (1774: 2) as preferable to the author's words. In 1780 William Enfield in the same periodical rehearsed the common complaint that Blower's *Parsonage House* printed by James Macgowan was a 'small Novel' but 'by the aid of the printer's art it is drawn out into three volumes'.[273] Macgowan was a bankrupt by the end of the season; the novel appears not to have survived.

Two cautions do need emphasis here. First, praise was given as well as dismissal, offering benchmarks for expected standards of print-shop work. Second, even caustic comment should be considered with care and judged—where it survives— against the original text. Many Lane novels contain very few obvious inaccuracies and Strahan and the other printers seem to have corrected Longman publications to very high standards. High correction charges from the printers are recorded in all fourteen entries for new novels in the Longman ledgers that provide full printing accounts. They range from about 1 per cent of total production costs (1797: 62; 1799: 78) to nearly 3 per cent (1797: 68; 1799: 77).[274] Another case in point is the reaction to Francis Noble's *Gilham Farm* published in mid October 1780 (although typically given a 1781 date in the imprint to prolong its shelf-life). According to the *Critical* (in a typical denunciation of the spun-out novel), *Gilham Farm* (1781: 9) was 'more conspicuous for the size of the type, and the extent of the intermediate spaces, than for anything it derives from the imagination of the writer'.[275] Samuel Badcock in the *Monthly* deemed the publication a 'trifling novel, which for the size of type and the extent of spaces, hath few equals, even in this book-making age'.[276] Consideration of the actual text, however, raises doubts about the reviewers' verdicts. The novel averages 130 words per page with sixteen lines per page in a two-volume text of 40,000 words (or perhaps a total of some four hours of reading at a slow pace). The delinquent 'intermediate spaces' are not interlineal. The leading, if not always consistent, does not seem excessive nor inappropriate for the long primer type. It is certainly true that a slightly smaller size of type would have allowed more acceptable justification, with less reliance on thick spaces, and that hyphenation of words, offering one way out of this composing dilemma, was employed somewhat chaotically. Despite the reviewers' castigation of one of their favourite bookselling targets, it is not, however, perhaps as outrageous an example of poor design as that embodied by other novels listed in this bibliography.

These inadequates are numerous. The translated *Cyanna of Athens* (1792: 30), published by Thomas Axtell was printed in Caslon English with a rough average of fifty-five words per page, or a total of just under 20,000 words in the whole large octavo two-volume text. Axtell, established at the Royal Exchange since 1774 and also operating from 1784 in Finch Lane, Cornhill, was a prominent and controversial printer, imprisoned for three months in 1776 for printing a seditious pamphlet. As a member of the Tinplate Workers Company by 1792, Axtell operated outside

273 CR 36 (1773): 477; MR 63 (1780): 70.
274 Longman Archives, impression book, H4, ff. 18, 42, 44, 46.
275 CR 51 (1781): 318.   276 MR 64 (1781): 71.

the Stationers' Company, alongside, indeed, most of those booksellers and printers recorded in this bibliography. Examples of badly executed printing are also common. Only a single (British Library) copy survives of Judith Alexander's *The Young Lady of Fortune* (1789: 32), printed in two volumes 'for the Author' by Levy Alexander, Bishopsgate-Street. Levy Alexander was a Jewish printer, later of Whitechapel Road, and related to Alexander Alexander, printer of Hebrew liturgical books. Miss Alexander's novel offers no plot besides the heroine doing good by alleviating seemingly endless examples of distress, all of which are spread generously over many pages. Apparent reluctance to split words by hyphens left some five words per line. The *Critical* was uncompromising: 'We have seen nothing so trifling and insignificant; nor can we say in what respect this novel is most contemptible; in its insignificancy, improbability, neglect of grammar, which even glares in the title, or the extravagant expansion by which it is extended to two volumes, loosely printed, containing together but two hundred pages.'[277] The printing is execrable. At the beginning of every gathering the pages are illegible, suggesting a damaged printing press at that position on the forme. Some signatures (notably L in the first volume) are also entirely illegible.

This sort of unreadable print marks the cheaper range of novels and those published by novice and particularly humble presses, but it was most common amongst the hurriedly printed Irish editions. Some three-quarters of all novels of the period were reprinted in Dublin and design differences between London and Irish versions were often extreme. With some notable exceptions, Dublin presswork was usually poor, especially when the text from two or three London volumes was fitted into a single volume. Even where the printed impression was satisfactory, other evidence of rushed production can be found from almost all booksellers. Somehow, the Lowndes bookshop managed to transpose some final gatherings from one volume to the other when sewing and (at least in the case of the British Library copy) binding Miss Elliott's *Relapse* (1780: 16). 'The printer's blunders, added to the author's, render the story often unintelligible', wrote the *Critical* of *The Ill Effects of a Rash Vow* (1789: 13).

Other horrors resulted from accidents in the press room or from the ill-conceived intervention of editing booksellers. Samuel Badcock reported that Lady Mary Hamilton had complained that seventy-five pages of the original manuscript for what proved to be her last novel, *The Life of Mrs Justman* (1782: 16) had been accidentally burnt by the printer. 'We have seldom seen any thing so mangled and mutilated' lamented Badcock.[278] William Enfield, the *Monthly's* reviewer of *The Maiden Aunt* (1776: 4) took to task its 'publisher', John Bew, for his 'carelessness' and 'grossest blunders', but Enfield also reported that he had received a complaint from the author (still unidentified) that the letters had been changed after delivery to the press. The alterations caused havoc with 'sense, grammar and spelling', and included the insertion of fifteen new letters unauthorized by the author.[279] There is

---

[277] CR 68 (1789): 328.   [278] MR 66 (1782): 474.   [279] MR 54 (1776): 161–2.

no way now of authenticating the author's claim (or his relationship with Enfield) but it fuels curiosity about the 'manufacture' of fiction in the period and poses further questions about the nature of authorship for many of these novels so speedily produced. The author here claimed that the additional letters were inserted 'merely to spin out the work', again, the common ploy by booksellers to package a novel in three 2s 6d volumes. One wonders who the hack was that dashed off the required padding—could it have been Bew himself?

In such instances, the bookseller–printers and their presses were assumed to be at fault, but in other cases it is extremely difficult to measure precise responsibilities. Mrs Gomersall was one of several novelists whose characters inadvertently changed names—was this her fault or that of poor and then uncorrected work by the compositor? We know all too little about print-room processes and the supervision of composing, verification of the imposition, and the arrangements for correcting. Almost all details of manuscript delivery and print-shop production have disappeared. We do have some glimpse of the process from a few surviving letters by popular authors, but we can only guess at how representative they are. As a result of their poverty, Phebe Gibbes (with her claim of having written twenty-two novels) and Mary Julia Young (nine novels and two translations between 1791 and 1807) begged assistance from the Royal Literary Fund and both have left some account of their novel writing experience. Their labours did not yield distinguished literature. *Zoraida* (1786: 25), which Gibbes claimed as hers, and which was printed in three volumes by Axtell, chronicles the plight of an Indian orphan, marooned in a Devon village, and so 'touched in her brain by over learning' as to threaten her conveyance to 'an untimely grave by over knowledge'. Most reviews were damning of the writing, but all also remarked upon the bad printing and book-making. In the words of the *Critical*, this latest Axtell offering was 'ill-written, worse printed; without ingenuity, novelty, or pathos'.[280]

The original writing must often have contributed to production failures. Both characteristics and idiosyncrasies of the delivered form of the manuscript novel—dialogue, short letters, attempts to bolster weak plots by stylistic extravagance—caused difficulties in the press work. Attempts to emulate rural dialect, for example, seem to have caused confusion in composition and correction. Innovative speech patterning provoked similar trials. Phebe Gibbes also provides another clue about the difficulties facing compositors and correctors. Many of her handwritten submissions to the Royal Literary Fund are illegible, and she herself admitted 'I have manuscripts by me, that would render my declining days comfortable, if it was but Enabled to transcribe them, my first copies being alone legible to my self.'[281] The haste with which many manuscripts were prepared could hardly have helped. Speed was emphasized by booksellers and authors alike, but aside from calculating the intervals between publications of prolific authors like Parsons, Smith, and A. M. McKenzie, little evidence survives of the time taken to complete a novel. We do

---

[280] CR 62 (1786): 394.   [281] Gibbes to the Royal Literary Fund, 17 Oct. 1804 (RLF 2: 74).

know that William Godwin wrote *Damon and Delia* (1784: 15) and *Italian Letters* (1784: 17) in three weeks apiece. If we are to judge by the dates of contract and of final payment, then William Hooper took just under three months to translate Mercier's *L'An deux mille quatre cent quarante* (1772: 36).

Although all this moves us a little closer to recovering schedules and procedures, we still do not know whether or how these authors suggested printing instructions (and how extensive the intervention of a Francis Noble, William Lane or J. F. Hughes actually was). How did the authors indicate use of italics or the proposed setting out of dialogue and other features of their work? The total £158 13s cost of production for Clara Reeve's *Destination* (1799: 77), listed in Longman's accounts, includes correction charges of £4s 6d by Strahan the printer, but excludes a listed charge of £2 16s for 'correcting proofs'. It suggests that Strahan was sent the bill for mistakes identified from galleys, but we have no indication of whether the inspecting reader was the author. The account for Mrs Parsons's *Old Friend with a New Face* includes payment of £1 2s 6d to Mr Woodbridge as corrector ('for Reading').[282] We must presume then, that where a manuscript had been sold outright, later access was denied the author unless specified in the agreement. Certainly, if we are to judge by Mary Julia Young's experience, then Eliza Parsons, Phebe Gibbes and their fellow writers did not get to correct proofs of their own novels. This does not mean that authors of these novels were unaware of the printing problems associated with the genre. In her plea to the literary establishment, Young insisted on her popularity and on her production of moral work. But she thought that she had better defend herself against the charge that such works were badly printed:

Most of my Originals and all my translations have been committed but once to paper, and sent sheet by sheet as I finished them to the press without time even to reperuse them, such is the fate of those who write for a maintenance, and tormented with a thousand apprehensions from the moment the pages went out of my hands I have felt thankful when they returned to me in print to find them what they are, even with the errors of the press for which I hoped the readers would make allowance as few books escape them.[283]

Examination of the texts themselves often remains the only available evidence of composition and correction performance. The errors that we can identify from *Zoraida* (1786: 25), for example, suggest different origins. Misuses included use of 'there' for 'their' and 'their' for 'there', 'set' for 'sat', 'vigor' for 'rigor', 'childish' for 'childless', and 'an offending creature' for 'unoffending creature'. These might well have derived from handwriting problems, particularly as Gibbes had the habit of splitting her words by random spaces. Other errors, such as 'sumputary laws' and 'setimal' for 'sentimental', are more likely to have been simple composing errors. Such examples do suggest that despite the paucity of real printshop and reception evidence, future examination of texts now brought together in this bibliography might better reconstruct writing and printing processes. We might be able to

---

[282] Longman archives, impression book H4, ff. 42, 46.
[283] Young to the Royal Literary Fund, 20 Mar. 1808 (RLF 6: 216).

explain the origins of the problems faced by readers confronted not only by particular design decisions but by their poor and erratic execution.

What, indeed, Miss Young also voiced was her concern that somehow her readers 'should make allowance for these errors as very few [novels] escape them'. Authors were obviously aware that their novels were modish publications and it follows that they pursued or acquired an interest in presentation. As the writing treadmill became increasingly remorseless, correction time seems to have become increasingly limited. Take, for example, the spirallingly work-load of Young as crudely but perhaps effectively measured by a page count of her novels. Her first novel, *The Family Party* (1791: 74), has 559 pages in total over its three volumes; there are 810 pages over the three volumes of *Rose-mount Castle* (1798: 75); and 1,171 pages for the four volumes of *The East Indian* (1799: 99), even with its generous twenty-three lines per page. Authors met constant appeals to write more to fill multiple volumes, only then to face the scorn of the critics:

We wish . . . that the lady had not thought it necessary to write *four* volumes. There is no *law* in favour of that number; and the business of this novel might have been dispatched in two volumes with more advantage to the author, and less weariness on the part of her readers.[284]

In the absence of further evidence of what these authors thought about what the booksellers and printers did to their work, Young's almost unique commentary suggests that she had no control whatsoever. She just waited for the pages to come back in a published printed form, bound in the set. Her later bookseller, Hughes, seems to have cut down on the correction time which allowed the Nobles (and sometimes Lane) to offer certain revisions. Some novels do have errata slips in. And again this is to the credit of the much-maligned Nobles and the early novels. Many Nobles titles carried errata lists. In *Gilham Farm* (1781: 9), for example, seven spelling errors are listed at the end of the second volume, and in the first volume a separate insert gives page and line numbers where readers can correct errors (and many surviving copies have these carefully marked in). Last minute correction here was telling. As the note for page twelve, line fourteen, says, 'for volubility read volatility'. All, of course, points to the close re-reading of the manuscript either by a corrector or by the author, and was something, perhaps, more easily achieved in the earlier than later decades of the novel print boom.

Reception, Readers and Reviewers

Both the high price of new novels and the limits of literacy determined readership boundaries, but these can never be clear cut. Purchases of non-essential goods depend upon individual taste as much as supply, opportunity, alternative spending attractions, and the fundamental level of income. Nor is literacy bounded and invariant, but is best considered as a compound of literacies, changing with aptitude

[284] CR n.s. 23 (1798): 233 on *Eloise de Montblanc* (1796: 5).

and experience. Associations with specific forms of texts also encouraged self-referential audiences, and what have been characterized as the 'widening circles' of readers in this period were sustained by the increased purchase and circulation of newspapers and prints as well as *belles-lettres*. In time, cost bars to new novels were breached by the second-hand market, as well as by library circulation and by other means of acquisition including gift and simple inheritance. Most aspirants to these circles placed a premium on access to the latest literature, and the novel typified modern publication. Nevertheless, the fashionable novel remained largely the luxury possession of a narrow section of society.[285]

Membership fees and borrowing charges for commercial circulating and proprietary libraries were hardly affordable for most. In late 1766 'The Reputable Circulating Libraries' of John and Francis Noble, William Bathoe, Thomas Lowndes, Thomas Vernor and J. Chater, Thomas Jones, and William Cooke, jointly announced new levies of 12s a year or 4s a quarter, a rise (from the charges, for example, by the Nobles for the previous twenty years) of 1s quarterly and 1s 6d annually.[286] These were the first increases since the reduction in rates after the first generation of libraries in the early 1740s, and in 1773 the *Critical* still assumed 10s 6d to be the normal annual subscription to a circulating library.[287] Over the next three decades quarterly charges increased to 5s or more and it was not unusual for an annual subscription to cost up to a guinea by 1800. Whatever the actual costs, however, the agreement between leading proprietors to fix standard rates proved just as significant as any increased charges.

The identity of particular readers for novels inevitably relies upon eclectic evidence. As detailed above, subscription lists, prefaced to novels or separately published, do give the names and sometimes addresses and professions of supporters,[288] but these, of course, are not simply proof of readership. Many subscribers signed up as a form of charity—and very public charity—to indigent friends and neighbours. Other subscribers were sought for social cachet; a quality name to lend distinction to an otherwise lacklustre list. More helpful in identifying individual readers are the fragmentary remains of circulating library subscription records (and we have none for the major London circulating libraries of the period with the exception of some ledgers from Hookham and Carpenter in the 1790s[289]). A few provincial libraries

---

[285] Discussion of eighteenth-century novel readers since Helen Sard Hughes, 'The Middle-Class Reader and the English Novel', *Journal of English and Germanic Philology* 25 (1926): 362–78, includes Roy McKeen Wiles, 'The Relish for Reading in Provincial England Two Centuries Ago' in Paul J. Korshin, *The Widening Circle: Essays on the Circulation of Literature in Eighteenth-Century Europe* (Philadelphia, 1976): 87–115, Jan Fergus, 'Women, Class, and the Growth of Magazine Readership in the Provinces, 1746–1780', *Studies in Eighteenth-Century Culture* 16 (1986): 41–56; Isabel Rivers, ed., *Books and their Readers in Eighteenth-Century England* (Leicester, 1982); Raven, Small and Tadmor, eds., *Practice and Representation of Reading*, chs. 1, 9–12, and Raven, *British Fiction*, pp. 25–32.

[286] A copy of this notice survives bound in the BL copy of the Nobles' *History of Mrs Drayton and her Two Daughters*, 1767 (JR 1079).

[287] CR 36 (1773): 397 in a review of 1773: 32. [288] See pp. 55–56.

[289] See Fergus and Thaddeus, 'Women, Publishers, and Money'.

give some indication; most notably James Marshall's library at Bath lists 1,779 names with 3,000 payments between 1793 and 1800 (usually 5s), from a very elite and largely female clientele.[290] A small selection of the orders and purchases from bookshops also survives, although almost none in London. The most studied are probably the bookselling records surviving up to 1780 of the Clays of Daventry, Rugby, Lutterworth, and Warwick. They have even been mined for the information they reveal about purchases by named servants, many of whom appear to have bought in their own right as well as acting as intermediaries for their mistresses and masters.[291] The diaries and memoirs of particular readers, if rare, assist in gauging reactions and identifying common responses. Many of these have been examined, ranging from the diary of Mrs Thrale, reading fiction in bed, to the journal of Anna Larpent, pious daughter of a diplomat and wife of the Inspector of Plays.[292] In her diary kept between 1773 and 1828, Larpent read more novels than any other form of literature. She recorded reading forty-six English novels and twenty-two French works of fiction. She abandoned *Anna St Ives* (1792: 38) as paltry, and found from reading *Desmond* that Charlotte Smith, despite what seemed obvious genius, was a 'wild leveller'. Like so many of her fellow novel readers, Anna Larpent insisted that she read novels for self-improvement.[293]

Attention to women readers, as customers of bookshops and libraries, as keepers of memoirs, or as imagined by the reviewers, should not overwhelm, however. In 1808 Mary Julia Young reflected on 'the works of fancy which I have written' and marked down 'novels as a species of literature sought after with avidity by the younger part of *both* sexes'.[294] Young wanted to emphasize her appeal to both men and women, but her stress upon age is just as significant. There can be no doubt that the majority of novels in this bibliography appealed to the youth market. The tender years of many readers were matched by the numerous boy and girl novelists already discussed, and the notion of under-twenties communicating with each other through the pages of inconsequential novels proved too much for many critics. The novel proved a fashionable form, however, adopted even by those who wished to intervene to curtail excesses or introduce to adolescents of good families the voice of mature responsibility.

Probably the best indication of the narrowness of the new novel audience, however, is the limited production of most first editions of these titles and the extremely high non-survival rate today. The audience for novels and *belles-lettres* naturally encompassed well-established popular titles, with circulation hugely boosted by

[290] Cited in Kaufman, *Community Library*, p. 10.

[291] Jan Fergus, 'Provincial Servants' Reading in the Late Eighteenth Century', in Raven et al., eds., *Practice and Representation of Reading*, pp. 202–25.

[292] Katherine C. Balderston, ed., *Thraliana: The Diary of Mrs Hester Lynch Thrale (later Mrs Piozzi) 1776–1809*, 2 vols. (Oxford: Clarendon Press, 1942); Huntington Library, HM 31201, Diary of Anna Larpent, 17 vols.

[293] For a full discussion see John Brewer, 'Reconstructing the Reader: prescriptions, texts and strategies in Anna Larpent's reading', in Raven et al., eds., *Practice and Representation of Reading*, pp. 226–45.

[294] Young to the Royal Literary Fund, 20 Mar. 1808 (RLF 6: 216).

the reprints of Bell and others and by the development of magazine and part-issue fiction. The volumes sold by the Clays or bought by Mrs Thrale furnished a popular canon of fiction. In the popular literary current new works were additional tributaries, not the mainstream. Manifestly, it was the successive reprinting of novel titles that created a more general readership. The cheaper library series and the eventual second-hand market swelled the audience for Burney, Mackenzie, and Radcliffe, but also for the strong supporting cast identified in Table 5. It would be quite false to try to isolate any audience for new novels alone.

Nevertheless, the market for and readership of *new* novels has enjoyed relatively modest historical attention, especially given the extent of contemporary alarm about indecencies that were precisely said to be modish and parvenu. Both then and in retrospect, the readership for the new novel is linked to contemporary concerns about its public life and influences, and in this the published criticism of the periodical reviews played an illustrious part. This bibliography gives some sense of this response, even though further research is required to identify other accounts, both public and private, of the particular reception for novels of the period. The available review criticism, however, certainly influenced many fiction writers and must have affected the actual reading of the novels. Popular novel readers, insisting, like Anna Larpent, on the improving qualities of their occupation, usually constructed defensive explanations for novel consumption. In response, the reviewers often entered a resigned protest that the public ignored their injunctions against novels and popular literature.[295]

Against this, the power of the reviewers was acknowledged by many of the novelists. *Adeline* (1790: 1) was one of several novels dedicated to the reviewers or begging in prefaces for critical leniency. *The Follies of St James's Street* (1789: 10) opened with the declaration that 'the Author of the following sheets is well aware, that the Critics will condemn her work, and the Reviewers murder it without mercy'. The author, still anonymous, was proved exactly right. More successfully, Mrs Roche directly addressed the critics in her *Vicar of Lansdowne* (1789: 64), imploring them to allow her novel 'to pass by in unheeded insignificance'. A discussion of the practice of reviewing was even included by Holcroft in his *Adventures of Hugh Trevor* (1794: 29).[296] In turn, the reviewers occasionally turned promoters, casting aside their usual pessimism about the attempts of learned and discerning men to educate a giddy public. William Enfield in the *Monthly* wrote that Mary Robinson's *Vancenza* (1792: 50) was 'a tale, which, we venture to predict, will be much read and admired'.[297] A few seasons later, Mary Robinson dedicated by return her *Widow* (1794: 51) to 'that Public, and those Liberal Critics, who have so highly distinguished my Former Productions'.

The influence of the periodical reviewers was pervasive, as has been clear in every

---

[295] MR 48 (1773): 71, on the continuation volumes of Wynne's *Man of Honour*, a Noble production (1771: 60).
[296] *Adventures of Hugh Trevor*, 3: 184–5.   [297] MR n.s. 7 (1792): 299.

section of this introduction. Their new critical influence dates from the foundation of the *Monthly* in 1749 and the *Critical* in 1756. Long reviews of novels were rare, but very few of the novels listed below were missed by the 'Catalogue' sections of the *Monthly* and *Critical*, and most were also noticed by other main periodicals and magazines. Many reviews were extremely unfavourable, to the extent that reviewing a novel became something of a sport. Critics often seemed to compete for the most insulting or sarcastic dismissal. These verdicts, as sent down from the two leading reviewing periodicals, were copied in other journals and magazines, notably the *Town and Country* and the *Lady's*, but as most novels were noticed in the also-ran, end sections of the *Monthly* and *Critical*, the plagiarism was not too demanding. On several occasions, the *Critical* is also clearly derivative from the *Monthly*.

The exact procedures involved in reviewing remain unclear. If the correspondence of the editor of the *Monthly* is any guide, then the periodical reviews did not usually receive free copies of the novels (or any books reviewed), but bought or borrowed them from the publishing bookseller. *Monthly* reviewers returned copies of their books to the editor, Ralph Griffiths, who then usually sold the reviewed books back to the original booksellers. The Longman and Rees records of the 1790s, however, indicate that Longman sometimes (although not always) sent up to six free copies of each novel to the review editors. Four of the 500 copies of *Caroline de Montmorenci* (1794: 4), five of the 750 copies of *Love's Pilgrimage* (1796: 13), and six sets of Pratt's five-volume *Family Secrets* (1797: 68) were despatched to 'Reviews and Magazines', all written off against costs.[298] Names of the journals are not listed in the accounts, so it is not clear whether Griffiths's buy-and-return practice continued in the case of the *Monthly*. Nor is it clear why some titles were sent free to the reviews and others were not. Perhaps the decision to send out free copies was taken when Longman wished to ensure that the novel was received by all the major periodical reviews and so hoped to gain individual responses and independent assessments, rather than the borrowings from the first review published. In the case of both *Caroline de Montmorenci* and *Family Secrets*, the reviews, while not savage, were all distinctly chilly. In a review that must have confirmed the apprehensions of Longman senior, Arthur Aikin decided that *Love's Pilgrimage*, free or not to his editor, was in the main 'utterly repugnant to every idea of delicacy and honour'.[299]

Many reviewers lived at great distance from London and worked hard for their wages. Carriage costs were paid, it seems, by the review editor, but the reviewers paid for the return of the book to London. For every sheet of work (amounting to 16 printed pages in octavo) Percival Stockdale was paid two guineas by the *Critical* in 1770 and Robert Southey was paid three guineas between 1797 and 1804. William Godwin was paid two guineas per sheet by the *English*. Over the same period, *Monthly* reviewers received between two and four guineas per sheet.[300] On

---

[298] Longman archives, impression book H4, ff. 2, 18.   [299] MR n.s. 20 (1796), 346.

[300] Derek Roper, *Reviewing before the Edinburgh 1788–1802* (London: Methuen and Co., 1978), pp. 39, 273 n. 162.

occasions these rates were increased for special work, but such payments, of up to sixteen guineas by the turn of the century, were exceptional. William Taylor complained that critics' pay had not increased for half a century. It is also the case that although the by-the-sheet rates of pay might seem relatively generous when compared, say, to the average sale price for novel manuscripts, it often took many 'Catalogue' articles to fill each sheet. Andrew Becket, son of Thomas Becket the bookseller, complained that he had received only £45 for writing 280 reviews for the *Monthly*.[301]

All critical notices appeared without attribution, and the reviewers' anonymity was earnestly guarded by the periodical editors. Contributors to the *Critical* in this period remain unknown, but wherever possible entries in the following bibliography include the names of *Monthly* reviewers, using the run of the periodicals annotated with contributors' initials by Ralph Griffiths.[302] Identified are the authors of some 202 of the 315 *Monthly* novel reviews of the 1770s, the authors of 315 of the 404 novel reviews of the 1780s, and, less adequately, the authors of 292 of the 701 novel reviews of the 1790s. All the critics might, of course, have reviewed many more novels.

Either by design or accident, several of the unattributed critics became specialist novel reviewers. If the *Monthly*'s reviewers are representative, then the published critical notices of new novels were concentrated in surprisingly few hands. The specificity of the commentary, especially given its often resourceful brevity, is therefore all the more revealing. Many responses must have been mediated by the critics' writings even though few readers would have been aware of the reviewers' identities. The backgrounds and perspectives of six men chiefly responsible for the *Monthly* criticism of novels assume major importance in the broader public debate about new fiction. Their commentaries provide, as Antonia Forster puts it, 'a view of literary developments startlingly different to that created by literary history's hindsight'.[303]

In the middle of this period, the *Monthly*'s pre-eminent reviewer of fiction was Samuel Badcock. An associate of Priestley and a dissenting minister of Barnstaple in Devon from 1769, Badcock returned to his native South Molton in the same county in 1778. From then until 1786, the year, it happens, in which he abandoned Nonconformity for the Church of England, he wrote *Monthly* reviews for at least 110 of the new novels listed in this bibliography. The total of new novels known to be published between 1779 and 1786 numbers some 221; for seven years, therefore, a copy

---

[301] Forster, *Index to Book Reviews in England 1749–1774*, p. 16 n. 32, where similar examples are also given.
[302] A cast of critics first assessed by Benjamin Christie Nangle, *The Monthly Review, First Series, 1749–1789: Indexes of Contributors and Articles* (Oxford; Clarendon Press, 1934), and *The Monthly Review, Second Series, 1790–1815: Indexes of Contributors and Articles* (Oxford; Clarendon Press, 1955); and refined by Forster, *Index to Book Reviews in England 1749–1774* and *Index to Book Reviews in England 1775–1800*.
[303] Forster, *Index to Book Reviews 1775–1799*, p. xliii. See her introduction for a full discussion of the transformation of reviewing in this period.

of every other new novel published in London was despatched by the mail coach to a distant part of Devon to be publicly appraised by Badcock. His withdrawal from reviewing came two years before his death in 1788. His place was largely filled by the London-based Andrew Becket, reviewing at least 132 novels (or more than half of the 242 new novels published) in an intense four-year period between 1786 and 1789 (including thirty-six of the thirty-nine author-identified *Monthly* reviews of the fifty-one novels with 1787 imprints). Employed by Griffiths over a much longer period was William Enfield. The apparent stalwart of popular novel criticism, Enfield is known to have reviewed 203 novels from 1774 until his death in 1797. Like Badcock, a dissenting minister and working far from London, Enfield held the Rectorship of the Academy at Warrington from 1770 until its dissolution in 1783. After this he moved to Norwich, where he preached and eked out a living by his pen.

These three critics dominated novel reviewing in the *Monthly* in this period, but amongst other contributors Gilbert Stuart, historian, critic, and dissolute friend of John Murray, was renowned as a rapid reviewer. He wrote notices for forty-eight of the 180 novels known to have been published between 1770 and 1773. In that year, Stuart left London to return to Scotland, but after the failure of his *Edinburgh Magazine and Review*, he returned to London in 1782, thereafter reviewing for John Murray's *English Review*.[304] Well known as the author of the *New History of London*, John Noorthouck also worked for Griffiths, but anonymously like all his fellow critics. He reviewed sixty new novels in the *Monthly* between 1770 and 1792. Like Becket, the son of an eminent bookseller, Noorthouck was liveryman of the Stationers' Company, and a frequently employed corrector and indexer for the London trade. He finally wrote from a Peterborough fastness in 1793, asking to resign because of failing eyesight (Noorthouck was then forty-seven). He also complained of unkind deadlines, although he went on to complete a few more specialist reviews.[305]

Certain novelists also reviewed for the major journals. Thomas Holcroft assessed eleven novels for the *Monthly* in the 1790s, including Anna Maria Porter's *Artless Tales* (1793: 36), Henry Le Maire's *French Gil Blas* (1793: 25), Richard Cumberland's *Henry* (1793: 26), and Ann Yearsley's *Royal Captives* (1795: 50). In the same periodical, John Hawkesworth reviewed Richard Griffith's *Posthumous Works* (1770: 32), and John Langhorne reviewed ten novels in the 1770s. As mischievous as ever, John Trusler even contrived to review the second edition of his own novel *Modern Times* (1785: 46) for John Murray's *English*—and was paid for doing so.[306] Murray, like the *Monthly*'s editor, Ralph Griffiths, also reviewed novels. In Griffiths's case this was often in collaboration with (or perhaps correction of) another reviewer, and the impression is that his selection was deliberate. His largely encouraging reviews welcomed novels by Wieland, Nicolai, and Henry Brooke, as well as

[304] See William Zachs, *Without Regard to Good Manners: A Biography of Gilbert Stuart 1743–1786* (Edinburgh, 1992).

[305] Bod. MS Add.c.89, ff. 266, 267, Noorthouck to Ralph Griffiths, 15 Feb. 1792, 3 Oct. 1793.

[306] EngR 5 (1785) 274–7; Murray archives, Murray to Trusler 29 Mar., 8 Apr., 6 Oct. 1786.

unexpectedly impressive debuts by unknown writers (1775: 22; 1797: 29). Very few women reviewers are known in this period, the most prominent in these listings being Elizabeth Moody. A *Monthly* reviewer of four novels in the 1790s, her brief notices appear relatively sympathetic. In the case of the turgid *Sempronia* (1790: 26), she was decidedly generous.[307]

Poignantly, most of these critics were chained to the same treadmill as the novelists. William Enfield sought reviewing or any other 'literary commission' that might sustain him, and in 1791 proposed a 'regular plan of business' to the *Monthly*'s editor. Griffiths acceded, granting Enfield what amounted to an annual salary or retainer of about £20 to write to order. The number of sheets he was obliged to complete under this agreement is not recorded in the correspondence, but he was clearly expected to produce the short Catalogue notices along with the more prestigious and sheet-filling reviews proper.[308] Within a few years, however, Enfield was complaining about the fare he received, pleading with Griffiths to send him as few novels as possible:

I shall be glad, now and then, when it may be worth while, to bestow some pains upon a good novel; nor will I ask to decline *my share* of the trash; but, at my time of life [fifty-four], *moderate novels* are very tedious reading; I must add, too, What is to me very material, they are of all articles the most *unproductive.*[309]

Nine months later he wrote that

I have done the novels briefly because I did not think they deserved a more particular notice. By the way, from the great number of novels sent me in the *two last* parcels, I conclude that a hint I dropt sometime ago has escaped your attention. I have no objection to lounging now and then an hour in Lane's shop: but to be shut up for several days together in his warehouse is to an old man an irksome confinement.[310]

Readers and writers must have been affected by positive recommendations as well as by the more sensational dismissals. Examples of reviewers' arbitration on novels' content, form and genre have already been given. The entries provide many further examples of positive guidance, whether or not this was ever accepted by the authors themselves. The clerical credentials of so many novel reviewers helps explain, perhaps, the sermonizing tendency in novel reviewing and the strictures offered in evaluating good and bad approaches. General metaphors and comparisons introduced by the reviewers also reveal much about attitudes and assumptions. The press is viewed as groaning with novel productions. The notion of literary 'manufacture' and of mass production is apparent even in favourable contexts. As Ralph Griffiths wrote of Cradock's *Village Memoirs* (1775: 22), 'the

---

[307] All identified reviewers are listed in the Notes index. Moody's other reviews were of 1790: 69, 1799: 41, and 1799: 64.

[308] Bod. MS Add.c.89, ff. 58, 60, Enfield to Ralph Griffiths, 3 Jan. 1791, 5 Aug. 1791.

[309] Bod. MS Add.c.89, f. 86, Enfield to Ralph Griffiths, 7 Jan. 1795.

[310] Bod. MS Add.c.89, f. 93, Enfield to Ralph Griffiths, 4 Oct. 1795.

Novel-Manufactory is not yet wholly abandoned to the lower orders of Grub-street'.[311] The language of production paralleled the insistent emphasis on consumption. Novels were digested, and like bad food, resulted in physical damage. Reviewers commented on poor cultivation, cooking and eating, and even described themselves as 'caterers for the Public'.[312] The 'poison' of the novelist featured in numerous reviews. Becket predicted, in this novel-food preparation industry, that the future of *Emma Dorvill* (1789: 5) was as paper for pastry cooks.[313]

As will already be plain, many of these published verdicts were contemptuous. How was an author and her existing and would-be readers to react to the *Critical*'s demand that she should take black hellebore, or by the *Monthly*'s conclusion that she had supplied 'the ravings of a deranged imagination'?[314] The best that the *Critical* reviewer could say about Regina Maria Roche's (now lost) *Maid of the Hamlet* (1793: 38) was that it might at least distract from a toothache. The enigmatic *Princess Coquedoeuf and Prince Bonbon* (1796: 37) was thought to be a 'good companion for the gout'.[315] Of Baculard D'Arnaud's *History of Count Gleichen* (1786: 13) the *Critical* decreed that

this is a modern sentimental novel, plentifully adorned with ahs! and ohs! with little real pathos, and less interest. Alice at last dies, in a fortunate moment; fortunate for Gleichen, for the reader, and supremely fortunate for the reviewer.[316]

Other 'Catalogue' review notices of the novels were short and pungent, but many also distilled an opinion rather than opting for the unmediated extracts offered in many of the longer reviews. It is true that in appraising much minor first-time fiction, reviewers used the notice more to demonstrate wit than to provide a measured verdict (or indeed, to take the time to read the novel), but in the majority of cases words were chosen carefully and always meant to influence. Insisting upon their moral duty, the periodical reviewers forged critical values as well as offering memorable publicity. Longer critical evaluations offered positive advice, as was the case, for example, in reviews of Minifie's *Count de Poland* (1780: 20), Elliott's *History of the Hon. Mrs Rosemont and Sir Henry Cardigan* (1781: 17), Godwin's *Italian Letters* (1784: 17) and Macdonald's *The Independent* (1784: 19). Sporadic rave reviews such as that from both the *Monthly* and the *Critical* for Elizabeth Keir's *History of Miss Greville* (1787: 43), sanctioned the didactic combination of instruction with entertainment.[317] The community was also a related one in which, for example, Enfield hears from Griffiths that Holcroft was pleased with Enfield's reviews of *Hugh Trevor* and Godwin's *Caleb Williams*.[318]

Acting as guardians of literary style, many reviewers commented—almost

---

[311] MR 52 (1775): 139–43. Cf. MR n.s. 2 (1790): 463–4 on 1789: 34.
[312] MR 77 (1787): 495–6, on 1787: 1.   [313] MR 81 (1789): 285.
[314] CR 32 (1771): 240 and MR 45 (1771): 156, on Mary Latter, *Pro and Con* (1771: 44).
[315] CR n.s. 10 (1794): 472–3; CR n.s. 21 (1797): 90.   [316] CR 62 (1786): 235–6.
[317] CR 64 (1787): 200–1; MR 77 (1787): 80.
[318] Bod. MS Add.c.89, f. 86, Enfield to Ralph Griffiths, 7 Jan. 1795.

always unfavourably—on the language and construction of the novel. Failures of 'composition' headed the concerns. Amongst many other identified solecisms were the 'ladyisms' of Elizabeth Blower in *Features From Life* (1788: 44), and, in one season alone, the 'vulgarisms' of the anonymous *Fair Hibernian* (1789: 6) and William Hayley's *The Young Widow* (1789: 44), other 'inelegant provincialisms' (1789: 29), and numerous attacks on bad or neglected grammar (including 1789: 9, 31, 32). Critics lambasted botched pretentions such as Lane's inaccurate and incorrectly printed French in *The Weird Sisters* (1794: 15). In the next season, the *Critical* reviewer begged novelists to 'avoid corrupting the language' with 'a confusion of words, resembling a wilderness of flowering weeds, which it would be impossible to separate or disentangle'.[319]

On several occasions, the reviewers disagreed about the quality of the novels sent to them. Clara Reeve, trusting to the periodical reviewers as arbiters of taste, still noted that their discernment clashed on certain occasions.[320] Where critical disagreement was marked, care has been taken to represent the differences in the entries below. The *Monthly* praised the *History of Eliza Warwick* (1778: 3), but the *Critical* was scornful and insisted that the author should never write again. In 1785 the *Critical* and *Monthly* disagreed about the merits of *The Liberal American*. Four years later, the *Critical* enjoyed the Misses Purbeck's *Honoria Sommerville* (1789: 60) which 'soars far above the common flight', but the *Monthly* condemned this 'tissue of adventures' as clichéd nonsense. In 1790 *Louisa; or, The Reward of an Affectionate Daughter* delighted the *Monthly*, but the *Critical* reviewer believed that he had rarely seen anything more 'trifling and uninteresting'. Other disparities include, for all the author's gratitude to her critics, the negative *Critical* and the positive *Monthly* notices of Mary Robinson's *The Widow* (1794: 51). Even recognized authors did not escape. The major reviews disagreed completely, for example, about whether Frances Brooke's *Excursion* (1777: 9) and Pratt's *Travels for the Heart* (1777: 15) were worthy of their authors.[321]

Clearly, many of the warnings against the novel were to be taken seriously. At the beginning of this period the 'romance' might be regarded as an 'old exploded sort',[322] but during the next thirty years anxiety about the new novel focused on the effects of reading seditious and damaging sentiments.[323] At best, argued critics, the poorest novels were a waste of time for young minds, but at worst they offered temptation to indecency and even madness. As the *Critical* thundered of Mary Robinson's 'fashionably vicious' *Widow* (1794: 51): 'O! for a warning voice to prevent those, at least, in whom age has not yet destroyed the capabilities of improvement, from dreaming away their hours in turning over publications like these.'[324]

[319] CR n.s. 15 (1795): 236 on 1795: 10.   [320] Reeve, *Progress of Romance*, 2: 22–4.
[321] CR 44 (1777): 61–3, and MR 57 (1777): 141–5; CR 44 (1777): 349–52, and MR 58 (1778): 85–6.
[322] MR 43 (1770): 400, on *The Captive* (1771: 7).
[323] Standard accounts are offered by John Tinnon Taylor, *Early Opposition to the English Novel: The Popular Reaction from 1780 to 1830* (New York, 1943); W. F. Gallaway Jun., 'The Conservative Attitude Toward Fiction 1770–1830', *PMLA* 55 (1940): 1041–59.
[324] CR n.s. 12 (1794): 102.

Moral panic about the social consequences of novel-reading intensified in times of social and political upheaval, much like the modern debate about sex and violence on the screen or the internet. Scarce able to believe that it had been written by a woman, the *English* denounced Mrs Morris's *Illicit Love* (1791: 52), lamenting that 'it is not harmless', and that it 'can only serve to corrupt and vitiate the female mind'.[325]

In this context, the reviewers maintained low estimations of those to be found reading new novels. According to the critics, lower-class readers might be satisfied with John Potter's *Curate of Coventry* (1771: 49), when it was clearly to be dismissed by people of superior ability, 'who can distinguish the strokes of genius'.[326] Milliners' apprentices and 'junior misses' featured amongst those likely to be sub-verted by inappropriate fiction.[327] More generally still, the abilities of novel readers might correspond to the abilities of novel writers. Producers and consumers were people of matching inadequacy. Samuel Badcock in the *Monthly* did not hesitate to attribute the anonymously published *History of the Hon. Mrs Rosemont and Sir Henry Cardigan* (1781: 17, by Miss Elliott) to a lady:

from the freedom and vivacity with which it is written, and from several glaring deficiencies even in common grammatical construction. This fault we have often observed in the com-position of ladies, who, notwithstanding, have acquired all the elegant graces of language: and have almost instinctively caught at elegance without giving themselves the trouble of pursuing the strict forms of grammar.[328]

Above all, however, genuine distinction and literary merit risked being lost in the flood of novels that seemed to teem from the press, overwhelming imaginations by the sheer number of new and foolish titles. No matter that most of these volumes were published in small editions and that many of them were quickly confined to the shelves of modest—and expensive—circulating libraries. These images of mass novel manufacture, of irresponsible, indiscriminate consumption, left a powerful legacy in literary history. Dismissive notices by eighteenth-century critics were compounded by the disappearance and unavailability of so many of these novels, but even more so by the continuing inadequacies of historical bibliography. Most of these productions were, after all, poor imitations of the more assured fiction of the period, and many were no more than self-consciously slight efforts designed to amuse or to keep poverty at bay. This has created a disordered literary history, one in which few have attempted to identify the full range of popular authors, novel genres, writing styles, booksellers, and the distributors and readers of the literature. The first stage in recovering a new historical and sociological profile of the popular novel and popular novelist of the period is attempted by this bibliography. In intro-ducing its entries, this essay has retraced the ambition of Clara Reeve. And as she declared in a self-critical dialogue in her *Progress of Romance*:

---

[325] EngR 19 (1792): 231.   [326] Gilbert Stuart, MR 44 (1771): 418.
[327] MR 44 (1771): 262, on *The Brother* (1771: 6).   [328] MR 64 (1781): 468–9.

It is now that I begin to be sensible in how arduous an undertaking I have engaged, and to fear I shall leave it unfinished . . . This is one of the circumstances that frightens me. If I skim over the subject lightly it will be doing nothing; and if I am too minute I may grow dull and tedious, and tire my hearers.[329]

It is hoped that the following bibliography will be sufficiently *minute* but also that it will encourage others to add further discoveries by which we might continue to rewrite the broader history of the English prose novel.

[329] Reeve, *Progress of Romance*, 1: 108.

An Historical Bibliography of Prose Novels in English First Published in the British Isles 1770–1799

ANTONIA FORSTER

and

JAMES RAVEN

with the assistance of Stephen Bending

ADVENTURES OF A BANK-NOTE
See BRIDGES, Thomas

THE ADVENTURES OF AN ACTOR
See 1782: 1

1770: 1   ANON.
CONSTANTIA; OR THE DISTRESSED FRIEND. A NOVEL.
> London: Printed for W. Johnston, Numb. 16. in Ludgate-street, 1770.
> 272p. 12mo. 3s (CR, MR).
> CR 29: 364–6 (May 1770); MR 43: 152 (Aug 1770); AF I: 494.
> C 7720.d.1002; ESTC t165381 (BI O).

Notes. 'An Allegorical, Moral, Dramatic, Musical Entertainment. By Way of Epithalamium' pp. [265]–72. Epistolary.
Further edn: Dublin, 1769/1770 (Printed for the author by Dillon Chamberlaine, 2 vols. in 1, 12mo), ESTC n005320. ESTC says vol. 2 is dated 1769.
   CR: 'The first part of the story is so perplexed, that we do not know what the author would be at: the winding up of it, however, is clear and commendable' (p. 364).
   MR [John Noorthouck]: 'This Novel merits some distinction from the common perform-ances of the kind. . . . it is full of business; and . . . might, with ease, have been spun into *four* [volumes].—The sentiments it contains are chaste and laudable. . . .'

THE DANGER OF THE PASSIONS
See THIBOUVILLE, Henri-Lambert d'Erbigny, marquis de

1770: 2   ANON.
THE DISTRESSED DAUGHTER: OR, THE HAPPY RECONCILIATION; A NOVEL.
> London: Printed for G. Riley, and A. Cooke, at their Circulating Library, Queen Street,
>   Berkley [*sic*] Square, 1770.
> 300p. 12mo. 2s 6d sewed (LC).
> BL RB 23a.8682; ESTC t224759.

Notes. BL copy lacks several leaves; in original blue boards.
Adv. LC 29: 16 (1–3 Jan 1771).

1770: 3   ANON.
FATAL FRIENDSHIP; A NOVEL. IN TWO VOLUMES. BY A LADY.
> London: Printed for T. Lowndes, at No. 77, in Fleet-Street, 1770.
> I 252p; II 239p. 12mo. 5s (CR), 5s sewed (MR).

CR 30: 397 (Nov 1770); MR 42: 488 (June 1770); AF I: 852.
BL 12614.ff.13; EM 191: 4; ESTC t107804.

Notes. Epistolary. 10 pp. advs. end vol. 2.
KM 4817: Printing completed by Bowyer 17 Mar 1770; 750 copies.
Extract published LC 27: 396 (24–26 Apr 1770).
Further edn: Dublin, 1771 (Printed for H. Saunders, D. Chamberlaine, J. Potts. W. Sleater, J. Williams, and 3 others, 2 vols., 12mo), ESTC t212490. Facs: FN.

CR: 'There is nothing in this novel to distinguish it from the common run of circulating productions.—To enter into a critique upon its literary merit would be to waste both time and paper.'

MR [John Noorthouck]: '. . . the catastrophe is affecting, while the letters are written in a lively agreeable style.'

1770: 4   ANON.

FEMALE FRIENDSHIP: OR THE INNOCENT SUFFERER. A MORAL NOVEL.

London: Printed for John Bell, at his Circulating Library near Exeter Exchange in the Strand, and C. Etherington, at York, 1770.
I iv, 226p; II 220p. 12mo. 5s sewed (CR, MR).
CR 29: 148 (Feb 1770); MR 42: 70 (Jan 1770).
BL 12611.de.1; EM 64: 4; ESTC t057439 (NA CtY).

Notes. 2 pp. advs. (dated 1 Jan 1770) end vol. 1.
Adv., 'On Monday next will be published', LC 26: 619 (26–28 Dec 1769).
Further edns: Dublin, 1770 (Printed for J. Williams, J. Porter, and T. Walker, 2 vols. in 1, 12mo), ESTC n009756; Hallowell, Me., 1797, ESTC w012118.

CR: '. . . the characters in these volumes are so loosely marked, the adventures are so tiresome from the commonness of them, and the language is so inelegant, that we cannot venture to recommend them to readers of sentiment or taste.'

1770: 5   ANON.

THE FORTUNATE BLUE-COAT BOY: OR, MEMOIRS OF THE LIFE AND HAPPY ADVENTURES OF MR. BENJAMIN TEMPLEMAN; FORMERLY A SCHOLAR IN CHRIST'S-HOSPITAL. BY AN ORPHANOTROPHIAN. IN TWO VOLUMES.

London: Printed for J. Cooke, at No. 17, in Pater-noster-Row, 1770 [vol. 2: Pater-Noster-Row].
I viii, 228p; II 218p. 12mo. 6s (CR, MR), 5s sewed or 6s neatly bound (LC).
CR 29: 149–50 (Feb 1770); MR 42: 71–2 (Jan 1770); AF I: 944.
BL C.175.bb.2; EM 7449: 5; ESTC t132228 (NA CtY-BR, MH-H).

Notes. 8 pp. 'Notes' end vol. 1; 2 pp. 'Notes' end vol. 2.
Adv., 'In a few Days will be published', LC 26: 559 (7–9 Dec 1769); adv. as published LC 26: 576 (12–14 Dec 1769).
Further edn: London, 1789, ESTC n047887.

CR: 'As this extraordinary history contains chiefly the insignificant transactions of the hospital, and the empty, very often illiberal, conversation of the nurse, the steward, the porter, the boys, the widow Getall's servants, Jack the vintner, &c. &c. it cannot afford any entertainment to readers of a higher class.'

MR: 'What will become of the Reviewers, if this numerous band of charity-boys should follow their comrade's example, and run their callow heads against the press. Mercy on us! what a deluge of histories, memoirs, lives and adventures, shall we have!'

1770: 6   ANON.
THE GENUINE MEMOIRS OF MISS FAULKNER; OTHERWISE MRS. D***L**N OR COUNTESS OF H*****X, IN EXPECTANCY. CONTAIN-ING THE AMOURS AND INTRIGUES OF SEVERAL PERSONS OF HIGH DISTINCTION, AND REMARKABLE CHARACTERS: WITH SOME CURIOUS POLITICAL ANECDOTES, NEVER BEFORE PUB-LISHED.

> London: Printed for William Bingley, at No. 31, in Newgate-Street, 1770.
> 338p. 12mo. 3s (CR), 3s sewed (MR, LC).
> CR 30: 240 (Sept 1770); MR 42: 251 (Mar 1770); AF I: 1055.
> BL G.14249; EM 7: 3; ESTC t073915 (BI C, O; NA CtY, CSmH, IU, MH-H, NjP, PU &c.).

Notes. Adv., 'In a Neat Pocket Volume', LC 27: 180 (20–22 Feb 1770).
MR includes under heading 'Novels'; CR does not classify. Mrs D***l**n is Mary Anne Donellan, niece of George Faulkner, the Dublin printer, and mistress to the Earl of Halifax, Viceroy of Ireland.

CR: 'The anecdotes which fill this volume have been gleaned with wonderful industry, to destroy the peace of a woman who has been cautious of giving public offence, and a noble-man who has deserved well of his country.'

MR: 'A great deal of fable grafted on a very small stock of truth.'

THE HISTORY OF CHARLES WENTWORTH, ESQ.
See BANCROFT, Edward

1770: 7   ANON.
THE HISTORY OF MISS HARRIOT MONTAGUE. IN TWO VOLUMES.

> London: Printed for J. Roson, No. 54, St. Martin's-Le Grand, near Newgate-Street, 1770.
> I 208p; II 204p. 12mo. 6s (CR), 5s (MR).
> CR 29: 149 (Feb 1770); MR 42: 250–1 (Mar 1770).
> PU Singer-Mend PR.3291.A1.H6315.1770; ESTC n007882.

Notes. Imprint date in vol. 1 is misprinted as MDCCLX. 4 pp. advs. end vol. 2.
CG records as 'The Inhuman Stepmother; or, The History of Miss Harriot Montague'.
Further edn: Dublin, 1770 (Printed for T. Todd, 2 vols. in 1, 12mo), xESTC.

MR [John Noorthouck]: 'Those who read the astonishing adventures of Miss Harriot Montague and her friends with a proper frame of mind, will be puzzled to determine whether to laugh at the ridiculous bundle of unnatural fictions crouded into two small volumes, or to detest the impiety of the Writer in so frequently admiring the ways of Providence in bringing to pass the forgeries of his own brain.'

1770: 8   ANON.

THE HISTORY OF MR. CHARLES FITZGERALD, AND MISS SARAH STAPLETON. IN FIVE BOOKS.

Dublin: Printed by James Hoey, Jun. at the Mercury in Parliament-Street, 1770.
258p. 12mo.
C Hib.8.770.3; ESTC n007818 (BI D; NA CtY-BR, PU).

Notes. ESTC: Sometimes attributed to Daniel Marley.
Both C and PU copies have lost pp. 1–2. New t.p. on p. [175] announcing 'Fugitive Pieces By The Author of the Preceding Memoirs', Dublin: Printed in the Year 1770. Pp. [175]–258: verse, comprising *The Bachelor* nos. 157, 172, 185, 190, 212, 271, 284, 291, 465.

1770: 9   ANON.

THE HISTORY OF SIR CHARLES DORMER AND MISS HARRIET VIL-LARS: IN WHICH ARE EXEMPLIFIED, FROM A LATE CATASTROPHE IN REAL LIFE, THE CONTRAST OF VIRTUE AND VICE, AND THE DANGEROUS AND FATAL CONSEQUENCES ARISING FROM CONFIDANTS AND INTERMEDDLARS IN FAMILY AFFAIRS. BY A LADY.

London: Printed for J. Roson, No. 54. St. Martin's le Grand, 1770.
I iii, 191p; II 224p. 12mo. 6s (CR), 5s sewed (MR), 5s sewed or 6s bound (adv).
CR 30: 302–5 (Oct 1770); MR 42: 489 (June 1770); AF I: 1281.
CtY-Walpole 53.A2.770H; xESTC.

Notes. Epistolary.
Adv. end vol. 3 of *The Noble Lovers* (1772: 19).

CR: 'This is one of the prettiest novels we have lately perused: the authoress of it discovers delicacy, sensibility, and taste.—Her ingenious performance should be carefully read by all those young married ladies who wish to keep the affections of their husbands.'

MR [John Noorthouck]: 'The story is terminated so absurdly as not to be worth attention; and tho' it is said to be written by a lady, it is hardly probable a lady (of any decency, which indeed was not added) would defile her pen with such detestable sentiments, and such prophane exclamations, as those which mark the character of this Miss Thornton; unless, indeed, we first suppose that there may be *such ladies* as Miss Thornton existing.'

1770: 10   ANON.

LETTERS BETWEEN AN ENGLISH LADY AND HER FRIEND AT PARIS. IN WHICH ARE CONTAINED, THE MEMOIRS OF MRS. WILLIAMS. BY A LADY. IN TWO VOLUMES.

London: Printed for T. Becket and P. A. De Hondt, in the Strand, 1770.
I vi, 241p; II 287p. 8vo. 6s (CR), 5s sewed (MR, LC).
CR 29: 294–9 (Apr 1770); MR 42: 330 (Apr 1770); AF I: 1608.
BL 244.g.23; EM 5898: 7; ESTC t146241 (BI E; NA CtY, DLC, NjP &c.).

Notes. By same author as *Anecdotes of a Convent* (1771: 3).
Epistolary. The Letters are between the fictitious Mrs Charlotte Williams and Mademoiselle D'Angeville.
Adv., 'In a few Days will be published', LC 27: 239 (8–10 Mar 1770).

Further edns: Dublin, 1770 (Printed for J. Williams, J. Porter, R. Moncrieffe and T. Walker, 2 vols., 12mo), ESTC n034179; London, 1771, EM 136: 2, ESTC t066909. Serialized as 'Memoirs of Mrs Williams', *Universal Magazine*, 1770, RM 884. French trans. Amsterdam, 1770 (*Lettres d'une dame angloise et de son amie à Paris*) (BGR); German trans. Leipzig, 1770 (*Geschichte der Frau Williams*) (Price).

CR: 'The story is told in a very agreeable manner: there is ease, and even elegance, in the language; and the piece abounds with fine sentiments, strikingly expressed' (p. 299).

MR: 'An air of reality, without the least intermixture of any appearance of fiction, runs through the whole, both of the letters and the memoirs; so that if, possibly, every circumstance related, be not strictly fact, this is more than the candid Reader will suspect, in the perusal: for every thing wears the face of nature and probability. Here we have nothing of wonderful adventure, no extravagant achievements, no romantic incidents.'

1770: 11   ANON.
LIFE, ADVENTURES AND AMOURS OF SIR R P WHO SO RECENTLY HAD THE HONOUR TO PRESENT THE F—— ADDRESS AT THE ENGLISH COURT.

London: Printed and Sold by J. Brough, in the Strand, near Temple Bar, 1770.
iv, 70p. 8vo. 1s 6d (CR, MR).
CR 29: 237 (Mar 1770); MR 42: 251 (Mar 1770); AF I: 1627.
BL 1419.e.27; EM 7021: 12; ESTC t065764 (BI E, LVu, MRu; NA CtY, CLU-S/C, CSmH &c.).

Notes. Sir R P = Sir Richard Perrot. F—— = Flintshire.
Dedication to 'His G— the D- of G—'. 2 pp. advs. end vol.
Extract published LC 27: 223 (3–6 Mar 1770).
MR includes under the heading 'Novels'; CR does not classify.
Facs: FN.

CR: 'This production can be considered in no other light than a *Grub-street catchpenny*, as it contains little more than a compilation of some letters which appeared in the Newspapers relative to this extraordinary adventurer, hashed up by the writer into the form of an *eighteen-penny touch*.'

THE LIFE AND ADVENTURES OF THE PRINCE OF SALERMO
See DE VERE, Marquis [pseud.]

THE LIFE AND EXTRAORDINARY ADVENTURES . . . OF TIMOTHY GINNADRAKE
See FLEMING, Francis

LUCILLA: OR THE PROGRESS OF VIRTUE
See RÉTIF DE LA BRÉTONNE, Nicolas-Edme

1770: 12   ANON.
THE MAID OF QUALITY: OR, THE HISTORY OF LADY LUCY LAYTON. IN TWO VOLUMES.

London: Printed for T. Vernor, at his Circulating Library, No. 86, in Bishop's-Gate-Street Without; and Sold by J. Chater, at his Circulating Library, in King's-Street, Cheapside, 1770.
I ii, 260p; II 310p. 12mo. 5s (CR), 6s (MR), 5s sewed or 6s bound (LC).
CR 29: 47–9 (Jan 1770); MR 42: 487 (June 1770); AF I: 1724.
PU Singer-Mend PR.3291.A1.M156.1770; ESTC n004075 (NA RPB-JH).
Notes. Epistolary.
Adv. LC 27: 39 (9–11 Jan 1770).
Further edn: Dublin, 1770 (Printed for S. Powell, P. & W. Wilson, H. Bradley, S. Watson, J. Hoey jun., J. Williams, J. Porter and T. Walker, 2 vols.) (BLC). French trans. Londres, 1770 (*Histoire de lady Lucie Fenton*) (HWS); German trans. Breslau and Leipzig, 1772 (*Das seltene Kammermädchen*) (Price).

CR: 'We have given the outlines of this curious performance because we would not be accused of proceeding to execution before the trial is over: we cannot, however, help thinking that it will be *transported* in a little while to the regions of *oblivion*' (p. 49).

1770: 13   ANON.
THE MALE-COQUETTE; OR, THE HISTORY OF THE HON. EDWARD ASTELL. IN TWO VOLUMES.

London: Printed for Robinson and Roberts, No. 25, Pater-noster-Row, 1770.
I 236p; II 226p. 12mo. 5s sewed (MR).
CR 28: 450–2 (Dec 1769); MR 42: 72 (Jan 1770); AF I: 2749.
BL 12614.d.19; EM 275: 3; ESTC t072172 (BI MRu; NA ICU).

Notes. ESTC attributes to Jane Timbury, author of *The Male Coquet* (1788: 76), probably because of similarity of title, but this novel has a very different form and content to the *Male Coquet* which has Timbury's name on t.p.
2 pp. advs. end vol. 2. Epistolary.
JR 1342.
Post-dated; adv., 'Tuesday next will be published', LC 26: 559 (7–9 Dec 1769); adv. as published LC 26: 567 (9–12 Dec 1769).
Further edn: London, 1788, ESTC n004439.

MR: '. . . a light and flimsy performance, that differs little from the rest of those mushroom romances which our expert novel Spinners will manufacture in a week, with as much ease as that with which Ambrose Phillips could "turn a Persian tale for half a crown."'

1770: 14   ANON.
THE MEMOIRS OF MISS ARABELLA BOLTON. CONTAINING A GENU-INE ACCOUNT OF HER SEDUCTION, AND THE BARBAROUS TREATMENT SHE AFTERWARDS RECEIVED FROM THE HON-OURABLE C— L——, THE PRESENT SUPPOSED M——R FOR THE COUNTY OF MIDDLESEX. WITH VARIOUS OTHER MISFORTUNES AND EMBARRASSMENTS, INTO WHICH THIS UNHAPPY YOUNG WOMAN HAS BEEN CRUELLY INVOLVED THROUGH THE VICISSI-TUDES OF LIFE, AND THE VILLAINY OF HER SEDUCER. THE WHOLE TAKEN FROM THE ORIGINAL LETTERS OF THE SAID

C—L——TO DR. KELLY, WHO ATTENDED HER IN THE GREATEST MISFORTUNES AND DISTRESSES UNDER WHICH SHE LABOURED; AND ALSO FROM SEVERAL ORIGINAL LETTERS FROM DOCTOR KELLY AND MISS BOLTON, AND FROM OTHER AUTHENTICATED PAPERS IN THE HANDS OF THE PUBLISHER.

> London: Printed for I. Fell, No. 14, Pater-noster Row, 1770.
> I xxii, 213p; II xi, 228p. 12mo. 5s (CR), 2s 6d each vol. (MR).
> CR 30: 240 (Sept 1770) both vols.; MR 42: 251 (Mar 1770) vol. 1; MR 43: 65 (July 1770) vol. 2; AF I: 1808, 1809.
> NjP Ex3633.79.363; ESTC n021983 (NA CaOHM, CtY-BR, PU).

Notes. Vol. 2 t.p.: 'from the Hon. Colonel L-l'.

Based on an Oxford scandal at the time of Luttrell's Middlesex election.

ESTC t069916 cites 2 copies of another version: one held at ViU with the same date and imprint but apparently without the variant vol. 2 title, and the other at BL even though this copy lacks vol. 2.

CR classes this with *Genuine Memoirs of Miss Faulkner* (1770: 6) and comments sarcastically that it has been 'published with an equally laudable intention.'

MR classifies as novel and comments that 'the present wretched production; in which it is difficult to pronounce whether the hero of the tale, or the tale-teller, makes the worst figure' is based on letters published in a newspaper.

1770: 15   ANON.
*THE MODERN COUPLE; OR, THE HISTORY OF MR. AND MRS. DAVERS. IN A SERIES OF LETTERS.

> London: Printed for F. and J. Noble, in Holborn, and St. Martin's Court (LC), 1770 (SJC). 2 vols. 12mo. 5s sewed (CR, MR).
> CR 31: 76 (Jan 1771); MR 43: 500 (Dec 1770) .
> No copy located.

Notes. Epistolary.

Adv. SJC 27–29 Nov 1770 and PA 20 Dec 1770; adv. LC 29: 55 (12–15 Jan 1771).

Adv. in *The Way to Lose Him* 1773: 21.

MR has sub-title as *or the History of Miss Davers.*

Further edn: Dublin, 1776 (Printed by and for J. A. Husband, 1 vol., 12mo), EM 92: 5, ESTC t055917.

CR: 'By husbands who take too great liberties after their marriage, and by wives who are apt to carry their resentment too far, this novel should be read with attention; because it may be read with advantage, if properly regarded.'

MR: 'Matrimonial infidelity forms the basis of this pretty, interesting novel; the story of which is told in a natural, easy manner.'

NATURE
See TREYSSAC DE VERGY, Pierre Henri

THE PLACID MAN
See JENNER, Charles

1770: 16   ANON.
THE PORTRAIT OF LIFE, OR THE VARIOUS EFFECTS OF VIRTUE AND VICE DELINEATED; AS THEY DAILY APPEAR ON THE GREAT THEATRE OF THE WORLD. IN A COLLECTION OF INTERESTING NOVELS. IN TWO VOLUMES.

> London: Printed for John Bell, at his Circulating Library near Exeter-Exchange in the Strand and C. Etherington at York, 1770.
> I 224p; II 234p. 12mo. 5s sewed (CR, MR).
> CR 29: 149 (Feb 1770); MR 42: 71 (Jan 1770); AF I: 2246.
> BL 12316.ccc.37; EM 770: 27; ESTC t095294 (NA NcD, ViWc [vol. 1 only]).

Notes. 2 pp. advs. end vol. 2. Vol. 1 contains 19 novelettes, and vol. 2, 17.

Adv., 'On Monday next will be published', LC 26: 69 (26–28 Dec 1769); adv. as published LC 27: 27 (6–9 Jan 1770).

CR: 'These volumes contain several stories which have been already published in Magazines, and other periodical productions, and therefore cannot be entitled to much attention. There are, indeed, some books of this kind which may be admitted into the politest library without disgracing it; but we do not think that the compiler of the sheets before us has made a happy selection; a *fair* selection he certainly has not; for he has taken the liberty to republish some of Marmontel's Moral Tales, which have been read over and over by every reader of sentiment and taste.'

MR [John Noorthouck]: 'These volumes are a much cheaper bargain than most of those of a like nature that have been published for some time past. Here are near forty novels, some of them very tolerable, and not ill-selected; and any one of them, by filling up the outlines, and enlarging the descriptions, with a due share of colloquies, might be expanded into two passable volumes of *modern memoirs*.'

THE POSTHUMOUS WORKS OF A LATE CELEBRATED GENIUS
See GRIFFITH, Richard

1770: 17   ANON.
*THE PREDICTION; OR, THE HISTORY OF MISS LUCY MAXWELL. BY A LADY.

> London: Chater and Vernor (CR) Chater &c (MR).
> 3 vols. 12mo. 7s 6d (CR), 7s 6d sewed (MR).
> CR 30: 306–9 (Oct 1770); MR 43: 326 (Oct 1770); AF I: 2270.
> No copy located.

Notes. CR: 'The perusal of these volumes, written by a lady, cannot afford great entertainment to readers who are capable of relishing the writings of a Sheridan, a Montague, a Lennox, and a Brooke; those, however, who take up a new book merely to kill time, will not be disappointed' (p. 306). 'The history contains many uninteresting adventures, inartificially huddled together; there is not a single character strongly marked through the whole; and the story of the heroine might have been comprized in a very small compass' (p. 309).

MR: 'There is more of *Novel* than of *Nature* in this work.—But we forbear to criticise the production of a *Lady*'s pen; especially as, whatever are its defects, it is friendly to the cause of virtue and morality: which is more than can be said in favour of many of the romances of this age and country.'

1770: 18   ANON.
THE SALLIES OF GENIUS, AND WANDERINGS OF YOUTH: OR, THE ADVENTURES OF COURSILLAC AND DORIGNI. TAKEN CHIEFLY FROM THE FRENCH.
> London: Printed for T. Lowndes, in Fleet-Street; and T. Slack, in Newcastle. 1770.
> vi, 181p. 12mo.
> MH-H *EC75.A100.770s; EM 3509: 9; ESTC n021302.

Notes. Drop-head title 'The Wanderings of Youth'. Pp. [183]–[184] table of contents with chapter titles and page numbers.

SENTIMENTAL LUCUBRATIONS, BY PETER PENNYLESS
See WORSLEY, Robert

A SERIES OF GENUINE LETTERS, BETWEEN HENRY AND FRANCES
See GRIFFITH, Elizabeth and Richard

1770: 19   ANON.
THE STORY OF THE METHODIST-LADY: OR THE INJUR'D HUS-BAND'S REVENGE. A TRUE HISTORY.
> London: Printed for John Doughty, near St. Paul's, n.d. [ESTC: 1770?].
> 51p. 8vo.
> BL 12611.cc.16; EM 237: 2; ESTC t055920 (NA CLU-S/C, ICU, IU).

A TRUE NARRATIVE
See SIMES, Thomas

1770: 20   ANON.
THE UNHAPPY WIFE, A SERIES OF LETTERS. BY A LADY. IN TWO VOLUMES.
> London: Printed for F. Newbery, the corner of Ludgate Street, St Paul's Church yard,
>   and J. Smith, No. 15. Paternoster-Row, 1770.
> I 165p; II 141p. 12mo. 5s (CR), 5s sewed (MR, LC).
> CR 29: 474–5 (June 1770); MR 42: 250 (Mar 1770); AF I: 2828.
> BL 012612.e.10; EM 165: 5; ESTC t067637.

Notes. 3 pp. advs. end vol. 2. Epistolary.
Adv., 'On Thursday next will be published', LC 27: 123 (3–6 Feb 1770).
   CR: '. . . we cannot help declaring that we think our *authoress* might employ her time more *usefully* with her *needle* than with her *pen*' (p. 475).
   According to MR, 'another scandalous catchpenny, founded on the same story with that of De Vergy's book' [i.e. *The Lovers*, 1769, JR 1344, AF I: 2772]. MR continues: 'Of all the worthless productions of this kind which have been imposed upon the public, we never perused any so totally uninteresting and unentertaining as the present; which, at the same, into the bargain, is, in a great measure, unintelligible also.'

1770: 21   ANON.
THE YOUNGER BROTHER, A TALE.
London: Printed for the Author, and sold by F. Newbery, at the Corner of St. Paul's
Church-Yard, 1770/72.
I (1770) iv, 208p; II (1772) iii, 208p. 12mo. 5s sewed (MR, SJC).
CR 34: 77 (July 1772); MR 46: 540 (May 1772); AF I: 3019.
BL 12611.aa.23; EM 196: 6; ESTC t054995 (NA CtY-BR, CLU-S/C, PU &c.).
Notes. Imprint date to vol. 1 possibly erroneous. Revs. give no date.
Extracts given in LC vol. XXXI pp. 413 and 433 (28–30 Apr and 5–7 May 1772).
Adv., with quotation of the MR's praise, SJC 16–19 Jan 1773.
   MR [Gilbert Stuart]: 'When we consider the imperfection and demerit of the works of this
class, we cannot but bestow our commendation on the present volumes. They are written
with a degree of humour, and a knowledge of life, that render them both interesting and
agreeable.'

THE YOUNGER SISTER
See DAWE, Anne

1770: 22   [BANCROFT, Edward].
THE HISTORY OF CHARLES WENTWORTH, ESQ. IN A SERIES OF
LETTERS. INTERSPERSED WITH A VARIETY OF IMPORTANT REF-
LECTIONS, CALCULATED TO IMPROVE MORALITY, AND PRO-
MOTE THE OECONOMY OF HUMAN LIFE.
London: Printed for T. Becket, in the Strand, 1770.
I 263p; II 284p; III 220p. 12mo. 7s 6d (CR), 7s 6d bound (MR).
CR 29: 358–64 (May 1770); MR 43: 67 (July 1770); AF I: 141.
BL N.2051–2053; EM 4582: 6; ESTC t144798 (BI E; NA ICN).
Notes. 1 p. advs. end vol. 1. Epistolary.
Further edn: Dublin, 1770 (Printed for W. Sleater, J. Potts, J. Williams, W. Colles, J. Porter,
and T. Walker, 2 vols., 12mo), ESTC t193541. German trans. Nuremberg, 1776 (*Geschichte
Karl Wentwort*) (Price). Facs: FN.
   CR: 'The History of Charles Wentworth is full of instruction: every page of it immediately
relating to the hero is particularly so: and those young men whose lively passions hurry them
to dangerous indiscretions, may receive excellent lessons from *his* letters: they may also
receive the greatest encouragement to act upon every occasion with honour and with prudence' (p. 363).
   MR: 'There is more of good sense, and of nature, in this novel than we find in fifty of such
productions as are continually obtruded upon the public, under this denomination; yet
there are in it some things to which we have strong objections, particularly in the extraordinary account here given of Mr Gordon, the Scotch Deist, who is said to live in a state of
nature among the Indians in Guiana.'

1770: 23   [BRIDGES, Thomas].
THE ADVENTURES OF A BANK-NOTE. IN TWO VOLUMES. / VOL-
UME THREE. / VOLUME FOUR.

London: Printed for T. Davies, in Russel-street, Covent-garden, 1770/71.

I (1770) 210p; II (1770) 204p; III (1771) 204p; IV (1771) 204p. 12mo. 5s sewed [for each pair of vols.] (MR), 5s sewed [vols. 1–2] (CR), 5s [vols. 3–4] (CR, LC).

CR 30: 395 (Nov 1770), MR 43: 152 (Aug 1770) vols. 1–2; CR 31: 475 (June 1771), MR 44: 333 (Apr 1771) vols. 3–4; AF I: 232, 233.

BL 12614.c.23; EM 230: 3; ESTC t071294 (BI C, O [vols. 1–2 only]; NA CLU-S/C, CSmH, CSt [vols. 1–2 only], CtY [vols. 3–4 only], ICN [vols. 1–2 only], MH-H, NjP [vols. 1–2 only], TxU [vols. 1–2 only] &c.).

Notes. Extract (from vol. 3) published LC 30: 305 (26–28 Sept 1771).

Vols. 3 and 4 adv., 'In the Press, and will be published in a few Days', LC 29: 211 (28 Feb 1771).

Further edns: Dublin, 1771 (Printed for H. Saunders, D. Chamberlaine, J. Hoey, Jun., J. Williams, R. Moncrieff, T. Walker, and J. Porter, 2 vols. in 1, 12mo), ESTC n004798; London, 1772, ESTC t073509. German trans. Frankfurt and Leipzig, 1771/72 (*Die Begebenheiten einer Banko-Note*) (EAG). Facs: FN.

CR 30: 'Not to allow some compassion to laborious dulness, would be cruel and inhuman; but when a writer of ability does not exert himself for the entertainment of the public, he deserves to be severely reprehended.—The author before us is not unacquainted with human nature; and exposes, with humour, the vices and follies of the age; but is too often hurried, by a lively imagination, into a negligence of composition, and looseness of expression.'

MR 43 [John Noorthouck]: 'Some parts of this work are very laughable, others are licentious; and the whole, as the good old Baxter would have said, shews that the Writer has more genius than grace.'

CR 31: 'In these volumes our author exhibits many remarkable characters, for the entertainment of his readers, in a strain of humour not inferior to the part formerly published.'

1770: 24   BROOKE, [Henry].
THE FOOL OF QUALITY; OR, THE HISTORY OF HENRY EARL OF MORELAND. VOLUME V. BY MR BROOKE.

London: Printed for W. Johnston, 1770.

V 300p. 12mo. 3s (CR, MR).

CR 30: 459–60 (Dec 1770) vols. 3–5; MR 42: 330 (Apr 1770) vol. 5 only; AF I: 266.

BL 838.b.8; EM 7371: 2; ESTC t147805 (BI AWu, BMp, D &c.; NA AzU, CaNfSM, CaOHM &c.).

Notes. Final vol. of the novel. Vols. 1–2 published by Johnston in 1766, JR 993, AF I: 263; with vol. 3, 1768, JR 1202, AF I: 264; and vol. 4, 1769, JR 1300, AF I: 265. Vol. 5 exists in at least 2 variant impressions.

Extracts published LC 27: 325 and 329 (3–5 and 5–7 Apr 1770).

Further edns: Dublin, 1765–69, with 5th vol., 1770 (Printed for the Author by Dillon Chamberlaine), EM 2373: 1, ESTC t059854; 15 further edns, variants & abridged edns in ESTC; WC has 15 entries between 1800 and 1850; NSTC lists edns in 1808/9, 1810, 1814/15 and 1818. German trans. Frankfurt am Main, 1776 (*Der vornehme Thor oder Heinrichs Grafen von Moreland Geschichte*) (EAG); French trans. Paris, 1789 (*Le Fou de Qualité*) (HWS). Facs: FN.

CR: 'We have perused these volumes with a mixture of admiration and contempt of their author. Many parts of them are such as provoke tears which cannot be restrained, and inspire horror which is not easy to be shaken off. The effects, however, of this magic are not of long duration. To scenes most happily copied from nature herself, succeed others which never yet appeared within the circle of her various combinations. Characters so perfectly good, and so irrecoverably bad, are displayed before us, as we cannot, without over-rating or depreciating humanity, suppose to have ever had existence. At one time the author appears religious even to madness, and we are almost ready to adore the splendid errors of his mind; at others, he becomes superstitious even beneath contempt, and we turn from his page at once with pity and disgust' (p. 459).

MR rev. of this vol. calls for 'an abridgment of this work, cleared from the sanctimonious rubbish by which its beauties are so much obscured.'

BROOKE, Mrs
See FRAMÉRY, Nicolas-Étienne

1770: 25   CRÉBILLON, [Claude-Prosper Jolyot de].
THE NIGHT AND MOMENT. A DIALOGUE. TRANSLATED FROM THE
FRENCH, OF M. CREBILLON.

> London: Printed for the Translator, and Sold by Richardson and Urquhart, under the
> Royal Exchange, 1770.
> 195p. 12mo. 2s (CR).
> CR 29: 396 (May 1770).
> C 7735.d.544; ESTC t182205.

Notes. Trans. of *La Nuit et le moment* (Londres [i.e. Paris], 1755).

CR: 'The translation appears to be too well executed. It is, in one sense of the words, neither immodest nor indelicate, but is, perhaps, only the more dangerous on that score. If it gives a faithful picture, as from other accounts it seems to do, of the manners of French people of quality, they are such as, we hope, never will be imitated, like their other fashions and follies, by those of the same class in this country.'

1770: 26   [DAWE, Anne].
THE YOUNGER SISTER.

> London: Printed for T. Lowndes, at No.77, Fleet-Street, 1770.
> I [266]p; II 201p. 12mo. 5s sewed (CR, MR), 5s sewed or 6s bound (LC).
> CR 30: 143–6 (Aug 1770); MR 42: 487–8 (June 1770); AF I: 590.
> BL 12611.aa.4; EM 7823: 2; ESTC t031407.

Notes. Drop-head title: 'The Younger Sister: or The History of Miss Somerset'. Running Title: 'The History of Miss Somerset'.

Epistolary. Last 2 pp. of vol. 1 misnumbered 183 and 184. 1 p. advs. end vol. 2.

Anne Dawe received 20 gns. for the copyright to *The Younger Sister*, 21 July 1769, GM n.s. 94 (1824): 136.

Adv., 'In a few Days will be published' and with title *The Younger Sister; or, the History of Miss Somerset*, LC 27: 184 (20–22 Feb 1770).

Further edn: Dublin, 1772 (Printed and Sold by R. Marchbank, 2 vols. in 1, 12mo), ESTC t183172. German trans. Leipzig, 1780 (*Leiden der Miss Meliora Somerset*) (EAG).

CR: 'Are the characters well sustained, and properly discriminated? Are the situations interesting? Are the sentiments striking? Is the style elegantly flowing, and pleasingly varied? We reply, with Mrs. Circuit, in the Lame Lover, *Certainly, no'* (p. 146).

D'ERBIGNY, Henri Lambert, marquis de Thibouville
See THIBOUVILLE, Henri-Lambert d'Erbigny, marquis de

1770: 27   DE VERE, Marquis [pseud.].
THE LIFE AND ADVENTURES OF THE PRINCE OF SALERMO: CON-
TAINING AN ACCOUNT OF HIS ADVENTURES AT VENICE, AND IN
HUNGARY; HIS CAPTIVITY AT DAMAS, AND AMOUR WITH AN
OTTOMAN PRINCESS, TOGETHER WITH HIS RETURN TO ITALY:
WITH MANY ENTERTAINING DESCRIPTIONS OF THE LAWS, CUS-
TOMS, AND MANNERS OF THE SEVERAL COUNTRIES THROUGH
WHICH HE TRAVELLED. BY THE MARQUIS DE VERE, A VENETIAN
NOBLEMAN.

London: Printed for J. Roson, No. 54 St Martin's Le-Grand, 1770.
xxii, 187p. 12mo. 3s (CR), 2s 6d sewed (MR).
CR 29: 148–9 (Feb 1770); MR 42: 251 (Mar 1770).
BL 012611.1.21; EM 98: 7; ESTC t067319 (BI O; NA CSmH, MH-H, PPL).

Notes. 3 pp. advs. end vol.
CR: 'The author of this novel appears to have heated his brain by the perusal of old Italian romances' (p. 148).
Reviewed in MR [by John Noorthouck] as a novel.

DE VERGY
See TREYSSAC DE VERGY, Pierre Henri

1770: 28   DU BOIS, Lady Dorothea.
THEODORA, A NOVEL. BY THE RIGHT HONOURABLE LADY-
DOROTHEA DU BOIS, IN TWO VOLUMES.

London: Printed for the Author, by C. Kiernan, in Fullwood's-Rents, Holborn, 1770.
I iii, 250p; II 306p. 12mo. 6s (CR, MR).
CR 29: 474 (June 1770); MR 43: 65–6 (July 1770); AF I: 692.
BL 1417.b.26; EM 2771: 1; ESTC t106576 (NA CtY-BR, CSmH).

Notes. CR: 'We sincerely pity lady Dorothea as a woman of distinction in distress; but, as impartial reviewers, we must own, that we cannot think the emolument arising from the publication of her novel will be adequate to her wishes.'
MR has 'sold by Nicoll, &c.', points out that Lady Dorothea, 'being in necessitous cir-
cumstances, has industriously endeavoured to mend them, in some small degree, by telling and embellishing her hapless tale' although 'she is not a very correct writer', and adds 'N.B. The story is not yet brought to a conclusion', but apparently no further vols. were published.

FAULKNER Miss
See GENUINE MEMOIRS OF

1770: 29   [FLEMING, Francis].
THE LIFE AND EXTRAORDINARY ADVENTURES, THE PERILS AND
CRITICAL ESCAPES OF TIMOTHY GINNADRAKE, THAT CHILD OF
CHECQUERED [*sic*] FORTUNE. IN THREE VOLUMES [vols. 1 and 2].
THE THIRD VOLUME OF THE LIFE AND ADVENTURES OF TIMO-
THY GINNADRAKE, CONTAINING A CONCISE ACCOUNT OF THE
CITY OF BATH, FROM THE YEAR 1670, TO THE PRESENT TIME
[vol. 3].

> Bath: Printed by R. Cruttwell, for the Author; And Sold by W. Frederick, H. Leake, W.
> Taylor, W. Bally, and A. Tennent, Booksellers, in Bath; and Mr. Dodsley, Pallmall,
> London. n.d. [MR: 1770].
> Vol. 3: Bath: Printed by R. Cruttwell, for the Author; And Sold by W. Frederick, L. Bull,
> W. Taylor, W. Bally, and A. Tennent, Booksellers, in Bath; and Mr. Dodsley, Pallmall,
> London, 1771.
> I [1770] xviii, 168p; II [1771] 204p; III (1771) xiv, 239p. 12mo. Vol. 1 3s 6d sewed (MR,
> LC), 3 vols. 9s (MR).
> CR 34: 51–4 (July 1772), MR 42: 488 (June 1770) vol. 1; CR 47: 239 (Sept 1772) all 3 vols.
> but without ref. to earlier rev.; MR 47: 239 (Sept 1772) all 3 vols. but without ref. to
> earlier rev.; AF I: 912, 913.
> BL 12654.f.46; EM 485: 4; ESTC t098989 (BI C, O; NA CaOHM, CtY, CLU-S/C).

Notes. 14 pp. subscriptions begin vol. 1; 12 pp. subscriptions end vol. 3.
Vol. 1 adv. LC 27: 140 (8–10 Feb 1770).

   MR 47: 'His adventures (most of which seem to have had their foundation in fact) are
chiefly of the humourous cast. Some of them are laughable enough; though all are rather of
low degree. They may serve to set the *alehouse* tables in a roar, but will hardly contribute much
to the entertainment of better company.'

1770: 30   FRAMÉRY, [Nicolas-Étienne]; BROOKE, [Frances] (*trans.*).
MEMOIRS OF THE MARQUIS DE ST. FORLAIX. TRANSLATED FROM
THE FRENCH OF MONS. FRAMERY. BY MRS. BROOKE.

> London: Printed for J. Dodsley, in Pall-Mall, 1770.
> I xii, 191p; II 189p; III 259p; IV 215p. 12mo. Vols. 1–4 12s (CR) Vols. 1–2 5s (MR);
> vols. 3–4 5s sewed (MR).
> CR 30: 417–20 (Dec 1770), MR 43: 362–5 (Nov 1770) vols. 1–2; MR 44: 48–51
> (Jan 1771) vols. 3–4; AF I: 259, 260.
> BL 1607/1753; EM 2222: 2; ESTC t118938 (BI C, O, MRu; NA CaQQLa, CLU-S/C,
> InU-Li &c.).

Notes. Trans. of *Mémoires de M. le Marquis de S. Forlaix* (Paris, 1770).
Epistolary.
KM 4884: vols. 1–2, printing completed by Bowyer 18 Sept 1770, and vols. 3–4 completed
28 Nov 1770; 750 copies.
Adv., 'Next Week will be published, The third and fourth Volumes', SJC 24–27 Nov 1770 and
PA 30 Nov 1770.
Further edn: Dublin, 1770–71 (Printed for J. Exshaw, H. Saunders, W. Sleater, D. Chamber-
laine, J. Potts [& 2 others], with vols. 3–4 variant, 4 vols., 12mo), ESTC n004095.

CR: 'We have read many novels more sentimental than the present; but very few more interesting to the heart. The story abounds with incidents which are extremely affecting, and is worked up in a very masterly manner. Love, the life and soul of romance, is the great spring which actuates almost all the parties concerned in these Memoirs, and involves them in various perplexities and distresses' (p. 417).

MR 43 [Gilbert Stuart]: 'In this species of composition, there are few publications more entertaining than the Memoirs of the Marquis de St. Forlaix. They are written in the form of letters, which succeed each other in proper order; and the incidents on which they turn are natural and probable' (p. 363).

GINNADRAKE, Timothy
See FLEMING, Francis

1770: 31   [GRIFFITH, Elizabeth and Richard].
A SERIES OF GENUINE LETTERS, BETWEEN HENRY AND FRANCES.
VOLUME V / VOLUME VI.
> London: Printed for W. Johnston in Ludgate-street, 1770.
> V viii, 280p; VI 288p. 12mo. 6s (CR), 5s sewed (MR), 5s sewed or 6s boards (SJC).
> CR 30: 460–1 (Dec 1770) 'vols. 4 & 5' acc. to rev. title, but actually of vols. 5 & 6; MR 43: 490 (Dec 1770); AF I: 1151.
> C S.727.d.76.35- [vols. 1–2, 1767 edn., vols 3–4, 1772 edn.]; ESTC t154222 (NA MA).

Notes. 1st 2 vols. published 1757, then 1760 and 1761 (as original 2 vols.), JR 412, 573, 651, 1013, 1102; AF I: 1149, 1150.
Epistolary. This edn. extended the text by the equivalent of 3 vols. These vols., 5 & 6, also in a 12mo set with title cancels as Printed for W. Richardson and L. Urquhart, 1770, ESTC t111106. Also vols. 3 & 4, new edn., Printed for W. Johnston, 1772, 12mo, ESTC t154223; and 6-vol. new edn., Printed (by assignment from E. Johnston) for J. Bew, 1786, 12mo, ESTC t111101.
Adv. SJC 24–27 Nov 1770. German trans. Leipzig and Berlin, 1790 (*Briefe zwischen Heinrich und Franziska*) (EAG).
CR: 'We find ourselves by no means disposed to retract any part of the praise which we formerly bestowed on the first and second, third and fourth parts of the same correspondence. . . . We never are better pleased than when we honestly have it in our power to recommend any performance to the perusal of our fair readers, whose vivacity so many pens are busy to mislead, and whose virtues so many hirelings are employed to undermine: for one book written on a useful subject or for a blameless purpose; with a view to interest their passions in the cause of humanity, or enlarge their understandings with materials supplied from the stores of reason; there are at least twenty produced which serve to render their lives less happy, by inspiring notions of romantic felicity which are no where to be realized on earth' (p. 460).
MR reviews under the heading 'Miscellaneous', although there is a 'Novels' category in this month's number.

1770: 32   [GRIFFITH, Richard].
THE POSTHUMOUS WORKS OF A LATE CELEBRATED GENIUS, DECEASED. IN TWO VOLUMES.

London: Printed by W. and J. Richardson: and sold by J. Almon, in Piccadilly; Robinson and Roberts, Paternoster Row; and G. Pearch, in Cheapside, 1770.

I viii, 216p; II xi, 214p. 8vo. [MR has 12mo] 5s sewed (CR, LC), 5s (MR).

CR 29: 102–9 (Feb 1770); MR 42: 360–3 (May 1770); AF I: 1153.

BL 12614.bbb.16; EM 3560: 6; ESTC t044094 (BI AWn, C, O; NA CtY-BR, CLU-S/C, MH-H &c.).

Notes. A spurious autobiography of Laurence Sterne by Richard Griffith the elder. Some claim it to be by Richard Griffith the younger although he was only seventeen when it was published.

Another 1770 version (BL 1607/5665, EM 3603: 6, ESTC t120275) appears identical apart from the imprint (Printed by W. and J. Richardson: and sold by T. Becket and P. A. De Hondt in the Strand, 1770) and the placing of the unnumbered 3-pp. table of contents (between p. viii and p. 1, as opposed to following the title-page in 12614.bbb.16). 1 p. adv. end vol. 2. Half-title in vols. 1 & 2, 'The Koran: Or, The Life, Character, and Sentiments of Tria Juncto in Uno M.N.A. or Master of No Arts'. Dedication to the Earl of Charlemont signed 'The Editor' 1, iii–iv, 'The Editor to the Reader' v–viii, 'A Private Letter from the Author to the Editor' 1–4; text, with drop-head title 'The Koran', begins on p. 5. 'The Author to the Reader' 2, v–xi. Pagination continuous Roman-Arabic in vol. 2; text of novel starts on p. 13. BL 12614.bbb.16 has handwritten copy of 24-line poem 'By Mr Samwell' at end of vol. 2: 'On Visiting the Grave of Sterne in company with a Welsh Bard, (Mr Edward Williams)'.

Adv., 'Next Week will be published', LC 27: 87 (23–25 Jan 1770).

Extract published LC 27: 117–18 (1–3 Feb 1770).

Further edns: Dublin, 1770 (Printed for J. Exshaw, H. Saunders, W. Sleater, D. Chamberlaine, J. Potts, J. Williams, and C. Ingham, 2 vols., 12mo), EM 5520: 2, ESTC t120274; London, 1775, ESTC n020946; 2 further edns. (entitled *The Koran*) in ESTC. German trans. Leipzig, 1771 (*Yoriks nachgelassne Werke*) (EAG).

CR: 'Authors of note commonly leave in the sweepings of their desks more that ought to be suppressed than published, and it is a cruelty to the memory of the deceased to send both kind into the world together; as the unhealthy can only serve to corrupt the sound' (p. 102). CR accepts the volume as Sterne's work and comments further that '... nudities ought not to be exposed merely because they are those of a deceased genius' (p. 109).

MR [John Hawkesworth] describes the *Posthumous Works* as 'manifestly spurious, a fraudulent imposition upon the Public, and a flagrant injustice to the memory of the dead' and points out that they 'allude to many facts and circumstances which did not happen till Sterne was dead...' (pp. 360–1).

1770: 33   [JENNER, Charles].

THE PLACID MAN: OR, MEMOIRS OF SIR CHARLES BEVILLE. IN TWO VOLUMES.

London: Printed for J. Wilkie, in St. Paul's Church-Yard, 1770.

I viii, 219p; II viii, 251p. 12mo. 6s (CR, MR), 6s bound (LC).

CR 29: 42–3 (Jan 1770); MR 42: 43–6 (Jan 1770); AF I: 1402.

BL 12611.g.8; EM 127: 2; ESTC t057338 (NA CtY, CLU-S/C, CSmH &c.).

Notes. Post-dated; adv., 'In a few Days will be published', LC 26: 511 (23–25 Nov 1769); adv. as published LC 26: 552 (5–7 Dec 1769).

1773 'Second Edition, with Additions' published by Dodsley adv. SJC 16–18 Mar 1773. Further edns: Dublin, 1770 (Printed for J. Exshaw, H. Saunders, D. Chamberlaine, J. Potts, W. Sleator [*sic*], S. Watson, and J. Williams, 2 vols., 12mo), ESTC n011482; London, 1773, EM 5597: 2, ESTC t070731; Chiswick, 1828 (WC, NSTC). German trans. Leipzig, 1770/71 (*Der sanftmüthige Mann; oder Nachrichten von Sir Carl Bevillens Begebenheiten* (EAG).

CR: 'There is not much contrivance in the story: it is carried on by starts, and in a desultory manner: the digressions are too numerous, tho' many of them are instructive and entertaining' (p. 43).

MR [John Noorthouck]: '. . . the aim of the Writer has been to unite the method of our celebrated novelist, Fielding, with the negligence of Sterne; and it is of course one of those novels in which a great deal is said and very little is done. But if the incidents are not many, the Author, in his dialogues and remarks, proves himself acquainted with the world, and conversant in literature; and, without absolutely determining how far he may have succeeded in the species of composition he has chosen, we need not scruple to pronounce that his style is lively and agreeable.'

LANGHORNE, John, **LETTERS TO ELEONORA**
See 1771: 43

MARLEY, Daniel
See **THE HISTORY OF MR. CHARLES FITZGERALD, AND MISS SARAH STA-PLETON**

PENNYLESS, Peter
See WORSLEY, Robert

1770: 34   [RÉTIF DE LA BRÉTONNE, Nicolas-Edme].
LUCILLA: OR THE PROGRESS OF VIRTUE. TRANSLATED FROM THE FRENCH.

London: Printed for T. Lowndes, N° 77 in Fleet-street, and G. Kearsley N° 1 in Ludgate-street, 1770.
viii, 241p. 12mo. 3s (CR, MR), 3s bound (LC).
CR 29: 366–7 (May 1770); MR 42: 70–1 (Jan 1770); AF I: 2351.
BL C.124.e.24; EM 3710: 6; ESTC t124724 (NA MH-H, NjP).

Notes. Trans. of *Lucile ou les progrès de la vertu* (Paris, 1768).
1 p. adv. end vol. Preface iii–vi; table of contents vii–viii.
JR 1326.
Post-dated; adv., 'Tuesday next will be published', LC 26: 583 (14–16 Dec 1769); adv. as published LC 26: 589 (16–19 Dec 1769).

CR: 'The design of this novel is more to be commended than the execution of it: some of the characters are engaged in romantic, and rather unnatural adventures; but notwithstanding the extravagance in several parts of the volume, the whole may be safely put into the hands of that class of readers, for whose perusal it seems to be calculated' (p. 366).

MR [John Noorthouck]: 'The progress of virtue is very injudiciously traced in the professed abode of vice; whereas in the present instance, its escape (beyond all credibility) is a matter of meer contingence; and can illustrate no principle of conduct.'

1770: 35   [SIMES, Thomas].
A TRUE NARRATIVE OF AN UNFORTUNATE ELOPEMENT, IN A
SERIES OF LETTERS. BY xxxxxx Sxxxx, ESQ.
>   London: Printed for W. Holdsworth, No. 7, Red-Lion Court, Fleet-Street, 1770.
>   83p. 8vo. 1s 6d (MR).
>   MR 42: 328 (Apr 1770).
>   BL 1086.h.23(3); ESTC t053844 (BI O; NA IaU, MnU, TxU).

Notes. Dedication 'To the Public' dated 28 Feb 1770.

MR reviews under the 'Miscellaneous' heading, although there is a 'Novels' category in
this month's number.

1770: 36   [THIBOUVILLE, Henri-Lambert d'Erbigny, marquis de].
*THE DANGER OF THE PASSIONS; OR, SYRIAN AND EGYPTIAN
ANECDOTES. TRANSLATED FROM THE FRENCH OF THE AUTHOR
OF THE SCHOOL OF FRIENDSHIP.
>   London: Printed for T. Evans, No. 54, Paternoster Row (PA), 1770 (MR).
>   2 vols. 12mo. 5s sewed (CR, MR), 5s sewed or 6s bound (LC).
>   CR 31: 160 (Feb 1771); MR 44: 173 (Feb 1771).
>   No copy located.

Notes. Trans. of *Le Danger des passions, ou Anecdotes syriennes et égyptiennes* (Paris, 1757).
Adv. PA 12 Jan 1771 and LC 29: 64 (15–17 Jan 1771).

CR: 'These little volumes contain one of the most dull and uninteresting stories that ever
yet were submitted to our judgments. We know not why in the second title they are called
Syrian and Egyptian *Anecdotes*, but that *anecdotes* is at present a fashionable term, and might
tempt a purchaser who expected to meet with a collection of lively, curious, and distinct particulars, instead of one long, perplexed and unentertaining narrative, branching out occasionally into a few episodical relations. That this work is translated from some indifferent
French writer, we are inclined to believe, on the score of some idiomatic baldnesses in the
stile. We do not, however, desire to meet with the original....'

MR [Gilbert Stuart]: 'These anecdotes are so frivolous, and so insipid, that they cannot, we
apprehend, greatly excite the attention, or contribute to the entertainment, of even the most
insignificant reader.'

TIMBURY, Jane, **THE MALE-COQUETTE**
See 1770: 13

1770: 37   TREYSSAC DE VERGY, [Pierre Henri].
HENRIETTA, COUNTESS OSENVOR; A SENTIMENTAL NOVEL IN A
SERIES OF LETTERS TO LADY SUSANNAH FITZROY. BY MR
TREYSSAC DE VERGY, COUNSELLOR IN THE PARLIAMENT OF
PARIS, AND EDITOR OF THE LOVERS.
>   London: Printed for J. Roson, at No. 54. in St. Martin's le Grand, 1770.
>   I ix, 227p; II 255p. 12mo. 6s (CR), 6s bound (t.p., MR), 5s sewed or 6s bound (adv.).
>   CR 30: 316 (Oct 1770); MR 42: 488 (June 1770).
>   O Vet.A5f.426–7; EMf; ESTC t190933 (BI BL).

Notes. Dedication to Lady Harr**t Stan***e, signed Treyssac de Vergy. Preface vii–ix. Epistolary. 2 pp. advs. [x]-[xi].

Adv. end vol. 3 of *The Noble Lovers* (1772: 19).

Further edns: Dublin, 1770 (Printed for J. Williams, J. Porter, and T. Walker, 2 vols in 1, 12mo), ESTC n007200; London, 1785, EM 2383: 1, ESTC t036092. Reprinted *Novelists Magazine*, 1785, RM 501.

CR: 'The novel before us is truly a *sentimental* one; the principal characters are strongly marked, the language tolerable, and the incidents are naturally introduced.'

MR: 'Mr de Vergy has for once, tried his hand at a *decent* novel. Here is no lewdness; nothing vicious nor favourable to vice: yet, in truth, the Author seems to be gotten so far out of his element, that he has given us a work in which, at the same time that there is little to censure, there is nothing to praise.'

TREYSSAC DE VERGY, Pierre Henri, **THE LOVERS**
See 1772: 40

1770: 38   [TREYSSAC DE VERGY, Pierre Henri].
NATURE, A NOVEL, IN A SERIES OF LETTERS.

London: Printed by and for G. Scott, and J. Murdoch, opposite Salisbury-street, Strand, 1770.
211p. 12mo. 3s (CR, MR), 3s bound (LC).
CR 30: 316 (Oct 1770); MR 42: 250 (Mar 1770); AF I: 2776.
PU PR3291.A1.N38.1770; xESTC.

Notes. 2 pp. advs. end vol. Epistolary.

Adv. for 'Nature: or, The School for Deni-Repts [*sic*]. A New Edition, revised and altered by the Author', 1 vol., and listed as by de Vergy at beginning of vol. 2 of de Vergy, *The Lovers* (1772: 40).

Adv. LC 27: 235 (8–10 Mar 1770); 'Printed for J. Murdoch, opposite the New Exchange Coffee House, Strand'.

CR: 'The author of these volumes very naturally paints the havock which the passions make in the human heart, when they are not under the correction of reason and virtue; but his writings are rather calculated to render that havock more extensive than to stop its progress.'

MR: 'A licentious performance, fitted to inflame the passions, to desecrate virtue, and to serve as a *pander* to the mind of an amorous Reader.'

1770: 39   TREYSSAC DE VERGY [Pierre Henri].
*****THE SCOTCHMAN: OR, THE WORLD AS IT GOES. A NOVEL. BY THE CHEVALIER TREYSSAC DE VERGY, COUNSELLOR IN THE PARLIAMENT OF PARIS, AND EDITOR OF THE LOVERS.**

London: Brough, 1770 (MR).
2 vols. (CR, MR). 12mo (MR). 6s (CR), 5s sewed (MR).
CR 30: 316–7 (Oct 1770); MR 43: 66 (July 1770); AF I: 2778.
No copy located.

Notes. Dedication to John Wilkes, but, according to CR, this was 'to forward the sale of his [de Vergy's] *Scotchman*'. CR continues, 'of all the dedications we have read this is the most absurd'.

MR expected 'a satire on the *Scotch*' but comments that de Vergy deviates 'all at once into his old lascivious path, which appears to be his natural and favourite walk of authorship....' MR says 'a 3rd volume is to finish the work' and *The Scotchman* is given as 3 vols. in adv. beginning vol. 2, *The Lovers* (1772: 40). A further vol., if published, was not reviewed.

1770: 40   [?WORSLEY, Robert].
SENTIMENTAL LUCUBRATIONS, BY PETER PENNYLESS.

> London: Printed for T. Becket and P. A. de Hondt, in the Strand, 1770.
> 196p. 8vo. 2s 6d (CR), 2s 6d sewed (MR, LC).
> CR 29: 110–13 (Feb 1770); MR 42: 180–5 (Mar 1770); AF I: 2157.
> BL 12612.aa.26; EM 127: 5; ESTC t066393 (NA CtY, IU).

Notes. Adv., 'In a few Days will be published', LC 26: 565 (9–12 Dec 1769); adv. as published LC 27: 91 (25–27 Jan 1770).
Extract published LC 27: 101 and 113–14 (27–30 Jan and 1–3 Feb 1770).
Further edns: Dublin, 1770 (Printed for J. Williams, and J. Porter, 1 vol., 12mo), ESTC n021964; Philadelphia, 1793, ESTC w022129. German trans. Leipzig, 1770 (*Empfindsame Gedanken bey verschiedenen Vorfällen von Peter Pennyless*) (EAG).

CR: 'This same lady Sentimentality, of whom we are apt to hear so much in modern publications, we are sorry to say is but too apt to quarrel with her elder brother Common-sense; and we are afraid our friend Peter Pennyless has a strong hankering to take her part' (p. 110).
MR [Ralph Griffiths]: 'A Crude imitation of Shandy's Crudities.'

1771

1771: 1   ANON.
THE ADVENTURES OF A JESUIT INTERSPERSED WITH SEVERAL REMARKABLE CHARACTERS, AND SCENES IN REAL LIFE.

> London: Printed by George Bigg, for G. Riley, (successor to Mr. Cooke) at his circulating library in Queen-Street, Berkeley-Square, 1771.
> I 244p; II 276p. 12mo. 5s (CR), 5s sewed (MR, LC).
> CR 30: 481 (Dec 1770); MR 44: 92 (Jan 1771); AF I: 15.
> BL 12612.df.8; EM 207: 2; ESTC t066882 (BI O; NA InU-Li).

Notes. 4 pp. advs. vol. 1; vol. 1 p. 189 misnumbered 188. Quotation on t.p. of vol. 1 'Sunt hic etiam sua praemia laudi. Virg. Aen. I'.
Post-dated; adv. as published SJC 4–6 Dec 1770 and PA 5 Dec 1770 with title extended: *Interspersed with many interesting Accounts of the Inquisition, with Remarks on the Manners and Customs of the French and Spanish Nations. The Whole displaying several remarkable Characters, and Scenes in real Life.*
Adv. LC 29: 16 (1–3 Jan 1771).
Extract published LC 30: 441–2 (5–7 Sept 1771).
Facs: FN.

MR: 'The adventures of this Jesuit may well serve as a second part to the adventures of Luke Anthony Gavin, as recorded in his famous *Master-key to Popery*.' Gavin, fl. 1726.

1771: 2   ANON.
THE AFFECTED INDIFFERENCE, A NOVEL.

London: Printed for F. and J. Noble, at their respective Circulating Libraries, near Middle Row, Holborn, and Saint Martin's Court, near Leicester Square, 1771.
I 250p; II 234p. 12mo. 5s sewed (CR, MR).
CR 32: 312 (Oct 1771); MR 45: 503 (Dec 1771).
PU Singer-Mend. PR 3291.A1.A44.1771; ESTC n029406 (NA CtY-BR).

Notes. 2 pp. advs. end vol. 1 and 1 p. advs. end vol. 2. Epistolary.
Adv. LC 30: 384 (17–19 Oct 1771).
Further edn: Dublin, 1781 (Printed for C. Jackson, 2 vols, 12mo), ESTC n063841 [with title *The Affected Indifference. A Sentimental Novel, in a Series of Letters*].

MR [Gilbert Stuart]: 'The novel before us, is not void of interesting scenes; and when we reflect on the load of obscene or insipid performances of this class, with which the press abounds, we cannot justly refuse our suffrage to it. In a listless interval, it may furnish a tolerable entertainment to even a cultivated mind.'

1771: 3   ANON.
ANECDOTES OF A CONVENT. BY THE AUTHOR OF MEMOIRS OF MRS. WILLIAMS. IN THREE VOLUMES.

London: Printed for T. Becket and P. A. De Hondt, in the Strand, 1771.
I viii, 271p; II 243p; III 236p. 8vo. 7s 6d (CR, MR), 7s 6d sewed (LC).
CR 31: 483–4 (June 1771); MR 45: 144–8 (Aug 1771).
BL N.1651–53; EM 3804: 5; ESTC t071897 (BI E; NA CaAEU, MH-H, PU &c.).

Notes. Sometimes incorrectly attributed to Helen Maria Williams.
Epistolary.
Letters Between an English Lady and Her Friend at Paris. In which are contained, the Memoirs of Mrs. Williams 1770: 10.
Adv., 'Speedily will be published', LC 29: 396 (23–25 Apr 1771); adv. as published LC 29: 572 (3–15 June 1771).
Further edn: Dublin, 1771 (Printed for J. Potts and T. Walker, 2 vols., 12mo), ESTC n030248.
German trans. Leipzig, 1772 (*Erzählung von Klosterbegebenheiten*) (Price).

CR: 'Among several agreeable passages in these volumes, there are some which startle *probability*.'
MR [Gilbert Stuart]: 'In the novel before us, we observe a degree of merit, rarely to be met with in publications of the same class. It discovers an enlarged acquaintance with the human heart, and exhibits a beautiful picture of real manners' (p. 144).

AUTHENTIC MEMOIRS OF THE COUNTESS DE BARRÉ
See TREYSSAC DE VERGY, Pierre Henri

1771: 4   ANON.
*BELLE GROVE; OR, THE FATAL SEDUCTION.

London: Printed for F. Noble, at his Circulating Library, near Middle Row, Holborn; and J. Noble, at his Circulating Library, in St. Martin's Court, near Leicester Fields (LC), 1771 (CR).

2 vols. 12mo (CR). 6s (CR), 5s sewed (MR, LC).

CR 31: 232–3 (Mar 1771); MR 44: 262 (Mar 1771); AF I: 162.

No copy located.

Notes. Epistolary.

Adv. LC 29: 247 (9–12 Mar 1771).

Adv. beginning of 1781 Dublin edn *The Parsonage-House* (1780: 12).

CR: 'A very flimsy performance indeed' (p. 232).

MR suggests novel by same author as *The Brother* (1771: 6), 'but the manufacture seems to be of rather a more substantial texture, the fabric somewhat finer, and the pattern richer.'

1771: 5   ANON.

*BETSY; OR, THE CAPRICES OF FORTUNE.

London: Printed for T. Jones, at his Circulating Library, in the Strand (PA), 1771 (PA).

3 vols. 12mo. 7s 6d (CR), 7s 6d sewed (MR, PA), 9s 'printed on a fine writing paper' (adv.).

CR 31: 484 (June 1771); MR 44: 333 (Apr 1771).

No copy located.

Notes. Adv. PA 15 Mar 1771.

Adv. end vol. 1 of *The Involuntary Inconstant* (1772: 13).

German trans. Frankfurt, 1770 (*Betsi oder Der Eigensinn des Schicksals*) (Price).

CR: 'While this author endeavours to interest the heart, and amuse the imagination, he frequently loses sight of probability, which gives his performance, in many parts, a ridiculous appearance.'

MR: 'All improbability; yet not entirely destitute of interesting scenes.'

1771: 6   ANON.

THE BROTHER. A NOVEL. BY A LADY.

London: Printed for T. Lowndes, No. 77. in Fleet-Street, 1771.

I 204p; II 182p. 12mo. 5s sewed (CR, MR), 5s sewed or 6s bound (LC).

CR 31: 315 (Apr 1771); MR 44: 262 (Mar 1771); AF I: 270.

BL Cup.404.b.16; EMf; ESTC t140109 (NA CLU-S/C, TxU).

Notes. 1 p. advs. beginning vol. 1. 11 pp. advs. end vol. 2. Epistolary.

ESTC suggests author also wrote *Louisa: a Sentimental Novel* (1771: 24); *The Brother* adv. on verso of t.p. of *Louisa*.

Adv. LC 29: 167 (14–16 Feb 1771).

CR: 'This little novel seems to be adapted to the capacity of the junior misses at a boarding school; but is so extremely insipid as not to gratify even the most puerile taste.'

MR: 'Prattling letters—scraps of songs—ends of verse—and *la belle passion*, to captivate the milliners apprentices; with a dismal tale at the end, to dissolve their pretty eyes in a pearly shower.'

1771:7   ANON.

THE CAPTIVE; OR, THE HISTORY OF MR. CLIFFORD. TRANSLATED FROM THE FRENCH. IN TWO VOLUMES.

> London: Printed for the Editor, and sold by J. Roson, no. 54, St. Martin's Le-Grand, 1771.
>
> I 220p; II 204p. 12mo. 5s (CR), 5s sewed (MR).
>
> CR 30: 397–8 (Nov 1770); MR 43: 400 (Nov 1770); AF I: 329.
>
> BL 12612.bb.6; EM 168: 1; ESTC t064711.

Notes. Dated 1771, but revs. suggest post-dating.

MR: 'A romance, of the old exploded sort.—A Moorish captivity, seraglio intrigues, and hair-breadth escapes: all extravagance, improbability, and absurdity.'

1771:8   ANON.

THE CAPTIVES: OR, THE HISTORY OF CHARLES ARLINGTON, ESQ; AND MISS LOUISA SOMERVILLE. IN THREE VOLUMES.

> London: Printed for T. Vernor, at his Circulating Library, in St. Michael's Alley, Corn-hill; and J. Chater, at his Circulating Library, in King-street, Cheapside, 1771.
>
> I 227p; II 233p; III 158p. 12mo. 7s 6d (CR), 7s 6d sewed (MR, LC June), 9s bound (LC May).
>
> CR 31: 483 (June 1771); MR 45: 153 (Aug 1771); AF I: 330.
>
> BL C.124.e.22; EMf; ESTC t124528 (NA MH-H).

Notes. BL copy in original blue paper and boards.

Adv., 'This Month will be published . . . *The History of Charles Arlington, Esq.*', LC 29: 490 (21–23 May 1771); adv. as published LC 29: 555 (1771).

CR: '. . . full of uninteresting characters feebly drawn, and of insipid adventures flimzily related. . . .'

MR [Gilbert Stuart]: 'We are here presented with adventures that shock probability by their extravagance; while the history of them possesses no advantages of style or manner to recommend it.'

THE CONTEMPLATIVE MAN
See LAWRENCE, Herbert

1771:9   ANON.

*THE CONTRAST; OR, HISTORY OF MISS WELDON AND MISS MOSELY.

> London: Printed for F. and J. Noble, in Holborn, and St. Martin's Court (LC), 1771 (LC).
>
> 2 vols. 12mo. 5s (CR), 5s sewed (MR, LC).
>
> CR 31: 232 (Mar 1771); MR 44: 173 (Feb 1771).
>
> No copy located.

Notes. Adv. LC 29: 55 (12–15 Jan 1771).

CR: 'Mr. Noble is a very industrious purveyor for his fair readers; and as his provisions are at present wholesome, we shall not complain of their coarseness. We do not, however, suspect Miss Weldon's and Miss Mosely's biographer of having kept what is called the best company, as he introduces cold ham, pickled oysters, and arrack punch, as part of the refreshment given at a rout.'

MR: 'The adventures in which these contrasted heroines are involved, are interesting and exemplary; and their story, upon the whole, though not of the highest rank in this species of literature, deserves commendation for its good tendency.'

1771: 10   ANON.
*COQUETILLA; OR, ENVY ITS OWN SCOURGE: CONTAINING THE ADVENTURES OF SEVERAL GREAT PERSONAGES. FROM A MANU-SCRIPT LATE IN THE POSSESSION OF A GENTLEMAN FAMOUS FOR HIS ACQUAINTANCE WITH THE GREAT WORLD.

> London: Printed for S. Leacroft, (Successor to Mr. March) opposite Spring Gardens, Charing Cross (SJC), 1771 (SJC).
> 1 vol. 12mo. 2s 6d (CR, MR), 2s 6d sewed or 3s bound (SJC).
> CR 31: 482 (June 1771); MR 45: 152 (Aug 1771).
> No copy located.

Notes. Adv., 'On Thursday next will be published', SJC 16–18 May 1771.

CR: 'The volume before us is so uninteresting, that we cannot help looking upon it as a slovenly translation from a very indifferent French original.'

MR [Gilbert Stuart]: 'This novel is introduced to the public with great modesty; and, on that account, we are sorry that it cannot boast of more important claims to attention and favour.'

CUCKOLDOM TRIUMPHANT OR, MATRIMONIAL INCONTINENCE VINDICATED
See WILMOT, Frederick

1771: 11   ANON.
THE DISGUISE, A DRAMATIC NOVEL.

> London: Printed for J. Dodsley, in Pall-Mall. 1771.
> I xi, 261p; II 239p. 12mo. 5s sewed (CR, MR).
> CR 31: 315 (Apr 1771); MR 44: 334 (Apr 1771); AF I: 641.
> BL 12612.ccc.5; EM 205: 4; ESTC t066891 (NA IU).

Notes. Written in the style of a play. CR reviews under 'Novels' and MR under 'Novels, &c.'.
Adv., 'In a few Days will be published', LC 29: 111 (29–31 Jan 1771); adv. as published LC 29: 141 (7–9 Feb 1771).
Further edn: Dublin, 1771 (Printed for J. Williams; and R. Moncrieffe, 2 vols., 12mo), ESTC n046223.

CR: '. . . truth compels us to declare that we have experienced *the Disguise* to be more nar-cotic than *poppy or mandragora, or all the drowsy syrups of the world.*'

MR [Gilbert Stuart]: 'The Author of this performance apologizes to his Reader for deviat-ing from the forms in which novels have usually been written; but this circumstance is, per-haps, the only one for which he deserves commendation. In the hands of a man of genius the dramatic form may certainly be employed in a novel with the greatest advantages; but our Author is not to be ranked in this class.'

1771: 12   ANON.
*THE DIVORCE. IN A SERIES OF LETTERS TO AND FROM PERSONS OF HIGH RANK.

London: Printed for R. Baldwin, in Paternoster Row (SJC), 1771 (SJC).
2 vols. 12mo. 5s sewed (CR, MR).
CR 31: 315 (Apr 1771); MR 44: 497–8 (June 1771).
No copy located.

Notes. Epistolary. Based upon the divorce case of Richard Lord Grosvenor (see also *Harriet* 1771: 18 and cf., on the same subject, *Free Thoughts on Seduction, Adultery, and Divorce,* London: J. Bell, 1771, EM 1207: 18, ESTC t117150).
Adv., 'In a few Days will be published', SJC 7–19 Jan 1771; 'Dedicated to the Duke of G——n'.
  CR: 'The author of this performance has availed himself of the temper of the times, and launched it into the world with a dedication to a nobleman, the repudiation of whose wife made no little figure in the annals of gallantry. The work is not without its merit, and may certainly be classed with those which are more distinguished by regularity and decency of conduct, than variety or splendor of invention.'
  MR [John Noorthouck]: '. . . we are firmly convinced of the bad tendency of putting such decorated pictures of vice into the hands of young persons, whose passions are more mature than their powers of reflection, and whose dispositions are pliable to the most alluring bias.'

THE ELOPEMENT
See COLTON, Henry

THE EXPEDITION OF HUMPHRY CLINKER
See SMOLLETT, Tobias

1771: 13   ANON.
THE FALSE STEP; OR THE HISTORY OF MRS. BRUDENEL. A NOVEL. IN TWO VOLUMES.

London: Printed for J. Almon, opposite Burlington House, Piccadilly, 1771.
I 218p; II 205p. 12mo. 5s sewed (CR, MR), 5s sewed or 6s bound (SJC).
CR 31: 160 (Feb 1771); MR 44: 91–2 (Jan 1771).
BL 012618.df.21; EM 277: 5; ESTC t108167 (NA InU-Li).

Notes. Vol. 1 imperf. wanting pp. 59–62; p. 94 misnumbered 96 and seq. Vol. 1 p. 216 misnumbered 214; vol. 2 p. 38 misnumbered 37. Epistolary.
Adv., 'In a few Days will be published', PA 26 Dec 1770; adv. as published PA 1 Jan 1771.
  CR: 'In point of language, sentiment and moral, this novel is superior to many that have been published this season: yet it must in justice be observed, that the phraseology is often affected, and that frequent and absurd gallicisms render the piece disgusting to a reader of taste.'
  MR: 'The work, if not a brilliant performance, is a moral one; which ought not to be considered as a slight commendation.'

1771: 14   ANON.
*THE FATAL COMPLIANCE; OR, THE HISTORY OF MISS CONSTANTIA PEMBROKE.

London: Printed for T. Jones, at his Circulating Library, in the Strand (PA), 1771 (PA).
2 vols. 12mo. 5s (CR), 5s sewed (MR), 6s (adv.), 5s sewed or 6s bound (PA).
CR 31: 483 (June 1771); MR 44: 499 (June 1771); AF I: 850.
No copy located.

Notes. Epistolary.
Adv., 'in a few Days will be published', PA 22 Mar 1771; adv. as published PA 26 Apr 1771.
Adv. end v. 1 of *The Involuntary Inconstant* (1772: 13) which is 'By the editor of The Fatal Compliance'.

CR: 'There is nothing in the composition of this novel, either with regard to invention or stile, to raise it above that sort of mediocrity so conspicuous in most productions of a similar nature which have lately swarmed from the press.'

MR: 'Her story is told in natural, easy language; some of the *letters* (for the epistolary form is become the high mode of modern romance) are sprightly; and none of them are ill written.'

THE FAULT WAS ALL HIS OWN
See NICHOLS, Elizabeth Eyton

1771: 15   ANON.
THE FAVOURITE. A MORAL TALE. WRITTEN BY A LADY OF QUALITY. IN TWO VOLUMES.

London: Printed for R. Baldwin, in Pater-noster Row, 1771.
I iv, 203p; II 228p. 12mo. 5s sewed (CR, MR).
CR 31: 159 (Feb 1771); MR 44: 497 (June 1771).
BL 1607/4668; EM 2658: 9; ESTC t119660 (BI O).

Notes. Adv., 'In a few Days will be published', SJC 7–9 Jan 1771; adv. as published PA 9 Feb 1771.

CR: 'The volumes now under consideration may be fairly said to deserve some preference to the great majority of those which are published every day for the emolument of circulating libraries. They are written with good sense, no inconsiderable knowledge of the world, and a delicacy not often to be met with even in performances of the same tendency. Most of the characters are well marked, and the passions are always directed to their true end and purpose. The old and considerate may peruse them without disgust, and the young and inexperienced without danger.'

MR [John Noorthouck]: 'If one of these compositions will afford an afternoon's amusement to a novel-reader, and do her no harm, it is as much good as can be expected from it.'

1771: 16   ANON.
THE GENEROUS HUSBAND; OR, THE HISTORY OF LORD LELIUS AND THE FAIR EMILIA. CONTAINING LIKEWISE THE GENUINE MEMOIRS OF ASMODEI, THE PRETENDED PIEDMONTESE COUNT, FROM THE TIME OF HIS BIRTH, TO HIS LATE IGNOMINIOUS FALL IN HYDE PARK.

London: Printed for W. Wheeble, oppposite the New Church in the Strand, 1771.
viii, 138p. 8vo. 2s 6d (CR, MR).

CR 32: 232 (Sept 1771); MR 45: 73 (July 1771); AF I: 1035.
BL 12614.ee.15; EM 418: 10; ESTC t072454.

Notes. Edward Ligonier (later Earl Ligonier) and his first wife Penelope are represented fictionally as Lord Lelius and Emilia; 'Count Asmodei' was the known pseudonym of Vittorio Amadeo Alfieri.

CR: 'This is one of those productions which is a disgrace to the press: it contains nothing which can entitle it to a favourable reception from the public.'

MR [Gilbert Stuart]: 'in the highest degree, disgusting'.

1771: 17 ANON.
THE GENEROUS INCONSTANT. A NOVEL. IN TWO VOLUMES. BY A LADY.

London: Printed for W. Nicol, No. 51, St Paul's Church-Yard, 1771.
I 246p; II 214p. 12mo. 5s (CR) 5s sewed (MR, PA).
CR 31: 232 (Mar 1771); MR 44: 498 (June 1771); AF I: 1036.
CLU-S/C PR3991 A6L1415; ESTC n018237.

Notes. Epistolary.
Adv. PA 4 Feb 1771; adv., with quotation from LM, LC 29: 275 (19–21 Mar 1771).

CR: 'The hero of this novel is a wretch whose sole employment is to excite hopes which he never means to gratify, and to embitter the anguish of disappointment by proceeding in a new courtship with the next deluded fair whom he meets. After having deserved the gallows ten times in the course of the present insipid narrative, the author has thought proper to reward him with a young, rich, and amiable wife.'

THE GENEROUS LOVER
See CHIARI, Pietro

1771: 18 ANON.
HARRIET: OR, THE INNOCENT ADULTRESS.

London: Printed for R. Baldwin, No. 47, Pater-noster-Row, 1771.
I xxviii, 163p; II 176p. 8vo. 5s (CR, MR), 5s sewed (PA).
CR 31: 484 (June 1771); MR 44: 418 (May 1771); AF I: 1172.
C Syn.8.77.12; ESTC n007138 (NA MnU).

Notes. 'Address to the Twelve wise men not of Goat'em' i–xxv; 'The Editor's Advertisement' xxv–xxviii.
Novel based upon the Grosvenor divorce case of the previous year. See also *The Divorce* 1771: 12.
Adv., 'In a few Days will be published', LC 29: 288 (21–23 Mar 1771); adv. as published PA 3 Apr 1771.
Adv. end vol. 2 of *Arville Castle* (1795: 1).
Further edn: London, 1779, EM 2580: 8, ESTC t116622.
1779 edn. adv., with 4 other Baldwin and Bew re-publications (including 1771: 35, 1774: 9 and 1775: 6), SJC 6–9 Mar 1779 under the heading 'The Approbation these Performances have met with from the Monthly and Critical Reviewers cannot fail to attract the publick Attention, and to place them in a Rank superiour to most of our modern Novels, as it is well

known those Goliahs of Literature are much less prone to compliment than condemn such Publications.'

CR: 'The *professed* design of this performance is to shew the danger, in these times, of presuming a lady guilty of adultery, *upon the strongest circumstances*, when there is not irresistible and precise evidence to convict her. Though the author takes his fable from the late trial between the D— of C— and L— d G—, he means to combat the principle of convicting upon equivocal evidence, rather than condemning *seriously* the verdict given in that trial.'

MR: has 'too much the air of an apology for that heinous though fashionable crime....'

1771: 19   ANON.
THE HISTORY OF MR. CECIL AND MISS GREY. IN A SERIES OF LETTERS. IN TWO VOLUMES.
> London: Printed for Richardson and Urquhart, under the Royal-Exchange, 1771.
> I 240p; II 264p. 12mo. 5s sewed (CR, MR), 5s sewed or 6s bound (LC).
> CR 31: 484 (June 1771); MR 44: 262 (Mar 1771).
> CLU-S/C PR 3991.A1.H62; ESTC n007805 (NA TxHR).

Notes. Epistolary.
Adv. LC 29: 247 (9–12 Mar 1771); booksellers' addresses expanded to No. 91, Royal Exchange, and No. 46, Paternoster Row, and title continues: 'In a Series of Letters; through which are interspersed original Remarks on the French Nation.'

CR: 'This little piece abounds with so much good sense, and so many virtuous sentiments, that it ought to be exempted from censure for any defects which may be discovered in regard to taste and variety.'

MR: 'To those... who can think good sense and virtuous sentiments a sufficient compensation for any deficiency in point of taste, or of spirit, this honest and not wholly uninteresting work, may be acceptable.'

1771: 20   ANON.
THE HISTORY OF SIR WILLIAM HARRINGTON WRITTEN SOME YEARS SINCE, AND REVISED AND CORRECTED BY THE LATE MR. RICHARDSON, AUTHOR OF SIR CHARLES GRANDISON, CLARISSA, &C. NOW FIRST PUBLISHED IN FOUR VOLUMES.
> London: Printed for John Bell, at his Extensive Circulating Library near Exeter Exchange in the Strand, and C. Etherington at York, 1771.
> I 251p; II 250p; III 257p; IV 263p. 12mo. 10s sewed (CR, MR).
> CR 31: 147–8 (Feb 1771); MR 44: 262–3 (Mar 1771); AF I: 1330.
> C 7720.d.77.16; EM 6459: 4; ESTC t033244 (BI BL, O; NA CSmH, CtY-BR, NjP, TxU &c.).

Notes. Sometimes attributed to Anna Meades and Thomas Hull.
4 pp. advs. end vol. 1, 6 pp. advs. end vol. 2, 6 pp. advs. end vol. 3.
Imitation of Richardson.
Adv., 'To the Admirers of Mr. Richardson's Works, This Week will be published', SJC 15–17 Jan 1771; adv. as published SJC 31 Jan–2 Feb 1771.
Still adv., 'just published', SJC 11–13 Mar 1777.

2nd edn. adv. WFA 18 Jan 1787; 'first published in 1771, since which time it hath met with a very successful sale, and acquired a degree of estimation only to be equalled by Mr. Richardson's Works, to which these volumes have been greatly recommended as a valuable supplement.' Further edns: Dublin, 1771 (Printed for J. Exshaw, H. Saunders, W. Sleator, and 7 more, 4 vols., 12mo), ESTC n033215; London, 1772, ESTC t127675; London, 1797, ESTC t222170. German trans. Leipzig, 1771 (*Geschichte Sir Wilhelm Harrington*) (EAG); French trans. Amsterdam, 1772 (*Les Moeurs du jour ou histoire de sir William Harrington*) (BGR).

CR: 'We have read it with a great degree of attention and pleasure. Though we cannot absolutely determine whether it was revised by the late Mr. Richardson or not, we make no scruple to assert that its author has been a diligent studier of his works' (p. 148).

MR: 'Notwithstanding it has been (not very satisfactorily indeed) *contradicted* in an advertisement (To which the publisher of this work made a very proper and decent reply) published by the widow and daughters of Mr Richardson, yet it will by no means follow, that Mr Richardson *thought* it, or by his corrections *made* it, a work of extraordinary merit.'

1771: 21 ANON.
*THE JEALOUS MOTHER; OR, INNOCENCE TRIUMPHANT.

> London: Printed for Robinson and Roberts, No. 25, Paternoster Row (PA), 1771 (PA). 2 vols. 12mo. 6s (CR, MR), 5s sewed (SJC).
> CR 31: 480–2 (June 1771); MR 45: 152 (Aug 1771).
> No copy located.

Notes. Adv., 'In a few Days will be published', SJC 14–16 Mar 1771 and PA 22 Mar 1771.
MR [Gilbert Stuart]: '. . . superior to the common run of publications of the same class.'

1771: 22 ANON.
JESSY; OR, THE BRIDAL DAY. A NOVEL. WRITTEN BY A LADY, AFTER THE MANNER OF THE LATE MR. RICHARDSON, (AUTHOR OF CLARISSA, &C.) BUT NOT REVISED BY THAT CELEBRATED WRITER. IN TWO VOLUMES.

> London: Printed for F. and J. Noble, at their respective circulating Libraries, near Middle Row, Holborn, and Saint Martin's Court, near Leicester Square, 1771.
> I ii, 200p; II 176p. 12mo. 4s (CR), 4s sewed (MR, LC).
> CR 31: 479–80 (June 1771); MR 45: 73 (July 1771); AF I: 1428.
> BL 12611.df.16; EM 92: 9; ESTC t057444.

Notes. 2 pp. advs. end vol. 2.
Adv., 'Next Week', LC 29: 391 (20–23 Apr 1771); adv. as published SJC 30 Apr–2 May 1771 and LC 29: 447 (7–9 May 1771).

CR: 'Ye credulous fair ones, and ye loose, licentious fellows of the age! by you this piece may be read to some purpose, if it is read with proper attention.'

MR [Gilbert Stuart]: 'To imitate, with any degree of success, the manner of Richardson, it is necessary to possess some proportion of his genius.'

1771: 23 ANON.
LETTERS FROM CLARA: OR, THE EFFUSIONS OF THE HEART.

London: Printed for J. Wilkie, No. 71, in St. Paul's Church Yard, 1771.
I x, 144p; II 147p. 8vo. 5s sewed (CR, MR).
CR 31: 484 (June 1771); MR 44: 418 (May 1771); AF I: 1609.
PU Singer-Mend.PR.3291.C52.L47.1771; ESTC n011333.

Notes. Preface iii–x, signed 'The Editor'. Epistolary.
Adv., 'Next Thursday will be published.... Written by a Young Lady', LC 29: 363 (13–16 Apr 1771); adv. as published LC 29: 374 (16–18 Apr 1771).

CR: 'Dull, frigid effusions, neither flowing from the heart, nor possessing the power of affecting it; and which even the unexceptionable morality they contain cannot preserve from oblivion.'

MR [Gilbert Stuart]: 'Cold, insipid, and devoid of circumstances....'

LETTERS FROM THE MARCHIONESS OF POMPADOUR
See BARBÉ-MARBOIS, François, Marquis de, App. B: 1

LETTERS TO ELEONORA
See LANGHORNE, John

THE LIFE OF LAMENTHER
See WALL, Anne

1771: 24   ANON.
LOUISA: A SENTIMENTAL NOVEL.

London: Printed for T. Lowndes, in Fleetstreet; and G. Kearsley, in Ludgate-street, 1771.
234p. 12mo. 3s (MR), 3s bound (SJC, LC).
MR 44: 173 (Feb 1771); AF I: 1679.
C 7720.d.1345; EM 5093: 9; ESTC t126674 (BI BL; NA NjP, PU, CLU-S/C).

Notes., 4-pp. prefatory advertisement signed, as editor, T. M. Epistolary.
ESTC suggests author also wrote *The Brother* (1771: 6), adv. on verso of t.p.
Adv., 'On the 1st of February will be published', SJC 24–26 Jan 1771; adv., 'To-morrow will be published', LC 29: 111 (29–31 Jan 1771).

MR: 'It does not seem, to us, entitled to stand in the first rank of this order of books of entertainment....'

THE MAN OF FEELING
See MACKENZIE, Henry

THE MAN OF HONOUR OR, THE HISTORY OF HARRY WATERS, ESQ.
See WYNNE, John Huddlestone

1771: 25   ANON.
MEMOIRS OF LADY WOODFORD. WRITTEN BY HERSELF, AND ADDRESSED TO A FRIEND. IN TWO VOLUMES.

London: Printed by George Bigg, For F. and J. Noble, at their respective Circulating

Libraries, near Middle-Row, Holborn, and St. Martin's-Court, near Leicester-Square, 1771.

I 232p; II 214p. 12mo. 5s (CR), 5s sewed (MR, PA).

CR 31: 482 (June 1771); MR 44: 498 (June 1771).

MH-H *EC75.A100.771m; EM 3012: 4; ESTC n010548 (BI O).

Notes. T.p. to vol. 2 omits 'In Two Volumes'.

Adv. PA 17 Apr 1771 and LC 29: 391 (20–23 Apr 1771).

Further edn: Dublin, 1782 (Printed by William Spotswood, 2 vols., 12mo), ESTC t175112.

CR: 'Lady Woodford tells her tale in a decent manner, and does not surfeit her reader with those violent egotisms, by which the majority of memoir-writers render their narrations extremely disgusting. Her ladyship relates the most interesting parts of her life, from her early youth, to the consummation of her felicity in the marriage state, (during which period she is thrown into many trying situations) without paying any gross compliments to her own understanding; without concealing her imperfections: and we will venture to recommend her mode of behaviour to every young lady who finds herself in similar circumstances.'

MR: 'Tenderness and simplicity are the principal characteristics of this innocent novel.'

1771: 26 ANON.
THE MEMOIRS OF MISS WILLIAMS: A HISTORY FOUNDED ON FACTS. IN TWO VOLUMES.

London: Printed for E. Johnson, in Ave Mary Lane; and A. Bell, near the Stone Pump, Aldgate, 1771.

I 274p; II 294p. 12mo. 5s sewed (CR, MR).

CR 33: 498 (June 1772); MR 46: 457 (Apr 1772); AF I: 1813.

AWn PR 4091.M53; ESTC t211566

Notes. Preface vol. 1; table of contents both vols.

CR reviews under the heading 'Miscellaneous' and judges it to be 'The whimsical lucubrations of a weak, religious enthusiast.'

MR [Gilbert Stuart] reviews as a novel and comments: 'We have here the reveries of a pious and well disposed, but weak religionist.'

1771: 27 ANON.
MEMOIRS OF MR. WILSON: OR, THE PROVIDENTIAL ADULTERY. IN TWO VOLUMES.

London: Printed for Francis Hall, at his circulating library, near the New Church, in The Strand, 1771.

I 175p; II 178p. 12mo. 5s sewed (CR, MR), 5s sewed or 6s bound (SJC).

CR 31: 160 (Feb 1771); MR 44: 92 (Jan 1771); AF I: 2294.

BL 12611.df.3; EM 237: 7; ESTC t095751 (BI O; NA PU).

Notes. Vol. I p. 87 misnumbered 67; vol. 2 p. 5 misnumbered 125, pp. 121–44 wanting. 2 pp. advs. end vol. 2.

Adv. SJC 18–20 Dec 1770.

CR gives title as *The Providential Adultery.*

CR: 'The writer of this piece is not deficient in fancy or imagination; but he appears to be destitute of judgment, and seems totally to have rejected probability from the composition of his novel, which may be termed a romance, in the strictest sense of the word.'

MR: 'Although this romance abounds with the grossest absurdities, and most ridiculous flights of imagination, it is not, however, a dull performance.'

MISS MELMOTH
See BRISCOE, Sophia

MISTAKES OF THE HEART
See TREYSSAC DE VERGY, Pierre Henri

1771: 28   ANON.
THE NUN; OR, THE ADVENTURES OF THE MARCHIONESS OF BEAUVILLE.

> London: Printed for J. Roson, No. 54, St. Martin's Le Grand; And sold by T. Shepherd, No. 147, in the Minories, 1771.
> 196p. 12mo. 2s 6d (CR, MR).
> CR 31: 315–16 (Apr 1771); MR 44: 262 (Mar 1771); AF I: 2033.
> BL 12654.ee.84; EM 485: 2; ESTC t107027 (NA CSmH).

Notes. 4 pp. advs. end vol.

CR: 'An indecent recital of such adventures as are supposed to happen in convents; calculated to inflame the passions of youthful readers, and to supply the wants of an abandoned and shameless writer.'

MR: 'Like most of the tales of nuns and convents, this narrative abounds with scenes of lewdness and complicated wickedness, unfit for the eye or ear of a modest and virtuous reader....'

1771: 29   ANON.
THE NUNNERY FOR COQUETTES.

> London: Printed for T. Lowndes, at No. 73, in Fleet-Street, 1771.
> viii, 239p. 12mo. 3s (CR, MR).
> CR 30: 476–7 (Dec 1770); MR 43: 489 (Dec 1770); AF I: 2034.
> BL 12612.df.24; EM 98: 2; ESTC t066913 (NA CtY, IU, MH-H, NjP &c.).

Notes. Consists of a collection of tales taken from other sources, such as the *Tatler*, *Spectator*, *Rambler* &c. with editorial comment in between. Signature on last page 'The Invisible Spy'. Reviewed as miscellany.

Adv. SJC 24–26 Jan 1771.

Further edn: Dublin, 1771 (Printed for W. and W. Smith, J. Exshaw, H. Saunders, and 7 more, 1 vol., 12mo), EM 4506: 8, ESTC t131564.

CR calls the work a 'wretched patchwork' and treats with contempt the 'wretched compiler of this pirated work' (p. 477).

1771: 30   ANON.
THE OXONIAN: OR, THE ADVENTURES OF MR. G. EDMUNDS, STUDENT OF BRAZEN-NOSE COLLEGE, OXFORD. DEDICATED, BY HIS

LORDSHIP'S PERMISSION, TO THE RIGHT HON. THE EARL OF — BY A MEMBER OF THE UNIVERSITY.

> London: Printed for J. Roson, No. 54, St. Martin's Le Grand, 1771.
> I vi, 212p; II 208p. 12mo. 5s (MR), 5s sewed (LC), CR has no price.
> CR 32: 154 (Aug 1771); MR 46: 78 (Jan 1772).
> CtY Im.Ox2.771; ESTC n062540 (NA ICN).

Notes. Dedication to the Earl of — i–vi.
Adv., 'On the First of September will be published', LC 30: 159 (13–15 Aug 1771).

CR: 'We cannot bring ourselves to believe that these volumes were written by a member of the university of Oxford. If the writer is really a member of it, he certainly, in his literary character, deserves expulsion. The perusal of the first page of these volumes gave us no encouragement to imagine that our progress through them would be pleasing: we soon found it, indeed, painful. There is not, in our opinion, throughout the whole performance a strong-marked character, a striking incident, an interesting situation, or an uncommon thought elegantly expressed.'

MR notes that this publication is 'partly stolen from *The Adventures of Charles Careless Esq*' [*The Amours and Adventures of Charles Careless*, 1764, JR 805, AF I: 71] and goes on to speculate that 'the Bookseller has been *taken-in* for these pretended *new pieces*, by some genius who, perhaps, would have *out-curl'd* Curl himself, had they been co-temporaries.'

1771: 31   ANON.
*THE PERPLEXITIES OF RICHES.

> London: Printed for Robinson and Roberts, No. 25, Paternoster Row (LC), 1771 (MR).
> 2 vols. 12mo. 5s (CR), 5s sewed (MR, LC).
> CR 33: 84 (Jan 1772); MR 46: 79 (Jan 1772).
> No copy located.

Notes. Adv., 'This Month will be published', LC 30: 599 (19–21 Dec 1771).

CR: 'We are not so little acquainted with the world as to suppose that the *moral* of this story will have such an effect upon the minds of those who read it, while they feel themselves in affluent circumstances, as to excite in them the smallest desire to have their splendid income diminished; but some of those who are moderate in their wishes, and placed in the middle state of life, may, possibly, during the perusal of Sir Charles Trent's distresses, feel a keener relish for the blessings of *mediocrity*.'

MR [Gilbert Stuart]: '. . . we can find in it no circumstances that render it in the smallest degree interesting or valuable.'

PROVIDENTIAL ADULTERY
See MEMOIRS OF MR WILSON

1771: 32   ANON.
THE SAMIANS, A TALE.

> London: Printed for J. Dodsley, in Pall-Mall, 1771.
> 89p. 8vo. 1s 6d (half-title, CR, MR).
> CR 31: 477–8 (June 1771); MR 45: 156 (Aug 1771); AF I: 2433.
> BL 1607/5284(3); ESTC t138549.

Notes. A prose retelling of the tale of Euryale and Evander, taken from Ovid's Metamorphoses (ESTC).

MR & CR review under 'Miscellaneous'.

Adv. LC 29: 391 (20–23 Apr 1771).

French trans. Paris, 1781 (*Les Samiens*) (BGR)

CR: 'The stile in which it is related is flowery and elaborate.'

MR [John Langhorne]: 'Written in the false taste of the Arcadian, heroi-comi-tragi-pastoral stuff that now pesters France; and in that kind of style which we have often condemned, prose titupping on a Parnassian poney.'

SENTIMENTAL TALES
See RUSSELL, William

THE SHIPWRECK AND ADVENTURES OF MONSIEUR PIERREVIAUD
See DUBOIS-FONTANELLE, Joseph-Gaspard, App. B: 2

THE TUTOR
See KELLY, Hugh

1771: 33   ANON.
THE UNDUTIFUL DAUGHTER; OR, THE HISTORY OF MISS GOODWIN. IN A SERIES OF LETTERS. IN THREE VOLUMES.

London: Printed for F. Noble, at his Circulating Library, near Middle-Row, Holborn. and
    J. Noble, at his Circulating Library, in St. Martin's Court, near Leicester-Square, 1771.
London: Printed by T. Baldwin, No. 42, Fleet-street.
I viii, 231p; II 228p; III 213p. 12mo. 7s 6d sewed (MR), 7s 6d sewed or 9s bound (SJC).
CR 30: 396–7 (Nov 1770); MR 43: 400 (Nov 1770); AF I: 2821.
NN ncv; ESTC n051009 (NA IU).

Notes. 1 p. adv. end vol. 1. Epistolary.

Post-dated; adv. as published SJC 1–3 Nov 1770.

Adv. LC 29: 55 (12–15 Jan 1771).

Further edn: Dublin, 1773 (Printed for T. Walker, 1 vol., no format), xESTC.

MR: 'This work is cast in the *form*, though not written in the *manner* of Richardson's novels. . . .'

1771: 34   ANON.
*THE UNGUARDED MOMENT.

London: Almon, 1771 (MR) [CR has no date].
2 vols. 12mo (CR). 5s (CR), 5s sewed (MR).
CR 31: 482 (June 1771); MR 45: 74 (July 1771).
No copy located.

Notes. French trans. London and Paris, 1776 (*L'Erreur d'un moment*) (BGR).

CR: 'The laudable design with which this novel seems to have been written is sufficient to rescue it from a severe scrutiny as a literary composition. It is particularly calculated by the author for the married part of his readers, and it merits a careful perusal from husbands as well as from wives.'

MR [Gilbert Stuart]: 'This publication, unexceptionable in its moral, is not so with regard to execution. It can boast of no elegance of expression; and the incidents it describes are often extravagant and improbable.'

1771: 35 ANON.
THE VICAR OF BRAY: A TALE.

London: Printed for R. Baldwin, at No. 47, Pater-Noster Row, 1771.
I vi, 231p; II vii, 216p. 12mo. 5s sewed (CR, MR), 5s sewed or 6s bound (SJC).
CR 32: 78 (July 1771); MR 44: 334 (Apr 1771); AF I: 2852.
BL 1154.k.18; EM 2901: 5; ESTC t117343 (BI O; NA CtY-BR, CSmH, MH-H &c.).

Notes. The Vicar of Bray ballad appears vol. 2, pp. 215–16.
Adv., 'In a few Days will be published', SJC 7–9 Feb 1771; adv. as published 1–5 Mar 1771.
Further edns: Dublin, 1771 (Printed for J. Williams, W. Wilson, and T. Walker, 2 vols. in 1, 12mo), ESTC t177069; London, 1779, ESTC t181284, and praised in SJC adv.; see *Harriet* (1771: 18).

CR: 'The ground-work of this tale is an extravagant fiction which the author has absurdly attempted to support, by warping it with the political history of late years.'

MR [John Noorthouck]: 'A ridiculous story ridiculously blended with the political history of the last fourteen or fifteen years, in order to give an air of secret history to a scandalous improbable fiction.'

1771: 36 AUSTIN, Mrs.
THE NOBLE FAMILY, A NOVEL; IN A SERIES OF LETTERS; BY MRS AUSTIN.

London: Printed for G. Pearch, No. 12, Cheapside, 1771.
I 190p; II 191p; III 179p. 12mo. 5s (CR), 9s (MR).
CR 31: 482 (June 1771); MR 45: 74 (July 1771).
InU-Li Spec. Pr4045.A9.N7; ESTC n064179 (NA PU, ICU)

Notes. Evidence of leaf missing at end vols. 2 and 3. Epistolary.
Adv., 'On Thursday next will be published', PA 6 May 1771; adv., 'Tomorrow will be published', PA 8 May 1771; adv. as published PA 9 May 1771. No price given; Pearch's full name, George, appears in advs.

CR: 'Humanity prompts us to hope that Mrs. Austen of Clerkenwell, does not trust to her pen for her subsistence.'

MR [Gilbert Stuart] says that the novel 'is replete with business and incident; but it wants nature and probability; and its Author is little acquainted with the art of composition.'

BARBÉ-MARBOIS, François, Marquis de, LETTERS FROM THE MARCHIONESS OF POMPADOUR
See App. B: 1

1771: 37 [BRISCOE, Sophia].
MISS MELMOTH; OR, THE NEW CLARISSA. IN THREE VOLUMES.

London: Printed for T. Lowndes, No. 77, in Fleet-Street, 1771.
I 309p; II 282p; III 287p. 12mo. 9s (CR, MR), 9s bound (LC).
CR 31: 479 (June 1771); MR 45: 74 (July 1771).
O Vet.A5e.1354–56; ESTC n034944 (NA IU).

Notes. By the same author as *The Fine Lady* (1772: 31).
Running title: 'The History of Miss Melmoth'. 3 pp. advs. for plays end vol. 1. Epistolary.
Adv., 'In a few Days will be published', LC 29: 396 (23–25 Apr 1771); adv. as published LC 29: 447 (7–9 May 1771).
Extract published LC 29: 559 (8–11 June 1771).
Further edn: Dublin, 1772 [*The History of Miss Melmoth*] (Printed for James Williams, 2 vols., 12mo), ESTC n033043. German trans. Leipzig, 1774, *Geschichte der Miss Melmoth* (Price).

CR: 'The history of Miss Melmoth . . . deserves the perusal of the fair part of a circulating librarian's customers, more than many of the histories, memoirs, and anecdotes which they, liberally, put into their hands. There is much *business* in it, and of an interesting nature; several parts of it are affecting; and it contains, upon the whole, a pleasing mixture of instruction and entertainment.'
MR: 'The good-natured and benevolent reader will receive more pleasure from the perusal of this work than the critic.'

1771: 38   CHIARI, Abbé Pietro.
THE GENEROUS LOVER: OR THE ADVENTURES OF THE MAR-
CHIONESS DE BRIANVILLE. IN THREE VOLUMES. TRANSLATED
FOM THE ORIGINAL ITALIAN OF THE ABBÉ PIETRO CHIARI.

London: Printed for D. Steel, on Little Tower-Hill, 1771.
I 228p; II 232p; II 120p. 12mo. 7s 6d sewed (CR).
CR 32: 229–30 (Sept 1771).
CtY Hd48.78g; ESTC n065734 (NA PU).

Notes. CR reviews under heading 'Novels'.
6 pp. advs. end vol. 1 and 1 p. advs. end vol. 2. 6 pp. list of contents end each vol.

CR: 'The lovers of variety will be sufficiently gratified by the perusal of this performance: the incidents in it are numerous, and the rapid succession of them, rapid as the revolutions in a pantomime, must be highly delightful to the hasty reader who seizes a new book merely to kill time, and who wishes not, on his arrival at the conclusion of it, to remember a syllable in the pages through which he has scampered, with the expedition of a post-boy through a country town, and with a similar vacancy of mind.'

1771: 39   CHIARI, [Abbé] Pietro.
ROSARA; OR, THE ADVENTURES OF AN ACTRESS: A STORY FROM
REAL LIFE TRANSLATED FROM THE ITALIAN OF PIETRO CHIARI.

London: Printed for R. Baldwin and S. Bladon, in Paternoster Row, 1771.
I viii, 228p; II 239p; III 228p. 12mo. 7s 6d sewed (CR, MR).
CR 32: 231–2 (Sept 1771); MR 44: 498 (June 1771).
BL 12472.aa.12; EM 3: 1; ESTC t083490 (BI D; NA InU-Li, PU, TxU &c.).

Notes. Trans. of *La Commediante in Fortuna* [n.d.]. MR and CR review under the heading 'Novels.'

Paternoster-Row hyphenated in t.p. to vol. 2.

Adv., 'In a few Days will be published', SJC 12–14 Mar 1771; adv. as published 26–28 Mar 1771.

CR: 'If Rosara's narrative, written by herself, is to be relied on, it is a curiosity of the kind; it has very little merit if it is fictitious.'

MR: 'If the narrative be true, it is curious, from that circumstance; if it be a mere fiction, it has little merit. . . .'

1771: 40   [COLTON, Henry].
*THE ELOPEMENT; OR PERFIDY PUNISHED.

London: Printed for F. and J. Noble, in Holborn, and St. Martin's Court (LC), 1771 (LC).

3 vols. 12mo. 7s 6d sewed (CR, MR).
CR 32: 392 (Nov 1771); MR 45: 503 (Dec 1771).
No copy located.

Notes. Adv. LC 30: 499 (21–23 Nov 1771).
Further edn: Dublin, 1772 (Printed for D. Chamberlaine, W. Colles, and T. Walker, 3 vols.), ESTC n054261.

DUBOIS-FONTANELLE, Joseph-Gaspard, THE SHIPWRECK AND ADVEN-TURES OF MONSIEUR PIERRE VIAUD
See App. B: 2

FLEMING, Francis, LIFE AND EXTRAORDINARY ADVENTURES . . . OF TIMOTHY GINNADRAKE
See 1770: 29

1771: 41   GRIFFITH, [Elizabeth].
THE HISTORY OF LADY BARTON, A NOVEL, IN LETTERS, BY MRS GRIFFITH. IN THREE VOLUMES.

London: Printed for T. Davies, in Russel-Street, Covent-garden; and T. Cadell, in the Strand. 1771.

I xv, 272p; II 296p; III 308p. 12mo. 7s 6d sewed (MR), 7s 6d (CR, LC).
CR 32: 372–7 (Nov 1771); MR 46: 165 (Feb 1772); AF I: 1145.
BL 12614.cc.7; EM 335: 3; ESTC t071307 (NA MH-H, NjP, PU &c.).

Notes. Epistolary.
Adv., 'Thursday, Nov. 14, will be published', LC 30: 391 (19–22 Oct 1771).
Extract published LC 30: 489 (19–21 Nov 1771).
Further edn: London, 1773, ESTC n017659. German trans. Leipzig, 1772 (Geschichte der Lady Barton) (Price); French trans. in 1788: Histoire de Lady Barton (Londres [Paris?], 2 vols., 12mo) ESTC t200399, and Delia, ou histoire d'une jeune héritiere (Londres et se trouve en Paris, 3 vols., 12mo) ESTC n016962.

CR: 'Upon the whole, this novel is equally ingenious and sentimental, and contains a natural delineation of the passions through scenes the most interesting, and difficult to support with propriety' (pp. 376–77).

MR: '... the work abounds with affecting incidents, interesting situations, and such rational observations as may be expected from a person who converses with, and knows, the world.'

HULL, Thomas
See THE HISTORY OF SIR WILLIAM HARRINGTON

1771: 42   [?KELLY, Hugh].
THE TUTOR; OR, THE HISTORY OF GEORGE WILSON AND LADY FANNY MELFONT. IN TWO VOLUMES.

> London: Printed for T. Vernor, at Garrick's-Head, St. Michael's-Alley, Cornhill: and J. Chater, No. 39, King-Street, Cheapside, 1771.
> I 211p; II 235p. 12mo. 5s (CR), 5s sewed (MR, LC June), 6s bound (LC May).
> CR 32: 153–4 (Aug 1771); MR 45: 332 (Oct 1771).
> ICU PR3991.T9 1771; ESTC n024384.

Notes. Attributed to Hugh Kelly (ESTC).
Prefatory address 'To the Reader'. Epistolary.
Adv., 'This Month will be published', LC 29: 490 (21–23 May 1771); adv. as published LC 29: 555 (8–11 June 1771).

MR [Gilbert Stuart]: 'The benevolent and virtuous sentiments which abound in this performance are a great recommendation of it. They soften the severe brow of the critic; and, while they induce him to respect the heart of its Author, they excite in him a regret, that he cannot express the highest admiration of his genius.'

1771: 43   [LANGHORNE, John].
LETTERS TO ELEONORA. IN TWO VOLUMES.

> London: Printed for T. Becket, and P. A. De Hondt, in the Strand, 1770/71.
> I (1770) 173p; II (1771) 187p. 8vo. 5s sewed (CR, MR).
> CR 32: 230–1 (Sept 1771); MR 45: 73 (July 1771).
> BL 838.a.7; EM 2389: 2; ESTC t115420 (BI E).

Notes. Letters from John Langhorne to Ann Cracroft (ESTC). Epistolary. 1771 is most likely publication date. 1-p. prefatory advertisement claims that the letters were written during the reign of Queen Anne. 2 pp. advs. end vol. 2.
Adv., 'Speedily will be published', LC 29: 95 (24–26 Jan 1771) and PA 29 Jan 1771; adv. as published LC 29: 427 (2–4 May 1771). Adv., as *Letters to Leonora. Written in the Reign of Queen Anne*, PA 8 May 1771.
CR and MR review under 'Novels'.

CR: 'In these letters the author endeavours to express the sentiments of love agreeably to the emotions of nature, and to exhibit a picture of tender passion in the justest as well as the most lively colours. A man of sense may write *about* that passion; a man of feeling only can paint it.'

MR [Gilbert Stuart]: 'These letters attempt to express the natural sentiments of love, and to exhibit a lively and genuine portrait of that passion. They speak not, however, to the heart. Their Author has preposterously ventured to impress his Reader with sensations and emotions which he himself did not feel.'

1771: 44   LATTER, [Mary].
PRO & CON; OR, THE OPINIONISTS: AN ANCIENT FRAGMENT. PUB-
LISHED FOR THE AMUSEMENT OF THE CURIOUS IN ANTIQUITY.
BY MRS LATTER.

> London: Printed for T. Lowndes, in Fleet-Street; and sold also by the Author at Read-
> ing, 1771.
> viii, 172p. 12mo. 2s (CR), 2s sewed (MR), 2s sewed or 2s 6d bound (LC).
> CR 32: 240 (Sept 1771); MR 45: 156 (Aug 1771); AF I: 1573.
> BL 1208.g.3; EM 2730: 3; ESTC t078294 (NA DFo).

Notes. Leaves C6 and C7 should be pp. 27/28 and 29/30 but they are 27/29 and 28/30; the text
of p. 27 leads on to p. 28, 28 to 29, and 29 to 30 but these pages are in the wrong order; p. 166
misnumbered 165.

Adv., 'Next Tuesday will be published', LC 29: 504 (23–25 May 1771); adv. as published
LC 29: 509 (25–28 May 1771).

MR & CR review under 'Miscellaneous'.

CR: 'An ancient physician would have recommended to the author of this production the
use of black hellebore. What a pity that any thing should be published without the *impri-
matur* of common sense!'

MR [Gilbert Stuart]: 'The Author of this production mistakes for wit, the ravings of a
deranged imagination.'

1771: 45   [?LAWRENCE, Herbert].
THE CONTEMPLATIVE MAN. OR THE HISTORY OF CHRISTOPHER
CRAB, ESQ; OF NORTH WALES.

> London: Printed for J. Whiston, Fleet-Street, 1771.
> I xi, 247p; II viii, 243p. 8vo. 5s (CR), 5s sewed (MR).
> CR 32: 448–53 (Dec 1771); MR 46: 263–4 (Mar 1772); AF I: 1575.
> BL 12613.b.15; EM 223: 1; ESTC t068746 (BI C, D, O; NA CtY-BR, CSmH, DLC, IU,
> NjP, PU &c.).

Notes. ESTC notes as sometimes attributed to Herbert Lawrence, but Lawrence not in author
line of ESTC entry.

Extract published LC 30: 521 (28–30 Nov 1771).

Further edn: Dublin, 1772 (Printed for W. Sleater, D. Chamberlaine, J. Williams, J. A. Husband, W. Colles, T. Walker, 2 vols. in 1, 12mo), EM 7581: 1, ESTC t084648. German trans.
Bern, 1789 (*Der betrachtende Müssiggänger*) (EAG). Facs: FN.

CR: '. . . his present performance is inferior to the *Adventures of Common Sense*. It would
be unjust not to own, at the same time, that the *Contemplative Man* affords more entertainment in the perusal, than there is reason to expect from the title. The Crab family are very
laughable people, and their situations are whimsically described; though the author has
made too rapid a progress from chapter to chapter, and shifted the scenes too frequently'
(pp. 448–9).

MR: '. . . it is not to be ranked with the productions of Fielding, Coventry, Smollett, or
Sterne; of the last of which it is somewhat of an imitation:—it may, rather, be placed on the
same shelf with the Vicar of Wakefield, Arthur O'Bradley, and the Adventures of a Bank
Note.'

[*The Vicar of Wakefield*, 1766, JR 1007, AF I: 1094; *The History and Aventures of Arthur O' Bradley*, 1769, JR 1324, AF I: 2250; *Adventures of a Bank Note* 1770: 23.]

1771: 46   [MACKENZIE, Henry].
THE MAN OF FEELING.
London: Printed for T. Cadell, in the Strand, 1771.
viii, 268p. 12mo. 2s 6d (CR), 2s 6d sewed (MR, LC).
CR 31: 482–3 (June 1771); MR 44: 418 (May 1771); AF I: 1709.
BL 12604.bb.6; EM 91: 2; ESTC t038895 (BI E, O; NA CtY-BR, IU, MH-H, NjP, PU &c.).

Notes. Pp. 162 and 165 are unnumbered and pp. 163 and 164 are misnumbered 164 and 163.
Adv., 'Speedily will be published', LC 29: 263 (14–16 Mar 1771); adv. as published LC 29: 375 (16–18 Apr 1771).
Extract published LC 30: 189–90 (22–24 Aug 1771).
Adv. by W. Strahan and T. Cadell PA 4 Nov 1777 refers to recent newspaper reports ascribing authorship of *The Man of Feeling*, *The Man of the World* (1773: 36), *Julia de Roubigné* (1777: 13) and Mackenzie's poem *The Pursuits of Happiness* to the late Mr Eccles of Bath; Strahan and Cadell declare that they have 'long been intimately acquainted with' Mackenzie and have printed his works from manuscripts in his own hand, have paid him for the copyrights and have reprinted some from Mackenzie's corrected copies.
Further edns: London, 1771, EM 6571: 14, ESTC t118918; Dublin, 1771 (Printed for W. Sleater, D. Chamberlaine, J. Hoey, jun., J. Williams, J. Potts and R. Moncrieffe, 1 vol., 12mo), ESTC t170829; Dublin, 1771, ESTC t170830; London, 1773, EM 91: 2, ESTC t038896; London, 1775, ESTC t038897; 22 further entries in ESTC; 24 post-1800 entries in WC, including Italian trans. Milan, 1818 (*L'uomo di sentimento*); NSTC lists edns in 1801, 1803, 1805, 1807, 1810, 1815, 1820, 1823, 1824, 1826, 1839 and [1850?]. Extracts from *The Man of Feeling*, 'Emily Atkins', 'The Story of Old Edwards' and 'Old Edwards', published in 4 magazines between 1778 and 1810, RM 363, 1199. German trans. Danzig, 1774 (*Der Mann von Gefühl*) (Price); French trans. Londres [Paris], 1775, ESTC t120532. Facs: FN.
   CR: 'By those who have feeling hearts, and a true relish for simplicity in writing, many pages in this miscellaneous volume will be read with satisfaction. There is not indeed fable enough in this volume to keep up the attention of the majority of novel readers; there is not business enough in it for a million: but there are several interesting situations, several striking incidents, several excellent reflections, which sufficiently discover the author's invention and judgment, delicacy and taste.'
   MR [Gilbert Stuart]: 'This performance is written after the manner of Sterne; but it follows at a prodigious distance the steps of that ingenious and sentimental writer.'

1771: 47   MARTEN, Thomas (trans.).
*THE MARRIAGE: OR, HISTORY OF FOUR WELL-KNOWN CHARACTERS. TRANSLATED FROM THE CELEBRATED FRENCH NOVEL OF THE SAME TITLE. BY THOMAS MARTEN, A.M.
London: Wheble, 1771.
2 vols. 12mo. 5s sewed (CR, MR).
CR 32: 231 (Sept 1771); MR 45: 73 (July 1771); AF I: 1760.
ICU PQ1950.M301M3 [missing]; xESTC.

Notes. CR: 'The caprices of love are . . . minutely described in these volumes, but we frequently wish to see delicacy guiding the author's hand.'

MR [Gilbert Stuart]: 'It does not seem to us that the original merited translation.'

MASTERMAN, Miss
See SKINN, Ann Emelinda

MEADES, Anna
See THE HISTORY OF SIR WILLIAM HARRINGTON

N, Sir Francis
See TREYSSAC DE VERGY, Pierre Henri, AUTHENTIC MEMOIRS

1771: 48   [NICHOLS, Elizabeth Eyton].
THE FAULT WAS ALL HIS OWN. IN A SERIES OF LETTERS. BY A
LADY.

>London: Printed for G. Riley, (Successor to W. Cooke,) at his Circulating Library, in
>   Queen Street, May Fair 1771.
>I 239p; II 206p. 12mo. 5s (CR), 5s sewed (MR, LC).
>CR 31: 397 (May 1771); MR 44: 333 (Apr 1771); AF I: 854.
>PU EC75.N5156.771f; ESTC n047311 (BI O; NA CSmH [vol. 1 only]).

Notes. Epistolary.
PU copy has ms. annotation facing t.p.: 'The book was set up by the hands of the Rev. William Tooke FRS . . . who afterwards married in 1771 its author Miss Eyton. In the same year—that of its publication, he gave this copy to my grandfather, who has written his name at the head of the titlepage John Gough Nichols.'
Adv., 'In a few Days will be published', LC 29: 235 (7–9 Mar 1771); adv. as published SJC 14–6 Mar 1771.

CR: 'The writer seems to have taken little pains either in planning or executing her work. The story is irregular, and productive of few interesting events. The characters are imperfectly delineated, and the business assigned them seldom has importance enough to excite the reader's curiosity or concern. Yet these letters are not destitute of merit. They are interspersed with many sprightly sentiments and sensible reflections, and bear the marks of a promising genius. They are the production of a young lady, who is lately married, and now resides at Cronstadt in Russia.'

MR: 'We are told that this is the production of a *young* Lady, of a promising genius; and the work bears sufficient testimony that we are not misinformed; for it abounds with the marks of an immature judgment, and yet affords proofs of a fine imagination. It is defective in plan, characters, and style; but many good sentiments are interspersed in it; and we meet with reflections that would do honour to the pen of a more experienced writer.'

NOGARET, François Félix
See TREYSSAC DE VERGY, Pierre Henri, AUTHENTIC MEMOIRS

1771: 49   POTTER, John.
THE CURATE OF COVENTRY: A TALE. BY JOHN POTTER, AUTHOR

OF THE HISTORY AND ADVENTURES OF ARTHUR O'BRADLEY. IN TWO VOLUMES.

> London: Printed for F. Newbery, the Corner of St. Paul's Church-Yard, 1771.
>
> I 219p; II 263p. 12mo. 5s (CR), 5s sewed (MR, LC).
>
> CR 31: 301–6 (Apr 1771); MR 44: 418 (May 1771); AF I: 2249.
>
> BL 1607/4333; EMf; ESTC t119354 (BI BMu, DBL [vol. 2 only]; NA CtY, MH-H, PU).

Notes. 2 vols. bound in 1.

The History and Adventures of Arthur O'Bradley, 1769, JR 1324, AF I: 2250.

Adv., 'In the Press, and speedily will be published, In Two Volumes in Twelves, Adorned with elegant Frontispieces, designed and engraved by the best Masters', PA 1 Dec 1770; adv. 'In a few Days will be published', LC 29: 295 (23–26 Mar 1771); adv., 'next Monday will be published' LC 29: 343 (6–9 Apr 1771).

CR: 'The novel is, undoubtedly[,] superior to the common run of romances. Though the characters are generally trite, and an uniformity prevails among several of them, yet they are supported in an agreeable manner, and the reader's curiosity is kept awake through the whole narration.'

MR [Gilbert Stuart]: 'Readers of the lower classes may find something to please them in it; but for those who have sensibility, and who can distinguish the strokes of genius, it will have fewer charms.'

1771: 50   RENWICK, William.
THE GENUINE DISTRESSES OF DAMON AND CELIA: IN A SERIES OF LETTERS BETWEEN THE LATE GENERAL CRAUFURD, SIR JOHN HUSSEY DELAVAL, BART. SIR FRANCIS BLAKE DELAVAL, K.B. AND TWO UNFORTUNATE LOVERS. BY WILLIAM RENWICK.

> Bath: Printed by R. Cruttwell, for the Author; And sold by Mr Dodsley, Pall-Mall; Mr Almon, Piccadilly; Mr Griffin, Strand; Mr F. Newbery, Ludgate-Street; and Messrs. Richardson and Urquhart, Royal Exchange, London, 1771.
>
> I x, 222p; II 251p. 12mo. 6s sewed (CR), 6s (MR, LC).
>
> CR 32: 311–12 (Oct 1771); MR 45: 331–2 (Oct 1771); AF I: 2347.
>
> BL Cup.404.b.20; ESTC t140071 (NA PU, TxHR).

Notes. Renwick was promised a commission for voting for Sir John Hussey Delaval in the by-election of Jan 1765 but the reward never materialised.

6-pp. list of subscribers (unn.). Introduction iii–x, signed 'The Author', Wokingham, 29 May 1771. Text of novel starts on p. 3. Epistolary.

Adv., 'By Subscription. In the Press, and will be published some Day in May, Handsomely printed on a fine Paper, and ornamented with an elegant engraved Frontispiece', LC 29: 308 (28–30 Mar 1771); adv. as published LC 30: 324 (1–3 Oct 1771).

Extract published LC 30: 465 (2–14 Nov 1771).

Both review journals are doubtful about whether this is a work of fiction, although both review under the heading 'Novels'.

CR: 'Considered as literary compositions, the letters contained in these volumes are no objects of criticism: and even those written by the unfortunate lovers themselves, excite not so much compassion as they would otherwise have done, perhaps, if there had been more of the pathetic and less of the lamentable in them.'

MR: 'Although we have classed this publication with those works of invention usually ranged under the denomination of *Novels*, it contains nevertheless a recital of facts relating to the unhappy Author, William Renwick, a young apothecary, formerly a surgeon's mate in one of our regiments, but at present reduced to the humble station of a journeyman, in a shop at Wokingham.'

1771: 51   [RUSSELL, William].
SENTIMENTAL TALES, IN TWO VOLUMES.

> London: Printed by John Dixcey Cornish, at Number 4, Printinghouse-yard, Black Friars; and sold by J. Wilkie in St Paul's Churchyard, 1771.
> I 204p; II 200p. 12mo. 5s sewed (CR, MR).
> CR 31: 231–2 (Mar 1771); MR 44: 333 (Mar 1771); AF I: 2426.
> BL RB.23.a.6834; EMf; ESTC t223119.

Notes. 3-pp. preface. Vol. 1 contains 'The Progress of Love', 'The Extravagance of Passion' and 'The Freethinker'; vol. 2 contains 'The Rake in Love' and 'The Lapse of the Heart'.
CR includes under heading 'Novels' and MR under 'Novels, &c.'.
Adv. LC 29: 159 (12–14 Feb 1771); more elaborate adv. LC 29: (19–21 Feb 1771) points out that 'The Extravagance of Passion' is a continuation of 'the celebrated Story of Madame de L***, from the Sentimental Journey'. Re-adv., with quotation from LM, LC 29: 347 (9–11 Apr 1771): 'The Author of the SENTIMENTAL TALES takes this opportunity of telling Malignitas the Critical Reviewer, that he scorns his impotent Malice, while favoured with the Approbation of the Public, and supported by the Testimony of every other literary Journal.'
Extracts published LC 29: 212 and 245 (28 Feb–2 Mar and 9–12 Mar 1771).
Further edn: London, 1772, ESTC n021973.

   CR: 'If these two volumes, which we have endured the labour of perusing, should be weighed in opposition to any work that can boast the merit of affording the least instruction, they would appear but as a few floating atoms which fall unheeded into the scale, without the power to shake it. Such light, such fluttering stuff, such pages of inanity are seldom seen; and the lover may truly be said *to bestride the Gossamour* who trusts his conduct to the guidance of a Palinurus like this.'

   MR: 'In these *sentimental* productions are comprehended some very warm ideas, and allusions to situations rather *sensual* than sentimental. The Author, in some parts of his work, imitates Sterne, with the usual success of imitators.'

1771: 52   SKINN, [Ann Emelinda].
THE OLD MAID; OR, HISTORY OF MISS RAVENSWORTH. IN A SERIES OF LETTERS BY MRS SKINN, LATE MISS MASTERMAN, OF YORK, IN THREE VOLUMES.

> London: Printed for J. Bell, at his Circulating-Library, near Exeter-Exchange, in the Strand; and C. Etherington, at York, 1771.
> I 200p; II 195p; III 154p. 8vo. 7s 6d (CR), 7s 6d sewed (MR, LC).
> CR 30: 478–9 (Dec 1770); MR 43: 500 (Dec 1770); AF I: 2558.
> BL 12611.df.24; EM 163: 4; ESTC t057368 (NA CaOTU, MH-H, PU &c.).

Notes. 14 pp. advs. end vol. 2. Epistolary.
Post-dated; adv. as published SJC 1–4 Dec 1770; 'A New Novel, elegantly printed, in three neat Pocket Volumes, on a fine Writing Paper. . . . Those Gentlemen and Ladies in different

Parts of the Kingdom, who so earnestly recommended the Publication and subscribed their Names, may be immediately supplied with the Books, by sending their Orders, and second Subscription Money to the Publishers.' Adv. LC 29: 99 (26–29 Jan 1771).

Further edn: Dublin, 1771 (Printed by J. Potts, 3 vols. in 1, 12mo), ESTC n041546; London, 1790 (WC), xESTC.

Adv. as new SJC 11–13 Nov 1790.

MR: 'Although there are defects in this work gross enough to disgust a critical reader, there are parts of it that will be far from disagreeable to a good-natured one, who is fond of novels, and not too nice in the choice of them.'

1771: 53   [SMOLLETT, Tobias].
THE EXPEDITION OF HUMPHRY CLINKER. BY THE AUTHOR OF RODERICK RANDOM. IN THREE VOLUMES.

London, Printed for W. Johnston, in Ludgate-Street; and B. Collins, in Salisbury, 1771. I xv, 250p; II 249p; III 275p. 12mo. 9s (CR), 7s 6d sewed (MR), 9s bound (LC).

CR 32: 81–8 (Aug 1771); MR 45: 152 (Aug 1771); AF I: 2595.

C S727.d.77.16-; EM 5094: 6; ESTC t055323 (BI BL, E, MRu &c.; NA AzU, CaOHM, CLU-C &c.).

Notes. Misdated 1671 in vol. 1.

The Adventures of Roderick Random 1748.

Adv., 'In the Press, and speedily will be published, in Two Volumes', LC 29: 71 (17–19 Jan 1771); adv., 'Next Month will be published', LC 29: 408 (25–27 Apr 1771); adv., 'Next Monday will be published', LC 29: 555 (8–11 June 1771); adv. as published LC 29: 582 (5–18 June 1771).

Extract published LC 29: 580 (5–18 June 1771). Epistolary.

Further edns: London, 1771, ESTC t055324; Dublin, 1771 (Printed for A. Leathley, J. Exshaw, H. Saunders, & 12 others, 2 vols., 12mo), EM 3743: 5, ESTC t055326; London, 1772, EM 218: 6, ESTC t055327; Dublin, 1774, EM 164: 2, ESTC t055328; Dublin, 1775, ESTC t185980; 21 further entries in ESTC; WC has 20 entries between 1800 and 1850. Reprinted *Novelist's Magazine*, 1785, RM 380. German trans. Leipzig, 1772 (*Humphry Klinke Reisen*) (EAG); French trans. Paris, 1826 (*Voyage de Humphry Clinker*) (HWS).

CR: 'The celebrated author of this production is one of those few writers who have discovered an original genius. His novels are not more distinguished for the natural management of the fable, and a fertility of interesting incidents, than for a strong, lively, and picturesque description of characters. The same vigour of imagination that animates his other works, is conspicuous in the present, where we are entertained with a variety of scenes and characters almost unanticipated' (p. 81).

MR [Gilbert Stuart]: 'Some modern wits appear to have entertained a notion that there is but one kind of *indecency* in writing; and that, provided they exhibit nothing of a lascivious nature, they may freely paint, with their pencils dipt in the most odious materials that can possibly be raked together for the most filthy and disgustful colouring.'

1771: 54   [TREYSSAC DE VERGY, Pierre Henri].
*THE AUTHENTIC MEMOIRS OF THE COUNTESS DE BARRÉ, THE FRENCH KING'S MISTRESS, CAREFULLY COLLATED FROM A MANU-

SCRIPT IN THE POSSESSION OF THE DUCHESS OF VILLEROY, BY SIR
FRANCIS N——.

> London: Roson, 1771 (MR).
> 1 vol. 12mo. 3s bound (MR, PA).
> MR 44: 92 (Jan 1771); AF I: 120.
> No copy located.

Notes. Not by the Countess de Barré [Jeanne Bécu, comtesse du Barry]. Author attribution
from MR. ESTC: Sometimes attributed to François Félix Nogaret.
Adv., 'Speedily will be published.... Printed for J. Roson, No. 45, St. Martin's Le Grand', PA
11 Dec 1770; adv. as published PA 15 Dec 1770.
Adv. SJC 25–27 Dec 1770.
Further edn: London, 1771, EM 5602: 2, ESTC t067755. 1772 'French' edn 'Traduits de
l'Anglois' Printed for J. Roson and G. Reily, ESTC n035159; German trans. Cologne and
Leipzig, 1772 (*Glaubenswürdige Nachrichten von der Gräfin von Barre*) (Price).
   MR: 'Another heap of rubbish swept out of Mons. de Vergy's garret. This foreigner, who
has so impudently thrust himself into the English Grubean society, appears determined to fill
all our booksellers shops, stalls, and circulating libraries, with lies and obscenity; the only
studies in which he seems ambitious of excelling. In truth, we are sorry to see the Chevalier
so grossly misapplying his talents; for he certainly is capable of better things.'

1771: 55   [TREYSSAC DE VERGY, Pierre Henri].
*THE MISTAKES OF THE HEART: OR, MEMOIRS OF LADY CARO-
LINE PELHAM, AND LADY VICTORIA NEVIL.

> London: Shatwell, 1771 (CR, MR).
> 'Vol. IV. and last'. 12mo. Shatwell (CR, MR); 2s 6d sewed (MR), 3s sewed (CR).
> CR 33: 182 (Feb 1772); MR 46: 164 (Feb 1772).
> No copy located.

Notes. This vol. is a continuation of the 3 vols., 1769, JR 345, AF I: 2774.
   CR: 'This volume is not equal to the foregoing ones in point of spirit, but it is superior to
them in point of decency.'
   MR: 'If Monsieur de Vergy had ever been really acquainted with persons of distinction in
this country, or had seen any of their letters, he could not have so egregiously mistaken their
style and manner.'

1771: 56   TREYSSAC DE VERGY, [Pierre Henri].
THE PALINODE: OR, THE TRIUMPHS OF VIRTUE OVER LOVE: A
SENTIMENTAL NOVEL IN WHICH ARE PAINTED TO THE LIFE THE
CHARACTERS AND MANNERS OF SOME OF THE MOST CELE-
BRATED BEAUTIES IN ENGLAND. BY MR. TREYSSAC DE VERGY.

> London: Printed for G. Woodfall, Charing-Cross, and T. Evans, No. 54, Paternoster-
>   Row, n.d. [1771].
> I 242p. II 210p. 12mo. 5s sewed (CR, MR).
> CR 32: 230 (Sept 1771); MR 45: 73 (July 1771); AF I: 2777.
> PU Singer-Mend PR3736.T734.P3.1771; ESTC n038118.

Notes. ESTC date: 1770?

Vol. 1 dedication 'To the English Ladies' signed Treyssac de Vergy.

Adv., 'This Month will be published', SJC 1–5 Mar 1771.

CR: 'The Palinode is, in general, a decent performance: if a few passages, of an inflammatory nature, were expunged, it would be an unexceptionable one. There are several scenes drawn in it with a delicate hand, and which sufficiently prove the author to be acquainted with the inmost recesses of the female heart. How much fair fame does he lose, whenever he sends a volume to the press unfit for the perusal of the fair sex!'

MR [Gilbert Stuart]: 'This novel is by much the most decent and unexceptionable that has fallen from the pen of Mons. De Vergy.'

VOLTAIRE, François Marie Arouet de, **THE PUPIL OF NATURE**

first trans. as *L'Ingenu; or the Sincere Huron*, 1768, JR 1239.

1771: 57　　[WALL, Anne].

THE LIFE OF LAMENTHER: A TRUE HISTORY. WRITTEN BY HERSELF. IN FIVE PARTS. CONTAINING A JUST ACCOUNT OF THE MANY MISFORTUNES SHE UNDERWENT, OCCASIONED BY THE ILL TREATMENT OF AN UNNATURAL FATHER.

London: Printed for the Proprietor, 1771.

vii, 221p. 8vo. 4s 6d sewed (CR), 5s half bound (MR).

CR 32: 471 (Dec 1771); MR 46: 77–78 (Jan 1772); AF I: 2894.

BL 1416.k.60; EM 2771: 11; ESTC t040958 (BI E, O [imperf.], SAN; NA CSmH, DLC, ICN, PU).

Notes. ESTC quotes author's statement that 'none of these books printed or sold by the author's leave, but what have the initials of her name annexed, in her own hand-writing' on the prefatory advertisement/errata leaf. One of the BL's copies [992.h.16(3)] lacks this leaf. 'To the Reader' iii–v; 'A Short Epistle to the Curious' (in verse) vi–vii; 2-pp. list of subscribers; 1 p. adv. at end for subscription edn of the same author's poems.

Note in BL copy: 'Lamenther i.e. Ann Wall 13 October 1771'.

CR and MR give bookseller as Evans.

CR, despite some belief in the story, reviews as a novel; MR reviews under 'Miscellaneous' and treats it as a true, if possibly exaggerated, story.

1771: 58　　WIELAND, [Christoph Martin]; WINTERSTED, Mr (*trans.*).

SOCRATES OUT OF HIS SENSES: OR, DIALOGUES OF DIOGENES OF SINOPE. TRANSLATED FROM THE GERMAN OF WIELAND, BY MR. WINTERSTED.

London: Printed for T. Davies, in Russel-Street, Covent-Garden, 1771.

I xxvii, 115p; II 134p. 8vo. 4s sewed (CR, SJC), 4s bound (MR).

CR 33: 216–18 (Mar 1772); MR 46: 624 (June 1772).

BL 12331.aaa.32; EM 939: 15; ESTC t099053 [BI C, Dt, Owo; NA CaOHM, CLU-S/C, TxU &c.).

Notes. Trans. of *Sokrates mainomenos oder die Dialogen des Diogenes von Sinope* (Leipzig, 1770).

2 pp. advs. end both vols.

Adv., 'In Two neat Pocket Vols. with Frontispieces to each Vol.', with quotations from CR
and MR, SJC 6–8 Aug 1772; additional booksellers are J. Ridley, in St. James's-Street and R.
Baldwin, Pater-noster-Row.

Further edn: Newburgh, N.Y., 1797, ESTC w022294. French trans. Dresden and Paris, 1772
(*Socrate en délire*) (BGR).

MR: 'An ingenious writer has given the above whimsical title to a work abounding with
delicate satire, pleasant humour, and excellent sentiments; in which he seems frequently to
have had his eye upon our admirable STERN. But why he has given the name of Socrates the
lead, in his title-page, we are at a loss to conceive, since Diogenes is the hero of this performance, and Socrates is never personally introduced.'

1771: 59   [WILMOT, Frederick].
CUCKOLDOM TRIUMPHANT OR, MATRIMONIAL INCONTINENCE VINDICATED. ILLUSTRATED WITH INTRIGUES PUBLIC AND PRI-VATE, ANCIENT AND MODERN. BY A GENTLEMAN OF DOCTORS COMMONS. TO WHICH IS ADDED, A LOOKING-GLASS FOR EACH SEX.

London: Printed for T. Thorn, in Pater-noster Row. n.d. [1771].
I 203p; II 192p. 12mo. 5s sewed (CR, MR).
CR 32: 154 (Aug 1771); MR 45: 153 (Aug 1771); AF I: 564.
BL 1489.r.4; EM 2962: 8; ESTC t062268.

Notes. Dedication 'To the British Nobility and Gentry' signed 'Cornuto'. Vol. 1 has 'Finis' at
end. Vol. 2 drophead title, 'Horn Tales. Tit for Tat: or, the Cuckolds Reconciled'.

CR: 'We are certainly ashamed to say that we have read the volumes before us; for among
the numbers which have been poured in upon us since the commencement of this prolific,
scriblerian year, they are much the worst in many respects which we have perused. By these
volumes, indeed, replete with bad language, and bad reasoning, crude conceits, and clumsy
irony, to say nothing of the indelicacies and indecencies scattered through them with a liberal hand, the public is more than imposed upon—it is insulted.'

MR [Gilbert Stuart]: 'This impudent apology for matrimonial incontinence unites excessive dulness with obscenity, and is, in the highest degree, detestable.'

CR states that bookseller is Roson, but this is because the vols. were re-issued (and reviewed)
with a new title page as:

CUPID TURNED SPY UPON HYMEN; OR, MATRIMONIAL INTRIGUES IN POLITE
LIFE, BOTH PUBLIC AND PRIVATE, A NOVEL, BY FREDERICK WILMOT ESQ. (Lon-
don: Printed for J. Roson, No. 54, St. Martin's le Grand. n.d. [ESTC: 1777?]), rev. CR 32: 230
(Sept 1771); MR 45: 153 (Aug 1771), ESTC n003826 (NA CLU-S/C call no. PR3765.W547c).
Adv. LC 30: 24 (4–6 July 1771): 'Printed for J. Roson, at No. 54, in St. Martin's le-Grand; and
may be had of all the Booksellers in Town and Country.'

MR points out: 'The foregoing worthless production [i.e. *Cuckoldom Triumphant*]
vamped with a new title-page'. The t.p. is added to the Thorn vol. CR also comments on
Roson's 'endeavouring to impose upon the public, by re-advertising the same production
under a new title'.

1771: 60   [WYNNE, John Huddlestone].
THE MAN OF HONOUR OR, THE HISTORY OF HARRY WATERS, ESQ.

London: Printed for F. and J. Noble, at their respective Circulating Libraries, near Middle-Row, Holborn; and St Martin's Court, near Leicester Square, 1771.

I 241p; II missing; III missing. 12mo. Vol. 1 2s 6d sewed (CR, MR); vols. 2–3 5s sewed (MR).

CR 32: 311 (Oct 1771), MR 45: 503 (Dec 1771) vol. 1; CR 34: 473 (Dec 1772) vols. 2–3; MR 48: 71 (Jan 1773) vols. 2–3; AF I: 1735, 1736.

ViWC PR 3991.A1 M36 177 Spec Coll—Webb-Prentis Coll [vol. 1 only]; xESTC.

Notes. Adv. LC 30: 384 (17–19 Oct 1771): 'By J. H. Wynne'.

CR 32: 'We cannot, as men of honour, recommend the History of Harry Waters, esq. as a composition which will stand the test of criticism; we do not remember to have met with a more contemptible personage than the hero of this piece, nor can we discover the propriety of his historian's calling him "the Man of Honour," characteristically.'

CR 34: 'By the way too, this same history of 'Squire Waters is an egregious imposition on the public, as a great part of the second volume, and almost all of the last, have no sort of connection with the first part'.

MR 48: 'Vain were the hopes we expressed, on reading the first of these stupid volumes, that we should never be troubled with any more of them. The public, or the circulating librarians, have formed a different judgment of the merit of this work, and, lo! the sequel is before us.'

1772

1772: 1   ANON.
THE ADVANTAGES OF DELIBERATION; OR, THE FOLLY OF INDISCRETION. IN TWO VOLUMES.

London: Printed for Robinson and Roberts, No. 25, Paternoster-Row, 1772.

I 235p; II 222p. 12mo. 5s (CR), 5s sewed (MR, LC).

CR 33: 83 (Jan 1772); MR 46: 79 (Jan 1772); AF I: 12.

PU Singer-Mend.PR3291.A1.A24.1772; EM 1015: 1; ESTC n002708 (BI BL [imperf: lacks 2 pp. in vol. 1]; NA CSmH, MH-H).

Notes. Epistolary.

Adv., 'This Month will be published', LC 30: 599 (19–21 Dec 1771).

German trans. Leipzig, 1778 (*Unglückliche Folgen eines Fehlers aus übereilung, eine moralische Geschichte*) (Price).

CR: 'These volumes are evidently written with a design to deter thoughtless women from beholding libertines in too favourable a light, and to induce them to believe that conjugal felicity cannot be expected from men of a roving disposition.'

MR [Gilbert Stuart]: 'To render his performance interesting, our Author has ventured beyond the bounds of probability and nature: But though, by this means, he may create the surprize, and rouse the curiosity, of vulgar readers, the extravagance of the events he has produced will necessarily disgust those who can judge of what may happen in real life, and who know the principles and motives of human conduct.'

1772: 2   ANON.
THE BIRMINGHAM COUNTERFEIT; OR, INVISIBLE SPECTATOR. A SENTIMENTAL ROMANCE. IN TWO VOLUMES.

> London: Printed for S. Bladon, at No. 28, in Paternoster-Row, 1772.
> I 268p; II 280p. 12mo. 6s (MR).
> CR 33: 325–7 (Apr 1772); MR 46: 540 (May 1772); AF I: 192.
> BL N.2510; EM 1500: 1; ESTC n015638 (NA CtY, IU, MH-H, PU &c.).

Notes. Further edns. (chapbooks, as *The Adventures of a Halfpenny: commonly called a Birmingham Halfpenny, or, Counterfeit*): Banbury, 1820 (WC); Banbury, c.1830 (WC). Facs: FN.

CR: 'The epithet *sentimental* is used now so frequently, that we are at a loss to guess what idea some writers have of it. We have here a *sentimental* Romance. What sort of a romance, gentle reader, do you expect this to be?—Why a romance that has sentiment.—The arch rogue of an author!' (p. 325).

MR: 'A Birmingham Shilling recites its travels and adventures, on the hacknied and worn-out plan on which the *Adventures of a Guinea*, with a multitude of other Invisible Spies, have been written.'

1772: 3   ANON.
THE CAUTIOUS LOVER; OR, THE HISTORY OF LORD WOBURN. BY A YOUNG GENTLEMAN OF OXFORD. IN TWO VOLUMES.

> London: Printed for T. Davies, in Russel-Street, Covent-Garden; and T. Cadell, in the Strand, 1772.
> I 245p; II 247p. 12mo. 5s sewed (CR, MR).
> CR 33: 180–1 (Feb 1772); MR 46: 265 (Mar 1772); AF I: 353.
> CU-A PR 3991.A6.Y6; xESTC.

Notes. Epistolary.
Adv., 'In the Press, and speedily will be published', LC 30: 583 (14–17 Dec 1771); adv. 'will be published in a few Days', LC 31: 20 (4–7 Jan 1772).
Further edn: Dublin, 1773 (Printed for James Williams, 2 vols. in 1, 12mo), ESTC n026925.

CR: '. . . we are of opinion that it affords many lessons to the youth of both sexes; that it consists of characters well drawn, distinguished and sustained; situations interesting and affecting; and of incidents unexpected, yet natural.'

MR [Gilbert Stuart]: 'This is one of those insipid performances which we take up without pleasure, and lay aside without regret.'

1772: 4   ANON.
THE EGG, OR THE MEMOIRS OF GREGORY GIDDY, ESQ: WITH THE LUCUBRATIONS OF MESSRS. FRANCIS FLIMSY, FREDERICK FLORID, AND BEN BOMBAST. TO WHICH ARE ADDED, THE PRIVATE OPINIONS OF PATTY POUT, LUCY LUSCIOUS, AND PRISCILLA POSITIVE. ALSO THE MEMOIRS OF A RIGHT HONOURABLE PUPPY. OR, THE BON TON DISPLAY'D: TOGETHER WITH ANEC-DOTES OF A RIGHT HONOURABLE SCOUNDREL. CONCEIVED BY A CELEBRATED HEN, AND LAID BEFORE THE PUBLIC BY A FAMOUS COCK-FEEDER.

London: Printed for S. Smith, in Pater-Noster-Row, and sold by all other Booksellers in Town and Country. n.d. [ESTC: 1772?].

3, 232p. 12mo. 3s (CR, MR), 2s 6d or 3s neatly bound (SJC).

CR 34: 472 (Dec 1772); MR 47: 411 (Nov 1772); AF I: 717.

BL 12330.d.36; EM 836: 11; ESTC t096811 (Bl MRu [imperf.—lacks 2 pp.]; NA CSmH, MH-H, NjP &c.).

Notes. Adv., 'In a handsome Pocket Volume, adorned with a humourous Frontispiece', SJC 1–3 Oct 1772.

Facs: FN.

CR: 'This *funny* author has given us so ample a specimen of his wit in the title page, that little remains to be said. The *Egg* is a vile egg, and the *Cockfeeder* is a vile cockfeeder: the *Hen* likewise is of a bad breed; and this precious pair of fowls have made the most disagreeable *cackling* we ever remember to have heard. Ribaldry is always disgusting, but low ribaldry is intolerable.'

MR: 'The title-page is enough.'

THE ELOPEMENT
See COLTON, Henry (1771: 40)

1772: 5   ANON.
ERMINA; OR, THE FAIR RECLUSE. A NOVEL. IN A SERIES OF LET-TERS BY A LADY, AUTHOR OF DORINDA CALSBY [*sic*], &C. TWO VOLUMES.

London: Printed for S. Bladon, No 28, Pater-noster-Row, 1772.

I 267p; II 173p. 12mo. 6s (MR).

MR 47: 324 (Oct 1772); AF I: 790.

CSmH 446849; ESTC n045862.

Notes. By same author as *The History of Lord Aimworth* (1773: 7).

7 pp. advs. end vol. 2. Epistolary.

The History of Miss Dorinda Catsby 1772: 11.

Further edn: London, 1789, EM 289: 5, ESTC t064189.

MR [Gilbert Stuart]: 'A most insupportable languor and heaviness crawls through these volumes; in which we are struck with no novelty of incidents, or of character; we are surprized with no unexpected or interesting situations; nor are we charmed with any delicacy of sentiment, or of manner.'

1772: 6   ANON.
THE FEELINGS OF THE HEART: OR, THE LETTERS OF A COUNTRY GIRL. WRITTEN BY HERSELF, AND ADDRESSED TO A LADY OF QUALITY. IN TWO VOLUMES.

London: Printed for F. and J. Noble, at their respective Circulating Libraries, near Middle Row, Holborn, and Saint Martin's Court, near Leicester Square, 1772.

I 240p; II 205p. 12mo. 5s sewed (CR), 5s (MR).

CR 33: 255 (Mar 1772); MR 46: 625 (June 1772); AF I: 873.

MH-H *EC75.A100.772f; EM 1102: 11; ESTC n008060 (NA NIC).

Notes. 3 pp. advs. end vol. 2. Epistolary.

CR: 'The Country Girl tells her story agreeably enough; but few of her readers will, we imagine, give credit to it, as she deals more in the marvellous than the probable. Staggered with the improbabilities in some parts, and perplexed by the intricacies in others, they will often find themselves disposed to exclaim, with Sir Gregory Gazette, "Good now! wonderful! wonderful."'

MR [Gilbert Stuart]: 'It is conducted with a good deal of art, expressed with tolerable purity, and may be read with some degree of pleasure.'

1772: 7 ANON.
FEMALE FRAILTY; OR, THE HISTORY OF MISS WROUGHTON.

> London: Printed for F. and J. Noble, at their respective Circulating Libraries, near Middle Row, Holborn, and Saint Martin's Court, near Leicester Square, 1772.
> I 239p; II 222p. 12mo. 6s (MR), 5s sewed (CR, LC).
> CR 32: 393 (Nov 1771); MR 46: 78–9 (Jan 1772).
> PU Singer-Mend. 823.F347; ESTC n006603 (NA DLC).

Notes. 1 p. adv. end vol. 1; 10 pp. advs. end vol. 2.
Post-dated; adv. as published LC 30: 499 (21–23 Nov 1771).

MR [Gilbert Stuart]: 'To judge from this performance, one would imagine, that women were mere objects of luxury and voluptuousness; and that both the sexes had nothing to which they should attend but the glory of conquests[,] the rivalship of beauty, the garniture of dress, and the arts of seduction; and, in fine, to practice all the allurements that work upon the senses.'

THE FINE LADY
See BRISCOE, Sophia

1772: 8 ANON.
FREDERIC: OR, THE FORTUNATE BEGGAR. WHEREIN IS DISPLAYED THE VARIOUS EVENTS IN HUMAN LIFE, IN A SERIES OF LETTERS, COPIED FROM THE ORIGINALS.

> London: Printed for J. Roson, at No. 54, in St. Martin's le Grand, and sold by S. Bladon, and W. Goldsmith, in Pater-noster-row, n.d. [1772?].
> I 191p; II 208p. 12mo. 6s (CR, MR), 5s sewed or 6s bound (SJC).
> CR 35: 79 (Jan 1773); MR 47: 487 (Dec 1772); AF I: 968.
> O Vet.A5f.287,288; EMf; ESTC t182796.

Notes. ESTC gives date as 1777?
Epistolary.
Adv. SJC 8–10 June 1773.

CR: 'The originals from which these letters are said to be copied, ought to have remained in perpetual oblivion. They seem to have been printed only to receive condemnation, for they are destitute of the smallest pretensions to afford entertainment.'

MR [Gilbert Stuart]: 'These volumes offer nothing that is new, or that is interesting. They contain only a dull repetition of dull scenes.'

1772: 9   ANON.

GENUINE MEMOIRS OF MISS HARRIET MELVIN AND MISS LEONORA STANWAY; IN A SERIES OF LETTERS: BY A YOUNG LADY OF GLOCESTER.

London: Printed for J. Fuller, in Ave-Maria-Lane, 1772.
215p. 12mo. 2s 6d sewed (CR), 3s (MR).
CR 33: 182 (Feb 1772); MR 46: 264–5 (Mar 1772); AF I: 1056.
BL 12604.cc.9; EM 128: 9; ESTC t124403 (NA CLU-S/C, MH-H).

Notes. 1 p. advs. end vol. Epistolary.

CR: 'The story is uninteresting, and told in so spiritless a manner, that we cannot compliment the young lady of Gloucester on her literary abilities. We are always sorry to be under the necessity of condemning the production of a female pen; but when ladies, not contented with handing about their manuscripts among their flattering friends, submit them to the public press, they must expect to hear disagreeable truths, if their writings are not calculated to engage the public attention.'

MR: 'This novel is *decent*, at least, though not a very important performance. The language is easy and correct; and the sentiments, though trite, are just.'

THE HERMITAGE
See HUTCHINSON, William

THE HISTORY OF FEMALE FAVOURITES
See LA ROCHE-GUILHEM, Anne de

1772: 10   ANON.

*THE HISTORY OF MISS CAROLINA MANNERS: IN A SERIES OF GENUINE LETTERS TO A FRIEND.

London: Printed for the Author, and sold by T. Evans, 1772.
3 vols. 12mo. 7s 6d sewed (CR, MR).
CR 33: 256 (Mar 1772); MR 46: 265 (Mar 1772); AF I: 1258.
No copy located.

Notes. Epistolary.
CR quotes from the prefatory advertisement and says that 'compassion is strongly excited, and, at the same time, criticism is excluded.'
MR questions whether it is fiction, and suggests that a sequel may be forthcoming.

1772: 11   ANON.

THE HISTORY OF MISS DORINDA CATSBY, AND MISS EMILIA FAULKNER; IN A SERIES OF LETTERS.

London: Printed and sold by S. Bladon, Pater-noster-Row, 1772.
I 188, 2p; II 130p. 12mo. 6s (CR), 5s sewed (MR, SJC), 5s sewed, 6s bound (adv.).
CR 34: 77 (July 1772); MR 47: 151 (Aug 1772); AF I: 1261.
BL 12611.aa.6; EM 7266: 6; ESTC t031414 (NA CSmH).

Notes. By same author as *Ermina; or, the Fair Recluse* (1772: 5) and *The History of Lord Aimworth* (1773: 7).

3 pp. advs. end vol. 1 and 10 pp. end vol. 2. Epistolary.

Adv. SJC 9–11 July 1772.

Adv. end vol. 3 of *The Noble Lovers* (1772: 19).

CR: 'Invention, judgment, and taste, are all wanting to rescue these volumes from oblivion. They will be probably forgotten as soon as they are read. None of the characters in them are strikingly marked, or happily varied: the incidents, though not unnatural, are so common as to be tiresome, particularly from the poverty of the language in which they are related.'

MR [Gilbert Stuart]: 'Some romance-writing female (as we guess, from the style) with her head full of love scenes,—shady groves, and purling streams, honourable passion and wicked purposes,—has here put together a flimsy series of such adventures and descriptions as we usually meet with in the amorous trash of the times.'

THE HISTORY OF SIDNEY AND VOLSAN
See BACULARD D'ARNAUD, François-Thomas-Marie de

1772: 12   ANON.
THE INDISCREET CONNECTION; OR, THE HISTORY OF MISS LESTER. IN TWO VOLUMES.

> London: Printed for F. and J. Noble, at their respective Circulating Libraries, near Middle-Row, Holborn, and St. Martin's-Court, near Leicester-Square, 1772.
> I 238p; II 226p. 12mo. 5s sewed (CR, MR).
> CR 33: 256 (Mar 1772); MR 46: 539 (May 1772); AF I: 1362.
> O 249.s.610–611; xESTC.

Notes. Epistolary. 1p. adv. verso of half-title vol. 2; 10 pp. advs. end vol. 2.

Adv. in *The Way to Lose Him* 1773: 21.

CR: 'The moral of this piece merits the attention of girls who are ambitious of emulating their superiors in a station of life they have no reasonable pretensions to assume.'

MR [Gilbert Stuart]: 'In these volumes the fair sex will meet with some of those lessons of prudence, which many of them are too apt to neglect.'

1772: 13   ANON.
THE INVOLUNTARY INCONSTANT; OR, THE HISTORY OF MISS FRANCFORT. A NOVEL. BY THE EDITOR OF THE FATAL COMPLIANCE.

> London: Printed for T. Jones, at his Circulating Library in the Strand, opposite Hungerford-Street. And B. Jones, at his Circulating Library, in Oxford-street, the Corner of Berwick-street, 1772.
> I 208p; II 222p. 12mo. 5s sewed (CR, MR).
> CR 33: 256 (Mar 1772); MR 46: 456 (Apr 1772); AF I: 1376.
> BL 012611.g.16; EM 8424: 1; ESTC t064740.

Notes. 3 pp. advs. end vol. 1; 2 pp. end vol. 2. Epistolary.

BL copy in original paper wrappers.

Fatal Compliance 1771: 14.

CR: 'It was unnecessary for the author of this Novel to tell us that it is a Novel; as nothing can induce us to believe that the characters drawn in it ever existed, or that the events related ever happened.'

MR [Gilbert Stuart]: 'There are scenes of distress in these volumes, but they fail to affect the heart: we cannot sympathise with what is extravagant, and out of the order of nature.'

1772: 14   ANON.
*THE IRISHMAN; OR THE FAVOURITE OF FORTUNE. A SATIRICAL NOVEL FOUNDED UPON FACTS.

London: Printed for W. Goldsmith, No. 24, Pater-noster-Row (SJC), 1772 (SJC).

2 vols. 12mo. 6s (CR), 6s bound (MR, SJC).

CR 34: 472 (Dec 1772); MR 47: 487 (Dec 1772); AF I: 1379.

No copy of 1st edn. located.

Notes. Dedicated to George, Lord Viscount Townsend, late Lord Lieutenant of Ireland (SJC).

Adv. SJC 3–5 Dec 1772.

Further edn: London, 1772, ESTC n016832.

Trans. into French in 1779 by Jean-Baptiste-René Robinet and BL has imperf. copy (lacks vol. 2) of 1784 'Amsterdam' reissue [ESTC t209211]. German trans. (from the French) Breslau, 1780 (*Günstling des Glücks*) (Price).

CR: 'This novel will neither instruct nor entertain the reader. The *facts* are destitute of probability, and the narration is without humour.'

MR: 'Unnatural, frivolous, and indelicate; and much in the manner of M. de Vergy's worst performances.'

LETTERS FROM THE MARCHIONESS OF POMPADOUR
See BARBÉ-MARBOIS, François, Marquis de, App. B: 1

1772: 15   ANON.
*LOVE IN A NUNNERY: OR, THE SECRET HISTORY OF MISS CHARLOTTE HAMILTON, A YOUNG LADY; WHO AFTER A VARIETY OF UNCOMMON INCIDENTS, WAS FORCED INTO A CONVENT, &C, &C.

London: Printed for Roson. n.d. (MR).

2 vols. 12mo. 5s (MR).

MR 46: 78 (Jan 1772); AF I: 1694.

No copy located.

Notes. MR: 'A shameless catch-penny jobb, meanly pilfered from old novels, and nunnery-tale books. The story of the pretended Miss Hamilton is wholly transcribed from the English translation of a well-known French Romance, by the Chevalier de Monchy [ie de Mouhy], entitled *The Fortunate Country Maid.*'

THE LOVERS
See TREYSSAC DE VERGY, Pierre Henri

THE MAN OF HONOUR: OR THE HISTORY OF HARRY WATERS, ESQ.
See 1771: 60

1772: 16   ANON.
THE MARRIED VICTIM: OR, THE HISTORY OF LADY VILLARS. A NARRATIVE FOUNDED ON FACTS.

> London: Printed for T. Hookham, at his Circulating Library, in New-Street, Hanover-Square, 1772.
> I 184p; II 160p. 12mo. 5s sewed (CR, MR), 6s bound (SJC, adv.), 5s sewed or 6s bound (LC).
> CR 32: 471 (Dec 1771); MR 46: 79 (Jan 1772).
> CLU-S/C PR3991.A1M337; ESTC n004516.

Notes. Epistolary.
Adv. LC 30: 599 (19–21 Dec 1771); adv. SJC 1–4 May 1773.
Adv. end vol. 2 *The History of the Hon. Mrs. Rosemont* (1781: 17).
French trans. Londres [Paris?], 1775, ESTC t133438.

   CR: 'The History of Lady Villars is, in our opinion, written in a pretty, easy, unaffected style; but considered as a literary composition, there is more delicacy than strength in it.'

   MR [Gilbert Stuart]: 'In these volumes the reader is presented with scenes of distress; but, as they are pourtrayed without passion, they make no impression on his heart. The Author, without sensibility or genius, should not have entered on the task of describing the human mind under the agitation of anxieties and emotions which he could not feel. Sentiments destitute of delicacy, adventures distressful but unnatural, and without propriety, and expressions coarse and inelegant, can never awake the affections, and excite a tender sympathy.'

MEMOIRS OF AN HERMAPHRODITE
See TREYSSAC DE VERGY, Pierre Henri

1772: 17   ANON.
MEMOIRS OF FRANCIS DILLON, ESQ; IN A SERIES OF LETTERS WRITTEN BY HIMSELF.

> London: Printed for T. Hookham, New-Street, Hanover-Square; and J. Roson, No. 54, St. Martin's le Grand, 1772.
> I vi, 240p; II 206p. 12mo. 6s (CR, MR).
> CR 33: 327 (Apr 1772); MR 46: 457 (Apr 1772).
> ICU PR3991.M533.1772 Rare Bk.; xESTC.

Notes. Dedication to the Duchess of Cumberland, signed Francis Dillon. Epistolary.

   CR: 'The characters he introduces are feebly drawn, and they are engaged in no business sufficiently important to interest the reader in their affairs. There is nothing striking in the descriptive, or sentimental parts; but every reader of taste will be shocked with the poverty of the language in general, and with the vulgarity of the style.'

   MR [Gilbert Stuart]: 'The details in this performance are most insufferably tedious, and are mixed with a vulgarity which is disgusting in the highest degree.'

THE MEMOIRS OF MISS WILLIAMS
See 1771: 26

MEMOIRS OF THE YEAR TWO THOUSAND FIVE HUNDRED
See MERCIER, Louis-Sébastien

MEMOIRS RELATING TO THE QUEEN OF BOHEMIA
See ERSKINE, Lady Frances

1772: 18   ANON.
THE NEW MODERN STORY-TELLER; IN A VARIETY OF ORIGINAL
TALES AND NOVELS, IN VERSE AND IN PROSE. AMONG WHICH IS
NOW FIRST PUBLISHED, BY DESIRE, THE CELEBRATED TALE OF
THE LAWYER AND HIS INKHORN. WITH A NEW EPILOGUE.
> London: Printed for J. Williams, No. 38, Fleet-Street, 1772.
> I vi, 216p; II 225p. 12mo.
> BL 12316.e.38; EM 635: 3; ESTC t131135 (NA PU).

Notes. Vol. 1 i–vi 'A Short Tractate of Story Telling' (in verse); pp. 89–216 14 separate prose
'novels'; vol. 2 15 separate. 2 pp. advs. end vol. 2.

1772: 19   ANON.
THE NOBLE LOVERS; OR THE HISTORY OF LORD EMELY AND MISS
VILLARS; CONTAINING SOME CHARACTERS OF THE MOST CELE-
BRATED PERSONS IN HIGH LIFE. IN THREE VOLUMES.
> London: Printed for S. Bladon, Paternoster-Row, 1772.
> I missing; II 216p; III 178p. 12mo. 7s 6d sewed (CR, MR).
> CR 34: 76–7 (July 1772); MR 47: 151 (Aug 1772); AF I: 2020.
> BL RB.23.a.8670 [Imperf—vols. 2 and 3 only]; ESTC t224761.

Notes. 2 pp. advs. end vol. 3.
Adv. SJC 9–11 July 1772.

CR: 'The history of lord Emely and miss Villars might have been very well contained in the
third volume, thin as it is. The author has shewn some ingenuity in bringing his Noble Lovers
together, after some unexpected, though not unnatural discoveries: but he has not, we think,
drawn his principal characters in such a manner as to interest us extremely in their
affairs.'

MR [Gilbert Stuart]: 'In fine, his work is a compound of malignity and dullness.'

1772: 20   ANON.
THE PRECIPITATE CHOICE: OR, THE HISTORY OF LORD OSSORY
AND MISS RIVERS. A NOVEL. IN TWO VOLUMES. BY A LADY.
> London: Printed for T. and B. Jones, at their respective Circulating Libraries, in the
> Strand, opposite Hungerford Street; and Oxford Street, the Corner of Berwick Street,
> 1772.
> I 219p; II 184p. 12mo. 5s sewed (CR, MR).
> CR 33: 255 (Mar 1772); MR 46: 456–7 (Apr 1772); AF I: 2269.
> BL 12612.df.17; EM 276: 1; ESTC t066525.

Notes. 7 pp. advs. end vol. 2. Epistolary.
Adv. end vol. 1 of *The Involuntary Inconstant* (1772: 13).
Further edns: Dublin, 1772 (Printed by Peter Hoey, 2 vols. in 1, 12mo), EM 3604: 1, ESTC
t107042; Boston, 1783, ESTC w026868.

CR: 'There is some contrivance in this novel, and it is, upon the whole, ingeniously conducted. The principal characters, tho' not very striking, are properly marked, and not injudiciously sustained. The melancholy scenes and situations occasioned by the infernal contrivances of lord Ossory, are related in an affecting manner. We would advise the author of these volumes to confine herself to the pathetic; as we think, notwithstanding the exuberance of the vivacity which she discovers in some places, that the pathetic is her forte.'

MR [Gilbert Stuart]: 'A variety of incidents, fancied without propriety, and expressed without elegance, cannot furnish entertainment to a mind, in the smallest degree cultivated by study or reflection. We should pity those readers to whom this production presents any thing interesting.'

THE RAMBLES OF MR. FRANKLY
See BONHOTE, Elizabeth

1772: 21 ANON.
*THE RECLAIMED PROSTITUTE: OR, THE ADVENTURES OF AMELIA SIDNEY.
London: Roson, [1772].
2 vols. 12mo. 5s (CR, MR).
CR 33: 84 (Jan 1772); MR 46: 165 (Feb 1772); AF I: 2327.
No copy located.

Notes. CR: 'The Adventures of Amelia Sydney are the most uninteresting we have ever met with, and related in the least entertaining manner. Tritenesses, vulgarisms, and improbabilities appear in almost every page, and nothing can equal—but the volumes will be forgotten before we go to the press!'

MR: 'Another despicable and scandalous attempt to impose on the public, by a wretched piece of patch-work, the shameless plunder of superannuated and worthless novels.' Also suggests that the novel is largely taken from a Curll publication, *Spanish Amusements* [English version begun 1680 and completed 1717, according to 2nd edn., London, 1727, ESTC t089212].

1772: 22 ANON.
THE STORM; OR, THE HISTORY OF NANCY AND LUCY. IN TWO VOLUMES.
London: Printed for F. and J. Noble, at their respective Circulating Libraries, near Middle Row, Holborn, and Saint Martin's Court, near Leicester Square, 1772.
I 240p; II 208p. 12mo. 5s (CR), 6s bound (MR).
CR 33: 83 (Jan 1772); MR 46: 164 (Feb 1772); AF I: 2675.
MH-H *EC75.A100.772s; EM 2140: 13; ESTC n023407 (BI O).

Notes. CR: 'This novel begins and ends with a storm, and there is a great deal of changeable weather in the middle of it; some foul, some fair, much in the April way.'

MR: 'This production is in the narrative form; and there is a vivacity in it which renders it more interesting than the common run of novels.'

THE TEST OF FILIAL DUTY
See SCOTT, Sarah

1772: 23   ANON.
THE TRIAL: OR THE HISTORY OF CHARLES HORTON ESQ. IN THREE VOLUMES. BY A GENTLEMAN.

> London: Printed for T. Vernor; and M. Chater, 1772.
> I 228p; II 228p; III 204p. 12mo. 7s 6d (CR), 9s (MR), 9s bound (t.p.), 7s 6d sewed (LC).
> CR 33: 83 (Jan 1772); MR 46: 79 (Jan 1772); AF I: 2781.
> BL 1508/463; ESTC t087714.

Notes. By same author as *The History of Lord Stanton* (1774: 10).
Epistolary.
Adv., 'Monday, Dec. 30, will be published', LC 30: 595 (19–21 Dec 1771).
Extract given in LC 31: 9 (2–4 Jan 1772).
Further edns: London, n.d. [1775?], ESTC n007573; Dublin, 1772 (Printed for H. Saunders, W. Sleater, J. Potts, J. Williams, T. Walker, R. Moncrieffe, C. Jenkins, 2 vols., 12mo), ESTC t086147.

CR: 'The volumes before us are among those which we have read with some degree of pleasure. They contain many sensible reflections, well-supported characters, unexpected turns, and trying situations; they are, at once, entertaining and instructive.'

MR [Gilbert Stuart]: 'This performance recommends itself by the chastity of its sentiments, the variety of its characters, and the propriety of its expression. It is, indeed, a beautiful display of the judgment and sensibility of its Author.'

1772: 24   ANON.
THE TRIUMPH OF BENEVOLENCE: OR, THE HISTORY OF FRANCIS WILLS. IN TWO VOLUMES.

> London: Printed for T. Vernor, at Garrick's Head, in St. Michael's Alley, Cornhill; and
>   M. Chater, in King Street, Cheapside 1772.
> I 252p; II 274p. 12mo. 5s sewed (CR, MR).
> CR 33: 255 (Mar 1772); MR 46: 457 (Apr 1772); AF I: 2786.
> BL Cup.403.bb.10; EM 6424: 2; ESTC t138879.

Notes. ESTC notes as variously attributed to Oliver Goldsmith or Arthur Murphy; BGR attributes to Samuel Jackson Pratt.
Final 2 pp. of vol. 1 ([251]–252) are advs.
Further edns: Dublin, 1772 (Printed for J. Potts, W. Sleater, D. Chamberlaine, J. Williams, T. Walker, and C. Jenkins, 2 vols., 12mo), ESTC n021546; Berlin, 1786, EM 2961: 7, ESTC t131913; Uppsala, 1799, EM 4372: 5, ESTC t066921. French trans., Amsterdam, 1773 (*Histoire de François Wills*) (BGR); German trans. Breslau, 1776 (*Geschichte des Herrn Franz Wills oder der Triumph der Mildthätigkeit*) (EAG).

CR: 'The pleasure which the author of these volumes evidently takes in recommending benevolence, will not suffer us to examine them with a critical severity. We cannot say that his history is a masterly performance; but as we applaud the design, we will not condemn the execution of it.'

MR [Gilbert Stuart]: 'In these volumes there is some knowledge of life, with a considerable portion of humour, tenderness, and sentiments.'

1772: 25   ANON.
THE UNEQUAL ALLIANCE; OR, THE HISTORY OF LORD ASHFORD. IN TWO VOLUMES.

London: Printed for F. and J. Noble, at their respective Circulating Libraries, near Middle-Row, Holborn, and St. Martin's-Court, near Leicester-Square, 1772.
I 232p; II 240p. 12mo. 5s sewed (CR, MR).
CR 33: 411 (May 1772); MR 46: 539 (May 1772); AF I: 2822.
NIC Rare PR3219.A1U56; ESTC n051011.

Notes. Epistolary
CR: 'The author's view is plainly to be perceived; and there are, doubtless, many married couples in the kingdom unsuitably enough joined, to feel that his piece is not, upon the whole, *overcharged*.'
MR [Gilbert Stuart]: 'This production is replete with romantic folly, and offers not one circumstance that can recommend it to attention.'

1772: 26 ANON.
THE UNFASHIONABLE WIFE. A NOVEL. IN TWO VOLUMES.

London: Printed for T. Lowndes, at his Circulating Library, in Fleet-Street, 1772.
I 240p; II 240p. 12mo. 5s sewed (CR), 6s (MR), 5s sewed or 6s bound (LC).
CR 32: 392 (Nov 1771); MR 46: 78 (Jan 1772).
MH-H *EC75.A100.772u; EM 1493: 24; ESTC n014498 (NA DLC, IU).

Notes. Drop-head title, 'The Unfashionable Wife: A Moral History'. 8 pp. advs. end vol. 2. Epistolary.
Post-dated: adv., 'Next Friday will be published', LC 30: 416 (26–29 Oct 1771); adv. as published LC 30: 428 (31 Oct-2 Nov 1771).
Further edn: Dublin, 1772 (Printed for James Williams, 2 vols., 12mo), ESTC t220101.
MR [Gilbert Stuart]: 'These volumes contain so much intrigue and business, that they cannot fail of being highly acceptable to a multitude of readers.'

1772: 27 ANON.
*VIRTUE IN DISTRESS: OR THE HISTORY OF MISS SALLY PRUEN, AND MISS LAURA SPENCER; BY A FARMER'S DAUGHTER IN GLO-CESTERSHIRE.

London: Fuller, 1772 (MR).
12mo. 3s (CR, MR).
CR 33: 327 (Apr 1772); MR 46: 264 (Mar 1772); AF I: 2861.
No copy located.

Notes. CR: 'When a farmer's daughter sits down to *read* a novel, she certainly mispends her time, because she may employ it in such a manner as to be of real service to her family: when she sits down to *write* one, her friends can have no hopes of her. The rustic authoress of this volume before us, having her head *overheated* by the perusal of some of Mr. Richardson's *intoxicating* stories, has totally mistaken the use of her hands: we have never seen her hands indeed, but we will venture to say, that she may turn them to a better account by making *butter*, than by making *books*.'
MR: 'A good tidy girl seems to have been spoilt by reading Pamela, and then taking it into her head that she could also *write* Pamelas. But this Farmer's Daughter of Gloucestershire would, surely, be much better employed in plying the churn-staff, than in brandishing a goose-quill; in the first of these occupations she could hardly fail of doing *some* good; in the

latter, she must certainly expose herself to ridicule, perhaps even among the rustics in her father's neighbourhood: unless they, too, have been reading Pamala [sic], and are all bewitched, like the Farmer's Daughter.'

1772: 28   ANON.
THE VOYAGES AND ADVENTURES OF THE CHEVALIER DUPONT.
IN FOUR VOLUMES. TRANSLATED FROM THE FRENCH.

> London: Printed for T. Jones, at his Circulating Library, opposite Hungerford Market, in the Strand; And B. Jones, at his Circulating Library, in Oxford-Street, at the Corner of Berwick Street, 1772.
> I (1772) 297p ; II (1772) 274p; III (1772) 259p; IV (1762 [1772]) 214p. 12mo. 10s 6d sewed (CR), 10s sewed (MR, adv.).
> CR 33: 411 (May 1772); MR 46: 625–6 (June 1772); AF I: 2889.
> BL 10408.aa.25; EM 828: 2; ESTC t110174 (NA CaOONL, CaQMBN, ViU &c.).

Notes. Trans. of Voyages et adventures du Chevalier de *** (Londres [Paris], 1769).
2 pp. advs. end vol. 4. Vol. 4 misdated 1762.
Adv., 'Speedily will be published', end vol. 2 The Involuntary Inconstant (1772: 13).

CR notes that the advertisements say it is 'an authentic narrative of facts' and that nothing suggests it was made up: 'As the representation delivered of these places [America and the West Indies] appears to be faithful, this work may at least be attended with the advantage of conveying useful information to such readers as confine their attention chiefly to works of entertainment; and in this view, the author has not improperly substituted truth in the room of ingenious fiction.'

MR: 'Although we have classed this work with the Novels, it has rather the appearance of a narrative of real adventures, occurring in a series of trading voyages, through various parts of America and the West Indies.'

THE YOUNGER BROTHER, A TALE
See 1770: 21

1772: 29   [BACULARD D']ARNAUD, [François-Thomas-Marie de].
THE HISTORY OF SIDNEY AND VOLSAN. TRANSLATED FROM THE
FRENCH OF THE CELEBRATED ARNAUD.

> Dublin: Printed for James Vallance, Bookseller, in Suffolk-Street, 1772.
> 110p. 12mo.
> BL 12330.aaa.13(4); EM 634: 23; ESTC t036453 (BI D).

Notes. Trans. of 'Sidney et Volsan, histoire anglaise' in vol. 2 of Les Epreuves du sentiment (Paris, 1772).

BARBÉ-MARBOIS, François, Marquis de, LETTERS FROM THE MAR-
CHIONESS OF POMPADOUR
See App. B: 1

1772: 30   [BONHOTE, Elizabeth].
THE RAMBLES OF MR. FRANKLY. PUBLISHED BY HIS SISTER. IN
TWO VOLUMES.

London: Printed for T. Becket and P. A. Dehondt in the Strand, 1772.
I 164p; II 171p. 8vo. 5s sewed (CR, MR).
CR 34: 472 (Dec 1772); MR 48: 71–2 (Jan 1773); AF I: 206.
C 7720.e.184-; EM 2998: 8; ESTC n013410 (BI MRu, O; NA CtY, DLC, IU &c.).
Notes. Vols. 3 & 4 1776: 9.
Adv., 'Speedily will be published', SJC 14–16 July 1772; adv. as published SJC 15–17 Dec 1772.
Further edn: Dublin, 1773 (Printed for Messrs. Sleater, Lynch, Williams, Potts, Chamberlaine [and 5 others], 2 vols., 12mo), EM 6563: 11, ESTC t010034. French trans. Paris, 1773 (*Les Promenades de M. Frankly*) (HWS); German trans. [of all 4 vols.] Leipzig, 1773/76 (*Die Wanderungen des Herrn Frankly*) (WC).

CR: 'We shall be very glad to see a new performance of this author's in the same style of composition, as we think he would shine in the pathetic; but we shall be sorry to find him continuing to tread upon the heels of Sterne.'

MR: 'The justly admired *Sentimental Journey*, has evidently given birth to *Sentimental Rambles*. Imitations are generally read with disadvantage to the Author; and this will probably prove to be the case with regard to the pair of Shandy-volumes before us.—Yet this little slight performance obviously shews that Mr. Frankly is very capable of walking alone if he pleases, and of pursuing his ramble to the temple of fame, without leaning on the arm of Sterne, or any other conductor.'

1772: 31   [BRISCOE, Sophia].
THE FINE LADY A NOVEL BY THE AUTHOR OF MISS MELMOTH. IN TWO VOLUMES.

London: Printed for T. Lowndes, No. 77, in Fleet-Street, 1772.
I 264p; II 266p. 12mo. 5s sewed (CR, MR).
CR 33: 181–2 (Feb 1772); MR 46: 457 (Apr 1772); AF I: 242.
BL 12614.ff.12; EM 326: 1; ESTC t080601 (NA CSmH, NjP, PU &c.).
Notes. 6 pp advs. end vol. 2. Epistolary.
Sophia Briscoe sold the copyright to *The Fine Lady* for 20 gns., Dec. 1771, GM n.s. 94 (1824): 136.
Miss Melmoth 1771: 37.
Further edn: Dublin, 1772 (Printed for J. Potts, J. Hoey, jun. James Williams, T. Walker, Stewart and Co. and C. Jenkin, 2 vols., 12mo), ESTC t212628. German trans. Leipzig, 1771 (*Die Frau nach der Mode*) (Price).

CR: 'The volumes now under our consideration deserve not to be classed with the lowest, nor to be ranked with the highest productions in this species of writing. They are not destitute of character, incidents, and situations: and it is not easy to read the catastrophe, of which the Fine Lady is the eventual cause, without feeling powerful emotions.'

MR [Gilbert Stuart]: 'The vivacity of this novel gives it a degree of interest with the reader, which the Author has agreeably heightened by the art with which the story unfolds itself.'

1772: 32   [ERSKINE, Lady Frances].
MEMOIRS RELATING TO THE QUEEN OF BOHEMIA. BY ONE OF HER LADIES.

n.p., n.d. [ESTC: London? 1772?].

162p. 8vo.

O Vet.A5e.890; EM 922: 7; ESTC t110270 (Bl BL; NA CtY-Walpole, DFo, NcD).

Notes. Martin classifies as 'a kind of historical novel' and 'evidently a private production' (p. 47).

Text starts on p. 3. 4-pp. handwritten note at end of Bodleian copy concerns Lady Frances Erskine and her family background and says that this 'Fragment of Memoirs', begun in 1753, is all that was published; the 'continuation of it, in manuscript, was lost in the fire at the Tower of Alton, the family Seat 28th August 1800' after Lady Frances's death.

1772: 33   HALLER, [Albrecht von].
USONG. AN EASTERN NARRATIVE. WRITTEN IN GERMAN BY BARON HALLER. IN TWO VOLUMES.

> London: Printed for the Translator; and sold by F. Newbery in Ludgate Street, and
>   J. Walter at Charing Cross, 1772.
> I viii, 256p; II 307p. 8vo. 5s sewed (PA).
> MR 48: 160–1 (Feb 1773); AF I: 1164.
> BL 241.e.24,25; EM 6953: 7; ESTC t133185 (Bl MRu, O; NA CaOHM, CaSSU, PU &c.;
>   EA GOT).

Notes. Preface vol. 1, iii–viii, signed 'Haller' and dated 29 Aug 1771.

Adv. PA 9 Jan 1773.

Further versions with different titles published in London in 1773 (*Usong. An Oriental History*, ESTC t106289), and 1784 (*The Virtuous Prince*, ESTC n052660). CR 35: 195–8 (Mar 1773) reviews the 1773 version. French trans. Lausanne, 1772 (*Usong, histoire orientale*) (BN).

MR [William Woodfall]: 'The life and adventures of this hero afford ample room for the play of a warm imagination; but a warm imagination happens not to be the talent of this celebrated Author; and therefore these two volumes, though they are innocent and useful in their precepts and instructions, will rather, through the tameness and coldness of the Writer, serve to exercise the Reader's patience, than contribute to his entertainment.'

1772: 34   [HUTCHINSON, William].
THE HERMITAGE; A BRITISH STORY.

> York: Printed by C. Etherington, for the author; and sold by John Bell, Bookseller in the
>   Strand, London; and C. Etherington, York, 1772.
> I (1772) 260p; II (1773) missing. 12mo. 3s vol. 1 (CR, MR), 6s both vols. (CR).
> CR 35: 78–9 (Jan 1773) vol. 1; CR 36: 236 (Sept 1773) both vols.; MR 48: 320 (Apr 1773)
>   vol. 1; AF I: 1348, 1349.
> BL 1207.a.29 vol. 1 only; EM 2471: 7; ESTC t117937 (Bl O [vol. 1 only]).

Notes. Further edns: London, 1773, ESTC n028677 [with title *Dumont: or, the Hermitage. A British Story*]; London, 1775, EM 7166: 11, ESTC t190584 [*The Hermitage of Du Monte*].

CR: 'The Story is, we really think, sufficiently romantic, and rendered far less interesting than it might have been made, with all its extravaganzas, by a less affected mode of composition' (p. 79).

MR [Thomas Pearne]: 'The Author of the Hermitage deals so much in supernaturals, and writes in such a fustian strain, that it was impossible for us, on perusing his work, not to rec-ollect the famous dramatic piece, entitled *Hurlothrumbo*, written about thirty years ago, by one Johnson, a mad dancing master. This "British story" is the very Hurlothrumbo of Romance: and like Johnson's performance, too, it contains some sentiments, and exertions of imagination, which would do honour to more rational and more regular productions.'

1772: 35   [LA ROCHE-GUILHEM, Anne de].
THE HISTORY OF FEMALE FAVOURITES. OF MARY DE PADILLA, UNDER PETER THE CRUEL, KING OF CASTILE; LIVIA, UNDER THE EMPEROR AUGUSTUS; JULIA FARNESA, UNDER POPE ALEXANDER THE SIXTH; AGNES SOREAU, UNDER CHARLES VII. KING OF FRANCE; AND NANTILDA, UNDER DAGOBERT, KING OF FRANCE.
> London: Printed for C. Parker, the Upper End of New Bond-Street, 1772.
> 324p. 8vo. 5s bound (MR).
> MR 46: 265 (Mar 1772); AF I: 1568.
> C 7450.c.24; EMf; ESTC t060642 (BI AWn, BL; NA DLC, IU, NjP, PU &c.).

Notes. Trans. of *Histoire des favorites* (Amsterdam, 1697).
Prefatory advertisement to the reader, p. [i], signed 'the Editor'.
Further edn: Dublin, 1772 (Printed for J. Exshaw, H. Saunders, W. Sleater, D. Chamberlaine, J. Potts, J. Hoey, jun. and R. Moncrieffe, 1 vol., 12mo), ESTC n017544.

MR [Gilbert Stuart]: 'This production is replete with anecdotes which have a slender foundation in truth; but which are extremely licentious. It is to the last unworthy circum-stance that they owe their publication.'

1772: 36   [MERCIER, Louis-Sébastien]; HOOPER, W[illiam] (*trans.*).
MEMOIRS OF THE YEAR TWO THOUSAND FIVE HUNDRED. TRANS-LATED FROM THE FRENCH BY W. HOOPER, M.D. IN TWO VOLUMES.
> London: Printed for G. Robinson, in Pater-noster-Row, 1772.
> I viii, 224p; II 248p. 12mo. 6s (CR), 5s sewed or 6s bound (SJC).
> CR 33: 468–76 (June 1772); CR 34: 7–18 (July 1772); AF I: 1307.
> BL 12510.dd.12; EM 89: 1; ESTC t072976 (BI C, E, O, &c.; NA CtY-BR, CSmH, IU &c.).

Notes. Trans. of *L'An deux mille quatre cent quarante. Rêve s'il en fut jamais* (Londres [Paris], 1772). [See also Darnton.]
Robinson contract with William Hooper for £28.17.6 on 19 Mar 1772 (receipt 5 June) for translating *L'An Deux Mille Quatre Cent Quarante* (RA).
Adv. SJC 29 Sept–1 Oct 1772.
Further edns: Dublin, 1772 (Printed for W. Wilson, 2 vols., 12mo), ESTC n004081; Philadel-phia, 1795, EM 4851: 7, ESTC w020742; Richmond, VA, 1799, EM 5685: 12, ESTC w029913; Liverpool, 1802 (WC); NSTC lists edns in 1802 and 1808. Facs: FN.

CR 33: '. . . it is evident, that the author possesses taste, and a fund of natural and just obser-vation. From the pleasing character of the visionary age which he affects to describe, he has chosen an advantageous situation for a retrospective view of the political imperfection of the present times; and it would tend to the happiness of mankind, that the government of every country would endeavour to remedy the defects in legislation and manners which are cen-sured in the course of this work.'

CR 34: 'The contrast exhibited in this work, between the periods which are the object of this author's comparison, is happily conducted for placing his satirical observations on the present times in the most conspicuous point of view' (p. 18).

1772: 37　RICCOBONI, [Marie-Jeanne Laboras de Mézières]; MACEUEN, Mr (*trans.*).
LETTERS FROM ELIZABETH SOPHIA DE VALIERE TO HER FRIEND LOUISA HORTENSIA DE CANTELEU. BY MADAM RICCOBONI. TRANSLATED FROM THE FRENCH BY MR. MACEUEN. IN TWO VOLUMES.

> London: Printed for T. Becket; and P. A. De Hondt, Strand, 1772.
> I 252p; II 242p. 12mo. 6s (CR), MR gives no price.
> CR 34: 62–5 (July 1772); MR 47: 8–13 (July 1772); AF I: 1708.
> BL 12510.c.17; EM 15: 6; ESTC t131027 (BI C, O; NA CSmH, NjP, TxU &c.).

Notes. Trans. of *Lettres d' Elisabeth-Sophie de Vallière* (Paris, 1772).
2 pp. advs. end vol. 2. Epistolary.
Rev. of French edn. [Gilbert Stuart], MR 46: 697 (June 1772).
Further edn: Dublin, 1772 (Printed for J. Potts, J. Williams, T. Walker, and C. Jenkins, 2 vols., 12mo), ESTC n018907.

CR: 'The Letters appear to be the genuine emanations of a mind endued with great sensibility, and strongly agitated with the disastrous events of fortune. Being dictated by the heart, they are calculated to interest the passions; and, exclusive of the sympathetic emotions excited by incidents of an affecting nature, and which are described with energy, the attention of the reader is engaged in the perusal of them by an almost uninterrupted profusion of ingenious sentiments' (pp. 62–3).

MR [Gilbert Stuart]: 'The public has been, for some years, indebted to this agreeable writer, for several ingenious performances, and for none more entertaining than the present letters. They are conceived with much art and sensibility; they abound with excellent observations on manners and life; and they discover a penetration which can never be exerted but by those who have mixed much in society' (p. 8).

1772: 38　[SCOTT, Sarah].
THE TEST OF FILIAL DUTY. IN A SERIES OF LETTERS BETWEEN MISS EMILIA LEONARD, AND MISS CHARLOTTE ARLINGTON. A NOVEL. IN TWO VOLUMES.

> London: Printed for the Author, and Sold by T. Carnan, at Number Sixty-Five, in St Paul's Church-Yard, 1772.
> I xii, 263p; II 232p. 12mo. 5s sewed (CR), 6s bound (MR, LC), 5s 'The Two Volumes bound in one, in the Vellum Manner' (SJC, PA).
> CR 33: 182 (Feb 1772); MR 46: 165 (Feb 1772); AF I: 2476.
> BL Cup.403.l.22; EM 6421: 19; ESTC t139130 (NA CaAEU, CaOHM, DFo).

Notes. Epistolary.
Adv. LC 31: 20 (4–7 Jan 1772). Adv., with 16-line statement of the author's motive for publication, SJC 2–4 Feb 1773 and PA 10 Feb 1773.
Further edn: Dublin, 1772 (Printed for D. Chamberlaine, J. Potts, J. Mitchell, J. Williams, T.

Walker, and C. Jenkin, 2 vols., 12mo [ESTC: final printer's name is 'C. Jenkins'), ESTC n050663. German trans. Hamburg, 1774 (*Die kindlichen Pflichten auf der Probe*) (EAG).

CR: 'We have received some pleasure from the perusal of these letters. . . . In short, though there is something to blame, there is also something to commend, and as they are printed for the author, we hope that his pecuniary expectations will be answered.'

MR [Gilbert Stuart]: 'The excellent lessons of morality, which this work inculcates, will not be able to save it from oblivion.'

1772: 39   SEALLY, {John}.
MORAL TALES, AFTER THE EASTERN MANNER: BY MR SEALLY.

> London: Printed for W. Goldsmith, No. 24, Paternoster Row, n.d. [1772?].
> I iv, 204p; II 202p. 12mo. 6s (SJC).
> BL 12611.c.30; EM 208: 6; ESTC t055924 (NA CtY, CLU-S/C, DLC &c.).

Notes. ESTC has 1780?
Imprint to vol. 2 has 'Poternoster'.
Dedication to the Hon. Miss Mary Tryon, Maid of Honour to the Queen, p. [i], signed John Seally; 'Address to the Reader' ii–iv.
Adv., 'will be published in a few Days', SJC 3–5 Dec 1772.

1772: 40   [TREYSSAC DE VERGY, Pierre Henri].
THE LOVERS: OR THE MEMOIRS OF LADY MARY SC——AND THE HON. MISS AMELIA B——: VOLUME TWO.

> London: Printed for the Editor, and sold by all the Booksellers in Great-Britain, 1772.
> II [248]p. 8vo. 5s sewed (CR), 5s (MR).
> CR 33: 83 (Jan 1772); MR 46: 263 (Mar 1772).
> BL 836.d.36; EM 2443: 4; ESTC t115338 (BI O; NA CLU-S/C, CSmH, &c.).

Notes. CR gives Evans as bookseller. Epistolary. Vol. 1 (1769) has 'The End' on final page.
Vol. 2 1 p. advs. for 6 novels written by de Vergy follows preface. Last numbered page is 247.
Adv. at end of p. [248]: 'The THIRD VOLUME will be published some time next month. It will contain the whole Love-Intrigue between Captain SUTH—— and Lady Mary Sc——, from the day of her Marriage to the scene at Barnet'. If published, no copy located.
Vol. 1: THE LOVERS; OR THE MEMOIRS OF LADY SARAH B— AND THE COUNTESS P—: PUBLISHED BY MR. TREYSSAC DE VERGY, COUNSELLOR IN THE PARLIA-MENT OF PARIS, London: Printed for the Editor, and sold by J. Roson, No. 54, St. Martin's le Grand; and all the Booksellers in Great Britain, 1769. [JR 1344].

CR: 'The volume before us does not indeed contain so many gross unexceptionable passages as are to be found in most of our lively author's licentious compositions; but there are too many indelicacies scattered through it to suffer us to recommend it to the perusal of a modest woman.'

MR: 'In the 41st volume of our Review, p. 480, we endeavoured to express the indignation and the contempt with which we perused the 1st volume of this vile effusion of De Vergy's dissolute pen.'

1772: 41   [?TREYSSAC DE VERGY, Pierre Henri].
*MEMOIRS OF AN HERMAPHRODITE. INSCRIBED TO THE CHEVALIER D'EON.

London: Roson (CR, MR).

12mo. 2s (CR, MR).

CR 33: 336 (Apr 1772); MR 46: 265 (Mar 1772); AF I: 1796.

No copy located.

Notes. Author attribution from Summers.

CR: 'The production, in all probability, of indigence and personal resentment.'

MR: 'It is, possibly, the work of his old friend, and countryman, the Chevalier de V——, with whom he had some variance. If so, here was a double inducement: revenge, and the mammon of unrighteousness.'

1773

THE ADVENTURES OF A FOOTMAN
See THE SENTIMENTAL SPY

1773: 1   ANON.

THE ANCHORET. A MORAL TALE, IN A SERIES OF LETTERS.

London: Printed for Francis Newbery, at the Corner of St Paul's Church Yard, 1773.

I 216p; II 215p; III 171p. 12mo. 9s (CR), 7s 6d sewed (MR, SJC).

CR 34: 471–2 (Dec 1772); MR 48: 71 (Jan 1773); AF I: 75.

BL C.123.fff.20; EM 5096: 3; ESTC t124781 (NA CaQMM, CSmH, CU-Riv &c.).

Notes. Epistolary.

Adv. SJC 14–16 Jan 1773.

Further edn: Dublin, 1779 (Printed by and for S. Colbert, 3 vols., 8vo), ESTC t185631.

CR: 'Not one tale, but many tales, in the true strain of modern romance, filled with love, courtship and marriage.'

MR [Thomas Pearne] believes that its readers will be 'chiefly females' and that the author 'seems to be one of their own sex'.

CECILIA; OR, THE EASTERN LOVERS
See CARRA, Jean-Louis

EMMA: OR THE UNFORTUNATE ATTACHMENT
See CAVENDISH, Georgiana

1773: 2   ANON.

THE EXPLANATION; OR, AGREEABLE SURPRISE. IN TWO VOLUMES. BY A YOUNG LADY.

London: Printed for F. and J. Noble, at their respective Circulating Libraries, near Middle Row, Holborn, and Saint Martin's Court, near Leicester Square, 1773.

I 206p; II 149p. 12mo. 6s (CR, adv.), 5s sewed (MR), 5s sewed or 6s bound (SJC).

CR 34: 397 (Nov 1772); MR 47: 324 (Oct 1772); AF I: 818.

BL 12611.a.26; EM 173: 8; ESTC t108470 (NA CSmH).

Notes. 1 p. advs. end vol. 2. Epistolary.

Post-dated; adv. as published SJC 8–10 OCt 1772.

Adv. end vol. 2 of *The Assignation* (1774: 2).

Further edn: Dublin, 1778 (Printed by P. Hoey, 2 vols. in 1, no format), xESTC (WC).

MR [Gilbert Stuart]: 'We have seldom met with a performance more insipid than the present; which offers nothing to excite applause or attention.'

1773: 3   ANON.
*FALSE GRATITUDE: A NOVEL; BY A LADY.

> London: Noble, 1773.
> 2 vols. 12mo. 6s (CR); MR gives no price.
> CR 34: 473 (Dec 1772); MR 48: 243–4 (Mar 1773); AF I: 838.
> No copy located.

Notes. Adv. in Nobles' *Way to Lose Him* (1773: 21) as *False Gratitude; or The History of Charles Melville.* Adv. in Nobles' *Sketches from Nature* (1778: 6) as *False Gratitude; or, the History of Miss Rosemont.*

German trans. Danzig, 1774 (*Die falsche Dankbarkeit*) (Price).

CR: 'As this novel appears, from some feminine strokes scattered through it, to be the real production of a lady, we shall not dissect it with a critical exactness, especially as it appears to be the fair writer's first production.'

MR [Thomas Pearne]: 'Although this performance is not crowded with interesting events, yet it contains incidents sufficient to keep the Reader's attention awake; and some passages in it will not fail to excite the tender and sympathetic passions. The characters are consistent, the sentiments delicate, and the language easy, and not incorrect.—Among the numerous publications of the kind, this female production may be ranked, with respect to its merit, in the middle class.'

THE FASHIONABLE FRIEND
See BONHOTE, Elizabeth

1773: 4   ANON.
THE FATAL EFFECTS OF DECEPTION. A NOVEL. IN THREE VOLUMES.

> London: Printed for T. Jones, at his Circulating Library, in the Strand, opposite Hungerford Street, 1773.
> I 211p; II 216p; III 231p. 12mo. 9s sewed (CR), 7s 6d sewed (MR).
> CR 36: 74 (July 1773); MR 49: 232 (Sept 1773); AF I: 851.
> MH-H *EC75.A100.773f; EM 1110: 3; ESTC n006609 (NA PU).

Notes. 1-p. prefatory advertisement vol. 1; 1 p. advs. end vol 2. Epistolary.

CR: 'This novel is every way superior to the foregoing [*The History of Lord Ashborn*, 1773: 8], both with regard to the matter which it contains, and the manner in which it is fabricated.'

MR: 'Although there is nothing very extraordinary in the composition of this novel, it is not unentertaining or uninteresting; and the moral inference, as implied in the title-page, is important, and can never be too strongly impressed on the minds of young readers.'

1773: 5   ANON.
THE FRIENDS: OR, ORIGINAL LETTERS OF A PERSON DECEASED.
NOW FIRST PUBLISHED, FROM THE MANUSCRIPTS, IN HIS COR-
RESPONDENT'S HANDS. IN TWO VOLUMES.

> London: Printed for J. Bell, near Exeter-Exchange, in the Strand; and C. Etherington, at
> York, 1773.
> I 287p; II 296p. 12mo. 6s (CR, MR), 6s bound (SJC).
> CR 36: 236 (Sept 1773); MR 48: 321 (Apr 1773); AF I: 983.
> BL 1608/2962; EM 8510: 2; ESTC t121492 (BI C; NA CWhC, MH-H, PU &c.).

Notes. The 8-pp. introduction 'The Editor to the Reader' is misplaced and is divided at end of
vol. 2 as: 290, vii, viii, v, vi, 291, 292, 293, 294, iii, iv, [i], ii, 295, 296. Epistolary. BL copy has
'F. Brooke M.S. 1773' handwritten on the original blue paper covers of both vols; it is not
clear whether this is Frances Brooke.
Adv., 'will be published in the Course of a few Days', SJC 23–25 Feb 1773.
Still adv., 'just published', SJC 11–13 Mar 1777.
   CR: 'The letters in these volumes have, in general, no small degree of merit. They abound
with judicious observations, strongly, and often happily expressed. If all the epistolary pro-
ductions of this scribbling age were as unexceptionable, the reviewing of them would be
rather a pleasant than a painful employment.'
   MR [William Woodfall] suggests that the letters are so dull that they must be genuine.

1773: 6   ANON.
HADLEIGH GROVE; OR, THE HISTORY OF SIR CHARLES DAVERS,
AND THE FAIR JESSICA. A NOVEL. IN TWO VOLUMES.

> London: Printed for J. Roson, No. 54, St Martin's le Grand; and sold by R. Snagg,
> No. 29, Paternoster-Row. n.d. [1773 CR, MR].
> I 237p: II 200p. 12mo. 5s sewed, or 6s neatly bound (t.p. both vols., SJC), 6s (CR, MR).
> CR 36: 397 (Nov 1773); MR 49: 508 (Dec 1773); AF I: 1162.
> BL Cup.402.k.30; EM 6424: 1; ESTC t138880.

Notes. 3 pp. advs. end vol. 1; 4 pp. advs. end vol. 2. Epistolary.
Adv. SJC 16–19 Oct 1773; adv. under 'New Books' SJC 1–3 Nov 1774.
German trans. Leipzig, 1775 (*Du schöne Gärtnerinn, oder Geschichte des Sir Carl Davers*)
(EAG).
   CR: 'This novel, apparently the production of a *female hand*, is superior to the foregoing;
though it cannot be said to merit a very extraordinary encomium.'
   MR [John Noorthouck]: 'If the reader has patience enough to peruse these very slender
volumes, he will find a crude jumble of improbabilities, too hastily huddled together to
afford him the satisfaction which results from the being well beguiled into a temporary belief
of the adventures related.'

1773: 7   ANON.
THE HISTORY OF LORD AIMWORTH, AND THE HONOURABLE
CHARLES HARTFORD, ESQ. IN A SERIES OF LETTERS. A NOVEL. BY
THE AUTHOR OF DORINDA CATESBY, AND ERMINA, OR THE FAIR
RECLUSE.

London: Printed for J. Roson, No. 54, in St. Martin's Le Grand; T. Shepherd, in the
Minories; and T. Lewis, Russel-street, Covent-Garden, 1773.
I 222p; II 188p; III 156p. 12mo. 9s (MR), 7s 6d sewed (SJC).
MR 48: 416 (May 1773); AF I: 1252.
OAU PR3991.A1 H5x; xESTC.

Notes. Epistolary.
Ermina; or, the Fair Recluse 1772: 5; *The History of Miss Dorinda Catsby* 1772: 11.
Adv. SJC 8–10 June 1773.
MR: 'All improbability and absurdity!'

1773: 8   ANON.
THE HISTORY OF LORD ASHBORN, AND THE HONOURABLE MISS
HOWE; OR, THE RECLAIMED LIBERTINE. IN THREE VOLUMES. BY
THE AUTHOR OF FREDERICK, OR THE FORTUNATE BEGGAR.

London: Printed for J. Roson, No. 54, St. Martin's Le-Grand; T. Shepherd, in the
Minories; and T. Lewis, Russel-street, Covent-Garden, n.d. [1773 (MR)].
I vii, 192p; II 212p; III 211p. 12mo. 9s sewed (CR), 9s (MR), 7s 6d sewed or 9s bound (SJC).
CR 36: 74 (July 1773); MR 49: 69 (July 1773); AF I: 1253.
CtY-BR Im.H62694.773; ESTC n007879 (NA PU).

Notes. 5 pp. advs. end vol. 3. Epistolary.
Frederic: or, the Fortunate Beggar 1772: 8.
Adv. SJC 8–10 June 1773.
German trans. Lübeck, 1780 (*Die glückliche Besserung oder Geschichte des Lord Ashburn und
Miss Howe*) (EAG).

CR: 'If any thing can save these volumes from critical damnation, it must be the avowed
design with which they are written: they are manufactured in so slovenly a manner, that they
deserve no praise as literary productions.'

MR [John Noorthouck]: 'When we read an ill-written novel and reflect, as we are led to
do, on the misapplication of a writer's talents, we cannot help recollecting the exclamation of
an honest illiterate carman, (in Joe Miller, perhaps) on seeing one of his acquaintance in the
pillory for forgery,—"This comes of your *reading* and *writing*, you foolish rascal!".'

1773: 9   ANON.
THE HISTORY OF MISS PAMELA HOWARD. BY THE AUTHOR OF
INDIANA DANBY. IN TWO VOLUMES.

London: Printed for T. Lowndes, No. 77, in Fleet-Street, 1773.
I 215p; II 228p. 12mo. 6s (CR, MR).
CR 34: 473 (Dec 1772); MR 48: 154 (Feb 1773); AF I: 1270.
BL 12612.bb.10; EM 168: 2; ESTC t066373 (NA CtY, IU, MiU).

Notes. Epistolary, but framed by narrator's introduction and conclusion.
Indiana Danby (1765/67), JR 884 and 1071, AF I: 1265–1266; 'By a Lady'.
Further edn: Dublin, 1773 (Printed for James Williams, 2 vols., 12mo), EM 4687: 3; ESTC
t126295.

CR: 'The *catastrophe* is melancholy in the highest degree, but it is not so affecting as it
would be if the *pathetic* was more striking than the *horrible*.'

MR: 'Comedy and Tragedy have here joined to furnish an entertainment with which the Ladies in general will be pleased; and even the Gentlemen, (the *sentimental* Gentlemen, we mean) may make tolerable shift to *while away* a vacant hour on the perusal of a story, pregnant with that kind of horrible distress which humanity will think *too much.*—It is not a finished piece; but there are touches in it which prove the writer possessed of abilities for this kind of writing. It seems to be the product of a female pen. This branch of the literary *trade* appears, now, to be almost entirely engrossed by the Ladies.'

1773: 10   ANON.

THE HISTORY OF MR STANLY AND MISS TEMPLE. A RURAL NOVEL.

> London: Printed for J. Johnson at No. 72, St. Paul's Church-yard, n.d. [1773].
> I 249p; II 221p. 12mo. 5s sewed (CR, MR).
> CR 35: 320 (Apr 1773); MR 48: 181–3 (Mar 1773); AF I: 1275.
> BL 12604.bb.4; EMf; ESTC t181281 (BI O; NA ICN, NIC).

Notes. 1 p. advs. end vol.; 3 pp. advs. end vol. 2. Epistolary.
CR and MR note that the story is based on that of Eudoxus and Leontine in the *Spectator*.
Adv. PA 26 Jan 1773.
German trans. Leipzig, 1775 (*Geschichte des Herrn Stanly und der Miss Temple*) (Price).

CR: 'The architect concerned in this literary edifice has not discovered much skill or taste in the adjustment of the several parts, and the materials of which the whole is composed seem to be too slight to promise it duration. It is, in some respects, like an old Gothic building, as it is loaded with little ornaments; it is in others, like a modern one, as it makes a showy appearance, but proves, on a near view, nothing but a deception.'

MR [William Woodfall]: 'It is written in the manner of Sir Charles Grandison, and has more merit than most imitations' (p. 181). 'All the letters are evidently written by one hand; the same quaint expressions are used by different characters, and the exclamations or interjections of males and females, are all in the same manner' (p. 183).

THE HISTORY OF RHEDI
See DUFF, William

THE HISTORY OF TOM RIGBY
See CHATER, John

1773: 11   ANON.

LOVE AT FIRST SIGHT: OR THE HISTORY OF MISS CAROLINE STANHOPE. IN THREE VOLUMES.

> London; Printed for T. Jones, at his Circulating Library in the Strand, opposite Hungerford-street, 1773.
> I 218p; II 221p; III 199p. 12mo. 9s (CR) 7s 6d sewed (MR).
> CR 35: 78 (Jan 1773); MR 48: 155 (Feb 1773); AF I: 1690.
> BL 12614.h.9; EM 191: 5; ESTC t074445.

Notes. 3 pp. advs. end vol. 1; 1 p. advs. end vol. 3. Epistolary.
German trans. Liegnitz and Leipzig, 1781 (*Liebe auf den ersten Anblick; oder Geschichte der Miss Caroline Stanhope*) (EAG).

CR: 'The characters introduced in this history are common, and the incidents trite; but the former are so properly kept up, and the latter so naturally related, that the reader is imperceptibly drawn on, without having his patience severely exercised during the perusal.'

MR [John Noorthouck]: 'A tolerable story, delivered in the usual familiar epistolary stile; but bearing all the marks of haste and inattention.'

THE MAN OF NATURE
See GUILLARD DE BEAURIEU, Gaspard

THE MAN OF THE WORLD
See MACKENZIE, Henry

THE MEMOIRS OF AN AMERICAN
See DELACROIX, Jacques-Vincent

1773: 12   ANON.
*MEMOIRS OF THE CELEBRATED MISS ANN C——Y: CONTAINING A SUCCINCT NARRATIVE OF THE MOST REMARKABLE INCIDENTS OF THAT LADY'S LIFE; WITH MANY CURIOUS ANECDOTES; NEVER BEFORE MADE PUBLIC.

> London: Printed for J. Roson, No. 54, St. Martin's le Grand; and T. Sheppard, in the Minories (SJC), 1773 (SJC).
> 2 vols. 12mo. 5s (CR, MR), 5s sewed or 6s bound (SJC).
> CR 36: 396–7 (Nov 1773); MR 48: 417 (May 1773); AF I: 1821.
> No copy located.

Notes. Adv. SJC 8–10 June 1773 with title given as *Memoirs of the celebrated Miss Ann Catley; containing a succinct Narrative of that Lady's Life, with an elegant Frontispiece, representing Miss Catley, in the Character of Leonora, in the Padlock.*
CR and MR review under 'Novels'.

CR: 'This lady's memorialist has *made* a little volume by picking up all the anecdotes he could find relating to his heroine in Newspapers and Magazines, and putting them together without any regular order in the arrangement. They may, however, prove amusing to those who love such reading—on a rainy day'.

MR [John Noorthouck] notes that it 'would have been strange if a character so notorious as that which is here celebrated, had escaped the vigilance of our dirty fabricators of scandalous memoirs', pointing out in a footnote: 'This Lady is equally celebrated for her *singing* and her *amours.*'

1773: 13   ANON.
THE MERCENARY MARRIAGE; OR, THE HISTORY OF MISS SHENSTONE.

> London: Printed for F. and J. Noble, at their respective Circulating Libraries, near Middle Row, Holborn, and Saint Martin's Court, near Leicester Square, 1773.
> I 231p; II 208p. 12mo. 6s (CR, MR), 5s sewed (SJC Jan), 6s bound (SJC Apr).
> CR 35: 78 (Jan 1773); MR 48: 154 (Feb 1773); AF I: 1839.
> O Vet.A5e.5158; EM 1008: 10; ESTC n003926 (NA MH-H).

Notes. 4 pp. adv. in defence of *The Way to Lose Him* and *The Way to Please Him* (1773: 21 and 22), recently attacked in the *London Magazine,* beginning vol. 1; 1 p. adv. end vol. 1; 7 pp. advs. end vol. 2. Epistolary.

Adv., 'With an appeal to the Publick from the Aspersions of the anonymous Editor of the London Magazine', SJC 21–23 Jan 1773.

Also adv. with different version of price SJC 10–13 Apr 1773 at end of adv. for *The Self-Deceived* (1773: 17).

German trans. Breslau, 1776 (*Die eigennützige Heurath*) (Price).

MR [William Woodfall]: 'This work is written in the general manner of modern novels. It is well intended; for it aims at combating the vanity and avarice of young people in the most important event of life. We wish it had merit enough to make its way to the notice of those high and mighty offenders, who might profit by the lessons which it affords.'

1773: 14   ANON.
THE PRUDENTIAL LOVERS, OR THE HISTORY OF HARRY HARPER. IN TWO VOLUMES.

> London: Printed for the Author, and sold by John Bell, in the Strand, 1773.
> I 8, 208p; II 201p. 12mo. 6s (CR, MR).
> CR 36: 397 (Nov 1773); MR 49: 150 (Aug 1773); AF I: 2295.
> BL 012613.f.17; EM 186: 5; ESTC t114124 (NA CLU-S/C, MnU).

Notes. 1 p. advs. verso of t.p. vols. 1 and 2 (same advs. in both vols.). Introduction vol. 1, 3–8 refers to the 'immorality, as well as filthiness of the generality' of novelists and says that these volumes 'were thought of, begun, and finished in the course of three months'.

CR: 'Your prudential lovers are generally very dull lovers, and those under our considera- tion are not the brightest we have met with.'

MR: [After quoting the author's prefatory promise to give up writing if this novel is unsuc- cessful] ''Ere this time, we doubt not, the public voice hath announced to him the fate of this poor history; and we hope he will have resolution enough to keep his word with his readers.'

1773: 15   ANON.
*THE RAKE: OR, THE ADVENTURES OF TOM WILDMAN; EXHIBIT-ING STRIKING PICTURES OF LIFE, IN ALL ITS VARIEGATED SCENES; INTERSPERSED WITH THE HISTORIES OF SEVERAL PER-SONAGES OF EITHER SEX, WELL KNOWN IN THE POLITE WORLD; WRITTEN BY HIMSELF.

> London: Printed for J. Williams, at No. 39, next the Mitre Tavern, Fleet-Street (SJC).
> 2 vols. 12mo. 5s (MR), 5s sewed (SJC).
> MR 49: 231–2 (Sept 1773).
> No copy located.

Notes. Adv. SJC 3–5 June 1773 with title given as *The Rake; or, the Adventures of Tom Wildman. Containing the Histories of several Personages well known in the Polite World.*

MR: 'Some parts of this history of a strolling player are fit only for *rakes* and libertines, of *either* sex, to read. But, although the cheek of modesty would be frequently crimson'd by the unchaste details which frequently occur, particularly in the first volume, it must be

acknowledged that, towards the conclusion, the story grows moral, sober, and exemplary.'
MR goes on to observe that the author 'plentifully abuses the Reviewers'.

1773: 16   ANON.
THE ROYAL ADVENTURERS; OR, THE CONFLICT OF LOVE. A
NOVEL.

> London: Printed for G. Allen, No. 59. in Pater-noster-Row, 1773.
> vii, xi, 202p. 12mo. 3s (MR), 2s 6d sewed, or 3s bound (SJC).
> MR 48: 320 (Apr 1773); AF I: 2721.
> PU Singer-Mend. PR.3991.A1.R63.1773; ESTC n049133.

Notes. Preface to the Reader i–vii; Contents i–xi. Drop-head title, not amongst headings in
Contents: 'The Test of Friendship, &c.'
MR title: *The Test of Friendship; or the Royal Adventurers.*
Adv. SJC 11–13 Mar 1773.

MR [Thomas Pearne]: 'A tale truly romantic, and narrated in the unnatural, bombast style
of the old chivalry books. We cannot conceive what could be the Author's view in adopting
this antiquated mode of writing, which has been exploded ever since fringed gloves and
basket-hilted swords went out of fashion: and we are the more puzzled to account for the
appearance of such a phænomenon, as he seems capable of producing something better.'

THE SCOTCH PARENTS
See CARTER, John

1773: 17   ANON.
THE SELF-DECEIVED: OR, THE HISTORY OF LORD BYRON.

> London: Printed for F. and J. Noble, at their respective Circulating Libraries, near
>   Middle Row, Holborn; and Saint Martin's Court, near Leicester Square, 1773.
> I 239p; II 195, 35p. 12mo. 6s sewed (CR) 5s (MR), 5s sewed (SJC).
> CR 35: 395 (May 1773); MR 48: 416 (May 1773); AF I: 2493.
> BL 12613.g.4; ESTC t070099 (NA MiDW, NjP). Not EM 275: 5 as stated in ESTC.

Notes. 1 p. advs. end vol. 1. 35 pp. 'Appeal to the public, (By F. and J. Noble, booksellers) from
the aspersions cast on them by the anonymous editor of the London Magazine' end vol. 2
(pp. 30–31 missing in BL copy). Epistolary.
Adv. SJC 13–16 Mar 1773 as *The Self-Deceived; or, the History of Lord Biron. To which will be
added, An Appeal to the Publick, in two Parts, from the Aspersions of the anonymous Editor of
the London Magazine: Together with some Strictures on the Conduct of Mr. Baldwin, the
Publisher.*

CR: 'This novel is of a different texture from the foregoing one [*The Sentimental Spy,* 1773:
18], and manufactured in a much better manner. It is written in an easy style, and the title-
page is ingeniously enough contrived *to carry double,* as the lord and the lady are both, in different shapes, *self-deceived.*'

MR [John Noorthouck]: 'A tender epistolary tale, though written by a bloody-minded
Author, who before he makes his hero happy in a second marriage, makes him put his first
wife, with her gallant, to the sword; he then brings a furious ravisher to destroy the lover of
his second spouse in order to leave the coast clear for him; and finally dismisses the said

ravisher with a stump arm. A novelist may kill and maim as many of his personages as he chuses, upon paper, with impunity; but the names of his heroes ought to be as fictitious as their adventures; without endeavouring to ensnare the public attention by undue liberties of appellation.'

1773: 18   ANON.
THE SENTIMENTAL SPY: A NOVEL. IN TWO VOLUMES.

> London: Printed for T. Lowndes, No. 77, in Fleet-street, 1773.
> I 238p; II 257p. 12mo. 6s sewed (CR), 5s (MR), 5s sewed or 6s bound (SJC).
> CR 35: 394 (May 1773); MR 48: 417 (May 1773); AF I: 2495.
> BL 12611.aa.18; EM 236: 2; ESTC t107866.

Notes. 1 p. adv. end vol. 2; running-title, 'The Adventures of a Footman'. William Warren received 8 gns. in Jan 1773 for the copyright to a novel, 'The Adventures of a Footman', GM n.s. 94 (1824): 224. Warren might have been an intermediary rather than the original author.
Adv., 'In a few days will be published', SJC 27 Feb-2 Mar 1773.
Extract published LC 33: 308 (30 Mar-1 Apr 1773).

   MR: 'Contains the adventures of a footman; and it is not improbable that a footman is the Author.'

THE SPIRITUAL QUIXOTE
See GRAVES, Richard

THE TEST OF FRIENDSHIP: OR THE ROYAL ADVENTURERS
See THE ROYAL ADVENTURERS

1773: 19   ANON.
'TWAS WRONG TO MARRY HIM; OR THE HISTORY OF LADY DURSLEY.

> London: Printed for F. and J. Noble, at their respective Circulating Libraries, near
>   Middle-Row, Holborn; and Saint Martin's Court, near Leicester Square, 1773.
> I 236p; II 219p. 12mo. 6s (CR, MR), 5s sewed (SJC Jan), 5s bound (SJC Apr).
> CR 35: 78 (Jan 1773); MR 48: 320 (Apr 1773); AF I: 2806.
> MH-H *EC75.A100.773t2; EM 1493: 4; ESTC n014103 (NA PU).

Notes. CR suggests by same author as *'Twas Right to Marry Him* (1774: 23).
15 pp. 'Appeal to the Public', a defence of the Nobles' publications and circulating library, and 2 pp. advs. end vol. 2.
Adv., 'With an appeal to the Publick from the Aspersions of the anonymous Editor of the London Magazine', SJC 21–23 Jan 1773.
Also adv. with different version of price SJC 10–13 Apr 1773 at end of adv for *The Self-Deceived* (1773: 17).
German trans. Leipzig, 1775 (*Sie that Unrecht, ihn zu heirathen, oder Geschichte der Lady Dursley*) (EAG).

   CR: '. . . the regard we have to the fair sex strongly induces us to hope that no unmarried female will consider Lady Dursley as a pattern for imitation.'
   MR [Thomas Pearne]: ' *'Twas wrong to write it,* would have been a title as suitable to the

merits of this Novel as that which it bears is to the moral of the story. The work contains many things which will disgust the sensible and delicate mind, and yet it will afford very little to interest or entertain those Readers who are less difficult to please.'

1773: 20   ANON.
THE VICISSITUDES OF FORTUNE: OR, THE HISTORY OF MISS SEDLEY. IN TWO VOLUMES.

> London: Printed for T. Jones, At his Circulating Library, in the Strand, opposite Hungerford-Street, 1773.
> I 306p; II 244p. 12mo. 5s (CR), 5s sewed (MR).
> CR 34: 473 (Dec 1772); MR 48: 320 (Apr 1773); AF I: 2854.
> MH-H *EC75.A100.773v; ESTC n063120 (NA CaOHM).

Notes. Epistolary.

CR: 'These volumes contain a good deal of business, or rather unimportant bustle. It is not, however, of an interesting nature. The characters are neither strongly drawn, nor strongly supported.'

MR [Thomas Pearne]: 'Whoever has the ill fortune to throw away their time in the perusal of this nonsensical production, will find it to be a strange jumble of incoherent incidents, vilely detailed in about one hundred of the worst-written letters that ever disgraced the press. But the press is pretty well even with the pen. Between the wretched writing, and the miserable printing, it is as difficult to discover the meaning as the sense of the Author, except where the Reader would wish not to understand him: but the indecent and even shocking freedoms which are taken with that name which should ever be sacred, are every where too obvious.'

1773: 21   ANON.
THE WAY TO LOSE HIM; OR, THE HISTORY OF MISS WYNDHAM: BY THE AUTHOR OF THE WAY TO PLEASE HIM.

> London: Printed for F. and J. Noble, at their respective Circulating Libraries, near Middle Row, Holborn, and Saint Martin's Court, near Leicester Square, 1773.
> I 238p; II 226p. 12mo. 6s (CR); 5s (MR).
> CR 34: 398 (Nov 1772); MR 48: 155 (Feb 1773); AF I: 2910.
> BL 12653.aaa.32; EM 364: 1; ESTC t107630.

Notes. 6 pp. advs. end vol. 2. Epistolary.
CR rev. suggests post-dating.
Further edn: Dublin edn. with title *How She Lost Him; or, the History of Miss Wyndham* adv. beginning of 1781 Dublin edn. of *The Parsonage-House* (1780: 12). German trans. Leipzig, 1774 (*Der Weg, ihn zu verlieren*) (EAG); French trans. Amsterdam, 1775 (*Henriette Wyndham, ou la coquette abusée*) (BL).

CR considers it 'calculated to be of service to the unmarried fair ones'.

MR [Thomas Pearne] reviews *The Way to Lose Him* and *The Way to Please Him* together, judging them to be 'of very useful tendency.'

1773: 22   ANON.
THE WAY TO PLEASE HIM: OR THE HISTORY OF LADY SEDLEY: BY THE AUTHOR OF THE WAY TO LOSE HIM. IN TWO VOLUMES.

London: Printed for F. and J. Noble, at their respective Circulating Libraries, near Middle Row, Holborn,. and Saint Martin's Court, near Leicester Square, 1773.

I 248p; II 247, 15, 22p. 12mo. 6s (CR), 5s (MR).

CR 34: 398 (Nov 1772); MR 48: 155 (Feb 1773); AF I: 2911.

BL C.107.e.58; ESTC n025232 (NA PU).

Notes. End vol. 2: 1 p. adv., followed by 'An Appeal to the Public, (By F. and J. Noble, Booksellers) From the aspersions cast on them by the anonymous editor of the London Magazine' 1–15, 1 more p. adv., 'A Continuation of the Appeal to the Public, (By F. and J. Noble, Booksellers) From the aspersions cast on them by the editor of the London Magazine' [1]–22, and 1 final p. adv. Publication date Nov. 1772 given in the Nobles' 'Appeal to the Public' (1773) in *'Twas Wrong to Marry Him* (1773: 19).

German trans. Leipzig, 1774 (*Der Weg, ihm zu gefallen*) (Price).

CR describes Lady Sedley as 'indeed, an exemplary wife' who 'may serve as a pattern to married ladies in similar circumstances.'

MR [Thomas Pearne] reviews *The Way to Lose Him* and *The Way to Please Him* together, judging them to be 'of very useful tendency.'

1773: 23   ANON.
WOODBURY: OR THE MEMOIRS OF WILLIAM MARCHMONT, ESQ.
AND MISS WALBROOK; IN LETTERS; IN TWO VOLUMES.

London: Printed for J. Bell, near Exeter Exchange, Strand, 1773 [vol. 1].

London: Printed for J. Bell, near Exeter-Exchange, in the Strand; and C. Etherington, at York, 1773 [vol. 2].

I 281p; II 360p. 12mo. 6s sewed (CR), 6s (MR), 6s bound (SJC).

CR 35: 395 (May 1773); MR 48: 417 (May 1773); AF I: 2983.

CLU-S/C PR3991.A1W798; ESTC n036058.

Notes. 2 pp. advs. end vol. 1. Epistolary.

Adv., 'will be published in the Course of a few Days', SJC 23–25 Feb 1773. Still adv., 'just published', SJC 11–13 Mar 1777.

Further edn: Dublin, 1781 (Printed by C. Jackson, 2 vols., 12mo), EM 5067: 3, ESTC t119381 [t.p. includes 'By the author of The Suspicious Lovers', 1777: 8]. German trans. Leipzig, 1779 (*Woodbury, oder Nachrichten in Briefen von Wilhelm Marchmont*) (EAG).

CR: 'This is one of the prettiest novels which we have lately seen; the story is carried on in an interesting manner, and there is a general ease in the language—The parts which merit reprehension are few, compared with those which deserve approbation.'

MR [Thomas Pearne]: 'Surely the youthful part of the fair sex have as keen a relish for novels, as they have for green apples, green gooseberries, or other such kind of crude trash, otherwise it would not be found worth while to cultivate these literary weeds, which spring up, so plenteously, every month, even under the scythe of criticism! If such is the case, the ladies must be gratified; but we would advise them to be least free with those that are of a pernicious tendency. As to the above-mentioned performance, though somewhat insipid, it is, at least, innocent.'

1773: 24   [BACULARD D']ARNAUD, [François-Thomas-Marie de]; MURDOCH, John (*trans.*).
THE TEARS OF SENSIBILITY, NOVELS: NAMELY, 1. THE CRUEL FATHER.

2. ROSETTA; OR, THE FAIR PENITENT REWARDED. 3. THE RIVAL
FRIENDS. 4. SIDNEY AND SILLI; OR, THE MAN OF BENEVOLENCE AND
THE MAN OF GRATITUDE. TRANSLATED FROM THE FRENCH OF M.
D'ARNAUD, BY JOHN MURDOCH.

> London: Printed for Edward and Charles Dilly, in the Poultry, 1773.
> I 164p; II 182p. 8vo. 4s sewed (CR), 5s bound (MR), 4s sewed or 5s bound (SJC).
> CR 35: 233 (Mar 1773); MR 48: 319–20 (Apr 1773); AF I: 1942.
> E Vts.2.f.19.1–2; ESTC t177443.

Notes. A trans. of part of *Épreuves du sentiment* (Paris 1772–3; later vols., 1775–80).

Adv., 'On the first of January will be published, Beautifully printed on a fine Writing Paper',
SJC 24–26 Dec 1772; adv. as published SJC 2–5 Jan 1773; additional booksellers are J. Roson
in New Bond-Street and J. Walter, at Charing Cross.

Extracts from *The Tears of Sensibility*, 'The History of Rosetta', published in *London* and
Hibernian Magazines, 1773, RM 638.

CR: 'The first, second and fourth novels are truly pathetic, and we have not been able to
peruse them without feeling compassion for the sufferers. We should be better pleased were
not some of the incidents beyond the reach of probability. . . .'

MR [William Woodfall]: 'The Author aims, for the most part, to keep his Readers on the
rack. He deals only in those virtues and vices which astonish and exercise our sensibility in
the extreme. He therefore defeats his own purpose. A tale made up wholly of wonders, never
excites admiration; and a novel, which in every page is to harrow up the soul, leaves it in great
quietness.'

1773: 25   [BONHOTE, Elizabeth].
THE FASHIONABLE FRIEND: A NOVEL. IN TWO VOLUMES.

> London: Printed for T. Becket and P. A. Dehondt, in the Strand, 1773.
> I 182p; II 178p. 16mo. 6s (CR) 5s sewed (MR, SJC).
> CR 36: 235–6 (Sept 1773); MR 49: 69 (July 1773); AF I: 205.
> MH-H *EC75.B6415.773f; EM 1002: 7; ESTC n004640 (NA CtY, PU).

Notes. 1 p. adv. end vol. 1; 6 pp. advs. end vol. 2. Epistolary.

Adv., 'In Two Pocket Volumes', SJC 22–25 May 1773.

Further edn: Dublin, 1774 (Printed for J. Potts, J. Williams, J. A. Husband, T. Walker and
C. Jenkin, 1 vol., 12mo), EM 239: 7, ESTC t068062. German trans. Leipzig, 1775 (*Der Freund
nach der Mode*) (EAG).

CR: 'When the ancient romances were exploded, and the pictures of real life were substituted in their stead, such a variety of characters and incidents presented themselves, that
novel-writers easily met with materials; a wide field was opened for them to range in, and
they might avoid treading in each others steps. But since almost every track is become beaten,
authors are obliged to make the most of what is left them; for this reason most of our later
novels are very barren of incidents, and the writers seem to aim less at diversifying their tales,
than at working up a single circumstance in the most striking manner. In that before us we
have little variety; but the author of it endeavours to interest us in behalf of injured innocence, by painting the misfortunes of his heroine in the strongest colours. In this he certainly
succeeds, as the reader who is susceptible of pity will scarcely peruse this little tale without
emotions of sympathy.'

MR [John Noorthouck]: 'Nature and probability have had no concern in the production of this trifle.'

1773: 26 [CARRA, Jean-Louis].
CECILIA; OR, THE EASTERN LOVERS. A NOVEL. TRANSLATED FROM THE FRENCH.

> London: Printed for the Author, and sold by S. Bladon in Pater-noster Row, and G. Lister, No. 46, in the Old Bailey, 1773.
> 187p. 12mo. 3s (CR), 3s bound (MR).
> CR 36: 397 (Nov 1773); MR 49: 150 (Aug 1773); AF I: 357.
> BL 1154.i.12; EM 2903: 3; ESTC t117297 (NA CLU-S/C, TxHR).

Notes. Trans. of *Odazir, ou le jeune Syrian* (La Haye, 1772).

CR: '*Eastern* Lovers? The author might as well have called them *Northern, Southern,* or *Western* lovers, for he has not distinguished them by any striking marks of *Orientalism.* The truth is they are mere *French* lovers: but it is by no means clear that they will figure away with much *eclat* in England.'

MR: 'Those who love a melancholy story, may here indulge themselves to the utmost of their heart's discontent.—We have nothing to add in the commendation of this piece.'

1773: 27 [CARTER, John].
THE SCOTCH PARENTS: OR, THE REMARKABLE CASE OF JOHN RAMBLE, WRITTEN BY HIMSELF, (IN THE MONTH OF FEBRUARY, 1773); EMBELLISHED WITH ELEGANT COPPERPLATES OF THE SINGULAR AND UNCOMMON SCENES CONTAINED IN THIS NARRATIVE.

> London: Printed, and sold by all the Booksellers in Great-Britain and Ireland, 1773.
> 212p. 12mo. 3s 6d (MR), 3s sewed (SJC).
> MR 49: 69 (July 1773); AF I: 347.
> BL 1418.c.36; EM 3406: 3; ESTC t082663 (BI E).

Notes. Annotation on t.p. 'M^r. Carter—son of a Statuary in Piccadilly'. MR reviews under 'Novels'.

MR and SJC give Bladon as bookseller.

Adv., 'Embellished with elegant Engravings, and Metzotinto [*sic*] Copper-Plates, of the singular and uncommon Scenes contained in this Narrative', SJC 17–19 June 1773. The adv. has this additional note: 'The Author has been put under the disagreeable Necessity of laying before the World his most singular Amour with Miss Eleonora Macpherson, in order to vindicate his own Character from the cruel Aspersion of her Parents; and to set this Affair, which has been so variously related, in its true Light.'

MR: 'A ridiculous, low, ill-written story of the Author's illicit and unfortunate amour with the daughter of a shop-keeper in a market not far from St. James's. John Ramble appears, from his own account (which has, to give him his due throughout, the air of *truth*) to be a very indiscreet man, and to have not only involved himself in distress, by his misconduct; but also to have occasioned the ruin of the poor girl whom he seduced. Miss M——'s parents, too, seem to have made but a sorry use of their authority over their unhappy daughter.'

1773: 28 [?CAVENDISH, Georgiana, Duchess of Devonshire].
EMMA: OR THE UNFORTUNATE ATTACHMENT; A SENTIMENTAL
NOVEL; IN THREE VOLUMES.

London: Printed for T. Hookham, at his Circulating Library, in New-Street, Hanover-Square, 1773.

I v, 274p; II 295p; III 330p. 12mo. 9s (CR, MR), 7s 6d sewed or 9s bound (SJC).

CR 35: 475 (June 1773); MR 49: 69 (July 1773); AF I: 758.

BL 12611.ee.18; EM 203: 9; ESTC t057436 (NA CSmH, IU, MH-H, NjP &c.).

Notes. Dublin edn. claims to be 'By the Author of the Sylph', i.e. Georgiana Cavendish, Duchess of Devonshire? [*The Sylph* 1779: 8].

Dedication to Lady Camden vol. 1, iii–v, followed by 4-pp. list of subscribers. In vol. 2 1 p. adv. recto of leaf after t.p. Epistolary.

Adv., 'In a few Days will be published', SJC 1–4 May 1773. Still adv. as 'This Day was published' SJC 15–17 Dec 1774.

Further edns: Dublin, 1784 (Printed by S. Colbert, 2 vols., 12mo) (BRu ENC), xESTC; London, 1787, EM 2261: 9, ESTC t075741; London, 1789 (Summers).

CR: 'We heartily recommend the perusal of these three volumes to those who are in want of a soporific, and we do it very confidently, as we have experienced its effects. The story of the Unfortunate Attachment is told in a series of letters; a mode of writing which Richardson and Rousseau have indeed practised with the greatest success, but which requires too great a share of talents for every dabbler in novel-writing to adopt. Although we seldom commend novels, it is not because we are so nice as to condemn every one which is not *very* excellent, but because we very rarely meet with any we can honestly praise. The novel now before us is very insipid, and all we can in [*sic*] its commendation is, that no part of it has any immoral tendency.'

MR: 'Innocent, but not excellent:—yet not contemptible. We have characterised fifty such; and are sick of *repetition.*'

1773: 29 [CHATER, John].
THE HISTORY OF TOM RIGBY. IN THREE VOLUMES.

London: Printed for T. Vernor, in St. Michael's Alley, Cornhill; and J. Boosey, King-Street, Cheapside, 1773.

I 250p; II 240p; III 258p. 12mo. 9s (CR), 7s 6d sewed (MR).

CR 34: 472 (Dec 1772); MR 48: 154 (Feb 1773); AF I: 368.

BL 12613.d.25; EM 233: 4; ESTC t070081 (NA PU).

Notes. Imprint date in vol. 1 misprinted as 1733.

Further edn: Dublin, 1773 (Printed by A. Mitchell, for the booksellers, 2 vols., 12mo), EM 4869: 2, ESTC t119332. German trans. Lübeck and Leipzig, 1775 (*Geschichte des Herrn Thomas Rigby*) (WC).

CR: 'The author of these volumes is possessed of tender feelings, and of abilities to describe them: but his characters are not drawn with sufficient variety: they resemble each other, and seem to be of the same family.'

MR [Thomas Pearne]: 'A plentiful but homely entertainment, ill-suited to the delicate taste of those who are accustomed to the literary dainties provided by your Cervanteses, your Marivauxs, your Fieldings, and other celebrated cooks.—It may, however, go down well enough with those who only gape and swallow: and to whom, like the ostrich, it is immaterial whether you are treating them with biscuits or hobnails.'

1773: 30   [DELACROIX, Jacques-Vincent].
THE MEMOIRS OF AN AMERICAN. WITH A DESCRIPTION OF THE
KINGDOM OF PRUSSIA, AND THE ISLAND OF ST. DOMINGO.
TRANSLATED FROM THE FRENCH. IN TWO VOLUMES.

> London: Printed for F. and J. Noble, at their respective Circulating Libraries, near
> Middle Row, Holborn, and Saint Martin's Court, near Leicester Square, 1773.
> I xx, 216p; II 225. 12mo. 6s (CR), 5s sewed (MR), 5s sewed or 6s bound (SJC).
> CR 34: 397 (Nov 1772); MR 47: 411 (Nov 1772); AF I: 1795.
> BL C.142.a.36; ESTC n035329 (NA CLU, DLC, NIC &c.).

Notes. Trans. of *Mémoires d'un Américain* (Paris, 1771). 3 pp. advs. end vol. 2.
Post-dated; adv. as published SJC 8–10 Oct 1772.

CR: 'You are at a loss to know when [the author] writes in the character of the *Novellist*,
and when he assumes the dignity of the *Historian*; when he is a fabricator of fables, or when
he is a narrator of true occurrences.'

MR [Gilbert Stuart]: 'These volumes are intitled to rank immediately above the common
class of novels. But though they possess, in some degree, the power of interesting the Reader,
they are confused in their manner, and furnish an imperfect entertainment. The historical
parts of them, though seemingly relative to matters of fact, are trifling, and want precision.'

1773: 31   [DUFF, William].
THE HISTORY OF RHEDI, THE HERMIT OF MOUNT ARARAT: AN
ORIENTAL TALE.

> London: Printed for T. Cadell, in the Strand, 1773.
> 307p. 12mo. 3s (CR, MR, SJC).
> CR 36: 283–86 (Oct 1773); MR 49: 410 (Nov 1773); AF I: 695.
> BL 245.f.9; EM 6294: 10; ESTC t130068 (BI ABu, C, O; NA CSmH, MH-H, NjP).

Notes. Adv., 'In a few Days will be published', SJC 19–22 June 1773.
Further edn: Dublin, 1781 (Printed by Brett Smith, for C. Jackson, 1781), EM 4298: 19, ESTC
t059652 and includes in t.p. 'Written by Mr. Mackenzie', but ESTC is quite clear: 'In fact by
William Duff.' French trans. Londres [Versailles?], 1777 (*Histoire de Rhedy*), ESTC n033032.
Facs: FN.

CR: 'This tale is written in the figurative style of oriental composition. The narration,
though sometimes unequal, is in general supported with an uniform luxuriance of ornament, the sentiments are virtuous, and the incidents are described in a lively and affecting
manner. In these, however, there is not much novelty; and we may discover in the work some
trivial marks of inadvertency' (p. 286).

MR: 'A few Scotticisms discover this Eastern Tale to be the production of North Britain;
and it is a pity that they were not corrected before the publication of the book. Defects of this
kind, however, but rarely occur; and they are not here mentioned with a view to detract from
the merit of a work which, without being a first rate performance, is both moral and entertaining.'

1773: 32   FOGERTY, Mrs.
*THE FATAL CONNEXION: BY MRS. FOGERTY.

> London: Printed for R. Snagg, No. 29, Pater-noster-Row (SJC), 1773 (MR).

2 vols. 12mo. 5s (CR, MR), no price (SJC).

CR 36: 397 (Nov 1773); MR 49: 150 (Aug 1773); AF I: 916.

No copy located.

Notes. Adv. SJC 2–5 Oct 1773.

CR cites Bladon as the bookseller.

CR: 'Whether Mrs. Fogerty is a real or a fictitious personage, is of no sort of consequence to the public; of less consequence is the production under her name, which has very little to recommend it to their attention.'

MR: 'Surely Mrs. Fogerty was begotten, born, nursed, and educated in a circulating library, and sucked in the spirit of romance with her mother's milk! Novel-writing seems quite natural to her; and while she lives there is no fear that the reading Misses and reading Masters who cultivate this profitable study at the easy rate of ten shillings and six-pence per ann. will ever want a due supply of adventures, memoirs, and genuine histories of Lady this, and Lord that, and Colonel t'other thing. In the manufacturing of all which, the greatest difficulty seems to be—the hitting off a new title-page: for as to the stories told, and the characters drawn, they are all echoes of echoes, and shadows of shades.'

1773: 33 FOGERTY, Mrs.
*MEMOIRS OF COLONEL DIGBY AND MISS STANLEY: BY MRS. FOGERTY.

London: Printed for R. Snagg, No. 29, Pater-noster-Row (SJC).

2 vols. 12mo. 5s (CR, MR), 5s sewed or 6s neatly bound (SJC).

CR 36: 397 (Nov 1773); MR 49: 319 (Oct 1773); AF I: 917.

No copy located.

Notes. Adv. SJC 2–5 Oct 1773.

CR: 'Mrs. Fogerty certainly has a prolific brain, but she breeds so fast, that the brats which she produces are not very likely to live, having but *washy* constitutions. To write *fast*, and to write *well* are two very different things; but many readers who have voracious appetites, and who are contented with *mere business* in works of this kind, may meet with amusement in the two volumes now under our inspection: but those who expect that business of an interesting nature, and conducted in a masterly manner, will be, most probably, disappointed.'

1773: 34 [GRAVES, Richard].
THE SPIRITUAL QUIXOTE: OR, THE SUMMER'S RAMBLE OF MR. GEOFFRY WILDGOOSE. A COMIC ROMANCE. IN THREE VOLUMES.

London: Printed for J. Dodsley, Pall-Mall, 1773.

I xx, 352p; II vi, 287p; III xii, 322p. 12mo. 7s 6d sewed (CR, SJC) 7s 6d (MR).

CR 35: 275–86 (Apr 1773); MR 48: 384–8 (May 1773); AF I: 1112.

BL 12614.eee.20; EM 191: 2; ESTC t072189 (BI BMp, C, DE, MRu; NA CaOONL, CtY-BR, CLU-S/C).

Notes. KM 4980: Printing completed by Bowyer 6 Mar 1773; 1000 copies. KM 4998: 2nd edn., printing completed by Bowyer 16 Dec 1773; 1250 copies.

Adv., 'Speedily will be published', SJC 18–20 Feb 1773, and as 'Next Week will be published' 4–6 Mar 1773.

Extracts published LC 33: 269 and 277 (18–20 and 20–23 Mar 1773).

Further edns: Dublin, 1774 (Printed for W. Sleater, D. Chamberlaine, J. Potts, J. Williams, T. Walker, and C. Jenkin, 2 vols., 12mo), EM 6293: 4, ESTC t055927; London, 1774, EM 5528: 7, ESTC t057374; London, 1783, EM 4826: 3, ESTC t072188; London, 1792, EM 5530: 4, ESTC t067326; London, 1816 (WC); WC has entries for 1 or more further post-1800 edns (exact number unclear); NSTC lists edns in 1805, 1808, 1810, 1816, [1820], 1827 and [1830?]. Extract published in *Literary Register*, 1773, RM 1175. German trans. Leipzig, 1773 (*Der Geistliche Don Quixote*) (Price). Facs: FN.

CR places 'this entertaining romance' in tradition of *Don Quixote*.

MR [William Woodfall]: 'There is something singular in this production, and it deserves to be distinguished from the common trash of modern novels. The subject, however, is mean, and unworthy the talents of this Writer. The adventures of a frantic enthusiast (a Methodist preacher) cannot be supposed to afford the materials of an entertaining romance' (p. 384).

1773: 35   [GUILLARD DE BEAURIEU, Gaspard]; BURNE, James (*trans.*).
THE MAN OF NATURE. TRANSLATED FROM THE FRENCH BY JAMES BURNE. VOLUME I. SOLITUDE.
THE MAN OF NATURE. TRANSLATED FROM THE FRENCH BY JAMES BURNE. VOLUME II. SOCIETY.

London: Printed for T. Cadell, in the Strand, 1773.
I 256p; II 260p. 12mo. 6s (CR) 5s (MR), 5s sewed (SJC).
CR 35: 188–91 (Mar 1773); MR 48: 179–81 (Mar 1773); AF I: 291.
BL 12510.cc.7; EM 56: 5; ESTC t038906 (NA CaOHM, MnU).

Notes. Trans. of *L'élève de la nature* (The Hague and Paris, 1763).
Adv., 'In the Press and speedily will be published', SJC 3–5 Sept 1772; adv. 'On Tuesday the 19th inst. will be published, Adorned with Frontispieces elegantly engraved', SJC 5–7 Jan 1773. Extracts published LC 33: 85 and 121 (23–26 Jan and 4–6 Feb 1773).
Further edn: Dublin, 1773 (Printed for J. Potts, J. Williams, J. Husband, T. Walker, R. Moncrieffe, and C. Jenkin, 2 vols., 12mo), ESTC t171060.

CR: 'In this novel, the great developement [*sic*] of ideas in the human mind, and the reflexions occasioned by the first sight of objects with which it is totally unacquainted, are, *sometimes*, described in a natural and pleasing manner; but we cannot consider the history of the Man of Nature as peculiarly qualified for affording moral instruction, nor seems there to be reason for concluding from observations made on the most uncultivated people, that mankind are more strongly attached to virtue in the state of simple and untutored nature, than in that of civilized and social life' (p. 191).

MR [William Woodfall]: '. . . the Writer has merit, though it does not rise to excellence: nor is the plan of his work, in its primary idea, absolutely new.'

HUTCHINSON, William, DUMONT: OR, THE HERMITAGE: A BRITISH STORY
See 1772: 34

1773: 36   [MACKENZIE, Henry].
THE MAN OF THE WORLD: IN TWO PARTS.

London: Printed for W. Strahan; and T. Cadell, in the Strand, 1773.
I 340p; II 251p. 12mo. 6s (CR) 5s sewed (MR), 6s bound (SJC).
CR 35: 269–74 (Apr 1773); MR 48: 268–9 (Apr 1773); AF I: 1710.
BL 243.h.7,8; EM 6332: 1; ESTC t038918 (BI C, E, O &c.; NA CtY, CtY-BR, CSmH, ICN, MH-H, NjP, PU, TxU &c.; EA Pm, SU, TaLn &c.).
Notes. Adv., 'In the Press, and speedily will be published', SJC 30 Jan-2 Feb 1773.
Adv. by Strahan and Cadell PA 4 Nov 1777 refers to recent newspaper reports ascribing authorship of *The Man of Feeling* (1771: 46), *The Man of the World, Julia de Roubigné* (1777: 13) and Mackenzie's poem *The Pursuits of Happiness* to the late Mr. Eccles of Bath; Strahan and Cadell declare that they have 'long been intimately acquainted with' Mackenzie and have printed his works from manuscripts in his own hand, have paid him for the copyrights and have reprinted some from Mackenzie's corrected copies.
Further edns: London, 1773, EM 4231: 3, ESTC t120999; Dublin, 1773 (Printed for Messrs. Sleater, Potts, Williams, Chamberlaine, Husband, Walker, Moncrieffe, and Jenkin, 2 vols., 12mo), EM 4584:4, ESTC t062655; London, 1783, ESTC n022566; Dublin, 1787 (Printed for T. Heery, 2 vols., 12mo), ESTC t205810; London, 1787, ESTC n022564; 4 further entries in ESTC; NSTC lists edns in 1802, [1803], 1806, 1809 and 1818. German trans. Leipzig, 1773 (*Sir Thomas Sindal oder der Mann nach der Welt*) (Price); French trans. Paris, 1775 (*L'Homme du monde*) (BN). Facs: FN. Extract from *The Man of the World*, 'The Adventures of Wm. Annesley', published in *Harvest Home*, 1807, RM 65.
CR: 'In the first volume of this novel the characters are strongly marked; there are delicate and interesting situations, excellent moral precepts, and such sentiments as can arise only in a mind that is habituated to observation and reflexion on life and manners. The second, however, is not entitled to equal praise; and the story concludes with a juncture of improbable incidents' (p. 274).
MR [William Woodfall]: 'The Author of this work is known to the public from the *Man of Feeling*, and the *Pursuits of Happiness*. The Reader will find that he continues to write in character. There is the same improbability in his fable, the same affectation in some of his *sentiments*, and the same quaintness in some of his phrases,—the same love of virtue, the same philanthropy, and the same pathetic and happy touches which distinguished his Man of Feeling' (p. 268).

1773: 37   SADI [MUSHARRIF OD-DĪN MUŞLIH OD-DĪN]; SULIVAN, Stephen (*trans.*).
SELECT FABLES FROM GULISTAN, OR THE BED OF ROSES. TRANSLATED FROM THE ORIGINAL PERSIAN OF SADI.
London: Printed in the Year 1773.
82p. 8vo.
O Vet.A5e.2729; ESTC t175669 (BI E).
Notes. Translator's name appears on t.p. of 1774 edn.
The Gulistan by Sadi (d. 1291) was written in Persian in 1258.
Extracts published LC 36: 17 and 37 (5–7 and 9–12 July 1774).
Further edns: London, 1774, ESTC t147765; n.p., 1780 (WC), xESTC; London, 1785, ESTC t177902.
1774 edn. rev. MR 51: 485 (Dec 1774).
MR [John Langhorne]: 'Though we have read these Fables with attention, we have met

with nothing particularly striking, either in the delineation of character or in the deduction of moral. They have, in general, a political tendency, recommending justice and humanity to princes, which, in the regions of the East, can never be too much inculcated.'

1773: 38   WIELAND, C[hristoph] M[artin].
THE HISTORY OF AGATHON, BY MR. C. M. WIELAND. TRANS-
LATED FROM THE GERMAN ORIGINAL, WITH A PREFACE BY THE
TRANSLATOR.

> London: Printed for T. Cadell, in the Strand, 1773.
> I xxxi, 248; II iii, 327; III 275p; IV 235p. 12mo. 12s (CR, MR), 12s bound (SJC).
> CR 37: 196–9 (Mar 1774); MR 50: 176–82 (Mar 1774); AF I: 2950.
> BL 243.k.9; EM 6220: 1; ESTC t099052 (BI BMp, C, Ota; NA CtHT, DLC, IU &c.).

Notes. Trans. of *Geschichte des Agathon* (Frankfurt and Leipzig [ie Zurich], 1766/67).
ESTC also records same title, printed in London for C. Heydinger, 1773, 4 vols., 12mo,
ESTC n033040.
Publication possibly delayed: adv., 'In a few Days will be published', SJC 27–29 Jan 1774.

CR: 'His descriptions are picturesque, his reasoning is in general just, and the satire, in which he abounds, is well aimed; but his allusions are sometimes indelicate, and he has not restrained his imagination from frequently painting in too seducing and agreeable colours those objects which ought to be marked with the reprehension of a moral writer' (p. 199).

MR [Ralph Griffiths]: 'A romance, or a novel, like other fables, usually ends with a moral deduction; and it is proper that this should always be the case, not only because the moral is the main object and end of the piece, but because the farewell impression left on the Reader's mind when he closes the book, is generally that which strikes the deepest, and lasts the longest. Now, although the balance obviously inclines in favour of morality, throughout the whole of Agathon's history, there is no exemplary inference of this kind at the conclusion of the work . . .' (p. 181).

1773: 39   WIELAND, C[hristoph] M[artin].
REASON TRIUMPHANT OVER FANCY: EXEMPLIFIED IN THE SIN-
GULAR ADVENTURES OF DON SYLVIO DE ROSALVA. A HISTORY IN
WHICH EVERY MARVELLOUS EVENT OCCURS NATURALLY.
TRANSLATED FROM THE GERMAN ORIGINAL OF MR. C. M.
WIELAND. IN THREE VOLUMES.

> London: Printed for J. Wilkie, at No. 71, St. Paul's Church-Yard; S. Leacroft, at the
> Globe, at Charing-Cross, and C. Heydinger, No. 274, in the Strand, 1773.
> I 247p; II 231p; III 211p. 12mo. 7s 6d sewed (CR), 9s (MR), 7s 6d sewed or 9s bound
> (SJC).
> CR 35: 143–7 (Feb 1773); MR 48: 126–9 (Feb 1773); AF I: 2951.
> BL 12556.a.21; EM 138: 6; ESTC t129736.

Notes. Trans. of *Der Sieg der Natur über die Schäwrmerey, oder die Abentheuer* [*sic*] *des Don Sylvio von Rosalva* (Ulm, 1764), but re-issued as *Die Abenteuer des Don Sylvio von Rosalva* (Leipzig, 1772) (EAG).
Adv., 'In the Press, and in a few Days will be published', SJC 12–15 Dec 1772; adv. as pub-
lished SJC 24–26 Dec 1772.

CR places the novel in the *Don Quixote* tradition and says of the hero's adventures, '... as they generally end in the disappointment of his ridiculous hopes, we have been frequently led to laugh at them...' (p. 144).

CR 36: 80 (July 1773) notes in 'Correspondence': 'The History of Don Sylvio de Rosalva we have seen in French but we have no reason to believe, that the translation we received was not made from the German Original.'

MR [William Woodfall] reviews positively, but then writes of one episode: 'It is extravagant enough for the purpose intended by it; but it is indecent in many places. No man should write a novel, or any book of entertainment, which a gentleman cannot read aloud in a company of ladies' (p. 129).

1774

1774: 1   ANON.
ALL'S RIGHT AT LAST: OR, THE HISTORY OF MISS WEST.

> London: Printed for F. and J. Noble, at their respective Circulating Libraries, near Middle Row, Holborn, and Saint Martin's Court, near Leicester Square, 1774.
> I 224p; II 215p. 12mo. 6s (CR, MR), 5s sewed or 6s bound (SJC).
> CR 36: 397 (Nov 1773); MR 49: 409 (Nov 1773); AF I: 255.
> BL 12612.bb.27; EM 131: 1; ESTC t064708 (NA IU).

Notes. 1 p. advs. end vol. 2. Epistolary.
Post-dated; adv. as published SJC 2–5 Oct 1773.
German trans. Leipzig, 1775 (*Der Schein betrügt*) (Price); French trans. Rotterdam, 1777 (*Histoire de Miss West, ou l'heureux dénouement*) (BGR).

CR: 'This novel is agreeably written. The *authoress* seems to have endeavoured to imitate the style and manners of the ingenious lady who has so agreeably entertained the public with her Julia Mandeville, and Emily Montague.'

MR suggests it is by the same author as *Emily Montague* (1769, JR 1298, AF I: 256), i.e. Frances Brooke, principally because it too describes Canada.

1774: 2   ANON.
THE ASSIGNATION; A SENTIMENTAL NOVEL, IN A SERIES OF LETTERS. IN TWO VOLUMES.

> London: Printed for F. and J. Noble, at their respective Circulating Libraries, near Middle Row, Holborn, and St. Martin's Court, near Leicester Square, 1774.
> I 236p; II 208p. 12mo. 6s (CR, MR), 5s sewed (SJC).
> CR 36: 477 (Dec 1773); MR 50: 234 (Mar 1774); AF I: 115.
> BL 1507/333; EM 2601: 1; ESTC t084646.

Notes. End vol. 2 has 3 pp. advs. for the Nobles' publications, followed by 1 p. 'Advertisement To the Country Booksellers' regarding the Nobles' contest with Baldwin. Epistolary.
Post-dated; adv. as published SJC 4–7 Dec 1773.

CR: 'These volumes are written in a pretty easy manner, and they are, upon the whole, not destitute of entertainment.'

MR [John Cleland?]: 'It is impossible to read over these volumes without remarking the quantity of blank paper which meets the eye at almost every page of this *sentimental* work: a circumstance, however, which we mention not as a *blemish*; but, on the contrary, as the greatest possible excellence attending most writings of this stamp.'

1774: 3   ANON.
LA BELLE PHILOSOPHE; OR THE FAIR PHILOSOPHER. IN TWO VOLUMES.

London: Printed for T. Lowndes, N°. 77, in Fleet-street, 1774.
I 248p; II 240p. 12mo. 5s sewed (CR) 6s (MR), 5s sewed or 6s bound (SJC).
CR 37: 76 (Jan 1774); MR 50: 234 (Mar 1774); AF I: 163.
BL C.192.a.188; ESTC t227111.

Notes. Epistolary.
Adv., *The Fair Philosopher. A Novel*, SJC 18–20 Jan 1774.
Further edn: Dublin, 1775 [*The Fair Philosopher: or the history of the hon. Miss Eloisa Howard*] (Printed by Thomas Walker, 2 vols., long 12mo), ESTC n047378.

CR: 'These volumes contain many characters, many situations, many sentiments, much business, and not a little bustle. This novel cannot be ranked among the drowsy productions of a similar kind, for the attention is sufficiently kept awake to prevent the reader from taking a nap.—The catastrophe is confessedly an imitation of Clarissa.' [Samuel Richardson's *Clarissa* 1748.]

MR [John Cleland?]: 'In reading over these two volumes, we probably imbibed so much of the philosophy of the fair heroine of the piece, as to render us less susceptible than ordinary to tender impressions; for we can truly say, we felt not one sensation either of pain or pleasure, during the whole of the time which we passed in conversation with this pretended philosopher in petticoats: who, by the way, is not much of a philosopher neither; for her history is as mere a novel-book, as any of the Miss Jessamys, or Delia Daintys, or Lady Flirts, or Sophy Slamakins, that ever the circulating libraries produced.'

1774: 4   ANON.
THE DISINTERESTED MARRIAGE: OR THE HISTORY OF MR. FRANK-LAND.

London: Printed for F. and J. Noble, at their respective Circulating Libraries, near Middle Row, Holborn; and Saint Martin's Court, near Leicester Square, 1774.
I 248p; II 227p. 12mo. 6s (CR, MR), 5s sewed or 6s bound (SJC).
CR 36: 398 (Nov 1773); MR 49: 409–10 (Nov 1773); AF I: 642.
PU Singer-Mend. PR.3991.A1.D57.1774; ESTC n028531 (BI O).

Notes. ESTC notes 'With reference to Charles Frankland'.
8 pp. advs. end vol. 2 and final page of vol. 2 is 'Advertisement To the Country Booksellers' regarding the Nobles' contest with Baldwin. Epistolary.
Post-dated; adv. SJC 2–5 Oct 1773.
German trans. Breslau, 1776 (*Die uneigennützige Heurath*) (Price).

CR: 'If the author of this novel expects to make his readers act in a disinterested manner, when matrimony engages their attention, he will be, in all human probability, very much disappointed; however, as he has endeavoured to shew the ill consequences resulting from a conjugal connection, without the existence of love on both sides, his laudable efforts deserve commendation; and if his fictitious scenes are perused with attention, they may prove serviceable to many personages, both of the masculine and feminine gender in real life.'

MR: 'Whatever may be objected against the sentimental comedy, the sentiments conveyed in novels are perhaps of more importance; as they are the chief study of the youthful part of the female sex. The principles inculcated in this narrative may indeed cover many imperfections, and render it *innocent* reading, at least; it might be added, *profitable* too, were it not known how eagerly young Misses skip from incident to incident; carefully overlooking every observation or reflection that might impede the immediate gratification of their eager curiosity.'

1774: 5   ANON.
THE DOUBLE DISAPPOINTMENT; OR, THE HISTORY OF CHARLES MARLOW. IN A SERIES OF LETTERS. IN TWO VOLUMES.

> London: Printed for T. Hookham, at his Circulating Library, Hanover Street, Hanover Square, 1774.
> I 214p; II 225p. 12mo. 6s bound (adv.).
> O 249.s.612,613; EM 999: 2; ESTC n000753 (NA MH-H, PU [vol. 1 only]).

Notes. 1 p. advs. end vol. 2. Epistolary.
Adv. end vol. 2 of *The History of the Hon. Mrs. Rosemont* (1781: 17).
Adv. PA 16 Jan 1781 as *History of Charles Marlow Esq and Miss Hastings.*

1774: 6   ANON.
EDWARD. A NOVEL. DEDICATED (BY PERMISSION) TO HER MAJESTY.

> London: Printed for T. Davies, Russell-Street, Covent-Garden; Bookseller to the Royal Academy, 1774.
> I 216p; II 224p. 12mo. 6s (CR, MR), 5s sewed (SJC).
> CR 37: 475 (June 1774); MR 51: 72 (July 1774); AF I: 716.
> BL 12613.e.4; EM 275: 5; ESTC t070086 (BI O; NA CtY, MH-H, PU &c.).

Notes. Epistolary.
Adv., 'Speedily will be published', SJC 29–31 Mar 1774; title given as *The History of Edward.*
Re-adv., 'On Saturday next will be published' and as *Edward. A Novel,* SJC 3–5 May 1774. Imprint in both forms of the adv. includes the additional 'and sold by J. Bew, in Paternoster-Row; and J. Walter, Charing-Cross'.
German trans. Leipzig, 1774 (*Eduard, eine Geschichte*) (Price).

CR: 'The general tendency of the work before us is to recommend virtue; the story is told in a serious strain, and the author frequently inserts very grave moral reflexions on the events related. Some of the characters are pretty strongly marked, and the work is superior to the *general run* of novels.'

MR: 'Another of the cluster; but not destitute of sentiment. . . .'

1774: 7   ANON.
EDWIN AND JULIA: A NOVEL IN A SERIES OF LETTERS. BY A LADY. IN TWO VOLUMES.

London: Printed for J. Wilkie, No. 71, St. Paul's Church-Yard, n.d. [vol. 1].
London: Printed for J. Wilkie, No. 71, St. Paul's Church-Yard, 1774 [vol. 2].
I 291p; II 272p. 12mo. 5s sewed (CR), 5s (MR), 5s sewed or 6s bound (SJC).
CR 39: 163 (Feb 1775); MR 52: 361 (Apr 1775); AF II: 1221.
ICU Rare PR3291.E26; ESTC n065417 (NA CtY).
Notes. 4 pp. advs. end vol. 2. Epistolary.
Adv., 'On Thursday next will be published', SJC 8–10 Dec 1774; additional bookseller is
J. Robson, in Bond-Street. Also adv. LC 37: 127 (4–7 Feb 1775).
German trans. Leipzig, 1775 (Edwin und Julia, eine Geschichte im Briefen) (EAG).
    CR: 'However plentiful the follies and vices of mankind are, the numerous representations
which have been made of them seem to have almost exhausted the subject; at least in the present Novel, as in many others which we have lately perused, we have met with scarcely any
thing but what is grown thread-bare by repetition.'
    MR [William Enfield]: '... to invent incidents at once natural, interesting and instructive;
to exhibit characters distinguished by peculiar traits and uniformly supported; to express a
variety of passions in the language proper to each; and, by the whole narrative, to fix virtuous
impressions upon the heart of the reader, without the aid of sententious reflections and a formal application; requires the hand of no mean artist. Such a hand, we think, we plainly discover in the novel before us.'

THE FASHIONABLE DAUGHTER
See TURNER, Daniel

1774: 8   ANON.
*FATAL AFFECTION; OR THE HISTORY OF HENRY AND CAROLINE.
London: Printed for F. and J. Noble, in Holborn and St. Martin's-Court, 1774 (SJC).
2 vols. 12mo. 6s (CR, MR), 6s bound (SJC).
CR 37: 76 (Jan 1774); MR 50: 234 (Mar 1774); AF I: 849.
No copy located.
Notes. Adv., 'Next Thursday will be published', SJC 8–11 Jan 1774.
    CR: 'Caroline is the heroine of the piece, and generally appears in an amiable light. We
cannot say so much in favour of the hero; for Henry is a very contemptible and censurable
character. The other personages of the piece are but indifferently drawn, and the situations
into which they are thrown are barely within the bounds of probability.'

THE FATAL EFFECTS OF INCONSTANCY
See DORAT, Claude-Joseph

1774: 9   ANON.
THE FORTUNE TELLER. IN TWO VOLUMES.
London: Printed for J. Bew, in Pater-noster-Row, 1774.
I xii, 200p; II 207p. 12mo. 5s sewed (CR), 6s (MR), 5s sewed or 6s bound (SJC).
CR 38: 157 (Aug 1774); MR 50: 326–7 (Apr 1774); AF I: 946.
ViU PR 3291.AIF 6 1774; xESTC.
Notes. Preface iii–xii. Table of contents in each vol.

Adv., 'On the first of Feb. will be published', SJC 27–29 Jan 1774.

Adv. SJC 17–[19] Feb 1774: *The Fortune-Teller; a Novel. Being a faithful Display of the Magic Arts practised in and about this Metropolis.*

Further edns: London, 1774, EM 2685: 5, ESTC t117773; London, 1779, EM 4646: 3, ESTC n032721.

Further edn. adv., with 4 other Baldwin and Bew re-publications, SJC 6–9 Mar 1779; see *Harriet* (1771: 18).

CR: '. . . we are pretty confident we are not mistaken in predicting some reputation to the Fortune-teller before us, who, besides possessing the very desirable talent of telling a story agreeably, has no inconsiderable knowledge of mankind.'

MR [John Cleland?]: 'These little volumes are distinguished by a vein of good sense and morality, which runs through the whole performance, and renders it far from being wanting either in entertainment or improvement.'

THE HISTORY OF ARSACES, PRINCE OF BETLIS
See JOHNSTONE, Charles

1774: 10   ANON.
THE HISTORY OF LORD STANTON. A NOVEL. BY A GENTLEMAN OF THE MIDDLE TEMPLE. AUTHOR OF THE TRIAL, OR HISTORY OF CHARLES HORTON.

London: Printed for T. Vernor, in St. Michael's Alley, Cornhill, n.d. [ESTC: 1775?].

I 235p; II 260p; III 260p; IV 264p; V 274p. 12mo. 12s bound (t.p., vols. 1–3), 15s bound (t.p., vols. 4–5), 3 vols. 9s (MR), vols. 4–5 6s (MR), 5 vols 15s (CR), 3 vols. 7s 6d sewed (SJC), 5 vols. 12s 6d (SJC).

CR 37: 318 (Apr 1774); MR 50: 172–6 (Mar 1774), vols. 1–3; MR 50: 327 (Apr 1774), vols. 4–5; AF I: 1255.

MH-H *EC75.A100.774h; EM 1107: 16; ESTC n007573.

Notes. Vols. 1–2 have 'In Four Volumes' on t.p. Epistolary.

The Trial 1772: 23.

Vols. 1–3 adv., 'On Thursday the 20th inst. will be published', SJC 11–13 Jan 1774.

5-vol. version adv. SJC 5–8 Mar 1774.

German trans. Lübeck and Leipzig, 1775 (*Geschichte des Lord Stanton*) (Price).

CR: 'Whatever the malice of disappointed authors may prompt them to alledge, we are always desirous of saying as much in favour of the publications which comes under our notice as they deserve. Actuated by this inclination, we declare, that these five volumes are well printed, on good paper, contain a reasonable number of pages, and may afford amusement to many of the subscribers to Circulating Libraries.'

MR [John Cleland?]: '. . . much superior to the common run of those romances that are daily published under the title of *Novels*; and we will venture to assure those of our Readers, who have a taste for writings of this kind, that they will not find the time employed in perusing the present work wholly thrown away' (p. 173).

1774: 11   ANON.
IDEAL TRIFLES. PUBLISHED BY A LADY.

London: Printed by John Boosey, Bookseller, at No. 39 King-Street, Cheapside, 1774.

vi, 266p. 12mo. 3s (CR, MR).

CR 38: 474 (Dec 1774); MR 51: 487 (Dec 1774); AF I: 1350.

BL 12331.ee.27; EM 837: 14; ESTC t063971 (NA CLU-S/C, DLC).

Notes. Epistolary. CR reviews under 'Novels'; MR under 'Miscellaneous'.

CR: 'A collection of letters, said to have been the real correspondence of a society of friends, indifferently written, and little interesting.'

MR [John Langhorne]: 'We have been many times deceived by title-pages, but *this* is honest and just. The deception lies not there; but in a new artifice of persuading the Reader, and making him verily believe through half a score of preliminary pages, that he is to meet with some substantial fare at a wholesome meal of reason and philosophy; when, all on a sudden, instead of being seated at so desirable a board, he is ushered into a roomful of romantic girls, Almiras, Eudocias, Hypatias, and Sir Harrys, and tormented with a most dismal and tragical love tale.'

1774: 12　ANON.
THE JOURNEY TO LONDON: OR, THE HISTORY OF THE SELBY-FAMILY.

London: Printed for F. and J. Noble, at their respective Circulating Libraries, near Middle Row, Holborn; and Saint Martin's Court, near Leicester Square, 1774.

I 236p; II 210p. 12mo. 6s (CR, MR), 6s bound (SJC).

CR 37: 77 (Jan 1774); MR 50: 233–4 (Mar 1774); AF I: 1461.

PU Singer-Mend. PR.3291.A1.J68; ESTC n052505.

Notes. 3 pp. advs. end vol. 2, followed by 1-p. 'Advertisement To the Country Booksellers' regarding the Nobles' contest with Baldwin.

Adv., 'Next Thursday will be published', SJC 8–11 Jan 1774.

German trans. Danzig, 1775 (*Geschichte der Familie Selby*) (Price).

CR: 'The Selby-family, Mr. Selby himself excepted, are all of the race of Wrongheads; and are, by their ignorance of the world, of the town at least, thrown into ruinous situations.'

MR [John Cleland?]: 'This history, without one incident that is new to recommend it, is not very ill written.—If the Author will accept this as any compliment, we mean it particularly in favour of the second volume' (p. 234).

THE KINSMAN OF MAHOMET
See FROMAGET, Nicolas

1774: 13　ANON.
THE LIBERTINE HUSBAND RECLAIMED; AND VIRTUOUS LOVE REWARDED.

London: Printed for J. Bew, at No. 28, in Pater-noster Row, 1774.

I 227p; II 234p. 12mo. 5s sewed (CR) 6s (MR), 5s sewed or 6s bound (SJC).

CR 38: 455–60 (Dec 1774); MR 360: 52 (Apr 1775).

CLU-S/C PR3991.A1L61; EMf; ESTC n011296 (NA CSmH).

Notes. Epistolary.

Adv. SJC 10–13 Dec 1774.

German trans. Leipzig, 1775 (*Der treulose Ehemann bekehrt; und die tugendhafte Liebe belohnt*) (EAG).

CR: 'To preach grave doctrines of morality, without intermixing something of entertainment, and to give precepts without examples, are methods so unlikely to succeed, in competition with that which mixes the useful with the agreeable, that it is not surprising we meet with so many attempts at the latter: and that novels in particular, a species of writing which aims strongly to unite instruction and entertainment, fall so frequently under our inspection. Among these it is, indeed, seldom that we have the opportunity to compliment the writers on their success; but this is the fault of the workmen, and not of the species of employment' (p. 455). CR also notes: 'His tale is interesting, and agreeably told, and the lessons he inculcates are such as a rigid moralist would approve' (p. 455).

MR: 'A simple narrative, agreeably related, and conveying a good moral.'

1774: 14   ANON.
THE LOCKET; OR, THE HISTORY OF MR. SINGLETON. A NOVEL. IN TWO VOLUMES. BY THE AUTHOR OF EMILY; OR, THE HISTORY OF A NATURAL DAUGHTER.

London: Printed for R. Snagg, No. 29, Pater-Noster-Row, 1774.
I 226p; II 228p. 12mo. 6s (MR).
MR 51: 72 (July 1774).
MH-H *EC75.A100.774l; EM 1012: 22; ESTC n010753 (NA ICN).

Notes. Emily: or, the History of a Natural Daughter, 1756, JR 349, AF I: 757.

MR: 'One of that numerous cluster of novels which, as the Author of *Juliet Grenville* [1774: 24] says, rarely seem to have any intention, but to waste or kill the time of those who are enemies to sentiment and reflection.'

1774: 15   ANON.
MEMOIRS OF A CLERGYMAN; OR THE CHARACTER AND IDEAS OF THE REV. MR. CLEGG. A SENTIMENTAL HISTORY, FOUNDED UPON FACTS.

London: Printed for T. Becket, in the Strand, 1774.
vii, 186p. 8vo.
NjP Ex 3600.001.625; ESTC n036423.

Notes. Preface and unn. table of contents.
Extracts published LC 43: 553–4 and 561–2 (9–11 and 11–13 June 1778).
Adv. PA 30 May 1778.
Further edn: London, 1778, ESTC t219334.
This edn. not rev.; 1778 London edn. rev. CR 46: 318 (Oct 1778); MR 59: 392 (Nov 1778); AF II: 2821.

CR: 'By some expressions of warmth and acrimony, it appears to be, what the author represents it, a history founded on fact. But this, we apprehend, is a point of more importance to the author, than the reader.'

MR [William Enfield]: 'We have too often been deceived by title-pages, to be greatly surprized, that, after having laboured through the tedious leaves of this insipid volume, we found ourselves incapable of discovering in it either *ideas, characters,* or *sentiment.*'

MEMOIRS OF A GENTLEMAN, WHO RESIDED SEVERAL YEARS
See W., C.

1774: 16   ANON.
MEMOIRS OF AN UNFORTUNATE LADY OF QUALITY.
> London: Printed for R. Snagg, No. 29, Pater-Noster-Row, 1774.
> I viii, 176p; II 167p; III 144p. 12mo. 7s 6d (MR).
> MR 51: 322–3 (Oct 1774).
> MH-H 17438.59.36.10*; EM 1115: 12; ESTC n010690.

Notes. MR: 'A romance founded, chiefly, on the story of Lady Jane Douglas, sister to the late Duke of Douglas. It is a poor performance, affording little of sentiment, and less of character; and yet the Author, (or pretended Editor) has the assurance to style it "an entertaining work, not unworthy a place on the shelf with the productions of a Fielding, a Smollett, or a Goldsmith." Thus a draggle-tailed nymph, from Billingsgate, cries about the streets "Sprats as big as herrings, ho!"—but then she is not so silly as to imagine that any body believes her.'

1774: 17   ANON.
THE MODERN FINE GENTLEMAN, A NOVEL, IN TWO VOLUMES.
> London: Printed for T. Lowndes, at No. 77, in Fleet-Street, 1774.
> I 240p; II 232p. 12mo. 5s sewed (CR), 6s (MR), 6s bound (SJC).
> CR 38: 473 (Dec 1774); MR 52: 275–6 (Mar 1775).
> BL 12611.aa.9; EM 235: 2; ESTC t108474 (NA CtY).

Notes. In vol. 2 text of novel starts on p. 3. Epistolary.
Adv., 'On Thursday next will be published', SJC 12–15 Nov 1774.
Facs: FN.

CR: 'Of the various novels which we have lately perused, The Modern fine Gentleman is far from being the most exceptionable. Its characters are tolerably well supported; its incidents are natural and amusing; and it contains nothing in the least offensive to decency and good manners.'

MR [William Enfield]: '. . . where characters are nothing more than a compound of scepticism and stupidity, licentiousness without taste or generosity, and the affectation of passion with an heart capable of every thing base and cruel, we must despise and detest them: we cannot think that such characters are proper to be contemplated by young minds, or exhibited before them, even in fiction.'

1774: 18   ANON.
THE NEWS-PAPER WEDDING; OR, AN ADVERTISEMENT FOR A HUSBAND. A NOVEL; FOUNDED ON INCIDENTS WHICH WERE IN CONSEQUENCE OF AN ADVERTISEMENT THAT APPEARED IN THE DAILY ADVERTISER OF JULY 29, 1772. INCLUDING A NUMBER OF ORIGINAL LETTERS ON THE SUBJECT OF LOVE AND MARRIAGE.
> London: Printed for R. Snagg, No. 29, Paternoster-Row, 1774.
> I xii, 179p; II 191p. 12mo. 6s (CR, MR), 4s sewed or 5s bound (SJC).
> CR 37: 318–19 (Apr 1774); MR 50: 327 (Apr 1774); AF I: 2013.
> O 249.s.509; EMf; ESTC n011125 (NA CLU-S/C, ICU, PU &c.).

Notes. Dedication 'To the Generous and candid Public' 1, v–vi; preface vii–xii. 2 pp. advs. end vol. 2.
Adv. SJC 5–8 Nov 1774.

CR: 'We have taken the trouble to read [the letters] through, in order, had we met with one which would have been worthy of our reader's notice, to have transcribed it. Our search has, however, been in vain; and we should be sorry that any other lady, who may think proper to advertise for a husband, should, by publishing the letters she may receive on that account, subject us to the like disagreeable task.'

MR [John Cleland?]: 'This curious collection chiefly consists of a number of ridiculous letters, supposed to be sent to the publisher in consequence of the above-mentioned advertisement; the whole appears to be a most unmeaning catch-penny performance.'

1774: 19   ANON.
THE ORPHAN SWAINS: OR, LONDON CONTAGIOUS TO THE COUNTRY. A NOVEL. BY A YOUNG LIBERTINE, REFORM'D. IN TWO VOLUMES.

> London: Printed for R. Snagg, No. 29, Paternoster-Row, n.d. [1774].
>
> I 158p; II 135p. 8vo [MR and CR have 12mo]. 6s (CR), 5s (MR), 4s sewed or 5s bound (SJC).
>
> CR 37: 318 (Apr 1774); MR 50: 327 (Apr 1774); AF I: 2110.
>
> MH-H *EC75.A100.774o; xESTC.

Notes. Adv. SJC 5–8 Nov 1774.

CR: 'If writing such novels as the present be the best effect of this young libertine's reformation, he might, for any good his reformation has produced, have remained unreformed still.'

MR [John Cleland?]: 'High-flown prose, and grovelling verse, compose this ridiculous performance.'

THE PERUVIAN LETTERS
See GRAFIGNY, Françoise d'Issembourg d'Happoncourt, Mme de

1774: 20   ANON.
*THE PRUDENT ORPHAN; OR, THE HISTORY OF MISS SOPHIA STANLEY.

> London: Sold at J. Roson's Circulating Library, No. 54, St Martin's le Grand, near Newgate Street; and R. Lea, the Corner of King's-Street, St. Ann's, Soho (SJC), 1774 (SJC).
>
> 2 vols. 12mo. 5s sewed (CR, MR), 5s sewed or 6s bound (SJC).
>
> CR 39: 510 (June 1775); MR 52: 186 (Feb 1775); AF II: 3630.
>
> No copy located.

Notes. Adv. SJC 1–3 Nov. 1774; 'By a Lady'.
CR reviews with 1775: 2, 1775: 13, and 1775: 7; see 1775: 2 for comment.

MR [William Enfield]: 'He who sits down to write, with a "consciousness that he shall acquire but little credit as an Author" will not be much surprised when he finds that the fact agrees with his pre-sentiment. . . . in our judgment, the story is confused and uninteresting, the characters ill supported, the expression childish and incorrect, and the moral—nothing.'

1774: 21   ANON.
THE SCHOOL FOR HUSBANDS. WRITTEN BY A LADY.

London: Printed for J. Bew, at No. 28. in Paternoster-Row, 1774.
I 242p; II 253p. 12mo. 6s (CR, MR), 5s sewed or 6s bound (SJC).
CR 37: 317–18 (Apr 1774); MR 50: 327 (Apr 1774); AF I: 2450.
O 256f.2753-2754; ESTC n036331 (NA ICU).

Notes. Epistolary.
Adv. SJC 29 Jan–1 Feb 1774.
Further edn: Dublin, 1776 (Printed for S. Price, W. Whitestone, W. Watson, J. Sheppard, D. Chamberlaine [and 22 others in Dublin], 2 vols., 12mo), EM 2599: 17, ESTC t119281. French trans. Amsterdam and Paris, 1776 (*L'école des maris*) (BGR); German trans. Leipzig, 1777 (*Die Männerschule*) (Price).

CR: 'We are not without suspicion that in anonymous publications, the words *written by a lady* are sometimes made use of to preclude the severity of criticism; but as Reviewers are generally churls and greybeards, this piece of *finesse* very seldom answers.—Whether or not the work before us be really written by a lady, is neither known to us, nor of the least consequence. Had it been destitute of merit, justice to our readers would have prevented our suffering it to pass uncensured; but as it possesses no small share of useful entertainment we cannot deny it that tribute of praise to which it is justly entitled.' The reviewer concludes: '. . . our sensibility has been greatly affected by the perusal of this performance, which is calculated to promote the interests of virtue.'

MR [John Cleland?]: 'As the ladies are generally acknowledged to be superior to our sex in all works of the imagination and fancy, we doubt not this is deemed a sufficient reason for placing their names in the title-page of many a dull, lifeless story which contains not a single female idea, but has been hammered out of the brainless head of a Grubstreet hireling. We quote not, however, the present work as an instance of this imposition, nor do we doubt, from many of the scenes which it describes, the *femality* of its Author. The story is lively, natural, and affecting; well told, and free from those frequent episodes which are so often introduced in works of this kind, and which are too much for even the patience of a Reviewer.'

THE SENTIMENTAL EXHIBITION
See LONG, Edward

1774: 22   ANON.
THE TRINKET. A NOVEL. BY A LADY.

London: Printed for T. Lowndes, No. 77, in Fleet-Street, 1774.
271p. 12mo. 3s sewed (CR) 3s (MR), 2s 6d sewed or 3s bound (SJC).
CR 37: 475 (June 1774); MR 50: 327 (Apr 1774); AF I: 2782.
BL 12613.bb.13; EM 223: 7; ESTC t108021 (NA NjP, PU).

Notes. 1 p. adv. end vol. Epistolary.
Adv., 'in a few Days will be published', SJC 22–24 Feb 1774.

CR: 'As this novel is said to be written by a lady, and really appears to comes from a female hand, we are too polite to point our critical cannon against her. Could we believe it to be the composition of a man, we should not scruple to say that it contains a crude and indigested heap of characters, incidents, and adventures, tossed and thrown together without much meaning, and less moral; we shall also add that the unravelling of the plot makes us not sufficient amends for the perplexities in which the piece is involved, from its commencement to its conclusion.'

MR [John Cleland?]: 'If Mr. Lowndes has taken the trouble to look over this novel, he must have thought the Lady very extravagant in this Trinket of hers, as she has crowded *story* and *plot* enough in the last twenty pages, to have formed, with the least degree of management, another whole volume of this valuable species of writing.'

1774: 23   ANON.
'TWAS RIGHT TO MARRY HIM; OR, THE HISTORY OF MISS PET-WORTH; IN TWO VOLUMES.

London: Printed for F. and J. Noble, at their respective Circulating Libraries near
   Middle-Row, Holborn, and St. Martin's Court, near Leicester-Square, 1774.
I iv, 226p; II 231p. 12mo. 6s (CR, MR).
CR 36: 476 (Dec 1773); MR 50: 233 (Mar 1774); AF I: 2805.
BL 12613.bb.21; EM 7415: 7; ESTC t107706.

Notes. 4-pp. prefatory address to the Nobles concerns their feud with the *London Magazine* and its publisher, as does an advertisement at the end of both volumes addressed 'To the Country Booksellers'. 1 further p. advs. end vol. 1; 7 pp. end vol. 2. Epistolary.
German trans. Leipzig, 1775 (*Sie that Recht, ihn zu heirathen, oder Geschichte der Miss Petworth*) (EAG).
CR: 'On the first opening of this novel, we fancied it was written by the author of '*Twas Wrong to marry Him* [1773: 19 above]; and as we proceeded, our conjectures were confirmed. The marks of the same manufacture are sufficiently visible in the fabrication of them both.'
MR [John Cleland?]: 'In a letter addressed to Messrs. Noble, and placed at the beginning of this work, the Author declares himself solicitous of being ranked rather among the dull, than the dangerous novel-writers of the age: and as, in our opinion, there unfortunately appears a necessity of referring him to one or the other of these classes, we readily subscribe to his choice, and pronounce the "History of Miss Petworth" perfectly innocent.'

THE VIZIRS: OR, THE ENCHANTED LABYRINTH
See FAUQUE DE LA CÉPEDE, Marianne-Agnès Pillement

1774: 24   BROOKE, [Henry].
JULIET GRENVILLE: OR, THE HISTORY OF THE HUMAN HEART. IN THREE VOLUMES. BY MR BROOKE.

London: Printed for G. Robinson, in Pater-Noster Row, 1774.
I 288p; II 240p; III 222p. 12mo. 9s (CR), 7s 6d sewed (MR), 7s 6d sewed or 9s bound
   (SJC).
CR 36: 443–53 (Dec 1773); MR 50: 15–20 (Jan 1774); AF I: 267.
BL 243.i.5–7; EM 7641: 1; ESTC t130243 (BI BMp, C, MRu; NA CSmH, ICN, IU &c.).

Notes. Contract between Robinson and Brooke of 13 Aug 1773 specifies a first edition of 2,000 copies 'to be sold to the public at the price of nine shillings per Sett bound' with 7/8 of the net profits (after the deduction of printing and publishing costs) to be paid to Brooke, with a similar arrangement for subsequent edns (RA); Bentley mistakes the figure for 1,000 and the copies as 'in boards'.
Adv., to be published on 16 Dec, SJC 9–11 Dec 1773.

Extracts published LC 35: 401 and 409–10 (26–28 and 28–30 Apr 1774).
Further edn: Dublin, 1774 (Printed for James Williams, 3 vols., 12mo), ESTC t107653;
Philadelphia, 1774, ESTC w027542. Extracts under a variety of titles published in 7 magazines, 1774–1804, RM 1317. German trans. Leipzig, 1774 (*Julie Grenville oder Die Geschichte
des menschlichen Herzens*) (Price); French trans. Paris, 1801 (*Juliette Granville, ou Histoire du
coeur humain*) (BN)

CR: 'Its principal merit consists in the strong and lively description with which it presents
us of the emotions of the heart; and in this entertaining and instructive field of representation, it may be admitted to vye with the most masterly productions of the kind. A few religious peculiarities may be observed in the work, but they are of such a nature as not to call for
animadversion, and will be considered by some persons as a foil to the exertion of descriptive
talents, almost every where conspicuous in this interesting novel.'

MR [Ralph Griffiths]: 'We have so frequently given our opinion of the merit of this Writer,
as a novelist, and the two works which he has published of this kind are so uniformly characteristic, that we have little to add, on the present occasion, either of panegyric or of censure.
Mr. Brooke's heroes and heroines are still saints, or angels on earth; too exalted, we apprehend, for mere sinful mortals to presume to emulate, and we fear too, that they have so much
of the old-fashioned form of piety about them, and talk so solemnly, in the style and phrase
of the scriptures, that they will not generally be looked upon as *fit* models for imitation, in
this age of freedom and gaiety' (p. 15).

CRADOCK, Joseph, VILLAGE MEMOIRS
See 1775: 22

1774: 25   [DORAT, Claude-Joseph]; [GRIFFITH, Elizabeth] (*trans.*).
THE FATAL EFFECTS OF INCONSTANCY; OR LETTERS OF THE MAR-
CHIONESS DE SYRCÉ, THE COUNT DE MIRBELLE, AND OTHERS.
TRANSLATED FROM THE FRENCH.

London: Printed for J. Bew, No. 28, Pater-Noster-Row, 1774.
I xiv, 270; II 233p. 12mo. 5s sewed (CR, MR), 5s sewed or 6s bound (SJC).
CR 38: 393 (Nov 1774); MR 51: 238 (Sept 1774); AF I: 668.
BL Cup.403.z.45; EM 6466: 1; ESTC t140062 (NA PU).

Notes. Trans. of *Les Malheurs de l' inconstance* (Amsterdam and Paris, 1772).
Vol. 1 t.p. has 'MIRBEELE'. Engraved frontispiece vol. 1. Epistolary.
Adv., 'Embellished with two elegant Frontispieces, Engraved by Collyer', SJC 11–14 June
1774. Still adv. as 'This Day was published' SJC 18–20 June 1776 and as 'Lately published' SJC
4–6 Mar 1777.
RG notes 'Mrs. Griffith' as the translator's name; 1777 SJC adv. confirms this with 'Translated from the French by Mrs. Griffith'.

CR: 'While . . . we compliment the writer on his art, we cannot recommend the choice of
his subject, and would sooner put into the hands of our sons and daughters Prior's loosest
tales, than the soft, enchanting descriptions which are to be met with in the present performance.' Also compares this work with the good effects of *The Child of Nature* (1774: 29).

MR: 'The fatal effects of criminal indulgences in amorous pursuits, are here displayed, in
a striking and exemplary light. The Author has ability, and the Translator judgment; though,
perhaps, the latter is somewhat deficient in taste.'

1774: 26 [FAUQUE DE LA CÉPEDE, Marianne-Agnès Pillement].
THE VIZIRS: OR, THE ENCHANTED LABYRINTH. AN ORIENTAL TALE.
BY MADE. FAUQUES DE VAUCLUSE.

> London: Printed for G. Riley, Bookseller, at Sterne's Head, Curzon-Street, May-Fair,
> 1774.
> I 6, xix, 224p; II 5, 266p; III 2, 274p. 12mo. 7s 6d sewed (CR) 9s (MR), 7s 6d sewed or 9s
> bound (SJC).
> CR 38: 157 (Aug 1774); MR 51: 401 (Nov 1774); AF I: 837.
> BL N.1672; EM 1924: 1; ESTC t071893 (BI O; NA CaAEU, MH-H, NjP &c.).

Notes. Small engraving set in t.p. 2 pp. advs. end vol. 2; 1 p. advs. end vol. 3.

Adv., 'On Monday at Noon will be published, In three Volumes, Duodecimo, embellished
with Frontispieces, finely executed', SJC 26–28 Apr 1774. A fuller adv. in the SJC for 5–7 May
1774 includes this extension of the title: 'In which are displayed the Characters of a good, and
of a bad Minister; the former of whom, by a noble, intrepid and wise Conduct, causes a rash
Monarch to become the Glory of his People; while the other, by his crafty and oppressive
Administration, having alienated the Hearts of the Subjects, involves his peaceful, Sovereign,
in a Maze of Difficulties. The Whole interspersed with several striking Examples of Female
Virtue and Heroic Love.'

Extract published LC 36: 108 (30 July–2 Aug 1774).

German trans. Leipzig, 1775 (*Die Veziere*) (Price).

CR: 'Those who are fond of this kind of reading, may not think their time thrown away in
the perusal of these volumes. We have very little relish for the affected imitations of Eastern
eloquence, which are now so frequent; and the Vizirs has not contributed much to the alteration of our taste.' Also notes that a new book is promised, *The Transmigration of Hermes, or
the Laws of Nature, a Philosophical Romance*, and remarks, 'We hope, that the style of it will
be less *fantastical* than that of the present work, as we cannot read without disgust such language as the following: "While the Vizir was stringing the ungenuine pearls of feigned counsel on the thread of insincerity, the cheeks of Kishtasb were discoloured with various
passions, and his heart was too large for the purple walls that confined it." '

MR: 'Mademoiselle de Vaucluse is a genius, and would certainly succeed in novel-writing,
if, following Nature, and copying the living manners of those nations with which she has
been personally conversant, she could totally divest herself of the Oriental ideas which she
has collected from D'Herbelot [Barthélemy d'Herbelot, author of the *Bibliothèque Oriental*,
1697], and from the imitators of Eastern sublimity. Such imitators rarely succeed in this
country. What is deemed *pomp* in the Persic and Arabic writers, is, in their European copyists, generally regarded as mere *bombast:* and the cool, reasoning northern reader is more apt
to be disgusted than charmed with the perpetual glare of brilliant images, the eternal round
of laboured allegories and metaphors, and the crowd of incredible events, enchantments,
and prodigies:—where the meaning, if there be any (as this ingenious and learned Lady
expresses herself, in her preface) is concealed under a superfluity of words, or lost in a maze
of unnatural fictions.'

1774: 27 [FROMAGET, Nicolas].
THE KINSMAN OF MAHOMET; OR, MEMOIRS OF A FRENCH SLAVE,
DURING HIS EIGHT YEARS CAPTIVITY IN CONSTANTINOPLE:
INCLUDING MANY CURIOUS PARTICULARS RELATIVE TO THE

RELIGION, HISTORY, POLICY, CUSTOMS, AND MANNERS OF THE
TURKS; AND INTERSPERSED WITH A VARIETY OF ADVENTURES IN
THE SERAGLIOS OF THE EAST. WRITTEN BY HIMSELF. AND
TRANSLATED FROM THE ORIGINAL FRENCH.

> London: Printed for D. Culver, in Little Bridges-Street, near Drury-Lane Theatre, 1774.
> I viii, 195p; II 216p. 12mo. 6s (MR).
> MR 50: 71 (Jan 1774); AF I: 985.
> BL C.123.k.15; EM 5070: 15; ESTC t124782 (BI Dp; NA CSmH, MH-H).

Notes. Trans. of *Le Cousin de Mahomet et la folie salutaire* (Leide, 1742).

MR reviews under the heading 'Novels and Memoirs'.

MR: 'Adulteries, fornications, murders; in a word, almost every species of debauchery and wickedness, are comprehended in these execrable adventures; which for the honour of human nature, we hope are wholly fictitious.'

1774: 28   [GRAFIGNY, Françoise d'Issembourg d'Happoncourt, Mme de] and
ROBERTS, R. (*trans.* vol. 1).
THE PERUVIAN LETTERS, TRANSLATED FROM THE FRENCH.
WITH AN ADDITIONAL ORIGINAL VOLUME. BY R. ROBERTS,
TRANSLATOR OF SELECT TALES FROM MARMONTEL, AUTHOR OF
SERMONS BY A LADY, AND TRANSLATOR OF THE HISTORY OF
FRANCE, FROM THE ABBÉ MILLOT.

> London: Printed for T. Cadell, in the Strand, 1774.
> I vi, 225p; II 171p. 12mo. 5s sewed (CR, SJC) 6s (MR).
> CR 39: 473–8 (June 1775); MR 51: 161–2 (Aug 1774).
> BL 636.d.19; EM 4365: 7; ESTC t114350 (BI E, O; NA CLU-S/C, ICU, MH, &c.).

Notes. Vol. 1 trans. of *Lettres d'une Péruvienne* (Paris 1747). MR quotes Roberts' prefatory explanation that she wrote 2nd vol. as she was unhappy with conclusion of the 1st.

Preface iii–vi. Epistolary.

Adv. SJC 15–17 Mar 1774.

WC has 20 entries for *Lettres d'une Peruvienne* before 1850, most English trans. and only 1 Roberts's version; NSTC lists edn (different trans.) in 1805.

CR: '... Mr. Roberts has translated them with freedom and spirit' (p. 473).

MR: '... there is considerable merit in the Peruvian Letters; and we shall not, in any probability, ever have a better translation of them, than the present.'

1774: 29   HELVETIUS, Mr [pseud].
THE CHILD OF NATURE, IMPROVED BY CHANCE. A PHILOSOPHI-
CAL NOVEL. BY MR. HELVETIUS. IN TWO VOLUMES.

> London: Printed for T. Becket, Corner of the Adelphi, in the Strand, 1774.
> I vi, 303p; II 350p. 12mo. 5s sewed (CR, SJC), 6s bound (MR).
> CR 38: 270–4 (Oct 1774); MR 51: 323 (Oct 1774); AF I: 1209.
> BL 837.d.4; EM 2444: 4; ESTC t100245 (BI E, O; NA CSmH, IaU, IU; EA P).

Notes. ESTC suggests probably not by Helvetius [Claude-Adrien Helvétius, 1715–1771], and Grieder believes attribution 'is of course false' (p. 100).

WC: Represented as a translation but actually an original work.
'Preface of Mr. Helvetius' iii–vi; 'The Translator to the Public' [vii].
Adv., 'In a few Days will be published', SJC 11–14 June 1774.
Extract published LC 36: 33–4 (9–12 July 1774).
German trans. Leipzig, 1776 (*Das Kind der Natur*) (EAG). Facs: FN.

CR: 'It must, indeed, be confessed, that the pictures are drawn with a luxurious fancy, and prudery, it is probable, will condemn them; but they are too well intended to be neglected on that account' (p. 270).

MR: 'We were not acquainted with the imposture of this title page (the book will not impose on any body) till it had wrought all the effect it is likely to have. Those who have read this philosophical novel, as it is called, need not be told that it was not written by the late celebrated Helvetius*. It consists of characters not well drawn, and very improperly placed; and the morality and language of it is probably *designed* to injure the principles and manners of the Public.' Footnote: '*It is now supposed to have been the work of a noted writer lately deceased; and who seems to have formed an artful scheme not only to impose on the Public, but to *take in* even the bookseller.'

1774: 30 [JOHNSTONE, Charles].
THE HISTORY OF ARSACES, PRINCE OF BETLIS. BY THE EDITOR OF CHRYSAL. IN TWO VOLUMES.

> London: Printed for T. Becket, Corner of the Adelphi, in the Strand, 1774.
> I xx, 303p; II viii, 278p. 12mo. 5s sewed (CR, SJC), 6s bound (MR).
> CR 38: 274–7 (Oct 1774); MR 51: 237–8 (Sept 1774); AF I: 1443.
> BL 243.i.3; EM 7656: 8; ESTC t117967 (BI E, O; NA CtY, ICN, IU, MH-H, NjP, PU, TxU &c.).

Notes. Adv., 'In a few Days will be published', SJC 25–28 June 1774.
Chrysal 1760, JR 577, AF I: 1440.
Further edns: Dublin, 1774 (Printed for the United Company of Booksellers, 2 vols., 12mo), ESTC n007597; Dublin, 1774–75, EM 5438: 1, ESTC t064759; London, 1775, xESTC (WC). Extracts from *The History of Arsaces*, 'The Travels of Himilco', published in *Universal Magazine*, 1774, RM 1261. German trans. Leipzig, 1775 (*Geschichte Arsaces, des Prinzen von Betlis*) (Price). Facs: FN.

CR: 'There is great knowledge of mankind displayed in this work, which therefore does not derogate from the reputation its author acquired by the Adventures of a Guinea' (p. 277).

MR: 'A romance, rather than a novel. It is a kind of political fiction, subjected to the severest laws of morality' (p. 237).

1774: 31 [LONG, Edward].
THE SENTIMENTAL EXHIBITION; OR, PORTRAITS AND SKETCHES OF THE TIMES.

> London: Printed for T. Lowndes, No. 77, in Fleet-Street, 1774.
> iv, 133p. 8vo. 2s 6d (CR), 2s sewed (LC).
> CR 38: 400 (Nov 1774).
> MH-H *EC75.St455S.H774l; EMf; ESTC n021867 (NA MnU, NjP).

Notes. A collection of sketches.
Adv. LC 12–14 July 1774.
Extract published LC 36: 41 (12–14 July 1774).

CR: '*Dulce est desipere in loco* would have been no improper motto for this satyrical Exhibition of modern manners, this farrago of descriptions and remarks, some humorous, and some (saving the author's resentment) but one degree remote from nonsense. Several of the sections are, it must be confessed, very grave, consisting of lessons for behaviour in so sober a style, that we are apprehensive it was owing to their soporific power, that we fell asleep during the perusal of them.'

SADI
See 1773: 37

1774: 32   [TURNER, Daniel, of Woolwich].
THE FASHIONABLE DAUGHTER. BEING A NARRATIVE OF TRUE AND RECENT FACTS. BY AN IMPARTIAL HAND. IN FOUR PARTS.

> London: Printed for W. Domville, under the Royal Exchange, Cornhill; and J. Knox,
> No. 148, near Somerset-House, in the Strand, 1774.
> xiv, 318p. 12mo. 2s 6d (CR), 3s (MR), 2s 6d sewed and 3s bound (SJC).
> CR 37: 77 (Jan 1774); MR 50: 234–5 (Mar 1774); AF I: 2804.
> BL 12604.bb.32; EM 92: 4; ESTC t108363.

Notes. Adv. SJC 4–6 Jan 1774.

CR: 'This volume can only be interesting, we think, to those who are acquainted with the characters or the facts contained in it, and seems better calculated for the meridian of Edinburgh than of London.'

MR [John Noorthouck]: 'This story, from the minuteness of the detail, from the earnestness with which the transactions are related, and from the description of the characters introduced, appears to be really according to the professions of the Writer, a relation of "*true facts.*" It does not indeed contain adventures enough for a professed novel; and it is to be viewed rather as a narrative than as a literary composition.'

VAUCLUSE, Mademoiselle Fauques de
See FAUQUE DE LA CEPEDE, Marianne-Agnès Pillement

1774: 33   VOLTAIRE, [François-Marie Arouet].
LE TAUREAU BLANC: OR THE WHITE BULL. FROM THE FRENCH. TRANSLATED FROM THE SYRIAC, BY M. DE VOLTAIRE.

> London: Printed for J. Murray, No. 32, Fleetstreet, 1774.
> 75p. 8vo. 1s 6d (t.p., CR).
> CR 38: 290–3 (Oct 1774), reviewing both trans., this and 33B.
> ICU PQ2083.T21 1774 Rare; ESTC n021547 (NA DLC).

Notes. In fact an original work by Voltaire (ESTC); trans. of *Le Taureau blanc* (Geneva, 1774).
See also entry below.
Text begins on p. 5.
2nd edn. adv. SJC 23–26 July 1774.

Further edns: London, 1774, ESTC t068094; London, 1788, ESTC n025617. Extracts of trans. entitled 'The White Ox', *Sentimental Magazine*, 1774, RM 1344.

CR thinks this translation 'not of equal merit' with the other (p. 290).

French original reviewed MR 50: 584 (App [June/July 1774).

1774: 33B   VOLTAIRE, [François-Marie Arouet]; [BENTHAM, Jeremy (trans.)].

THE WHITE BULL, AN ORIENTAL HISTORY. FROM AN ANCIENT SYRIAN MANUSCRIPT, COMMUNICATED BY MR. VOLTAIRE. CUM NOTIS EDITORIS ET VARIORUM: SC. THE WHOLE FAITHFULLY DONE INTO ENGLISH.

London: Printed for J. Bew, Pater-Noster Row, 1774.

cxliv, 168p. 8vo. 3s sewed (CR, SJC).

CR 38: 290–3 (Oct 1774).

BL 837.b.10; EMf; ESTC t137651 (BI O; NA CaOHM, ICN, NIC).

Notes. In fact an original work by Voltaire (ESTC). See also 33A above.

Adv., 'In the Press and speedily will be published' SJC 16–18 June 1774; no price given. Adv., 'Handsomely printed in Twelves, on a fine Writing Paper', SJC 30 June–2 July 1774; title as above until, after Voltaire's name, *With Notes and a Preface, in which several bloody Transactions are brought to Light.*

French original reviewed MR 50: 584 (App [June/July 1774]).

CR: '. . . neither servilely copies the phrase of the original, nor, however free, too far deviates from the sense of it. The notes are pertinent and satirical, and, as well as the preface, show the translator to be a man after the author's *own* heart' (p. 290).

1774: 34   {W., C}.

MEMOIRS OF A GENTLEMAN, WHO RESIDED SEVERAL YEARS IN THE EAST INDIES DURING THE LATE REVOLUTIONS, AND MOST IMPORTANT EVENTS IN THAT PART OF THE WORLD; CONTAINING SEVERAL ANECDOTES OF A PUBLIC AS WELL AS OF A PRIVATE NATURE, NEVER BEFORE PUBLISHED. WRITTEN BY HIMSELF.

London: Printed for J. Donaldson, Corner of Arundel-Street, Strand, 1774.

ii, 237p. 12mo. 3s (CR, MR).

CR 36: 477 (Dec 1773); MR 50: 71 (Jan 1774); AF I: 1791.

BL 583.b.14; EM 1334: 3; ESTC t096514 (BI C, MRu, O; NA CtY-BR, MH-H).

Notes. Dedication to Dr. D****, signed C. W.

Ends with (p. [238]) an 'Explanation of the Names used in the East Indies, and mentioned in this Work'.

CR reviews under 'Novels'; MR reviews under 'Novels and Memoirs'.

CR: 'As pitiful, miserable a romance as we remember to have read; with false English in the first page.'

MR [John Noorthouck]: ' "*Never before published!*" There are two reasons to be given why they ought not to have been published at all. The *Gentleman*, who declares himself to be a German, is not qualified to write in English, or perhaps in any other language; and his memoirs, whether true or false, were not worth writing.'

1774: 35 WHITE, J{oseph}.
CHARLES AND TERESA. AN ORIGINAL NOVEL. IN A SERIES OF LETTERS, FOUNDED ON TRUTH. BY J. WHITE.

Dublin: Printed by Messrs. J. Williams, J. A. Husband, T. Walker, and C. Jenkin, 1774. vi, 244p. 12mo.

BL 1487.aaa.5; EM 2374: 12; ESTC t064458 (BI Dt; NA CSmH).

Notes. Preface v–vi identifies the factual basis of the novel as *Anecdotes of the Reigns of Henry III of France, and Henry of Navarre* [No book with this title or one like it has been identified in French or English; the closest is Louis Laurent Prault's *L'Esprit d'Henri IV, ou Anecdotes les plus intéressantes* . . . (Paris, 1770)]. Dedication to Mrs. Christmas signed 'Joseph White'. Epistolary.

WIELAND, C. M., THE HISTORY OF AGATHON
See 1773: 38

1775

1775: 1 ANON.
THE ADVENTURES OF A CORK-SCREW; IN WHICH, UNDER THE PLEASING METHOD OF A ROMANCE, THE VICES, FOLLIES AND MANNERS OF THE PRESENT AGE ARE EXHIBITED AND SATIRI-CALLY DELINEATED. INTERSPERSED WITH STRIKING ANEC-DOTES, CHARACTERS AND ACTIONS OF PERSONS IN REAL LIFE; ALL DRAWN TO PROMOTE VIRTUE, EXPOSE VICE, AND LAUGH FOLLY OUT OF COUNTENANCE.

London: Printed for and Sold by T. Bell, No 26, Bell Yard, Temple-Barr [*sic*], 1775. xv, 170p. 12mo. 3s sewed (CR), 3s (MR), 2s 6d sewed (SJC).

CR 39: 510 (June 1775); MR 52: 557 (June 1775); AF II: 23.

BL 12611.g.3; EM 224: 6; ESTC t057421 (BI O; NA CtY, IU, MH-H, PU &c.).

Notes. Adv. SJC 15–18 Apr 1775.
Further edn: Dublin, 1776 (Printed for W. Whitestone, 1 vol., 12mo), ESTC n004799. German trans. Leipzig, 1776 (*Abendtheuer eines Korkenziehers, eine lehrreiche Erzählung*) (EAG). Facs: FN.

CR: 'Though this production cannot be admitted to any uncommon degree of merit, it may prove equally entertaining with others of the kind, which have not been ill received by the public.'

MR [John Noorthouck]: 'This corkscrew is made of bad metal, ill tempered, and of coarse manufacture.'

THE ADVENTURES OF ALONSO
See DIGGES, Thomas Atwood

THE BENEVOLENT MAN

See BICKNELL, Alexander

1775: 2 ANON.
*THE CAPRICIOUS FATHER, OR, THE HISTORY OF MR MUTABLE AND HIS FAMILY.

London: Printed for F. Noble, near Middle Row, Holborn; and J. Noble, in St Martin's Court, near Leicester Fields (LC), 1775.

2 vols. 12mo. 5s sewed (CR), 6s (MR).

CR 39: 510 (June 1775); MR 52: 360 (Apr 1775); AF II: 601.

No copy located.

Notes. Adv. LC 37: 148 (11–14 Feb 1776).

German trans. Leipzig, 1776 (*Der eigensinnige Vater*) (Price).

CR reviews with 1774: 20, 1775: 13, and 1775: 7, and says that to 'give an account of each of these productions separately would be to bestow on them a degree of attention to which they have not any claim' since 'with respect to fable, sentiment, description, or other circumstances, they are exposed to the reprehension, if not the contempt, of criticism.'

MR [William Enfield]: 'We seldom have met with a novel, in the whole course of our labours, in which the characters of dulness and insipidity have been more uniformly and perfectly supported than in the present. The Writer's head seems to have been so fully possessed by the single idea of fickleness and caprice, that he has not been able to find room for any other. . . . In short, if we were to characterize this novel in two words, we could not do it more justly, than by adopting one of the Author's own phrases, and pronouncing it— *immensely silly.*'

1775: 3 ANON.
THE CORRESPONDENTS, AN ORIGINAL NOVEL; IN A SERIES OF LETTERS.

London: Printed for T. Becket, corner of the Adelphi, in the Strand, 1775.

264p. 12mo. 2s 6d sewed (CR), 3s bound (MR).

CR 39: 341 (Apr 1775); MR 52: 430–7 (May 1775); AF II: 863.

BL N.2201; EM 4373: 2; ESTC t144478 (BI C, E, Lnt; NA CtY, CtY-BR, ICN, NjP, ViU &c.).

Notes. Based on alleged correspondence between Lord Lyttelton and Mrs Peach (widow of the Governor of Bombay). Blakey (p. 39) points out that even Horace Walpole at first believed the correspondence to be genuine. Summers (p. 285) reports that a 'contemporary MS. note in a copy of the first edn., 1775, states that the book was from the pen of Miss Berry, the friend of Horace Walpole, who revised and edited her work.'

Note in MR 55 (1776) 'To Our Readers': 'Having received repeated assurances from the friends of the late Lord Lyttelton, that the work entitled "*The Correspondents*, an original Novel" is *not genuine*, we take this opportunity of undeceiving the Public, so far as regard may have been paid to the opinion we had formed, of the authenticity of the Letters in question.' We are now satisfied that those Letters do *not* contain a *real* Correspondence between 'the NOBLE Poet and Historian lately deceased, and Mrs. Peach.'

Extract published LC 8: 281 (19–21 Sept 1775).

Adv. SJC 11–14 Mar 1775.

Further edns: London, 1775, EM 160: 4, ESTC t068747; Dublin, 1775 (Printed by John Exshaw, 1 vol., 12mo), ESTC n001997; London, 1776, EM 6333: 2, ESTC t144516; Dublin, 1778, ESTC n001998; London, 1784, EM 3834: 9, ESTC t066889; one further entry in ESTC. German trans. Leipzig, 1776 (*Der Briefwechsel*) (EAG).

CR: 'In this novel, no female laments that the tyranny of her parents prevents her from eloping with the dear, dear man she loves; no cooing turtle pours forth her soul in tender epistles, which the faithful chambermaid conveys to the favourite swain; no rake triumphs over, and forsakes, the fair one he has deceived; in short, no intrigue is carried on; and, for that reason alone, a true novel reading girl would not give sixpence for the book. Thus far for its negative merit; and negative merit is all we can allow it. Without plot, without connexion, and with very little sentiment, it is one of the most uninteresting, insipid, futile productions, which has ever come under our notice'.

MR [George Colman, the elder]: 'The title, as well as some other parts of this little work, appear calculated to mislead the Reader, unless by "an *original* novel" is implied, by a kind of contradiction in terms, that the personages are not only real, but also that the epistles here exhibited are their original letters. They bear indeed, notwithstanding a similarity of style that runs through the whole series, many marks of originality, several touches relative to time, place, and circumstance, not likely to be founded on fiction' (p. 430).

THE DAUGHTER
See COOPER, Maria Susanna

1775: 4   ANON.
THE DELICATE OBJECTION: OR, SENTIMENTAL SCRUPLE.

> London: Printed for W. Lane, N°. 33, Leaden-Hall-Street, 1775.
> I vii, 216p; II 214p. 12mo. 5s (MR).
> CR 41: 241 (Mar 1776); MR 53: 184 (Aug 1775).
> CaAEU PR 3991.A1.D35 1775; ESTC n006270 (BI BL [vol.2 only]; NA TxHR).

Notes. Prefatory advertisement v–vii, signed 'The Editor'. 2 pp. advs. end vol. 2. Epistolary.

MR [William Enfield]: 'We confess ourselves disappointed in every particular; having met with no incidents to surprise us, except for their absurdity; nor any thing in the sentiment or language, to excite our admiration or give us pleasure. To us it appears, like many other very delicate sentimental productions of our modern novelists, insupportably insipid.'

EDWIN AND JULIA: A NOVEL
See 1774: 7

1775: 5   ANON.
THE EMBARRASSED LOVERS OR, THE HISTORY OF HENRY CAREY, ESQ. AND THE HON. MISS CECILIA NEVILLE. IN A SERIES OF LETTERS. IN TWO VOLUMES.

> London: Printed for W. Lane, N°. 33, Leadenhall Street, 1775.
> I 238p; II 278p, 12mo. 6s (CR, MR).
> CR 41: 241 (Mar 1776); MR 53: 185 (Aug 1775).
> CSmH 125650; ESTC n065434.

Notes. 2 pp. advs. end vol. 2. Epistolary.

CR: ' . . . we can seldom get through a score of pages of performances of this sort without being heartily tired, and we generally drudge through the remainder with aching heads. Habit inures us to this in some degree, and our patience lasts tolerably well through the first volume; a second we are apt to look on with an evil eye; but a third or fourth are almost enough to make us forswear our employment.'

MR [William Enfield]: 'Though the Reviewer sat down to this Novel with his eyes open, and all his faculties awake; before he had dragged through fifty pages, his attention began to droop; the lead descended upon his eye-lids; and a drowsy listlessness crept through his whole frame. In this comfortable state of half-slumber, which left him just strength enough to turn over the leaves, while the soft ideas of *tender attachment, delicacy, embarrassment,* and the like, played in confusion about his fancy, he continued, till he had almost reached the end of the first volume; when, at length, the book dropped to the ground and he fell into a profound sleep. Thus totally vanquished, it would be presumption in him to attempt to rally; nor will he venture to draw a single arrow out of his quiver, against a writer thus defended by the impenetrable shield of the "Mighty Mother." He will only take the liberty of advising the readers of the Monthly Review, when all the *other* opiates fail, and even their seat at church refuses them their accustomed nap, to send for a dose of *soporiferous reading,* from the circulating library, under the name of *The embarrassed Lovers.*'

1775: 6 ANON.
THE GENERAL ELECTION. A SERIES OF LETTERS CHIEFLY BETWEEN TWO FEMALE FRIENDS. IN TWO VOLUMES.

> London: Printed for J. Walter, at Homer's Head, Charing-Cross, 1775.
> I 239p; II 248p. 12mo. 5s sewed (CR, SJC), 6s (MR).
> CR 39: 510 (June 1775); MR 53: 185 (Aug 1775).
> BL 12614.bbb.17; EM 289: 2: ESTC t071395.

Notes. Epistolary.
Adv. SJC 6–9 May 1775.
Extracts published LC 37: 529 and 549 (3–6 and 8–10 June 1775).
Further edn: London, 1779, ESTC n006689, and praised in SJC adv.; see *Harriet* (1771: 18).

CR: 'If this novel becomes a favourite with our usual novel-readers, we should congratulate them on their change of taste. Though Miss Sidney and Miss Fielding, the writers of the letters before us, deals [*sic*] chiefly in politics, it must be confessed, that the discussion of such subjects is to be preferred to that of the tender ones so plentifully dispersed throughout most of the modern novels.'

MR [John Noorthouck]: 'A composition of small politics and love, which if it is not an improvement, is at least a variation, in the ingredients of a modern novel.'

1775: 7 ANON.
HE IS FOUND AT LAST: OR, MEMOIRS OF THE BEVERLEY FAMILY. IN TWO VOLUMES.

> London: Printed for F. and J. Noble, at their respective Circulating Libraries, in Holborn, and St Martin's Court, near Leicester-Fields, 1775.
> I 221p, II 221p; 12mo. 5s sewed (CR), 6s (MR), 5s sewed or 6s bound (SJC).

CR 39: 510 (June 1775); MR 52: 187 (Feb 1775); AF II: 1865.

BL 12612.bb.3; EM 167: 6; ESTC t066370 (BI O).

Notes. Vol. 1, final 1-p. 'Advertisement to the Country Booksellers', regarding the Nobles' contest with Baldwin; 3 pp. advs. end vol. 2. Epistolary.

Adv. SJC 15–17 Nov 1774.

Further edn: Dublin, 1781 (Printed for C. Jackson, 2 vols., 12mo), EM 3515: 14, ESTC n032704. CR reviews with 1775: 2, 1774: 20, 1775: 13; see 1775: 2 for comment.

MR [William Enfield]: 'We have met with incidents, plain indeed and simple, but natural and interesting; entertaining journals; lively reflections on places and things; agreeable characters; and, at last, a discovery and a union which have given us no small pleasure.'

THE HISTORY OF FANNY MEADOWS
See COOPER, Maria Susanna

THE HISTORY OF MADEMOISELLE DE BELEAU (London, 1775) is a variant of Defoe's Roxana (1724)

1775: 8   ANON.
THE IRISH GUARDIAN. A PATHETIC STORY. IN FOUR VOLUMES. BY A LADY.

London: Printed for Joseph Johnson, No. 72, St. Paul's Church-yard, 1775.

I 204p; II 210p; III 252p; IV 285p. 12mo. 10s sewed (CR, MR, LC).

CR 40: 260–2 (Oct 1775); MR 53: 515 (Dec 1775); AF II: 2211.

C Hib.8.775.3–6; ESTC t167034 (NA ViUC).

Notes. Following vol. 2, p. 210 are 2 pp. of errata numbered 205 and 206; following vol. 4, p. 285 are 2 pp. of errata numbered 207 and 208 followed by 2 unn. pp. advs. In both vols. errata page nos. in square brackets; preceding page nos. in parentheses. Epistolary.

Adv. LC 37: 575 (15–17 June 1775).

Further edn: Dublin, 1776 (Printed for W. Whitestone, 2 vols., 12mo), ESTC t212443. German trans. Leipzig, 1776 (*Der irländische Vormund*) (Price).

CR: 'The plan on which novels are usually written is to deliver the history of some particular personage, who is distinguished as the principal character in the fictitious narrative. . . . The author of The Irish Guardian has deviated from the beaten path. . . . Instead of any particular favourite, we are presented with several, whose amiable portraits almost equally engage our partiality. Agreeably discriminated by their endowments, however, as well as their situations in life, and contrasted by the sexual distinction, with a natural diversity of manners, we survey the select assemblage without being disgusted by similitude, and in attending to each of the characters experience the pleasure of novelty. The title of the work, indeed, seems to have no immediate relation to the subject: but where we are so well entertained, to revolt at a nominal impropriety, might justly be considered as uncandid and fastidious criticism' (p. 260).

MR [William Enfield]: 'The Writer does not so much as attempt the pathetic, till she is pretty far advanced in the third volume, and then only in the way of episode. . . . Sometimes we find the unadorned and unimpassioned narrative of the traveller; sometimes the Author takes up the poet's pencil, and paints the beautiful or romantic scenes of nature in not unpleasing colours; sometimes she assumes the gravity of the philosopher and moralist, and makes just observations and useful reflections; and here and there the tale is enlivened with agreeable strokes of humour. But the narrative is not sufficiently uniform and connected; the characters are not delineated with adequate strength; nor are the incidents sufficiently striking, to produce any great effect upon the Reader's feelings. If therefore the work be allowed the merit of an agreeable miscellany, or an entertaining novel, it must by no means, claim that of a pathetic story.'

1775: 9   ANON.
*JULIA BENSON; OR THE SUFFERINGS OF INNOCENCE; IN A SERIES OF LETTERS, FOUNDED ON WELL-KNOWN FACTS, TENDING TO GUARD THE MIND FROM INDULGENCE OF ILLICIT PLEASURES, AND THE FATAL EFFECTS OF FEMALE RESENTMENT.
  London: Printed for W. Goldsmith, at No. 24, in Paternoster-Row (LC), 1775.
  I 137p; II 90p. 12mo. 6s (CR, MR), 5s sewed (LC).
  CR 41: 241 (Mar 1776); MR 53: 184 (Aug 1775); AF II: 2329.
  No copy located.
Notes. FB suggests by Arthur Young.
Epistolary.
Adv., 'may be had in a few days', LC 37: 163 (16–18 Feb 1775); title is given as *Julia Benson; or, the Flutterings of Innocence: In a Series of Letters: Founded on Facts.*
Further edn: Dublin, 1784 (Printed by Charles Lodge, 2 vols., 12mo), EM 3521: 4, ESTC n032764. German trans. Leipzig, 1776 (*Julie Benson, oder Die leidende Unschuld*) (Price); French trans. Rotterdam, 1780 (*Julie Benson, ou l'Innocence opprimée*) (BGR).
  CR: 'Thus it is with the world.—Every one complains of his own sufferings, heedless of what he inflicts on his neighbour. —Miss Benson, we dare say, however sensible to her own misfortunes, cares not a farthing about the irrecoverable loss of time, and the fatigue to which the publication of these volumes has subjected the Reviewers.'
  MR [William Enfield]: 'The variety of interesting incidents which are crowded into these two volumes, sufficiently prove that the Author possesses the powers of invention in no inconsiderable degree; and some of his characters, particularly that of the heroine of the piece, are conceived with boldness, and supported with propriety. The eye of criticism will, however, discover several improbabilities in the course of the story; and the tender and generous heart will be wounded by the catastrophe, in which the principal persons, through the whole distinguished by their virtues, after having surmounted a series of difficulties, and reached the summit of enjoyment, are on a sudden plunged into the deepest distress, and fall a sacrifice to malice and revenge.'

1775: 10   ANON.
*THE MARRIED LIBERTINE; OR, HISTORY OF MISS MELVILLE.
  London: Printed for F. Noble, near Middle Row, Holborn; and J. Noble, in St Martin's Court, near Leicester Fields (LC), 1775 (LC).
  2 vols. 5s sewed (LC).
  No copy located.
Notes. Adv. LC 37: 148 (11–14 Feb 1775).

1775: 1ʰ ANON.

MEMOIRS OF A DEMI-REP OF FASHION; OR, THE PRIVATE HIS-
TORY OF MISS AMELIA GUNNERSBURY. CONTAINING CURIOUS
ANECDOTES OF PERSONS OF THE FIRST RANK, WHICH ILLUS-
TRATE MANY CELEBRATED AND EMINENT CHARACTERS. IN TWO
VOLUMES.

> London: Printed for J. Dix, N°. 22, near St. John's Gate, 1775.
> I vi, 232p; II vi, 243p. 12mo. 6s (MR), 5s sewed (SJC).
> MR 54: 162 (Feb 1776); AF II: 2822.
> MnU WILS RAR 825G959 OM; ESTC n010973 (NA CLU-S/C).

Notes. Table of contents i–vi each vol.
Adv. LC 38: 564 (9–12 Dec 1775) and SJC 16–19 Dec 1775.
Further edn: Dublin, 1776 (Printed for the United Company of Booksellers, 2 vols. in 1,
12mo), EM 329: 1, ESTC t072461.

MR [John Noorthouck]: 'Some worthy successor to the celebrated *Treysac* [*sic*] *de Vergy*,
has coined or dressed up, a number of ill-digested tales of licentious love, in hopes that the
public avidity for scandalous anecdotes may give them a welcome reception: but when we
cannot approve a writer's motive, there is some consolation in finding his abilities unequal
to his intentions.'

1775: 12 ANON.

MEMOIRS OF MAITRE JACQUES, OF SAVOY.

> Bath: Printed by S. Hazard; for W. Owen, at Homer's-Head, in Fleet-Street, London,
> 1775.
> I iv, 188p. 12mo. 2s sewed (CR, MR).
> CR 41: 159 (Feb 1776); MR 54: 197–202 (Mar 1776).
> BL RB.23.a.7519; ESTC t223568.

Notes. Preface iii–iv.
Vol. 2 1783: 6.
CR reviews under 'Miscellaneous'; MR does not classify.
Adv. SJC 18–21 Nov 1775.
Extracts published LC 38: 553 and 561 (7–9 and 9–12 Dec 1775).
Further edn: London, 1779, EM 173: 1, ESTC t066877 [combines 2nd edn. of vol. 1 with
1st edn. of vol. 2]. German trans. Leipzig, 1776 (*Memoiren Meister Jakobs aus Savoyen*)
(Price).

CR: 'It would appear from the conclusion of the volume that Maitre Jacques has an
intention of continuing his Memoirs to a later period; and as he is a lively, terse, excentric
kind of biographer, we doubt not of his furnishing amusement to a particular class of
readers.'

MR [John Langhorne]: 'Master Jacques of Savoy is no unentertaining companion. He is
the biographer of his own very curious and comical being, and, in a manner that is at once
arch and unaffected, sets forth the variety of that whim and caprice wherewith *Fortune* had
vouchsafed to treat him' (p. 197). 'The only objection we have to this little performance, is
the Author's disregard to delicacy, in a few instances, which might well have been spared'
(p. 202).

1775: 13   ANON.
THE MORNING RAMBLE; OR, HISTORY OF MISS EVELYN. IN TWO VOLUMES.

London: Printed for F. and J. Noble, at their respective Circulating Libraries, in Holborn, and St Martin's Court, near Leicester-Fields, 1775.

I 208p, II 191p; 12mo. 5s sewed (CR), 6s bound (MR), 5s sewed or 6s bound (SJC).

CR 39: 510 (June 1775); MR 52: 186–7 (Feb 1775); AF II: 2957.

BL 1607/331; EM 4334: 11; ESTC t118483.

Notes. BL copy vol. 2, has imperfect final 1 p. advs. Epistolary.

Adv. SJC 15–17 Nov 1774.

Adv. on verso of t.p. to vol. 2 of *Capricious Father* (1775: 2).

CR reviews with 1775: 2, 1774: 20, and 1775: 7; see 1775: 2 for comment.

Sarcastic MR rev. [William Enfield] concludes: 'A very pretty, *romantic, sentimental* morning's entertainment for *Miss in her Teens.*'

MR. BENTLEY, THE RURAL PHILOSOPHER
See MAN, Henry

THE PALACE OF SILENCE
See ARCQ, Philippe-Auguste de Sainte-Foix, chevalier d'

THE PHILOSPHER IN BRISTOL
See COMBE, William

THE PILGRIM: OR, A PICTURE OF LIFE
See JOHNSTONE, Charles

THE PRUDENT ORPHAN
See 1774: 20

1775: 14   ANON.
THE SCHOOL FOR DAUGHTERS: OR, THE HISTORY OF MISS CHARLOTTE SIDNEY: IN A SERIES OF ORIGINAL LETTERS BETWEEN PERSONS IN GENTEEL LIFE. IN TWO VOLUMES.

London: Printed for J. Bew, No. 28, Pater-Noster-Row, 1775.

I 220p; II 216p. 12mo. 5s sewed (CR, MR), 5s sewed or 6s bound (SJC).

CR 39: 341 (Apr 1775); MR 52: 505–6 (June 1775); AF II: 3968.

ICN Y155.S362; ESTC n052904.

Notes. Epistolary. Last letter ends on p. 212, followed by 'The Conclusion'.

Adv. SJC 14–16 Mar 1775; additional booksellers are J. Walter, J. Ridley, W. Brown, G. Kearsly, and W. Davenhill.

German trans. Leipzig, 1775 (*Die Schule für Töchter*) (Price).

CR: 'We shall take care to keep our daughters from this School; or rather, this School from our daughters.'

1775: 15   ANON.
THE TENDER FATHER. A NOVEL. IN TWO VOLUMES.
London: Printed for G. Riley, in Curzon-street, May-Fair, 1775.
I xv, 253p, II 228p. 12mo. 5s sewed (CR), 6s (MR), 5s sewed or 6s bound (SJC).
CR 40: 164 (Aug 1775); MR 53: 274 (Sept 1775); AF II: 4391.
BRu ENC; ESTC n013443 (NA MH-H).

Notes. Dedication to H.R.H. the Duchess of Cumberland iii–vi, signed 'The Author'; introduction vii–xv.
Adv. SJC 25–27 Apr 1775.
German trans. Lübeck and Leipzig, 1776 (*Der zärtliche Vater*) (Price).
   CR: 'A collection of tales, chiefly abridgements of, and extracts from, other publications,
tacked together in an artless and uninteresting manner.'
   MR [William Enfield]: [After quoting the author's opening sentence concerning the care
authors should take not to 'disgrace both themselves and their country by unworthy performances'] 'If this Writer had paid proper attention to his own reflection in its full extent, either
the several stories which are tacked together to make up a work, would have been more
interesting, the reflections would have been more striking, and the composition more
masterly—or the work would not have been suffered to make its appearance.'

THE TRIFLER
See MAN, Henry

TRIUMPH OF TRUTH
See LEPRINCE DE BEAUMONT, Marie

VILLAGE MEMOIRS
See CRADOCK, Joseph

1775: 16   ANON.
*THE WAITING MAID; OR, THE GALLANTRIES OF THE TIMES.
Printed for the Author, and sold by J. Robins, near Paternoster-Row (SJC), 1775 (SJC).
2 vols. 12mo. 5s sewed (CR, SJC), 6s (MR).
CR 40: 164 (Aug 1775); MR 53: 185 (Aug 1775); AF II: 4649.
No copy located.

Notes. Adv. SJC 25–27 May 1775 as *The Waiting-Maid; or, The Gallantries of the Times; con-
taining many secret Amours, soft Scenes, and tender Situations, between the principal living
Characters in the Kingdom.*
A further adv. SJC 29–31 Aug 1775 adds: 'N.B. This Book may be considered as a Counter-
Part to the Tete-a-Tetes delivered in the Town and Country Magazine. In that Work, the
Amours of our most gallant Noblemen and Gentlemen, with their Favourites of inferior
Condition, have been related in a Manner that has given general Satisfaction: In the Waiting-
Maid, on the other Hand, the Female Closet is opened; and the Amours of our most libertine
Ladies of Rank and Fashion, with their Paramours of all Conditions, are painted with a
Warmth of Pencil, which, it is hoped, will do Justice to the Luxury of their Feelings; and at
the same Time with a Truth which calumny cannot controvert.'

CR: 'We have frequently had occasion to lament the ill tendency of such novels as impress young minds with romantic notions of love. The work before us is in some measure liable to the same censure, and in another particular deserves the most severe reprehension. It contains a frequent and minute description of amorous intrigues, tending to excite the most lascivious ideas, and is therefore highly improper for the perusal of those into whose hands novels generally fall.'

Single word rev. in MR: 'Obscenity'.

A WEEK AT A COTTAGE
See HUTCHINSON, William

1775: 17   [ARCQ, Philippe-Auguste de Sainte-Foix, chevalier d'].
THE PALACE OF SILENCE: A PHILOSOPHIC TALE. TRANSLATED FROM THE FRENCH BY A LADY.

London: Printed for J. Bew, at Number 28, in Pater-Noster-Row, 1775.
I lix,141p; II 215p. 12mo. 5s sewed (CR), 5s (MR), 4s sewed or 5s bound (SJC).
CR 39: 509–10 (June 1775); MR 53: 184–5 (Aug 1775).
BL 12548.aa.24; EM 554: 4; ESTC t129730 (BI Owo; NA CLU-S/C [vol. 1], MnU).
Notes. Trans. of *Le Palais du Silence* (Amsterdam, 1754).
Preface falsely claims that it is a trans. from the Greek of Cadmus the Milesian, 'the only production of his that is extant'. 1 p. adv. end vol. 2.
Adv. SJC 8–10 June 1775; booksellers listed include, with addresses, Almon, Ridley, Walter, Brown, Kearsley, and Davenhill.

CR: 'This Philosophic Tale, we are assured in the Preface, is a translation of a Greek manuscript, sold by a Greek of Navarino, a town in the Morea, to the commander of a Leghorn privateer. We shall not take the trouble to enquire when or by whom it was written, as we cannot lavish praise on the author of it, either for the entertainment or the instruction he has afforded us. The story contains little variety, if the marvellous part of it be extracted, and we have not found ourselves much interested for the hero of it, although he is represented as the dupe of execrable fraud and the victim to hopeless love.'

MR [William Enfield]: 'It is sufficient for our purpose, to inform our readers, that, in the romantic and extravagant cast of the story, it bears a much greater resemblance to an Arabian or Fairy Tale, than to a modern novel; and that in the sentiments, and style of the dialogues, it approaches nearer to the flimsy texture of French romance, than to the substantial fabric produced by the genius of ancient Greece.'

BACULARD D'ARNAUD, François-Thomas-Marie de
See TENCIN, Claudine-Alexandrine Guérin de

BEAUMONT, Jeanne Marie le Prince de
See LEPRINCE DE BEAUMONT, Marie

1775: 18   [BICKNELL, Alexander].
THE BENEVOLENT MAN; OR, THE HISTORY OF MR. BELVILLE; IN WHICH IS INTRODUCED, THE REMARKABLE ADVENTURES OF

CAPTAIN MACLEAN, THE HERMIT. IN TWO VOLUMES. DEDICATED
TO THE EARL OF DARTMOUTH.

> London: Printed for J. Lewis, at his Circulating Library, in Charles Street, near Parlia-
> ment Street, Westminster, 1775.
>
> I 240p; II 223p. 12mo. 5s (CR), 5s sewed (MR), 5s sewed or 6s neatly bound (LC).
>
> CR 40: 263–4 (Oct 1775); MR 53: 515–16 (Dec 1775); AF II: 330.
>
> PU Singer-Mend.PR3318.B42B4 1775; ESTC n031944 (NA InU-Li, IU).

Notes. Dedication to the Earl of Dartmouth. 1 p. advs. end vol. 2. InU-Li copy has table of
contents at beginning of both volumes.

Adv. LC 37: 620 (29 June–1 July 1775); adv. adds parenthetically in the title the information
that Captain Maclean is 'a Gentleman of North Britain'.

Extract published LC 38: 53 (13–15 July 1775).

German trans. Leipzig, 1777 (*Der Wohlthätige, oder Geschichte des Herrn Belville* (EAG).
Facs: FN.

CR: 'Very good lessons for the conduct of life may be selected from these little volumes,
but there is scarcely any adventure described in them, which can claim the merit of
novelty. . . . [This author] more particularly merits censure, as he ridicules the *poor author*
who, in conformity to the taste of the pretty misses, must write of dukes, lords, and baronets,
and must make his hero and heroine happy at last; yet submits to please those pretty misses
by doing exactly what he condemns in others, and that in contradiction to his own
sentiments.'

COMBE, William, **LETTERS FROM ELIZA TO YORICK**
See App. B: 3

1775: 19 [COMBE, William].
THE PHILOSOPHER IN BRISTOL.

> Bristol: Printed by G. Routh, in the Maiden-Tavern, 1775.
>
> I 110p; II 159p. 8vo. 5s (MR).
>
> CR 42: 477–9 (Dec 1776); MR 55: 238 (Sept 1776); AF II: 822.
>
> BL 12330.bb.29; EM 633: 3; ESTC t128693 (BI C [vol. 1 only], O; NA CaOHM, CSmH,
> CtY &c.).

Notes. 1 p. adv. end vol. 2. 'Part the Second', t.p. to vol. 2. Dedication vol. 1 'To the Inhabitants of Bristol' and to Charles Hayward Esq. of St James's Square, London, and vol. 2 'To
the Inhabitants of Bristol'.

Vol. 1 published 12 June and vol. 2, 26 July (Hamilton). Berg Collection, NN, has a bill to
Combe from George Routh including printing, paper, and labour costs of £28.8.6 for 700
copies of the 2 vols. and a further charge of £5.4s for a total of 19 advs. in 4 local and regional
newspapers and a total of 8 advs. in 4 London newspapers (bill reproduced in Hamilton,
pp. 35–6).

CR reviews under 'Miscellaneous', MR under 'Novels and Memoirs'.

Further edn: Dublin, 1784 (Printed for T. Jackson at his Circulating Library, 1 vol., 8vo), EM
3810: 4, ESTC t118196.

MR [John Noorthouck]: 'As these volumes were published at two different times, the first
half of the second part is occupied by discoursing on the merits of the former volume, and in
retorting contempt on those who dared to censure it.'

1775: 20   [COOPER, Maria Susanna].
THE DAUGHTER: OR THE HISTORY OF MISS EMILIA ROYSTON, AND MISS HARRIET AYRES; IN A SERIES OF LETTERS. BY THE AUTHORESS OF THE EXEMPLARY MOTHER.

London: Printed for J. Dodsley in Pall-mall, 1775.
vi, 280p. 12mo. 3s (CR), 2s 6d sewed (MR, SJC).
CR 39: 426–7 (May 1775); MR 53: 274 (Sept 1775).
BL Huth 89; EMf; ESTC t081163 (NA InU-Li, ICN).

Notes. Dedication to Lady Beauchamp Proctor i–iv. Epistolary. As the author points out in her preface (v–vi), this is a revision of Letters Between Emilia and Harriet (London, 1762, JR 708, AF I: 520) which she saw as in need of improvement; she describes the earlier novel as 'the ground-work' of The Daughter.
The Exemplary Mother, 1769, JR , AF I: 519.
Adv. SJC 15–18 Apr 1775.
Further edn: Dublin, 1775 (Printed by D. Chamberlaine, for the United Company of Booksellers, 1 vol., 12mo), ESTC n028419. German trans. Leipzig, 1776 (Die Tochter oder Geschichte der Miss Emilie Royston und der Miss Henriette Ayres in Briefen) (EAG).

CR: 'While the province of romance-writing is generally usurped by mercenaries, who inflame the passions and corrupt the minds of young readers, it is with much pleasure that we meet with a novel calculated to enforce any of the moral duties. To draw a perfect pattern of filial obedience is the grand object of the present performance . . . ' (p. 426).

MR [William Enfield]: 'The Author, perceiving many material defects in the original work, particularly that the story was too simple to be very interesting, too concise to admit of much exemplification of character, and too much in the usual strain of romantic love, to conduct the reader to the temple of truth, has attempted to improve both the plan and exe-cution of the work; endeavouring to draw a perfect pattern of filial obedience, and female delicacy, with a view to interest the affections, modulate the passions, and mend the heart. By these alterations the moral of the piece is doubtless improved; but with respect to the com-position, we still do not think ourselves authorised to place it above the line of mediocrity, or to allow it a degree of merit equal to that of the Author's later productions.'

1775: 21   {COOPER, Maria Susanna}.
THE HISTORY OF FANNY MEADOWS. IN A SERIES OF LETTERS. BY THE AUTHOR OF THE EXEMPLARY MOTHER. IN TWO VOLUMES.

London: Printed for T. Becket, the Corner of Adelphi, in the Strand, 1775.
I iv, 202p; II 178p. 8vo. 5s sewed (CR, SJC), 6s (MR).
CR 39: 509 (June 1775); MR 53: 183–4 (Aug 1775).
BL Cup.402.k.29; EM 8177: 234; ESTC t138868 (NA CtY, IU, MH-H).

Notes. Dedication to Edward Jerningham Esq. Preface signed Maria Susanna Cooper. 2 pp. advs. end vol. 1. Epistolary.
The Exemplary Mother, 1769, JR , AF I: 519.
Adv. SJC 20–23 May 1775.
Further edn: Dublin, 1776 (Printed for John Beatty, 2 vols., 12mo), ESTC t209952. German trans. Leipzig, 1775 (Geschichte der Fanny Meadows) (Price).

CR: ' . . . the author has executed her task with taste and judgment'.

MR [William Enfield]: 'The History of Fanny Meadows ... raises no romantic ideas of life; ministers no fuel to illicit passion; furnishes no hints for the successful management of intrigues; gives no encouragement to clandestine and imprudent amours: It is written with the laudable design of warning the inexperienced fair, of the dangers of forming hasty connections with such as are greatly their superiors in rank and fortune, and pointing out to them the behaviour, which, in such a situation, discretion, delicacy, and a refined sense of propriety would suggest. This good lesson is conveyed in a manner well adapted to touch the heart. The story, though simple, is sufficiently interesting; the style is agreeably diversified, always correct, and sometimes elegant: the characters are distinctly marked, and the catastrophe is highly pleasing.'

1775: 22   [CRADOCK, Joseph].
VILLAGE MEMOIRS: IN A SERIES OF LETTERS BETWEEN A CLERGY-MAN AND HIS FAMILY IN THE COUNTRY, AND HIS SON IN TOWN.
> London: Printed for T. Davies, in Russel-street, Covent-Garden, MDCCLXV [ESTC: 1774?].
> xii, 180p. 8vo. 2s 6d sewed (CR, SJC Dec), 3s (MR), 5s sewed (SJC June).
> CR 38: 449–55 (Dec 1774); MR 52: 139–43 (Feb 1775); AF II: 923.
> BL 244.e.14; EM 3631: 4; ESTC t130067 (BI O; NA CSmH, DLC, NjP &c.).

Notes. Epistolary.
Adv., 'Speedily will be published, In two neat Pocket Volumes', SJC 11–14 June 1774. Adv., 'Saturday the 10th of Dec. will be published', SJC 1–3 Dec 1774.
Extracts published LC 37: 245 and 277 (11–14 and 21–23 Mar 1775); extracts published LC 37: 245 and 277 (11–14 and 21–23 Mar 1775).
Further edns: Dublin, 1775 (Printed for P. Wilson; and M. Mills, 1 vol., 12mo), EM 4173: 4, ESTC t118358; London, 1775, EM 126: 6, ESTC t070709; London, 1775, ESTC t178717; London, 1776, ESTC t195333. Further edns. reviewed in CR 40: 165 and 42: 157–8. German trans. Leipzig, 1775 (*Dorfmemoiren in einer Reiche von Briefen zwischen einem Geistlichen und seiner Familie auf dem Lande und seinem Sohne in der Stadt*) (EAG).

CR: 'On the whole, these Memoirs abound with precepts and examples of the greatest utility in the conduct of life. At the same time, that they treat of various subjects relative to literature and the polite arts, they warmly interest the heart in the fortune of an amiable family, whose instructive correspondence we would be glad to see continued in a future publication' (p. 455).

MR [Ralph Griffiths]: 'The Novel-Manufactory is not yet wholly abandoned to the lower orders of Grubstreet. Writers of superior degree are sometimes still induced to tread this inviting walk of literature; and there are few readers who delight not to follow their steps.

The *Village Memoirs* are not to be ranked with the *first* compositions of this kind; they will not rival a JOSEPH ANDREWS, or a TOM JONES, in the esteem of the Public; but they far excel the common productions of the circulating libraries. The unknown Author is evidently a man of genius, learning, and taste; but he seems to want the application necessary to produce a finished piece' (p. 139).

1775: 23   [?DIGGES, Thomas Atwood].
THE ADVENTURES OF ALONSO: CONTAINING SOME STRIKING ANECDOTES OF THE PRESENT PRIME MINISTER OF PORTUGAL.

London: Printed for J. Bew, No. 28, Paternoster-Row, 1775.
I 148p; II 129p. 8vo. 4s sewed (CR), 5s bound (MR), 4s sewed or 5s bound (LC).
CR 40: 163–4 (July 1775); MR 53: 274 (Sept 1775); AF II: 28.
BL 12612.aa.8; EM 166: 9; ESTC t067327 (NA ICU, MWA, NN &c.).

Notes. ESTC: Sometimes attributed to T. A. Digges.
The Prime minister is the Marquês de Pombal (1699–1782).
Adv., 'Next Week will be published, Neatly printed on a fine writing paper', LC 37: 543 (6–8 June 1775).
Extract published LC 37: 617 (29 June-1 July 1775).
Further edn: London, 1785 (CR), xESTC. German trans. Leipzig, 1787 (*Alonzos Abenteuer*) (Price).

CR: 'The writer of this work amuses himself with too much political matter (especially as it relates chiefly to a foreign kingdom,) to render his book a favourite with the readers of novels' (p. 163).

MR [William Enfield]: 'The Author of this Novel has contrived to mix just so much political anecdote and reflection with his love-tale, as to make it dull and tedious.'

1775: 24   [HUTCHINSON, William].
A WEEK AT A COTTAGE, A PASTORAL TALE.

London: Printed for Hawes, Clarke & Collins, in Pater-noster-row, 1775.
222p. 8vo. 2s (CR, MR).
CR 41: 325–7 (Apr 1776); MR 55: 77 (July 1776).
BL 4410.g.3; EM 4850: 3; ESTC t079362 (BI MRu; NA ViU).

Notes. Engraved t.p.
MR reviews under 'Miscellaneous' but CR under 'Novels'.

CR: 'What a deal of business our author executes in one short week!.... To speak the truth (and we never are ashamed of veracity) we conceived no small dislike to him in our Sunday's excursion in his company; the quaintness of his expressions, and the affectation in his style, we could by no means relish, and although in the course of the week we grew better acquainted with him and his manners, we cannot yet eradicate the notion we first conceived, that his phrases border on fustian; and, not being poetry, are prose run mad.'

1775: 25   [JOHNSTONE, Charles].
THE PILGRIM: OR, A PICTURE OF LIFE. IN A SERIES OF LETTERS, WRITTEN MOSTLY FROM LONDON BY A CHINESE PHILOSOPHER, TO HIS FRIEND AT QUANG-TONG. CONTAINING REMARKS UPON THE LAWS, CUSTOMS, AND MANNERS OF THE ENGLISH AND OTHER NATIONS. ILLUSTRATED BY A VARIETY OF CURIOUS AND INTERESTING ANECDOTES, AND CHARACTERS DRAWN FROM REAL LIFE. BY THE EDITOR OF CHRYSAL.

London: Printed for T. Cadell, in the Strand; and W. Flexney in Holborn, 1775.
I iv, 287p; II 267p. 8vo. 5s sewed (CR, MR), 5s sewed or 6s bound (SJC).
CR 40: 231–3 (Sept 1775); MR 53: 362–3 (Oct 1775); AF II: 2312.
BL 245.f.7–8; EM 978: 4; ESTC t118158 (BI LEu [vol. 2 only], O; NA CSmH, IU, MH-H, PU &c.).

Notes. 'End of Volume Two' final p. of vol. 2, indicating possibility of continuation. Epistolary.

Chrysal 1760, JR 577, AF I: 1440.

Adv. SJC 23–25 May 1775.

Extract published LC 37: 497 (25–27 May 1775).

Further edns: Dublin, 1775 (Printed for J. Potts, J. Williams, W. Colles, R. Moncrieffe, C. Jenkin [and 5 others in Dublin], 1 vol., 12mo), EM 551: 11, ESTC t116306; variant CtY copy (xESTC) 'Printed by T. Carnan [*sic*], in the Strand; and W. Flexnet [*sic*], in Holborn n.d.' German trans. Leipzig, 1775 (*Der Pilgrim*) (EAG). Facs: FN.

CR: 'Our Pilgrim has the good fortune to be acquainted with several extraordinary personages, and his account of them enables us to determine what originals sat for the pictures' (p. 233).

MR [William Enfield]: 'His former works, at the same time that they have exhibited their Author in the character of a severe and angry satirist, have afforded many proofs of inventive genius, and a cultivated understanding. In the present publication he so nearly pursues the same line of writing, and so exactly preserves his former rough manner, and peculiar turn for exaggeration and caricature, that it is unnecessary to enter into a particular critique on his work.'

1775: 26   LEPRINCE DE BEAUMONT, [Marie].
MORAL TALES. TRANSLATED FROM THE FRENCH OF MDE LE PRINCE DE BEAUMONT. IN TWO VOLUMES.

> London: Printed for J. Nourse, in the Strand, Bookseller to His Majesty, 1775.
> I 304p; II [222]p. 12mo. 5s (CR), 5s sewed or 6s bound (SJC).
> CR 39: 125–9 (Feb 1775); MR 52: 360–1 (Apr 1775); AF II: 2486.
> BL 12614.h.5; EM 290: 4; ESTC t073531 (NA CLU-S/C).

Notes. Trans. of *Contes moraux* (Lyons and Paris, 1774).

Last p. of vol. 2 is misnumbered 220. 2 pp. advs. end vol. 2.

Adv. SJC 8–10 Dec 1774.

Further edn: Dublin, 1776 (Printed for Messrs. Price, Whitestone, Chamberlaine, Sleator, W. Watson [and 20 others in Dublin], 2 vols., 12mo), ESTC t169554.

CR: 'These histories may be read both with profit and pleasure. While destitute of the extravagance, they are interspersed with the agreeable incidents of romance; the persons introduced are marked with natural and discriminating features, and every narrative is conducted in such a manner as to promote the interest of morality and virtue' (p. 129).

MR [William Enfield]: 'On the whole, these Moral Tales are, in our opinion, adapted to furnish more entertainment, and better instruction to young persons, than most of the modern productions of this kind. Yet, perhaps, with respect to some of her fair readers, a caution may not be wholly unnecessary, concerning the partiality which, in the midst of her just zeal for religion, she sometimes discovers in favour of the life of a devotee.'

1775: 27   [LEPRINCE DE BEAUMONT, Marie]; ROBERTS, R. (trans.).
THE TRIUMPH OF TRUTH; OR, MEMOIRS OF MR. DE LA VILLETTE, TRANSLATED FROM THE FRENCH. BY R. ROBERTS. IN TWO VOLUMES.

London: Printed for T. Cadell, in the Strand, 1775.

I xvi, 168p; II 142p. 12mo. 5s sewed (CR), 6s (MR), 5s sewed or 6s bound (LC).

CR 39: 283–7 (Apr 1775); MR 52: 506–8 (June 1775); AF II: 3808.

BL 1607/4543; EM 6456: 9; ESTC t120763 (BI MRu).

Notes. Trans. of *Le Triomphe de la Vérité* (Nancy, 1748).

Dedication to the Duchess of Devonshire, by R. Roberts, 12 Jan. 1775, St Paul's Church-yard.

Engraving on t.p. of vol. 1.

BL copy imprint line cut out in vol. 1 and additional t.p. without engraving before properly printed t.p. in vol. 2.

Adv., 'On Saturday next will be published, Neatly printed in two pocket volumes, . . . embellished with two engraved Vignettes adapted to the work', and adds that the trans. 'was undertaken at the request of the late Dr. Hawkesworth, who revised and corrected the Translator's manuscript', LC 37: 159 (14–16 Feb 1775).

Further edn: Dublin, 1775 (Printed for T. Armitage, 1775, 2 vols. 12mo), ESTC t175313.

CR: 'This instructive novel, which was originally written by a lady, and is translated by a person of the same sex, is a production of the moral and sentimental kind, in which the powers of the human understanding are ingeniously developed, and natural and revealed religion established on the obvious principles of reason' (p. 285).

MR [William Enfield]: 'The Author of this work has united two species of writing, which have certainly no natural alliance,—systematic divinity and fictitious narrative; and might very properly have entitled his piece, a theological novel. However, the union is by no means unpleasing; and may serve to give young persons some general ideas of the grounds of religious faith, in a form which will be likely to make a strong impression upon the memory, and thus by an innocent artifice to cheat them into instruction, where they expected nothing but entertainment' (p. 506).

1775: 28   [MAN, Henry].

MR. BENTLEY, THE RURAL PHILOSOPHER: A TALE. IN TWO VOLUMES.

London: Printed for W. Goldsmith, in Pater-Noster-Row, 1775.

I vii, 219p; II 235p. 12mo. 5s sewed (CR), 6s (MR), 5s sewed or 6s bound (LC).

CR 39: 478–81 (June 1775); MR 52: 361–4 (Apr 1775); AF II: 2697.

PU Singer-Mend. PR.4972.M6.M5.1775; EM 6570: 5; ESTC t142951 (BI BL; NA CtY).

Notes. Adv. LC 37: 163 (16–18 Feb 1775).

Further edn: Dublin, 1777 (Printed for W. Whitestone [successor to the late Mr Ewing], 2 vols. in 1, 12mo), EM 3516: 2, ESTC n035215. German trans. Leipzig, 1775 (*Mr. Benthely, der Philosoph auf dem Lande*) (Price).

CR: 'There are so many snares laid in the paths of virtue, and so many temptations to draw the inexperienced aside, that he who takes pains to caution the unwary of their danger is certainly entitled to thanks. This is the case with the author of the Rural Philosopher, who, although in some instances his sentiments are singular, and his opinions ill founded, holds forth to observation many useful lessons for the conduct of life' (p. 478).

MR [William Enfield]: 'In the midst of the endless variety of love-stories which our office calls us to peruse, it is a great relief and pleasure to us, sometimes to meet with a novel-writer, who ventures out of the beaten track, and employs a narrative and fiction, for other purposes than merely to cherish the flame, which nature is sufficiently able to kindle and keep alive without the help of art' (p. 361).

1775: 29   [MAN, Henry].
THE TRIFLER: OR, A RAMBLE AMONG THE WILDS OF FANCY, THE
WORKS OF NATURE, AND THE MANNERS OF MEN.

> London: Printed for R. Baldwin, at No. 47, in Pater-Noster-Row, 1775/77.
> I (1775) 241p; II (1775) 222p; III (1777) 223p; IV (1777) 230p. 8vo. 12s sewed (CR),
>   Vols. 1–2 6s (MR), 5s half bound (SJC); vols. 3–4 5s sewed (MR, SJC).
> CR 44: 64 (July 1777) 4 vols.; MR 53: 269–70 (Sept 1775), vols. 1–2, MR 56: 483–4 (June
>   1777), vols. 3–4; AF II: 2698, 2699.
> BL 12330.aaa.26; EM 639: 17; ESTC t128851 (NA MChB [vols. 2 & 4 only]).

> *Notes.* Vols. 1–2 adv. SJC 25–27 Apr 1775. Vols. 3–4 adv. SJC 23–25 Jan 1777.
> MR reviews under 'Miscellaneous'; CR does not classify.
> Further edns: Dublin, 1779 (Printed for W. Colles, G. Burnet, T. Walker, C. Jenkin,
> W. Hallhead, W. Gilbert, L. L. Flin, and J. Beatty, 1 vol., 12mo), EM 2816: 7, ESTC t129028;
> 2nd edn. vols. 1–2 adv., with quotation from 'The Reviewers', PA 16 Jan 1778. German trans.
> Leipzig, 1778 (*Der Tändler, oder Streiferey in die Wildnisse der Einbildungskraft*) (EAG).

> CR: 'The Trifler is desirous to free his countrymen from the insipid constraints of fashion,
> to impress them with a disgust of the vices and follies of the age, and above all to initiate them
> into the rational enjoyments which arise from giving a free course to the warm, impassioned
> feelings of the heart. Sensible of the taste of the times, the author of the Trifler has clothed his
> reflexions in a pleasing variety of little incidents which keep the reader's attention awake . . .
> among the numerous volumes of amusement which fill our monthly catalogues, we seldom
> meet with any, which have so much merit as the Trifler.'

> MR 53 [William Enfield]: ' . . . although some of his rambles appear to us to border upon
> nonsense, (particularly the chapter upon breakfast, dinner and supper,) and others to
> approach towards ribaldry, (more especially the chapter upon honour) in several of them, he
> exhibits lively pictures of manners, makes sensible and sprightly remarks, and satirizes folly
> with much boldness and with some humour' (p. 270).

MELMOTH, Courtney
See PRATT, Samuel Jackson

1775: 30   [PRATT, Samuel Jackson].
LIBERAL OPINIONS, UPON ANIMALS, MAN, AND PROVIDENCE. IN
WHICH ARE INTRODUCED, ANECDOTES OF A GENTLEMAN.
ADDRESSED TO THE RIGHT HON. LADY CH***TH. BY COURTNEY
MELMOTH . [vols. 1–2]
LIBERAL OPINIONS, IN WHICH IS CONTAINED THE HISTORY OF
BENIGNUS. WRITTEN BY HIMSELF. AND PUBLISHED BY COURT-
NEY MELMOTH. [vols. 3–6].

> London: Printed for G. Robinson, and J. Bew, in Paternoster-Row; and Sold by J. Wal-
>   ter, Charing-Cross, 1775/77.
> I (1775) viii, 228p; II (1775) 186p; III (1776) xi, 218p; IV (1776) 227p; V (1777) xii,
>   184p; VI (1777) 221p. 12mo. Vols. 1–2 5s sewed (CR), 5s sewed or 6s bound (SJC);
>   vols. 3–4 6s (MR), 5s sewed or 6s bound (SJC); vols. 5–6 5s sewed or 6s bound (WEP).
> CR 39: 277–83 (Apr 1775), MR 52: 468–72 (June 1775), vols. 1–2; CR 41: 383–7 (May

1776), MR 55: 319–20 (Oct 1776), vols. 3–4; CR 42: 443–7 (Dec 1776), MR 56: 231 (Mar 1777), vols. 5–6; AF II: 3577–3579.

BL 1081.d.18–20; EM 6861: 2; ESTC t146992 (BI C, O; NA CaAEU, CaOHM, CSmH, CtY &c.).

Notes. Vol. 2 Dedication to Thomas Lord Lyttelton. Vol. 3 Dedication to Duchess of Devonshire.

Vols. 1–2 adv., 'In the Press, and speedily will be published, Neatly printed on a fine Writing Paper', SJC 16–18 Mar 1775. Vols. 3–4 adv., 'Handsomely printed in small 8vo, on a fine Writing-Paper', SJC 21–23 May 1776. Vols. 5–6 adv., 'Handsomely printed on a fine Writing-Paper', WEP 19–21 Nov 1776.

Extracts published LC 37: 377–378 and 385 (20–22 and 22–25 Apr 1775), WEP 10–12 Dec 1776.

Further edn: London, 1777, ESTC n011295; London, 1783, EM 90: 1, ESTC t066928. German trans. Leipzig, 1777/78 (*Freymütige Gedanken über die Thiere*) (Price).

CR 39: 'By the aid of fanciful invention, he has rendered the animal kingdom subservient to moral entertainment, and amidst a picturesque description of scenes, laid before us a lively representation of several characters. We wish, however, that he had preserved, through the whole of his narrative, the same uniformity of design, which he has supported in the character of his hero; for in his excursions into the field of philosophy, though he often treads in unbeated paths, he rather wanders deviously, in search of objects that may gratify the imagination, than of such as inform the understanding' (p. 277).

MR 52 [William Enfield]: 'From several lively narratives occasionally introduced in this miscellany, our Author appears to be capable of delineating manners and characters, especially in low life, with a degree of spirit and humour, which, under the regulation of a correct taste, might render him an agreeable novelist. But, not content to follow the natural bent of his genius, and confine himself to the walk of low humour, in which he would probably make some figure, he, at once, labours to climb the steep ascent of Parnassus, and is ambitious to enrol himself among the philosophers. . . . The spirit and tendency of his work evidently appears to be nothing less than to bring the principles and practice of Benevolence into contempt, and to attack the strong-holds of Virtue' (p. 468).

MR 55 [William Enfield]: ' . . . we find little in the present volumes either to offend our moral feelings, or call for our critical censure' (p. 320).

SAINTE-FOIX, Philippe-Auguste de, Chevalier d'Arcq
See ARCQ, Philippe-Auguste de Sainte-Foix, Chevalier d'

1775: 31   [TENCIN, Claudine-Alexandrine Guérin de].
MEMOIRS OF THE COUNT OF COMMINGE. FROM THE FRENCH OF MONSIEUR D'ARNAUD.

London: Printed for G. Kearsley, at No. 46, opposite Fetter Lane, Fleet-Street, 1774.
181p. 2s 6d (CR), 2s 6d boards (MR), 2s 6d sewed or 3s bound (SJC).
CR 39: 163 (Feb 1775); MR 52: 339–41 (Apr 1775).
DLC PQ2067.T2A7313; ESTC n022058 (BI Dt; NA CLU-S/C, CtY-Walpole).

Notes. Not a trans. of Baculard d'Arnaud's play *Les amans malheureux, ou le comte du Comminge* but of the original work by C. A. Guérin de Tencin (ESTC); trans. of *Mémoires du comte de Comminge* (La Haye, 1735).

Adv., 'Translated from the Third Edition of the French', SJC 30 May–1 June 1775 with much fuller title: *Memoirs of the Count of Comminge; or, The Unhappy Lovers. With a Sketch of the Abbey of La Trappe, in Normandy, the Members of which are enjoined perpetual Silence.*
Further edn: Dublin, 1781 (Printed for C. Jackson, 1 vol., 12mo), ESTC t190872. Later French version Londres, 1784, EM 4253: 23, ESTC n035165.

CR: 'Stories of romantic love carried on beyond the bounds of probability, and inferior to some of the productions of M. d'Arnaud.'

MR [William Enfield]: 'In this novel, which has obtained a high degree of reputation, and passed through several editions in the original, we discover many traces of an inventive genius and a feeling heart. If the incidents border on the extravagant, it is, however, an extravagance which will please; for they are adapted at once to excite surprise, and to interest the passions. The sentiments are such as will touch the heart without danger of corrupting it; and the expression is natural and animated' (p. 339).

1776

1776: 1   ANON.
DISINTERESTED LOVE; OR THE HISTORY OF SIR CHARLES ROYSTON AND EMILY LESSLEY: IN A SERIES OF LETTERS.

> London: Printed for John Wilkie, No. 71, St Paul's Church-Yard, n.d. [1776].
> I 263p; II 213p. 12mo. 5s (MR), 5s sewed or 6s bound (SJC).
> MR 55: 66 (July 1776).
> BL 12611.e.18; EM 58: 10; ESTC t057433 (NA RPB-JH).

Notes. Epistolary. ESTC gives incorrect EM ref. (238: 3).
Adv., 'In a few Days will be published', SJC 19–21 Mar 1776.
Further edn: Dublin, 1776 (Printed for S. Price, D. Chamberlaine, J. Hoey, W. Whitestone, J. Sheppard [and 14 others in Dublin], 2 vols., 12mo, ESTC n006543. German trans. Leipzig, 1776/77 (*Die uneigennützige Liebe*) (EAG).

MR: 'Refinement and delicacy of sentiment, and elevated ideas of honour and generosity, are so strongly marked in these letters, that they must prove an agreeable entertainment to those who read with the same moral feelings and principles with which the Author appears to have written. The characters are evidently chosen, and the plot contrived, with a view to display the most amiable virtues of the heart. It is not without regret that we observe in the execution of so laudable a design, a feebleness of expression, and a redundancy and confusion of incident, which in a great measure prevent the effect the Author meant to produce.'

1776: 2   ANON.
EMMA; OR, THE CHILD OF SORROW. A NOVEL. IN TWO VOLUMES.

> London: Printed for T. Lowndes, No. 77, in Fleet-street, 1776.
> I 247p; II 239p. 12mo. 6s (MR), 5s sewed or 6s bound (SJC).
> MR 54: 341–2 (Apr 1776).
> BL 12604.df.37; EM 52: 1; ESTC t108372 (NA PU).

Notes. Epistolary.

Adv. SJC 28–30 Dec 1775.

Further edns: Dublin, 1776 (Printed for S. Price, D. Chamberlaine, W. Watson, J. Potts, W. Sleater [and 21 others in Dublin], 2 vols, 12mo), ESTC n050813 [ESTC notes vol. 2 with 'J. Beatty' added as the 22nd name]; Dublin, 1777, ESTC 212583. German trans. Leipzig, 1776 (*Emma oder das Kind des Kummers*) (EAG); French trans., Londres [Paris?], 1788 (*Histoire de Lady Cleveland*), ESTC n033086; also, Paris, 1788 (*Emma, ou l'enfant du malheur*) (HWS).

MR [William Enfield]: 'This is, indeed, as the title intimates, a tale of woe. The fair sufferer is placed in situations, and meets with events, of the most distressful nature: nor is the Reader, at the close, relieved from the pain which the story has given him, by a sudden reverse of fortune. Emma lives and dies the child of sorrow.'

THE HISTORY OF LADY ANNE NEVILLE
See BICKNELL, Alexander

THE HISTORY OF LADY SOPHIA STERNHEIM
See LA ROCHE, Marie Sophie von

1776: 3 ANON.
THE HUSBAND'S RESENTMENT; OR, THE HISTORY OF LADY MAN-CHESTER. A NOVEL. IN TWO VOLUMES.

London: Printed for T. Lowndes, No. 77, in Fleet-street, 1776.

I 224p; II 223p. 12mo. 6s (CR, MR), 5s sewed or 6s bound (SJC).

CR 41: 242 (Mar 1776); MR 54: 341 (Apr 1776).

BL 12614.aaa.20; EM 228: 1; ESTC t070923 (BI AWn; NA CtY, PU; EA QSL).

Notes. 13 pp. advs. end vol. 2, which omits 'In Two Volumes' from t.p. Epistolary.

Adv. SJC 21–24 Oct 1775.

German trans. Dresden, 1780 (*Geschichte der Lady Manchester*) (Price).

CR: 'Lady Manchester visits us in somewhat of a slatternly dress; the literary mantua maker and milliner not having set her off to advantage. Her real merit, it is true, is not thereby diminished, but of this her stock does not give much room for boasting.'

MR [William Enfield]: ' . . . a tale, sufficiently *natural* indeed, but neither capable of interesting the passions, nor improving the heart.'

ISABELLA, OR THE REWARDS OF GOOD NATURE
See BICKNELL, Alexander

JOHN BUNCLE, JUNIOR, GENTLEMAN
See COGAN, Thomas

LETTERS FROM THE DUCHESS DE CRUI
See HAMILTON, Lady Mary

1776: 4 ANON.
THE MAIDEN AUNT. WRITTEN BY A LADY. IN THREE VOLUMES.

London: Printed for J. Bew, Pater-Noster-Row, 1776.
I vi, 221p; II 216p; III 264p. 12mo. 9s (MR), 7s 6d sewed or 9s bound (SJC, LC).
MR 54: 161–2 (Feb 1776); AF II: 2691.
PU Singer-Mend. PR3291.A6.L33.1776; ESTC n034765 (NA CLU-S/C).

Notes. Not by Menella Bute Smedley who wrote a novel of the same title, published London, 1849. Prefatory advertisement v–vi declares: 'With a heart anxiously trembling for the success it may meet with, does the authoress venture this, her first performance.' Epistolary.
Post-dated; adv. SJC 28–31 Oct 1775 and LC 28–31 Oct 1775; booksellers include Almon, Ridley, Walter, Sewell and Davenhill.
German trans. Leipzig, 1776–77 (*Die unverheirathete Tante*) (Price).

MR [William Enfield]: 'We observe, in this novel, evident traces of a cultivated mind, and a feeling heart; and think we may venture to recommend it to the perusal of our fair Readers, as not only perfectly inoffensive, (which may be said of many very insignificant performances of this class) but as capable of affording them rational and elegant entertainment. . . . We should have thought ourselves under the necessity of censuring this female Writer for the incorrect manner in which her work appears before the Public, had we not received *information* [from the author] . . . that since the copy passed out of the Author's hands, the beginning of every letter in the first volume was altered, many of them in the most absurd and vulgar manner;—that the carelessness of the publisher has suffered the grossest blunders in sense, grammar, and spelling to pass into print, for which the copy was not answerable, and that he has added fifteen letters just before the conclusion, beginning with the 42d, and ending with the 56th, which the Author entirely disclaims, and considers as a compound of inconsistency, added merely to spin out the work.'

MEMOIRS OF MAITRE JACQUES OF SAVOY
See 1775: 12

MEMOIRS OF MISS SOPHY STERNHEIM
See LA ROCHE, Marie Sophie von

MISPLACED CONFIDENCE
See RENWICK, William

THE PUPIL OF PLEASURE
See PRATT, Samuel Jackson

THE RAMBLES OF MR. FRANKLY
See BONHOTE, Elizabeth

1776: 5   ANON.
THE RIVAL FRIENDS; OR, THE NOBLE RECLUSE: A NOVEL. IN THREE VOLUMES.

London: Printed for T. Vernor, in St. Michael's-Alley, Cornhill, 1776.
I 224p; II 214p; III 231p. 12mo. 7s 6d sewed (CR, LC, SJC), 9s (MR).
CR 41: 241 (Mar 1776); MR 54: 413–14 (May 1776).
CtY Im.R521.776; ESTC n065946.

Notes. 1 p. advs. end vol. 3. Epistolary.

Adv., 'on Monday, Nov. 13, will be published', LC 38: 462 (9–11 Nov 1775). Also adv. SJC 14–16 Nov 1775.

ESTC has 2 Dublin (1779 and 1784, t070918, EM 244: 4, and t119120) and 1 London (1784, n034328) edns. of *Reginald du Bray: an Historic Tale,* a reprint of vol. 2 of *The Rival Friends.* Further edn: Dublin, 1784 (Printed by S. Colbert, 1 vol., 12mo), EM 7473: 2, ESTC t119120. *Reginald du Bray* serialised, *Berwick Museum,* 1785–86, RM 1049. German trans. Leipzig, 1777 (*Die beyden Freunde und Nebenbühler oder Der edle Klausner, eine Erzählung in Briefen*) (EAG).

CR: 'The Rival Friends, if comprized in two volumes, might have passed in peace; the weight of three must bear it down, and the pastry-cooks will have the more plentiful cargo.'

MR [William Enfield]: 'Though this novel is barren of incident, and makes but a feeble attack upon the heart, it is not altogether destitute of merit. The principal character is drawn with propriety and strength; many just and sensible reflections are interspersed through the piece; a tolerable imitation of ancient romance is introduced by way of episode; and the whole is written in an agreeable style.'

1776: 6 ANON.
A SELECT COLLECTION OF ORIENTAL TALES. CALCULATED TO FORM THE MINDS OF YOUTH TO THE LOVE OF VIRTUE AND TRUE WISDOM.

Edinburgh: Printed for W. Gordon, J. Bell; W. Creech; C. Elliot, Edinburgh; T. Caddel [*sic*], London; and R. Taylor, Berwick, 1776.

viii, 258p. 12mo.

BL 1608/1330; EM 2118: 5; ESTC t132020 (BI C, E; NA CLU-S/C, PPL).

Notes. Frontispiece. Dedication to the Duchess of Buccleugh, signed 'The Editor'. Preface v–vi; table of contents vii–viii.

1776: 7 [BICKNELL, Alexander].
THE HISTORY OF LADY ANNE NEVILLE, SISTER TO THE GREAT EARL OF WARWICK: IN WHICH ARE INTERSPERSED MEMOIRS OF THAT NOBLEMAN, AND THE PRINCIPAL CHARACTERS OF THE AGE IN WHICH SHE LIVED. IN TWO VOLUMES.

London: Printed for T. Cadell, in the Strand, 1776.

I xii, 263p; II 306p. 12mo. 5s sewed (CR), 5s (MR), 5s sewed or 6s bound (SJC).

CR 41: 240–1 (Mar 1776); MR 55: 66 (July 1776).

BL 1076.m.27; EM 5502: 1; ESTC t071411 (BI BMp, MRu, O; NA CSmH, ICN, MH-H, PU &c.).

Notes. Based in part on Antoine François Prévost's *Histoire de Marguerite d'Anjou* (Grieder). Dedicated to the Duchess of Kingston.

Adv., 'In the Press, and speedily will be published', SJC 27–30 Jan 1776; adv., with quotation from LR for Feb, PL 12 Apr 1776.

German trans. Leipzig, 1777 (*Geschichte der Lady Anne Neville*) (EAG).

CR: 'This work is a strange inconsistent mixture of history, romance, and improbability, written in an affected, poetical, or rather bombastic style. There are, however, a number of reflections interspersed throughout, which might intitle it rather to be called a moral history, than a simple novel. . . . This writer appears not to have so critically distinguished between a *fable* and a *falsehood*, as he ought to have done, in a composition of this kind, where it is only permitted to create imaginary personages, by way of *machinery*. . . . But to belie historic records and characters . . . is to use a liberty beyond the laws either of the novelist, the dramatist, or any other dealer in fiction.'

MR [John Langhorne] also complains about the blending of history and fiction.

1776: 8   [BICKNELL, Alexander].
ISABELLA: OR, THE REWARDS OF GOOD NATURE. A SENTIMENTAL NOVEL. INTENDED CHIEFLY TO CONVEY UNITED AMUSEMENT AND INSTRUCTION TO THE FAIR-SEX. BY THE AUTHOR OF THE BENEVOLENT MAN, AND THE HISTORY OF LADY ANNE NEVILLE.

> London: Printed for J. Bell, near Exeter Exchange, Strand; and C. Etherington, in York, 1776.
> I 127p; II 132p. 8vo [MR has 12mo]. 6s (MR), 6s bound (SJC), 5s bound (PL).
> MR 55: 157 (Aug 1776).
> BRu ENC; ESTC n016833 (NA CaQQLa [vol. 2 only]).

Notes. 1 p. adv. end vol. 1 and 10 pp. advs. end vol. 2.
Adv., 'In a few Days will be published', SJC 9–11 Apr 1776; adv. as published PL 2 Apr 1776.

MR [John Langhorne]: 'Death! duels! adulteries! fornications! burning livers, and breaking hearts! what would the present race of novelists do without you, ye horrid train? yet, notwithstanding all this *terrible business* and the diffuse and ill modulated language in which these volumes are written,—the work has some merit.'

1776: 9   [BONHOTE, Elizabeth].
THE RAMBLES OF MR. FRANKLY. PUBLISHED BY HIS SISTER. VOL. III/ VOL. IV.

> London: Printed for T. Becket, the Corner of the Adelphi, in the Strand, 1776.
> III 183p; IV 230p. 8vo. 5s sewed (CR, MR).
> CR 42: 155 (Aug 1776); MR 55: 67 (July 1776); AF II: 404.
> O 256.f. 2879–2880; EM 2998: 9; ESTC n013411 (BI MRu; NA PU).

Notes. Vols. 1 and 2 1772: 30.
Adv., 'Next Week will be published', SJC 23–25 Apr 1776.
German trans. [of all 4 vols.] Leipzig, 1773–76 (*Die Wanderungen des Herrn Frankly*) (WC).

CR: 'These two additional volumes seem to complete the Rambles of Mr. Frankly, who merits our approbation on account of the moral tendency of the work; though he seems to have paid less attention to probability than entertainment, in the course of these excursions of fancy.'

MR : ' . . . the principles of virtue, and especially of benevolence, so plentifully sown in these literary rambles, may produce a valuable crop in the minds of young readers: and to such, it seems probable, this performance will be most acceptable. Those who have more experience of human life and manners, will think it romantic.'

1776: 10   [COGAN, Thomas].
JOHN BUNCLE, JUNIOR, GENTLEMAN.
> London: Printed for J. Johnson, in St. Paul's Church-Yard, 1776/78.
>
> I (1776) 280p; II (1778) 307p. 12mo. vol. 1 3s (CR, MR), 3s sewed (SJC); vol. 2 3s sewed (CR, MR, LC).
>
> CR 42: 319–20 (Oct 1776), MR 55: 160 (Aug 1776) vol. 1; CR 45: 239 (Mar 1778), MR 58: 312–3 (Apr 1778) vol. 2; AF II: 741, 742.
>
> C 7720.d.1582-; EMf; ESTC t144130 (BI BL, MRu, O; NA CtY-BR, CSmH, DLC, IU &c.).

Notes. 'St. Paul's Church Yard' has no hyphen on t.p. to vol. 2. Epistolary.
A sequel to Thomas Amory's *The Life of John Buncle* (1756, JR 362, 990; AF I: 68, 69).
CR 42 and MR 58 review under 'Miscellaneous'.
Vol. 1 adv. SJC 20–23 Apr 1776; vol. 2 adv. LC 43: 243 (10–12 Mar 1778).
Further edn: Dublin, 1776 [vol. 1] (Printed by W. Kidd, for W. Whitestone, B. Corcoran, D. Chamberlaine, J. Potts [and 9 others in Dublin], 1 vol., 12mo), EM 169: 6, ESTC t055914.
German trans. Leipzig, 1778 (*Johann Buncle der jüngere, ein Mann ehrbaren Standes*) (Price).

CR 42: '... by no means ill calculated for amusing a few leisure hours' (p. 320).

CR 45: '... a fund of good sense, often enlivened with a strain of pleasantry peculiar to this author.'

MR 55 [John Langhorne]: 'Another Sentimental Journey maker, mounted on one of the milky mothers, and wofully galling her, after the nobly wanton course of Sterne.'

MR 58: 'We, at first, regarded this gentleman merely as an individual in the crowd of Sterne's imitators; but the more we see of him, the more worthy does he appear of some distinction. There are many entertaining, and some *good* things in this volume.'

1776: 11   GRIFFITH, [Elizabeth].
THE STORY OF LADY JULIANA HARLEY. A NOVEL. IN LETTERS. BY MRS. GRIFFITH.
> London: Printed for T. Cadell, in the Strand, 1776.
>
> I 259p; II 270p. 12mo. 5s sewed (CR, SJC), 6s (MR).
>
> CR 42: 155 (Aug 1776); MR 55: 238–9 (Sept 1776); AF II: 1741.
>
> BL 12612.e.6; EM 231: 4; ESTC t066937 (BI O; NA CSmH, CU-A, IU, &c.; EA Pm).

Notes. Epistolary.
Adv. SJC 13–15 June 1776. Extract published WEP 22–24 Aug 1776.
Further edn: Dublin, 1776 (Printed for S. Price, B. Corcoran, W. Sleater, W. Whitestone, R. Cross [and 20 others in Dublin], 2 vols., 12mo), EM 3558: 7, ESTC t107620. French trans. Paris, 1777 (*Histoire de lady Julie Harley*) (BN); German trans. Leipzig, 1777 (*Geschichte der Lady Juliana Harley*) (Price).

CR: 'The productions of this ingenious lady have so often obtained our approbation that she may claim a kind of prescriptive right to the favour of criticism. We do not, however, exceed the bounds of impartiality when we remark, that in elegance of style, chasteness of sentiment, and moral tendency, the present novel merits an equal degree of encomium with those which have formerly proceeded from the same agreeable and interesting writer.'

MR [John Noorthouck]: '... it may be characterized as a sorrowful love tale, compounded of the usual distressful incidents, disappointed inclinations, a forced marriage, dove like tenderness, a little blood, conjugal infidelity, with unbounded generosity and liberality.'

1776: 12   [HAMILTON, Lady Mary].
LETTERS FROM THE DUCHESS DE CRUI AND OTHERS, ON SUBJECTS MORAL AND ENTERTAINING, WHEREIN THE CHARACTER OF THE FEMALE SEX, WITH THEIR RANK, IMPORTANCE, AND CONSEQUENCE, IS STATED, AND THEIR RELATIVE DUTIES IN LIFE ARE ENFORCED. BY A LADY.

> London: Printed for Robson, New Bond-Street; Walter, Charing-Cross; and Robinson, Pater-noster Row, 1776.
>
> I ii, iv, 222p; II 240p; III 224p; IV 222p; V 243p. 8vo. 12s 6d sewed (CR), 15s (MR), 12s 6d sewed or 15s bound (SJC).
>
> CR 41: 204–8 (Mar 1776); MR 55: 403–4 (Nov 1776).
>
> BL 1085.h.10–12; EM 1913: 1; ESTC t080472 (NA CSmH, KU-S, PU, &c.).

Notes. Lady Mary Leslie became by her two marriages first Walker and then Hamilton (see FC). Epistolary.

MR reviews under 'Miscellaneous'; CR does not classify.

Adv. SJC 30 May–1 June 1776.

2nd edn., 'corrected and enlarged', adv. SJC 15–17 May 1777.

Further edns: Dublin, 1776 (Printed for S. Price, W. and H. Whitestone, R. Fitzsimons, T. Wilkinson, J. Williams [and 13 others in Dublin], 2 vols., 12mo), EM 6031: 6, ESTC t080460; London, 1777, ESTC n003684. German trans. Leipzig, 1776/77 (*Briefe der Herzogin von Crui, und andrer Personen*) (EAG).

CR: 'These Letters in general discover the author to have great knowledge of the world, and that her observations have been made with much discernment. She seems to have improved a natural acuteness of judgment both by reading and reflection. Considered as a female writer, (we beg pardon of the ladies for this distinction) her acquaintance with ancient authors is extraordinary, and the solidity of her remarks might do honour to those of the other sex' (pp. 207–208).

MR [William Enfield]: 'We are at a loss to know whether these Letters should be classed under the head of novels or moral essays. A story is interwoven with the piece; but it makes so small a part of the whole, that we are afraid, if we recommend it as one of the least faulty of our modern novels, those who turn over as blank paper all such matter as does not carry on the plot, will think they have a dear bargain. On the other hand, if we recommend it under the notion of a course of moral and prudential instruction for young females, probably many novel readers will conclude it is not one of their books, and so lose the benefit of much wholesome advice.'

1776: 13A   [LA ROCHE, Marie Sophie von]; {COLLYER, Joseph (trans.)}.
THE HISTORY OF LADY SOPHIA STERNHEIM. ATTEMPTED FROM THE GERMAN OF MR. WIELAND.

> London: Printed for Mr. Joseph Collyer, and sold by T. Jones, at Clifford's-Inn-Gate, Fetter-Lane, near Fleet-Street, 1776.
>
> I viii, 252p; II 212p, 12mo. 6s (MR), 6s bound (SJC).
>
> MR 55: 157 (Aug 1776).
>
> BL 837.c.21; EM 2371: 9; ESTC t100449 (BI E, O).

Notes. Trans. of *Geschichte des Fräuleins von Sternheim*, originally edited and corrected with a preface by C. M. Wieland (Leipzig, 1771). See also trans. by Edward Harwood (below).

4 pp advs. end vol 2. Epistolary. Translator's Preface signed Joseph Collyer.

Adv., 'For the Benefit of the Widow and Children of the late Mr. Collyer,' SJC 30 May–1 June 1776.

RG: 'N.B. M^r. Wieland was only Editor of Lady Sternheim, wch. was written by a Lady,— Mad^m. de la Roche, of Coblentz.'

Serialised as 'The Adventures of Miss Sophia Sternheim' in 4 magazines in 1776–77, RM 53.

French trans. La Haye, 1773 (*Mémoires de mademoiselle de Sternheim*) (BGR).

MR [William Enfield]: 'If a Writer has genius enough to rise above the barrenness and insipidity of modern novels, it requires no small share of good sense and taste to avoid extravagance and improbability. The present work, like the former productions of Mr. Wieland, is faulty in this respect. We observe many just and striking sentiments; much bold-ness of colouring; and a great variety of characters and incidents; but we every where meet with violations of nature and propriety. The virtuous characters are elevated to a degree of perfection, and the vicious sunk to a depth of villainy, scarcely to be supposed: incidents are related too extraordinary to be credited; and events are brought about, which, though they surprise by their novelty, evidently appear to be the creation of fancy.'

1776: 13B   [LA ROCHE, Marie Sophie von]; HARWOOD, E[dward] (trans.).
MEMOIRS OF MISS SOPHY STERNHEIM. FROM THE GERMAN OF
MR. WIELAND. BY E. HARWOOD, D.D. IN TWO VOLUMES.

> London: Printed for T. Becket, Corner of the Adelphi, in the Strand, 1776.
> I vi, 214p; II 170p. 6s (MR), 5s sewed (WEP).
> MR 55: 319 (Oct 1776); AF II: 1826.
> IU x833.L32.OgEh; ESTC n035384 (NA MiU, MA).

Notes. Trans. of *Geschichte des Fräuleins von Sternheim*, originally edited and corrected with a preface by C. M. Wieland (Leipzig, 1771). Also translated by Joseph Collyer (see above) as *The History of Lady Sophia Sternheim*.

Preface signed E. Harwood and dated March 25, 1776. Epistolary.

Adv., 'In the Press, and speedily will be published' with the title given only as 'A Translation of *de Mademoiselle de Sternheim*', SJC 4–6 Jan 1776. Adv. WEP 8–10 Oct 1776.

Further edn: Dublin, 1777 (J. Beatty and J. Jackson, 1 vol., no format) (WC), xESTC [WC also has an entry for an apparently identical edn. with the second bookseller C. Jackson].

MR [William Enfield]: 'Dr. Harwood judged very properly in making choice of an agree-able Novel for his Exercise book, when he undertook the tedious task of learning German; and is doubtless to be commended for having so happily provided for his own amusement and improvement during the long evenings in January and February: but we are surprised to find that he has ventured to publish his Exercise, as Miss Sophy Sternheim has already appeared in an English dress, and therefore could not be expected to gain much additional notice from any embellishments which Dr. Harwood could give her. We must, however, allow the new Translator the merit of exhibiting this lady in a more pleasing form than that in which the [*sic*] first appeared; and to such of our Readers as are fond of German beauties, we beg leave to introduce her as an agreeable sentimental companion.'

MELMOTH, Courtney
See PRATT, Samuel Jackson

1776: 14   [PRATT, Samuel Jackson].
THE PUPIL OF PLEASURE: OR, THE NEW SYSTEM ILLUSTRATED. INSCRIBED TO MRS. EUGENIA STANHOPE, EDITOR OF LORD CHESTERFIELD'S LETTERS. BY COURTNEY MELMOTH.

London, Printed for G. Robinson, and J. Bew, in Pater-Noster-Row. 1776.
I xv, 230p; II 252p. 12mo. 5s sewed (CR), 6s (MR), 5s sewed or 6s bound (SJC).
CR 42: 447–51 (Dec 1776); MR 56: 231–2 (Mar 1777); AF II: 3584.
BL 245.f.2; EM 3771: 2; ESTC t124435 (NA CtY-BR, CSmH, ICN, MH-H, PU &c.).

Notes. Epistolary. Adv. SJC 4–7 Jan 1777.
Further edns: Dublin, 1781 (Printed for C. Jackson), 1 vol., 8vo), n019791; London, 1783, ESTC t070717; Philadelphia, 1778, ESTC w030655; Boston, [1780], ESTC w025005. French trans. Amsterdam, 1787 (*L'Élève du plaisir*) (BN); German trans. Leipzig, 1789 (*Der Freudenzögling*) (RS).

CR: 'The hero of the present work . . . is represented as conducting himself according to Lord Chesterfield's maxims. An unlimited indulgence in pleasure he regards as the greatest happiness; to the attainment of which he sacrifices truth, sincerity, virtue, conscience, and every moral consideration' (pp. 447–8). 'Independent, however, of any allusion [to Chesterfield], the work, as a novel, is calculated to afford entertainment; and though the author may have sometimes painted vice in colours too alluring to the fancy, he makes in the end a retribution conformable to the interests of morality' (p. 451).

MR [William Enfield]: ' . . . the scenes of seduction are painted in such glowing colours, that some readers may be apt to question whether Mr Melmoth's preparation will operate as an antidote against the poison of lord Chesterfield's writings.'

1776: 15   [RENWICK, William].
MISPLACED CONFIDENCE; OR, FRIENDSHIP BETRAYED.

London: Printed for the Author; and sold by E. and C. Dilly, in the Poultry, 1776.
I xxiv, 196, 110p; II 203p; III 218p. 12mo.
OU PS700.A1 M54; ESTC n022165.

Notes. Continuation of Renwick's *Genuine History of two Unfortunate Lovers* (ESTC).
Dedication to the Duke of Northumberland. Page numbering in vol. 2 begins with p. 111; preceding part appears to conclude vol. 1. Epistolary.
Further edn: London, 1777 (Fielding and Walker), EM 98: 3, ESTC t066925.
This edn. not reviewed; 1777 London edn. rev. CR 44: 158 (Aug 1777); MR 57: 80 (July 1777). Fielding and Walker edn. adv., 'elegantly printed', 6s sewed or 7s 6d bound, SJC 24–26 June 1777.

CR: 'If a controversy with various persons concerning a former publication of the author's, could be offered to the world as a book of entertainment, the present volumes might have some claim to the specious title-page which seems to promise very different contents. If scurrility and gross illiberal abuse, without the addition of wit or humour, may be relished, the author may hope for success.'

MR [John Langhorne]: 'Compassion alone makes us attend to his story, and it is only from the same motive that we recommend his book to our readers.'

1776: 16   SEALLY, John.
THE LOVES OF CALISTO AND EMIRA; OR, THE FATAL LEGACY. PUBLISH'D FROM THE ORIGINALS, BY JOHN SEALLY, GENT.

London: Printed for T. Becket, Corner of the Adelphi, in the Strand, 1776.
10, 262p. 12mo. 2s 6d sewed (CR, SJC), 3s (MR).
CR 41: 324–5 (Apr 1776); MR 55: 66 (July 1776).
BL 12611.g.18; EM 225: 1; ESTC t057366 (NA CtY, CSmH, PU).

Notes. 1 p. advs. end vol.
Epistolary. 'To the Reader' 3–10. Dedication (first in French and then in English) to Comtesse Elizabeth Messerati) signed Jean Seally in the French version and John Seally in the English. Page numbering begins again at 1 with first page of novel.
Adv., 'In a few Days will be published', SJC 24–27 Feb 1776.
French trans. [Londres; probably Paris] 1777 (*Les amours d'Émire et Calisto, ou la fatale succession*) ESTC t162776; German trans. Leipzig, 1777 (*Calisto's und Emirens Liebe oder die unglückliche Erbschaft*) (EAG).
CR: ' . . . a very trifling and uninteresting performance; barren of incident, and deficient in character. The language is below criticism, at once affectedly obscure, and familiarly vulgar . . . ' (p. 324).
MR [William Enfield]: 'His merit is to be determined in a court where our opinion will be little regarded, and in which he would not be the less applauded on account of any censure we might pass on the plan or execution of his work. In the court of love, Reviewers are not allowed a voice.'

1776: 17   VOLTAIRE, [François-Marie Arouet].
YOUNG JAMES OR THE SAGE AND THE ATHEIST. AN ENGLISH STORY FROM THE FRENCH OF M. DE VOLTAIRE.

London: Printed for J. Murray, No. 32, Fleet Street, 1776.
ii, 130p. 8vo. 1s 6d (CR), 2s 6d sewed (SJC).
CR 41: 487–8 (June 1776); AF II: 4642.
BL 012548.eeee.44; EM 94: 7; ESTC t137638 (NA CaOHM, CLU-S/C, CSmH &c.).

Notes. Trans. of *Histoire de Jenni, ou le sage et l'athée* (Londres [Geneva], 1775). CR reviews under 'Miscellaneous'.
Adv., 'Adorned with an original Frontispiece, finely engraved', SJC 9–11 Apr 1776; Murray's address is expanded to 'No. 32, facing St. Dunstan's Church, Fleet Street'.
Further edns: Dublin, 1776 (Printed for D. Chamberlaine, W. Whitestone, J. Sheppard, J. Potts, S. Watson [and 15 others in Dublin], 1 vol., 8vo), ESTC t177717; London, 1776, ESTC t179133; London, 1795, ESTC t212649.
CR: 'This production is written with the same vivacity which distinguishes the other works of the celebrated author, and contains the strongest proof of his disavowing those principles that he had been supposed to entertain' (p. 488).

WALKER, Lady Mary
See HAMILTON, Lady Mary

WIELAND, Mr
See LA ROCHE, Marie Sophie von

THE CHAMPION OF VIRTUE
See REEVE, Clara

CHARLES AND CHARLOTTE
See PRATT, Samuel Jackson

1777: 1 ANON.
THE HISTORY OF AMELIA HARCOURT AND LOUISA DARLINGTON. IN TWO VOLUMES.

> London: Printed for H. Gardner, opposite St Clement's Church, in the Strand; C. Parker, in New Bond-Street; and J. Bew, in Pater-noster-Row, 1777.
> I 160p; II 141p. 8vo. 6s bound (MR), 5s sewed or 6s bound (half-title, SJC).
> MR 57: 74–5 (July 1777); AF II: 1954.
> BL 12611.aa.24; EM 162: 1; ESTC t107714.

Notes. 4-pp. table of contents beginning each vol. Text in both vols. begins on p. 17.
Adv., 'In Two neat Pocket Vols.', SJC 11–13 Mar 1777.
German trans. Leipzig, 1778 (*Amelie Harcourt und Louise Darlington*) (Price).

MR [William Enfield]: 'It is a common remark, that when people are disposed to be pleased, they will be pleased with a little. Novels are perhaps generally read (except by Reviewers) with this advantage: and yet we think there are few readers so exceedingly good humoured, or moderate in their expectations, as to be capable of being pleased with the present insipid tale, or of discovering in it any portion of invention, fancy, or sentiment.'

1777: 2 ANON.
THE HISTORY OF MELINDA HARLEY, YORKSHIRE.

> London: Printed for G. Robinson, No. 25. Paternoster-Row, and J. M'Cliesh, Edinburgh, 1777.
> iv, 180p. 12mo. 2s 6d sewed (CR, MR), 3s bound (adv.).
> CR 44: 478 (Dec 1777); CR 45: 474 (June 1778); MR 58: 395 (May 1778); AF II: 1967, 1968.
> PU Singer-Mend.PR.3991.A1.H5734.1777; ESTC n008474.

Notes. Epistolary.
Adv. end vol. 2 of *The History of the Hon. Mrs. Rosemont* (1781: 17).
Further edn: London, 1779, EM 7725: 7, ESTC t127667.

CR 45: 'It is a general character of many romances that they are *good for nothing*; but we must except the History of Melinda Harley from this censure, for we can affirm, from our own experience, that it is admirably calculated—to procure sleep.'

MR [William Enfield]: 'A very inoffensive, but a very dull and ill-written book, which, short as it is, the author has been under the necessity of *ekeing out* with—a sermon. If this piece of clumsy patch-work was put together by a fair sempstress, we wish her better success in the labours of her needle, to which we would advise her for the future to confine her ambition.'

1777: 3   ANON.

THE HISTORY OF MISS MARIA BARLOWE. IN A SERIES OF LETTERS. IN TWO VOLUMES.

> London: Printed for Fielding and Walker No. 20, Pater-Noster-Row, 1777.
> I 246p; II 233p. 12mo. 5s sewed (CR), 6s (MR).
> CR 44: 397–8 (Nov 1777); MR 58: 395–6 (May 1778); AF II: 1969.
> BL 12612.ccc.12; EM 129: 5; ESTC t066902.

Notes. Epistolary.

CR refers to the book-writing machine encountered by Gulliver in Balnibarbi and concludes: '. . . the machine by which our modern novels are written, and especially this before us, does appear, as well as we can collect from the description and engraving, to be most clearly and evidently borrowed from the famous machine of this Balnibarbian, to whom, if he be still living, or to his descendants, we sincerely think his majesty of Great Britain should immediately transmit his royal letters patent, which might be conveyed by the first vessel which the company sends to Tonquin and China.'

MR [William Enfield]: 'This tale is so perfectly insipid, and related in such vulgar language, that it cannot, we imagine, afford a moment's gratification to the most eager devourer of novels. If it can be read at all, it may however be read with safety, for its stupidity renders it perfectly inoffensive' (p. 395).

THE HISTORY OF MISS TEMPLE
See ROGERS, A.

1777: 4   ANON.

*THE HISTORY OF PHILARIO AND CLEMENTINA.

> London: Printed for the Author; and sold by B. Law, in Ave-Maria Lane, and all other
>   Booksellers (SJC), 1777 (SJC).
> 2 vols. 12mo. 6s bound (MR), 5s sewed or 6s bound (SJC).
> MR 57: 75 (July 1777); AF II: 1970.
> No copy located.

Notes. Adv. SJC 9–11 Jan 1777; title has added 'A Novel'.

MR [William Enfield]: ' . . . too stupid, and vulgar, for particular criticism.'

1777: 5   ANON.

*THE HISTORY OF THE CURATE OF CRAMEN. TAKEN FROM REAL LIFE. BY AN UNBENIFICED CLERGYMAN OF THE CHURCH OF ENGLAND.

> London: Johnson, 1777.
> 2 vols. 12mo. 5s sewed (CR, MR).
> CR 43: 314 (Apr 1777); MR 57: 248–9 (Sept 1777).
> No copy located.

Notes. CR reviews under 'Novels'; MR reviews under 'Novels & Memoirs'.

Adv. SJC 23–25 Mar 1775 announces that this novel 'About the Beginning of next May will be published, By Subscription, In two Volumes, Price 5s. sewed in blue'. Adv. continues: 'They who choose to favour the above Publication are requested to send their Names to

Mr Dodsley, Pall-Mall, or to Mr George Keith, Gracechurch-Street, some before the beginning of next April, as but a few Copies more than are subscribed for will be printed.

No Money is desired till the Work is published. A List of the Subscribers' Names will be prefixed to the first Volume.

However ridiculed of late Years a Regard for the Public may be, yet I will venture to affirm that is my principal Motive for the above Publication, but not my sole Motive; I wish to be paid for my Trouble; and if the Generosity of the Public shall exceed that, and make me some Amends for the Untowardness of Fortune, I shall receive the Obligation with Gratitude. The AUTHOR.'

German trans. Leipzig, 1778 (*Der Substitut von Craman*) (Price).

CR: 'The narrative is interspersed with a variety of episodical digressions, and some little effusions in poetry. From the whole there is ground to expect, that by such productions as the present, this unbeneficed clergyman may be enabled to keep himself in a tight gown and cassock, and a clean band on Sundays, till he becomes a beneficed member of the church, which we wish may soon be the case.'

MR [William Enfield]: 'This narrative exhibits a striking picture of the difficulties which obstruct the way of promotion in the church of England, and the hardships to which the inferior clergy are liable. The tale is simple and interesting, and is sometimes enlivened with humorous incidents.'

JULIA DE ROUBIGNÉ
See MACKENZIE, Henry

1777: 6   ANON.
LETTERS FROM HENRIETTA TO MORVINA. INTERSPERSED WITH ANECDOTES, HISTORICAL AND AMUSING, OF THE DIFFERENT COURTS AND COUTRIES THROUGH WHICH SHE PASSED. FOUNDED ON FACTS. IN TWO VOLUMES.

London: Printed for J. Bew, No. 28, Paternoster Row, 1777.

I iv, 206p; II 230p. 12mo. 5s sewed (CR), 6s bound (MR), 5s sewed or 6s bound (LC).

CR 46: 267–71 (Oct 1778); MR 59: 392 (Nov 1778); AF II: 2536.

BL 12613.g.9; EM 227: 7; ESTC t070913 (NA PU).

Notes. Epistolary.

Possibly misdated? No. 1777 adv. located but adv. LC 43: 492 (21–23 May 1778), GND 20 May 1778 and PA 22 May 1778.

German trans. Leipzig, 1779 (*Briefe von Henriette an Morvina*) (Price).

CR: 'A Novel which is founded on facts, though it may not always prove so entertaining, in respect of incidents, is free, however, from those blemishes which arise from the extravagance of ungoverned invention. In that before us we are presented with the correspondence of an accomplished and amiable young lady, who describes to her sister several characters, which she occasionally accompanies with various particulars concerning them' (p. 267). 'These Letters in general discover the sentiments of a virtuous and well educated mind, that retains a taste unvitiated either by the fashionable gaieties of life, or an increased acquaintance with the world; and in point of composition, they are superior to common novels' (p. 271).

MR [William Enfield]: 'This novel discovers some marks of ability, and contains several entertaining anecdotes; but its narrative is too much broken, and unconnected, to be interesting; it discovers a great degree of partiality to the national character and manners of the French; and its language is so inlaid with French words and phrases, that it is impossible for a mere Englishman to understand it.'

MEMOIRS OF THE MARCHIONESS DE LOUVOI
See HAMILTON, Lady Mary

MISPLACED CONFIDENCE; OR, FRIENDSHIP BETRAYED
See RENWICK, William (1776: 15)

MODERN SEDUCTION
See GIBBES, Phebe

1777: 7   ANON.
THE MUTABILITY OF HUMAN LIFE; OR, MEMOIRS OF ADELAIDE, MARCHIONESS OF MELVILLE. BY A LADY. IN TWO VOLUMES.

London: Printed for J. Bew, in Pater-Noster-Row, 1777.
I 256p; II 273p; III 232p. 12mo. 7s 6d sewed (CR), 9s bound (MR), 7s 6d sewed or 9s bound (SJC).
CR 44: 154 (Aug 1777); MR 57: 319 (Oct 1777); AF II: 3022.
C S727.d.77.39-; EM 1100: 8; ESTC n010299 (NA CSmH, MH-H, NjP).

Notes. Epistolary.
Adv. SJC 26–28 June 1777.
Further edn: Dublin, 1777 (Printed for S. Price, W. Sleater, W. Whitestone, W. Watson, D. Chamberlaine [and 11 others in Dublin], 2 vols., 12mo), ESTC n022585. German trans. Leipzig, 1778 (*Die Abwechselungen des menschlichen Lebens*) (Price).
    CR: 'Improbable events in vulgar language.'
    MR [William Enfield]: 'Though in our court of criticism we always wish to treat the Fair with lenity, we cannot think that this indulgence should proceed so far as to exempt their productions from every kind of critical censure. Insipidity of sentiment and vulgarity of style are faults which we cannot easily pardon, where we naturally expect their contrary excellencies. For these faults we must therefore condemn the present work, though written *by a Lady*.'

THE OFFSPRING OF FANCY
See 1778: 4

1777: 8   ANON.
THE SUSPICIOUS LOVERS: A NOVEL. IN THREE VOLUMES. BY THE AUTHOR OF WOODBURY.

London: Printed for J. Wilkie, St Paul's Church-Yard; and E. and C. Dilly, in the Poultry, 1777.
I 227p; II 191p; III 233p. 12mo. 6s (MR), 6s sewed (GND).
MR 57: 319 (Oct 1777); AF II: 4310.
CtY Im.Su82.777; xESTC.

Notes. Epistolary.

Woodbury 1773: 23.

Adv. GND 11 Apr 1777.

German trans. Leipzig, 1778 (*Die misstrauischen Verliebten*) (Price).

MR [John Langhorne]: 'A lively, sensible series of letters; calculated not merely to *do away* an idle hour, but to inspire love of honour, and a contempt of vicious principles.'

THE THOUGHTLESS WARD
See FERGUSS, Miss

TRAVELS FOR THE HEART
See PRATT, Samuel Jackson

THE TRIFLER
See MAN, Henry (1775: 29)

1777: 9   BROOKE, [Frances].
THE EXCURSION. IN TWO VOLUMES. BY MRS. BROOKE; AUTHOR OF THE HISTORY OF LADY JULIA MANDEVILLE, AND OF EMILY MONTAGU.

> London: Printed for T. Cadell, in the Strand, 1777.
> I 215p; II 267p. 12mo. 5s sewed (CR, MR).
> CR 44: 61–3 (July 1777); MR 57: 141–5 (Aug 1777); AF II: 480.
> BL 12612.cc.9; EM 129: 8; ESTC t066365 (BI C, O; NA CSmH, MH-H, NjP, PU &c.).

Notes. The History of Lady Julia Mandeville, 1763, JR 769, AF I: 257; *The History of Emily Montague,* 1769, JR 1298, AF I: 256.

Adv., 'In a few Days will be published', SJC 28 June–1 July 1777; adv. as published SJC 10–12 July 1777.

Further edns: Dublin, 1777 (Printed for Messrs. Price, Whitestone, Corcoran, R. Cross, Sleater [and 18 others in Dublin], 2 vols., 12mo), ESTC t060973; London, 1785, ESTC n007041. French trans. Serialised, *Universal* and *Hibernian* Magazines, 1777, RM 378. Lausanne, 1778 (*L'Excursion, ou l'Escapade*) (BN); German trans. Leipzig, 1778 (*Die Lustreise*) (EAG).

CR: 'There is that delicacy of satire, that liveliness of imagination, that warmth of expression, that beautiful variety of colouring in this performance, which distinguish the former publications of this agreeable author' (p. 63).

MR [David Garrick]: 'We cannot approve of this strange method of blending *pretendedly real* anecdotes, with such as are *professedly imaginary*; and the artful ambiguity of giving an injurious falsehood the air of a fact, and yet weaving it in, as part of a work of invention, is a mode of writing prejudicial both to morals and letters' (p. 141).

1777: 10   [FERGUSS, Miss].
THE THOUGHTLESS WARD. A NOVEL. BY A LADY.

> London: Printed for T. Lowndes, N° 77, in Fleet-Street, 1777.
> 283p. 12mo. 3s sewed (CR), 3s (MR), 3s bound (SJC).

CR 44: 153–4 (Aug 1777); MR 57: 319 (Oct 1777); AF II: 1424.

DFo PR3447.F8.T4.Cage; xESTC (NA MB).

Notes. Author attribution from NUC. Epistolary.

GM n.s. 94 (1824): 224 notes that Rhoda Woodington was paid 10 gns. in Feb 1777 for this novel 'wrote by Miss Ferguss, of Bugden, Huntingdonshire.'

Adv. SJC 16–18 Sept 1777.

German trans. Leipzig, 1778 (*Das unbehutsame Mündel*) (Price).

CR: 'The plot, the characters, and the style, seldom rise above that degree of mediocrity, which readily gains admittance into circulating libraries. The last scenes are, however, affecting, and finished with more care than the rest' (p. 154).

MR [William Enfield]: 'A plain story, told in very plain language; and may be read without the trouble of laughing, crying, or thinking.'

1777: 11   [GIBBES, Phebe].

*MODERN SEDUCTION, OR INNOCENCE BETRAYED: CONSISTING OF SEVERAL HISTORIES OF THE PRINCIPAL MAGDALENS, RECEIVED INTO THAT CHARITY SINCE ITS ESTABLISHMENT. VERY PROPER TO BE READ BY ALL YOUNG PERSONS; AS THEY EXHIBIT A FAITHFUL PICTURE OF THOSE ARTS MOST FATAL TO YOUTH AND INNOCENCE; AND OF THOSE MISERIES THAT ARE THE NEVER-FAILING CONSEQUENCES OF A DEPARTURE FROM VIRTUE. BY THE AUTHOR OF LADY LOUISA STROUD.

London: Printed for F. Noble, near Middle-Row, Holbourn; and J. Noble, in St Martin's Court, near Leicester-Square (SJC).

2 vols. 12mo. 6s (MR, LC), 5s sewed or 6s bound (SJC).

MR 57: 75 (July 1777); AF II: 1606.

No copy located.

Notes. The History of Lady Louisa Stroud, 1764, JR 836, AF I: 1250.

Adv. SJC 1–4 Mar 1777.

Adv. LC 15–17 Feb 1780.

MR [William Enfield] reviews under 'Novels and Memoirs' and notes, 'The several narratives are related in an easy and agreeable manner; and with a considerable variety of incident and character.'

1777: 12   [HAMILTON, Lady Mary].

MEMOIRS OF THE MARCHIONESS DE LOUVOI. IN LETTERS. BY A LADY. IN THREE VOLUMES.

London: Printed for Robson, New Bond-Street; Walter, Charing-Cross; and Robinson, Paternoster-row, 1777.

I vii, 199p; II 203p; III 187p. 8vo. 7s 6d sewed (CR, MR).

CR 43: 303–6 (Apr 1777); MR 57: 249 (Sept 1777); AF II: 1793.

BL C.175.l.4; EM 4789: 18; ESTC t127871 (NA CSmH, MH-H, NjP &c.).

Notes. Lady Mary Leslie became by her two marriages first Walker and then Hamilton (see FC). 1 p. adv. end vol 3 (adv. for 2nd edn. of *Letters of the Duchess De Crui* [1776: 12] by Lady Mary Walker). Epistolary.

CR and MR suggest same author as *Letters of the Duchess de Crui*, i.e. Lady Mary Hamilton. Adv. SJC 22–24 Apr 1777; adv. LC 43: 237 (7–10 Mar 1778). LC adv. mentions that *Letters from the Duchess de Crui* is by the same author.

German trans. Leipzig, 1778 (*Nachrichten der Marquise von Louvois in Briefen*) (Price).

CR: 'When literary correspondence is maintained with sentiment and vivacity, it may justly be considered as a species of writing well adapted to the purpose both of entertainment and instruction; especially if the subject of it be the history of persons to whose characters we are previously introduced. We then regard the several parties, in some degree, as of our acquaintance, and become the more interested in whatever concerns them. The production now before us is happily founded upon this plan, with the additional advantage, that it contains the correspondence of persons of merit, elegance, taste, and discernment, exemplified not only in the narrative of domestic life, but in the description of some celebrated places, and in historical anecdotes' (p. 303).

MR [William Enfield]: 'To communicate knowledge, and wisdom, in an easy and agreeable manner to those who have hitherto been accustomed only to read for immediate entertainment, is an important design: and we cannot but recommend these letters as well calculated to answer this good purpose.'

1777: 13   [MACKENZIE, Henry].
JULIA DE ROUBIGNÉ, A TALE. IN A SERIES OF LETTERS. PUBLISHED BY THE AUTHOR OF THE MAN OF FEELING, AND THE MAN OF THE WORLD. IN TWO VOLUMES.

London: Printed for W. Strahan, and T. Cadell; and W. Creech, Edinburgh, 1777.

I xii, 195p; II vii, 202p. 12mo. 5s sewed (MR, SJC).

MR 57: 248 (Sept 1777); AF II: 2663.

C S727.d.77.6-; EM 1009: 20; ESTC n002740 (NA MH-H, ILfC).

Notes. 1 p. advs. end vol. 2.

Adv., 'In a few Days will be published', SJC 1–3 Apr 1777; adv. as published SJC 8–10 Apr 1777. 1,000 copies printed Feb. 1777 (Strahan 16 f. 21).

2nd edn., 'speedily will be published', adv. SJC 8–11 Nov 1777; adv. as published SJC 20–23 Dec 1777.

Adv. by Strahan and Cadell PA 4 Nov 1777 refers to recent newspaper reports ascribing authorship of *The Man of Feeling* (1771: 46), *The Man of the World* (1773: 36), *Julia de Roubigné* and Mackenzie's poem *The Pursuits of Happiness* to the late Mr Eccles of Bath; Strahan and Cadell declare that they have 'long been intimately acquainted with' Mackenzie and have printed his works from manuscripts in his own hand, have paid him for the copyrights and have reprinted some from Mackenzie's corrected copies.

Also issued with imprint, London: Printed for W. Strahan, and T. Cadell, 1777, 2 vols., 12mo, EM 6881: 1, ESTC t029274. Further edns: Dublin, 1777 (Printed by James Byrn, and Son, for the Company of Booksellers, 2 vols., 12mo), ESTC t029275; London, 1778, ESTC n029290; Edinburgh, 1781/82, ESTC t186938; Philadelphia, 1782, ESTC w027541; Dublin, 1783, ESTC t107273; 6 further entries in ESTC; WC has 5 entries between 1800 and 1850; NSTC lists edns in 1805, 1809, 1810, 1823 and 1824. German trans. Leipzig, 1778 (*Julie von Roubigné*) (EAG); French trans. Rotterdam, 1779 (*Histoire de Julie de Roubigné*) (BN). Facs: N.

MR [William Enfield]: ' . . . we can with pleasure assure our readers, that they will find in *Julia de Roubigné*, the same richness of invention, pathos of sentiment and simplicity of language, which distinguished the Author's former productions. We have found so much to admire in these natural effusions of genius and feeling, that it is with great regret we learn from the preface, that this may, probably, be the last time that the Author will contribute, in this way, to the amusement of the Public.'

MAN, Henry, **THE TRIFLER**
See 1775: 29

1777: 14   [PRATT, Samuel Jackson].
CHARLES AND CHARLOTTE. IN TWO VOLUMES.
>   London: Printed for William Lane, Leadenhall-Street, 1777.
>   I 240p; II 250p. 8vo. 5s sewed (CR), 6s (MR).
>   CR 43: 314 (Apr 1777); MR 57: 74 (July 1777); AF II: 3565.
>   BL 1489.cc.90; EM 2265: 4; ESTC t060939 (NA PU, ViU; EA ZWTU).

Notes. Ornamented t.p. Epistolary.
German trans. Vienna and Leipzig, 1784 (*Karl und Charlotte*) (EAG).

   CR: 'A collection of letters between different persons, but containing chiefly the correspondence of Charles and Charlotte, after the latter had, from motives of penitence, renounced an illicit connection in which they had lived some time.'

   MR [William Enfield]: 'The writer of this novel has the merit of giving, in some degree, an air of originality to a tale which has already been told in a thousand different forms, by making choice of incidents and situations not commonly introduced in works of this kind. . . . The expression is easy and natural, and the narrative interesting and tender.'

1777: 15   [PRATT, Samuel Jackson].
TRAVELS FOR THE HEART. WRITTEN IN FRANCE, BY COURTNEY MELMOTH. IN TWO VOLUMES.
>   London: Printed for John Wallis, No. 16, Ludgate-Street, 1777.
>   I xlvii, 205p; II xvi, 239p. 8vo. 6s sewed (CR), 5s sewed (MR, SJC).
>   CR 44: 349–52 (Nov 1777); MR 58: 85–6 (Jan 1778); AF II: 3588.
>   BL 302.a.10–11; EM 3205: 2; ESTC t124428 (BI BMp, C; NA CtY, MH-H, NjP &c.).

Notes. Imitation of Sterne. Dedicated 'To the heart of his excellency Lord Stormont, Ambassador at the Court of France'. MR reviews under 'Miscellaneous' (immediately following *The Champion of Virtue*, 1777: 16).
Adv., 'In a few Days will be published', SJC 16–19 Aug 1777; still adv, 'In a few Days will be published', PA 29 Sept 1777.
Further edn: Dublin, 1777/78 (Printed for S. Price, W. Whitestone, T. Wilkinson, J. Williams, W. Colles, [and 4 others in Dublin], 2 vols., 12mo), ESTC t177522. German trans. Leipzig, 1778 (*Reisen für das Herz*) (Price).

   CR: 'These volumes contain the effusions of a lively imagination, apparently well acquainted with those delicate sensibilities which mark the human heart in various characters' (p. 352).

   MR [William Enfield]: 'We do not hesitate to pronounce this hasty production, an unsuccessful attempt to imitate the Shandyan manner. The work is indeed sufficiently irregular, and the Author has said enough about his irregularities. . . . If Mr. Melmoth knew his own *talents*, he would employ himself chiefly in the humourous delineation of characters; of his abilities for which, he has given us an agreeable specimen or two, in the course of these volumes.'

1777: 16   [REEVE, Clara].
THE CHAMPION OF VIRTUE. A GOTHIC STORY. BY THE EDITOR OF THE PHOENIX; A TRANSLATION OF BARCLAY'S ARGENIS.

> Colchester: Printed for the Author, by W. Keymer, and sold by him; sold also by G. Robinson, No. 25 Pater-noster-Row, London. 1777.
> vii, 190p. 12mo. 3s sewed (CR, MR), 3s (half-title, SJC).
> CR 44: 154 (Aug 1777); MR 58: 85 (Jan 1778).
> BL 12611.f.5; EM 175: 3; ESTC t056188 (NA CtY-BR, MH-H, ViU &c.).

Notes. Adv., 'With an elegant Frontispiece, designed and engraved by an ingenious Friend, from an interesting Scene in the Story', SJC 3–5 June 1777; additional booksellers are J. Shave of Ipswich and Gray and Frost of Chelmsford.
Further edn. with this title: London, 1795, EM 4374: 3, ESTC t056189.
Reissued 1778 as *The Old English Baron: A Gothic Story.* By Clara Reeve ESTC t172453, rev. CR 45: 315–16 (Apr 1778); MR 58: 476 (June 1778). 750 copies printed Mar 1778 (Strahan 16 f. 31).
Further edns: London, 1778, EM 7448: 18, ESTC t129762; Dublin, 1778 (Printed by John Exshaw, 1 vol., 12mo), ESTC t060970; London, 1780, ESTC n011369; London, 1784, ESTC n041555; 6 further entries in ESTC; WC has 4 entries between 1800 and 1850; Summers lists 14 edns. 1800–1850. Serialised as 'The Champion of Virtue', *Berwick Museum*, 1785–86, RM 201. French trans. in 1787 (both Paris): *Le Champion de la Vertu, ou le Vieux Baron Anglais* (Lévy) and *Le Vieux baron anglais, ou les Revenants vengés* (BN); German trans. Nuremberg, 1789 (*Der altenglische Baron*) (EAG).
The Old English Baron adv., 'Tuesday the 31st Instant, will be published, Handsomely printed in Crown Octavo', LC 43: 276 (19–21 Mar 1778).
CR 44: 'The author of this novel proposes to interest the imagination of his reader, by going into the marvellous, without transgressing the bounds of credibility . . . he succeeds to captivate the attention of his readers; and the story being well contrived, agreeably told, and not very long, may be ranked among those which afford a tolerable degree of amusement without any dangerous tendency. How far it may be excusable, in our times, to encourage a belief concerning the existence of ghosts, we shall not here determine; but it may be said that if the dramatic poet is allowed to introduce them with impunity, the novel writer has a claim to the like indulgence.'
CR 45: 'This is no common novel—it may, in some respects, claim a place upon the shelf with The Castle of Otranto, which has its faults as well as The Old English Baron.—The *Baron* will probably live as long as the *Castle* stands, but he should never forget that he was *born* in the Castle of Otranto' (p. 316).
[*Castle of Otranto*, 1765 {1764}, JR 868, AF I: 2898].
MR 58: 85 [William Enfield]: 'This writer has imitated with tolerable success, the style and manner of ancient romance. The story is enlivened with an agreeable variety of incidents; the narrative is plain and simple; and the whole is adapted to interest the feelings of the reader,— provided that he has either faith, or fancy, enough to be interested in the appearance of ghosts.'

1777: 17   {ROGERS, A}.
THE HISTORY OF MISS TEMPLE. IN TWO VOLUMES. BY A YOUNG LADY.

London: Printed for the author; and sold by Wallis, No. 16, Ludgate Street; Flexney,
   Holborn; Davenhill, No. 30, Cornhill; and Fielding and Walker, Pater-noster Row,
   1777.
I vii, 228p; II 259p. 12mo. 5s sewed (CR, SJC), 5s (MR).
CR 43: 473 (June 1777); MR 57: 174 (Aug 1777); AF II: 3856.
MH-H *EC75.R6311.777h; EM 1495: 47; ESTC n007821 (BI BL, O; NA CaOTU, NjP,
   PU).

Notes. Dedication to Mr Aikin 1, v–vii, signed 'A. Rogers Dronfield, Derbyshire, June 1st.
1777'. Epistolary.
Adv., with title *Painful Pre-Eminence; or, the History of Miss Temple. By a Young Lady*, SJC
24–26 June 1777.
Further edn: Dublin, 1777 (Printed for Messrs. Price, Whitestone, W. Wilson, R. Cross,
Chamberlaine [and 14 others in Dublin], 2 vols., 12mo), ESTC n007822. German trans.
Leipzig, 1778 (*Geschichte der Miss Temple*) (Price).
   CR: 'The abuse of novel writing is so great, that it has almost brought that species of entertainment into discredit. Meagre stories, flatly told, and drawled through many tedious volumes with no other view than a little dirty emolument, have overwhelmed us like a flood; and
the manes of Richardson, Fielding, and Smollett have often been cruelly tortured by their
imitators. Those authors, who stand the test of criticism, and a few others, who appear from
time to time, prevent the better part of mankind from condemning novels and romances in
general. Among the authors of this kind, who have laid their volumes at the shrine of virtue,
we now behold a young lady timidly approaching to make her first offering. We prepared to
be indulgent to the sex and youth of this fair writer, but the History of Miss Temple is of that
stamp, which renders such allowances unnecessary.'
   MR [William Enfield]: 'The manner in which she unfolds the sentiments of elegant love,
will be pleasing to all, whom nature has not forbidden to feel, or system instructed to despise
them. . . . The incidents are well conceived, the characters are distinctly marked, and the diction is easy and correct.'

1777: 18   THISTLETHWAITE, [James].
THE CHILD OF MISFORTUNE; OR, THE HISTORY OF MRS. GILBERT.
BY MR. THISTLETHWAITE. IN TWO VOLUMES.

London: Printed for John Murray, N° 32, opposite St. Dunstan's Church, Fleet-street,
   1777.
I 307p; II 287p. 12mo. 6s (CR, MR), 5s sewed (WEP).
CR 44: 398 (Nov 1777); MR 57: 74 (July 1777); AF II: 4412.
IU x823.T348c; EMf; ESTC n027800 (BI O; NA CLU-S/C, MnU, PU).

Notes. Postdated; adv., 'On Monday next will be published, Handsomely printed in Two
Pocket Volumes', WEP 3–5 Dec 1776; adv. as published WEP 10–12 Dec 1776.
Published in partnership with William Richardson; 800 copies printed; production costs
£33.17s.6d (Zachs 168).
Further edn: Dublin, 1777 (Printed for S. Price, W. Watson, W. Whitestone, R. Cross J. Potts
[and 14 others in Dublin], 2 vols., 12mo), ESTC t190454.
   CR: 'The Child of Misfortune has contrived to get our hearts on her side; but the author,
by distracting our passions, has less command over them. The stream of sentiment and feeling is diminished by being turned into so many channels within so small a circle.'

MR [William Enfield]: 'We observe in this novel a fertility of invention and command of language, which raise it above the common run of these productions.... But the work would have been more perfect, if the writer had been more attentive to unity of design, and introduced few incidents by way of episode, which, however proper in large works, a story comprised in two small volumes will scarcely admit.'

WALKER, Lady Mary
See HAMILTON, Lady Mary

1778

EVELINA OR, A YOUNG LADY'S ENTRANCE INTO THE WORLD
See BURNEY, Frances

1778: 1   ANON.
THE EXAMPLE: OR THE HISTORY OF LUCY CLEVELAND. BY A YOUNG LADY.
> London: Printed for Fielding and Walker, No. 20, Pater-Noster-Row, 1778.
> I viii, 259p; II 235p. 12mo. 5s sewed (CR, MR).
> CR 46: 297–9 (Oct 1778); MR 59: 391–2 (Nov 1778); AF II: 1338.
> BL 12611.d.16; EM 237: 4; ESTC t057438; (NA MH-H, OU, PU).

Notes. 1 p. advs. end vol. 2. Epistolary.
Adv. GND 17 Dec 1778; adv. SJC 2–5 Jan 1779.
German trans. Leipzig, 1780 (*Das Beyspiel oder Geschichte der Lucie Cleveland*) (EAG).

CR: 'What is the subject of this novel? Love.——What its story? Love.——What is it calculated to promote? Love, almighty love' (p. 297). 'If to *put together* a bundle of incidents which the wildest child of romance can never believe—if to draw an extravagant picture which would soften the heart of the softest beholder—if to tell a tedious tale of love, with the perusal of which Love herself would be fatigued—if these be to "hold out a good example to female readers," [the author's prefatory claim] then is Lucy Cleveland the most complete example of morality, wrapped up in the most engaging dress, which we remember to have seen' (p. 299).

MR [William Enfield]: 'It is an unfortunate circumstance for the reputation of this novel, that it fails in the circumstance on which alone the Author ventures to rest its merit, that of holding out a good example to the female sex.'

FRIENDSHIP IN A NUNNERY
See GIBBES, Phebe

1778: 2   ANON.
*GREENWOOD FARM. WRITTEN BY A WARRANT OFFICER BELONGING TO THE NAVY.

London: Printed for F. Noble, near Middle-Row, Holborn; and J. Noble, in St Martin's-court, St. Martin's Lane (PA), 1778 (PA).

2 vols. 12mo. 5s sewed (CR), 6s (MR), 6s bound (PA).

CR 45: 316 (Apr 1778); MR 58: 395 (May 1778); AF II: 1730.

No copy located.

Notes. Adv. PA 10 Feb 1778.

Further edn: Dublin, 1784 (Pat. Higly, 2 vols., 8vo), ESTC n031209. German trans. Leipzig, 1779 (*Grünwald eine Erzählung*) (EAG).

CR: 'They who visit *Greenwood Farm*, though they may not find there the richest and most beautiful prospects, or company the most refined and elegant, will yet meet with much to entertain and please them, and nothing to hurt their morals, or their feelings.'

MR [William Enfield]: 'The piece is so extremely defective in incident, sentiment and language, that we apprehend he will find few readers who will think him entitled to praise as an author, whatever claims he may have upon the public as a naval officer.'

1778: 3 ANON.
THE HISTORY OF ELIZA WARWICK. IN TWO VOLUMES.

London: Printed for J. Bew, in Pater-Noster-Row, 1778.

I vii, 278p; II 258p. 8vo [CR, MR have 12mo]. 5s sewed (CR), 6s (MR), 5s sewed or 6s bound (PA).

CR 44: 477–8 (Dec 1777); MR 58: 394 (May 1778); AF II: 1957.

O 249.s.638-639; ESTC n047427 (NA CSt).

Notes. Dedication v–vii 'To the Reviewers' mentions that the author is 'a female, and a very young one' (p. vi). 2 pp. advs. end vol. 2. Epistolary.

Post-dated; adv. as published PA 9 Dec 1777; 'By a Lady'. Adv., with quotation from MR, LEP 7–9 Feb 1786.

Further edns: Dublin, 1778 (Printed for S. Price, W. Whitestone, R. Feitzsimmons, D. Chamberlaine, J. Sheppard [and 17 others in Dublin], 2 vols., 12mo), ESTC n007998; London, 1791, ESTC t127651. German trans. Leipzig(?), 1779 (*Die Geschichte der Elise Warwick*) (EAG); French trans. Amsterdam and Paris, 1781 (*Histoire de Miss Elise Warwick*) (BGR).

CR: 'In this age of petit-maitres and *chevaliers*, there is no such thing as distinguishing men from women.—If this novel be really written by a lady, and "from a motive the most virtuous would approve;" we counsel her never to write any more novels, except from the same motive.—Is it of the masculine gender?—then we admire the gentleman's artifice as little as his work' (p. 478).

MR [William Enfield]: 'This is an entertaining tale, related in easy and agreeable, and where the occasion requires, in pathetic language: it is calculated to touch the springs of tender sympathy; and, notwithstanding its distressing catastrophe, is better adapted to produce a good moral effect, than many of those *agreeable* stories in which virtue is made at last triumphant.'

LEARNING AT A LOSS
See WAY, Gregory Lewis

MEMOIRS OF A CLERGYMAN
See 1774: 15

MEMOIRS OF THE COUNTESS D'ANOIS
See MURAT, Henriette Julie de

MUNSTER VILLAGE
See HAMILTON, Lady Mary

1778: 4   ANON.
THE OFFSPRING OF FANCY, A NOVEL. BY A LADY. IN TWO VOLUMES.
> London: Printed for J. Bew, Pater-noster-Row, 1778.
> I 245p; II 244p. 12mo. 6s (CR, MR), 5s sewed or 6s bound (SJC).
> CR 45: 474 (June 1778); MR 58: 395 (Oct 1778); AF II: 3130.
> TxHR PR 3291. A6 L22 1778; xESTC.

Notes. Post-dated; adv., 'In a few Days will be published, Neatly printed on a fine Writing-Paper', SJC 22–25 Nov 1777; adv. as published PA 9 Dec 1777.

CR: 'This novel discovers neither much regularity of design, nor attention to embellishment, as is necessary to give the stamp of genius to a literary production. It may however serve in some degree to amuse those readers whose taste is chiefly for what is new, and who prefer variety to excellence.'

MR [William Enfield]: 'We find too much confusion in the plan, and negligence in the execution of this novel, to allow it any considerable share of merit.'

THE OLD ENGLISH BARON
See REEVE, Clara, THE CHAMPION OF VIRTUE (1777: 16)

1778: 5   ANON.
THE SENTIMENTAL CONNOISSEUR: OR, PLEASING AND ENTER-TAINING NOVELIST. BEING AN ELEGANT AND NEW ASSEMBLAGE OF LIVELY EFFUSIONS OF FANCY, POLITE TALES, DIVERTING ESSAYS, DROLL ADVENTURES, PLEASING STROKES, ENTERTAIN-ING NOVELS, COMIC CHARACTERS, FACETIOUS HISTORIES, AFFECTING EXAMPLES, STRIKING REMARKS, POINTED SATIRES, &C. &C. ENTIRELY CALCULATED TO FORM IN THE MIND THE MOST VIRTUOUS SENTIMENTS: AND ADAPTED TO PROMOTE A LOVE OF VIRTUE AND AN ABHORRENCE OF VICE.
> London: Sold by R. Newton, J. Murdell, M. Cooper, and D. Midwinter, 1778
> 192p. 12mo.
> BL 12316.cc.13; EM 7482: 3; ESTC t128586.

Notes. Frontispiece. Preface pp. 3–6.

A SENTIMENTAL DIARY
See PHILLIPS, Peregrine, App. B: 4

1778: 6   ANON.
SKETCHES FROM NATURE; OR, THE HISTORY OF HENRY AND EMMA, AND OF FANNY AND LUCY STANLEY. IN THREE VOLUMES.

London: Printed for F. Noble, near Middle Row, Holborn; and J. Noble, in St. Martin's
    Court, St. Martin's Lane, 1778.
I viii, 232p; II 236p; III 176p. 12mo. 9s (MR), 7s 6d sewed or 9s bound (SJC, PA).
MR 58: 475–6 (June 1778); AF II: 4115.
LVu Y77.2.6-8; ESTC t160118 (NA MdBJ, NjP).

Notes. By a woman; see *The Wedding Ring* (1779: 5)
Half-title vol. 1, with a quotation from Job xv, has the title 'The History of Fanny and Lucy
Stanley: a Narrative, Founded on a late Melancholy Event'. Prefatory advertisement v–viii.
First half-title vol. 2: 'The History of Fanny and Lucy Stanley Continued'; p. [91] new half-
title: 'Henry and Emma. A Moral History Founded on real Facts'; pp. 93–96 are a further
'Address to the Reader' and then begins 'Henry and Emma. A Moral History'. Half-title
vol. 3: 'Henry and Emma. A Moral History Founded on real Facts. Continued'. 12 pp. advs.
end vol. 3.
Adv. SJC 26–28 Mar 1778 and PA 3 Apr 1778.
Reissued as *Female Sensibility; or, the History of Emma Pomfret. A Novel. Founded on Facts.*
London: Printed for W. Lane, 1783, 1 vol., 8vo, ESTC n031405.
German trans. Leipzig, 1779 (*Skizzen nach der Natur*) (Price).
    MR [William Enfield]: 'If we were to call in question this Writer's abilities for drawing
Sketches from Nature, we are apprehensive that a numerous train of female advocates would
appear, with tears in their eyes, to plead his cause. Rather than risk so unequal a contest, we
therefore pronounce these tales *natural* and *pathetic*.'

1778: 7   ANON.
THE TRAVELS OF HILDEBRAND BOWMAN, ESQUIRE, INTO CARNOVIRRIA, TAUPINIERA, OLFACTARIA, AND AUDINANTE, IN NEW-ZEALAND; IN THE ISLAND OF BOHMOMMICA, AND IN THE POWERFUL KINGDOM OF LUXO-VOLUPTO, ON THE GREAT SOUTHERN CONTINENT. WRITTEN BY HIMSELF; WHO WENT ON SHORE IN THE ADVENTURE'S LARGE CUTTER AT QUEEN CHARLOTTE'S SOUND NEW-ZEALAND, THE FATAL 17TH OF DECEMBER 1773; AND ESCAPED BEING CUT OFF, AND DEVOURED, WITH THE REST OF THE BOAT'S CREW, BY HAPPENING TO BE A-SHOOTING IN THE WOODS; WHERE HE WAS AFTERWARDS, UNFORTUNATELY LEFT BEHIND BY THE ADVENTURE.

London: Printed for W. Strahan; and T. Cadell, in the Strand, 1778.
xv, 400p. 8vo. 5s boards (CR, MR).
CR 45: 367–71 (May 1778); MR 59: 409–10 (Dec 1778); AF II: 4518.
BL 12614.dd.15; EM 275: 4; ESTC t060861 (BI C; NA CLU-S/C, CSmH, NcD; EA GOT,
    SRGS, ZDUHO &c.).

Notes. Adv. PA 5 May 1778.
    CR: '... we think that like his predecessor Gulliver, of whimsical memory, he has indirectly
satirized several follies, which are too common to be reckoned exotics in the northern hemi-
sphere; and that he has at least afforded new matter for the entertainment of the public'
(p. 371).
    MR [William Bewley]: '... Though Lemuel Gulliver, it is now well known, was married, it

does not appear that he ever had any legitimate offspring. Be that, however, as it may, we cannot honestly afford Squire Bowman any higher praise than that he may possibly be one of his distant kin' (p. 410).

1778: 8   ANON.
A TRIP TO MELASGE; OR, CONCISE INSTRUCTIONS TO A YOUNG GENTLEMAN ENTERING INTO LIFE WITH HIS OBSERVATIONS ON THE GENIUS, MANNERS, TON, OPINIONS, PHILOSOPHY, AND MORALS, OF THE MELASGENS.
> London: Printed for B. Law No. 13, Ave-Mary Lane, Ludgate Street, 1778.
> I viii, 232p; II 251p. 8vo. 6s (CR), 5s sewed (MR, SJC).
> CR 45: 232–3 (Mar 1778); MR 58: 315 (Apr 1778); AF II: 4526.
> BL 8407.aaa.17; EM 356: 8; ESTC t124827 (NA CSmH, ICN).

Notes. CR reviews under 'Novels'; MR under 'Novels and Memoirs'.
Adv., 'Next Week will be published', SJC 9–11 Dec 1777; adv. as published SJC 23–25 Dec 1777.
Same work published (with same number of pages) as THE SENTIMENTAL TRAVELLER, OR A DESCRIPTIVE TOUR THROUGH LIFE, FIGURATIVELY AS A TRIP TO MELASGE, IN WHICH IS INCLUDED THE ADVENTURES OF A GENTLEMAN IN THE EAST-INDIES: THE WHOLE FORMING A SYSTEM OF EDUCATION WITH INSTRUCTIONS TO A YOUNG GENTLEMAN, ENTERING INTO LIFE. IN TWO VOLUMES. (London: Printed for S. Brown, Strand. n.d. [ESTC: 1780?]), EM 2145: 5, ESTC n021226.

CR: 'After having waded through two volumes of affected language, incorrect expressions, ridiculous metaphors, and insufferable allusions, we are still at a loss to discover the author's idea, and totally unable to give any account of his meaning. . . . In friendship to our Readers, we advise them never to think of a Trip to Melasge.'

MR [William Enfield]: 'The Writer's design seems to have been, to convey lessons of instruction, and exhibit pictures of manners, in a fictitious narrative; and as far as we are able to decypher his meaning, we think we discover some traces of ability both as a moralist and a satyrist; but we are so frequently at a loss for the sense, that we do not deem ourselves qualified absolutely to decide concerning the merit of the work. Before this Author can expect to be received as an agreeable or useful writer by common readers, he must learn to lower his style to the level of common understandings.'

1778: 9   ANON.
THE UNFORTUNATE UNION: OR, THE TEST OF VIRTUE. A STORY FOUNDED ON FACTS, AND CALCULATED TO PROMOTE THE CAUSE OF VIRTUE IN YOUNGER MINDS. WRITTEN BY A LADY.
> London: Printed for Richardson and Urquhart, under the Royal Exchange, and at No. 46, Pater-Noster-Row, 1778.
> I 197p; II 226p. 12mo. 6s (CR), 6s bound (MR), 6s sewed (PA).
> CR 45: 473–4 (June 1778); MR 58: 395 (May 1778); AF II: 4579.
> MH-H *EC75.A100.778u; EM 1281: 34; ESTC n014503.

Notes. Epistolary.
Adv. PA 14 Feb 1778.

Further edn: Dublin, 1779 (Printed for Messrs. Price, W. Whitestone, Corcoran, R. Cross, Sleater [and 12 others in Dublin], 1 vol., 12mo), ESTC n035417. German trans. Leipzig, 1779 (*Die unglückliche Verbindung*) (Price).

CR: 'This novel is written with a better intention and a better pen than the generality of such publications. The same story might have been told more agreeably by the same writer in smaller compass. It is something, however, in a modern novel, to find *half* of it worth reading.'

MR [William Enfield]: 'There is something so exceedingly disgusting in the exhibition of characters, which have no tints of elegance or virtue, to soften the coarse lines of vulgar manners, or enliven the dark shades of abandoned libertinism—there is something so extremely painful, in seeing such characters employed in harassing, tormenting, and defaming an innocent and gentle spirit—that it is surprising such representations should be thought capable of affording entertainment, or calculated to promote the cause of virtue in young minds.'

ANOIS, COUNTESS D'
See MURAT, Henriette Julie de

AULNOY, MARIE CATHERINE DE LA MOTTE, BARONNE D'
See MURAT, Henriette Julie de

BOWMAN, HILDEBRAND
See THE TRAVELS OF...

1778: 10   [BURNEY, Frances].
EVELINA, OR, A YOUNG LADY'S ENTRANCE INTO THE WORLD.
London: Printed for T. Lowndes, No 77, in Fleet-Street, 1778.
I xv, 235p; II 263p; III 263p. 12mo. 7s 6d sewed (CR), 9s (MR), 7s 6d sewed or 9s bound (LC).
CR 46: 202–4 (Sept 1778); MR 58: 316 (Apr 1778); AF II: 549.
BL C.117.b.80; EMf; ESTC t145413 (BI E, O, WIS; NA CtY-BR, CSmH, ICN, IU, MH-H, NjP, NN, TxU &c.).

Notes. 1 p. advs. end vols. 1, 2, and 3. Epistolary.
Lowndes wrote on 11 Nov 1777 offering Burney 20 gns. for *Evelina*; Burney was disappointed—'... I should not have taken the pains to Copy & Correct it for the Press, had I imagined that 10 Guineas a Volume would have been more than its worth'—but she accepted it and later expressed herself as 'satisfied' (Troide 2: 287–288 and 3: 54). Lowndes claimed to have printed 500 copies but Burney later gave the figure as 800 (Troide 3: 43n).
Adv., 'In a few Days will be published', LC 43: 75 (20–22 Jan 1778); adv. as published LC 43: 103 (27–29 Jan 1778). A 'new Edition' adv. PA 30 Oct 1778.
Further edns: Dublin, 1779 (Printed for Messrs. Price, Corcoran, R. Cross, Fitzsimons, W. Whitestone [and 12 others in Dublin], 2 vols., 12mo), ESTC t200766; London, 1779, ESTC t107606; London, 1779, EM 222: 2, ESTC t081094; London, 1779, ESTC t113895; Dublin, 1780, ESTC t186175; 17 further entries in ESTC; WC has 17 entries between 1800 and 1850; NSTC lists edns. in 1804, 1805, 1808, 1810, 1812, 1820, 1821, 1822, 1829, 1832, 1835, 1838, 1845 and 1850. French trans. Paris and Amsterdam, 1779 (*Evelina, ou l'Entrée d'une jeune personne dans le monde*) (BN); German trans. Leipzig, 1779 (*Evelina, oder eines jungen Frauenzimmers Eintritt in die Welt*) (EAG).

CR: 'This performance deserves no common praise, whether we consider it in a moral or literary light. It would have disgraced neither the head nor the heart of Richardson' (p. 201).

MR [William Enfield]: 'This novel has given us so much pleasure in the perusal, that we do not hesitate to pronounce it one of the most sprightly, entertaining, and agreeable productions of this kind, which has of late fallen under our notice. A great variety of natural incidents, some of the comic stamp, render the narrative extremely interesting. The characters, which are agreeably diversified, are conceived and drawn with propriety, and supported with spirit. The whole is written with great ease and command of language. From this commendation, however, we must except the character of a son of Neptune, whose manners are rather those of a rough uneducated country 'squire, than those of a genuine sea-captain.'

1778: 11   [GIBBES, Phebe].
FRIENDSHIP IN A NUNNERY; OR, THE AMERICAN FUGITIVE. CONTAINING A FULL DESCRIPTION OF THE MODE OF EDUCATION AND LIVING IN CONVENT SCHOOLS, BOTH ON THE LOW AND HIGH PENSION; THE MANNERS AND CHARACTERS OF THE NUNS; THE ARTS PRACTISED ON YOUNG MINDS; AND THEIR BANEFUL EFFECTS ON SOCIETY AT LARGE. BY A LADY. IN TWO VOLUMES.

London: Printed for J. Bew, in Pater-Noster-Row, 1778.
I 262p; II 255p. 12mo. 5s sewed (CR), 6s (MR), 5s sewed or 6s bound (PA).
CR 46: 300–1 (Oct 1778); MR 60: 324 (Apr 1779); AF II: 1604.
BL 1607/3460; EMf; ESTC t126084.

Notes. Author attribution: MR, FC.
1 p. advs. end vol 2. Epistolary.
Adv., 'Neatly printed', PA 18 Sept 1778.
Further edns: Dublin, 1784 [The American Fugitive: or, Friendship in a Nunnery] (Printed for John Cash, 1 vol., 12mo), EM 3678: 3, ESTC t141142; Dublin, 1784 [ESTC: imprint is false], ESTC t141143. German trans. Leipzig, 1779 (Die junge Nordamerikanerin oder Klosterfreundschaft) (Price).

CR calls 'its style and language . . . of a superior order', dislikes its political aspect, which 'would make a capital figure in the most conspicuous column of a republican print', and comments on the author's claimed age (14): 'What may not be expected from the old men and sages of that happy continent, when its maidens, its babes and sucklings talk, and write, and reason thus!' (p. 301).

MR [William Enfield]: 'The picture here exhibited of convent-manners is perhaps too deeply shaded; it is, however, marked with such peculiar traits, as to shew the Author to have drawn from the life; and there is so much truth, as well as execution in the piece, that it merits some attention in an age, in which it is become too fashionable for females to receive the last finishing of their education in a convent.'

1778: 12   [HAMILTON, Lady Mary].
MUNSTER VILLAGE, A NOVEL. IN TWO VOLUMES.

London: Printed for Robson and Co. New Bond Street; Walter, Charing Cross; and Robinson, Paternoster Row, 1778.

I 202p; II 260p. 8vo. 6s (CR, MR), 6s bound (LC).
CR 45: 300–2 (Apr 1778); MR 58: 396 (May 1778); AF II: 1794.
O Vet.A5f.530,531; ESTC n021991 (NA OU).

Notes. Lady Mary Leslie became by her two marriages first Walker and then Hamilton (see FC).
1 p. advs. end vol. 1.
Adv. LC 43: 371 (16–18 Apr 1778); adv. GND 6 June 1778; additional booksellers are E. and
C. Dilly, in the Poultry.
Further edn: Dublin, 1779 (Printed by Peter Hoey, 2 vols., 12mo), EM 1279: 6, ESTC
n010236. German trans. Leipzig, 1779 (*Münsterdorf, eine Erzählung*) (EAG); French trans.
Paris and Rotterdam, 1782 (*Le Village de Munster*) (BGR).

CR: 'These two little volumes are written in the form of narrative, with several letters interspersed. The incidents are not numerous nor very striking, but the characters are naturally
drawn, and supported with consistency' (p. 300). 'This agreeable Novel, the author of which
appears to be a person of extensive reading, abounds with pertinent observations on life and
manners. A variety of subjects, instructive as well as entertaining, is occasionally introduced;
and we have only to suggest, that this writer would pay a little more regard to correctness of
composition, in any future work' (p. 302).

MR [William Enfield]: 'It abounds with just reflections, discovers extensive reading, and
is written in an agreeable style. The story is not uninteresting; but its chief value is, that it is
the vehicle of much entertaining information, and of useful moral instruction.'

1778: 13   [MURAT, Henriette Julie de Castelnau, comtesse de].
**MEMOIRS OF THE COUNTESS D'ANOIS: WRITTEN BY HERSELF
BEFORE HER RETIREMENT. IN TWO VOLUMES.**

London: Printed for F. Noble, near Middle Row, Holborn; and J. Noble, in St Martin's
Court, Leicester Fields, 1778.
I 240p; II 241p. 12mo. 5s sewed (CR), 6s (MR), 6s bound (PA).
CR 45: 316 (Apr 1778); MR 58: 394 (May 1778); AF II: 2998.
BL 1608/4505; EM 2893: 2; ESTC t130488.

Notes. Trans. of *Mémoires de Mme la comtesse de *** avant sa retraite* (Lyon, 1697).
Adv. PA 10 Feb 1778.
2-pp. preface (unn.); 3 pp. advs. end vol. 2.

CR: 'We can discover no ground on which to recommend her countess-*ship* to our female
readers. We suspect that Madame la Comtesse may be found in some British garret; without
breeches perhaps, but yet not in petticoats.'

MR [William Enfield]: 'When books that have long been forgotten are revived, it is to be
supposed, either that they have extraordinary merit, or are peculiarly seasonable. Neither of
these reasons can however be assigned, for the revival of these memoirs.'

PHILLIPS, Peregrine, **A SENTIMENTAL DIARY**
See App. B: 4

REEVE, Clara, **THE OLD ENGLISH BARON**
See **THE CHAMPION OF VIRTUE** (1777: 16)

1778: 14   RICCOBONI, [Marie-Jeanne Laboras de Mézières]; STOCKDALE, Percival (*trans.*).
LETTERS FROM LORD RIVERS TO SIR CHARLES CARDIGAN, AND TO OTHER ENGLISH CORRESPONDENTS, WHILE HE RESIDED IN FRANCE. TRANSLATED FROM THE ORIGINAL FRENCH OF MADAME RICCOBONI, BY PERCIVAL STOCKDALE. IN TWO VOLUMES.

> London: Printed for T. Becket, Adelphi, Strand; Bookseller to their Royal Highnesses the Prince of Wales, Bishop of Osnaburgh, Prince William, and Prince Edward, 1778.
> I xx, 192p; II viii, 234p. 12mo. 5s sewed (CR, PA), 6s (MR).
> CR 46: 186–8 (Sept 1778); MR 59: 233–4 (Sept 1778).
> BL 12510.c.18; EM 93: 4; ESTC t131026 (BI MRu; NA DLC).

Notes. Trans. of *Lettres de Mylord Rivers à Sir Charles Cardigan* (Paris, 1777).
Dedication to Mrs. Shipley v–viii, signed Percival Stockdale, Lleweny, 13 Sept 1777. Table of contents xvii–xx, followed by preface ix–xvi. (EM corrects the page order.) Epistolary.
Adv., 'In a few Days will be published, . . . with a Preface by the Translator', PA 24 Apr 1778; also adv. GND 14 May 1778.
Further edn: Dublin, 1785 (Printed by S. Colbert, 2 vols., 12mo), ESTC t205581.

CR: 'The style, in which these Letters are written, is lively and animated; the sentiments are just and delicate; the moral unexceptionable: but the story does not abound with interesting events, sufficient to excite the reader's curiosity, or to warm and interest his affections with energy and spirit' (p. 188).

MR [William Enfield]: 'These Letters discover genius, and taste, of an order superior to those which are usually employed in novel-writing. They unfold, with delicacy, many of the finer feelings of the heart, are enriched with just sentiments and reflections, and are written with no inconsiderable degree of elegance and animation. In one of the most essential excellencies of this kind of writing, novelty and variety of incident, they are, however, materially defective.'

1778: 15   THISTLETHWAITE, [James].
THE MAN OF EXPERIENCE; OR, THE ADVENTURES OF HONORIUS. IN TWO VOLUMES. By MR. THISTLETHWAITE.

> London: Printed for John Boosey, at his Circulating Library, No. 39, King Street, Cheapside, 1778.
> I 263p; II 250p. 12mo. 6s (MR), 6s sewed (CR), 5s sewed (LC).
> CR 45: 234 (Mar 1778); MR 58: 404 (May 1778); AF II: 4415.
> BL 012618.ee.13; EM 367: 2; ESTC t085457 (NA IU).

Notes. 4-pp. dedication (unn.) to the Earl of Chesterfield vol. 1, 4 pp. advs. end vol. 2; p. 217 misnumbered 271 in vol. 1.
Adv. LC 43: 212 (28 Feb–3 Mar 1778).

CR: 'Sterne and Goldsmith seem to have been intimate acquaintances of our author—but from the latter he has not learnt the art of working up incidents naturally, nor from the former the ability of relating them ludicrously or affectingly. We question whether "The Man of Experience" may not rather induce the reader to think ill, than well, of the world—a doctrine which, as men of experience, we cannot fail to condemn.'

MR [John Langhorne]: 'An unmeaning, unnatural, and ill written satire on mankind.'

WALKER, Lady Mary
See HAMILTON, Lady Mary

1778: 16   [WAY, Gregory Lewis].
LEARNING AT A LOSS, OR THE AMOURS OF MR. PEDANT AND MISS HARTLEY. A NOVEL. IN TWO VOLUMES.
>London: Printed for the Author, And sold by H. Gardner, opposite St. Clements's Church in the Strand; and J. Bew, Paternoster-Row, 1778.
>I 158p; II 163p. 8vo [MR has 12mo]. 5s bound (MR).
>MR 59: 392 (Nov 1778).
>BL 1156.i.16; EM 5530: 2; ESTC t097491 (NA CSmH, MnU, PU).

Notes. 'Dedication, Preface, &c. to all the Circulating Librarians In the Kingdom of Great-Britain' 1–25, signed 'The Author'; text of novel starts on p. 27. Epistolary.

MR [William Enfield]: 'An illiberal attack upon the learned; the Author of which seems to have mistaken *vulgarity* for ease;—*fun* for humour, and *pertness* for wit.'

1779

1779: 1   ANON.
CHARLES; OR, THE HISTORY OF A YOUNG BARONET AND A LADY OF QUALITY. A NOVEL IN TWO VOLUMES.
>London: Printed for J. Bew, in Pater-Noster-Row, 1779.
>I 214p; II 230p. 12mo. 6s bound (MR), 5s sewed or 6s bound (SJC).
>MR 60: 398 (May 1779); AF II: 667.
>PU Singer-Mend.PR3991.A1.C42 1779; ESTC n052435.

Notes. 1 p. advs. end each vol. Epistolary.
Adv. SJC 27 Feb–2 Mar 1779.

MR [William Enfield]: 'This novel has such mediocrity of merit, that to discover and enumerate its faults or its excellencies, would be a task attended with equal difficulty. If it has any leading character, it is that of insipidity; a quality which the readers of modern novels are tolerably well accustomed to endure.'

COLUMELLA
See GRAVES, Richard

1779: 2   ANON.
THE COUNT DE RETHEL: AN HISTORICAL NOVEL. TAKEN FROM THE FRENCH. DEDICATED (BY PERMISSION) TO THE LADY VISCOUNTESS HEREFORD. IN THREE VOLUMES.
>London: Printed for T. Hookham, at his Circulating Library, the Corner of Hanover-Street, Hanover-Square, 1779.

I ii, iii, 276p; II 276p; III 286p. 12mo. 9s bound (MR), 7s 6d sewed or 9s bound (adv.).
MR 60: 481 (June 1779); AF II: 877.
BL 1154.1.2; EM 2907: 4; ESTC t117379 (BI O; EA Ps).

Notes. Adv. SJC 21–23 Sept 1779; adv. includes comments from CR and LR and twice gives name as 'Bethel'. In fact the quotation said to be from the CR for July is from the MR for June (no CR rev. located for this novel).
Adv. end vol. 2 of *The History of the Hon. Mrs. Rosemont* (1781: 17).

MR [William Enfield]: 'This novel is sufficiently enriched with variety of incident and sentiment to raise it above the character of insipidity. It is written in an easy style, and, without calling for any vigorous exertions of the understanding, or producing any violent agitations of the heart, may afford an agreeable amusement for a leisure hour.'

1779: 3 ANON.
COXHEATH-CAMP: A NOVEL. IN A SERIES OF LETTERS. BY A LADY. IN TWO VOLUMES.

London: Printed for Fielding and Walker, No. 20, Pater-Noster-Row, 1779.
I 270p; II 274p. 12mo. 6s (MR), 6s sewed or 7s bound (GND, SJC).
MR 60: 239 (Mar 1779); AF II: 916.
C S727.d.77.46-; EM 3003: 2; ESTC t167111 (BI MRu).

Notes. 1-p. dedication (unn.) vol. 1 'To the Ladies, both nobility and commoners, who, during the late campaign, disdained not to share, in order to soften the inconveniencies of their husbands' situation.' Epistolary.
Post-dated; adv. GND 17 Dec 1778; 'Neatly printed on a fine paper . . . And embellished with a half-sheet Perspective View, engraved by Walker, of the Royal Review of the Encampment.' Adv. SJC 5 Jan 1779.
Further edn: Dublin, 1779 (Printed for Messrs. Price, Whitestone, Wilkinson, Williams, Walker [and 12 others in Dublin], 2 vols., 12mo), EM 6422: 3, ESTC t140103.

MR [William Enfield]: 'The title of this novel led us to expect, what the relation of the adventures of an encampment in the hands of a master might have produced, wit and satire; instead of which we meet with nothing but that kind of sentimental narrative, which, though in itself not unpleasant, has been served up in such a variety of ways by the present race of novelists, that we are almost sick of the dish.'

THE HERMIT OF THE ROCK
See LE PILEUR D'APLIGNY

LETTERS TO AND FROM THE COUNTESS DU BARRY
See PIDANSAT DE MAIROBERT, Mathieu-François

MODERN ANECDOTE OF THE ANCIENT FAMILY OF THE KINKVER-VANKOTSDARSPRAKENGOTCHDERNS
See CRAVEN, Elizabeth, Margravine of Brandenburgh-Anspach and Bayreuth

PRINCE ARTHUR
See BICKNELL, Alexander

SHENSTONE GREEN
See PRATT, Samuel Jackson

THE SORROWS OF WERTER
See GOETHE, Johann Wolfgang von

1779: 4   ANON.
SUTTON-ABBEY. A NOVEL. IN A SERIES OF LETTERS, FOUNDED ON FACTS.

>London: Printed for Richardson and Urquhart, under the Royal Exchange, 1779.
>I viii, 211p; II 168p. 12mo. 6s bound (MR).
>MR 62: 324 (Apr 1780); AF II: 4301.
>C 7720.d.1297-; EM 3051: 11; ESTC n024956 (NA MH-H).

Notes. Has been attributed to Henry Summersett.
Epistolary.
Further edn: Dublin, 1780 (Printed by James Williams, for the Company of Booksellers, 1 vol., 12mo), ESTC n024957. German trans. Leipzig, 1781 (*Sutton Abtey*) (EAG).

   MR [Edmund Cartwright]: 'In Sutton-Abbey we meet with nothing sufficiently excellent or defective to distinguish it from the common run of second rate novels.'

THE SYLPH
See CAVENDISH, Georgiana

THE TUTOR OF TRUTH
See PRATT, Samuel Jackson

1779: 5   ANON.
THE WEDDING RING; OR THE HISTORY OF MISS SIDNEY. IN A SERIES OF LETTERS. IN THREE VOLUMES.

>London: Printed for F. Noble, near Middle Row, Holborn; and J. Noble, in St Martin's Court, St. Martin's Lane, 1779.
>I viii, 220p; II 235p; III 230p. 12mo. 7s 6d sewed (CR), 9s (MR), 7s 6d sewed or 9s bound (PA).
>CR 47: 477 (June 1779); MR 60: 324 (Apr 1779); AF II: 4725.
>BL C.141.bb.6; EM 4790: 5; ESTC t126827 (NA MH-H [imperf.], PU).

Notes. 6 pp. advs. end vol. 3. Epistolary.
Post-dated; adv. as published PA 7 Nov 1778; second publisher is 'P. Desbrow, successor to J. Noble'; by the same author as *Sketches from Nature* (1778: 6).
Further edn: Dublin, 1779 (Printed for S. Price, W. and H. Whitestone, T. Wilkinson, R. Fitzsimons, J. Williams [and 9 others in Dublin], 2 vols., 12mo), ESTC n035690. German trans. Breslau, 1780 (*Der Trauring*) (Price).

   CR: 'This work, as we are told in the preface, is the production of a female pen. . . . Had every novel the same tendency to promote the interests of truth and virtue with the present, they might form a valuable part of the female library.'

   MR [William Enfield]: 'The character of an abandoned libertine, who commits the vilest offences against decorum, humanity, and religion, is so disgusting, that nothing is more astonishing than that novels, in which such characters are *minutely* described, should pass with innocent female readers for books of agreeable entertainment: unless it be the ignorance or presumption of their writers, who recommend them to the public as books of excellent moral tendency. The bad effect of the exhibition of such characters, is by no means counterbalanced by the good impression that may arise from the execution of poetic justice in the catastrophe of the tale, in which the contemptible hero is punished, and the innocent object of his machinations escapes into the arms of a virtuous lover. We must therefore add the Wedding Ring to the long catalogue of unprofitable novels.'

1779: 6   [BICKNELL, Alexander].
PRINCE ARTHUR: AN ALLEGORICAL ROMANCE. THE STORY FROM SPENSER. IN TWO VOLUMES.
>London: Printed for G. Riley, Curzon-Street, May-Fair; And sold by F. Newbery, Corner of St. Paul's Church Yard, 1779.
>I vii, ix, 237p; II xii, xi, 238p. 12mo. 6s (CR), 6s bound (MR), 5s sewed or 6s 6d bound (PA).
>CR 46: 461–4 (Dec 1778); MR 60: 324 (Apr 1779); AF II: 335.
>BL 12410.bbb.19; EM 1: 7; ESTC t134638 (BI C; NA CtY-BR, CSmH, IU, PU &c.).

Notes. A paraphrase in prose of Edmund Spenser's *Faerie Queene* (ESTC).
2-pp. (unn.) dedication 'To the Honourable Lady Howe' vol. 1; 2 pp. advs. end vol. 2.
Post-dated; adv. as published PA 4 Nov 1778. Adv. under heading 'Presents for Youth at School' and with 'or, Portraits of Virtue and Vice' inserted after 'Prince Arthur:', SJC 6–8 Apr 1779.

CR: 'The last six books of Spenser having been lost, the author of these volumes has endeavoured to supply the defect by lengthening the narrative from his own fancy; at the same time that he has made considerable alterations in various parts, to preserve uniformity, and bring the story to a regular conclusion' (p. 461). 'In a work of this kind, it may be presumed that poetical embellishments will be often sacrificed to the less figurative nature of prose composition; but if the narrative loses in point of ornament, it gains in that of perspicuity; and we doubt not, that this romance will afford entertainment to those who would trace the luxuriant invention of Spenser, divested of the antiquity of his language' (pp. 463–4).

MR [William Enfield]: 'At a period when the generality of Writers, under pretence of adhering to nature, are forsaking the paths of fancy, and in avoiding extravagance, are sinking into insipidity, there is some share of merit in recalling the attention of the age to the sacred relics of genius, transmitted from ancient times. . . . Those who are already well acquainted with the admired original, will not perhaps relish the idea of modernizing and *prosaicising* Spenser; but Readers of another class will probably find entertainment, perhaps instruction, in this imperfect reflection of the images, sentiments, and characters of the Fairy Queen.'

BRANDENBURGH-ANSPACH AND BAYREUTH, Elizabeth, Margravine of
See CRAVEN, Elizabeth

BRISCOE, Sophia
See CAVENDISH, Georgiana, Duchess of Devonshire, THE SYLPH

1779: 7   CARTWRIGHT, Mrs [H.].
THE GENEROUS SISTER. A NOVEL. IN A SERIES OF LETTERS. BY
MRS. CARTWRIGHT. IN TWO VOLUMES.

> London: Printed for J. Bew, No. 28, Pater-Noster-Row, 1779.
> I 218p; II 297p. 12mo. 5s sewed (CR), 5s (MR), 5s sewed or 6s bound (SJC).
> CR 49: 75 (Jan 1780); MR 60: 324–5 (Apr 1779); AF I: 623.
> TxHR WRC PR3339.C42A63 1779; ESTC n002410.

Notes. 3 pp. advs. advs. end vol. 2. Epistolary.

Adv. SJC 5–7 Jan 1779.

German trans. Leipzig, 1780 (*Die grossmüthige Schwester*) (EAG).

CR: 'The artifices and horrors of the Stanhopean system are emphatically described in the story of miss Donaldson, miss Warburton, and sir William Dunbar.'

MR [William Enfield]: 'When the Reader has half an hour to spare, and finds himself disinclined, either to be fatigued with thinking, or to be disturbed by emotion, he cannot pass it in more indolent amusement, than in turning over these little volumes.'

CARTWRIGHT, Mrs. [H.], **MEMOIRS OF LADY ELIZA AUDLEY** is retrans. of *Memoires de Miledi B****. *Par Madame R**** by Charlotte Marie-Anne Charbonnier de La Guesnerie, first trans. as *Memoirs of Lady Harriot Butler*, 1761/2, JR 663, AF I: 1804.

1779: 8   [?CAVENDISH, Georgiana, Duchess of Devonshire].
THE SYLPH; A NOVEL. IN TWO VOLUMES.

> London: Printed for T. Lowndes, No. 77, Fleet-Street, 1779.
> I 258p; II 200p. 12mo. 6s sewed (CR), 5s (MR), 5s sewed or 6s bound (PA).
> CR 48: 319 (Oct 1779); MR 60: 240 (Mar 1779); AF II: 648.
> MH-H *EC75.D4985.779s; EM 2141: 8; ESTC n023232 (NA CtY-BR, CSmH, MnU).

Notes. Some doubt on authorship is cast by a receipt for 12 gns. paid by Lowndes on 29 Oct 1778 to S. Briscoe; the word 'Sylph' is written in the lower left-hand corner (BM Add. Mss. 38,728 fol. 35). Possibly Sophia Briscoe, author of *Miss Melmoth* (1771: 37) and *The Fine Lady* (1772: 31), also published by Lowndes. In private but never in public the Duchess admitted authorship of the autobiographical *Sylph*, according to Amanda Foreman (*Georgiana Duchess of Devonshire* [London: HarperCollins, 1998], pp. 59–60). Foreman also reports that the Burneys were outraged when Lowndes advertised *The Sylph* together with *Evelina* (1778: 10) and implied that they were by the same author (p. 411).

4 pp. advs. end vol. 1, 14 pp. advs. end vol. 2. Epistolary.

Post-dated; adv. PA and GND 4 Dec 1778.

Further edns: London, 1779, ESTC n024431; Dublin, 1779 (Printed for S. Price, J. Williams, W. Colles, W. Wilson, T. Walker [and 9 others in Dublin], 1 vol., 12mo), EM 173: 4, ESTC t067335; Dublin, 1780, EM 3457: 14, ESTC t119338; London, 1783, EM 3410: 11, ESTC t117371; Dublin, 1784, ESTC n024428; NSTC lists edns. in 1804. German trans. Leipzig, 1779 (*Der Sylphe*) (EAG); French trans. Paris, 1784 (*La Sylphe*) (HWS).

CR: 'There is ingenuity in the plan of this novel, and a sufficient variety of events, but several improbabilities in the subordinate circumstances.'

MR [William Enfield]: 'This story has the uncommon merit of some originality in its plan; the story is agreeably related; and many good moral reflections are suggested in the course of the narrative.'

1779: 9   [CRAVEN, Elizabeth, Margravine of Brandenburgh-Anspach and Bayreuth].
MODERN ANECDOTE OF THE ANCIENT FAMILY OF THE KINKVER-VANKOTSDARSPRAKENGOTCHDERNS: A TALE FOR CHRISTMAS 1779. DEDICATED TO THE HONOURABLE HORACE WALPOLE, ESQ.

> London: Printed for the Author; and sold by M. Davenhill, No. 13, Cornhill; J. Bew, Pater-Noster-Row; and the Booksellers in Town and Country. n.d. [ESTC: 1779].
> 84p. 8vo. 2s sewed (CR), 1s 6d (MR).
> CR 49: 122–3 (Feb 1780); MR 62: 368–70 (May 1780); AF II: 930.
> BL 1079.i.12(4); EM 1877: 11; ESTC t068887 (NA CtY-Walpole, CtY-BR, NjP &c.).

Notes. 10-pp. dedication to Horace Walpole.
Further edns: London, n.d. [1779?], ESTC t073214; Dublin, 1781 (Luke White, 1 vol., 12mo), ESTC n004740; London, 1781, ESTC t069518; Anspac [sic], 1787, ESTC n004741. German trans. Leipzig, 1781 (Anekdote aus der alten Familie der Kinkvervankotsdarspraken-gotschderns) (EAG).

CR: 'Why it should be called both an Anecdote and a Tale in the title page does not appear: it might as well indeed have been styled a Novel or a History. Call it by what name you please, it is prettily written, and will afford as agreeable an hour's amusement as any thing of this kind which we have lately met with.'

MR [Samuel Badcock]: 'This is the production of a sprightly mind, somewhat of the Rabelaic cast. The story itself is rather a simple one, and required very little invention as to plot, machinery, or denouëment. It is called a Tale for Christmas, and a person with a lively fancy and a voluble tongue might have told it extempore for the amusement of a company over a good fire, on a Christmas evening' (p. 368).

1779: 10   [GOETHE, Johann Wolfgang von]; [MALTHUS, Daniel or GRAVES, Richard? (trans.)].
THE SORROWS OF WERTER: A GERMAN STORY.

> London: Printed for J. Dodsley, Pall-Mall, 1779.
> I viii, 168p; II 172p. 8vo. 5s sewed (CR, MR).
> CR 47: 477 (June 1779); MR 61: 74 (July 1779).
> BL 12555.a.34; EM 174: 3: ESTC t096191 (BI Gu, Ota; NA MH-H, NjP, ViU &c.).

Notes. Trans. of Die Leiden des jungen Werthers (Leipzig, 1774) apparently from the French trans. Werther, traduit de l'Allemand by G. Deyverdun (Maastricht, 1776).
Epistolary.
Adv. SJC 27–29 Apr 1779; title continues: 'founded on Fact'.
Further edns: Dublin, 1780 (Printed for C. Jackson, 2 vols., 12mo), EM 3811: 6, ESTC t155711; London, 1782, EM 5164: 7, ESTC t096194; London, 1783, EM 5589: 4, ESTC t155713; London, 1785, EM 3915: 6, ESTC t096190; Dublin, n.d. [1785?], EM 3881: 18, ESTC t062637; 20 further entries in ESTC (including various translations); WC has 10 entries between 1800 and 1850; NSTC lists edn. in 1826. Trans. by J. R. Green ('John

Gifford') published *Novelist's Magazine*, 1789, RM 1169. Different French trans. Erlangen, 1776 (*Les Souffrances du jeune Werther*) (BN).

CR: 'Notwithstanding the translator attempts in his preface to palliate the pernicious tendency of the work before us, we cannot but agree with those who consider Mr. Goethé, its original author, as the apologist of suicide.'

MR [William Enfield]: 'In this little work is drawn, by a masterly hand, a lively picture of the horrors of a mind disordered by the phrensy of a disappointed passion, and at length abandoning itself to despair, and seeking refuge from its sorrows in a voluntary death. An excellent moral may be deduced from it—if the reader pleases.'

1779: 11 [GRAVES, Richard].
COLUMELLA; OR, THE DISTRESSED ANCHORET. A COLLOQUIAL TALE BY THE EDITOR OF THE SPIRITUAL QUIXOTE.

London: Printed for J. Dodsley, Pall-Mall, 1779.
I iv, 240p; II 248p. 12mo. 5s sewed (CR, MR).
CR 47: 454–7 (June 1779); MR 61: 315–6 (Oct 1779); AF II: 1691.
C 7720.d.1311–12; EM 2601: 5; ESTC t010229 (BI MRu, O, Oa &c.; NA CtY, CSmH, DLC, ICN, IU, MH-H, NjP, PU &c.; EA ZWTU).

Notes. Adv., 'adorned with frontispieces', SJC 6–8 Apr 1779.
German trans. Leipzig, 1780 (*Kolumella; oder der geplagte Annakoret*) (EAG).

CR: 'The design of this publication is to expose the folly and imprudence of retiring from the world and deserting our duty in it, before we have done any thing to merit a discharge from its services' (p. 454). 'Though it must be confessed our ingenious author has made the most of his argument, yet we cannot help thinking that chearfulness and tranquility of mind depend more upon *disposition* than *situation*, provided that situation be unattended with positive evils' (p. 457).

MR [Edmund Cartwright]: 'So far from shewing any disposition to injure society by retiring from the world, it seems to be the general study of all ranks to obtrude themselves as much as possible upon the Public, and to dissipate in active idleness, if we may so express ourselves, that time which ought to have been devoted to their own private concerns.... His characters are, in general, drawn with truth and humour, and his wit, if we except a few stale jokes, and a feeble attempt to ridicule Dr. Priestley and his fixed air, is neither unclassical nor inelegant.'

1779: 12 KEATE, George.
SKETCHES FROM NATURE; TAKEN, AND COLOURED, IN A JOURNEY TO MARGATE. PUBLISHED FROM THE ORIGINAL DESIGNS. BY GEORGE KEATE, ESQ.

London: Printed for J. Dodsley, Pall-Mall, 1779.
I vii, 207p; II 223p. 8vo. 5s sewed (CR, MR).
CR 47: 376–9 (May 1779); MR 61: 111–17 (Aug 1779).
C Oates 475–6; EMf; ESTC t122134 (BI E, L [imperf.], KIK; NA CtY, CSmH, IU, PU, TxU &c.).

Notes. Adv., 'In a few Days will be published, Elegantly printed in Two Vols.', SJC 1–4 May 1779.

Further edns: London, 1779, ESTC t119885; Dublin, 1779 (Printed for S. Price, J. Sheppard, R. Cross, J. Potts, J. Williams [and 11 others in Dublin], 2 vols., 12mo), ESTC t213942; London, 1782, ESTC t160117; Dresden, 1784, ESTC t149388; London, 1790, ESTC t072181; 1 further entry in ESTC; NSTC lists edn. in 1802. German trans. Leipzig, 1780 (*Skizzen aus der Natur auf einer Reise nach Margathe entworfen*) (EAG).

CR: 'The work we are now considering, though formed in some measure on the plan of the Sentimental Journey, has that share of originality, and contains those agreeable Sketches of Nature, which cannot fail of rendering it acceptable to those who read for amusement' (p. 377). 'This work has one circumstance to recommend it, which is of no small importance in compositions of this kind: and that is, it contains no effusions of spleen or ill humour; nor any thing that can offend the morals of the reader' (p. 379).

MR [Ralph Griffiths]: 'Yorick left many natural children, or, in more familiar phrase, *bye-blows*, but Mr Keate is the legitimate offspring of that singular and celebrated writer; and it is with peculiar satisfaction we recognise the father's features in the son' (p. 111). 'These Sketches from Nature are enlivened with a variety of entertaining anecdotes, real or figured, together with some episodical stories, well told, and naturally introduced' (p. 117).

1779: 13   [LE PILEUR D'APLIGNY].
THE HERMIT OF THE ROCK; OR, THE HISTORY OF THE MAR-CHIONESS DE LAUSANNE, AND THE COMTE DE LUZY. TRANS-LATED FROM A FRENCH MANUSCRIPT. IN THREE VOLUMES.

> London: Printed for F. Noble, at his Circulating Library in Holborn; and B. Desbrow, Succesor to J. Noble, at his Circulating Library, in St Martin's Court, near Leicester Square, 1779.
> I viii, 260; II 232p; III 211p. 12mo. 9s bound (MR, LC).
> MR 60: 325 (Apr 1779); AF II: 1907.
> O 249.s.491–493; ESTC n051274 (NA ICN).

Notes. According to Bodl., trans. from Le Pileur d'Apligny; BN has only later (Paris, 1820) edn. of his *L'Ermite de la Roche-Noire, ou la Marquise de Lausanne.* No record of earlier French original in BLC or NUC.
Dedication to the Hon. Lady Priscilla Bertie v–viii, signed 'The Translator'. 9 pp. advs. end vol. 3. Epistolary.
Adv. LC 47: 163 (15–17 Feb 1780).
Further edns: Dublin, 1779 (Printed for Messrs. Price, R. Cross, Williams, Walker, E. Cross [and 10 others in Dublin], 3 vols., 12mo), ESTC n006773; London, 1789, t126576. German trans. Leipzig, 1780 (*Der Einsiedler auf dem Felsen*) (Price).

MR [William Enfield]: 'The emotions of the gentle passions of love are in this novel unfolded, through a series of tender and interesting incidents, in language so natural and pathetic, that it cannot fail of being read with pleasure by such as are capable of feeling, and have not learned to despise the refinements and delicacies of a sentimental attachment.'

MELMOTH, Courtney
See PRATT, Samuel Jackson

1779: 14   NUGENT, Miss, and Miss TAYLOR of Twickenham.
*THE INDISCREET MARRIAGE; OR HENRY AND SOPHIA SOMERVILLE.

IN A SERIES OF LETTERS. BY MISS NUGENT AND MISS TAYLOR OF
TWICKENHAM.
>London: Dodsley, 1779.
>3 vols. 12mo. 7s 6d sewed (CR, PA), 9s bound (MR).
>CR 49: 76 (Jan 1780); MR 60: 480 (June 1779); AF II: 3089.
>No copy located.

Notes. Epistolary.

Adv., 'Now in the Press, and speedily will be published by Subscription', PA 30 Nov 1778; by 'Miss Nugent, Daughter to Captain Walter Nugent, who was killed in the present War in America; and Miss Taylor, of Twickenham'; 'Subscriptions are taken in at the Circulating Library, Twickenham; and at the following Booksellers, viz. Dodsley, in Pall-mall; Ridley, in St James's Street; Walter, at Charing-cross; Robinson and Evans, in Pater-noster Row; and T. Jones, in Minster Street, Reading.'

German trans. Leipzig, 1781 (*Die unüberlegte Heirath*) (EAG).

CR: 'Surprisingly well! for two ladies, "whose ages together do not exceed thirty years." To masters and misses about their own age, the work will probably appear not a little entertaining.'

MR [William Enfield]: 'A novel which appears before the Public under the sanction of two female names, seems entitled, if not to favour, at least to lenity. Instead, therefore, of entering into a particular enumeration of the defects of this work, we shall only express a wish, that those females who think themselves possessed of sufficient genius and invention to write for the entertainment of the Public, would not content themselves with that moderate share of literary reputation which a tolerable facility in the art of epistolary writing may have obtained among the circle of their friends, but by conversing intimately with the best models of good writing, acquire that elegance and refinement of taste, which will neither be capable of being pleased with, nor expect to please by, *mediocrity*.'

1779: 15   PENN, James.
THE SURRY COTTAGE. BY JAMES PENN, VICAR OF CLAVERING
CUM LANGLEY, ESSEX; CHAPLAIN TO THE RIGHT HON. EARL OF
GOWER, AND LECTURER OF ST. ANN'S, ALDERSGATE.
>London: Printed for, and sold by the Author in Wilderness Row, Goswell Street, and
>   Mr Bladon in Paternoster-Row, 1779.
>iv, 267p. 12mo. 3s bound (CR 48), 3s (CR 51, MR), 2s 6d unbound, and 3s bound (t.p.).
>CR 48: 398–9 (Nov 1779), CR 51: 319 (Apr 1781); MR 63: 467 (Dec 1780); AF II: 3294.
>BL N.1654; EM 6666: 6; ESTC t070714 (BI O; NA NjR).

Notes. CR 48: 'The story is related in a series of conversations, supposed to have passed in a little society, which occasionally met at a cottage, where one of the company resided. The narrative is diversified by a variety of observations on political, moral, and sentimental subjects. The story has a laudable tendency; but is full of improbabilities. We have likewise observed a number of little inaccuracies in the language . . . (p. 398).

CR 51: 'If this cottage be not distinguished for variety of entertainment, it at least abounds with good-sense, and with lessons of morality, which may render it more profitable in the perusal than many other productions of the novel kind.'

MR [Edmund Cartwright]: 'The materials of which the Surry Cottage is composed, though neither elegant nor curious, are at least sound and useful. To speak without a metaphor; much plain sense, and many practical aphorisms, may be collected from this unostentatious little volume, for which, in more splendid performances, the Reader will frequently look in vain.'

1779: 16   [PIDANSAT DE MAIROBERT, Mathieu-François].
LETTERS TO AND FROM THE COUNTESS DU BARRY, THE LAST MISTRESS OF LEWIS XV, OF FRANCE; CONTAINING HER CORRESPONDENCE WITH THE PRINCES OF THE BLOOD, MINISTERS OF STATE, AND OTHERS: INCLUDING THE HISTORY OF THAT FAVOURITE, AND SEVERAL CURIOUS ANECDOTES OF THE COURT OF VERSAILLES DURING THE LAST YEARS OF THAT REIGN. WITH EXPLANATORY NOTES. TRANSLATED FROM THE FRENCH.

London: Printed for G. Kearsley, No. 46, Fleet-street 1779.
iv, iv, 167p. 8vo. 3s (CR, SJC), 3s sewed (MR).
CR 49: 128–32 (Feb 1780); MR 62: 491 (June 1780).
BL T.987(8); EM 5146: 2; ESTC t038545 (NA CSmH, MoSW, NjP, &c.).

Notes. Trans. of Lettres originales de Madame la Comtesse Du Barry (Londres, 1779). [See also Darnton.]
1 p. advs. end vol.
Adv. SJC 20–23 Nov 1779; 'The Booksellers of Paris knew the Danger of publishing this Collection (which exposed the Folly of the King, and the Infamy of his Mistress) too well, to risque an open Sale. They knew also, that the Countess du Barry had many Enemies at Court, particularly amongst the Ladies; these they confidentially employed in circulating several thousand Copies. So general has been the Demand, that, at a remote Place, Geneva, it has been printed no less than six Times in less than as many Weeks!!!'
Further edns: London, 1779, ESTC n019196; London, 1779, ESTC t179972; Dublin, 1780 (Printed by P. Higley. For the Company of Booksellers, 1 vol., 12mo), ESTC t110907; London, 1780, ESTC n011322. 3rd edn. adv. MC 22 Jan 1780; this adv. is headed: 'Those who are desirous of acquiring an elegance of stile, and a pleasing familiarity, particularly in the epistolary line, will receive considerable benefit by an attentive perusal of the following collection, which consists of One Hundred and Sixty-four Letters upon a great variety of Subjects.' Probable German trans. (catalogue announcement) London, 1779 (Die Geschichte der Gräfinn von Barry in Originalbriefen) (EAG).
CR is doubtful about the authenticity of the letters but pronounces them 'entertaining'.
   MR [William Enfield]: 'Perhaps there is no part of the globe where female influence is so extensive as in France. Madame Du Barry is only one instance, among several, in which the mistress of a King of France has been in fact his prime minister. In this capacity she acted for many years: and whether these letters be genuine or not (which is a point we do not undertake to determine), they exhibit, in a lively and entertaining manner, the amours and political intrigues of this celebrated woman.'

1779: 17   [PRATT, Samuel Jackson].
SHENSTONE-GREEN; OR, THE NEW PARADISE LOST. BEING A HISTORY OF HUMAN NATURE. IN THREE VOLUMES. WRITTEN BY THE PROPRIETOR OF THE GREEN. THE EDITOR COURTNEY MELMOTH.

London: Printed for R. Baldwin, at No. 47, in Pater-Noster-Row, 1779.
I 216p; II 210p; II 191p. 8vo. 7s 6d sewed (CR, MR).
CR 47: 207–10 (Mar 1779); MR 61: 73–4 (July 1779); AF II: 3586.
C 7720.e.287-; EM 98: 5; ESTC t057352 (BI BL, Dt, NOu; NA ICN, MH-H, NjP, PU, ViU &c.).

Notes. Adv., 'Thursday next will be published, in Three neat Pocket Volumes', SJC 11–13 Feb 1779; adv. as published SJC 16–18 Feb 1779.
Further edns: London, 1780, EM 4506: 1, ESTC t120260; London, 1787, ESTC n022333. German trans. Mannheim and Leipzig, 1780 (*Shenstone-Grün oder Das neue verlorene Paradies*) (Price).

CR: 'Besides a variety of incidents, this novel contains a picturesque description of several characters, which are well supported; and the author has adhered to nature in delineating the progress and the series of events' (p. 210).

MR [William Enfield]: 'The narrative discovers no inconsiderable powers of invention; the style is in general more correct, and at the same time more easy and inartificial than that of some of the Author's former works; and several of the characters are conceived with boldness, and drawn with lively strokes of humour: Mr. Melmoth has, however, suffered his favourite idea, maintained at large in his *liberal opinions,* "that to be good is not the way to be happy" to give a general tincture to the work. . . . '

1779: 18   [PRATT, Samuel Jackson].
THE TUTOR OF TRUTH BY THE AUTHOR OF THE PUPIL OF PLEAS-URE &C &C. IN TWO VOLUMES.

London: Printed for Richardson and Urquhart, under the Royal Exchange, 1779.
I xiv, 225p; II 291p. 12mo. 5s sewed (CR), 6s bound (MR), 5s sewed or 6s bound (SJC).
CR 49: 63–5 (Jan 1780); MR 62: 324 (Apr 1780); AF II: 3591.
MH-H *EC75.p8896.779t; EM 1471: 15; ESTC n014258 (BI O; NA InU-Li, ICU [vol.1 only], ViU).

Notes. Dedicated to Lady Miller of Bath-Easton Villa.
Adv. SJC 9–11 Dec 1779.
Further edns: Dublin, 1781 (Printed for C. Jackson, 2 vols., 12mo), ESTC n045635; Dublin, 1781, ESTC n019791; London, 1787, ESTC t223479. German trans. Leipzig, 1781 (*Der Vormund der Rechtschaffenheit*) (Price).

CR: 'There is a great variety of characters and incidents interwoven into this agreeable novel, which not only contribute to render the fable interesting, but to enforce the moral . . . ' (p. 63). 'The characters . . . on the whole, are well supported, and the Tutor of Truth is a pleasant and instructive companion' (p. 65)

MR [William Enfield]: 'Though this piece is, perhaps, more inoffensive than any of the former productions of this Writer, it must also be said, that it is less entertaining. In the humorous characters which are introduced, we can discover little of the true comic. The wit of these characters consists almost entirely in the false pronunciation or spelling of words, or in the use of vulgar or pedantic language.'

1780: 1   ANON.

THE AFFECTING HISTORY OF TWO YOUNG GENTLEWOMEN, WHO
WERE RUINED BY THEIR EXCESSIVE ATTACHMENT TO THE AMUSE-
MENTS OF THE TOWN. TO WHICH ARE ADDED, MANY PRACTICAL
NOTES, BY DR. TYPO, P. T. M.

> London: Printed by T. Baldwin in Great-May's Buildings; And sold by W. Bingley, in
> the Strand, And H. Woodgate, in St Paul's Church-Yard, n.d. [ESTC: 1780?].
> viii, 86p. 8vo. 1s (t.p.).
> BL 1079.i.12(5); EM 1877: 12; ESTC t068883. WC also lists TxHR.

Notes. Preface iii–viii.

ALWYN: OR THE GENTLEMAN COMEDIAN
See HOLCROFT, Thomas

1780: 2   ANON.

CHARACTERS OF THE PRESENT MOST CELEBRATED COURTEZANS:
INTERSPERSED WITH A VARIETY OF SECRET ANECDOTES NEVER
BEFORE PUBLISHED.

> London: Printed for M. James, Pater-noster Row, 1780.
> 212p. 8vo. 2s 6d sewed (PA).
> BL Cup.403.pp.1; EM 1083: 4; ESTC t067809 (BI E; NA CtY-BR, CLU-S/C).

Notes. Adv. PA 13 May 1780.

A DIARY KEPT IN AN EXCURSION TO LITTLE HAMPTON
See PHILLIPS, Peregrine, App. B: 5

EMMA CORBETT
See PRATT, Samuel Jackson

1780: 3   ANON.

HARCOURT; A SENTIMENTAL NOVEL. IN A SERIES OF LETTERS. BY
THE AUTHORESS OF EVELINA.

> Dublin: Printed for C. Jackson by J. and R. Byrn, 1780.
> I 135p; II 114p. 12mo.
> BL Cup.403.z.53; EM 6363: 12; ESTC t140056 (BI C, Dt; NA PU).

Notes. Not by Frances Burney, author of *Evelina* (1778: 10).
In vol. 2 text of novel starts on p. 3. Epistolary.

THE HISTORY OF LADY BETTESWORTH AND CAPTAIN HASTINGS
See M., E.

1780: 4   ANON.
THE HISTORY OF MISS HARRIOT FAIRFAX, CONTAINING I. THE
DEATH OF HER PARENTS, SHE IS LEFT AN ORPHAN, TAKEN HOME
BY AN OLD MAIDEN AUNT, WITH AN EXTRAORDINARY ACCOUNT
OF THAT LADY'S CROSSES IN LOVE, WHICH IS THE REASON SHE
DESPISES MANKIND IN GENERAL. II. HARRIOT'S BEAUTY, HOW
HER AUNT MAKES HER BEHAVE AT CHURCH, A GENTLEMAN
FALLS IN LOVE WITH HER AT HER WINDOW, MAKES PROPOSALS
TO MARRY HER, IS REFUSED BY HER AUNT, &C. III. ANOTHER
FAMILY INTRODUCED, A PARTICULAR FRIENDSHIP BETWEEN
LOUISA BEESLEY AND HARRIOT, A GENTLEMAN FALLS IN LOVE
WITH HER IN THE PUBLIC WALKS. IV. MR. BEESLEY INTERCEDES
FOR MR. TOWNLEY, IS REFUSED BY MISS BLACKBOURN, WHICH
OCCASIONS A GREAT STORM, THE INTERESTING HISTORY OF
MISS AMELIA WILLIS, THE SUDDEN ARRIVAL OF TWO WEST INDI-
ANS, WHO THEY ARE, AND FOUR HEARTS ENTANGLED IN LOVE'S
SNARE V. FRANKLIN, A YOUNG MERCHANT, INTRODUCED, PART-
ING SCENE BETWEEN THE FOUR LOVERS, WITH THAT OF
BEESLEY'S PARENT, MUTUAL PROMISES TO BE ETERNALLY CON-
STANT, &C. VI. FRANKLIN MAKES LOVE TO HARRIOT AFTER THE
DEPARTURE OF HER ADORED CHARLES, THE DEATH OF LOUISA'S
MOTHER, &C. VII. OLD MR. BEESLEY MARRIES MISS BLACK-
BOURN, HARRIOT IS COURTED BY A LORD, BUT REFUSES HIM
ON ACCOUNT OF HER LOVE FOR YOUNG BEESLEY, WHO IS GONE
TO THE WEST INDIES. VIII. A LETTER IS FORGED TO MAKE
HARRIOT BELIEVE HER LOVER IS DEAD, WHICH PUTS THE
WHOLE FAMILY IN TEARS. IX. THE YOUNG LOVERS ARRIVE AT
BARBADOS, GET THEIR FRIENDS CONSENT TO RETURN TO ENG-
LAND TO MARRY THE TWO YOUNG LADIES, WITH SOME
ACCOUNT OF THE BEAUTIFUL MARIA, THEY EMBARK FOR ENG-
LAND TOGETHER, AND ARRIVE AT MR. BEESLEY'S, AN APPAR-
ITION SUPPOSED, FAINTING, SIGHING, BUT A DEAL OF JOY AFTER
SORROW. X. MARIA IS MARRIED TO LORD L——, A DUEL, THE
TWO COUPLE ARE MARRIED, PREPARATIONS FOR LEAVING
ENGLAND, FARTHER ACCOUNT OF AMELIA WILLIS, AND MR.
TOWNLEY, WHO HAD FOLLOWED HIM THROUGH MOST PARTS
OF EUROPE IN DISGUISE. XI. A PARTING BETWEEN ALL FRIENDS,
THE LOVERS ARRIVE SAFE AT BARBADOES, EVERY THING IS
SETTLED TO THEIR MINDS, A HAPPY CONCLUSION. WRITTEN BY
A LADY.

London: Printed by T. Sabine and Sons, 81, Shoe Lane, Fleet Street, n.d. [BLC: 1780?;
   ESTC: 1800?].
64p. 8vo. 6d (t.p.).
BL 12331.d.32(1); EM 802: 28 and 4814: 3; ESTC t064195.

1780: 5   ANON.
HOW SHE LOST HIM; OR, THE HISTORY OF MISS WYNDHAM. IN TWO VOLUMES.

Dublin: Printed and sold by S. Colbert, at his Circulating Library, No. 69, Stephen-
   Street, six doors from George's-Street, 1780.
I 113p; II 216p. 12mo. British Half Crown bound (t.p.).
C Hib.7.780.41; ESTC t200329.

Notes. Pagination continuous between the 2 vols.; vol. 2 (no t.p.) begins on p. 115. 1 p. advs.
facing t.p. to vol. 1 and 1 p. advs. end vol. 1. Epistolary.

1780: 6   ANON.
THE INDIAN ADVENTURER; OR THE HISTORY OF MR. VANNECK, A NOVEL, FOUNDED ON FACTS.

London: Printed for W. Lane, No. 33, Leadenhall-Street, 1780.
237p. 12mo. 3s (CR, half-title), 3s bound (MR).
CR 51: 319 (Apr 1781); MR 63: 233 (Sept 1780).
BL 1154.c.29; EM 2381: 9; ESTC t117481 (NA NjP).

Notes. Last page [238] contains 'Explanation of the Names used in the East Indies, and mentioned in this Work'.
   CR: 'Equally mean and uninteresting with the preceding [*Alwyn*, 1780: 18], but yet more
vulgar and indelicate.'
   MR [William Enfield]: 'Still more insipid and vulgar than the preceding article [*Alwyn*,
1780: 18], and withal insufferably coarse and indelicate.'

1780: 7   ANON.
JULIA STANLEY: A NOVEL. IN A SERIES OF LETTERS. PUBLISHED BY THE AUTHOR OF THE MAN OF FEELING, MAN OF THE WORLD, ROUBIGNE, &C. IN TWO VOLUMES.

Dublin: Printed for C. Jackson, 1780.
I viii, 167p; II 152p. 12mo.
BL C.175.c.9; ESTC t127869 (BI D; NA MH-H).

Notes. Not by Henry Mackenzie, author of *The Man of Feeling* [1771: 46] (ESTC).
2 pp. advs. following t.p. vol. 1, and 'Advertisement to this Edition' signed C. Jackson,
Dublin, 28 Sept 1780, vii–viii. Epistolary.

1780: 8   ANON.
LETTERS BETWEEN CLARA AND ANTONIA: IN WHICH ARE INTER-SPERSED THE INTERESTING MEMOIRS OF LORD DES LUNETTES, A CHARACTER IN REAL LIFE. IN TWO VOLUMES.

London: Printed for J. Bew, in Pater-Noster-Row, 1780.

I viii, 238p; II 260p. 12mo. 5s sewed (CR), 6s bound (MR), 5s sewed or 6s bound (SJC).

CR 50: 239 (Sept 1780); MR 62: 323–4 (Apr 1780); AF II: 2533.

BL 12611.a.8; EM 4826:13; ESTC t031409 (NA CSmH, ICN).

Notes. Dedication to 'That Pattern of Perfection, the Right Hon. Earl —' v–viii signed 'The Editor', Edinburgh, 9 Nov 1779. 4 pp. advs. end vol. 2. Epistolary.

Adv. SJC 25–28 Dec 1779.

German trans. Leipzig, 1780 (*Briefwechsel zwischen Clara und Antonia*) (EAG).

CR: 'There is nothing in these Letters either very entertaining or instructive.'

MR [Edmund Cartwright]: 'To those who read merely for amusement, and who look no higher for it than to the novelist, we may recommend the Letters between Clara and Antonia. The time that will be bestowed on them, if not very usefully employed, will, at least, be spent innocently.'

1780: 9   ANON.

LOUISA WHARTON. A STORY, FOUNDED ON FACTS: WRITTEN BY HERSELF, IN A SERIES OF LETTERS TO A FRIEND. WHEREIN IS DIS-PLAYED SOME PARTICULAR CIRCUMSTANCES WHICH HAPPENED DURING THE BLOODY CONTEST IN AMERICA. I. LOUISA'S FATHER AND MOTHER GO TO BATH; THE AMUSEMENTS OF THAT PLACE DESCRIBED, &C. II. SOME ACCOUNT OF CAPTAIN TRUMAN AND HIS FAMILY; HE FALLS IN LOVE WITH LOUISA; HER BROTHER ARRIVES FROM PHILADELPHIA, AND CONFIRMS THE WAR HAV-ING BROKE OUT. III. CAPTAIN TRUMAN IS ORDERED WITH HIS REGIMENT TO AMERICA; LOUISA IS GREATLY ALARMED, &C. IV. TRUMAN TAKES LEAVE OF LOUISA WITH THE GREATEST TENDER-NESS; SHE GIVES HIM HER PICTURE IN MINIATURE; HE GIVES HER A RING, AND THEY VOW MUTUAL CONSTANCY. V. LOUISA'S FATHER GOES TO LONDON, FROM THENCE, WITH GEORGE HIS SON, SETS OUT FOR PHILADELPHIA. VI. A LETTER FROM YOUNG TRUMAN, FULL OF TENDER EXPRESSIONS, &C. VII. A LETTER FROM HER BROTHER, RELATES THE DEATH OF HER FATHER, AND THE CONFISCATION OF ALL THEIR PROPERTY; THEY ARE GREATLY DISTRESSED; AND LOUISA IS SLIGHTED BY SIR JAMES, &C. VIII. THE HISTORY OF CHARLOTTE MODISH, AND LORD SQUANDER. IX. LOUISA AND HER MOTHER IN A DEPLORABLE SITU-ATION; SHE GETS SOME NEEDLEWORK TO DO, AND IS ADMIRED FOR HER SINGING: LORD SQUANDER TRIES TO SEDUCE HER, &C. X. FANNY IS VERY KIND, BUT GOES INTO THE COUNTRY; LOUISA HEARS THE DISMAL NEWS THAT TRUMAN IS TAKEN BY THE ENEMY, AND CONDEMNED BY WAY OF RETALIATION, &C. XI. A LETTER FROM FANNY, GIVES AN ACCOUNT OF AN UNCLE, WHO IS VERY RICH BY ACCIDENT: HE GIVES THEM MONEY, COMES TO TOWN, &C. XII. SHE HEARS THAT YOUNG TRUMAN IS RELEASED;

HE COMES TO ENGLAND WITH HER BROTHER; THEY ALL MEET AT THE HOUSE OF LOUISA, AND ALL PARTIES ARE MADE HAPPY BY MARRIAGE.

> London: Printed and sold by T. Sabine, No. 81, Shoe Lane, Fleet Stree [*sic*], n.d. [1780?]. 64p. 8vo. 6d (t.p.).
> BL 12612.aaa.2; EM 124: 5; ESTC t066379.

Notes. Frontispiece. Text begins on p. 3. Epistolary.

LOVE AND MADNESS
See CROFT, Sir Herbert

1780: 10   ANON.
MASQUERADES; OR, WHAT YOU WILL. BY THE AUTHOR OF ELIZA WARWICK, &C. IN FOUR VOLUMES.

> London: Printed for J. Bew, in Pater-Noster-Row, 1780.
> I 232p; II 248p; III 288p; IV 299p. 12mo. 12s (CR), 12s bound (MR).
> CR 52: 155 (Aug 1781); MR 65: 74–5 (July 1781); AF II: 2747.
> O Vet. A5f.185–188; ESTC t174950 (NA CtY). WC also lists PU.

Notes. 5 pp. advs. end vol. 3. Epistolary.
The History of Eliza Warwick 1778: 3.
Adv., 'This day was published', LEP 7–9 Feb 1786.
Further edn: Dublin, 1781 (Printed for Messrs. Price, Sleater, W. Watson, Ennis [and 9 others in Dublin], 2 vols., 12mo), EM 3768: 2, ESTC t118993. German trans. Leipzig, 1782–84 (*Maskeraden, oder was euch beliebt*) (RS).

CR: 'This novel . . . may justly lay claim to entertainment, which is, however sometimes precluded by an unpleasing prolixity. But its principal blemishes are a levity of sentiment that occasionally breaks forth in opposition to moral restraint.'

MR [Samuel Badcock]: 'Perhaps it will be deemed tedious and prolix; and here and there the tautology of love may disgust the cold and more critical reader. But with all its redundancies and imperfections, we think this is a very interesting and entertaining Novel' (p. 74). Rev. goes on to point out some objections to the work's 'moral tendency'.

THE OLD ENGLISH BARON
See REEVE, Clara, THE CHAMPION OF VIRTUE (1777: 16)

THE PARSONAGE HOUSE
See BLOWER, Elizabeth

THE RELAPSE, A NOVEL
See ELLIOTT, Miss

1780: 11   ANON.
THE SCHOOL FOR MAJESTY: AN ORIENTAL TALE.

> Dublin: Printed and sold (for the author) by S. Colbert, [no. 69,] Stephen-Street, 1780.

141p. 12mo. 2 British shillings bound (t.p.).
BL 012646.bbb.20; EM 498: 7; ESTC t107629.

Notes. Dedication to Lady Louisa Conolly. 1 p. adv. verso of dedication, facing p. 1. 7 pp. advs. end vol.
Further edns: Dublin, 1781 (Printed and sold, for the author, by S. Colbert, 1 vol., 12mo), ESTC t212585; London, 1783 [*School for Majesty; or the Sufferings of Zomelli*], EM 2146: 2, ESTC n021579.
This edn. not reviewed; 1783 London edn. rev. CR 57: 235 (Mar 1784); MR 71: 224–5 (Sept 1784).

THE SENTIMENTAL TRAVELLER, OR A DESCRIPTIVE TOUR THROUGH LIFE
See **A TRIP TO MELASGE** (1778: 8)

1780: 12   [BLOWER, Elizabeth].
*THE PARSONAGE HOUSE. A NOVEL BY A YOUNG LADY. IN A SERIES OF LETTERS.

London: Printed for J. Macgowan, Paternoster-Row (LC), 1780 (LC).
3 vols. 12mo. 6s sewed (CR), 7s 6d (MR), 6s sewed or 7s 6d bound (LC).
CR 50: 373–6 (Nov 1780); MR 63: 70 (July 1780); AF II: 385.
No copy located.

Notes. Epistolary.
Further edn: Dublin, 1781 (Printed and sold by S. Colbert, 3 vols., 12mo), ESTC t194672.
French trans. n.p., n.d. (*La Maison du Curé*) (HWS); German trans. Leipzig, 1781 (*Das Pfarrhaus*) (Price).
Adv., 'In a few days will be published', LC 47: 403 (25–27 Apr 1780).

CR: '. . . we shall readily acknowledge that the Parsonage House is possessed of no inconsiderable share of real merit, as it is written in an easy and unaffected style, abounds in good and virtuous sentiments, and conveys some useful lessons of instruction. The incidents, though not numerous, are natural; the characters of the persons concerned, in general, well supported; and the story sufficiently interesting to engage the attention, without too deeply affecting the hearts and passions of its readers' (p. 373).

MR [William Enfield]: 'This *small* Novel (for so it must be called, though by the aid of the printer's art it is drawn out into three volumes) contains several distinct narratives, chiefly to show the hazard of female credulity, written on the whole in an agreeable manner, and adapted to afford entertainment, without leaving any improper impression.'

CARTWRIGHT Mrs. H., THE GENEROUS SISTER
See 1779: 7

1780: 13   CARTWRIGHT, Mrs [H].
LETTERS MORAL AND ENTERTAINING. BY MRS. CARTWRIGHT.

London: Printed for J. Macgowan, No. 27, Paternoster-Row, 1780.
xii, 275p. 8vo. 3s sewed (MR).
MR 64: 469 (June 1781); AF II: 624.
ICN B 692.152; ESTC n035032 (NA CaOHM).

Notes. List of subscribers iii–vii; table of contents ix–xii. Epistolary.

MR includes under heading 'Novels'.

MR [Samuel Badcock]: 'These Letters are more moral than entertaining; though perhaps they have enough of the latter quality, to recommend them to that class of readers for whom they were meant. The stories interspersed shew little fancy or ingenuity.'

1780: 14   [CROFT, Sir Herbert].
LOVE AND MADNESS. A STORY TOO TRUE. IN A SERIES OF LET-
TERS BETWEEN PARTIES WHOSE NAMES WOULD PERHAPS BE
MENTIONED WERE THEY LESS WELL KNOWN OR LESS LAMENTED.

> London: Printed for G. Kearsley, at No. 46, near Serjeants Inn, Fleet Street, 1780.
> 296p. 8vo. 3s 6d sewed (MR), 3s 6d (LC).
> MR 62: 326 (Apr 1780).
> BL 12651.ff.21; EM 193: 3; ESTC t113654 (BI BMu, E, O; NA CtY, CtY-Walpole, CSmH, DLC, IU, MH-H, PU &c.).

Notes. Adv. LC 9–11 Mar 1780.

Further edns: London, 1780, ESTC t143247; London, 1780, t120250; London, 1780, ESTC t113655; Dublin, 1786 (Printed for the Proprietor, 1 vol., 12mo), ESTC n003112; London, 1786, ESTC t057348; WC has 3 entries between 1800 and 1850; NSTC lists edn. in 1809. French trans. n.p., n.d. (*Les Fureurs de l'Amour, ou hist. et corr. authentique de J. Hackman et de Miss Marthuroy, assasinée d'un coup de pistolet par son amant*) (HWS).

'A New Edition, But with as little Injustice as possible to the Purchasers of the first' since the 'Corrections are principally of the Press; the Additions are only two or three Notes, and a fuller Table of Contents', adv. PA 14 Apr 1780.

MR reviews under 'Miscellaneous' and confesses inability to decide whether the letters are genuine.

For a brief account of the factual basis of this work, the 'most unprecedented murder . . . committed on the person of Miss Ray by the Rev. Mr. Hackman', see GM 49: 210 (Apr 1779). See also Maximillian E. Novak, 'The Sensibility of Sir Herbert Croft', *The Age of Johnson* 8 (1997) pp. 189–207.

1780: 15   EDWARDS, Miss.
OTHO AND RUTHA: A DRAMATIC TALE. BY MISS EDWARDS.

> Edinburgh: Printed, by Murray & Cochran, For, and sold by, the Author. Sold also by Mr Elliot, and other Booksellers, 1780.
> viii, 269p. 8vo. 3s (CR), 2s 6d (MR).
> CR 52: 159 (Aug 1781); MR 66: 309–10 (Apr 1782).
> BL 1459.b.18; EM 5166: 5; ESTC t145728.

Notes. A prose pastoral. Prefatory advertisement 'Written by a Friend' iii–vi; dramatis personae (headed 'Speakers') vii–viii.

CR and MR review under 'Miscellaneous'.

Further edn: Dublin, 1787 (Printed by H. Colbert, 1 vol., 12mo), ESTC n042279.

CR: 'This Tale is written in a style, which resembles blank verse. The lessons of morality, which it suggests, are edifying and important.'

MR [Samuel Badcock]: 'The design is commendable; we wish the execution had been more worthy of it. But as justice to the Public is of more importance than complaisance to a Lady, we are compelled, by the necessity of duty, to pronounce this work deficient in almost every requisite of a *Dramatic Tale*. The language is disgustingly tumid; full of solecisms and grammatical inaccuracies. The narrative is insufferably tedious: and we are never more inclined to laugh, than when the Author is *violently* bent on making us weep!' (p. 310).

1780: 16   [ELLIOTT, Miss].
THE RELAPSE, A NOVEL. IN TWO VOLUMES.
> London: Printed for T. Lowndes, No.77, Fleet-Street, 1780.
> I 223p; II 223p. 12mo. 5s sewed (CR), 5s (MR), 5s sewed or 6s bound (SJC).
> CR 49: 75–6 (Jan 1780); MR 62: 244 (Mar 1780); AF II: 1257.
> BL 12611.aaa.28; EM 169: 4; ESTC t077667 (NA IU, MH-H, PU &c.).

Notes. Author attribution: FC.
Leaves L2–L4 of the 2 vols. have been transposed, i.e. the final 3 leaves of vol. 2 are in vol. 1 and vice versa. 2 pp. advs. following t.p. vol. 1; 1 p. advs. end each vol. Epistolary.
Post-dated; adv. as published SJC 21–23 Oct 1779.
Further edn: Dublin, 1780 (Printed for S. Price, W. and H. Whitestone, W. Sleater, C. Jenkin, P. Higley [and 4 others in Dublin], 2 vols., 12mo), EM 7584: 11, ESTC t110029 [vol. 1 n.d.; imprint in vol. 2 reads 'Dublin: Printed by S. Colbert, for the United Company of Booksellers']. German trans. Leipzig, 1780 (*Der Råckfall*) (Price).
   CR: 'A lively description of the wanderings of an inconstant heart, with the miseries that flow from conjugal infidelity and the gratification of criminal desires.'
   MR [William Enfield]: 'There has of late been such an uncommon dearth of this kind of food, that, at this time, no doubt, many thousand eager appetites are craving for *something new*, to whom a dish prepared by the author of *Indiana Danby* [1765/67, JR 884 and 1071, AF I: 1265–1266] will be a delicious morsel.'

GOLDSMITH, Oliver
See GRIFFITH, Elizabeth, NOVELLETTES

1780: 17   GRIFFITH, [Elizabeth], [Oliver] GOLDSMITH, and [Mr McMILLAN].
NOVELLETTES, SELECTED FOR THE USE OF YOUNG LADIES AND GENTLEMEN; WRITTEN BY DR. GOLDSMITH, AND MRS. GRIFFITH, &C. AND ILLUSTRATED BY ELEGANT ENGRAVINGS.
> London: Printed for Fielding and Walker, Pater-noster-row, 1780.
> viii, 328p. 8vo.
> BL RB.23.a.5917; EM 2511: 28; ESTC n005867 (NA CtY-BR, CSmH, IU, NjP &c.).

Notes. Frontispiece (portrait of Griffith) and illustrations. Preface i–[iv]; table of contents vii–viii; [iv]–[vi] misnumbered vi–viii. Contains 16 tales, 13 by Griffith, 2 by Goldsmith, and 1 by Mr McMillan.
Further edn: Dublin, 1784 (Printed for John Cash, 2 vols., 12mo), EM 4686: 2, ESTC t131769.

1780: 18   [HOLCROFT, Thomas].
ALWYN: OR THE GENTLEMAN COMEDIAN. IN TWO VOLUMES.

> London: Printed for Fielding and Walker, Pater-noster-Row, 1780.
> I xv, 192p; II x, 235p. 12mo. 6s (CR, MR).
> CR 51: 319 (Apr 1781); MR 63: 233 (Sept 1780); AF II: 1998.
> O Vet.A5e.1053,1054; EM 287: 2; ESTC t010038 (BI BL; NA CtY-BR, CSmH, IU,
> MH-H, TxU &c.).

Notes. Dedication to R. B. Sheridan. Preface 1, i–viii concerns the development of fiction and
the definitions of romance and novel. Epistolary; tables of contents ix–xv in vol. 1 and i–x in
vol. 2 list the recipients and contents of every letter. 4 pp. advs. end vol. 2.
German trans. Leipzig, 1781 (*Alwyn*) (Price).
> CR: 'A narrative of frivolous incidents in the life of a strolling player.'
> MR [William Enfield]: 'A vulgar narrative of uninteresting incidents in the peregrinations
of a strolling player.'

1780: 19   {M, E}.
HISTORY OF LADY BETTESWORTH AND CAPTAIN HASTINGS. IN A
SERIES OF LETTERS. IN TWO VOLUMES.

> London: Printed for F. Noble, in Holborn, 1780.
> I vii, 232p, II 227p. 12mo. 6s (CR, MR) 5s sewed (LC).
> CR 51: 319 (Apr 1781); MR 63: 151 (Aug 1780); AF II: 1963.
> BL 12612.ccc.10; EM 219: 6; ESTC t066899.

Notes. 'The Editor to the Reader' iii–vii signed 'E. M.' 8 pp. advs. end vol. 2. Epistolary.
Adv. LC 15–17 Feb 1780.
Further edn: Dublin, 1780 (Printed for S. Price [and 9 others], 1 vol., 12mo), xESTC (WC).
> CR: 'Extremely trifling and insipid.'
> MR [William Enfield]: '. . . we pronounce this history, trifling in incident, confused in
method, inelegant in language, and in short, (as the Author of a late *Tour* would say) insipid
"to a degree."'

McMILLAN, Mr
See GRIFFITH, Elizabeth, NOVELLETTES

1780: 20   MINIFIE, M[argaret].
THE COUNT DE POLAND, BY MISS M. MINIFIE, ONE OF THE AUTHORS
OF LADY FRANCES AND LADY CAROLINE S—.

> London: Published for the Author, and sold by J. Dodsley, Pall-Mall, R. Baldwin, Pater-
> noster-Row, London; and Pratt and Clinch, Bath, 1780.
> I 234p; II 261p; III 311p; IV 287p. 12mo. 12s (CR), 10s sewed (MR).
> CR 50: 168–73 (Sept 1780); MR 63: 388 (Nov 1780); AF II: 2882.
> BL 243.h.10–11; EM 1004: 9; ESTC n005671 (NA CLU-S/C, CSmH, MH-H &c.; EA WA)

Notes. Often incorrectly attributed to Susanna Minifie (later Mrs Gunning).
In vols. 2 and 3 text of novel starts on p. 5. Epistolary.
Margaret and Susanna Minifie's *The Histories of Lady Frances S—, and Lady Caroline S—,*
1763, JR 785 and 856, AF I: 1867–1868.

Further edn: Dublin, 1780 (Printed by J. and R. Byrn. For Messieurs Price, Whitestone, Sleater, W. Watson, R. Cross [and 6 others in Dublin], 4 vols., 12mo), ESTC t167287. German trans. Leipzig, 1781 (*Der Graf von Polen in Briefen*) (EAG).

CR: '. . . we may venture to recommend the piece before us, which, though far inferior to the compositions of Richardson and Fielding, may boast no inconsiderable share of real merit; the style being in general easy and unaffected, the characters not ill sustained, the narrative in most parts interesting, and the moral resulting from the whole unexceptionable' (p. 168).

MR [William Enfield]: 'We have been so much amused by the perusal of this Novel, that we scruple not to recommend it as one of the most pleasing productions of this kind which has lately come under our notice. The incidents are well conceived, and the tale constructed in a manner properly adapted to interest the feelings of the Reader: there is an agreeable variety in the characters; the language is easy, and diversified; and for the moral, it is a very good one—as the Reader will find, if he will take the pains to search for it.'

1780: 21   PALMER, Miss.
FEMALE STABILITY; OR THE HISTORY OF MISS BELVILLE. IN A SERIES OF LETTERS. BY THE LATE MISS PALMER.

London: Printed for F. Newbery, the Corner of St Paul's Church-Yard, 1780.
I 268p; II 274p; III 285p; IV 262p; V 213p. 12mo. 15s (MR).
MR 66: 394 (May 1782); AF II: 3198.
BL N.1782–1786; EM 3804:2; ESTC t070713 (NA CtY, DLC, MH-H, PU).

Notes. 'The late Miss Palmer' sometimes wrongly identified with Charlotte Palmer, who was the author's sister. Charlotte wrote the preface, describing the novel as the juvenile work of her sister.
Prefatory advertisement refers to the death of the author. In vols. 2–5 text of novel starts on p. 5. Epistolary.
Further edns: London, 1781, ESTC n006429; Dublin, 1785 (Printed by S. Colbert, 4 vols., 8vo), ESTC n031392. Extracts from *Female Stability* published in *London Magazine and Edinburgh Weekly Magazine*, 1781, RM 411. German trans. Leipzig, 1783–85 (*Die weibliche Beständigkeit*) (Price).

MR [Samuel Badcock]: 'As a composition it is defective; and as a picture of real life it is erroneous. It is in its morality alone that it is unexceptionable. The eager visitors of a circulating library will however find an amusing, if not an highly interesting story. . . .'

PHILLIPS, Peregrine, A DIARY KEPT IN AN EXCURSION TO LITTLE HAMPTON
See App. B: 5

1780: 22   PORNEY, Mr. (*trans.*).
A NEW AND COMPLETE COLLECTION OF INTERESTING ROMANCES AND NOVELS; TRANSLATED FROM THE FRENCH, BY MR PORNEY, TEACHER OF THE FRENCH LANGUAGE AT RICHMOND, SURRY. DESIGNED FOR INSTRUCTION AS WELL AS ENTERTAINMENT, BEING CALCULATED TO CONVEY A GENERAL

KNOWLEDGE OF THE WORLD; AND CONSISTING OF THE MOST
VALUABLE AND IMPORTANT ROMANCES, NOVELS, FABLES, ALLE-
GORIES, MEMOIRS, ADVENTURES, HISTORIES, ANECDOTES, &C.
NOT TO BE FOUND IN ANY OTHER WORK WHATEVER IN ENGLISH.
EMBELLISHED WITH AN ELEGANT SET OF COPPER-PLATE PRINTS,
DESIGNED BY THE CELEBRATED MR. DODD AND THE INGENIOUS
MR. DIGHTON, AND ENGRAVED IN A SUPERIOR STYLE OF EXCEL-
LENCE BY THOSE EMINENT ARTISTS, MESSRS. WELLS, HOW, AND
MEARS—THE IMPRESSIONS OF WHICH BEING ALL EXCEEDINGLY
FINE, AND EXECUTED IN THE BEST MANNER ON FRENCH PAPER.

> London: Printed for the Proprietors, and Sold by Alex. Hogg, No. 16, Paternoster-Row,
> n.d. [ESTC: 1780?].
> 392p. 8vo.
> C 7735.c.29; EM 5835: 18; ESTC t107271 (BI BL, O; NA CLU-S/C, OU).

Notes. 1-p. preface by the translator; on verso of this is a list of the 10 plates. 2-pp. table of contents end vol. Plates dated 1780.

1780: 23   [PRATT, Samuel Jackson].
EMMA CORBETT; OR, THE MISERIES OF CIVIL WAR. FOUNDED ON
SOME RECENT CIRCUMSTANCES WHICH HAPPENED IN AMERICA.
BY THE AUTHOR OF LIBERAL OPINIONS, PUPIL OF PLEASURE,
SHENSTONE GREEN, &C.

> Bath: Printed for Pratt and Clinch; and R. Baldwin, London, 1780.
> I vi, 204p; II 210p; III 211p. 8vo. 7s 6d (CR), 9s bound (MR), 7s 6d sewed or 9s bound
> (PA).
> CR 49: 460–2 (June 1780); MR 63: 310–11 (Oct 1780); AF II: 3566.
> BL RB.23.a.9234; EM 1490: 51; ESTC n006237 (NA CSmH, DLC, IU, MH-H, ViU &c.).

Notes. Epistolary. Dedication to Dr Delacour iii–vi, signed 'The Author', Bath, April 1, 1780.
In vol. 2 text of novel starts on p. 5; in vol. 3 text of novel starts on p. 3.
Liberal Opinions 1775: 30; *Pupil of Pleasure* 1776: 14; *Shenstone Green* 1779: 17.
Adv., 'Printed on a Superfine Writing Paper', PA 2 May 1780.
Extract published LC 48: 84 (25–27 July 1780).
Further edns: Bath, 1780, ESTC n006239; Dublin, 1780 (Printed for Price, Messrs. W. and H.
Whitestone, Sleater, Burnett, Walker [and 11 others in Dublin], 1 vol., 16mo), EM 98: 1,
ESTC t032635; London, [1781], ESTC t202511; London, 1781, ESTC n006229; London, n.d.
[1781?], EM 5168: 13, ESTC t068565; 9 further entries in ESTC. German trans. Leipzig, 1781
(*Emma Korbet*) (Price); French trans. Londres [Paris], 1783, ESTC n037845.
2nd edn. adv., with substantial quotations from CR, LR and LM, PA 18 July 1780. 5th edn.
adv. SJC 29–31 May 1783: '. . . with a beautiful Frontispiece to each volume, after the Designs
of Angelica Kauffman. . . . Gratitude to the Publick, for the favourable Reception this Work
has aleady been honoured with, has induced the Proprietor to reduce this Edition to two Volumes only. . . .'
    CR: 'The heroine of the work is formed upon the models of Clarissa and Eloisa; possess-
ing, however, less prudery than one, and, perhaps, more delicacy than the other; at the same

time that in point of literary composition she is hardly inferior to either of those characters' (p. 460). '. . . in general, the work discovers the same vivacity, and that natural flow of imagination, which we have formerly observed in the several productions of this ingenious author' (p. 462).

MR [William Enfield]: 'Of all the productions of his versatile pen, this is perhaps the least exceptionable in sentiment, and the least faulty in composition. And besides this negative kind of merit, which, in a Writer who has so frequently and egregiously offended, ought not to pass unnoticed, this novel has some claim to praise, on account of the variety of interesting incidents which fill up the narrative, and the lively, and sometimes pathetic, manner in which it is related.'

1780: 24   {RICH, W. P.}.
THE HISTORY OF LEWIS DE MARCHMENT, OR WONDERFUL EVENTS.

Norwich: Printed for G. Alfred Stephens, by J. Payne, Market-Place, n.d. [ESTC: 1780?]. 68p. 12mo.
BL 12611.ee.14; EM 175: 2; ESTC t057363.

Notes. 'W. P. Rich, Author' printed on verso of t.p. Text starts on p. 3. 1 p. (unn.) following p. 168 contains 12 lines of verse, followed by 'Finis' and the printer's colophon.

SEALLY, John, **MORAL TALES**
See 1772: 39

TYPO, Dr.
See **THE AFFECTING HISTORY OF TWO YOUNG GENTLEWOMEN**

1781

1781: 1   ANON.
THE ADVENTURES OF A HACKNEY COACH.

London: Printed for G. Kearsly [*sic*], No 46, Fleet-street, 1781.
I 6, 150p; II vi, 168p. 8vo. 2s 6d sewed (CR), 2s 6d (MR), 1s (PA) (vol. 1); 2s 6d (MR), 2s 6d (PA) vol. 2.
CR 51: 284–7 (Apr 1781), MR 64: 468 (June 1781) vol. 1; CR 52: 159 (Aug 1781), MR 65: 389–90 (Nov 1781) vol. 2; AF II: 24–25.
IU x823.Ad964 [vol. 1], CLU-S/C Delta PR4839.K55a 1781 v.2 [vol. 2]; ESTC n042509 [vol. 1] (NA CSt), n051029 [vol. 2], n049999 [vol. 2] (NA PU), t227285 (BI BL) [vol. 2].

Notes. PU/ESTC: Sometimes attributed to Dorothy Kilner.
ESTC has 3 entries for vol. 2, apparently identical except that t227285 is described as having 167, [1] p. and n051029 and n049999 168p.

ESTC: Vol. 2 an 'opportunistic follow-up to "The Adventures of a Hackney Coach"'.
Vol. 2 imprint omits 'No. 46'. Vol. 1 dedication to Lady Craven, signed 'The Author', London 11 Mar 1781; 1 p. adv. at end. Vol. 2 dedication to Mary Isabella, Duchess of Rutland v–vi, signed 'The Author', London, 25 July 1781; 1 p. adv. recto of leaf following t.p.; adv. on p. 168 following end of novel text.
Vol. 1 adv. PA 21 Mar 1781. Vol. 2 adv., 'This Morning at Eleven will be published', PA 26 July 1781.
Further edns: London, 1781, ESTC n049998; London, 1781, ESTC n004300; London, 1781, ESTC n005091; Dublin, 1781 (Printed for C. Jackson and P. Byrne, 1 vol., 12mo), EM 172: 7, ESTC t068054; London, 1783, EM 7899: 4, ESTC t191390; Philadelphia, 1783, ESTC w027322; 3 further entries in ESTC. German trans. Leipzig, 1782 (*Abentheuer einer Mietkutsche*) (Price).
    CR 51: '. . . though the subject might, in the hands of an able writer, afford an ample field for wit, humour, and a knowledge of mankind, this is, after all the pains which the author has taken, but a flimsy performance: our coachman's fares (as the reader, who takes the trouble to ride with him, will easily perceive) are too short; and before any interesting story can be told, or any good character drawn of one person, he stops on a sudden, and takes up another' (p. 284). 'A servile copy of *Sterne*'s peculiarity of expression, his sudden transitions, exclamations, &c. without his force, spirit, and sensibility, will never recommend a writer to public attention' (p. 286).
    MR 64 [Samuel Badcock]: 'The Author says, that "he has found an old pen belonging to Sterne." We wish he had found the spirit which animated it. But that is exhausted, and nought remains here but the dull, lifeless *residuum!*'
    CR 52: 'This is as execrable a hack as any private gentleman would wish to be drove in; being nothing but a heap of uninteresting ill-written adventures, in a pompous and turgid style.'
    MR 65 [Samuel Badcock]: '. . . this second volume is, *if possible*, more contemptible than the first. It hath the same glaring affectation; the same unnatural and disgusting attempt at pathos; with more than usual absurdity, and a double portion of inaccuracies' (p. 390).

1781: 2   ANON.
COLONEL ORMSBY; OR THE GENUINE HISTORY OF AN IRISH NOBLEMAN, IN THE FRENCH SERVICE.

    London: Printed for J. Macgowan, No. 27 Pater-Noster-Row, 1781.
    I 183p; II 211p. 12mo. 5s sewed (MR).
    MR 67: 69 (July 1782).
    PU Singer-Mend. 823.C718; EM 1275:9; ESTC n014767 (NA MH-H).

Notes. By same author as *Les Delices du Sentiment* (1781: 3) and *Young Philosopher* (1782: 11). 4 pp. advs. end vol. 2. Epistolary.
Further edn: Dublin, 1781 (Printed for Messrs. Price, Whitestone, Sleater, W. Watson, Sheppard [and 8 others in Dublin], 2 vols., 12mo), EM 11: 7, ESTC t055922. German trans. Leipzig, 1781 (*Der Oberste Ormsby, oder eine wahre Geschichte eines Irlaendischen von Adel in französischen Diensten*) (EAG).
    MR [William Enfield]: 'A tale *simple* without innocence, and *warm* without sentiment.'

1781: 3   ANON.
LES DELICES DU SENTIMENT; OR THE PASSIONATE LOVERS: IN A

SERIES OF LETTERS WHICH HAVE RECENTLY PASSED BETWEEN TWO CELEBRATED CHARACTERS, WELL KNOWN IN POLITE LIFE FOR THEIR VIRTUES, TALENTS, AND ACCOMPLISHMENTS. WITH A TRANSLATION FROM THE ORIGINALS. WRITTEN IN CYPHER.

London: Printed for J. Macgowan, No. 27 Pater-noster-Row, 1781.
176p. 8vo. 3s 6d (CR, MR).
CR 54: 320 (Oct 1782); MR 67: 70 (July 1782).
BL 12510.f.25; EM 5: 4; ESTC t131511 (NA CaOHM, ICU, PU).

Notes. Text in French and English. Epistolary.
By the author of *Young Philosopher* (1782: 11) and *Colonel Ormsby* (1781: 2).

CR: 'This is one of the many *misnomers* which we meet with in our literary examination; for instead of *passion*, we find in it nothing but the dregs of prurient *insipidity*.'

MR [William Enfield]: 'Of all the pap that was ever prepared in the nursery of Venus, for the use of her pretty babes, this is the most insipid.'

1781: 4 ANON.
THE DÉNOUEMENT: OR, HISTORY OF LADY LOUISA WINGROVE. BY A LADY.

Dublin: Printed by John Exshaw, No. 86, Dame-street, 1781.
211p. 12mo.
BL 12611.e.17; EM 208: 2; ESTC t057432 (NA PU).

Notes. Epistolary.
Further edn: London, 1784, ESTC n028179.
This edn. not reviewed; 1784 London edn. reviewed CR 57: 397–8 (May 1784); MR 72: 233 (Mar 1785).

1781: 5 ANON.
DISTREST VIRTUE; OR, THE HISTORY OF MISS HARRIET NELSON. IN WHICH IS INCLUDED THE UNHAPPY STORY OF MISS CAROLINE LENOX. IN A SERIES OF LETTERS. IN THREE VOLUMES.

London: Printed for F. Noble, at his Circulating Library, opposite Gray's Inn Gate, Holborn, 1781.
I 252p; II 240p; III 239p. 12mo. 9s (CR, MR), 9s bound (PA).
CR 52: 155 (Aug 1781); MR 65: 75 (July 1781).
PU EC75.A100.781d3.1781; ESTC n049960.

Notes. Dedication 'To the Reader' signed 'The Author' pp. [5]–[8]. 1 p. advs. end vol. 3. Epistolary.
Post-dated; adv. as published PA 9 Dec 1780.
German trans. Leipzig, 1782 (*Geschichte der Miss Henriette Nelson*) (EAG).

CR: 'Virtue in distress is an interesting object; but its effects are totally frustrated by the incapacity of this writer.'

MR [Samuel Badcock]: '"I am aware (says the Author), that many, on reading this little Work, will throw it aside with much disdain." We are very much of the Author's opinion.'

1781:6   ANON.
EDAL VILLAGE: OR, THE FORTUNATE LOTTERY TICKET. IN TWO VOLUMES.

> London: Printed for T. Lowndes, No. 77, in Fleet-Street, 1781.
>
> I 222p; II 210p. 12mo [CR and MR have 8vo]. 5s sewed (CR, MR), 5s sewed or 6s bound (LC).
>
> CR 51: 319 (Apr 1781); MR 64: 121–9 (Feb 1781); AF II: 1206.
>
> CLU-S/C PR3991.A1E25; EMf; ESTC n007302 (BI BL; NA NIC).

Notes. Vol. 1 lacks t.p. 8 pp. advs. end vol. 2.

Post-dated; adv. as published LC 48: 488 (18–21 Nov 1780).

German trans. Leipzig, 1782 (*Das Dorf Edal*) (EAG).

CR: 'The hero of this novel is Jerry Last, a shoemaker, whose history is related in an easy familiar style, interspersed with some pertinent reflections. Considered as a work of invention, however, it deserves to be ranked among the productions of the meaner kind; being not sufficiently interesting either in the plot or in sentiment to engage the attention of the reader.'

MR [Samuel Badcock]: 'This little novel relates, in a strain somewhat lively and uncommon, the adventures of an honest and benevolent shoemaker, to whom fortune had been particularly liberal, by a prize of ten thousand pounds in the lottery' (p. 121). 'The Author of this performance is doubtless a man of ingenuity and observation. We perceive in his reflections a ray or two of Shandean genius. He possesses a quickness of perception; and his mode of expressing himself is lively and entertaining. But his genius wants force and extent. His invention is narrow; and his wit superficial and trifling' (p. 129).

FASHIONABLE FOLLIES
See VAUGHAN, Thomas

1781:7   ANON.
FASHIONABLE LIFE; OR, THE HISTORY OF MISS LOUISA FERMOR. A NOVEL. BY A LADY.

> Dublin: Printed by C. Jackson, Anglesea-Street, 1781.
>
> 244p. 12mo.
>
> ICN Y155.F263; ESTC n031314.

Notes. 4-pp. prefatory advertisement (unn.) signed T. M. but not as author. Running-title: 'Louisa Fermor'. Epistolary.

1781:8   ANON.
THE FEMALE MONITOR, OR THE HISTORY OF ARABELLA AND LADY GAY.

> London: Printed and sold by W. Richardson in the Strand, and sold also By J. Bew, Bookseller, in Paternoster-Row, 1781.
>
> vi, 86p. 8vo. 2s (t.p.), 2s stitched (CR, MR).
>
> CR 52: 480 (Dec 1781); MR 65: 390 (Nov 1781).
>
> BL RB.23.b.1590; ESTC n031372 (NA CaOHM).

Notes. Dedication to the Duchess of Hamilton, the Countess of Percy, Lady Algernon Percy and Mrs Bennet iii–vi, signed 'The Author'. Work is signed Peter M'Dermott on p. 86.

CR: 'The title of this production might suggest the idea, that it possesses at least some moral merit; but at the same time that it bears the marks of great affectation, it is far too frivolous to be useful.'

MR [Samuel Badcock]: 'Equally frivolous and affected! . . . . Such Writers, it is our office to *twist* in the *bud*; and, as literary pruners, to *amputate* from the *wild proximity* of scribbling.'

FRIENDSHIP AND MATRIMONY
See MANSEL, Henry (1782: 17)

1781: 9 ANON.
GILHAM FARM; OR, THE HISTORY OF MELVIN AND LUCY. IN A SERIES OF LETTERS. IN TWO VOLUMES.

> London: Printed for F. Noble, in Holborn, 1781.
> I 211p; II 240p. 12mo. 5s sewed (CR, MR), 6s bound (LC, PA).
> CR 51: 318 (Apr 1781); MR 64: 71 (Jan 1781).
> C S727.d.78.19-20; ESTC t199529.

Notes. Preface v–viii. Table of contents 1, ix–xvi; 2, v–viii. Epistolary.
Post-dated; adv. as published LC 48: 378 (19–21 Oct 1780) and PA 23 Oct 1780. German trans. Leipzig, 1782 (*Gilhalm oder Geschichte von Melvin und Luzie*) (EAG).

CR: 'This novel is more conspicuous for the size of the type, and the extent of the intermediate spaces, than for any thing it derives from the imagination of the writer.'

MR [Samuel Badcock]: 'This trifling novel, which for the size of the type, and the extent of the spaces, hath few equals even in this book-making age, is fabricated to introduce some seemingly original accounts of India. Allured by the success of Emily Montague, and the pleasing descriptions of Canada in that agreeable novel, the Author hath followed his original with unequal steps. The descriptions are meagre and scanty, with little colouring; and the reflections vague and trite, without novelty or acuteness.'

THE HISTORY OF JOHN JUNIPER, ESQ.
See JOHNSTONE, Charles

THE HISTORY OF THE HONOURABLE MRS. ROSEMONT
See ELLIOTT, Miss

LETTERS BETWEEN TWO LOVERS, AND THEIR FRIENDS
See COMBE, William

LETTERS OF AN ITALIAN NUN
See COMBE, William

1781: 10 ANON.
*LITERARY AMUSEMENTS; OR, EVENING ENTERTAINER. BY A FEMALE HAND. CONTAINING, THE HISTORY OF MR. ALLEN. THE LIFE OF AN AUTHORESS. THE ENCHANTED ROSE. HISTORY OF NOUZHATEL. FATAL CURIOSITY. THE FOX-HUNTERS. EFFECTS OF

SEDUCTION. LETTER ON SUICIDE. ON THE STUDIES OF WOMEN.
WILLIAM AND PHEBE. THOUGHTS ON FRIENDSHIP. ON RURAL
SIMPLICITY. IN TWO VOLUMES.

> London: Printed for F. Noble, at his Circulating Library, opposite Gray's Inn Gate, Holbourn (PA), 1781 (PA).
> 12mo. 6s. (MR), 5s sewed (PA, LC), 7s (adv.).
> MR 66: 476 (June 1782).
> No copy located.

Notes. Adv. PA 30 Nov 1781; adv. LC 50: 611 (25–27 Dec 1781).
Adv. end vol. 2 of *The Young Widow* (1785: 21).
Further edn: Dublin, 1782 (Printed by T. Henshall, for S. Price, W. & H. Whitestone, T. Walker, J. Beatty, E. Cross and R. Burton, 2 vols., 12mo), EM 635: 1, ESTC t097316.

> MR [Samuel Badcock]: 'Amusements for the *illiterate!*'

LUCINDA; OR, THE SELF-DEVOTED DAUGHTER
See MANTE, Thomas

THE MASQUED WEDDINGS
See ELLIOTT, Miss

1781: 11   ANON.
THE NEW ELOISA; OR THE HISTORY OF MR. SEDLEY, AND MISS
WENTWORTH. IN A SERIES OF LETTERS. BY A LADY. IN TWO VOLUMES.

> Dublin: Printed for C. Jackson, Anglesea-Street, 1781.
> 236p. 12mo.
> BL C.192.a.174; ESTC t226780 (BI Dt).

Notes. Not a version of Jean-Jacques Rousseau's *Nouvelle Héloïse.*
2 vols in 1; pagination continuous. 3 pp advs. end vol. Epistolary.
Further edn. (perhaps identical): Dublin, 1781, ESTC t212754.

REVERIES OF THE HEART
See App. B: 6

1781: 12   ANON.
*THE REVOLUTION. A NOVEL IN FOUR VOLUMES.

> London: J. Fielding, No. 23, Paternoster-Row, (PA), 1781 (PA).
> 1 vol. 12mo. 2s 6d (CR, MR).
> CR 52: 76 (July 1781); MR 65: 390–2 (Nov 1781); AF II: 3751.
> No copy located.

Notes. It appears that although 4 vols. were intended, only 1 was published.
Adv. PA 6 June 1781: 'The First Volume of the Novel of the Revolution, was published by the Editors by way of Experiment; and the others were not intended to be printed, unless the First was well received. The great and unexpected Demand for it already enables the Editors to assure the Public, That the remaining Volumes will now be published with all convenient

Speed. . . . The Moral of the Work is founded on the Situation of this Kingdom with Respect to America, and the common Enemy'.

Adv. LC 50: 15 (3–5 July 1781); 'N.B. This work is written on the plan of an epic poem; and the moral of it is founded on the situation of this kingdom with respect to America and the common enemy.'

PA 24–26 Jan 1782 re-adv. of what appears to be just the 1st vol. as it is 2s 6d.

Based on the novel's prefatory advertisement, CR reports that the author died in 1774, was under 18, had no classical education and was a labourer. '. . . the work discovers an invention far beyond what might be expected from the youth and situation of the author; and which, if employed on a more interesting subject, under the judgment of a maturer age, might have procured his name a monument among those who have been distinguished by genius.'

MR [Samuel Badcock]: 'This work is improperly stiled a novel. It was intended for an epic poem, and at first was adorned with machinery, which was afterwards omitted.' MR also comments with compassion on the author's circumstances.

1781: 13   ANON.
A SKETCH OF THE TIMES; OR, THE MEMOIRS OF LORD DERVILLE. IN TWO VOLUMES.

> London: Printed for J. Bew, Paternoster-Row; and E. Macklew, opposite the Opera-House, Hay-Market, 1781.
> I 192p; II 195p. 8vo. 5s sewed (CR, MR), 5s sewed or 6s bound (PA).
> CR 51: 318 (Apr 1781); MR 64: 71–2 (Jan 1781).
> BL 12654.f.53; EM 269: 1; ESTC t100496. WC shows also NNC.

Notes. 1 p. adv. end vol. 2. Epistolary.

Post-dated; adv. as published PA 16 Nov 1780.

German trans. Leipzig, 1782 (Ein Gemälde unserer Zeit) (Price).

MR reviews under the title Sketches of the Times: the History of Lord Derville (1780); MR's mistake is copied, along with the review's contents, by CR.

CR: 'O Tempora! O mores!—If the tempora be bad, the mores, according to this description, are equally liable to censure. But we wish that the author, while he painted both in strong colouring, had not also deservedly incurred the blame of exciting the vices which he delineates.'

MR [Samuel Badcock]: 'If the times are in reality so bad as they are here represented, we shall no longer condemn the gloomy pictures drawn by discontented moralists and splenetic divines; nor attribute to the dictates of disappointment what may have been the effect of observation. This infamous story is well told: but in its vicious tendency every other merit is totally lost.'

1781: 14   ANON.
THE TRIUMPH OF PRUDENCE OVER PASSION: OR, THE HISTORY OF MISS MORTIMER AND MISS FITZGERALD. BY THE AUTHORESS OF EMELINE. IN TWO VOLUMES.

> Dublin: Printed (for the Author) by S. Colbert, No. 136, Capel-street, opposite Abbey-street, M,DCC,XXI [ESTC: 1781].
> I 229p; II 195p. 12mo.
> BL Cup.403.pp.30; EM 6424: 5; ESTC t135343 (BI Dt; NA CLU-S/C).

Notes. By same author as *The Fairy Ring* (1783: 2)?

Text of novel starts on p. 3 in vol. 1 and p. 5 in vol. 2. 3 pp. advs. end vol. 2. Drop-head title vols. 1 and 2: 'The History of Miss Moreton and Miss Fitzgerald'. Epistolary.

Further edn: London, 1783 (*The Reconciliation; or, the History of Miss Mortimer and Miss Fitzgerald*), (BRu ENC), xESTC. In fact this edn. pub. by Lane was from same sheets.

London edn. rev. CR 56: 74 (July 1783); MR 68: 457–8 (May 1783).

MR [Samuel Badcock]: 'Why an "*Hibernian* novel?" We know not, unless it hath this distinction given it for the sake of two or three Irish names that chiefly figure in it. We have no discriminating representations of Hibernian manners, or Hibernian scenes. We do not even meet with blunders—those happy and truly laughable blunders, fortuitously struck out "beyond the reach of art;" which have for so long been characteristic of Hibernian conversation, as to become proverbial' (p. 457).

1781: 15 ANON.

THE UNFORTUNATE CALEDONIAN IN ENGLAND; OR, THE GENUINE MEMOIRS OF AN IMPRESSED YOUNG GENTLEMAN, IN THE YEAR 1779. WRITTEN BY HIMSELF.

London: Printed for J. Wade, No. 163, Fleet Street, 1781.

138p. 8vo. 2s 6d sewed (CR), 2s (MR).

CR 52: 159 (Aug 1781); MR 67: 152 (Aug 1782).

BL 12613.c.5; EM 279: 6; ESTC t108182.

Notes. CR reviews under 'Miscellaneous' and MR under 'Novels'.

CR: 'Whether these Memoirs of an Impressed young Gentleman be genuine or fictitious, they certainly afford entertainment. The incidents are interesting; the characters well delineated; and several places accurately described.'

MR [Samuel Badcock]: 'We know not what motives could have tempted the Author to have assumed a borrowed character: but we have little scruple in declaring, that the Author, instead of *having never left Scotland* till *January* 1st, 1779, was, probably, *never in* it.'

1781: 16 [COMBE, William].

LETTERS BETWEEN TWO LOVERS, AND THEIR FRIENDS. BY THE AUTHOR OF LETTERS SUPPOSED TO HAVE BEEN WRITTEN BY YORICK AND ELIZA. IN THREE VOLUMES.

London: Printed for J. Bew, in Pater-Noster-Row, 1781.

I vii, 199p; II 200p; III 217p. 8vo [MR has 12mo]. 7s 6d (MR), 7s 6d sewed or 9s bound (PA).

MR 65: 65–6 (July 1781).

C Oates.479-; ESTC n011338 (NA PU).

Notes. Authorship attribution: Hamilton p. 312; ESTC is doubtful.

Epistolary. Dedication to Lady Monson iii–vii, signed 'The Author'. 3 pp. advs. end vol. 3.

Adv. PA 29 Jan 1781.

Further edn: Dublin, 1781 (Printed by Brett Smith, for Messrs. Price, Sleator, Sheppard, E. Cross, Jenkin [and 8 others in Dublin], 3 vols., 12mo), ESTC n011339. German trans. Leipzig, 1782 (*Briefe zweier Liebenden und ihrer Freunde*) (Price).

MR [Samuel Badcock]: These volumes '. . . are less affected, and much more interesting and entertaining [than the author's former publication]. They have a story, or rather two or three stories interwoven very naturally with each other,—which excite curiosity, and keep the attention awake, on objects of interest both to the affections and understanding.... these Letters have a moral tendency that will make them acceptable to the lovers of virtue; and though they are not enlivened by the brilliance of wit, yet they are supported by good sense, and solid experience' (p. 66).

1781: 17   [COMBE, William].
LETTERS OF AN ITALIAN NUN AND AN ENGLISH GENTLEMAN. TRANSLATED FROM THE FRENCH OF J. J. ROUSSEAU.
> London: Printed for J. Bew, Pater-Noster-Row, 1781.
> xiv, 176p. 8vo. 2s sewed (MR), 2s 6d sewed or 3s bound (LC, SJC).
> MR 67: 314 (Oct 1782); AF II: 2538.
> O G.Pamph.1315(4); ESTC n003816 (BI BL; NA DLC, MH-H, NIC, &c).

Notes. Attribution to Combe: Hamilton, p. 312; ESTC is doubtful. The t.p. attribution to Rousseau is spurious.
Epistolary.
Adv. LC 51: 539 (4–6 June 1782); adv. SJC 23–25 July 1782.
Further edns: Dublin, 1782 (Printed for C. Jackson, 1 vol., 12mo), ESTC t060901; London, 1784, EM 6184: 11, ESTC t136491; London, 1789, ESTC n034125; Dublin, 1790, ESTC n002737; Philadelphia, 1794, ESTC w041525; 3 further entries in ESTC; WC has 4 entries between 1800 and 1850; NSTC lists edns. in 1806 and 1817. German trans. Leipzig, 1784 (*Briefe einer Italienischen Nonne und eines Engländers*) (EAG); French trans. Rome and Paris, 1787 (*Maria ou lettres d'un gentilhomme anglois à une religieuse*) (BGR).

MR [Samuel Badcock]: 'Not Rousseau's, but in many respects worthy of his exquisite pen. The story is interesting and pathetic: and the letters are written with spirit and elegance.'

1781: 18   [ELLIOTT, Miss].
THE HISTORY OF THE HON. MRS. ROSEMONT, AND SIR HENRY CARDIGAN, IN A SERIES OF LETTERS. IN TWO VOLUMES.
> London: Printed for T. Hookham, at his Circulating-Library, No. 147 New Bond-Street, n.d. [1781].
> I 251p; II 250p. 12mo [CR and MR have 8vo]. 5s sewed (CR, MR), 5s sewed or 6s bound (PA).
> CR 52: 155 (Aug 1781); MR 64: 468–9 (June 1781).
> Ps L.E.ar 56–1 and 56–2; ESTC t213216.

Notes. Author attribution: FC.
2 pp. adv. for Hookham's Circulating Library end vol. 2, followed by 2 pp. advs. for "Books published by Thomas Hookham" and 6 pp. advs. for "Livres vendu Par T. Hookham". Epistolary.
Adv. PA 16 Jan 1781. German trans. Leipzig, 1782 (*Geschichte der Frau Julia Rosemont und des Herrn Heinrich Cardigan*) (EAG).

CR: 'Though this novel be founded on some improbable circumstances, and the narrative be, in several places, destitute of natural connection, it discovers many traces of a lively fancy; the characters are not only well supported, but happily contrasted with each other; and the whole, if we except some grammatical inaccuracies, is written in an easy and agreeable manner.'

MR [Samuel Badcock]: 'This is a sprightly entertaining Novel. Its plot is somewhat romantic and improbable, and its events are linked by circumstances too artificial and arbitrary to deceive the reader: yet it is on the whole conducted with spirit and address:—the story is well told; and the different characters are properly discriminated. . . . It appears to have been the composition of a Lady well versed in the nicer points and mysteries of love. We say a *Lady*, and for two reasons do we attribute it to a female pen:—from the freedom and vivacity with which it is written, and from several glaring deficiencies even in common grammatical construction. This fault we have often observed in the composition of ladies, who, notwithstanding, have acquired all the elegant graces of language: and have almost instinctively caught at elegance without giving themselves the trouble of pursuing the strict forms of grammar.'

1781: 19   [ELLIOTT, Miss].
THE MASQUED WEDDINGS, A NOVEL IN A SERIES OF LETTERS. IN TWO VOLUMES.

> London: Printed for T. Hookham, at his Circulating-Library, New Bond Street, Corner of Bruton Street, 1781.
>
> I 251p; II 255p. 8vo. 6s (CR), 5s (MR), 5s sewed or 6s bound (PA).
>
> CR 52: 480 (Dec 1781); MR 65: 392 (Nov 1781).
>
> DLC PR4699.E44M3 Rare Bk Coll; xESTC. WC shows also MH-H, TxHR.

Notes. WC gives author's name as Gertrude Elliott Espenscheid.
Epistolary. 2 leaves advs. end vol. 2.
Adv. PA 18 May 1781.
Further edn: Dublin, 1781 (Printed by George Bonham, for Messrs. Price, Burnet, Moncrieffe, Walker, Beatty, Higly, and Byrn, 2 vols., 12mo), ESTC t205932. German trans. Leipzig, 1783 (*Die maskierte Heurath*) (Price).

CR: 'Whether this novel was written in haste, we know not; but from the uninterrupted flow of the language, it must be read with precipitation. To compensate this inconvenience, however, it abounds with vivacity, and cannot fail of affording entertainment.'

MR [Samuel Badcock]: 'The Letters are written with spirit and vivacity. The rapidity of the language hurries on the reader too fast, and scarcely leaves him a resting-place on which to sit down and draw breath. But the lovers of novels will find entertainment in these volumes. . . .'

1781: 20   [JOHNSTONE, Charles].
THE HISTORY OF JOHN JUNIPER, ESQ. ALIAS JUNIPER JACK. CONTAINING THE BIRTH, PARENTAGE, AND EDUCATION, LIFE, ADVENTURES, AND CHARACTER OF THAT MOST WONDERFUL AND SURPRIZING GENTLEMAN. BY THE EDITOR OF THE ADVENTURES OF A GUINEA.

> London: Printed for R. Baldwin, in Pater-Noster Row, 1781.
>
> I 269p; II 257p; III 282p. 12mo. 10s 6d (CR), 9s sewed (MR, PA).
>
> CR 52: 480 (Dec 1781); MR 66: 131–3 (Feb 1782); AF II: 2311.
>
> BL N.2054-56; EM 2018: 6; ESTC t073521 (BI E; NA CtY-BR, MH-H, PU, ViU &c.; EA ZWTU).

Notes. 2 pp. advs. end vols. 1 & 2.

Adv., 'In the Press and speedily will be published', PA 25 Apr 1781; adv. as published PA 18 June 1781.

Further edn: Dublin, 1781 (Printed for S. Price, J. Sheppard, R. Cross, T. Wilkson, W. Gilbert [and 10 others in Dublin], 2 vols., 12mo), ESTC n008001.

CR mentions the pre-publication rumour that this novel 'contained the *true* history' of John Wilkes, 'a circumstance which naturally raised the curiosity of the public, whose sanguine expectations will be miserably disappointed, when they discover, as we have found by a painful perusal, that, instead of exhibiting any entertaining traits of that great phænomenon, the reader will meet with little more than a series of uninteresting vulgar occurrences, and an aukward affectation of humour.'

MACNALLY, Leonard, SENTIMENTAL EXCURSIONS TO WINDSOR
See App. B: 7

1781: 21 [?MANTE, Thomas].
LUCINDA; OR, THE SELF-DEVOTED DAUGHTER.

> London: Printed for T. Hookham, at his Circulating-Library, New Bond Street, Corner of Bruton Street, 1781.
> 286p. 12mo [CR, MR have 8vo]. 3s (CR, MR), 3s sewed (PA).
> CR 52: 480 (Dec 1781); MR 65: 390 (Nov 1781); AF II: 2706.
> CSmH 357932; EMf; ESTC n034009 (NA DLC).

Notes. ESTC: Attributed to Thomas Mante.
1 p. advs. verso of final leaf (p. [288]).
Adv. PA 6 July 1781.

CR: 'An extravagant assemblage of terrible incidents, recited in bombastic narrative.'
MR [Samuel Badcock]: 'This is, in truth, a super-tragical story! related in a style, which may be called, super-sublime! Like most of these stories, it begins with love: as it proceeds, it takes in perfidy, seduction, adultery, jealousy, rage, madness—and, at last, ends in *battle, murder, and sudden death!* "Oh horrible! most horrible!" '

ROUSSEAU, Jean-Jacques, LETTERS OF AN ITALIAN NUN
See COMBE, William

1781: 22 [VAUGHAN, Thomas].
FASHIONABLE FOLLIES. A NOVEL. CONTAINING THE HISTORY OF A PARISIAN FAMILY. IN TWO VOLUMES.

> London: Printed for, and sold by J. Dodsley, Pall-Mall, 1781.
> I 311p; II 424p. 12mo. 6s (MR), 6s sewed (PA).
> MR 66: 395 (May 1782); AF II: 4594.
> BL N.2515; EM 4583: 16; ESTC t073516 (NA CtY-BR, ICN, IU, MH-H &c.; EA GDAs).

Notes. Adv. PA 8 Dec 1781. Re-adv. SJC 20–22 Mar 1783 with this note: 'N.B. At which Time will be ready to be delivered to the former and present Purchasers, a most elegant Design, selected from the Work, by that much-admired Artist, Mr. DE LUTHERBOURGH, and presented by him to the Authour, and executed under his Inspection, in a very masterly Stile, by Mr. RUOTTE. The Print may be had separately, Price 1s.'

Further edns: London, 1781, ESTC n048969; Dublin, 1782 (Printed by D. Graisberry, for Messrs. Price, Whitestone, Walker, White, E. Cross, Burton, and P. Byrne, 2 vols., 12mo), ESTC n031300; London, 1810 (BRU ENC).

MR [Samuel Badcock]: 'The number of follies recorded in this work is 301! *one* more might have been added to the catalogue, and that is the *folly* of a sensible author in recording the most detestable crimes under so gentle a title; and in relating with gaiety what ought never to be thought of without abhorrence.'

1782

THE ADVENTURES OF A RUPEE
See SCOTT, Helenus

1782:1   ANON.
THE ADVENTURES OF AN ACTOR, IN THE CHARACTERS OF A MERRY-ANDREW, A METHODIST-PREACHER, AND A FORTUNE-TELLER. FOUNDED ON FACTS.

London: Printed for the Author; and sold by the Book-sellers, n.d. [1782].
334p. 12mo.
BL 12653.aaa.38; EM 222: 6; ESTC t086016 (BI O; NA ICN, NIC, TxU &c.).

Notes. ESTC date: 1770? WC suggests 1778, based on datable events in novel.
Ornamented t.p.
Adv. SJC 21–24 Dec 1782; *The Adventures of an Actor. Founded on Facts*; London: Printed for the Authour; and sold by Scatcherd and Whitaker Successors to Mr E. Johnson, Ave-Maria-Lane.

1782:2   ANON.
ANNA: A SENTIMENTAL NOVEL. IN A SERIES OF LETTERS. IN TWO VOLUMES.

London: Printed for T. Hookham, at his Circulating Library, New-Bond-Street, the Corner of Bruton-Street, 1782.
I 272p; II 254p. 12mo. 5s (CR), 5s sewed (MR, SJC).
CR 54: 320 (Oct 1782); MR 67: 70 (July 1782); AF II: 110.
BRu ENC; xESTC.

Notes. EurM attributes to Miss Nugent and Miss Taylor, authors of *The Indiscreet Marriage* (1779: 14).
4 pp. advs. end vol. 1 and 6 pp. advs. end vol. 2. Epistolary.
Adv. SJC 14–16 Feb 1782.
Further edn: Dublin, 1782 (Printed by P. Higly, for Messrs. Price, Whitestone, R. Cross, Walker, Gilbert, Higly, Beatty, Burton, and Parker, 2 vols., 12mo), EM 4159: 1, ESTC t089118.

MR [William Enfield]: 'This novel is written with a kind of vivacity and smartness which sometimes approaches the borders of humour, but which much oftener steps into the walks of affectation and pertness. The tale has animation enough to engage some degree of attention, but is too deficient in connection and probability to interest the passions.'

1782: 3   ANON.
BLANDFORD RACES: A NOVEL. IN TWO VOLUMES.

> London: Printed for J. Bew, in Pater-noster Row, 1782.
> I 213p; II 230p. 12mo [CR and MR have small 8vo]. 6s (CR), 6s bound (MR), 5s sewed or 6s bound (LC, SJC).
> CR 54: 152 (Aug 1782); MR 67: 314 (Oct 1782); AF II: 377.
> PU Singer-Mend. PR3991.A1.B52.1782; ESTC n032284.

Notes. Epistolary.
Adv., 'By a Lady', LC 51: 539 (4–6 June 1782); adv. SJC 23–25 July 1782.

CR: 'There is no harm in these two volumes, which is more than can be said of half the novels that make their monthly appearance for the entertainment of masters and misses in this reading age.'

MR [Samuel Badcock]: 'This is one of those neutral things whose "generation is so equivocal," that it would puzzle Aristotle himself to characterize them.'

CECILIA, OR MEMOIRS OF AN HEIRESS
See BURNEY, Frances

1782: 4   ANON.
*EXTRACT FROM THE LIFE OF LIEUTENANT HENRY FOLEY, OF HIS MAJESTY'S—REGIMENT OF FOOT.

> London: Printed for G. Robinson, Pater-noster-Row; and Richard Fisher, Newcastle (SJC), 1782 (SJC).
> 1 vol. 2s 6d sewed (MR, SJC).
> MR 68: 358 (Apr 1783); AF II: 1345.
> No copy located.

Notes. Adv., 'In a neat Pocket Volume. . . . The First Volume . . . . By an Officer', SJC 3–5 Dec 1782.
An extract appears in *Moral Tales* (Ludlow, 1799), ESTC n035227.

MR [Samuel Badcock]: 'One more added to the long—long list of Sterne's imitators! This Author, however, is not so unfortunate in his adventure, as most of his brethren who have gone before him in this wild goose chase—and are now, with their works, at an everlasting rest. . . . A vein of sprightly sentiment runs through this little work; and the features of some characters are hit off very happily.'

1782: 5   ANON.
THE FORTUNATE SISTERS; OR, THE HISTORY OF FANNY AND SOPHIA BEMONT.

> London: Printed for Francis Noble, at his Circulating Library, opposite Gray's Inn Gate, Holborn, 1782.

I 236p; II 236p. 12mo. 6s (CR, MR), 6s bound (PA).
CR 54: 320 (Oct 1782); MR 66: 474 (June 1782); AF II: 1485.
BL 1210.m.42; EM 2679: 1; ESTC t099726 (NA MH-H).

Notes. Post-dated; adv. as published PA 14 Nov 1781.

German trans. Leipzig, 1785 (*Die glücklichen Schwestern oder Geschichte der Miss Fanny und Sophie Belmont*) (EAG).

CR: 'A common-place novel, patched up in the very pink of insipidity.'

MR [Samuel Badcock]: 'The hacknied cant of a novel-writer by profession!'

1782: 6   ANON.
*FRAILTIES OF FASHION, OR THE ADVENTURES OF AN IRISH SMOCK, INTERSPERSED WITH WHIMSICAL ANECDOTES OF A NANKEEN PAIR OF BREECHES; CONTAINING AMONG A GREAT VARIETY OF CURIOUS CONNEXIONS BETWEEN THE MOST CELEBRATED DEMI REPS AND BEAUX GARÇONS UPON THE TON. THE SECRET MEMOIRS OF MADAME D'EON, AS RELATED BY HERSELF. AMOURS OF COUNT D'ARTOIS. PRIVATE INTRIGUES OF LADY W——Y AND MRS. N——N.; NEVER BEFORE PUBLISHED. THE FROLICS OF BOARDING SCHOOL MISSES. THE GAMBOLS OF MAIDS OF HONOUR, &C. &C. (EngR).

London: Lister, 1782 (MR).
1 vol. 12mo. 2s 6d sewed (CR), 2s 6d (MR).
CR 55: 234 (Mar 1783); MR 68: 358 (Apr 1783); AF II: 1501.
No copy located.

Notes. CR: 'One of those pernicious incentives to vice that are a scandal to decency. A common pander, who confines his infamous occupation to the service of the stews, is less injurious to society than such prostituted miscreants as devote their time and attention to corrupt the imaginations of youth. The most ignominious punishment prescribed by our laws is infinitely too slight for offences of so heinous a nature.'

MR [Samuel Badcock]: 'This publication is equally remarkable for its stupidity and obscenity. The only circumstance in favour of so wretched a performance, is its more than ordinary dulness and absurdity; which may counteract its bad tendency, and make what was bad in its design, abortive in its effect.'

FRIENDSHIP AND MATRIMONY
See MANSEL, Henry

1782: 7   ANON.
GENUINE ANECDOTES AND AMOROUS ADVENTURES OF SIR RICHARD EASY, AND LADY WAGTAIL: CONTAINING THE HISTORY OF THE POLITE WORLD FOR THE LAST FIVE YEARS; ALSO INCLUDING THE TETES A TETES, INTRIGUES, AND CONNECTIONS OF THE BEAUX GARCONS AND DEMIREPS UPON THE TON; WITH THEIR CHARACTERS, DISPOSITIONS, AND PURSUITS. BY A MAN OF FASHION.

London: Printed for M. Goadby, Pater-noster-Row, 1782.

164p. 8vo [MR has 12mo]. 2s 6d (MR).

MR 66: 475 (June 1782).

BL 1578/3931; EMf; ESTC t204450.

Notes. 2-pp. dedication to 'all the Cuckolds of every Rank, Dignity, Profession, Persuasion, and Description in Europe'. Introduction pp. 1–14.

MR [Samuel Badcock]: 'An obscene and most wretched catchpenny, written from principles which must excite the detestation of all men of goodness, and in a manner which must provoke the contempt of all men of sense.'

GEORGE BATEMAN
See BLOWER, Elizabeth

1782: 8 ANON.
AN INTERESTING SKETCH OF GENTEEL LIFE. BY A LADY.

Southampton: Printed by Linden & Cunningham. Sold by Shelton & Mills, Southampton, and by B. Law, Avemary Lane, London, 1782.

I 160p; II 157p; III 152p. 8vo [MR has 12mo]. 7s 6d (CR), 6s sewed (MR, SJC).

CR 53: 234 (Mar 1782); MR 66: 474 (June 1782).

PU Singer-Mend. PR3991.A6.L319 1782; ESTC n008582.

Notes. Epistolary.

Adv. SJC 10–12 Jan 1782.

Further edn: Dublin, 1782 (Printed by J. and R. Byrn, for Messrs. Price, Whitestone, Walker, Burton, and N. Cross, Booksellers, 2 vols., 12mo), ESTC n008581.

CR: 'There is in these volumes much business with little incident; and a great many persons without interest. The author has no invention; the characters are not discriminated with art or knowledge; and the language, though easy, is often colloquial and vulgar.'

MR [Samuel Badcock]: 'This "interesting sketch" is one of the most tedious and *un*interesting things imaginable: unless (as in this fair lady's estimation!) love and marriage should be deemed the only ends of our existence.'

THE LIFE OF MRS. JUSTMAN
See HAMILTON, Lady Mary

LITERARY AMUSEMENTS; OR, EVENING ENTERTAINER
See 1781: 10

MEMOIRS OF THE RIGHT HONOURABLE LORD VISCOUNT CHERINGTON
See MULLER, Richard

MOUNT HENNETH, A NOVEL
See BAGE, Robert

MUTUAL ATTACHMENT; OR, THE MEMOIRS OF VICTORIA DE PONTY
See BASTIDE, Jean-François de

1782: 9   ANON.
THE PHILOSOPHICAL QUIXOTE; OR, MEMOIR OF MR. DAVID WILKINS. IN A SERIES OF LETTERS.

> London: Printed for J. Johnson, in St. Paul's Church-yard, 1782.
> I vi, 174p; II 164p. 12mo. 6s (CR, MR).
> CR 54: 438–42 (Dec 1782); MR 68: 273 (Mar 1783); AF II: 3330.
> BL 12654.i.1; EM 269: 2; ESTC t107041 (NA MH-H, PU).

Notes. Epistolary.

CR: 'This is a very laughable attack on some of the late philosophical discoveries, and on the attempts which have been made to apply them to the purposes of medicine' (p. 438). 'On the whole, we have been much entertained with these letters, and earnestly wish for their continuation' (p. 442).

MR [Samuel Badcock]: '*Intended* for a satire on certain whimsical adventurers in philosophy and physic. The ridicule of it is only calculated to strike *professional* men. There is little in it to interest general readers, and still less to amuse them.'

THE SIEGE OF AUBIGNY
See USSIEUX, Louis d'

1782: 10   ANON.
WILMOT; OR THE PUPIL OF FOLLY. IN FOUR VOLUMES.

> London: Printed for William Lane, Leadenhall-Street, 1782.
> I xv, 207p; II 187p; III 198p; IV 166p. 8vo. 12s (CR), 10s (MR), 10s sewed (PA).
> CR 54: 319 (Oct 1782); MR 67: 238 (Sept 1782); AF II: 4847.
> BRu ENC; ESTC n066163 (NA CtY).

Notes. Dedication 'To the Monthly and Critical Reviews' v–viii; 'Apology for a Preface' ix–xv. Pagination continuous Roman-Arabic; text of novel starts on p. 17. Epistolary.
Post-dated; adv. as published PA 5 Dec 1781: *Wilmot, or the Pupil of Folly: A Novel, in a Series of Letters. By a Lady.*
Further edn: Dublin, 1782 (Printed for Messrs. S. Price, W. Whitestone, T. Walker, J. Beatty, E. Cross, and R. Burton, 4 vols. [pagination continuous in vols. 1–2 & 3–4], 12mo), ESTC t175164.

CR: 'Though this novel cannot boast of much ingenuity, it is distinguished from the greater part of those productions by one quality, that of not being immoral; a circumstance particularly commendable in such publications as are intended chiefly for the juvenile class of readers.'

MR [Edmund Cartwright]: 'Though this novel may not be distinguished from the general herd of such publications either by originality of incident or character, it has a property which, in works of this kind, is not always to be met with—it is perfectly harmless; and may, therefore, with safety be indulged in by such readers as, labouring under a mental chlorosis, make a practice of gratifying their appetite with every thing that comes in their way.'

1782: 11   ANON.
THE YOUNG PHILOSOPHER, OR THE NATURAL SON. A DRAMATIC NOVEL. IN TWO VOLUMES.

London: Printed for and sold by J. Bowen, No. 40, New Bond-street, And at his Circulating Library on the Steyne, Brighthelmstone, 1782.

I ix, 256p; II 203p. 8vo [MR has 12mo]. 7s (CR), 6s (MR).

CR 53: 234 (Mar 1782); MR 66: 394–5 (May 1782); AF II: 4977.

BRG 823.69 YOU; ESTC t212354.

Notes. ESTC: 'Possibly by Charlotte Turner Smith' [n046067] / 'Apparently not by Charlotte
Turner Smith' [t212354].

EurM gives author as Mr Seally.

Table of contents i–ix. 1 p. advs. end vol. 2.

Adv. LC 50: 619 (27–29 Dec 1781); adv. also lists as by the same author *Delices du Sentiment*
(1781: 3), *Colonel Ormsby* (1781: 2) and *The Woman of Quality* (not identified; the only
known work of this title is 1786: 13).

Further edn: Dublin, 1782 (Printed by George Bonham, for W. Sleater, S. Price, T. Walker,
W. and H. Whitestone, W. Gilbert [and 3 others in Dublin], 1 vol., 12mo), ESTC n046067.

CR: 'This novel is evidently borrowed from a French original; yet, it is not given to the public as a translation, or as an imitation. . . . The story is unequal; and the conclusion, which
ought to have been laboured and artful, is abrupt and unsatisfactory.'

MR [Samuel Badcock]: 'This seems to be a translation from the French; as there are some
errors in grammar not very consistent with the lively and acute arguments observed in other
parts of the performance. . . . There are some characters in this novel that are drawn with a
lively though careless hand' (p. 394).

1782: 12   [BAGE, Robert].
MOUNT HENNETH, A NOVEL. IN TWO VOLUMES.

London: Printed for T. Lowndes, No. 77, Fleet-Street, 1782.

I vi, 286p; II 310p. 12mo. 7s (CR), 6s (MR), 6s sewed (PA, LC).

CR 54: 152 (Aug 1782); MR 66: 129–31 (Feb 1782); AF II: 195.

LEu Novello-Cowden Clarke Collection; ESTC n004283 (NA ICN, IU, NjP, PU &c.).

Notes. Preface i–vi jokes about the reviewers' complaints about reading novels. Epistolary.
LEu copy lacks t.p. to vol. 2.

Bage sold *Mount Henneth* to Lowndes for £30 (Tompkins 9).

Post-dated; adv., 'On Tuesday next will be published', LC 50: 474 (15–17 Nov 1781); adv. as
published LC 50: 492 (20–22 Nov 1781); adv. PA 6 Dec 1781.

Further edns: Dublin, 1782 (Printed for Messrs. Price, Whitestone, Sleater, Moncrieffe,
Walker, Mills, Beatty, E. Cross, and Burton, 2 vols., 12mo), ESTC n004284; London, 1824
(WC, NSTC). German trans. Leipzig, 1783 (*Henneth Castle*) (Price); London, 1788, EM 199:
4, ESTC t108066. Facs: N (Dublin edn.).

CR: 'In this performance there are strokes of vivacity and wit. It is interesting, and, in many
instances, tends to promote virtue. The stories it relates, however, arise not always with sufficient art; and they produce not their effect in that progressive form which corresponds with
real life.'

MR [Samuel Badcock]: We recommend it, 'with the most sincere conviction of its superior merit, to the perusal of our Readers: for we do not remember that we have, for many years,
had the satisfaction of reviewing a work of this kind, that abounds with more lively strokes of
wit, or sallies of fancy; with more judicious reflections, or pleasing and interesting characters.
Its sentiments are liberal and manly, the tendency of it is perfectly moral; for the whole design

is to infuse into the heart, by the most engaging examples, the principles of honour and truth, social love, and general benevolence' (pp. 129–30).

1782: 13 [BASTIDE, Jean-François de].
*MUTUAL ATTACHMENT; OR, THE MEMOIRS OF VICTORIA DE PONTY. A NOVEL. TRANSLATED FROM THE FRENCH.

> London: Printed for W. Lane, Leadenhall-Street (SJC), 1782 (SJC).
> 1 vol. 12mo. 3s (CR, adv.), 2s 6d sewed (SJC).
> CR 57: 233 (Mar 1784); AF II: 3023.
> No copy located.

Notes. Trans. of *Les Aventures de Victoire Ponty* (Amsterdam and Paris, 1758).
Adv. SJC 21–23 Nov 1782.
Adv. end vol. 3 of *The Myrtle* (1784: 5).
   CR: '... the present work is certainly not a translation. It is however a very good little book, if it be not very entertaining.'

1782: 14 [BLOWER, Elizabeth].
GEORGE BATEMAN: A NOVEL. IN THREE VOLUMES.

> London: Printed for J. Dodsley, Pall-Mall, 1782.
> I vi, 243p; II 226p; III 223p. 12mo. 9s sewed (CR), 7s 6d sewed (MR, SJC).
> CR 54: 152 (Aug 1782); MR 66: 237 (Mar 1782); AF II: 383.
> CaOHM; ESTC n067407 (BRu ENC).

Notes. Prefatory advertisement v–vi; 1-p. dedication to Viscountess Mahon (unn.), signed 'The Authoress'. Adv., 'In a few Days will be published', MC 14 Jan 1782; adv. SJC 19–22 Jan 1782.
Further edn: London, 1788 (Bodl.), xESTC. French trans. n.p., 1804 (*Bateman*) (HWS).
   CR: '... some of the characters are well drawn, and several parts of the story are interesting and amusing. We cannot but at the same time remark, in this performance, a too laborious, and even servile, imitation of the two great novelists, Richardson and Fielding. ...'
   MR [Samuel Badcock]: 'The Author*ess* (for so she styles herself, though the distinction was unnecessary, since many "*minutias*" concurred to evince her sex) hath related a plain and simple tale, in an agreeable style. She attempts, however, the bow of Ulysses, without the strength to bend it to advantage, by endeavouring sometimes to imitate Fielding, and at other times the Author of "Evelina" [1778: 10].'

1782: 15 [BURNEY, Frances].
CECILIA, OR MEMOIRS OF AN HEIRESS. BY THE AUTHOR OF EVELINA. IN FIVE VOLUMES.

> London: Printed for T. Payne and Son at the Mews-Gate, and T. Cadell, in the Strand, 1782.
> I 293p; II 263p; III 365; IV 328p; V 398p. 12mo. 15s (CR), 15s bound (MR), 12s 6d sewed (SJC).
> CR 54: 414–20 (Dec 1782); MR 67: 453–8 (Dec 1782); AF II: 548.
> BL 94.a.5-9; EM 5365: 3; ESTC t102228 (BI LEu, MRu, O &c.; NA CSmH, DLC, ICN, MH-H, NjP, PU, TxU &c.; EA GDAs, Ps, ZWTU &c.).

Notes. Evelina 1778: 10.

Burney sold *Cecilia* to Payne and Cadell for £250 (Tompkins 9). In 1795 Burney writes of being told at third-hand that *Cecilia* '*cleared* 1500 pounds *the first Year!*' (Burney, *Journals*, 140).

Adv., 'In a few Days will be published', SJC 22–25 June 1782; adv. as published SJC 11–13 July 1782.

Extract published LC 53: 33 (9–11 Jan 1783).

Further edns: Dublin, 1783 (Printed for Messrs. Price, Moncrieffe, Wilson, Walker, and Byrne, 3 vols., 12mo), EM 4776: 2, ESTC t107625; London, 1783, EM 3805: 3, ESTC t065256; London, 1783, EM 4286: 1, ESTC t120783; Dublin, 1784, EM 4675: 1, ESTC t108068; London, 1784, EM 4432: 1, ESTC t057309; 6 further entries in ESTC; WC has 15 entries between 1800 and 1850; NSTC lists edns. in 1820, 1822, 1823 and [1825?]. Extracts from *Cecilia* published in *Universal Magazine* and *Hibernian Magazine*, 1783, RM 197. French trans. Neufchâtel, 1783 (*Cécilia, ou Mémoires d'une héretière*) (BN); German trans. Leipzig, 1783–84 (*Cecilia, oder Geschichte einer reichen Waise*) (EAG).

CR: 'Upon the whole, we think it but justice to class this work among the first productions of the kind; and recommend it to our readers as worthy their attention, and replete with instruction and rational amusement' (p. 420).

MR [Samuel Badcock]: '... we are at a loss, whether to give the preference to the design or the execution: or which to admire most, the purity of the Writer's heart, or the force and extent of her understanding. We see much of the dignity and pathos of Richardson; and much of the acuteness and ingenuity of Fielding. The attention is arrested by the story; and in general, expectation is gratified by the several events of it. It is related in a style peculiarly nervous and perspicuous, and appears to have been formed on the best model of Dr Johnson's' (p. 453). 'The Novel is protracted to too great a length; and some parts of it are uninteresting. Every part should not be brilliant; but no part should be languid: and if the mind is not awakened, or kept attentive by events of importance, it should be so far amused as not to be indifferent even in the most trivial scenes' (p. 457).

1782: 16   [HAMILTON, Lady Mary].
*THE LIFE OF MRS. JUSTMAN.

> London: Lewis, 1782.
> 2 vols. 12mo. 6s (MR).
> MR 66: 474 (June 1782).
> No copy located.

Notes. Author attribution: Todd. Lady Mary Leslie became by her two marriages first Walker and then Hamilton (see FC).

MR [Samuel Badcock]: 'The Author, we understand, complains of the negligence of the printer, as we think with reason; for we have seldom seen any thing so mangled and mutilated. Seventy-five pages of the original MS. have, we find, been burnt by some accident! But on this occasion, instead of offering our condolence, we present our congratulations both to the Author and the Reader.'

1782: 17   MANSEL, Henry.
FRIENDSHIP AND MATRIMONY; OR, THE HISTORY OF EMILIA AND HENRY; OF LORD AND LADY P——; AND OF FREDERICK AND

FANNY. NOW FIRST PUBLISHED FROM THE SEVERAL ORIGINALS, AS FOUND AMONG THE PAPERS OF THE LATE HENRY MANSEL, ESQ; WITH AN OCCASIONAL PREFACE, BY THE EDITOR. IN A SERIES OF LETTERS. IN TWO VOLUMES.

London: Printed for F. Noble, at his Circulating Library, opposite Gray's Inn Gate, Holborn, 1782.
I xx, 220p; II 212p. 12mo. 6s (CR, MR), 6s bound (PA).
CR 54: 319–20 (Oct 1782); MR 66: 474–5 (June 1782); AF II: 1535.
BRu ENC; xESTC.

Notes. Vol. 1, 'The Editor to the Reader' 5–xx [Arabic 5, then Roman vi–xx], incorporating a letter 'To the writers of the Monthly, Critical and London Reviews' xvii–xx. 4 pp. advs. end vol. Epistolary. Vol. 2 of BRu copy lacks some pages before p. 7.
Post-dated; adv. as published, 'By Henry Mansel, Esq;', PA 14 Nov 1781.

1782: 18   [MULLER, Richard].
MEMOIRS OF THE RIGHT HONOURABLE LORD VISCOUNT CHER-INGTON, CONTAINING A GENUINE DESCRIPTION OF THE GOV-ERNMENT, AND MANNERS OF THE PRESENT PORTUGUESE.

London: Printed for J. Johnson, No. 72, St Paul's Church-Yard, 1782.
I xviii, 190p; II v, 384p. 12mo. 5s sewed (MR, SJC).
MR 67: 388–90 (Nov 1782).
BL N.1804; EM 5603: 3; ESTC t070710 (BI C, BMu; NA DLC).

Notes. 2 vols. in 1, continuous pagination. Dedication to Master General of the Ordnance I, vii, signed 'The Editor'; Editor's Preface viii–xv, London, 21 June 1781.
Adv. SJC 25–27 Apr 1782.
Further edn: Dublin, 1782 (Printed by John Parker, for Messrs. R. Cross, Walker, Beatty, Burton, and Webb, 2 vols., 12mo), ESTC t212832.

1782: 19   ROBINSON, [John].
LOVE FRAGMENTS. A SERIES OF LETTERS NOW FIRST PUBLISHED BY MR. ROBINSON.

London: Printed for J. Wallis, Ludgate-Street, and J. Binns, Leeds, 1782.
xi, 150p. 12mo [MR has small 8vo]. 2s 6d boards (CR, MR).
CR 55: 246 (Mar 1783); MR 68: 275 (1783); AF II: 3817.
BL 12611.d.18; EM 207: 6; ESTC t057812.

Notes. Introduction ('By the Editor') v–xi. Letters end on p. 139; 'Elegy on the Death of the Lady' pp. 141–150. Epistolary.
Adv. SJC 14–17 Dec 1782.
    CR: 'The Letters, supposed originals, are highly affecting; and the heart must be indeed hardened, which can dare to incur reproaches, that even in a fictitious tale chills the blood.'
    MR [Samuel Badcock]: 'These Fragments possess something of the tender and pathetic.'

1782: 20   [SCOTT, Helenus].
THE ADVENTURES OF A RUPEE. WHEREIN ARE INTERSPERSED VARIOUS ANECDOTES ASIATIC AND EUROPEAN.

London: Printed for J. Murray, No. 32, Fleet-Street, 1782.

ix, viii, 264p. 12mo. 3s sewed (half-title, CR), 3s boards (MR), 3s boards or 3s 6d bound (LC, SJC).

CR 52: 477–80 (Dec 1781); MR 66: 395–6 (May 1782); AF II: 3977.

BL N.1880; EM 5371: 17; ESTC t071896 (BI C [imperf.], DBL, O &c.; NA CaAEU, CSmH, CtY-BR &c.).

Notes. Post-dated; adv. as published LC 50: 583 (15–18 Dec 1781); p. 245 misnumbered as 249. Murray paid Scott 5 gns. for copyright (Zachs 320).

Adv. SJC 14–16 Feb 1782 with quotations from CR and TCM.

Further edns: London, 1782, ESTC n003860; Dublin, 1782 (Printed by W. Spotswood, for Messrs. Price, Whitestone, Walker, White [and 4 others in Dublin], 1 vol., 12mo), EM 3769: 4, ESTC t119119; London, 1783, ESTC t077688; Philadelphia, 1783, ESTC w004639. German trans. Berlin, 1788 (*Die Rupie, mit untermischten asiatischen und europäischen Anekdoten*) (Price).

CR: 'This mode of making up a book, and styling it the Adventures of a Cat, a Dog, a Monkey, a Hackney-coach, a Louse, a Shilling, a Rupee, or—any thing else, is grown so fashionable, that few months pass which do not bring one of them under our inspection. It is indeed a convenient method to writers of the inferior class, of emptying their common-place books, and throwing together all the farrago of public transactions, private characters, old and new stories, every thing, in short, which they can pick up, to afford a little temporary amusement to an idle reader. This is the utmost degree of merit which the best of them aspire to; and, small as it is, more than most of them ever arrive at.'

MR [Samuel Badcock]: 'These *Adventures of a Rupee* are somewhat formed on the model of the *Adventures of a Guinea*: but they have neither the shrewd reflections nor the varied entertainment of the latter.'

1782: 21   [USSIEUX, Louis d']; [MANTE, Thomas (*trans.*)].
THE SIEGE OF AUBIGNY. AN HISTORICAL TALE.

London: Printed for T. Hookham, at his Circulating Library, New Bond-Street, Corner of Bruton-Street, n.d. [ESTC: 1782].

iv, 120p. 8vo. 2s (MR), 2s sewed (SJC).

MR 66: 310 (Apr 1782).

ICN Case Y.155.U8; ESTC t212078 (BI E; NA CLU-S/C, MH-H).

Notes. Trans. of *Clémence d'Entragues ou le siège d'Aubigny*, from *Le décaméron françois* [*Le décameron* published Paris, 1772–73; this tale from part 4, 1773].
'The Address' iii–iv.
Adv. SJC 14–16 Feb 1782. Hookham published a *Siege of Aubigny* in 1791, probably the same work, rev. CR n.s. 3: 235 (Oct 1791).

MR [John Noorthouck]: 'A little tale of female heroism, from the history of Henry IV, of France dressed up *à la mode de Paris*, for the transient amusement of our young country-women, who love to read with rapidity; any one of whom would require three or four such *tomes* as this, to fill up the gap between dinner and tea time.'

1782: 22   {YEO, James}.
OMAR AND ZEMIRA: AN EASTERN TALE. FOUNDED ON THE PIETY OF THE ASIATICS. IN TWO VOLUMES.

London: Printed for H. Goldney, Pater-Noster-Row, 1782.
I xxvii, 195p; II 174p. 8vo.
BL 012635.de.2; EM 364: 5; ESTC t108018 (NA NjP).

Notes. Frontispiece in both vols. Dedication to Mrs Roddam v–vi, signed James Yeo; preface vii–xxvii. In vol. 2 text of novel starts on p. 5.
Further edn: Portsmouth, 1791, ESTC n010412. 1791 edn. rev. EngR 21: 226–7 (Mar 1793).

1783

BURTON-WOOD
See MACKENZIE, Anna Maria

COOMBE WOOD. A NOVEL
See MINIFIE, Margaret

1783: 1   ANON.
THE DOUBLE SURPRISE: A NOVEL. IN A SERIES OF LETTERS. IN TWO VOLUMES.

London: Printed for T. Hookham, Corner of Bruton-Street, New Bond-Street, 1783.
I ii, 240p; II ii, 252p. 12mo. 5s sewed (CR), 6s bound (MR), 5s (MC).
CR 56: 477 (Dec 1783); MR 70: 382 (May 1784); AF II: 1127.
BL RB.23.a.8162; ESTC n008086 (NA MnU, ICU).

Notes. Table of contents i–ii in each vol. Epistolary.
Adv. MC 2 Apr 1784.

CR: 'One well-imagined, well-conducted surprize would be fairly worth a thousand such duplicates as the present. These volumes consist of the common materials which are to be found in the store-room of every novellist; but they are not manufactured with any degree of ingenuity. If they cannot afford much entertainment to the fancy, they are, however, not calculated to corrupt it.'

MR [Samuel Badcock]: 'Better than the common offspring of this most common Muse:—who having been so long on the town, we can scarcely expect any thing from her but shapeless abortions, or a still-born issue. A living child creates *surprize*; and a healthy one *doubles* it.'

ERRORS OF NATURE
See WALWYN, B.

EXTRACT FROM THE LIFE OF LIEUTENANT HENRY FOLEY
See 1782: 4

1783: 2   ANON.
THE FAIRY RING, OR EMELINE, A MORAL TALE, BY A LADY.

London: Printed for W. Lane, Leadenhall-Street, 1783.

135p. 12mo. 2s 6d (CR), 1s 6d (MR), 1s 6d sewed (SJC), 2s (adv.).

CR 57: 233 (Mar 1784); MR 68: 358 (Apr 1783); AF II: 1361.

ICN Case Y 154.28; ESTC n047307.

Notes. Text of novel starts on p. 13.

Post-dated; adv. as published SJC 21–23 Nov 1782.

Adv. end vol. 3 of *The Myrtle* (1784: 5).

CR: 'The Fairy, in this little tale, performs her office with wonderful dexterity. She is always ready to support the heroine, and chearfully engages in the cause of virtue and religion. Besides, we find excellent lessons for princes and ministers; but unfortunately in a place where they will do little service, as they probably will be never read.'

MR [Samuel Badcock]: 'This little trifle is distinguished by that pleasing train of imagery, and those romantic situations which usually characterise this visionary class of productions.'

FEMALE SENSIBILITY; OR, THE HISTORY OF EMMA POMFRET
See SKETCHES FROM NATURE (1778: 6)

THE HISTORY OF SANDFORD AND MERTON
See App. A: 1

1783: 3   ANON.
THE HISTORY OF THE MISS BALTIMORES; IN A SERIES OF LETTERS.

London: Printed for T. Hookham, At his Circulating Library, New Bond-street, Corner of Bruton-street, 1783.

I 222p; II 264p. 12mo. 6s (CR, MR), 5s sewed or 6s bound (SJC).

CR 56: 477 (Dec 1783); MR 69: 439 (Nov 1783); AF II: 1973.

BL 12611.aaa.11; EM 7264: 5; ESTC t054972 (NA PU).

Notes. Vol. 2 lacks t.p. In vol. 2 text of novel starts on p. 5. Epistolary.

Adv. SJC 1–3 Apr 1783.

CR: 'A more frivolous and insipid production than these two volumes has, we believe, seldom issued from the press. Without incident, without sentiment, without passion, without character, that deserve to be called such; and hardly less exceptionable in point of morality than of dullness.'

MR [Samuel Badcock]: 'The mental imbecility which requires food of so very tender a nature, as is here set before us, is almost, if not entirely, past even the hope of cure! But it is not enough to observe, that these volumes are trifling, insipid, and tedious in the extreme; they are also defective in their moral tendency.'

1783: 4   ANON.
THE INCOGNITA: OR, EMILY VILLARS. A NOVEL. IN TWO VOLUMES.

London: Printed for W. Lane, Leadenhall-Street, 1783.

I 240p; II 214p. 12mo. 5s sewed (CR, MR), 6s (adv.).

CR 56: 477 (Dec 1783); MR 71: 150 (Aug 1784); AF II: 2183.

BRu ENC; xESTC (EA AUG).

Notes. Epistolary.

Adv. SJC 13–16 Dec 1783.

Adv. end vol. 3 of *The Myrtle* (1784: 5): *The Incognita, or Emily Willis, a Novel, in a Series of Letters.*

CR: 'We meet not here with any remarkable display of imagination; but as little does the author offend the judgment with any thing mean, indelicate, or immoral. So far is he meritorious as to inculcate to his readers the wholesome precept of filial duty; and it would be unjust not to allow him likewise a talent superior to common novellists, in the contrivance of incident, the ingenuity of reflection, and the delineation of character.'

MR [Samuel Badcock]: 'There is some sprightliness in this novel. It has however too much of that sort of vivacity which is kept up by pertness, and *snip-snap*, and saying smart things. Grave readers will be offended at its friskiness; and readers of taste will be disgusted at descriptions which enter too minutely into vulgar scenes, and at dialogues which are degraded by the cant of provincial speech.'

JOSEPH
See App. B: 8

1783: 5   ANON.
A LESSON FOR LOVERS. OR THE HISTORY OF COLONEL MELVILLE, AND LADY CHARLOTTE RICHLEY.

> London: Printed for Francis Noble, at his Circulating Library, opposite Gray's-Inn-Gate, 1783.
> I iv, 260p; II 241p. 12mo. 6s (CR), 6s sewed (MR, LC).
> CR 55: 234 (Mar 1783); MR 68: 91 (Jan 1783); AF II: 2525.
> C S727.d.78.21–2; ESTC n019506 (NA PU).

Notes. T.p. to vol. 2 has comma instead of full stop after 'Lovers'. 6 pp. advs. end vol. 2.

Post-dated; adv. as published LC 52: 475 (4–16 Nov 1782) and SJC 16–19 Nov 1782.

CR: 'Neither the plan nor the execution of this novel is well calculated to procure it admirers among those who have taste for elegant composition, or will admit that fictitious productions have a moral effect on the minds of those who read them. At the same time that the incidents are trite, the story is, with regard to the author's design, injudiciously conducted; and, considering that the story is so tragical, its operation on the passions is extremely disproportioned.'

MR [Samuel Badcock]: 'A very tragical story, but not a very interesting one. . . . Its incidents are all of the trite and hackneyed kind; and the observations that accompany them are flimzy and superficial.'

THE MAGDALEN, OR HISTORY OF THE FIRST PENITENT, first published in shorter version as *The Histories of Some of the Penitents in the Magdalen-House,* 1760 [1759], JR 56, AF I: 1233. William Dodd is sometimes given as author.

THE MAN IN THE MOON
See THOMSON, William

1783: 6   ANON.
MEMOIRS OF MAITRE JACQUES, OF SAVOY. VOL. II.
London: Printed for W. Owen, in Fleet-Street, 1783.
180p. 8vo. 2s sewed (CR, SJC), 2s 6d sewed (MR).
CR 55: 234 (Mar 1783); MR 68: 274 (Mar 1783); AF II: 2826.
RB.23.a.7519; EM 173: 1; ESTC t066877 (NA CLU-S/C, DLC, MdBJ &c.).

Notes. Vol. 1 1775: 12.
This vol. post-dated; adv. as published SJC 3–5 Dec 1782.

CR: 'We recognize in him the same lively and eccentric character as formerly; and it is therefore not improbable that he will afford his readers farther entertainment by the continuation of his narrative.'

MR refers to rev. of vol. 1 of 'these entertaining memoirs' and asks 'Where has this pleasant fellow been ever since?'

MEMOIRS OF THE MANSTEIN FAMILY
See HAWEIS, Thomas

THE ORPHAN. A NOVEL
See ELLIOTT, Miss

PEGGY AND PATTY
See WARTON, Jane

THE PORTRAIT
See ELLIOTT, Miss

THE RECESS
See LEE, Sophia

SIBERIAN ANECDOTES
See HAWEIS, Thomas

THEMIDORE
See GODARD D'AUCOR, Claude

THE TWO MENTORS
See REEVE, Clara

WILLIAM SEDLEY
See App. A: 2

D'AUCOR, Claude Godard
See GODARD D'AUCOR, Claude

DAY, Thomas, THE HISTORY OF SANDFORD AND MERTON
See App. A: 1

1783: 7   [ELLIOTT, Miss].
THE ORPHAN. A NOVEL. IN TWO VOLUMES.

> London: Printed for T. Hookham, At his Circulating Library, New Bond-street, Corner
> of Bruton-Street, 1783.
> I 238p; II 224p. 12mo. 6s (CR), 6s bound (MR), 5s sewed or 6s bound (SJC).
> CR 56: 119 (Oct 1783); MR 69: 262–3 (Sept 1783); AF II: 1255.
> IU x823.EI 583o; ESTC n041719 (NA DLC, ICU).

Notes. Epistolary.
Adv. SJC 1–3 Apr 1783.

CR: 'This novel is not destitute of agreeable qualities, though it abounds with defects. The incidents in general are neither interesting nor new, and the attention is frequently fatigued with a similarity of description.'

MR [Samuel Badcock]: 'There is a prettiness in this Novel; but it wants seasoning. It consists too much of insipid relations of uninteresting adventures, and tedious repetitions of raptures and terrors, and doubts and fears, and so on, through the whole generation of sensibility.'

1783: 8   [ELLIOTT, Miss].
THE PORTRAIT. A NOVEL. IN TWO VOLUMES.

> London: Printed for T. Hookham, At his Circulating Library, New Bond-street, Corner
> of Bruton-street, 1783.
> I 250p; II 243p. 12mo. 6s (CR, MR), 6s bound (SJC).
> CR 56: 477 (Dec 1783); MR 69: 439–40 (Nov 1783).
> BL 12612.bbb.20; EM 133: 6; ESTC t067650.

Notes. Epistolary. Text of novel starts on p. 3 in both vols. 4 pp. advs. end vol. 2.
Adv. SJC 1–3 Apr 1783.

CR: 'This is such a portrait as evinces the author to be no Apelles. It were well if he could even claim a rank among the menial servants of the dilettanti.'

MR [Samuel Badcock]: 'The babes and sucklings of literature, who are supported by this light kind of food, may find in these little volumes provision, if not much better seasoned, yet of a less pernicious quality than what was served up in the former mess.'

1783: 9   GENLIS, [Caroline-Stéphanie-Félicité Ducrest de Mézières],
comtesse de.
**ADELAIDE AND THEODORE; OR LETTERS ON EDUCATION: CON-
TAINING ALL THE PRINCIPLES RELATIVE TO THREE DIFFERENT
PLANS OF EDUCATION; TO THAT OF PRINCES, AND TO THOSE OF
YOUNG PERSONS OF BOTH SEXES. TRANSLATED FROM THE
FRENCH OF MADAME LA COMTESSE DE GENLIS.**

> London: Printed for C. Bathurst, in Fleet-street; and T. Cadell, in the Strand, 1783.
> I 304p; II 295p; III 288p. 12mo. 9s boards (CR), 9s sewed (MR, SJC).
> CR 56: 300–3 (Oct 1783); MR 70: 338–45 (May 1784); AF II: 508.
> BL 1031.1.4-6; EM 6665: 26; ESTC t144082 (BI C, E, O &c.; NA AzU, IU, ViU &c.).

Notes. Trans. of *Adèle et Théodore* (Paris, 1782).
Translator is female and was later to translate *Zelia in the Desert* (1789: 38A).
Epistolary.

Adv., 'In the Press and speedily will be published', SJC 25–27 Mar 1783; adv. as published SJC 5–7 June 1783.

Extract published LC 54: 433 (1–4 Nov 1783).

Further edns: Dublin, 1783 (Printed for Luke White, 3 vols., 12mo), ESTC n016021; London, 1784, ESTC t144531; Dublin, 1785, EM 7868: 8, ESTC t153143; London, 1788, ESTC t153144; London, 1796, ESTC t144661; 2 further entries in ESTC. Extracts in different translations published in 8 magazines between 1782 and 1810, RM 9, 12, 68, 421, 888.

CR: '. . . is much superior to the usual novels, in the general strictness and purity of its precepts, and the exquisite delicacy with which the most important lessons are inculcated' (p. 301).

MR [William Enfield]: '. . . though it may not be practicable to follow the track marked out in these letters, a great variety of hints may be drawn from them, which will be found exceedingly useful to parents and other instructors: and these hints are conveyed in a manner well adapted to interest the reader,—the whole plan being unfolded, at large, in a lively fictitious narrative. Several instructive and pathetic tales are introduced in the way of episode, and entertaining descriptions of domestic manners in the French nation, are interwoven with the work' (pp. 338–9).

1783: 10   [GODARD D'AUCOR, Claude].
THEMIDORE. A NOVEL. TRANSLATED FROM THE FRENCH, BY A CITIZEN OF THE WORLD.

London: Printed for J. Cattermoul, No. 376 Oxford-Street, near Wardour-street, 1783. 8, 220p. 12mo. 3s (MR).

MR 69: 172 (Aug 1783); AF II: 1643.

MH-H *FC7.G5403.Eg 783t; EM 1279: 5; ESTC n014250.

Notes. Trans. of *Thémidore* (The Hague, 1745).

ESTC has 2 entries for Londres [i.e. Paris] edns: 1781 (ESTC t115747, EM 2450: 8) and 1785 (ESTC t222071).

CR 56: 160 (Aug 1783) reviews Themidore and Rozette; or, Authentic Anecdotes of a Parisian Counsellor and Courtezan.

MR: 'Low obscenity, &c. calculated for St. Giles's and Rag Fair.'

1783: 11   [HAWEIS, Thomas].
MEMOIRS OF THE MANSTEIN FAMILY. PATHETIC, SENTIMENTAL, HUMOUROUS, AND SATIRICAL. IN TWO VOLUMES.

London: Printed for T. and W. Lowndes, No. 77, Fleet-Street, 1783. I 228p; II 260p. 12mo. 6s (CR), 6s bound (MR), 5s sewed or 6s bound (SJC).

CR 56: 319 (Oct 1783); MR 69: 261–2 (Sept 1783); AF II: 1830.

BL Cup.401.c.19; EMf; ESTC t133516 (NA CSmH, MH-H).

Notes. ESTC gives name as Haweis; BB gives details of the Rev. Thomas Hawies of Aldwinkle, Northants. BL Add. Mss 38, 728 fol. 111 has the two different forms: the caption to a portrait spells it 'Hawies' and his own signature on a receipt spells it 'Haweis'.

Adv., 'In the Press and speedily will be published', SJC 10–12 Apr 1783; adv. as published SJC 17–19 Apr 1783.

Extract published LC 54: 321 (30 Sept–2 Oct 1783).

Further edn: Dublin, 1783 (Printed for Messrs. Price, Sheppard, Burnet, Gilbert, Moncrieffe [and 6 others in Dublin], 2 vols., 12mo), ESTC n011309. German trans. Leipzig, 1784 (*Mansteinische Familiennachrichten in Erzählungen und Briefen*) (Price).

CR: 'An interesting narrative, accompanied with virtuous sentiments, renders this novel superior to the common productions of the kind.'

MR [Samuel Badcock]: 'This Novel possesses a considerable degree of merit; and is, in almost every view, superior to the general run of productions of this sort. It interests us ... in the fortunes of the principal personages who figure in it: we realize the scene, and take a share in the event. To the merit of keeping us awake, it adds the merit of keeping us pure. As its graver instructions do not fatigue the mind, so its lighter sallies do not taint the fancy. The feelings it communicates are chaste, and the affections it would inspire are benevolent' (p. 261).

1783: 12   [?HAWEIS, Thomas].
SIBERIAN ANECDOTES, A NOVEL. IN THREE VOLUMES. CONTAINING REAL HISTORIES AND LIVING CHARACTER.

> London: Printed for T. Lowndes and Son, No. 77, Fleet-Street, 1783.
> I 238p; II 234p; III 185p. 12mo. 9s (CR), 9s bound (MR), 7s 6d sewed or 9s bound (LC, SJC).
> CR 57: 316 (Apr 1784); MR 68: 273–4 (Mar 1783); AF II: 4088.
> BL 12613.f.5; EM 217: 1; ESTC t070100 (BI C, Ct; NA DLC, NjP, ViU &c.).

Notes. ESTC attributes to 'Hawers', but this seems to be a mistake or alternative for 'Hawies' or 'Haweis' (see 1783: 11).
Historical novel with some basis in fact.
Imprint in vol. 1 omits 'and Son'.
Adv. LC 52: 622 (26–28 Dec 1782); adv. SJC 7–9 Jan 1783. Also adv. several times in SJC in Apr 1783 as footnote to adv. for Thomas Hawies's *Memoirs of the Manstein Family* [see above].
Further edn: Dublin, 1783 (Printed for S. Price, W. Gilbert, T. Walker, W. Wilson, L. White [and 3 others in Dublin], 2 vols., 12mo), ESTC t174159. German trans. Leipzig, 1785 (*Sibirische Anekdoten*) (Price).

CR: 'Among the various furniture of a circulating library, these little volumes were for some time overlooked; yet they ought to be mentioned with respect. There is a semblance of true history in some parts of them; and others are distinguished by a luxuriance of imagination, corrected by a knowledge of the country which is described, and of the manners of its inhabitants.'

MR [Samuel Badcock]: 'The vestiges of Siberian customs, and the analogy, though remote, which they bear to real history, render these little volumes, in a considerable degree, amusing and interesting. The design is meritorious, and the tendency such as to warrant our cordial recommendation. . . . The story is naturally conducted; and the anecdotes will afford both entertainment and instruction to a candid reader.'

1783: 13   HOLCROFT, Thomas.
THE FAMILY PICTURE; OR, DOMESTIC DIALOGUES ON AMIABLE AND INTERESTING SUBJECTS; ILLUSTRATED BY HISTORIES, ALLEGORIES, TALES, FABLES, ANECDOTES, &C. INTENDED TO

STRENGTHEN AND INFORM THE MIND. BY THOMAS HOLCROFT, AUTHOR OF DUPLICITY, A COMEDY.

London: Printed for Lockyer Davis, in Holborn; Printer to the Royal Society, 1783.
I 260p; II 280p. 12mo. 6s sewed in boards (SJC).
EngR 1: 255 (1783); AF II: 2007.
BL 12611.df.2; EM 238: 2; ESTC t057335 (BI O; NA CLU-S/C, MnU, MdBJ; EA COR).

Notes. 2 pp. advs. vol. 2 between the table of contents and the first page of the text.
Adv., 'On Tuesday next will be published', SJC 23–25 Jan 1783.
Further edn: Dublin, 1783 (Printed by R. Rhames, for J. Potts, T. Walker, J. Beatty, L. White, and R. Burton, 2 vols., 12mo), ESTC t190524.

1783: 14   JOHNSON, Theophilus.
PHANTOMS: OR, THE ADVENTURES OF A GOLD-HEADED CANE. CONTAINING A GENERAL DESCRIPTIVE AND PICTURESQUE VIEW OF HUMAN LIFE. BY THE LATE THEOPHILUS JOHNSON, PROMPTER TO SADLER'S-WELLS. IN TWO VOLUMES.

London: Printed for William Lane, Leadenhall-Street, 1783.
I 226p; II 212p. 12mo. 6s (CR, adv. 1784), 5s sewed (MR, adv. 1786).
CR 57: 234–5 (Mar 1784); MR 71: 150–1 (Aug 1784).
O Hope 8° 537, 538; ESTC n011396 (NA CtY, MH-H).

Notes. Vol. 1, 1-p. dedication to Thomas King, Comedian; 3-pp. preface; 4-pp. table of contents.
Adv. end vol. 3 of The Myrtle (1784: 5); adv. end vol. 3 of Zoriada (1786: 24).

CR: 'Every thing has had its adventures, from a Bank Note to a Shilling, from a Coach to a Sedan, from a Star to a Gold-Headed Cane. This mode of conveying political censures, private scandal, or general satire, is almost exhausted; and the spirit and good sense which animated the imaginary Chrysal, was lost in the Hackney Coach, and scarcely breathe in the "Phantoms." . . . They are the hasty productions of the glowing hand of an author, who sometimes painted from his own reflections, and sometimes, we fear, from his own misfortune.'

MR [Samuel Badcock]: '. . . it is nothing but a dirty, rotten broomstick, thrown away by the scavenger, and picked up in the kennel.'

KILNER, Mary Ann, WILLIAM SEDLEY
See App. A: 2

1783: 15   [LEE, Sophia].
THE RECESS; OR, A TALE OF OTHER TIMES. BY THE AUTHOR OF THE CHAPTER OF ACCIDENTS.

London: Printed for T. Cadell, in the Strand, 1783.
256p. 12mo. 3s 6d (CR), 3s sewed (MR, PA).
CR 55: 233–4 (Mar 1783); MR 68: 455–6 (May 1783); AF II: 2503.
PU Singer-Mend.PR3451.L2R4 1783; ESTC n048409 (NA ICU, ViU).

Notes. Re-published with 2 additional vols. 1785: 37.
The Chapter of Accidents (1780) is a play.

Adv., 'In a few Days will be published', PA 1 Feb 1783; adv. as published PA 12 Feb 1783.
Further edn: Dublin, 1783 (Printed for T. Walker, J. Beatty, H. Whitestone, R. Burton, J. Cash, and W. Sleater, 2 vols. in 1, no format) (WC), xESTC; rest of further edns all of 3-vol. version. German trans. Leipzig, 1786 (*Die Ruinen, eine Geschichte aus den vorigen Zeiten*) (EAG). Facs: N.

CR: 'This little volume is full of surprising and yet not improbable events. The author, Miss Lee, properly observes, that the age of Elizabeth was that of romance, and she has accordingly chosen it for the era of her heroines. . . . It is new; it is instructive; it is highly interesting; and we wish that this mode of writing were more frequent' (p. 233).

MR [Samuel Badcock]: '*The Tale of other Times* is a romantic title. It awakens curiosity; it sets us at once on *fairy* land—while Fancy, equipped for adventure, sallies forth in quest of the castle, the giant, and the dragon. . . . The Preface, however, soon broke the *charm* of the title; and we were brought back to our sober senses by an assurance, that the ground we had before us was real and not imaginary: it was founded on fact and not on fiction; and that what we took for a romance was only a history!' (p. 455).

1783: 16   [MACKENZIE, Anna Maria].
BURTON-WOOD. IN A SERIES OF LETTERS. BY A LADY.

> London: Printed for the Author, by H. D. Steel, No. 51, Lothbury, near Coleman Street: and sold by W. Flexney, Bookseller, Holborn, 1783 [vol. 1].
> London: Printed for the Author, by H. D. Steel, No. 51, Lothbury, near Coleman Street, 1783 [vol. 2].
> I 132, 7p; II 158p. 8vo. 5s sewed (CR, MR).
> CR 56: 74 (July 1783); MR 68: 457 (May 1783); AF II: 2653.
> C S727.e.78.4-; ESTC t167329.

Notes. Preface in form of address to the subscribers at end of vol. 1. Epistolary.
MR gives Dodsley as bookseller.
Adv., 'In Two neat Pocket Volumes', PA 18 Jan 1783; Printed for the Author and sold by Mr. Dodsley, Bookseller, Pall-mall; Mr Flexney, Bookseller, Holborn; Mr. Fielding, Paternoster-Row; Mr. Steel, Bookseller, Star Alley, Fenchurch-street; Mr. Tomlinson, Bookseller, Whitechapel; and the other Booksellers in Town and Country.'
Further edn: Dublin, 1783 (Printed by J. A. Husband, for W. Sleater, S. Price, T. Walker, J. Beatty, R. Burton [and 4 others in Dublin], 2 vols., 12mo), EM 160: 7, ESTC t079541.

MR [Samuel Badcock]: 'As this is a *first* attempt, and especially the first attempt of a *female* author, candour should repress the vigour of criticism, even though impartiality could not compliment with the warmth of applause.—The story of this novel is natural and pathetic; and it hath still the higher merit of encouraging the virtuous propensities of the human heart: nor doth it slight the sanctions of religion, in enforcing and recommending the obligations of morality.'

MACKENZIE, Anna Maria, **JOSEPH**
See App. B: 8

1783: 17   [MINIFIE, Margaret].
COOMBE WOOD. A NOVEL: IN A SERIES OF LETTERS. BY THE AUTHOR OF BARFORD ABBEY AND THE COTTAGE.

London: Printed for R. Baldwin, Pater-Noster-Row, 1783.
I 216p; II 172p. 12mo. 6s (CR), 5s sewed (MR, SJC).
CR 55: 333 (Apr 1783); MR 68: 456–7 (May 1783); AF II: 2881.
PU Singer-Mend. PR.3505.G85.C66.1783; ESTC n027373 (BI O).

Notes. Often incorrectly attributed to Susannah Minifie Gunning, but see FC pp. 469, 744.
Epistolary.
Barford Abbey, 1768, JR 1121, AF I: 1870; *The Cottage,* 1769, JR 1322, AF I: 1871.
Adv., 'On Tuesday next will be published', SJC 23–25 Jan 1783; adv. 'To morrow at Noon will
be published', PA 27 Jan 1783.
Further edn: Dublin, 1783 (Printed by T. Henshall, for W. Sleater, J. Potts, T. Walker,
J. Beatty, J. Exshaw, R. Burton, J. Parker, P. Byrne, and T. Webb, 1 vol., 12mo), ESTC
n014789.
  CR: '. . . the present volumes are some of the most uninteresting we ever perused.'
  MR [Samuel Badcock]: 'We have no high encomiums to bestow on this performance. The
story is meagre; the incidents are few; and the characters have been long worn out in the service of the novel writers. We must, however, pay some tribute of acknowledgment to the style
and manner of the letters, which make up the story of *Coombe Wood.* They are written with
ease, and contain no inconsiderable portion of the *agreeable*' (p. 457).

1783: 18   MURDOCH, John.
PICTURES OF THE HEART, SENTIMENTALLY DELINEATED IN THE
DANGER OF THE PASSIONS, AN ALLEGORICAL TALE: THE ADVEN-
TURES OF A FRIEND OF TRUTH, AN ORIENTAL HISTORY, IN TWO
PARTS: THE EMBARRASSMENTS OF LOVE, A NOVEL: AND THE
DOUBLE DISGUISE, A DRAMA, IN TWO ACTS. BY JOHN MURDOCH.
IN TWO VOLUMES.

London: Printed for the Authour; and sold by J. Bew, Pater-noster-Row; J. Stockdale,
  Piccadilly; J. Millidge, Maiden-Lane, Covent-Garden; and by the Authour, No. 9.
  Green-Park-Row, near Down-Street, Piccadilly, 1783.
I x, 212p; II 219p. 12mo. 6s (CR), 5s sewed (MR), 5s sewed or 6s bound (SJC).
CR 56: 75–6 (July 1783); MR 69: 343 (Oct 1783); AF II: 2999.
BL 12611.bbb.18; EM 235: 7; ESTC t108512 (BI BMu, E; NA CSmH, MH-H).

Notes. 1 p. advs. end vol. 2. Dedicated to John Earl of Galloway. A series of tales and a play.
Part published in 1769 in *Universal Museum* as 'The Danger of the Passions', RM 284. Part
published in 1773 in *Westminster Magazine* as 'The Embarrassments of Love'; this part later
republished in *New Novelist's Magazine* and *Caledonian Magazine* in 1786–87, RM 359.
Extracts from *Pictures of the Heart* also published in *Universal Magazine* and *Hibernian
Magazine,* 1783, RM 541.
CR reviews under 'Miscellaneous' and MR under 'Novel'.
Adv. SJC 17–20 May 1783.
Further edn: Dublin, 1783 (Printed by J. Rea, for Messrs. Gilbert, Walker, Beatty, Exshaw,
Burton, White, Byrne, and Mackenzie, 2 vols., 12mo), ESTC n020697.
  CR: 'This *pretty* title page introduces some entertaining adventures, which will agreeably
amuse during the fashionable tortures of the frizeur. We can promise nothing more; but, if
an attentive reader should probably think them worth his perusal, he will find the Adven-
tures of a Friend to Truth superior to the other works.'

MR [Samuel Badcock]: 'Neither entitled to much censure, nor deserving of much praise. The merit of these pictures is of the negative kind. Some will be amused and perhaps instructed by them. But others will soon grow tired, and turn from them either with disgust or indifference.'

1783: 19   [REEVE, Clara].
THE TWO MENTORS: A MODERN STORY. BY THE AUTHOR OF THE OLD ENGLISH BARON.

> London: Printed for Charles Dilly, 1783.
> I 308p; II 315p. 12mo. 6s (CR), 5s sewed (MR, SJC).
> CR 55: 333–4 (Apr 1783); MR 68: 539 (June 1783); AF II: 3716.
> BL N.1703; EM 1924: 3; ESTC t070737 (BI C, IPSr, O; NA CSmH, CtY-BR, ICN, MH-H, NjP, ViU &c.; EA Ps).

Notes. Epistolary.
For *The Old English Baron* see *The Champion of Virtue* 1777: 16.
Adv., 'Wednesday the 26th inst. will be published', SJC 13–15 Feb 1783.
Extract published LC 53: 473–4 (17–20 May 1783).
Further edns: London, 1783, EM 6463: 7, ESTC t118919; Dublin, 1783 (Printed for S. Price, W. and H. Whitestone, W. Colles, W. Gilbert, R. Moncrieffe [and 7 others in Dublin], 2 vols., 12mo), ESTC t076282; London, 1803 (Bodl., WC). French trans. Amsterdam and Paris, 1784 (*Les Deux Mentors, ou Mémoires pour servir à l'histoire des moeurs anglaises au 18e siècle*) (BN); German trans. Leipzig, 1784 (*Die zween Mentor*) (Price).

CR: 'To exhibit virtue in its pleasing native hue should be the business of genius and taste; but it often falls to the lot of those who are little qualified to adorn it with their fancy, or recommend it by their representations. On the whole, our author has succeeded in her attempt, and deserves our approbation' (p. 334).

MR [Samuel Badcock]: 'If strict morality can recommend a work, the present hath a claim to public attention.'

1783: 20   ROUSSEAU, J[ean]-J[acques].
EMILIUS AND SOPHIA; OR, THE SOLITARIES. BY J. J. ROUSSEAU. BEING A SEQUEL TO EMILIUS. ALSO SOME ADDITIONS TO ELOISA. BY THE SAME AUTHOR. BOTH FOUND AMONGST HIS PAPERS AFTER HIS DECEASE.

> London: Printed by H. Baldwin. Sold by T. Becket in Pallmall; and R. Baldwin, in Paternoster-Row, 1783.
> 104p. 12mo [CR has 8vo]. 2s 6d (CR, MR).
> CR 55: 108–9 (Feb 1783); MR 68: 396–8 (May 1783).
> BL RB.23.a.6894; ESTC n045664 (BI Ct).

Notes. Trans. of *Émile et Sophie, ou les solitaires. Suite d'Émile* (Geneva, 1780).
'The Editor's Preface' pp. 3–6; text begins on p. 7.
Adv., 'In the Press, and speedily will be published', SJC 22–24 Oct 1782; entitled only 'A Translation of Mons. Rousseau's Sequel to his Emilius' and without the Baldwins' names.
Adv., 'Tomorrow will be published, (Now first printed in English)' with full title and both booksellers' names, SJC 14–17 Dec 1782.

Extract published LC 53: 569 (14–17 June 1783).

Extracts (possibly different trans.) from *Emilius and Sophia* published in *Universal Magazine*, 1810, RM 361.

CR: 'These additions are in the spirit of Rousseau, and said to have been found among his papers after his decease. It would not be easy to detect a careful imitator of this visionary and inconsistent author, because, while there is nothing too elevated for his more sublime flights, there is nothing so absurd and contradictory that his conduct and writings will not in some measure countenance. . . . On the whole, we have little doubt of the authenticity of the present continuation; and this will be a sufficient recommendation of it to the admirers of this visionary reformer' (p. 108).

MR [Samuel Badcock]: 'These fragments are undoubtedly authentic. Every page speaks the pen of Rousseau—that wild but original pen, which he sometimes dipped in the pure fount of nature and sometimes in the mingled stream of fancy and folly' (pp. 396–97).

1783: 21   {SMYTH, Maria}.
THE WOMAN OF LETTERS; OR, THE HISTORY OF MISS FANNY BEL-TON. IN TWO VOLUMES.

> London: Printed for Francis Noble, at his Circulating Library, opposite Gray's-Inn-Gate, Holborn, 1783.
> I xii, 248p; II 279p. 12mo. 6s (CR, MR), 6s sewed (SJC), 7s bound (adv.).
> CR 56: 74 (July 1783); MR 68: 456 (May 1783); AF II: 4168.
> BRu ENC; EM 8814: 2; ESTC n025043 (BI MRu; NA TxHR; EA WAu).

Notes. Preface to the reader i–viii; 'Advertisement to the Reader. By the Editor', signed Maria Smyth, ix–xii. 5 pp. advs. end vol. 2. Epistolary.
Adv. SJC 2–4 Jan 1783.
Adv. end vol. 1 of *The Young Widow* (1785: 21).

CR: 'Whether this novel was meant to have any particular allusion, we shall not determine; but the moral of it seems not to be such as is often verified in female life. It inculcates, that genius and a learned education united, are insufficient to procure a woman a decent subsistence, or to prevent her from being entangled in the mazes of a plausible hypocrite. The novel, however, is undoubtedly superior to the common productions of the kind; and should it be attended with the effect of inducing ladies to cultivate the qualifications of domestic life rather than literary talents, it may prove of considerable advantage.'

MR [Samuel Badcock]: 'This interesting Narrative we suspect to be something more than the fiction of a lively imagination: but whether fictitious or real, we think it in many respects superior to the usual furniture of a circulating library. It inculcates a very useful lesson,—That all the fire of genius, all the advantages of a learned education, are of themselves insufficient to procure a female a decent subsistence, or secure her from falling a victim to the artifices of a hypocrite.

1783: 22   [THOMSON, William].
THE MAN IN THE MOON; OR, TRAVELS INTO THE LUNAR REGIONS, BY THE MAN OF THE PEOPLE.

> London: Printed for J. Murray, No 32, Fleet Street, 1783.
> I 178p; II 214p. 8vo. 6s (CR), 5s sewed (MR, SJC).
> CR 55: 470–3 (June 1783); MR 69: 405–10 (Nov 1783); AF II: 4462.

BL N.1809, 10; EM 2010: 1; ESTC t070735 (BI E; NA CaQMM, CtY, CSmH, PU &c.; EA WaU).

Notes. 6 pp. advs. end vol. 1; 2 pp. advs. end vol. 2.

Adv., 'In the Press and speedily will be published, In Two small Pocket Volumes', SJC 5–8 Apr 1783; adv., 'To-morrow will be published', SJC 26–29 Apr 1783.

CR: 'This ingenious and eccentric performance seems to have been written under the full influence of the planet whose solitary inhabitant it so whimsically describes; yet the term Lunatic will not disgrace the author, if we follow his opinion of the powers of the planet. The Man of the People, Mr. C. F. [Charles Fox] in a solitary walk at midnight, full of reflexions on his complicated disappointments both in politics and play, is accosted by the Man in the Moon, and carried by him to the lunar regions. The particular appearance of the planet and its inhabitants are described with fancy and ingenuity; so that the work, as may be expected, is a vehicle both for literary and political satire. Though we have praised these volumes for their ingenuity, yet we must confess, that we were not much interested in the event. The discussions, though sometimes lively and frequently severe, are not always so particularly appropriated, as to fix the attention' (pp. 470–1).

1783: 23   [WALWYN, Mr. B.].
THE ERRORS OF NATURE: OR, THE HISTORY OF CHARLES MANLEY. IN THREE VOLUMES.

London: Printed for B. Pownall, Bookseller, N°. 6, Pall-Mall, 1783.
I 266p; II 244p; III 240p. 12mo. 9s bound (MR), 7s 6d (LEP), 7s 6d sewed (adv.).
MR 70: 163 (Feb 1784); AF II: 4695.
BMu r PR 3757.W65; ESTC t222336;

Notes. Love In A Cottage (1785: 47) is, according to MR, 'By B. Walwyn, Author Of The Errors Of Nature'.

Epistolary. T.p. to vol. 3 omits 'In Three Volumes' and vol. 3 not dated. In vol. 3 p. [214] misnumbered 114 and p?[215] misnumbered 151.

Adv. SJC 12–14 Aug 1783.

Adv., as 'by Mr. Walwyn' and with Cass as bookseller, LC 57: 376 (16–19 Apr 1785). Adv. LEP 12–15 Aug 1786; 'Printed for J. Bew, Pater-noster-Row; and H. D. Symonds, facing Stationers-Hall'.

Extract published LC 54: 167 (14–16 Aug 1783).

Adv. end vol. 3 of *Camilla* (1785: 4).

MR [Samuel Badcock]: 'This Novel shews the *error* of the Author in imitating a corrupt model. The admirers of some late performances in this line may think the present work interesting and pathetic; but those who look for nature and simplicity, good sense, or nice discernment, entertaining relations, or instructive and judicious reflections, will find very little to gratify their taste in these volumes.'

1783: 24   [WARTON, Jane].
PEGGY AND PATTY; OR THE SISTERS OF ASHDALE. IN FOUR VOLUMES.

London: Printed for J. Dodsley, Pall-Mall, 1783.
I vii, 164p; II 183p; III 172p; IV 171p. 8vo [MR has 12mo]. 10s sewed (CR, MR).

CR 56: 476 (Dec 1783); MR 69: 440 (Nov 1783); AF II: 4703.

CSmH 421352; EM 5555: 1; ESTC n038510 (NA CtY-BR, PU, TxU).

Notes. Author attribution: Todd.

'Advertisement to the Reader' vol. 1, pp. v–vii. Epistolary.

Adv., 'In a few Days will be published', PA 13 June 1783; adv. as published PA 21 June 1783. Further edns: Dublin, 1783 (Printed for T. Walker, P. Byrne [etc.], 2 vols. in 1, no format) (WC), xESTC; Dublin, 1784, ESTC n019881; London, 1784, EM 167: 2, ESTC t066388; London, 1805 (WC); London, 1810 (WC).

CR: 'This novel, we find, is the production of a lady, and bears evident marks of a chasteness and delicacy of imagination, as well as of pathetic and moral sentiment. It refines while it moves the tender emotions of sympathetic affliction; and where the narrative assumes a strain less remote from gaiety, it is always by agreeable transitions, and with adventures that never fail to prove interesting.'

MR [Samuel Badcock]: 'This pathetic, and in many respects instructive novel, is . . . distinguished for its delicacy and morality. In the *outlines* there is a striking resemblance of "*The Sisters*," a novel by the late Dr Dodd [1754, JR 233, AF I: 656], of unfortunate memory. But the resemblance is in the outlines only.'

1784

BARHAM DOWNS
See BAGE, Robert

1784: 1   ANON.
THE BASTARD; OR, THE HISTORY OF MR. GREVILLE. BY A LADY. DEDICATED, BY PERMISSION, TO HIS ROYAL HIGHNESS THE PRINCE OF WALES. IN TWO VOLUMES.

London: Printed for T. Hookham, At his Circulating Library, New Bond Street, Corner of Bruton Street, 1784.
I 256p; II 246p. 12mo. 6s (CR), 5s sewed (MR, MC).
CR 58: 227 (Sept 1784); MR 71: 387 (Nov 1784); AF II: 231.
P Y².16497/8; ESTC t213837 (NA NNU).

Notes. By same author as *Death's a Friend* (1788: 11).

Text spread thinly; only 14 lines on each full page. Dedication to H.R.H. the Prince of Wales missing. 2 pp. adv. for Hookham's Library end vol. 2.

Adv. MC 8 July 1784; 'Printed for Thomas Hookham, (Agent to the New Fire-Office, Lombard Street) at his Circulating Library, New Bond-street, corner of Bruton-street'.

French trans. Amsterdam and Paris, 1786 (*Le Fils Naturel ou mémoires de Gréville*) (BGR).

CR: 'The first volume of this novel is somewhat interesting; but the second is much inferior, though the author endeavours to "harrow up the soul" by a pathetic, but hackneyed catastrophe. . . . We think that the whole of this work is familiar to us; but these passing shades do not make a sufficient impression on the mind's eye, to enable us to recollect the particular form in which it has appeared.'

MR [Samuel Badcock]: 'Though this cannot be numbered amongst the finer and more elegant productions of sensibility, yet it is at least entitled to the honourable claim of a *legitimate* birth; and this is no trifling boast, considering how the literary world, and especially the region of novels, hath of late been over-run with a spurious issue.'

DAMON AND DELIA
See GODWIN, William

DANGEROUS CONNECTIONS
See LACLOS, Pierre-Antoine-François Choderlos de

THE DÉNOUEMENT; OR, THE HISTORY OF LADY LOUISA WINGROVE
See 1781: 4

1784: 2   ANON.
THE HISTORY OF LORD BELFORD, AND MISS SOPHIA WOODLEY. IN A SERIES OF LETTERS.

London: Printed for Francis Noble, opposite Gray's Inn Gate, Holborn, 1784.
I xii, 227p; II 236p; III 224p. 12mo. 9s (CR), 7s 6d (MR), 7s 6d sewed (LC), 9s bound (MC).
CR 58: 397 (Nov 1784); MR 72: 234 (Mar 1785); AF II: 1966.
BL 12611.c.11; EM 235: 8; ESTC t055912 (NA MH-H, PU).

Notes. 1 p. advs. end vol. 1. Epistolary.
Adv. LC 56: 380 (16–19 Oct 1784). Adv. MC 18 Nov 1784.

CR: 'The little merit in this History is borrowed from Richardson. Lord Belford is a poor copy of Grandison, Sophia of his Harriet, and Julia of Clementina. Even the lower characters have little originality; but the story is amusing and exemplary. On the whole, this performance deserves no great commendation: the sentiments are trite, the situations common, and the plot is conducted with so little artifice, that expectation is gratified almost as soon as it is raised.'

MR [Samuel Badcock]: 'A sprightly, amusing, and sensible novel, in which the several characters are happily distinguished; and the whole is calculated to impress the mind with the purest sentiments of virtue, and teach it, in the hour of trial, to bear afflictions and disappointments with patience and fortitude, that it may be prepared to enjoy prosperity with calmness and dignity; ever considering that the lot of life is not at our disposal nor subject to our controul; and that virtue only is in the power of man.'

IMOGEN; A PASTORAL ROMANCE
See GODWIN, William

THE INDEPENDENT
See McDONALD, Andrew

ITALIAN LETTERS
See GODWIN, William

LAURA AND AUGUSTUS
See BROMLEY, Eliza Nugent

LETTERS TO HONORIA AND MARIANNE, ON VARIOUS SUBJECTS
See WARTON, Jane

1784: 3   ANON.
LOYOLA. A NOVEL.

> London: Printed for T. and W. Lowndes, No. 77, Fleet-street; B. Law, in Ave-Maria-Lane; G. Wilkie, in St. Paul's Church-Yard; Messrs. Richardson and Urquhart, under the Royal Exchange, 1784.
> 230p. 8vo.
> BL 12613.d.12; EM 201: 9; ESTC t070094.

Notes. Epistolary.

MARIA, OR THE GENEROUS RUSTIC
See BERKELEY, George Monck

1784: 4   ANON.
THE MODERN ATALANTIS; OR, THE DEVIL IN AN AIR BALLOON. CONTAINING THE CHARACTERS AND SECRET MEMOIRS OF THE MOST CONSPICUOUS PERSONS OF HIGH QUALITY, OF BOTH SEXES, IN THE ISLAND OF LIBERTUSIA, IN THE WESTERN OCEAN. TRANSLATED FROM THE LIBERTUSIAN LANGUAGE.

> London: Printed for G. Kearsley, at No. 46, Fleet Street, 1784.
> iv, 125p. 12mo. 2s 6d (MR, MC)
> MR 71: 231 (1784); AF II: 2899.
> BL 1081.f.18; EM 1993: 11; ESTC t061075 (NA CtY-Walpole, CSmH, MH-H, PU &c.).

Notes. Dedication to J*** W*****, Esq. [John Wilkes] iii–iv. 6 pp. advs. end vol.
MR reviews under 'Miscellaneous'.
Adv., 'By permission of the Professor of Modern Languages in the Island of Libertusia. Tomorrow will be published, in a pocket volume', MC 12 Mar 1784.

MR [Samuel Badcock]: 'The characters here exhibited are well known; and what is related of them needed no *devil* to reveal. The Writer had no secret communication with supernatural intelligences. The news-papers and the common fame of the day, supplied him with the whole fund of private and personal scandal, which he hath here retailed.'

MUTUAL ATTACHMENT; OR, THE MEMOIRS OF VICTORIA DE PONTY
See 1782: 13

1784: 5   ANON.
THE MYRTLE: OR, EFFECTS OF LOVE. A NOVEL, IN A SERIES OF LETTERS. BY A LADY. IN THREE VOLUMES.

London: Printed for William Lane, Leadenhall-Street, 1784.
I 200p; II 190p; III 197p. 12mo. 7s 6d sewed (MR, adv., SJC), 9s (CR).
CR 59: 66 (Jan 1785); MR 73: 236 (Sept 1785); AF II: 3025.
MnU WILS RAR 824M99 0; ESTC n026582.

Notes. 6 pp. advs. end vol. 3. Running-title: 'Effects of Love'. In vols. 2 and 3 text begins on p. 5. Epistolary.
Adv. SJC 18–20 Jan 1785.
Adv. end vol. 3 of *Zoriada* (1786: 24).
Further edn: Dublin, 1785 (Printed for S. Price, R. Moncrieffe, C. Jenkin, L. White, J. Beatty [and 4 others in Dublin], 3 vols., 12mo), ESTC 035271.

CR: 'We peruse so many trifling performances of this kind, that we want a variety of language to characterise them; but, in future, when we meet with any thing unusually trifling, we may say, that it is as trite as insignificant, and as uninteresting as the Myrtle.'

MR [William Enfield]: 'The story trifling, the language pertly familiar, and the moral—nothing.'

ORIGINAL LOVE-LETTERS
See COMBE, William

REGINALD DU BRAY: AN HISTORIC TALE
See THE RIVAL FRIENDS (1776: 5)

THE RENCONTRE
See GWYNN, Albinia (1785: 33)

1784: 6   ANON.
THE RING: A NOVEL: IN A SERIES OF LETTERS. BY A YOUNG LADY. IN THREE VOLUMES.

London: Printed for J. Stockdale, opposite Burlington-House, Piccadilly, 1784.
I iv, 264p; II 243p; III 191p. 12mo. 9s (CR, MR), 7s 6d sewed or 9s bound (SJC).
CR 56: 477 (Dec 1783); MR 71: 150 (Aug 1784); AF II: 3793.
BL 012635.df.3; EM 366: 3; ESTC t107702 (BI O; NA CLU-S/C, MH-H; EA P, WAu).

Notes. By same author as *The False Friends* (1785: 7) and *Agitation* (1788: 3).
Running-title: 'The history of Lady Jemima Guzman'. Vol. 3 imprint date MDCCCLXXXIV. Epistolary.
Post-dated; adv., 'On the 1st of November next will be published', SJC 23–25 Oct 1783; adv. as published SJC 15–18 Nov 1783.
Further edns: Dublin, 1784 (Printed for S. Price, W. and H. Whitestone, R. Moncrieffe, T. Walker, G Burnet [and 5 others in Dublin], 3 vols., 12mo), ESTC n012822. German trans. Leipzig, 1785 (*Der Ring*) (Price); French trans. Paris, 1789 (*L'anneau ou Jemima Gusman*) (BGR).

CR: 'This novel, which is said to be the production of a lady, introduces us to the acquaintance of such a number of personages that we are almost bewildered in the crowd. The discrimination of character is lost in the multiplicity and mutual resemblance of the objects; and we are every moment astonished with something marvellous. The language, nevertheless, is perfectly chaste, and the situations unexceptionable in point of morality.'

MR [Samuel Badcock]: 'This is said to be the production of a *very* young Lady. She appears, however, to be so well acquainted with the tricks of the profession, that one would be led to imagine that she had been an old practitioner.'

THE RIVAL BROTHERS, A NOVEL
See MORRIS, Mrs

1784: 7 ANON.
ST. RUTHIN'S ABBEY: A NOVEL. IN THREE VOLUMES.

> London: Printed for Francis Noble, opposite Gray's Inn Gate, Holborn, 1784.
> I 240p; II 236p; III 232p. 12mo. 9s (CR, MR), 7s 6d sewed (SJC), 9s bound (adv.).
> CR 57: 236 (Mar 1784); MR 71: 150 (Aug 1784); AF II: 3931.
> IU x823.Sa242; ESTC n037167.

Notes. Direct narrative to I, 80; then epistolary.
Post-dated; adv. as published SJC 22–25 Nov 1783.
Adv. end vol. 1 of *The Young Widow* (1785: 21).
German trans. Leipzig, 1785 (*Abtey St. Ruthin*) (Price).

CR: 'This is a pretty plaintive story, deducing a series of misfortunes from one false step in the beginning. . . . it will fill the shelves of a circulating library and beguile some tender fair one of her tears.'

MR [Samuel Badcock]: 'The tale of Ruthin's Abbey was, it seems, at all events, to be a tragedy; though we confess (such is the dulness of Reviewers!) that we had not the slightest suspicion of a tragedy being meant from the conduct of the drama, or the characters that were meant to figure in it. However, as matters were destined by the Author to take this woful turn, just as the whole was about to be wound up, it was judged necessary to hang the conclusion in as deep mourning as possible. We were fairly taken in. We expected a marriage; but behold—a murder! "Oh horrible! most horrible!" '

1784: 8 ANON.
THE SENTIMENTAL DECEIVER: OR HISTORY OF MISS HAMMOND. A NOVEL, IN A SERIES OF LETTERS. BY A LADY.

> London: Printed for William Lane, Leadenhall-Street, 1784.
> 233p. 12mo. 3s (CR, MR), 2s 6d sewed (adv., SJC).
> CR 58: 312 (1784); MR 71: 77–8 (July 1784); AF II: 4018.
> MnU WILS RAR 824Se59 I; ESTC n021866.

Notes. Prefatory address (unn.) concentrates many of the most common prefatory claims into its one sentence: 'This novel respectfully claims the favour of the *Public*, being the first essay of a *Female Pen*, and of one, who from a situation of affluence and elegance, is unfortunately reduced to a reliance on the generosity of her friends, for maintenance and support; and as this work has only been the employment of her leisure hours, it is hoped the kind reader will accept this apology, and candidly view its errors and imperfections.' Epistolary.
Adv. SJC 18–20 Jan 1785.
Adv. end vol. 3 of *Zoriada* (1786: 24).

CR quotes the author's description of her sad circumstances and adds: 'At this relation, Criticism must drop her pen, and smooth her wrinkles: every fault is softened into a kindred excellence, and every beauty magnified. We know not whether it is owing to the author's own story, but we think we perceive in this little volume some tenderness and delicacy: a moral tendency enforced by examples, perhaps too common, but certainly interesting and entertaining.'

MR [Samuel Badcock]: 'Another virgin pen!—Though, unless we took the lady's words for it, we should rather have supposed that this was *not the first time*' (p. 77).

1784: 9   ANON.
UNFORTUNATE SENSIBILITY; OR, THE LIFE OF MRS. L******. WRITTEN BY HERSELF. IN A SERIES OF SENTIMENTAL LETTERS. DEDICATED TO MR. YORICK, IN THE ELYSIAN FIELDS. IN TWO VOLUMES.

>London: Printed for Mess. Richardson and Urquhart, under the Royal Exchange, 1784.
>I ix, 213p; II 199p. 8vo [MR has 12mo]. 6s (CR), 5s sewed (MR), 5s sewed or 6s bound (LC).
>CR 57: 397 (May 1784); MR 71: 149–50 (Aug 1784); AF II: 4578.
>MH-H *EC75.A100.784u; ESTC n014500 (NA PU).

Notes. Epistolary. Dedication signed 'Octavia'. An imitation of Sterne.
Adv. LC 55: 565 (10–12 June 1784).

CR: 'From the title we were led to expect misfortunes, acute sensibility, and sentiment, with a hint of something Shandean, either in the manner or the matter; but, in the perusal, we find a crude uninteresting attempt, which we know not how to characterize but by negatives. It is not entertaining, it is not affecting, it is not instructive.'

MR [Samuel Badcock]: 'The numerous adventurers, who have put to sea on the light bottom of *sentiment* (and this Author among the rest of the *crew*) will be swallowed up and lost in the Stygian gulph, long before they arrive in sight of the Elysian Fields: and out of a thousand packets "*addressed to Mr. Yorick*," scarcely one will reach him.'

1784: 10   BACON, Theophilus James.
THE MAID OF THE FARM; OR MEMOIRS OF SUSANNAH JAMES: CONTAINING, I. THE CHARACTER OF LORD THALEY, AND HIS PERFIDIOUS FRIEND SIR THO. THOWARD. II THE EDUCATION AND CHARACTER OF THE GOOD FARMER JAMES, AND HIS BEAU-TIFUL DAUGHTER SUSANNAH. III. THE PARTICULARS OF LORD THALEY FALLING IN LOVE WITH THE AMIABLE SUSANNAH, AND THE GROWTH OF THEIR MUTUAL PASSION FOR EACH OTHER. IV. LORD THALEY COMES UP TO LONDON, TO CURE THE WOUND SUSANNAH HAD MADE IN HIS HEART. V. FARMER JAMES USES EVERY MEANS TO PERSUADE LORD THALEY FROM MARRYING HIS DAUGHTER SUSANNAH. VI. BY THE TREACHERY OF SIR THOMAS THOWARD, SUSANNAH IS POSSESSED BY THALEY, UNDER THE MASK OF A FALSE MARRIAGE. VII. LORD THALEY RUINS AND ABANDONS THE BEAUTIFUL SUSANNAH. VIII. THE PERFIDIOUS THOWARD AND LORD THALEY COME UP TO TOWN, AND GIVE INTO ALL SCENES OF RIOT AND DEBAUCHERY. IX. LORD THALEY

MARRIES A RICH LADY, WITH WHOM HE GOES ABROAD AND IS MISERABLE. X. FARMER JAMES AND HIS FAMILY REDUCED TO THE MOST SHOCKING STATE OF POVERTY AND DISTRESS. IX. LADY THALEY DIES, WHEN HE AND THOWARD RETURN AGAIN TO LONDON, TO THEIR USUAL HAUNTS OF RIOT AND DISSIPATION. XII. THE PERFIDIOUS THOWARD IS KILLED IN A DUEL, BY AN OFFICER, WHO REVENGES THE CAUSE OF THE UNFORTUNATE SUSANNAH. XIII. LORD THALEY REPENTS OF HIS CRIMES, AND GOES IN PURSUIT OF SUSANNAH. XIV. AFFECTING SCENE AT THE MEETING OF LORD THALEY AND SUSANNAH. XV. LORD THALEY AND SUSANNAH ARE MARRIED, AND SPEND THE REMAINDER OF THEIR DAYS IN HAPPINESS. BY THEOPHILUS JAMES BACON, ESQ.

> London: Printed in the Year 1784.
> 60p. 8vo. 6d (t.p.)
> BL 12611.ee.32(6); EM 58: 9; ESTC t057313.

1784: 11   [BAGE, Robert].
BARHAM DOWNS. A NOVEL. IN TWO VOLUMES. BY THE AUTHOR OF MOUNT HENNETH.

> London: Printed for G. Wilkie, No. 71, St. Paul's Church-Yard, 1784.
> I 355p; II 355p. 12mo. 6s (CR), 6s sewed (MR, LC).
> CR 58: 75–6 (July 1784); MR 71: 223–4 (Sept 1784); AF II: 189.
> BL 12611.bb.5; EM 52: 3; ESTC t033005 (BI C, LEu, O; NA CtY-BR, MH-H, NjP, PU, ViU &c.; EA P).

Notes. Epistolary.
Mount Henneth 1782: 12.
Adv. LC 55: 494 (20–22 May 1784); adv. MC 20 Aug 1784, with mention of CR's rev.
Further edns: Dublin, 1786 (Printed by S. Colbert, 2 vols., 12mo), ESTC n043386; London, 1821/24 (WC); London, 1824 (WC, NSTC). German trans. Züllichau, 1787/88 (*Die Brüder Ein Roman*) (EAG); French trans. Paris, 1810 (*Anna Bella, ou les Dunes de Barham*) (BN). Facs: N.

CR: 'The author seems to have profited by our former sentiments. Without losing any share of his vivacity or brilliancy, his story is better connected, and the incidents more conformable to those of real life. . . . our author's lively manner, his good sense, and his just but sarcastic reflections, obscure his errors, and render his present work highly agreeable. His style is still distinguished by its strength rather than its elegance; but his dialogue is less licentious, and his story is in every respect strictly moral.'

MR [Samuel Badcock]: 'Some of the characters exhibited in this novel are the most execrable and abandoned that can disgrace human nature . . . but they are contrasted by others which are peculiarly amiable and excellent, and shine with more than common lustre. . . . The leading principle of this Author's novels is *good sense*, animated by a spirit of freedom and benevolence, and expressed in a style peculiarly pointed and sprightly. But we see nothing original either in his characters or plots, though there is a novelty in the *manner*. . . . In a work of entertainment, designed for general reading, every thing which hath a tendency to infuse loose ideas into the mind, and to unsettle religious principles, should be carefully avoided by every one who hath the real interests of virtue and the welfare of society at heart.'

1784: 12   [BERKELEY, George Monck].
MARIA, OR THE GENEROUS RUSTIC.

> London: Printed for T. Cadell, London, and C. Elliot, Edinburgh, 1784.
> ix, 135p. 8vo. 2s 6d (CR, MR).
> CR 58: 75 (July 1784); MR 71: 387 (Nov 1784); AF II: 308.
> O Vet.A5f.2928; ESTC n004372 (NA AaU, CaOHM, PU).

Notes. Dedication to Almeria. Pagination continuous Roman-Arabic; text of novel begins on p. 11. Unn. last page [136] contains verse 'Epitaph On the Tomb of Clerville and Maria. Written by the Baron Fitzou.'

CR: 'This little tale affords a melancholy satisfaction; for it is a tale of woe. We may reason on the probability of its truth, but we feel its influence; and while it affects, it may amend the heart. . . . The story is told with simplicity and neatness; the author depended on nature, and had little reason to look for the effects of artifice and refinement.'

MR [Samuel Badcock]: 'A tale may be romantic, and yet not amuse the fancy: it may be dismal, and yet not affect the heart. If examples were needed (which we are sorry to say is very far from being the case) we should produce the present novel. . . .'

1784: 13   [BROMLEY, Eliza Nugent].
LAURA AND AUGUSTUS, AN AUTHENTIC STORY; IN A SERIES OF LETTERS. BY A YOUNG LADY. IN THREE VOLUMES.

> London: Printed for W. Cass, Lambs-Conduit-street, Holborn, 1784.
> I vii, 160p; II 180p; III 155p. 8vo [CR has 12mo]. 9s (CR), 7s 6d (MR, MC), 7s 6d sewed (adv.).
> CR 57: 233–4 (Mar 1784); MR 71: 77 (July 1784); AF II: 477.
> C S727.d.78.16–18; EM 6958: 2; ESTC t119086 (BI L (-t.p. vol. 1); NA ICU, IU, MH-H &c.).

Notes. Vols. 2 and 3 have a comma after 'Letters' in title. Dedicated to the Dowager Countess Spenser. Epistolary.

Adv. MC 9 Feb 1784.

Adv. end vol. 3 of *Camilla* (1785: 4).

Further edn: Dublin, 1784 (Printed for R. Moncrieffe, G. Burnet, T. Walker, R. Marchbank, R. Burton [and 5 others in Dublin], 3 vols., 12mo), ESTC n020617.

CR: 'If the young lady did not announce herself in the title, she would betray the author, by the warmth, the tenderness, and the unaffected modesty of her descriptions. She will excuse us for adding, that she would betray herself, by a few inaccuracies in language, and a little improbability in some of the incidents; but these faults are really few . . . . the story is told with elegance, and is frequently interesting.'

MR [Samuel Badcock]: 'This Novel is said to be "the production of a *virgin* pen." The epithet is neither new nor striking. . . . Give us something worth reading, something that really interests us by the entertainment it affords, or the instruction it furnishes, and call you her by any name you please—virgin or not, just as it may suit your purpose, or gratify your taste.'

1784: 14   [COMBE, William].
ORIGINAL LOVE-LETTERS, BETWEEN A LADY OF QUALITY AND A PERSON OF INFERIOR STATION.

London: Printed for J. Bew, in Pater-Noster-Row, 1784.
I viii, 149p; II 174p. 12mo. 5s sewed (MR), 5s sewed or 6s bound (MC).
MR 71: 225 (Sept 1784); AF II: 820.
NjP Ex 3686.7.368; ESTC n011038 (ICN, NNU).

Notes. Preface signed 'The Editor'. 1 p. advs. end vol. 2. Epistolary.
Adv., 'Neatly printed on a fine Writing-Paper, in Two Pocket Volumes', MC 24 Aug 1784.
Further edns: Dublin, 1784 (Printed by J. Rea, for Messrs. Moncrieffe, R. Cross, Exshaw, Wilson [and 11 others in Dublin], 2 vols., 12mo), EM 133: 2, ESTC t064750; NSTC lists edns in 1811.

The 'editor' claims not to have written the letters and MR [Samuel Badcock] notes, 'These artifices are become so very common, that they have lost the power of imposition. We have no doubt but that the Editor and the Author are the same person. . . . [The letters] are, however, elegant, moral, and sentimental; and may be read with pleasure, whether they are considered as original or fictitious.'

1784: 15   [GODWIN, William].
DAMON AND DELIA: A TALE.

London: Printed for T. Hookham, at his Circulating Library, New Bond-Street, Corner of Bruton-Street, 1784.
182p. 8vo. 3s (CR, MR).
CR 57: 473 (June 1784); MR 71: 78 (July 1784); AF II: 1645.
BL C.136.ee.24; EMf; ESTC t182841.

Notes. 2 pp. advs. end vol.
Marshall (p. 61) says that Godwin wrote *Damon and Delia* in 3 weeks in Nov 1783 and was paid 3 gns. by Hookham.
Adv. MC 2 Apr 1784.

CR: 'This is an amusing little story, without any very considerable pretensions to novelty or elegance. There is however some reason to think it is the production of no common author; for we sometimes meet sentiments, which are not the usual ornaments of a novel, and a strength of language fitted for higher pursuits. It is, on the whole, superior to those tales which commonly fall in our way.'

MR [Samuel Badcock]: 'The Author makes an effort, sometimes to be witty and sometimes to be pathetic. But his wit is too insipid to amuse, and his pathos is too dull to affect.'

1784: 16   [GODWIN, William].
IMOGEN; A PASTORAL ROMANCE. IN TWO VOLUMES. FROM THE ANCIENT BRITISH.

London: Printed for William Lane, Leadenhall-Street, 1784.
I xxiv, 178p; II 175p. 12mo. 5s (CR), 5s sewed (MR, MC, adv.).
CR 58: 312 (Oct 1784); MR 72: 233–4 (Mar 1785); AF II: 1646.
MdBJ Cage PO4722.I5 1784; ESTC n061141.

Notes. Frontispiece to vol. 1; table of contents [iii]–viii; preface ix–xxiv. 1 p. advs. end vol. 2. Some pp. of MdBJ copy mutilated.
Marshall (p. 64) says that Godwin wrote *Imogen* in the first 5 months of 1784 and was paid £10 for it by Lane.

Adv., 'Adorned with an elegant Frontispiece', MC 26 July 1784.

Adv. end vol. 3 of *Zoriada* (1786: 24).

CR: 'Whether this be really a translation from the Welsh, and the original of that great antiquity, as the editor affirms, it is impossible for us to determine without farther evidence. But we do not hesitate to pronounce that it abounds with tender sentiments, pleasing description, and an innocent simplicity of manners.'

MR [Samuel Badcock]: 'Though Romance rises beyond the level of common life, yet it should not shock probability; and though its language may be highly figurative and splendid, yet it should not be turgid and extravagant. . . . The wildness of fancy may amuse for a few moments; but it will soon grow tiresome, and perhaps disgusting, unless enlivened by acute observation, and supported and dignified by solid judgment, where nature supplies the ground, and experience directs the pencil.

These little volumes, however, are of a chaste and virtuous tendency; and those who are fond of this style of composition, will find both entertainment and instruction from the perusal of them.'

1784: 17   [GODWIN, William].

ITALIAN LETTERS: OR, THE HISTORY OF THE COUNT DE ST. JULIAN. IN TWO VOLUMES.

> London: Printed for G. Robinson, No. 25, Pater-noster-Row, 1784.
>
> I 170p; II 202p. 8vo. 5s sewed (CR, MR).
>
> CR 58: 211–13 (Sept 1784); MR 71: 386 (Nov 1784); AF II: 1647.
>
> CU-BANC PR4722.I93.1784; ESTC n016834 (BI BL, BRu).

Notes. Epistolary.

Godwin was paid 21 gns. by Robinson on 5 Jan 1784 for *Italian Letters* (RA).

Marshall (p. 62) says that immediately after *Damon and Delia* (1784: 15) Godwin wrote *Italian Letters* in 3 weeks and was paid 20 gns. by George Robinson.

Adv., 'In Two Pocket Volumes', MC 10 July 1784.

Further edn: Dublin, 1785 (Printed by J. M. Davis, for Messrs. Marchbank, Colbert, Cash, and W. Porter, 2 vols., 12mo), ESTC n016835. French trans. n.p., 1788 (*L'amitié trompée*) (BGR).

CR: 'This is a novel which interests rather by a faithful and accurate description of the feelings of a wounded mind, than by incident, bustle, or intrigue. They are called, with propriety, Italian Letters, independent of the scene and country of the persons introduced. The sentiments are refined and delicate; the distress rises to horror, and inspires fury and revenge. The language is suitable to the situations; it is spirited and forcible in some parts, and more placidly elegant in others; but it is deformed by foreign idioms, and words which with particular meanings are scarcely yet naturalized' (p. 211).

MR [Samuel Badcock]: 'These Letters are written in a chaste, easy, and perspicuous style; and intermixed with reflections equally sensible benevolent, and moral.'

1784: 18   [LACLOS, Pierre-Antoine-François Choderlos de].

DANGEROUS CONNECTIONS: OR, LETTERS COLLECTED IN A SOCIETY, AND PUBLISHED FOR THE INSTRUCTION OF OTHER SOCIETIES. BY M. C***. DE L***.

> London: Printed for T. Hookham, at his Circulating Library, New Bond Street, Corner of Bruton Street, 1784.

I xix, ii, viii, 343p; II 240p; III 226p; IV 254p. 12mo. 12s (CR), 10s (MR), 10s sewed (MC, LEP, adv.).

CR 57: 473–4 (June 1784); MR 71: 149 (Aug 1784); AF II: 693.

BL 1093.h.6; EM 5614: 1; ESTC t111575 (NA CSmH, DLC, MH-H, PU; EA P).

Notes. Trans. of *Liaisons dangereuses* (Amsterdam and Paris, 1782). Epistolary.

Adv. MC 2 Apr 1784.

Adv. LEP 18–21 Mar 1786 with Hookham's name given as 'Hookman'.

Adv. end vol. 3 of *Edelfrida* (1792: 7).

Further edn: Dublin, 1784 (Printed for Messrs. Sheppard, Moncrieffe,Walker, Jenkin, Wilson, White, Burton, Byrne, and Cash, 4 vols. in 2, no format), xESTC (WC).

CR: 'An improper story, or the insinuations of a depraved heart, infuse a slow and secret poison, whose effects are more fatal as the approach is more delusive and secret. . . . The whole is delusive and dangerous in a great degree; nor is the poetical justice a sufficient antidote.'

MR [Samuel Badcock]: 'The story is conducted with great art and address; but it is almost too diabolical to be realized. The pretence of "*instruction*" is an insult on the understanding of the Public, as the work itself is a daring outrage on every law of virtue and decorum.'

1784: 19   [McDONALD, Andrew].
THE INDEPENDENT. A NOVEL. IN TWO VOLUMES.

London: Printed for T. Cadell, London; and C. Elliot, Edinburgh, 1784.
I ix, 188p; II viii, 181p. 8vo. 6s (CR), 5s boards (MR, MC).
CR 58: 226–7 (Sept 1784); MR 71: 225–6 (Sept 1784); AF II: 2647.
BL N.1655; EM 3809: 1; ESTC t071891 (BI C, E; NA CSmH, MiU, NjP).

Notes. 1 p. adv. end vol. 1, repeated vol. 2.
Adv. MC 27 Apr 1784.
Further edn: Dublin, 1784 (Printed for Messrs. Price, Sheppard, Moncrieffe, Walker, Exshaw [and 9 others in Dublin], 2 vols., 12mo), ESTC n007758. French trans. London, 1788 (*L'Indépendant*) (BN); German trans. Strasbourg, 1789 (*Der Unabhängige*) (Price).

CR: 'The story is pleasing and simple; more interesting in the manner of relating, than by the novelty of the adventures. The end is not merely to add to the entertainment of those who would destroy time rather than employ it. Our author's object is to render attempts to violate conjugal fidelity ridiculous.'

MR [Samuel Badcock]: 'In many places the language of this Novel is too inflated and poetical to be either natural or elegant; and on this very account a prejudice will be conceived against this Novel at its first outset. . . . [It] is the production of a lively, acute, and sensible writer. Its moral is chaste. The spirit it breathes is generous and manly; and the reflections scattered through it are pertinent and judicious.'

1784: 20   [MORRIS, R. P. Mrs].
THE RIVAL BROTHERS, A NOVEL. IN A SERIES OF LETTERS, FOUNDED ON FACTS. BY A LADY.

[London]: Printed for the Authoress; And Sold by H. D. Symonds, No. 4, Stationers-Court, Ludgate-Street, 1784.
I iv, 140p; II 121p. 12mo. 6s (CR, MR), 5s sewed or 6s bound (MC, SJC).

CR 58: 155 (Aug 1784); MR 71: 224 (Sept 1784); AF II: 2960.
MdBJ PO3291.R61 1784; ESTC n055916.

Notes. Preface 1, [i]–iv; p. iii misnumbered ii.
Adv. MC 17 Apr 1784; adv., with quotation from EngR, SJC 8–11 Jan 1785.
'A New Edition' adv., 'A Composition truly Original' (5s sewed or 6s bound), LEP 29 Apr–2 May 1786.

CR: 'The execution of this novel is entitled to little praise; but even merit would be obscured, when compared with the feelings excited by the subject, and motives for the publication.'

MR [Samuel Badcock]: 'If this performance be considered merely as a *novel*, it is inartificial, uninteresting, and inelegant. If it be (as the Preface very seriously declares) "a narrative founded on absolute fact," the publication of it can answer no end, but to gratify a love of scandal, and give vent to a malign and revengeful disposition. . . .'

OCTAVIA
See UNFORTUNATE SENSIBILITY

1784: 21   PARRY, Catherine.
EDEN VALE. A NOVEL. IN TWO VOLUMES. DEDICATED, BY PERMISSION, TO LADY SHELBURNE. BY MRS. CATHERINE PARRY.

London: Printed for John Stockdale, opposite Burlington-House, Piccadilly, 1784.
I v, 180p; II 172p. 8vo. 6s (CR), 5s sewed (MR, MC).
CR 58: 155 (Aug 1784); MR 71: 149 (Aug 1784); AF II: 3229.
BL 1154.h.1; EM 2555: 11; ESTC t117004 (BI AWn; NA CtY-BR, ICN).

Notes. Dedication to Lady Shelburne. Preface i–v. Epistolary.
Adv. MC 3 June 1784.

CR: 'This is a harmless little novel, with a very good moral: we cannot pronounce it interesting or entertaining.'

MR [Samuel Badcock]: 'A few flowers are scattered through this vale; but they are all of the lowest order—*primroses*, and *daisies*, and *daffodils*. Its productions are perfectly harmless; and the vale of *Eden* doth not, like the antient garden of that name, tempt us with the fruit of the tree of *knowledge*.'

1784: 22   POTTER, John.
THE VIRTUOUS VILLAGERS, A NOVEL. IN A SERIES OF LETTERS. BY JOHN POTTER, M.B. AUTHOR OF THE CURATE OF COVENTRY, &C. &C. IN TWO VOLUMES.

[London]: Printed for W. Cass, Lamb's Conduit Street, Holborn, 1784.
I 174p; II 191p. 12mo. 6s (CR), 5s sewed (MR, MC).
CR 58: 476–7 (Dec 1784); MR 72: 391 (May 1785); AF II: 3545.
MH-H *EC75.P8533.784v; ESTC n066765 (NA PU).

Notes. 1-p. prefatory advertisement end vol. 1. 1 p. advs. p. [192] of vol. 2. Epistolary.
The Curate of Coventry 1771: 49.
Adv. MC 12 Nov 1784.

CR: '. . . this novel is addressed more to the judgment than to the fancy; and to the feelings of the heart, rather than to the eagerness of curiosity. There is a calm repose in the picture, very different from the active scenes which other novellists have delineated. . . . Our author is cool, sedate, and judicious. His reflections are generally accurate; and, though his language is not always finished with the highest elegance, yet it is neat, clear, and exact' (p. 477).

MR: 'Mr. Potter possesses abilities, which, we think, may be more successfully employed than in Novel-writing; in which he does not, in our apprehension, seem to excel.'

1784: 23   RICCOBONI, [Marie Jeanne de Heurles Laboras de Mezières].
THE HISTORY OF CHRISTINA, PRINCESS OF SWABIA; AND OF ELOISA DE LIVAROT. TRANSLATED FROM THE FRENCH OF MADAME RICCOBONI. IN TWO VOLUMES.

London: Printed for J. Stockdale, opposite Burlington House, Piccadilly, 1784.
I 216p; II 144p. 8vo. 6s (CR), 5s sewed (MR).
CR 57: 474 (June 1784); MR 71: 150 (Aug 1784).
OU PQ2027.R45H51 1784; ESTC n033062 (NA NIC).

Notes. Trans. of Histoire de Christine, reine de Suabe (Paris, 1783).
Running-title vol. 1 'History of Christina, Princess of Swabia' and vol. 2 'The History of Eloisa de Livarot'.
Adv., 'In a few Days will be published, neatly printed in Two Pocket Volumes', MC 7 Feb 1784.
Further edn: Dublin, 1784 (Printed by J. Rea for Messrs. Price, Moncrieffe, Exshaw, Wilson [and 9 others in Dublin], 2 vols., 12mo), EM 2225: 5, ESTC t118941.

CR: 'This is a very pleasing and interesting novel. It is undoubtedly a translation, for the idiom of the language every where obtrudes, and probably it is the production of the ingenious author mentioned in the title. Its moral tendency is unquestionable; yet we fear it may arm the enthusiasm of youth with a fresh weapon, and contribute to conquer the tender heart already prepared to yield.'

MR [Samuel Badcock]: 'Elegant and tender; but too romantic to be of much use in the direction of human conduct in the general scenes and occurrences of life. We awake from it, as from a dream which leaves an indistinct lustre on the imagination; but when we look around us, we see other objects; and behold a milder, but a more certain and a more constant light.'

1784: 24   [WARTON, Jane].
LETTERS TO HONORIA AND MARIANNE, ON VARIOUS SUBJECTS. IN THREE VOLUMES.

London: Printed for J. Dodsley, Pall-Mall, 1784.
I 164p; II 159p; III 144p. 8vo [MR has 12mo]. 9s (CR), 7s 6d (MR), 7s 6d sewed (LC).
CR 57: 209–11 (Mar 1784); MR 71: 155 (Aug 1784).
CSmH 356400; ESTC n011284 (BI E (-vol. 1); NA CtY, ICU, TxHR &c.).

Notes. In Todd, John A. Vance cites ms. evidence that Warton is the author of Peggy and Patty (1783: 24); LC adv. says by same author as Peggy and Patty.
Epistolary, each letter on a topic relating to conduct. Letters signed Emilia.
MR reviews under 'Miscellaneous'; CR does not classify.
Adv. LC 55: 157 (12–14 Feb 1784).

CR: 'Though there are few letters in these volumes, which can engage the attention of a learned or a well-informed reader, yet, on the other hand, there is nothing but what is consistent with delicacy of sentiment, and the strictest morality. The author's observations are very proper; but most of them are obvious and trite. The judgment approves, but curiosity is seldom awakened' (p. 209).

MR [Jabez Hirons]: 'The reader will find, in these little volumes, many just remarks on human life, together with wise and useful directions for its proper conduct.... The Author's style is plain and easy, and the observations are interspersed with numerous characters, anecdotes, quotations in prose and verse, &c. adapted to gain attention, and render the performance more agreeable and beneficial to the reader.'

1785

1785:1   ANON.
ADELAIDE; OR, CONJUGAL AFFECTION. A NOVEL, TRANSLATED FROM THE FRENCH.

> London: Printed for W. Lane, Leadenhall-Street, 1785.
> 242p. 12mo. 2s 6d (MR), 2s 6d sewed (SJC).
> MR 73: 391 (Nov 1785); AF II: 19.
> BL RB.23.a.8977; ESTC t225032.

Notes. ESTC: French original not traced. Sometimes attributed to Nicolas Masson de Morvilliers.
Grieder gives Masson de Morvilliers as author (and title as *Adelaide, ou l'amour et le repentir*, Paris, 1769) but says 'attribution is due to comments in the November 1785 *Monthly*', a puzzle since the MR's whole comment is quoted below.
2½ pp. advs. beginning on p. 242.
Adv. SJC 5–7 Apr 1785.
> MR [Samuel Badcock]: 'No matter whence *she* comes, who brings nothing with her that can tempt one to wish for her stay.'

ADVENTURES OF THE SIX PRINCESSES OF BABYLON
See PEACOCK, Lucy

1785: 2   ANON.
THE AEROSTATIC SPY: OR, EXCURSIONS WITH AN AIR BALLOON. EXHIBITING A VIEW OF VARIOUS COUNTRIES, IN DIFFERENT PARTS OF THE WORLD; AND A VARIETY OF CHARACTERS IN REAL LIFE. BY AN AERIAL TRAVELLER.

> London: Printed by Edmund Fawcett, at the Bible, Shoemaker-Row, Black-Friars. And
>   sold by H.D. Symonds, Stationer's-Court, Ludgate-Street, 1785.
> I vii, 220p; II 216p. 12mo. 6s (MR, CR).

CR 60: 234 (Sept 1785); MR 73: 466 (Dec 1785); AF II: 38.

DLC PZ3.A2523; ESTC n029408 (NA KU-S, PU).

Notes. MC 7 Jan 1784 has adv., 'Speedily will be published, in Three Vols. 12mo, *The Air-Balloon; a Novel*' for R. Dodsley, Pall-Mall; adv. has 27 lines of verse describing the novel's content. Appears not to have been further mentioned in MC in 1784 [The 'R. Dodsley' appears to be a mistake for James Dodsley, as Robert had been dead for 20 years.]

Adv., 'In the Press, and speedily will be published' by Lane, *Balloon: a Novel* SJC 1–4 Oct 1785. Full title given in adv. in SJC 1–3 Aug 1786: *Balloon; or Aerostatick Spy, with the Adventures of an Aerial Traveller.*

Further edn: London, 1786 [*The Balloon or Aerostatic Spy*], EM 52: 4; ESTC t055911. German trans. Leipzig, 1787 (*Der aerostatische Zuschauer*) (EAG).

CR: 'This little work is superior to many attempts of the same kind. It contains some amusing adventures, just reflections, and well drawn characters: it is not even deficient in its philosophical observations, if we except a sanguine partiality for aerial machines, and too great expectations of their utility.'

MR [Samuel Badcock]: 'Though this balloon is launched too far into the ocean of extravagance, and the course it takes is not of sufficient interest to excite much attention, or gain much applause, yet the hand that constructed and guides the machine, wants neither skill nor power for greater exertions, and more important enterprises, than this work delineates.'

ANNA; OR, MEMOIRS OF A WELCH HEIRESS
See BENNETT, Anna Maria

1785: 3   ANON.
BELMONT GROVE: OR, THE DISCOVERY. A NOVEL, IN A SERIES OF LETTERS, BY A LADY. IN TWO VOLUMES.

London: Printed for W. Lane, Leadenhall-Street, 1785.

I 271p; II 257p. 12mo. 6s (CR), 5s sewed (MR, SJC, adv.).

CR 59: 475 (June 1785); MR 73: 466 (Dec 1785); AF II: 284.

CSmH 446751; ESTC n046551.

Notes. Dedication to the Countess of Westmorland. 3 pp. advs. end vol. 2. Epistolary.

Adv. SJC 12–14 Apr 1785.

Adv. end vol. 3 of *Zoriada* (1786: 24).

CR: 'The whole is a very insipid, insignificant performance; and if this "lady" had been debarred from pen and ink, the Reviewers would have had cause to bless the friendly hand which saved them from "honest anguish and an aching head."'

MR [Samuel Badcock]: 'A lifeless and insipid composition, affording neither entertainment nor instruction, in any degree answerable to the fatigue of reading it.'

1785: 4   ANON.
CAMILLA; OR, THE CORRESPONDENCE OF A DECEASED FRIEND. IN THREE VOLUMES.

London: Printed for W. Cass, Lamb's-Conduit-Street, Holborn, 1785.

I vi, 196p; II 213p; III 191p. 12mo. 9s (CR), 7s 6d (MR), 7s 6d sewed (SJC, adv.).

CR 59: 475 (June 1785); MR 73: 466 (Dec 1785); AF II: 588.

BL 12612.b.18; EM 133: 1; ESTC t071889 (NA CSmH, MH-H, PU).

Notes. ESTC: Falsely attributed to [Samuel de] Constant de Rebecque by F. G. Black.
Preface v–vi. 1 p. advs. end vol. 3. Epistolary.
Adv., 'In a few Days will be published', SJC 26–29 Mar 1785.
Adv. end vol. 3 of *Zoriada* (1786: 24).
Further edn: London, 1788 (WC), xESTC.

CR: 'This correspondent presents herself to us in the negligent undress of the closet, and tells her artless tale with simplicity, and probably with truth. Though frequently deceived by the pretensions to authenticity, we think there is much reason to consider these letters as original: the language is unequal, often incorrect; the characters and situations are not uncommon. Perhaps what we gain on the side of truth we lose on that of entertainment; for many things have really happened, though they would raise little interest in the relation: yet we feel for the misfortunes of Camilla, and are pleased at her temporary success.'

MR [Samuel Badcock]: 'If these Letters had been consigned to the grave with the supposed writer of them, the world would have had no reason to regret the loss.'

THE CASKET; OR, DOUBLE DISCOVERY
See HIGGS, Henry

1785: 5   ANON.
THE CONFESSIONS OF A COQUET. A NOVEL. IN A SERIES OF LETTERS.

> London: Printed for W. Lane, Leadenhall-Street, 1785.
> viii, 175p. 12mo. 2s 6d sewed (MR, SJC).
> MR 73: 391 (Nov 1785); AF II: 833.
> O 249.r.4; ESTC n026857 (NA PU).

Notes. 1 p. advs. end vol. Preface iii–viii says work is a trans. but has no clue to original. Epistolary.
Adv., 'in the Press, and speedily will be published', SJC 21–23 Apr 1785.
Adv. end vol. 3 of *Zoriada* (1786: 24).

MR [Samuel Badcock]: 'The sins of the Marchioness and Lady Fanny are very great; but we could sooner forgive their *coquetry* than their *confessions*. Confession, designed to lessen guilt, increases theirs: and it is *those* that do *penance*, who are obliged to hear it.'

THE CONQUESTS OF THE HEART
See TOMLINS, Elizabeth Sophia

CONSTANCE: A NOVEL
See MATHEWS, Eliza Kirkham

1785: 6   ANON.
EDWIN AND ANNA, A NORTHUMBRIAN TALE. FOUNDED ON FACTS. WRITTEN BY EDWIN HIMSELF.

> London: Printed for Messrs. Scatcherd and Whittaker, Ave-Maria-Lane; and J. Parsons,
>   No. 21, Pater-noster-Row, 1785.
> I 192p; II 194p; III 212p. 12mo. 7s 6d (CR), 7s 6d sewed (MR).

CR 61: 235 (Mar 1786); MR 75: 153 (Aug 1786); AF II: 1221.
CLU-S/C PR3991.E3E26; ESTC n006607.

Notes. German trans. Leipzig, 1792 (*Edwin und Mariane. Erzählung einer angenehmen Begebenheit*) (Price).

CR: 'This is a confused medley of modern and ancient anecdotes . . . . We suspect the Tale to be a new edition, with *additions*, of an older story.

The author is frequently in a humorous vein, but his attempts are unsuccessful; and he is sometimes pathetic, without the power of drawing a tear.'

MR [Samuel Badcock]: 'His descriptions are inelegant, his humour is coarse and insipid; his style is spiritless; and his observations are trite and superficial.'

ELEONORA
See BURKE, Anne

EUGENIUS: OR, ANECDOTES OF THE GOLDEN VALE
See GRAVES, Richard

1785: 7 ANON.
THE FALSE FRIENDS. A NOVEL. IN A SERIES OF LETTERS. BY THE AUTHOR OF THE RING. IN TWO VOLUMES.

London: Printed for J. Barker, near the Pit-Door, in Russell-Court, Drury Lane, 1785.
I iv, 262p; II 274p. 12mo. 5s sewed (MR), 6s (CR), 6s bound (adv.).
CR 60: 73 (July 1785); MR 73: 466 (Dec 1785); AF II: 1368.
MH-H *EC75.A100.785f2; ESTC n008325.

Notes. 'A Young Lady' given as author on t.p. of *The Ring* (1784: 6). Also by same author: *Agitation* (1788: 3).
Preface signed 'The Author' vol. 1, iii–[v]; 1 p. advs. [vi]. Epistolary.
Adv. beginning of *Stella* (1791: 36).

CR: 'We are told in the preface, that the "author is young, unexperienced, and a female." We readily believe it; and only wish that she had been more advantageously employed. The characters, the language, and the sentiments, if we except a strict morality, are below mediocrity. We endeavour, however, to learn something from every book which we read; and we find a lady's idea of a handsome man to consist in "black piercing eyes, a brown complexion, and white teeth."'

MR [Samuel Badcock]: 'Flimsy sentiments, dressed up in stiff and formal language.'

FANNY, A NOVEL
See HOLFORD, Margaret

1785: 8 ANON.
THE FATAL MARRIAGE: A NOVEL. IN TWO VOLUMES.

London: Printed for T. Hookham, At his Circulating Library, New Bond Street, Corner of Bruton Street, 1785.
I 237p; II 259p. 12mo. 6s (CR, MR), 5s sewed (SJC).
CR 59: 475 (June 1785); MR 73: 236 (Sept 1785); AF II: 1387.
BL 1509/2455(1-2); EM 1845: 4; ESTC t092913.

Notes. Epistolary. 2 pp. advs. (for Hookham's circulating library and fire insurance) end vol. 2.

Adv. SJC 15–17 Mar 1785.

CR: 'A pathetic story; but contains little novelty of character and sentiment. The tale is somewhat interesting; and the conclusion is affecting.'

MR [William Enfield]: 'The silly small talk of two giddy girls, who have determined to fall in love as soon as they have an opportunity, that they may have great secrets to tell one another, and charming things to write about.'

A FRAGMENT OF THE HISTORY OF THAT ILLUSTRIOUS PERSONAGE, JOHN BULL
See POLESWORTH, Humphrey

FRANCIS, THE PHILANTHROPIST
See JOHNSON, Mrs. (1786: 27)

1785: 9   ANON.
THE HISTORY OF SIR HENRY CLARENDON.

> London: Printed for R. Baldwin, in Pater-noster Row; and W. Richardson, at the Royal-Exchange, 1785.
> I 310p; II 328p. 12mo. 6s (CR), 6s sewed (MR).
> CR 59: 316 (Apr 1785); MR 73: 153 (Aug 1785); AF II: 1971.
> BL 12613.cc.3; EM 201: 3; ESTC t070091 (NA CSmH).

Notes. Epistolary.

Adv. SJC 18–20 Jan 1785.

CR mocks 'the skeleton of a modern novel': 'sentiments, character, or language, are of little consequence; and such is the flimsy texture of sir Henry Clarendon, with a very scanty share of merit in these necessary additions.'

MR [William Enfield]: 'The struggles of innocence and virtue, through a succession of misfortunes and injuries, are here represented in a truly pathetic tale, which will not be read without tears by those who are inclined to indulge the amiable sensibilities of sympathy.'

HISTORY OF THE HONOURABLE EDWARD MORTIMER
See GWYNN, Albinia

INTERESTING MEMOIRS. BY A LADY
See KEIR, Elizabeth

1785: 10   ANON.
LETTERS BETWEEN AN ILLUSTRIOUS PERSONAGE AND A LADY OF HONOUR AT B*******.

> London: Printed at the Logographic Press, and sold by J. Walter, Printing-house Square, Black-Friars, J. Stockdale, Piccadilly, Scatchard and Whitaker, Ave-Maria-lane, W. Richardson, Royal Exchange, and M. Wilson, No. 45, Lombard Street, n.d. [ESTC: 1785].

xv, 87p. 8vo. 2s sewed (CR, MR).
CR 60: 399 (Nov 1785); MR 73: 73 (July 1785); AF II: 2532.
C 7720.d.1592; EM 5148: 1; ESTC t064797 (BI BL; NA CSmH).

Notes. Epistolary. Introduction i–xv.
Illustrious personage is George, Prince of Wales; Lady of Honour is Mrs Fitzherbert;
B******* is Brighton.

CR: 'A frivolous but inoffensive production, founded upon the late frequent excursions of
the P—— of W—— to Brighthelmstone.'

MR: 'The P. of W. having lately amused himself by repeated excursions to Brighthelmstone, and frequently appearing there in the company of ladies, seems to have furnished a
hint to one of the sons or daughters of literary industry: of which this Shandyan volume is the
fruit.—It is a frivolous, but innocent production.'

1785: 11   ANON.
THE LIBERAL AMERICAN. A NOVEL, IN A SERIES OF LETTERS, BY A LADY. IN TWO VOLUMES.

London: Printed for William Lane, Leadenhall-Street, 1785.
I 197p; II 276p. 12mo. 5s sewed (MR, SJC, adv.), 6s (CR).
CR 61: 154 (Feb 1786); MR 73: 466 (Dec 1785).
BL 012611.e.11; EM 239: 1; ESTC t064737 (NA CtY, MH-H, PU, &c.).

Notes. In vol. 2 text of novel starts on p. 5. Epistolary.
Adv., 'in a few Days will be published', SJC 12–14 Apr 1785; adv. as published SJC 21–23 Apr
1785.
Adv. end vol. 3 of *Zoriada* (1786: 24).
French trans. Amsterdam, Leiden, Rotterdam and Utrecht, 1788 (*Elliott ou le généreux
Américain*) (BGR); German trans. Quedlinburg, 1790 (*Der edle Amerikaner, eine Novelle in
Briefen von einem Frauenzimmer*) (Price).

CR: 'We often suspect these professional ladies, when the title is not supported by internal
evidence. The only proof in the narrative before us, is the number of marriages.... It is a dull,
insipid narrative, related in uninteresting letters.'

MR [Samuel Badcock]: 'The few imitations of Richardson which we meet with in these
volumes set the writer in a light somewhat unfavourable, as they bring to our remembrance
an author of such superior abilities. Nevertheless, the *Liberal American* is far more deserving of the public favour than the generality of the present Novels. There is considerable
warmth and force in the sentiments; and the language is easy, perspicuous, and unaffected.'

MARIA: A NOVEL
See BLOWER, Elizabeth

1785: 12   ANON.
*MARIA; OR, THE OBSEQUIES OF AN UNFAITHFUL WIFE.

London: Printed for the Author; and sold by J. Bew, No. 28, Paternoster-Row; T. W.
Swift, Charles-street, St James's square; W. Forty, Chippenham; and the principal
Booksellers in Town and Country (SJC), 1785 (SJC).
12mo. 2s 6d (CR, MR), 2s sewed (SJC).

CR 60: 318 (Oct 1785) MR 74: 390 (May 1786); AF II: 2712.
No copy located.

Notes. Adv. SJC 2–5 Apr 1785: 'This moral work is, in its principal incidents, truly historical: it was occasioned by a Lady of high rank, who, since her divorcement, resided with her gallant at his country seat near Bath; a Lady whose conjugal infidelity (the circumstances of which transpired about two years since at Doctors Commons) was not more remarkable than her end was melancholy.'

CR: 'We have often given our opinion on this poetical prose, which wants only measure to constitute verse. It is not the least of the objections to it that it soon swells into bombast, or, *sermoni propior,* creeps in humble prose; that without a cultivated taste, and sound judgment, it cannot be with ease and propriety sustained. This work, which seems to be founded on a modern event, is subject to both these faults; nor is the conduct of the story unexceptionable; but the lessons are salutary, and the moral just.'

MR: 'This tale would, perhaps, have been more pathetic, had the author taken less trouble to make it so. It is written in that sort of flowery, poetical prose, which borders on bombast; and is apt to become insufferably tedious. Much good sentiment is injuriously represented, by appearing with such unnatural ornaments. We have often expressed our dislike of this mongrel style of composition; but it still has its admirers, and will, like other fashions, have its day. Nothing, however, can last, which has not its foundation in nature.'

1785: 13   ANON.
MATILDA: OR, THE EFFORTS OF VIRTUE. A NOVEL, IN A SERIES OF LETTERS, BY A LADY. IN THREE VOLUMES.

London: Printed for William Lane, Leadenhall-Street, 1785.
I 240p; II 216p; III 257p. 12mo. 7s 6d sewed (MR, SJC, adv.), 9s (CR).
CR 59: 395 (May 1785); MR 73: 465–6 (Dec 1785); AF II: 2773.
ICU PR3991.M43 1785; ESTC n061339.

Notes. In vols. 2 and 3 text of novel starts on p. 5. 3 pp. advs. end vol. 3. Epistolary.
Adv., 'In a few Days will be published . . . By a Lady', SJC 27–29 Jan 1785.
Adv. end vol. 3 of *Zoriada* (1786: 24).

CR: 'These young ladies write very prettily and sentimentally: every man has a "fine understanding," and every lady is very handsome, and much in love. Their lovers too are all accomplished.—Yet here and there we perceive a few "purple shreds," seemingly cut from a more valuable garment, and one more substantial than the flimsy gauze of which this summer-robe is composed.'

MR [Samuel Badcock]: 'The language of this Novel is forcible and elegant; and the sentiments are in general just and manly. We think, however, that the work is defective in the most difficult part of composition—the *delineation of character.*

The characters in this work are not marked with sufficient boldness, or discrimination, to rouse or fix the reader's attention. There are, nevertheless, such strokes both of sentiment and expression, as convince us that the pencil was held by a skilful and experienced artist.'

1785: 14   ANON.
MEMOIRS AND ADVENTURES OF A FLEA; IN WHICH ARE INTERSPERSED MANY HUMOROUS CHARACTERS AND ANECDOTES. IN TWO VOLUMES.

London: Printed for T. Axtell, 1785.
I 231p; II 232p. 12mo. 5s sewed (CR, MR).
CR 60: 318 (Oct 1785); MR 73: 391 (Nov 1785); AF II: 2819.
O Hope 8° 395, 396; EMf; ESTC t177275.

Notes. CR: 'There is some originality, humour, and good sense, in these volumes; yet they are obscured by indelicacies, perhaps inseparable from the nature of the Adventurer, but not, on that account, less disgusting.'

MR [Samuel Badcock]: 'The execution is worthy of the subject: the hero of the story and the historian who records his adventures, seem made for one another.'

MEMOIRS OF A PYTHAGOREAN
See THOMSON, Alexander

1785: 15 ANON.
THE MISFORTUNES OF LOVE. A NOVEL. TRANSLATED FROM THE FRENCH. IN TWO VOLUMES.

London: Printed for W. Lane, Leadenhall-Street, 1785.
I 212p; II 262p. 12mo. 6s (CR), 5s sewed (MR, SJC, LC).
CR 59: 395 (May 1785); MR 73: 466 (Dec 1785); AF II: 2895.
CtY-BR Im.M687.785; ESTC n065197.

Notes. Adv., 'From a Paris Edition', LC 57: 162 (15–17 Feb 1785); adv., 'Translated from the last Paris edition', SJC 26–29 Mar 1785.
Adv. end vol. 3 of *Zoriada* (1786: 24).
Further edn: London, n.d. [1800?], EM 4298: 25, ESTC t131892.

CR: 'If this be a translation, for in this age of literary imposition we always doubt; but if it be really so, as from some internal evidence we have reason to suppose, it will only prove that our neighbours are equally craving after novelty with ourselves, and satisfied with the same unsubstantial fare. Is invention at so low an ebb in this island, that we must make every crudity, every trifling publication of the continent our own?'

MR [Samuel Badcock]: 'Eugenia's story takes up too large a portion of this Novel, and diverts the attention of the reader too much from the principal object. In other respects, this little piece is entitled to our recommendation: it is sensible and pathetic.'

MODERN TIMES, OR THE ADVENTURES OF GABRIEL OUTCAST
See TRUSLER, John

1785: 16 ANON.
THE NABOB. A NOVEL. IN A SERIES OF LETTERS. BY A LADY. IN TWO VOLUMES.

London: Printed for William Lane, Leadenhall-Street, 1785.
I xvi, 240p; II 256p. 12mo. 6s (CR), 5s sewed (MR, LC, SJC).
CR 59: 395–6 (May 1785); MR 74: 72 (Jan 1786); AF II: 3027.
PU Singer-Mend.PR 3991.A6.L326.1785; ESTC n009990 (BI AWn; NA CtY-BR).

Notes. By same author as *Arpasia* (1786: 4).
Epistolary.

Adv., 'Addressed to the Sons of the East', LC 57: 179 (19–22 Feb 1785); adv. SJC 31 Mar–2 Apr 1785.

Adv. end vol. 3 of *Zoriada* (1786: 24).

CR: 'Amidst hackneyed scenes, and the usual characters with which such productions abound, there is novelty in the situations, spirit in the language, and a proper discrimination of style. The moral is just, and the conduct of the different parties frequently exemplary' (p. 395).

MR [Samuel Badcock]: 'In this performance we sometimes meet with inelegant expressions, and the writer frequently approaches the borders of vulgarity. This is the more inexcusable, because the characters which he describes required more delicate language. But, overlooking these defects, the *Nabob* is entitled to attention; and the justness and vivacity of his observations, place him in a rank superior to that of his brother novel-writers.'

1785: 17   ANON.
THE NEW ENTERTAINING NOVELLIST; BEING A SELECTION OF STORIES, FROM THE MOST APPROVED MODERN AUTHORS.

>Glasgow: Printed for the Booksellers, 1785.
>107p. 12mo.
>BL 12612.df.16; EM 136: 6; ESTC t066912.

Notes. Text starts on p. 3. Table of contents pp. [106]–107.

THE OMEN; OR, MEMOIRS OF SIR HENRY MELVILLE
See GIFFORD, Arthur

1785: 18   ANON.
ORIGINAL TALES, HISTORIES, ESSAYS AND TRANSLATIONS. BY DIFFERENT HANDS.

>Edinburgh: Printed for Charles Elliot; And Thomas Dobson Bookseller, Philadelphia, 1785.
>441p. 8vo. 5s boards (see below).
>BL 12271.c.1; EMf; ESTC t073670 (BI E; NA MdBJ, PPL).

Notes. Possibly a reissue of an existing publication. Letter of 22 Aug 1785 from Elliot to Dobson reports, 'I bought them with a view for your sale [—] there was only about 150 [—] you'll observe new Titles [—] it sold at 5/- in bd formerly' (AJM, Elliot Letter-Books).

1785: 19   ANON.
THE QUAKER. A NOVEL. IN A SERIES OF LETTERS, BY A LADY. IN THREE VOLUMES.

>London: Printed for William Lane, Leadenhall-Street, 1785.
>I 209p; II 193p; III 175p. 12mo. 7s 6d sewed (CR, MR).
>CR 60: 395 (Nov 1785); MR 74: 306 (Apr 1786); AF II: 3667.
>BL 1490.l.20; EM 2770: 2; ESTC t075764 (NA CaAEU).

Notes. 3 pp. advs. end vol. 1 and vol. 2; 1 p. advs. end vol. 3. Text of novel starts on p. 5 in vols. 2 and 3. Epistolary.

Adv., 'In the Press, and speedily will be published', SJC 1–4 Oct 1785; adv. as published SJC 25–27 Oct 1785.

CR: 'There is little merit in the management of the story, or novelty in the characters. . . . On the whole this is, in our opinion, an indifferent performance.'

MR [Samuel Badcock]: 'Though the diction of this performance is in general too splendid for the title it assumes, and too much ornamented for epistolary writing, yet on the whole, it possesses merit, and is entitled to recommendation for its virtuous and moral tendency.'

THE RECESS
See LEE, Sophia

THE RENCONTRE
See GWYNN, Albinia

1785: 20   ANON.
SENTIMENTAL MEMOIRS: BY A LADY.

> London: Printed by H. Trapp, No. 1. Pater-noster-Row; and sold by Mr Hookham, Bond-Street, 1785.
> I xvi, 287p; II 283p. 8vo. 6s (MR, SJC), 7s (CR).
> CR 60: 232–33 (Oct 1785); MR 73: 465 (Dec 1785); AF II: 4019.
> BL 12613.bbb.17; EM 200: 4; ESTC t064188 (NA CtY, IU, MH-H &c.)

Notes. 'Address to the Public' iii–xvi. 24-pp. list of subscribers end of vol. 2. Epistolary.
Adv. SJC 12–14 July 1785.

CR: 'These Memoirs may indeed instruct, for the conduct of the personages is often exemplary; but we fear they will not entertain. We respect good intentions: we would be candid, and even complaisant, if it were in our power; but as we cannot praise we will be silent.'

MR [Samuel Badcock]: 'These Memoirs appear to have been written with the best and most laudable intentions; and if their *moral and religious tendency* can recommend them, we would not impede their success by exposing their defects.'

THE VALE OF GLENDOR
See CARTWRIGHT, Mrs H.

1785: 21   ANON.
THE YOUNG WIDOW; OR, THE HISTORY OF MRS LEDWICH. WRITTEN BY HERSELF. IN A SERIES OF LETTERS TO JAMES LEWIS, ESQ. IN TWO VOLUMES.

> London: Printed for the Editor; and Sold by F. Noble, near Middle Row, Holborn, 1785.
> I 223p; II 216p. 12mo. 6s (CR), 5s sewed (MC).
> CR 59: 67 (Jan 1785); MR 72: 391 (May 1785); AF II: 4978.
> MH-H *EC75.S100.785y; xESTC.

Notes. 2-pp. prefatory advertisement 'To the Reader' (unn.), signed H. S. 1 p. advs. end vol. 1 and 8 pp. advs. end vol. 2. Epistolary.
Post-dated; adv. as published MC 18 Nov 1784.
Further edn: Dublin, 1785 (Printed for Messrs. Moncrieffe, Jenkin, Walker, Burton, White [and 3 others in Dublin], 2 vols., 12mo), EM 234: 2, ESTC t067636.

CR: '. . . the tale is trite, uninteresting, and insipid: the young widow's virtues and frailties, her pleasures and remorse, are buried in a country retirement: we wish not to disturb her repose, nor to rouse her from the oblivion in which she will soon be involved.'

MR [Samuel Badcock]: 'Her story is not badly related; but there is little in it to amuse, and still less to instruct. Expectation is frequently excited: but it is seldom gratified; and where the disappointment can be least borne, we meet with it in the strongest force; and that is at the conclusion.'

1785: 22   [BENNETT, Anna Maria].
ANNA; OR, MEMOIRS OF A WELCH HEIRESS, INTERPERSED WITH ANECDOTES OF A NABOB. IN FOUR VOLUMES.

Printed for William Lane, Leadenhall-Street, 1785.

I xii, 242p; II 264p; III 270p; IV 280p. 12mo. 10s sewed (MR, SJC), 12s (CR).

CR 59: 476 (June 1785); MR 73: 153 (Aug 1785); AF II: 296.

BL 12614.c.8; EM 4968: 7; ESTC t021920 (BI BMu, MRu, O; NA CtY-BR, ICN, IU, MH-H, NjP, ViU &c.; EA P).

Notes. FC: Name often given incorrectly as Agnes Maria.

Dedication to H.R.H. Princess Charlotte-Augusta-Matilda, Princess Royal of England iii–xii.

Adv., 'In the Press, and speedily will be published', SJC 26–29 Mar 1785; adv. as published LC 57: 328 (2–5 Apr 1785) and SJC 9–12 Apr 1785.

Further edns: Dublin, 1785 (Printed for Luke White, 2 vols., 12mo), ESTC n030254; London, 1786, EM 7274: 2, ESTC t076268; Dublin, 1786, ESTC t188040; London, 1796, EM 7280: 1, ESTC t101270; NSTC lists edns. in 1804. Serialised, *Town and Country Weekly Magazine*, 1785–86, RM 110. French trans. Paris, 1788 (*Anna; ou l'héretière galloise*) (BN).

CR: 'This is one of those histories which entertains by an intricate, rather than a very artful series of events, without any pretensions to exact discrimination of manners or any very intimate acquaintance with the human heart. In the conduct of the story we have little to praise or blame; similar characters have often been displayed, and the adventures are not uncommon. The mind is sometimes affected, and sometimes interested; but the principal attraction is a soothing melancholy, which pervades the whole, with a happy termination not highly improbable or greatly forced. In some parts of it the incidents are scarcely within the verge of probability; and the language is generally incorrect. We have seen many worse novels; more dull in their progress, and more pernicious in their tendency.'

MR [William Enfield]: 'These volumes, though by no means written with the elegance or spirit of Cecilia [1782: 15], of which they appear to be an imitation, have a sufficient variety of character and incident to keep up the reader's attention, and make them in some degree interesting.'

1785: 23   [BLOWER, Elizabeth].
MARIA: A NOVEL. IN TWO VOLUMES. BY THE AUTHOR OF GEORGE BATEMAN.

London: Printed for T. Cadell, in the Strand, 1785.

I iii, 258p; II 272p. 12mo. 6s (CR), 5s sewed (SJC), MR gives no price.

CR 60: 233–34 (Sept 1785); MR 73: 392 (Nov 1785); AF II: 384.

BL 12611.aa.3; EM 6996: 1; ESTC t031394 (BI E, O; NA ViU).

Notes. Dedication to the Honourable Mrs Ward i–iii signed 'E. B.'

George Bateman 1782: 14.

Adv. SJC 17–20 Sept 1785.

Further edn: Dublin, 1787 (Printed by James Moore, 2 vols., 12mo), ESTC n034803. German trans. Berlin, 1785/86 (*Marie, eine Geschichte*) (Price); French trans. Rome and Paris, 1787 (*Maria, ou Lettres d'un gentilhomme anglois à une religieuse*) (HWS).

CR: 'Her judgment is accurate, her discernment quick, and her language ready. Her attempts at humour and ridicule frequently succeed; but, probably from a slight acquaintance with situations of active life, we perceive inconsistencies which, in some degree, destroy the interest of her tale. We were, however, pleased with the work in general, and much affected with particular parts of it. . . .'

MR [Samuel Badcock]: 'Lovely Maria, you are welcome!—you are doubly welcome. Your own merit entitles you to a cordial reception; and after such company as that we are just parted from [*The Omen* and *Adelaide* (1785: 30 and 1)], we shall relish your conversation the better.'

1785: 24   BOYS, Mrs [S].

*THE COALITION; OR FAMILY ANECDOTES. A NOVEL. BY MRS BOYS.

> London: Printed for the Authour, and sold by J. Bew, No. 28, Pater-noster-Row; and to be had also at her House, No. 38, Berner's Street (SJC), 1785 (SJC).
> 2 vols. 12mo. 6s (CR), 6s sewed (MR), 6s sewed or 7s bound (SJC).
> CR 59: 475–76 (June 1785); MR 73: 153 (Aug 1785); AF II: 452.
> No copy located.

Notes. In Dublin edn. dedication to Mrs Hastings is signed 'S. Boys'.

Adv. SJC 14–16 Apr 1785.

Further edn: Dublin, 1785 (Printed for Messrs. Price, White, Cash, H. Whitestone, and Marchbank, 2 vols., 12mo), EM 4789: 12, ESTC t119004.

CR: 'The events in this novel are amusing, though the denouement is improbable. The story is told with a sufficient share of elegance; but the language of each character is nearly the same. It is the language of the author, and her sentiments are frequently repeated without sufficient regard to the persons to whom they are attributed. This is consequently not a picture of real life, but bears nearly the same resemblance to it which a puppet shew does to a well written comedy. This fault excepted, for which we may be thought to have looked too narrowly, as well as the improbability of some of the incidents, the work is not without merit; and it is not the least, that we never meet with the slightest hint which may tend to raise an indelicate idea.'

MR [William Enfield]: 'Neither the labour of the Author, nor the ingenuity of the Printer, will, we apprehend, be able to preserve this tedious tale from oblivion.'

1785: 25   [BURKE, Anne].

ELEONORA: FROM THE SORROWS OF WERTER. A TALE.

> London: Printed for G. G. J. and J. Robinson, Pater-Noster Row, 1785.
> I iv, 147p; II 168p. 8vo [MR has 12mo]. 5s sewed (CR, MR).
> CR 60: 141–2 (Aug 1785); MR 73: 392 (Nov 1785); AF II: 541.
> CtY-BR Speck Coll.z.Jo4a.A14.785; xESTC.

Notes. Johann Wolfgang von Goethe's *Die Leiden des jungen Werthers* (Leipzig, 1774). See 1779: 10.

Preface 1, iii–iv. In vol. 2 text of novel starts on p. 3. Epistolary.

Adv. SJC 21–23 July 1785; 2nd edn. 'corrected' adv. LC 59: 219 (4–7 Mar 1786).

CR: 'There is no work more captivating than the Sorrows of Werter. . . . [but] it is poison to a mind diseased; and may contribute with the "proud man's contumelies," or the "pangs of despised love," to hurry a despairing wretch to the extreme verge. The volumes before us seem to be designed as an antidote to the poison; but, like other antidotes, may come too late: they are certainly not dangerous; and they possess a power of attraction by the same means, and in a degree little inferior, to the Sorrows of Werter' (p. 141).

MR [Samuel Badcock]: 'Fair maid! thou bringest with thee the countenance of woe; but religion dignifies, and resignation softens it. Relate thy *tale*, and we will weep where thou mournest: and while its pathetic scenes melt our bosoms, its instructive moral shall teach us how to act, and how to suffer, when virtue is put to its most rigid test.'

1785: 26   CARTWRIGHT, Mrs [H].

THE DUPED GUARDIAN: OR, THE AMANT MALADE. A NOVEL. IN A SERIES OF LETTERS. BY MRS CARTWRIGHT. IN TWO VOLUMES.

London: Printed for W. Cass, Lamb's Conduit-Street, Holborn, 1785.
I 230p; II 221p. 12mo. 5s sewed (MR, SJC), 6s (CR).
CR 60: 396 (Nov 1785); MR 74: 306 (Apr 1786).
BL 12611.e.8; EM 4019: 1; ESTC t057316 (NA CtY, CSmH, DeGE).

Notes. Epistolary.

Adv. SJC 29 Sept–1 Oct 1785. Re-adv. SJC 27–29 Apr 1786 for Bew and Symon[d]s: 'N.B. This Novel is full of Business, very well conducted, and contains a Variety of entertaining, sensible, and pertinent Remarks'.

CR: 'The English, the French, and the Latin of these little volumes are equally exceptionable; and the greater part of the story is that of Mrs. Cowley's last comedy, viz. "More Ways than One:" we mean so far as relates to the artless niece of the artful physician. . . . The characters are the threadbare personages of a modern novel.'

MR [Samuel Badcock]: 'The construction is inartificial, and the catastrophe is particularly confused; but the work is neither tedious nor insipid; it may afford amusement to please an idle mind, and instruction to warn a thoughtless one.'

1785: 27   [CARTWRIGHT, Mrs. H].

THE VALE OF GLENDOR; OR, MEMOIRS OF EMILY WESTBROOK. IN TWO VOLUMES.

London: Printed for F. Noble, near Middle Row, Holborn, 1785.
I 236p; II vii, 219p. 12mo. 6s (CR), 5s sewed (MR, SJC).
CR 59: 317 (Apr 1785); MR 73: 152–3 (Aug 1785); AF II: 628.
BRu ENC; ESTC n068264 (EA AMu).

Notes. Author attribution: FC.
'To the Reader' vol. 2, pp. v–vii. 1 p. adv. end vol. 2.
Adv. SJC 5–8 Mar 1785.

CR: 'This is a pleasing little history; but with few striking excellencies. It is "a simple tale, in simple guise," and contains a very useful lesson.'

MR [William Enfield]: 'We here meet with a novel, which both in design and execution, has a considerable share of merit. In a correct and pleasing style, it relates an interesting tale, adapted to afford a useful warning to young females, at their entrance upon the world, against hasty and incautious confidence.'

CHILCOT, Harriet
See MEZIERE, Harriet

CONSTANT DE REBECQUE
See CAMILLA; OR, THE CORRESPONDENCE OF A DECEASED FRIEND (1785: 4)

1785: 28   DENT, John.
THE FORCE OF LOVE. A NOVEL. IN A SERIES OF LETTERS. BY JOHN DENT, AUTHOR OF TOO CIVIL BY HALF, &C. &C. IN TWO VOLUMES.
> London: Printed for W. Cass, Lamb's Conduit Street, Holborn, 1785.
> I 173p; II 176p. 12mo. 5s sewed (MR, SJC), 6s (CR).
> CR 60: 318 (Oct 1785); MR 74: 306 (Apr 1786).
> O 256.e.15425; ESTC t219589.

Notes. Epistolary.
Adv. SJC 3–6 Sept 1785.
Adv. end vol. 3 of *Zoriada* (1786: 24).
    CR: 'This novel is entitled to little praise; the story and the characters are not beyond the usual personages of that most respectable mansion, a circulating library. The incidents are usually trifling, and the situations uninteresting.'
    MR [Samuel Badcock]: 'This little piece is sprightly and ingenious; though as it possesses none of the higher qualities, it hath no *force* to withstand the tide which is perpetually carrying down the progeny of modern genius to the gulph of oblivion.'

1785: 29   GENLIS, [Caroline-Stéphanie-Félicité Ducrest de Mézières, comtesse de]; HOLCROFT, Thomas (trans).
TALES OF THE CASTLE: OR, STORIES OF INSTRUCTION AND DELIGHT. BEING LES VIELLEES DU CHATEAU, WRITTEN IN FRENCH BY MADAME LA COMTESSE DE GENLIS, AUTHOR OF THE THEATRE OF EDUCATION, ADELA AND THEODORE, &C. TRANSLATED INTO ENGLISH BY THOMAS HOLCROFT.
> London: Printed for G. Robinson, N° 25, Pater-Noster-Row, 1785.
> I 324p; II 295p; III 308p; IV 279p; V 286p. 12mo. 15s boards (CR), 15s sewed (MR, MC).
> CR 59: 99–104 (Feb 1785); MR 73: 92–6 (July 1785); AF II: 2021.
> BL C.175.l.6; EM 3815: 6; ESTC t150150 (BI BMp [vols. 2–4 only], O, Ota &c.; NA CSmH, IU, MH-H, NjP, PU, TxU &c.).

Notes. Trans. of *Les Veillées du château* (Paris, 1782).
4-pp. prefatory advertisement (unn.) vol. 1.
Adelaide and Theodore 1783: 9.
Post-dated; adv., 'In the press, and speedily will be published', MC 1 Dec 1784; adv. as published MC 10 Dec 1784.
Further edns: London, 1785, ESTC t172930; Dublin, 1785 (Printed for Messrs. Price,

Moncrieffe, Jenkin, Walker, Burton [and 6 others in Dublin], 4 vols., 12mo), EM 3558: 1, ESTC t144991; London, 1787, EM 3640: 2, ESTC t147160; Dublin, 1789, ESTC t172932; London, 1793, ESTC t147161; 1 further entry in ESTC; WC has 17 entries between 1800 and 1850; NSTC lists edns. in 1806, 1817, 1819 and abridged edn. in 1824. Several extracts from *Tales of the Castle* published in 5 magazines between 1785 and 1806, RM 165, 406. Other trans. from *Les Veillées du château* published in *New Lady's Magazine* in 1792 and *New Gleaner* in 1810, RM 291 and 347.

CR: '... her stories are adapted with judgment, and wound up with exquisite art; with art the more excellent, because unperceived. She is mistress of the utmost recesses of the human heart, and reaches it by winding passages, to some imperceptible, and by others with difficulty explored' (p. 100).

MR [William Enfield]: 'In the invention of a connected series of probable and striking incidents—a task which, though often attempted by writers of the lower order, requires no small exertions of genius—this lady is peculiarly happy: and her pieces are, for the most part, very judiciously adapted to the design of impressing virtuous sentiments upon young minds.... The present work cannot fail to add fresh celebrity to her name. It is written in a manner that must captivate every heart, whose virtuous sensibility has not been damped by a fastidious philosophy, or debased by criminal passions' (p. 92).

1785: 30   [GIFFORD, Arthur].
THE OMEN; OR, MEMOIRS OF SIR HENRY MELVILLE AND MISS JULIA EASTBROOK. A NOVEL. IN TWO VOLUMES.
London: Printed for W. Lowndes, No. 77, Fleet-street, 1785.
I 272p; II 234p. 12mo. 5s sewed (MR), 6s (CR), 6s bound or 5s sewed (LC, SJC).
CR 60: 234 (Sept 1785); MR 73: 391 (Nov 1785); AF II: 1613.
NjP Extran 3752.67.368; ESTC n011255 (NA PU).

Notes. 6 pp. advs. end vol. 2.
Arthur Gifford was paid 10 gns. for the copyright of *The Omen*, on (18 Oct 1784), GM n.s. 94 (1824): 136.
Adv. LC 58: 53 (14–16 July 1785) and SJC 23–25 Aug 1785; 'by a Lady'.

CR: 'Neither the design nor the execution of this novel is very happy. Many improbabilities occur in both; and we are not recompensed by the brilliancy of wit, justness of remark, well drawn characters, or interesting situations.'

MR [Samuel Badcock]: '... we would not wish our enemy a greater punishment, than to be doomed to read and to review bad novels.

Reviewers are a sort of augurs; but the fate of these Memoirs may be foretold without the help of divination.'

1785: 31   [GRAVES, Richard].
EUGENIUS: OR, ANECDOTES OF THE GOLDEN VALE: AN EMBELL-ISHED NARRATIVE OF REAL FACTS.
London: Printed for J. Dodsley, Pall Mall, 1785.
I 184p; II 192p. 12mo. 5s sewed (CR, MR).
CR 60: 199–202 (Sept 1785); MR 73: 392 (Nov 1785); AF II: 1692.
BL 12614.ff.6; EM 191: 3; ESTC t073514 (BI O, Ota; NA CtY-BR, CLU-S/C, MH-H &c.; EA ZWTU).

Notes. Frontispiece to vol. 1. Dedication 'To the Fair Reader' i–iv.

Adv., 'adorned with frontispieces', LC 57: 588 (18–21 June 1785) and SJC 18–20 Aug 1785.

Further edns: London, 1786, ESTC n002459; Dublin, 1786 (Printed for Messrs. Burnett, Wilson, Byrne, Whitestone and Parker, 2 vols., 12mo), ESTC n031143. German trans. Leipzig, 1787 (*Eugenius oder Anekdoten aus dem goldnen Thale*) (Price).

CR: 'The story, in general, is simple, pleasing, and tender. The author calls it an embellished narrative; it is not above truth; it is not ornamented with splendid imagery, or refined by an affected delicacy; it seems to contain real facts in disguise. We have read the anecdotes with pleasure: they speak to the heart; and the heart which can feel will applaud them' (pp. 201–202).

MR [Samuel Badcock]: 'The benevolence of Eugenius's heart, his moral qualities, and his good understanding, render him a very proper companion for *Maria* and *Eleonora* [1785: 12 and 25]. . . .'

1785: 32   [GWYNN, Albinia].

HISTORY OF THE HONOURABLE EDWARD MORTIMER. BY A LADY.

> London: Printed for C. Dilly, Poultry; G. Wilkie, St. Paul's Church-Yard; and T. Hookham, Bond-Street, 1785.
>
> I viii, 163p; II 171p. 12mo. 6s (CR), 6s sewed (MR, SJC).
>
> CR 60: 316–17 (Oct 1785); MR 73: 465 (Dec 1785); AF II: 1769.
>
> MnU WILS RAR 824G996 OH; ESTC n008482 (NA NjP).

Notes. 1-p. dedication to the Duchess of Devonshire, signed 'The Author', Bath; introduction vii–viii; 13-pp. list of subscribers. In vol. 2 text begins on p. 3.

Adv., 'Printing by Subscription, In Two Volumes, neatly printed in small Octavo, best Paper', SJC 14–16 July 1785; 'Subscriptions received by Mr. Cruttwell, Printer, and the several Booksellers in Bath; and by Mr Dilly, Poultry; Mr. Hookham, Bond-Street; and Mr Wilkie, St. Paul's Church-Yard, London.' Adv. as published SJC 25–27 Aug 1785. Re-adv., with quotations from CR and GM, LC 59: 403 (27–29 Apr 1786).

Further edn: Dublin, 1786 (Printed for Messrs. White, Byrne, Parker, and Cash, 2 vols., 12mo), EM 2486: 6, ESTC n001522.

CR: 'We have been greatly interested and entertained by this novel. The author possesses much knowlege of the human heart, and some acquaintance with fashionable manners. The story is pleasing; the strokes of satire are well introduced, and the pathos is tender without affectation. But all is not perfect; some little improbabilities in the story occasionally discover the deception, and the denouement is too much crowded to be quite intelligible. On the whole, however, these volumes are greatly superior to those which have been lately added to the circulating library, and will deserve the attention of those who owe their entertainment to such collections' (p. 316).

MR [Samuel Badcock]: 'We cannot say that this Novel is happy for the perspicuity of its plot, or the contrivance of its incidents:—we cannot say that the heart takes a warm interest in the story, or feels itself much delighted, or affected, by the characters or events that compose it: but we can say, and we say it with equal sincerity and satisfaction, that a vein of sprightliness and good sense runs through this Novel, that cannot fail of gratifying those who chiefly read for amusement. . . .'

1785: 33   [GWYNN, Albinia].
THE RENCONTRE: OR, TRANSITION OF A MOMENT. A NOVEL, IN A
SERIES OF LETTERS. BY A LADY. IN TWO VOLUMES.

> London: Printed for William Lane, Leadenhall-Street, 1785.
> I xi, 239p; II 246p. 12mo. 6s (CR), 5s sewed (MR, SJC).
> CR 58: 397 (Nov 1784); MR 72: 233 (Mar 1785); AF II: 1770.
> BRu ENC; xESTC (NA CLU-S/C).

Notes. Preface v–xi. Epistolary.
Adv. SJC 18–20 Jan 1785.
Adv. end vol. 3 of The Myrtle (1784: 5).
Further edn: Dublin, 1785 (Printed for Messrs. Price, White, Moncrieffe, Jenkin, Beatty
[and 5 others in Dublin], 1 vol., 12mo), EM 192: 2; ESTC t069359.

CR: 'There is no great novelty in the story of this work, and little correctness in the execution; but the conduct of the heroine is striking and exemplary: her letters abound with just
morality and true religion.'

MR [Samuel Badcock]: 'Though this seems to be the production of a sensible and virtuous
mind, and contains many just reflections, and inculcates the purest precepts of morality, yet
the Transition of a Moment will have an existence almost as short; and will soon pass away and
be heard of no more.'

1785: 34   [HIGGS, Henry].
THE CASKET; OR, DOUBLE DISCOVERY: A NOVEL. BY THE AUTHOR
OF HIGH LIFE. IN TWO VOLUMES.

> London: Printed for W. Lowndes, No. 77, Fleet-street, 1785.
> I 207p; II 195p. 12mo. 6s (CR, MR), 5s sewed or 6s bound (LC, MC).
> CR 59: 66–7 (Jan 1785); MR 72: 391 (May 1785); AF II: 634.
> BRu ENC; xESTC.

Notes. 5 pp. advs. end vol. 1 and 18 pp. advs. end vol. 2. Epistolary.
High Life, 1767, JR 1105, AF I: 1218.
Post-dated; adv., 'will soon be published', LC 56: 372 (14–16 Oct 1784); adv. MC 9 Dec 1784;
'By the Author of High Life'.
Further edn: Dublin, 1785 (Printed by J. Rea, for Messrs. Price, Moncrieffe, Jenkin, Walker,
Exshaw [and 7 others in Dublin], 2 vols., 12mo), ESTC t212646.

CR: 'We meet with the hackneyed adventures, and the usual catastrophes, of novels in these
volumes, without an uncommon incident, a peculiar character, or new language. The work
is one of those equivocal beings, without the spirit and dignity of man; yet not so far debased
by trifling effeminacy, as to belong to the other sex. It is a milk and water production; and
we shall leave it to the babes and sucklings, for whose weak organs it is peculiarly adapted.'

MR [Samuel Badcock]: 'The wiles and the detection of an hypocrite, and the trials and
constancy, together with the rewards of virtue, form the general outline of this sensible, animated, and well-written novel.'

1785: 35   [HOLFORD, Margaret, the elder].
FANNY: A NOVEL; IN A SERIES OF LETTERS. WRITTEN BY A LADY.
IN THREE VOLUMES.

London: Printed for W. Richardson, under the Royal Exchange, 1785.
I 261p; II 251p; III 273p. 12mo. 5s sewed (MR), 7s 6d sewed (CR), 9s sewed (SJC).
CR 61: 235 (Mar 1786); MR 75: 314–15 (Oct 1786); AF II: 2030.
BL 12614.f.4; EM 329: 5; ESTC t064554 (NA CtY-BR, CSmH, IU, MH-H &c.).

Notes. Epistolary.
Adv. SJC 7–9 Feb 1786.
Further edn: Dublin, 1786 (Printed for Messrs. Colles, Parker, Byrne, Whitestone, Cash [and 4 others in Dublin], 2 vols., 12mo), ESTC t203191.

CR: 'This is an interesting little story, related in a pleasing manner, without the degree of perfection which will enable it to bear the approach of the torch of criticism, without revealing some considerable imperfections.'

MR [William Enfield]: 'This novel, besides that it is agreeably written, and exhibits a variety of characters in interesting situations, has the uncommon merit of conveying, in its story, a useful lesson to young women. . . .'

1785: 36   [KEIR, Elizabeth].
INTERESTING MEMOIRS. BY A LADY. IN TWO VOLUMES.

London: Printed for A. Strahan, and T. Cadell in the Strand; J. Balfour, and W. Creech,
    Edinburgh, 1785.
I viii, 242p; II 267p. 12mo. 5s sewed (MR, SJC).
CR 61: 78 (Jan 1786); MR 74: 307 (Apr 1786); AF II: 2347.
BL 837.d.5; EM 6553: 6; ESTC t094663 (BI E, MRu, O; NA CaOHM, CSmH).

Notes. ESTC : 'erroneously attributed to Susanna Harvey Keir'.
Dedication to the Queen v–vi, signed 'The Author'; preface vii–viii. 3 pp. advs. end vol. 2.
Adv. LC 58: 597 (20–22 Dec 1785) and SJC 22–24 Dec 1785; 3rd edn. adv. LC 59: 171 (18–21 Feb 1786).
BL copy has before t.p. unsigned handwritten dedication (dated January 1786) by the author to an unnamed recipient; an owner's name, Anna Yorke, is written on the t.p.
Further edns: London, 1785, ESTC n008578; London, 1786, EM 4109: 11, ESTC t119346; New York, 1792, ESTC w012871; Boston, 1802 (WC). French trans. London and Paris, 1788 (*Mémoires intéressants, par une lady*) (BGR).

CR notes that novel is now first published in England, following a previous edn. 'in a remote part of the kingdom'; 'In many respects these Memoirs are really interesting, for the duties of morality and religion are of the highest importance. They are in different parts of this work inculcated with a zeal that deserves success. In other respects, the Memoirs are amusing, with little novelty either of sentiment or character; but the different parts are well proportioned to each other; and we are never long detained by our author's instructions, without some relief from the narrative.'

MR [William Enfield]: 'The reader will meet in these volumes with entertainment of a kind much superior to that which is commonly afforded by novels. Several amiable characters are drawn with discrimination, and exhibited in situations truly interesting. The sentiments of piety, of paternal and filial affection, of gratitude, friendship, and love, are, by turns, agreeably unfolded.'

1785: 37   [LEE, Sophia].
THE RECESS; OR, A TALE OF OTHER TIMES. BY THE AUTHOR OF THE CHAPTER OF ACCIDENTS.

London: Printed for T. Cadell, in the Strand, 1785.

I 263p; II 298p; III 356p. 8vo. 7s (CR) [vols. 2 and 3], 10s 6d boards (MR).

CR 61: 214–18 (Mar 1786); MR 75: 131–6 (Aug 1786); AF II: 2504.

BL 635.a.11-13; EM 2554: 1; ESTC t113816 (BI C, E, O, &c.; NA CtY, CSmH, ICN, IU, MH-H, NjP, PU, TxU, ViU &c.).

Notes. Dedication to Sir John Eliot, Baronet, signed Sophia Lee, Bath. 2-pp. prefatory advertisement (unn.).

Vol. 1 first published 1783 (1783: 15).

Adv., 'In a few Days will be published, Elegantly printed in 3 Vols . . . The second and third Volumes will be sold separate', SJC 6–8 Dec 1785.

Extract published LC 59: 385–6 (22–25 Apr 1786).

Further edns: London, 1786, ESTC n021489; Dublin, 1786 (Printed for Messrs. G. Burnet, R. Moncrieffe, J. Exshaw [and 10 others in Dublin], 2 vols., 12mo), EM 3003: 9, ESTC t170600; London, 1787, EM 3663: 1, ESTC t069142; Dublin, [1790?], ESTC t170601; Dublin, 1791, ESTC t119360; ESTC has 1 further entry; WC has 4 entries between 1800 and 1850; Summers has 5 edns. between 1800 and 1850; NSTC lists edns. in 1804, 1821, [1825?] and 1826. Extract from *The Recess* published in *Marvellous Magazine*, 1802, RM 1042. German trans. Leipzig, 1786 (*Die Ruinen eine Geschichte aus den vorigen Zeiten*) (WC); French trans. Hamburg and Paris, 1793 (*Le Soutterain, ou Matilde*) (Lévy). Facs: GNI (vol. 1 1783 edn.).

CR: '. . . the artificial contexture of the several incidents, the near approaches to romance, without trespassing on probability, as well as the accumulation of unexpected distress, fix the eager attention, and gratify the imagination, without an insult to the judgment' (p. 214). 'We think our author has been too uniformly gloomy: the mind sinks under continued distress in real life; it escapes from the imaginary misfortunes; and the attention fails, when there is no respite for the wounded feelings.'

MR [Samuel Badcock] identifies several faults, principally the fact that 'fiction is indeed too lavishly employed to heighten and embellish some well-known and distinguished facts in the English history', a problem because 'Romance and History are at perpetual variance with one another', and some resulting from 'a want of skill, or at least of attention, in the writer' (p. 134), but concludes that '. . . with all its faults, the Recess is a very ingenious and pathetic novel. The Author possesses a copious fund of imagination. Her powers of description are very great; and there is a richness in her style which shows that her genius is ardent and vigorous' (p. 135).

1785: 38   [MATHEWS, Eliza Kirkham].
CONSTANCE: A NOVEL. THE FIRST LITERARY ATTEMPT OF A YOUNG LADY. IN FOUR VOLUMES.

London: Printed at the Logographic Press, for Thomas Hookham, at his Circulating-Library, New Bond-Street, corner of Bruton-Street, 1785.

I xi, 290p; II 267p; III 261p; IV 256p. 12mo. 10s sewed (MR), 12s (CR), 12s sewed (SJC, LEP).

CR 60: 394 (Nov 1785); MR 74: 306 (Apr 1786); AF II: 2755.

BL 12612.ccc.18; ESTC t066880 (NA CtY, CSmH, DLC, PU, ViU &c.; EA P, Ps).

Notes. Dedication to 'Mrs. ********* ******, of ******, an example of every female virtue and elegance' signed 'The Author'. Prefatory advertisement 1, [vii]; preface ix–xi.

Adv. SJC 29 Sept–1 Oct 1785 with contents listed in triple columns of single words (except for 'Paternal Affection' and 'Cross Purposes'): 'Contents of the First Volume. Retirement Novelty Staring Loquacity Sincerity Difficulty Vexation Intrusion Discretion Paternal Affection Generosity Distress Perplexity Indifference Obstinacy Justification Surprise Explanation Disappointment Anger Entreaty Despair Sensibility Honour Acquiescence Pacification Resolution Communication Determination Supposition Cross Purposes. Contents of the Second Volume. Hospitality Protection Supplication Endurance Conscientiousness Self-consideration Grief Scheming Assurance Accommodation Monarchy Ascendency Reiteration Confabulation Inquisitiveness Malice Zeal Suspense Catechism Sarcasm Accident Eloquence Assistance Restitution Sickness Bounty Politeness Initiation Education. Contents of the Third Volume. Dependence Inebriety Error Rencontre Revenge Integrity Sunday Discovery Melancholy Concealment Caution Cordiality Peace Compliance Introduction Defence Exculpation Confession Dissuasion Obduracy Warning Manoeuvre Alternative Aid Temporising News Deception Argument Retracting Liberation. Contents of the Fourth Volume. Meeting Acquittal Revelation Discordance Farewell Submission Attachment Perfidy Exile Reception Bribery Diligence Plain Truth Wretchedness Mystery Charity Deliverance Compunction Reprehension Conflict Misconstruction Reference Hope Denouement Resignation Banter Repentance Expectation Surrender Finale.'

Adv. LEP 25–28 Mar 1786 (Hookham as 'Hookman') with the contents in a different double-columned list of single words, not divided into volumes: 'Justification, Surprize, Anger, Entreaty, Sensibility, Honour, Acquiescence, Pacification, Resolution, Communication, Determination, Supposition, Catechising, Sarcasm. Accident, Eloquence, Assistance, Restitution, Sickness, Bounty, Politeness, Initiation, Education, Exculpation, Confession, Dissuasion, Obduracy, Warning, Manoeuvre, Alternative, Aid, Temporising, News, Deception, Argument, Retracting, Liberation, Deliverance, Compunction, Reprehension, Conflict, Misconstruction, Reference, Hope, Denouement, Resignation, Ranter, Repentance, Expectation, Surrender, Finale'.

CR: 'In this artless narrative, the incidents are numerous and striking, the situations interesting and pathetic, the morality unexceptionable. The story is intricate without confusion; and the mistakes are explained without violence. We have felt, in the perusal, the author's power to harrow up the soul, or, in turn, to expand it by the warmest, the most benevolent and social feelings: in many of these respects our "young lady" does not yield to female novellists of the highest rank. It is, however, from incidents and situations, that our greatest interest and entertainment are derived: the story is common almost to triteness, and the characters are not new.'

MR [Samuel Badcock]: 'The characters in this novel are discriminated with a considerable degree of spirit and propriety; but they are not thrown into situations so various or interesting as wholly to prevent languor. It is, however, one of the best written productions of this sort that hath appeared since CECILIA' [1782: 15].

1785: 39   MEZIERE, Harriet.
MORETON ABBEY; OR THE FATAL MYSTERY. A NOVEL, IN TWO
VOLUMES. BY THE LATE MISS HARRIET CHILCOT, OF BATH.
(AFTERWARDS MRS. MEZIERE.) AUTHORESS OF ELMAR AND ETH-
LINDA, A LEGENDARY TALE, &C. &C.

Southampton: Printed and sold by T. Baker, Sold also by J. Bew, Pater-Noster-Row,
London, n.d. [1785].

I viii, 191p; II 232p. 12mo. 3s sewed (MR), 5s sewed (SJC).

MR 75: 153 (Aug 1786); AF II: 687.

BL 12612.a.11; EM 166: 4; ESTC t070063 (BI C).

Notes. ESTC date 1786.

Preface 'To the Public' v–viii. In vol. 2 text of novel starts on p. 5. Epistolary.

Elmar and Ethlinda (1783) is verse.

Adv., 'Neatly printed, in two Volumes', LC 58: 588 (17–20 Dec 1785) and SJC 20–22 Dec 1785.

MR [Samuel Badcock]: '*Moreton Abbey* is but little superior to *Melwin Dale* [1786: 9]. If it
be more instructing, it is also more extravagant: and if it is contended that the language is
more elegant, many will think it more affected.'

1785: 40   {PEACOCK, Lucy}.

THE ADVENTURES OF THE SIX PRINCESSES OF BABYLON, IN THEIR TRAVELS TO THE TEMPLE OF VIRTUE. AN ALLEGORY. DEDICATED BY PERMISSION, TO HER ROYAL HIGHNESS THE PRINCESS MARY.

London: Printed for the Author, by T Bensley; and sold by J. Buckland, Pater-Noster-
Row J. Pridden, Fleet-Street, and by the Author at A. Perfetia's, No. 91, Wimpole-
Street, Cavendish-Square, 1785.

xxxi, 131p. 8vo. [MR and CR, apparently reviewing large-paper edn., have 4to]. 3s
(CR), 3s 6d (MR).

CR 60: 221–22 (Sept 1785); MR 74: 313 (Apr 1786); AF II: 3272.

BL 635.f.18(1); EM 2447: 8; ESTC t116126 (BI O; NA CaOTP, MnU, NjP).

Notes. ESTC: Adaptation for children of Spenser's *Faerie Queene*.

List of subscribers ix–xxiv.

Signed in ms. at foot of p. 131 (of BL and MnU editions) by the author.

Further edns: London, 1785, EM 1494: 17, ESTC n002727 [large-paper edn.]; London, 1785,
ESTC n051177; London, 1785, ESTC n051179; London, 1786, ESTC t095878; London, 1790, EM
7275: 5, ESTC t145071; WC has 4 entries between 1800 and 1850; NSTC lists edns. in 1805 and
1820. German trans. Hamburg, 1787 (*Abentheuer der sechs Prinzessinnen von Babylon*) (Price).

CR: 'The age of allegory is now past, for it approaches too nearly to positive precept; and
we wish to be allured into virtue and cheated into health. . . . These objections are not
intended to depreciate the pleasing performance before us, but to animate the exertions of
the author in a more successful line. There is much fancy in the descriptions, and much
wholesome instruction from the events: the wonders of fairy land, calculated to engage the
imagination, are employed to fix the lessons more firmly on the heart' (p. 221).

MR [Samuel Badcock]: 'Under the veil of allegory the ingenious writer recommends the
practice of virtue, and contrasting its difficulty with its advantages, shows the infinite superiority of the latter to the former. . . . If this performance be, as we have heard, the production
of a very young female, it may well be considered as a work of considerable merit.'

1785: 41   POLESWORTH, Humphry (pseud).

A FRAGMENT OF THE HISTORY OF THAT ILLUSTRIOUS PERSONAGE, JOHN BULL, ESQ; COMPILED BY THE CELEBRATED HIS-

TORIAN SIR HUMPHRY POLESWORTH. LATELY DISCOVER'D IN THE REPAIRS OF GRUB-HATCH, THE ANCIENT SEAT OF THE FAMILY OF THE POLESWORTHS; NOW FIRST PUBLISHED FROM THE ORIGINAL MANUSCRIPT, BY PEREGRINE PINFOLD, OF GRUB-HATCH, ESQ;.

London: Printed for the Editor, By T. Wilkins, No. 45, Cow Lane, Snow Hill. And Sold by Mr Debrett, opposite Burlington-house, Piccadilly; Mr Bew, Pater-noster-Row; Mr Kearsley, Fleet treet [sic], and all the Pamphlet Shops, at the Royal Exchange, n.d. [ESTC: 1785].

xxx, 118p, 8vo. 2s 6d (half-title).

BL 8133.aa.18; EM 572: 24; ESTC t109550.

Notes. ESTC: Erroneously attributed to John Arbuthnot.

Preface v–xv, signed Peregrine Pinfold, Grub-Hatch, 30 Apr, 1785; Dedication to William Pitt xvi–xxiii, signed Peregrine Pinfold; table of contents xxv–xxx. Contents are 'Part IV' and 'Part V'.

Further edn: London, 1791 (BN); NSTC lists edns. in 1820 and 1820/21.

1785: 42   POTTER, John.

THE FAVOURITES OF FELICITY. A NOVEL. IN A SERIES OF LETTERS. BY JOHN POTTER, MB. AUTHOR OF THE CURATE OF COVENTRY, THE VIRTUOUS VILLAGERS, &C. &C.

London: Printed for W. Cass, Lamb's-Conduit-Street, Holborn; T. Becket, Pall-mall; and Messrs. Baldwin, Robinson, and Bew, Pater-noster-Row, 1785.

I viii, 180p; II 187p; III 195p. 12mo. 7s 6d (MR), 7s 6d sewed (SJC, adv.), 6s sewed (CR).

CR 60: 233 (Sept 1785); MR 73: 466–7 (Dec 1785); AF II: 3542.

PU Singer-Mend. PR3639.P445F3 1785; ESTC n006378 (NA CaOHM).

Notes. Dedication 'To the Fair-Sex of Great Britain'. 1 p. advs. end vol. 3. Epistolary.

Curate of Coventry 1771: 49; Virtuous Villagers 1784: 22.

Adv., 'Next Month will be published', SJC 14–17 May 1785; adv. as published SJC 19–21 July 1785.

Adv. end vol. 3 of Zoriada (1786: 24).

CR: 'In this work, as well as in the Virtuous Villagers [1784: 22], the author instructs by precept rather than adventures; and, if there be more incident in the Favourites of Felicity than in the volumes just mentioned, there is somewhat less of that luxuriance of language which we reprehended, though some colloquial vulgarities are admitted.'

MR [William Enfield]: 'The Author of this Novel undertakes to remove the prejudices justly entertained against Novels, by writing one, which shall refine female delicacy, discriminate real and pretended characters, and direct his fair readers to those desirable sources of permanent felicity, which arise from domestic pleasure, moral improvement, and artless truth. The design is good, but, in the execution, he has, in our opinion, essentially failed.'

1785: 43   POTTER, T.

NOVELLETTES MORAL AND SENTIMENTAL PARTLY ORIGINAL AND PARTLY COMPILED BY THE LATE, T. POTTER. SURGEON AT NORTH SHIELDS, NEAR NEWCASTLE UPON TYNE.

London: Printed for the Editor, 1785.
vi, 241p. 12mo. 3s boards (t.p.).
BL 12356.aa.21(3); EM 907: 3; ESTC t073606 (NA MH-H, PU).
Notes. ESTC: Edited by A. M. Potter.
Table of contents v–vi. Introduction (pp. 1–2) is followed by 12 stories.
Attached before the half-title is a folded sheet, printed to resemble handwriting and signed in ink 'A. M. Potter', orphan daughter of the compiler, begging for the recipient's 'Patronage, for the little Volume which accompanies this address'. A portrait of Mr T. Potter is a frontispiece.

1785: 44   [THOMSON, Alexander].
MEMOIRS OF A PYTHAGOREAN. IN WHICH ARE DELINEATED THE MANNERS, CUSTOMS, GENIUS, AND POLITY OF ANCIENT NATIONS. INTERSPERSED WITH A VARIETY OF ANECDOTES. IN THREE VOLUMES.

London: Printed for G. G. J. and J. Robinson, Pater-Noster Row, 1785.
I viii, 204p; II iv, 163p; III iv, 168p. 8vo. [MR has 12mo]. 7s 6d sewed (MR, SJC).
MR 73: 391 (Nov 1785); AF II: 4453.
BL G.16517; EM 4877: 2; ESTC t101857 (NA CSmH).

Notes. Robinson paid 25 gns. on 18 Mar 1785 to Alexr. Thomson for *Memoirs of a Pythagorean* (RA).
Editor's preface 1, iii–vi; table of contents vii–viii. Table of contents 2, iii–iv and 3, iii–iv.
Adv. LC 57: 535 (2–4 June 1785) and SJC 21–23 July 1785.

MR [Samuel Badcock]: 'Too learned for the general readers of Novels; too dull and superficial for the learned; —too stiff and formal to amuse corrupt hearts; and too impure to please the chaste.'

1785: 45   [TOMLINS, Elizabeth Sophia].
*THE CONQUESTS OF THE HEART. A NOVEL. BY A YOUNG LADY.

London: Printed for R. Baldwin, No. 47, Pater-noster-Row (SJC), 1785 (SJC).
3 vols. 12mo. 9s (CR), 9s sewed (MR, SJC).
CR 59: 316 (Apr 1785); MR 74: 472–3 (June 1786); AF II: 4491.
No copy located.

Notes. Adv., 'In three neat Pocket Volumes', SJC 18–20 Jan 1785.
Further edn: Dublin, 1785 (Printed for Messrs. Price, S. Watson, Moncrieffe, Jenkin, Walker [and 9 others in Dublin], 3 vols., 12mo), ESTC t204519. Extracts from *Conquests of the Heart* published in *London Magazine*, 1785, RM 242.

CR: 'This young lady endeavours to assist "the cause of morality and virtue" with success. The tale indeed is not very new or interesting; though it be a little superior to the common class. . . . We wish to cherish this tender bud; for we guess that it may expand with a more varied foliage, and more vivid colours, when time shall have advanced it to greater maturity.'

MR [Charles Burney the younger]: 'The Conquests of the Heart, though not an extraordinary effort of genius, is entitled to a degree of praise. The Author possesses some knowledge of nature, and, perhaps, more of modern life. The story is interesting, but sometimes it verges on *the improbable*. To originality it has few claims, for the ground work and colouring are evidently borrowed from Evelina [1778: 10] and Cecilia [1782: 15]; yet still we will recommend it—for it pleads the cause of virtue.'

1785: 46   [TRUSLER, John].
MODERN TIMES, OR THE ADVENTURES OF GABRIEL OUTCAST.
SUPPOSED TO BE WRITTEN BY HIMSELF. IN IMITATION OF GIL
BLAS. IN THREE VOLUMES.
> London: Printed for the Author, by the Literary Society, At the Logographic Press, and
> sold by J. Walter, Printing-House-Square, Blackfryars, 1785.
> I viii, 238p; II 220p; III 238p. 12mo. 9s (CR), 9s sewed (MR, MC).
> CR 59: 65–66 (Jan 1785); MR 73: 298 (Oct 1785); AF II: 4548.
> BL 1208.f.1-3; EM 4338: 12; ESTC t098935 (NA CtY-BR, CSmH, IU &c.; EA ZCMU).

Notes. Prefatory advertisement 1, v–viii. Pagination continuous Roman-Arabic; text of novel starts on p. [9] of vol. 1. Text of novel starts on p. 5 in vols. 2 and 3. 1-p. address 'To Literary Men' concerning the publication arrangements of the Literary Society is p. [239] of vol. 3.

Post-dated; adv. as published MC 2 Dec 1784; 'Printed for the Author, and sold by J. Walter, Printing House-square, Blackfriar's; where may be had, gratis, the plan of this society, associated for the encouragement of literature, who propose to print and publish, at their own risk and expence, such original works as they may approve of, and give their authors all profits arising from the same.' Letter signed 'Lector' in MH 13 Mar 1786 praises the novel extravagantly in terms close to those used in later advs.

Further edns: London, 1785, ESTC t100116; Dublin, 1785 (Printed by J. M. Davis, for Messrs. Moncrieffe, Jenkin, Walker, White [and 5 others in Dublin], 3 vols., 12mo.), ESTC t169112; London, 1786, t153576; London, 1789, ESTC t169105; London, 1789, ESTC n059914. Serialised, *Ulster Repository*, 1785, RM 910. German trans. Leipzig, 1786 (*Gemälde aus der heutigen Welt*) (Price).

2nd edn., 'very much improved and enlarged, of that celebrated Novel (published under the Patronage of the Literary Society) . . . Sold by J. Murray, Fleet-Street', adv. SJC 15–17 Nov 1785, with quotations from EngR and CR.

4th edn. adv. SJC 5–7 Apr 1791 with this claim: 'This celebrated Novel is universally allowed to far exceed both for humour and character, any thing published since the days of Fielding. It is a keen satire on the times; lays open the deceptions of the age in all professions of life; is a proper book for youth, teaching more knowledge of the World in once reading than 26 years experience.'

CR: 'We think that our author has acted injudiciously in obtruding this excellent work [*Gil Blas*] on our notice; and, by that means, suggesting a comparison very unfavourable to his own. . . . his portraits are often distorted likenesses; and, though we perceive some original traits, the colouring frequently disguises the resemblance. He seems to have observed and copied the picture in the worst light; and to have copied the characters of professions from the lowest of its professors' (p. 65). 'Many of the characters introduced into these volumes are drawn with spirit, and preserved with consistency; though, when we catch a living likeness, we think the picture, as usual, is overcharged. The different situations are described with pleasantry, and we are led through the train of adventures without languor or listlessness. The author is generally in a good humour himself, except where he speaks of booksellers or reviewers; and his strokes of ridicule are sometimes so poignant, and generally so transitory, that we forget our own lashes, to contemplate the punishment of our neighbours, who seldom fare better' (p. 66).

MR: 'A strange kind of a—*St. Giles's* Gil Blas. The Author has talents for scene-painting in low life; but the objects he exhibits are unpleasing. He seems to view mankind in a very degrading light. All are knaves, cheats, and rascals; nor does he make much exception in favour of himself—the hero of the tale. He passes through almost every rank of human society; and he behaves like a sorry fellow in most of them.'

1785: 47   WALWYN, Mr. B.
LOVE IN A COTTAGE: A NOVEL. WRITTEN BY B. WALWYN, AUTHOR OF THE ERRORS OF NATURE.

> London: Printed at the Logographic Press, Black-Friars. For Messrs. Shepperson and
>   Reynolds, Booksellers, No. 139 [sic], Oxford-Street (SJC), 1785 (SJC).
> I 196p; II 190p. 8vo. [CR, MR have 12mo]. 5s (CR), 5s sewed (MR, SJC).
> CR 60: 395–96 (Nov 1785); MR 74: 472 (June 1786); AF II: 4696.
> Bmu rPR 5708.W8. ESTC t230778.

Notes. 1-p. prefatory adv. (unn.); pp. 3–18 vol. 1 missing. T.p. to vol. 2 has 'Volume II' at end of title and has no comma after 'Booksellers' in imprint. Adv. SJC 25–27 Oct 1785.
Errors of Nature 1783: 23.

CR: 'This is an interesting little story, though some of the incidents are scarcely within the bounds of probability. The ladies are, however, little obliged to Mr Walwyn for the examples of the weakness and mutability of their sex. . . . These volumes are not very full of incident and intrigue, and the morality is less exceptionable than the language: there are no very great errors or inelegancies in the latter, yet we think it is not polished with sufficient care.'

MR [Charles Burney the younger]: 'The events of this novel are few, but they are such as interest the Reader. . . . The scene lies in America.'

1786

THE ADVENTURES OF ANTHONY VARNISH
See JOHNSTONE, Charles

THE ADVENTURES OF GEORGE MAITLAND, ESQ. (London, 1786) first
published as *The Life and Adventures of James Ramble, Esq.* by Edward Kimber, (London, 1755, JR 320, AF I: 1521).

1786: 1   ANON.
THE ADVENTURES OF LUCIFER IN LONDON. EXHIBITED IN A SERIES OF LETTERS TO THE RIGHT HONOURABLE THE LORD PRESIDENT OF THE STYGIAN COUNCIL OF PANDÆMONIUM.

London: Printed for H. D. Symonds, No. 4, Stationer's Court, Ludgate-Street, 1786.
220p. 12mo. 1s 6d (CR), 3s 6d (MR).
CR 62: 155 (Aug 1786); MR 75: 230 (Sept 1786); AF II: 34.
Lg; EM 2072:4; ESTC t066523 (BI BL [imperf—lacks all before p. 5]).

Notes. Text of novel starts on p. 5. Some pages possibly missing following t.p. Epistolary.
ESTC date: 1799? (based on BL copy which lacks t.p.).

CR: 'These are not the adventures of Lucifer, but one of the lowest class of demons, who endeavours to compensate for trite satire and dull narrative, by personalities and obscenity. But his arm is nerveless, and the weapon will do no injury. We hope the next devil who attempts to write will be previously taught English.'

MR [Andrew Becket]: 'This book is undoubtedly the production of the devil himself, and he has honestly subscribed it with his name. (We would not be thought to insinuate that Mr Lucifer in any respect resembles the pleasant devils of Le Sage and Samuel Foote. No—he is one of the *dull* devils.)

1786: 2 ANON.
ALBINA, A NOVEL, IN A SERIES OF LETTERS, IN TWO VOLUMES.

London: Printed for William Lane, Leadenhall-Street, 1786.
I missing; II 256p. 12mo. 5s sewed (MR, CR).
CR 62: 149 (Aug 1786); MR 75: 394 (Nov 1786); AF II: 55.
WAu 17.20.4.2[2] (Imperf; wanting vol. 1); ESTC t201277.

Notes. Uncut and bound in the original wrappers (ESTC). Epistolary.
Adv., 'in the Press, and speedily will be published', LEP 14–16 Feb 1786.
Further edn: Dublin, 1786 (Printed by Mary Graisberry, for Messrs. Moncrieffe, Gilbert, White, H. Whitestone, Cash [and 5 others in Dublin], 1 vol., 12mo), ESTC n029631.

CR: '. . . it is some of the vilest trash, in every respect, that probably ever disgraced [circulating libraries'] shelves.'

MR [Andrew Becket]: 'Though the present performance has nothing to do with *poetry*, we still pronounce it to be "prose run mad." '

AN AMOUROUS TALE OF THE CHASTE LOVES OF PETER THE LONG
See BILLARDON DE SAUVIGNY, Edme-Louis

1786: 3 ANON.
APPEARANCE IS AGAINST THEM, IN A SERIES OF LETTERS, IN THREE VOLUMES, BY THE AUTHOR OF EMILY HERBERT, OR PERFIDY PUNISHED.

London: Printed for Thomas Jones, at his Circulating Library, Bridge-Street, Westminster, 1786.
I 216p; II 213p; III 176p. 12mo. 5s sewed (CR), 7s 6d sewed (MR, SJC).
CR 62: 236 (Sept 1786); MR 75: 393 (Nov 1786); AF II: 130.
BL RB.23.a.9495; ESTC t225547.

Notes. 1 p. adv. (for *Emily Herbert* [1786: 5]) verso of t.p. vol. 1 and vol. 3. Epistolary.
Adv. (with *Emily Herbert*) PA 7 June 1786 and SJC 11–13 July 1786.
CR reviews this novel with *Emily Herbert*: 'It would be wrong to separate these conjoined

supports of the author's mighty fame; for we can truly say, that we have never seen anything so flimzy as the first, except the second;—we have never seen any work more ridiculous and uninteresting than Emily Herbert, if it be not Appearance is against them.'

MR [Andrew Becket]: 'The main incident in this novel is borrowed, but without acknowledgment, from *L'Ecossaise*, a well-known comedy of Voltaire's. The story, which is an interesting one, is considerably heightened by the present writer, but his language is poor and weak.'

AN ARABIAN TALE
See BECKFORD, William

1786: 4   ANON.
ARPASIA; OR, THE WANDERER. A NOVEL. BY THE AUTHOR OF THE NABOB. IN THREE VOLUMES.

London: Printed for William Lane, Leadenhall-Street, 1786.
I 216p; II 216p; III 232p. 12mo. 7s 6d sewed (CR, MR), 7s 6d (LEP).
CR 61: 399–400 (May 1786); MR 75: 394 (Nov 1786); AF II: 145.
O Vet.A5e.475-477; ESTC n029923 (NA CtY-BR, OU, PU &c.).

Notes. The Nabob. A Novel (1785: 16) has 'By a Lady' on t.p.
Adv., 'in the Press, and speedily will be published', LEP 14–16 Feb 1786: 'In the manner, taste, and style of Cecilia'. Adv. as published LEP 23–25 Feb 1786: 'Written in the manner, taste, and style of Cecilia, Evelina, &c.' [*Evelina* 1778: 10; *Cecilia* 1782: 15].
Adv. end vol. 3 of *Zoriada* (1786: 24).
Further edn: Dublin, 1786 (Printed by J. Moore Davis, for Messrs. Colles, Moncrieffe, White, Byrne, Cash [and 4 others in Dublin], 2 vols., 12mo), EM 2115: 26, ESTC t100472. French trans. London and Paris, 1787 (*Arpasie*), ESTC t133459 [ESTC identifies as trans. of *Aspasia* {1791: 30}].

CR: 'This is a common story, but related with some art, and in many passages highly interesting. Hurried on by events, there is not much time to detect the numerous improbabilities which occur; and, affected by the situations, we are sometimes led to overlook inconsistencies in the characters.'

MR [William Enfield]: '. . . though not abounding with reflection, or remarkable for elegance of language, [it] is a busy, and not uninteresting tale.'

BARON MUNCHAUSEN'S NARRATIVE
See RASPE, Rudolph Erich

CAROLINE OF LICHTFIELD
See MONTOLIEU, Jeanne-Isabelle-Pauline Polier de Bottens

THE CHILD OF CHANCE; OR, THE ADVENTURES OF HARRY HAZARD
See WYNNE, John Huddlestone

CLERIMONT, OR, MEMOIRS OF THE LIFE AND ADVENTURES OF MR B******
See BRISCOE, C. W.

THE CONVENT: OR, THE HISTORY OF SOPHIA NELSON
See FULLER, Anne

ELFRIDA: OR PATERNAL AMBITION
See GIBBES, Phebe

1786: 5   ANON.
EMILY HERBERT; OR PERFIDY PUNISHED. A NOVEL. IN A SERIES
OF LETTERS. BY THE AUTHOR OF APPEARANCE IS AGAINST
THEM.
> London: Printed for Thomas Jones, at his Circulating Library, Bridge-Street, Westmin-
> ster, 1786.
> I 225p; II 218p; III 224p. 12mo. 7s 6d sewed (MR, CR), 7s 6d (adv., SJC).
> CR 62: 236 (Sept 1786); MR 75: 393–94 (Nov 1786); AF II: 1271.
> ICU PR3291.E5.1786; ESTC n065435.

Notes. Not by Elizabeth Inchbald, author of the farce *Appearance is Against Them* but by the
anonymous author of the novel *Appearance is Against Them* (1786: 3).
Text of novel starts on p. 3 in each vol. Epistolary.
Adv. (with *Appearance Is Against Them*) SJC 11–13 July 1786 as *Emily Horbert* but corrected
in next issue of SJC.
Adv. verso of t.p. to vol. 1 of *Appearance is Against Them.*
Further edn: Dublin, 1787 (Printed by William Porter, for Mess. White, Colbert, Cash,
W. Porter [and 3 others in Dublin], 1 vol., 12mo), ESTC t107739.
CR reviews this novel with *Appearance Is Against Them.* For rev. see 1786: 3.
  MR [Andrew Becket]: 'The style is pert and flippant, and the story improbable.'

THE ERRORS OF INNOCENCE
See LEE, Harriet

FRANCIS, THE PHILANTHROPIST
See JOHNSON, Mrs

THE GAMESTERS. A NOVEL
See MACKENZIE, Anna Maria

HENRIETTA OF GERSTENFELD
See BEUVIUS, Adam

THE HISTORY OF SANDFORD AND MERTON
See DAY, Thomas, App. A: 3

1786: 6   ANON.
THE INNOCENT RIVALS, A NOVEL, TAKEN FROM THE FRENCH,

WITH ALTERATIONS AND ADDITIONS. BY A LADY. IN THREE VOLUMES.

London: Printed for the Proprietor; and sold by J. Bew, Pater-Noster-Row, and H. D.
Symonds, facing Stationers-Hall, 1786.
I x, 243p; II 256p; III 208p. 12mo. 7s 6d sewed (MR, CR).
CR 62: 149 (Aug 1786); MR 75: 314 (Oct 1786); AF II: 2193.
NjP 3600.001.491; ESTC n009468 (NA CtY, CLU-S/C).

Notes. ESTC: Original French version not traced.
Translator's preface. Epistolary.
Adv., 'In a few Days will be published', SJC 15–17 June 1786. Re-adv. with quotation
from EngR SJC 7–10 Oct 1786; a more elaborate version of this adv. appears in the semi-
editorial columns of the SJC 12–14 Oct 1786, beginning 'The Innocent Rivals, a Novel taken
from the French, but considerably altered and enlarged by a Lady, deservedly merits the
Estimation it is held in; indeed was it not approved of by the Fair-Sex, they would not only be
professed Enemies to Delicacy of Sentiment, but devoid of Sympathy, two of their greatest
Ornaments.'
    CR: 'A set of dull sentimental letters, with little to instruct or entertain. This work, which
is said to be taken from the French, is one of the most useless captures which has occurred
during the present literary *hostilities.*'
    MR [William Enfield]: '. . . this novel affords a striking example of the danger of indulging
an illicit passion. It is a lesson which has been taught in many different forms; but it comes
with peculiar weight, as the moral of an interesting tale, agreeably written.'

JULIANA. A NOVEL
See JOHNSON, Mrs

JUVENILE INDISCRETIONS
See BENNETT, Anna Maria

THE KENTISH CURATE; OR THE HISTORY OF SAMUEL LYTTELTON
See LEMOINE, Henry

1786: 7   ANON.
THE LADY'S TALE; OR, THE HISTORY OF DRUSILLA NORTHINGTON. IN TWO VOLUMES.

London: Printed for F. Noble, in Holborn, 1786.
I 190p; II 170p. 12mo. 5s sewed (CR, MR).
CR 60: 470 (Dec 1785); MR 74: 307 (Apr 1786).
BL 12613.aaa.23; EM 199: 5; ESTC t068749 (NA InU-Li).

Notes. 2½ pp. advs. end vol. 2, beginning on p. 170.
Post-dated; adv. as published LC 58: 540 (3–6 Dec 1785) and SJC 10–13 Dec 1785.
    CR: 'This is an insipid story, with little merit in any respect; but we suspect that it has been
part of a larger work. A late detection of plagiarism has made us cautious; and the abrupt
beginning and conclusion of the history seems to support our suspicions.'

MR [Charles Burney the younger]: '. . . by no means so quaint in its style as the title seems to promise.'

1786: 8   ANON.
LANE'S ANNUAL NOVELIST. A COLLECTION OF MORAL TALES, HISTORIES, AND ADVENTURES, AMUSING AND INSTRUCTIVE SELECTED FROM THE MAGAZINES & OTHER PERIODICAL PUBLI-CATIONS FOR THE YEAR. TO BE CONTINUED ANNUALLY.
London: Printed for W. Lane, n.d. [ESTC: 1786].
I 240p; II 244p. 12mo. 6s (CR), 5s sewed (MR, LEP).
CR 63: 78 (Jan 1786); MR 76: 82 (Jan 1787); AF II: 2455.
MRu SC 11983A [vol. 1 only], CaAEU PR 1297.L26 [vol. 2 only]; ESTC t200478.

Notes. Engraved t.p. both vols. Preface 1, i–ii; table of contents iii–iv.
Adv., 'in the Press, and will be speedily published', LEP 23–25 Feb 1786; adv. 'Next Week will be published, Calculated for a Genteel Present', LEP 23–25 Mar 1786.
Adv. LC 59: 338 (8–11 Apr 1786); 'This selection has been made with care and attention, the stories are formed to inspire virtue, and to regulate our passions and conduct; consequently this book is well calculated for a genteel present.'
   CR: 'A collection of tales, histories, and adventures, from Magazines and other periodical publications.'
   MR: 'We are here presented with several pleasing tales. Some of them are even excellent. . . .'

THE LETTERS OF CHARLOTTE
See JAMES, William

1786: 9   ANON.
MELWIN DALE, A NOVEL, IN A SERIES OF LETTERS, BY A LADY. IN TWO VOLUMES.
London: Printed for William Lane, Leadenhall-Street (LEP), 1786.
I 191p; II 181p. 12mo. 5s (CR), 5s sewed (MR, adv.), 7s sewed (LEP).
CR 61: 235 (Mar 1786); MR 75: 153 (Aug 1786); AF II: 2818.
ZWTU REng.MELWIN.1786; ESTC t213994.

Notes. 1 p. advs. end vol. 1 and 3 pp. advs. end vol. 2. Epistolary.
Adv. LEP 28–31 Jan 1786.
Adv. end vol. 3 of Zoriada (1786: 24).
CR has 'Melwyn'; adv. SJC 11–14 Mar 1786 has 'Melvin'.
   CR: 'The usual characters, trite sentiments, and an expected catastrophe, will characterise this novel. Is it new? or is it old? We confess we know not. We suspect it to be a literary patch-work, and consign it to the oblivion which it deserves.'
   MR [Samuel Badcock]: 'Trifling and dull.'

1786: 10   ANON.
RAJAH KISNA, AN INDIAN TALE. IN THREE VOLUMES.

London: Printed for P. Mitchell, at his Circulating Library, North Audley-Street, Grosv.
   Square, 1786..
I 183p; II 208p; III 199p. 8vo. 9s sewed (MR, SJC).
MR 75: 394 (Nov 1786); AF II: 3681.
BL 838.b.13; EM 2385: 3; ESTC t092435 (BI E; NA DLC).

Notes. Adv. SJC 25–28 Feb 1786 with title *Rajah Kima* and additional booksellers: J. Fielding,
Scatcherd & Whitaker, and Debret [sic]. MR gives Debrett as bookseller.
Further edn: London, 1788 [*The Wonderful Adventurer, or, Rajah Kisna*] (WC).

   MR [William Enfield]: 'A wild rhapsody, that tells of Indian gods and goddesses, of incan-
tations high, and powerful spells; of giants vast, and fiery monsters; of royal loves, and groves
of paradise, and beds of roses, and—of a thousand wondrous things, in words of swelling
sound, and dark import.'

THE RAMBLES OF FANCY
See PEACOCK, Lucy

ST. BERNARD'S PRIORY
See HUGILL, Martha

1786: 11   ANON.
TALES, ROMANCES, APOLOGUES, ANECDOTES, AND NOVELS; HUMOROUS SATIRIC, ENTERTAINING, HISTORICAL, TRAGICAL, AND MORAL; FROM THE FRENCH OF THE ABBE BLANCHET, M. BRET, M. DE LA PLACE, M. IMBERT, M. SAINT LAMBERT, AND THE CHEVALIER DE FLORIAN.

London: Printed for G. G. J. and J. Robinson, Pater-Noster-Row, 1786.
I iv, xxiv, 260p; II 243p. 12mo. 6s sewed (CR, MR).
CR 62: 236–237 (1786); MR 75: 316–317 (1786); AF II: 4343.
O Douce T 127-8; ESTC t178169 (NA CSmH, DLC, NjP &c.).

Notes. Table of contents 1, iii–iv; preface i–xxiv.
Adv., 'Thursday next, the 29th instant, will be published', LEP 20–22 June 1786.
Extract published LC 60: 241–2 (7–9 Sept 1786).
Stories by Florian from this collection reprinted numerous times in various magazines
between 1791 and 1809, RM 144, 244, 1202. Many other trans. of these stories published in
various magazines between 1791 and 1814, RM 143, 164, 198, 199, 824.

   CR: 'We have read them with much pleasure; but more than one is the work of the last age,
in a modern dress; though this is not mentioned to lessen their merit, nor ought it to have
that effect.'

   MR [William Enfield]: 'This is an interesting medley from French Novellists; but it was, to
say the least, *unnecessary* to swell the volumes with the addition of *five* of the tales of Florian,
already so well translated by the Editor of the preceding article [*The Works of M. le Chevalier
de Florian*].'

THE TOUR OF VALENTINE
See POTT, Joseph Holden

VATHEK
See BECKFORD, William

VICTORIA. A NOVEL
See ROWSON, Susanna

WARBECK: A PATHETIC TALE
See BACULARD D'ARNAUD, François-Thomas-Marie de

1786: 12   ANON.
THE WOMAN OF QUALITY; OR, THE HISTORY OF LADY ADELINDA
BELLEMONT, IN A SERIES OF LETTERS. IN TWO VOLUMES.

> London: Printed for William Lane, Leadenhall-Street, 1786.
> I 184p; II 192p. 12mo. 5s sewed (CR, SJC, adv.).
> CR 60: 470 (Dec 1785); AF II: 4921.
> BL Cup.404.b.42; EMf; ESTC t140106 (NA NcU).

Notes. Epistolary.
Adv., 'In the Press, and speedily will be published', SJC 1–4 Oct 1785.
Adv. end vol. 3 of *Zoriada* (1786: 24).
   CR: 'We suspect this to be a translation; if it be so, the translator need not have been eager
to appropriate a novel like this to his own nation. The story is contradictory and confused; perplexed without interest, and terrible without pathos. The language too—but we need not
enlarge—it will buz [*sic*] through its short life unheeded, and be forgotten without a parting sigh.'

ZORIADA: OR VILLAGE ANNALS
See HUGHES, Anne

1786: 13   [BACULARD D']ARNAUD, [François-Thomas-Marie].
THE HISTORY OF COUNT GLEICHEN, A GERMAN NOBLEMAN, WHO
RECEIVED PERMISSION FROM POPE GREGORY IX. TO HAVE TWO
WIVES AT THE SAME TIME. TRANSLATED FROM THE FRENCH OF
ARNAUD.

> London: Printed for T. Hookham, New Bond Street, 1786.
> 220p. 12mo. 3s (CR).
> CR 62: 235–6 (Sept 1786).
> C 7735.d.214; EM 6517: 5; ESTC t142925 (BI BL; NA CSmH, DLC).

Notes. Trans. of 'Le comte de Gleichen' in vol. 3 of *Nouvelles Historiques* (Paris, 1777).
4 pp. advs. for French books, 'Livres Vendu Par. T. Hookham', end vol.
   CR: '. . . this is a modern sentimental novel, plentifully adorned with ahs! and ohs! with
little real pathos, and less interest. Alice at last dies, in a fortunate moment; fortunate for
Gleichen, for the reader, and supremely fortunate for the reviewer.'

1786: 14   [BACULARD D'ARNAUD, François-Thomas-Marie de]; [LEE,
Sophia (trans.)].
WARBECK: A PATHETIC TALE. IN TWO VOLUMES.

London: Printed for William Lane, Leadenhall-Street, 1786.
I 203p; II 194p. 12mo. 5s sewed (MR, SJC, adv.).
CR 60: 395 (Nov 1786); MR 75: 153 (Aug 1786).
PU Singer-Mend. PQ.1954.A7.A73 1786; ESTC n035568 (BI BL; NA CSt).

Notes. Trans. of 'Varbeck' from vol. 1 of *Nouvelles historiques* (Paris, 1774).
9-pp. preface followed by 9-pp. introduction (unn.). 2 pp. advs. end vol. 2.
Post-dated; adv. as published SJC 1–4 Oct 1785. Re-adv. as new SJC 24–26 Oct 1786.
Adv. end vol. 3 of *Zoriada* (1786: 24).
Further edns: Dublin, 1786 (Printed by S. Colbert, 2 vols., 12mo), EM 5: 5, ESTC t131492;
Dublin, 1786, ESTC n035567. Earlier trans. serialised in *Sentimental Magazine* (1774–76)
and *Monthly Miscellany* (1777), RM 1329.

CR: 'The conduct of the novel closely imitates the real events; but the force is weakened by
exclamations, by conversations, and reflections. Some parts are related with address; but the
whole is not very interesting. English literature would have sustained little loss, if the French
work had been still neglected.'

MR [Samuel Badcock]: 'Fiction is here made to embellish some historical facts; and the
Author hath executed his design with considerable address. It is indeed a *pathetic* tale; and the
Reader of sensibility will be instructed and entertained by it.'

1786: 15   [BECKFORD, William]; [HENLEY, Samuel (trans.)].
[VATHEK]. AN ARABIAN TALE, FROM AN UNPUBLISHED MANU-
SCRIPT: WITH NOTES CRITICAL AND EXPLANATORY.

London: Printed for J. Johnson, in St. Paul's Church-Yard, and entered at the Station-
ers' Hall, 1786.
vii, 334p. 8vo. 4s sewed (MR, CR).
CR 62: 37–42 (July 1786); MR 76: 450 (May 1787); AF II: 258.
C S727.d.78.15; EM 2444: 2; ESTC t062055 (BI BL, E, O &c.; NA CtY-BR, CtY-Walpole,
CSmH, ICN, IU, MH-H, NjP, PU, TxU, ViU &c.).

Notes. Written in French in 1782 and revised version trans. into English and with notes by
Samuel Henley. Earlier (but not original) French version published in Lausanne several
months later in late 1786, dated 1787 (for further information see Roger Lonsdale's 1970
OUP edn. and Kenneth W. Graham's 1975 article '*Vathek* in English and French' in *Studies
in Bibliography* 28).
Running-title: *The History of the Caliph Vathek.*
Preface iii–iv. Text of novel ends on p. 211; the notes start on p. 213.
Adv., 'In a few days will be published', LEP 25–27 May 1786; title *The History of the Caliph
Vathek; An Arabian Tale; from an unpublished Manuscript, with Notes Critical and Explan-
atory.* Adv. (also as forthcoming) as *The History of Kaliph Vathec* SJC 30 May–1 June 1786;
adv. as published LC 59: 558 (10–13 June 1786).
Further edns: London, 1809 (WC); London, 1834 (WC); [Paris], 1834 (WC); London, 1836
(WC); London, 1849 (WC); NSTC lists edns in 1816, 1823, 1845 and 1849. German trans.
Leipzig, 1788 (*Der Thurm von Samarah*) and Mannheim, 1788 (*Vathek, eine arabische Erzäh-
lung*) (Price).

CR admires the work and its moral and suggests that the notes 'though extensive' are 'too
short' (p. 39).
MR [William Enfield]: 'Though there are in this work too many ideas and sentiments of

European growth, to admit of its passing for a translation of an Eastern manuscript, the piece has all the wildness of Eastern fable: we will add, too, that it preserves the peculiar character of the Arabian Tale, which is not only to overstep nature and probability, but even to pass beyond the verge of possibility, and suppose things, which cannot be for a moment conceived.'

1786: 16   [BENNETT, Anna Maria].
JUVENILE INDISCRETIONS. A NOVEL. IN FIVE VOLUMES. BY THE AUTHOR OF ANNA, OR THE WELCH HEIRESS.

London: Printed for W. Lane, Leadenhall-Street, 1786.
I xi, 228p; II 213p; III 212p; IV 244p; V 248p. 12mo. 15s (MR, LEP May), 12s 6d sewed (CR, adv., LEP Oct).
CR 62: 68–69 (July 1786); MR 75: 315 (Oct 1786); AF II: 299.
BL 12614.cc.12; EM 368: 5; ESTC t071400 (NA CtY, NjP, PU, ViU &c.; EA Ps).

Notes. FC: Name often given incorrectly as Agnes Maria.
Prefatory address 'To the Reviewers' i–iii, signed 'The Author'; Dedication to H.R.H. Prince William Henry v–xi, signed 'the Author'.
Anna; or, Memoirs of a Welch Heiress 1785: 22.
Adv. 'shortly, by the same Author', in adv. for Anna, PA 23 Feb 1786; adv. as published LEP 25–27 May 1786. Re-adv. LEP 14–17 Oct 1786 with extension of title—' Containing several real Characters, genuine Anecdotes, Adventures, &c. of distinguished Personages in the City and at the Court end of the Town'. The contents of the novel are described in a double-columned list: 'A Modern Academy, Pursardo the Master, Gentlewoman in Conceit, A Young Runaway, Apprehended for a Robber, Committed to Bridewell, Examin. by Sir Benjamin, Doctor Orthodox described, Advent. with a Dairy Maid, The Female Republican, Landlady at the Buck's Head, Blue Coat Boy trans. to D.D., Lavy the Country fine Lady, Orthodox and Rotundity, Money in Mar. the Ne plus, Effect of a B. School Educa. Distress of a Country Curate, Love-sick Old Maid, Wisdom of Forty-five, Wife and 40,000l., Mrs Crape, Barber's Lady, Royal Fam. on the Terrace, Midnight Scene at an Inn, Very near a Rape, Honest Tars of Old Engl., Navy Office Clerks descri., Demi-Rep in the Boxes, The Insect described, Box Loungers, Citizen and Clapham Villa, Nobility of Dowgate-hill, A Boxing Match, Love in A Bagnio, City Ladies a La Noblesse, Mayor of Plymouth, Lord, Lady, & L'Eau de Vie, Water, Place and Gallant, Watch house Scene, Spunging-house and Bailiff, The new Irish Howl, Merchant in St Helen's, London Tavern Assembly, Theatrical Rencontre, Party at Vauxhall, Italian Fidler and Singers, Le Dames de Plaisirs [sic], Beau Peter on Ludgate Hill, A Greek-street Lady, Lying dangerous in Public, The Lost Child restored, Meeting of the Lovers, Wisdom of an Old Maid, E. India Capt. Generosity, Terrible J. Doe and R. Roe, Play-house Bustle, Our Hero in Limbo, Juvenile Indis. of a Quaker, Pursardo and a Lecture, The Pawnbroker's Discov., the Kept Mistress, Concludes in Marriage, The Denouement, Containing many curious Rencontres, &c.'
Adv. end vol. 3 of Zoriada (1786: 24).
Further edns: Dublin, 1786 (Printed for Messrs. Moncrieffe, Gilbert, White, Beatty, H. Whitestone [and 8 others in Dublin], 5 vols., 12mo), EM 2954: 1, ESTC t121162; London, 1805 (Summers, NSTC). French trans. Londres [ESTC: i.e. Paris?], 1788 (Les imprudences de la jeunesse), ESTC t133447; German trans. Berlin, 1791 (William oder Geschichte jugendlicher Universichtigkeiten, vol. 1 of Romanen-Magazin von Friedrich Schülz) (EAG, RS).

CR: 'The story of this work is not a very unusual one, and its more remarkable incidents not very numerous; yet we are interested in the tale, and, by many artless, pleasing strokes, the heart is engaged, and the attention led away captive. The characters are well drawn, and the change of fortune equally unexpected and pleasing. So far may panegyric proceed; but there is a reverse, which must be displayed with equal fidelity. The improbability of the story is frequently disgusting; and the lady so often indulges her fancy in describing improper scenes, that we suspect the cap is assumed to palliate other errors, and to obtain that interest which the author could not, with equal confidence, expect in his proper dress.'

MR [William Enfield]: '. . . the characters are more numerous than was necessary, and are strained beyond real life. The plot is confused, and in many particulars extravagant. The tale is drawn out to an immoderate length, and the reader is fatigued without being interested. The writer is culpable too, in adopting and proceeding upon an idea of a pernicious tendency, namely, that *juvenile indiscretions* are rather to be regarded as indications of genius and spirit, than as proofs of an ill-principled or irresolute mind.'

1786: 17   [BEUVIUS, Adam].
HENRIETTA OF GERSTENFELD. TRANSLATED FROM THE GERMAN OF MR WIELAND [vol. 1].
HENRIETTA OF GERSTENFELD; A GERMAN STORY [vol. 2].

> Dublin: Printed for the Translatour [*sic*]; And sold by H. Chamberlaine, No. 5, College-Green, T. Heery, No. 20, Chapel-Street, And by the Company of Booksellers, 1786 [vol.1].
> London: Printed for William Lane, Leadenhall-Street, 1788 [vol. 2].
> I viii, 240p; II 292p. 12mo.
> BL 1490.d.57 [vol. 1], ; EM 3813: 5 [vol. 1], EM 95: 6 [vol. 2]; ESTC t073960 [vol. 1], ESTC t073946 [vol. 2].

Notes. Trans. of *Henrietta, oder der Husarenraub* (Berlin and Leipzig, 1779). Falsely attributed to Christoph Martin Wieland.
Epistolary. Dublin edn. of vol. 1 apparently anticipates 2nd vol. but none survives. London Lane edn. of vol. 1 published 1787 (292p 12mo). Dublin vol. 1: Preface 1, v–viii, Dublin 1 Dec, 1786; pp. 25–6 missing, cancellandum and cancellans leaves B1 both remain, one with the drop-head title *Henrietta of Gerstenfeld* and the other with *The Force of Nature*. 4 pp. advs. end vol. 2.
1787 London edn. adv. LC 61: 253 (13–15 Mar 1787): 'A German Story, in manner of Sorrows of Werter'.
Both London vols. adv. LC 63: 124 (2–5 Feb 1788); 'The Publisher of this Work, the former part of which has been received so very favourably as to be universally read and approved, flatters himself the Public will excuse the delay of this second part, which has arose from some unforeseen circumstances. He however presumes to hope the uncommon merit of this book will make amends for the delay.'
French trans. Paris, 1782 (*Henriette de Gerstenfeld*) (BGR).
Dublin edn. of vol. 1 apparently not reviewed; reviews are of 1787–88 London edn: CR 63: 389–90 (May 1787); MR 77: 79 (July 1787) [vol. 1]; MR 80: 168–9 (Feb 1789) [vol. 2].
    CR: 'The story, so far as it goes, is well told; the reflections are judicious, and the moral unexceptionable' (p. 390).

MR 77 [Andrew Becket]: '... on the score of morality it is truly excellent.—But it is greatly wanting in those delicate and pathetic *touches*, which so particularly distinguish the writings of a Gesner, and a Klopstock....'

1786: 18   [BILLARDON DE SAUVIGNY, Edme-Louis]; HOLCROFT, Thomas (trans.).
AN AMOUROUS TALE OF THE CHASTE LOVES OF PETER THE LONG, AND OF HIS MOST HONOURED DAME BLANCHE BAZU, HIS FEAL FRIEND BLAIZE BAZU, AND THE HISTORY OF THE LOVER'S WELL. IMITATED FROM THE ORIGINAL FRENCH BY THOMAS HOLCROFT.
> London: Printed for G. G. J. and J. Robinson, Paternoster Row, 1786.
> iv, 236p. 8vo [MR has 12mo] 3s 6d sewed (MR, LEP).
> MR 76: 521–2 (June 1787); AF II: 1999.
> C 7720.e.166; EM 1922: 4; ESTC t075771 (BI BL, E; NA IU, MH-H, PU &c.).

Notes. ESTC: A free translation.
Trans. of *Histoire Amoreuse, de Pierre le Long* (Londres [i.e. Paris], 1765).
Prefatory address headed 'Nota Bene' iii–iv.
Adv., 'On the First of November will be published, Beautifully printed upon a fine Writing Paper', LEP 12–14 Oct 1786.
    MR [Andrew Becket]: '... our Author's *matter* is as uninteresting as the generality of novels,—but his *manner* will frequently induce a smile.'

1786: 19   [BRISCOE, C. W.].
CLERIMONT, OR, MEMOIRS OF THE LIFE AND ADVENTURES OF MR B******. (WRITTEN BY HIMSELF.) INTERSPERSED WITH ORIGINAL ANECDOTES OF LIVING CHARACTERS.
> Liverpool: Printed by Charles Wosencroft, 1786.
> vi, 351p. 12mo.
> BL 12613.cc.10; EM 291: 5; ESTC t068953 (BI LVp, O; NA CtY).

Notes. Dedication to 'his most potent, Puissant, High and Mighty Serene Highness, The Lord Oblivion' iii–iv; address 'To the Public' v–vi. Pagination continuous Roman-Arabic; text of novel starts on p. 7.

1786: 20   CARTWRIGHT, Mrs. [H.].
THE PLATONIC MARRIAGE: A NOVEL, IN A SERIES OF LETTERS. BY MRS. CARTWRIGHT.
> London: Printed at the Logographic Press, by J. Walter, Printing-House-Square, Black-
>   fryers, and sold by J. Hookham, Bond-street; R. Baldwin, Paternoster-Row; and W.
>   Richardson, under the Royal-Exchange, 1786.
> I 263p; II 225p; III 274p. 12mo. 7s 6d sewed (MR), 9s (CR).
> CR 63: 310 (Apr 1787); MR 76: 530–31 (June 1787); AF II: 626.
> CSmH 354874; EM 5553: 2; ESTC n025495.

Notes. 'Blackfryers' is spelt 'Blackfriars' in imprints to vols. 2 & 3. 2 pp. advs. end vol. 3. Epistolary.

Further edn: Dublin, 1787 (Printed by William Porter, for Messrs. W. Watson, Colles, Burton, White, Byrne [and 8 others in Dublin], 2 vols., 12mo [Imprint to vol. 2 gives printer's name as John Exshaw]), ESTC n020287. French trans. Amsterdam, and Paris, 1789 (*Le mariage platonique*) (BGR).

CR: '... the "Platonic Marriage" is an entertaining novel; and, among some commonplace trifles, we meet with interesting situations.'

MR [Andrew Becket]: '... there is something of novelty in the story, which is conducted with tolerable skill and address.—The work, however, is incorrectly written, and several vulgarisms are scattered through it.'

DAY, Thomas, **THE HISTORY OF SANDFORD AND MERTON**
See App. A: 3

1786: 21   {FULLER, Anne}.
ALAN FITZ-OSBORNE, AN HISTORICAL TALE. IN TWO VOLUMES.
> Dublin: Printed by P. Byrne, (108) Grafton-Street, 1786.
> I x, 288p; II 378p. 12mo.
> ICN Y155.F947; ESTC n029520 (NA NjP).

Notes. Dedication to Mrs Newenham of Maryborough, signed Anne Fuller, 1, iii–vi [2 pp. numbered as v]; Preface vii–x. 8pp unn. List of subscribers begin. vol. 1. Pagination in vol. 1 continuous Roman-Arabic; text of novel starts on p. 11. Text in vol. 2 starts on p. 3.

London edn. adv. SJC 28 Apr–1 May 1787: 'The Second Edition (the first being taken off by the Nobility and Gentry of Ireland.'

Further edns: Dublin/London, 1787, EM 2011: 1, ESTC t074659; London, 1787, EM 4994: 12; ESTC t119103. French trans. Amsterdam and Paris, 1789 (*Alan Fitz'Osborne, roman historique*) (Lévy).

This edn. not reviewed; London edn. rev. CR 65: 235–6 (Mar 1788); MR 77: 190–2 (Sept 1787); AF II: 1541.

CR compares it to Lee's *The Recess* (1783: 15 and 1785: 37): 'These volumes possess great merit; but they do not interest us by events so uncommon; they do not harrow up the soul by distress so accumulated, or rouse the attention by events so unexpected as occur in the work just quoted. Miss Fuller's merit is of an humbler kind; she connects the outline of history with a chain of events in domestic life; and interests us as much by the tender affection of Gertrude, as she dazzles by the splendid heroism of Edward.'

MR [Andrew Becket]: 'The history of Alan Fitz-Osborne may perhaps dispute the claim to *excellence*, with any similar production extant. The fable is highly interesting and affecting; and though the historian has certainly furnished the outline of the principal personages in it, yet as they are generally placed by Miss Fuller either in a more pleasing, or a more striking point of view, than that in which they have been usually presented to us, we now regard them with a proportionate satisfaction and delight.'

1786: 22   [FULLER, Anne].
THE CONVENT: OR, THE HISTORY OF SOPHIA NELSON. IN TWO VOLUMES. BY A YOUNG LADY.

London: Printed by T. Wilkins, No. 23, Aldermanbury, 1786.

I 293p; II 320p. 12mo. 6s sewed (CR, SJC), 5s sewed (MR).

CR 62: 469–70 (Dec 1786); MR 76: 449–50 (May 1787); AF II: 1542.

BL N.2316; EM 5603: 4; ESTC t146879 (NA AzU, ICU, MH-H; EA P).

Notes. According to Todd, author attribution is doubtful (but see SJC advs. below).
Epistolary.
Vol. 1 not dated.

Adv. SJC 26–29 Aug 1786; title continues, after 'Sophia Nelson', 'in Letters to and from several Persons of England, France, and Ireland', bookseller list is expanded—'Printed by T. Wilkins, Aldermanbury, for the Authour; sold by Mr Fuller, New George-Street; No. 43, Surrey Side of Black-Friars; Murray, Fleet-Street; Symonds, Stationer's Court; Jones, Westminster-Bridge; and J. Hookham, New Bond Street'— and there is a final note: 'N.B. Entered at Stationer's-Hall, by Mr Fuller, who has the Disposal of the Copy-Right.'
CR gives Murray as bookseller.

Adv., with *Alan Fitz-Osborne*, SJC 28 Apr–1 May 1787 as 'the first Attempt of the same young Lady' [Anne Fuller's name is given in the heading].

German trans. Leipzig, 1788 (*Sophie Nelson, eine Geschichte nach dem Leben*) (Price); French trans. Paris, 1790 (*Le Couvert, ou Histoire de Sophie Nelson*) (Summers); French trans. Neuwied, 1792 (*Histoire de Miss Nelson*) (Price).

CR: 'This pleasing writer treads in the footsteps of miss Burney with considerable success. . . . The story is told in the fashionable form of letters, in which the style is not skilfully discriminated, though it is, at times, sufficiently varied to raise it above uniformity. The language is, in general, easy, correct, and sometimes, in spite of numerous press errors, even elegant. The story is well managed; the situations generally interesting, and the characters well copied' (p. 469).

MR [Andrew Becket]: 'Long and painful have been our wanderings in the misty regions of fiction and romance. A performance like the present, therefore, has nearly the same effect upon us as the splendid luminary of the heavens upon the weary and dejected traveller; it cheers, enlivens, and encourages us to pursue our way. . . . The fair Writer has evidently taken the Author of Cecilia for a model. Could she have chosen a better?' [*Cecilia* 1782: 15].

1786: 23   [GIBBES, Phebe].
ELFRIDA; OR, PATERNAL AMBITION. A NOVEL. IN THREE VOLUMES. BY A LADY.

London: Printed for J. Johnson, No. 72, St. Paul's Church-Yard, 1786.

I 264p; II 223p; III 236p. 12mo. 7s 6d sewed (MR, CR).

CR 62: 68 (July 1786); MR 76: 360 (Apr 1787); AF II: 1603.

MH-H *EC75.A100.786e; EM 1100: 7; ESTC n006605 (NA CtY, OU [vol. 1 lacks t.p.]).

Notes. In her petition to the Royal Literary Fund declaring authorship of this novel, Gibbes wrote to the bookseller, Joseph Johnson, for authentication (RLF 2: 74, letter of 15 Oct 1804).

Adv., 'In a few Days will be published', LEP 11–13 May 1786; adv. as published LC 59: 558 (10–13 June 1786).

Further edn: Dublin, 1786 (Printed by John Rea, for Messrs. White, Byrne, Brown, Moore, Lewis and Halpen, 2 vols., 12mo), ESTC t123792. German trans. Leipzig, 1788 (*Elfriede oder Das Opfer väterlicher Vorurtheile*) (Price); French trans. n.p., 1792 (*Elfrida, ou l'ambition paternelle*) (HWS).

CR: 'The novel is, in general, pathetic and interesting: the story and the characters are in many respects new, and drawn faithfully from nature: the language, however, is not finished with elegance, nor sometimes with sufficient exactness.'

MR [Andrew Becket]: 'A very old story, and dull as a "Comical fellow." '

HASWELL, Susanna
See ROWSON, Susanna

1786: 24   [?HUGHES, Anne, or Phebe GIBBES].
ZORIADA: OR, VILLAGE ANNALS. A NOVEL. IN THREE VOLUMES.
London: Printed for T. Axtell, Royal Exchange, 1786.
I 196p; II 160p; III 165p. 12mo. 7s 6d (MR, CR), 7s 6d sewed (LEP, adv.).
CR 62: 394 (Nov 1786); MR 76: 265 (Mar 1787); AF II: 2103A.
O 256f.1848-50; ESTC t219607 (NA InU-Li).

Notes. In a letter of 18 Oct 1804 (RLF 2: 74) Phebe Gibbes claimed authorship of this novel.
3½ pp. advs. end vol. 3, beginning on p. 165.
Adv. LEP 26–28 Sept 1786.
Adv. end vol. 2 of Darnley Vale (1789: 33).
Further edn: Dublin, 1786 (Printed for Messrs. Colles, Gilbert, White, Byrne, Cash [and 3 others in Dublin], 3 vols., 12mo), ESTC t212001. French trans. London and Paris, 1787 (Zoraïde, ou Annales d'un Village) (BGR); German trans. Vienna, 1791 (Zoraide, oder Jahrbücher eines Dorfs) (DBI).

CR: 'One of our associates, the natural historian, a great admirer of systems, and an idolater of the Linnaean definitions, contend that every work is a species, and may be exactly characterised in the concise language of the naturalists. If this scheme be ever conveniently followed, it must be in the work before us; let us try.

Genus, Novel; Species, N. Zoriada, three volumes, ill-written, worse printed; without ingenuity, novelty, or pathos.'

MR [Andrew Becket]: 'This Novelist is superior to most of his brethren at story-telling. His portraits likewise have really something striking in them. . . . The fable of this Novel, as we have already hinted, is not unentertaining; we wish, indeed, we could say any thing in praise of its language,—but justice obliges us to remark, that the whole is written in a very incorrect and faulty manner. Some of the errors, however, are possibly typographical.'

1786: 25   [HUGILL, Martha].
ST. BERNARD'S PRIORY. AN OLD ENGLISH TALE; BEING THE FIRST LITERARY PRODUCTION OF A YOUNG LADY.
London: Printed for the Authoress, and sold at Swift's Circulating Library, 1786.
xi, 117p. 4to.
MH-H *EC75.H8727.786s; EM 2141: 15; ESTC n023109 (BI BL; NA CaBVaU, CLU-S/C).

Notes. Dedication to the Duchess of Devonshire v–vi; introduction vii–viii; list of subscribers ix–xi.
Further edn: London, [1789], EM 4543: 8, ESTC t127660 [Priory of St. Bernard]. German trans. Gera, 1791 (Die Priorey St. Bernhardt) (Price); French trans. Paris, 1798 (Le Prieuré de Saint Bernard, ou l'Usurpateur puni) (Lévy). Facs: GN II (1829 edn.).

1786 edn. not reviewed; 1789 edn. rev. CR 68: 75–6 (1789) and two other journals; AF II: 2110.

1786: 26   [JAMES, William].
THE LETTERS OF CHARLOTTE, DURING HER CONNEXION WITH WERTER.

> London: Printed for T. Cadell, in the Strand, 1786.
> I x, 159p; II 170p. 8vo [MR has 12mo]. 5s sewed (CR, MR), 5s sewed or 6s bound (SJC).
> CR 61: 357–9 (May 1786); MR 75: 153 (Aug 1786); AF II: 2243.
> BL 1607/1723; EM 4789: 17; ESTC t128494 (BI Gu, O, Ota; NA CLU-S/C, IU, ViU &c.).

Notes. ESTC: Based on *Die Leiden des jungen Werthers* [Johann Wolfgang von Goethe's *Die Leiden des jungen Werthers* (Leipzig, 1774)].
Dedication to the Queen, signed 'The Editor'; preface vol. 1, i–x. Epistolary.
Adv., 'In the Press, and speedily will be published,' PA 10 Feb 1786; adv. 'Elegantly printed . . . with a Preface by the Editor', SJC 14–16 Mar 1786.
Further edns: Dublin, 1786 (Printed for Messrs. Chamberlaine, Colles, Moncrieffe, Walker, White [and 11 others in Dublin], 2 vols., 12mo), EM 2210: 8, ESTC t060898; New York, 1797, ESTC w020676; New York, 1797, ESTC w013556; New York, 1797, ESTC w013555; WC has 3 entries between 1800 and 1850; NSTC lists edn. in 1813. French trans. Paris, 1786 (*Lettres de Charlotte à Caroline son amie pendant sa liaison avec Werther*) (BGR) German trans. Berlin and Stettin, 1788 (*Lottens Briefe an eine Freundin während ihrer Bekanntschaft mit Werthern*) (Price).
CR approves of '. . . these Letters, which we think contain the seducing tenderness of Werter, without its danger; which raise the feelings in a whirlwind, without hurrying the judgment along with them, and driving the reader, perhaps smarting from recent, from similar disappointments, into the same destructive abyss' (p. 359).
MR [Samuel Badcock]: 'This Novel is in general both interesting and pathetic; but the judgment of the Author is not equal to his feelings. The texture is too flimsy, and the imagery is frequently extravagant.'

1786: 27   [JOHNSON, Mrs].
FRANCIS, THE PHILANTHROPIST: AN UNFASHIONABLE TALE. IN THREE VOLUMES.

> London: Printed for William Lane, Leadenhall Street, 1786.
> I xii, 222p; II 209p; III 201p. 12mo. 7s 6d sewed (MR, SJC), 9s (CR).
> CR 60: 395 (Nov 1785); MR 74: 306 (Apr 1786); AF II: 2291.
> CSmH 285050; EMf; ESTC n031627.

Notes. Blakey: 'By the same author: *Juliana* (1786), attributed by a Minerva Library Catalogue of 1814 to Mrs. Johnson'.
Dedication to Lady Williams-Wynne pp. v–viii, signed 'The Author', Aug 1785; 'Advertisement to the Public' pp. ix–xii on the pros and cons of epistolary and narrative fiction.
Post-dated; adv., 'In the Press, and speedily will be published', SJC 1–4 Oct 1785; adv. as published SJC 25–27 Oct 1785.
Adv. PA 4 Feb 1786; 'The Publisher of this Novel is happy to find that it is received with universal Approbation; but he cannot avoid remarking, that it would have been rather more candid, if the Editor of the Town and Country Magazine had given a Note of Reference to the

Story, which he has thought fit to extract from it in the Supplement to that Magazine.'
Adv. end vol. 3 of *Zoriada* (1786: 24).
Further edn: Dublin, 1786 (Printed for L. White, 1 vol., 12mo), EM 3515: 15, ESTC n018525.
German trans. Zeitz and Nuremburg, 1793 (*Der Menschenfreund Franz Fairborn*) (EAG).

CR: 'This is a scyon from a venerable stock, which sprouts with vigour, if not with luxuriance. In plainer English, the author has left the fashionable mode of expanding his story, by
the uninteresting exclamations of insipid correspondents, and adopted that of discriminated
description, and interesting situation. His language is free and easy; his observations neither
tritely superficial, nor affectedly philosophical; and his drawings preserve a roughness, not
perhaps essential to good pictures, but not unsuitable to characteristic sketches. The author
chiefly excels in shrewd, unexpected remarks; but good sense animates the whole, and he is
occasionally pathetic and moral. We have been much entertained with the work before us;
and wish to see the author again engaged in a similar undertaking.'

MR [Samuel Badcock]: 'Considering the present state of novel-writing, this author is entitled to more applause than we can honestly bestow on the generality of the profession. His
language is not inelegant, and his observations bespeak good sense, if not acute penetration.
He is sometimes pathetic, but his tenderness too often degenerates into puerility; and in several passages where he evidently exerted himself to awake our sensibility, he only excited a
smile.'

1786: 28   [JOHNSON, Mrs].
JULIANA. A NOVEL. BY THE AUTHOR OF FRANCIS THE PHILAN-THROPIST. IN THREE VOLUMES.

London: Printed for William Lane, Leadenhall-Street, 1786.
I 223p; II 216p; III 222p. 12mo. 7s 6d sewed (MR, CR), 7s 6d (LEP Feb).
CR 61: 496–70 (June 1786); MR 76: 82 (Jan 1787); AF II: 2292.
BL 12604.ccc.16; EM 91: 6; ESTC t108460 (NA CtY, PU).

Notes. Blakey: 'Attributed by a Minerva Library Catalogue of 1814 to Mrs Johnson'.
Dedication to Mrs Hastings i–ii, signed 'The Author'. 2½ pp. advs. end vol. 3, beginning on
p. 222. Epistolary.
Adv., 'in the Press, and speedily will be published', LEP 14–16 Feb 1786; adv., 'This Week will
be published', LEP 25–28 Mar 1786.
Adv. inaccurately, as *Justiana*, with dedicatee given as Mr Hastings and author's other novel
as *Frances, the Philanthropist,* SJC 1–4 Sept 1787.

CR: 'There is an error in the title-page: read "by a very distant Relation" of the Author, &c.
for we can find very little resemblance between the works.'

MR: 'Various episodes are introduced, by which the writer evidently intended to arrest
attention; but his labours have a totally different effect. By a multiplicity of incidents
and characters the interest is broken and divided, and the hero and heroine are lost in the
crowd.'

1786: 29   [JOHNSTONE, Charles].
THE ADVENTURES OF ANTHONY VARNISH; OR, A PEEP AT THE MANNERS OF SOCIETY. BY AN ADEPT. IN THREE VOLUMES.

London: Printed for William Lane, Leadenhall-Street, 1786.
I xii, 240p; II 240p; III 269p. 12mo. 7s 6d sewed (MR, CR).

CR 62: 149 (Aug 1786); MR 76: 83 (Jan 1787); AF II: 2307.

BL 12612.dd.5; EM 231: 3; ESTC t066944 (BI O; NA CtY-BR, PU).

Notes. Dedication to George Colman, Esq. v–vii, signed 'The Author'; prefatory advertisement ix–xii. In vols. 2 and 3 text of novel starts on p. 5. 7 pp. advs. end vol. 3.

Adv., 'in the Press, and speedily will be published', LEP 14–16 Feb 1786.

French trans. Londres [ESTC: i.e. Paris?], 1788, ESTC t149929; German trans. Leipzig, 1789 (*Peregrine Pickel der Zweyte oder Tragisch-komische Abenteuer von Anton Varnish*) (Price).

CR: 'A view of the manners of Grub-street and St Giles's, probably copied from a former sketch. . . .'

MR: 'Made up entirely of scenes in low life. And it must be acknowledged that the Author, in describing them, appears to be perfectly *at home.*'

1786: 30   [LEE, Harriet].

THE ERRORS OF INNOCENCE, IN FIVE VOLUMES.

London: Printed for G. G. J. and J. Robinson, No. 25, Pater-Noster-Row, 1786.

I 264p; II 263p; III 260p; IV 252p; V 252p. 12mo [LEP and CR have 8vo]. 15s (CR), 15s sewed (MR).

CR 61: 234 (Mar 1786); MR 75: 230 (Sept 1786); AF II: 2492.

BL 12601.g.1; EM 5598: 3; ESTC t108510 (BI O; NA IU, MH-H).

Notes. Epistolary.

Adv., 'In the Press and speedily will be published', LEP 17–20 Dec 1785; adv. as published LEP 28–31 Jan 1786.

Further edn: Dublin, 1786 (Printed for Messrs. Burnet, Moncrieffe, Burton, Exshaw, White [and 7 others in Dublin], 2 vols., 12mo), EM 2509: 5; ESTC n006788. German trans. Leipzig, 1787–88 (*Die Irrthümer aus Unschuld*) (EAG); French trans. Edimbourg [ESTC: i.e. Paris], 1788 (*Herbert, ou Adieu Richesses, ou les Mariages*), ESTC n033191.

CR: 'The different parts of this novel are of very unequal merit. An obscurity in the conduct of the story, at first perplexes the reader, and the connection of the several events is at last traced with difficulty. On the other hand, good sense, strict morality, and the most guarded propriety of conduct, in many of the characters, render a salutary lesson to those who eagerly pursue similar productions. Vice and folly are also exposed to censure and ridicule. The author seems capable of commanding the heart, and all its finer sensations; of harrowing up the soul with distress, of softening it with pity, or expanding it with joy. We can only attribute her failure, in some parts, to haste, perhaps to inexperience. In the beginning she seems to have had no regular plan, and consequently could not provide for the succeeding events.'

MR [Samuel Badcock]: 'The general complexion of this novel is various. In some parts it is tedious and redundant; and in others animated, interesting and pathetic. . . . . The Writer discovers a very intimate acquaintance with the manners of fashionable life: and some striking scenes of it are drawn with a spirited and elegant pencil. The tendency of this Novel deserves our warmest praise; and though there are faults in the execution, yet where there is so much to commend, we censure with reluctance.'

1786: 31   LEGRAND [D'AUSSY, Pierre-Jean-Baptiste].

TALES OF THE TWELFTH AND THIRTEENTH CENTURIES. FROM THE FRENCH OF MR LE GRAND.

London: Printed for Egerton, Hookham, Kearsley, Robinson, Bew and Sewel, 1786.
I xxxii, 239p; II 240p. 12mo. 6s sewed (CR, MR).
CR 62: 76–77 (July 1786); MR 76: 59–61 (Jan 1787); AF II: 2513.
BL 12511.ee.26; EMf; ESTC t160021 (BI AWn; NA NNC).

Notes. Trans. of *Fabliaux ou contes du XIIe et du XIIIe siècle* (Paris, 1779).
Adv., 'Next Week will be published', LEP 11–13 May 1786; adv. notes, 'These Volumes comprehend Thirty-Seven Original Stories, serious and comic; with an account of the imitations and uses that have since been made of them, by Boccase [Boccacio], Moliere, Bossuet, La Fontaine, Racine, Corneille, Voltaire, Rousseau, and other modern authors.'
Adv. SJC 10–13 Mar 1787 with the heading 'Upon the following singular Collection several of our modern Romances, Novels, and dramatick Pieces are founded' and the titles of 19 of the stories listed in double columns.
Further edn: London, 1789 [*Norman Tales*], ESTC t147716; London, 1796 [*Tales of the Minstrels*] (Mayo) xESTC; London, n.d. [1800?] [*Tales of the Minstrels*], ESTC t230121; London, n.d. [1800?] [*Tales of the Minstrels*], ESTC n063227. Extracts from *Tales of the XIIth and XIIIth Centuries*, 'Aucassin and Nicolette', published in *Lady's Magazine*, 1796, RM 128.
CR: '. . . many of them have been so often told, in prose and verse, that they want even the charms of novelty. To elegance and delicacy they cannot pretend; for they are the faithful pictures of an age emerging from barbarism, where the artificial refinements of chivalry were introduced as a powerful bulwark against oppression or tyranny, and supernatural aid was required to cut the knot, which eluded the dexterity of those who were not yet taught the art of untying it' (p. 76).
MR [Samuel Badcock]: 'These Tales shock probability. We cannot realise many of the incidents, yet they discover a vigorous and wild imagination. They awaken curiosity; and as they are generally short, they are seldom tedious: and we easily suffer ourselves to be carried away by the pleasing illusion into the land of inchantment [*sic*]' (p. 61).

1786: 32   [LEMOINE, Henry].
THE KENTISH CURATE; OR, THE HISTORY OF LAMUEL LYTTLE-TON, A FOUNDLING. WRITTEN BY HIMSELF.

London: Printed for J. Parsons, No. 21, Pater-noster-Row, 1786.
I v, 250p; II 234p; III 215p; IV [244]p. 12mo. 12s (CR), 10s sewed (MR), 12s sewed (PA).
CR 63: 77–8 (Jan 1787); MR 77: 496–7 (Dec 1787); AF II: 2520.
BL 012618.df.11; EM 370: 2; ESTC t106128 (NA MH-H).

Notes. Introduction i–v. Drop-head title: *The Adventures of Lamuel Lyttleton, the Kentish Curate*. Pagination continuous Roman-Arabic; text of novel starts on p. 7. Pp. 245–248 of vol. 1 missing in BL copy. Last page of vol. 4 misnumbered 222.
Adv. PA 7 Nov 1786.
CR: 'As it is the indispensible duty of a reviewer to encourage merit, we must praise the Kentish Curate, for his new, laborious, and tedious history' (p. 77).
MR [Andrew Becket]: 'A series of uninteresting, ill-written adventures. The scene is for the most part in prisons and spunging-houses, and the principal characters are rogues and vagabonds. . . . If *dulness* will recommend a man to a benefice; and a wicked wit has insinuated that it seldom fails,—the Kentish curate may reckon on something *great*.'

1786: 33   [MACKENZIE, Anna Maria].
THE GAMESTERS: A NOVEL. IN THREE VOLUMES. BY THE AUTHO-
RESS OF BURTON-WOOD AND JOSEPH.

> London: Printed by H. D. Steel, Nº. 51, Lothbury, and sold by R. Baldwin, Nº. 47, Pater-
> Noster-Row, 1786.
> I 222p; II 192p; III 210p. 8vo [MR and CR have 12mo]. 7s 6d sewed (MR, CR).
> CR 61: 154 (Feb 1786); MR 75: 230 (Sept 1786); AF II: 2657.
> BL 1154.i.3; EM 2450: 1; ESTC t064282 (NA InU-Li, PU, TxHR).

Notes. 1-p. prefatory advertisement (unn.). Epistolary.
Adv. SJC 22–24 Dec 1785; 'In which is delineated the fatal Consequences of the prevailing
Habit of Gaming, in their most glaring Colours'. Re-adv., 'Lately published', 28–31 Oct 1786.
Further edn: Dublin, 1786 (Printed for Messrs. Burnet, Moncrieffe, Burton, White, Cash,
Byrne, Marchbank, Moore, 2 vols., 12mo), ESTC n003370. German trans. Leipzig, 1787 (Die
Spieler, eine Erzählung in Briefen) (Price); French trans. Geneva and Paris, 1789 (Les joueurs)
(BGR).

CR: 'Though we trace our author in the footsteps of some of her predecessors, we must still
allow her considerable merit. The characters are not less distinguished by their bold and
faithful outlines, than by a warmth of colouring, and spirited attitude. In some respects they
are superior to their originals; for they rise to a distorted caricature, though somewhat
removed from real life. The language is animated and easy; frequently elegant: the pathos is
well managed, and properly contrasted. We would not, however, be understood too generally: the story has faults in its conduct, and, in some instances, improbability; nor are its merits, even when perspicuous, always unalloyed. . . .'

MR [Samuel Badcock]: 'This Novel is entitled to our recommendation, on account of the
moral it means to inculcate, as well as the ingenious conduct of the plot from which it arises.
A considerable knowledge of the ways of the world is discovered in it: and characters are
marked with a happy discrimination. There is a delicacy of sentiment that frequently places
the fair author in an amiable light. She is sometimes pathetic; but we were most entertained
by her wit and vivacity in the more comic scenes.'

MEZIERE, Harriet (née Chilcot), MORETON ABBEY; OR THE FATAL
MYSTERY
See 1785: 39

1786: 34   [MONTOLIEU, Jeanne-Isabelle-Pauline Polier de Bottens, dame de
Croussaz, baronne de]; HOLCROFT, Thomas (trans.).
CAROLINE OF LICHTFIELD; A NOVEL. TRANSLATED FROM THE
FRENCH. BY THOMAS HOLCROFT.

> London: Printed for G. G. J. and J. Robinson, Paternoster-Row, 1786.
> I 298p; II 301p; III 293p. 12mo. 9s sewed (CR, MR).
> CR 62: 199–203 (Sept 1786); MR 76: 265–6 (Mar 1787); AF II: 2001.
> BL C.175.a.17; EMf; ESTC t129168 (BI MRu; NA IU, MH-H, PU, TxU &c.).

Notes. Trans. of Caroline (Lausanne, 1786), later titled Caroline de Lichtfield. Mayo (pp.
450–1) reports that this novel is based on 'Albertine', a short story by Nicolas Bonneville
from his adaptation of German originals in Choix de petits romans, imités de l'allemand

(1786). 'Albertine' itself was published in translation several times, with and without acknowledgment of its source, in magazines between 1786 and 1805, RM 76–78, 815.
4 pp. advs. end vol. 3.
Adv., 'Thursday next the 29th instant, will be published', LEP 20–22 June 1786.
Further edns: London, 1786, EM 3634: 3, ESTC t129190; Dublin, 1786 (Printed by M. Graisberry, for Messrs. W. Watson, Gilbert, Moncrieffe, Exshaw [and 11 others in Dublin], 2 vols., 12mo), ESTC n026677; Dublin, 1795, ESTC n003099; London, 1797, EM 3634: 5, ESTC t129191; New York, 1798, ESTC w037318; ESTC has 8 entries for French versions claiming (probably falsely) 'Londres' and Dublin as places of publication; WC has 7 entries between 1800 and 1850; NSTC lists edn. in 1817.

CR: 'A Romance which differs, in its progress and its events, from the volumes which crowd and disgrace a circulating library, forms a new era in literature. To interest, and attract, it is necessary to avoid the usual trait of incident; to diversify the faces to which we have been so much accustomed to survey; at the same time, to avoid what is only uncommon, if destitute of probability or the resemblance of nature; to neglect absurd refinements, and superficial reflections.

The author of Caroline has started from vulgar bounds, and her narrative is natural, interesting, and in some degree new' (p. 199).

MR [Samuel Badcock]: 'In this beautiful and interesting novel, the lights and shades of character are blended with great ingenuity: and in every part of it we discover the hand of an elegant and skilful artist. With wonderful energy and address, the Authoress unfolds the secret springs and complex movements of the human heart; and so forcibly are the different feelings that agitate the soul, delineated by her magic pencil, that they strongly awaken the sympathy of the reader, and interest him in the distress of the story.'

1786: 35   [PEACOCK, Lucy].
THE RAMBLES OF FANCY; OR MORAL AND INTERESTING TALES. CONTAINING, THE LAPLANDER, THE AMBITIOUS MOTHER, LETTERS FROM—LINDAMIRA TO OLIVIA, MIRANDA TO ELVIRA, FELICIA TO CECILIA, THE AMERICAN INDIAN, THE FATAL RESOLUTION, THE CREOLE. BY THE AUTHOR OF THE ADVENTURES OF THE SIX PRINCESSES OF BABYLON. IN TWO VOLUMES.

London: Printed by T. Bensley, for the author; And Sold by J. Buckland, Paternoster-Row; T. Hookham, New Bond-Street; T. Becket, Pall Mall; J. Pridden, Fleet-Street; A. Perfetti, Nº 91, Wimpole-Street; and by the Author, No. 28, Warwick-Street, Golden-Square, 1786.
I 177p; II 177p. 12mo. 5s sewed (CR, MR).
CR 62: 393–4 (Nov 1786); MR 75: 468–9 (Dec 1786); AF II: 3277.
BL N.2057; EM 2068: 30; ESTC t073532 (NA CSmH, NNPM).

Notes. The Adventures of the Six Princesses of Babylon 1785: 40.
Extracts from *The Rambles of Fancy*, 'The Ambitious Mother' and 'The Creole', published in 3 magazines, 1786–87, RM 95, 263.

CR: 'These little Tales are really moral and interesting: the story is often conducted with skill, and the catastrophe frequently, perhaps too frequently, pathetic. If miss Peacock had not called them the *Rambles* of Fancy, we should have styled them too fanciful. The descriptions are romantic, the situations often improbable: instead of the scenes of nature, we are presented with magical groups of imaginary views. For the glaring scenery of romance, our young author loses the empire of nature, and is content to lose it' (p. 393).

MR [Andrew Becket]: 'Take care, fair lady! you are by no means safely mounted—Fancy is a runaway tit, and stands in particular need of the curb. Without a figure, we would recommend it to Miss Peacock, in her future writings, to keep a little more within the line of nature and probability. Her stories are too romantic to affect us, and her language much too pompous to please' (p. 468).

1786: 36   [POTT, Joseph Holden].
THE TOUR OF VALENTINE.

> London: Printed for J. Johnson, No. 72, St Paul's Church-Yard, 1786.
> vi, 242p. 8vo. 3s 6d (CR), 3s sewed (MR, SJC).
> CR 61: 236–7 (Mar 1786); MR 75: 315 (Oct 1786).
> BL 12613.a.36; EM 173: 5; ESTC t067647 (NA CaOHM, NjP, PU &c.).

Notes. Address 'To the Reader' iii–vi.
Adv., 'In a few Days will be published', SJC 29–31 Dec 1785; adv. as published MC 10 Jan 1786.
Further edn: London, 1791, ESTC t104760.

CR: 'The design of this work is to mix instruction with entertainment; but the chief object is to instruct the ignorant both in their religious and moral duties. . . . The author has made some apology for cloathing his precepts in the dress of fancy; but we think it was unnecessary. The little narrative interspersed shews no inconsiderable acquaintance with the heart; and, if the author had followed it still farther, and evinced the force of his precepts by other errors of conduct, his work might have been more useful.'

MR [Jabez Hirons]: 'The scenes and adventures, if not so numerous, or wrought up with so much art and passion as other novels display, are yet interesting, instructive, and friendly to virtue; giving rise to just and useful reflections and conversations on subjects of the greatest importance.'

PRÉVOST, Antoine-François, **MANON L'ESCAUT** (London, 1786) trans. Charlotte Smith, first trans. 1767 as *The History of the Chevalier des Grieux*, JR 1124, AF I: 2273.

1786: 37   PYE, [Jael-Henrietta].
THEODOSIUS AND ARABELLA, A NOVEL, IN A SERIES OF LETTERS, BY THE LATE MRS. HAMPDEN PYE. IN TWO VOLUMES.

> London: Printed for William Lane, Leadenhall-Street, 1786.
> I 240p; II 207p. 12mo. 5s sewed (MR, CR).
> CR 61: 399 (May 1786); MR 75: 394 (Nov 1786); AF II: 3665.
> BL Cup.501.aaa.32; EMf; ESTC t137673 (NA PU).

Notes. Epistolary. Note on verso of t.p. to vol. 1: 'This Novel was intended by the Author to have been call'd MARY and FRANCIS GREY, but from a Similarity of Title to another Publication, is altered to THEODOSIUS and ARABELLA.'
Adv., 'in the Press, and speedily will be published', LEP 14–16 Feb 1786; adv. as published 11 Mar 1786.

CR: 'Novelty must be very captivating, since it is purchased so dearly; for, with extensive modern margins, and a large letter, as in the volumes before us, it is sold at two shillings for each hour's entertainment.—We thought we had reached the bottom of the bathos; but Theodosius and Arabella were yet behind.'

MR [William Enfield]: 'This is so poor and trifling a performance, that it has only one circumstance to recommend it, which is, that it is very short.'

1786: 38   [RASPE, Rudolph Erich].
BARON MUNCHAUSEN'S NARRATIVE OF HIS MARVELLOUS TRAV-
ELS AND CAMPAIGNS IN RUSSIA. HUMBLY DEDICATED AND REC-
OMMENDED TO COUNTRY GENTLEMEN; AND, IF THEY PLEASE,
TO BE REPEATED AS THEIR OWN, AFTER A HUNT, AT HORSE
RACES, IN WATERING-PLACES, AND OTHER SUCH POLITE ASSEM-
BLIES; ROUND THE BOTTLE AND FIRE-SIDE.

> Oxford: Printed for the Editor and sold by the Booksellers there and at Cambridge, also
> in London by the booksellers of Piccadilly, the Royal Exchange, and M. Smith, at
> No. 46, in Fleet-street, 1786.
> iv, 49p. 12mo. 1s (t.p., SJC).
> CR 60: 479 (Dec 1785).
> BL T.471(4); ESTC t000508 (NA CtY-BA, ICN, NjP).

Notes. Based on a selective trans. of vol. 8 (1781) and vol. 9 (1783) of August Mylius (ed.) *Vade Mecum für lustige Leute* 10 vols. (Berlin, 1764–92). Raspe himself expanded the 2nd edn. to include the sea adventures of Munchhausen, and Gottfried August Bürger published anonymously in London in 1786 a trans. and expansion of the 2nd edn. as *Wunderbare Reisen zu Wasser und zu Lande, Feldzüge und lustige Abenteuer des Freiherrn von Münchhausen.*
Preface i–iv. Pagination continuous Roman-Arabic; text starts on p. 5.
Adv. SJC 21–24 Jan 1786; 'The Baron is supposed to relate those extraordinary Adventures over his Bottle, when surrounded by his friends'.
Further edns. (many with title *Gulliver Revived*): London, 1786, ESTC n007449; London, 1786, ESTC n032363; London, 1786, ESTC t152234; London, 1786, ESTC n007451; Dublin, 1788 (Printed by P. Byrne, 12mo), ESTC n030808; 12 further entries in ESTC. WC has 95 pre-1851 entries, the majority of versions in English but many in German and some in French.
With additional material, the work became longer; the 3rd edn. is 136p.
4th edn. adv. SJC 10–12 Aug 1786: 'All the Reviewers, and other monthly Publications, unite in speaking of these entertaining Adventures in Terms of the greatest Approbation; and upon the Continent it is, at this Time, more read, particularly in France, Germany, and Holland, where the Authour is well known, than any Production that has appeared for some Years.'

CR: 'This is a satirical production, calculated to throw ridicule on the bold assertions of some parliamentary declaimers. If rant may be best foiled at its own weapons, the author's design is not ill-founded; for the marvellous has never been carried to a more whimsical and ludicrous extent.'

1786: 39   [ROWSON], Susanna.
VICTORIA. A NOVEL. IN TWO VOLUMES. THE CHARACTERS TAKEN
FROM REAL LIFE, AND CALCULATED TO IMPROVE THE MORALS

OF THE FEMALE SEX, BY IMPRESSING THEM WITH A JUST SENSE OF THE MERITS OF FILIAL PIETY. BY SUSANNAH HASWELL.

> London: Printed by J. P. Cooke, for the Author, at No. 38, Tavistock-street, Covent-Garden. And sold by J. Bew, No. 28, Pater-Noster-Row, and T. Hookham, New Bond-street, 1786.
> I vii, viii, 247p; II 185p. 12mo. 5s boards (CR), 5s sewed (MR, LEP).
> CR 63: 76–7 (Jan 1787); MR 76: 83 (Jan 1787); AF II: 3887.
> InU-Li PS2736.R3V64 vault; ESTC n063203.

Notes. Dedication to the Duchess of Devonshire 1, [v]–vii, signed Susannah Haswell; list of subscribers [i]–viii.

Adv. LEP 19–21 Dec 1786; gives author's address as 38 Tavistock street, Covent-garden.

CR: 'The author wishes to inculcate filial piety; and she has executed her design in a number of well-chosen pathetic tales.—In such a cause Criticism smooths his brow, and takes off his spectacles, willing to see no fault. She who would support the cause of piety and virtue *cannot* err.'

MR: 'It is so far to be commended, that it exhibits the ill effects of filial disobedience and thoughtless libertinism, in striking colours: the language is neither good nor bad; it is too much in the common style of modern novels to deserve great commendation, though, when ranked in that numerous class of productions, the lowest place must not be assigned to this first-born of a young writer's brain.'

WIELAND, Christoph Martin
See BEUVIUS, Adam

1786: 40   [WYNNE, John Huddlestone].
THE CHILD OF CHANCE; OR, THE ADVENTURES OF HARRY HAZARD.

> London: Printed for T. Hookham, New Bond Street, 1786.
> I iv, 258p; II iv, 224p. 8vo [MR and CR have 12mo]. 6s (CR), 5s sewed (MR, MC).
> CR 63: 307 (Apr 1787); MR 76: 265 (Mar 1787); AF II: 4956.
> CtU Dodd A931-1 and A931-2; ESTC n027833.

Notes. T.p. to vol. 1 gives date as M.DCC.LXXXXVI. Table of contents iii–iv in each vol.
Adv. MC 21 Dec 1786.

CR: 'This is a pleasing little novel, with a good moral. The adventures are varied, and occasionally contrasted with skill; through the whole, we feel an interest for the hero; and, in the lowest situations, find reasons, if not for excusing, for palliating his conduct. The author, however, injudiciously destroys the suspence, which uncertainty would occasion, by a prognosticating dream.'

MR [Andrew Becket]: 'The work is not ill written, and displays a fertile imagination.'

1787: 1   ANON.
THE ADVENTURES OF JONATHAN CORNCOB, LOYAL AMERICAN REFUGEE. WRITTEN BY HIMSELF.

> London: Printed for the author; and sold by G. G. J. and G. Robinson, Paternoster-Row; and R. Faulder, New Bond-Street, 1787.
> 213p. 12mo. 2s 6d (CR), 2s 6d sewed (MR, SJC).
> CR 65: 150 (Feb 1788); MR 77: 495–6 (Dec 1787); AF II: 33.
> BL 12612.df.18; EM 164: 7; ESTC t066885 (NA CtY-BR, ICN, MH-H &c.).

Notes. Adv. SJC 3–6 Nov 1787.

CR: 'Harkee, Mr. Jonathan Corncob! leave your indecorums, and preserve your genuine humour, unpolluted by improper language, or indecent descriptions.'

MR: 'On the whole, we have been alternately pleased and disgusted with this story, whether real or feigned, of an adventurer, whose motley production contains much to divert one kind of readers, and many things which will meet the disapprobation of those who are not fond of low humour, and who cannot tolerate licentious details, and scenes of impurity; too many of which, we are sorry to add, occur in this work, disgracing the less exceptionable parts of it; and of which, as caterers for the Public, we cannot avoid taking notice.'

THE ADVENTURES OF MONSIEUR PROVENCE
See RUTLIDGE, James

AUGUSTA; OR, THE FEMALE TRAVELLERS
See ANDREWS, Dr

1787: 2   ANON.
BLENHEIM LODGE, A NOVEL. IN TWO VOLUMES.

> London: Printed for W. Lane, Leadenhall-Street, 1787.
> I 240p; II 248p. 12mo. 5s (CR), 5s sewed (MR, SJC).
> CR 64: 392–93 (Nov 1787); MR 78: 249 (Mar 1788); AF II: 379.
> O 256.e.14406, 14407; EM 1590: 3; ESTC n015184 (NA MH-H [vol. 2 pp. 71–72 mutilated], NjP).

Notes. Epistolary.

Adv., 'By a Lady', SJC 27–30 Oct 1787.

Adv. LEP 10–13 Nov 1787 as the lead item in a list of novels and with the heading 'A New Novel, Descriptive and Entertaining'.

Further edn: Dublin, 1788 (Printed by John Rea, for Messrs. Wogan, Byrne, Colbert, Halpen, and Dornin, 2 vols., 12mo), ESTC t200743.

CR: 'This is a lively, entertaining novel, though we fear, if we examine it too closely, we should discover, that a little spirit in the dialogue, like rouge on an antiquated lady's face, covered some wrinkles and defects.'

MR [Andrew Becket]: '. . . the liveliness which runs through many of the pages, evinces a capacity for better things; but then it is to be objected, that this sprightliness often degenerates into flippancy—and thus have we finally perused these volumes with disgust. The fable has nothing striking or interesting in it; the characters are not sufficiently discriminated; and as to the moral, we cannot find it.'

CAROLINE; OR THE DIVERSITIES OF FORTUNE
See HUGHES, Anne

1787: 3 ANON.
CAROLINE: OR, THE HISTORY OF MISS SEDLEY. BY A YOUNG LADY. IN TWO VOLUMES.

Dublin: Printed by W. Sleater, 1787.
I 142p; II 273p. 12mo.
PU Singer-Mend.PR3991.A6.Y676 1787b; ESTC n043727.

Notes. Pagination continuous; vol. 2 begins with p. 145. Epistolary. Vol. 2 lacks t.p.
On t.p. 'Caroline: or, the' is followed by ms. comment 'Greatest nonsense I have ever met under so modest a title' and 'By a Young Lady' is followed by 'who I hope will never write again'.

1787: 4 ANON.
THE CONTRAST: OR THE OPPOSITE CONSEQUENCES OF GOOD AND EVIL HABITS, EXHIBITED IN THE LOWEST RANKS OF RURAL LIFE, FOR THE BENEFIT OF INTELLIGENT SERVANTS, AND THE BEST PROFICIENTS IN SUNDAY SCHOOLS.

London: Printed for T. Longman; G. G. J. & J. Robinson, Paternoster-Row; J. Johnson, St. Paul's Church-Yard; and T. Cadell, Strand, 1787.
xi, vii, 291p. 12mo. 3s 6d (CR), 3s 6d boards (MR), 3s 6d sewed (SJC).
CR 65: 159 (Feb 1788); MR 78: 77 (Jan 1788); AF II: 849.
BL 04410.l.50; EMf; ESTC t105098 (NA CSmH, MH-H, NjP &c.).

Notes. Prefatory apology 'To the Candid Reader' iii–xi; table of contents i–vii. Frontispiece and illustrations. Two parts: 'The Bright Side of the Contrast. The Happy Effects of a Docile Disposition and Orderly Conduct, exhibited in the Life of Sarah Meanwell' (pp. 1–161) and 'The Dark Side of the Contrast. The Wretched Effects of a Perverse Disposition and Disorderly Conduct, exhibited in the Life of Richard Coreworm' (pp. 163–291). Each part has its own running title: 'The Life of Sarah Meanwell' and 'The Life of Richard Coreworm'.
Adv., 'illustrated with a Number of Engravings', SJC 4–6 Sept 1787.
Adv., 'For the Benefit of intelligent Servants, and the best Proficients in Sunday Schools. . . . Illustrated by 17 Copper-plates, expressive of the most interesting passages of the two Moral Tales', LC 63: 204 (26–28 Feb 1788).
Extract published LC 65: 388 (21–23 Apr 1789).
Further edn: London, 1812 (WC). German trans. Nuremberg, 1793 (*Lebensgeschichte der Rosine Meyerin oder Die glücklichen Folgen eines guten Verhaltens*) (EAG).
   MR [William Enfield]: 'Many very important moral instructions are here conveyed through the medium of a natural and interesting story, in a manner well adapted to the understandings of those for whose benefit it is designed.'

THE CURSE OF SENTIMENT
See DODD, Charles

1787: 5 ANON.
THE DISINTERESTED NABOB, A NOVEL INTERSPERSED WITH GENUINE DESCRIPTIONS OF INDIA, ITS MANNERS AND CUSTOMS.

> London: Printed by S. Hazard, for G. G. J. and J. Robinson, No. 25, Pater-Noster-Row, 1787.
> I iii, 224p; II 235p; III 225p. 12mo. 9s sewed (MR, LEP), 7s 6d sewed (CR).
> CR 63: 309 (Apr 1787); MR 76: 447–8 (May 1787); AF II: 1102.
> IU x823.B917e; ESTC n008221 (BI Gu; NA CtY, ICU, ViU).

Notes. ESTC describes this as by the same author as *Arpasia* (1786: 4), but this appears to be a confusion of titles. *Arpasia*'s t.p. claims authorship of *The Nabob* (1785: 16), not *The Disinterested Nabob*, and both 1785 and 1786 novels were published by Lane.
Dedication 'To Their High Mightinesses, The Reviewers'. Epistolary.
Adv., 'In the Press, and speedily will be published', LEP 13–16 Jan 1787; adv. quotes 4 lines from the author's prefatory address to the reviewers.
Further edns: Dublin, 1787 (Printed by J. Exshaw, 2 vols., 12mo), ESTC n006850; [London], 1788, ESTC n047423.

CR: 'The description of India appears to be new and genuine; from the little circumstances which naturally arise, the reader may acquire more exact ideas of the appearance of that country, and the manners of its inhabitants, than from many laboured descriptions. On the whole, it is a pleasing work, with a very good moral. Little inaccuracies occur; but we have had so many novellists, only female *in name*, that we are rather apt to suspect our present author, in disguise, to be really one.'

MR [Andrew Becket]: '. . . the author must pardon us if we give it as our opinion that the "Letters from India" were written by his fire-side at home. Mrs. Kindersley's publication [Jemima Kindersley's *Letters from the Island of Teneriffe, Brazil, the Cape of Good Hope, and the East Indies*, 1777], and others of the like kind, appear to have furnished him with his *genuine* description of the East. Be this, however, as it may, there is nothing in his account of the country that can boast the smallest pretension to novelty; all that is to be found concerning it in the present publication having been related by other writers, and in a much more pleasing style.'

1787: 6 ANON.
EDWARD AND SOPHIA. A NOVEL. IN TWO VOLUMES. BY A LADY.

> [London]: Printed for William Lane, Leadenhall Street, 1787.
> I 242p; II 275p. 12mo. 5s sewed (MR, SJC), 6s (CR).
> CR 64: 392 (Nov 1787); MR 77: 496 (Dec 1787); AF II: 1215.
> BL 1608/3444; EM 5160: 1; ESTC t120637 (NA MH-H).

Notes. By same author as *Eliza Cleland* (1788: 14); *Powis Castle* (1788: 30); *The Predestined Wife* (1789: 22); *Benedicta* (1791: 3); *Ashton Priory* (1792: 2); and *Mariamne* (1793: 8).
2 pp. advs. end vol. 1. Sigs. F10 and K2 of vol. 2 are mutilated.
Adv., 'A First-Rate Novel, enriched with Genuine Characters', SJC 9–11 Oct 1787.
Adv. end vol. 2 of *The School of Virtue* (1787: 23).
French trans. Londres [ESTC: i.e. Paris?], 1788 (*Edouard et Sophie*), ESTC t151634.

CR: 'Without much novelty of incident or character, there is a sprightliness in this narrative which engages the attention, and a pathos occasionally in the situations which interests the heart. The novel is undoubtedly superior to the general herd; but we ought also to remark, that there is a levity, when the author speaks on sacred subjects, which we greatly disapprove.... These volumes are said to be written by a lady, and indeed there are many ladylike errors to be found in it. ...'

MR [Andrew Becket]: 'The old story.... The moral, however, is excellent; and it must be acknowleged that this novel is, on the whole, superior, in point of writing, to may which we are fated to read. ...'

ELA: OR, THE DELUSIONS OF THE HEART
See BURKE, Anne

EXCESSIVE SENSIBILITY; OR, THE HISTORY OF LADY SAINT LAURENCE
See THOMSON, Anna

THE FAIR SYRIAN, A NOVEL
See BAGE, Robert

1787: 7   ANON.
FAVOURITE TALES, TRANSLATED FROM THE FRENCH.

London: Printed for G. G. J. and J. Robinson, Paternoster-Row, 1787.
iii, 171p. 8vo [CR, MR and LEP have 12mo]. 2s 6d (CR), 3s sewed (MR, LEP).
CR 65: 157 (Feb 1788); MR 78: 531 (June 1788); AF II: 1390.
C Oates.504; EMf; ESTC t184987 (BI O; NA ICU).

Notes. Adv. LEP 24–27 Nov 1787.

CR: 'We wish they had remained in their original state, for indecorum and infidelity can never be pleasing.'

MR [Andrew Becket]: 'Productions like the present are extremely numerous on the continent, but we wish not to see them encouraged here. The *verbiage*, the frothiness of a Parisian *petit-maitre*, is no way suitable to honest John Bull.'

1787: 8   ANON.
THE GENEROUS ATTACHMENT; A NOVEL, IN A SERIES OF LETTERS.

London: Printed for the Proprietor, and sold by J. Bew, Paternoster-Row, 1787.
I viii, 215p; II 214p; III ?; IV ?. 12mo. 10s sewed (MR, LC), 12s (CR).
CR 63: 310 (Apr 1787); MR 76: 450 (May 1787); AF II: 1587.
CaOHM new acquisition (imperf.; vols. 1–2 only).

Notes. p. [i] Dedication to Major Halliday by 'The Author' n.d. Adv. LC 61: 213 (1–3 Mar 1787). Preface I: vi notes 'Having in the third volume been already elaborate on the subject of *Novel writing....*' Preface suggests a male author. Epistolary.

CR: 'In the story of these volumes there is little probability, and less interest: in many parts the author betrays great ignorance, not only in the common affairs of life, but of the more elegant arts; and the whole, as may be expected, is heavy, dull, and insipid.'

MR [Andrew Becket]: 'There is nothing in the fable or conduct of this Novel to entitle it to much consideration or regard: neither does the work merit our commendation with respect to language.'

1787: 9   ANON.
*GENUINE AND ENTERTAINING MEMOIRS OF A WELL-KNOWN WOMAN OF INTRIGUE. WRITTEN BY HERSELF.

> London: Printed for J. Ridgeway, 1787.
> 2 vols. 12mo. 5s sewed (MR).
> MR 77: 327 (Oct 1787).
> No copy located.

Notes. Further edn: London, 1787, ESTC t186932.

MR: 'The sign sufficiently intimates the entertainment within.' MR reviews as a novel.

GEORGINA: OR MEMOIRS OF THE BELLMORE FAMILY
See BOUVERIE, Georgina

1787: 10   ANON.
THE HAPPY ART OF TEAZING: A NOVEL.

> London: Printed for R. Jameson, no. 227, Strand, 1787.
> 212p. 8vo [CR has 12mo]. 3s 6d boards (half-title, MR), 3s 6d (CR).
> CR 64: 309 (Oct 1787); MR 78: 82 (Jan 1788); AF II: 1804.
> CLU-S/C PR3991.A1H214; ESTC n008771.

Notes. Epistolary.

Post-dated; adv. as published MC 21 Dec 1786.

CR: '. . . unintelligible nonsense, too dull to excite resentment at the licentiousness of the author, and too absurd, as well as too insipid, to be injurious.'

MR [Andrew Becket]: 'The Author of the work before us is an adept in the art of teazing and fatiguing his reader. He, therefore, who is obliged to follow him thro' the whole of the ridiculous story here related, may surely reckon it among his *labours*, and even consider it as none of the least.'

1787: 11   ANON.
*THE HAPPY RELEASE; OR THE HISTORY OF CHARLES WHARTON AND SOPHIA HARLEY. A NOVEL. IN A SERIES OF LETTERS.

> London: Printed for F. Noble, Holborn (LEP), 1787 (CR).
> 3 vols. 12mo. 9s 6d (CR), 3s 6d sewed (MR), 7s 6d (LEP), 7s 6d sewed (LC).
> CR 62: 391 (Nov 1786); MR 76: 82–3 (Jan 1787); AF II: 1806.
> No copy located.

Notes. Epistolary.

Adv. LEP 26–28 Aug 1786, PA 13 Sept 1786 and LC 60: 381 (17–19 Oct 1786). CR gives publication date of 1787.

CR: 'By an ingenious contrivance, this novel will continue to be a new one till the end of next year; for it is dated in 1787, a method not peculiar to the editor, but so unreasonably extended, as to require being noticed with a slight reprimand. . . . this novel requires little to be said: there are several very good persons, and there are some villains, or these good people would not find employment. They labour in the usual style, through three volumes, and then the villains die or are reformed, and the good ones marry: a consummation that *we* devoutly wished for more early.'

MR: 'Contains some *excellent* instructions for seducing females from the bosoms of their parents, or for carrying them off by force, and deserting them at a proper time. Such kind of productions must no doubt be highly pleasing to the would-be Jupiters of the day . . . and to their perusal the performance now before us will probably be chiefly confined.'

HENRIETTA OF GERSTENFELD; A GERMAN STORY
See BEUVIUS, Adam (1786: 17)

1787: 12   ANON.
THE HISTORY OF CAPTAIN AND MISS RIVERS. IN THREE VOLUMES.

> London: Printed for T. Hookham, New Bond Street, 1787.
> I viii, 230p; II 255p; III 244p. 12mo. 7s 6d sewed (CR, MR), 9s sewed (SJC).
> CR 63: 309 (Apr 1787); MR 76: 529 (June 1787); AF II: 1955.
> PU Singer-Mend. 823.H635; EM 1291: 2; ESTC n007574 (NA MH-H).

Notes. Dedication to Miss Ashby, 20 Dec 1786, iii–viii. 2 pp. advs. end vol. 1.
Adv. PA 19 Jan 1787 and SJC 30 Jan–1 Feb 1787; 'By a Lady'.
Further edn: Dublin, 1787 (Printed by John Rea, for Messrs. Colles, Burton, H. Whitestone, Byrne, W. Porter, Lewis, Moore, and Halpen, 2 vols., 12mo), EM 135: 3, ESTC t108924.

CR: 'This novel is sufficiently entertaining, without any striking merit. Its chief fault is the misrepresenting, in some slight instances, the customs of the countries to which the different persons are conveyed; and the fault is of greater consequence, since, if the costume were perfectly preserved, the fair readers of the circulating libraries might have some chance of instruction.'

MR [Andrew Becket]: 'This Author seems so highly delighted with his performance, that we imagine he will scarcely believe us when we tell him that it is greatly wanting in *essentials*, i.e. in character, style and sentiment. . . .'

1787: 13   ANON.
THE HISTORY OF CHARLES FALKLAND, ESQ. AND MISS LOUISA SAVILLE. A NOVEL. IN A SERIES OF LETTERS. IN WHICH IS INTRODUCED, THE HISTORY OF JULIA HARWOOD.

> [London]: Printed for Francis Noble, at his Circulating Library, Holborn, 1787.
> I viii, 239p; II 207p. 12mo. 5s (CR), 5s sewed (MR, LEP).
> CR 62: 392 (Nov 1786); MR 76: 529 (June 1787); AF II: 1956.
> BL 12604.bb.16; EM 91: 5; ESTC t072038 (NA CtY-BR, NjP).

Notes. Epistolary. Introduction iii–viii. Pagination continuous Roman-Arabic; text of novel starts on p. 9. In vol. 2 text of novel starts on p. 5. 1 p. advs. cut out and glued to verso of p. 207 of vol. 2.
Post-dated; adv. as published LEP 17–19 Oct 1786 and PA 17 Oct 1786.

CR: 'These volumes contain love, in excess, a due proportion of murder, unfaithful friends, and heroic constancy; yet with all these ingredients, we have seldom read any thing less interesting or affecting. The ahs! and ohs! leave sufficient openings for every particle of distress to escape.'

MR [Andrew Becket]: 'It was formerly the practice to finish every novel with a wedding. It is now become the fashion to conclude them, generally, with a funeral.—The heroes and heroines must all be buried. In the performance now before us (which by the way is nothing more than the old and hacknied story of a violated female and an injured friend) the dead are quite as numerous as in the mock-heroics of Chrononhotonthologos, and Tom Thumb.'

1787: 14   ANON.
*THE HISTORY OF HENRIETTA MORTIMER; OR, THE FORCE OF FILIAL ENTHUSIASM.

> London: Printed for T. Hookham, New Bond-street (PA), 1787 (PA).
> 2 vols. 12mo. 6s (CR), 5s sewed (MR, PA).
> CR 63: 308 (Apr 1787); MR 77: 80 (July 1787); AF II: 1960.
> No copy located.

Notes. Adv. PA 16 Feb 1787.

Adv. SJC 28–31 July 1787 with quotation from CR.

Adv. end of *The Minstrel* (1793: 10) as *The History of Henrietta Mortimer, or the Force of Filial Affection, a Novel. By a Lady.*

CR: 'There is a complication in the arrangement of the several incidents in this novel, which fixes the attention and the manners of the different personages interest the reader. The story is conducted with art, and unfolded with skill; the incidents are numerous and well connected; and the work, on the whole, will afford amusement for an idle hour: it is much superior to many novels of the present annual crop.'

MR [Andrew Becket]: 'Were the merits of a novel to lie in its *intrigo*, as Mr. Bayes expresses it, in the heaping of incident on incident, and that in defiance of established rules, the history of Henrietta Mortimer would be a capital performance indeed!'

1787: 15   ANON.
THE HISTORY OF LADY EMMA MELCOMBE, AND HER FAMILY. BY A FEMALE. IN THREE VOLUMES.

> London: Printed for G. G. and J. Robinson, Pater-Noster-Row, 1787.
> I xv, 170p; II 190p; III 179p. 12mo. 7s 6d (CR), 7s 6d sewed (MR, LEP).
> CR 63: 77 (Jan 1787); MR 76: 448 (May 1787); AF II: 1964.
> MH-H *EC75.A100.787h; EM 1268: 3; ESTC n007827 (ICU, NjP).

Notes. ESTC: Sometimes attributed to Mrs Winifred Marshall Gales.

Vol. 1 dedication to Miss Eleanor Gordon v–ix; preface xi–xv; text begins on p. 3. Vol. 2 text begins on p. 5; vol. 3 text begins on p. 3.

Adv., 'will speedily be published', LEP 7–9 Dec 1786; adv. as published LEP 21–23 Dec 1786.

Further edn: Dublin, 1787 (Printed for Messrs. Gilbert, Whitestone, Byrne, Lewis and Moore, 3 vols., 12mo), ESTC n007829.

CR: 'In truth this pleasing narrative is frequently interesting, and inculcates some useful moral lessons. It engages the attention, though it does not captivate the fancy by any intricate arrangement of adventures, or any uncommon description of characters or events.'

MR [Andrew Becket]: 'We will tell [the author] that her novel, in point of style and grammar, abounds with faults; and this we are the rather induced to do, as she appears to be of a good and ingenuous disposition, and one who is likely to profit by our hint.—When acquainted with the rules of composition, and when her judgment shall have ripened, she may possibly produce a better work than the history of Lady Emma Melcombe.'

THE HISTORY OF MISS GREVILLE
See KEIR, Elizabeth

1787: 16   ANON.
*LORD WINWORTH; OR, THE MEMOIRS OF AN HEIR; A NOVEL DEDICATED, BY PERMISSION, TO HER GRACE THE DUCHESS OF DEVONSHIRE.

> London: Printed for and sold by G. Allen, Long Acre; C. Stalker, Stationers-court; and by every Bookseller in Great-Britain and Ireland (LC), 1787 (LC).
> 3 vols. 12mo. 7s 6d (CR), 7s 6d sewed (MR), 7s 6s sewed or 9s neatly bound (LC, SJC).
> CR 63: 225–26 (Mar 1787); MR 76: 266 (Mar 1787); AF II: 2602.
> No copy located.

Notes. By same author as *Maria Harcourt* (1788: 22); *Phoebe* (1788: 28); *William and Charles* (1789: 29); *Lucinda Hartley* (1790: 17); and *Frederick and Alicia* (1791: 12).
Dedication to the Duchess of Devonshire (LC, SJC). Epistolary.
Adv., 'On Thursday January 4, will be Published', WFA 3 Jan 1787.
Adv., 'On Thursday last was published', LC 61: 87 (23–25 Jan 1787): 'On account of the very great demand for this original Novel, which has so far exceeded the Publisher's expectations, G. Allen humbly solicits his friends, who wish to be possessed of so valuable a Work, to be as early as they can in their application'.
Adv. SJC 27 Feb–1 Mar 1787; 'N.B. So exceedingly rapid has been the Sale of this very affecting Novel, that an Impression of 1,500 has been nearly sold in little more than one Month, a Circumstance scarcely to be equalled in the Memory of Man.'
BL has 1-sheet adv. for this novel: 937.f.2/8 (ESTC t032784).
Further edn: London, 1787, ESTC 033874.

CR: 'This is said to be the author's first production, and, so far as he knows, on an entire new plan. There is indeed some novelty in the conduct of the story, and in the delineation of the characters. . . . The plot is also unfolded with great dexterity; and the denouement is an interesting part of the work.'
MR [Andrew Becket]: 'Dedicated to her grace of Devonshire—and with that noble lady's permission too! Is it possible?—Those who read these memoirs, and also are acquainted with the good sense, and cultivated taste, of the duchess of Devonshire, will be staggered by this assertion. . . .'

LOUISA; OR THE COTTAGE ON THE MOOR
See HELME, Elizabeth

1787: 17   ANON.
*LUCINDA OSBORN. A NOVEL. BY A YOUNG LADY.

London: Printed for, and sold by C. Geary, at his Circulating Library, No. 27, Great
Marlborough-street, near Oxford-street (WFA), 1787 (WFA).
2 vols. 12mo. 5s sewed (CR, MR), 7s sewed (WFA).
CR 63: 226 (Mar 1787); MR 77: 246 (Sept 1787); AF II: 2631.
No copy located.

Notes. By same author as *The Modern Husband* (1789: 19).
Adv., *Lucinda Osborn, a pleasing and entertaining Novel, in Letters, By a Lady*, WFA 8 Jan
1787.
Further edn: Dublin, 1787 (Printed for Messrs. Whitestone, Byrne, Lewis, Jones, and
Halpen, 2 vols., 12mo), ESTC n034006. French trans. London and Paris, 1788 (*Miss Lucinde
Osburn*) (BGR).

CR: '. . . we cannot highly praise this novel. The story and the characters are common, the
language never rises to elegance, and the events are anticipated.'

MR [Andrew Becket]: 'Lucinda Osburn is not a first-rate beauty: neither can her air and
manner properly be considered as her own.'

1787: 18   ANON.
LUMLEY-HOUSE: A NOVEL. THE FIRST ATTEMPT OF A YOUNG
LADY. IN THREE VOLUMES.

London: Printed for W. Lane, Leadenhall-Street, n.d. [1787].
I vii, 208p; II 199p; III 236p. 12mo. 7s 6d sewed (CR, LEP), 7s 6d (MR).
CR 63: 391 (May 1787); MR 77: 162–3 (Aug 1787); AF II: 2638.
BL 12653.a.21; EM 193: 4; ESTC t125054 (NA CSmH).

Notes. 'Author's Address to the Public' v–vii. 1 p. advs. end vol. 2.
Adv., 'New and Entertaining Novel', LEP 27 Feb–1 Mar 1787. Re-adv., with heading 'An
Approved Novel, with the Reviewers Opinion' and quotations from EngR and CR, LEP
12–14 July 1787.
Adv. end vol. 2 of *The School of Virtue* (1787: 23).

CR: 'The young lady attempts to walk in the footsteps of miss Burney: it would be injudicious praise, as well as injurious to her "fair fame," to say that she has equalled Cecilia [1782:
15] or Evelina [1778: 10]. As a first attempt, this work deserves praise: it is the luxuriant
herbage which promises an ample harvest in due season. The story is well conducted; the
characters properly supported; and the denouement is rendered interesting.'

MR [Andrew Becket]: 'Almost every female of sensibility (and we observe it with much
regret, is apt to imagine herself a Burney, and to believe that she cannot be better employed
than in *favouring the public with a pretty novel.* . . . We discover in it, indeed, the traces of an
elegant mind; but the work has no discriminating feature. Not a single incident is to be found
in it which we have not met with an hundred times before: not a sentiment that is new or
striking.'

OLIVIA; OR, DESERTED BRIDE
See BONHOTE, Elizabeth

ORLANDO AND SERAPHINA: A TURKISH STORY
See NICHOLSON, Mr

1787: 19   ANON.
THE PERPLEXITIES OF LOVE.

> London: Printed for W. Lane, Leadenhall-Street, 1787.
> vii, 180p. 12mo. 2s 6d sewed (CR, MR).
> MR 77: 246 (Sept 1787); AF II: 3309.
> MH-H *EC75.A100.787p5; EM 1285: 4; ESTC n012156 (NA ICN, MH-H, NjP &c.).

Notes. Preface iii–vii. 4 pp. advs. end vol.
Adv. LEP 9–12 June 1787.
Adv. SJC 30 Oct–1 Nov 1787; 'In which is delineated the tender Passion from historick Traits.'
> MR [Andrew Becket]: 'This novel is not ill-written; but its tendency is pernicious.'

THE PLATONIC GUARDIAN
See JOHNSON, Mrs

1787: 20   ANON.
*THE RATTLE. A NOVEL. IN A SERIES OF LETTERS.

> London: Printed for F. Noble, No. 324, Holbourn (SJC), 1787.
> 2 vols. 12mo. 5s (CR), 5s sewed (MR), 5s sewed or 7s calf, lettered (SJC).
> CR 64: 392 (Nov 1787); MR 78: 165–6 (Feb 1788); AF II: 3697.
> No copy located.

Notes. Adv. SJC 27–29 Sept 1787; as *The Rattle; or, Modern Life. A Novel.*
> CR: 'In the little narrative which we have discovered in these dreary leaves, there is some attempt at a spirited delineation of high-life, and an endeavour to contrast it: but the spirit is a momentary glare; the contrast faint and insipid. We consider this work, however, as of some importance, since it shows with how little substance two volumes of modern novels may be formed.'

> MR [Andrew Becket]: '"The Rattle." To signify, we presume, that the book is intended for the amusement of children. This Writer is at least *ingenuous*; he tells the purchaser of his volumes what he is to expect. There is, however, some good morality in the work.'

THE RECLUSE. A FRAGMENT
See HEATH, Henry Feron, Junior

1787: 21   ANON.
REUBEN, OR, THE SUICIDE. IN TWO VOLUMES.

> London: Printed for W. T. Swift, Charles-street, St James's-Square; and J. Bew, Paternoster-Row, 1787.
> I xvi, 150, 2p; II 182, 2p. 8vo [MR and CR have 12mo]. 5s sewed (MR), 6s (CR).
> CR 63: 308–9 (Apr 1787); MR 76: 448 (May 1787); AF II: 3746.
> BL 12612.aa.27; EM 124: 3; ESTC t066389.

Notes. Epistolary. Dedication to H.R.H. Anne, Duchess of Cumberland iii–iv, signed 'The Editor'; preface v–xvi. 2 pp. advs. end both vols. 1 and 2.
> CR: 'The editor's laboured Preface, and his confident assertions of the authenticity of the Letters, have led us to examine them minutely. The examination has not ended advantageously for the editor.'

1787: 22   ANON.

THE RICH YOUNG COUNTRY 'SQUIRE; IN A SERIES OF LETTERS, A NOVEL: CHIEFLY IN THE LUSCIOUS TASTE.

[London]: Printed in the year 1787.

149p. 8vo. 2s 6d (t.p.).

BL 012640.m.37; EM 498: 5; ESTC t093369.

Notes. Frontispiece. Epistolary.

ROSA DE MONTMORIEN. A NOVEL

See HOWELL, Ann

1787: 23   ANON.

THE SCHOOL OF VIRTUE. A NOVEL, ON A NEW PLAN, INSCRIBED TO HER MAJESTY, BY A GENTLEMAN OF THE TEMPLE. IN TWO VOLUMES.

London: Printed for William Lane, Leadenhall-Street, 1787.

I xii, 171p; II 155p. 12mo. 5s sewed (MR, LEP), 6s (CR).

CR 64: 480 (Dec 1787); MR 78: 249–50 (Mar 1788); AF II: 3974.

O Antiq.f.E.1787.1-2; ESTC n021653 (BI BL; NA CSt, NjP).

Notes. Dedication to the Queen signed 'The Author' and dated from Temple, 1787. Preface vii–xii. 5 pp. advs. end vol. 1 and 1 p. adv. end vol. 2.

Adv., 'A Novel of Sensibility', LEP 3–6 Nov 1787.

Further edns: London, 1787, ESTC t226689; Philadelphia, 1790, ESTC w022085.

CR: 'This gentleman dislikes, with some reason, the novels which commonly appear: but his new plan is not deserving of our praise. Adventures, without probability;—characters, without discrimination;—language ungrammatical;—style full of affectation, and frequently obscure, are what he would substitute in their place:—Indeed, good sir, we would "rather bear the ills we have." '

MR: 'We have here a very singular production. A novel written, as we take it, by a Methodist, or at least by some one of a fanatical cast:—a farrago, in short, of religion, ravishment, philosophy, and love.—The whole set forth in a style which will no doubt be approved of by the good people of Moorfields and Tottenham Court Road.'

1787: 24   ANON.

SEDUCTION, OR THE HISTORY OF LADY REVEL. A NOVEL. IN TWO VOLUMES.

London: Printed for T. Axtell, Cornhill, 1787.

I 160p; II 192p. 12mo. 5s sewed (MR, LEP), 6s (CR).

CR 64: 152 (Aug 1787); MR 77: 326–7 (Oct 1787); AF II: 3998.

O 249.s.56, 57; xESTC.

Notes. Epistolary.

Adv. LEP 31 May–2 June 1787; adv. spells protagonist's name as 'Revell' and adds: 'By the Widow of an Officer in the Army'.

French trans. Lausanne, 1795 (*La séduction ou histoire de lady Revel*) (BGR).

CR: 'An insipid work! There is scarcely any attempt to seduce; and the History of Lady

Revel is little more than an Appendix, subjoined to the work. The author seems to have framed a title before he wrote the book; and therefore was obliged to introduce something which had any relation, though a remote one, to his first design.'

MR [Andrew Becket]: 'The "History of Lady Revel" is one of those productions of which it would be highly ridiculous in us to enter into a particular account. We shall therefore content ourselves with observing, that scarcely a page of it is tolerably written. . . .'

THE SORROWS OF THE HEART
See HERIOT, John

SPANISH MEMOIRS
See BERKELEY, George Monck

THE VICTIM OF FANCY
See TOMLINS, Elizabeth Sophia

THE VILLAGE OF MARTINDALE
See NICHOLSON, Mr

1787: 25   ANON.
*THE WEST INDIAN; OR, THE MEMOIRS OF FREDERIC CHARLTON.
London: Axtell, 1787.
2 vols. 12mo. 5s sewed (MR, CR).
CR 65: 150 (Feb 1788); MR 78: 250 (Mar 1788); AF II: 4749.
No copy located.

Notes. CR: 'There is too great similarity in this story to the Adventures of Roderick Random, and his Narcissa; yet there is some dexterity in the manner of dishing up the repast before us; and the first morsel is not wholly unpalatable.'

1787: 26   ANON.
WILLIAM OF NORMANDY. AN HISTORICAL NOVEL. IN TWO VOLUMES.
London: Printed for T. Axtell, Leadenhall-Street, 1787.
I 191p; II 152p. 8vo [CR has 12mo]. 5s sewed (MR, LEP), 6s (CR).
CR 63: 307 (Apr 1787); MR 76: 531 (June 1787); AF II: 4815.
BL Cup.403.pp.26; ESTC t102031 (BI BMu; NA CtY-BR, MH-H).

Notes. In vol. 2 p. 151 misnumbered 152; last p. also numbered 152.
Adv. LEP 16–18 Jan 1787; adv. is headed 'Historical Romance'.

CR: 'This is a very imperfect attempt: historical novels are a pleasing species of composition, when well executed; but William of Normandy wants the support of history, of probability, of interest, and even of typographical accuracy. These are the spurious insects, produced by the sunshine which has illumined the "Recess."' [Sophia Lee's The Recess 1783: 15 and 1785: 37].

MR [Andrew Becket]: 'A monstrous and mis-shapen birth; and such as criticism turns from in terror and disgust.'

1787: 27   [ANDREWS, Dr].
AUGUSTA; OR, THE FEMALE TRAVELLERS. A NOVEL. IN THREE VOLUMES.

> London: Printed for William Lane, Leadenhall-Street, 1787.
> I 231p; II 214p; III 210p. 12mo. 7s 6d (CR), 7s 6d sewed (MR, LC).
> CR 65: 237 (Mar 1788); MR 78: 530–1 (June 1788); AF II: 97.
> BL 1607/428; EM 5793: 7; ESTC t118783.

Notes. 2 pp. advs. end vol. 3.
Adv. LC 63: 285 (20–22 Mar 1788) and SDA 6 June 1788.
Further edn: Dublin, 1788 (Printed for Messrs. Wogan, Lewis, Moore, Dornin and Halpen, 1 vol., 12mo), ESTC n004385. German trans. Leipzig, 1828 (*Auguste, oder die Gefahren der grossen Welt*) (RS).

> MR [Andrew Becket]: '. . . however faulty this performance may be in point of composition, it will, no doubt, be approved by many readers, on account of the variety of incidents of which it is composed, and which are managed with some degree of skill. It is much more easy to twist and entangle a story, than to instruct or improve us by just and noble sentiments, or to present us with faithful images of men and things.'

1787: 28   [BAGE, Robert].
THE FAIR SYRIAN, A NOVEL. BY THE AUTHOR OF MOUNT HENNETH AND BARHAM DOWNS. IN TWO VOLUMES.

> London: Printed for J. Walter, Charing-Cross; J. Bew, Pater-noster-Row; and P. Sandford, Shrewsbury, 1787.
> I 342p; II 370p. 12mo. 7s (CR), 6s sewed (MR, LEP).
> CR 63: 109–112 (Feb 1787); MR 76: 325–29 (Apr 1787); AF II: 190.
> CSmH 408887; ESTC n009659 (NA NNU, NjP, PU &c.).

Notes. Epistolary.
Mount Henneth 1782: 12; *Barham Downs* 1784: 11.
Adv. LEP 19–21 Dec 1786.
Further edns: Dublin, 1787 (Printed for Mess. Gilbert, Byrne, H. Whitestone, Heery, Lewis, Moore, Jones, and Halpen, 2 vols., 12mo), EM 3919: 1, ESTC t126825. French trans. London and Paris, 1788 (*La belle Syrienne*) (BN). Facs: N.

> CR: 'There are many improbabilities in the story: there are some insipid pages, and a few events are neither explained, or connected with the general plan. The epistolary and narrative style are little varied; for almost every correspondent is shrewd, witty or sarcastic, in the author's own manner. . . . In the Fair Syrian there is great merit: many parts of it are conducted very happily; and these volumes abound with just reflections, acute sarcasms, and lively wit.'

> MR [Andrew Becket]: '. . . it is no little satisfaction to us . . . to meet with a writer like the present, who to ease and correctness of expression unites that very essential requisite of a novelist,—a talent for nice and accurate delineation of character: who contrasts his several personages with considerable skill and ability: who gives to them their appropriate language, spirit and manners; and who finally presents us with a fable or story, tolerably harmonious in all its parts' (pp. 325–326).

1787: 29   [BERKELEY, George Monck].

SPANISH MEMOIRS; IN A SERIES OF ORIGINAL LETTERS. CON-
TAINING THE HISTORY OF DONNA ISABELLA DELLA VILLAREA,
NIECE TO DON JOHN, TWENTIETH AND LAST DUKE OF ARAND-
INA. PUBLISHED BY THE AUTHOR OF MARIA, OR THE GENEROUS
RUSTIC. IN TWO VOLUMES.

> London: Printed for C. Elliot, T. Kay, and Co. Nº 332, opposite Somerset-House,
> Strand, London; And C. Elliot, Edinburgh, 1787.
> I 205p; II 188p. 12mo. 5s (CR), 5s sewed (MR, SJC), 5s boards (LC).
> CR 64: 152 (Aug 1787); MR 77: 162 (Aug 1787); AF II: 311.
> C 7720.d.804–805; EM 2385: 4; ESTC t115132 (BI BL).

Notes. Epistolary, with some added material. Dedication to 'The Lady L***m of the Kingdom
of Ireland' [5], signed 'The Editor'; prefatory advertisement 7–12. Text of novel starts on p. 5
in vol. 2. 1 p. adv. end vol. 2. In BL copy 1 p. advs. beginning vol. 2 before half-title.
Maria; or the Generous Rustic 1784: 12.
Adv. LC 61: 550 (7–9 June 1787); adv. SJC 19–21 June 1787.

CR: 'This is a pleasing history, but the story is conducted with so little probability that it
often disgusts:—we are told, however, that it is true. The narrative is in the form of letters,
and so much expanded, that one half of these little volumes might have contained it, almost
in the author's words.'

MR [Andrew Becket]: 'Some good and virtuous sentiments are scattered through the
pages of this performance. But why an ordinary love-story should be dignified with the title
of "Spanish *Memoirs*," we have not been able to discover.'

1787: 30   [BONHOTE, Elizabeth].

OLIVIA; OR, DESERTED BRIDE. BY THE AUTHOR OF HORTENSIA,
THE RAMBLES OF FRANKLY, AND THE FASHIONABLE FRIEND.

> London: Printed for W. Lane, in Leadenhall-Street, 1787.
> I xi, 303p; II 199p; III 190p. 12mo. 7s 6d (CR), 7s 6d sewed (MR, LEP, adv.).
> CR 62: 468–9 (Dec 1788); MR 76: 529 (June 1787); AF II: 403.
> C S727.d.78.29-31; EM 52: 6; ESTC t107650 (BI BL, O; NA CtY, MH-H, ViU).

Notes. Preface v–xi. 2 pp. advs. end vol. 3.
Hortensia, 1769, JR 1277; *The Rambles of Mr Frankly* 1772: 30 and 1776: 9; *The Fashionable
Friend* 1773: 25.
Adv., 'In the Press, and speedily will be published', LEP 21–24 Oct 1786.
Adv., with quotations from EngR and CR, SDA 3 May 1788: 'An Approved Novel'.
Adv. end vol. 3 of *Darnley Vale* (1789: 33).
French trans. Paris, 1788 (*Olivia*) (DBI).

CR: 'The modest merit displayed in the Introduction, and the general tenor of these volumes, which are calculated to show that a consciousness of having acted right will support
the mind under the greatest misfortunes, deserve our commendations. The story and the
incidents are not uncommon, and demand little praise or censure.'

MR [Andrew Becket]: 'The incidents in this novel bear, in particular, so strong a resemblance to those of Elfrida [1786: 23], that we think it scarcely possible such resemblance
should be accidental.'

1787: 31   [BOUVERIE, Georgina].
GEORGINA: OR MEMOIRS OF THE BELLMOUR FAMILY. BY A YOUNG LADY. IN FOUR VOLUMES.

> London: Printed for the Author; and sold by R. Baldwin, Paternoster-Row; J. Robson; New Bond-Street; P. Elmsly, Strand; and J. Walter, Charing-Cross, 1787.
> I viii, 214p; II 247p; III 261p; IV 248p. 12mo. 12s (CR), 10s sewed (MR, PA, LEP).
> CR 63: 389 (May 1787); MR 77: 163 (Aug 1787); AF II: 429.
> BL N.1831,32; EM 2010: 2; ESTC t072360 (NA CtY-Walpole, CLU-S/C, NjP &c.; EA GOT).

Notes. Dedication to Lavinia, Countess Spencer 1, i–ii; Introduction addressed to Mrs Montague iii–viii. Epistolary.
Adv. PA 15 Mar 1787 and LEP 20–22 Mar 1787.
French trans. [claiming to be by Frances Burney] Geneva and Paris, 1788 (*Georgina, histoire véritable*) (BGR); German trans. [claiming to be by Frances Burney] Tübingen, 1790–92 (*Georgina Eine wahre Geschichte*) (EAG).

CR: 'It is as dull as a homily, and as uninteresting as sir Richard Baker's Chronicle. We hope the young lady had learned the art of making pies and puddings, with a long etcetera of female accomplishments, before she was initiated into this idle trade.'

MR [Andrew Becket]: 'This novel exhibits a good deal of fancy, and it is written, for the most part, in a correct and pleasing manner; but the fair Author introduces too many characters on the scene, and all of nearly the same importance: so that her work, in fact, becomes so many separate histories.'

1787: 32   [BURKE, Anne].
ELA: OR, THE DELUSIONS OF THE HEART. A TALE, FOUNDED ON FACTS.

> London: Printed for G. G. J. and J. Robinson, Paternoster Row, 1787.
> 261p. 12mo. 2s 6d (CR), 3s sewed (MR, LEP).
> CR 65: 75 (Jan 1788); MR 78: 166 (Feb 1788); AF II: 540.
> MnU WILS RAR 824B907 OE; ESTC n001249 (NA IU).

Notes. Attributed to Mrs Burke by Bristol B6908; and to Ann Burke by Rink 254.
Robinson paid 5 gns. to Anne Ustick (or Urtick?) for *Ella* [*sic*] *or the Delusions of the Heart*; the receipt is annotated 'N.B. I am to have five guineas more, when the profits from the sale of the above amount to that sum' (RA).
Epistolary.
Adv. LEP 27–29 Nov 1787.
Further edns: Dublin, 1788 (Printed by William Porter, for Mess. Chamberlaine, W. Watson, White, Byrne, Wogan, Jones, and Halpin, 1 vol., 12mo), EM 1289: 13, ESTC n009096; Philadelphia, [1789], ESTC w009401; Wilmington, Delaware, [1789], ESTC w001500; London, 1790, ESTC n001250; Boston, [1790], ESTC w035217; 1 further entry in ESTC. French trans. Paris, 1788 (*Ela ou les illusions du coeur*) (BGR).

CR: 'This little Tale is truly simple and pathetic; and while its distress for a time pains, its moral mends the heart. The conduct of the story renders it interesting, and differs from the frequent narratives which, in this season of the year, the press sends forth in abundance; and it is the conduct and the reflections on the different incidents, rather than the novelty of the story, that distinguish the Delusions of Ela.'

MR [Andrew Becket]: 'This Novel represents, in very lively colours, the fatal effects which may arise to the female who indulges the tender passion uncontrolled; who listens not to the voice of reason, nor to the admonitions of her relations and friends. It is indeed a moral, and *truly pathetic* tale. We therefore pass over the few objections which might be urged against it in point of *style*.'

1787: 33　CARTWRIGHT, Mrs [H.].

RETALIATION; OR, THE HISTORY OF SIR EDWARD OSWALD, AND LADY FRANCES SEYMOUR. A NOVEL. IN A SERIES OF LETTERS. IN FOUR VOLUMES. BY MRS. CARTWRIGHT, AUTHOR OF THE VALE OF GLENDOR.

> London: Printed for F. Noble, at his Circulating Library, near Middle Row, Holborn, 1787.
>
> I 240p; II 236p; III 236p; IV 235p. 12mo. 10s sewed (MR), 12s (CR), 10s sewed or 14s in calf, lettered (LEP).
>
> CR 63: 390–91 (May 1787); MR 77: 326 (Oct 1787); AF II: 627.
>
> PU Singer-Mend. PR 4452.C55.R4.1787; ESTC n013254 (NA CaOLU [vols. 1 and 3 only]).

Notes. Epistolary. 5 pp. advs. end vol. 4.

The Vale of Glendor 1785: 27.

Adv. LEP 22–24 Mar 1787.

CR: '. . . this novel's chief claim to applause arises from the incident in the fourth volume, which is conducted with great address. The rest is trite, insipid, and common.'

MR [Andrew Becket]: 'This Novel is full of improbabilities. It is perhaps as absurd and inartificial in its conduct as any in the round of romance.'

1787: 34　[DODD, Charles].

THE CURSE OF SENTIMENT.

> London: Printed for G. G. J. and J. Robinson, Pater-noster-Row, 1787.
>
> I xix, 240p; II 224p. 12mo. 5s sewed (MR, LEP 21–23 Dec), 6s sewed (LEP 7–9 Dec).
>
> CR 63: 389 (May 1787); MR 76: 448–49 (May 1787); AF II: 1112.
>
> BL 12611.aa.28; EM 52: 2; ESTC t100634 (NA CtY, RPB-JH).

Notes. Contract between Robinson and Charles Dodd for 20 gns., 17 Apr 1786 (RA).

Vol. 1 2-pp. unsigned dedication to the Marchioness of Buckingham [iii]–[iv]; introduction v–xix. 2 pp. advs. end vol. 2 (catchword suggests that at least 1 leaf of advs. is missing at end). Epistolary.

Adv., 'Next Week will be published', LEP 7–9 Dec 1786; adv. as published LEP 21–23 Dec 1786.

Further edn: Dublin, 1787 (Printed for Messrs. Colles, H. Whitestone, Lewis, Colbert and Moore, 1 vol., 12mo), ESTC t183800. French trans. Geneva and Paris, 1789 (*Les malheurs du sentiment*) (BGR).

MR [Andrew Becket]: 'A very simple tale, and told in a particularly simple manner. The story, indeed, is much too ridiculous for us to enter into an examination of it' (p. 448).

1787: 35   ÉPINAY, [Louise-Florence-Pétronille Tardieu d'Escalavelle, dame de La Live, marquise d']; [LYONS, Lewis (*trans.*)].
THE CONVERSATIONS OF EMILY. TRANSLATED FROM THE FRENCH OF MADAME LA COMTESSE D'EPIGNY. IN TWO VOLUMES.

 London: Printed and Sold by John Marshall and Co. of No. 4, Aldermary Church Yard, in Bow-Lane, 1787.
 I xxiv, 357p; II 355p. 12mo. 7s bound (MR).
 MR 76: 261–2 (Mar 1787).
 BRu ENC; EM 7278: 2; ESTC t133441 (BI BL, E, O; NA CaOHM, CaOTP, CtY).

Notes. Trans. of *Les conversations d'Émilie* (Leipzig, 1774).
Robinson paid 5 gns. on 19 Feb 1783 to Lewis Lyons for translating *Conversations of Emily* (RA).
'To my Young Pupils', signed 'The Translator', London, 20 Dec 1786; 'The Translator's Preface' vii–xiii; 'Advertisement to the Second French Edition' xv–xxii; 'Letter from the Author to the Editor of the First French Edition' xxiii–xxiv.

 MR [George Edward Griffiths]: 'The dialogues are carried on between a young lady and her mother; they are enlivened with little stories, anecdotes, &c. and are well adapted to instil into young minds, a desire for knowledge, a due deference to their superiors, a becoming condescension to their inferiors, and a polite behaviour to all. The work does not seem to be ill translated; which is as much as we can say, without seeing the original . . .' (p. 261).

1787: 36   FLORIAN, [Jean-Pierre Claris de].
THE ADVENTURES OF NUMA POMPILIUS, SECOND KING OF ROME. TRANSLATED FROM THE FRENCH OF M. DE FLORIAN. IN TWO VOLUMES.

 London: Printed for C. Dilly, in the Poultry; J. Stockdale, Piccadilly; and W. Creech, Edinburgh, 1787.
 I iv, 267 p; II iii, 290p. 8vo. 6s sewed (MR), 6s boards (LEP).
 MR 78: 82 (Jan 1788); AF II: 707.
 BL 634.b.34; EM 5348: 4; ESTC t113862 (BI C; NA CSmH, KU-S, MnU &c.).

Notes. Trans. of *Numa Pompilius, second roi de Rome* (Paris, 1786).
Dedication by the translator to 'His Excellency Baron Nolcken, Envoy Extraordinary and Minister Plenipotentiary from His Majesty the King of Sweden'; table of contents i–iv. Vol. 2 table of contents i–iii. 2-pp. proposals for printing John Gaspard Lavater's *Essays on Phsiognomy* [*sic*] end vol. 2.
Adv., 'On Monday, the 25th instant, will be published, Beautifully printed on Writing Paper, in Two Pocket Volumes, Crown 8vo', LEP 12–14 June 1787; adv. quotes EngR's views on the French original [rev. EngR 9: 135–40 (Feb 1787)] and refers the reader to the MR's comments in the App to vol. 56 [June/July 1777].
Further edns: London, 1788, ESTC n050007; London, 1798, EM 7: 8, ESTC t131198; Brussels, 1790, ESTC t165126. Different trans. by Elizabeth Morgan (pub. Cadell), London, 1787, ESTC t117009; NSTC lists edn. in 1813. Serialised as 'Account of Numa Pompilius', *Town and Country Magazine*, 1791–93, RM 962.
 MR originally reviewed the French version of 'this truly elegant romance' in vol. 75: 513–4 (App. [Dec 1786/Jan 1787]).

FULLER, Anne, ALAN FITZ-OSBORNE
See 1786: 21

1787: 37　[HEATH, Henry Feron, Junior].
THE RECLUSE. A FRAGMENT.
South-Shields: Printed by James Churnside, for the author, 1787.
vii, 159p. 8vo.
MH-H *EC75.A100.787r3; EM 1493: 8; ESTC n012839.

Notes. ESTC: Attribution from an advertisement in the *Newcastle Chronicle* 31 Mar 1787.
Dedication to the Rev. Mr Farrer, of Witton-le-Wear iii–vii.

1787: 38　[HELME, Elizabeth].
LOUISA; OR, THE COTTAGE ON THE MOOR. IN TWO VOLUMES.
London: Printed for G. Kearsley, at Johnson's Head, No. 46, Fleet-Street, 1787.
I x, 208p; II 248p. 12mo. 6s (CR), 6s sewed (MR, LEP).
CR 63: 308 (Apr 1787); MR 76: 449 (May 1787); AF II: 1890.
BL 1489.cc.91; EM 3879: 2; ESTC t060935 (BI O; NA IU, MH-H, PU).

Notes. Preface v–x.
Adv., 'Next Week will be published', LEP 20–22 Mar 1787; adv. has heading 'How extraordinary and unmerited soever the distresses of the Heroine of the following Work may appear, all the Circumstances are well known in the County of C-mb-rl-d'.
Further edns: Dublin, 1787 (Printed by Brett Smith, for Messrs. Moncrieffe, Colles, Burnet, Gilbert, Wogan [and 10 others in Dublin], 2 vols., 12mo), EM 3605: 6, ESTC 129034; London, 1787, ESTC n018987; London, 1787, EM 4652: 11, ESTC n033439; London, 1787, ESTC n018988; London, 1787, EM 2069: 7, ESTC t073523; 4 further entries in ESTC; WC has 8 entries between 1800 and 1850; NSTC lists edn. in 1840. French trans. London and Paris, 1787 (*Louise, ou la Chaumière dans les marais*) (BN); German trans. Leipzig, 1789 (*Luise oder die Bauerhütte* [sic] *im Marschlande*) (EAG).
Adv. LEP 26–28 Apr 1787: 'The Publisher of Louisa, or the Cottage on the Moor, Two Volumes, begs leave respectfully to inform those who have been disappointed that he has, in order to expedite the New Edition, distributed it to four different Printing Houses, who have engaged to complete it by Monday next, when a large impression will be ready to supply the increasing demand for this favourite Production.
To remove from this Advertisement the suspicion of a puff, the Printers who have undertaken to expedite this New Edition (which will be considerably improved and divided into Chapters) are here inserted, viz. Messrs. Woodfall, Spilsbury, Bensley, and Thorne and Harrison.'
New edn. adv., 'now printed and ready for delivery', SJC 28 Apr–1 May 1787: 'The Improvements in this Edition are considerable, and the Number printed is supposed to be sufficient to supply the increasing Demand for this favourite Narrative, the principal Occurrences of which are founded on Facts, well known to the Friends of the Families who are the Subjects of it.'
3rd edn. adv., 'On Monday will be published', LEP 19–22 May 1787; adv. adds 'Two large Impressions of this favourite Production have been sold within this Month'.
CR: 'This is a pleasing little artless tale, much superior, both in its plan and conduct, to the

numerous productions of this class. Curiosity is skilfully excited, expectation kept momen-
tarily alive, and, at last, the intricacies are unravelled very satisfactorily. We believe, as is
asserted, that the story may be true, in its outline; but much must have been added to attract
and to adorn.'

MR [Andrew Becket]: 'A not unpleasing, but rather improbable tale. . . . The narrative,
some passages excepted, is prettily written.'

1787: 39   [HERIOT, John].
THE SORROWS OF THE HEART. A NOVEL. IN TWO VOLUMES.

> London: Printed for J. Murray, No. 32, Fleet-Street, 1787.
> I iv, 209p; II 205p. 12mo. 5s sewed (MR, CR).
> CR 63: 225 (Mar 1787); MR 76: 531 (June 1787); AF II: 1906.
> BL N.2058; EM 2069: 31; ESTC t073503 (BI E; NA MA, PU; EA Pm).

Notes. Dedication to Francis John Hartwell, Esq., Captain in the Royal Navy. 3 pp. advs. end
vol. 2.
Murray paid author £10 for copyright (Zachs 593).
Adv., 'This day, at noon, was published', LEP 11–13 Jan 1787.
French trans. Londres [ESTC: i.e. Paris?], 1789 (Horton et Mathilde), ESTC t152029; German
trans. Leipzig, 1788 (Die Leiden des Herzens in Briefen) (Price).

CR: 'The editor tells us that these letters are original ones; and we see no reason to distrust
his account. The letters are well written; and, though the adventures are such as may be supposed to happen frequently, yet they are related in a manner that renders the story interesting and affecting.'

MR [Andrew Becket]: 'The modern novel affords us nothing like variety. "Soup for breakfast, soup for dinner, and soup for supper," as the libertine in the comedy observes of his
wife. We are very fairly tired of it.'

HILDITCH, Ann
See HOWELL, Ann

1787: 40   [HOWELL, Ann].
ROSA DE MONTMORIEN. A NOVEL. BY MISS ANN HILDITCH. IN
TWO VOLUMES.

> London: Printed for William Lane, Leadenhall-Street, 1787.
> I 176p; II 155p. 8vo [MR, CR, LEP have 12mo]. 5s sewed (MR, CR).
> CR 64: 480 (Dec 1787); MR 79: 171 (Aug 1788); AF II: 2085.
> BL 12612.aa.20; EM 331: 8; ESTC t064757 (NA MB).

Notes. 1 p. of advs. end vol. 2.
Adv., 'in the Press, and speedily will be published', LEP 3–6 Nov 1787.

CR: 'There is little to recommend these volumes: some parts are sentimental, and some are
romantic; but, while we feel little interest for the heroine, we are disgusted with improbabilities and anachronisms.'

MR [Andrew Becket]: 'Rosa de Montmorien is a lively and agreeable lass. Let her not,
however, imagine that she is a goddess, because we allow her to be in possession of some personal charms. There is a degree of beauty both in the physical and moral world, which may

be intitled to a favourable report, though not to particular and absolute praise. In other words, the story of this novel is trifling; and, from a bad arrangement of the incidents, it is somewhat obscure.—But the language is often pretty, and might, with a little attention, have been rendered correct.'

1787: 41   [HUGHES, Anne].
*CAROLINE; OR THE DIVERSITIES OF FORTUNE. A NOVEL.

London: Printed for William Lane, Leadenhall-Street (LEP), 1787 (LEP).
3 vols. 12mo. 9s (CR), 7s sewed (LEP), 7s 6d sewed (MR, adv.).
CR 63: 390 (May 1787); MR 77: 162 (Aug 1787); AF II: 2099.
No copy located.

Notes. Adv., 'A Novel in the Style, Taste, and Manners of Miss Burney', LEP 28 Apr–1 May 1787; 'In this admired work is exhibited many interesting scenes in various situations of real life'.
Adv. twice in SJC 1–4 Sept 1787 (one adv. immediately following the other), the first headed 'A Novel, replete with Incident and Adventure'.
Adv. end vol. 2 of *The School of Virtue* (1787: 21).
Further edns: London, 1787, ESTC n043698; London, 1787, ESTC n002976; Dublin, 1787 (Printed by M. Graisberry, for Messrs. Gilbert, White, Byrne, and H. Whitestone, 2 vols., 12mo), EM 3634: 1, ESTC t118781; London, 1787, ESTC n002976. French trans., *Caroline, ou les vicissitudes de la fortune*, Londres [ESTC: i.e. Paris?], 1789, ESTC t204157; 1 further entry in ESTC; German trans. Leipzig and Leignitz, 1790 (*Karoline oder der Wechsel des Glücks*) (EAG).

CR: 'This is a pleasing and interesting story: though made up of "shreds and patches" of the scenes and characters of similar works; yet they are well arranged, and the attention is so closely fixed, that we want not the charm of novelty. The incidents are, however, rather too artificial; and we see too plainly the finger of contrivance.'
MR [Andrew Becket]: 'A pleasing and well-wrought story.'

1787: 42   [JOHNSON, Mrs].
*THE PLATONIC GUARDIAN; OR THE HISTORY OF AN ORPHAN. BY A LADY.

London: Printed for William Lane, Leadenhall-Street (LEP), 1787 (LEP).
3 vols. 12mo. 7s 6d (CR), 7s 6d sewed (MR, LEP, adv.).
CR 64: 392 (Nov 1787); MR 78: 250 (Mar 1788); AF II: 3399.
No copy located.

Notes. Blakey: attributed to Mrs Johnson in a Minerva Catalogue of 1814.
Epistolary.
Adv., 'A New Entertaining Novel', LEP 6–9 Oct 1787, with 'Platonic' spelt 'Plantonic'.
Adv. end vol. 2 of *The School of Virtue* (1787: 23).
Further edn: Dublin, 1788 (Printed for Messrs. P. Byrne, P. Wogan, H. Colbert, and J. Halpen, 1 vol., 12mo), ESTC n038671. French trans., *Le tuteur platonique*, Londres [ESTC: i.e. Paris], 1789, ESTC t078762.

CR: 'We trace our author so often in the footsteps of Miss Burney, that we must at least deny her the praise of originality. . . . If we except a few incorrectnesses, peculiar to a lady, the story is told in a manner not unpleasing; and is, by no means, deficient in entertainment.'

MR [Andrew Becket] believes it to be written by the author of *Caroline; or the Diversities of Fortune* (Anne Hughes?, 1787: 41).

1787: 43   [KEIR, Elizabeth].
THE HISTORY OF MISS GREVILLE. IN THREE VOLUMES. BY THE AUTHOR OF INTERESTING MEMOIRS.

> London: Printed and Sold for the Author at Mr Carruthers's, N° 36, Cheapside, and by T. Cadell, Strand, 1787.
> I vii, 270p; II 308p; III 283p. 12mo. 7s 6d sewed (CR, MR).
> CR 64: 200–1 (Sept 1787); MR 77: 80 (July 1787); AF II: 2346.
> BL N.2317-9; EMf; ESTC t145510 (BI E; NA IU, MH-H, NjP &c.)

Notes. Dedication to the Countess of Glasgow v–vii, signed 'The Author', Edinburgh, 20 Apr 1787. Epistolary.
Interesting Memoirs 1785: 36.
Adv. SJC 5–7 June 1787; Carruthers's address is given as 'Mrs. Carruther's Lace Warehouse, No. 36, Cheapside'.
Further edns: Edinburgh, 1787, ESTC n007334; Dublin, 1787 (Printed by P. Byrne, 2 vols., 12mo), ESTC n053226. German trans. Leipzig, 1802 (*Anna Grenwil, das tapfere Mädchen aus Schottland*) (EAG).

CR: 'These volumes are truly valuable: if we do not meet with new characters, we find the most salutary lessons: if we are not entertained with numerous adventures, we see frequent proofs of judicious reflection; we read the decisions of a well informed mind, and listen to the dictates of a well regulated heart.'

MR [Samuel Rose]: 'We have seldom perused a novel with which we have been better pleased, or more affected, than with the present. . . . Some of the scenes are drawn with exquisite tenderness and pathos, the sentiments are pure and virtuous, and the language in which they are clothed is for the most part elegant.'

1787: 44   [NĀRĀYANA BHATTA, after VISHNUSARMÁ]; WILKINS, Charles (trans.).
THE HĔĔTŌPĂDĒS OF VĔĔSHNŎŎ-SĂRMĀ, IN A SERIES OF CON-NECTED FABLES, INTERSPERSED WITH MORAL, PRUDENTIAL, AND POLITICAL MAXIMS; TRANSLATED FROM AN ANCIENT MANU-SCRIPT IN THE SANSKREET LANGUAGE. WITH EXPLANATORY NOTES, BY CHARLES WILKINS.

> Bath: Printed by R. Cruttwell, and sold by C. Nourse, in the Strand, London, and J. Marshall, Milsom-Street, Bath, 1787.
> xvii, 356p. 8vo. 6s boards (EngR, SJC), a few copies 'printed upon a fine wove Royal Paper' 10s 6d boards (SJC).
> EngR 11: 114–19 (Feb 1788); AF II: 4799.
> MH-H 27244.8; EM 8437: 5; ESTC t112180 (BI BL, C, E, O &c.; NA C-S, CSmH, &c.; EA Pm).

Notes. The Hitopadeśa, or the four books of good counsels, was extracted by Nārāyana Bhatta from the Pañchatantra by Vishnusarmá (fl. 1060). This is the first English trans., two years after that of the Bhagavadgita.

Dedication v–vi to Nathaniel Smith, signed Charles Wilkins, Queen's Square, Bloomsbury, 1 Nov 1787; preface, signed C. W., [vii]–xvii. P. [vii] misnumbered 6.

Adv. SJC 22–24 Nov 1787; 'N.B. The Original of this Work is the supposed Prototype of that Collection of Fables, which, through Persian and Turkish Mediums, has appeared in almost every Language in Europe, as the Composition of Pilpay, or Ridpai [Bīdpā'ī].'

The model indicated was The Fables of Pilpay, or the Anwār-I Suhaili, a Persian version of Kalīlah wa-Dimnah by Husain Wāiz Kāshifi, with a first complete trans. in 1747 but with versions since the 17ᵗʰ c. (see notes to ESTC t143267).

Further edns: NSTC lists edns. in 1830 and 1844.

EngR sees as the fables' chief defect 'one which distinguishes compositions of the same kind among all nations, viz. attributing human faculties and passions to the inferior and unintelligent animals' (p. 117) but the overall verdict is favourable: 'Upon the whole the *Heetopades of Veshnoo-Sarma* is a curious monument of Asiatic genius, and a valuable addition to European literature' (p. 119).

1787: 45   [NICHOLSON, Mr].
ORLANDO AND SERAPHINA: A TURKISH STORY.

> London: Printed for William Lane, Leadenhall-Street, 1787.
> I xvi, 160p; II 167p. 8vo [MR, CR and LEP have 12mo]. 5s sewed (MR, CR, adv.).
> CR 63: 391 (May 1787); MR 76: 528 (June 1787); AF II: 3180.
> BL 012618.df.25; EM 290: 5; ESTC t108186 (NA CU-Riv, MH-H, PU &c.).

Notes. Blakey: attributed to Mr Nicholson by a Minerva Library catalogue of 1814.

Preface v–xvi explains that the story was suggested by an episode in Hume's *History* about Colonel Kirke. In vol. 2 text of novel starts on p. 5. 1 p. advs. end vol. 2. Epistolary.

Adv., 'In a few Days will be published . . . Elegantly printed on fine Writing-Paper', SJC 13–15 Feb 1787; 'In which is included the pathetick History of two Lovers'.

Adv. LC 61: 172 (17–20 Feb 1787); 'A Tale affecting instructive, and historical. Containing a description of the manners of the Turks, account of the Serail, &c. &c.'

Adv., 'A Pathetic and Well-Told Tale', LEP 1–3 Mar 1787; 'in a Series of Letters. In which is described the Turkish Seraglio'.

Adv. end vol. 2 of *Darnley Vale* (1789: 33).

German trans. Leipzig, 1787 (*Orlande und Seraphine, eine türkische Geschichte*) (Price); French trans. Brussels, Dujardin and Paris, 1788 (*Roland et Séraphine, histoire turque*) (BGR).

CR: 'The narrative is well conducted; the changes, though sometimes at the extreme verge of probability, are yet, on the whole, sufficiently credible; the language is correct, forcible, and often elegant; the characters varied and well discriminated. The termination differs from the event as it occurs in Hume: it is a happy one.'

MR [Andrew Becket]: 'When a *Turkish* story is presented to us, we naturally look for something respecting the *Porte*, and the manners and customs of the people. In the performance before us, however, nothing of the kind is to be met with. It is simply a tale for the ladies; as plentifully interlarded with *ohs!* and *ahs!* as the prayers of an old puritanic divine.'

1787: 46   [NICHOLSON, Mr].
THE VILLAGE OF MARTINDALE: A NOVEL. IN TWO VOLUMES.

> London: Printed for W. Lane, Leadenhall-Street, 1787.

I 176p; II 196p. 8vo [MR has 12mo]. 5s sewed (MR, LEP, adv.), 6s (CR).

CR 63: 390 (May 1787); MR 76: 528 (June 1787); AF II: 3068.

O Vet.A5f.428-9; EMf; ESTC t174926 (BI BL, C [vol. 1 only]; NA IU, NjP, PU &c.).

Notes. Blakey: attributed to Mr Nicholson by a Minerva Library catalogue of 1814.

LEP adv. mentions *Orlando and Seraphina* (1787: 45 above) as 'by the same Author'.

Frontispiece. Dedication to the Duchess of Portland signed 'The Author'. 2-pp. introduction (unn.). In vol. 2 text of novel starts on p. 5. Half-page adv. on p. 176 of vol. 1.

Adv., 'In the Press, and speedily will be published . . . Neatly printed on a fine Paper, and adorned with an elegant Frontispiece, depicting a remarkable Part of the story', LEP 10–13 Mar 1787; adv. has heading 'Humanity and Excellence' and extends title: 'in which is pourtrayed that universal Philanthropist, Mr Howard'.

Adv. end vol. 2 of *Darnley Vale* (1789: 33).

Further edn: Dresden, 1789 [in English] (Price). German trans. Leipzig, 1797 (*Das Dorf Martinsthal, eine historische Novelle*) (EAG).

CR: 'The author promised us novelty, and he has not disappointed us. . . . The story is conducted with skill: we were interested in the progress, and pleased with the conclusion.'

MR [Andrew Becket]: 'This gentleman's talent is indisputably the *humorous* and *burlesque*; as he has here manifested in a very lively and agreeable tale.'

1787: 47   [?RUTLIDGE, Chevalier James].
THE ADVENTURES OF MONSIEUR PROVENCE, BEING A SUPPLEMENT TO THE ENGLISHMAN'S FORTNIGHT AT PARIS. TRANSLATED FROM THE FRENCH.

London: Printed for G. Kearsley, at Johnson's Head, No. 46, in Fleet-Street, 1787.

I viii, 338p; II viii, 298p. 12mo. 6s (CR), 6s sewed (half-titles, MR).

CR 64: 310 (Oct 1787); MR 77: 192–4 (Sept 1787); AF II: 3902.

CLU-S/C Delta PR3671.R65a; ESTCn061440.

Notes. Trans. of *Supplément à la Quinzaine angloise ou mémoires de monsieur Provence* (London and Paris, 1787).

BN gives name as RUTLIDGE, James, *dit* Jean-Jacques.

Possibly not by Rutlidge; development of the story of one of the characters in Rutlidge's *La Quinzaine anglois à Paris* (1776), itself pretending to be 'ouvrage posthume du Dr Stearne, traduit de l'anglois'.

Adv. for 1-vol. edition of *La Quinzaine anglois à Paris* published by Durham and Kearsley (SJC 22–25 Feb 1777) mentions that an 'English Translation . . . is in the Press, and will be published in a few Days'; trans., *The Englishman's Fortnight in Paris; or, the Art of ruining himself there in a few Days*, adv. SJC 10–12 Apr 1777.

Vol. 1 prefatory advertisement [i]–[iii], contents [v]–viii; vol. 2 contents [v]–viii.

Adv., 'Next Week will be published', LEP 3–5 July 1787; title begins *Memoirs of M. Provence*, and adv. has an added note: 'This Work, which is written after the manner of Gil Blas, and is by many esteemed superior to that favourite Romance, has already gone through several editions at Paris'. Re-adv. with title now *Adventures of M. Provence* LEP 5–7 July 1787.

CR: '. . . we have seldom seen a work less attracting even to the libertine, and more disgusting to every serious or attentive reader. The Adventures might have remained in their native garb, without exciting in us the smallest wish to have procured them in the English language.'

MR [Andrew Becket]: '. . . the Author exhibits the example of a man of real merit, who, notwithstanding the united advantages of birth, education and talents, could never arrive at eminence or wealth' (p. 192). 'This Author sometimes exhibits human nature *as it is*, and sometimes as *it ought to be*; but much more frequently to *disadvantage*' (p. 194).

1787: 48   SHELDON, Ann.
AUTHENTIC AND INTERESTING MEMOIRS OF MISS ANN SHELDON; (NOW MRS. ARCHER:) A LADY WHO FIGURED, DURING SEVERAL YEARS, IN THE HIGHEST LINE OF PUBLIC LIFE, AND IN WHOSE HISTORY WILL BE FOUND, ALL THE VICISSITUDES, WHICH SO CONSTANTLY ATTEND ON WOMEN OF HER DESCRIPTION. WRITTEN BY HERSELF.

> London: Printed for the Authoress, No. 2, St George's-Place, St George's Fields; and sold by all the Booksellers, 1787/88.
> I 240p (1787); II 262p (1788); III 250p (1788); IV 247p (1788). 12mo. 10s sewed (MR).
> MR 78: 532 (June 1788).
> BL 1202.a.4, 5; EM 2047: 5; ESTC t133187 (BI E, O; NA CtY-Walpole, IU, MnU).

Notes. In vols. 3 and 4 text starts on p. 5.
MR reviews under 'Novels'.
Further edn: London, 1790, ESTC t153211 [ESTC: a reissue of the 1787/88 edn. with cancel titlepages]. German trans. Leipzig, 1789 (*Galanterien der grossen Welt in England, aus dem Englischen der Miss Anna Sheldon*) (Price).
  MR [Andrew Becket]: 'Miss Anne Sheldon, who was formerly of considerable note in the pleasurable circles, has here presented the public with her *adventures*; and the scenes she brings to view excite at once our pity and disgust.'

1787: 49   SMITH, Charlotte.
THE ROMANCE OF REAL LIFE. BY CHARLOTTE SMITH. IN THREE VOLUMES.

> London: Printed for T. Cadell, in the Strand, 1787.
> I xi, 212p; II 205p; III 170p. 8vo [CR has 12mo]. 9s (CR), 9s boards (SJC).
> CR 64: 309–10 (1787); AF II: 4145.
> C 7720.e.222-; EM 129: 7; ESTC t057369 (BI BL, O; NA CtY, CSmH, IU, MH-H, NjP, PU TxU, ViU &c.).

Notes. ESTC: A collection of tales based on *Causes célèbres et intéressantes* by François Gayot de Pitaval [Paris, 1734–1743].
Preface v–xi signed Charlotte Smith. 2-pp. table of contents.
Adv., 'In a few Days will be published, elegantly printed in three Volumes', SJC 24–26 May 1787: 'a Selection of singular Stories from Les Cavres [*sic*] Celebres'; adv. as published SJC 31 May–2 June 1787.
Further edns: Dublin, 1787 (Printed by John Rea, for Messrs. Gilbert, Burton, White, Byrne, H. Whitestone, and Moore, 2 vols., 12mo), ESTC n013230; Philadelphia, 1799, ESTC w022012; Baltimore, 1799, ESTC w000221; Aberdeen, 1847 (WC, NSTC). Extracts from *the Romance of Real Life*, 'The Pretended Martin Guerre', published in 3 magazines between

1787 and 1790, RM 1022. German trans. Leipzig, 1789 (*Gemälde menschlicher Schwächen und Leidenschaften*) (Price).

CR: 'Few romances furnish any thing more incredible than some of these histories; but, as they are real transactions, whether we trust implicitly to the stories, as they are told, or suppose them to have originated from the artifices and impostures of villains, they become extremely interesting, and confirm the opinion, that nothing is so improbable, if it be within the bounds of possibility, but what may sometimes occur.'

1787: 50   [THOMSON, Anna].
EXCESSIVE SENSIBILITY; OR, THE HISTORY OF LADY ST. LAURENCE. A NOVEL.

> London: Printed for G. G. J. and J. Robinson, Paternoster-Row, 1787.
> I 238p; II 220p. 12mo. 6s (CR), 5s sewed (MR, LEP).
> CR 63: 389 (May 1787); MR 76: 529–30 (June 1787); AF II: 4445.
> BL 1507/1249; EM 2116: 13; ESTC t129340 (NA IU, PU).

Notes. For more information about author's name, see note to *Labyrinths of Life* (1791: 70); t.p. to this work claims authorship of *Excessive Sensibility*.
Dedication to Viscountess Fairford iii–iv, dated March 1787. Epistolary.
Adv., 'Thursday the 28th instant will be published', LEP 17–20 Mar 1787; adv. as published LEP 22–24 Mar 1787.
Re-adv., 'On Saturday next will be published', SJC 7–9 Aug 1787.

CR: 'This novel has no very distinguishing qualities: the arrangement is sufficiently artificial to interest the reader; and the events are so much within probability as not to disgust him.'

MR [Andrew Becket]: '. . . it must be acknowledged that some of this gentleman's characters are delineated with a bold and glowing pencil, and in a manner that sufficiently indicates his acquaintance with the human heart. . . . The Author's style, however, is frequently faulty and inelegant . . . .'

1787: 51   [TOMLINS, Elizabeth Sophia].
THE VICTIM OF FANCY. A NOVEL. BY A LADY, AUTHOR OF THE CONQUESTS OF THE HEART.

> London: Sold By R. Baldwin, Pater-noster row; and G. and T. Wilkie, St Paul's Church-
>   yard, 1787.
> I 186p; II 152p. 8vo [MR has 12mo]. 5s sewed (MR, SJC), 6s (CR).
> CR 63: 107–9 (Feb 1787); MR 76: 446–7 (May 1787); AF II: 4495.
> OU PQ 3736.T4V5 1787; ESTC n063119.

Notes. Vol. 1 2-pp. dedication to William Hayley (unn.), followed by 2-pp. adv. for *The Sorrows of Werter* (1779: 10). 1 p. adv. [for *The Conquests of the Heart* (1785: 45)] end vol. 1. Epistolary.
Post-dated; adv. SJC 19–21 Dec 1786. Re-adv., with quotation from CR, SJC 15–17 Mar 1787.
French trans. Paris, 1795 (*La Victime de l'imagination, ou l'enthousiaste de Werther*) (HWS).

CR: These volumes 'contain many just remarks, in a neat, and generally a correct style. It seems a circumstance of some importance in female life, and we think it a natural one, that the fancy is corrected in proportion as the heart is attached to an object worthy of it' (p. 109).

MR [Andrew Becket]: 'A new kind of *Female Quixote* but bearing no resemblance to any former work of the sort, that we have seen. We imagine it to be the production of a young Authoress, whose head and heart abound, or rather overflow with sentiment, fancy, feeling, and delicacy,—but all tinctured too strongly with the *extravagant*, and the *romantic*' (p. 446).

[Charlotte Lennox, *The Female Quixote*, 1752, JR 138–141, AF I: 1588.]

VISHNUSARMÁ
See NĀRĀYANA BHATTA, THE HĔĔTŌPĂDĒS OF VĔĔSHNŎŎ-SĂRMĀ (1787: 44)

WILKINS, Charles
See NĀRĀYANA BHATTA, THE HĔĔTŌPĂDĒS OF VĔĔSHNŎŎ-SĂRMĀ (1787: 44)

1788

1788: 1   ANON.
THE ADVENTURES OF A WATCH!
> London: Printed for G. Kearsley, at Johnson's Head, No. 46, Fleet Street, 1788.
> 211p. 12mo. 3s sewed (MR, half-title, MC).
> MR 80: 88 (Jan 1789).
> C 7700.d.745; ESTC n004800 (NA ICN, MH-H, NjP, PU, TxU &c.).

Notes: 3-pp. table of contents. Opening sentence of novel presents a pedigree: 'As Authors have made lap-dogs, fleas, lice, bank notes, guineas, nay even Birmingham half-pence, though of very roguish appearance, give the history of their lives, why not adopt the example?'
19½ pp. advs. at end, beginning on p. 211.
Adv. MC 28 Apr 1788.
MR [Andrew Becket] describes it as a 'very clumsy piece of workmanship'.

1788: 2   ANON.
*THE ADVENTURES OF CHRISTOPHER CURIOUS; IN A SERIES OF RAMBLES, AMOROUS AND ENTERTAINING. BY A MODERN RAMBLER.
> London: Printed for R. Randall, No. 1, Shoe-Lane; and sold by all other booksellers (MC), 1788 (MC).
> 12mo. 2s 6d (EngR, MC).
> EngR 14: 470 (Dec 1789).
> No copy located.

Notes. Adv., with heading 'Modern Gallantry', 'Consisting of Domestick History, New Characters[,] Accidents, Female Frailty, Night Scenes, Humorous Mistakes, Pleasing Explanations, Distressing Incidents', MC 12 Jan 1788: 'It will be found in the course of this Novel, that the pleasure of incident is preferable to the dulness of reasoning; the weakness and the frailty of human nature is forcibly depicted, and the contrivances of curiosity cannot fail to amuse and entertain.'

EngR: 'This is a publication that would disgrace the police of any civilised country upon earth. The mind who could rake together from brothels such a nauseous collection of filth, must be yet more depraved than even the miscreant he would describe. Here, however, the garb of vice is not attractive. The painter no doubt wished to render her charming, but she appears in her own likeness, ugly, vulgar, and detestable.'

1788: 3   ANON.
AGITATION: OR, MEMOIRS OF GEORGE WOODFORD AND LADY EMMA MELVILL. A NOVEL. DEDICATED (BY PERMISSION) TO THE HONOURABLE MRS. LIONEL DAMER. BY THE AUTHOR OF THE RING, AND THE FALSE FRIENDS. IN THREE VOLUMES.

> London: Printed for J. Barker, Russell-Court, Drury-Lane, 1788.
> I ii, 220p; II 215p; III 217p. 12mo. 7s 6d sewed (CR), 9s bound (MR), 9s neatly bound (adv.).
> CR 65: 150 (Feb 1788); MR 81: 460 (Nov 1789); AF II: 45.
> CU-BANC PR3291.A2A4; ESTC n029535 (EA Ps [vols. 1–2 only]).

Notes. Dedication to the Honourable Mrs Lionel Damer, signed 'The Authoress', vol. 1, pp. i–ii.

Text of novel starts on p. 9 in vol. 1 and p. 5 in vols. 2 and 3. 4 pp. advs. end vol. 1 and 1 p. advs. end vol. 3.

The Ring 1784: 6; *The False Friends* 1785: 7.

Adv. beginning of *Stella* (1791: 36).

Further edns: London, n.d. [1788?], EM 4239: 3, ESTC n033432; London, 1790, xESTC (WC).

CR: 'Like her former works, this novel, if it raise no admiration, will escape contempt; and, to continue in her own manner,—may never any novellist hold up worse examples, or inculcate less salutary lessons, than we find in the Memoirs of George Woodford and Lady Emma Melvill!'

MR [Andrew Becket]: '. . . the love-scenes in this performance—and it is composed of nothing else—are so coarsely, so very inelegantly delineated, that instead of inspiring a tender and delicate passion, they can only awaken disgust.'

1788: 4   ANON.
*ALFRED AND CASSANDRA, A ROMANTIC TALE.

> London: Lane, 1788 (MC).
> 2 vols. 12mo. 5s (CR), 4s sewed (MC).
> CR 66: 577 (App [Dec 1788/Jan 1789]); AF II: 59.
> No copy located.

Notes. Adv. MC 16 Dec 1788.

CR: 'One of the vamped-up productions of other times, to supply the literary vacuum of an unusually dull summer. Much of the story we have already seen, but where our memory cannot at present inform us. . . . In every view, these volumes are "the meanest of their tribe." '

1788: 5   ANON.
*THE AMERICAN HUNTER, A TALE. FROM INCIDENTS WHICH HAPPENED DURING THE WAR WITH AMERICA. TO WHICH IS ANNEXED A SOMERSETSHIRE STORY.

> London: Kearsley, 1788.
> 12mo. 2s 6d (CR), 2s 6d sewed (MR).
> CR 67: 154 (Feb 1789); MR 79: 170–1 (Aug 1788); AF II: 83.
> No copy located.

Notes. MR [John Noorthouck]: 'The writer understands human nature well. . . . The style of these tales is easy, but the language grossly incorrect; and a page and a half of *errata*, though they proclaim a shameful number, do not contain all the typographical errors in this small volume: these circumstances persuade us that it is the production of some writer not familiar with the press.'

1788: 6   ANON.
THE AMICABLE QUIXOTE; OR, THE ENTHUSIASM OF FRIENDSHIP. IN FOUR VOLUMES.

> London: Printed for J. Walter, Charing-Cross, 1788.
> I vii, 222p; II 206p; III 238p; IV 198p. 8vo [MR and CR have 12mo]. 10s sewed (MR, LC, MC), 12s (CR).
> CR 67: 77–8 (Jan 1789); MR 80: 60–2 (Jan 1789); AF II: 84.
> BL 12613.b.31; EM 279: 5; ESTC t068744 (BI E [vols. 2–3 only]; NA CtY, MH-H, NjP [vols. 2–3 only], PU &c.).

Notes. Preface v–vii.
Adv., 'Handsomely printed, in four pocket volumes', LC 64: 5 (28 June–1 July 1788) and MC 12 July 1788.

CR: 'We have seldom seen a more peculiar work, or one amidst much merit, checkered with so many errors. . . . As a novel, this work is very exceptionable; the plot is improbable, the characters are overcharged, and the events inconsistent. Yet the characters are sometimes the bold sketches of a master-hand, that, like the good knight changed to a Saracen, still preserve enough of nature to please and to interest. . . . The whole is a cento of sketches, struck out with carelessness, sometimes coloured with extravagance, and sometimes left in the meagre state of an outline. In the work there is, however, merit of a better kind: the author has read with attention and his quotations are sometimes well adapted, and generally pleasing, since they are chosen from the best authors. Just sentiments are frequently intermixed, and judicious reflections are not uncommon' (p. 77).

MR [Samuel Rose]: 'The very singular work now before us . . . possesses considerable merit. Much ingenuity is displayed in the delineation of the characters. The author shews great experience in the ways of men; and there is humour in the manner in which some of the incidents are conducted. We observed, however, with regret, several puns, which, though fairly and aptly applied, add little to the merit of these volumes; and notwithstanding all the allowance that we can reasonably make for *Quixotism*, many situations into which some of the personages are introduced, are unnatural; and some of the characters partake more of caricatura than of real life.... the errors we have noted, are not, in our opinion, the errors of a common writer; they proceed from an exuberance of imagination that hurries its possessor along, without permitting him to consult his judgment. Beside shrewd remark, which is the offspring of good sense, we discover much information and learning' (p. 61).

1788: 7   ANON.
*THE APPARITION. A TALE. BY A LADY.

> London: Printed for T. Hookham, New Bond-street (SDA), 1788.
> 2 vols. 12mo. 4s sewed (MR, SDA), 5s (CR).
> CR 65: 236 (Mar 1788); MR 79: 466–7 (Nov 1788); AF II: 128.
> No copy located.

Notes. Adv. SDA 20 Dec 1788.

CR: 'This is a pretty little story; but the invention of the author is superior to her powers.— The desk, the ring, and the apparition, are well conceived; but, from a want of force, their effects are inconsiderable.'

MR [Andrew Becket]: 'A simple, yet agreeable story. The writer is evidently of the Walpolian school. The "broad hand" which was seen on the staircase, as described in the *Castle of Otranto*, is no doubt in the memory of several of our Readers. The visits of the *Apparition* remind us of this and some other circumstances in that admired Romance. But the pupil is at many removes behind the master.' [*Castle of Otranto* 1764/65, JR 868; AF I: 2898]

1788: 8   ANON.
AUGUSTA; OR, THE DEPENDENT NIECE: IN LETTERS. IN TWO VOLUMES.

> London: Printed for T. Vernor, No. 10, Birchin-lane, Cornhill, 1788.
> I 181p; II 208p. 12mo. 5s sewed (MR, LEP), 6s (CR).
> CR 65: 76 (Jan 1788); MR 78: 530 (June 1788); AF II: 174.
> BL 12612.aaa.21; EM 124: 6; ESTC t064709 (NA CtY; EA Pm).

Notes. Epistolary.

Adv., 'On Friday, the 28th of December, will be published', LEP 18–20 Dec 1787.

CR: 'One of those productions which neither excite admiration nor contempt. There is not an atom in these volumes which some former novellist might not claim.'

MR [Andrew Becket]: 'These productions, while they contribute to the ruin of half our women, are the encouragers of foppery in the men.'

AUGUSTA; OR THE FEMALE TRAVELLERS
See ANDREWS, Dr (1787: 27)

1788: 9   ANON.
BEATRICE, OR THE INCONSTANT, A TRAGIC NOVEL. IN TWO VOLUMES.

> London: Printed for William Lane, Leadenhall-Street, 1788.
> I 216p; II 180p. 12mo. 5s sewed (MR, MC, adv.).

CR 66: 577 (App [Dec 1788/Jan 1789]); MR n.s. 2: 463 (Aug 1790); AF II: 242.
MRu R.54261; EM 7166: 1; ESTC t189111.

Notes. Epistolary.
Adv. MC 16 Dec 1788.
Adv. end vol. 1 and vol. 3 of *Darnley Vale* (1789: 33).

CR: 'Beatrice is one of those hackneyed productions which elude criticism, because there is hardly a fault or an excellence to excite remark. These volumes are extremely dull; and if there were not many errors, perhaps of the press, to keep the attention a little awake, no impression would remain.'

MR [John Noorthouck]: 'A pleasing and affecting tale, calculated to show the fatal consequences of giddy women marryings [*sic*] for promotion, with a total indifference as to their interested choice; and flirting afterward with the object of new attachments. It contains, throughout, sentiments that we apprehend are not very congenial with the feelings and taste of the generality of subscribers to circulating libraries.'

THE CASTLE OF MOWBRAY, AN ENGLISH ROMANCE
See HUGILL, Martha

CATHARINE; OR, THE WOOD OF LLEWELLYN
See NICHOLSON, Mr

1788: 10   ANON.
*THE CLANDESTINE LOVERS. A NOVEL. IN A SERIES OF LETTERS.

London: Printed for F. Noble, at his Circulating Library, No. 324, Holborn (SDA), 1788 (SDA).
2 vols. 12mo. 5s (CR), 5s sewed (MR, SDA).
CR 66: 577 (App [Dec 1788/ Jan 1789]); MR 81: 564 (Dec 1789); AF II: 706.
No copy located.

Notes. Adv. SDA 5 Dec 1788 and LC 64: 580 (13–16 Dec 1788).

CR: 'Many letters, like those before us, have, we know, passed, and many such correspondences have succeeded happily, though by means less violent and improbable than in these volumes. We ought, however, to add, that there is some variety of character in this work, and some attempt to display characteristic sentiments in the different correspondents.'

MR [Andrew Becket]: 'This is a trifling and flimsy story, but the language is tolerably correct and flowing; and if it may afford the writer any kind of satisfaction, we will say to him in the words of the poet,—"Sir, you have a style." But this is far from being sufficient. A printed performance must be possessed of some small portion of *matter* as well as *manner....*'

CONTINUATION OF YORICK'S SENTIMENTAL JOURNEY
See App. B: 9

THE CORRESPONDENCE OF TWO LOVERS
See LÉONARD, Nicolas-Germain

1788: 11   ANON.

DEATH'S A FRIEND, A NOVEL. BY THE AUTHOR OF THE BASTARD, &C. &C.

> London: At the Mary-le-bone printing office, by J. P. Cooke, And sold by J Bew, Pater-noster-Row; T. Hookham, New Bond-street; and T. & J. Egerton, Charing-Cross, 1788.
> I 163p; II 137p. 12mo. 4s sewed (MR), 5s sewed (CR).
> CR 65: 324 (Apr 1788); MR 79: 467 (Nov 1788); AF II: 1027.
> BL 12612.aa.15; EM 167: 1; ESTC t074653 (BI C; NA PU).

Notes. Epistolary.
The Bastard 1784: 1.

CR: 'From the author's first publication we expected better things: but in style, con-trivance, execution, and moral, this novel is truly contemptible. In one respect, it deserves a severer reproof, and may be styled detestable.'

MR [Andrew Becket]: '*Felo de se.* What may have induced the unhappy gentleman to com-mit so rash an action, we cannot pretend to say. 'Tis pity, however, that his friends did not hin-der him from seizing on that dreadful weapon—a pen*. [footnote]* The hero of this novel, after taking a dose of poison, writes a paltry letter to his friend in justification of the heinous act.'

1788: 12   ANON.

DISINTERESTED LOVE; OR, THE MODERN ROBIN GREY, IN A SERIES OF LETTERS, FOUNDED ON FACTS. IN TWO VOLUMES. BY A WIDOW LADY.

> London: Printed for the Benefit of the Author and Family, and sold by T. Hookham, New Bond Street, 1788.
> I 148p; II 171p. 12mo. 4s sewed (MR), 5s (CR).
> CR 66: 165 (Aug 1788); MR 79: 466 (Nov 1788); AF II: 1101.
> BL 12611.ee.10; EM 175:1; ESTC t057434 (NA CtY, NjP).

Notes. Epistolary.

CR: 'With all our tenderness for these fluttering butterflies of the moment, we are com-pelled to consign the Widow's work to oblivion. With all our regard to disinterested love, we must condemn the present example as the most trifling insipid series of adventures that we ever read.'

MR [Andrew Becket]: 'The story here presented to us is not very interesting: neither is the language at all times sufficiently correct. The performance, however, has the merit of being written in the cause of virtue, and we may therefore recommend it with safety to the youth-ful Reader.'

1788: 13   ANON.

EDWARD AND HARRIET, OR THE HAPPY RECOVERY; A SENTIMEN-TAL NOVEL. IN TWO VOLUMES. BY A LADY. DEDICATED BY PER-MISSION TO HER GRACE THE DUCHESS OF DEVONSHIRE.

> London: Printed for G. Allen, Bookseller, at his Circulating Library, No. 19, Duke's Court, St Martin's Lane; C. Stalker, Stationer's Court, and may be had at every Circulating Library in the Kingdom, 1788.

I 177p; II 181p. 12mo. 5s (CR), 5s sewed (MR), 6s bound (adv.).
CR 65: 324 (Apr 1788); MR 79: 467 (Nov 1788); AF II: 1214.
BL 12611.aaa.17; EM 162: 6; ESTC t080585.

Notes. Epistolary. Prefatory address from the publisher to the reader 1, v–vii. 5 pp. advs. end vol. 2.
Adv. end *The Freaks of Fortune* (1790: 13).

CR: 'These pages of trifling insipidity would deserve contempt only, if their loose morality did not render the offence capital. To confine them to oblivion is a mild punishment; they are already hastening to it. We must condemn them as one of the worst productions, in every view, that we have lately seen.'

MR [Andrew Becket]: 'How long, *O Novelist!* wilt *thou* abuse our patience? How long wilt thou continue to persecute us by the publication of "Nothings," and those too in "so strange a style"—So nonsensically, so stupidly written, that even Laughter is unable to exercise his functions on them.'

THE EFFECTS OF THE PASSIONS
See DUBOIS-FONTANELLE, Joseph-Gaspard

1788: 14   ANON.
ELIZA CLELAND, A NOVEL. IN THREE VOLUMES.

London: Printed for W. Lane, Leadenhall-Street, 1788.
I 205p; II 200p; III 184p. 12mo. 7s 6d (CR), 7s 6d sewed (MR, SDA).
CR 65: 486 (June 1788); MR 81: 183 (Aug 1789); AF II: 1248.
PU Singer-Mend.PR 3991.A1.E436.1788; ESTC n006974.

Notes. By same author as *Edward and Sophia* (1787: 6); *Powis Castle* (1788: 30); *The Predestined Wife* (1789: 22); *Benedicta* (1791: 3); *Ashton Priory* (1792: 2); and *Mariamne* (1793: 8). 2 pp. advs. end vol. 2. Epistolary.
Adv. SDA 3 May 1788.

CR: 'One of the buzzing insects which has received a temporary life from the warmth of a circulating library.... We can find no merit, but a harmless disposition, to induce us to foster and cheer the creature—to bid it live another hour.'

MR [Andrew Becket] confesses to an inability to 'convey to the reader a thorough and competent idea of the *nihility* of this performance'.

EMILIA DE ST AUBIGNE. A NOVEL
See BURKE, Anne

1788: 15   ANON.
FAIRY TALES, SELECTED FROM THE BEST AUTHORS. IN TWO VOLUMES.

London: Printed for W. Lane, Leadenhall-Street, 1788
I 288p; 306p. 12mo. 5s (CR), 5s sewed (MR, LC).
CR 65: 157 (Feb 1788); MR 78: 531 (June 1788); AF II: 1362.
CtY Ib82.T788F; xESTC.

Notes. Frontispiece and ill. both vols; 1-p. table of contents and 1-p. 'Directions for placing the cuts' both vols. 2-pp. introduction (unn.) vol. 1. 2 pp. advs. end vol. 2.

Adv., 'In the Press, and speedily will be published, . . . A Collection of Entertaining Tales of the Fairies; tending to inspire Youth with a Love of Virtue', LC 63: 45 (10–12 Jan 1788); adv. 'Ornamented and enriched with the most elegant and superb engravings, from the original designs of the first masters', LC 63: 140 (7–9 Feb 1788); adv. SDA 3 May 1788.

Further edns: London, 1788, ESTC n008279; London, 1794, ESTC n008278.

MR [Andrew Becket]: 'While we readily acknowlege, with the editor, that these histories are selected from amongst the most considerable of the dealers in *diminutives*, we have little to say in their praise. Fairy Tales were formerly thought to be the proper and almost the only reading for children; it is with much satisfaction, however, that we find them gradually giving way to publications of a far more interesting kind, in which the instruction and entertainment are judiciously blended, without the intermixture of the marvellous, the absurd, and things totally out of nature.'

FATAL FOLLIES
See THOMSON, Anna

FEATURES FROM LIFE; OR, A SUMMER VISIT
See BLOWER, Elizabeth

FREDERIC, OR THE LIBERTINE
See POTTER, John

THE HALF-PAY OFFICER; OR MEMOIRS OF CHARLES CHANCELEY
See HERIOT, John

1788: 16   ANON.
HELENA, A NOVEL. BY A LADY OF DISTINCTION.

> London: Printed for W. Richardson, Royal Exchange, 1788.
> 281p. 12mo. 2s 6d sewed (MR, MC), 3s (CR).
> CR 66: 419 (Nov 1788); MR 80: 169–70 (Feb 1789); AF II: 1880.
> BL N.2205; EM 2071: 5; ESTC t074436 (NA MH-H).

Notes. Adv. MC 14 July 1788.

Further edn: Dublin, 1788 (Printed by Wilson, 1 vol., 12mo), ESTC t210987. German trans. Leipzig and Coburg, 1799 (*Helene oder die Wirkungen der gesunden Vernunft*) (Price).

CR: 'The editor speaks highly of this work; but we cannot follow him in the profusion of his commendations. It is generally unaffected; sometimes interesting; but often dull, and in a few instances, a little improbable.'

MR [Andrew Becket]: 'No! *said we, mentally*, on a perusal of it, this is not the production of a woman of fashion. . . . there is no little degree of merit in this Novel: we mean not in the delineation and force of the characters, but in the several pleasing and truly moral reflections which are scattered through it. We wish this *Lady of distinction* would allow herself a greater portion of time in the finishing of her compositions, so as to give them the correctness they undoubtedly want.'

HELOISE; OR, THE SIEGE OF RHODES
See BERKELEY, George Monck

HENRY AND ISABELLA; OR, A TRAITE THROUGH LIFE
See HUGHES, Anne

1788: 17 ANON.
HISTORIC TALES. A NOVEL. IN TWO VOLUMES.
Dublin: Printed by P. Byrne, (108) Grafton-street, 1788.
I iv, 99p; II 240p. 12mo.
ICN Y155.H61; ESTC t212454.

Notes. Dedication to Lord Carbery 1, iii–iv. Pagination continuous Roman-Arabic; text of vol. 1 begins on p. 5. Paginatiion also continuous between volumes; vol. 2 begins with p. 103. ESTC lists CSmH copy but this is London edn.
Further edn: London, 1790, EM 7473: 11, ESTC t127176.
Dublin edn. not reviewed; 1790 London edn. rev. MR n.s. 2: 464–465 (Aug 1790); AF II: 1951.

MR [John Noorthouck]: 'The same easy plan of making a portion of true history the vehicle of fiction, which we could not commend in the former instance [*The Adventures of John of Gaunt*, 1790: 72], is here pursued. . . . The writer offers this performance as his first essay, and the public will sustain no great loss if it proves to be his last, in this department of writing' (p. 464).

THE HISTORY OF LEONORA MEADOWSON
See HAYWOOD, Eliza

THE HISTORY OF LITTLE JACK
See App. A: 4

THE HISTORY OF SIR CHARLES BENTINCK, BART.
See BROMLEY, Eliza Nugent

1788: 18 ANON.
ILLUSIONS OF SENTIMENT, A DESCRIPTIVE AND HISTORIC NOVEL.
London: Printed for T. Axtell, Cornhill, 1788.
168p. 12mo. 2s sewed (MR).
MR 80: 169 (Feb 1789); AF II: 2153.
O Vet.A5f.2334; ESTC n007616 (BI BL; NA PU).

Notes. Epistolary.
MR [Andrew Becket]: 'Trifling and frothy.'

1788: 19 ANON.
THE INTERESTING STORY OF EDWIN AND JULIA; BEING A RATIONAL AND PHILOSOPHICAL ENQUIRY INTO THE NATURE OF THINGS. IN A SERIES OF LETTERS. BY A DOCTOR OF PHYSIC, M.A. &C.
London: Printed for the Author; and sold by G. Kearsley, Fleet Street, n.d. [1788?].
202p. 12mo. 3s (MR), 3s stitched (t.p.).

MR n.s. 2: 351–2 (July 1790).

BL 12612.df.25; EM 164: 8; ESTC t066908.

Notes. Dedication to 'The Ladies' signed 'A Bachelor'. Text begins on p. 5. Epistolary. Not the same work as *Edwin and Julia* (1774: 7).

Adv. SDA 6 June 1788; sold by G. Kearsley, Fleet-street; Symmons, Paternoster-row; Darton, Birchin-lane; Faulder, bookseller to his Majesty; Booker and Moore, New Bond-street; and H. Jackson and Kerby, Oxford-street; and all other booksellers.

MR [Thomas Ogle]: 'Never did we toil through a more ridiculous compilation of inconsistent and incoherent stuff: a thing without beginning, and without end; equally devoid of form and usefulness' (p. 351).

ISMENE AND ISMENIAS, A NOVEL
See EUSTATHIUS MACREMBOLITES

JAMES WALLACE, A NOVEL
See BAGE, Robert

JULIA DE GRAMONT
See HAWKE, Cassandra

1788: 20   ANON.
*JULIET; OR THE COTTAGER: IN A SERIES OF LETTERS, BY A LADY.

London: W. Lane, Leadenhall-Street (MC), 1788 (MC).

2 vols. 12mo. 5s (CR), 5s sewed (MR and adv).

CR 67: 238 (Mar 1789); MR n.s. 4: 91 (Jan 1791); AF II: 2331.

No copy located.

Notes. Adv. MC 16 Dec 1788; adv., 'New Novel of Sympathy and Affection', SDA 1 Jan 1789. Adv. end of vol. 2 of *The Baron of Manstow* (1790: 4).

CR: 'The adventures are trite, hackneyed, trifling, and insipid: the language is often inaccurate; and, from the whole, we cannot extract a word, a character, or a sentiment that we can commend. There is much faultless dulness, and the morality is sufficiently pure; but "no farther this deponent sayeth."'

MR [John Noorthouck]: '. . . worked up with the old threadbare materials of obdurate unnatural parents, and obstinate cruel guardians, thwarting juvenile attachments, in favour of interested connexions; consequent distresses, and wonderful discoveries, terminating in happy consummations. The *dramatis personae* of these narrations are no sooner brought forward, and their situations unfolded, than a person who is used to them can conjecture the outline of the whole fabrication, and foresee the catastrophe of the piece.'

LAURA: OR LETTERS FROM SOME PERSONS IN SWITZERLAND
See CONSTANT DE REBECQUE, Samuel de

1788: 21   ANON.
THE LIFE OF MISS CATLANE; OR, THE ILL EFFECTS OF A HASTY MARRIAGE. IN A SERIES OF LETTERS. BEING A COMPLETE NARRA-

TIVE OF REAL CHARACTERS. TO WHICH IS ADDED, AN ESSAY ON FALSE FRIENDSHIP; OR SATAN'S EYE TOOTH.

London: Printed for the Author, 1788.
215p. 12mo. 4s 6d half-bound (MR).
MR 80: 442–3 (May 1789).
MH-H *EC75.A100.78812; EM 1284: 16; ESTC n010453 (NA PU).

Notes. Preface iii–iv; introduction v–vii; 16-pp. list of subscribers. Pp. 208–215 are verse. Epistolary.

MR [John Noorthouck] gives Boyter as bookseller and reviews under 'Memoirs': 'So little art is used in working up this story, and we perceive so little of what dramatic writers call plot, that we are induced to suppose it to be formed on a ground-work of truth. . . . The volume is not badly written on the whole; and the prose is much better than some few scattered attempts at poetry.'

MARIA CECILIA
See LAVALLÉE, Joseph

1788: 22 ANON.
MARIA HARCOURT. A NOVEL. IN TWO VOLUMES. WRITTEN IN DAILY JOURNALS. (NEVER BEFORE ATTEMPTED.) BY THE AUTHOR OF LORD WINWORTH, PHEBE, &C.

London: Printed for C. Stalker, Stationers-Court, 1788.
I v, 216p; II 223p. 12mo. 6s (CR), 5s sewed (MR, MC).
CR 66: 576 (App [Dec 1788/Jan 1789]); MR 81: 183 (Aug 1789); AF II: 2711.
BL 12612.aa.18; EM 331: 7; ESTC t064741.

Notes. Lord Winworth 1787: 16; *Phoebe; or Distressed Innocence* 1788: 28. Also by same author: *William and Charles* (1789: 29); *Lucinda Hartley* (1790: 17); and *Frederick and Alicia* (1791: 12).
Prefatory address to readers (iii–v) mentions the success of the author's previous works and the 'many commendations . . . received from the majority of REVIEWERS . . . .' 5 pp. advs. end vol. 2.
Adv. MC 26 Nov 1788.
Further edn: Dublin, 1789 (Printed by John Parker, for Messrs. P. Byrne, P. Wogan, J. Moore, and J. Halpen, 2 vols., 12mo), ESTC n034800.

CR: 'We cannot greatly approve of this plan. If it were new we should condemn it; but Miss Byron's and Clarissa Harlowe's Journals will rise in judgment against the novelty which the title promises. The volumes before us are full of business, without being interesting; they consist of adventures without probability; and of some traits of character, seemingly sketched from the life, without being, in the whole, natural.'

MARY, A FICTION
See WOLLSTONECRAFT, Mary

MELISSA AND MARCIA; OR THE SISTERS
See HERVEY, Elizabeth

1788: 23   ANON.
THE MINOR; OR HISTORY OF GEORGE O'NIAL, ESQ. IN TWO VOLUMES.

>London: Printed for W. Lane, Leadenhall-Street. 1788.
>I 240p; II 240p. 12mo. 5s sewed (MR, LEP), 6s (CR).
>CR 63: 307–8 (Apr 1787); MR 77: 80 (July 1787); AF II: 2883.
>BL 12613.cc.4; EM 291: 4; ESTC t070098 (NA CaAEU, CtY-BR, PU).

Notes. Dedication to A****** D****, Esq; signed 'The Author'.
Greatly post-dated; adv. as published LEP 10–12 Oct 1786.
Further edn: Dublin, 1787 (Printed for Messrs. W. Watson, L. White, S. Colbert, J. Moore and J. Halpen, 2 vols. in 1, no format) (WC), xESTC.

   CR: 'In the middle of the year 1786 we reprehended a publisher for dating his work in 1787 [See 1787: 11]. On this day, the first of April, 1787, we peruse a book of 1788. The editor is right; for few will read it through, and, those who have read it will wish to forget it: of course it will be new in every year of every century. The author seems to design being witty, licentious, and irreligious: we say "seems;" for though we have carefully read this work, in which few will follow us, we cannot be certain of the author's real design.'

   MR [Andrew Becket]: 'In this ill-written book, the Author has represented human nature in the most ugly and unseemly shapes. His persons can only be compared, in filthiness, with the fauns and satyrs of poetic days.'

MISOGUG: OR, WOMEN AS THEY ARE
See CUBIERES-PALMEZEAUX, Michel

THE NEW ROBINSON CRUSOE
See CAMPE, Joachim Heinrich

1788: 24   ANON.
THE NEW SYLPH, OR, GUARDIAN ANGEL. A STORY.

>London: Printed for W. Lane, Leadenhall-Street, 1788.
>196p. 12mo. 2s 6d (CR), 2s 6d sewed (MR, LC).
>CR 65: 486 (June 1788); MR 79: 557 (Dec 1788); AF II: 3053.
>BL G.17719; EM 7375: 2; ESTC t145694 (BI C, REu; NA CtY).

Notes. Text of novel starts on p. 5.
Adv., 'A Novel, on a plan entirely new', LC 63: 285 (20–22 Mar 1788); adv. SDA 3 May 1788.

   CR: 'The whole is too obviously artificial.—Yet the surprizes are sometimes well contrived, and not badly explained, though, in general, this Story has little real merit.'

   MR [Andrew Becket]: 'This little story displays a tolerable share of invention; but the *denouement* is much too easily and too early foreseen. *Ars est celare artem*: the business of art is to conceal art; an observation that holds with respect to every work of fancy, though very rarely attended to.'

ORIGINAL STORIES, FROM REAL LIFE
See WOLLSTONECRAFT, Mary

1788: 25   ANON.

OSWALD CASTLE, OR MEMOIRS OF LADY SOPHIA WOODVILLE; A
NOVEL. IN TWO VOLUMES. BY A LADY.

London: Printed for T. Hookham, New Bond-Street, 1788.
I 319p; II 167p. 12mo. 6s (CR), 6s sewed (MR, SDA).
CR 66: 503 (Dec 1788); MR 80: 169 (Feb 1789); AF II: 3186.
DLC PR3991.A6L32; ESTC n011086 (NA CU-SB).

Notes. Adv. SDA 20 Dec 1788.
Further edn: Dublin, 1789 (Printed for Messrs. Burnet, Gilbert, Byrne, Wogan, Moore,
Halpen and Dornin, 1 vol., 12mo), ESTC n011087.

CR: 'Oswald Castle is a production of the Cecilia school, and so nearly allied to it, that we
cannot pronounce it very new or interesting. The events are not artfully interwoven, nor is
the series always well preserved; the characters are seldom relieved by peculiar features; and
in one or two solitary instances only, do we meet with what was unexpected. Yet with these
faults there is calm dignity in the narrative, and a purity in the sentiments and conduct of the
heroine, that demand our applause: if the work be not very entertaining, it is inoffensive; and,
if not animated, is strictly moral.' [*Cecilia* 1782: 15]

MR [Andrew Becket]: 'Character and incident, the principal and *indubitable* requisites in
novel-writing are not to be found in this performance. The elegant and the tender, however,
are happily blended in it. It is, in short, a very pretty love-story; a story from which our
women may learn, as in a mirrour, to deck themselves with the jewels of virtue and
morality—*the brightest which they can possibly wear.*'

1788: 26   ANON.

THE PALACE OF ENCHANTMENT, OR, ENTERTAINING AND IN-
STRUCTIVE FAIRY TALES: CONTAINING FORTUNIO, PERFECT
LOVE, PRINCESS ROSETTA, WHITE MOUSE, PRINCESS VERENATA,
FLORIO AND FLORELLO, GOLDEN BOUGH, QUEEN & COUNTRY
GIRL, WONDERFUL WAND, KING AND FAIRY RING, PRINCESS
FAIR STAR AND PRINCE CHERY.

London: Printed for W. Lane, Leadenhall-Street, 1788.
ii, 306p. 12mo.
CLU-S/C CBC 77329; ESTC n011188 (BI O; NA MH-H).

Notes. Engraved frontispiece; preface i–ii. 2 pp. advs. end vol.
Further edn: London, 1794, ESTC n011189.

1788: 27   ANON.

*THE PENITENT PROSTITUTE: OR, THE HISTORY OF MISS JULIA
FRANK; WRITTEN BY HERSELF.

London: Scatcherd and Whitaker, 1788.
1 vol. Crown 8vo (LC), 12mo (CR, MR). 2s 6d (CR, MR).
CR 66: 576 (App [Dec 1788/Jan 1789]); MR 80: 87–8 (Jan 1789); AF II: 3293.
No copy located.

Notes. Adv., with comment from MR, LC 65: 598 (20–23 June 1789).

CR: 'A common tale, we fear too common, eked out with trite hackneyed reflections, news-paper essays, and trifling episodes. But the author enlists on the side of virtue; and we respect the meanest pioneer of that camp.'

MR [John Noorthouck]: 'Though the subject of this tale may not be the most delicate to put into a young lady's hand, a novel-reading lady may peruse it with more profit than many of those that exhibit vices in too favourable a light' (p. 88).

1788: 28   ANON.
*PHOEBE; OR DISTRESSED INNOCENCE.

> London: Printed for C. Stalker, No. 4, Stationers-Court, Ludgate-street; Kirkman and
>   Oney, No. 79, Fleet-street, and sold by all other booksellers (MC), 1788 (MC).
> 2 vols. 12mo. 5s sewed (MR, CR), 6s bound (adv.).
> CR 65: 150–51 (Feb 1788); MR 80: 169 (Feb 1789); AF II: 3332.
> No copy located.

Notes. By same author as *Lord Winworth* (1787: 16); *Maria Harcourt* (1788: 22); *William and Charles* (1789: 29); *Lucinda Hartley* (1790: 17); and *Frederick and Alicia* (1791: 12).

Adv., with heading 'Interesting Sorrow' and title *Phebe: or, Distressed Innocence. A Novel. In Two Volumes*, MC 12 Jan 1788: 'The circumstances which gave birth to the above novel, are founded on facts which lately occurred. A young Lady is involved in all the horrors of disappointment, her fortitude under which must delightfully entertain and agreeably instruct.'

Adv., as *Phoebe, a Novel*, at end *The Freaks of Fortune* (1790: 13).

CR: 'The reader, who can pursue the adventures of Phoebe in this strange and intricate contexture of events, must be capable of much patient attention; and, for those who can employ the necessary time in the enquiry, we anxiously wish a better employment. After much care, and a scrupulous examination, we gave up the cause as hopeless: of course, we cannot decide on the probability of the narrative. Every thing is designed, as Bayes says, to elevate and surprize.'

MR [Andrew Becket]: 'What a jumble of absurdity is here!'

1788: 29   ANON.
THE PLEASING COMPANION, A COLLECTION OF FAIRY TALES, CALCULATED TO IMPROVE THE HEART: THE WHOLE FORMING A SYSTEM OF MORAL PRECEPTS AND EXAMPLES, FOR THE CONDUCT OF YOUTH THROUGH LIFE: CONTAINING PRINCESS HEBE & ANGUILETTA GRACIOSA AND PERCINET STORY OF FINETTA PRINCESS CARPILONA STORY OF THE WHITE CAT YELLOW DWARF PIDGEON AND DOVE YOUNG AND HANDSOME ORNAMENTED WITH ELEGANT CUTS.

> London: Printed for W. Lane, Leadenhall-Street, 1788.
> 288p. 12mo.
> MH-H *EC75.A100.788p2; EM 1284: 19; ESTC n012176.

Notes. ESTC: Some tales are from Marie Catherine La Mothe, Countess d'Aulnoy's *Contes de fees.*

Illustrations. 2-pp. preface (unn.).

Further edns: London, n.d. [1790?], ESTC t137687; London, 1794, EM 7445: 4, ESTC 077513.

1788: 30   ANON.
POWIS CASTLE, OR ANECDOTES OF AN ANTIENT FAMILY. IN TWO VOLUMES.

London: Printed for W. Lane, Leadenhall-Street, 1788.
I 216p; II 208p. 12mo. 5s (CR), 5s sewed (MR, SDA).
CR 65: 484 (June 1788); MR 81: 182 (Aug 1789); AF II: 3562.
MH-H *EC75.A100.788p; EMf; ESTC n020868 (BI AWn; NA IU, ViU).

Notes. By same author as *Edward and Sophia* (1787: 6); *Eliza Cleland* (1788: 14); *The Predestined Wife* (1789: 22); *Benedicta* (1791: 3); *Ashton Priory* (1792: 2); and *Mariamne* (1793: 8).
Adv. SDA 3 May 1788.

CR: 'The first volume is artless and pleasing: the second is of very inferior value. . . . There are many trifling errors in language and circumstances, which leads us to think that the author's knowlege and experience have received very little cultivation.'

MR [Andrew Becket]: 'It is . . . composed of such flimsy materials, that should the artillery of criticism be brought to bear against it, the place would be immediately demolished.'

1788: 31   ANON.
THE PUPIL OF ADVERSITY, AN ORIENTAL TALE. IN TWO VOLUMES.

London: Printed for W. Lane, Leadenhall-Street, 1788.
I 166p; II 170p. 12mo. 5s (CR), 5s sewed (MR, adv.).
CR 66: 420 (Nov 1788); MR 81: 564–5 (Dec 1789); AF II: 3639.
BL 12653.aaa.20; EM 222: 5; ESTC t107619.

Notes. Adv. end vol. 3 of *Darnley Vale* (1789: 33).
German trans. Gera, 1792 (*Der Zögling des Unglücks; eine arabische Erzählung*) (EAG).

CR: 'This is a fairy tale, an allegorical history, with some political reflections, applicable to the present period. Together it affords an olio neither very consistent, interesting, or pleasing.'

MR [Andrew Becket]: 'Under colour of an *Oriental*Tale, we are here presented with a view of some political *manoeuvres* which, *in this country*, have been played off with success. . . . This performance, however, is not political throughout. The chapters which speak of the power of the *Fairy of Adversity* exhibit a considerable portion of fancy: and had the judgment of the author been equal to it, he would not have *scattered* the real and the fictitious through his pages, in the way that he has done—but rather have endeavoured to *blend* them so as to give a kind of verisimilitude to the whole.'

THE RAMBLE OF PHILO, AND HIS MAN STURDY
See NIXON, Capt

RETRIBUTION. BY THE AUTHOR OF THE GAMESTERS
See MACKENZIE, Anna Maria

1788: 32   ANON.
SAINT JULIAN'S ABBEY. A NOVEL. IN A SERIES OF LETTERS. IN TWO VOLUMES.

London: Printed for W. Lane, Leadenhall-Street, 1788.

I 237p; II 220p. 12mo. 5s (CR), 5s sewed (MR, MC, adv.).

CR 66: 255 (Sept 1788); MR n.s. 4: 91 (Jan 1791); AF II: 3929.

BL 12611.a.17; EM 4373: 9; ESTC t107707 (NA CaOTU, IaU, PU).

Notes. Epistolary.

Adv. MC 16 Dec 1788.

Adv. end vol. 2 of *Darnley Vale* (1789: 33).

CR: 'These volumes are in the modern dress, but the story is old; the manners are those of the last century. Though there is much murder, there is scarcely any pathos: St. Julian's abbey may amuse a winter's evening, if the reader looks not for probability, and is not disgusted by absurdity.'

MR [John Noorthouck]: '. . . there may be novel-readers who can relish any trumpery about love, ratsbane, and daggers.'

THE SCHOOL CANDIDATES, A PROSAIC BURLESQUE
See CLARKE, Henry

1788: 33   ANON.
THE SCHOOL FOR FATHERS; OR, THE VICTIM OF A CURSE. A NOVEL. CONTAINING AUTHENTIC MEMOIRS AND ANECDOTES, WITH HISTORICAL FACTS. IN THREE VOLUMES.

London: Printed for G. G. J. and J. Robinson, Paternoster Row, 1788.

I 255p; II 264p; III 288p. 12mo. 7s 6d sewed (MR), 9s (CR), 9s sewed (LEP, SJC).

CR 65: 74–5 (Jan 1788); MR 78: 250–2 (Mar 1788); AF II: 3969.

BL 12614.bb.23; EM 288: 6; ESTC t071390 (BI O, BMu; NA ICN, MH-H, NjP, ViU &c.).

Notes. Robinson paid 15 gns. to S. (or F.?) Boldero on 18 Oct 1787 for *The Victim of a Curse, a Novel* (RA).

Epistolary.

Adv., 'will speedily be published', LEP 27–29 Nov 1787; adv. as published SJC 22–25 Dec 1787.

Further edn: Dublin, 1788 (Printed for Messrs. Chamberlain, Moncrieffe, Byrne, Lewis, Moore and Halpen, 2 vols., 12mo), ESTC n021573.

CR: 'It is perhaps, as the editor observes, of no great consequence whether a novel be really authentic: it is read with avidity, and while it gives a faithful picture of real life, the authenticity of its materials are of little comparative importance. The letters, however, of which these volumes in a great degree consist, we believe to be genuine. They are simply elegant and neat, without adventitious ornaments' (p. 74).

MR [Andrew Becket]: 'This publication is very improperly styled a novel. It almost wholly consists of the letters of two unfortunate lovers, who are separated by the ill-timed ambition of their friends. . . . were some of the letters rejected, and the volumes, which now are three in number, compressed into one, the book might be deserving of public attention; but to wade through two or three hundred pages of such trifling and puerility . . . requires all the patience of a Reviewer.'

1788: 34   ANON.
THE SCHOOL FOR TUTORS. CONSISTING OF A SERIES OF CORRESPONDENCE CHIEFLY BETWEEN A YOUNG GENTLEMAN AND HIS

TUTOR. WRITTEN BY A LADY, SINCE DECEASED, THE AUTHORESS OF SEVERAL FORMER PUBLICATIONS.

> London: Printed for William Flexney, Holborn, 1788.
> xvi, 208p. 8vo [MR has 12mo]. 2s 6d sewed (MR, MC).
> MR 79: 466 (Nov 1788).
> BL 1608/5418; EM 6534: 4; ESTC t121203 (NA IU, PPL).

Notes. Preface v–xvi. Epistolary.
Adv. MC 31 May 1788.

   MR [Andrew Becket]: 'This little volume is said to be the production of a lady, and there is no sort of reason to question it. It is written in the slight and extravagant style so fashionable with the modern female novelist.... To the *morality* of this performance we must give our praise.'

THE SOLICITUDES OF ABSENCE
See RENWICK, William

1788: 35   ANON.
*SOPHIA; OR, THE EMBARRASSED WIFE. CONTAINING THE HISTORY OF MIRA, THE NEW FOUNDLING. A NOVEL. BY A LADY. BEING HER FIRST LITERARY ATTEMPT. DEDICATED TO HER GRACE THE DUCHESS OF DEVONSHIRE.

> London: Printed for G. Allen, 1788.
> 2 vols. 12mo. 5s (CR), 5s sewed (MR).
> CR 65: 486–87 (June 1788); MR 80: 88 (Jan 1789); AF II: 4185.
> No copy located.

Notes. Epistolary.
Further edn: London, 1788, ESTC n046408.

   CR: 'Is this then, madam, your *first* attempt? It is indeed, gentlemen; I hope that it has met with your approbation: what think you of its execution? Our opinion of its execution is such, that we sincerely hope you never will make a second trial. You have punished us sufficiently, by leading us through two volumes of insipid trifling.'

   MR [Andrew Becket]: '*Noli me tangere:* Touch me not—I shall be nothing the better for handling. Criticism, too, should be otherwise employed.'

1788: 36   ANON.
*SYDNEY PLACE; OR THE BRACELET.

> London: William Lane, Leadenhall-street (SDA), 1788.
> 2 vols. 12mo. 5s (CR), 5s sewed (MR, LC).
> CR 65: 236–7 (Mar 1788); MR 79: 466 (Nov 1788).
> No copy located.

Notes. Adv. LC 63: 285 (20–22 Mar 1788) and SDA 3 June 1788: *Sidney Place.*

   CR: 'This novel is, in many respects, superior to the numerous race of its companions; yet the author stoops with too much servility to the usual inartificial expedients of common authors.'

   MR [Andrew Becket] gives a sarcastic summary of the plot and concludes: 'It is but justice to acknowlege, that this production is superior, in point of composition, to the motley, we had almost said the undefinable tribe to which it belongs.'

1788: 37   ANON.
*TALES: ENTERTAINING AND SYMPATHETIC: INSCRIBED TO THE
HEART.

> London: Lane.
> 2 vols. 12mo. 5s (CR), 5s sewed (MR, advs.).
> CR 66: 255 (Sept 1788); MR n.s. 1: 331 (Mar 1790); AF II: 4337.
> No copy located.

Notes. Adv., as *Tales Entertaining and Pathetic; Inscribed to the Heart*, end of *Memoirs and Opinions of Mr Blenfield* (1790: 20) and as by the same author. Adv., as *Tales of Sympathy, Inscribed to the Heart*, end vol. 3 of *Darnley Vale* (1789: 33).

CR: 'We suspect that these tales are collected from some old Magazines: we can describe them only by negatives. They are not entertaining or sympathetic; they can neither affect the heart or the head: in short, we have scarcely ever seen a collection so insipid and uninteresting.'

MR [William Enfield]: 'These volumes are not improperly characterized in their title. The tales, though short and unconnected, are written in a manner well adapted to amuse the fancy, and interest the feelings.'

A TOUR, SENTIMENTAL AND DESCRIPTIVE
See App. B: 10

1788: 38   ANON.
THE TWIN SISTERS; OR, THE EFFECTS OF EDUCATION: A NOVEL;
IN A SERIES OF LETTERS. BY A LADY.

> [London]: Printed for T. Hookham, New Bond Street, 1788/89.
> I (1788) 252p; II (1788) 235p; III (1788) 237p; IV (1789) 240p. 12mo. 7s 6d sewed (CR),
>   9s sewed (MR, MC) vols. 1–3; 2s 6d (CR) vol. 4.
> CR 66: 419 (Nov 1788) vols. 1–3; MR 80: 88–9 (Jan 1789) vols. 1–3; CR 68: 495 (App
>   1789) vol. 4; AF II: 4557, 4558.
> CLU-S/C PR 3991.A6L 1437; EMf; ESTC n026331 (NA CtY, DLC, MH-H &c.).

Notes. On first recto following t.p. vol. 4: 'The three first Letters (owing to the publication of this, after the other volumes) are not properly disposed; they should have been placed between the last Letters in the Third Volume.' Epistolary.
Adv., 'In Three Volumes', MC 9 June 1788.
Further edn: Dublin, 1792 (Printed for H. Colbert, 3 vols., 12mo), EM 278: 2, ESTC t064187.

CR 66: 'So far as we have seen, the work is not written by a common hand. There is novelty in the remarks, and a neatness in the language, which seems to imply an author out of the usual line.'

MR 80 [Andrew Becket]: 'The production of a young woman fresh from the perusal of Pamela and Clarissa. There is a good deal of fancy, and many indications of real abilities both in the conduct of the fable and in the drawing of the characters' (p. 88).

CR 68: 'To return to a former work, where repetition has blunted the edge of curiosity, and a knowledge of the event has weakened the interest, is an unpleasing task: the author's delay of the fourth volume of this work must be consequently pronounced an impolitic measure. Perhaps it may be owing to these circumstances that we found the volume before us heavy, languid, and uninteresting. . . .'

THE UNFORTUNATE LOVERS
See WRIGHT, George

1788: 39   ANON.
*THE VICTIM OF DECEPTION.
> London: Printed for W. Lane, Leadenhall-street (LC), 1788 (LC).
> 2 vols. 12mo. 5s sewed (MR, LC).
> MR 79: 172 (Aug 1788).
> No copy located.

Notes. Epistolary.
Adv., 'A Tale of Woe and Sympathetic Distress LC 63: 116 (31 Jan–2 Feb 1788); *The Victim of Deception. A Novel. In a Series of Letters.*

MR [Andrew Becket]: '. . . the woman who rises from the study of his pages with an unheated imagination, may safely sit down to the perusal of *Therese Philosophe.*'
[For more information about the famed French pornographic novel *Thérèse Philosophe*, see Darnton, *Forbidden Best-Sellers.*]

1788: 40   ANON.
THE WIDOW OF KENT; OR, THE HISTORY OF MRS ROWLEY. A NOVEL. IN TWO VOLUMES.
> London: Printed for F. Noble, No. 324, Holborn, 1788.
> I 236p; II 250p. 12mo. 6s (CR), 5s sewed (MR).
> CR 64: 481 (Dec 1787); MR 79: 171–2 (Aug 1788); AF II: 4792.
> BL 12611.aaa.23; EM 125: 3; ESTC t108472 (NA CLU-S/C, PU).

Notes. CR: 'The author of this novel excels, if he excels at all, in the pathetic. The characters are not always drawn from nature, and the conduct of the story is highly improbable. Yet a few pathetic strokes interspersed, some little knowledge of the human heart, and a connected train of events, arrest the attention, and interest the feelings, in spite of the judgment.'

MR: 'This novel may be perused with advantage by every woman in the situation of our heroine. . . .'

1788: 41   ATKINS, Harriot Westrop.
THE VALE OF IRVIN; OR, MEMOIRS OF THE COUNTESS OF DOU-GLASS. IN A SERIES OF LETTERS TO MISS CHARLOTTE ALDERSEY, ALDERSEY CASTLE, WALES. BY MISS HARRIOT WESTROP ATKINS.
> Cork: Printed for the Authoress, by James P. Trant No. 3, Academy-Street, 1788.
> I 74p; II 68p. 12mo.
> D I 6551 Cork Vol. 1 and 2 1788; ESTC t193197.

Notes. 2-pp. preface (unn.). Epistolary.

1788: 42   [BAGE, Robert].
JAMES WALLACE, A NOVEL, BY THE AUTHOR OF MOUNT-HENNETH, BARHAM-DOWNS, AND THE FAIR SYRIAN. IN THREE VOLUMES.
> London: Printed for William Lane, Leadenhall-Street, 1788.
> I [288]p; II [287]p; III 272p. 12mo. 9s (CR), 9s sewed (MR, CR, adv.).

CR 67: 76–7 (Jan 1789); MR 80: 499–502 (June 1789); AF II: 192.
BL C.192.a.152; EM 8836: 4; ESTC t118424 (NA ICU, NjP, NNU).

Notes. Pages missing in BL copy after p. 284 in vol. 1 and p. 286 in vol. 2 (checked against facsimile from ICU copy). Epistolary.
Mount Henneth; 1782: 12 *Barham Downs* 1784: 11; *The Fair Syrian* 1787: 28.
Adv. MC 16 Dec 1788.
Adv. end vol. 3 of *Darnley Vale* (1789: 33).
Further edns: French trans. Brussels and Paris, 1789 (*La constance dans l'adversité ou l'histoire de James Wallace*) (BGR); London, 1821/24 (WC); NSTC lists edn. in 1824. Facs: N.

CR: '. . . it is interesting, well conducted, and generally pleasing; but we must add, that if the author does not vary his manner, we would advise him to be contented with his former reputation, and urge his fate no further. Few have possessed more genius, and few have exhausted their strength sooner; though, perhaps, there is as great a distance between Fielding's Amelia and Tom Jones, as between this work and Barham Downs' (p. 77).

MR [Andrew Becket]: 'There is much eccentricity about him. It may be remarked, moreover, that he paints with boldness; but sometimes, and more especially in the present instance, rather too coarsely.—In a word, there is evidently more of *genius* in his compositions than of *taste*. But, notwithstanding the objection . . . as to the *finishing* of this performance, the story of it is not uninteresting, and it is conducted with no little degree of art' (p. 500).

1788: 43   [BERKELEY, George Monck].
HELOISE: OR, THE SIEGE OF RHODES. A LEGENDARY TALE. BY THE AUTHOR OF MARIA: OR, THE GENEROUS RUSTIC.

London: for T. Forbes, C. Elliot and T. Kay, P. McQueen, T. and J. Egerton, Shepperdson and Reynold, C. Stalker, C. Rann, Oxford; Todd. York; and C. Elliot, Edinburgh, 1788.
I x, 109p; II 139p. 8vo. 3s 6d (CR), 3s 6d boards (MR); CR has 'vol. 1'.
CR 65: 485 (June 1788); MR 79: 84 (July 1788); AF II: 307.
CSmH 356494; ESTC n033118 (NA CtY).

Notes. Dedication to the Honourable Mrs Ward. Preface i–ix, Oxford, 21 Dec 1787. Text of novel ends on p. 137, followed by blank verso and 1 p. advs. for books sold by Forbes. Vol. 2 lacks t.p.
Maria, or the Generous Rustic 1784: 12.
Further edns: London, 1788, ESTC n033119; London, 1788, ESTC t074656; London, 1788, EM 5520: 3, ESTC t144577; Dublin, 1789 (Printed by P. Byrne, 2 vols., 12mo), ESTC t182126. German trans. Leipzig, 1789 (*Heloise oder Die Belagerung von Rhodus*) (Price).

CR: 'Legendary Tales are seldom executed very happily; and we cannot highly commend the Siege of Rhodes. The narrative is sometimes interesting, but it hurries too hastily along to be very affecting, while the story of the siege has been admirably told already in the page of history. There are a few brilliant passages, and a few anachronisms, interspersed, though the latter are not very glaring, nor do they greatly lessen the pleasure of the reader.'

MR [Christopher Lake Moody]: 'The practice of virtue is here inculcated, and the truth of imitation preserved. The scene is laid in the days of chivalry, and the adventures are such as might happen in feudal times. The incidents are contrived with art; the diction is elegant, yet natural; the sentiments are always interesting, often pathetic, and sometimes sublime.'

1788: 44 [BLOWER, Elizabeth].
FEATURES FROM LIFE; OR, A SUMMER VISIT. BY THE AUTHOR OF GEORGE BATEMAN, AND MARIA. IN TWO VOLUMES.

> London: Printed for G. Kearsley, 46, Fleet-Street, 1788.
> I ii, 252p; II 192p. 12mo. 5s sewed (CR), 6s sewed (MR), 6s (MC).
> CR 66: 73–4 (July 1788); MR 78: 531 (June 1788); AF II: 382.
> BL 1607/1992; EM 3323: 1; ESTC t118914 (NA CLU-S/C, IU).

Notes. Vol. 1 of BL copy lacks t.p. Dedication to Mrs Hastings i–ii, signed 'The Author'. Half-page adv. concludes p. 252 of vol. 1.
George Bateman 1782: 14; *Maria* 1785: 23.
Adv., 'This morning will be published', MC 16 Feb 1788.
Further edns: London, 1788 (Bodl.); Dublin, 1788 (Printed for Messrs. Byrne, Wogan, Halpen, Moore, Jones, and Dornin, 2 vols., 12mo), ESTC n031352. German trans. dated as Leipzig, 1787 (*Der Sommerbesuch*) (Price); French trans. Paris, 1788 (*La Visite d'été, ou portraits modernes*) (BN).

CR: 'The author has sketched an outline from fashionable features, and delineated the conjugal misfortunes which arise from the fascination of novelty, joined to want of confidence. Her outline may be, and we believe is real; but it is coloured by fancy, and sometimes finished unequally.'

MR [Andrew Becket]: 'The moral inculcated in this performance—*a steady and undeviating perseverance in the path of honour*—deserves particular praise; and the language, some few *ladyisms* excepted, is sufficiently pleasing and correct.'

1788: 45 [BROMLEY, Eliza Nugent].
THE HISTORY OF SIR CHARLES BENTINCK, BART. AND LOUISA CAVENDISH. A NOVEL, IN THREE VOLUMES. BY THE AUTHOR OF LAURA AND AUGUSTUS.

> London: Printed for T. Hookham, New-Bond Street, n.d. [ESTC: 1785?].
> I 239p; II 245p; III 244p. 12mo. 7s 6d (CR), 7s 6d sewed (MR).
> CR 67: 237–38 (Mar 1789); MR 81: 182 (Aug 1789); AF II: 477.
> O 256f.2558-2560; ESTC n053305 (NA CLU-S/C).

Notes. Author attribution: FC. ESTC: Sometimes attributed to Eliza Nugent Bromley.
2-pp. adv. for Hookham's circulating library end vol. 2. Epistolary. Text of novel starts on p. 13 in vol. 1 and p. 5 in vols. 2 and 3.
Laura and Augustus 1784: 13.
Adv., 'In a few days will be published', SDA 20 Dec 1788.

CR: 'We can perceive nothing in this history but a series of improbabilities, which constantly disgust, and of those trite hackneyed adventures which have been often related, and which have often lulled us to rest.'
MR [Andrew Becket]: 'A trifling, ill-written work.'

1788: 46 [BURKE, Anne].
EMILIA DE ST AUBIGNE. A NOVEL. BY THE AUTHOR OF ELA, OR THE DELUSIONS OF THE HEART.

London: Printed for C. Elliot, and T. Kay, opposite Somerset-Place, Strand, and C. Elliot, Edinburgh, 1788.

221p. 12mo. 2s 6d (CR), 3s sewed (MR, SJC).

CR 65: 484 (June 1788); MR 80: 364 (Mar 1789); AF II: 542.

BL 1607/2504; EM 4366: 12; ESTC t119153 (NA NcU).

Notes. Post-dated; adv. as published SJC 11–13 Dec 1787.

Re-adv., 'On Monday next, will be published . . . Elegantly printed on a superfine paper', MC 11 Apr 1788 and LC 63: 356 (10–12 Apr 1788).

Ela 1787: 32.

Further edn: Dublin, 1788 (Printed for P. Byrne, P. Wogan, J. Jones, J. Halpen, and B. Dornin, 1 vol., 12mo), EM 1001: 10, ESTC n001568. French trans. London and Paris, 1789 (*Emilie Fairville ou la philosophie du sentiment*) (BGR).

CR: 'We cannot highly commend the moral tendency of the conduct of this work. Some parts contain natural and unaffected descriptions; but the story is sometimes improbable, and often obscure.'

MR [Andrew Becket]: 'The author, apparently without intending it, is an advocate, or apologist, for vice. . . . The story comes not within the line of probability; but the sentiments arising from the situations of the several personages, are sometimes forcible and just.'

1788: 47	[CAMPE, Joachim Heinrich].

THE NEW ROBINSON CRUSOE; AN INSTRUCTIVE AND ENTER-TAINING HISTORY, FOR THE USE OF CHILDREN OF BOTH SEXES. TRANSLATED FROM THE FRENCH. EMBELLISHED WITH THIRTY-TWO BEAUTIFUL CUTS.

London: Printed for John Stockdale, opposite Burlington House, Piccadilly, 1788.

I 173p; II 156p; III 137p; IV 177p. 12mo. 6s sewed (MR).

MR n.s. 1: 108 (Jan 1790); AF II: 597.

BL 635.c.27–28; EM 6121: 4; ESTC t144879 (NA CaOTP, CLU-S/C, IU, &c.; EA ZWTU).

Notes. Translated from *Le Nouveau Robinson* (Paris, 1785), a French version of the German original, *Robinson der Jüngere* (Hamburg, 1779–80).

Preface 1, 5–22; text of novel starts on p. 23. In vols. 2, 3 and 4 text of novel starts on p. 3. Illustrations. 9 pp. advs. end vol. 4.

Further edns: London, 1789, EM 4441: 3, ESTC t153079; London, 1789, ESTC t138331; London, 1789, ESTC n020062; Dublin, 1789 (Printed by W. Colles, 1 vol., 12mo), ESTC n020064; Boston, 1790, ESTC w030128; 4 further entries in ESTC; WC has 25 entries between 1800 and 1850; NSTC lists abridged edns. in 1822 and 1827.

MR [George Edward Griffiths]: 'Mr Campe is of opinion, that the original life of Robinson Crusoe is particularly defective in allowing him, when cast on the desart island, European tools, instruments and necessaries. He, therefore, in this work, throws his hero on an island entirely destitute of those aids; and thence places, in a striking point of view, the ingenuity of man in overcoming the greatest difficulties. In this idea we certainly agree with Mr Campe. . . . we think ourselves warranted in recommending it to parents and instructors of youth; at the same time remarking, that it ought not to be skimmed over, as a book of entertainment only, but *studied* as a work uniting that quality with a very considerable degree of instruction.'

1788: 48   [CLARKE, Henry].
THE SCHOOL CANDIDATES, A PROSAIC BURLESQUE: OCCASIONED BY THE LATE ELECTION OF A SCHOOLMASTER. AT THE VILLAGE OF BOUDINNOIR.

Utopia [ESTC: i.e. Manchester]: Printed in the Year 1788.
103p. 12mo. MR gives no price.
MR 81: 375 (Oct 1789).
BL 12330.aa.17; EM 634: 13; ESTC t128839 (BI C, MRu, O; NA CSmH, MH-H).

Notes. 3-leaf folding plate frontispiece. Dedication 'To the Honourable and Learned Fraternity of Pedagogues'. 5 pp. of 'Fabulae Interlocutores', table of contents and 'Hoq Quid Sit?'. Text starts on p. 7. 2 pp. advs. end.

MR: 'Learned wit, but too obscure, both in subject and satire, for the generality of readers:—to confess the truth, the work is not very clearly understood, even by US!!'

1788: 49   [CONSTANT DE REBECQUE, Samuel de].
*LAURA: OR LETTERS FROM SOME PERSONS IN SWITZERLAND. BY THE AUTHOR OF CAMILLE.

London: Printed for T. Hookham, New Bond-street (SDA), 1788.
4 vols. 12mo. 10s (CR), 10s sewed (MR, SDA, adv.).
CR 65: 239 (Mar 1788); MR 78: 442 (May 1788); AF II: 2473.
No copy located.

Notes. Trans. of *Laure, ou Lettres de quelques femmes de Suisse* (Geneva and Paris, 1786). *Camille, ou lettres de deux filles de ce siècle* (Paris, 1785?) is not, as F. G. Black states erroneously, the same work as *Camilla; or, the Correspondence of a Deceased Friend* (1785: 4).
Adv. SDA 20 Dec 1788.
Adv. end vol. 3 of *Edelfrida* (1792: 7).

CR: 'In the original, we thought these Letters agreeable and entertaining: in the translation they lose much of their power to please, from the aukwardness rather than the incorrectness of the language. The translator cannot, however, deprive the reader of many judicious reflections; nor will his unskilfulness, on the whole, prevent these Letters from being read with some satisfaction and information. The characters and manners, though they may appear to be peculiar, are faithfully drawn, and well supported: to young ladies, in particular, these volumes afford many salutary lessons.'

MR [Andrew Becket]: 'Wrapped in the clouds of a faulty and inelegant version, it is scarcely possible to determine on the particular merits of the work. The hand of a master, however, is discoverable in it. We do not remember to have seen the progress of love in the female breast so delicately and artfully represented since the productions of Richardson and J. J. Rousseau. ... Some excellent political reflections are likewise scattered through these volumes, not unworthy the attention of lawgivers, and rulers of states.'

1788: 50   [CUBIERES-PALMEZEAUX, Michel].
MISOGUG: OR, WOMEN AS THEY ARE. A CHALDEAN TALE. TRANSLATED FROM THE FRENCH. IN TWO VOLUMES.

London: Printed for C. Elliot and T. Kay, No. 332, Strand; and C. Elliot, Edinburgh, 1788.

I 252p; II 247p. 12mo. 6s (CR), 5s sewed (MR, MC).
CR 66: 577 (App [Dec 1788/Jan 1789]); MR n.s. 5: 226 (June 1791); AF II: 948.
BL 12614.cc.9; EM 230: 4; ESTC t071298 (BI E; NA CLU-S/C).

Notes. Trans. of *Misogug, ou les femmes comme elles sont* (Paris, 1787).
Adv. SDA 27 Oct 1788; adv. MC 29 Oct 1788.

CR: 'The oriental tales in French are obvious disguises to conceal satire, irreligion, and indecency. The latter only in this work is violated, and not very offensively. The different adventures are related with some pleasantry, though with great improbability; and some anecdotes of the late king of Prussia, as well as other eminent men, are inserted. Their speeches and actions are attributed to Misogug.'

MR [William Enfield]: 'The writer, with more invention than delicacy, carries his hero through a series of adventures, in order to convince him, from experience, of the frailty of the female sex. The work is *not* one of those novels which we should recommend to our young readers, for the improvement of their morals.'

DAY, Thomas, **THE HISTORY OF LITTLE JACK**
See App. A: 4

1788: 51   [DUBOIS-FONTANELLE, Joseph-Gaspard].
THE EFFECTS OF THE PASSIONS, OR MEMOIRS OF FLORICOURT.
FROM THE FRENCH. IN THREE VOLUMES.

London: Printed for the Proprietor; and sold by T. Vernor, Bookseller, Birchin-Lane,
    Cornhill, 1788.
I 202p; II 284p; III 214p. 12mo. 9s (CR), 9s sewed (MR), 9s (LEP).
CR 65: 150 (Feb 1788); MR 79: 83–4 (July 1788); AF II: 1162.
BL 12518.aaa.2; EM 55: 2; ESTC t129714.

Notes. Trans. of *Les effets des passions* (London and Paris, 1768).
ESTC gives name as Jean-Gaspard; BN as Joseph-Gaspard.
Adv., 'Next Week will be published', LEP 18–20 Dec 1787; adv. adds 'A Remark made by a Person who perused this Work: "he who wishes to trace the Workings of the Passions, and the Effects produced by them, let him read FLORICOURT."'
Further edn: Dublin, 1789 (Printed for Messrs. H. Chamberlaine, P. Byrne, P. Wogan, J. Halpen, and B. Dornin, 2 vols., 12mo), ESTC t203507.

CR: 'There is ... no considerable merit in the whole; and the work can only appear in a very advantageous light, when placed near the miserable trash which we have received under the title of Novels.'

MR [Andrew Becket]: 'Our friends and neighbours the French (we date our friendship from the settling of the commercial treaty), have ever, in their writings, represented the passions with a more than ordinary degree of skill. In proof of this we may refer to the romances of J. J. Rousseau, Crebillon, le Jeune, the Abbé Prevost, &c. &c. In the present performance, the wild and ungovernable impulses of youth, together with their consequences, are delineated with considerable fire and spirit. The writer is evidently a person of sensibility, and a nice observer of the conduct of mankind.'

1788: 52   [EUSTATHIUS MACREMBOLITES]; LE MOINE, L. H. (*trans.*).
ISMENE AND ISMENIAS, A NOVEL TRANSLATED FROM THE FRENCH

BY L. H. LE MOINE, ESQ: FIRST VALET DE CHAMBRE OF HIS MOST CHRISTIAN MAJESTY.

London: Et se trouve a Paris, Chez Cazin, rue des Maçons, N°. 31, 1788.
xi, 199p. 12mo.
BL 12410.c.2; EM 1: 8; ESTC t112791 (BI O; NA CLU-S/C, CSmH; EA P).

Notes. ESTC: Probably printed in Paris; the original is *To Kath' Husmenen kai Husmenian drama.*
French version, *Les amours d'Ismene et d'Isémenias* (1783), trans. by P. F. Godart de Beauchamps.
Prefatory advertisement v–viii; dedication to the Queen ix–xi, signed Le Moine.

1788: 53   GIBBES, P[hebe].
THE NIECE; OR, THE HISTORY OF SUKEY THORNBY. A NOVEL. IN THREE VOLUMES. BY MRS P. GIBBES. AUTHOR OF THE HISTORY OF LADY LOUISA STROUD.

London: Printed for F. Noble, At his Circulating Library, No. 324, Holborn, 1788.
I 239p; II 240p; III 211p. 12mo. 9s (CR), 9s sewed (MR), 7s 6d sewed or 10s 6d calf lettered (LEP).
CR 64: 481 (Dec 1787); MR 78: 441 (May 1788); AF II: 1607.
BL 12611.bbb.12; EM 7939: 2; ESTC t154849 (NA CaOHM, PU).

Notes. 1-p. (unn.) list of 'Names of the Characters in this Novel' beginning each vol. 2-pp. preface vol. 1, signed P. Gibbes, claims 'a plan *entirely new*': 'it would not be any impropriety if it were called "A Dramatic Novel"'. 1 p advs. end vol. 1; 5 pp. advs. end vol. 3.
Post-dated; adv. as published LEP 13–15 Nov 1787.
The History of Lady Louisa Stroud, 1764, JR 836, AF I: 1250.
French trans. Paris, 1789 (*La jeune nièce ou l'histoire de Suckei Thornby*) (BGR).

   CR: 'Another attempt at a new plan, but . . . weak and abortive . . . . The present work is chiefly of a dramatic kind: the conversations are long and numerous; and we at least perceive one advantage in the mode—an advantage beyond that of tedious repetitions in the form of letters, viz. that, by its assistance, a story which could not be expanded to one volume, now requires three.'
   MR [Andrew Becket]: 'The design is undoubtedly good; but we can say little in praise of its execution.'

1788: 54   H[AWKE, Cassandra], Lady.
JULIA DE GRAMONT. BY THE RIGHT HONOURABLE LADY H***.

London: Printed by T. Bensley: for B. White and Son, at Horace's Head, Fleet-Street, 1788.
I 273p; II 324p. 8vo [MR has 12mo]. 6s (CR), 7s sewed (MR).
CR 66: 145–6 (Aug 1788); MR 80: 498–9 (June 1789); AF II: 1831.
BL N.1882, 83; EM 2011: 3; ESTC t070730 (BI C, O; NA NjP, PU, TxU &c.).

Notes. Further edn: Dublin, 1788 (Printed by John Parker, for L. White, P. Wogan, H. Colbert, J. Moore, J. Jones and J. Halpen, 2 vols., 12mo), ESTC t205256. French trans. Londres [ESTC: i.e. Paris?], 1788, ESTC t212647; German trans. Leipzig, 1790 (*Julie de Grammont,* [sic] *eine rührende Geschichte*) (RS).

CR: 'The story is conducted with great skill; intricately entangled, without too much perplexity; and artfully unravelled, without improbability. The language is generally elegant, the characters well drawn, and the situations interesting and affecting . . . If we found it sometimes exceptionable, it was from too great a profusion of ornamental description . . .' (p. 145).

MR [Andrew Becket]: 'This novel reflects particular honour on its author. It is moral, pathetic, and interesting. The fable is made up of a pleasing diversity of incidents; and is so artfully constructed, that attention is kept alive till the close of the work. The narrative is generally animated; but the style is in some places rather too flowery and pathetic' (p. 498).

1788: 55   [HAYWOOD, Eliza]
THE HISTORY OF MISS LEONORA MEADOWSON. A NOVEL. IN TWO VOLUMES. BY THE AUTHOR OF BETSY THOUGHTLESS.

> London: Printed for F. Noble, At his Circulating Library, No. 324, Holborn, 1788.
> I 192p; II 192p. 12mo. 5s sewed (adv.) 5s (CR).
> CR 65: 236 (Mar 1788).
> [Location to come] (uncut in original boards).

Notes. Vol. 2 p. 8 misnumbered 6. G. F. Whicher held this to be one of two novels 'ready for the press' and 'presumably of her composing' at Haywood's death in 1756 (the other being *Clementina* 1769 JR 1213, but also that this novel, like Clementina was 'a recombination of materials already familiar to the reading public', *The Life and Romances of Mrs Eliza Haywood* (New York, 1915), pp. 26, 169. The CR reviewer noted that parts of the novel, 'The History of Melinda Fairfax' and 'The Tale of Cornaro and the Turk', had been printed before, and more than once, and that the main plot was suspiciously similar to both Betsy Thoughtless and Cleomelia?

See commentary by Patrick Spedding, 'A Bibliography of Eliza Haywood,' Ph.D. dissertation Monash University, Melbourne, Ab.73.1.

CR: 'The spirit which dictated Betsy Thoughtless is evaporated; the fire of the author scarcely sparkles'.

1788: 56   HELME, [Elizabeth].
CLARA AND EMMELINE; OR, THE MATERNAL BENEDICTION. BY MRS HELME, AUTHORESS OF LOUISA; OR THE COTTAGE ON THE MOOR.

> [London]: Printed for G. Kearsley, at Johnson's Head, No. 46, Fleet Street, 1788.
> I iv, 208p; II 264p. 12mo. 6s sewed (t.p., CR, MR).
> CR 64: 480 (Dec 1787); MR 78: 531 (June 1788); AF II: 1883.
> BL N.2204; EM 2070: 4; ESTC t011251 (BI C; NA ICN, ICU, ViU &c.).

Notes. Epistolary.
Louisa 1787: 38.
Adv., 'On Friday next will be published', SJC 24–27 Nov 1787; adv. as published 27–29 Nov 1787. No price given.
French trans. Londres [ESTC: i.e. Paris?], 1788, ESTC t209248; French trans. Londres [ESTC: i.e. Paris?], 1788, ESTC t209250; French trans. Paris, 1788 (*Clare et Emmeline, ou la Bénédiction maternelle* (BN); German trans. Leipzig, 1789 (*Clara und Emmeline, oder der mütterliche Segen*) (EAG).

CR: '. . . Clara and Emmeline rise above the common rank, and are distinguishable for their tenderness and their affection, as well as for the various and interesting situations in which they are placed.'

MR [Andrew Becket]: 'Clara and Emmeline, as a *moral* production, may be placed foremost in the list of novels. The incidents, however, are trite and common; a few of the sentiments are strained and affected; and the language, to use a lady-like expression of the author's, is frequently faulty and inelegant '*to a degree!*'

1788: 57   [HERIOT, John].
THE HALF-PAY OFFICER; OR, MEMOIRS OF CHARLES CHANCELEY: A NOVEL. IN THREE VOLUMES.

> London: Printed For The Author, by T. Bensley, and sold by G. G. J. And J. Robinson, Pater-Noster-Row, 1788.
>
> I xx, 175p; II 179p; III 195p. 12mo. 7s 6d sewed (MR, MC).
>
> MR 79: 172 (Aug 1788); AF II: 1905.
>
> DLC PR4785.H75H3 1788; ESTC n051017 (NA ICU).

Notes. Dedication to Charles Ross, Esq. M.P. signed 'The Author', London 22 Apr 1788.
Adv., 'Next week will be published', MC 10 May 1788; adv. as published MC 17 May 1788. Re-adv., with quotation from MR, MC 8 Sept 1788.
French trans. London and Paris, 1788 (*L'officier réformé*) (BGR).
MR [Andrew Becket]: 'Though not remarkable for variety of incidents, or strength of character, yet, on account of its truly moral tendency, the manly sentiments it breathes, and the agreeable manner in which it is written, this performance is entitled to a considerable share of praise.'

1788: 58   [HERVEY, Elizabeth].
MELISSA AND MARCIA; OR THE SISTERS: A NOVEL. IN TWO VOLUMES.

> London: Printed for W. Lane, Leadenhall-Street, 1788.
>
> I 294p; II 320p. 12mo. 6s sewed (MR, MC), 5s (CR).
>
> CR 65: 486 (June 1788); MR 80: 168 (Feb 1789).
>
> CLU-S/C PR 4786.H38m; EM 1286: 1; ESTC n010312 (BI BL, MRu; NA CSmH, IU, MH-H, PU, TxU &c.; EA Ps).

Notes. Adv. MC 22 Apr 1788.
Further edn: London, 1796, ESTC n064744. French trans. London and Paris, 1788 (*Mélise et Marcia ou les deux soeurs*) (BGR).
CR: 'With little novelty to recommend the fable, with nothing very interesting in the various characters, or the conduct of the work, we have yet been entertained with the present volumes. If, in each of these respects, the novel does not rise to excellence, yet, in all, it soars above the usual attempts in this department; and the fair Sisters came to us in such company, that the darkest complexion would have appeared an agreeable brunette, a giantess only majestic, and a dwarf elegantly little.'
MR [Andrew Becket]: 'This performance has a more than ordinary degree of merit, both with respect to the strength of its characters, and its style.'

1788: 59 [HUGHES, Anne].
HENRY AND ISABELLA; OR, A TRAITE THROUGH LIFE. BY THE
AUTHOR OF CAROLINE, OR THE DIVERSITIES OF FORTUNE. IN
FOUR VOLUMES.
London: Printed for William Lane, Leadenhall-Street, 1788.
I 194p; II 218p; III 234p; IV 255p. 12mo. 12s (CR), 10s sewed (MR, MC).
CR 65: 485 (June 1788); MR 80: 443–4 (May 1789); AF II: 2100.
BL 12614.f.3; EM 290: 1; ESTC t072180 (BI BMp, O; NA CSmH, ICN, MH-H &c.).
Notes. 2 pp. advs. end vol. 1, 2 pp. advs. end vol. 3, and 1 p. advs. end vol. 4.
Caroline 1787: 41.
Adv. MC 22 Apr 1788.
Further edns: Dublin, 1788 (Printed for Luke White, 2 vols., 12mo), ESTC n007246;
London, 1811 (WC). French trans. Paris, 1789 (*Isabelle et Henri*), ESTC t149770.

CR: '. . . Henry and Isabella is a novel from the Burney-school. . . . On the whole, we think
Henry and Isabella much inferior to Cecilia [1782: 15] or Evelina [1778: 10]: yet these volumes may without great danger be compared with either: the story is well told; the catastrophe concealed and developed with tolerable skill; the characters are new, and sufficiently
discriminated.'

MR [Andrew Becket]: 'This work gives us a truly agreeable picture, coloured according to
nature. . . . We do not remember to have seen, for a considerable time past, a performance in
which the characters are more pleasingly grouped, or which presents a more perfect and regular *whole.* A greater boldness of pencil is, indeed, occasionally to be wished for; but this the
fair designer will, probably, in time, and when she shall have acquired a suitable degree of
confidence, be able to display.'

1788: 60 [HUGILL, Martha].
THE CASTLE OF MOWBRAY, AN ENGLISH ROMANCE. BY THE
AUTHOR OF ST BERNARD'S PRIORY.
London: Printed for C. Stalker, in Stationers'-Court; and H. Setchell, in King-Street,
Covent-Garden, 1788.
256p. 12mo. 2s 6d (CR), 3s sewed (MR, MC).
CR 66: 577 (App [Dec 1788/ Jan 1789]); MR 81: 183 (Aug 1789); AF II: 2107.
BL 12611.aa.17; EM 235: 5; ESTC t031408 (NA CtY-BR, MH-H, ViU).
Notes. Dedication 'To the Public' i–ii.
St. Bernard's Priory 1786: 25.
Adv. MC 26 Nov 1788.
Further edn: Dublin, 1789 (Printed by William Porter, for P. Wogan, P. Byrne, J. Parker, J.
Jones, J. Moore, and J. Archer, 1 vol., 12mo), ESTC n036095. German trans. Erfurt,
1799–1800 (*Die Geheimnisse des Schlosses Mowbray*) (EAG).

CR: 'The heroic novel, where characters are taken from real life, is a pleasing kind of composition; but it is the bow of Ulysses and requires strength as well as address to bend it. Our
author possesses neither. He has mutilated history, is unacquainted with the human heart,
and deficient in judgment; yet with these defects, he enters the lists as the rival of Horace Walpole, and Miss Lee.' [Horace Walpole's *The Castle of Otranto* 1765, JR 868, AF I: 2898; Sophia
Lee's *The Recess* 1783: 15 and 1785: 37]

MR [Andrew Becket]: '... the present performance, as some of its incidents are borrowed from history, is not contemptible; but it is so full of what is usually, though improperly, styled *business*, that all is confusion and perplexity. There is no discrimination of character—nothing that can lay hold of, or arrest, the attention; and the mind, grown weary with tracing a series of improbabilities, quickly "roams and expatiates" in search of other and more interesting persons and scenes.'

1788: 61   [LAVALLÉE, Joseph, marquis de Bois-Robert].
MARIA CECILIA: OR LIFE AND ADVENTURES OF THE DAUGHTER OF ACHMET III. EMPEROR OF THE TURKS. FROM THE FRENCH. IN TWO VOLUMES.
> London: Printed for W. Lane, Leadenhall-Street, 1788.
> I 222p; II 226p. 12mo. 5s (CR), 5s sewed (MR, MC).
> CR 66: 503 (Dec 1788); MR 81: 563 (Dec 1789); AF II: 2478.
> BL 1487.a.29; EM 1843: 1; ESTC t065261.

Notes. Trans. of *Cécile, fille d'Achmet III, empereur des Turcs* (Constantinople and Paris, 1787).
Half-page address 'To the Reader' signed 'The Editor' claims that the story is true.
Adv. MC 16 Dec 1788.
Further edns: Dublin, 1789 (Printed for P. Byrne, P. Wogan, J. Moore, J. Jones, J. Halpen, and J. Archer, 2 vols., 12mo), EM 4251: 6, ESTC n034802; Philadelphia, 1790, ESTC w027327.
CR: 'These adventures are said to have their foundation in truth; and we remember to have heard some confused tales of a similar kind. There is no great merit, and no very capital defects in this novel: the tale is told with some spirit; the improbabilities are concealed with address; and there is love enough, with "hair-breadth 'scapes," to please the romantic readers of lives and adventures.'
MR [Andrew Becket]: 'The editor asserts that the narrative, as far as it respects the history of Maria Cecilia, is founded in truth. It may be so; but, to us, the whole is romantic and improbable in the highest degree.'

1788: 62   [LÉONARD, Nicolas-Germain].
THE CORRESPONDENCE OF TWO LOVERS, INHABITANTS OF LYONS. PUBLISHED FROM THE FRENCH ORIGINALS. IN THREE VOLUMES.
> London: Sold by T. Hookham, New Bond Street; and G. G. J. Robinson, Paternoster-Row, 1788.
> I ii, 222p; II 177p; III 216p. 12mo. 7s 6d (CR), 7s 6d sewed (MR) [RG has altered this to 9s].
> CR 66: 165 (Sept 1788); MR 81: 50–3 (July 1789); AF II: 862.
> BL 837.b.11; EM 2449: 6; ESTC t106165 (EA P).

Notes. Trans. of *Lettres de deux amans, habitans de Lyon* (London, 1783).
ESTC: edited by John Seymour.
Dedication to Lady Anne Lindsay 1, i–ii. Epistolary.
Novel ends on p. 185 of vol. 3; what follows are a note from the English Editor, Original

Letters of Captain Von Arenswald from Maty's *Review*, and quoted passages from Spenser, Warton and Pope.

Extract published LC 66: 249 (10–12 Sept 1789).

Further edns: Dublin, 1789 (Printed by Zachariah Jackson, for Grueber and M'Allister, 2 vols., 12mo), EM 4633: 3, ESTC n001909; London, 1790, ESTC t106782.

CR: 'These pernicious volumes are copied in their style and manner from the Sorrows of Werter. They are worked up with equal passion, equal violence, but not equal interest. We can therefore let them pass, as the danger is not very considerable, though their tendency and design demand the severest censure.' [*The Sorrows of Werter* 1779: 10].

MR [Andrew Becket]: 'They contain a well-written detail of love-adventures, intermingled with admirable observations on the several propensities of the human heart. The catastrophe of the story—no other than the destruction of the lovers by each other's hands—and which is said to be founded in fact, is truly horrible. The accompanying reflections on that act, are, however, such as must awaken in every bosom a sense of its enormity. There is, therefore, nothing of pernicious tendency in this publication, as many might at first, and from a simple relation of the event, be led to imagine' (pp. 50–51).

1788: 63   [MACKENZIE, Anna Maria].
RETRIBUTION: A NOVEL. BY THE AUTHOR OF THE GAMESTERS, &C. IN THREE VOLUMES.

> London: Printed for G. G. J. and J. Robinson, Pater-Noster Row, 1788.
> I 228p; II 196p; III 154p. 8vo [MR has 12mo]. 9s sewed (MR, LEP), 7s 6d (CR).
> CR 65: 149–50 (Feb 1788); MR 78: 441–2 (May 1788); AF II: 2661.
> PU Singer-Mend.PR.4971.M42.R4.1788; ESTC n048792 (NA CtY-BR, InU-Li).

Notes. Robinson paid 20 gns. on 10 Oct 1787 to Anna Maria Johnson for *Retribution*.
At end of vol. 3 is a 26-pp. 'Contents' section (unn.), giving a précis of each chapter.
The Gamesters 1786: 33.
Adv., 'will speedily be published', LEP 27–29 Nov 1787.
French trans. London and Paris, 1788 (*La rétribution ou histoire de miss Prescott*) (BGR).

CR: 'The author's genius is superior to his art, and his knowlege of the human mind more conspicuous than his invention. His story is managed with very little address; and the frequent changes, the reference to the adventures of the other personages of the novel, weaken the feelings, and destroy the interest' (p. 149). Compares several of the characters to their counterparts in Burney's *Cecilia* (1782: 15).

MR [Andrew Becket]: '. . . this artist is not sufficiently attentive to *harmony* in his drawing. He seems to be fully sensible of the value of the several beauties he has borrowed, but wanting in judgment to blend them, so as to compose an excellent and unexceptionable *whole.*'

1788: 64   [NICHOLSON, Mr].
CATHARINE; OR, THE WOOD OF LLEWELLYN: A DESCRIPTIVE TALE. BY THE AUTHOR OF THE VILLAGE OF MARTINDALE, &C. IN TWO VOLUMES.

> London: Printed for W. Lane, Leadenhall-Street, 1788.
> I 132p; II 141p. 8vo [MR and CR have 12mo]. 5s sewed (MR, CR, adv.).
> CR 65: 75 (Jan 1788); MR 78: 530 (June 1788); AF II: 643.
> MH-H *EC75.A100.788c3; EM 1590: 5; ESTC n014842 (NA CaOHM, CLU-S/C).

Notes. Blakey: attributed to Mr Nicholson by a Minerva Library catalogue of 1814.

Frontispiece. Dedication to the Honourable Miss Howe, signed 'The Author'. 3 pp. advs. end vol. 2. Epistolary.

Village of Martindale 1787: 46.

Post-dated; adv.,'An Interesting and Affecting Novel . . . Embellished with an Elegant Frontispiece', LEP 18–20 Dec 1787.

Adv. end vol. 2 of *Darnley Vale* (1789: 33).

Further edn: Dublin, 1788 (Printed by John Parker, for Messrs. Byrne, Wogan, 2 vols. in 1, no format), xESTC (WC). French trans. Paris, 1792 (*Catherine, ou la Forêt de Lewelyn*) (HWS).

CR makes an obscurely phrased accusation of 'abuse of clemency' but most of the rest of the review is favourable: 'These volumes contain a simple and pathetic Tale.—Pure description sometimes holds the place of sense; and instead of new characters, we meet with situations somewhat uncommon, and occasionally improbable. . . . On the whole, however, the unity of the plan, the artificial concealment of the event, with the neatness of the language, render this novel more estimable than the "every day publications," designed for the circulating libraries.'

MR: 'A somewhat romantic, but not uninteresting tale.'

1788: 65   [NIXON, Capt.].
THE RAMBLE OF PHILO, AND HIS MAN STURDY.

London: Printed for W. Lane, Leadenhall-Street, 1788.

I iv, 282p; II 272p. 12mo. 6s (CR), 6s sewed (MR, MC, adv. *Darnley*), 5s sewed (adv. *Follies*).

CR 66: 419 (Nov 1788); MR 81: 181–82 (Aug 1789); AF II: 3682.

BL 1154.g.9; EM 2555: 14; ESTC t117087 (BI O).

Notes. Blakey: attributed to Capt. Nixon in a Minerva Library catalogue of 1814.

Table of contents iii–iv both vols.

Adv. MC 16 Dec 1788.

Adv. end vol. 3 of *Darnley Vale* (1789: 33); adv. end vol. 1 of *The Follies of St. James's Street* (1789: 10).

Further edn: Dublin, 1789 (Printed for W. Gilbert, P. Byrne, P. Wogan, J. Jones, and J. Halpen, 1 vol., 12mo), ESTC t168150.

CR: 'We expected much, and were disappointed. The plan was good, and the characters seemed at first to be interesting; but the author's strength soon failed, and we found nothing to entertain, or to instruct.'

MR [Andrew Becket]: '. . . though the present production is a mere abortion of the brain, we must at the same time acknowlege, that it is written with a tolerable degree of correctness; and, in that respect, it seems to give a warrant for better things. But . . . to succeed in the line of writing which he has here attempted, requires not only the pen but the judgment of a Fielding or a Le Sage.'

1788: 66   PASTORELLA, Sylvania [pseud.].
THE COTTAGE OF FRIENDSHIP. A LEGENDARY PASTORAL. BY SYLVANIA PASTORELLA.

London: Printed for J. Bew, Pater-Noster-Row, and H. G. Pridden, Fleet-Market, 1788.

vii, 254p. 12mo. 2s 6d sewed (MR).

MR 81: 79 (July 1789); AF II: 3252.

BL 12613.bb.3; EM 223: 5; ESTC t068753 (BI MRu, O).

Notes. Preface v–vii.

MR [William Enfield]: 'It is wonderful to observe the progress of genius. In the days of our Richardsons and Fieldings, such was the poverty of invention, that it was thought necessary to spin out a single story through six or eight volumes, in which the reader was so far from being surprised with new characters in almost every page, that he was obliged to converse with the same people, volume after volume, till he was, perhaps, as much tired of their company as if he had been one of the family. But in these more inventive days, our novellists find nothing more easy, than to weave three or four different stories into one small volume, and connect them by shutting up the parties together, no matter how, in a little snug cottage, till they have told their tender tales. All this hath Sylvania Pastorella done!'

1788: 67   [POTTER, John].
FREDERIC, OR THE LIBERTINE; INCLUDING MEMOIRS OF THE FAMILY OF MONTAGUE. A NOVEL. IN TWO VOLUMES.

London: Printed for W. Lane, Leadenhall-Street, 1788.

I 173p; II 168p. 8vo [CR and MR have 12mo]. 5s (CR), 5s sewed (MR, MC).

CR 66: 74 (July 1788); MR n.s. 3: 90–1 (Sept 1790); AF II: 3543.

CSmH 389195; EM 5552: 13; ESTC n031670 (NA CtY).

Notes. Adv. MC 16 Dec 1788.

CR: 'The train of adventures in these volumes is amusing, and not wholly destitute of probability. The language is sufficiently correct, and poetical justice is dispensed with tolerable propriety. There is, however, little positive merit in other respects. The reflections are jejune and trifling; the adventures a literary patchwork, from different volumes of modern histories; and the characters hackneyed in the pages of the novellists.'

MR [William Enfield]: 'Under the stale pretence of exposing the deformity of vice, in order to recommend the practice of virtue, this novellist conducts his reader through a succession of profligate amours' (p. 90).

1788: 68   REEVE, Clara.
THE EXILES; OR, MEMOIRS OF THE COUNT DE CRONSTADT. BY CLARA REEVE, AUTHOR OF THE OLD ENGLISH BARON, TWO MENTORS, &C. &C. IN THREE VOLUMES.

London: Printed for T. Hookham, New Bond Street, 1788.

I xxiv, 209p; II 293p; III 277p. 12mo. 9s (CR), 9s sewed (MR, SDA).

CR 67: 75 (Jan 1789); MR 80: 88 (Jan 1789); AF II: 3712.

BL 838.b.15-17; EM 2638: 3; ESTC t109367 (NA CtY-BR, DLC, IU, MH-H, PU &c.).

Notes. Based on François-Thomas-Marie Baculard d' Arnaud's 'D'Almanzi' in vol. 4 of *Suite des épreuves du sentiment* (Paris, 1776) (Grieder).

Epistolary. Dedication 'To Peter-Pertinax Puff, Esq.' iii–xiii, signed 'The Author'; preface [xiii]–xxiv. 3 pp. advs. end vol. 1 and vol. 2; 7 pp. advs. end vol. 3.

The Old English Baron (original title *The Champion of Virtue*) 1777: 16; *The Two Mentors* 1783: 19.

Adv. SDA 20 Dec 1788.

Further edn: Dublin, 1789 (Printed for P. Byrne, P. Wogan, C. Lewis, J. Moore, and J. Halpen, 2 vols., 12mo), EM 7468: 4, ESTC t072185. French trans. Paris, 1789 (*Mémoires du comte de Cronstadt*) (BGR).

CR: '... much is new; the whole is probable, correct and interesting.'

MR [Andrew Becket]: 'An interesting and well conducted story.... The principal incidents appear to be borrowed from a novel of the justly admired *M. D'Arnaud.*'

1788: 69   {RENWICK, William}.
THE SOLICITUDES OF ABSENCE. A GENUINE TALE.
London: Printed for the Author and sold by C. Forster, No. 41, Poultry; and by all other Booksellers, 1788.
xvi, 306p. 12mo. 3s (CR), 3s sewed (MR, MC).
CR 65: 484 (June 1788); MR 79: 443–5 (Nov 1788); AF II: 3741.
BL N.1817; EM 2009: 4; ESTC t070701 (BI C; NA MoU, PU).

Notes. Dedication (signed William Renwick) to the Duchess of Rutland iii–iv; Address to the British Parliament v–xiii; verse 'Exordium' xv–xvi.
Adv., with heading 'The following Tale is literally related, and will excite compassion while a spark of humanity exists in the World', 'In a large 12mo Volume (Containing 320 full pages, elegantly printed on a fine Demy', MC 12 May 1788: '*The Solicititudes of Absence: including Memoirs of two unfortunate English Lovers, authenticated by the correspondence of several exalted Personages, and interwoven with many sonnets, and other occasional poems*... printed for the author by Richie and Sammells, No. 14, Albion-Buildings, Bartholomew-Close; and sold by J. Stockdale, Piccadilly; and C. Forster, No. 41, Poultry.'

CR: 'His mind seems to be well regulated and well-informed: his language is elegant; his poetry pleasing, tender, and pathetic.'

MR [Ralph Griffiths] refers to rev. of Renwick's *Unfortunate Lovers* (1771: 50; title is *The Genuine Distresses of Damon and Celia*) and says that the same comments apply to *The Solicitudes of Absence.*

1788: 70   ROWSON, {Susanna}.
THE INQUISITOR; OR, INVISIBLE RAMBLER. IN THREE VOLUMES. BY MRS. ROWSON, AUTHOR OF VICTORIA.
London: Printed for G. G. J. and J. Robinson, Paternoster Row, 1788.
I 176p; II 184p; III 183p. 8vo [MR has 12mo]. 7s 6d sewed (MR, MC 28 Apr), 9s sewed (MC 17 Apr).
MR 79: 171 (Aug 1788); AF II: 3882.
BL 12611.d.19; EM 208: 5; ESTC t057365 (NA MWA).

Notes. Robinsons paid Rowson £30, 4 Mar 1783 (Bentley). Dedication to Lady Cockburne, signed Susanna Rowson. Preface vii–xvi. 1 p. adv. end vol. 3.
Victoria 1786: 39.
Adv., 'Saturday, the 26th instant, will be published', MC 17 Apr 1788; adv. as published MC 28 Apr 1788.
Further edns: Philadelphia, 1793, ESTC w013033; Philadelphia, 1794, EM 6995: 8; ESTC w020538.

MR [Andrew Becket]: 'There is nothing of novelty in the idea, nor any thing particularly striking in the execution of the work. It may, however, be perused with profit by our youthful friends, as in some of the stories here presented to us, the duplicity and dishonesty so frequently to be found in the world, are exhibited with a tolerable degree of skill. The Authoress is evidently in possession of a feeling heart. But *style*, and the various graces of composition, are yet to come.'

1788: 71   SAINT PIERRE, Jacques-Henri-Bernardin de.
PAUL AND VIRGINIE. BY JACQUES-BERNARDIN-HENRI DE SAINT-PIERRE. WITH PLATES.

> London: 1788.
> 218p. 12mo.
> MH-H *FC7.Sa283.Eg788p; EM 1280: 23; ESTC n010942 (NA CSmH).

Notes. Trans. of 'Paul et Virginie', first published in vol. 4 of *Études de la Nature* (Paris, 1788). Engraved t.p. Running-title: 'Paul and Virginia'. Printer's colophon p. 218: 'W. Blackader, Printer, 10, Took's Court, Chancery-Lane'.
Further edns. (with varying titles and translators): London, 1789, EM 3809: 2; ESTC t070721; London, 1789, ESTC t139008; Dublin, 1789 (Printed for Messrs. P. Byrne, Grueber, and McAlister, J. Jones, J. Moore, and William Jones, 1 vol., 12mo), EM 6188: 10, ESTC t118414; Philadelphia, 1794, ESTC w027590. ESTC shows 17 English forms of this work between 1795, when Helen Maria Williams's *Paul and Virginia* was published, and 1800; all but 4 of these are Williams's translation. The others, by Henry Hunter, D.D., were published in 1796, 1798, 1799 and 1800 in Boston; Exeter, NH; Baltimore; and Wrentham, MA. WC has 126 records for versions of this work before 1851, most in English or French, a few in Spanish and one in Armenian. Williams's trans. serialised in *Weekly Entertainer*, 1797, RM 626.
This edn. not reviewed; 1789 London edn. reviewed MR n.s. 1: 332 (Mar 1790); AF II: 2694.
  MR [Andrew Becket]: 'This beautiful little novel is translated from Mons. de St Pierre's work, entitled *Études de la Nature*. The scene is laid in the southern island called the Isle of France. The author represents the natural beauties of the climate, with great brilliancy of colouring; draws a charming picture of innocence and happiness in pastoral life; and relates a tale which few young persons will read without shedding a tear.'

SEYMOUR, John
See LEONARD, Nicolas Germain, **THE CORRESPONDENCE OF TWO LOVERS**

1788: 72   SMITH, Charlotte.
EMMELINE, THE ORPHAN OF THE CASTLE. BY CHARLOTTE SMITH. IN FOUR VOLUMES.

> London: Printed for T. Cadell, in the Strand, 1788.
> I 292p; II 268p; III 319p; IV 393p. 12mo; 12s boards (MR), 12s sewed (MC).
> MR 79: 241–4 (Sept 1788); AF II: 4138.
> BL N.2029–32; EM 2012: 3; ESTC t073502 (BI BMu, C, COCu &c.); NA CSmH, DLC, ICN, IU, MH-H, NjP, PU, TxU, ViU &c.; EA Pm).

Notes. Verse dedication 'To my Children'.
Adv. MC 21 Apr 1788.
Further edns: London, 1788, ESTC n006219; Dublin, 1788 (Printed for Messrs. White, Wogan, Byrne, Moore, Jones, and Halpen, 2 vols., 12mo), ESTC t212504; Dublin, 1789,

ESTC n050808; London, 1789, ESTC n006221; Belfast, 1799, EM 4852: 5, ESTC t138544; WC has 5 entries between 1800 and 1850. French trans. (*Emmeline, ou l'orpheline du chateau*) Londres [ESTC: i.e. Paris], 1788, ESTC t138542; French trans. (*L'orpheline du chateau, ou Emmeline*), Londres [ESTC: i.e. Paris?], 1788, ESTC t197176; German trans. Vienna, 1790 (*Emmeline, oder Die Waise des Schlosses*) (EAG).

MR [Andrew Becket]: 'Possessing a nice and accurate judgment, her drawing is elegant and correct. All is graceful and pleasing to the sight: all, in short, is simple, femininely beautiful and chaste. . . . the whole is conducted with a considerable degree of art; . . . the characters are natural, and well discriminated: . . . the fable is uncommonly interesting; and . . . the moral is forcible and just' (pp. 242–3).

1788: 73   SPENCER, Sarah Emma.
MEMOIRS OF THE MISS HOLMSBYS. BY SARAH EMMA SPENCER. (LATE MISS JACKSON, OF MANCHESTER.) AUTHORESS OF POETICAL TRIFLES, &C. IN TWO VOLUMES.

> London: Printed for S. Smith, Paternoster-Row, 1788.
> I xii, 225p; II 200p. 12mo. 5s sewed (MR).
> MR 80: 169 (Feb 1789); AF II: 4212.
> CtY Im Sp34.788; ESTC n063979.

Notes. Preface 1, v–viii, signed Sarah Emma Spencer; list of subscribers ix–xii. Epistolary. Some pages containing verse are missing end vol. 1 between pp. [217] and 225.
2nd edn. adv. MC 31 Mar 1789.

MR [Andrew Becket]: '. . . the writer stands not in need of the indulgence which she solicits. Her Novel is generally interesting. There is a happy contrast of character in it; and the more prominent features of virtue and vice are depicted with considerable skill and judgment.'

1788: 74   STEVENS, George Alexander.
THE ADVENTURES OF A SPECULIST; OR, A JOURNEY THROUGH LONDON. COMPILED FROM PAPERS WRITTEN BY GEORGE ALEXANDER STEVENS, (AUTHOR OF A LECTURE UPON HEADS) WITH HIS LIFE, A PREFACE, CORRECTIONS, AND NOTES, BY THE EDITOR. EXHIBITING A PICTURE OF THE MANNERS, FASHIONS, AMUSEMENTS, &C. OF THE METROPOLIS AT THE MIDDLE OF THE EIGHTEENTH CENTURY: AND INCLUDING SEVERAL FUGITIVE PIECES OF HUMOUR, BY THE SAME AUTHOR, NOW FIRST COLLECTED AND PUBLISHED. IN TWO VOLUMES.

> London: Printed for the Editor: and sold by S Bladon, no. 13, Paternoster-Row, 1788.
> I xxvi, 268p; II 286p. 12mo. 7s sewed (MR, LC).
> MR 79: 557–8 (Dec 1788); AF II: 4247.
> C 7720.d.1207-1208; EMf; ESTC t160622 (BI BL; NA MiU, MB, MH-H).

Notes. Preface 1, iii–xiii; 'Account of the Life of Geo. Alex. Stevens' xv–xxvi. 2-pp. table of contents (unn.) in each vol.
Adv., 'Entered at Stationers Hall, LC 63: 421 (29 Apr–1 May 1788); additional booksellers are J. Debrett, Piccadilly; and J. Sewell, Cornhill.

MR [Andrew Becket] 'If it be true, that "Vice, to be hated, needs but to be seen," the present volumes may go far toward rendering it generally detestable. They exhibit nature in some of her ugliest and most unseemly shapes: in the persons of highwaymen, gamblers, female prostitutes, and bawds. . . . we are of opinion that such publications are attended with danger; and that the writer, while thinking to warn by *precept*, may encourage by the *example* which he exhibits.'

1788: 75   [THOMSON, Anna].
FATAL FOLLIES: OR THE HISTORY OF THE COUNTESS OF STAN-MORE. IN FOUR VOLUMES.

London: Printed for G. G. J. and J. Robinson, Paternoster-Row, 1788.
I 238p; II 232p; III 240p; IV 244p. 12mo. 10s sewed (CR), 12s sewed (MR, LEP).
CR 65: 149 (Feb 1788); MR 78: 441 (May 1788); AF II: 4446.
BL 12611.b.17; EM 135: 4; ESTC t107743 (NA CLU-S/C, DLC, MH-H).

Notes. For more information about author's name, see note to *Labyrinths of Life* 1791: 70; t.p. to this work claims authorship of *Fatal Follies*.
Robinson paid 50 gns. on 8 Nov 1787 to William Thomson (the author's husband, also a novelist—see 1783: 22; 1789: 69) for *Fatal Follies* (RA); Bentley treats the novel as William Thomson's.
Epistolary.
Adv., 'will speedily be published', LEP 27–29 Nov 1787; adv. as published LC 63: 77 (19–22 Jan 1788).
Further edn: Dublin, 1788 (Printed for P. Byrne. P. Wogan, J. Halpen, and J. Moore, 2 vols., 12mo), ESTC t203204.

MR notes 'some read Strathmore,' concluding 'a late *démêlé* in the fashionable world has furnished this work with several *embellishments*'. A brief account of the 1786–7 scandals concerning the Countess of Strathmore was given in her obituary, GM 70: 488 (May 1800), which also noted that 'Her Ladyship's remains were deposited in Westminster Abbey, dressed in a superb bridal dress'.

CR: '. . . without any great novelty of sentiment or character, these volumes are interesting and entertaining. The author is well acquainted with the human heart: he is acquainted too with the several places where his scenes are laid, and with the manners of their inhabitants. Our young ladies may learn, from this novel, something besides an ah! and an oh!—these delightful decorations of a female correspondence.'

MR [Andrew Becket]: 'The seeming pleasures of a life of dissipation, and the miseries usually attendant on it, together with the influence which the manners of the rich and great will necessarily have on the surrounding multitude, who are seldom given to thought and reflection, are in these volumes delineated with tolerable spirit.'

1788: 76   TIMBURY, Jane.
THE MALE COQUET. A NOVEL. IN TWO VOLUMES. BY JANE TIMBURY, AUTHOR OF TOBIT.

London: Printed for J. Murray, No. 32, Fleet-Street, 1788.
I iv,166p; II iv, 150p. 12mo. 4s (Zachs); 5s sewed (MR, CR).
CR 66: 420 (Nov 1788); MR 81: 564 (Dec 1789); AF II: 4482.
CLU-S/C PR 5671.T222m; EMf; ESTC n004439 (BI E; NA CtY, MH-H).

Notes. 2 pp. advs. end vol. 2. Epistolary.

Murray paid the author 5 gns. 20 Mar 1788 (Zachs 698).

The History of Tobit (1787) is a poem.

Further edn: London, 1789 (CtY).

CR: 'The Male Coquet has been the object of so much satire, ridicule, and sober animadversion, that we fear these weak inefficient pages will be of no great service in reforming him. As a novel, we can say little of this work, but that it is a slight summer silk, easily frayed by the touch of criticism, and through which we can every moment see that the scene is fictitious.'

MR [Andrew Becket]: 'The Male Coquet (a truly despicable character) is here exposed to ridicule with some degree of success.'

1788: 77   TODD, Elizabeth.

THE HISTORY OF LADY CAROLINE RIVERS, IN A SERIES OF LETTERS. IN TWO VOLUMES. BY MISS ELIZABETH TODD.

London: Printed for the Author, 1788.

I vii, 11, 209p; II 233p. 12mo. 5s sewed (MR, CR), 5s (MC).

CR 65: 487 (June 1788); MR 81: 183 (Aug 1789); AF II: 4488.

BL N.2059; EM 2069: 1; ESTC t073505 (BI C, O; NA PU).

Notes. Epistolary. Dedication 'To the Ladies' I, v–vii; list of subscribers 5–11; text of novel starts on p. 1 in vol. 1 and p. 5 in vol. 2.

Adv. MC 26 May 1788; 'Printed for the Author, and may be had at No. 21, Queen-street, Westminster; and of most of the booksellers.'

CR: 'We should not have reprehended this young authoress of seventeen so severely, if she had not discovered, in the progress of her work, that she was totally unacquainted with life and manners, that she could not draw even a tolerably correct copy of characters, or paint with fidelity the conduct necessary in such situations.—Perhaps her end is sufficiently answered by an extensive list of subscribers.'

MR [Andrew Becket]: '. . . why should . . . nonsense be transmitted to the press? Why should the public be pestered with it?.'

1788: 78   [WOLLSTONECRAFT, Mary].

MARY, A FICTION.

London: Printed for J. Johnson, St. Paul's Church-Yard, 1788.

187p. 8vo [CR and MR have 12mo]. 3s (CR), 3s sewed (MR, MC).

CR 66: 74 (July 1788); MR n.s. 2: 352–3 (July 1790); AF II: 4917.

C 7100.d.638; EM 4967: 4; ESTC t039008 (BI BL; NA CtY-BR, CSmH, ICN, MH-H, NjP, TxU &c.).

Notes. 4-pp. prefatory advertisement.

Adv., 'In a few days will be published', MC 24 May 1788: 'In delineating the Heroine of this Fiction, the Author attempts to develope a character different from those generally pourtrayed. In an artless tale, the mind of a woman who has thinking powers, is displayed: in a Fiction, such a being may be allowed to exist, whose grandeur is derived from the operations of its own faculties, not subjugated to opinion, but drawn by the individual from the original source.'

Facs: FC, RWN.

CR: 'This is no common work. Various observations evince a pretty considerable acquaintance with different subjects; and these are not impertinently obtruded, but occur seemingly without design.... It is ... a pleasing tale: those who are fond of developing the minute traits of the human mind, will find in "Mary" a source of some reflection.' CR thinks that the author may have tried, but failed, to show that women's 'minds want sufficient force'.

MR [Thomas Pearne]: 'This little tale certainly possesses the merit of being well written: but that the author has succeeded in his attempt to delineate an original character, is not so certain.... there is nothing so striking, marked, or characteristic in the manners of Mary, as to make her a very close copy of any particular model. She is too much like the crowd, to resemble an individual; and toward this side chiefly, the author has deviated from original-ity.... This fiction is of the cast which is called moral; that is, good principles and a love of virtue are inculcated throughout: but we very much doubt whether these tender and pathetic moral tales ever do, in fact, contribute to promote virtue and morality in the world. They are too apt to enervate young minds; to cherish propensities which are better checked; to make them affect what they do not feel; to give them false and romantic notions of life; to teach them to expect characters and incidents which are rarely, if ever, to be found; to disgust and put them out of humour with such as actually occur.'

1788: 79   [WOLLSTONECRAFT, Mary].
ORIGINAL STORIES, FROM REAL LIFE; WITH CONVERSATIONS, CALCULATED TO REGULATE THE AFFECTIONS, AND FORM THE MIND TO TRUTH AND GOODNESS.

> London: Printed for J. Johnson, No. 72, St. Paul's Church-Yard, 1788.
> xii, 174p. 12mo. 2s 6d (MR), 2s 6d sewed (MC).
> MR 79: 271–2 (Sept 1788); AF II: 4918.
> MH-H *EC75.G5495.788o2; EM 1279: 7; ESTC n010598 (NA CSmH, PU, TxU &c.).

Notes. Preface v–x; introduction xi–xii.
Adv. MC 12 Apr 1788: *Original Stories from real Life: with Conversations between Mrs. Mason and her young Friends: calculated to regulate the affections, and form the mind to truth and goodness, as well as to furnish useful assistance to those who have the care of Children.*
Further edns: London, 1788, t043448; London, 1791, EM 4968: 6, ESTC t043449; Dublin, 1792 (Printed for J. Jones, 1 vol., 12mo), ESTC t178632; London, 1796, EM 2726: 9, ESTC t043450; Dublin, 1799, EM 4441: 7, ESTC t133855; ESTC has 1 further entry; WC has 3 entries between 1800 and 1850. German trans. Schnepfenthal, 1795 (*Erzählungen für Kinder*) (Price).

> MR [Jabez Hirons] '... we suspect it to be the production of a female pen, which has very lately contributed to instruct and entertain us on the subject of education. The present col-lection forms an agreeable and useful addition to the former.'

1788: 80   [WRIGHT, George].
THE UNFORTUNATE LOVERS, ABRIDGED FROM THE SORROWS OF WERTER. TO WHICH IS ADDED, THE LADIES COUNSELLOR; RES-PECTING LOVE, COURTSHIP, MARRIAGE, &C. IN PROSE AND VERSE; WITH ORIGINAL NOTES. BY THE AUTHOR OF RETIRED PLEAS-URES, &C.

> London: Printed for C! Stalker, Stationers-Court, Ludgate Street, n.d. [c.1788].
> 146p. 12mo. 1s 6d (adv.).

GlM 2: 308 (June 1788).

BL RB.23a.8495; ESTC t224669.

Notes. Frontispiece dated 1788. Partly verse; less than 100 pages of prose.

ESTC: An abridgment in English of Johann Wolfgang von Goethe's *Die Leiden des jungen Werthers* (Leipzig, 1774).

Retired Pleasures published in 1787.

Adv. end vol. 2 of *Arville Castle* (1795: 1).

Further edn: London, 1792 (WC), xESTC.

GlM: 'The celebrated story of Werter and Charlotte is here rendered more immediately subservient to religious purposes; and the "Ladies' Counsellor" is no improper addition, containing many useful cautions, and necessary reflections to secure propriety of conduct before, and permanent happiness after, marriage.'

1789

THE ADVENTURES OF CHRISTOPHER CURIOUS
See 1788: 2

1789: 1 ANON.
ALBERTINA. A NOVEL.

London: Printed for S. Crowder, Pater-Noster-Row, 1789.

I 204p; II vi, 207p. 12mo. 5s (CR).

CR 68: 494–5 (Dec 1789); AF II: 55.

Ot Danson; ESTC n029630 (NA NSbSU).

Notes. Preface (v–vi) bound at beginning of vol. 2 in Ot copy. Epistolary.

CR: 'This novel is a little too full of "hair-breadth 'scapes," and somewhat deficient in probability; but to a reader, not very nice and attentive, will appear interesting and entertaining' (p. 494).

ALFRED AND CASSANDRA, A ROMANTIC TALE
See 1788: 4

ALMERIA BELMORE
See O'CONNOR, E.

ARGUS; THE HOUSE-DOG AT EADLIP
See MATHEWS, Eliza Kirkham

ARUNDEL
See CUMBERLAND, Richard

1789: 2   ANON.

THE BASTILE: OR, HISTORY OF CHARLES TOWNLY, A MAN OF THE WORLD. IN FOUR VOLUMES.

London: Printed for William Lane, Leadenhall-Street, 1789.

I 310p; II 286p; III 263p; IV 239p. 12mo. 12s (CR), 10s sewed (SDA).

CR 67: 475 (June 1789); AF II: 232.

O 256.f.1934,1935; EMf; ESTC n015681 (NA CLU-S/C, CtY, MH-H &c.).

Notes. 1 p. advs. end vol. 2 and 1½ pp. advs. end vol. 4, starting on p. 239.

Adv. as 'in the press' MC 30 Dec 1788; still adv. as 'in the press' MC 3 Apr 1789; adv. as published SDA 23 May 1789.

Further edns: Dublin, 1789 (Printed by George Grierson, 3 vols., 12mo), ESTC t171548; Dublin, 1789, EM 5290: 2, ESTC t129036; Dublin, 1789, EM 4145: 1, ESTC t055926. All three Dublin edns. have the title *Memoirs of Charles Townly. Written by Himself.* German trans. Leipzig, 1790 (*Die Bastille, oder Carl Townly, ein Mann aus der grossen Welt*) (EAG).

CR: 'The style and manner of this work are not unlike those of Roderick Random. The fable is arranged and unfolded without intricacy, and without confusion. The personages are more than usually characteristic; events often uncommon and entertaining, though not in the extreme of low humour. When we compare these volumes with the novels of Fielding and Smollett, we cannot arrange them in the same line, yet we think they may safely be put in the first rank of the second class.'

BELINDA, OR, THE FAIR FUGITIVE
See C., Mrs

THE BELLE WIDOWS
See RUDD, Margaret Caroline

CALISTA, A NOVEL
See MACKENZIE, Anna Maria

THE CASTLES OF ATHLIN AND DUNBAYNE
See RADCLIFFE, Ann

THE CLANDESTINE LOVERS
See 1788: 10

THE COUNTESS OF HENNEBON
See HUGILL, Martha

THE DEATH OF CAIN
See HALL, William Henry, App. B: 11

1789: 3   ANON.

*THE DUEL, OR NATURE WILL PREVAIL. A NOVEL. IN THREE VOLUMES.

London: Printed by J. S. Barr, at the Printing-Office, Oxendon-street, near the Hay-
market; and may be had of the different Booksellers (LC), 1789 (AR).

3 vols. 716p (AR). 12mo. 716p. 9s (EngR), 9s sewed (AR, adv.).

AR 5: 579 (1789); AF II: 1179.

No copy located.

Notes. Epistolary.

Adv. LC 66: 517 (26–28 Nov 1789) under heading 'New Novel': 'This novel is replete
with sentiments not inelegant, characters drawn from life, and incidents real, comic, and
interesting.'

Adv. end of vol. 2 of *Arley; or, the Faithful Wife* (1790: 2) where this description is added:
'Replete with Sentiments not inelegant, Characters drawn from Life, and incidents real,
comic, and interesting'.

EngR gives a brief plot summary and says that the heroine's story 'is pleasing and affecting,
and will probably be read when many of our modern novels are forgotten.'

1789: 4   ANON.
THE DUKE OF EXETER: AN HISTORICAL ROMANCE. IN THREE VOLUMES.

London: Printed for W. Lane, Leadenhall-Street, 1789.

I iv, 181p; II 185p; III 204p. 8vo [CR has 12mo]. 7s 6d (CR), 7s 6d sewed (MC).

CR 67: 476 (June 1789); AF II: 1181.

BL 12611.bbb.11; ESTC n045768 (NA CSmH).

Notes. 3 pp. advs. end vols. 1 and 2. Epistolary.

German trans. 1791 (*Lord Heinrich Holland, Herzog von Exeter, oder irre geleitete Grossmuth*)
(EAG).

Adv., 'In the press, and next week will be published', MC 19 Mar 1789.

CR: 'As an historical romance, this novel is contemptible, since not one trait of history or
of the manners of the times is preserved. The story is, however, well wound up, and the catastrophe concealed with some art: we see occasionally traces of a French extraction; but the
brat is too insignificant for rival nations to contend for the honour of having produced it.'

EARL STRONGBOW
See WHITE, James

ELEONORA, A NOVEL
See GOMERSALL, Ann

1789: 5   ANON.
EMMA DORVILL. BY A LADY.

London: Printed for T. Hookham, New Bond-Street, 1789.

178p. 12mo. 3s (CR), 2s 6d sewed (MR), 3s sewed (adv.).

CR 68: 328 (Oct 1789); MR 81: 285 (Sept 1789).

BL 12612.bb.12; EM 137: 7; ESTC t064736 (NA CaAEU, ICU).

Notes. Adv., 'Speedily will be published', MC 9 Apr 1789.

Adv. end vol. 4 of *Edelfrida* (1792: 7).

CR: 'This is a pleasing interesting little story, but does not rise in the scale. It is made up of adventures gleaned from former works, and in no instance does our fair author soar above the footsteps of her predecessors.'

MR [Andrew Becket]: 'This is one of those performances which, in a very little time, must pass from the shop of the bookseller to that of the trunk-maker or the pastry-cook.'

1789: 6   ANON.
THE FAIR HIBERNIAN. IN TWO VOLUMES.
> London: Printed by John Crowder for G. G. J. and J Robinson, Pater-Noster-Row, 1789.
> I 234p; II 255p. 12mo. 6s sewed (MR, DWR).
> MR n.s. 2: 465 (Aug 1790); AF II: 1358.
> BL 1607/4499; EM 6292: 5; ESTC t119711.

Notes. Epistolary.
Adv. DWR 7 Nov 1789.
Further edns: Dublin, 1790 (Printed by W. Porter, for P. Byrne, P. Wogan, B. Dornin, J. Halpin, J. Jones [and 2 others in Dublin], 1 vol., 12mo), ESTC n008161; Newburyport, MA, 1794, ESTC w012185.

MR [Thomas Ogle]: 'We . . . could not fail to be surprized at the many vulgarisms, and grammatical errors, which were mixed with some very good writing; nor were we less astonished at the indelicacies which we observed in the conduct and letters of some of the female characters. . . . there still remained something good; and that too in sufficient quantity to justify us in giving a higher degree of praise to this work, than can belong to most of its feeble, fluttering brethren and sisters.'

1789: 7   ANON.
*FAMILY SKETCHES: A NOVEL. IN TWO VOLUMES. WRITTEN BY A LADY.
> London: Lane.
> 2 vols. 12mo. 5s sewed (MR).
> MR n.s. 1: 449 (Apr 1790); AF II: 1372.
> No copy located.

Notes. Further edn: Dublin, 1789 (Printed for Messrs. P. Byrne, P. Wogan, J. Jones, and J. Halpen, 2 vols., 12mo), ESTC t203189.

MR [Andrew Becket]: 'The *pencillings* in these sketches is so very faint, that it is not a little difficult to discover what sort of beings they are intended to represent. For *ourselves,* we shall not attempt it farther. The out-lines in general, indeed, are so extremely imperfect, that scarcely any one, we believe, will ever be at the trouble of filling them up.'

1789: 8   ANON.
FANNY VERNON, OR THE FORLORN HOPE; A TALE OF WOE: CONTAINING SCENES OF HORROR AND DISTRESS THAT HAPPENED DURING THE WAR IN AMERICA.
> London: Printed for T. Axtell, Cornhill, 1789.
> iv, 237p. 12mo. 3s (CR), 2s 6d sewed (SDA).
> CR 68: 251 (Sept 1789); AF II: 1376.
> MH-H *EC75.A100789f2; EM 1110: 2; ESTC n008353.

Notes. 'Introduction. An Allegory.' 1 p. advs. end vol.

AR says that *Fanny Vernon* is same work as *The American Hunter* (1788: 5); no copy of the latter survives.

Adv., 'Distress and Woe', SDA 23 Jan 1789.

CR: 'Fanny Vernon cannot alone fill the eye, the mind, or perhaps more properly the volume: she is accompanied by the Somersetshire story. Yet we are sorry to see, that talents for what is really natural, interesting, and pathetic, should be driven to such attempts. If the stories are not (long experience has made us suspicious) republications from *Magazines*, or *vamped* up from *older volumes*, they would deserve our attention, our regard, and our commendation.'

1789: 9   ANON.
FASHIONABLE INFIDELITY, OR THE TRIUMPH OF PATIENCE. IN THREE VOLUMES.

> London: Printed for T. Hookham, New-Bond Street, 1789.
> I xiv, 238p; II vii, 236p; III vii, 245p. 12mo. 9s sewed (MR, DWR).
> MR 81: 364 (Oct 1789); AF II: 1385.
> BL 12613.aa.16; EM 240: 2; ESTC t068748 (NA CLU-S/C, DLC).

Notes. Prefatory address 1, v–viii; table of contents ix–xiv. Table of contents v–vii in vols. 2 and 3. 1 p. advs. end vol. 3. Epistolary.

Adv., 'Speedily will be published', MC 19 Mar 1789; adv. as published DWR 21 May 1789. Still adv. as new SDA 24 Nov 1792.

MR [Andrew Becket]: '... we have nothing to commend in a writer who seems unacquainted with almost every rule of grammar—but his "good intentions." The volumes may, however, on account of the morality which generally pervades them, be perused by the younger part of the community with some advantage.'

1789: 10   ANON.
THE FOLLIES OF ST. JAMES'S STREET. IN TWO VOLUMES.

> London: Printed for William Lane, Leadenhall-Street, 1789.
> I xi, 126p; II iv, 180p. 8vo [MR and CR have 12mo]. 5s (CR), 5s sewed (MR, SDA).
> CR 67: 554 (App [June/July 1789]); MR n.s. 4: 92 (Jan 1791); AF II: 1467.
> BL 1607/2521; EM 5873: 9; ESTC t118947 (NA CtY, IU).

Notes. Dedication 1, iii–iv to Duchess Dowager of Ancaster, signed The Author; 'To the Public' v–vii, identifying author as a woman 'neither young nor prosperous'; table of contents ix–xi; table of contents 2, iii–iv. Dedication is 'without permission ... for the Author, wishing to be concealed, does not presume to ask.' 2 pp. advs. end vol. 1. Large sections are epistolary.

Adv., 'In the Press', SDA 20 Dec 1788; adv. as published, 'A Fashionable Work, shewing the errors of dissipation', SDA 14 May 1789.

Adv. end vol. 3 of *Darnley Vale* (1789: 33).

CR: 'We have seen nothing more trifling and insipid than these volumes; they are the lowest of their rank, and we consign them with hearty good will—to oblivion.'

MR [John Noorthouck]: 'This title does not fully express the complexion of a performance, which is a natural sentimental tale, related in a pleasing manner. ... The writer, who professes to be of the feminine gender, knows how to interest, and to insinuate herself into her reader's good opinion, without having recourse to those wonderful turns of good or ill luck, which novelists always have ready at their elbows to introduce *just* when they are wanted; and which lose all effect, excepting with giddy readers, who surrender their understanding to the flights of fancy.'

1789: 11   ANON.
FORTESCUE; OR, THE SOLDIER'S REWARD: A CHARACTERISTIC NOVEL. IN TWO VOLUMES.

> London: Printed for W. Lane, Leadenhall-Street, 1789.
> I vii, 202p; II 216p. 12mo. 5s (CR), 5s sewed (MC).
> CR 67: 397 (May 1789); AF II: 1483.
> CSmH 285054; EMf; ESTC n031846 (NA CtY).

Notes. Dedication to Lord Heathfield, Governor of Gibraltar v–vii. 1 p. adv. facing t.p. Epistolary.

Adv. as 'in the press' MC 30 Dec 1788; adv., 'In a few Days will be published', MC 26 Jan 1789; adv. as published, 'A New Characteristic Novel', with text of dedication reprinted, SDA 25 Feb 1789.

Further edn: Dublin, 1789 (Printed for Mess. P. Byrne, P. Wogan, J. Moore, and B. Dornin, 1 vol., 12mo), ESTC t121007.

CR: 'These volumes have no claim to be distinguished from the common herd, either on account of the language, characters, or situation. But there is occasionally a passage, which seems to say, that the author is not one of the hackneyed tribe which regularly furnish the circulating library.'

A FRIEND OF VIRTUE
See MOUHY, Charles de Fieux, Chevalier de

1789: 12   ANON.
*HARRIET AND SOPHIA; OR, THE TEST OF LOVE: INCLUDING SEVERAL ENTERTAINING AND AFFECTING NARRATIVES, NEVER BEFORE MADE PUBLIC. WRITTEN BY A LADY OF DISTINCTION.

> London: Allen.
> 2 vols. 12mo. 5s (CR).
> CR 68: 408 (Nov 1789); AF II: 1819.
> No copy located.

Notes. CR: 'We remember the substance of these narratives, which, instead of being included in one story, are independent of each other. We do not know what kind of "distinction" the lady who wrote, or more properly transcribed them, deserves; but in the republic of letters it is not a very honourable one.'

HARTLY HOUSE, CALCUTTA
See GIBBES, Phebe

HEERFORT AND CLARA
See NAUBERT, Christiane Benedicte Eugenie

THE HERMIT OF SNOWDEN
See RYVES, Elizabeth

HONORIA SOMMERVILLE
See PURBECK, Elizabeth and Jane

1789: 13 ANON.
THE ILL EFFECTS OF A RASH VOW; A NOVEL, IN A SERIES OF LETTERS.
London: Printed for William Lane, Leadenhall–Street, 1789.
I 239p; II 239p. 12mo. 5s (CR), 5s sewed (MR, adv., SDA), 7s 6d sewed (MC).
CR 67: 153 (Feb 1789); MR 81: 563 (Dec 1789); AF II: 2152.
MH-H *EC75.A100.789i2; EM 1109: 30; ESTC n007617.

Notes. 1 p. advs. end vol. 2. Epistolary.
Adv. MC 16 Dec 1788; adv. as 'in the press' MC 30 Dec 1788; adv. as published, 'A Truly Affecting Tale', SDA 22 Jan 1789.
Adv. SDA 20 Dec 1788:'The Author of the above pleasing Tale, who favoured the Publisher with her correspondence some time since, under the signature of MATILDA, is respectfully informed, that the Novel is now nearly finished; the Execution, both as to excellence of paper, neatness and accuracy in printing, will, he presumes, meet her approbation—and as it is his intention to publish the Work the ensuing week, he would be happy in presenting a few Copies prior to the Publication. Leadenhall-street, Dec. 12, 1788.'
Adv. end vol. 1 of Darnley Vale (1789: 33).
CR: 'We have found so little to commend in these volumes that we should have passed them in silence, if it were not necessary to guard against deception and error. From the beginning to the end, if we except the moral, the whole is almost beneath contempt. Even the English is replete with solecisms; and the printer's blunders, added to the author's, render the story often unintelligible.'
MR [Andrew Becket]: 'The lovers of stultiloquence have here an admirable opportunity of perfecting themselves in that, at present, much-admired and much cultivated art. A performance better suited to their purpose, will not be easily found.'

THE INNOCENT FUGITIVE
See JOHNSON, Mrs

JULIET; OR THE COTTAGER
See 1788: 20

JULIUS; OR, THE NATURAL SON
See LOAISEL DE TRÉOGATE, Joseph-Marie

1789: 14 ANON.
THE LIFE AND ADVENTURES OF ANTHONY LEGER, ESQ; OR, THE MAN OF SHIFTS. IN THREE VOLUMES.
London: Printed and Sold by T. Wilkins, Aldermanbury: Sold also by J. Bew, Paternoster-Row; and T. Hookham, New Bond-Street, 1789

I xii, 279p; II viii, 296p; III viii, 284p. 12mo. 7s 6d sewed (CR), 9s sewed (MR).
CR 67: 397 (May 1789); MR 81: 285 (Sept 1789); AF II: 2564.
BL 1507/1345; EM 7586: 1; ESTC t129465 (NA DLC, PU).

Notes. German trans. Leipzig, 1790 (*Leben und Thaten Anton Legers, des Schlaukopfs*) (EAG).

CR: 'The work is Ferdinand Count Fathom in another form, and in different situations: it is entitled both to praise and censure, for many of the adventures are well conducted; some of them display much knowledge of the human heart; and a few of the characters possess the peculiar features of nature. But, on the other hand, we feel a constant disgust, even at the success of the hero; the work is a series of distinct, unconnected, and generally unfinished adventures; and we scarcely see any character in which we are interested, but he is left in distressed or at least doubtful circumstances.'

[Tobias George Smollett's *Ferdinand Count Fathom* 1753, JR 192, AF I: 2592]

MR [Andrew Becket]: 'The style of this performance is suited to the subject.'

LORD WALFORD
See LEWIS, L.

LOUIS AND NINA; OR, AN EXCURSION TO YVERDUN
See GORJY, Jean-Claude

1789: 15   ANON.
LOUISA FORRESTER; OR, CHARACTERS DRAWN FROM REAL LIFE. IN THREE VOLUMES.

London: Printed for W. Lane, Leadenhall-Street, 1789.
I iii, 222p; II 192p; III 218p. 12mo. 7s 6d (CR), 7s 6d sewed (MR, adv.).
CR 67: 76 (Jan 1789); MR n.s. 3: 91 (Sept 1790); AF II: 2605.
BL 12612.aa.17; EM 331: 6; ESTC t066377 (NA CtY).

Notes. Dedication to Lady Middleton, of Middleton i–iii.
Adv. MC 16 Dec 1788.
Adv. end vol. 3 of *Darnley Vale* (1789: 33).

CR: 'Two amiable old women, two pair of insipid, sentimental lovers, with a gay, vain, thoughtless heroine, are the principal personages of this novel. We are glad to find that there are such characters in real life; but we can add, that we have, on average, found them, in fifteen novels of every season, for these last fifteen years.'

MR [William Enfield]: 'The tales of benevolence and tenderness, which are crowded together in these three busy volumes, are, on the whole, pleasing: but there is too little unity of plan, and the characters pass before the reader's fancy in too rapid a succession, to produce any great effect. The gentle fluctuations of sentiment, which are excited by the various incidents of the piece, all terminate, as usual, in joy on the happy union of a worthy pair.'

MAMMUTH; OR, HUMAN NATURE DISPLAYED
See THOMSON, William

1789: 16   ANON.
THE MAN OF BENEVOLENCE.

London: Printed for the Author; and sold by Hughes and Walsh, Inner Temple Lane; Morgan, Ludgate Hill; Buckland, Paternoster-Row, and Raithby, St. Michael's Alley, Cornhill, 1789.

xii, 200p. 12mo. 2s 6d (CR), 3s boards (MR), 3s bound (SJC).

CR 68: 407 (Nov 1789); MR 81: 460–1 (Nov 1789); AF II: 2700.

Gu Z6–i.11 [2]; ESTC n034732 (NA CtY, PU).

Notes. Dedication to Miss W—— (identifying the author as her brother) iii–vi; preface vii–xii. Pagination continuous Roman-Arabic; text of novel starts on p. 13.

Adv. SJC 29 Nov–1 Dec 1791.

CR: 'The exertion of Benevolence procures the hero a rich and amiable wife—The reader will not want the application of the fable: "Go and do thou likewise." In other respects this novel scarcely rises above mediocrity.'

MR [Andrew Becket]: 'This little work is at once pathetic and pleasing. The only objection which can be raised against it is, that its incidents bear too close a resemblance to those of the before mentioned performance [*The Man of Feeling*, 1771: 46].'

1789: 17 ANON.
THE MAN OF FAILING: A TALE, IN TWO VOLUMES.

London: Printed for William Lane, Leadenhall Street, 1789.

I 238p; II 249p. 12mo. 5s (CR), 5s sewed (MR, MC, adv.).

CR 67: 237 (Mar 1789); MR n.s. 3: 90 (Sept 1790); AF II: 2701.

MH-H *EC75.A100.789m; EM 3030: 2; ESTC t038893 (BI BL).

Notes. Text of novel starts on p. 5 in both volumes. 1 p. advs. end vol. 2.

Adv. MC 16 Dec 1788.

Adv. end vol. 1 of *Darnley Vale* (1789: 33).

CR: 'This Man of Failing, who, by the way, is supposed to be a natural son of Sterne, commits many faults against his better judgment, and is, notwithstanding his errors, happy at last. His temporary sufferings are his only punishment. The author's manner is a little uncommon, in this age, and resembles that of the unsuccessful imitators of Fielding. In other respects this work deserves neither praise nor blame. It is too insignificant to draw on itself the vengeance of criticism for its faults, and too trifling to demand praise when no faults can be discovered.'

MR [William Enfield]: 'Vulgar amours, vulgarly related; and fit only to lie in the corner of the powdering room, for the hair-dresser's amusement, while he is waiting for his master.'

1789: 18 ANON.
*THE MENTAL TRIUMPH, A SENTIMENTAL NOVEL. BY A LADY, INSCRIBED, BY PERMISSION, TO THE PLAINEST OF HER SEX.

London: Printed at the Logographic Press; and orders for the Work will be received by Mr. J. Walter, No. 169, Piccadilly; and Mr. Richardson, under the Royal Exchange (DWR), 1789 (MR).

3 vols. 12mo. 7s 6d sewed (MR, DWR).

CR 68: 327–8 (Oct 1789); MR n.s. 1: 108–9 (Jan 1790); AF II: 2833.

No copy located.

Notes. Adv., 'In a few days will be published', DWR 19 June 1789.
New edn. adv. SJC 11–13 Feb 1790.

CR: 'On the whole, in many respects, these volumes rise above the ground; but they do not soar to any height, or preserve a continued flight' (p. 328).

MR [Andrew Becket]: 'In the letters of this lady, "so richly *decked in* mental charms," we discover nothing but the most common thoughts and expressions; and of her correspondents, we may observe the same. . . . With respect to the story, it is highly improbable.'

1789: 19   ANON.
*THE MODERN HUSBAND, A NOVEL, IN A SERIES OF LETTERS. BY THE AUTHOR OF LUCINDA OSBORN.

> London: Printed for and sold by J. P. Bateman, No. 21, Devonshire-street; Queen Square; T. Hookham, New-Bond-street; and J. Bew, Pater-noster Row (DWR), 1789 (MR).
> 2 vols. 12mo. 5s (CR), 5s sewed (MR, DWR).
> CR 68: 408 (Nov 1789); MR n.s. 1: 224 (Feb 1790).
> No copy located.

Notes. Lucinda Osborn (1787: 17).
Adv. DWR 1 June 1789.

MR [Andrew Becket], quoting Pope, describes the novel as one of those 'half-formed insects' but one not worth crushing.

MOUNT PELHAM. A NOVEL
See HOWELL, Ann

1789: 20   ANON.
THE PARSON'S WIFE. A NOVEL. WRITTEN BY A LADY.

> London: Printed at the Logographic Press, and sold by J. Walter, No. 169, Piccadilly; and W. Richardson, under the Royal Exchange, 1789.
> I 283p; II 287p. 12mo. 6s (CR), 6s sewed (DWR).
> CR 68: 251 (Sept 1789); AF II: 3245.
> BL 12611.aaa.7; EM 162: 4; ESTC t065823.

Notes. Adv., 'A New and Interesting Novel', DWR 20 July 1789.

CR: 'This is a pleasing, interesting tale, without novelty of sentiment or character, without any artful series of adventures, broad humour, or intrigue. The lady is, however, partial to matrimony, and, with very little exception, puts all characters to bed.'

1789: 21   ANON.
*PLEASING VARIETY; CONSISTING OF A COLLECTION OF ORIGINAL TALES, COMIC, SENTIMENTAL, AND INTERESTING.

> London: Allen.
> 2 vols. 12mo. 5s (CR), 5s sewed (MR).
> CR 67: 79 (Jan 1789); MR n.s. 4: 343 (Mar 1791).
> No copy located.

Notes. CR: 'The author, or the editor, seems much pleased with his Variety; but though we own, that variety may be charming, a variety of dulness has scarcely the negative merit of enabling us to escape *ennui*. Our hopes are kept alive by the change, but our disappointment, as in the present instance, is the greater.'

MR [William Enfield]: 'This disgusting medley has treated us with no very *pleasing* variety. Instead of comic humour, and laudable sentiment, we have been regaled with scarcely any thing but folly and insipidity.'

1789: 22 ANON.
THE PREDESTINED WIFE; OR FORCE OF PREJUDICE; A NOVEL. IN A SERIES OF LETTERS. BY THE AUTHOR OF EDWARD AND SOPHIA, POWIS CASTLE, AND ELIZA CLELAND. IN TWO VOLUMES.

> London: Printed for J. Kerby, at his Circulating Library, No. 190, Oxford-Street, 1789.
> I iv, 236p; II 233p. 12mo. 5s (CR), 6s sewed (MR, MC).
> CR 68: 328 (Oct 1789); MR n.s. 1: 109 (Jan 1790); AF II: 3592.
> PU Singer-Mend. PR.3991.A7.E436.1789; ESTC n020400 (NA TxU).

Notes. Epistolary. 'Advertisement to the Reader' 1, iii–iv.
Edward and Sophia 1787: 6; *Powis Castle* 1788: 30; *Eliza Cleland* 1788: 14. Also by same author: *Benedicta* (1791: 3); *Ashton Priory* (1792: 2); and *Mariamne* (1793: 8).
Adv. MC 4 Mar 1789; additional bookseller: C. Stalker, in Stationer's Court; adv. SS 31 Mar 1789 also lists Mess. Robinson, Paternoster-Row.

> CR: '. . . the story is trite, trifling, and in the highest degree improbable.'
> MR [Andrew Becket] describes it as 'tedious' and 'soporific'.

1789: 23 ANON.
THE PROGRESS OF LOVE; OR, THE HISTORY OF STEPHEN ELLIOT. IN THREE VOLUMES.

> London: Printed by L. Wayland, for T. Vernor, Birchin Lane, Cornhill, 1789.
> I 240p; II 240p; III 233p. 12mo. 9s sewed (MR, DWR).
> MR 81: 459–60 (Nov 1789).
> MH-H *EC75.A100.789p3; EM 1285: 6; ESTC n012036 (BI C).

Notes. Text of novel starts on p. 3 of each vol.
Adv. DWR 30 Apr 1789.

> MR [Andrew Becket]: '. . . by no means a contemptible performance. The story, indeed, is neither new nor interesting; but the observations which occasionally arise from the situations of the several personages, are such as bespeak a competent knowledge of the world, while they reflect no little honour on the writer as a man' (p. 459).

1789: 24 ANON.
THE RELAPSE: OR, MYRTLE-BANK. A NOVEL. IN TWO VOLUMES.

> London: Printed for C. Stalker, Stationers-Court, Ludgate Street, 1789.
> I 195p; II 175p. 12mo. 5s sewed (MR), 6s (adv.).
> MR n.s. 4: 91–2 (Jan 1791); AF II: 3733.
> DLC PR 3991.A1.R425. 1789; ESTC n065079.

Notes. 3 pp. advs. end vols. 1 and 2. Epistolary.
Adv., as *Myrtle Bank, a Novel,* end *The Freaks of Fortune* (1790: 13).

MR: 'To give us variety, characters and situations are here strained to extravagance and absurdity.'

ROSENBERG: A LEGENDARY TALE
See HOWELL, Ann

1789: 25   ANON.
THE SELF-TORMENTOR, A NOVEL. IN THREE VOLUMES.

London: Printed for G. and T. Wilkie, St. Paul's Church-Yard, 1789.
I 254p; II 263p; III 255p. 12mo. 9s (CR), 9s sewed (MR, MC).
CR 67: 554 (App [June/July 1789]); MR n.s. 1: 448–9 (Apr 1790); AF II: 4010.
BL 012601.aa.61; EM 241: 6; ESTC t108371 (NA MH-H).

Notes. ESTC: Sometimes erroneously attributed to Hannah More.
Epistolary. 500 copies printed Apr 1789 (Strahan 15 f. 111).
Adv. MC 14 Apr 1789; 'Written by a Lady'.

CR: 'If we allow for a little improbability resulting from the blindness of the self-tormentor, we can praise the general conduct of the novel before us. . . . There are many marks of address in the conduct of the story; and the language, as well as the conversations, show the author to be much above the tribe of hackneyed novel-writers. Much of this work is in the style of Evelina.' [*Evelina* 1778: 10]

MR [Andrew Becket]: 'This is a lively and ingenious work. We find in it a nice discrimination of character; together with a pleasing variety of incident, *sentimentality*, and humour. The author is not sufficiently correct in his language: but if he does not deserve to be ranked in the first class of modern novelists, he is certainly entitled to a place in the second.'

SENTIMENTAL LOVE ILLUSTRATED
See JACOBI, Johann Georg

1789: 26   ANON.
SEYMOUR CASTLE, OR THE HISTORY OF JULIA & CECILIA, AN ENTERTAINING AND INTERESTING NOVEL. IN TWO VOLUMES.

London: Printed for H. D. Symonds, Paternoster-Row, 1789.
I 214p; II 190p. 12mo. 5s (CR).
CR 70: 219 (Aug 1790); AF II: 4032.
BL 12611.aa.25; EM 162: 2; ESTC t054993.

Notes. Further edn: Dublin, 1789 (Printed by H. Colbert, 2 vols., 12mo), EM 5075: 8, ESTC t100483.

CR: 'We thought we had already sunk into the "extreme profound["] of insipid nonsense: but Seymour Castle lurked at the bottom. If the old motto were altered, and detur pessimo was the direction, every critical Paris would give the apple to the author of this "entertaining and interesting novel." '

THE SOLITARY CASTLE
See NICHOLSON, Mr

THE SPECTRE
See PYE, Henry James

THE TEST OF HONOUR
See ROWSON, Susanna Haswell

1789: 27   ANON.
**THE TRIUMPHS OF FORTITUDE: A NOVEL. IN A SERIES OF LET-
TERS. IN TWO VOLUMES.**
> London: Printed for William Richardson, Royal Exchange, 1789.
> I 245p; II 236p. 5s (CR), 6s sewed (SDA, DWR).
> CR 68: 407 (Nov 1789); AF II: 4539.
> PU Singer-Mend.PR3991.A1.T75 1789; ESTC n048329.

Notes. Epistolary.
Adv. SDA 29 June 1789; DWR 5 Dec 1789.
   CR: 'Some very young lady seems to have "dipped her fingers" in ink for the first time. Her production contains much romantic love, little probability, and less interest.—Fye, miss! indeed these pretty fingers may be better employed.'

1789: 28   ANON.
**THE TYRANNY OF LOVE; OR MEMOIRS OF THE MARCHIONESS
D'AREMBERG.**
> London: Printed for C. Elliot and T Kay, No. 332 Strand; and Charles Elliot, Edinburgh,
>   n.d. [1789].
> I 205p; II 184p. 12mo. 6s (CR), 6s sewed (MR, MC), 5s sewed (SJC).
> CR 68: 494 (Dec 1789); MR n.s. 1: 333 (Mar 1790); AF II: 4567.
> BL 12611.ccc.19; EM 165: 3; ESTC t057458.

Notes. ESTC date 1790, based on Heavisides's 1790 catalogue.
Dedication to Mrs. Fitzherbert signed 'The Authoress'. 2 pp. advs. beginning vol. 2, between t.p. and p. 1. Epistolary.
Adv., 'Handsomely printed in Two Volumes. . . . By a Lady,' MC 6 Apr 1789; adv. SJC 22–25 Jan 1791.
   CR: 'We think these volumes may be very useful, though in a way which the author probably did not intend. The stories are so closely and confusedly intermixed, that the work will exercise the powers of reflection, discrimination, and memory. We therefore recommend it for this purpose, since the mind cannot easily be gratified while it labours; nor will those who come for entertainment, remain to labour. In other respects, the novel is very trifling. . . .'
   MR [Andrew Becket]: 'This performance is either translated from the French, or formed on the models of this species of composition produced by that nation. They who are pleased with the extravagant and flighty manner of those writers will here meet with considerable gratification. We cannot say that their efforts, in this line of authorship, are altogether agreeable to us: but we must, at the same time, acknowlege that the present production, with all its romantic expression, is not uninteresting in its story; and that some of the characters are drawn in a bolder and far more animated style than those which usually fall under our notice.'

1789: 29   ANON.
WILLIAM AND CHARLES: OR, THE BOLD ADVENTURERS. A NOVEL.
IN TWO VOLUMES. WRITTEN IN LETTERS AND NARRATIVE. BY
THE AUTHOR OF LORD WINWORTH, MARIA HARCOURT, PHOEBE,
&C. &C.

London: Printed for C. Stalker, No. 4, Stationers Court, Ludgate Street, 1789.
I 212+p; II 232p. 12mo. 5s (CR), 5s sewed (MC).
CR 68: 494 (Dec 1789).
BL 1578/3655 [imperf.]; EM 8705: 2; ESTC t210087.

Notes. Some pages missing end vol. 1. Epistolary.
Lord Winworth 1787: 15; *Phoebe; or Distressed Innocence* 1788: 28; *Maria Harcourt*
1788: 22. Also by same author: *Lucinda Hartley* (1790: 17) and *Frederick and Alicia*
(1791: 12).
Adv. MC 16 Mar 1789.

CR: 'We know not whether the design, the conduct, or the language of this work be more
contemptible. The whole is in a high degree absurd and improbable, deformed by inelegant
provincialisms.'

THE WONDERFUL TRAVELS OF PRINCE FAN-FEREDIN
See BOUGEANT, Guillaume-Hyacinthe

THE YOUNG WIDOW; OR, THE HISTORY OF CORNELIA SEDLEY
See HAYLEY, William

ZELIA IN THE DESERT, OR, THE FEMALE CRUSOE
See DAUBENTON, Marguerite

ZELUCO
See MOORE, John

1789: 30   ALEXANDER, Judith.
THE YOUNG LADY OF FORTUNE, OR HER LOVER GAINED BY
STRATAGEM. A NOVEL, IN TWO VOLUMES. BY MISS JUDITH ALEX-
ANDER.

[London]: Printed for the Author by L. Alexander, Bishopsgate-Street, and Sold by
C. Stalker, No. 4, Stationers-Court, Ludgate-Street, 1789.
I 96p; II 104p. 5s (CR), 3s sewed (DWR).
CR 68: 328 (Oct 1789); AF II: 58.
BL N.1704(1); EM 1924: 4; ESTC t070723.

Notes. Text of novel starts on p. 3 in vol. 1 and p. 5 in vol. 2.
Adv. DWR 7 July 1789.

CR: 'We have seen nothing so trifling and insignificant; nor can we say in what respect this
novel is most contemptible; in its insignificancy, improbability, neglect of grammar, which
even glares in the title, or the extravagant expansion by which it is extended to two volumes,
loosely printed, containing together but two hundred pages.'

1789: 31   BENNETT, [Anna Maria].
AGNES DE-COURCI, A DOMESTIC TALE. IN FOUR VOLUMES. BY
MRS. BENNETT, AUTHOR OF THE WELCH HEIRESS, AND JUVENILE
INDISCRETIONS.

> Bath: Printed and Sold, for the Author, By S. Hazard: Sold also by G. G. J. and J. Robin-
> son, Paternoster-Row, and T. Hookman [sic], New Bond-Street, London; Shiercliff,
> Bristol; and all other Booksellers, 1789.
> I 12, 250p; II 257p; III 264p; IV 296p. 12mo. 10s sewed (MR), 12s (CR), 10s 6d
> (MC).
> CR 67: 474–75 (June 1789); MR n.s. 1: 215–18 (Feb 1790); AF II: 295.
> BL 1608/3854; EM 2378: 2; ESTC t120073 (BI C; NA TxU).

Notes. FC: Name often given incorrectly as Agnes Maria.
Epistolary. Dedication to Colonel Hunter 5–12, signed 'The Author'.
Juvenile Indiscretions 1786: 16; *Anna; or, Memoirs of a Welch Heiress* 1785: 22.
Adv., 'In the Press, and speedily will be published', MC 4 Dec 1788; adv. as published MC
13 Jan 1789.
Further edns: London, 1797, ESTC t164856; Dublin, 1789 (Printed for Messrs. Burnet,
Wogan, Byrne, Colbert, Moore, Jones, and Dornin, 2 vols., 12mo), EM 7101: 1, ESTC
t119105. French trans. Paris, 1799 (*Agnès de Courci*) (BN); NSTC lists French trans. in 1806.

> CR: 'The principal merit of this work . . . consists in the artful contrivance of an intricate
> series of events, well connected, without improbability, without confusion, and without a
> redundant perplexity. There is also some pathos, we mean independent of the conclusion
> which we wholly disapprove; much humour; and some well-conducted incidents. In the
> characters we see nothing very new, and nothing outré or unnatural; the different person-
> ages, and they are pretty numerous, are well distinguished, without the force of contrast. On
> the whole, if the author had known where to have stopped, she would have done well. . . . The
> arrangement of the convent is surely detailed in colours too captivating; and the sin of
> escaping from a vowed celibacy as too enormous.'

> MR [Andrew Becket]: '. . . as a well-wrought story, it is entitled to particular regard. The
> *inventive* faculty of its authoress is not to be disputed: but *character*, that great, that almost
> indispensable requisite in all such performances as the present, is seldom to be found in it.
> The reader's attention is so much taken up by the events, that the *personages*, who should
> undoubtedly be the *first*, become the *secondary*, consideration with him; and thus the very
> *essence* of such a composition (which, like the dramatic, consists in a faithful display of *man-
> ners*) is, in some degree, destroyed' (p. 216). MR disagrees with the argument that the novel
> is 'open to censure' for being favourable to Catholicism (p. 216).

1789: 32   BICKNELL, Alex[ander].
DONCASTER RACES; OR THE HISTORY OF MISS MAITLAND; A TALE
OF TRUTH; IN A SERIES OF LETTERS, PUBLISHED FROM THE ORI-
GINALS, WITH INTERESTING ADDITIONS. BY ALEX. BICKNELL,
AUTHOR OF THE HISTORY OF LADY ANNE NEVILLE; ISABELLA,
OR THE REWARDS OF GOOD NATURE; THE PATRIOT KING, A
TRAGEDY; &C. &C. &C. AND EDITOR OF MRS. BELLAMY'S APOL-
OGY, CAPTAIN CARVER'S TRAVELS, &C. &C. IN TWO VOLUMES.

London: Printed for C. Stalker, Stationer's Court, Ludgate-Street, n.d. [ESTC: 1790?].
I 272p; II 275p. 12mo. 6s sewed (MR), 6s neatly bound (adv.), 5s sewed or 6s bound
(DWR).
CR 68: 75 (July 1789); MR n.s. 2: 463–4 (Aug 1790); AF II: 331.
BL 1487.aaa.13; EM 2261: 1; ESTC t064470 (BI O; NA CtY InU-Li).

Notes. 2-pp. prefatory advertisement claims that the letters are genuine and embellished by
the editor. 8 pp. advs. end vol. 1. Epistolary.
Adv. DWR 20 Apr 1789.
Adv. end of vol. 1 of Martha Hugill's *Prince of Leon* (1794: 31).

CR: '. . . we know not how much is real, and how much may be styled "interesting additions;" but the whole is trite, flimsy, and improbable.'

MR [John Noorthouck]: 'The manufacture of novels has been so long established, that in
general they have arrived at mediocrity; and the similarity in the usual economy of the inun-
dation that still continues to pour on us, renders it difficult to discriminate and decide on
their comparative merit.'

1789: 33   BONHOTE, {E}[lizabeth].
DARNLEY VALE; OR, EMELIA FITZROY. A NOVEL, BY MRS. BON-
HOTE. AUTHOR OF PARENTAL MONITOR, &C. IN THREE VOLUMES.

London: Printed for William Lane, Leadenhall-Street, 1789.
I iv, 239p; II 214p; III 233p. 12mo. 9s (CR), 7s 6d sewed (MR, SDA).
CR 68: 407 (Nov 1789); MR n.s. 1: 223–4 (Feb 1790); AF II: 401.
CtY Im.B641.789; ESTC n047439 (EA TALn R/V 7088 [vol. 2 only]).

Notes. Dedication to the Rev. Dr Cooper and Mrs Cooper, Yarmouth, 1, i-iv, signed E. Bonhote, Bungay, May 1789. 1 pp. advs. end vol. 1, 2 pp. advs. end vol. 2, 3 pp. advs. end vol. 3.
Epistolary.
Adv. as 'in the press' MC 30 Dec 1788; still adv. as 'in the press' MC 3 Apr 1789; adv. as published SDA 23 May 1789.

CR: 'This is a very interesting and pleasing novel; it may be placed in the first rank, and
probably might be arranged at an equal distance from the first and the last of that rank. The
author, particularly towards the conclusion, steps too nearly in the steps of Cecilia [1782: 15].
The whole, we have said, is pleasing and interesting; and we may add also, that the story is
well conducted, strictly moral, and unfolded with skill.'

MR [Andrew Becket]: 'The volumes are pleasingly, and, with some few exceptions, very
correctly written; and the lessons in virtue and morality do the greatest honour to the writer's
heart' (p. 223).

1789: 34   [BOUGEANT, Guillaume-Hyacinthe].
THE WONDERFUL TRAVELS OF PRINCE FAN-FEREDIN, IN THE
COUNTRY OF ARCADIA. INTERSPERSED WITH OBSERVATIONS,
HISTORICAL, GEOGRAPHICAL, PHYSICAL, CRITICAL, AND MORAL.
TRANSLATED FROM THE ORIGINAL FRENCH.

Northampton: Printed by T. Dicey and Co. For T. and J. Evans, Pater-noster-Row,
London, n.d. [1789 (AR)].
vii, 224p. 12mo. 2s 6d sewed (AR).

AR 4: 352 (July 1789).

MH-H 40516.65*; xESTC.

Notes. Trans. of *Voyage merveilleux du prince Fan-Férédin* (Paris, 1735).

Dedicatory epistle to Madame C** B** vi–vii; table of contents [viii]; text begins on p. 9.

Further edns: Dublin, 1789 (Printed by Zachariah Jackson, for Messrs. W. Gilbert, Grueber and M'Allister, and J. Jones, 1 vol., 12mo), ESTC t197398; London, 1794, xESTC, AF II: 425; London, 1799, xESTC, AF II: 423.

AR: 'This is professedly a satirical work; but so feebly written, that it wants a sting to send the ridicule home.'

1789: 35   BROOKS, Indiana.

ELIZA BEAUMONT AND HARRIET OSBORNE: OR, THE CHILD OF DOUBT. WRITTEN BY INDIANA BROOKS. IN TWO VOLUMES.

London: Printed for G. J. J. and J. Robinson, Pater-Noster-Row, 1789.

I 250p; II 232p. 12mo. 6s (CR), 6s sewed (MR), 5s sewed (MC), 12s sewed (adv.).

CR 67: 397–8 (May 1789); MR n.s. 2: 465 (Aug 1790); AF II: 486.

MH-H *EC75.B7915.789e; EM 1102: 3; ESTC n007073 (NA NjP).

Notes. Epistolary.

Adv., 'In a few days will be published', MC 13 Feb 1789; adv. as published MC 17 Feb 1789. Adv. end vol. 1 of *The Son of Ethelwolf* (1789: 40).

CR: 'The adventures, which the fair authoress has interwoven into one tale, seem to be independent sketches, probably copied from nature. There are many characteristic traits, and nothing is greatly exaggerated, or raised beyond credibility. The language is also clear, natural, and easy. We have read these volumes with some pleasure, and think they rise much beyond the common herd, though we cannot style them excellent.'

MR [Thomas Ogle]: 'We cannot compliment the authoress on her success in these volumes. The story is incoherent and improbable; and the actors are always inconsistent, and at variance with themselves; but we must not be too severe with a lady, whose intentions appear to be good, whatever her book may be.'

1789: 36   C., Mrs

BELINDA, OR, THE FAIR FUGITIVE. A NOVEL. BY MRS. C—. DEDICATED TO HER GRACE THE DUCHESS OF MARLBOROUGH. IN TWO VOLUMES.

London: Printed for G. Allen, at his Circulating Library, Duke's Court, St Martin's Lane, 1789.

I iv, 201p; II 216p. 12mo. 5s (CR).

CR 68: 250 (Sept 1789); AF II: 271.

MH-H *EC75.C100.789b; EM 1606: 1; ESTC n015622 (NA CLU-S/C [vol. 1 only]; EA COR).

Notes. Dedication to the Duchess of Marlborough. 1 p. advs. beginning vol. 1 and 3 pp. advs. end vol. 1.

Adv. LC 65: 182 (19–21 Feb 1789).

Further edns: London, 1789, EM 5069: 2, ESTC t033007; Dublin, 1789 (Printed for Mess. P. Byrne, P. Wogan, J. Moore, J. Jones, and J. Halpen, 1 vol., 12mo), ESTC t223082; Halle,

1789, ESTC t211450; Görliz, 1795, ESTC t149041. German trans. Halle, 1789 (*Belinda, oder der Schöne Flüchtling*) (RS).

CR: 'This Novel is a little fascinating, for it has kept us nearly an hour from better employment, without novelty of sentiment, character, or situation.'

1789: 37   [CUMBERLAND, Richard].
ARUNDEL. BY THE AUTHOR OF THE OBSERVER.

London: Printed for C. Dilly, in the Poultry, 1789.
I 296p; II 300p. 12mo. 6s (CR), 5s sewed (MR, MC).
CR 67: 78–9 (Jan 1789); MR 80: 332–5 (Mar 1789); AF II: 955.
BL 838.b.18; EM 2385: 5; ESTC t011253 (BI O; NA CtY-BR, CSmH, MH-H, NjP, PU, TxU &c.; EA P, Pm).

Notes. Pp. 296–300 of vol. 2 are an address 'The Editor to the Reader', signed R.C. Epistolary. Adv., 'Tuesday next will be published', MC 20 Dec 1788; adv. as published MC 26 Dec 1788. Further edns: Dublin, 1789 (Printed for Messrs. G. Burnet, R. Moncrieffe, L. White, P. Byrne, P. Wogan, C. Lewis, J. Moore, J. Jones, J. Halpen, and B. Dornin, 2 vols., 12mo), ESTC t162113; London, 1791, EM 5166: 8, ESTC t066026; London, 1795, EM 4969: 14, ESTC t064720. French trans. Brussels and Paris, 1789 (*L'Heureuse révolution, ou histoire de M. Arundel*) (BN); German trans. Leipzig, 1790–91 (*Arundel oder Der Sieg des Edilmuths*) (EAG).

CR: 'Perhaps we expected too much, for we confess our disappointment.... the story and the conduct are in a great measure new.... The conduct of the story in general deserves our commendation; but it is occasionally stopped by dissertations, which impede the progress, and whose intrinsic merit does not compensate for the defect.... we may commend Arundel, as an interesting and entertaining companion' (p. 78).

MR [Andrew Becket]: 'The characters (with the exception of Arundel) are only faint and imperfect sketches, and such as we have long been accustomed to see. The sentiments which are put into the mouths of the principal personages, it must be owned, are often manly and spirited, tender and pathetic; they manifest a considerable knowlege of the human heart, yet what we have to complain of is, that these personages are not sufficiently drawn out or called into action. They talk about virtue and vice, and they describe the effects of the passions sometimes with considerable energy: but in performances in this line of writing, which considerably partakes of the nature of the drama, we expect to see the characters brought forward in a bold and spirited manner: we expect to see them virtuous or wicked, as different circumstances may operate on their different inclinations and tempers; and we likewise expect to be left, for the most part, to our own reflections on the matter. This is what we are desirous of seeing; and if this be neglected, the novel loses its distinguishing feature, and becomes didactic.—It instructs by *precept* instead of *example*' (pp. 332–3).

DALTON, Regina Maria
See ROCHE, Regina Maria

1789: 38A   [DAUBENTON, Marguerite].
ZELIA IN THE DESERT. FROM THE FRENCH. BY THE LADY WHO TRANSLATED "ADELAIDE AND THEODORE;" AND "ANECDOTES OF HENRY IV. OF FRANCE." IN THREE VOLUMES.

London: Printed for G. and T. Wilkie, Nº 71, St Paul's Church-Yard, 1789.

I 12, 224p; II 244p; III 285p. 12mo. 9s sewed (MR).

MR 81: 363–4 (Sept 1789); AF II: 999.

BL 12517.aaa.31; EM 3: 2; ESTC t102664 (NA CtY-Walpole).

Notes. Trans. of *Zélie dans le désert* (London and Paris, 1786–87).
List of subscribers vol. 1, 5–12. 750 copies printed May 1789 (Strahan 15 f. 111).
Same translator as 1783: 9, *Adelaide and Theodore.*
Adv., 'In the Press, and speedily will be published', LC 65: 243 (10–12 Mar 1789); adv. 'In the press, and in a few days will be published', MC 14 Apr 1789.
Further edns: Dublin, 1789 (Printed for Messrs. P. Byrne, L. White, P. Wogan, Grueber and M'Allister, H. Colbert [and 2 others in Dublin], 2 vols., 12mo), ESTC t212294; New Haven, CT, 1812 (WC). See also B below.

MR [Andrew Becket]: 'This performance is evidently founded on the *Isola Disabitata* of Metastasio,—a circumstance which we think the writer should, in justice to his distinguished prototype, have acknowledged by a line or two in the way of a preface: many of the situations in the *Novel* being exactly the same as those in the *Drama.* The incidents, however, are here considerably multiplied, and the amplification of the whole evinces a further degree of imagination, tempered by a suitable judgment' (p. 363). [Metastasio's play *Isola disabitata* trans. Arthur Murphy as *The Desert Island* in 1760.]

1789: 38B   [DAUBENTON, Marguerite].
ZELIE IN THE DESERT: OR, THE FEMALE CRUSOE. TRANSLATED FROM THE FRENCH.

London: Printed for C. Forster. No. 41, Poultry, 1789.

I 236p. 12mo. 2s 6d (CR).

CR 67: 397 (May 1789); AF II: 999.

ICN Case Y1565.D26; ESTC n060675 (NA PU).

Notes. Trans. of *Zélie dans le désert* (London and Paris, 1786–87).
Advs. pp. 231–236.
Further edns: London, 1789, ESTC n051811, and see A above. Extract published *Tell-Tale,* 1805, RM 1369.

CR: 'Instead of "the Female Crusoe, from the French," this work should be entitled, the French Crusoe; for the lady has all the refinements of that nation; and, instead of being alone obliged to her invention and her labour for her support, every necessary and many luxuries are provided. . . . In the delineation of English manners, the author is very faulty, and the translator has not corrected the errors.'

DAY, Thomas, THE HISTORY OF SANDFORD AND MERTON
See App. A: 5

1789: 39   FINGLASS, Esther.
THE RECLUSE: OR, HISTORY OF LADY GERTRUDE LESBY. IN TWO VOLUMES. DEDICATED (BY PERMISSION) TO HER GRACE THE DUTCHESS OF RUTLAND. BY MISS ESTHER FINGLASS.

London: Printed for J. Barker, Russell-Court, Drury-Lane, 1789.

I 226p; II 228p. 12mo. 6s (CR), 5s sewed (MR), 6s neatly bound (advs.).
CR 67: 153–4 (Feb 1789); MR n.s. 3: 90 (Sept 1790); AF II: 1444.
MH-H *EC75.F4945.789r; EM 1494: 22; ESTC n012840.

Notes. Dedication to the Duchess of Rutland 1, iii–vi; 'Remarks On the following Work, by a Gentleman of Eminence in the Literary World', signed R. Lewes, vii–viii. Pagination continuous Roman-Arabic; text of novel starts on p. 9. In vol. 2 text of novel starts on p. 5. Epistolary. Adv. beginning of *Stella* (1791: 36) and end of vol. 2 of Martha Hugill's *Prince of Leon* (1794: 31).
Further edn: Dublin, 1789 (Printed for P. Wogan, P. Byrne, J. Moore, and J. Halpen, 2 vols., 12mo), EM 4850: 4, ESTC t119662.

CR: 'Miss Esther Finglass is neither qualified by her knowledge of the human heart, of the manners of the world, nor the country where her scene is occasionally laid, to write a novel. We would, therefore, advise her to desist from the office. Her present work is deficient in each of these respects, and we would recommend to her the housewifely cares, where she may be useful and respectable; where, if she does not enchant by her wit, or her humour, she may secure esteem by being employed advantageously.'

MR [William Enfield]: 'A series of incidents arising from a clandestine marriage, contrived with some ingenuity, and told in the usual impassioned style, may give these volumes some title to a place in the list of interesting Novels.'

1789: 40　　{FULLER, Anne}.
THE SON OF ETHELWOLF: AN HISTORICAL TALE. IN TWO VOLUMES. BY THE AUTHOR OF ALAN FITZ-OSBORNE, &C.

London: Printed for G. G. J. and J. Robinson, Paternoster-Row, 1789.
I vii, 235p; II 209p. 12mo. 6s (CR), 6s sewed (MR, LC).
CR 68: 74 (July 1789); MR 81: 239–41 (Sept 1789); AF II: 1543.
BL 1608/1320 (t.p. vol. 1 mutilated); EM 2118: 4; ESTC t120826 (BI C; NA CSmH, ICN, MH-H, PU &c.).

Notes. Dedication to H.R.H. George Prince of Wales iii–vii (mutilated in BL copy; checked in ICN), signed Anne Fuller. 19-pp. list of subscribers (unn.) following dedication. 4 pp. advs. end vol. 1.
Alan Fitz-Osborne 1786: 21.
Adv. LC 65: 420 (30 Apr–2 May 1789); adv. DWR 13 May 1789. Rev. DWR 1 June 1789.
Further edns: Dublin, 1789 (Printed for Messrs. L. White, P. Byrne, P. Wogan, H. Colbert, A. Grueber and M'Allister, C. Lewis, J. Jones, and J. Moore, 1 vol., 12mo), ESTC t155651; London, 1800, ESTC n037137. French trans. Paris, 1789 (*Le fils d' Ethelwolf*) (BGR); German trans. Bremen, 1794 (*Alfred, König in England*) (EAG).

CR: 'The Son of Ethelwolf is inferior to his predecessor; and though Alfred calls for all the veneration of an Englishman, yet his obscurity and his adventures afford little that is not well known, and that has not been often repeated in modern times. . . . Miss Fuller engages attention by her pleasing language, and generally interests the reader by a varied contexture of adventures.'

MR [Andrew Becket]: '. . . never, we believe, have moral and historical truths been more nicely and intimately blended, than in the present performance. The story is interesting; and the rude and boisterous manners of the times are, in general, preserved with fidelity and care' (p. 239).

1789: 41   [GIBBES, Phebe].
HARTLY HOUSE, CALCUTTA. IN THREE VOLUMES.

> London: Printed for J. Dodsley, Pall-Mall, 1789.
> I 167p; II 167p; III 168p. 8vo [MR has 12mo]. 7s 6d (CR), 7s 6d sewed (MR, LC).
> CR 68: 164 (Aug 1789); MR n.s. 1: 332 (Mar 1790); AF II: 1605.
> BL 1425.b.16; EM 1834: 4; ESTC t117366 (BI E; NA CLU-S/C, CSmH, MH-H; EA
>   GOT)

Notes. Author attribution: FC.
Epistolary.
Adv. LC 65: 432 (2–6 May 1789).
Further edn: Dublin, 1789 (Printed for William Jones, 1 vol., 12mo), EM 6419: 3, ESTC
t057441. German trans. Leipzig, 1791 (*Hartlyhaus, oder Schilderungen des häuslichen und
gesellschaftlichen Lebens in Ostindien*) (EAG).

CR: 'We have been much pleased with these volumes; for, in the guise of a novel, they will
convey much information. They contain a pleasing, and, we think, an accurate description of
Bengal and its capital, Calcutta.'

MR [William Enfield]: 'These volumes contain a lively and elegant and, as far as we are
informed, a just picture of the manners of the Europeans residing in the East Indies. . . . Without affording any thing sufficiently novel for selection, they contain much pleasing description, and many smart observations.'

1789: 42   [GOMERSALL, Ann].
ELEONORA, A NOVEL, IN A SERIES OF LETTERS; WRITTEN BY A FEMALE INHABITANT OF LEEDS IN YORKSHIRE.

> London: Printed for the Authoress, by the Literary Society at the Logographic Press, and
>   sold by J. Walter, No. 169, Piccadilly, and W. Richardson, n.d. [ESTC: 1789].
> I vii, 261p; II 206p. 12mo. 6s sewed (MR), 6s (CR, MC).
> CR 68: 163 (Aug 1789); MR 80: 552 (June 1789); AF II: 1665.
> BL 1153.l.16; EM 2382: 4; ESTC t117008 (BI C; NA CLU-S/C).

Notes. Although burial records in Newport, Isle of Wight, imply that Mrs Gomersall's name
was Anna (see Raven, *Judging New Wealth*), evidence from petitions made to the Royal Literary Fund (RLF 9: 332) now suggest 'Ann'.
Dedication to Viscountess Irwin of Temple Newsam, Yorkshire, signed 'The Author', 1,
iii–vii; prefatory poem 'To ***** of *******'. 10-pp. list of subscribers end vol. 2.
Epistolary.
Adv. MC 27 Feb 1789.

CR: 'It is, on the whole, a work highly creditable to the good sense and the benevolence of
the author. The story is not perplexed by an artificial plot unravelled with skill; but an artless
tale, told in an easy pleasing style, enlivened by the occasional introduction of humorous personages and laughable events, and rendered instructive by the excellent morality which pervades every page of these volumes.'

MR [William Enfield]: 'These volumes are rendered interesting by a great variety of natural incidents, and are enlivened by an easy and often humourous delineation of characters.
The former are indeed such as often happen in life; and the latter are chiefly taken from the
middle or the lower classes of society; but the general effect is pleasing, and the writer certainly possesses a vein of comic humour.'

1789: 43   [GORJY, Jean-Claude].
**LOUIS AND NINA; OR, AN EXCURSION TO YVERDUN. IN TWO VOL-
UMES.**
> London: Printed for W. Lane, Leadenhall Street, 1789.
> I 152p; II 125p. 8vo. 5s (CR), 5s sewed (MR, SDA).
> CR 68: 251 (Sept 1789); MR n.s. 1: 109 (Jan 1790); AF II: 1678.
> ViU *PZ2.G66L.1789; ESTC n034058.

Notes. Original unidentified; not in AC or BN.
6 pp. advs. end vol. 2.
Adv., 'in the press', MC 30 Dec 1788; adv. as published, 'Laughter, Mirth, and Sentiment . . .
This Work has been translated into almost all the European Languages', SDA 7 Feb 1789.

CR: 'In this French, or rather Swiss story, there is some pathos, some sentiment, and no
little affectation of both. Probability is left at a distance, while our modern Sterne indulges in
the finer feelings of the heart, without reflecting, that intoxication often succeeds satiety.'

MR [Andrew Becket]: 'This performance is conceived in the strain of our more fashionable and sentimental tourists; and it must be acknowleged that it contains some tender and
pathetic strokes. . . . But the *prettinesses*, the *sensibilities* exhibited in the present production
are, by far, too many: we are absolutely overpowered by them.'

HALL, William Henry, **THE DEATH OF CAIN**
See App. B: 11

1789: 44   [HAYLEY, William].
**THE YOUNG WIDOW; OR, THE HISTORY OF CORNELIA SEDLEY, IN
A SERIES OF LETTERS.**
> London: Printed for G. J. J. and J. Robinson, Paternoster-Row, 1789.
> I 242p; II 267p; III 297p; IV 378p. 8vo [MR has 12mo]. 12s (CR), 12s sewed (MR,
> DWR).
> CR 68: 74–5 (July 1789); MR n.s. 1: 332–3 (Mar 1790); AF II: 1861.
> CHIr Crookshank Lib. 244–46 [vols. 1–3 only], ICN Y155.H33; EMf; ESTC t177867
> (NA CtY, ICN, IU, MH-H, PU &c.)

Notes. CHIr copy lacks vol. 4; details of that vol. from ICN copy. Epistolary.
Hayley's *Memoirs* report that he sold *The Young Widow* for £200 (1: 377).
Adv., 'On the 1st of May will be published, In Four Volumes, Crown Octavo', LC 65: 389
(21–23 Apr 1789); adv. DWR 30 Apr 1789.
Further edn: Dublin, 1789 (Printed for Messrs. L. White, P. Byrne, P. Wogan, H. Colbert, A.
Grueber [and 3 others in Dublin], 2 vols., 12mo [ESTC misspells 2 names in vol. 2 imprint]),
EM 6453: 4, ESTC t127663. French trans. Londres [i.e. Paris?], 1789, ESTC t152090; German
trans. Weissenfels and Leipzig, 1794 (*Leidenschaft und Delikatesse oder Geschichte einer jun-
gen Engländerin*) (EAG).

CR: 'This work is the production of no common author; to an extensive knowledge of
modern literature, he unites a very particular acquaintance with different parts of the continent; and our young ladies have some chance of improving their minds, as well as of amusing
their fancies. . . .'

MR [Andrew Becket]: 'This performance is scarcely to be placed in the class of *novels*;

though such was evidently the intention of its author. It is deficient in character and in contrivance: but this is compensated, in a great degree, by excellent observations on men and things; together with some exquisitely pathetic touches.... The present volumes are eked out by needless and tiresome repetitions. This, it may be remembered, was the fault of Richardson: but can the admirers of Richardson equal him in nothing but his faults? Many of the pages, too, are disgraced by *vulgarisms*, and by a poverty of expression' (p. 332).

1789: 45   [HOWELL, Ann].
MOUNT PELHAM. A NOVEL. IN TWO VOLUMES. BY THE AUTHOR OF ROSA DE MONTMORIEN.
London: Printed For William Lane, Leadenhall-Street, n.d. [ESTC: 1789].
I 181p; II [186]p. 8vo [MR has 12mo]. 5s (CR), 5s sewed (MR, MC).
CR 66: 577–8 (App [Dec 1788/Jan 1789]); MR n.s. 1: 109–10 (Jan 1790); AF II: 2084.
IU x823.H54m; ESTC n035200.

Notes. 1 p. advs. end vol. 1. Final p. vol. 2 misnumbered 86.
Rosa de Montmorien 1787: 40.
Adv. MC 16 Dec 1788; adv. as 'in the press' MC 30 Dec 1788; adv. as published, 'Novel of Incident and Adventure', SDA 22 Dec 1788.
   CR: 'It is not easy to discern, or to point out in what respects this novel rises above the common herd. It is not in character, in situation, in adventure, or in reflections.... it has amused an idle, a painful hour, and we owe our thanks to the author, for the favour. If we were to examine more closely, the verdict might be more unfavourable.'
   MR [Andrew Becket]: 'We have climbed, with no little difficulty, to the summit of this mount; and with nothing, alas! to cheer us by the way. The prospect is dreary and desolate around' (p. 109).

1789: 46   [HOWELL, Ann].
ROSENBERG: A LEGENDARY TALE. BY A LADY. IN TWO VOLUMES.
London: Printed for W. Lane, Leadenhall-Street, 1789.
I 158p; II 142p. 8vo [CR has 12mo]. 6s (CR).
CR 68: 408 (Nov 1789); AF II: 2086.
MH-H *EC75.H839; EM 1497: 3; ESTC n012944 (BI BL; NA CaAEU, InU-Li, ViU [vol. 1 only]).

Notes. 2 pp. advs. end vol. 2.
   CR: 'From the title of this tale, professedly *legendary*, we were led to expect that the imagination and the fancy would be more attended to than the judgment, and that the wonderful would be more predominant than the probable. We were not greatly deceived; yet the imagination is strongly and forcibly interested, particularly in the tale of the Haunted Castle.... the young lady's tale is interesting and amusing: the wilder horrors astonish; and the more familiar scenes entertain us.'

1789: 47   [HUGILL, Martha].
*THE COUNTESS OF HENNEBON, AN HISTORICAL NOVEL, IN THREE VOLUMES. BY THE AUTHOR OF THE PRIORY OF ST. BERNARD.
London: Printed for William Lane, Leadenhall-street (SDA), 1789 (CR).

3 vols. 12mo. 7s 6d (CR), 7s 6d sewed (SDA).
CR 68: 408–9 (Nov 1789).
No copy located.

Notes. St. Bernard's Priory (1786: 25).
Adv. as 'in the press' MC 30 Dec 1788; still adv. as 'in the press' MC 3 Apr 1789; adv. 'On Tuesday next will be published', SDA 30 May 1789.

CR: 'We have owned our predilection for historical novels, chiefly because the idle readers of these works might, in this way, have some remote chance of information. But where history and geography are so repeatedly violated; where probability can scarcely be found; where names and titles are constantly mutilated and disfigured, the whole must be pronounced contemptible.'

1789: 48   [?JACOBI, Johann Georg]; [LUDGER, Conrad (trans.)].
SENTIMENTAL LOVE ILLUSTRATED IN CHARMIDES AND THEONE, AND ASE-NEITHA, TWO ANCIENT TALES. TO WHICH IS ADDED, ELYSIUM, A PRELUDE. THE WHOLE TRANSLATED FROM THE GERMAN.

> London: Printed by D. Brewman, for J. Searle, Corner of Warwick Street and Brewer Street, Golden Square; Riley, No. 33, Ludgate Hill; Appleyard, in Wimpole Street; and Parsley, at the Dunciad, Surrey Side of Blackfriars Bridge, near Christ Church, 1789.
> 204p. 8vo. 2s sewed (adv.).
> NcD RBR Jantz no.937; ESTC n062258 (NA CSmH, DLC).

Notes. NcD copy presentation copy signed by 'the Translator C: Ludger'. NcD notes first and third works as attributed to Johann Georg Jacobi (*Elysium* [Königsberg, 1774] and *Charmides und Theone* [Halberstadt, 1774]).
ESTC: Original not traced.
Frontispiece and 1 other plate; 1-p. prefatory adv. (unn.) following t.p. concerns plates. Running title pp. 2–10 'Charmides and Theone', pp. 114–62 'Ase-Neitha', pp. 166–9 'Prologue' and pp. 172–204 'Elysium'. 'Elysium' in dramatic form.
Adv. end of vol. I of Martha Hugill's *Prince of Leon* (1794: 31).

1789: 49   [JOHNSON, Mrs].
THE INNOCENT FUGITIVE; OR MEMOIRS OF A LADY OF QUALITY.

> London: Hookham, 1789.
> 2 vols. 12mo. 5s (CR), 5s sewed (MR, adv.).
> CR 68: 164 (Aug 1789); MR n.s. 1: 332 (Mar 1790); AF II: 2192.
> DLC PZ3.I583 [missing]; xESTC.

Notes. Adv. end vol. 3 of *Edelfrida* (1792: 7) as 'By the Author of the Platonic Guardian' (1787: 41). Blakey: *Platonic Guardian* attributed to Mrs Johnson in a Minerva Catalogue of 1814.
Adv., 'Speedily will be published', MC 9 Apr 1789; adv. as published DWR 5 May 1789.

CR: 'The present story, and particularly the hinge on which it turns, is in some degree improbable; but it is pleasing, and often interesting. The characters are neither pointed, nor discriminated with much address.'

MR [Andrew Becket]: 'This production is principally to be commended on account of its *story*. The incidents are new and striking: but as to the personages, they are such as we have long been accustomed to see, and without any discriminative *traits*. The style is sometimes animated, and the sentiments are good.'

JOHNSON, Mrs, CALISTA
See MACKENZIE, Anna Maria

1789: 50   L[EWIS], L.
LORD WALFORD. A NOVEL. IN TWO VOLUMES. BY L. L. ESQ.

> London: Sold by T. Hookham, Bond-Street; T. and J. Egerton, Whitehall; J. Evans, Pater-Noster-Row; and W. Richardson, under the Royal Exchange, 1789.
> I 194p; II 208p. 8vo [CR and MR have 12mo]. 5s (CR), 6s sewed (MR, LC).
> CR 68: 328 (Oct 1789); MR n.s. 1: 449 (Apr 1790); AF II: 2544.
> BL 12612.aa.22; EM 137: 3; ESTC t064738.

Notes. MR has 'By L. Lewis, Esq.' after title; 2nd edn. adv. LC 67: 396 (24–27 Apr 1790): 'By L. Lewis, Esq.'.
Introduction vol. 1, 9–14; text of novel starts on p. 15. In vol. 2 text of novel starts on p. 5.
Adv. LC 65: 517 (28–30 May 1789).

CR: 'The Author of Lord Walford delights "in hair breadth 'scapes," for the different personages are often near death, though they never die. This, we suppose, is intended to elevate and surprise. In other respects the work is a motley mixture, composed of shreds and patches, without much regard to consistency or probability. . . . It is not, however, unentertaining, or occasionally uninteresting: it will supply the "something new" the incessant call of idle young ladies, antiquated dowagers, or neglected virgins.'

MR [Andrew Becket]: 'There is little to commend in this production. The incidents are common and trifling. The author sometimes attempts to soar into the *heaven of sentiment*: but his pinions are weak, and he presently falls to the ground.'

1789: 51   [LOAISEL DE TRÉOGATE, Joseph-Marie].
*JULIUS; OR, THE NATURAL SON: TRANSLATED FROM THE FRENCH.

> London: Ridgway, 1789.
> 2 vols. 12mo. 5s (CR), 5s sewed (MR).
> CR 69: 356 (Mar 1790); MR n.s. 2: 462–3 (Aug 1790); AF II: 2332.
> No copy located.

Notes. Trans. of *Le fils naturel* (Geneva and Paris, 1789); also issued as *Jules et Sophie, ou le fils naturel* (Grieder).
Further 2 vol. Longman edn. of 500 copies (LA), *The Natural Son*, with t.p. claim 'Translated from the French of M. Diderot' (for comment on the claim, see Grieder, p. 103), London, 1799, EM 1003: 39; ESTC n003973.

CR: 'Julius is the victim of sensibility: it seems to be his lot to be always in agonies or in raptures, and each are excited by causes which we think (but perhaps we are cold speculators) are unequal to the effect. . . . the novel is amusing, and the author seems to have had Werter in his eye, though he does not proceed to suicide.'

MR [John Noorthouck]: 'As the common occurrences in life are too insipid to bear reading, the composers of novels, regardless of probability, describe remarkable accidents, calculated to entertain and surprize; every novel that appears, therefore, renders the task of this species of writing more arduous, and requires invention to be racked for new situations and adventures, more extraordinary than have been yet conceived; and this necessity has produced the natural son. . . . The author endeavours to make it more pathetic by endowing his hero with exquisite sensibility; he is of course always in ecstasy or in agony; full of soliloquies and reflections, which, with a large print, extend a very short narrative to two scanty volumes. The work is said to be translated from the French, and is written with that kind of mediocrity that secures it from much censure, if it does not entitle it to great commendation.'

1789: 52   [MACKENZIE, Anna Maria].
*CALISTA, A NOVEL, BY MRS. JOHNSON, AUTHOR OF RETRIBU-
TION, GAMESTERS, &C.

> London: Printed for William Lane, Leadenhall-street (SDA).
> 2 vols. 12mo. 6s (CR), 5s sewed (SDA).
> CR 68: 327 (Oct 1789); AF II: 2654.
> No copy located.

Notes. Retribution 1788: 63; *The Gamesters* 1786: 33.
Adv., 'in the press', MC 3 Apr 1789; adv., 'In a few days will be published', SDA 30 May 1789; adv. as published 6 June 1789.
French trans. Paris, 1798 (*Histoire de Calixta, ou l'Amour conjugal*) (BN).
   CR: 'The characters displayed in this novel are supported with spirit and consistency. . . . In many parts there is much novelty, and the whole is very interesting, often pathetic, and generally amusing. The conduct of the story does not, however, show any great skill: the event is soon obvious; and though the catastrophe is varied beyond what may be at first expected, yet it is in effect foreseen. The wandering of Calista is perhaps a little too much like that of Cecilia; but this defect is compensated for by the artful arrangement of circumstances, by which she is prevented from returning to her husband, and by which she is rendered in appearance guilty. We have not in our late career, met with many better works, and few which possess so much merit, or which we can with less exception recommend.'

1789: 53   [?MATHEWS, Eliza Kirkham].
ARGUS; THE HOUSE-DOG AT EADLIP. MEMOIRS IN A FAMILY COR-
RESPONDENCE, BY THE AUTHOR OF CONSTANCE AND THE
PHAROS. IN THREE VOLUMES.

> London: Printed for T. Hookham, New Bond-Street, 1789
> I 261p; II 262p; III 225p. 12mo. 7s 6d (CR), 9s sewed (MR, MC).
> CR 67: 396–7 (May 1789); MR 81: 77–8 (July 1789); AF II: 2753.
> C 7720.d.1394; EM 230: 1; ESTC t071303 (BI BL; NA CtY-BR, IU, MH-H, PU, ViU &c.;
>   EA AMu, P)

Notes. FC says author attribution is doubtful.
2-pp. adv. for *L'Esprit des Journaux* at end of vol. 2. 3 pp. advs. end vol. 3, some including comments from revs., for books published by Hookham. Epistolary.
Constance 1789: 53.
Adv. MC 19 Mar 1789.
French trans. 1803 (NSTC).

CR: '... this novel is the meanest of its tribe; the tale is dull, the plot trite, the denouement hurried and improbable. Every character we have seen before; we have seen them in better dress and better situations.'

MR [Andrew Becket]: 'The present publication is so much superior to most of those performances which come under the denomination of *novels*, that we are not a little doubtful of its success.... when it is remembered that the ordinary *novel-reader* looks for nothing but a train of love adventures, with elopements, duels, and all the various *et cetera* thereunto belonging, and not for any thing like rational investigation, or philosophical truth; the justness of our observation will, scarcely, we think, be questioned.'

1789: 54   [MOORE, John].
ZELUCO. VARIOUS VIEWS OF HUMAN NATURE, TAKEN FROM LIFE AND MANNERS, FOREIGN AND DOMESTIC. IN TWO VOLUMES.

London: Printed for A. Strahan and T. Cadell, in the Strand, 1789.
I 482p; II 529p. 8vo. 12s boards (MR, CR).
CR 67: 505–6 (App [June/July 1789]); MR 80: 511–15 (June 1789); AF II: 2936.
O Vet.A5e.4606, 4607; EM 5901: 2; ESTC t123769 (BI BL, C, E &c.; NA CtY-Walpole, CtY-Med, CSmH, DLC, ICN, IU, PU, TxU, ViU &c.; EA Pm, PRTup).

Notes. Adv., 'This Month will be published', DWR 12 May 1789; adv. as published DWR 27 May 1789. 1,500 copies printed May 1789 (Strahan 15 f. 125).
Extracts published LC 65: 529–30, 537–8, 545–6, 561–2 and 569–70 (2–4, 4–6, 6–9, 11–13 and 13–16 June 1789).
Further edns: Dublin, 1789 (Printed for Messrs. Grueber and M'Allister, 2 vols., 12mo), ESTC t212538; Dublin, 1789, ESTC t180904; London, 1789, EM 2219: 1, ESTC t123768; Dublin, 1789, EM 4853: 16, ESTC t123770; New York, 1790, ESTC w011462; 3 further entries in ESTC; WC has 6 entries between 1800 and 1850; NSTC lists edn. in 1810. Extracts from *Zeluco* with various titles published in 4 magazines, 1789, RM 838, 1370, 1371. German trans. Liegnitz and Leipzig, 1791 (*Zeluko oder Schilderungen der menschlichen Natur*) (EAG); French trans. Paris, 1796 (*Zelucco, ou le vice trouve en lui-même son châtiment*) (HWS).

CR: 'If this work be, as fame has reported, the production of Dr Moore, we think it greatly inferior to his other labours.... The series of adventures is not, we think, conducted with such address as to keep the attention alive and interest the feelings in the event of the story, though the moral is constantly kept in view, and every page reminds us of the necessity of being virtuous if we would be happy.... The great merit of this work consists in the conversations and disquisitions...' (p. 505).

MR [John Gillies]: 'This is not a common novel. The author's mind is stored with useful knowlege, and adorned with elegant literature. He appears to have read the great book of life with attention and profit.... Unlike to most modern novels, which have little other merit but that of exciting curiosity, and which are thrown aside as soon as that curiosity is gratified, the story, or fable, in this performance, is to be considered merely as the canvas, on which this skilful observer of life and manners delineates such moral pictures as are likely to excite the attention of his age and country' (pp. 511–12).

1789: 55   [MOUHY, Charles de Fieux, Chevalier de].
A FRIEND OF VIRTUE. A NOVEL. FROM THE FRENCH. BY THE TRANSLATOR OF THE EFFECTS OF THE PASSIONS. IN THREE VOLUMES.

London: Printed for T. Vernor, Birchin-Lane, Cornhill, 1789.
I 210p; II 224p; III 226p. 12mo. 9s (CR, SJC); 7s 6d (adv.), 9s sewed (DWR).
CR 67: 554 (App [June/July 1789]); AF II: 1534.
BL RB.23.a.8929; ESTC n047383 (NA NjP).

Notes. Trans. Of *Le financier* (Amsterdam, 1755), later republished as *L'ami de la vertu ou mémoires et aventures de monsieur d'Argicourt* (Liège, 1764).
ESTC lists London edn. as anonymous and Dublin edn. as by Jean-Gaspard Dubois-Fontanelle; Fontanelle was the author, not the translator, of *The Effects of the Passions* (*Les Effets des passions*, London and Paris, 1768). Grieder, following Block, also lists as by the author of the earlier trans., given as Gaspar Moise Augustin de Fontanieu.
1 p. adv. end vol. 1; 1 p. end vol. 3.
Adv. DWR 30 Apr 1789: *The Friend of Virtue; Or Memoirs of D'Argicourt*; adv. SJC 22–24 Mar 1791 as *Friend of Virtue; or, Memoirs of D' Argicourt.*
Adv. end of *The Adventures of Henry Fitzherbert* (1794: 1) as *The Friend of Virtue; or the Memoirs of Dr Argincourt.*
Further edn: Dublin, 1789 (Printed for Messrs. H. Chamberlaine, P. Byrne, P. Wogan, J. Halpen, and B. Dornin, 2 vols., 12mo), ESTC t203507.

CR: 'The hero of this insipid tale scatters his money with all the profusion of some modern heroes of romance, and is at last very happy, and like Job, richer than before. If this work is of service to the cause of virtue, we shall rejoice: but we suspect that they will add little to the entertainment of their readers.'

1789: 56   [?NAUBERT, Christiane Benedicte Eugenie]; [POULIN, John (*trans.*)].
*HEERFORT AND CLARA. FROM THE GERMAN.

London: Printed for G. G. J. and J. Robinson, Paternoster-Row (DWR), 1789 (DWR).
3 vols. 12mo. 9s (CR), 9s sewed (MR, DWR).
CR 68: 494 (Dec 1789); MR n.s. 2: 465 (Aug 1790); AF II: 1878.
No copy located.

Notes. Trans. of *Heerfort und Klärchen* (Frankfurt, 1779).
ESTC: Attributed to Christiane Benedicte Eugenie Naubert.
Robinsons paid Poulin 18gns., 30 May 1789, and a further 18gns., 11 June 1789, for translating *Heetfort* [*sic*] *and Clara* (RA).
Adv. DWR 7 Nov 1789; has 'Heertfort'; adv. SJC 16–18 Feb 1790 has 'Heertford'.
French trans. Londres [ESTC: i.e. Paris?], 1789–90, ESTC t151922.

CR: 'We found this novel very interesting and entertaining: the characters are uncommon, and the situations frequently affecting; but, in the conduct of the plot we do not think the author skilful. The narrative is too frequently broken, and he returns to relate adventures, which a novellist of more address would have brought some of the other characters to explain. The moral is exemplary. . . .'

MR [Thomas Ogle]: 'When we first opened this book, it was with pleasure that we saw it was from the German. The original must have merit, we thought, to occasion a translation. Beside, we had been so much pestered with *novel* adventures in our own country, that we were heartily glad to change the scene. Alas! to our sorrow, we soon found that, whatever country gave it birth, a novel was a novel; that it was still the same unnatural, ridiculous, tedious, and stupid, composition.'

1789: 57   [NICHOLSON, Mr].
THE SOLITARY CASTLE, A ROMANCE OF THE EIGHTEENTH CEN-
TURY. BY THE AUTHOR OF THE VILLAGE OF MARTINDALE. IN
TWO VOLUMES.
>London: Printed for W. Lane, Leadenhall-Street, 1789.
>I ii, 172p; II 171p. 8vo [MR has 12mo]. 5s sewed (MR).
>MR n.s. 1: 449 (Apr 1790); AF II: 4173.
>BL 12611.a.23; EM 3409: 11; ESTC t031410 (NA MH-H)

Notes. Blakey: attributed to Mr. Nicholson in a Minerva Library catalogue of 1814.
Frontispiece. Preface i–ii.
The Village of Martindale 1787: 46.

MR [Andrew Becket]: 'Reader, thou hast, no doubt, observed the coruscations, the
streams of light, which sometimes play on the skirts of evening; and which throw a temporary brightness on the earth. Like to these, are the present pages. —A flash or two is seen; and
darkness again envelopes us.'

1789: 58   NORMAN, Elizabeth.
THE CHILD OF WOE. A NOVEL. BY MRS. ELIZABETH NORMAN. IN
THREE VOLUMES.
>London: Printed for H. D. Symonds, Pater-Noster-Row, 1789.
>I 188p; II 165p; III 167p. 12mo. 7s 6d (CR), 7s 6d sewed (MR, MC).
>CR 67: 237 (Mar 1789); MR 81: 364 (Oct 1789) ; AF II: 3076.
>PU Singer-Mend. PR.5112.N44.C5.1789; ESTC n027807.

Notes. Epistolary.
Adv. MC 16 Dec 1788; adv. as 'in the press' MC 30 Dec 1788; adv., 'just published, Dedicated
to George Colman, Sen. Esq.', SDA 22 Jan 1789.
Further edn: Dublin, 1789 (Printed for Messrs. P. Byrne, P. Wogan, J. Parker and J. Moore,
3 vols., 12mo), ESTC t212474.

CR: 'Though Mrs. Norman makes one of the correspondents say to Eliza, the Child of
Woe, that she tells her story elegantly and pathetically, we cannot join in the commendation.
The language is turgid, and in some passages it is prose almost run mad. The contrivance is
not greatly superior, and the characters are trifling and familiar. It is, on the whole, an
insignificant and insipid work.'

MR [Andrew Becket]: '. . . of all the woful productions which have lately come into our
hands, this is unquestionably the most *woful*—whether we consider it in point of character,
contrivance, sentiment, or style.'

1789: 59   [O'CONNOR, E.].
*ALMERIA BELMORE. IN A SERIES OF LETTERS. BY A LADY. (DWR).
>London: Printed for G. G. J. and J. Robinson, Paternoster-Row (DWR), 1789 (DWR).
>12mo. 3s sewed (MR, DWR).
>MR n.s. 1: 331 (Mar 1790); AF II: 3098.
>No copy located.

Notes. Authorship information is given in ESTC's entry for this author's *Emily Benson*
(1791: 54).

Epistolary.

German trans. Duisburg, 1792 (*Almeria Belmore, eine Novelle in Briefen*) (EAG).

MR [Andrew Becket]: 'Nonsense, *double refined*; and *sweetened* withal to the taste of the times,—*in Tavistock Street.*'

1789: 60   [PURBECK, Elizabeth and Jane].
HONORIA SOMMERVILLE: A NOVEL. IN FOUR VOLUMES.

> London: Printed for G. G. J. and J. Robinson, Pater-noster-Row, 1789.
> I 244p; II 234p; III 256p; IV 248p. 12mo. 12s (MR, CR), 12s sewed (MC, adv.).
> CR 67: 398 (May 1789); MR 81: 78–9 (July 1789); AF II: 3641.
> NjP 3600.001.476; EM 3359: 9, ESTC t166295.

Notes. Print missing at left edge of p. [256] of vol. 3 leaves page number as 56.

Adv., 'On Monday, the first of March will be published', MC 17 Feb 1789; adv. as published MC 4 Mar 1789.

Adv. end vol. 1 of *The Son of Ethelwolf* (1789: 40).

Further edns: London, 1789, ESTC n008357; Dublin, 1789 (Printed for Messrs. P. Byrne, P. Wogan, J. Moore, and J. Halpen, 2 vols., 12mo), ESTC t212420. German trans. Leipzig, 1791 (*Honorie Sommerville*) (RS).

CR: 'This Novel soars far above the common flight, and consists of a series of adventures well arranged; intricate without perplexity, unravelled without confusion, and the denouement is so carefully concealed, that, while each event seems natural, it contributes imperceptibly and apparently without design, to an unexpected conclusion. The characters are well drawn, and appear to be sometimes sketched from nature. . . . The language of the volumes is uniformly neat; it is the language of nature not refined into elegance, or stiffened by rounded periods.'

MR [Andrew Becket]: '. . . the production before us is nothing but a tissue of adventures which the writer has before presented to the public in a variety of shapes, although the materials and colouring are nearly the same in all.'

1789: 61   [PYE, Henry James].
THE SPECTRE. ORNAMENTED WITH A FRONTISPIECE.

> London: Printed for John Stockdale, opposite Burlington House, Piccadilly, 1789.
> I xvi, 171p; II 196p. 6s boards (MR), 6s sewed (LC).
> CR 68: 76 (July 1789); MR 80: 552 (June 1789); AF II: 4206.
> BL N.1658; EM 3809: 3; ESTC t071903 (BI O; NA CtY, CSmH, MH-H &c.).

Notes. Author attribution: RG, NCBEL.

Long dedication to James Petit Andrews, Esq. 1, iii–xvi. 8 pp. advs. end vol. 2. Epistolary.

Adv., 'Ornamented with a beautiful Frontispiece', LC 65: 188 (21–24 Feb 1789); adv. MC 26 Feb 1789.

CR: 'Our author's aim, in this novel, has been to mix general observation and more serious discussion with adventure. This plan has, however, as little novelty as the story of the Spectre, which, in substance, has been repeatedly detailed, particularly in the Sylph [1779: 8], and more closely in an old novel entitled the Apparition [1788: 7]. There is great improbability also in the conduct, and little that can interest in the character or situations.'

MR [William Enfield]: 'If this book be regarded as a Novel, it has little merit, for the incidents are few and unnatural: if it be considered as a series of letters on various topics, it deserves commendation.'

1789: 62   [RADCLIFFE, Ann].
THE CASTLES OF ATHLIN AND DUNBAYNE. AN HIGHLAND STORY.

London: Printed for T. Hookham, New Bond-Street, 1789.
280p. 12mo. 3s (CR), 3s sewed (MR, DWR).
CR 68: 251 (Sept 1789); MR 81: 563 (Dec 1789); AF II: 3671.
MH-H *EC75.R1163.789c; EM 1498: 30; ESTC n014983 (BI E; NA CtY-BR, CSmH, PU, ViU &c.).

Notes. 12 pp. advs. between t.p. and p. 1.
Adv., 'Speedily will be published', MC 9 Apr 1789; adv. as published, with title as *The Castles of Athlane and Dunbayne, A Highland Story*, DWR 28 May 1789.
Further edns: Dublin, 1792 (Printed for T. Jackson, 1 vol., 12mo), ESTC n029021; London, 1793, EM 269: 10, ESTC t114711; Dublin, 1794, ESTC t199967; Philadelphia, 1796, ESTC w037326; London, 1799, EM 6225: 7, ESTC t092043; WC has 8 entries between 1800 and 1850; Summers lists 8 edns. between 1800 and 1850; NSTC lists edns. in 1821, 1824, 1827, 1832, 1836 and 1841. French trans. Paris, 1797 (*Les Châteaux d'Athlin et de Dunbayne*) (Lévy). Facs: GN I (1821 edn.).

   CR: 'There is some fancy and much romantic imagery in the conduct of this story; but our pleasure would have been more unmixed had our author preserved better the manners and costume of the Highlands. He seems to be unacquainted with both.'

   MR [Andrew Becket]: 'To those who are delighted with the *marvellous*, whom wonders, and wonders only, can charm, the present production will afford a considerable degree of amusement. This kind of entertainment, however, can be little relished but by the young and unformed mind.... this little work is to be commended for its moral; as also for the good sentiments and reflections which occasionally occur in it.'

1789: 63   ROBINSON, Pollingrove [pseud?].
COMETILLA; OR VIEWS OF NATURE. BY POLLINGROVE ROBINSON, ESQ. VOL. I. BEING AN INTRODUCTION TO ASTRONOMY.

London: Printed for J. Murray, Fleet-Street, 1789.
262p. 8vo.
BL 49.a.24; EM 5631: 1; ESTC t140633 (NA CLU-S/C).

Notes. ESTC: Pollingrove Robinson may be a pseudonym. ESTC: No more published? 'Text book heavily disguised as a romantic novel.'
'Premonition' v–xv, dated 2 Apr 1789. Text of novel ends on p. 215; pp. 216–62 are an index.

1789: 64   [ROCHE], Regina Maria.
THE VICAR OF LANSDOWNE; OR, COUNTRY QUARTERS. A TALE. BY MARIA REGINA DALTON. IN TWO VOLUMES.

London: Printed for the Author: And sold by J. Johnson, No. 72, in St. Paul's Church-Yard, 1789.
I 298p; II 295p. 12mo. 6s (CR), 6s sewed (MR).
CR 67: 475 (June 1789); MR n.s. 1: 222–3 (Feb 1790); AF II: 3853.
BL N.1714; EM 1925: 2; ESTC t071894 (NA MnU, OU, ViU).

Notes. 3-pp. dedication to the Marchioness of Buckingham; 2-pp. address to the critics begging them to allow the work 'to pass by in unheeded insignificance....'

Further edns: London, 1800, EM 6993: 11, ESTC t108468; Baltimore, 1802 (WC); New York, 1802 (WC), London, 1825 (Summers). French trans. Paris, 1789 (*Le curé de Lansdowne, ou Les garnisons*) (WC); German trans. Leipzig, 1790 (*Der Landprediger von Landsdowne und seine Familie*) (Price).

CR: 'We see in many passages of this novel proofs of its having been written by an author unhackneyed in the tricks of the profession. The tale is natural, easy, pleasing and interesting.... The language is good, the characters, if not quite new, are not those usual personages which we meet with every day; the situations are interesting, and the moral unexceptionable.'

MR [Andrew Becket]: 'She aims, occasionally, at a display of *character*; and not unfrequently delineates it with tolerable success. This, as we have repeatedly observed, is the principal excellence in a novel, as in a dramatic production. Miss Dalton too, in a plain and simple tale (which we would always prefer to that which is complex, because the figures may consequently be drawn with a bolder hand) has contrived to interest us sufficiently in the event. Attention is kept awake, while the sentiments are such as every good and susceptible heart must thoroughly approve.'

1789: 65   [ROWSON, Susanna].
THE TEST OF HONOUR. A NOVEL. BY A YOUNG LADY.

> London: Printed by and for John Abraham, at his Circulating Library, St. Swithin's Lane, Lombard-Street, 1789.
> I viii, 192p; II 226p. 12mo. 5s (CR), 5s sewed (MR, SJC).
> CR 68: 408 (Nov 1789); MR n.s. 1: 331–2 (Mar 1790); AF II: 3885.
> MH-H *AC7.R7997.A789t; ESTC n013415 (NA MWA [vol. 1 only]).

Notes. ESTC: sometimes attributed to Rowson.
Preface 1, i–viii. Running title 'Mary; or, the Test of Honour'. 1 p. advs. end vol. 2.
Adv. SJC 29 May–1 June 1790.

CR: 'This little story is related in an artless style; but we cannot compliment the young lady on what appears to be her first attempt. There is little to commend in the conduct of the plot, or in the delineation of characters. The whole is generally trifling, and frequently improbable.'

MR [Andrew Becket]: 'The writer is evidently unaccustomed to the use of the pen: but the story is, in some parts, interesting, and, generally speaking, prettily told. The moral . . . is of the highest and most exemplary kind.'

1789: 66   [RUDD, Margaret Caroline].
THE BELLE WIDOWS: WITH CHARACTERISTIC SKETCHES OF REAL PERSONAGES AND LIVING CHARACTERS. A NOVEL, INSCRIBED TO THE BEAU-MONDE. WITH A PREFACE BY THE EDITOR OF THE LETTERS OF CHARLOTTE DURING HER CONNEXION WITH WERTER.

> London: Printed for J. Kerby, Stafford Street, Old Bond-Street, 1789.
> I xvi, 214p; II 199p. 12mo. 5s (CR), 6s sewed (DWR).
> CR 68: 495 (Dec 1789); AF II: 3893.
> CtY-Mudd Im.R831.789; ESTC n064579.

Notes. Preface 1, i–xvi.
Letters of Charlotte (by William James) 1786: 26.

Adv. DWR 17 Dec 1789; 'Printed for J. Kirby, No. 2, Stafford-Street, Old Bond-Street; and sold by Champante and Witrew [*sic*], Jurey-Street, and Scatchard and Whitaker, Ave-Maria-Lane.'

CR: 'These "real personages" and "living characters" are very trifling and insipid. If this be the Beau Monde, we shall retire contentedly to our garret, and congratulate ourselves on escaping from it: in truth the author has reached the climax of uninteresting nonsense.'

1789: 67   [RYVES, Elizabeth].
THE HERMIT OF SNOWDEN: OR MEMOIRS OF ALBERT AND LAVINIA. TAKEN FROM A FAITHFUL COPY OF THE ORIGINAL MANUSCRIPT, WHICH WAS FOUND IN THE HERMITAGE, BY THE LATE REV. DR. L—— AND MR. ——, IN THE YEAR 17**.

> London: Printed at the Logographic Press, (Under the Direction of the Literary Society,) and sold by J. Walter, No. 169, Piccadilly; C. Stalker, Stationers-Court, Ludgate-Street; and W. Richardson, under the Royal-Exchange, 1789.
>
> xvii, 230p. 12mo. 3s (CR), 3s sewed (DWR).
> CR 68: 163 (Aug 1789); AF II: 3910.
> BL 1608/2770; EM 3912: 15; ESTC t120591 (NA CSmH).

Notes. Introduction i–xvii. Pagination continuous Roman-Arabic; text of novel starts on p. 19.
Adv. DWR 21 May 1789.
Further edns: Dublin, 1790 (Printed by H. Colbert, and sold at the Established Circulating Library, 1 vol., 12mo), EM 5317: 6, ESTC t108168; London, 1793, EM 995: 17, ESTC n002674. Serialised in *Weekly Entertainer*, 1791, RM 507.

CR: 'Without pretending to examine the authenticity of the manuscript, or to develope the inconsistencies of a tale so trite as the discovery of a hermitage and the papers containing the story, we can safely say that the tale is written by no common author; is pleasing, and may be useful.'

SAINT PIERRE, Jacques-Henri-Bernardin de, PAUL AND MARY
See PAUL AND VIRGINIE (1788: 71)

1789: 68   SMITH, Charlotte.
ETHELINDE, OR THE RECLUSE OF THE LAKE. BY CHARLOTTE SMITH. IN FIVE VOLUMES.

> London: Printed for T. Cadell, in the Strand, 1789.
> I iii, 258p; II 292p; III 282p; IV 304p; V 338p. 12mo. 15s boards (CR), 15s sewed (MR, LC).
> CR n.s. 3: 57–61 (Sept 1791); MR n.s. 2: 161–5 (June 1790); AF II: 4139.
> BL Cup.403.i.8; EM 6535: 11; ESTC t138541 (BI O, MRu; NA CtY-BR, CSmH, ICN, IU, MH-H, NjP, PU, TxU, ViU &c.; EA QU)

Notes. Dedication to H.R.H. the Duchess of Cumberland, signed Charlotte Smith, i–iii.
BL copy has a quotation from MR copied onto leaf facing t.p. of vol. 1.
Adv. LC 66: 517 (26–28 Nov 1789).
Further edns: Dublin, 1790 (Printed for H. Chamberlaine, W. Watson, J. Sheppard, P. Wogan, L. White [and 11 others in Dublin], 3 vols., 12mo), ESTC n031110; London, 1790,

EM 186: 2, ESTC t070082; London, 1814 (WC, NSTC); London, 1820 (WC, NSTC). German trans. Leipzig, 1792 (*Ethelinde oder Die Einsiedlerinn am See*) (Price); French trans. Paris, 1796 (*Éthelinde, ou la Recluse du lac*) (BN). Extracts from *Ethelinde*, 'The Affecting History of Caroline Montgomery' or 'The History of Caroline Montgomery', published in 8 magazines between 1789 and 1791, RM 66.

CR: 'If we examine it, without a retrospect to the former attempt, we shall find the story in general interesting, various passages pleasing and affecting; the characters delicately shaded, supported with judgment and skill, more conspicuous in a minute examination, and more meritorious as the lines to be copied are less glaring. It cannot escape any reader that, in the third and fourth volumes, the conversations are too numerous, the same sentiments frequently repeated, and that the story is scarcely progressive: it will always occur, that the beautiful scenery and the affecting situations, in the first volume, have made so lasting an impression, that the future scenes are from this cause sometimes insipid' (p. 57). 'We . . . can truly tell Mrs Smith that her merits are great, her faults very few, and comparatively inconsiderable' (p. 61).

MR [Andrew Becket]: 'As she principally aims at a display of character, Mrs Smith is entitled to rank considerably above the crowd of novelists who have lately come under our Review. There is not, indeed, in this performance, that boldness of figure, that warmth of colouring, that thorough knowlege of men and manners, which can alone give the stamp of *superior excellence* to a novel: but there is a gentleness, that lovely simplicity, that nice sensibility, that true feminine beauty, as we have before observed of that lady's writings, which is sure to please, if it does not astonish; and which calls forth a train of agreeable sensations, more properly encouraged, perhaps, than the fierce and turbulent emotions of the soul; which, as they have their origin in *a local distinction*, are, frequently, from disappointment, the fatal causes of madness and despair' (p. 162).

1789: 69   [THOMSON, William].
MAMMUTH; OR, HUMAN NATURE DISPLAYED ON A GRAND SCALE: IN A TOUR WITH THE TINKERS, INTO THE INLAND PARTS OF AFRICA. BY THE MAN IN THE MOON. IN TWO VOLUMES.
London: Printed for G. and T. Wilkie, N° 71, St Paul's Church-Yard, 1789.
I 285p; II 320p. 12mo. 6s (CR), 6s sewed (MR).
CR 70: 97–8 (July 1790); MR n.s. 2: 338–9 (1790).
O 256.f.2265,2266; ESTC t219545 (NA MnU).

Notes. 2-pp. table of contents (unn.) following t.p. in each vol.
Another London, 1789 edn. (also 2 vols., 12mo, published by Murray), ESTC n004435. This edn. adv., 'Handsomely printed in Two Volumes', MC 31 Mar 1789: 'printed for J. Murray, No. 22, Fleet-Street'.
German trans. Leipzig, 1792 (*Mammuth, oder Darstellung der menschlichen Natur nach unverjüngtem Maasstabe*) (EAG).
CR: 'In this strange, whimsical, excentric, and unequal performance, we could find subject of both praise and blame, if it were of importance to discriminate its different features. The leading idea, of virtuous monsters and a race of giants, who are both just and benevolent, is not new; and, in the work before us, it is not expanded with skill, or rendered very interesting by additional situations, or new remarks.'
MR [John Gillies]: 'We approve not Dr Thomson's politics, nor his personalities. His

indelicacies he would probably justify by the examples of Lucian, of Apuleius, and of Swift,— authors from whom he seems to have learned the happy talent of being romantic without extravagance, and eccentric without absurdity; and whom, in the present work, he rivals in vigour of invention and depth of observation. . . . The tendency of the work is salutary, and its design is liberal . . .' (p. 338).

TIMBURY, Jane, **THE MALE COQUET**
See 1788: 76

1789: 70 TIMBURY, Jane.
*THE TRIUMPH OF FRIENDSHIP; OR THE HISTORY OF CHARLES
COURTNEY, AND MISS JULIA MELVILLE. BY JANE TIMBURY.

> London: Printed for J. Fox, at his Circulating Library, Dartmouth-Sreet, Westminster;
>   and C. Stalker, Stationer's Court (DWR), 1789 (MR).
> 2 vols. 12mo. 5s sewed (MR, DWR).
> CR 68: 251 (Sept 1789); MR 81: 364 (Oct 1789).
> No copy located.

Notes. Adv. DWR 1 Aug 1789.
  CR: 'Mrs Timbury's novel is strictly moral; and, though not humorous, is pleasing and interesting. She seems to entertain the truly laudable feminine fondness for matrimony, which is recommended not only by precept but by example.'
  MR [Andrew Becket]: 'Trifling and insipid "*to a degree.*"'

1789: 71 [WHITE, James].
EARL STRONGBOW: OR, THE HISTORY OF RICHARD DE CLARE
AND THE BEAUTIFUL GERALDA. IN TWO VOLUMES.

> London: Printed for J. Dodsley, Pall-Mall, 1789.
> I 224p; II 191p. 8vo [MR has 12mo]. 6s sewed (MR, CR).
> CR 67: 330–3 (May 1789); MR n.s. 2: 414–15 (Aug 1790); AF II: 4774.
> C 7720.d.169; EM 3454: 5; ESTC t033003 (BI BL, Di; NA CtY-BR, IU, NjP, PU, ViU
>   &c.).

Notes. Frontispiece to vol. 1.
Adv. MC 17 Feb 1789.
Further edns: Dublin, 1789 (Printed for Messrs. P. Byrne, L. White, P. Wogan, J. Parker, J. Moore, and J. Halpen, 2 vols., 12mo), ESTC t164126. French trans. Londres [ESTC: i.e. Paris?], 1789, EM 3459: 6, ESTC t133456; French trans. London and Paris, 1789 (*Le Comte Strongbow*) (EAG); German trans. Helmstedt, 1790 (*Graf Strongbow oder die Geschichte Richard's de Clare und der scönen Geralda*) (RS).
  CR: '. . . if we are not mistaken this is the production of a veteran; it is pretty certainly the work of a person well acquainted with ancient manners, and minutely attentive to every part of the costume' (p. 331). 'It is not an eventful story to please general readers; but we think many will be instructed in some points of history by it, and particularly in the manners of their ancestors' (pp. 332–3).
  MR [John Noorthouck]: 'History and fable have distinct merits, the one to inform us of past events, and the other to inforce wholesome principles by fictitious machinery. . . . While

these species of composition are kept distinct, they answer their respective purposes: but to blend them together, is to poison the sources of information to young readers; who, after feasting on history embellished with these meretricious ornaments, will not easily relish the dry details of truth . . . ' (p. 414). '. . . if we add that the novel is neatly written, and that the characters are well drawn and supported, we imagine these qualifications are as much as the readers of works of entertainment, generally, require' (p. 415).

1790

1790: 1   ANON.
ADELINE; OR THE ORPHAN. A NOVEL. IN THREE VOLUMES.
London: Printed for W. Lane, Leadenhall-Street, 1790.
I iii, 261p; II 268p; III 247p. 12mo. 7s 6d sewed (SJC).
MH-H *EC75.A100.790a3; EM 1283: 3; ESTC n015180 (NA CaSRU).

Notes. By same author as *Frederic and Louisa* (1792: 16).
Dedication to the Reviewers i–iii. 1 p. advs. end vol. 3.
Adv. SJC 2–4 Sept 1790.

ALMERIA BELMORE
See O'CONNOR, E. (1789: 59)

ANECDOTES OF THE LIFE, ADVENTURES, AND VINDICATION OF A MEDICAL CHARACTER
See ADAIR, James Makittrick

1790: 2   ANON.
ARLEY; OR, THE FAITHLESS WIFE. A NOVEL, IN TWO VOLUMES.
London: Printed by J. S. Barr, Oxendon-Street, Hay-Market, 1790.
I 208p; II 210p. 12mo. 5s (CR), 5s sewed (SJC).
CR 70: 96–7 (July 1790); AF II: 137.
BL 12611.b.3; EM 11: 5; ESTC t054970.

Notes. 2 pp. advs. end vol. 2.
Adv. SJC 5–8 June 1790; 'Printed by W. Barr, No. 15, Oxendon-Street, near the Hay-Market'.
    CR: 'The adventures of Arley are not without some contradictions and improbabilities. . . . When we have said that this novel is amusing, we have nothing farther to add in its praise.'

ARNOLD, ZULIG, A SWISS STORY
See MATHEWS, Eliza Kirkham

1790: 3   ANON.
ARULIA; OR, THE VICTIM OF SENSIBILITY: A NOVEL, BY A YOUNG
LADY. IN TWO VOLUMES.

> London: Printed for William Lane, Leadenhall-Street, 1790.
> I 199p; II missing. 12mo. 5s (CR), 6s (SDA).
> CR 69: 357 (Mar 1790); AF II: 148.
> WA BN.XVIII.1.18094 (imperf.—lacks vol. 2); ESTC t201213.

Notes. 1 p. advs. end vol. 1.
Adv. SDA 18 Mar 1791.

> CR: 'An amusing little love-story, where the heroine dies from excess of sensibility . . .'.

1790: 4   ANON.
THE BARON OF MANSTOW, A NOVEL, FROM THE GERMAN. IN
TWO VOLUMES.

> London: Printed for William Lane, at the Minerva, Leadenhall-Street, 1790.
> I 236p; II 166p. 12mo. 6s (CR), 5s sewed (SJC, SDA).
> CR n.s. 1: 350–1 (Mar 1791); AF II: 224.
> BL 12611.c.23; EM 11: 6; ESTC t055919.

Notes. 2 pp. advs. end vol. 1.
Adv., 'in the press', SJC 6–9 Nov 1790; adv. SDA 21 Jan 1791.

> CR: 'If the German novelists possess some knowledge of the human heart, they do not display much skill in interesting it. The pathetic scenes are ill arranged, and their force is weakened by improper management. The Novel before us, in better hands, would have been highly pleasing and forcibly interesting. At present, though it deserves great commendation, its merit is obscured by unskilful arrangement. The descriptions are often highly finished; but the sensibility is too refined, and the notions of honour are almost ridiculously romantic.'

BELMONT CASTLE
See TONE, Theobald Wolfe, Richard JEBB, and John RADCLIFF

BLANSAY; A NOVEL TAKEN FROM THE FRENCH
See GORJY, Jean-Claude

1790: 5   ANON.
*THE BRITISH KNIGHT ERRANT.

> London: Printed for W. Lane, Leadenhall-Street (SJC), 1790 (SJC).
> 2 vols. 12mo. 5s sewed (SJC).
> No copy located.

Notes. Adv., 'In the Press, and shortly will be published', SJC 3–5 Aug 1790; adv. SDA 21 Jan 1791.

1790: 6   ANON.
CAROLINE, THE HEROINE OF THE CAMP. A NOVEL. IN TWO VOL-
UMES.

London: Printed for W. Beilby, Pall-Mall, 1790.
I 154p; II 152p. 8vo [CR has 12mo]. 5s (CR), 5s sewed in blue paper (SJC).
CR 70: 97 (July 1790); AF II: 612.
BL C.175.i.14; EMf; ESTC t127136.

Notes. Small pages with large margins—most pages contain fewer than 100 words.
Adv., 'In a few Days will be published, neatly printed on Writing Paper', SJC 13–15 May 1790.
Further edn: NSTC lists edn. in 1830.

CR: 'This lady has no great right to the name of heroine, for she remains quietly at New York, in peace from all attacks but those of love. Though the story is told in a plain easy manner, and amuses for the time, we cannot avoid styling it a trite, hackneyed tale, while reflection does not furnish one hint or character to induce us to make a single effort to rescue it from oblivion.'

1790: 7   ANON.
CHARLES ALTMAN; OR THE SON OF NATURE. FROM THE GERMAN.
IN TWO VOLUMES.

London: Printed for W. Lane, Leadenhall-Street, 1790.
I 238p; II 236p. 12mo. 5s sewed (AR, SJC).
AR 7: 462 (Aug 1790).
MdBJ PO 135.G3 C4; ESTC n028826.

Notes. Trans. of *Karl Altmann, eine vaterländische Geschichte* (Leipzig, 1787).
5 pp. advs. end vol. 2.
Adv., 'In the Press, and shortly will be published', SJC 3–5 Aug 1790.

AR: 'There is a simplicity of manners and style in this story, which renders it very interesting, and induces us to recommend it, as we would the generality of German novels that have hitherto come under our eye, because it appears probable that they would act as a kind of antidote to the *deluge* of sentiment and gallantry, which, from time to time, have been translated from the French, and imitated in English. . . . A knowledge of human nature appears in some of the affecting scenes, and many just observations occur in the course of the tale, calculated to improve young people, whilst some moral lessons are more forcibly impressed by appeals to the heart.'

CHARLES HENLEY: OR, THE FUGITIVE RESTORED
See GREEN, Sarah

THE CONFIDENTIAL LETTERS OF ALBERT
See EDEN, Anna

DANGERS OF COQUETRY
See OPIE, Amelia Alderson

1790: 8   ANON.
*DE MONTMORENCY. A NOVEL FOUNDED ON A RECENT FACT, INTERSPERSED WITH A TRANSLATION OF AN ORIGINAL MANUSCRIPT FOUND IN THE BASTILE.

London: Printed by J. S. Barr, at the Printing-Office, Oxendon-Street, near the Hay-
Market; and may be had of the different Booksellers (LC), 1790 (LC).
2 vols. 12mo. 5s (CR), 9s (LC).
CR 69: 356–7 (Mar 1790); AF II: 1022.
No copy located.

Notes. Adv. LC 67: 69 (19–21 Jan 1790) under 'New Novels'.
CR: 'This is a pleasing little story. . . .'

DELIA, A PATHETIC AND INTERESTING TALE
See PILKINGTON, Miss

THE DEVIL UPON TWO STICKS IN ENGLAND
See COMBE, William

DINARBAS; A TALE
See KNIGHT, Ellis Cornelia

1790: 9   ANON.
*EDMUND; OR, THE CHILD OF THE CASTLE, A NOVEL.

London: Lane, at the Minerva (SDA), 1790 (CR).
2 vols. 12mo. 5s (CR), 5s sewed (SDA).
CR 70: 454 (Oct 1790); AF II: 1213.
No copy located.

Notes. By same author as *Sidney Castle* (1792: 26).
Adv. SDA 21 Jan 1791.
CR: 'The adventures before us are not only absurd and improbable, but almost wholly
unintelligible.'

1790: 10   ANON.
ELOISA DE CLAIRVILLE. AN HISTORICAL NOVEL, WRITTEN DUR-
ING THE REIGN OF PHILIP AUGUSTUS, KING OF FRANCE. IN TWO
VOLUMES.

London: Printed for William Lane, Leadenhall-Street, 1790.
I 226p; II 203p. 12mo. 5s (CR), 5s sewed (SJC).
CR 70: 454 (Oct 1790); AF II: 1260.
MH-H 40537.70; ESTC n008612 (NA ICU, NjP).

Notes. 1 p. advs. end vol. 2.
Adv. SJC 7–10 Aug 1790.
CR: 'This is a very uninteresting French story, perhaps translated from some work of an
earlier period.'

1790: 11   ANON.
THE FAIR CAMBRIANS. A NOVEL. IN THREE VOLUMES.

London: Printed for William Lane, Leadenhall-Street, 1790.
I 240p; II 240p, III 240p. 12mo. 9s (CR), 9s sewed (SDA), 10s 6d (SJC).

CR 69: 712 (June 1790); AF II: 1357.

BL 1489.i.4; EM 2773: 12; ESTC t061475 (NA AzU, MH-H).

Notes. Adv. SDA 21 Jan 1791; adv. SJC 17–20 Dec 1791.

CR: 'A pleasing interesting story, made up, however, of shreds and patches from other works of this kind, except in what regards one family, where some characteristic sketches seem to show that observation guided the pen. . . . The incidents are trite and common.'

THE FATE OF VELINA DE GUIDOVA
See RADCLIFFE, Mary Ann

1790: 12   ANON.
FOSCARI, A VENETIAN TALE, FOUNDED ON FACTS.

London: Printed for William Lane, at the Minerva, Leadenhall-Street, 1790.
143p. 8vo. [CR has 12mo]. 3s (CR), 2s 6d sewed (SDA).
CR n.s. 1: 350 (Mar 1791); AF II: 1488.
NcU RBC PQ4675.A1.F63; ESTC n068615 (NA CtY).

Notes. NcU copy has manuscript emendations.
Adv., 'in the press', SJC 6–9 Nov 1790; adv. SDA 21 Jan 1791; re-adv., 'A Tragic and Affecting Tale', SDA 2 Feb 1791.

CR: 'This tale is, we suspect, older than the present season, though modernised to fill up the vacuum which the secession of our best novel-writers has occasioned. It is interesting and pathetic; the costume is also well preserved; but we cannot cordially praise a tale where vice triumphs, and virtue suffers for faults not her own.'

1790: 13   ANON.
THE FREAKS OF FORTUNE; OR, MEMOIRS OF CAPTAIN CONYERS. A NOVEL.

London: Printed for C. Stalker, Stationers' Court, Ludgate-Street, MDCCXL [ESTC: 1790?].
186p. 12mo. 2s sewed (adv.).
BL 12611.aaa.12; EM 13: 8; ESTC t054971 (NA CaOTU, ICN).

Notes. 2 pp. advs. end vol.
Adv. end vol. 2 of *Arville Castle* (1795: 1).

1790: 14   ANON.
GABRIELLE DE VERGY, AN HISTORIC TALE. IN TWO VOLUMES. BY THE AUTHOR OF ANTHONY LEGER, ESQ; OR, THE MAN OF SHIFTS.

London: Printed by T. Wilkins, Aldermanbury; for T. Hookham, New Bond-Street, and J. Bew, Paternoster-Row, 1790.
I xxv, 249p; II 296p. 12mo. 6s (CR).
CR 70: 219–20 (Aug 1790); AF II: 1547.
BL 1154.i.10; EM 4686: 6; ESTC t117342.

Notes. ESTC: 'Not a translation of "Gabrielle de Vergy, tragédie" by Pierre Laurent Buyrette de Belloy'.

Preface 1, iii–xxv.
Life and Adventures of Anthony Leger (1789: 14).
    CR: 'This is a pleasing, well-conducted, historic tale. . . . Our author has not sufficiently brought forward the peculiar customs of that time, to give his novel the air of a tale of other times; but in those alluded to, he has been guilty of no gross or material error.'

HELENA: OR, THE VICISSITUDES OF A MILITARY LIFE
See SCOTT, Helenus

HISTORIC TALES
See 1788: 17

INTEGRITY, OR THE HISTORY OF SOPHIA FRANCOURT
See LA SALLE, Adrien-Nicolas, marquis de

JULIA, A NOVEL
See WILLIAMS, Helen Maria

LAURA; A NOVEL. BY THE AUTHOR OF THE INDEPENDENT
See McDONALD, Andrew (1791: 46)

1790: 15   ANON.
LAURA; OR, ORIGINAL LETTERS. IN TWO VOLUMES. A SEQUEL TO THE ELOISA OF J. J. ROUSSEAU, FROM THE FRENCH.
    London: Printed for W. Lane, Leadenhall-Street, 1790.
    I 147p; II 158p. 8vo [CR has 12mo]. 6s (CR), 5s sewed (SJC).
    CR 70: 218–19 (Aug 1790); AF II: 2474.
    CSmH 213172; ESTC n054219.

Notes. Not by Rousseau (see Grieder).
Sequel to Jean-Jacques Rousseau's *Lettres de deux amans* (Amsterdam, 1761), later better known as *La Nouvelle Héloise*; trans. as *Eloisa* by William Kenrick 1761, JR 666; AF I: 1497.
2 pp. advs. end vol. 2. Epistolary.
Adv., 'A Work in High Estimation', SJC 17–20 July 1790.
    CR refers to rev. of the French original and discusses only some omissions in the translation.

LAURENTIA. A NOVEL
See SABINA

THE LETTERS OF MARIA
See STREET, Miss

LOUISA. A NOVEL
See HERVEY, Elizabeth

1790: 16   ANON.
LOUISA; OR, THE REWARD OF AN AFFECTIONATE DAUGHTER. A NOVEL, IN TWO VOLUMES.

London: Printed for T. Hookham, New Bond-Street, 1790.
I 197p; II 199p. 12mo. 5s (CR), 5s sewed (MR, SJC).
CR 69: 118 (Jan 1790); MR n.s. 3: 475 (Dec 1790); AF II: 2607.
BL 12612.aaa.36; EM 167: 3; ESTC t066378 (NA TxU).

Notes. 3 pp. advs end vol. 1. Epistolary.
Adv. SJC 2–5 Jan 1790.

CR: 'We have seldom seen letters more trifling and uninteresting, except a few descriptive of places in Holland and Germany. The stories and the characters are equally trifling and insipid.'

MR [William Enfield]: 'We are here amused by some natural incidents. . . . related in correct and unaffected language. The tale is pleasing, and the moral is good.'

1790: 17   ANON.
*LUCINDA HARTLEY; OR, THE ADVENTURES OF AN ORPHAN, CONTAINING THE HUMOROUS HISTORY OF MR. GOODWIN. BY THE AUTHOR OF LORD WINWORTH, &C.

London: Allen (CR).
2 vols. 12mo. 5s (CR).
CR 69: 476 (Apr 1790); AF II: 2630.
No copy located.

Notes. Lord Winworth 1787: 16. Also by same author: *Maria Harcourt* (1788: 22); *Phoebe* (1788: 28); *William and Charles* (1789: 29); and *Frederick and Alicia* (1791: 12).
German trans. Leipzig, 1792 (*Lucinde oder Herrn Simon Goodwins medicinische Leiden*) (Price).

CR: 'The adventures of the orphan are a little improbable, and not very new or interesting; but the history of Mr Goodwin, a valetudinarian, affected with all disorders, and curing each by a quack medicine, is very humorous and entertaining.'

1790: 18   ANON.
LUCRETIA; OR, VIRTUE THE BEST DOWRY. IN TWO VOLUMES.

London: Printed by L. Wayland, for T. Vernor, Birchin-Lane, Cornhill, 1790.
I 207p; II 171p. 12mo. 5s sewed (MR, DWR), 5s (SJC).
MR n.s. 3: 475 (Dec 1790); AF II: 2632.
BL RB.23.a.7328; ESTC t223449.

Notes. 1 p. advs. end both vols.
Post-dated; adv. as published DWR 7 Dec 1789 and LC 66: 550 (5–8 Dec 1789).
Adv. SJC 22–24 Mar 1791.
German trans. Dresden, 1791 (*Lukretia Harris; oder, Tugend ist die beste Mitgabe*) (RS).

MR [William Enfield]: 'Low, miserable trash! on which it is scarcely worth while to waste a line—even of censure.'

1790: 19   ANON.
THE MAID OF KENT.

London: Printed for T. Hookham, New Bond-Street, 1790.

I 245p; II 248p; III 220p. 12mo. 9s (CR), 9s sewed (MR, SJC).

CR 69: 592 (May 1790); MR n.s. 3: 90 (Sept 1790); AF II: 2690.

BL 12613.aa.17; EM 160: 1; ESTC t068750 (BI O; NA CSmH, MBNEH, MnU).

Notes. 3 pp. advs. end vol. 1 and 4 pp. end vol. 3. BL copy lacks t.p. to vol. 1.

Hookham's adv. for this book at end vol. 1 of Eliza Kirkham Mathews' *Memoirs of a Scots Heiress* (1791: 50) says that *The Maid of Kent* is 'by the Author of Travelling Anecdotes'.

Adv. SJC 18–20 May 1790.

CR: 'This seems to be the work of a man unhackneyed in the profession of novel-writing, and with abilities to soar above it. There are traces of learning and knowledge occasionally scattered in this performance; but as a novel it is romantic, improbable, and uninteresting.'

MR [William Enfield]: 'Without any pretension to the merit of fine writing, this is an agreeable novel. Several of the characters are not destitute of humour; and the story, in which there is a pleasing variety of incidents, is told with spirit.'

1790: 20 ANON.
MEMOIRS AND OPINIONS OF MR. BLENFIELD. BY THE AUTHOR OF TALES OF SYMPATHY.

London: Printed for W. Lane, Leadenhall-Street, 1790.

I viii, 244p; II 249p. 12mo. 5s (CR), 6s sewed (SJC).

CR 69: 592 (May 1790); AF II: 2820.

MH-H *EC75.A100.790m2; EM 1011: 6; ESTC n010527 (BI BL; NA PPL).

Notes. Apology 1, v–viii. 1-p. adv. end vol. 2 for the same author's *Tales, Entertaining and Pathetic; Inscribed to the Heart* (1788: 37) quotes review comment.

Adv., 'In the Press, and shortly will be published', SJC 7–10 Aug. 1790.

CR: 'This Shandeyan performance aims at wit, humour, pathos, and eccentricity. Though more connected than the Life and Opinions of Tristram, it is inferior in every other respect; and we must confess that we have felt little mirth, little interest, and little instruction in perusing it.'

1790: 21 ANON.
MEMOIRS OF MARIA, A PERSIAN SLAVE.

London: Printed for G. G. J. and J. Robinson, Paternoster-Row, 1790.

I xiii, 176p; II 199p. 8vo [MR and CR have 12mo]. 5s (CR), 6s boards (MR), 5s boards (SJC 1790), 6s sewed (SJC 1791).

CR n.s. 1: 349–50 (Mar 1791); MR n.s. 4: 229 (Feb 1791); AF II: 2827.

BL 12612.aa.23; EM 332: 1; ESTC t067639 (BI C; NA CaAEU, CSmH, IU).

Notes. Dedication to Lady St George 1, v–viii; preface ix–xiii; unn. 12-pp. list of subscribers.

Adv., 'Next Week will be published', SJC 4–7 Dec 1790.

Adv. SJC 8–10 Mar 1791.

CR: 'There are many circumstances which lead us to think that these Memoirs are genuine, or at least have their foundation in truth. They are very interesting and entertaining. The little improbabilities which appear may arise from our ignorance of Eastern customs, or be owing to the European additions, *retouchings* which may have been supposed necessary to adapt them for the "English market." The second volume we were particularly pleased with.'

MR [John Noorthouck]: 'Similar distresses, and similar consummations, run through them all [new novels]; and though removing the scene to a distant country, where a familiarity with slavery countenances strange vicissitudes, is favourable to novelty, yet allowing a Persian girl the best Persian education, we cannot readily conceive her keeping a diary of all her adventures, like a Clarissa Harlow, or a Harriet Byron. . . . we cannot overcome our doubts of its being, at *best*, the product of a fertile imagination working on a very slender foundation of fact.'

THE NEGRO EQUALLED BY FEW EUROPEANS
See LAVALLÉE, Joseph

1790: 22 ANON.
NORMAN AND BERTHA; OR, EXALTED ATTACHMENT. A NOVEL. IN TWO VOLUMES. WRITTEN BY A LADY.

> London: Printed at the Logographic Press and sold by J. Walter No. 169. Piccadilly, 1790.
> I missing; II 204p. 12mo. 6s (CR), 6s sewed (SJC).
> CR 70: 97 (July 1790); AF II: 3077.
> PC-S [vol. 2 only]; ESTC t210623.

Notes. Owner reports that novel was taken by her great-grandmother from Yorkshire to South Australia in 1855; has bookplate of a previous owner, Capt. Spawforth of the 28th Light Dragoons.
Adv. SJC 5–8 June 1790.

CR: '. . . our present fair one delights in sudden deaths, and unexpected changes of character and conduct. In short, probability is violated at every moment, and we meet with nothing to reconcile the disgust which this inattention must necessarily produce.'

1790: 23 ANON.
*THE ORPHAN MARION: OR, THE PARENT REWARDED.

> London: Published for T. Vernor, No. 10, Birchin-Lane, Cornhill (SJC), 1790 (MR).
> 2 vols. 12mo. 5s (CR), 5s sewed (MR, SJC).
> CR n.s. 1: 469 (Apr 1791); MR n.s. 4: 228 (Feb 1791); AF II: 3182.
> No copy located.

Notes. Adv. SJC 25–27 Nov 1790.
German trans., said to be from the English, Weissenfels and Leipzig, 1791 (*Die Waise Marion*, vol. 1 of *Geist der neuesten ausländischen Romane*) (RS).

CR: 'This novel is of French manufacture, and is neither unpleasing nor uninteresting; but it is of a texture easily *seen through*, and incapable of bearing, without injury, even the lenient hand of criticism.'

MR [John Noorthouck]: 'This is at least a decent story. The orphan Marion, like the heroines of all novels, is the paragon of every female good quality. She is precipitated into wonderful distress, in order to be exalted to wonderful good fortune, by wonderful coincidences of lucky circumstances; and so all parties are left wonderfully happy!'

1790: 24 ANON.
THE PERFIDIOUS GUARDIAN; OR, VICISSITUDES OF FORTUNE,

EXEMPLIFIED IN THE HISTORY OF LUCRETIA LAWSON. IN TWO VOLUMES.

> London: Printed and sold by T. Wilkins, Aldermanbury. Sold also by J. Bew, Paternoster-Row; T. Hookham, New Bond-Street; J. Murray, Fleet-Street; and W. Richardson, Royal Exchange, 1790.
>
> I xi, 206p; II 237p. 12mo. 6s (CR).
>
> CR 70: 455 (Oct 1790); AF II: 3307.
>
> BL C.175.m.37; EM 5903: 7; ESTC t127127 (NA CSmH, PU).

Notes. Epistolary.

CR: 'The story of a youthful pen, abounding in love, rapes, rescues, and matrimony. It is very trite, very insipid, and very improbable. The young lady, for we are told in the preface that the author is an unexperienced female, talks too knowingly of bagnios, of various modes of seduction, of keeping, &c. But, as a blind poet has described visible objects, so we may suppose our young author speaks from imitation.'

1790: 25 ANON.

THE PERJURED LOVER, OR THE HISTORY OF THOMAS BEAUMONT, AN OXFORD STUDENT, AND MISS LUCIA BANNISTER, SHEWING HOW AFTER THE DEATH OF HER FATHER, SHE WAS UNDER THE GUARDIANSHIP OF MR. SLYMAN, WHO WISHING TO GET HER FORTUNE, (WHICH WAS FIVE THOUSAND POUNDS) INTO HIS POSSESSION, COURTED AND MARRIED HER MOTHER, AND IN A SHORT TIME, BY CRUEL USAGE, BROKE HER HEART. MISS LUCIA BECOMES ACQUAINTED WITH MR. FRIENDLY, HAS MANY SUITORS, BUT NONE OF THEM SUCCEED IN HER GOOD GRACES, AS HER FORTUNE SEEMS TO BE THEIR ONLY OBJECT. MR. BEAUMONT, A RELATION OF MR. FRIENDLY'S, ARRIVES FROM THE UNIVERSITY, HIS AGREEABLE CONVERSATION ENGAGES LUCIA, HE WRITES TO HER, AND TAKES EVERY METHOD WHICH CUNNING CAN MAKE USE OF TO RUIN HER; HE LEAVES HER AFTER MANY PROTESTATIONS TO MARRY HER, BUT IN THE END TOTALLY FORSAKES HER. SHE PROVES WITH CHILD, HER FATHER-IN-LAW DIES AFTER HAVING SQUANDERED AWAY HER FORTUNE AT A GAMING TABLE, LUCIA TAKES LODGINGS IN LONDON, IS DELIVERED OF A BOY, WHICH IS GOT INTO THE FOUNDLING HOSPITAL. LUCIA TAKES TO DRINKING; DIES OF A CONSUMPTION; AND BEAUMONT HAVING GOT A COMMISSION IN THE ARMY, IS KILLED IN A DRUNKEN BRAWL, AND CONFESSES IT IS DIVINE JUSTICE FOR HAVING BEEN GUILTY OF SEDUCTION AND PERJURY. TO WHICH IS ADDED, ORIGINAL LETTERS FOUND AFTER THE DEATH OF LUCIA, IN A BOX, IN HER APARTMENTS.

> London: Printed and sold by T. Sabine, at No. 81, Shoe Lane, Fleet-Street, n.d. [ESTC: 1790?]

35, 29p. 8vo. 6d (t.p.).
BL 12613.c.6; EM 200: 5; ESTC t077674.

Notes. Frontispiece. Text starts on p. 3. The title story occupies pp. 3–35; then the pagination starts again at 1 with 'The Generous Husband; or, the Amours of Arabella' (1–7) and several more short pieces (7–29).
A separate edn. London, n.d. [1790?], ESTC t224643 (Hambleton).

PICTURES OF LIFE: OR, A RECORD OF MANNERS
See RESTIF DE LA BRÉTONNE, Nicolas-Edme

PLEXIPPUS: OR, THE ASPIRING PLEBEIAN
See GRAVES, Richard

RADZIVIL. A ROMANCE
See RADCLIFFE, Mary Ann

RAYNSFORD PARK, A NOVEL
See PURBECK, Elizabeth and Jane

1790: 26   ANON.
SEMPRONIA. IN THREE VOLUMES.

> London: Printed for W. Lane, Leadenhall-Street, 1790.
> I 206p; II 222p; III 260p. 12mo. 9s sewed (MR, SJC), 9s (CR).
> CR 70: 698–9 (Dec 1790); MR n.s. 4: 343 (Mar 1791); AF II: 4013.
> BL 12622.pp.4; EMf; ESTC t205487.

Notes. By same author as *Elvira* (1796: 6).
ESTC: Author's presentation copy, with ms. corrections.
2 pp. advs. end vols. 1 and 2, and 4 pp. end vol. 3. Epistolary.
Adv. SJC 6–9 Nov 1790.

CR: 'Though there are incidental marks of knowledge and of polished life in these volumes, yet they are, on the whole, as insipid and uninteresting as the worst of their tribe. Their chief merit is the concealment of the principal event, but curiosity is so little awakened that we receive even the denouement with indifference.'

MR [Elizabeth Moody]: 'The style of these letters is, on the whole, elegant; and though incidents are not sufficiently numerous and various to make the narrative interesting, the reader may discern, throughout the work, the latent possibilities of excellence; and may infer, from the writer's style, that she is capable of painting a *good story* with all it's necessary embellishments.'

A SICILIAN ROMANCE
See RADCLIFFE, Ann

1790: 27   ANON.
*THE SLAVE OF PASSION: OR, THE FRUITS OF WERTER. A NOVEL.

> London: Richardson, 1790.
> 2 vols. 12mo. 5s (EngR).

EngR 16: 67 (July 1790).
No copy located.

Notes. Epistolary.
Die leiden des jungen Werthers (Leipzig, 1774) trans. as 1779: 10.
New edn. adv. SDA 6 Jan 1791 with quotation from EngR.
Further edns: Dublin, 1790 (CtY) xESTC; Philadelphia, 1802 (NUC, NSTC).

EngR: 'Much as we dislike imitations, this obvious copy of a very beautiful and interesting performance is not without its charms. There is nature and novelty enough in these volumes to reward a perusal. We are not sure, however, that the author's laudable intention of defeating the effects of Werter's principles will be answered by the means he adopts.'

1790: 28   ANON.
SYDNEY AND EUGENIA: A NOVEL. IN TWO VOLUMES. BY A LADY.

London: Printed and Sold by T. Wilkins, No. 23, Aldermanbury. Sold also by J. Bew, Paternoster-Row; J. Murray, Fleet-Street; W. Richardson, Royal Exchange; and T. Hookham, New Bond-Street, 1790.
I 304p; II 322p. 12mo. 6s (CR), 6s sewed (SJC).
CR 70: 97 (July 1790); AF II: 4328.
MRu R 54260; EMf; ESTC t198975.

Notes. Epistolary.
Adv. SJC 10–13 July 1790.

CR: 'We perceive neither novelty nor merit in these volumes: it is the hackneyed tale ten times told; told till it disgusts. As it is from a female pen, we can excuse the profusion with which Hymen scatters his favours; but we cannot excuse, from a lady, the great susceptibility of each fair one introduced. Every lady is quickly in love, and no lady scruples to own it: almost every one gives sufficient intimation of it to the gentleman she distinguishes.'

1790: 29   ANON.
*TALES OF IMAGINATION ON MORAL AND INTERESTING SUBJECTS: CONTAINING, THE DRUID. THE MANDARIN. THE HIGHLANDERS. THE HOTTENTOT. THE SWISS MINER. THE VENETIAN.

London: Walter.
2 vols. 12mo. 6s (CR).
CR 70: 220 (Aug 1790); AF II: 4340.
No copy located.

Notes. Further edn: Dublin, 1790 (Printed for R. White, 1 vol., 12mo), ESTC n049144.
Dedication in Dublin edn. (to Lady Caroline Paget) is signed 'Tamary Eliz. Hurrell' but ESTC notes that she is identified as the compiler's friend.

CR: 'The titles of these tales are, the Druid, the Mandarin, the Highlanders, the Hottentot, the Swiss Miner, and the Venetian. Mrs. Hurrel, whose name is annexed to the dedication, tells us, that she received them from a friend; that they are designed for the amusement of an idle hour, and that it has been the aim of the author to represent virtues as the most permanent good. In these respects she has not misled the reader. The stories are interesting, the manners of the different nations well preserved, and the moral in general unexceptionable.'

1790: 30   ANON.
A TRIP TO WEYMOUTH. A NOVEL. IN TWO VOLUMES.

London: Printed for W. Lane, Leadenhall-Street, 1790.
I 176p; II 159p. 8vo [CR has 12mo]. 6s (CR), 5s sewed (SJC).
CR n.s. 3: 235 (Oct 1791); AF II: 4528.
BL 012612.df.22; EM 227: 5; ESTC t067648 (NA CtY-BR).

Notes. 1 pp. advs. end vol. 2.
Adv. SJC 3–5 Aug 1790.

CR: 'The Trip to Weymouth is *a* Sentimental Journey, but without any offensive imitation of the Shandean manner, though without any very striking merit in that line. It is a pleasant resource in a warm afternoon, and may be read with ease and comfort in that half listless state, which warmth and fullness will occasion.'

1790: 31   ANON.
THE TRIUMPHS OF CONSTANCY: A NOVEL. IN A SERIES OF LETTERS.

London: Printed at the Logographic Press and sold by J. Walter, No. 169, Piccadilly, 1790.
I 215p; II 187p. 12mo. 6s (CR), 5s sewed (SJC).
CR n.s. 1: 471 (Apr 1791).
MdE PR5189.P8T839 1805; ESTC n048330.

Notes. Epistolary.
MdE catalogue notes attribution to Samuel Jackson Pratt.
Adv. SJC 26–28 Oct 1790.

CR: 'The most uninteresting, dry, improbable, trifling work that the novel-press, in its late laborious efforts, has produced. When will the dreary prospect be enlivened again by a work of real genius?'

1790: 32   ANON.
VALENTINE. A NOVEL. IN TWO VOLUMES.

London: Printed for W. Lane, Leadenhall-Street, 1790.
I iv, 160p; II 172p. 8vo [CR and adv have 12mo]. 5s (CR), 5s sewed (SJC).
CR 69: 477 (Dec 1790); AF II: 4587.
BL 12611.aa.20; EM 235: 6; ESTC t108467 (BI O).

Notes. Preface 1, i–iv. Epistolary.
Adv., 'In the Press, and shortly will be published', *Valentine; A Soldier's Tale*, SJC 3–5 Aug 1790
Adv. as *Valentine; A Soldier's Tale* at end of vol. 2 of Frances Brooke's *History of Charles Mandeville* (1790: 39).

CR: 'The story is interesting and pleasing; but the catastrophe melancholy, the denouement hastened too rapidly, and not a little improbable.'

1790: 33   ANON.
*THE VICTIM OF A VOW; OR THE DANGERS OF DUPLICITY.

London: Symonds (MR), the Literary Press (SJC).

2 vols. 12mo. 6s (CR), 6s sewed (MR, SJC) 1790 (MR).
CR n.s. 3: 356 (Nov 1791); MR n.s. 5: 467 (Aug 1791); AF II: 4612.
No copy located.

Notes. Adv., 'From the Literary Press . . . Sold at No. 62, Wardour-Street, Soho', SJC 5–7 Apr 1791.

CR: 'The foundation of a plot seems to us improbable and absurd; but the subsequent conduct of the story deserves our commendation.'

MR [John Noorthouck and George Edward Griffiths]: 'If there be any ingenuity manifested in the conduct of this story, it is over-balanced by the great improbability of the whole.'

VICTORINA, A NOVEL
See GORJY, Jean Claude

VILLEROY; OR, THE FATAL MOMENT
See WHITFIELD, Henry

1790: 34   ANON.
THE WHIM; OR, THE MUTUAL IMPRESSION. A NOVEL. IN TWO VOLUMES. BY A LADY.

London: Printed and sold (for the Author) by S. Ford, No. 42, Little Britain, 1790.
I 144p; II 107p. 12mo. 5s (CR), 4s sewed (adv.).
CR n.s. 2: 355 (July 1791).
CtY Im.W577.790; ESTC n066790.

Notes. 13-pp. list of subscribers end vol. 2. Epistolary.
CR gives Hookham as bookseller.
Adv. end vol. 4 of *Edelfrida* (1792: 7).

CR: 'We have many stories of love at first sight as well as of a man wishing to be loved for himself alone. Novelty cannot, therefore, be expected. The tale is pleasing and agreeable, without one interesting trait which can discriminate the features.'

1790: 35   ANON.
THE WREATH OF FRIENDSHIP; OR, A RETURN FROM INDIA. A NOVEL, IN A SERIES OF LETTERS. IN THREE VOLUMES.

London: Printed for William Lane, Leadenhall-Street, 1790.
I x, 240p; II 264p; III 283p. 12mo. 9s (EurM); 7s 6d sewed (adv.).
EurM 17: 344 (May 1790).
PU Singer-Mend.3991.A1.W74.1790; ESTC n025503.

Notes. Dedication to Mrs Montague. 2 pp. advs. follow preface, as pp. [xi]–[xii] in vol. 1. Epistolary.
Adv. end vol. 3 of *Sempronia* (1790: 26).
Further edn: Dublin, 1790 (Printed for P. Wogan, P. Byrne, J. Parker, W. M'Kenzie, J. Moore [and 4 others in Dublin], 2 vols., 12mo), EM 216: 3, ESTC t086190.

EurM: 'Those who love to have their hearts torn to tatters by the force of tender feelings, have an opportunity of enjoying the painful pleasure by the perusal of many parts of this novel. . . . these volumes may be safely perused, without giving offence to the understanding or corrupting the heart.'

YOUNG HOCUS, OR THE HISTORY OF JOHN BULL
See L., W.

1790: 36 [ADAIR, James Makittrick].
ANECDOTES OF THE LIFE, ADVENTURES, AND VINDICATION, OF A MEDICAL CHARACTER, METAPHORICALLY DEFUNCT. TO WHICH ARE PREFIXED OR SUBJOINED A DEDICATION TO CERTAIN RESPECTABLE PERSONAGES; A CURIOUS DRAMATIC DIALOGUE; AND AN APPENDIX, CONTAINING AN EXPOSTULATORY EPISTLE, ADDRESSED TO COUN-SELLOR ABSQUE, ON HIS CONDUCT AT A LATE TRIAL AT WINCHES-TER, SUNDRY VOUCHERS, AND SPECIMENS OF LATIN AND ENGLISH POETRY. PUBLISHED FOR THE BENEFIT OF THE TIN MINERS OF CORNWALL, BY BENJAMIN GOOSEQUILL AND PETER PARAGRAPH.

> London: Sold by P. J. Bateman, No. 21, Devonshire Street, 1790.
> xxxii, 370p. 8vo. 4s boards (AR).
> AR 8: 101–102 (Sept 1790).
> BL RB.23.a.8493; ESTC n030264 (NA DNLM).

Notes. 1 p. advs. on verso of t.p. Preface by Benjamin Goosequill and Peter Paragraph i–vii; Editor's Preface ix–xvi signed F.G; dedication to 'Mrs. Anna Taylor, Her Guardians, Lawyers, and Associates' xvii–xxxii Appendix 353–70.

AR: 'The work ... is in itself so trifling, redundant, and useless, that we cannot but consider Preface i–xvi, the perusal of it as a task imposed on such as may be deceived by the title-page. The age is far from averse to anecdotes, but those recorded here are unimportant, childish, and futile' (p. 102).

1790: 37 BALLIN, {Rossetta}.
THE STATUE ROOM: AN HISTORICAL TALE. BY MISS BALLIN. IN TWO VOLUMES.

> London: Printed for H. D. Symonds, Paternoster-Row, 1790.
> I x, 168p; II 145p. 8vo [CR has 12mo]. 5s (CR), 5s sewed (SJC).
> CR 69: 477 (Apr 1790); AF II: 205.
> BL 12611.bbb.5; EM 8143: 1; ESTC t033006 (NA ICN, TxHR).

Notes. Text of novel starts on p. 9 in vol. 1 and on p. 5 in vol. 2. Dedication to the Countess of Duncannon signed 'Rossetta Ballin, Swan Street, Jan. 24, 1790' 1, v–vi; preface also numbered v–vi followed by xi–x. Epistolary.
Adv. SJC 6–9 Feb 1790; *The Statue-Room, an Historical Tale. (Founded on the History of England during the Reign of Queen Elizabeth).*

CR: 'When we spoke with complacency of historical novels, we excepted those abounding with anachronisms, which contradicted history in its most material circumstances, and in every respect was insignificant.—Such is miss Ballin's very youthful work.'

1790: 38 BONHOTE, [Elizabeth].
ELLEN WOODLEY. A NOVEL, IN TWO VOLUMES. BY MRS. BON-HOTE, AUTHOR OF PARENTAL MONITOR. OLIVIA; OR, DESERTED BRIDE. AND DARNLEY VALE; OR, EMILIA FITZROY.

London: Printed for William Lane, Leadenhall-Street, 1790.

I 192p; II 192p. 12mo. 5s (CR), 5s sewed (MR).

CR 69: 592 (May 1790); MR n.s. 2: 351 (July 1790); AF II: 402.

MH-H *EC75.B6415 790e; EM 1002: 6; ESTC n000748 (NA CaAEU; EA TALn [vol. 2 only]).

Notes. Olivia 1787: 30; *Darnley Vale* 1789: 33.

French trans. Paris, 1795 (*Hélène Woudlei*) (DBI); German trans. Leipzig, n.d. (*Ellen Woodley*) (RS).

CR: 'The plan of this work is greatly superior to its execution. . . . In its present state, the tale is often pathetic, interesting and exemplary, though generally improbable.'

MR: 'If her productions do not excite our admiration by the splendor of exquisite language, by the strength or novelty of the characters which they exhibit, by traits of genuine humour, or by the brilliancy of wit; they have, nevertheless, the power of interesting her readers, by affecting circumstances, and incidents, in the story; and of touching their hearts by edifying examples, and improving sentiments.'

1790: 39   BROOKE, [Frances].
THE HISTORY OF CHARLES MANDEVILLE. IN TWO VOLUMES. A SEQUEL TO LADY JULIA, BY MRS. BROOKE.

London: Printed for W. Lane, Leadenhall Street, 1790.

I viii, 185p; II 181p. 12mo. 5s (CR), 5s sewed (SJC).

CR 69: 476 (Apr 1790); AF II: 481.

BL 1607/4026; ESTC t122953 (NA CtY-BR, MH-H, PU).

Notes. Vol. 1 pagination continuous Roman-Arabic; text of novel starts on p. 9 in both vols. 3 pp. advs. end both vols. Epistolary.

The History of Lady Julia Mandeville 1763, JR 769, AF I: 257.

Adv. SJC 14–17 Aug. 1790.

Further edn: Dublin, 1790 (Printed for Chamberlaine and Rice, P. Wogan, P. Byrne, H. Colbert, W. McKenzie [and 6 others in Dublin], 1 vol., 12mo), ESTC t120736.

CR: 'Julia Mandeville, notwithstanding its faults, is a pleasing, pathetic, interesting work; though perhaps every reader closes it with pain, disappointment, and regret.'

1790: 40   CAMBON, [Maria Geertruida] de; [HALL, John (trans.)].
YOUNG GRANDISON. A SERIES OF LETTERS FROM YOUNG PERSONS TO THEIR FRIENDS. TRANSLATED FROM THE DUTCH OF MADAME DE CAMBON. WITH ALTERATIONS AND IMPROVEMENTS. IN TWO VOLUMES.

London: Printed for J. Johnson, No. 72, St. Paul's Church-Yard, 1790.

I 305p; II 230p. 12mo. 6s sewed (MR), 5s sewed or 6s bound (SJC).

MR n.s. 3: 222–3 (Oct 1790); AF II: 1779.

C 7746.d.59; EM 2730: 4; ESTC t117994 (BI BL, E, Eu &c.; NA ICN, NcD, PU &c.; EA SU [vol. 1 only], ZWTU).

Notes. Trans. of *De Kleine Grandisson, of de gehoorzame zoon* (The Hague, 1782); 2nd edn., with 2 additional vols., *De jonge Grandisson* (The Hague, 1786). Johnson's adv. for various publications by Mary Wollstonecraft LC 77: 36 (8–10 Jan 1795) claims this trans. as hers;

BLC notes that the 'alterations and improvements' are by Wollstonecraft.

2-pp. prefatory advertisement beginning vol. 1. 3-pp. 'Catalogue of Books composed for the Use of Children and young Persons' end vol. 1. 1 p. advs. for school books end vol. 2. Epistolary.

Adv., 'Speedily will be published', MC 19 Jan 1788.

Adv. SJC 3–6 Apr 1790: 'This work is an abridgement of a more voluminous one, intended to fix, by a lively example of early virtue, social duties on the firmest basis in the tender hearts of youth, to form the temper, and open the understanding. For which last purpose the authour has interspersed some little introductory hints relative to Natural Philosophy.'

Further edn: Dublin, 1790 (Printed by William Jones, 2 vols., 12mo), ESTC t118809. 3 ESTC entries also for trans. of Arnaud Berquin's *Le petit Grandisson, traduction libre du hollandais* (trans. as *The History of Young Grandison*) itself a trans. of de Cambon, although ESTC does not note this: t089083, n052266 and t090040. NSTC lists French trans. in 1816.

   MR [William Enfield]: 'This publication is of that useful kind, which, while it awakens curiosity, and affords instruction, is calculated to expand the heart' (p. 222).

1790: 41   [COMBE, William].
THE DEVIL UPON TWO STICKS IN ENGLAND. BEING A CONTINUA-
TION OF LE DIABLE BOITEUX OF LE SAGE [vols. 1–4].
THE DEVIL UPON TWO STICKS IN ENGLAND: BEING A CONTINUA-
TION OF LE DIABLE BOITEUX OF LE SAGE. VOL. V / VOL. VI.

   London: Printed at the Logographic Press; and sold by J. Walter, No. 169, Piccadilly;
      and W. Richardson, under the Royal Exchange, 1790 [vols. 1–4].
   London: Printed at the Logographic Press; and sold by J. Walter, No. 169, Piccadilly;
      and The principal Booksellers in Town and Country, 1791 [vols. 5–6].
   I vii, 228p; II 243p; III 234p; IV 256p; V 271p; VI 239p. 12mo. Vols. 1–4 12s (CR, SJC),
      vols. 5–6 6s (SJC).
   Vols. 1–4 CR 70: 219 (Aug 1790); AF II: 805; vols. 5–6 AR 13: 216–18 (June 1792); AF II:
      806.
   C Rom.76.100- [vols. 1–4], BL 12613.bb.8 [vols. 5–6]; EM 2009: 2 [vols. 1–4], EM 200:
      3 [vols. 5–6]; ESTC t063646 (BI BL, D; NA CaOLU, PU, ViU &c.) [vols. 1–4], ESTC
      t129268 (BI C, D; NA CaAEU, CLU-S/C, NjP &c.) [vols. 5–6].

Notes. Preface 1, v–vii.

6 introductory parts first published in *Daily Universal Register* between 20 June and 8 Sept 1787 (Hamilton).

Vols. 5–6 adv. SJC 31 May–2 June, 1791.

Further edns: Dublin, 1790 (Printed by Zachariah Jackson, for W. Jones), ESTC n008911; London, 1790–91, ESTC n008914; London, 1791, EM 200: 2, ESTC t063645; London, 1811 (WC, NSTC); London, 1817 (WC). German trans. Berlin and Leipzig, 1792 (*Der Teufel Asmodi Hinkelstein und sein Befreyer in England*) (Price).

   CR: 'Though continuations often lose the race, the zest which delighted in the first part, yet we think the present attempt a very respectable one. The Devil preserves his pleasantry, and Don Cleofas his eager curiosity. The pictures are, however, too often portraits, and instead of satyrizing vices, our author frequently attacks individuals.'

   AR: 'Continuations seldom answer the expectations of the public; and in the eighth vol-ume of our Review we gave our opinion that even the *former* part of this publication, instead of being extended into four volumes, ought to have been condensed into two. Of the volumes before us we cannot say much in commendation. The subjects are exceedingly trite; and they are treated in the style which usually adorns the shelves of a circulating library. Most of the anecdotes which relate to real life have appeared in newspapers, &c. and have originally been picked up from footmen and waiters, and even in their present dress retain a cast of their primitive vulgarity' (p. 216).

1790: 42   [?EDEN, Anna].
THE CONFIDENTIAL LETTERS OF ALBERT; FROM HIS FIRST ATTACHMENT TO CHARLOTTE TO HER DEATH. FROM THE SORROWS OF WERTER.

> London: Printed by John Crowder, for G. G. J. and J. Robinson, Paternoster-Row, 1790.
> 222p. 12mo. 3s (CR), 3s sewed (MR, SJC).
> CR 69: 357–8 (Mar 1790); MR n.s. 3: 227 (Oct 1790); AF II: 1208.
> MH-H *EC75.Ar577.790c; EMf; ESTC n014782 (NA DLC, IU).

Notes. ESTC gives author as John Armstrong. Robinson paid 10 gns. on 3 Aug 1789 to Anna Eden for *Letters of Albert* (RA).
Epistolary.
Adv. SJC 16–18 Feb 1790.
   CR: '. . . interesting and palliative' (p. 358).
   MR [William Enfield]: 'It will be a sufficient recommendation, to say that these letters may be read with pleasure as a sequel to the Sorrows of Werter, by those with whom that work is a favorite.' [Johann Wolfgang von Goethe's *Die Leiden des jungen Werthers* (Leipzig, 1774), 1779: 10].

1790: 43   GOMERSALL, {A}[nn].
THE CITIZEN, A NOVEL. IN TWO VOLUMES, BY MRS. GOMERSALL OF LEEDS, AUTHOR OF ELEONORA.

> London: Printed for Scatcherd & Whitaker, Ave-Maria-lane; and sold by Binns, Leeds,
>   and Edwards and Son, Halifax, 1790.
> I x, 217p; II 211p. 12mo. 6s (CR), 6s sewed (MR).
> CR n.s. 2: 355 (July 1791); MR n.s. 3: 223 (Oct 1790); AF II: 1663.
> BL N.2353,2354; EM 8714: 1; ESTC t088969.

Notes. On author's name see note to 1789: 42.
Epistolary. Dedication to Viscountess Irwin, signed A. Gomersall. List of subscribers i–x. Text of novel starts on p. 5 in vol. 1 and p. 3 in vol. 2. 1 p. advs. end vol. 2.
Eleonora 1789: 42.
   CR: 'This Novel, like Eleonora, noticed in our review for August, 1789, is more interesting from the humourous scenes with which it is interspersed, than from any artful plot or dextrous developement. Some parts of it are very entertaining. . . .'
   MR [William Enfield]: 'The favourable idea which we formed of this female writer, from her Eleonora . . . is confirmed by this second attempt. Though she does not appear to possess any peculiar degree of refinement, either in sentiment or language, she represents the manners of middle life with great exactness, and has a happy facility in sketching familiar conversations. Her *citizen*, the hero of the piece, is an excellent character, and well supported.'

GOOSEQUILL, Benjamin
See ADAIR, James Makittrick

1790: 44   [GORJY, Jean-Claude].
BLANSAY. A NOVEL. TAKEN FROM THE FRENCH BY THE AUTHOR OF VICTORINA, LOUISA, AND NINA, &C. IN TWO VOLUMES.

> London: Printed for W. Lane, Leadenhall-Street, 1790
> I 175p; II 224p. 8vo [CR has 12mo]. 5s (CR and adv.).
> CR 69: 357 (Mar 1790); AF II: 1676.
> CU-BANC PQ1985.G8.B513 1790; xESTC.

Notes. Trans. of *Blançay* (London and Paris, 1788).
Victorina 1790: 45; *Louis and Nina* 1789: 43.
Adv. end vol. 2 of *The Baron of Manstow* (1790: 4) as *Blansay: a Tale of Incidents in Life. (From the French.).*
Adv., 'A Work of the first Merit in the Novel Line ever published at Paris ... In Two neat Volumes', SJC 26–28 Aug 1790: 'It would be too much to intrude on the Publick with the merit of this Book; Suffice it to say, so rapid was its sale in France, that an impression of near five thousand were sold in a week from its publication; and that the translation has been made in that stile that cannot fail to amuse and entertain the English reader. The characters are natural and well drawn, the plot entertaining, the circumstances such as are in common life, the language pleasing and affecting, and the denouement will not fail of interesting the mind— Upon the whole, in an entertaining kind, it is such as may be fully recommended for novelty, amusement, and variety.'
ESTC has 3 entries for French versions of *Blançay* probably printed in Paris but with false London imprints: 1788, EM 203: 4, ESTC t131171; 1789, EM 4583: 1, ESTC t131099; 1789, ESTC n015124.
    CR: 'The tale is interesting, and in the observations there is something singularly naïvé [*sic*] and amusing. Perhaps the characters and the manners, copied from nature in a different country, may render this work less generally pleasing. If the proper allowances are, however, made, we think Blansay will stand high in our catalogue of novels.'

1790: 45   [GORJY, Jean-Claude].
VICTORINA, A NOVEL. BY THE AUTHOR OF BLANSAY, LOUIS AND NINA, &C. TRANSLATED FROM THE FRENCH.

> London: Lane, Minerva, Leadenhall-Street (SJC), [1790].
> I 222p; II 179p. 12mo. 5s (CR, adv.), 7s (SJC).
> CR 69: 713 (June 1790); AF II: 1680.
> NN NKT; xESTC.

Notes. Trans. of *Victorine* (Paris, 1789).
T.ps. missing in both vols. 5 pp. advs. end vol. 2.
Blansay 1790: 44; *Louis and Nina* 1789: 43.
Adv. end vol. 2 *The Baron of Manstow* (1790: 4) as *Victorina: an interesting and incidental Tale. (From the French.)*
Adv. SJC 20–22 Dec 1791.
ESTC has a 1789 French version of *Victorine* with a false London imprint (probably French provincial printing): EM 2125: 18, ESTC t120286.

CR: 'We have already said that customs and manners so different from our own do not greatly interest us ... we wish this volume had continued in its native language. ...'

1790: 46   [GRAVES, Richard].
PLEXIPPUS: OR, THE ASPIRING PLEBEIAN.

London: Printed for J. Dodsley, Pall-Mall, 1790.
I xii, 220p; II 219p. 12mo. 6s (CR), 5s sewed (MR, SJC).
CR 70: 97 (July 1790); MR n.s. 5: 225 (June 1791); AF II: 1697.
BL 12612.bb.17; EM 133: 4; ESTC t064743 (BI C; EA ZWTU).

Notes. 'The Preamble; by the Editor' 1, iii–xii.
Adv. SJC 26–29 June 1790.
German trans. Weissenfels and Leipzig, 1793 (*Plexippus, oder der emporstrebende Bürgerliche*) (RS).

CR: 'There is no attempt at humour; and the author seems rather to aim at copying from nature, without distorting the features to render the pictures ridiculous, or the portraits caricatures. He has greatly entertained us, and it is a debt of gratitude, on our side, to recommend his work.'

MR [John Noorthouck]: 'These volumes are not so full of business as such stories generally comprehend: but they contain an unexceptionable decent tale; which is allowing as much praise as those publications deserve, where little beyond amusement is intended.'

1790: 47   [GREEN, Sarah].
*CHARLES HENLEY: OR, THE FUGITIVE RESTORED.

London: Lane.
2 vols. 12mo. 5s (CR), 5s sewed (MR).
CR 70: 219 (Aug 1790); MR n.s. 4: 92 (Jan 1791); AF II: 1712.
No copy located.

Notes. Author attribution: FC, Blakey.

CR: 'Charles Henly will fill his place for a time on the shelves, but he will soon reach the higher ranks, we mean not of fame, but of the library: ranks filled by many heroes equally trifling and insipid, who labour through two volumes of inanity, are read for a few weeks, and then disappear for ever.'

MR [John Noorthouck]: 'After all the labour which the writer has bestowed on the style of a jumble of improbabilities, he has worked it up, the latter part especially, into an affected kind of measured prose, that will be admired by no one but himself.'

1790: 48   {HERON, M}[ary].
THE CONFLICT. A SENTIMENTAL TALE IN A SERIES OF LETTERS.

Newcastle: Printed by Hall and Elliot, 1790.
I 161p; II 166p. 12mo.
NCp L823H562/XH14; ESTC t204297.

Notes. 2-pp. preface (unn.) signed M. Heron; the author proclaims that she has 'bestowed more attention on the *morality*, than either the *diction* or the *incidents* of the following pages'.
Epistolary.
Further edn: London, 1793 (MR, CR), xESTC.

Newcastle edn. not reviewed; 1793 London edn. (Deighton) rev. CR n.s. 9: 357–8 (Nov 1793); MR n.s. 11: 343 (July 1793).

MR [William Enfield]: 'A few ordinary incidents, which discover little invention in the contrivance or ingenuity in the arrangement, are here expanded through two small volumes, and rendered *sentimental* by the frequent insertion of violent exclamations.'

1790: 49   [HERVEY, Elizabeth].
LOUISA. A NOVEL. IN THREE VOLUMES. BY THE AUTHOR OF MELISSA AND MARCIA; OR, THE SISTERS.

> London: Printed for T. Hookham, New Bond-Street, 1790.
> I 251p; II 258p; III 271p. 12mo. 9s (CR), 9s sewed (SJC).
> CR 70: 96 (July 1790); AF II: 1928.
> MH-H *EC8.H4453.7901; EM 997: 2; ESTC n003033 (NA ViU).

Notes. Melissa and Marcia 1788: 58.
Adv. SJC 2–5 Jan 1790.
Further edn: Dublin, 1790 (Printed for P. Wogan, P. Byrne, J. Moore, J. Jones, Grueber and McAllister, and W. Jones, 2 vols., 12mo), EM 5093: 8, ESTC t118421.

CR: 'The author of this pleasing and interesting story has fixed her eyes on Cecilia [1782: 15], and from this charming model, founded her history. The changes of fortune are frequent; the characters well diversified, though not strongly marked or pointedly contrasted; and the interest most feelingly supported. If there is a fault it is perhaps in the *frequent* changes: the difficulties are scarcely started, but they are explained; and a misfortune seldom happens without a remedy being soon at hand.'

JEBB, Richard
See TONE, Theobald Wolfe

JOHNSON, Anna Maria
See MACKENZIE, Anna Maria

1790: 50   [KNIGHT, Ellis Cornelia].
DINARBAS; A TALE: BEING A CONTINUATION OF RASSELAS, PRINCE OF ABYSSINIA.

> London, Printed for C. Dilly, in the Poultry, 1790.
> xii, 336p. 12mo. 3s (CR), 3s boards (MR), 3s sewed (SJC).
> CR n.s. 3: 116 (Sept 1791); MR n.s. 8: 106 (May 1792); AF II: 2415.
> BL 635.c.30; EM 2440: 5; ESTC t127411 (BI ABu, BMp, O &c.; NA CtY, CtY-BR, DLC, MH-H, TxU &c.).

Notes. Dedication to the Queen signed 'The Author'. Introduction v–viii; table of contents ix–xii.
Samuel Johnson's *The Prince of Abissinia* (London, 1759), JR 495, AF I: 1436.
Adv. SJC 18–20 May 1790.
Further edns: Dublin, 1790 (Printed by John Rea, for Messrs. P. Byrne, J. Moore, J. Jones, Grueber and M'Allister, W. Jones, and R. White, 1 vol., 12mo), EM 3463: 8, ESTC t128959; Philadelphia, 1792, ESTC w019875; London, 1792, EM 3455: 13, ESTC t1227412; London,

1793, ESTC t064754; Greenfield, Mass., 1795, EM 3143: 1, ESTC w028990 (*Dinarbas* with *Rasselas*); 1 further entry in ESTC; WC has 10 entries between 1800 and 1850, 4 of them with *Rasselas*; NSTC lists edns. in 1803, 1811, 1817 and 1823. Extracts from *Dinarbas* published in GM and LM, 1790, RM 308.

CR: 'It is no slight undertaking to pursue the steps of Johnson, and to endeavour to complete what he has left unfinished. A writer, greatly superior to the common rank, engaging in such a task, under so many disadvantages, could scarcely expect to succeed: it is no little credit to our author, that he has succeeded so well. . . . It is a continuation which Johnson could not have disapproved, and which he probably would not have been ashamed to own.'

MR [Thomas Pearne]: 'The author . . . discovers . . . a comprehensive acquaintance with human life, and conveys many valuable precepts for the regulation of it, in easy and unaffected language; and the general impression which the perusal of Dinarbas leaves on the mind, is more pleasing and useful than that which results from reading Rasselas.'

1790: 51   L., Sir W.
YOUNG HOCUS, OR THE HISTORY OF JOHN BULL, DURING THE YEARS 1783, 1784, 1785, 1786, 1787, 1788, 1789. A NOVEL. BY SIR W—— L——, K——. WITH NOTES, CRITICAL AND EXPLANATORY, BY THE FOLLOWING PERSONS: DUKES. GL—C-ST-R, D-RS-T, GR-FT-N, L— DS, R-CHM-ND, ATH-L. MARQUESSES. B-CK-NGH-M, L-NDSD-WN-. LORDS. CH-ST-RF-LD, M-RN-NGT-N, W-STM-R-L-ND, F. C-MPB-LL, GR-SV-N-R, S-DN-Y, TH-RL-W, H-WK-SB-RY, G-LL-W-Y, B-LGR-V-, H-W-. M-LGR-V-, C-MD-N, W-NCH-LS—, H—D. BISHOP. DR. PR-TTYM-N. BARONETS. J. M-LL-R, J. M-WB-Y, W. H-W-, R. P. ARD-N, G. P. T-RN-R. KNIGHTS. W. CH-MB-RS, W. L-W-S, IS—C H—RD—. ESQUIRES. H. D-ND-S, W. GR-NV-LL-, B. W-TS-N, J. SC-TT, J. CH-RCH-LL, J. H. T—K-, J. R-LL-, J. R-B-NS-N, P. L. M-SUR—R, J. B-RR-, H. B—F-Y, G. R-S-, J. M'N-M—, J. W-LK-S, G. P-TT, A. ADD-NGT-N, J. P-TT, C. L-N-X, J. D-RNF-RD, J. B-T-S. LADIES. S-L-SB-RY, W-LL-CE, MRS. P—ZZ-, MAD. SCHW-LL-NB-RG, MRS. N-SB-TT, GENTLEMEN. MR. C-P-L. CHEESE-MONG. MR. P—RS-N, DOOR-KEEP. &C. &C. &C. &C.

London: Printed for J. Bird, n.d. [ESTC: 1790?].
ii, 4, xxiv, 137p. 12mo.
BL 12314.bb.32; EM 559: 14; ESTC t123234 (NA CLU-S/C, MBAt, MH-H).

Notes. 'Volume One' on t.p. and 'End of Vol. I' at end of p. 137 but ESTC says no more published. Editor's preface i–ii; contents [3]–4; dedication '(By Permission,) to Myself' signed W. L, iii–xxiv.

1790: 52   [LA SALLE, Adrien-Nicolas, marquis de].
INTEGRITY, OR THE HISTORY OF SOPHIA FRANCOURT. FROM THE FRENCH. IN TWO VOLUMES.

London: Printed for W. Beilby in Pall Mall, 1790.
I xii, 207p; II 216p. 12mo. 5s (CR), 5s sewed (SJC).
CR 69: 713 (June 1790); AF II: 2196.
NjP 3785.52.349.11 v.1–2; ESTC n008593.

Notes. Trans. of *Histoire de Sophie de Francourt* (Paris, 1768) (Grieder/Block).

ESTC: Sometimes erroneously attributed to Barbara Hofland. ESTC also notes that the French original has not been found.

Preface by the French editor.

Adv. SJC 18–20 Mar 1790 as forthcoming 'In a few Days': *Integrity; or, the History of Sophia Francourt, a Novel.*

CR: 'This is an entertaining little work, though it is not easy to ascertain its particular merits. We are amused with the events; but French manners are not so familiar to the generality of readers as to render the adventures of their novels very interesting. It would have been no great loss to English literature, if this work had remained in its original language.'

1790: 53   [LAVALLÉE, Joseph, marquis de Boisrobert].
THE NEGRO EQUALLED BY FEW EUROPEANS. TRANSLATED FROM THE FRENCH.

> London: Printed for G. G. J. and J. Robinson, Paternoster-Row, 1790.
> I 221p; II 261p; III 269p. 12mo. 9s (CR), 9s sewed (SJC).
> CR 70: 454 (Oct 1790); AF II: 2479.
> MH-H *FC7.L3825.Eg790n; EM 989: 7; ESTC n003974.

Notes. Trans. of *Le Negre comme il y a peu de blancs* (Madras and Paris, 1789).

Adv. SJC 4–7 Dec 1790.

Different trans. by J. Trapp with title *The Negro as there are Few White Men*, London, 1790, ESTC n041768.

Further edn: Dublin, 1791 (Printed for P. Byrne, A. Grueber, W. Jones, and R. White, 2 vols., 12mo), EM 4853: 25, ESTC t119347; Philadelphia, 1801 (WC). Extracts from *The Negro Equalled by Few Europeans* published in *Lady's Magazine* and *Hibernian Magazine*, 1790, RM 946.

CR refers to previous rev. of the original French edn. [CR 64: 324–8]: '. . . it is only necessary at present to observe, that it is translated with care and accuracy, and affords a pleasing variety in this department of our reading.'

1790: 54   LENNOX, Charlotte.
EUPHEMIA. BY MRS. CHARLOTTE LENNOX. IN FOUR VOLUMES.

> London: Printed for T. Cadell, in the Strand; and J. Evans, Paternoster-Row, 1790.
> I 237p; II 227p; III 226p; IV 267p. 12mo. 12s (CR), 12s sewed (MR, SJC).
> CR 70: 81–3 (July 1790); MR n.s. 3: 89–90 (Sept 1790); AF II: 2522.
> BL N.2349–52; EM 2070: 1; ESTC t073522 (BI O; NA CtY-BR, CSmH, IU, MH-H, PU &c.).

Notes. Text of novel starts on p. 3 in vol. 1. Epistolary.

Separate adv. 'Just published, price fourteen shillings bound, Euphemia, a novel' ESTC: t188184. Adv., 'In a few Days will be published', SJC 15–18 May 1790; adv. as published SJC 29 May–1 June 1790. Adv. SJC 17–19 Mar 1791; adv. quotes from EngR and refers to the 'very high character already given of Euphemia, both by the Monthly and the Critical Reviewers. . . .'

Further edn: Dublin, 1790 (Printed by Brett Smith, for Messrs. P. Wogan, P. Byrne, H. Colbert, J. Moore, W. M'Kenzie, J. Jones, B. Dornin, A. Grueber, W. Jones, J. Rice, G. Draper, and R. White, 4 vols., 12mo), ESTC n002321. Extracts from *Euphemia* published in 3 magazines, 1790–91, RM 374, 813. German trans. Berlin, 1791 (*Euphemia*) (RS). Facs: BWN.

CR: '. . . we think it uncommon in its construction, and interesting from some of its descriptions; accounts of a country which, though long in our possession, has scarcely ever been described in a picturesque narrative' (p. 81). 'The characters, . . . though drawn without any splendid traits, are sufficiently distinct, and very ably supported; indeed, in every part of these volumes we see characters delineated with so much apparent fidelity, and preserved with such strict consistency, that we almost forget we are reading a novel. This last work of Mrs Charlotte Lennox, if it should prove to be her last, will not sully her fame. If she does not shine with meridian splendor, she sets with a mild radiance, more pleasing and more attractive' (p. 83).

MR [Thomas Ogle]: 'We have been better pleased with Mrs. Lennox's Novel, than with many others of the same class, which have lately passed under our review; though indeed there is no prodigality of commendation in this sentence, as most of them have excited our displeasure. The language of Euphemia is easy, though not always accurate; the sentiments are, generally, just, though they may not entirely possess the recommendation of novelty; the incidents are frequently natural, though in some instances they are carried beyond the bounds of probability; and the characters are well preserved, though they are not drawn with any appearance of bold design or nice discrimination' (p. 89).

1790: 55   [MACKENZIE], Anna Maria.
MONMOUTH: A TALE, FOUNDED ON HISTORIC FACTS. INSCRIBED TO HIS GRACE THE DUKE OF BUCCLEUGH. BY ANNA MARIA JOHNSON, AUTHOR OF CALISTA, A NOVEL, &C. IN THREE VOLUMES.

> London: Printed for W. Lane, Leadenhall Street, 1790.
> I 216p; II 204p; III 176p. 12mo. 7s 6d sewed (EngR), 7s 6d (SDA), 9s (SJC).
> EngR 16: 68 (July 1790).
> AUG 02/III.9.8.165; xESTC (NA MB).

Notes. Adv. for *Calista* [1789: 52] end p. 176 of vol. 3.
Adv. SJC 8–10 June 1790 (no price); adv., 'In the Press, and shortly will be published, SJC 3–5 Aug 1790; adv. SDA 21 Jan 1791.

EngR: 'The story of the unfortunate Duke of Monmouth, who lost his life in aspiring to the throne, is here presented to the public in the form of an historic tale. There are, no doubt, affecting circumstances in the history and fate of that nobleman. With these, aided by fiction, our author has attempted to interest the feelings of her readers, while she has not failed properly to mark that fatal ambition which prompted her hero to attempts beyond his strength, and to which he owed his fall. The style is not always accurate; and, from a continued affectation of high-sounding words, the performance runs frequently into bombast. Other defects may be pointed out; but regard to a fair author softens the severity of criticism, and we recommend her production as entitled to some share of approbation.'

1790: 56   [MATHEWS, Eliza Kirkham].
ARNOLD ZULIG, A SWISS STORY. BY THE AUTHOR OF CONSTANCE, PHAROS, AND ARGUS.

> London: Printed for T. Hookham, New Bond Street, 1790.
> 281p. 12mo. 3s (CR), 3s sewed (MR).

CR 69: 593 (May 1790); MR n.s. 2: 353 (July 1790); AF II: 2754.

MH-H *EC75.M4227.790a; EM 995: 18; ESTC n002041 (NA DLC).

Notes. FC says author attribution is doubtful.

3 pp. advs. end vol.

Constance 1785: 38; *Argus* 1789: 53.

Further edn: Dublin, 1790 (Printed for R. White, 1 vol., 12mo), EM 4506: 3, ESTC t118929.

CR: '. . . this little novel is interesting, eventful, and exemplary. There are too many "hair-breadth 'scapes," and too many improbable circumstances; but as stepping out of the common path, abounding with unexpected changes of fortune, and the story being told often with elegance and propriety, the work deserves our commendation.'

MR [Thomas Ogle]: 'This . . . is one of those stories which we must allow to be well written; and this is the highest degree of commendation which we can allow it. It contains no discrimination of character; and, in the management of its incidents, probability is continually violated.'

1790: 57   [OPIE, Amelia Alderson].

DANGERS OF COQUETRY. A NOVEL. IN TWO VOLUMES.

London: Printed for W. Lane, Leadenhall-Street, 1790.

I 144p; II 131p. 8vo [EngR has 12mo]. 5s sewed (EngR).

EngR 17: 234–5 (Mar 1791); AF II: 3171.

BL C.142.c.2; ESTC n000341 (NA MH-H, NjP).

Notes. 1 pp. advs. end vol. 1.

EngR: 'The characters are well drawn; the incidents arising naturally from each other exhibit in their fatal catastrophe a solemn warning to the fair sex to avoid the dangers of coquetry.'

PARAGRAPH, Peter

See ADAIR, James Makittrick

1790: 58   PARSONS, {Eliza}.

THE HISTORY OF MISS MEREDITH; A NOVEL. DEDICATED BY PERMISSION, TO THE MOST NOBLE THE MARCHIONESS OF SALISBURY. BY MRS. PARSONS. IN TWO VOLUMES.

London: Printed for the Author; and sold by T. Hookham, New Bond-Street, 1790.

I vi, 24, 226p; II 205p. 12mo. 6s (CR), 6s sewed (MR).

CR 70: 219 (Aug 1790); MR n.s. 3: 90 (Sept 1790); AF II: 3234.

ICN Y155.P244; EM 2555: 12; ESTC t141206 (BI BL; NA CSmH, CtY, MH-H, NjP, ViU).

Notes. Roman and 1st set of Arabic pp. nos. continuous in vol. 1. Dedication to the Marchioness of Salisbury, signed Eliza Parsons, No. 15, East-place, Lambeth, 31 Mar 1790, 1, i–[iv]; preface v–vi; list of subscribers 7–[25]; followed by text from p. 1. 2 pp. advs. end vol. 1 and 3 pp. end vol. 2. Epistolary.

Further edns: London, 1790, ESTC n007435; Dublin, 1791 (Printed by J. Jones, 1 vol., 12mo), ESTC n007439.

CR: 'If we could have felt an inclination to be severe, Mrs Parsons has taken from criticism her sting; and when we find a work which is strictly moral and generally pleasing, from an author in similar circumstances, we must commend. We wish our circulating libraries were always so well supplied.'

MR [William Enfield]: 'A natural and interesting tale is related in neat and unaffected language; and the moral which it inculcates, is the reverse of those romantic notions, which most novels have a tendency to inspire. . . .'

1790: 59   [PILKINGTON, Miss].
DELIA, A PATHETIC AND INTERESTING TALE. IN FOUR VOLUMES.

London: Printed for William Lane, Leadenhall-Street, 1790.
I 262p; II 264p; III 288p; IV 279p. 12mo. 12s (CR, SDA).
CR 69: 118 (Jan 1790); AF II: 3341.
BL 12604.ccc.17; EM 132: 2; ESTC t107742 (BI MRu; NA CtY-BR, MH-H, OAU).

Notes. Not by Mary Pilkington; see FC.
1 p. advs. end vol. 4. Epistolary.
Adv. SDA 18 Mar 1791.
Further edn: Dublin, 1790 (Printed for Messrs. P. Byrne, P. Wogan, Grueber and M'Allister, J. Moore, J. Jones and W. Jones, 2 vols., 12mo), ESTC n006235.

CR: 'Though as an artful contexture of events, within the reach of probability, we cannot highly commend these volumes; yet we perceive some traits of genius and acquired knowledge in them, which shows the author to be unhackneyed in his profession, and to be, in reality, above it. At the same time, we ought to remark, that the conduct of the work is not very particularly defective; and the author's pathetic scenes are well worked up, and heightened by a judicious choice of incidents.'

1790: 60   [PURBECK, Elizabeth and Jane].
RAYNSFORD PARK, A NOVEL. IN FOUR VOLUMES.

London: Printed for G. Kearsley, no. 46, Fleet-Street, 1790.
I 232p; II 241p; III 210p; IV 236p. 12mo. 12s (CR, SJC).
CR 69: 357 (Mar 1790); AF II: 3643.
BL N.1715,16; CME 3–628–45150–7; EM 1925: 3; ESTC t070719 (NA CaAEU, IU, NjP &c.; EA COR).

Notes. Only vol. 3 dated. 4 pp. advs. end vol. 1. Epistolary.
Adv., 'On Wednesday next, will be published', SJC 14–16 Jan 1790, 'Printed for George Kearsley, at Johnson's Head, Fleet-Street'; adv. as published SJC 19–21 Jan 1790.
German trans. Hanover, 1794 (*Rainforts-Park*) (RS).

CR: 'We felt ourselves occasionally interested in this story, which, though written with more elegance than usual, is drawn out too far, and extended to a tiresome length. When we reflected on it, however, we found nothing artful in the series of adventures, no new characters, nicely discriminated personages, or uncommon situations. If it be, therefore, interesting, it must be owing to its general merit, and we fear it will be difficult to raise it higher in the scale of excellence.'

RADCLIFF, John
See TONE, Theobald Wolfe

1790: 61   [RADCLIFFE, Ann].
A SICILIAN ROMANCE. BY THE AUTHORESS OF THE CASTLES OF
ATHLIN AND DUNBAYNE. IN TWO VOLUMES.

> London, Printed for T. Hookham, [1790] [misdated MDCCLXC].
> I 239p; II 216p. 12mo. 6s (CR), 5s sewed (MR).
> CR n.s. 1: 350 (Mar 1791); MR n.s. 3: 91 (Sept 1790); AF II: 3676.
> C S727.d.79.21-; EM 7938: 2; ESTC t062068 (BI BL, O; NA CtY-BR, DLC, MH-H,
>   NjP &c.).

Notes. The Castles of Athlin and Dunbayne 1789: 62.
Further edns: Dublin, 1791 (Printed by B. Smith, for J. Moore, 2 vols., 12mo), ESTC
n023021; London, 1792, ESTC t127120; London, 1792, ESTC t127134; Baltimore, 1795,
ESTC w022281; London, 1796, ESTC t062065; WC has 8 entries between 1800 and 1850;
Summers has 8 edns. between 1800 and 1850; NSTC lists edns. in 1809, 1809/1796, 1818,
1826, 1830 and 1843. German trans. Hanover, 1791 (Die nächtliche Erscheinung im Schlosse
Mazzini) (Price); French trans. Paris, 1797 (Julia, ou les Souterrains du château de Mazzini)
(Lévy); Spanish trans. Mexico, 1835 (Julia, o, Los subterraneos del Castillo de Mazzini) (WC).
Facs: GNI (1821 edn.).

   CR: 'This very interesting novel engages the attention, in defiance of numerous im
probabilities and "hair-breadth 'scapes" too often repeated. Perhaps, on a second reading,
these might be still more disgusting; but it is an experiment that we can scarcely venture to try
but with modern novels of the first class. We found the tale, we have said, very entertaining,
and involved with art, developed with skill, and the event concealed with great dexterity.
If our author again engages in this task, we would advise her not to introduce so many
caverns with such peculiar concealments, or so many spring-locks which open only on one
side.'

   MR [William Enfield]: 'In this tale, we meet with something more than the alternate tears
and rapture of tender lovers. The writer possesses a happy vein of invention, and a correctness of taste, which enable her to rise above the level of mediocrity. Romantic scenes, and
surprizing events, are exhibited in elegant and animated language.'

1790: 62   [RADCLIFFE, Mary Ann(e)].
THE FATE OF VELINA DE GUIDOVA. A NOVEL. IN THREE VOLUMES.

> London: Printed for W. Lane, Leadenhall-Street, 1790.
> I 213p; II 207p; III 171p. 12mo. 9s (CR), 7s 6d (SJC).
> CR 70: 96 (July 1790); AF II: 3677.
> Corvey; CME 3-628-45037-3; ESTC n006620 (NA PU).

Notes. Author attribution: FC. For the problems concerning the name of this author or
authors see Todd and FC.
2 pp. advs. end vol. 1; 5 pp. advs. end vol. 2. Vol. 2 p. 185 misnumbered 18. Epistolary.
Letters end p. 147 of vol. 3.
Adv., 'In the Press, and shortly will be published', SJC 3–5 Aug 1790.

   CR: 'The Fate of Velina is a happy one; but it is brought about by common incidents, and
the characters differ only from the works whose scene is laid in England in the names and
titles.... The circumstances of the story are also improbable, and the denouement is improperly hurried.'

1790: 63   [RADCLIFFE, Mary Ann(e)].
RADZIVIL. A ROMANCE. TRANSLATED FROM THE RUSS OF THE
CELEBRATED M. WOCKLOW. IN THREE VOLUMES.

London: Printed for W. Lane, Leadenhall-Street, 1790.
I viii, 208p; II 200p; III 178p. 8vo [CR has 12mo]. 7s 6d (CR), 9s (SDA).
CR 69: 118 (Jan 1790); AF II: 3678.
BL 012590.c.7; EM 224: 4; ESTC t130407 (BI O; NA MH-H; EA WA [vol. 3 only]).

Notes. For the problems concerning the name of this author or authors see Todd and FC.
Author's preface 1, i–ii; Editor's Preface iii–viii. Text of novel starts on p. 13 in vol. 1 and on
p. 9 in vols. 2 and 3. 2 pp. advs. end vol. 3.
Adv. SDA 18 Mar 1791.
    CR: 'We found it very interesting, though, to a mere English reader, it will often appear
improbable.'

1790: 64   [RESTIF DE LA BRÉTONNE, Nicolas-Edme].
PICTURES OF LIFE: OR, A RECORD OF MANNERS, PHYSICAL AND
MORAL, ON THE CLOSE OF THE EIGHTEENTH CENTURY. TRANS-
LATED FROM THE FRENCH. IN TWO VOLUMES.

London: Printed for C. Dilly, Poultry, 1790.
I xvi, 217p; II 208p. 8vo. 6s (TCM).
TCM 22: 460–1 (Oct 1790); AF II: 3743.
BL 12510.aaa.13; EM 330:2; ESTC t131182 (BI MRu; NA ICN, MH-H, PU &c.).

Notes. Trans. of *Monument du costume physique et moral de la fin du dix-huitième siècle*
(Neuwied sur le Rhin, 1789).
Frontispiece in each volume. Prefatory advertisement of the Editors 1, i–xvi.
Further edn: London, 1793 (WC), xESTC.
TCM: 'These tales are spirited, entertaining, interesting, and characteristic, though
occasionally bordering on indecorum. The translation is elegant.'

1790: 65   SABINA (pseud?).
LAURENTIA. A NOVEL. IN TWO VOLUMES.

London: Printed for William Lane, at the Minerva, Leadenhall-Street, 1790.
I 239p; II [246]p. 12mo. 6s sewed (adv.), 5s sewed (SJC), 6s sewed (SDA).
BL 12611.bb.18; EM 3709: 5; ESTC t154605.

Notes. Epistolary. 2-pp. preface, signed 'Sabina', appeals to 'the Gentlemen Reviewers' to 'in
pity spare a simple maid' (and they seem to have done so). Last p. vol. 2 misnumbered 194.
Adv., 'in the press', SJC 6–9 Nov 1790; adv. SDA 21 Jan 1791; re-adv., 'A Tale of Incident and
Adventure', SDA 1 Feb 1791.
Adv. end vol. 2 of *Conscious Duplicity* (1791: 6).

1790: 66   {SCOTT, H}[elenus].
HELENA: OR, THE VICISSITUDES OF A MILITARY LIFE. IN TWO
VOLUMES. BY AN OFFICER'S DAUGHTER.

Cork: Printed by James Haly, King's Arms, North Main Street, 1790.

I xvi, 289p; II 291p. 12mo.

Dt OLS 189.r.47–48; EM 367: 3; ESTC t084550 (BI BL; NA MH-H).

Notes. Dedication to 'the Right Honourable Lady Eliz. Irving' signed H. Scott. List of subscribers vol. 1, v–xvi. Epistolary.

1790: 67   SQUIRREL, Harriett.
*ORIGINAL NOVELS, POEMS, AND ESSAYS. BY HARRIETT SQUIRREL.

> London: Sold by the Author, No. 7, Denmark-Street, Soho, 1790 (EngR).
> 3 vols. 12mo. 10s 6d (EngR).
> EngR 15: 466 (June 1790).
> No copy located.

Notes. EngR: 'These volumes, though not the production of extraordinary genius, contain both amusement and instruction for many readers. There are *babes* in literature as well as religion, who require to be *fed* with its *milk* and not its *strong meat*. To them the work before us may be acceptable. The *essays* will furnish them with morality, and even devotion; the *novels* will help them to kill their leisure hours; and the *poems*, which in truth are in some places very pretty, must be agreeable to all who have taste enough to relish them.'

1790: 68   [STREET, Miss].
THE LETTERS OF MARIA; TO WHICH IS ADDED, AN ACCOUNT OF
HER DEATH.

> London: Printed for G. Kearsley, No. 46, Fleet-Street, 1790.
> viii, 124p. 8vo [MR has 12mo]. 2s 6d (CR, MR).
> CR 70: 698 (Dec 1790); MR n.s. 4: 355 (Mar 1791); AF II: 4280.
> BL 12611.ee.26; EM 236: 6; ESTC t057446 (BI C; NA CaOGU, CtY-BR, CSmH &c.).

Notes. Founded on an incident in Laurence Sterne's *Sentimental Journey* (London, 1768), JR 1234, AF I: 2640.

Preface v–viii. 4 pp. advs. end vol. Epistolary.

Adv. SJC 21–23 Oct 1790; adv. SJC 8–11 Jan 1791 as *Letters of Maria, from the Sentimental Journey of Sterne.*

German trans. Weissenfels, 1791 (*Mariens Briefe nebst Nachricht von ihrem Tode*) (EAG).

CR: '... if the author and translator are not the same, the version must be styled unusually accurate, as many parts are so *truly English*, that we can scarcely suppose they ever appeared in any other language. In the few circumstances in Sterne the story is apparently built; but it is barren of other *incident*, and supported by the tender sentiment which dictated the short account of Yorick. In *his* Amber, it is enshrined and secured from all attack.'

MR [William Enfield]: 'Maria's tears were long ago consecrated by the genius of Sterne; and it is sacrilege for any unhallowed hand to attempt the wild and tender strains, which this "luckless maiden," in her wanderings, played upon her pipe. This Maria, it is true, has sighs and tears, and lamentations, in abundance: but these are all she has to boast. To the "something that was scarcely earthly," which Yorick's Maria possessed, she is entirely a stranger.'

1790: 69   THOMSON, Rev. James.
THE DENIAL; OR, THE HAPPY RETREAT. A NOVEL. BY THE REV.
JAMES THOMSON. IN THREE VOLUMES.

London: Printed for J. Sewell, No. 32, Cornhill, 1790.

I 224p; II 216p; III 198p. 12mo. 9s (CR), 9s sewed (MR, SJC).

CR n.s. 1: 471 (Apr 1791); MR n.s. 3: 400–2 (Dec 1790); AF II: 4460.

BL 12604.h.16; EM 227: 1; ESTC t095828 (NA CSmH).

Notes. 20-pp. preface (unn.). Epistolary.

Adv. SJC 23–26 Oct 1790 with quotation from rev. WEP 12 Oct 1790. Re-adv. SJC 11–13 Jan 1791 with quotations from AR, MR, EngR and 2 magazines.

Further edn: London, 1792, EM 4373: 8, ESTC t064729. German trans. Liegnitz and Leipzig, 1793 (*Die Stiefschwestern*) (RS).

CR: 'In the department of cooler reasoning, we have nothing to object; but in the little natural incidents, in the minor points of delicate incident, there is not a millener's [*sic*] apprentice who hastens with her literary first-born to Leadenhall-Street, but will excel not only Mr Thomson, but probably all the senior fellows of either University. As a novel, we think this work liable to some exceptions: as a string of dissertations on the parental authority and its abuse, these volumes deserve praise.'

MR [Elizabeth Moody and Ralph Griffiths] offers a 15-line 'sketch of what a novel should be' and, although criticising its language, deems this novel 'not void of merit' (p. 401) and 'entitled to a considerable degree of distinction above the common crowd—the *canaille* of modern romances and novels' (p. 402).

1790: 70 TIMBURY, Jane.
THE PHILANTHROPIC RAMBLER. BY JANE TIMBURY, AUTHOR OF TOBIT, THE MALE COQUET, AND THE TRIUMPH OF FRIENDSHIP.

London: Printed for and sold by the Author, Petty France, Westminster: Sold also by J. Southern, St James's Street; and W. Nicoll, St Paul's Church-yard, 1790.

148p. 12mo. 3s sewed (MR).

MR n.s. 5: 225–6 (June 1791); AF II: 4483.

BL N.1717(1); EM 1925: 4; ESTC t137255 (NA DFo).

Notes. List of subscribers v–xvii; prefatory 'Dialogue between the Author and a Friend' xix–xxiv.

The Male Coquet 1788: 76; *The Triumph of Friendship* 1789: 70.

Continued as *A Sequel to the Philanthropic Rambler* 1791: 71.

MR [John Noorthouck]: 'If the lady to whom we are indebted for the Philanthropic Rambler, had ever seen the Amicable Quixotte [1788: 6], or the Benevolent Quixotte [*William Thornborough, the Benevolent Quixote*, 1791: 57], we imagine this work might never have appeared. They are recent publications similar in nature to this; and it is rather unfortunate for the Philanthropic Rambler to come after them; since whatever merit that part of it now published may possess, has been anticipated by the others in a greater degree.... In the Philanthropic Rambler a dead gravity is preserved throughout; which, instead of enticing the novel reader into an approbation of moral conduct, may make even a moral reader yawn.'

1790: 71 [TONE, Theobald Wolfe, Richard JEBB, and John RADCLIFF].
BELMONT CASTLE: OR. SUFFERING SENSIBILITY. CONTAINING THE GENUINE AND INTERESTING CORRESPONDENCE OF SEVERAL PERSONS OF FASHION.

Dublin: Printed for P. Byrne, No. 108, Grafton-Street, 1790.
xi, 223p. 12mo.
O Vet.A5f.189; EM 7888: 3; ESTC t191367 (BI D).

Notes. Dedication to Mrs. Carden v–vii, signed 'The Editor', 17 Oct 1790; 'The Editor to the Reader' ix–xi. 5 pp. advs. end vol. Epistolary.

1790: 72   WHITE, James.
THE ADVENTURES OF JOHN OF GAUNT, DUKE OF LANCASTER. BY JAMES WHITE, ESQ. AUTHOR OF EARL STRONGBOW, CONWAY CASTLE, &C.

London: Printed by John Crowder, for G. G. J. and J. Robinson, Pater-Noster-Row, 1790.
I 259p; II 257p; III 250p. 12mo. 9s (CR), 9s sewed (MR, SJC).
CR 69: 713–14 (June 1790); MR n.s. 2: 416–22 (Aug 1790); AF II: 4771.
C 7720.d.166-168; ESTC n004252 (BI Dt; NA MH-H, NN, PU &c.).

Notes. Robinson paid 55 gns. on 27 Oct 1789 to James White for *John of Gaunt, a Romance* (RA). *Earl Strongbow* 1789: 71.
Adv. SJC 1–3 Apr 1790.
Further edn: Dublin, 1790 (Printed for J. Jones, W. Jones, Grueber and M'Allister, and R. White [imprint to vol. 2 begins 'Printed by Zachariah Jackson, for J. Jones, . . .'], 2 vols., 12mo), ESTC t107032. Extracts from *The Adventures of John of Gaunt* published under several titles in 5 magazines, 1790, RM 659, 660, 1010. German trans. Helmstedt, 1791 (*Johann von Gaunt, Herzog von Lancaster*) (RS).

CR: '. . . what purpose do these antique-modern tales answer? They are less entertaining (we speak for ourselves), less interesting, and less instructive than even the modern ones; for the evident fiction destroys the interest, and the mixture of ancient and modern customs, which cannot be discriminated by general readers, will mislead. . . . we ought to add, that, in many respects, the address of the author, his abilities, and the personages introduced, have for a time obviated all these disadvantages, and forcibly attracted our attention.'

MR [John Noorthouck]: '. . . if this curiosity does not tire, we may, in due time, be supplied with the whole history of England, loaded with fiction from his prolific imagination, into an enormous romance, that may turn the less amusing details of Rapin and Hume out of doors!' (p. 416). 'The adventures are all in the style of heroic errantry, and consist of tilting, succouring distressed damsels, punishing lawless caitiffs, and other events, of course, in the records of chivalry' (p. 418).

1790: 73   [WHITFIELD, Henry].
VILLEROY; OR, THE FATAL MOMENT: A NOVEL, IN THREE VOLUMES. BY A LADY.

London: Printed for W. Lane, Leadenhall Street, 1790/91.
I (1790) xiii, 237p; II (1791) 191p; III (1791) 184p. 12mo. 9s (CR), 9s sewed (SJC).
CR n.s. 3: 117 (Sept 1791); AF II: 4786.
BL Cup.403.l.16; EM 6467: 1; ESTC t139131 (BI AWu, O; NA CSmH; EA COR).

Notes. Vol. 1 pagination is continuous Roman-Arabic; text of novel starts on p. 15; in vols. 2 and 3 text starts on p. 5. Introduction 1, v–xiii. Epistolary.
Adv., 'in the press', SJC 6–9 Nov 1790; adv. SDA 21 Jan 1791.

CR: 'This novel is interesting and pleasing; but surely the error of Villeroy did not, by any statute in the code of poetical justice, deserve such a visitation on the head of his inoffending offspring.'

1790: 74   WILLIAMS, Helen Maria.
JULIA, A NOVEL; INTERSPERSED WITH SOME POETICAL PIECES. BY HELEN-MARIA WILLIAMS. IN TWO VOLUMES.
>   London: Printed for T. Cadell, 1790.
>   I iv, 263p; II 245p. 12mo. 6s (CR), 6s sewed (MR, SJC).
>   CR 69: 592–3 (May 1790); MR n.s. 2: 334–6 (July 1790); AF II: 4822.
>   BL N.2320; EM 4968: 1; ESTC t070026 (BI BMu; NA CtY, DLC, ICN, IU, MH-H, NjP, TxU, ViU &c.).

Notes. Prefatory advertisement 1, iii–iv.
Adv. SJC 6–9 Mar 1790.
Further edns: London, 1790, ESTC t070026; Dublin, 1790 (Printed for Chamberlaine and Rice, P. Wogan, P. Byrne, H. Colbert, W. M'Kenzie [and 7 others in Dublin], 2 vols., 12mo), ESTC t190916. German trans. Leipzig, 1791 (*Julie ein Roman*) (RS). Facs: FCy, RWN.

CR: 'The characters, the language, and the conduct of this novel are in no common style. The characters are well discriminated and supported; the story is probable and interesting; the language elegant and pleasing. Perhaps the lady uses others [*sic*] words too frequently, and prefers them too often to her own; but the quotations are chiefly from Shakspeare, and we have been so frequently culprits the same way, that we dare not censure the error.'

MR [Christopher Lake Moody]: 'We will not compliment the lady on an extensive and accurate knowledge of life; nor on having reached perfection in this species of writing: but we must give her the praise of having framed a simple, instructive, and affecting story' (p. 334).

1791

1791: 1   ANON.
***ADOLPHUS; OR, THE UNNATURAL BROTHER, A NOVEL.**
>   London: Printed and sold by T. Wilkins, Aldermanbury; Messrs. Robinsons, and H. D. Symonds, Paternoster-row, T. Hookham, New Bond-street; and W. Richardson, Royal Exchange (SJC), 1791 (SJC).
>   2 vols. 12mo. 6s (CR), 5s sewed (SJC), 5s (adv.).
>   CR n.s. 3: 117 (Jan 1791); AF II: 22.
>   No copy located.

Notes. Adv. SJC 2–4 June 1791.
Adv. end vol. 2 *Emily; or, the Fatal Promise* (1792: 11).

CR: 'No—we have not yet penetrated the depth of the bathos:—we have not yet seen folly and insipidity in their most disgusting forms. Adolphus sinks lower than any other work of this kind we have hitherto perused; and we can only suppose that there is something worse, because we have formerly thought ourselves at the bottom of the scale and been mistaken.'

1791: 2 ANON.
*THE ADVENTURES OF BOBBY LOUNGE; OR, THE UNFORTUNATE LEVEE HAUNTER. RELATED BY HIMSELF, AS A REAL FACT (2nd edn.).

> London: Printed and sold by W. Kemmish, Borough; also, sold by J. Parsons, Paternoster-Row; and all the Booksellers, 1791 (2nd edn.).
> No copy of 1st edn. located.

Notes. All details from 2nd edn. London, 1791, EM 164: 6, ESTC t066884 (BL).

ALVAREZ; OR, IRRESISTIBLE SEDUCTION
See CAZOTTE, Jacques

ASPASIA; OR, THE DANGERS OF VANITY
See BENOIT, Françoise Albine

1791: 3 ANON.
BENEDICTA, A NOVEL. IN TWO VOLUMES. IN TWO VOLUMES [*sic*].

> London: Printed for William Lane, at the Minerva, Leadenhall-Street, 1741 [SJC: 1791].
> I 264p; II 240p. 12mo. 6s sewed (SDA), 6s (SJC).
> BL 12612.bbb.2; EM 170: 2; ESTC t064710 (NA CaAEU, CSmH).

Notes. By same author as *Edward and Sophia* (1787: 6); *Eliza Cleland* (1788: 14); *Powis Castle* (1788: 30); *Predestined Wife* (1789: 22); *Ashton Priory* (1792: 2); and *Marianne* (1793: 8). Adv. SDA 15 July 1791; adv. SJC 17–20 Dec 1791.

THE BLIND CHILD
See PINCHARD, Elizabeth

1791: 4 ANON.
THE CARPENTER'S DAUGHTER, OF DERHAM-DOWN; OR SKETCHES ON THE BANKS OF WINDERMERE. IN TWO VOLUMES.

> London: Printed at the Minerva, for William Lane, Leadenhall-Street, 1791.
> I 260p; II 248p. 12mo. 6s (CR, SJC).
> CR n.s. 4: 236 (Feb 1792); AF II: 613.
> BL 12614.c.10; EM 289: 4; ESTC t071394 (NA CtY, MH-H).

Notes. By same author as *Count Roderic's Castle* (1794: 7).
Adv., 'In the Press', SDA 26 Oct 1791; adv. SJC 17–20 Dec 1791.
Further edn: Dublin, 1792 (Printed for Messrs. A. Grueber, W. Sleater, W. M'Kenzie, J. Moore, W. Jones, R. M'Allister, and J. Rice, 1 vol., 12mo), EM 3213: 6, ESTC t118780.

CR: 'The whole is entertaining and interesting; the characters diversified, and generally amiable. In the conduct of the story there are many improbabilities, and the changes are seldom skilfully introduced: we were much surprised that, with some knowledge of the manners of the world, and some skill in developing the intricacies of the human heart, there should be so great a defect in the mechanical business of arrangement.'

CHARLOTTE. A TALE OF TRUTH
See ROWSON, Susanna

1791: 5 ANON.
THE CHATEAU DE MYRELLE, OR LAURA. A NOVEL.

London: Printed for T. Hookham, Corner of Bruton Street: Bond Street, 1791.
vi, 221p. 12mo. 3s (CR), 3s sewed (SJC).
CR n.s. 2: 477 (Aug 1791); AF II: 673.
BL 12612.bb.14; EM 130: 3; ESTC t064712 (NA NcU).

Notes. Address 'To the Public' iii–vi. Pagination continuous Roman-Arabic; text of novel starts on p. 7. Epistolary.
Adv. SJC 24–27 Dec 1791.

CR: 'These Letters are descriptive and entertaining: as a story, the novel is not very probable, or well conducted.'

THE CIPHER
See LITTLEJOHN, P.

1791: 6 ANON.
CONSCIOUS DUPLICITY. A NOVEL. IN TWO VOLUMES.

London: Printed for William Lane, at the Minerva, Leadenhall-Street, 1791.
I 216p; II 231p. 12mo. 6s (CR), 5s sewed (SJC).
CR n.s. 2: 355 (July 1791); AF II: 840.
BL 12613.aaa.10; EM 199: 1; ESTC t068745.

Notes. 1 p. advs. end vol. 2. Epistolary.
Adv., 'in the press', SJC 6–9 Nov 1790.

CR: 'A pretty little entertaining story, of a lady running from Europe and the borders of Asia to America after her lover.... The hero and heroine are not very distinguishable, and the denouement is brought about a little too artificially.'

THE CYPHER
See LITTLEJOHN, P., THE CIPHER

DANISH MASSACRE, AN HISTORIC FACT
See MACKENZIE, Anna Maria

DELINEATIONS OF THE HEART
See RAITHBY, John (1792: 49)

DEVIL UPON TWO STICKS
See COMBE, William (1790: 41)

1791: 7 ANON.
THE DUCHESS OF YORK: AN ENGLISH STORY. IN TWO VOLUMES.

London: Printed for William Lane, at the Minerva, Leadenhall-Street, 1791.

I xii, 180p; II 180p. 8vo [MR, CR and SJC have 12mo]. 6s (CR), 6s sewed (MR), 5s sewed (SJC).

CR n.s. 3: 117 (Sept 1791); MR n.s. 8: 339–40 (July 1792); AF II: 1163.

PU Singer-Mend.PR3991.A1.D823.1791; ESTC n007620 (BI O).

Notes. 2 pp. advs. end vol. 2. PU copy in original blue covers. Epistolary.

Adv. SDA 21 Jan 1791; adv. SJC 21–23 June 1791.

Further edn: Dublin, 1791 (Printed for P. Byrne, H. Colbert, J. Parker, J. Moore, J. Halpen, J. Rice, and R. M'Allister, 2 vols., 12mo), EM 2594: 9, ESTC t119487.

CR: 'What can we say? The preface disarms criticism; and historical probability, so far as history goes, is not violated. Where history is silent, our author has supplied the narrative, not improperly, nor unartificially, and has at least formed a novel equal to the works of many of her cotemporaries.'

MR [John Noorthouck]: '. . . it may suffice to repeat our well-founded aversion to blending truth with fiction, so as to mislead the ignorant, by confounding the distinctions between them: but this expedient has been adopted, because invention seems to be, in a great measure, exhausted. To this remark, which is made with no invidious intention, we need only add, that the story is decently told, and might have appeared to better advantage, had it been more correctly printed.'

1791: 8 ANON.

EDWARD: OR, SORROWS FROM SEPARATION. AN INTERESTING NARRATIVE, FOUNDED ON FACTS. IN TWO VOLUMES.

London: Printed for W. Richardson, under the Royal Exchange, 1791.

I vii, 174p; II 162p. 12mo. 6s (CR), 5s sewed (SDA, SJC).

CR n.s. 2: 356 (July 1791).

CtY Im.Ed92.791; xESTC.

Notes. Preface 1, v–vii.

Adv. SDA 24 Mar 1791; adv. SJC 5–7 Apr 1791.

German trans. Weissenfels, 1793 (*Eduard oder die Leiden der Trennung*) (EAG).

CR: 'What is unnatural is seldom interesting; and the inflated poetical style in a prosaic narrative can seldom, but in the hands of a master, reach the heart. The tale is not an uncommon one, though we hope *such* sorrows are unusual. It has "beguiled us of a tear," and led us to regret that we were *"thus moved."* '

1791: 9 ANON.

EDWY; SON OF ETHELRED THE SECOND: AN HISTORIC TALE. BY A LADY. ADDRESSED (BY PERMISSION) TO THE RIGHT HON-OURABLE THE COUNTESS OF WESTMORLAND. IN TWO VOLUMES.

Dublin: Printed for the Authoress; by John Rice, College-Green: And Sold by G. G. J. & G. [*sic*] Robinson, Pater-Noster-Row, London, 1791.

I 175p; II 203p. 12mo.

MH-H *EC75.A100.791e; EM 1007: 30; ESTC n001241 (NA CSmH, NjP).

Notes. Dedication to the Countess of Westmorland signed 'The Authoress', Dublin, Aug 1791; followed by verse 'Address to the Countess of Westmorland' and 2-pp. preface (all unn.). Text of novel starts on p. 7 in vol. 1 and p. 3 in vol. 2. The novel is divided into books rather than chapters, 6 in vol. 1 and 10 in vol. 2.

Further edn. (possibly a reissue with cancel t.p.): Dublin, 1791 (Printed for the Authoress; by John Rice: and sold by G. G. J. & J. Robinson, London, 1791, 2 vols., 12mo), ESTC n034848.

ELEGANT TALES, HISTORIES, AND EPISTLES
See ADAMS, John

1791: 10   ANON.
*THE EMBARRASSED ATTACHMENT.

London: The Literary Press; Sold at No. 62, Wardour-Street, Soho (SJC), 1791 (SJC).
2 vols. 6s sewed (SJC).
No copy located.

Notes. Adv. SJC 5–7 Apr 1791; re-adv. SJC 13–15 Mar 1792.

EMILY BENSON
See O'CONNOR, E.

1791: 11   ANON.
EUGENIA AND ADELAIDE, A NOVEL. IN TWO VOLUMES.

London: Printed for C. Dilly, in the Poultry, 1791.
I iii, 237p; II 238p. 12mo. 6s (CR), 5s sewed (MR, SJC).
CR n.s. 1: 469 (Dec 1791); MR n.s. 8: 341 (July 1792); AF II: 1329.
BL N.2180; EM 2069: 5; ESTC t074438 (NA CtY).

Notes. Preface 1, i–iii.
Adv., 'On Saturday the 22nd instant will be published', LC 69: 44 (11–13 Jan 1791); adv., 'On Saturday the 29th Instant will be published', SJC 20–22 Jan 1791.
Adv. end vol. 2 of *Arville Castle* (1795: 1).
CR: '... though it is disgraced by no common faults, it is distinguished by few excellencies.' CR compares Eugenia to Viola in *Twelfth Night*.
MR [John Noorthouck]: 'The trifling distinctions observable in these compositions of love and the vicissitudes of its success, often prevent us from discriminating the merits of one from another; so that they might be bundled up by the dozen, under a general description. All that the present instance demands, is an acknowlegement that it is not one of the worst.'

THE FAMILY PARTY
See YOUNG, Mary Julia

FLIGHTS OF INFLATUS
See MAN, Henry

FOSCARI, A VENETIAN TALE
See 1790: 12

1791: 12   ANON.
*FREDERICK AND ALICIA; OR, THE SORROWS OF LOVE. A NOVEL.

CONTAINING THE CHARACTER OF AN HONOURABLE GENTLE-
MAN TOO WELL KNOWN BY THE NOBILITY AND OTHERS. BY THE
AUTHOR OF LORD WINWORTH, &C.

> London: Printed for Couch and Laking, No 44, Curzon-Street May-Fair; W. and J.
> Stratford, No. 112, Holbourn, Hill; Scatcherd and Whitaker, Ave-Maria-Lane,
> C. Stalker Stationers'-Court; and H. D. Symonds, No. 20, Pater-noster-Row (SJC),
> 1791 (SJC).
>
> 2 vols. 12mo. 1791 (CR), 6s (SJC).
> CR n.s. 1: 470 (Apr 1791); AF II: 1521.
> No copy located.

Notes. Lord Winworth 1787: 15. Also by same author: *Maria Harcourt* (1788: 22); *Phoebe*
(1788: 28); *William and Charles* (1789: 29); and *Lucinda Hartley* (1790: 17).
Adv. SJC 26–29 Mar 1791.

CR: 'The character of Colonel Prattle is well drawn and supported: it is the same, we suspect, that is alluded to in the title-page, and it is equally infamous and contemptible. The
other characters do not merit any particular distinctions; but the story is artfully inveloped,
well conducted, and dextrously unravelled.'

1791: 13   ANON.
*GEORGINA HARCOURT, A NOVEL.

> London: Printed for H. D. Symonds, Paternoster-row (SJC), 1791 (SJC).
> 2 vols. 12mo. 6s (CR), 5s sewed (SJC).
> CR n.s. 2: 477 (Aug 1791); AF II: 1596.
> No copy located.

Notes. Post-dated; adv. as published, 'To the Ladies . . . Ornamented with two neat Vignettes
. . . By a Lady', SJC 7–9 Dec 1790.

CR: 'A trifling insignificant, improbable story. Will the labour of reviewing novels be
never again compensated by a little rational entertainment?'

1791: 14   ANON.
GERTRUDE; OR, THE ORPHAN OF LLANFRUIST. A NOVEL. IN TWO
VOLUMES.

> London: Printed and Sold by T. Wilkins, Aldermanbury; Sold also by Messrs. Robin-
> sons, and H. D. Symonds, Paternoster-row, T. Hookham, Bond-Street; J. Murray,
> Fleet Street, and W. Richardson, Royal Exchange, 1791.
>
> I xii, 207p; II 269p. 12mo. 6s (CR, adv.).
> CR n.s. 2: 233 (June 1791); AF II: 1601.
> PPL O Eng Gert 49166.D; ESTC n016948 (NA CtY).

Notes. Introduction (1, [i]–xii) dated 4 May 1791. In vol. 2 p. [105] is misnumbered 10.
1 p. advs. end vol. 1 and 3 pp. advs. end vol. 2.
Adv. end vol. 2 *Emily; or, the fatal Promise* (1792: 11).

CR: 'The story consists of hackneyed incidents differently combined, and the characters
are neither new nor very interesting. The ladies have too great tendency to insanity, and the
gentlemen to suspicion: besides, since the aera of Roderic Random, going either to the East
or West Indies to find fathers has been too common an expedient. The author dedicates his

tale to the publisher; but though the nature of his obligations in general is concealed, we are convinced that carefully correcting the proof sheets is not one of them.'

HERMIONE, OR THE ORPHAN SISTERS
See LENNOX, Charlotte

1791: 15   ANON.
THE HISTORY OF GEORGINA NEVILLE; OR, THE DISINTERESTED ORPHAN. A NOVEL. IN TWO VOLUMES. BEING THE FIRST LITER-ARY ATTEMPT OF A YOUNG LADY. DEDICATED, WITH PERMIS-SION, TO THE HON. LADY WARREN.

> London: Printed for the Authoress: Sold by T. Hookham, No. 147, New, and No. 15, Old Bond Street; and J. Carpenter, No. 1, Charles Street, Grosvenor Square, 1791.
> I 252p; II 247p. 8vo [MR has 12mo]. 6s (CR), 6s sewed (MR).
> CR n.s. 2: 477 (Aug 1791); MR n.s. 7: 230 (Feb 1792); AF II: 1959.
> BL 12611.c.27; EM 208: 4; ESTC t055921 (NA CLU-S/C, ICU).

Notes. Dedication to the Hon. Lady Warren 1, 5–12; 12-pp. list of subscribers (unn.); text of novel starts on p. 13. 1 p. advs. end vol. 2.

CR: 'With all our partiality for female authors, and our anxiety to raise a drooping or a promising genius, we cannot commend this novel. Praise would be cruelty; and the young lady, who may possess numerous good qualities, in the end might condemn us, for tempting her to sacrifice more solid accomplishments, to the unprofitable labour of the pen.'

MR [William Enfield]: 'This "first literary attempt" of a young Lady is unquestionably intitled to some degree of indulgence, especially when it is made, as in the present case, under the protection of a long list of noble patrons. If the performance pleases Lords A. B. and C. and Ladies W. X. and Y. though it should not happen exactly to suit the notions of a few old-fashioned critics, who know little of the great world, it must please the ordinary class of read-ers; who, in judging of works of taste, certainly can wish for no better guides than people of the first fashion.'

THE HISTORY OF SIR GEOFFRY RESTLESS
See MAN, Henry

1791: 16   ANON.
IPHIGENIA, A NOVEL. IN THREE VOLUMES.

> London: Printed for William Lane, at the Minerva Press, 1791.
> I 256p; II 216p; III 228p. 12mo. 9s (CR), 9s sewed (SDA), 10s 6d (SJC).
> CR n.s. 4: 114 (Jan 1792); AF II: 2203.
> MH-H *EC75.A100.791Ii; EM 1114: 11; ESTC n006615.

Notes. Address to the Public signed 'A Female Writer'. List of subscribers. Epistolary.
Adv. SDA 30 Sept 1791; adv. SJC 17–20 Dec 1791.

CR: 'This Novel is the work of an author unhackneyed in the ways of men or of authorship. The tale is perplexed without interest, and the plot unravelled without pathos. She, for we suspect it is the work of a female pen, knows as little *what* to conceal, as in what manner the concealment should be discovered. In short, it is in every view a trifling and improbable story.'

THE LABYRINTHS OF LIFE
See THOMSON, Anna

1791: 17   ANON.
LADY JANE GREY: AN HISTORICAL TALE. IN TWO VOLUMES.
London: Printed for William Lane, at the Minerva, Leadenhall-Street, 1791.
I 169p; II 191p. 8vo [CR and SJC have 12mo]. 6s (CR, SJC), 5s sewed (SDA).
CR n.s. 3: 234–5 (Oct 1791); AF II: 2448.
BL 1507/867; EM 5480: 3; ESTC t128882 (BI O; NA CaAEU, CtY, ViU &c.).

Notes. Vol. 1 text begins on p. 7; vol. 2 text begins on p. 9. 1 p. adv. end vol. 2. Epistolary.
Adv. SDA 30 Sept 1791; adv. SJC 17–20 Dec 1791.

CR: 'The language and sentiments of this novel greatly excel the merits of the usual sale-work in this department. Historical truth, with one trifling exception, is also well preserved. There are, however, defects in the conduct of the story. Lady Jane Grey's merits and misfortunes are not sufficiently brought forward, and the fatal catastrophe is passed over too hastily to interest or assist us.'

THE LAKE OF WINDERMERE, A NOVEL
See STREET, Miss

LAURA; A NOVEL. BY THE AUTHOR OF THE INDEPENDENT
See McDONALD, Andrew

1791: 18   ANON.
LAURA VALMONT, A NOVEL WRITTEN BY A LADY.
London: Printed for Charles Dilly, in the Poultry, 1791.
v, 166p. 12mo. 2s 6d sewed (MR, LC).
MR n.s. 8: 339 (July 1792).
BL N.2063(1); EM 2072: 2; ESTC t066522 (BI E).

Notes. Epistolary.
Adv., 'On Saturday the 12th Inst. will be published', LC 70: 438 (3–5 Nov 1791); adv. as published LC 70: 464 (10–12 Nov 1791).

MR [John Noorthouck]: 'The volume comprizes two stories, that may have their due effect on young ladies of sensibility and sentiment.'

1791: 19   ANON.
*THE LIFE, ADVENTURES, AND HISTORY OF MISS MORETON, AND THE FAITHFUL COTTAGER.
London: Kerby, 1791.
2 vols. 12mo. 5s (CR).
CR n.s. 2: 355 (July 1791).
No copy located.

Notes. ESTC: Sometimes attributed to W. P. Rich.
Further edns. (under the title *The Authentic and Interesting History of Miss Moreton, and the*

Faithful Cottager): Nottingham, 1799, ESTC t164231; Birmingham, 1800?, ESTC n030694; Norwich, 1800, ESTC t163862; Nottingham, 1822 (Bodl.).

CR: 'The narrative is said to be true, and we cannot deny it; but we never saw truth in such an ungracious, uninteresting, and improbable form. Perhaps as virtue is its own reward, so truth always furnishes its own entertainment.'

LINDOR AND ADELAIDE, A MORAL TALE
See SAYER, Edward

1791: 20 ANON.
MAPLE VALE, OR THE HISTORY OF MISS SIDNEY. IN THREE VOLUMES.

London: Printed for T. Vernor, Birchin-Lane, Cornhill, 1791.
I 214p; II 216p; III 210p. 12mo. 7s 6d (CR), 9s sewed (MR, SJC).
CR n.s. 1: 349 (Mar 1791); MR n.s. 4: 229 (Feb 1791); AF II: 2709.
BL 12611.bbb.22; EM 7086: 2; ESTC t108625 (NA CtY).

Notes. Epistolary.
Post-dated; adv. as published SJC 25–27 Nov 1790.

CR: 'This is a pleasing chit-chat novel, unreasonably extended. We have said that souls have no sexes, yet we think that there is sufficient *internal* evidence to conclude that the author is a female. Are we, in this, inconsistent? We trust not: novels of this kind are constructed mechanically; the mind has no share in the business.'

MR [John Noorthouck]: 'The first of these three volumes opens in a lively agreeable manner, introducing a variety of characters, which are not ill described, and are properly supported; so that we proceed in the hope of being well entertained with them; and truly we were even to superabundance: for when their respective stories began to move forward, we found ourselves entangled in business enough to spin through two or three modern compositions of this nature.'

MEMOIRS OF A SCOTS HEIRESS
See MATHEWS, Eliza Kirkham

MEMOIRS OF ANTONINA
See GREEN, John Richards (trans.)

1791: 21 ANON.
MONIMIA. A NOVEL. IN TWO VOLUMES.

London: Printed for William Lane at the Minerva, Leadenhall-Street, 1791.
I 195p; II 254p. 12mo. 6s (CR), 5s sewed (SJC), 6s sewed (SDA).
CR n.s. 3: 235 (Oct 1791); AF II: 2913.
PU Singer-Mend.PR3991.A1.M65.1791; ESTC n005323.

Notes. 2 pp. advs. end vol. 2. Epistolary.
Adv., 'In the Press, and shortly will be published', SJC 3–5 Aug 1790; still adv. as 'in the press' SJC 6–9 Nov 1790 and SDA 18 Mar 1791; adv. as published SDA 15 July 1791.

CR: 'Monimia is more varied than almost any novel that we have lately read. The shortness of the letters, and the improbability of many parts of the story, indeed lessen the interest; nor is the denouement conducted with very great address or ability. On the whole, it possesses a share of merit which will place it in a respectable station in the second rank.'

1791: 22   ANON.
PERSIANA, THE NYMPH OF THE SEA. A NOVEL. IN THREE VOL-
UMES.
>   London: Printed for William Lane, at the Minerva, Leadenhall-Street, 1791.
>   I 172p; II 164p; III 152p. 12mo. 6s (CR), 7s 6d sewed (SJC), 9s (SDA).
>   CR n.s. 2: 356 (July 1791); AF II: 3315.
>   MH-H *EC75.A100.791p; EM 1284: 18; ESTC n011100 (NA PU).

Notes. Adv. SJC 21–23 June 1791; adv. SDA 18 Mar 1791.

CR: 'There is a romantic air in the various incidents of this little Novel that is pleasing and attractive: the conclusion too is well managed, and the characters properly discriminated. Yet, perhaps, among the wretched productions that have lately issued from the press in this department, it is no very great honour to be in the first line. Persiana is not the first of the line, though not far distant from the first.'

1791: 23   ANON.
THE POLITE REPOSITORY OR, AMUSING COMPANION: A SELEC-
TION OF TALES, ADVENTURES, HISTORIES, ANECDOTES, FROM
THE BEST MODERN PUBLICATIONS. WITH A VARIETY OF ORI-
GINALS.
>   London: Printed for William Lane, at the Minerva. Leadenhall Street, 1791/92.
>   I ii, 573p; II 574p. 4to.
>   O Vet.A5e.4691-4694; ESTC t196417.

Notes. Each vol. divided into 2 parts; only 1.1 dated 1791. Vol. 1.1 has frontispiece of 'The Genius of Taste introduced by MINERVA to the Novelist.' 'Introductory Address' 1, i–ii. Engraved t.ps. both vols; illustrations both vols; index end both vols.

POPULAR TALES OF THE GERMANS
See MUSÄUS, Johann Karl August

THE ROMANCE OF THE FOREST
See RADCLIFFE, Ann

1791: 24   ANON.
THE SIEGE OF BELGRADE: AN HISTORICAL NOVEL. TRANSLATED
FROM A GERMAN MANUSCRIPT. FOUR VOLUMES IN TWO.
>   London: Printed for H. D. Symonds, No. 20. Paternoster Row, 1741 [1791].
>   I vi, 180p; II 171p. 12mo. 6s (CR), 5s sewed (MR, SDA).
>   CR n.s. 2: 356 (July 1791); MR n.s. 5: 338–9 (July 1791); AF II: 4101.
>   BL N.1775; EM 3804: 1; ESTC t071902.

Notes. 1741, for 1791 (MR).

Dedication to Lord Rawdon. First line of text refers to events of 1789.

Adv. SDA 14 Apr 1791 and LC 69: 359 (12–14 Apr 1791).

CR: 'Though this Novel is a little defective in historical accuracy, it contains some local knowledge of Russian customs, and is very entertaining. In this scarcity of good novels we look upon the "Siege of Belgrade" as an acquisition.'

MR [John Noorthouck]: 'The *Siege of Belgrade* is a recent event; the words *translated from a German manuscript* insinuate *secret history*; and under these specious outlines, we apprehend that we have been reading as mere a circulating-library-story as ever was fabricated. Great liberties are taken with Imperial majesty: but who, in the full possession of their faculties, and with a common knowlege of the world, will take up private characters from such unknown hands?'

1791: 25 ANON.
SOMERVILLE BOWER; OR, THE ADVENTURES OF SOPHRONIA. IN A SERIES OF LETTERS. IN TWO VOLUMES.

London: Printed for S. Bladon, No. 13, Paternoster Row, 1791.

I 191p; II 184p. 12mo. 5s (CR), 5s sewed (SJC).

CR n.s. 1: 350 (Mar 1791); AF II: 4178.

ICN Case Y1565.S68; ESTC n047083.

Notes. Epistolary.

Post-dated; adv. as published SJC 25–27 Nov 1790.

CR: 'There is no little art conspicuous in the conduct of this Novel, not in the unexpected changes of events, contrast of characters, or a skilful arrangement of the story, but in spinning out such a meagre tale to the extent of two volumes.'

TERENTIA; A NOVEL
See JOHNSON, Mrs

1791: 26 ANON.
THE VALE OF FELICITY, OR SYLVAN HAPPINESS: POURTRAYED IN A SERIES OF LETTERS, MORAL AND ENTERTAINING. BY A LADY. IN TWO VOLUMES.

London: Printed for A. Hamilton, No. 5, Russel-Court, Covent-Garden, 1791.

I 211p; II 197p. 12mo. 5s (EngR).

EngR 19: 71 (Jan 1792).

BL 1607/1082; EMf; ESTC t118740 (NA PU).

Notes. Epistolary.

Further edn: Dublin, 1792 (Printed for Messrs. P. Byrne, P. Wogan, A. Grueber, J. Moore, W. Jones [and 2 others in Dublin], 1 vol., 12mo), EM 7242: 2, ESTC t181049.

EngR: 'We were extremely *happy* when we had made our escape from this *Vale of Felicity*, into which we are sorry we cannot advise any of our readers to enter.'

WANLEY PENSON
See SADLER, Robert

WILLIAM THORNBOROUGH, THE BENEVOLENT QUIXOTE
See PURBECK, Elizabeth and Jane

1791: 27   ANON.
*WOODLEY PARK; OR, THE VICTIMS OF REVENGE. BY A LADY.
> London: Wilkie, 1791.
> 2 vols. 12mo. 5s (CR).
> CR n.s. 1: 350 (Mar 1791); AF II: 4926.
> No copy located.

Notes. CR: 'In the whole course of our literary experience we have seen nothing more child-ish, trifling, and improbable, than the work before us.'

1791: 28   [ADAMS, John].
ELEGANT TALES, HISTORIES, AND EPISTLES OF A MORAL TEN-DENCY; ON LOVE, FRIENDSHIP, MATRIMONY, CONJUGAL FELIC-ITY, JEALOUSY, CONSTANCY, MAGNANIMITY, CHEERFULNESS, AND OTHER IMPORTANT SUBJECTS. BY THE AUTHOR OF WOMAN; OR, HISTORICAL SKETCHES OF THE FAIR SEX.
> London: Printed for G. Kearsley, at No. 46, Johnson's-Head, in Fleet-Street, 1791.
> ii, 480p. 12mo. 4s sewed (MR, SJC).
> MR n.s. 4: 93 (Jan 1791); AF II: 13.
> BL 012331.e.59; CME 3-628-51183-6; EM 804: 1; ESTC t073693 (BI O; EA COR).

Notes. 1-p. prefatory advertisement and 1 p. advs. for publications by Adams (unn.); table of contents i–ii.

Post-dated; adv. as published, with titles of 14 of the stories, SJC 23–26 Oct 1790.

Further edn: Dublin, 1791 (Printed for P. Wogan, H. Colbert, J. Jones, W. M'Kenzie, W. Jones, J. Halpen, G. Draper, and J. Rice, 1 vol., 12mo), ESTC n048883.

   MR [John Noorthouck]: 'This is a wholesale compiler, who cuts novels down to a proper size, and then bundles them into a faggot, to warm the imaginations of his readers.'

1791: 29   BACON, James.
THE LIBERTINE. A NOVEL. IN A SERIES OF LETTERS. BY JAMES BACON.
> London: Printed for W. Miller, Bookseller to His Royal Highness the Duke of Clarence,
>   No. 5, Old Bond-Street, 1791.
> x, 285p. 12mo. 3s (CR).
> CR n.s. 4: 352 (Mar 1792); AF II: 181.
> BL 1077.c.11; EM 3604: 5; ESTC t117405 (NA CtY).

Notes. Dedication to the Hon. Mrs Beresford.

Adv. SDA 12 Jan 1792: 'Lane, at the Minerva, Leadenhall-street, Having purchased the Copies of The Libertine, a novel, In a Series of Letters, By James Bacon, Price 3s. sewed, Informs Ladies and Gentlemen, As well as the Trade, who may be served Wholesale, That they may be supplied by him with this pleasing Publication.'

   CR: 'A great deal of love, many marriages, some seduction, much sentiment and poetical description, with a good moral. This is the farrago libelli of a book, that on the whole possesses too little merit to require a more ample examination.'

BECKFORD, William
See MUSÄUS, Johann Karl August

1791: 30   [BENOIT, Françoise Albine].
ASPASIA; OR, THE DANGERS OF VANITY. A FRENCH STORY, TAKEN
FROM REAL LIFE. IN TWO VOLUMES.
> [London]: Printed for J. Bew, No. 28, Paternoster Row, 1791.
> I 312p; II 319p. 12mo. 6s (CR), 6s sewed (LC, SJC).
> CR n.s. 2: 233 (June 1791); AF II: 157.
> BL N.2062; ESTC t142899 (BI O; NA NNU).

Notes. Trans. of *Les Aveux d'une jolie femme* (Paris, 1762).
Adv., 'will be published on Tuesday next', LC 69: 348 (9–12 Apr 1791). Adv. SJC 23–26 July
1791.
ESTC identifies *Aspasie* (London and Paris 1787, ESTC t133459) as a trans. of this work, but
it is a trans. of *Arpasia* (1786: 4).
  CR: 'The insipid memoirs of a French courtezan; love without passion, intrigues without
interest, characters sketched in water colours, equally incapable of exciting esteem or indignation. Why was this work translated? Is not folly the growth of our own soil? Must insipidity be imported? There are hot beds in this kingdom where it spreads already with too great
luxuriance.'

1791: 31   BREWER, George.
THE HISTORY OF TOM WESTON. A NOVEL, AFTER THE MANNER
OF TOM JONES. BY GEORGE BREWER, ESQ. OF THE ROYAL NAVY.
IN TWO VOLUMES.
> London: Printed for the Author; and published by T. Hookham, No. 147, New Bond
> Street, 1791.
> I xi, 228p; II 261p. 12mo. 6s (CR), 6s sewed (MR, SJC).
> CR n.s. 1: 469–70 (Apr 1791); MR n.s. 5: 465–6 (Aug 1791); AF II: 461.
> MH-H *EC75.N7585.791h; EM 1003: 8; ESTC n002714 (NA ICU).

Notes. Preface 1, v–viii. List of subscribers 1, ix–xi.
Adv. SJC 10–12 Feb 1791.
Further edn: Dublin, 1791 (Printed for P. Wogan, J. Rice, W. Jones, A. Grueber, R. White,
and G. Draper, 2 vols., 12mo), ESTC n007256. German trans. Leipzig and Halle, 1792
(*Geschichte Thomas Weston*) (Price).
  CR: 'The descriptions of characters and situations are new and entertaining; but the inci-
dents of the tale itself are parodies of those of Roderick Random, Tom Jones, and Booth in
Fielding's Amelia. On the whole, however, these volumes rise much above the common rank:
they are humorous, entertaining, and interesting.'
  MR [John Noorthouck and George Edward Griffiths]: 'This story is drawn up by a writer
who is evidently not unacquainted with human nature, life, and manners; which are in many
instances sarcastically and truly represented. It would have been better, therefore, if Mr
Brewer had not professedly given it as an imitation of a model, of which it certainly falls very
far short; and those abilities, which are now obscured by comparison, might have shone to
some advantage, if employed on an original task.'

1791: 32   [CAZOTTE, Jacques].
ALVAREZ; OR, IRRESISTIBLE SEDUCTION: A SPANISH TALE. DEDI-
CATED TO HIS ROYAL HIGHNESS THE PRINCE OF WALES.

> London: Printed for W. Richardson, Royal Exchange, 1791.
> viii, 258p. 8vo [CR has 12mo]. 3s (CR), 5s (half-title, SDA).
> CR n.s. 3: 118 (Jan 1791); AF II: 75.
> BL RB.23.a.10194; ESTC t226198.

Notes. Trans. of *Le Diable amoureux, nouvelle espagnole* (Naples, 1772).
Not identified as by Cazotte in ESTC, but later trans., *The Devil in Love*, is so identified.
Dedication to H.R.H. George, Prince of Wales v–viii.
Adv. SDA 7 Mar 1791, also sold at Mills's, Bookbinder, and at L. Bull's and W. Meyler's, Bath;
adv. SJC 5–7 Apr 1791.
Further edns. (different trans.): London, 1793, EM 54: 4, ESTC t071529 (*The Devil in Love*);
London, 1798, CME 3-628-45053-5, ESTC t210676 (*The Enamoured Spirit*); London, 1810
(*Biondetta, or the Enamoured Spirit*) (ViU); New York, 1810 (*The Devil in Love*) (WC).

> CR: 'The tale is humorous and interesting: it is the production of no common author, and
> the moral is a good one—Shun the first temptations to vice, however trifling they may
> appear.'

1791: 33   CHÉRENSI, B[enjamin] Frère de.
THE MODERN HERO IN THE KINGDOM OF CATHAI. IN THE YEAR
90000. TRANSLATED FROM THE FRENCH OF MR. B. FRERE, DE
CHERENSI.

> Hereford: Printed and Sold by W. H. Parker; J. Evans, London; Prince and Cook,
>   Oxford; Hazard and Bull, Bath, 1791.
> vi, 193p. 12mo. 3s (EngR).
> EngR 20: 70 (July 1792).
> BL 12511.ee.21; EM 7: 5; ESTC t098590 (BI O).

Notes. Trans. of *Les Prémices de ma jeunesse* (London and Paris, 1787).
Possibly a pseudonym. Dedication of the original signed D. F. D. Chérensi. BLC/ESTC
catalogue under Frère, apparently his later anglicized name.
Has both a translator's preface (v–vi) and an author's preface (1p., unn.).

> EngR: 'We must confess that we can discover very little merit in this work; we therefore
> consign it *to the family vault of all the Capulets.*'

1791: 34   CLARKE, Eliza[beth] [later COBBOLD].
THE SWORD; OR, FATHER BERTRAND'S HISTORY OF HIS OWN
TIMES, FROM THE ORIGINAL MANUSCRIPT: BY ELIZA CLARKE,
AUTHOR OF NARRATIVE POEMS, &C.

> Liverpool: Printed for the Author by A. Smith, and sold by R. Faulder, New Bond-street,
>   London, 1791.
> I xii, 213p; II 224p. 12mo.
> BL 12611.cc.11; EM 62: 1; ESTC t055915 (BI LVp, O; NA CSmH, NjP).

Notes. List of subscribers i–xii.

COMBE, William, **THE DEVIL UPON TWO STICKS**
See 1790: 41

1791: 35   FLORIAN, [Jean Pierre Claris de].
**GALATEA A PASTORAL ROMANCE, IMITATED FROM CERVANTES
BY M. DE FLORIAN. TRANSLATED BY AN OFFICER.**
>   Dublin: Printed by P. Byrne 108, Grafton Street, 1791.
>   lii, 253p. 8vo.
>   BL RB.23.a.8732; EM 4: 3; ESTC t131685 (BI BMp, C, D &c.; NA CaOHM, CaOLU,
>   DeGE &c.).

Notes. Trans. of *Galatée, roman pastoral imité de Cervantes* (Paris, 1783). First published in
English in *The Works of Mr. le Chevalier de Florian* (London, 1786), ESTC n025864.
Engraved t.p. 3-pp. (unn.) verse dedication to Caroline, Countess of Portarlington, Dublin,
10 Aug 1791; 16-pp. (unn.) list of subscribers; 'The Life of Cervantes' i–lii. Illustrations.
Mostly in prose but with some verse parts.
Adv. end vol. 3 of *Camilla* (1785: 4): 'Shortly will be published, Dedicated to her Grace the
Duchess of Devonshire, *Galatea, a Pastoral Romance. From the French of Mons. De Florian.*
Further edns. (various trans.): Boston, 1798, ESTC w024663; London, 1804, ECB 209, NSTC
F942; London 1813, NSTC C4063.

1791: 36   FLORIAN, [Jean Pierre Claris] de; MORGAN, Elizabeth (*trans.*).
**STELLA. A PASTORAL ROMANCE. TRANSLATED FROM THE
FRENCH OF MON. DE FLORIAN. DEDICATED, BY PERMISSION, TO
LADY BROUGHTON, BY MISS ELIZABETH MORGAN, AUTHORESS
OF NUMA POMPILIUS.**
>   London: Printed and Sold (for the Authoress) by J. Barker, Russell-Court, Drury-Lane,
>   1791.
>   I iii, xv, 128p; II 164p. 12mo.
>   BL 12512.aaa.25; EM 10: 9; ESTC t131212 (BI O; NA MH-H).

Notes. Trans. of *Estelle, roman pastoral* (Paris, 1788).
Dedication to Lady Broughton 1, i–iii signed Elizabeth Morgan, Stable-yard, St James's,
1 Feb 1791; 1 p. advs. verso of p. iii of dedication; list of subscribers i–xv. Text of novel begins
on p. 9 in both vols; text ends on p. 144 of vol. 2; notes begin on p. 145.
Further edns: [different trans.] London, 1798, EM 5348: 5, ESTC t114945; NSTC lists edns. in
1803, 1805 and 1811. Spanish trans. Barcelona, 1814 (*Estela: pastoral en prosa y verso*) (WC).
This edn. not reviewed; 1798 edn. rev. CR n.s. 25: 473 (Apr 1799); MR n.s. 25: 213
(Feb 1798); AF II: 979.

1791: 37   FOX, J[oseph].
**TANCRED. A TALE OF ANCIENT TIMES. BY J. FOX, JUN. IN TWO
VOLUMES.**
>   London: Printed for William Lane, at the Minerva, Leadenhall-Street, 1791.
>   I 160p; II 142p. 8vo [CR has 12mo]. 5s (CR), 6s (SDA).
>   CR n.s. 2: 355 (July 1791); AF II: 1498.
>   BL 12654.i.11; EM 269: 5; ESTC t107043 (NA CtY, CLU-S/C).

Notes. Dedication to the Duchess of Rutland 1, v–viii.

2 pp. advs. end vol. 2.

Adv., 'In the Press', SDA 18 Mar 1791.

   CR: 'The milder features of the Castle of Otranto are copied in this sketch, which is an humble imitation of the same story.' [*Castle of Otranto*, 1765 [1764], JR 868; AF I: 2898].

FRÈRE, Benjamin
See CHÉRENSI, Benjamin Frère

1791: 38   GORJY, [Jean Claude].
LIDORA; AN ANCIENT CHRONICLE. FROM THE FRENCH OF MONS.
DE GORGY, AUTHOR OF BLANSAY, VICTORINA, AND ST. ALMA. IN
TWO VOLUMES.
   London: Printed for W. Lane, at the Minerva, Leadenhall-Street, 1791.
   I viii, 182p; II viii, 184p. 12mo. 6s (CR), 5s sewed (adv.).
   CR n.s. 2: 116 (May 1791); AF II: 1677.
   CtY Hfd29.416w; xESTC.

Notes. Trans. of *Lidorie, ancienne chronique allusive* (Paris, 1790).

Table of contents iii–viii in both vols.

Blansay 1790: 44; *Victorina* 1790: 45; *St. Alma* 1791: 39.

Adv. SDA 21 Jan 1791.

Adv. end vol. 2 of *Leon, a Spartan Story* (1791: 66).

   CR: 'This Ancient Chronicle, like the Tales of other Times, is entertaining and interesting. It pretends not, however, to real antiquity, nor is it a successful imitation: modern refinements glare through the veil, and the political speculations of our reforming neighbours give a striking hue to the whole.'

1791: 39   GORJY, [Jean Claude]; [?HELME, Elizabeth (*trans.*)].
*ST. ALMA, A NOVEL, FROM THE FRENCH OF M. DE GORGY,
AUTHOR OF BLANSAY, &C.
   London: Lane, at the Minerva, Leadenhall-Street (SDA), 1791 (SDA).
   2 vols. 12mo. 5s (CR), 5s sewed (adv.).
   CR n.s. 1: 469 (Apr 1791); AF II: 1679.
   No copy located.

Notes. Trans. of *Saint-Alme* (Paris, 1790). Summers gives Helme as translator.

Blansay 1790: 44.

Adv. SDA 21 Jan 1791.

Adv. end vol. 2 of *Leon, a Spartan Story* (1791: 66).

   CR: 'A tender little story, interesting, but improbable. The author, in the second volume, approaches too near the splendor of Rousseau, not to appear in a disadvantageous situation. The most pleasing parts of this novel were, in our opinion, the artless picturesque descriptions of the habitations and inhabitants of the Alpine regions.'

1791: 40   [?GREEN, John Richards (trans.)]
MEMOIRS OF ANTONINA, QUEEN OF ABO. DISPLAYING HER

PRIVATE INTRIGUES, AND COMMON PASSIONS. WITH FAMILY
SKETCHES, AND CURIOUS ANECDOTES OF GREAT PERSONS.
TRANSLATED FROM THE FRENCH. TWO VOLUMES IN ONE.

London: Printed for E. Bently, [sic] No. 22, Fetter Lane, 1791.
I 78p; II 83p. 12mo. 2s 6d sewed (SJC).
GM 61: 361 (Apr 1791).
BL 12510.dd.23; EM 60: 5; ESTC t090063 (BI D; NA MH-H; EA ZWTU).

Notes. Trans. of *Essai historique sur la vie de Marie Antoinette* (Amsterdam and Paris, 1789),
variously attributed to P. E. A. Goupil and Jacques-Pierre Brissot de Warville.
Handwritten comments on verso of t.p. to vol. 1 in BL copy describe the work as a 'coarse,
false and infamous libel . . . published in Paris, early in the Revolution' with a 'share in producing the events which terminated in the murder of Louis 16 and the Queen'. This note also
says, on the authority of Cobbett in the *Political Register* for 1804, that the work was translated by 'John Giffard' [i.e. John Richards Green]. Text starts on p. 3 in vol. 1. Vol. 2 has half-
title only.
Adv. SJC 10–12 Mar 1791 as 'London: Printed and sold by Taylor and Co. Royal Exchange;
and all other Booksellers' with the heading 'Secret History of a Great Family' and 'Embellished with an elegantly engraved Head of the Heroine'; adv. claims huge sales in France,
Prussia, Holland, Germany and Russia.
    GM: 'If this be a translation, the original is a worthy specimen of the unbounded licen-
tiousness of the press in France, without the least regard to decency, delicacy, or morality.'

1791: 41   INCHBALD, [Elizabeth].
A SIMPLE STORY. IN FOUR VOLUMES. BY MRS. INCHBALD.

London: Printed for G. G. J. and J. Robinson, Pater-noster Row, 1791.
I vii, 233p; II 253p; III 157p; IV 209p. 8vo [MR has 12mo]. 12s sewed (MR, SJC).
CR n.s. 1: 207–13 (Feb 1791); MR n.s. 4: 434–8 (Apr 1791); AF II: 2175.
BL 243.h.21-24; EMf; ESTC t134770 (BI C, O; NA CtY, CtY-BR, CSmH, IU, MH-H,
    NjP, ViU &c.).

Notes. Preface 1, i–vii. 8 pp. advs. end vol. 4.
Robinson paid £200 for *A Simple Story* (Boaden 1: 273). In 1800 Inchbald was paid £600 by
'her bookseller' (Boaden 2: 35–36) which Tompkins presumes to be Robinson for *Nature
and Art* (1796: 57) and *A Simple Story*, although Inchbald had dealings with other booksellers
who published her plays. In 1810 Inchbald again sold the copyright to the two novels, to
Longman (Boaden 2: 164).
Adv., 'On Thursday, the 10th instant, will be published', SJC 1–3 Feb 1791.
Further edns: London, 1791, EM 7615: 7, ESTC t128226; Dublin, 1791 (Printed by William
Porter, for W. Wilson, P. Wogan, P. Byrne, W. McKenzie, J. Moore [and 7 others in Dublin],
2 vols., 12mo), EM 6851: 5, ESTC t128227; Philadelphia, 1793, ESTC w022283; London,
1793, ESTC n054040; London, 1799, ESTC t107614; WC has 14 entries between 1800 and
1850; Summers has 7 edns. between 1800 and 1850; NSTC lists edns. in 1804, 1808, 1810,
1820, 1824, 1833, 1840, 1843, 1845, 1848 and 1849. Extracts from *A Simple Story* published
in 3 magazines, 1791, RM 1148. French trans. Paris, 1791 (*Simple histoire*) (BGR); German
trans. Leipzig, 1791 (*Eine einfache Geschichte*) (RS); Spanish trans. Paris, 1837 (*Sencilla histo-
ria*) (BN).
    CR: 'Character is accurately delineated and faithfully preserved, with few exceptions: the

most delicate feelings are continually excited: the incidents are natural; and, what is more extraordinary in the present state of novel-writing, they are new' (p. 207). CR comments, however, on the introduction in the third volume of 'a totally new story' and says that 'nothing can be more disjointed than these two stories in the present mode of connecting them' (p. 208).

MR [George Edward Griffiths]: 'The style is in perfect unison with the title. A vein of elegant simplicity runs through the whole' (p. 435). 'The characters in this piece are drawn with a true and steady pencil. We are not presented, as is the case in many other novels, with an overcharged picture of prominent features, merely to introduce extravagant conduct afterward' (p. 436). 'The fable abounds with incidents, all following in a regular train, like effects springing from their causes; and yet expectation is kept alive, and, though probability is not violated, surprize is constantly awakened. The narrative is generally pleasing. The secret charm, that gives a grace to the whole, is the art with which Mrs Inchbald has made her work completely dramatic. The business is, in a great measure, carried on in dialogue' (pp. 436–7). MR comments, apparently in response to CR, that there is 'one unbroken narrative, not two stories woven together, which has been erroneously observed' (p. 436).

1791:42   [JOHNSON, Mrs].
TERENTIA; A NOVEL. BY THE AUTHOR OF THE PLATONIC GUARDIAN, &C. IN TWO VOLUMES.
> London: Printed for T. Hookham, and J. Carpenter, New and Old Bond-Street, 1791.
> I 211p; II 214p. 12mo. 6s (CR), 6s sewed (SDA, adv.).
> CR n.s. 4: 352 (Mar 1792); AF II: 4393.
> BL 12613.b.20; EM 223: 2; ESTC t068742 (NA CtY, DLC).

Notes. Blakey: *Platonic Guardian* (1787: 42) attributed to Mrs Johnson in a Minerva Catalogue of 1814.
2 pp. advs. end vol. 2.
Adv. SDA 14 Jan 1792.
Adv. end vol. 3 of *Edelfrida* (1792: 7).
Further edn: Dublin, 1792 (Printed by Wm. Hunter, for Mess. P. Byrne, A. Grueber, W. M'Kenzie, J. Halpen, R. M'Allister, and R. White, 1 vol., 12mo), EM 7901: 4, ESTC t175109.

CR: 'This is one of the few imitators of miss Burney that we can read with pleasure. Yet the work, though pleasing and interesting, neither deficient in character or situation, is pursued so rapidly as to leave us often to regret chasms which might be filled with advantage, and improbabilities which might have been prevented, or cleared. Terentia will hold her place on the second shelf, though the author, with more care, might have claimed a higher station.'

1791:43   [LENNOX, Charlotte].
HERMIONE, OR THE ORPHAN SISTERS. A NOVEL. IN FOUR VOLUMES.
> London; Printed for William Lane, at the Minerva, Leadenhall-Street, 1791.
> I iii, 278p; II 296p; III 303p; IV 264p. 12mo. 12s (CR), 5s sewed (SJC 1790), 12s sewed (SDA), 14s (SJC 1791).
> CR n.s. 2: 233 (June 1791); AF II: 2522.
> BL Cup.403.u.11; EMf; ESTC t140064 (NA CtY, DLC, MnU &c.).

Notes. Address 'To Ladies and Gentlemen, Patrons of Entertaining Literature' from the Minerva Printing Office 1, i–iii. 1 p. advs. end vol. 3. Epistolary.

Adv.,'in the press', SJC 6–9 Nov 1790; adv. SDA 21 Jan 1791; adv. SJC 17–20 Dec 1791.

Further edn: Dublin, 1791 (Printed by John Exshaw, 2 vols., 12mo), ESTC t140065. German trans. Hanover, 1792–93 (*Hermione oder die Rache des Schicksalds*) (EAG); French trans. n.p., 1803 (*Hermione, ou journal de deux orphelines*) (HWS).

CR: 'Though we trace our author too often in the tracts of miss Burney's Evelina [1778: 10], especially in the vulgar familiarity of Mrs Hindon, and in the embarrassments of Hermione, as well as in the denouement of her adventures, we must allow her much merit in raising the expectations and enhancing the interest. The characters are also well discriminated, and the catastrophe well explained.'

1791: 44   LESUIRE, [Robert-Martin].
THE FRENCH ADVENTURER; OR, MEMOIRS OF GREGOIRE MER-
VEIL, MARQUIS D'ERBEUIL. TRANSLATED FROM THE FRENCH OF
M. LE SUIRE. IN THREE VOLUMES.

> London: Printed for John Bew, No. 28, Paternoster Row, 1791.
> I 315p; II 258p; III 312p. 12mo. 9s (CR), 9s sewed (SJC, LC).
> CR n.s. 2: 234 (June 1791); AF II: 2488.
> BL N.1706-1708; EM 1924: 7; ESTC t072362 (EA COR).

Notes. Trans. of *L'aventurier françois, ou mémoires de Grégoire Merveil* (London and Paris, 1782, with continuations 1783, 1785–86 and 1788).

Adv., 'In the Press, and speedily will be published', SJC 24–26 Aug 1790; adv., 'will be published on Tuesday next', LC 69: 348 (9–12 Apr 1791).

CR: 'These are indeed adventurers and very extraordinary ones, they set probability and sometimes decorum at defiance. In short these volumes would be uniques, if we had not the extraordinary adventures of Munchausen; the marquis has, however, more ingenuity than the baron, and his adventures are not always contradictory to reason and common sense. The reader must have a spirit of perseverance to peruse the whole, notwithstanding the hairbreadth scapes, and the very singular changes of fortune.'

1791: 45   [LITTLEJOHN, P.].
THE CIPHER; OR, THE WORLD AS IT GOES.

> London: Printed for William Lane, at the Minerva Press, Leadenhall-Street, 1791.
> I 330p; II 322p; III 332p. 12mo. 9s (CR), 9s sewed (SJC).
> CR n.s. 2: 356 (July 1791); AF II: 986.
> CaAEU PR 4890.L5.C57 1791; ESTC n005138 (NA MnU).

Notes. In vol. 1 p. [71] misnumbered 41, p. [146] misnumbered 156, p. [290] misnumbered 291. Epistolary.

Adv. SDA 21 Jan 1791; adv. SJC 21–23 June 1791.

CR: 'The style of this work and its external appearance led us to think that it was not a new production; and even at this moment we are not satisfied that it is not one of those novels with which the press swarmed, after Dr Smollett had introduced a new aera of novel-writing. . . . The work is evidently an imitation of Smollett's manner, though not a happy one.'

1791: 46   [McDONALD, Andrew].
LAURA; A NOVEL. BY THE AUTHOR OF THE INDEPENDENT. IN
TWO VOLUMES.

> London: Printed for C. Elliot and T. Kay, No. 332, Strand and Charles Elliot,
> Edinburgh, n.d. [1791? SJC/LC].
> I 256p; II 290p. 12mo. 6s sewed (SJC).
> BL N.1705; EM 1924: 6; ESTC t070911 (NA CLU-S/C).

Notes. Adv., 'By the late A. McDonald, Esq. Authour of The Independent [1784: 19],
and of the Tragedy of Vimonda', published 'By Thomas Kay, No. 332, opposite
Burlington-House, Strand'; SJC 22–25 Jan 1791; adv. LC 69: 86 (22–25 Jan 1791). ESTC
has ?1790.

1791: 47   [MACKENZIE, Anna Maria].
DANISH MASSACRE, AN HISTORIC FACT. BY THE AUTHOR OF
MONMOUTH, A TALE. IN TWO VOLUMES.

> London: Printed for William Lane, at the Minerva Press, Leadenhall-Street, 1791.
> I 243p; II 295p. 12mo. 6s (CR), 6s sewed (SJC).
> CR n.s. 3: 117–18 (Sept 1791); AF II: 2655.
> MH-H *EC75.M1993.791d; EM 1268: 14; ESTC n000342.

Notes. Introduction 1, 1–27; text of novel starts on p. 29. 1 p. adv. end vols. 1 and 2.
Monmouth 1790: 55.
Adv. SJC 16–19 July 1791.
Further edn: Dublin, 1791 (Printed for Messrs. P. Byrne, P. Wogan, A. Grueber, J. Moore,
J. Jones [and 4 others in Dublin], 2 vols., 12mo), ESTC n028421.

   CR: 'This work is neither new nor old: it has not the interest of the one, nor the zest of the
other: it is generally insipid, and often disgusting from its improbability. The Danes too are
the heroes: though Etheldred was contemptible, Guiderius should not have been the only
respectable Englishman.'

1791: 48   [?MAN, Henry].
FLIGHTS OF INFLATUS; OR, THE SALLIES, STORIES, AND ADVEN-
TURES OF A WILD-GOOSE PHILOSOPHER. BY THE AUTHOR OF
THE TRIFLER. IN TWO VOLUMES.

> London: Printed for C. Stalker; and sold by Holl, & Smart, Worcester; Sharp, Warwick;
> Walford, Stratford; Luckman, Coventry; Sandford, Shrewsbury. And Swinney,
> Birmingham, 1791.
> I xii, 259p; II vii, 221p. 12mo. 5s sewed (CR, MR, adv.), 6s bound (SJC).
> CR n.s. 6: 561 (App [Dec 1792/Jan 1793]); MR n.s. 8: 110 (May 1792); AF II: 1462.
> BL 12604.aaa.3; EM 65: 4; ESTC t108368 (NA CLU-S/C, MH-H).

Notes. ESTC: Sometimes attributed to Henry Man.
Preface 1, v–vii; table of contents 1, ix–xii and 2, v–vii.
The Trifler 1775: 29.
Adv. SJC 13–15 Dec 1791.
Adv. end vol. 2 of *Arville Castle* (1795: 1).
Further edn: Birmingham, 1791, ESTC n006761.

CR: 'The stories and adventures of this novelist abound with improbabilities; and his sallies are conspicuous for indelicacy, as well as affectation.'

MR [Christopher Lake Moody]: 'Indelicacy, improbability, and affectation of wit, should meet, from impartial and honest Reviewers, an unqualified condemnation. Let then Mr Inflatus know, that we think his *Flights* do him no credit, and had better never have taken their flight from the press.'

1791: 49   [MAN, Henry].
THE HISTORY OF SIR GEOFFRY RESTLESS, AND HIS BROTHER CHARLES. BY THE AUTHOR OF THE TRIFLER. IN TWO VOLUMES.

> Birmingham: Printed by E. Piercy, in Bull Street, for W. Lowndes, Fleet Street, London, 1791.
> I xii, 184p; II vi, 195p. 12mo. 9s (CR), 5s sewed or 6s bound (LC, SJC).
> CR n.s. 4: 114 (Jan 1792); AF II: 2696.
> MH-H *EC75.N5374.791h; EM 3517: 7; ESTC t167697 (BI BMp).

Notes. Preface 1, iii–vii concerns *The Trifler.* Tables of contents 1, ix–xii and 2, iii–vi.
The Trifler 1775: 29.
Adv. LC 69: 504 (24–26 May 1791). Adv. SJC 31 May–2 June, 1791.

CR: 'We were pleased with the Trifler; but no prepossession in favour of an author can render personal satire agreeable. In every other view also the History of Sir Geoffry Restless is contemptible.'

1791: 50   [MATHEWS, Eliza Kirkham].
MEMOIRS OF A SCOTS HEIRESS. ADDRESSED TO THE RIGHT HONOURABLE LADY CATHARINE ******. BY THE AUTHOR OF CONSTANCE.

> London: Printed for T. Hookham, No. 147, New, and No. 15, Old Bond Street; and sold by J. Carpenter, No. 1, Charles Street, Grosvenor Square, 1791.
> I 262p; II 287p; III 268p. 12mo. 9s (MR), 9s sewed (SDA, SJC).
> CR n.s. 3: 356 (Nov 1791); MR n.s. 8: 340–1 (July 1792); AF II: 2757.
> C 7720.d.771-; EM 187: 2; ESTC t070917 (BI BL, KIK [vol. 3 only]; NA CLU-S/C, IU &c.).

Notes. 2 pp. advs. for Hookham end vol. 1.
Constance 1785: 38.
Adv., 'In a few Days will be published', SDA 14 May 1791; adv. SJC 16–19 July 1791.
Further edn: Dublin, 1791 (Printed by William Porter, for R. Cross, P. Wogan, P. Byrne, W. Sleater [and 9 others in Dublin], 2 vols., 12mo), ESTC n011104. Extracts from *Memoirs of a Scots Heiress* published in *Monthly Extracts,* 1791, RM 336, 1358.

CR: 'These Memoirs are in many respects singular: the author, in almost every step, wanders from the beaten path, occasionally elevates and surprises, is frequently interesting, and sometimes highly pathetic. The incidents are, nevertheless, often improbable, and the unexpected changes of fortune are, in one or two instances, disagreeably abrupt.'

MR [John Noorthouck]: 'This will be an agreeable novel to the generality of readers; the story being full of business, and conducted through many strange vicissitudes. In this author's former production [*Constance,* 1785: 38], we remarked her knowledge of human nature in pourtraying characters, but did not conceive them sufficiently exerted in the narrative; in the present, we have not only characters well described, but those characters are active throughout. The situations and conduct of the parties are diversified. . . .'

1791: 51   MILES, E.
VIOLET HILL: OR MEMOIRS OF CORDELIA, A FAIR FOUNDLING. BY E. MILES.

>London: Printed for Ogilvy and Speare, J. Wallis, and J. Binns, Leeds, 1791.
>250p. 12mo. Half a crown sewed (SJC).
>BL RB.23.a.10329; ESTC t226255.

Notes. Text of novel starts on p. 5. Running-title: 'Memoirs of Cordelia'.
Adv. SJC 29 Nov–1 Dec 1791.

1791: 52   MORRIS, Mrs {R. P.}.
ILLICIT LOVE: A NOVEL. BY MRS. MORRIS, AUTHOR OF THE RIVAL BROTHERS, A NOVEL; POEMS, &C. IN TWO VOLUMES.

>London: Printed for the Author; And sold by H. D. Symonds, Nº 20, Paternoster-Row; and W. Beilby, No 6, Pall Mall, 1791.
>I xii, 136p; II 154p. 8vo [EngR has 12mo]. 5s (EngR), 6s (SJC).
>EngR 19: 231 (Mar 1792).
>PU Singer-Mend.PR5059.M484.I5.1791; ESTC n016753 (NA TNJ).

Notes. Dedication to the Hon. Mrs Massey signed 'R. P. Morris'. PU copy in original blue covers and boards.
The Rival Brothers 1784: 20.
Adv. SJC 9–11 June 1791.
Further edn: London, 1793 (WC), xESTC.
   EngR: 'Trash, vile trash!—and sorry are we to say that it is not harmless. The plan is immoral and pernicious—and the chief character is an *unprincipled scoundrel.* We must lament that such a production, which can only serve to corrupt and vitiate the female mind, should proceed from the pen of a *woman.*'

1791: 53   [MUSÄUS, Johann Karl August]; [BEDDOES, Thomas (*trans.*)].
POPULAR TALES OF THE GERMANS. TRANSLATED FROM THE GERMAN. IN TWO VOLUMES.

>London: Printed for J. Murray, No 32, Fleet-Street, 1791.
>I xi, 264p; II 284p. 12mo. 6s sewed (MR), 6s boards (CR, SJC).
>CR n.s. 3: 56–7 (Sept 1791); MR n.s. 5: 467 (Aug 1791); AF II: 261.
>O Douce T 123-4; EMf; ESTC t178187 (BI C, BL, E &c.; NA CtY-BR, CSmH, IU, MH-H, NjP &c.).

Notes. Trans. of *Volksmärchen der Deutschen* (Gotha, 1787–88).
This trans. traditionally ascribed to William Beckford; Murray archives show that John Murray paid Beddoes 30 gns. for the translation with proviso for 10 gns. more if it went to a 2nd edn. (Zachs 842).
Vol. 1: A Dialogue, Consisting Chiefly of Soliloquies [running title: Introduction] (i–xi); Richilda; or, the Progress from Vanity to Vice; The Chronicles of the Three Sisters; The

Stealing of the Veil; or, The Tale a la Mongolfier. Vol. 2: Elfin Freaks; or, the Seven Legends of Number-Nip; The Nymph of the Fountain.

Extracts from *Popular Tales of the Germans* published in 4 magazines, 1791, RM 163, 522, 1063.

Adv. SJC 8–10 Feb 1791: 'These Tales are partly of the serious, and partly of the comick cast. They were eagerly read in Germany, and speedily passed through several editions. The applause of his country conferred upon the authour the Title of Musæus, from the popular Greek Poet who versified the favourite story of the Loves of Hero and Leander. The substance of these Tales is taken from the unaltered traditions of the Germans, concerning their Fairies and Heroes, &c. a kind of Mythology, which has been transmitted from Generation to Generation, and which has been found in its present dress, capable of interesting readers of every denomination from whom it was borrowed.'

Adv., 'printed upon a fine Medium Paper', with 23-line quotation from EngR, SJC 19–21 July 1792.

Further edn: Dublin, 1791 (Printed by William Porter, for P. Wogan, P. Byrne, W. Porter, W. McKenzie, J. Moore [and 6 others in Dublin], 1 vol., 12mo), ESTC t202432.

CR: 'There is great reason to suppose . . . that these Tales are the result of the traditionary legends of the nursery, and very slightly connected with Germany, except that the scene of these legendary narratives is laid in that country' (p. 56).

MR [William Enfield]: 'The contempt and *calumny* with which the courts of criticism are treated in the Introduction to these Tales, must not deter us from declaring the sentence which we hold ourselves bound, in virtue of our office, to pass on them. The Tales, whether domestic or foreign, are, in our judgment, extravagant in the extreme, without a sufficient portion of humour, satire, or sentiment, to repay the reader for the pain of putting his imagination on the rack. Powers of invention, directed to no good end, might as well be suffered to sleep; and at monsters of fiction, which only excite a momentary wonder, we gaze for a day, and forget them.'

1791: 54   [O'CONNOR, E.].
EMILY BENSON. A NOVEL. BY THE AUTHOR OF ALMERIA BELMORE.

> Dublin: Printed by P. Byrne, No. 108, Grafton-street, 1791.
> xi, 156p. 12mo.
> IU x823.Oc5e; ESTC t212437 (BI Dt).

Notes. Prefatory address 'To the Reader' concerns the 'bad tendency of Novels in general' and the need to 'raise those works of fancy, from the abject state into which they are sunk'. P. [134] misnumbered 143. Epistolary.
Almeria Belmore 1789: 59.

1791: 55   PARSONS, [Eliza].
ERRORS OF EDUCATION. IN THREE VOLUMES. BY MRS. PARSONS. DEDICATED (BY PERMISSION) TO THE RIGHT HON. THE COUNTESS OF HILLSBOROUGH.

> London: Printed for William Lane, at the Minerva Press, Leadenhall-Street, 1791.
> I vii, 243p; II 226p; III 279p. 12mo. 9s (CR), 9s sewed (SJC).
> CR n.s. 3: 234 (Oct 1791); AF II: 3233.
> BL 12651.i.4; EM 7098: 6; ESTC n009284 (NA CtY, CCC, DLC &c.).

Notes. Dedication to the Countess of Hillsborough.

Adv., 'In a few Days will be published', SDA 31 May 1791; adv. SJC 9–11 June 1791.

Further edn: Dublin, 1792 (Printed for T. Jackson, 2 vols., 12mo), EM 226: 3, ESTC t068574.

CR: 'This story is very defective in probability; but we cannot blame what is so strictly and exemplarily moral.'

1791: 56   [PINCHARD, Elizabeth].
THE BLIND CHILD, OR ANECDOTES OF THE WYNDHAM FAMILY.
WRITTEN FOR THE USE OF YOUNG PEOPLE. BY A LADY.

> London: Printed for E. Newbery, the Corner of St Paul's Church-Yard, 1791.
> I vii, 178p. 12mo. 2s (CR), 2s sewed (MR).
> CR n.s. 4: 116 (1792); MR n.s. 8: 340 (1792); AF II: 3368.
> BL Ch.790/32; EM 2731: 9; ESTC t066824 (BI AWn, BMu, C; NA CaOTP, CLU-S/C, NNPM).

Notes. Frontispiece. Preface iii–vii. Pagination continuous Roman-Arabic; text of novel starts on p. 9. 2 pp. advs. end vol.

Further edns: London, 1793, EM 7415: 1; ESTC t068892; London, 1795, EM 7132: 4, ESTC t084633; Philadelphia, 1793, ESTC w025010; Boston, 1795, ESTC w038400; Worcester, MA, 1796, ESTC w025007; 2 further entries in ESTC; WC has 7 entries between 1800 and 1850; NSTC lists edns. in 1802, 1809, 1814 and 1825. German trans. Leipzig, 1793 (*Das blinde Kind*) (Price).

CR: 'This is a pleasing and instructive little story.'

MR [John Noorthouck]: 'Giving all due credit to the upright intentions of this and other writers in the same benevolent line, to instil moral sentiments by apt incidents and examples, we apprehend that they may be, in some measure, undermining their own intentions, and undesignedly injuring the cause of morality, by giving their pupils a taste for novel-reading. . . . This, however, is a pretty book. . . .'

1791: 57   [?PURBECK, Elizabeth and Jane].
WILLIAM THORNBOROUGH, THE BENEVOLENT QUIXOTE. IN FOUR
VOLUMES.

> London: Printed for G. G. J. and J. Robinson, Paternoster-Row, 1791.
> I 234p; II 256p; III 190p; IV 218p. 12mo. 12s (CR), 12s boards (SJC).
> CR n.s. 1: 470–1 (Apr 1791).
> MH-H *EC75.P9703.791x; EM 3054: 14; ESTC n025266 (BI MRu, O; NA ICN, ICU).

Notes. Robinson paid 21 gns. on 23 Dec 1790 to Frances Eleanor Dalrymple for *The Benevolent Quixote* (RA).

Post-dated; adv. as published SJC 14–16 Dec 1790.

German trans. Leipzig, 1793–94 (*William Thornborough, der wohltätige Don Quixote*) (RS).

CR: 'We have found Quixotism in every passion and in every propensity of the human mind, and from many of the delineations on this plan we have drawn much entertainment. Since the period, however, of the Spiritual Quixote [1773: 34], the fairest game for the arrow of the satyrist, we have despaired of reaping any great pleasure from a similar attempt. . . . He has acquitted himself, however, with great success. The hero is amiable and respectable, and his foible is conducted so judiciously, that though it sometimes places him in a ridiculous light, it never renders him mean or despicable. This is the true point in which the Quixote should be placed, and the happy mean which some writers have not perceived, or disregarded' (p. 470).

1791: 58 [RADCLIFFE, Ann].
THE ROMANCE OF THE FOREST: INTERSPERSED WITH SOME PIECES OF POETRY. BY THE AUTHORESS OF "A SICILIAN ROMANCE," &C. IN THREE VOLUMES.

London: Printed for T. Hookham and J. Carpenter, New and Old Bond Street, 1791.
I 274p; II 286p; III 347p. 12mo. 9s sewed (CR, MR).
CR n.s. 4: 458–60 (Apr 1792); MR n.s. 8: 82–7 (May 1792); AF II: 3674.
C S727.d.79.1-3; EMf; ESTC t062067 (BI BL, O; NA CtY-BR, MH-H, NjP, PU, ViU &c.; EA ZWTU, ZWU).

Notes. Carpenter's initial is missing on the t.p. to vol. 1. 1 p. advs. end vol. 3.
A Sicilian Romance 1790: 61.
Adv. SDA 17 Dec 1791.
Further edns: London, 1792, EM 4059: 12, ESTC n013222; Dublin, 1792 (Printed for Messrs. P. Wogan, P. Byrne, A. Grueber, W. M'Kenzie, W. Sleater [and 10 others in Dublin], 2 vols., 12mo), ESTC n013221; London, 1792, ESTC t169437; Dublin, 1793, ESTC n013231; London, 1794, EM 236: 1, ESTC t059915; 5 further entries in ESTC; WC has 14 entries between 1800 and 1850; Summers has 12 edns. between 1800 and 1850; NSTC lists edns. in 1801, 1810, 1816, 1820, 1824, 1825, 1827, 1832, 1834, [1835], [1846] and 1848. Extracts from *Romance of the Forest*, 'Character of Pierre de la Motte' and 'Memoirs of the Faily of La Luc', published in *Monthly Extracts*, 1792, RM 205, 889. German trans. Leipzig, 1793 (*Adeline oder das Abentheuer im Walde*) (EAG); French trans. Paris, 1794 (*La Forêt ou l'abbaye de Saint-Clair*) (BGR); Italian trans. Pisa, 1813 (*La Foresta*) (BN). Facs: GN II (1827 edn.).

CR: 'The novel . . . engages the attention strongly, and interests the feelings very powerfully: the general style of the whole, as well as the reflections, deserve also commendation. The greater part of the work resembles, in *manner*, the old English Baron, formed on the model of the Castle of Otranto. . . . every thing is consistent, and within the verge of rational belief: the attention is uninterruptedly fixed, till the veil is designedly withdrawn. One great mark of the author's talents is, that the events are concealed with the utmost art, and even suspicion sometimes designedly misled, while, in the conclusion, every extraordinary appearance seems naturally to arise from causes not very uncommon. The characters are varied with skill, and often dexterously contrasted' (pp. 458–9).
[Clara Reeve, *The Old English Baron*, see *The Champion of Virtue* 1777: 16; Horace Walpole, *The Castle of Otranto* 1764, JR 868, AF I: 2898.]
MR [William Enfield]: 'The days of chivalry and romance being (ALAS! as Mr Burke says,) for ever past, we must hear no more of enchanted forests and castles, giants, dragons, walls of fire, and other "monstrous and prodigious things;"—yet still forests and castles remain, and it is still within the province of fiction, without overstepping the limits of nature, to make use of them for the purpose of creating surprise. By the aid of an inventive genius it may still be done, even in this philosophical age, to fill the fancy with marvellous images, and to "quell the soul with grateful terrors."
In this way, the authoress of the Romance of the Forest is no mean performer. . . . she has very skilfully contrived to hold the reader's curiosity continually in suspense, and at the same

time to keep his feelings in a state of perpetual agitation. . . . we have seldom met with a fiction which has more forcibly fixed the attention, or more agreeably interested the feelings, throughout the whole narrative' (pp. 82–3).

1791: 59   REEVE, Clara.
THE SCHOOL FOR WIDOWS. A NOVEL. IN THREE VOLUMES. BY
CLARA REEVE, AUTHOR OF THE OLD ENGLISH BARON, &C.
> London: Printed for T. Hookham, New Bond Street; Harrison and Co. Paternoster
> Row; and W. Miller, Old Bond Street, 1791.
> I x, 284p; II 320p; III 260p. 12mo. 9s (CR), 9s sewed (MR, adv., SDA).
> CR n.s. 2: 476–7 (Aug 1791); MR n.s. 5: 466–7 (Aug 1791); AF II: 3715.
> BL 12613.bbb.31; EM 577: 1; ESTC t068573 (BI IPSr, O; NA CLU-S/C, NjP, PU, ViU
> &c.).

Notes. Pagination continuous Roman-Arabic; text of novel starts on p. 11 of vol. 1. In vols. 2 and 3 text of novel starts on p. 5. Epistolary.
For *The Old English Baron* see *The Champion of Virtue* 1777: 16.
Adv., 'In a few Days will be published', SDA 14 May 1791; adv. as published SDA 18 June 1791.
Adv. end vol. 4 of *Edelfrida* (1792: 7).
Further edn: Dublin, 1791 (Printed by William Porter, for P. Wogan, P. Byrne, H. Colbert, J. Moore, J. Halpen [and 5 others in Dublin], 2 vols., 12mo), ESTC t175102. French trans. n.p., n.d. (*L'École des Veuves*) (HWS).
CR: 'These pleasing and interesting volumes contain two distinct stories; but not improperly blended or carelessly confused. . . . In the title we find a little fault, for this work is in reality the School for *Wives*.'
MR [John Noorthouck]: 'Richardson has illustrated the old fable of Cadmus, by sowing the seed of a most prolific generation, inevitably destructive to each other by their short lived competition . . .' (p. 466).

1791: 60   [ROWSON, Susanna].
CHARLOTTE. A TALE OF TRUTH. IN TWO VOLUMES.
> London: Printed for William Lane, at the Minerva, Leadenhall-Street, 1791.
> I viii, 169p; II 169p. 8vo [CR and SDA have 12mo]. 5s (CR), 5s sewed (SDA).
> CR n.s. 1: 468–9 (Apr 1791); AF II: 3880.
> ViU PS 2736.R3C5 1791; ESTC t224839 (BI BL [vol. 2 only]).

Notes. Vol. 1, i–iii address 'To Ladies and Gentlemen, Patrons of Entertaining Literature' signed 'Minerva Printing Office, Leadenhall-street'; preface v–viii explains that the novel is intended for 'the perusal of the young and thoughtless of the fair sex'. 3 pp. advs. end both vols. P. 128 of vol. 2 misnumbered 828.
Adv. SDA 21 Jan 1791.
Further edns: Philadelphia, 1794, EM 7582: 3, ESTC t139046; Philadelphia, 1794, ESTC w007579; Philadelphia, 1794, ESTC w004915; Philadelphia, 1797, ESTC w011855; WC has 130 pre-1851 records for this work.
CR: 'It may be a Tale of Truth, for it is not unnatural, and it is a tale of real distress. . . . The situations are artless and affecting; the descriptions natural and pathetic.'

1791: 61   ROWSON, [Susanna].
MENTORIA; OR THE YOUNG LADY'S FRIEND: IN TWO VOLUMES.
BY MRS. ROWSON, AUTHOR OF VICTORIA, &C. &C.

> London: Printed for William Lane, at the Minerva, Leadenhall-Street, n.d. [1791].
> I vii, 168p; II 198p. 12mo. 5s sewed (SDA).
> InU-Li PS 2736.R3M54 1791; ESTC n067680 (NA NNS, NN).

Notes. Vol. 1 preface [i]–vii, 4-pp. list of subscribers (unn.). Vol. 1 p. 95 misnumbered 59; vol. 2 p. 25 unn., p. 62 misnumbered 2, p. 86 misnumbered 89, p. 106 misnumbered 06, p. 146 misnumbered 247, pp. 169–192 misnumbered 193–216 and followed by 193–198.
Victoria 1786: 39.
Adv. SDA 15 July 1791.
Further edns: Dublin, 1791 (Printed by Thomas Morton Bates, for Messrs. P. Wogan, A. Grueber, J. Halpen, J. Moore, R. M'Allister [and 3 others in Dublin], 1 vol., 12mo), ESTC n034695; Philadelphia, 1794, ESTC w026005.

1791: 62   RUTLIDGE, Chevalier [James].
MEMOIRS OF JULIA DE M*****, A RECLAIMED COURTEZAN. FROM
THE FRENCH OF LE CHEVALIER RUTLEDGE, AUTHOR OF LA QUIN-
ZAINE ANGLAISE. IN TWO VOLUMES.

> London: Printed for Bentley and Co No. 22. Fetter-Lane; and C. Lowndes, No. 66, Drury-Lane, 1741 [1791].
> I vi, 165p; II v, 144p. 12mo. 5s sewed (MR, SJC).
> MR n.s. 5: 339 (July 1791); AF II: 3903.
> O Vet.A5e.5089; EM 7229: 3; ESTC t182182.

Notes. Trans. of *Mémoires de Julie de M* (1790) (Grieder).
BN gives author's name as RUTLIDGE, James, *dit* Jean-Jacques.
Table of contents 1, iii–vi and 2, iii–v.
MR gives date as 1741, for 1791.
Adv., 'A Pleasing Novel . . . elegantly printed', SJC 5–8 Mar 1791 and SDA 5 Mar 1791, with favourable comment from the *Journal Encyclopédique.*
   MR [John Noorthouck]: 'This work appears to be, according to its profession, a translation; it is full of business and intrigue; and like many other novels of French manufacture, represents depravity of manners in that country, as being reduced to system.'

1791: 63   [SADLER, Robert].
WANLEY PENSON; OR, THE MELANCHOLY MAN: A MISCELLA-
NEOUS HISTORY. IN THREE VOLUMES.

> London: Printed for C. and G. Kearsley, No. 46, Fleet-Street, 1791.
> I xxviii, 354p; II 386p; III ii, 280p. 8vo. 9s (CR), 13s 6d boards (MR, SJC).
> CR n.s. 4: 114–15 (Jan 1792); MR n.s. 7: 265–70 (Mar 1792); AF II: 3921.
> BL N.2369; EM 2071: 3; ESTC t074443 (BI C; NA CLU-S/C, CSmH, MH-H &c.).

Notes. 'Preface by the Curate' 1, iii–xxviii. Vol. 3 pagination continuous Roman-Arabic; text of novel resumes on p. 3.
Adv. SJC 4–6 Aug 1791; adv., with extensive quotation from AR, SDA 25 Nov 1791; new edn. adv., with quotations from CR and MR, SDA 2 May 1791.

Further edn: London, 1792, EM 229: 1, ESTC t086286 [a reissue of edn. of 1791 with cancel title-pages]. German trans. Berlin and Leipzig, 1795–96 (*Der Melancholische. Eine Geschichte*) (EAG).

2nd edn. adv. with substantial quotations from CR and MR on 1st edn. and mention of the AR having 'spoken very handsomely' of it, SJC 1–3 May 1792.

CR: '. . . it is not void of merit: but its peculiar nature; the various digressions; some of which at least are not very entertaining; a story frequently interrupted, without any artificial contexture of adventures, will not please the million. . . . Perhaps the great defect of this work is a want of originality: the images are too often borrowed, and the feelings are more weakly affected, because the impression has lost the force and the zest of novelty.'

MR [William Enfield]: 'This is one of the few novels which prove that it is possible to write an amusing as well as instructive fictitious story, with other materials than a series of love adventures. The hero of this work, though not without his tender attachments, chiefly interests the reader by the general benevolence and humanity of his character, and by the sufferings which were brought on him in consequence of his excessive sensibility. . . . The plan is executed with a degree of ability, which entitles the work to commendation' (p. 265).

1791: 64   SAINT PIERRE, [Jacques-Henri-Bernardin] de; [KENDALL, Edward Augustus (*trans.*)].
THE INDIAN COTTAGE. TRANSLATED FROM THE FRENCH OF MONSIEUR DE ST. PIERRE, AUTHOR OF ETUDES DE LA NATURE, PAUL ET VIRGINIE, &C. &C.

London: Printed for John Bew, No. 28, Paternoster-Row, 1791.
132p. 8vo. 2s sewed (SJC).
BL 635.c.31 (1); EM 2736: 2; ESTC t114946 (BI Gu; NA MH-H, IU).

Notes. Trans. of *La chaumière indienne* (Paris, 1791).
'Paul et Virginie', first published in vol. 4 of *Études de la Nature* (Paris, 1788), trans. as *Paul and Virginie* (1788: 71).
Adv. SJC 23–26 July 1791.
This edn. not reviewed; EngR 18: 307 (Oct 1791) reviews another 1791 edn. pub. by Lane (adv. SDA 14 Apr 1791).
Further edns: Dublin, 1791 (Printed for J. Parker, J. Jones, W. Jones, R. White, J. Rice, R. McAllister, 144p, 12mo), ESTC t188550; Philadelphia, 1794, ESTC w027590; London, 1797, ESTC t138761; Workington, 1797, EM 6164: 2, ESTC t131214; London, 1799, ESTC n031286; ESTC has one further entry; NSTC lists edn. in 1824. Extracts in two trans. published in *Harvest Home*, 1807, and *Bee*, 1795, RM 689, 690.

EngR: 'The Paria's story is novel, interesting, and pathetically told.'

1791: 65   [SAYER, Edward].
LINDOR AND ADELAÏDE, A MORAL TALE. IN WHICH ARE EXHIBITED THE EFFECTS OF THE LATE FRENCH REVOLUTION ON THE PEASANTRY OF FRANCE. BY THE AUTHOR OF "OBSERVATIONS ON DOCTOR PRICE'S REVOLUTION SERMON."

London: Printed for J. Stockdale, opposite Burlington House, Piccadilly, 1791.
vii, 358p. 12mo. 3s (CR), 3s 6d boards (MR, SJC).

CR n.s. 1: 349 (July 1791); MR n.s. 5: 280–4 (July 1791); AF II: 3954.
C S727.d.79.89; EM 1006: 15; ESTC n002912 (NA MH-H).

Notes. Not by Henry Goodricke, identified as author by BGR.
Prefatory advertisement (v–vii) concerns Burke. 2 pp. advs. end vol.
Post-dated; adv. as published SJC 25–27 Nov 1790.
French trans. Paris, 1792 (*Lindor et Adélaïde*) (BGR).

CR: '... he draws a gloomy picture of the inconveniences which have resulted from the late revolution: when the seigneur resembled the marquis d'Antin, his loss must be a misfortune; and for the credit of human nature we must hope that many did resemble him. In other respects, this tale is interesting and pleasing, interspersed with many judicious observations on that wild licentiousness which assumes the garb of liberty, and the irregular exertions of the spirit of innovation, under the guise of a reform.'

MR [Thomas Pearne]: 'This tale abounds more in argument, (such as it is,) than in incident. The characters, which are few, are of two descriptions, of very opposite complexion and cast of features. The enemies to the Revolution are made, in every way, amiable. Their persons are handsome and attracting, their manners are artless and engaging, and their morals are pure. The favourers of the Revolution, on the contrary, are distorted in body, and corrupted in mind' (p. 280). 'Deficient ... as this *argumentative* tale is, in sound reasoning, it is not destitute of good writing, nor of some interesting situations' (p. 284).

1791: 66   SIDDONS, Henry.
LEON A SPARTAN STORY: IN TWO VOLUMES. BY HENRY SIDDONS, AUTHOR OF WILLIAM WALLACE.

London: Printed at the Minerva, for William Lane, Leadenhall-Street, 1791.
I viii, 180p; II 178p. 8vo [CR and SJC have 12mo]. 5s (CR), 6s (SJC).
CR n.s. 4: 236 (Feb 1792); AF II: 4094.
REu Reserve 823.69 SID; ESTC t171492.

Notes. Vol. 1 unsigned prefatory advertisement [iii] and preface [iv]–viii. 2 pp. advs. end vol. 2.
William Wallace 1791: 67.
Adv. 'In the Press, and speedily will be published', SDA 9 May 1791; still 'In the Press', SDA 26 Oct 1791; adv. SJC 17–20 Dec 1791.
Further edn: Dublin, 1792 (Printed by Hugh Fitzpatrick, for Messrs. P. Byrne, A. Grueber, W. McKenzie, J. Moore, J. Halpen [and 4 others in Dublin], 2 vols., 12mo), ESTC t212459.

CR: 'A Spartan story! There is not the slightest resemblance of Spartan manners. Even the names are Saxon; and the manners the puling, maukish, resemblances of the veriest trash of modern novels.—Such crude absurdities are an insult on the public. ...'

1791: 67   SIDDONS, Henry.
WILLIAM WALLACE: OR, THE HIGHLAND HERO. A TALE, FOUNDED ON HISTORICAL FACTS. BY HENRY SIDDONS, AUTHOR OF MODERN BREAKFAST. IN TWO VOLUMES.

London: Printed for G. and T. Wilkie, Pater-noster-Row, 1791.
I x, 159p; II 176p. 8vo [CR has 12mo]. 6s (CR), 5s sewed (LC, SJC).
CR n.s. 3: 235 (Oct 1791); AF II: 4097.

C 7720.d.1185; CME 3-628-45185-X; EM 239: 10; ESTC t068571 (BI BL; NA ViU; EA COR).

Notes. Brief prefatory advertisement informs the reader that the deviations from historical fact are deliberate; this is said to 'avoid the disgust of those who are versed in the History of the Hero'. Dedication to Thomas Erskine. Preface apologises for the 'sorry meal' his volumes will make to 'all novel-reading young ladies'. 750 copies printed May 1791 (Strahan 15 f. 111).

Adv. LC 69: 515 (28–31 May 1791). Adv. SJC 2–4 June, 1791.

German trans. Leipzig, 1796 (*Wilhelm Wallace, oder der Held aus dem Hochlande*) (RS).

CR: 'Were even Mrs. Siddons to plead with all her pathos and persuasive powers, she could not alter the decrees of criticism, which condemn this novel as trifling, improbable, and absurd. . . . In short, it is the work of a school-boy, who ought to have been better employed, and to be severely reprehended for such idle engagements.'

1791: 68   SMITH, Charlotte.
CELESTINA. A NOVEL. IN FOUR VOLUMES. BY CHARLOTTE SMITH.

London: Printed for T. Cadell, in the Strand, 1791.
I 273p; II 313p; III 303p; IV 353p. 8vo [SJC has 12mo]. 12s boards (MR), 12s sewed (SJC, LC).
CR n.s. 3: 318–23 (Nov 1791); MR n.s. 6: 286–91 (Nov 1791); AF II: 4131.
BL N.2060,1; EM 2069: 2; ESTC t073501 (BI COCu; NA CSmH, CtY, ICN, IU, MH-H, NjP, PU, ViU &c.; EA PRTup, SU).

Notes. Adv., 'In the Press, and speedily will be published', SJC 31 May–2 June 1791. Adv. as published LC 70: 56 (14–16 July 1791).

Further edns: London, 1791, ESTC n014708; Dublin, 1791 (Printed for R. Cross, P. Wogan, P. Byrne, J. Moore, J. Halpen [and 11 others in Dublin], 3 vols., 12mo), EM 6874: 8; ESTC n014707. Extracts from *Celestina,* with various titles, published in 3 magazines, 1791–92, RM 706. German trans. Leipzig, 1792 (*Celestine*) (RS); French trans. Paris, 1795 (*Célestine, ou la Victime des préjugés*) (BN).

CR: 'In the modern school of novel-writers, Mrs. Smith holds a very distinguished rank; and, if not the first, she is so near as scarcely to be styled an inferior.' This novel is 'inferior in some respects to Emmeline, and less varied in characters than Ethelinde, yet scarcely less interesting or entertaining' (p. 318). [*Emmeline* 1788: 72; *Ethelinde* 1789: 68].

MR [William Enfield] classes the novel with 'such as possess superior merit' and thus deems it worthy of being reviewed at much greater length than is usually thought 'right to devote to productions of this class' (p. 287).

1791: 69   [STREET, Miss].
THE LAKE OF WINDERMERE, A NOVEL. BY THE EDITOR OF THE LETTERS OF MARIA.

London: Printed for W. Lane, at the Minerva, Leadenhall-Street, 1791.
I 236p; II [255]p. 8vo [CR has 12mo]. 6s (CR), 6s sewed (SJC).
CR n.s. 3: 117 (Sept 1791); AF II: 4279.
CaAEU PR3991.A7.L65 1791; ESTC n062376.

Notes. In vol. 2 p. 253 misnumbered 197, p. 254 misnumbered 252 and p. 255 misnumbered 253.

Letters of Maria 1790: 68.
'Adv., 'In the Press', SDA 18 Mar 1791; adv. SJC 18–21 June 1791.

CR: 'The story is a little too complicated; the denouement too abrupt; and the whole not very probable; yet it is an amusing and interesting novel: with the little corrections of a master-hand it might have ranked the foremost in the second line.'

1791: 70   [THOMSON, Anna].
THE LABYRINTHS OF LIFE. A NOVEL. BY THE AUTHOR OF EXCESSIVE SENSIBILITY, AND FATAL FOLLIES. IN FOUR VOLUMES.

London: Printed for G. G. J. and J. Robinson, Pater-Noster-Row, 1791.
I iv, 225p; II 227p; III 222p; IV 268p. 12mo. 12s (CR), 12s sewed (MR, SJC).
CR n.s. 2: 234 (June 1791); MR n.s. 5: 337–8 (July 1791); AF II: 4447.
PU Singer-Mend.PR5178.P66.L3 1791; ESTC n020615.

Notes. Robinson paid £20.0.0, £10.0.0, and £10.0.0 on 17 Sept 1790, 18 Jan 1791, and 18 Mar 1791 to Anna Thomson for *The Labyrinths of Life*; the receipt of 18 Jan 1791 says that the work is 'by me', Anna Thomson (RA).
Dedication to the Duchess of Leeds signed 'The Author'. 4 pp. advs. end vol. 4. Epistolary.
Excessive Sensibility 1787: 50 and *Fatal Follies* 1788: 75.
Adv., 'Next Saturday will be published', SJC 8–10 Mar 1791.
German trans. Dresden and Leipzig, 1792 (*Die Labyrinthe des menschlichen Lebens*) (RS).

CR: 'The best that we can say of this novel is, that we found it amusing; though, from the first volume, we expected more interest than we discovered in it. The events, the characters, and situations, are trite and hackneyed; and, if we wished to commend, we scarcely know where to find an object of praise.'

MR [John Noorthouck]: 'When a manufacture has been carried on long enough for the workmen to attain a general proficiency, the uniformity of the stuffs will render it difficult to decide on the preference of one piece beyond another; and this must be our apology for not entering into a discussion of the merits of the novel now before us, which, at the same time that it exhibits nothing to shock our feelings, affords nothing to attract particular attention, either as to materials or workmanship' (p. 337).

1791: 71   TIMBURY, Jane.
A SEQUEL TO THE PHILANTHROPIC RAMBLER. BY JANE TIMBURY, AUTHOR OF TOBIT, THE MALE COQUET, AND THE TRIUMPH OF FRIENDSHIP.

London: Printed for the Author; and sold by Messrs. G. G. J. and J. Robinson, Pater-noster-Row; R. Faulder, New Bond-street; and J. Southern, St James's-street, 1791.
152p. 12mo.
BL N.1717(2); EM 1925: 5; ESTC t137254 (BI Gu).

Notes. The Philanthropic Rambler 1790: 70; *The Male Coquet* 1788: 76; *The Triumph of Friendship* 1789: 70.

1791: 72   WHITE, J[ames].
THE ADVENTURES OF KING RICHARD COEUR-DE-LION. TO WHICH IS ADDED, THE DEATH OF LORD FALKLAND: A POEM. BY J. WHITE,

ESQ. AUTHOR OF EARL STRONGBOW, AND JOHN OF GAUNT. IN THREE VOLUMES.

> London: Printed for T. and J. Evans, Paternoster-Row, 1791.
> I xvi, 163p; II 180p; III 184p. 8vo. 9s sewed (MR, SJC).
> CR n.s. 2: 116 (May 1791); MR n.s. 6: 230–1 (Oct 1791); AF II: 4772.
> C 7720.d.1089; EM 237: 6; ESTC t057805 (BI BL, O; NA CaOTU, ICU, IU).

Notes. Novel ends on p. 175 of vol. 3; the rest is 'The Death of Lord Faulkland: a Poem'.
Earl Strongbow 1789: 71; *John of Gaunt* 1790: 72.
Adv., 'This Month will be published, Elegantly printed, in three Volumes, Crown Octavo, Price 9s. sewed, Ornamented with an elegant Frontispiece, designed by Burney, and engraved by Chesham', SJC 8–10 Feb 1791; author's name given as John.
Further edns: Dublin, 1791 (Printed by Zachariah Jackson, for Arthur Grueber, 2 vols., 12mo), ESTC t217606; Dublin, 1791, ESTC t208324.

CR: 'Mr White no longer employs the thread-bare story of old manuscripts, nor breaks the chain of the narrative by introductions as tedious as those of the Arabian Nights Entertainments. His volumes are consequently more entertaining. But if he wishes that this work should be considered as a supplement to the general history, an account of the minuter events, which history deigns to record, he should not contradict it.'

MR [John Noorthouck and Ralph Griffiths]: 'He still proceeds in his heterogeneous plan, of combining *History* with *Romance, Chivalry,* and burlesque *Ridicule:* by which last ingredient, the Dignity of Heroism is oddly caricatured, in almost every part of the composition. Nevertheless, in spite of every violation of the laws of Novel-writing, as generally observed by the best of our modern authors in that branch of literature, these adventures, (which never *could* have happened,) have afforded us a good deal of amusement: so that, after much laughing *with* the writer, and *at* him, we, on the whole, grew sorry to part with him, as we drew towards the close of his performance.'

1791: 73   WRIGHT, T[homas].
SOLYMAN AND FATIMA; OR, THE SCEPTIC CONVINCED. AN EASTERN TALE. BY T. WRIGHT.

> London: Printed for John Bew, No. 28, Paternoster-Row, 1791.
> I 166p; II 146p. 8vo [SJC has 12mo]. 5s sewed (MR, SJC).
> MR n.s. 9: 338 (Nov 1792); AF II: 4953.
> BL N.1807; EMf; ESTC t144977 (BI Gu).

Notes. 2 pp. advs. end vol. 2.
Adv., 'In a few Days will be published', SDA 23 July 1791; adv. SJC 10–13 Dec 1791.
Further edn: Dublin, 1792 (Printed for P. Byrne, J. Moore, J. Jones, J. Rice, R. White, and R. M' Allister, 1 vol., 12mo), ESTC n022768; Dublin, 1797 (WC), xESTC.

MR [William Enfield]: 'An Eastern tale ought to be at least a tolerable representation of Eastern manners, sentiments and language. The work now before us has no other pretensions to the title, than that the scene of the story is laid in Cassimire, and that its two principal characters are two young adventurers, who are led through various regions of the East, and, after many sudden and suprizing vicissitudes of fortune, meet at last at their native home. Except a few incidents . . . the reader might as easily fancy the the scene to pass on English as on Asiatic ground.'

1791: 74   [YOUNG, Mary Julia].
THE FAMILY PARTY. IN THREE VOLUMES.

London: Printed at the Minerva, for William Lane, Leadenhall-Street, 1791.
I 191p; II 171p; III 177p. 12mo. 7s 6d (EngR), 9s (SJC).
EngR 20: 69 (July 1792).
BL 12614.b.33; EM 189: 4; ESTC t076788 (NA NNS).

Notes. Attributed to Mary Julia Young by a Minerva Library catalogue of 1814 (Blakey). Not included in the list of her claimed works in letter to RLF 20 Mar 1808 (RLF 6: 216).
1 p. advs. end vol. 1; 1 p. advs. end vol. 2; 3 pp. advs. end vol. 3.
Adv. SDA 26 Oct 1791; adv. SJC 17–20 Dec 1791.

EngR: '*Mediocre*—The attention is not sufficiently excited—and the incidents are spun out to too great a length. The story might certainly be condensed into one volume without any injury. To do the author justice, however, we must confess that his characters are unexceptionable, and that he no where outrages the decent order of society.'

1792

1792: 1   ANON.
ANNA MELVIL. A NOVEL. IN TWO VOLUMES.

London: Printed for William Lane, at the Minerva Press, Leadenhall-Street, 1792.
I 207p; II 220p. 12mo. 5s sewed (EngR).
EngR 21: 147–8 (Feb 1793).
O Vet.A5f.620-621; EM 1280: 28; ESTC n014940 (NA CtY, MH-H).

Notes. Adv., 'In the Press', SDA 2 Dec 1791.

EngR: 'He is not entitled to a small degree of praise who, in the beaten path of literature, opens to the view of the beholder a perspective hitherto unseen or little noticed. Such praise belongs to the author of the novel before us, which contains incidents perfectly new. . . . We could have wished that the language had been a little more correct.'

ARABIAN TALES
See CAZOTTE, Jacques, and Denis CHAVIS

1792: 2   ANON.
*ASHTON PRIORY. A NOVEL.

London: Law, 1792 (CR).
3 vols. 8vo. 9s (CR).
CR n.s. 7: 357 (Mar 1793).
No copy located.

Notes. By same author as *Edward and Sophia* (1787: 6); *Eliza Cleland* (1788: 14); *Powis Castle* (1788: 30); *Predestined Wife* (1789: 22); *Benedicta* (1791: 3); and *Mariamne* (1793: 8).

Adv., 'In the Press' (Lane), SDA 2 Dec 1791.

Further edn: London, 1803 (Summers).

   CR: 'We do not think this novel free from faults, and in some places very gross ones; particularly in this leading instance, that the heroine, miss Overbery, a girl of sixteen, is supposed to reason and think like a woman of thirty; girls of that age never consider so deeply. The characters are, however, well drawn and supported. . . .'

1792: 3   ANON.
THE BARONESS OF BEAUMONT. A NOVEL. BY A LADY. A NARRATIVE FOUNDED ON OBSERVATION. THE OBJECT OF IT IS A PERFECT ACQUIESCENCE IN THE WILL OF THE GREAT DISPOSER OF EVENTS: WHILST IT SHEWS VIRTUE IN DIFFERENT CHARACTERS, IT WILL, IT IS HOPED, NOT BE FOUND DESTITUTE OF AMUSEMENT AND ORIGINALITY.

>   London: Sold by Messrs. Robinsons, Paternoster-Row, and Mr. Debrett, Piccadilly, 1792.
>   I iv, 279p; II 232p. 8vo. 6s sewed (MR, SJC).
>   MR n.s. 9: 107–8 (Sept 1792); AF II: 225.
>   CtY Im.B268.792; ESTC n063796.

Notes. Dedication to Mrs Bewly, of Swaffham, Norfolk, widow of William Bewley, 1, iii–iv, signed 'The Authoress'.

Adv. SJC 7–9 June 1792; 'A Narrative founded on observation, the object of it is a perfect acquiescence to the will of the great dispenser of events: whilst it shows virtue in different characters it will it is hoped, not be found destitute of amusement and originality.'

Further edns: London, 1793, ESTC n015668; Dublin, 1793 (Printed by Z. Jackson, 1 vol., 12mo), EM 2911: 8, ESTC t119271.

2nd edn. adv. SDA 8 Feb 1793: 'The rapid sale of the First has induced the Authoress to a Second Edition, which she trusts will be found corrected. The favourable mention of this work in the Monthly Review of September, as likewise in other periodical publications, has flattered her into a confidence, that it affords some entertainment.'

   MR [William Enfield]: 'We cannot finish our brief account of this pleasing novel without adding, that it is dedicated to the widow of a man whom we recollect with a mixture of veneration and affection, as one of the first and brightest ornaments of our board'.

1792: 4   ANON.
A BUTLER'S DIARY; OR, THE HISTORY OF MISS EGGERTON. A NOVEL. IN TWO VOLUMES.

>   London: Printed for William Lane, at the Minerva Press, Leadenhall-Street, 1792.
>   I 248p; II 194p. 12mo. 6s (CR, adv., SDA).
>   CR n.s. 4: 236 (Feb 1792); AF II: 572.
>   O 249.s.213,214; ESTC t149043 (NA CSmH; EA GOT).

Notes. By same author as *Weird Sisters* (1794: 15) and *Waldeck Abbey* (1795: 10).

Adv., 'In the Press', SDA 26 Oct 1791; adv. SDA 9 Mar 1792.

Adv. end vol. 1 of *The Child of Providence* (1792: 6).

   CR: 'There is a novelty in the style and manner of this story which renders it pleasing.

There is a discrimination of character also, with various little traces of knowledge and reflection, which seem to lift these volumes above the common rank: the situations and events are interesting and not improbable; but the language, from the printer's or author's inadvertence, is very inaccurate; we suspect both to be in fault.'

1792: 5   ANON.
THE CASTLE OF ST. VALLERY, AN ANCIENT STORY.

> London: Sold by G. G. J. and J. Robinson, Paternoster-Row; T. and J. Egerton, Charing-Cross; and J. Cooke, in Oxford, 1792.
> 77p. 8vo. 2s boards (MR, SDA).
> MR n.s. 9: 337–8 (Nov 1792); AF II: 640.
> NjP PR3991.A1C37 1792; xESTC.

Notes. Adv., 'Next Week will be published', SDA 19 June 1792; adv. as published SDA 7 July 1792.

German trans. Hanover, 1793 (*Das Schloss St. Vallery*) (RS).

MR [Thomas Holcroft]: 'This story is an imitation of the Castle of Otranto, Sir Bertrand, the Old English Baron, and others, in which the chief passion intended to be excited is fear. Of all the resources of invention, this, perhaps, is the most puerile, as it is certainly among the most unphilosophic. It contributes to keep alive that superstition which debilitates the mind, that ignorance which propagates error, and that dread of invisible agency which makes inquiry criminal. . . . The story of this work is told in that species of poetic prose, which cannot easily be reconciled to good taste. The incidents are too crowded to be prepared and explained with that consistency which should render them probable; and the common place events of a cruel uncle, a helpless child, a pitiful assassin, and an heir in disguise, are here repeated' (p. 337).

[*The Castle of Otranto* 1765 {1764}, JR 868, AF I: 2898; 'Sir Bertrand' first published 1773 in the Aikins' *Miscellaneous Pieces in Prose*; *The Old English Baron*, originally *The Champion of Virtue*, 1777: 16.]

1792: 6   ANON.
THE CHILD OF PROVIDENCE: A NOVEL, IN FOUR VOLUMES.

> London: Printed for William Lane, at the Minerva Press, Leadenhall-Street, 1792.
> I 274p; II 284p; III 272p; IV 232p. 12mo. 12s (CR), 12s sewed (SJC).
> CR n.s. 9: 118 (Sept 1793).
> PU Singer-Mend.PR.3991.A1.C45.1792; CME 3-628-45016-0; ESTC n044538 (BI BL; NA CaOHM, MiU, NNU; EA COR).

Notes. Drop-head title 'The Shipwreck; or, Child of Providence'. 2 pp. advs. end vol. 1.

Adv., 'In the Press', SDA 2 Dec 1791; adv. SJC 24–26 Oct 1793.

CR: 'Amidst much improbability, some expedients too artificial, and absurdities too glaring, our heroine at last reaches the goal of happiness, with the man of her choice. The mind is occasionally interested in her adventures, and sometimes agreeably amused; but the faults often disgust and generally draw aside the veil; so that this novel can never attain great celebrity.'

THE COUNT DE HOENSDERN
See MATHEWS, Eliza Kirkham

DELINEATIONS OF THE HEART
See RAITHBY, John

THE DOUBTFUL MARRIAGE
See HUTCHINSON, William

1792: 7   ANON.
EDELFRIDA, A NOVEL.

> London: Printed for T. Hookham, and J. Carpenter, Old and New Bond-Street, 1792.
> I ii, 282p; II 306p; III 278p; IV 243p. 12mo. 12s (CR), 12s sewed (SJC, SDA).
> CR n.s. 6: 560–1 (App [Dec 1792/Jan 1793]); AF II: 1207.
> BL 12613.f.10; EM 217: 2; ESTC t070085 (BI O; NA CtY, CSmH, DLC, MH-H).

Notes. Dedication to Miss M—— (i–ii). 2 pp. advs. end vol. 3 and 1 p. advs. end vol. 4.
Adv. SJC 5–7 Apr 1792; adv., 'By a Lady', SDA 23 May 1792.

CR: 'This novel, considered as a series of events artfully connected, deserves some praise. But the events are the common ones of novels; and the characters are seldom relieved by peculiar features, or rendered interesting by uncommon situations. In other respects this work deserves severe reprobation. The supposed force of rash vows, the softened features of the Roman Catholic religion may, each in different ways, have a dangerous tendency.'

1792: 8   ANON.
ELIZABETH PERCY; A NOVEL, FOUNDED ON FACTS. WRITTEN BY A LADY. IN TWO VOLUMES.

> London: Printed for A. Hamilton, near Gray's-Inn Gate, Holborn, 1792.
> I 196p; II 190p. 12mo. 6s sewed (EngR), 5s sewed (SJC).
> EngR 20: 389 (Nov 1792); AF II: 1249.
> BL 1154.f.37; EM 2578: 2; ESTC t063537.

Notes. 2 pp. advs. end vol. 2.
Adv., simply as *A Novel, founded on Facts. Written by a Lady*, SJC 24–26 May 1792. Adv., as *Elizabeth Pucy*, LC 71: 501 (24–26 May 1792).

EngR: 'If a person should be confined in one of the solitary *Scilly islands*—and if that same person should have no other books to peruse but the two volumes of Elizabeth Percy, he might perhaps be tempted to travel through them. In any other situation we are persuaded that he would not accomplish the perusal of the first *six* pages.'

1792: 9   ANON.
ELVINA; A NOVEL. IN TWO VOLUMES.

> London: Printed for William Lane, at the Minerva, Leadenhall-Street, 1792.
> I 175p; II 192p. 8vo [CR has 12mo]. 6s (CR).
> CR n.s. 5: 233 (June 1792); AF II: 1266.
> PU Singer-Mend. PR3991.A1.E44.1792; ESTC n008613.

Notes. Epistolary.
Adv., 'most elegantly printed . . . will be published in a few Days', SDA 6 Mar 1792.

CR: 'Elvina is a work which never rises above mediocrity, and sometimes sinks greatly below that standard. . . . The greater part is wire-drawn and insipid.'

1792: 10   ANON.
EMILY: A NOVEL. IN THREE VOLUMES.

> London: Printed for William Lane, at the Minerva, Leadenhall-Street, 1792.
> I 176p; II [210]p; III 190p. 16mo (ESTC has 12mo).
> PU Singer-Mend. PR.3991.A1.E444.1792; ESTC n030777 (NA CSt).

Notes. Final p. of vol. 2 misnumbered 110. 2 pp. advs. end vol. 2; 2 pp. advs. end vol. 3.
Adv. end vol. 2 of *Matilda Fitz-Aubin* (1792: 20); adv. reprints t.p.

1792: 11   ANON.
EMILY; OR, THE FATAL PROMISE. A NORTHERN TALE, IN TWO VOLUMES.

> London: Printed and Sold by T. Wilkins, No. 23, Aldermanbury. Sold also by H. D.
> Symonds, and J. Bew, Paternoster-Row; T. Hookham, New Bond Street; J. Murray,
> Fleet-Street; and W. Richardson, Royal Exchange; A. Hamilton, Holborn; W. Drury,
> St. Martin's Lane; and W. Oulton, No. 14, Oxford Street, 1792.
> I 204p; II 215p. 12mo. 6s. (CR).
> CR n.s. 5: 234 (June 1792).
> BL RB.23.a.9379; ESTC t225440 (NA CtY).

Notes. 2-pp. dedication to 'the Prettiest Women in the Kingdom'. Epistolary.
CR: 'A tale without interest, probability, or common sense.—Heaven defend us from such
trash; but Reviewers must wade through the most disgusting masses.'

1792: 12   ANON.
THE EXCURSION OF OSMAN, THE SON OF ABDALLAH, LORD OF THE VALLIES; A POLITICAL ROMANCE: INCLUDING SOME ANEC-DOTES RELATIVE TO A GREAT NORTHERN FAMILY.

> Liverpool: Printed by T. Schofield, Dale-Street, 1792.
> xii, 144p. 8vo. 2s 6d (AR).
> AR 17 (Oct 1793): 203–6.
> BL 12614.g.1; EM 277: 1; ESTC t107715 (BI LVu; NA C-S, ICN, MH-H &c.).

Notes. Dedication to Charles James Fox v–vi, signed 'The Author', Aug 1792; address to the
reader vii–xii.
AR: 'In this tale more is meant than meets the eye.... The author appears to possess a ready
invention; but with respect to the "*argument*," as we do not well understand it, we cannot
pretend to say there is "no offence in it"' (p. 203).

1792: 13   ANON.
THE EXPEDITION OF LITTLE PICKLE; OR, THE PRETTY PLOTTER.

> London: Printed for H. D. Symonds, no. 20, Paternoster-Row; and Champante and
> Whitrow, Jewry-Street, Aldgate, 1792.
> vi, 188p. 8vo. 2s 6d sewed (MR).
> MR n.s. 8: 340 (July 1792); AF II: 1343.
> BL Ch.790/67; EM 7277: 3; ESTC t133449 (NA CLU-S/C, MH-H, PU, &c.).

Notes. 1-sheet prospectus for the forthcoming *Whimsical Expedition of Little Pickle* ESTC t223397.
Not for small children; ch. xxi has 'A Serious Lesson to all Young Ladies'.

Although Little Pickle is not portrayed as an actress or in any other way associated with Dora Jordan, mistress of the Duke of Clarence, later William IV, her nickname 'Little Pickle' was certainly current when this novel was published. AR comments on the natural but mistaken assumption that the novel concerns 'a certain celebrated actress' and wonders whether 'the title was fixed upon as a false lure or accidentally popped into the author's head'.

Adv., 'in a neat pocket Volume', SJC 9–11 Feb 1792; additional bookseller is J. Owen, opposite Bond-street, Piccadilly.

Further edn: London, 1797 (WC), xESTC.

MR [John Noorthouck]: 'From the title and the size, we expected that Little Pickle had a reference to a *public* character currently known by that appellation: but in this supposition we were deceived. Little Pickle is a sprightly young lady, and her story is a common novel. The plot is indeed childish enough: but all circumstances being at the writer's command, it succeeds to admiration, and is conducted with some degree of humour.'

1792: 14   ANON.
THE FAIR IMPOSTOR. A NOVEL. IN THREE VOLUMES.

London: Printed for T. Hookham and J. Carpenter, Old and New Bond-Street, 1792.

I viii, 264p; II 262p; III 271p. 12mo. 9s sewed (adv., SJC).

BL 12613.f.11; EM 243: 3; ESTC t070089 (BI MRu; NA CtY, MH-H, NjP, PU, ViU &c.).

Notes. In 1799 Carpenter advertises the novel as by Reeve (Summers).

Epistolary. In vols. 2 and 3 text of novel starts on p. 3.

Adv. SJC 5–7 Apr 1792. Adv., 'Dedicated, by Permission, to the Right Hon. Lady Dacre, . . . By a Lady', 14 May 1792.

Adv. end of *The Minstrel* (1793: 10).

1792: 15   ANON.
FANNY; OR, THE DESERTED DAUGHTER. A NOVEL. BEING THE FIRST LITERARY ATTEMPT OF A YOUNG LADY. IN TWO VOLUMES.

London: Printed for J. Bew, no. 28, Paternoster-Row, 1792.

I xii, 284p; II 296p. 12mo. 6s sewed (MR, SJC).

MR n.s. 9: 212–13 (Oct 1792); AF II: 1375.

BL N.2033; CME 3-628-45046-2; EM 2014: 2; ESTC t072384 (BI E; EA COR).

Notes. Verse dedication to the Honourable Miss S——. 4 pp. advs. end vol. 2.

Adv., 'An Interesting Novel . . . In a few Days will be published', SJC 8–10 Mar 1792.

MR [William Enfield]: 'Though this production may not be possessed of sufficient excellence to ensure it a place in the first class of novels, it has too much merit to be thrown among the rubbish of the circulating libraries. . . . The language is easy and natural; without much ornament, but, at the same time, without any very culpable negligence. The chief excellence, however, of the work, consists in the lively and touching manner in which it represents the expression of emotions and passions.'

THE FILLE DE CHAMBRE
See ROWSON, Susanna

1792: 16   ANON.
*FREDERIC AND LOUISA; A NOVEL. IN FOUR VOLUMES. BY THE
AUTHOR OF ADELINE.

> London: Printed at the Minerva Press, for William Lane, 1792 (EngR).
> 12mo. 1110p. 12s sewed (EngR, SJC), 4s sewed (SDA).
> EngR 20: 389 (Nov 1792).
> No copy located.

Notes: Adeline 1790: 1.
Adv., 'In the Press', SDA 2 Dec 1791; adv. as published SDA 26 June 1792; adv. SJC 24–26 Oct 1793.

> EngR: 'The author seems to have set out with a wish to do good, and with sufficient judg-
> ment to direct him in the proper path. His *Frederic* and *Louisa* are well worthy of imitation.
> The other subordinate characters are drawn with no careless pencil; and, with respect to inci-
> dent, the author seems not *much* to have "o'erstepped the modesty of nature."'

1792: 17   ANON.
FREDERICA: OR THE MEMOIRS OF A YOUNG LADY. A NOVEL, IN
THREE VOLUMES. BY A LADY. DEDICATED TO HER ROYAL HIGH-
NESS THE DUTCHESS OF YORK.

> London: Printed for J. Ridgway, York-Street, St. James's-Square, 1792.
> I 264p; II 251p; III 245p. 12mo [MR has 8vo]. 9s (CR), 9s sewed (MR).
> CR n.s. 4: 472–3 (Apr 1792); MR n.s. 8: 460 (Aug 1792); AF II: 1518.
> NjP 3600.001.631; ESTC n006573. WC also shows TxHR.

Notes. Dedication to H.R.H. the Duchess of York.
Further edn: Dublin, 1792 (Printed for Messrs. P. Wogan, P. Byrne, A. Grueber, W. M'Kenzie, J. Moore [and 4 others in Dublin], 2 vols., 12mo), ESTC n031674.

> CR: 'We cannot approve of this novel: the tale is trite, hackneyed, and insipid: the events
> frequently improbable, and the characters of the common cast. We wish the lady some bet-
> ter employment.'
> MR [William Enfield]: 'If these volumes be taken up with no higher expectation than that
> of occupying a few tedious hours with light amusement, the reader will not be disappointed;
> for they contain a sufficient variety of incidents and characters to afford an easy exercise of
> attention, without burthening the understanding with a superfluity of reflection, or over-
> powering the heart with a deep-wrought tale of distress. More than this we cannot promise.'

1792: 18   ANON.
GENEROSITY. A NOVEL. IN THREE VOLUMES.

> London: Printed for William Lane, at the Minerva, Leadenhall-Street, 1792.
> I 216p; II 239p; III 238p. 12mo. 9s (CR, SDA).
> CR n.s. 4: 352 (Mar 1792); AF II: 1586.
> NNC 825G28 / O; xESTC.

Notes. 1 leaf advs. end vol. 3. Epistolary.
Adv., 'In the Press', SDA 26 Oct 1791.
Further edn: Dublin, 1792 (Printed for P. Byrne, A. Grueber, J. Halpin, J. Moore, W. Jones,
R. M'Alister, and J. Rice, 2 vols., 12mo), ESTC n006682.

CR rev. is a conversation between a 'flippant girl' and a reviewer; the girl thinks it charming but the reviewer remarks: 'It is one of the most trite, trifling, improbable, and absurd stories that I ever saw.'

THE GENEROUS BRITON [Edward KIMBER]. First published 1765, JR 924, AF I: 1517.

1792: 19   ANON.
*LADY ALMIRA GRANTHAM, IN A SERIES OF LETTERS, INTERSPERSED WITH SEVERAL INTERESTING STORIES, WRITTEN IN THE YEAR MDCCLXXXIX.
> Printed at Bath, by Hazard, 1792 (MR).
> 2 vols. 12mo. About 500 pp. in each. 5s sewed. (MR).
> MR n.s. 9: 213–4 (Oct 1792).
> No copy located.

Notes. Epistolary.

MR [John Noorthouck]: 'As this lady confesses that her first production, though candidly treated by the Reviewers, yielded but little profit, and as she disclaims all pretensions to fame; we mean kindly to her in asking, whether she cannot use a needle in any mode, turn a spinning wheel, knit, touch a keyed instrument, or handle a painting brush, or any brush, as well as a pen? To fill up *her own* vacant hours merely to furnish others with the means of misapplying *their* hours, is rendering a sad account of time: nor did we know that a narrow fortune afforded many vacant hours to an industrious hand, however it may be with an industrious mind. As this lady professes to understand the workings of the human heart, and the motives of human actions, so intimately, if she must exercise her pen, can she not use it more profitably than in fabricating idle tales eked out with old stories?' (p. 213).

MAN AS HE IS. A NOVEL
See BAGE, Robert

MARY DE-CLIFFORD. A STORY
See BRYDGES, Sir Samuel Egerton

1792: 20   ANON.
MATILDA FITZ-AUBIN, A SKETCH. IN TWO VOLUMES.
> London: Printed for William Lane, at the Minerva, Leadenhall-Street, 1792.
> I 257p; II 262p. 12mo. 6s (CR).
> CR n.s. 9: 117–18 (Sept 1793).
> CtY Im.M427.792; ESTC n064258.

Notes. 3 pp. advs. end vol. 1; 2 pp. advs. end vol. 2.

Further edn: Dublin, 1793 (Printed for Messrs. P. Wogan, P. Byrne, J. Moore, W. Jones, and J. Rice, 2 vols., 12mo), ESTC t124728.

CR: 'This is a *cento*, a patchwork from different novels. We always trace the author in the steps of Miss Burney or Mrs Smith—even her characters are in no instance original, and the only merit we can assign them, is that they are well contrasted—But these volumes are amusing: they will not implant a vice in the heart, nor raise a blush on the cheek of innocence.'

MEMOIRS OF A BARONESS
See TOMLINS, Elizabeth Sophia

1792: 21   ANON.
THE MODERN MINIATURE. A NOVEL. IN TWO VOLUMES.
>London: Printed for T. Hookham and J. Carpenter, Old and New Bond-Street, 1792.
>I xii, 288p; II 282p. 12mo. 6s sewed (MR).
>MR n.s. 9: 108 (Sept 1792); AF II: 2905.
>BL C.187.a.21; EM 6961: 14; ESTC n005041 (NA DLC, NjP, PU &c.).

Notes. List of subscribers v–xii.
According to EngR, a prefatory advertisement says that the author is female.
Adv., 'In the Press, and in a few days will be published.... Printed for the Author, and sold by Hookham and Carpenter, Bond-street', SDA 7 June 1792.

   MR [William Enfield]: 'The incidents and situations are sometimes interesting: but its chief merit consists in the easy and lively sketches of character, some taken from lower and some from higher life, which are given in *miniature* in the course of the story.'

1792: 22   ANON.
THE NOBLE ENTHUSIAST; A MODERN ROMANCE. IN THREE VOLUMES.
>London: Printed for William Lane, at the Minerva, Leadenhall-Street, 1792.
>I xiv, 221p; II 204p; III 202p. 8vo. 9s (EngR).
>EngR 20: 308 (Oct 1792).
>PU Singer-Mend.PR.3991.A1.N63.1792; ESTC n042164 (NA CtY).

Notes. Preface (pp. v–xiv) says that the author is female. 3 pp. advs. end vol. 1; 2 pp. advs. end vol. 3.
Adv., 'In the Press', *A Modern Romance*, SDA 26 Oct 1791.

   EngR: 'We cannot bestow much applause on this romance, which is by no means interesting. The language is inflated in the highest degree.'

1792: 23   ANON.
ORLANDO AND LAVINIA: OR, THE LIBERTINE. A NOVEL. IN FOUR VOLUMES. BY A LADY.
>London: Printed for L. Wayland, No. 2, Middle-Row, Holborn, 1792.
>I 167+p; II 147p; III 123, 2p; IV 98p. 8vo [CR has 12mo]. 10s (CR) 10s sewed (half-title).
>CR n.s. 5: 234 (June 1792).
>BL 012612.df.43; EM 165: 4; ESTC t064650.

Notes. Dedication to the Duke of Queensberry. Text of novel starts on p. 17 in vol. 1 and p. 5 in vols. 2, 3 and 4. Page(s) missing at end of vol. 1. 2 pp. book advs. end vol. 3, followed by numbered 2-pp. adv. for Dr Smith's Tonic Remedy.

   CR: 'We cannot deny that the lady possesses some talents: they gleam occasionally and faintly; but the whole is trite, trifling, and improbable.'

THE PATHETIC HISTORY OF EGBERT AND LEONORA
See HALL, William Henry

THE PEASANT; OR, FEMALE PHILOSOPHER
See FELL, Mrs

1792: 24   ANON.
*PHILARO AND ELEONORA; OR THE ORPHAN TWINS. DEDICATED
BY PERMISSION TO THE DUCHESS OF DORSET.

> London: Barker, 1792 (CR).
> 2 vols. 12mo. 6s (CR).
> CR n.s. 6: 561 (App [Dec 1792/Jan 1793]); AF II: 3326.
> No copy located.

Notes. CR: 'This little artless story is interesting; but probability is often violated, and history sometimes too much changed. We cannot, upon the whole, recommend these volumes, except as for the mere amusement of those who will not be disgusted by the errors.'

1792: 25   ANON.
*PREPOSSESSION; OR, MEMOIRS OF COUNT TOULOUSSIN. WRIT-
TEN BY HIMSELF. IN 2 VOLS.

> London: Forbes, 1792 (AR).
> 2 vols. 12mo. 442p. 6s (AR).
> AR 13: 70 (May 1792).
> No copy located.

Notes. AR: 'The narrative, which turns almost entirely upon the subject of love, or upon what the author calls *amours* and *amourettes*, appears, in the leading incidents at least, to have been founded on fact, and to agree very well with the state of French manners previous to the revolution.'

THE RECLUSE OF THE APPENINES, A TALE
See STREET, Miss

THE ROCK OF MODREC
See THELWALL, John

1792: 26   ANON.
*SIDNEY CASTLE: OR THE SORROWS OF DE COURCI, A NOVEL, BY
THE AUTHOR OF EDMUND, OR THE CHILD OF THE CASTLE.

> London: Lane (CR).
> 2 vols. 12mo. 6s (CR).
> CR n.s. 6: 561 (App [Dec 1792/Jan 1793]).
> No copy located.

Notes: Edmund 1790: 9.
Further edn: Dublin, 1793 (Printed for P. Wogan, P. Byrne, J. Moore, W. Jones and J. Rice, 2 vols., 12mo), ESTC n023084.

CR: 'The circumstances of this novel are not common; but the whole is so improbable and absurd, that it deserves not even the labour of pointing out its faults. The gulph of oblivion is already open to receive it.'

SLAVERY: OR, THE TIMES
See MACKENZIE, Anna Maria

1792: 27   ANON.
*SOMERSET; OR, THE DANGERS OF GREATNESS. A TALE, FOUND-
ED UPON HISTORIC TRUTHS.
> London: Lane, 1792 (EngR).
> 2 vols. 339p. 12mo. 5s sewed (EngR).
> EngR 21: 147 (Feb 1793).
> No copy located.

Notes. Advertised end of vol. 3 of Pilkington's *Rosina* (1793: 35).

EngR: 'The author ingenuously confesses in the preface that he aims not at novelty. Indeed he asserts that "to invent any thing entirely new, is now become almost an utter impossibility. The rapidity with which literature has *increased itself* for these two last centuries, and the voluminous authors in every department, have swallowed up every passage to novelty."—We will not enter into a discussion of this assertion at present—suffice it to say, that we do not coincide in opinion with the author. As all our readers are acquainted with the history of Somerset, we need say no more than that there are some agreeable episodes interwoven with the main plot, which attach an additional degree of interest to the whole.'

TALES OF A PARROT
See ZIYA UL-DIN NAKSHABI

THEODORE, A DOMESTIC TALE
See STREET, Miss

1792: 28   ANON.
*THE VILLAGE LOVERS; A NOVEL.
> London: Lane, Minerva, Leadenhall-Street (SJC), 1792 (EngR).
> 2 vols. 311p. 12mo. 5s (EngR, SJC).
> EngR 19: 232 (Mar 1792).
> No copy located.

Notes. Adv., 'In the Press', SDA 26 Oct 1791; adv. SJC 17–20 Dec 1791.

EngR: 'The author of the above novel declares that her wish in writing it was, "to blend the verisimilitude of the modern novel with the flowery scenes of the ancient pastoral; to paint nature in her romantic forms, and the human mind in its unsophisticated state." She has been sufficiently successful. The story, though neither new nor very eventful, is interesting; and the peaceful serenity of a life of retirement, is depicted in pleasing colours. The moral being unobjectionable, young people may derive from the perusal of it both amusement and instruction.'

THE WANDERING ISLANDER
See WILSON, Charles Henry

1792: 29   [BAGE, Robert].
MAN AS HE IS. A NOVEL. IN FOUR VOLUMES.

> London: Printed for William Lane, at the Minerva Press, Leadenhall-Street, 1792.
> I vii, 288p; II 243p; III 275p; IV 272p. 12mo. 12s sewed (MR, SDA 1792), 9s (SDA 1791).
> MR n.s. 10: 297–302 (Mar 1793); AF II: 193.
> BL N.2504; EM 2072: 5; ESTC t077679 (BI D, O; NA CtY-BR, CSmH, DLC, IU, MH-H, NjP, PU &c.).

Notes. Preface i–vii; 'Exordium' [viii]. 1 p. adv. end vol. 2 and 1 p. adv. end vol. 3.
Adv., 'In the Press', SDA 26 Oct 1791; adv. SDA 14 June 1792.
Further edns: Dublin, 1793 (Printed for P. Wogan; P. Byrne; B. Smith, 2 vols., 12mo), ESTC n004380; Dublin, 1793, ESTC t170817; London, 1796, EM 1002: 18, ESTC n004379; NSTC lists edn. in 1819. German trans. Berlin and Stettin, 1798 (*Der Mensch wie er ist*) (EAG). Facs: N.

> MR [Thomas Holcroft]: '. . . when a novel has the power of playing on the fancy, interesting the affections, and teaching moral and political truth, we imagine that we are capable of feeling these beauties, and that we have liberality enough to announce these to the world.
>
> Of this superior kind, is the novel now before us; which, though far from being without faults, gave us great pleasure, and is such as we can warmly recommend to readers of taste, science, and sentiment. In narrating his fabulous adventures, the author frequently leads us through the regions of metaphysics, politics, and even theology; in which, however, he seldom remains long enough to fatigue the attention, or to pall the appetite, of his reader' (p. 297).

1792: 30   BILDERBECK, [Ludwig Benedict Franz, Freiherr von].
CYANNA OF ATHENS. A GRECIAN ROMANCE. IN TWO VOLUMES. FROM THE FRENCH OF THE BARON DE BILDERBEC.

> London: Printed for T. Axtell, Cornhill, 1792.
> I viii, 163p; II 179p. 8vo. 5s (EngR).
> EngR 21: 227 (Mar 1793).
> BL 12518.ccc.17; EM 55: 3; ESTC t129707.

Notes. Trans. of *Cyane: roman grec* (Neuwied, 1790).
Large print on very small pages containing a maximum of about 80 words; most have fewer.
Adv., 'In the Press', SDA 2 Dec 1791.

> EngR: 'We cannot avoid wishing that the translator had employed himself in a more useful manner. There is very little novelty in the construction or conduct of the work; the language, evidently an imitation of that of Rousseau, is inflated, and removed, *longo intervallo*, from the delightful style of that great man.'

1792: 31   [BRYDGES, Sir Samuel Egerton].
MARY DE-CLIFFORD. A STORY. INTERSPERSED WITH MANY POEMS.

> London: Printed for H. D. Symonds, Paternoster-Row, 1792.
> vii, 231p. 8vo [CR has 12mo]. 3s (CR), 4s 6d sewed (SJC).

CR n.s. 4: 352–3 (Mar 1792); AF II: 519.

BL 1607/4156; EMf; BL microfilm PBMic 37282; ESTC t119344 (NA CLU-S/C, PPRF).

Notes. Adv., 'Embellished with two elegant Engravings, SJC 7–9 Feb 1792.

Further edns: London, 1800, ESTC t115448; Philadelphia, 1845 (WC); NSTC lists edns. in 1811, [1844] and 1854.

CR: 'This little novel is the work of no common author: the characters are varied and well discriminated; the language polished and elegant, while a minute knowledge of the human heart, and a pretty extensive acquaintance with some branches of science, not generally understood, may be traced in different parts of it.'

1792: 32   [CAZOTTE, Jacques, and Denis CHAVIS]; HERON, Robert (trans.). ARABIAN TALES: OR, A CONTINUATION OF THE ARABIAN NIGHTS ENTERTAINMENTS. CONSISTING OF STORIES RELATED BY THE SULTANA OF THE INDIES, TO DIVERT HER HUSBAND FROM THE PERFORMANCE OF A RASH VOW; EXHIBITING A MOST INTERESTING VIEW OF THE RELIGION, LAWS, MANNERS, CUSTOMS, ARTS, AND LITERATURE, OF THE NATIONS OF THE EAST; AND AFFORDING A RICH FUND OF THE MOST PLEASING AMUSEMENT, WHICH FICTITIOUS WRITINGS CAN SUPPLY. IN FOUR VOLUMES. NEWLY TRANSLATED FROM THE ORIGINAL ARABIC INTO FRENCH, BY DOM CHAVIS, A NATIVE ARAB, AND M. CAZOTTE, MEMBER OF THE ACADEMY OF DIJON. AND TRANSLATED FROM THE FRENCH INTO ENGLISH, BY ROBERT HERON.

> Edinburgh: Printed for Bell & Bradfute, J. Dickson, E. Balfour, and P. Hill, Edinburgh; and G. G. J. & J. Robinson, London, 1792.
>
> I xxiii, 288p; II 323p; III 340p; IV 357p. 12mo. 10s sewed (MR, SJC).
>
> CR n.s. 6: 297–306 (Nov 1792); MR n.s. 11: 153–60 (June 1793); AF II: 1924.
>
> BL 1608/5644; EM 4154: 2; ESTC t141145 (BI C, E; NA CLU-S/C).

Notes. Trans. of *Continuation des Mille et une nuits* (Geneva and Paris, 1788).

A compilation by Chavis edited and extended by Cazotte and unknown others; see BGR. Illustrations.

Adv., 'The Only Complete Edition, Ornamented with Twelve elegant Engravings', SDA 21 June 1792 and SJC 26–28 June 1792.

Further edns: Edinburgh, 1792, EM 3759: 1, ESTC t130077; Dublin, 1792 (Printed by Robert Rhames, for R. Cross, P. Wogan, P. Byrne, W. McKenzie, J. Moore [and 4 others in Dublin], 4 vols., 12mo), ESTC t141146; London, 1794, EM 5315: 2, ESTC t070116. Extracts from *Arabian Tales* published in 6 magazines, 1792–1803, RM 1019, 1033, 1066, 1147, 1207.

CR: 'If the contents of these four volumes had really belonged to the MSS. of the Arabian Nights Entertainments, M. Galland shewed his judgment in not translating what could only debase his enchanting work' (p. 306).

MR [Thomas Holcroft]: 'Accustomed as we are to consider the Arabians frequently as a wandering and wild, and but seldom as a schooled and scientific, people, we receive such tales from them as the genuine produce of the partial advances which they have made in knowledge: though, were they the works of Europeans, we should regard them as the indolent resources of authors, who were either unwilling, or unable, to awaken attention and

excite applause, by exhibiting accurate and well-contrasted characters of human Beings'
(p. 154).

1792: 33   [FELL, Mrs].
THE PEASANT; OR, FEMALE PHILOSOPHER. A NOVEL. IN TWO
VOLUMES.
> London: Printed for William Lane, at the Minerva, Leadenhall-Street, 1792.
> I 250p; II 312p. 12mo. 6s (CR).
> CR n.s. 7: 357 (Mar 1793).
> AUG 02/III.9.8.185; xESTC.

Notes. Blakey: Attributed to Mrs Fell by a Minerva Library Catalogue of 1814.
Adv. end vol. 1 of *Matilda Fitz-Aubin* (1792: 20); adv. reprints t.p.
   CR: 'This, though not acknowledged, is evidently a translation from the French, and a
scyon from the stock of the Paisanne Parvenue. But it contains more events and less sentiment. The translation is not very well executed. . . .'

1792: 34   FLORIAN, [Jean Pierre Claris de]; HERON, [Robert] (*trans.*).
GONSALVO OF CORDOVA: OR, THE CONQUEST OF GRENADA. BY M.
FLORIAN, MEMBER OF THE FRENCH ACADEMY, AND ALSO THE
ACADEMIES OF MADRID, FLORENCE, &C. TO WHICH IS PREFIXED, A
SKETCH OF THE HISTORY OF THE MOORS IN SPAIN. IN THREE VOL-
UMES. TRANSLATED FROM THE ORIGINAL FRENCH, BY MR. HERON.
> Perth: Printed by R. Morison Junior, for R. Morison and Son, Booksellers, Perth; and
>   sold by A. Guthrie, N° 25, South-Bridge, Edinburgh; and Tho. Vernor, Birchin-Lane,
>   London, 1792.
> I vi, 217p; II 221p; III 208p. 8vo.
> C S735.d.79.5-7; EMf; ESTC t163140 (BI E, BL, O; NA CSmH, MB, PPL &c.).

Notes. Trans. of *Gonzalve de Cordoue ou Grenada reconquise* (Paris, 1791).
Table of contents 1, iii–vi. The 'History of the Moors', with notes, takes up the whole of
vol. 1.
Further edns: London, 1793, EM 6842: 2, ESTC n018282; Dublin, 1793 (Printed for
P. Wogan, P. Byrne, J. Moore, W. Jones, and J. Rice, 2 vols., 12mo), ESTC n030611; Dublin,
1793, 12mo), ESTC n030612. Serialised in different trans. as 'Gonzalo de Cordova, or
Granada Recovered', *Lady's Magazine*, 1792–95, RM 472.
This edn. not reviewed; London, 1793 edn. rev. MR n.s. 12: 474 (Dec 1793); AF II: 708.
1793 London edn. adv., 'On the 15th Instant will be published,' SJC 8–10 Nov 1792; adv. as
published LC 72: 471 (13–15 Nov 1792).
   MR refers to rev. of original in App to n.s. vol. 7 [Apr/May 1792] pp. 529–38.

1792: 35   FLORIAN, [Jean Pierre Claris de].
NEW TALES. FROM THE FRENCH OF M. FLORIAN.
> London: Printed for T. and J. Egerton, Whitehall, 1792.
> 283p. 8vo [MR has 12mo]. 3s sewed (CR), 3s 6d sewed (MR, SJC).
> CR n.s. 6: 449–53 (Dec 1792); MR n.s. 12: 212–13 (Oct 1793); AF II: 709.
> BL 012550.k.16; EM 5950: 8; ESTC t144878 (NA DLC).

Notes. Trans. of *Nouvelles nouvelles* (Paris, 1792).

Adv., 'printed on Writing-Paper. . . . Translated from the French Edition just published in Paris', SJC 23–25 Aug 1792.

Further edn: Dublin, 1793 (Printed by William Porter, for P. Wogan, P. Byrne, W. Porter, J. Moore [and 2 others in Dublin], 1 vol., 8vo), ESTC t173399. Extracts from *New Tales* published in 14 magazines between 1792 and 1808, RM 175, 176, 222, 223.

CR: 'We cannot discover in any of these stories much power of invention; but they are narrated with some degree of elegance, and are strictly moral' (p. 449).

MR [John Noorthouck]: 'If stories of this nature possess no great merit, it may be pleaded, in behalf of those now before us, that they are not spun to a tedious length, and that they have all a moral tendency' (p. 213).

MR rev. French original in App to n.s. vol. 9, pp. 488–9 [Dec 1792/Jan 1793].

1792: 36 GUNNING, [Susannah].
ANECDOTES OF THE DELBOROUGH FAMILY. A NOVEL. IN FIVE VOLUMES. BY MRS. GUNNING.

> London: Printed for William Lane, at the Minerva Press, Leadenhall-Street, 1792.
> I 237p; II 228p; III 234p; IV 240p; V 256p. 12mo. 15s sewed (MR, SJC).
> CR n.s. 5: 234 (June 1792); MR n.s. 8: 316–19 (July 1792); AF II: 1760.
> BL 012612.df.14; EM 364: 4; ESTC t067336 (BI C, KIK; NA CtY-BR, IU, NjP, PU &c.).

Notes. Dedication to the Dowager Duchess of Bedford.

Adv., 'Mr Lane most respectfully informs Ladies and Gentlemen, as well as the Trade in general, who have made such numerous applications for this Work, that it is now nearly finished, and will be published in a few days', SDA 27 Feb 1792; adv. 'now printing at the Minerva Press . . . will be published in a few Days', SJC 13–15 Mar 1792; 'The Demand for this excellent Work is now so great, that the first Impression is nearly subscribed for amongst the Trade. Such Ladies and Gentlemen, therefore, as request this Novel, will be early in their Directions to the Booksellers, that they may not be disappointed.' Adv. as published SJC 27–29 Mar 1792.

Adv. at end of *Anna Melvil* (1792: 1) contains identical claim about 'The demand for this excellent Work' except that it is now the 'two first Impressions' that 'have been already subscribed for amongst the Trade'. Adv. SDA 8 Mar 1792 has a long list of additional booksellers.

Adv. SDA 20 Mar 1792 counters 'a most invidious, false report . . . spread by interested parties, founded on their opposition and envy of the rapid success' of Lane's publications, that Gunning is not the author of the book; Lane offers anyone interested a sight of the manuscript and his advertisement is signed by himself, his superintendent, twelve compositors, ten pressmen and his warehouseman.

Further edns: London, 1792, EM 4649: 1, ESTC n032716; Dublin, 1792 (Printed for Messrs. G. Burnet, P. Wogan, P. Byrne, A. Grueber, J. Halpen [and 9 others in Dublin], 3 vols., 12mo) ESTC n030239. German trans. Berlin, 1793 (*Leiden der Familie Delborough*) (RS).

CR: 'Mrs Gunning has been a novelist from her youth; but a more extensive career, greater experience in the manners of the world, and a fancy still warm and vivid, have rendered her last work greatly superior to all her former. The chief merit of the present volumes consists in the delineation of characters. . . . They preserve the distinguishing traits of nature; and, like well-drawn portraits, appear, from these circumstances, to be the representation of originals. In the conduct of the story, there is nothing to blame or praise particularly: in general it possesses merit, though not void of errors. . . .'

MR [William Enfield]: 'As a mere tale, it is not superior, either in invention or arrange-ment, to many other novels. If it be worthy of the praise of ease, sprightliness, and an agree-able diversity of language, it is frequently liable to censure for inaccuracy and redundancy:—but, as an exhibition of portraits freely sketched from real life, it will be perused with pleasure' (p. 316).

1792: 37   [HALL, William Henry].
*THE PATHETIC HISTORY OF EGBERT AND LEONORA. BY A YOUNG LADY, AUTHOR OF THE DEATH OF CAIN. FOUNDED ON REAL FACTS.
> London: Printed for C. Stalker, Stationers Court, Ludgate Hill, and Messrs. Bell, Oxford
>   Street (SDA), 1792 (SDA).
> 2 vols. 5s sewed (SDA).
> No copy located.

Notes: The Death of Cain (1789) App. B: 11.
Adv. SDA 14 May 1792.

1792: 38   HOLCROFT, Thomas.
ANNA ST. IVES: A NOVEL. BY THOMAS HOLCROFT.
> London: Printed for Shepperson and Reynolds, no. 137, Oxford-Street, 1792.
> I 210p; II 227p; III 240p; IV 239p; V 237p; VI 234p; VII 260p. 12mo. £1 1s sewed (MR),
>   £1 1s (CR, SJC, SDA).
> CR n.s. 4: 460–1 (Apr 1792); MR n.s. 8: 151–5 (May 1792); AF II: 2000.
> BL N.1886–88; EM 2012: 1; ESTC t139809 (BI E, NOu; NA CSmH, CtY, MH-H, ViU
>   &c.).

Notes. Epistolary.
Adv., 'On Tuesday next, February 7, will be published', SJC 2–4 Feb 1792; adv. SDA 10 Mar 1792.
Further edns: Dublin, 1792 (Printed for Messrs. P. Byrne, J. Parker, A. Grueber, J. Moore, J. Jones [and 4 others in Dublin], 3 vols., 12mo), ESTC n030252; London, 1800 (WC). German trans. Berlin, 1792–94 (*Anna St. Ives*) (Price).

CR reports with disgust that here 'a philosophic leveller becomes the hero of a novel' (p. 460) and thinks the story 'absurd, often insipid, and unreasonably extended' and its doctrines demanding 'the severest reprehension'.

MR [William Enfield]: 'Improbability on the one side, and triteness on the other, are the Scylla and Charybdis of novelists. . . . To convict a writer of occasionally overstepping the bounds of nature, if it be a reflection on his judgment, is at the same time a compliment to his talents. We may therefore be allowed, without fear of offending the very sensible author of this novel, or its numerous admirers, to give it as our opinion concerning the principal char-acter of his piece, that though it may merit the praise of originality, it is liable to critical cen-sure as a violation of probability' (p. 151). '. . . we readily admit most of the other characters to be natural; and we think the author entitled to great praise for the distinctness with which they are conceived, and for the spirit and energy with which they are expressed' (p. 153). 'The incidents . . . are, on the whole, well contrived, and arranged so as to keep awake the reader's attention. The narrative, though long, is never tedious: but, toward the close, the circum-stances of distress and horror are too minutely detailed' (p. 155).

1792: 39   HOLLOWAY, W[illiam].

DOVEDELL HALL; OR, THE FORTUNATE EXILES. A NOVEL. INTER-SPERSED WITH SOME ORIGINAL POETRY. BY W. HOLLOWAY.

Waymouth [*sic*]: Printed for J. Love, By S. Powell, and W. Holloway, 1792.
vi, 119p. 8vo.
MH-H *EC8.H7288 792d; EM 997: 11; ESTC n000747.

Notes. Dedication to Sir John Smith, Bart. p. [iii]; preface v–vi.
Extracts from *Dovedell Hall* published in *Lady's New and Elegant Pocket Magazine*, 1796,
RM 326.

1792: 40   HUNTER, Maria.

FITZROY; OR, IMPULSE OF THE MOMENT. A NOVEL. IN TWO VOL-UMES. BY MARIA HUNTER.

London: Printed for William Lane, at the Minerva Press, Leadenhall-Street, 1792.
I xii, 196p; II 251p. 12mo. 6s (CR), 6s sewed (SJC).
CR n.s. 5: 234–5 (June 1792); AF II: 2122.
C S727.d.79.82-83; EM 3461: 8; ESTC t129871 (BI BL; NA CtY, IU, MH-H,
PU &c.).

Notes. Dedication to John Doyle, M.P. 1, i–v; preface vii–xii. 1 p. adv. end vol. 2.
BL copy has pages missing between iv and ix of vol. 1.
Adv., 'In the Press', SDA 2 Dec 1791; adv., 'now printing at the Minerva Press . . . by Mrs
Hunter, of Titchfield-street . . . will be published in a few Days', SJC 13–15 Mar 1792; 'This
Novel, from its interesting Merit, is warmly recommended to the Patronage of the Publick,
as it contains Lessons of Life, blended with Entertainment, and is so far above Mediocrity,
that it may be ranked in the first Class of Works of a similar Nature.' In Lane adv. SDA 27 Feb
1792 author's name given as Anna Maria Hunter.
German trans. Leipzig, 1793 (*Lehrreiches Leben des Britten G. Fitzroy*) (RS).

CR: 'Mrs Hunter seems to possess talents and acquisitions much beyond modern
authoresses, or the ladies of the drama, with whom she ranks. Her language is easy and elegant; the adventures well conducted, and the denouement natural. Perhaps she has not
involved her tale with sufficient art to render it highly interesting; and the characters scarcely
start from the canvas with sufficient spirit. But, on the whole, her work is very pleasing and
entertaining, and the little disquisitions, with which the narrative is interspersed, shew much
ingenuity and no inconsiderable share of learning.'

1792: 41   [HUTCHINSON, William].

THE DOUBTFUL MARRIAGE A NARRATIVE DRAWN FROM CHAR-ACTERS IN REAL LIFE.

London: Printed for B. Law and Son, 1792.
I 212p; II 218p; III 173p. 12mo. 7s 6d (CR), 7s 6d sewed (LC).
CR n.s. 6: 561 (App [Dec 1792/Jan 1793]); AF II: 2138.
C 7720.d.734–736; ESTC t162923.

Notes. Epistolary.
Adv. LC 71: 422 (28 Apr–1 May 1792); Law's address, No. 13, Ave-Maria-lane, is given and
additional bookseller is F. Jollie, Carlisle.

Further edn: Dublin, 1793 (Printed for Messrs. P. Wogan, P. Byrne, W. Jones, R. McAllister, J. Rice, G. Folingsby, 1 vol., 12mo), ESTC n008296.

CR: 'This is an interesting and distressing tale, perhaps a narrative of real events, for they are not beyond the limits of probability. The characters are well drawn. . . .'

KIMBER, Edward, THE GENEROUS BRITON. First published 1765 JR 924, AF I: 1517.

1792: 42   KNIGHT, E[llis] Cornelia.
MARCUS FLAMINIUS; OR, A VIEW OF THE MILITARY, POLITICAL, AND SOCIAL LIFE OF THE ROMANS: IN A SERIES OF LETTERS FROM A PATRICIAN TO HIS FRIEND; IN THE YEAR DCC.LXII FROM THE FOUNDATION OF ROME, TO THE YEAR DCC.LXIX. BY E. CORNELIA KNIGHT. IN TWO VOLUMES.

> London: Printed for C. Dilly, in the Poultry, 1792.
> I xii, 402p; II 341p. 8vo. 10s 6d boards (MR, SJC).
> MR n.s. 9: 164–9 (Oct 1792); AF II: 2416.
> BL 803.e.8,9; EM 4427: 2; ESTC t092285 (BI INV, O; NA CtY, CSmH, DLC, IU, MH-H, TxU &c.; EA GOT).

Notes. Dedication to the Earl of Orford [i.e. Horace Walpole]. Epistolary.
Adv., 'The 21st of this Month will be published', SJC 10–12 Apr 1792.
Further edns: London, 1795, ESTC n022577; London, 1808 (WC, NSTC). Italian trans. Rome, 1794 (*Lettere di M. Flaminio a Settimio*) (BN); French trans. Paris, 1801 (*Vie privée, politique et militaire des romains*) (WC, NSTC).

MR [William Enfield]: 'To mix fictitious incidents with real facts so evidently tends to confound the reader's conceptions, that it may, without hesitation, be pronounced an injudicious method of communicating historical information to young persons. . . . Even a reader already well acquainted with history may find some difficulty in marking the exact line, which separates dramatic fiction from historic truth: to a tyro in historical learning, the task would be wholly impracticable. Still greater objections seem to lie against those prose writings which undertake at once to amuse by fiction, and to inform by a relation of facts; except when the narrative is authenticated by means of accurate and minute references to authorities. . . . Marcus Flaminius partakes more of the fictitious than the historical character' (p. 164). 'If the letters do not afford a perfect delineation of Roman manners, they nevertheless contain a very entertaining narrative of incidents ingeniously contrived; and they express, in elegant, and often animated, language, such sentiments as may be easily conceived to have arisen from the circumstances of the story' (p. 165).

1792: 43   [MACKENZIE, Anna Maria].
SLAVERY: OR, THE TIMES. IN TWO VOLUMES. BY THE AUTHOR OF MONMOUTH, THE DANISH MASSACRE, &C.

> London: Printed for G. G. J. and J. Robinsons [*sic*], Pater-Noster-Row; and J. Dennis, Middle-Row, Holborn, 1792.
> I 221p; II 238p. 8vo. 6s sewed (CR, MR).

CR n.s. 9: 194–7 (Oct 1793); MR n.s. 10: 224–6 (Feb 1793); AF II: 2662.
BL 1607/2636 [imperf.]; EM 7370: 2; ESTC t119024 (BI Lu).

Notes. Epistolary.
Monmouth 1790: 55; *Danish Massacre* 1791: 47.
Adv., with quotation from MR, SJC 13–16 Apr 1793.
Further edn: Dublin, 1793 (Printed for Messrs. P. Wogan, P. Byrne, J, Moore, W. Jones, and J. Rice, 1 vol., 12mo), EM 4267: 17, ESTC n033438.

CR: 'The best commendation we can fairly give this work is, that the feelings it raises are uniformly on the side of virtue, but its power of raising feelings is but feeble' (p. 194).

MR [William Enfield]: 'The reflections and feelings, which such situations may be supposed to excite, are expressed in natural and animated language. Other characters, both virtuous and vicious, are introduced and well supported; the present state of manners is, in many particulars, strongly delineated; and the general effect of the work is, to leave a forcible impression on the mind of the reader, that what is called education, in civilized countries, is often nothing better than corruption' (pp. 224–5).

1792: 44   MARMONTEL, [Jean-François].
THE TALES OF AN EVENING, FOLLOWED BY THE HONEST BRETON. TRANSLATED FROM THE FRENCH OF M. MARMONTEL. [VOL. I]. TALES. TRANSLATED FROM THE FRENCH OF M. MARMONTEL. CONSISTING OF THE VILLAGE BREAKFASTS, THE LESSON OF MISFORTUNE, THE ERROR OF A GOOD FATHER, PALAEMON, A PASTORAL, AND THE SOLITARY FUGITIVES OF MURCIA. VOL. II. NEW MORAL TALES; CONSISTING OF THE TRIPOD OF HELEN; THE SCHOOL FOR FRIENDSHIP; THERE WAS NO HELP FOR IT; AND THE WATERMAN OF BESONS. NOW FIRST TRANSLATED FROM THE FRENCH OF MARMONTEL. VOL. III. NEW MORAL TALES. NOW FIRST TRANSLATED FROM THE FRENCH OF M. MARMONTEL. IN FOUR VOLUMES. VOL. IV. CONTAINING THE CASKET, THEIR OWN RIVALS, AND THE RECOLLECTIONS OF THE FIRE-SIDE.

London: Printed for J. Bew, No. 28, Paternoster-Row, 1792 [vols. 1–2].
London: Printed for J. Bew, Paternoster-Row, 1793 [vol. 3].
London: Printed for Jane Bew, no. 28, Paternoster-Row, and Hookham and Carpenter, New Bond-Street, 1794 [vol. 4].
I 236p; II vii, 266p; III 233p; IV 135p. 12mo. 6s sewed (CR, MR)[vols. 1 and 2], 3s (ER) [vol. 3], 3s sewed each of vols. 1–3 (SJC), 1s 6d (SJC) [vol. 4].
CR n.s. 5: 53–60 (May 1792), MR n.s. 8: 339 (July 1792) vols. 1–2; EngR 21: 305–6 (Apr 1793) vol. 3; AF II: 2718–2720.
BL 634.e.12-13; EM 8117: 15 [vol. 1], EM 2551: 1 [vol. 2], EMf [vol. 3]; ESTC t090268, t090269 and t090270 (BI AWn [vols. 1–3 only]; NA CLU-S/C [vols. 1–3 only], NA CaOHM [vol. 3 only], PPL [vol. 1 only]).

Notes. Trans. of *Les déjeunés du village* (Liège, 1791), *L'erreur d'un bon père* (Liège, 1791), *L'école de l'amitié* (Liège, 1792) and tales from the 2 vols. of *Nouveaux Contes Moraux* (Liège, 1792), all different to *Nouveaux Contes Moraux* first pub. Paris, 1765.

2 pp. advs. end vol 2.

Vol. 1 adv. 'In the Press, and in a few Days will be published', SDA 11 Nov 1791; adv. as published SDA 10 Dec 1791 and SJC 10–13 Dec 1791; the second volume is mentioned as 'In the Press, and speedily will be published'.

Vol. 2 adv., 'In a few Days will be published', SJC 10–12 Jan 1792; adv. as published SJC 7–9 Feb 1792.

Vol. 3 adv., 'In a few Days will be published', SDA 8 Dec 1792 and SJC 31 Jan–2 Feb 1793; adv. quotes EngR and AR comments on the preceding vols.

3-vol. version adv. SDA 10 Aug 1793; 'The Public is cautioned against a spurious Edition printed at Perth, of which one part is a compleat piracy of the above translation, another consists of Tales that bear no resemblance to Marmontel's', and a third is very badly translated (adv. gives examples).

Vol. 4 adv., 'In the Press, and speedily will be published', SDA 10 Aug 1793; adv. as published SDA 26 Dec 1793; also adv. 2nd edn. of vols. 1–3, 'carefully improved and corrected': 'The two first volumes of the former Edition having been translated by different hands, and hastily brought out to avoid a threatened opposition, many inequalities of language occurred, and many errors escaped the pen and the press. In the present Edition great pains and considerable abilities have been bestowed in translating all the defective parts anew, and in rendering the whole of those two Volumes equal to the third, and as nearly so as may be to the excellent original.' The 'CAUTION to the PUBLIC and the TRADE' about the Perth 'spurious work under the same title' is expanded and the work 'said to be translated by a Mr Heron'.

Further edns: Dublin, 1792 (Printed for Messrs. P. Wogan, P. Byrne, A. Grueber, J. Moore, W. Jones, R. Macallister, and J. Rice, 2 vols., 12mo), ESTC n049122; London, 1799 [abridged], EM 4441: 4, ESTC t090961; NSTC lists edn. in 1825. ESTC has 3 entries for a different 3-vol. trans., *A New Collection of Moral Tales*, by Robert Heron, published in Perth in 1792: ESTC n060589, ESTC n060588 and ESTC t132833. Many extracts in different translations published in a variety of magazines between 1792 and 1810, RM 371, 665, 666, 751–753, 896, 1246, 1332.

CR: 'Though these Tales are not equal to the former volumes of Marmontel, and are sometimes prolix with the garrulity of old age, yet they have great merit; and, under the flower of amusement, present the fruit of morality' (p. 53). 'We must confess that we have perused few of them, without feeling those tears start from our eyes, which are sweeter than those of joy' (p. 54). 'The translation is tolerable, though sometimes quaint, and sometimes mistaken' (p. 60).

MR [William Enfield]: 'We confess that we have not perused these pieces with that degree of pleasure with which we read the author's former tales; they appear to us to want much of the vivacity and gaiety which have rendered Marmontel's tales so popular. Many of these are, however, interesting and pathetic, and adapted to impress the mind with good moral sentiments.'

EngR: 'Perhaps they are not equal to Marmontel's first productions of a similar nature— but they are by no means unworthy of him' (p. 305).

1792: 45   [MATHEWS, Eliza Kirkham].
THE COUNT DE HOENSDERN; A GERMAN TALE. BY THE AUTHOR OF
CONSTANCE, THE PHAROS, ARGUS, &C. &C. IN THREE VOLUMES.

> London: Printed for T. Hookham and J. Carpenter, Old and New Bond-Street, 1792.
> I 267p; II 258p; III 288p. 12mo. 9s sewed (MR, SDA).

MR n.s. 12: 337–8 (Nov 1793); AF II: 2756.

DLC PR 4987.M185C7; ESTC n028052 (NA IU, ViU).

Notes. FC says author attribution is doubtful.

Dedication to Lady ******, signed 'The Author'. 5 pp. advs. end vol. 1.

Constance 1785: 38; *Argus* 1789: 53.

Adv. SDA 6 Nov 1792; adv. SJC 17–20 Nov 1792.

Further edn: Dublin, 1793 (Printed for Messrs. P. Wogan, P. Byrne, J. Parker, W. Jones, and J. Rice, 2 vols., 12mo), EM 2729: 13, ESTC t119886.

MR [Thomas Holcroft]: 'That she can think, philosophize, and pourtray character with a certain degree of penetration and energy, we gladly discover: but we conceive that she may yet possess these faculties in much higher perfection. In general, she recollects but two species of character; the one unsuspectingly virtuous, the other trammelled in all the hypocrisy of vice. The principal incidents in the present tale are produced by this reiterated and palling machinery. . . . Her philosophy is no less erroneous. Her characters are virtuous or vicious *by nature.* . . . The morality of this ingenious writer is still more blameable. The continual tendency of the work before us is to persuade us that there is little else than misery on earth.'

1792: 46   PALMER, Charlotte.
INTEGRITY AND CONTENT, AN ALLEGORY; &C. &C. &C. BY CHARLOTTE PALMER.

> London: Printed by Hixon and Griffiths, Brydges-Street, Covent Garden, for Hookham and Carpenter, Old and New Bond Street, 1792.
>
> 44p. 4to. 2s (t.p., CR, MR).
>
> CR n.s. 6: 479 (Dec 1792); MR n.s. 9: 235 (Oct 1792); AF II: 3199.
>
> CU-BANC PR5115 P5515 1792; xESTC.

Notes. Dedication to Mrs Goodrich of Queen-Square, Bloomsbury pp. [3]–4, signed C. Palmer, Mill-Hill, Hendon, Middlesex; text begins on p. 5.

CR: 'We wish miss Palmer better employment: it is a barren field, where the best cultivation can produce few flowers, and our author is not particularly happy in her attempt.'

MR [William Enfield]: 'Without that rich variety of scenery and imagery which genius alone can supply, a moral allegory in prose is not likely to engage much attention. Of the present attempt, the chief recommendation is that it is neatly written; and that it teaches, in a way which may, perhaps, to some young minds, be more impressive than simple precepts, several important lessons of morality.'

1792: 47   PALMER, Charlotte.
IT IS AND IT IS NOT A NOVEL. IN TWO VOLUMES. BY CHARLOTTE PALMER.

> London: Printed for Hookham and Carpenter, Old and New Bond-Street, 1792.
>
> I ix, 337p; II 376p. 12mo. 6s (CR, adv.), 6s sewed (SDA).
>
> CR n.s. 4: 472 (Apr 1792); AF II: 3200.
>
> BL C.107.bb.54; EMf; ESTC t211729 (BI O; NA DLC).

Notes. Dedication to Mrs Douglas of St Alban's in Kent. Preface 1, v–ix, followed by 1 p. advs.; 2 pp. advs. end vol. 2. Text of novel starts on p. 5 in both vols. Epistolary.

BL copy vol. 2 pp. 365–76 duplicated.

Adv. SDA 7 Mar 1792.

Adv. end vol. 3 of *Edelfrida* (1792: 7).

CR: 'No, my dear,—"It is *not* a novel:" but be a good girl; do so no more; and we will say nothing about it this time.'

1792: 48 PERRIN, {Pierre}; [STREET, Thomas George (*trans.*)].
THE FEMALE WERTER. A NOVEL. TRANSLATED FROM THE FRENCH OF M. PERRIN. IN TWO VOLUMES.

London: Printed for G. G. J. and J. Robinson, 1792.

I iv, 216p; II 210p. 8vo [CR and MR have 12mo]. 6s (CR), 5s sewed (MR, SJC).

CR n.s. 4: 235–6 (Feb 1792); MR n.s. 8: 337–9 (July 1792); AF II: 3310.

ViU *PZ2.P47F 1792; ESTC n018697 (NA NjP, PU).

Notes. Trans. of *Werthérie* (Paris, 1791), an imitation of Johann Wolfgang von Goethe's *Die Leiden des jungen Werthers* (Leipzig, 1774).

Robinson paid 8 gns. on 11 Oct 1791 to Thomas George Street 'for the translation of a french Novel, entitled female Werter' (RA).

'Prefatory observation by the author' signed 'Pierre Perrin'. Epistolary.

Adv. SJC 21–24 Jan 1792.

Further edn: Dublin, 1792 (Printed for P. Wogan, P. Byrne, A. Grueber, J. Halpen, J. Moore, J. Jones, W. Jones, R. M'Allister, J. Rice, G. Draper, 1 vol., 12mo) ESTC n018771.

CR: 'The pernicious poison of the "Sorrows of Werter" wanted not a more general dissemination. But the present work is less dangerous, because it is less interesting; and when, as a concomitant motive to suicide, the little mortification of failing in the performance of a concerto from timidity is added, the whole is rendered ridiculous. . . . If we except the pernicious lesson, some parts of this work deserve our applause, as indicating a knowledge of the human heart, and containing various scenes elegantly descriptive.'

MR [William Enfield] mocks the 'extravagance of this tale' and describes it as 'sentimental trash; fit only to convert our boarding-school misses, first into melting Julias, "sighing like Furnace" for forbidden fruit, and then into frantic Elizas, ready whenever the occasion calls, to terminate an *unfortunate* attachment by a voluntary exit . . .' (pp. 338–9).

1792: 49 [RAITHBY, John].
DELINEATIONS OF THE HEART; OR, THE HISTORY OF HENRY BENNET. A TRAGI-COMI-SATIRIC ESSAY, ATTEMPTED IN THE MANNER OF FIELDING. IN THREE VOLUMES.

London: Printed for T. Hookham and J. Carpenter, Old and New Bond-Street; and sold by W. Bent, Paternoster-Row; J. Denis, No. 6, Middle-Row, Holborn; and G. Kearsley, No. 46, Fleet-Street, n.d. [1792].

I 276p; II 267p; III 274p. 12mo. 9s (CR), 9s sewed (MR, SJC).

CR n.s. 4: 472 (Apr 1792); MR n.s. 8: 107 (May 1792); AF II: 3680.

BL C.171.b.23; EMf; ESTC t187269 (BI C; NA DLC, IU).

Notes. 8-pp. list of subscribers.

Adv. SJC 24–26 Jan 1792. Adv. SDA 15 June 1793 and SJC 22–25 June 1793 as 'by Henry Bennet'.

Further edns: Dublin, 1792 (Printed for Messrs. P. Wogan, P. Byrne, A. Grueber, W. M'Kenzie, J. Moore [and 4 others in Dublin], 2 vols., 12mo), EM 2372: 2, ESTC t129538; London, 1793 (WC), xESTC. French trans. Paris, 1794 (*Henry Bennett et Julie Johnson, ou les esquisses du coeur*; t.p. claims A. M. Bennett as author) (BGR).

CR: 'It is the form of Fielding, and occasionally his semblance will rise for a moment, and the "eyes are made the fools of the other senses." But we want his spirit, his wit, that clue which leads to the inmost recesses of the heart, and which he almost exclusively possessed .... in spite of some humour and a few interesting scenes, we are compelled to dismiss this work with reprobation.'

MR [William Enfield]: 'He modestly professes ... rather to have attempted Fielding's style of composition, than the comic nature of the facts with which the works of that great comic writer abound:—but what is the manner of Fielding, without his lively delineation of character, his comic humour and wit, and the originality and shrewdness of his reflections? ... Except the character of a faithful and able preceptor, which is well sketched in the first part of the story, and the introductory chapters of general reflection, placed, *after the manner of Fielding*, at the head of each book, we find nothing in this novel to distinguish it from the ordinary run of love tales.'

1792: 50   ROBINSON, M[ary].
VANCENZA; OR, THE DANGERS OF CREDULITY. IN TWO VOLUMES. BY MRS. M. ROBINSON, AUTHORESS OF THE POEMS OF LAURA MARIA, AINSI VA LE MONDE, &C. &C.

> London: Printed for the Authoress; and sold by Mr. Bell, at the British Library, Strand, 1792.
> I 157p; II 151p. 8vo [MR and CR have 12mo]. 5s (CR), 5s sewed (MR, SJC).
> CR n.s. 4: 268–72 (Mar 1792); MR n.s. 7: 298–303 (Mar 1792); AF II: 3838.
> CtY Im R564.792v; xESTC (BI BRu ENC).

Notes. Vol. 2 of CtY copy is of 3rd edn. 2 pp. advs. end vol. 1; 2 pp. advs. end vol. 2.
Adv., 'In the Press, and on the 1st of February will be published', SJC 24–26 Jan 1792; adv. as published, 'The New Edition', SJC 4–7 Feb 1792.
3rd edn., 'with considerable Additions', adv. SDA 2 Mar 1792: 'The uncommon demand for this Work having already taken the whole of the Second Edition, the Third is now in the Press, and will be ready for delivery next week at Mr Bell's British Library, Strand.'
Further edns: London, 1792, ESTC n047868; London, 1792, EM 279: 3, ESTC t068572; Dublin, 1792 (Printed for P. Wogan, P. Byrne, A. Grueber, J. Moore, J. Jones [and 3 others in Dublin], 1 vol., 12mo), ESTC t212589; London, 1793, ESTC n046129; London, 1810 (WC). Extracts from *Vancenza* published in 4 magazines, 1792, RM 1008. French trans. Paris, 1793 (*Vancenza ou les dangers de crédulité*) (BGR); German trans. Berlin, 1793 (*Vancenza oder die Gefahren der Leichtgläubigkeit*) (EAG).

CR: '... we think this novel unworthy of the high reputation of its author ...' (p. 268). 'The language is in general highly and poetically laboured. It is refined into obscurity; and perspicuity of description is often sacrificed to a flowing period. There are many instances where, but from the future pages, it is difficult to discover the events in the blaze of description ...' (p. 269).

MR [William Enfield]: 'Vancenza ... is not written in the simple style: but it is written, and in our opinion well-written, in the style of elegance peculiar to Mrs R. The richness of fancy and of language, which the fair author had so successfully displayed in her poetical productions, . . . she has transferred to prose narration; and has produced a tale, which, we venture to predict, will be much read and admired' (p. 299). 'The authoress . . . often overcharges her language with luxuriant imagery: nevertheless, on the whole, it will not be an immoderate panegyric, to say of this elegant little work, that it is the pleasing production of a fertile fancy, and a feeling heart' (p. 303).

1792: 51   [ROWSON, Susanna].
THE FILLE DE CHAMBRE, A NOVEL, IN THREE VOLUMES, BY THE
AUTHOR OF THE INQUISITOR, &C. &C.
> London: Printed for William Lane, at the Minerva, Leadenhall-Street, 1792.
> I vi, 196p; II 180p; III 247p. 12mo. 9s (EngR), 9s sewed (SJC).
> EngR 22: 307 (Oct 1793).
> AUG 02/III.9.8.177; xESTC (NA InU-Li [vol. 2 only]).

Notes. Preface 1, i–vi. 1 p. adv. end vol. 3.
The Inquisitor 1788: 70.
Adv. SJC 24–26 Oct 1793.
Further edns: Philadelphia, 1794, ESTC w014479; Baltimore, 1795, ESTC w039052; Baltimore, 1795, ESTC w000234; Boston, 1814 (WC); Boston, 1831 (WC) [both Boston edns. *Rebecca, or the Fille de Chambre*].

EngR: 'The Fille de Chambre is a pleasing tale. The author has selected his heroine from that rank which impudent and upstart men, enriched by vicious practices, have dared to call the lower rank of life—the *canaille*, or "the swinish multitude."'

1792: 52   SMITH, Charlotte.
DESMOND. A NOVEL, IN THREE VOLUMES. BY CHARLOTTE SMITH.
> London: Printed for G. G. J. and J. Robinson, Pater-Noster-Row, 1792.
> I ix, 280p; II 296p; III 348p. 12mo. 9s sewed (CR, MR).
> CR n.s. 6: 99–105 (Sept 1792); MR n.s. 9: 406–13 (Dec 1792); AF II: 4132.
> BL N.2355; EM 3021: 7; ESTC t073500 (BI C, O; NA CSmH, CtY, ICN, IU, MH-H, NjP, PU, ViU &c.).

Notes. Robinson paid £135.5.0 between 7 Nov 1791 and 12 Apr 1792 to Charlotte Smith, possibly for *Desmond* (RA).
Preface i–ix signed Charlotte Smith, London, 20 June 1792. Epistolary.
Adv., 'Next Week will be published', SJC 19–21 June 1792; adv. as published SJC 28–30 June 1792.
Further edns: London, 1792, EM 7574: 5, ESTC t064731; Dublin, 1792 (Printed for P. Wogan, P. Byrne, J. Moore, W. M'Kenzie, H. Colbert [and 9 others in Dublin], 2 vols., 12mo), ESTC t064732. French trans. Paris, 1793 (*Desmond ou l'amant philanthrope*) (BGR); German trans. Hamburg, 1793 (*Desmond, eine Geschichte in Briefen*) (RS). Facs: Fcy.

CR: 'The principal novelty in the conduct of this tale is the introduction of French politics, and a more happy description of French manners than we usually meet with in similar publications. . . . in all her novels, the descriptions of scenery and situation are peculiarly excellent. Her politics we cannot always approve of. Connected with the reformers, and the revolutionists, she has borrowed her colouring from them, and represented their conduct in the most favourable light' (p. 100).

MR [William Enfield]: 'Mrs Smith, who has already favoured the public with several instructive as well as entertaining works of this kind, has, in the present publication, ventured beyond the beaten track, so far as to interweave with her narrative many political discussions. Being very justly of opinion, that the great events which are passing in the world are no less interesting to women than to men, and that in her solicitude to discharge the domestic duties, a woman ought not to forget that, in common with her father and her husband, her brothers and sons, she is a citizen; Mrs Smith introduces, where the course of the tale will easily admit of such interruptions, conversations on the principles and occurrences of the French revolution; and these conversations she enlivens with humorous strokes of character, which prove that she has observed the present state of society with an attentive and discriminating eye' (p. 406).

1792: 53   [STREET, Miss].
*THE RECLUSE OF THE APPENINES, A TALE, IN TWO VOLUMES. BY THE AUTHOR OF THE LAKE OF WINDERMERE.

> London: Printed for William Lane, at the Minerva-Press, Leadenhall-Street, 1792 (adv.).
> 2 vols.
> No copy located.

Notes. Epistolary.
The Lake of Windermere 1791: 69.
Adv. end vol. 1 of *Matilda Fitz-Aubin* (1792: 20); adv. reprints t.p.
Further edn: Dublin, 1793 (Printed for Messrs. P. Wogan, P. Byrne, J. Moore, W. Jones, and J. Rice, 1 vol., 12mo), EM 6150: 2; ESTC t119375.

1792: 54   [STREET, Miss].
THEODORE, A DOMESTIC TALE, IN TWO VOLUMES.

> London: Printed for William Lane, at the Minerva-Press, Leadenhall-Street, 1792.
> I 178p; II 168+p. 12mo. 6s sewed (SJC, adv.).
> Corvey; CME 3-628-45215-5; xESTC.

Notes. Blakey: attributed to Miss Street by a Minerva Library catalogue of 1814.
2 pp. advs. end vol. 1. Epistolary. Vol. 2 of Corvey copy ends with p. 168 (evidently not the end of the novel) and continues with repeats of pp. 169–78 of vol. 1 plus the 2 pp. advs. which end vol. 1.
Adv. SJC 24–26 Oct 1793; 'A pleasing Story, very well told.'
Adv. end vol. 5 of Pilkington's *Rosina* (1793: 35).

1792: 55   [THELWALL, John].
THE ROCK OF MODREC, OR, THE LEGEND OF SIR ELTRAM; AN ETHICAL ROMANCE. TRANSLATED FROM AN ANCIENT BRITISH MANUSCRIPT, LATELY DISCOVERED AMONG THE RUINS OF AN ABBEY IN NORTH WALES.

> London: Printed for W. Bent, Pater Noster Row, 1792.
> I 152p; II 199p. 8vo [EngR has 12mo]. 5s (EngR), 5s sewed (SJC).

EngR 19: 388 (May 1792); AF II: 3854.
BL N.1659; EMf; ESTC t070920 (BI AWn, E; NA OU, ICU).
Notes. Adv., 'Tuesday, Feb. 21, will be published', SJC 14–16 Feb 1792.
Adv., 'Lately published', SJC 13–15 Nov 1794: 'By John Thelwall'.
Further edn: Dublin, 1792 (Printed by Thomas Burnside, for Messrs. P. Wogan, P. Byrne, A. Grueber, W. M'Kenzie, J. Moore [and 4 others in Dublin], 1 vol., 12mo), ESTC n013279.

EngR: 'The author of this romance is an admirer of the age of knight errantry and chivalry. Whoever delights in the perusal of scenes of horror, will here find ample satisfaction.'

1792: 56 [TOMLINS, Elizabeth Sophia].
MEMOIRS OF A BARONESS. BY THE AUTHOR OF THE CONQUESTS OF THE HEART AND THE VICTIM OF FANCY. IN TWO VOLUMES.

London: Printed for G. G. J. and J. Robinson, Pater-Noster-Row, n.d. [ESTC: 1792?].
I vii, 175p; II 196p. 12mo. 5s sewed (MR, SJC).
MR n.s. 8: 460–1 (Aug 1792).
BL 12612.aaa.38; EM 124: 7; ESTC t066382.

Notes. Robinson paid 11 gns. on 15 June 1793 to Eliz. S. Tomlins 'in full for my Interest & Share in the Baroness D'Alantun' (RA).
Publication date has been erased on both t.ps. Prefatory advertisement (1, v–vii) notes that the novel is partly founded on a French original.
Conquests of the Heart 1785: 45; *Victim of Fancy* 1787: 51.
Adv. SJC 21–24 Jan 1792.
Further edn: Dublin, 1792 (Printed for P. Wogan, P. Byrne, A. Grueber, J. Halpen, J. Moore [and 4 others in Dublin], 1 vol., 12mo), ESTC n021927.

MR [William Enfield]: 'The scene of this novel is laid in the court of Henry IV. of France; and the principal incident, (that for which, indeed, the whole novel appears to have been written,) is the romantic attempt made by Mademoiselle de St Aubin to obtain a sight of Marshal Biron, whom she had long secretly loved, and who was now imprisoned for treason, and condemned to die. Beside this story, which is well related, the novel has little to fix the reader's attention.'

1792: 57 [WILSON, Charles Henry].
THE WANDERING ISLANDER; OR, THE HISTORY OF MR. CHARLES NORTH. IN TWO VOLUMES.

London: Printed for J. Ridgway, York-Street, St James's-Square, 1792.
I ii, xiv, 162p; II iii, 263p. 12mo. 5s sewed (CR, MR).
CR n.s. 8: 298–300 (July 1793); MR n.s. 12: 338–9 (Nov 1793); AF II: 4850.
BL 1155.i.4; EM 2899: 4; ESTC t117013 (BI O; NA IU, NjP).
Notes. Dedication to Lord Rawdon. Text of novel starts on p. 15 in vol. 1 and p. 5 in vol. 2.

CR: 'Like those of the celebrated Sterne, this eccentric production is a curious combination of the humourous with the pathetic; and contains a greater number of strange anecdotes, of singular and *outre* observations, and of humourous traits, than any publication of the kind, which has lately fallen under our notice. The author, indeed, appears to be not only conversant with the world, but possessed of a greater stock of uncommon miscellaneous reading than most modern writers—and has seldom failed to seize the most ludicrous and apposite passages, which with great dexterity he introduces into his letters' (pp. 298–9).

MR [William Enfield]: 'Had this writer entitled his work merely *the Wanderer*, it would have been impossible in one word more properly to express the character of his book. The author rambles from topic to topic with so much rapidity, that the reader never knows where to find him. It is impossible to refer the work to any class of writing, or to describe it under any of the characters which the laws of criticism have provided. It is not properly narrative, for it pursues no regular story; yet it contains tales of both the humorous and pathetic kind. It abounds too much in low jokes, or in dull small talk, to merit the general character of a witty, humorous, or satirical, work; yet it is not wholly destitute of humour and satire' (pp. 338–9).

1792: 58   [ZIYA UL-DIN NAKSHABI]; [GERRANS, B. (*trans.*)].
TALES OF A PARROT; DONE INTO ENGLISH, FROM A PERSIAN MANUSCRIPT, INTITLED, TOOTI NAMEH. BY A TEACHER OF THE PERSIC, ARABIC, HEBREW, SYRIAC, CHALDAIC, GREEK, LATIN, ITALIAN, FRENCH, AND ENGLISH LANGUAGES.

> London: Printed for the Translator, at the Minerva Press; and sold by Mess. Robson, New Bond-Street; B. Law, Ave-Maria Lane; and W. Lane, Leadenhall-Street, 1792.
> xiii, 188p. 8vo. 4s boards (CR), 4s sewed (MR).
> CR n.s. 6: 293–7 (Nov 1792); MR n.s. 10: 109 (Jan 1793).
> BL 635.f.18(3); EM 2447: 9; ESTC t117592 (BI E, O; NA CaOHM, CLU-S/C, NjR &c.).

Notes. Trans. by B. Gerrans from the Persian compilation *Tuti-nama.*
Following the Prolegomena (v–xiii) and 2 unn. contents pp. there is an advertisement by the editor addressed to those who want to learn various languages, including 'Gentlemen who are destined for India, who are desirous of learning the Persian, or Arabic Tongues'.
Further edns. [various translations]: Calcutta, 1792 (WC); London, 1801 (WC); London, n.d. [*c.*1810–1815] (WC); London, 1845 (WC).

> CR: '... we can hardly encourage the translator to proceed, though his translation be well executed, and to all appearance faithful. Some of the tales are amusing, but to a reader of the Arabian Nights most of them will appear insipid, and destitute of invention' (p. 295).

> MR [William Enfield]: 'It is of very little consequence to the public, whether extravagance and absurdity be of English or of Persian growth; and we apprehend that few persons will give themselves the trouble to ascertain the truth in the present case.'

1793

THE ADVANTAGES OF EDUCATION
See WEST, Jane

1793: 1   ANON.
ARGAL; OR THE SILVER DEVIL, BEING THE ADVENTURES OF AN EVIL SPIRIT, COMPRISING A SERIES OF INTERESTING ANECDOTES IN PUBLIC AND PRIVATE LIFE, WITH WHICH THE DEMON BECAME

ACQUAINTED IN VARIOUS PARTS OF THE WORLD, DURING HIS CONFINEMENT IN THE METALLINE SUBSTANCE TO WHICH HE WAS CONDEMNED. RELATED BY HIMSELF. IN TWO VOLUMES.

> London: Printed for T. Vernor, Birchin-Lane, Cornhill, and Rawson and Co. Hull, n.d. [ESTC: 1793?].
>
> I iv, xxiv, 216p; II iv, 205p. 12mo. 6s (CR), 6s sewed (MR, SDA).
>
> CR n.s. 9: 102–4 (Sept 1793); MR n.s. 12: 474–5 (Dec 1793); AF II: 134.
>
> BL 12611.i.20; EM 197: 2; ESTC t057426 (BI MRu; NA CLU-S/C, MH-H, PU &c.).

Notes. WC: sometimes attributed to George Hadley.

Vol. 1 table of contents i–iv; Preface iii–xxiv; then pagination continuous Roman-Arabic; text of novel starts on p. 25. Vol. 2 table of contents i–iv; text of novel starts on p. 3.

Adv. SDA 4 May 1793; adv. SJC 14–16 May 1793.

Further edns: Dublin, 1794 (Printed by Zachariah Jackson, 1 vol., 12mo), ESTC t066887; London, 1798 (WC), xESTC. Facs: SO.

CR: 'This is an attempt, but not a happy one, to interweave with some passages of history, particularly those which of themselves bear a romantic air, a number of imaginary adventures' (p. 102).

MR [Thomas Holcroft]: 'The plan of this novel, or this collection of anecdotes and adventures, rather resembles that of "Chrysal, or the Adventures of a Guinea," than that of *Le Diable Boiteux*; though it participates of both. It is not, however, executed with the animation, satire, or pleasantry of either' (p. 475). [Charles Johnstone's *Chrysal: or the Adventures of a Guinea* (1760/65), JR 577, AF I: 1440–1442; Alain René Le Sage's *Le Diable Boiteux* trans. Smollett as *The Devil Upon Crutches* (1750), JR 37.]

1793: 2   ANON.

BELLEVILLE LODGE, A NOVEL, IN TWO VOLUMES.

> London: Printed for William Lane, at the Minerva Press, Leadenhall-Street, n.d. [ESTC: 1793].
>
> I 284p; II 260p. 12mo. 6s (CR), 7s (adv.).
>
> CR n.s. 7: 357 (Mar 1793).
>
> Corvey; CME 3-628-47233-4; ESTC t200845.

Notes. Epistolary.

Adv. end vol. 1 of *The Romance of the Cavern* (1793: 44).

Further edn: Dublin, 1793 (Printed by Thomas Burnside, for Messrs. P. Wogan, P. Byrne, J. Moore, W. Jones, and J. Rice, 2 vols., 12mo), EM 192: 5, ESTC t101271.

CR: 'Belleville Lodge appears to be the production of some milliner's apprentice, whose mind, wonderfully rich in expedients, provides fathers, brothers, and husbands, rich and handsome, suddenly and unexpectedly for all her young ladies. Some ingenuity seems to be exerted in filling two volumes with a meagre story—but what is impossible to a mind fraught with the rich treasures, dispensed by Lane, Hookham, and Co.'

D'ARCY
See TODD, E.

THE DEVIL IN LOVE
See 1791: 32, ALVAREZ; OR, IRRESISTIBLE SEDUCTION

1793: 3 ANON.
THE ERRORS OF SENSIBILITY. A NOVEL. IN THREE VOLUMES.

London: Printed at the Minerva Press, for William Lane, Leadenhall-Street, 1793.
I 160p; II 143p; III 134p. 8vo [CR has 12mo]. 10s 6d sewed (CR).
CR n.s. 10: 473 (Apr 1794).
BL 012635.df.2; EM 216: 1; ESTC t107998 (BI O; NA ViU).

Notes. Epistolary.
Adv., 'now in the Press', SJC 24–26 Oct 1793.
CR: 'There is an *error* in the title: it should have been, the Absurdities and Follies of an unnatural affected Sensibility;—for such a title only the work demands.'

1793: 4 ANON.
FREDERICA RISBERG, A GERMAN STORY, IN TWO VOLUMES.

London: Printed for William Lane, at the Minerva Press, Leadenhall-Street; and sold by
E. Harlow, Bookseller to Her Majesty, Pall-Mall, 1793.
I 275p; II 323p. 12mo. 7s sewed (CR).
CR n.s. 10: 473 (Apr 1794).
ViU *PZ2.F745.1793; ESTC n018554 (NA PU).

Notes. 1 p. advs. end each vol. Epistolary.
Adv., 'now in the Press', SJC 24–26 Oct 1793.
Further edn: London, 1801 (Corvey), CME 3-628-47808-1.
CR: '... we cannot discover in Frederica Risberg, either novelty of character, or of situation; no peculiar elegance of language, or force of sentiment. Yet, in each respect, these volumes rise somewhat above mediocrity; and, if the generosity of the characters was not sometimes too highly strained, we should have thought the series of adventures natural and pleasing.'

1793: 5 ANON.
HARTLEBOURN CASTLE: A DESCRIPTIVE ENGLISH TALE. IN TWO VOLUMES.

London: Printed for J. Bell, no. 148, Oxford-Street, 1793.
I 279p; II 283p. 12mo [CR has 8vo]. 6s (CR, adv.), 6s sewed (SDA).
CR n.s. 10: 235–6 (Feb 1794); AF II: 1825.
BL RB.23.a.10090; ESTC n017270 (NA CaOHM, InU-Li, IU).

Notes. By same author as *Henry Somerville* (1797: 10).
Adv. SDA 2 May 1793.
Adv. end vol. 1 *The Emigrants: a Gallic Tale* (1794: 11).
CR: 'Mediocrity has become so general a characteristic of novels, that it must be our plea for dismissing them with a very brief notice. When a work, like the present, is so nicely balanced, that to find fault is as difficult as to bestow commendation, what is left for the reviewer? The incidents of Hartlebourn Castle are common, the personages common, and the fable common. .... there is nothing to engage the attention, or interest the affections, no ingenuity of plot, and but a moderate attention to consistency of character.'

HENRY, A NOVEL
See LITTLEJOHN, P.

HISTORY OF MAY-FLOWER
See HAMILTON, Anthony

THE HISTORY OF PHILIP WALDEGRAVE
See TOWERS, Joseph

JULIANA ORMESTON
See HUGILL, Martha

THE KNIGHT OF THE ROSE
See PEACOCK, Lucy

1793:6   ANON.
LETTERS FROM A FRENCH NOBLEMAN TO MADEMOISELLE DE
P——; WRITTEN IN THE MONTHS OF JUNE, JULY, AND AUGUST,
1792: WITH AN APPENDIX.
> London: Printed for the Author; and sold by J. Debrett, Piccadilly; and J. Downes,
> No. 240 Temple-Bar, Strand, 1793.
> I v, 17, 143p; II 165p. 12mo. 6s (BC), 5s sewed (SDA).
> BC 1: 453 (Aug 1793).
> IU x823L5691; ESTC n011332 (NA CLU-S/C).

Notes. Preface iii–v, signed 'The Translator', London, 2 May 1792. Pagination in preliminaries continuous Roman-Arabic; preface is followed by list of subscribers pp. 7–17. In vol. 1 text ends at p. 129, followed by appendix pp. [131]-143; in vol. 2 text ends at p. 148, followed by appendix pp. [149]–165.
Adv. SDA 4 June 1793.

   BC: 'These letters are professedly translated from French; but if we were never to exercise our powers of discrimination upon them, we should not hesitate to say, that they have never spoken any language but our own. . . . The little incidents and reflections seem by far too trifling for the situation; and some of the great incidents related are crowded too rapidly on each other; yet the book is not devoid of merit. The appendix is chiefly filled with the atrocities of popular fury in France.'

THE LIFE AND ADVENTURES OF THE CHEVALIER DE FAUBLAS
See LOUVET DE COUVRAY, Jean-Baptiste

LIFE; OR, THE ADVENTURES OF WILLIAM RAMBLE, ESQ
See TRUSLER, John

1793:7   ANON.
LOUISA MATHEWS. BY AN EMINENT LADY. IN THREE VOLUMES.
> London: Printed for J. Lackington, No. 46 & 47, Chiswell-street, Finsbury-square,
> Moorfields, 1793.

I 235p; II 236p; III 257p. 12mo. 9s (CR), 7s 6d sewed (MR), 7s 6d sewed or 9s bound (SJC).

CR n.s. 8: 120 (May 1793); MR n.s. 10: 459 (Apr 1793); AF II: 2606.

MH-H *EC75.A100.79312; EM 1108: 1; ESTC n010752.

Notes. 5-pp. preface (unn.). Text of novel starts on p. 5 in vols. 1 and 2 and p. 3 in vol. 3.

Adv. SJC 2–5 Feb 1793; 'J. Lackington assures the Publick, that the above very interesting Novel is the Production of a very respectable Lady;—is sorry that her Timidity should prevent her Name from appearing in the Title-page of a Work that does honour to her Judgment, her Taste, and her Feeling; and at the same Time discovers the Goodness of her Heart.'

Further edn: London, 1793 (WC) xESTC.

2nd edn. adv., with quotation from EngR, SDA 25 Sept 1793.

CR: 'The authoress of this production, if we regard the inaccuracies of it, is, we suspect, not much entitled to the appellation of eminent. Her novel, as usual, exhibits the most perfect virtue, and the most consummate vice; characters which, we apprehend, are little calculated for initiating her readers in a knowledge of real life. Dukes, marquisses, and noble ladies, are scattered with unbounded profusion through her work; while a damsel run away with, perfidious friends, and dying lovers, complete the group.'

MR [Thomas Holcroft]: 'This novel . . . on the whole, will certainly amuse and interest the reader: but we must farther observe, with respect to the language, that it might have been improved, throughout, by a careful revision.'

LUCIFER AND MAMMON
See MOSER, Joseph

1793: 8   ANON.
MARIAMNE: OR, IRISH ANECDOTES. A NOVEL. IN TWO VOLUMES. BY THE AUTHOR OF ASHTON PRIORY, BENEDICTA, POWIS CASTLE, &C. &C.

London: Printed for William Lane, at the Minerva Press, Leadenhall-Street; and Sold by E. Harlow, Pall-Mall, 1793.

I 197p; II 176p. 12mo. 5s. (CR), 5s sewed (SJC).

CR n.s. 9: 476 (Dec 1793).

Corvey; CME 3-628-45035-7; xESTC.

Notes: Ashton Priory 1792: 2; Benedicta 1791: 3; Powis Castle 1788: 30. Also by same author: Edward and Sophia (1787: 6); Eliza Cleland (1788: 14); and Predestined Wife (1789: 22).

3 pp. advs. end vol. 1.

Adv. SJC 24–26 Oct 1793.

Further edns: Dublin, 1794 (Printed by P. Wogan, P. Byrne, and B. Smith), ESTC t212268; Dublin, 1794, EM 4251: 7, ESTC n034819; London, 1801 (Summers).

CR: 'Some well-intended subjects of a political nature are . . . introduced; and a variety of sensible remarks on the uncultivated state, both of the lands and peasantry of our sister kingdom. Amidst these, however, the machinery of romance possesses its natural movements and the whole may reasonably be considered as an amusing composition.'

MAXIMS OF GALLANTRY
See BREWER, George

1793: 9   ANON.
MELASINA; OR THE FORCE OF PASSION. BEING A WELL AUTHEN-
TICATED FACT. IN A SERIES OF ORIGINAL LETTERS. IN TWO VOL-
UMES.

> London: Printed for J. Bell, No. 148, Oxford Street, Opposite Bond Street; T. Evans,
> Paternoster-Row; W. Stewart Opposite York-House, Piccadilly; and A. Hamilton,
> Gray's-Inn Gate, 1793.
> I 204p; II 165p. 12mo. 5s sewed (CR, SDA).
> CR n.s. 10: 348–9 (Mar 1794); AF II: 2816.
> DLC PR3991.A1M38; ESTC n065271.

Notes. Epistolary. Dedication to——— Esq., signed 'Editor', London, 10 Mar 1793.
Adv. SDA 28 Mar 1793: *Melasina, or the Force of Passion, being a well authenticated Fact, in a Series of Original Letters, interspersed with an impartial description of the people of Ireland, and some original Anecdotes, relative to a family in that kingdom;* Printed for the Author, and sold by J. Nunn, No. 48, Great Queen-street, Lincoln's-Inn Fields.

   CR: 'The heroine of this production is a frail female, who, after several incidents affecting her character, is at last married to the object of her attachment.... we are inclined to believe, from several circumstances, that the letters are genuine; and, as such, they may gratify the curiosity of those in particular who are acquainted with the parties, as well as afford general entertainment.'

1793: 10   ANON.
THE MINSTREL; OR, ANECDOTES OF DISTINGUISHED PERSON-
AGES IN THE FIFTEENTH CENTURY. IN THREE VOLUMES.

> London: Printed for Hookham and Carpenter, Bond-Street, 1793.
> I iv, 216p; II 237p; III 192p. 12mo. 9s sewed (CR), 7s 6d sewed (MR, SJC).
> CR n.s. 8: 316–19 (July 1793); MR n.s. 13: 192–6 (Feb 1794); AF II: 2886.
> C S727.d.79.67-69; EM 237: 3; ESTC t057451 (BI BL, E, O; NA CtY, DLC, IU, MH-H,
>   PU &c.; EA WA).

Notes. Preface i–iv. 2 pp. advs. end vol. 2; 17 pp. advs. end vol. 3.
Adv. SJC 11–13 Apr 1793.
Further edn: Philadelphia, 1802 (WC, NSTC)

   CR: 'The Preface to these volumes announces them to be the production of a lady; nor do we meet with any thing of internal evidence, which can be regarded as contradictory to the truth of that declaration. The title of *Anecdotes,* however, is evidently an exception to the ingenuousness of the fair author; as it seems to imply a reality, not properly corresponding with the fictitious nature of the narrative. The personages introduced are, for the most part, such as we know to have lived in the fifteenth century; and their characters are frequently described with historical veracity; but the parts assigned to them in this recitative drama, are founded upon no incidents immediately derived from record; and, in general, plausibility is a substitute adopted throughout the production' (p. 316).

   MR [William Enfield]: '... it brings before the reader's imagination the busy period of the English history in which the contest between the houses of Lancaster and York was at its height, and places its characters in the midst of the great events of that period. The incidents, indeed, as well as most of the persons, are fictitious: but the writer adheres with fidelity to the general spirit and manners of the times, and carries the Minstrel, whose character is strongly conceived and well supported, through a series of adventures well calculated to arrest our attention, and sufficiently interesting to awaken our sympathetic feelings' (p. 192).

MORTIMORE CASTLE; A CAMBRIAN TALE
See HOWELL, Ann

1793: 11 ANON.
THE ORPHAN SISTERS: A NOVEL. IN TWO VOLUMES.

> London: Printed for William Lane, at the Minerva Press, Leadenhall-Street, 1793.
> I 179p; II 169p. 8vo. 5s sewed (SJC).
> PU Singer-Mend.PR.3991.A1.083.1793; EMf; ESTC t108930 (BI BL [imperf.—lacks both t.ps.]; EA AUG).

Notes. 1 p. advs. end vol. 1; 3 pp. advs. end vol. 2.
Not in Blakey.
Adv. SJC 24–26 Oct 1793.
Further edn: NSTC lists edn. in 18—.

1793: 12 ANON.
THE PEACEFUL VILLA, AN EVENTFUL TALE. IN TWO VOLUMES.

> London: Printed for G. Sael, Strand, 1793.
> I 190p; II 244p. 12mo. 5s sewed (CR, MR).
> CR n.s. 10: 348 (Mar 1794); MR n.s. 10: 224 (Feb 1793); AF II: 3270.
> BL C.171.aa.17; ESTC n011996 (NA CLU-S/C, CtY, MnU).

Notes. 2 pp. advs. end vol. 2. Epistolary.
MnU copy has prefatory advertisement: 'The following NOVEL was some months ago received by the Publisher from an UNKNOWN HAND; which, after perusal, conceiving it cherished no sentiment that *chastity* could *blush* for, nor violated any *precept* that *religion* held *sacred*, he has obtruded on the public, at the same time expressing his gratitude for the distinction and favour shewed him.'
Post-dated; adv. as published, with heading 'Received from an Unknown Hand', SDA 20 Nov 1792 and SJC 20–22 Nov 1792.
CR: 'Some poor milliner's apprentice has probably scribbled the Peaceful Villa, we trust, to keep herself from harm.—Execrable as this novel is, she *might* have been *worse* employed.'
MR [William Enfield]: 'In this novel we find much business, but all so ill contrived and arranged, as to produce little effect; many incidents, but no unity of plot and action; many persons, but few characters; much external action, but little exposure of internal sentiment.'

1793: 13 ANON.
THE PENITENT FATHER: OR INJURED INNOCENCE TRIUMPHANT OVER PARENTAL TYRANNY.

> London: Printed for T. White, no. 22, Down Street, Piccadilly; and C. Stalker, Stationers Court, Ludgate Street, 1793.
> I 191p; II 175p. 12mo. 5s (CR), 5s sewed (SDA, SJC).
> CR n.s. 10: 235 (Feb 1794).
> O 249.r.76,77; ESTC n067086 (NA CLU-S/C).

Notes. Epistolary.

Post-dated; adv. as published 5 Dec 1792; adv. SJC 22–25 Dec 1792.

CR: 'Light summer reading!—plots and counter plots—sighing lovers, and parents with flinty hearts—after the newest taste!'

THE ROMANCE OF THE CAVERN
See WALKER, George

ROSINA: A NOVEL
See PILKINGTON, Miss

1793: 14   ANON.
STELLINS; OR, THE NEW WERTER. IN TWO VOLUMES.

London: Printed at the Minerva-Press, For William Lane, Leadenhall-Street, 1793.

I viii, 164p; II 170p. 8vo [EngR has 12mo]. 5s (EngR).

EngR 22: 307 (Oct 1793).

PU Singer-Mend.PR.3991.A1.S74.1793; ESTC n026583.

Notes. 'The Editor's Advertisement'[i]–[ii] followed by 'Letter from Mr de St. P. to the Editor' dated 'Rome Dec. 8 1790' (iii–viii) which says that the original ms. is by 'Mr. G. G. our common friend'. 2 pp. advs. end vol. 2. Epistolary.

Johann Wolfgang von Goethe's *Die leiden des jungen Werthers* (Leipzig, 1774).

Adv., 'In the Press, and speedily will be published', SDA 25 Apr 1791.

EngR: 'There is a degree of *pathos* which pervades this tale, and renders it extremely interesting. The author is conscious of its inferiority to the original Werter; and therefore any comparative remarks would be invidious. An assertion, however, is made in the preface, to which we do not give much credit, viz. that the subject of the first Werter was founded on real facts—we believe it to have been founded in fiction.'

1793: 15   B[REWE]R, G[eorg]e.
MAXIMS OF GALLANTRY, OR THE HISTORY OF THE COUNT DE VERNEY. BY G—E B—R.

London: Printed for the Author, and sold by Hookham and Carpenter, 1793.

xv, 198p. 8vo. 5s boards (CR, SDA).

CR n.s. 9: 478–9 (Dec 1793); AF II: 463.

O 12 theta 958(2); ESTC n004360 (NA PU).

Notes. Preface iii–iv; introduction v–xv.

Handwritten note on t.p. of Bodleian copy reads 'There never were but six copies of this work.'

Adv., 'In a few days will be published', SDA 3 June 1793.

Another apparently identical edn. has imprint 'Printed for the Author, and sold by J. Parsons' ESTC n047472 (NA CSt); adv. as published SDA 26 July 1793.

CR: 'This is a mingled cup of morality and wickedness, held to the lips of those youthful characters of this dissipated age, who will not fail to relish the *latter*. It is falsehood, hypocrisy, and lasciviousness, cloaked with the delusive coverings of fashion, elegance, and false honour. It contains the deleterious doctrines of Chesterfield *infernalised*, if we may be allowed the expression, and reduced to a system still more disgraceful to morals.'

CAZOTTE, Jacques, **THE DEVIL IN LOVE**
See 1791: 32, **ALVAREZ; OR, IRRESISTIBLE SEDUCTION**

1793: 16   DIBDIN, {C}[harles].
**THE YOUNGER BROTHER: A NOVEL, IN THREE VOLUMES, WRIT-
TEN BY MR. DIBDIN.**
>   London: Printed for the author, and sold at his warehouse, No. 411, Strand, opposite
>   the Adelphi, n.d. [ESTC: 1793].
>   I iv, xxviii, 250p; II 312p; III 336p. 8vo. 13s 6d (CR), 13s 6d boards, 18s 6d calf lettered
>   and 19s 6d calf gilt (LC).
>   CR n.s. 11: 467 (Aug 1794).
>   BL 836.d.35; EMf; ESTC t138147 (BI Dt, O &c.; NA CtY, CSmH, ICN, DLC, MH-H,
>   PU &c.).

Notes. Dedication to the Marquis of Salisbury i–iii, signed C. Dibdin, the Strand, 8 Jan 1793.
Preface i–xxviii. Text of novel starts on p. 5 in vols. 2 and 3.
Adv., 'in three handsome Octavo Volumes', LC 73: 282 (21–23 Mar 1793); 'As this Work has
been sought after with such avidity, that the first impression, though a very large one, is
already nearly bespoken, it is requested that those who wish to be supplied with it, would
leave or send their addresses, as it is intended to issue it as fast as it can be got ready by the
bookbinder, exactly in the order it has been applied for.'
Further edn: London, 1793 (SDA 6 Dec 1793), xESTC.
>   CR: 'The fable, in its progress, is conducted with probability; the conversations, though not
>   always interesting from their subject, are frequently managed with much humour; and the dif-
>   ferent persons are strongly marked, rather than contrasted by prominent features in their char-
>   acter. By a mixture of classical illusions [*sic*] and observations, the author has given the work,
>   in many places, an air of dignity superior to the common standard of novels. But what chiefly
>   distinguishes it, is a competent knowledge of the world; exhibited, for the most part, in delin-
>   eating such propensities as have their source in the numerous modifications of vice and folly.'

1793: 17   {FOX, Joseph}.
**THE BASTARD OF NORMANDY, A TALE, ON THE BANKS OF THE
SEINE. IN TWO VOLUMES. BY THE AUTHOR OF TANCRED, A TALE
OF ANCIENT TIMES.**
>   London: Printed for the author, and sold by Hookham & Carpenter, Bond-Street, 1793.
>   I 114p; II 116p. 12mo. 5s (CR), 5s sewed (SDA, SJC).
>   CR n.s. 10: 347–8 (Mar 1794).
>   BL C.171.d.4; EMf; ESTC t211732.

Notes. Vol. 1 undated. Dedication to Sir Francis Bourgeois, 14 Oct 1729 [*sic*], signed Joseph
Fox. 10 pp. advs. end vol. 1.
Tancred 1791: 37.
Adv. SDA 11 Feb 1793. Adv. SJC 23–26 Feb 1793 as *The Bastard of Normandy; or, the Funeral
Procession on the Banks of the Seine.*
>   CR: 'We have seldom read a production of this kind framed with less regard to nature and
>   probability, affording less of entertainment in the detail, or written in a style (if style it may
>   be called) so remarkably stiff and uncouth.'

1793: 18   FRANKLIN, William (trans.).
THE LOVES OF CAMARUPA AND CAMALATA, AN ANCIENT INDIAN
TALE. ELUCIDATING THE CUSTOMS AND MANNERS OF THE
ORIENTALS. IN A SERIES OF ADVENTURES OF RAJAH CAMARUPA,
AND HIS COMPANIONS. TRANSLATED FROM THE PERSIAN BY
WILLIAM FRANKLIN, LIEUTENANT ON THE HONOURABLE EAST
INDIA COMPANY'S BENGAL ESTABLISHMENT.
> London: Printed for T. Cadell, in the Strand, 1793.
> viii, 284p. 8vo. 3s 6d sewed (CR), 3s 6d boards (SDA).
> CR n.s. 9: 96–100 (Sept 1793); AF II: 1516.
> O 8°X 8 Art; EMf; ESTC t149313 (BI BL; NA CaAEU, CSmH, DLC &c.; EA GOT).

Notes. From a Persian text associated with Muhammad Kârim. ESTC: Written originally in
Hindustani.

Dedication to Sir William Jones, signed 'The Translator', Calcutta, 10 Nov 1790 [v]; 1 p. advs.
[vi]; preface vii–viii. Text of tale ends on p. 272; pp. 273–84 are a glossary of Sanscrit names.
Adv. SDA 1 May 1793.

German trans. Weimar, 1800 (*Geschichte des Prinzen Kamarupa und der schönen Kamalata*)
(RS).

CR: 'This tale, though not distinguished by that brilliant exuberance of imagination, nor
that fertility of incident, which characterize the Arabian Tales, translated by Galland, yet
affords a pleasing picture of oriental manners. But the adventures of Camarupa and his companions, though wildly and sometimes absurdly conceived, are too similar; and this want of
variety constitutes the chief defect of the work' (p. 96).

1793: 19   GUNNING, [Susannah].
MEMOIRS OF MARY, A NOVEL. BY MRS. GUNNING. IN FIVE VOLUMES.
> London: Printed for J. Bell, No. 148, Oxford-Street, 1793.
> I 226p; II 248p; III 251p; IV 265p; V 225p. 12mo. 15s sewed (AR), 15s bound (SDA).
> AR 18: 101 (Jan 1794); AF II: 1764.
> BL 12613.g.8; EM 187: 1; ESTC t070729 (BI BRu; NA CtY-BR, IU, MH-H, NjP, PU &c.).

Notes. 1 p. advs. end vol. 5. Novel ends on p. 178 of vol. 5; pp. 179–225 contain 'An Allegory'
in verse. Epistolary.

Adv., 'In the Press, and on the 1st of November will be published', SDA 22 Oct 1793;
adv. as published SDA 1 Nov 1793.

Further edns: London, 1794, ESTC n052541; London, 1794, EM 7137: 6, ESTC t073527;
Dublin, 1794 (Printed for P. Wogan, P. Byrne, W. Jones, J. Moore, and H. Colbert, 2 vols.,
12mo), ESTC n021982.

AR: '. . . she draws a very natural and lively picture of what passes in high life. Her design
appears to have been, not to astonish by improbable incidents, or to harrow up the soul by
scenes of distress which can barely be supposed to exist, but to interest and instruct, by representing persons, manners, and events, as they are exhibited in real life. And she has, we
think, executed this design very successfully. The incidents of the novel are natural; the characters are marked with that peculiarity of feature, which shows that they have been drawn
from actual observation; and the language possesses the ease and vivacity, though in some
instances the negligence too, of polite conversation.'

1793: 20 [HAMILTON, Anthony, known as Comte Antoine].
HISTORY OF MAY-FLOWER, A FAIRY TALE.

> London: Printed for G. and T. Wilkie, no. 57, Pater-Noster-Row, 1793.
> xi, 196p. 12mo. 2s 6d sewed (CR, MR).
> CR n.s. 11: 233–4 (June 1794); MR n.s. 15: 354 (Nov 1794); AF II: 1786.
> O Fic.27523f.34; ESTC t219333.

Notes. Trans. of *Histoire de fleur d'épine* (Paris, 1730).
1-p. prefatory advertisement. Table of contents v–xi.
Adv. SJC 7–9 Nov 1793.
Further edn: Salisbury, 1796, EM 203: 6, ESTC t098978.

   CR: '[Hamilton's *Contes*, of which this is one] are extremely amusing, as they join to the fanciful extravagance of the Arabian Tales, which he at once laughed at and imitated, the gaiety and lighter graces, the wit and pleasantry of the Parisian bel-esprit.'

   MR [William Enfield]: 'We . . . recommend the pretty tale of May Flower to the perusal of such of our readers as are disposed to enjoy an hour's light amusement, without calling themselves too strictly to account, when it is past. The work is elegantly translated. . . .'

HARLEY, Mrs
See HUGILL, Martha

HERON, Mary, **THE CONFLICT**
See 1790: 48

HOMESPUN, Prudentia
See WEST, Jane

1793: 21 [HOWELL, Ann].
MORTIMORE CASTLE; A CAMBRIAN TALE. IN TWO VOLUMES.

> London: Printed for William Lane, at the Minerva Press, Leadenhall-Street, 1793.
> I 164p; II 149p. 303p. 8vo. [EngR has 12mo]. 5s (EngR), 5s sewed (SJC).
> EngR 22: 307 (Oct 1793).
> AUG 02/III.9.8.175; xESTC.

Notes. Author attribution: Blakey (p. 302).
3 pp. advs. end vol. 2.
Adv. SJC 24–26 Oct 1793.
Further edn: London, 1809 (WC).

   EngR: 'As the quantity of novels with which Mr Lane deluges the public is very large, it must be expected that some of them will be indifferent. To this class does the present tale belong. The style is not reprehensible, but the incidents have been so often repeated that they not only cease to please, but begin almost to disgust.'

1793: 22 [HUGILL, Martha].
*****JULIANA ORMESTON: OR, THE FRATERNAL VICTIM. BY MRS. HARLEY, AUTHOR OF THE PRINCE OF LEON, ST. BERNARD'S PRIORY, &C. &C.**

London: Published by J. Barker, Russell-court, Drury-lane (adv.).
4 vols. 10s sewed (SDA, adv).
No copy located.

Notes. Martha Harley later became Hugill (see Todd).
The Prince of Leon 1794: 31; *St Bernard's Priory* 1786: 25.
Adv. as published SDA 7 Dec 1792.
Adv. end vol. 1 of *The Prince of Leon.*
Further edn: Dublin, 1793 (Printed by Brett Smith, for Messrs. P. Wogan, P. Byrne,
J. Moore, W. Jones, & J. Rice, 2 vols., 12mo), EM 4686: 1, ESTC t127679.
Prince of Leon is by 'the author of *Juliana Ormeston*'; *Juliana Ormeston* is by 'the author of
Prince of Leon'. If they came out simultaneously, the Dublin edn. precedes the London edn.

1793: 23   IMLAY, G[ilbert].
THE EMIGRANTS, OR THE HISTORY OF AN EXPATRIATED FAMILY;
BEING A DELINEATION OF ENGLISH MANNERS, DRAWN FROM
REAL CHARACTERS, WRITTEN IN AMERICA, BY G. IMLAY, ESQ.
AUTHOR OF THE TOPOGRAPHICAL DESCRIPTION OF ITS WEST-
ERN TERRITORY.

London: Printed for A. Hamilton, Near Gray's-Inn-Gate, Holborn, 1793.
I xii, 221p; II 222p; III 192p. 12mo. 9s sewed (CR, MR).
CR n.s. 9: 155–8 (Oct 1793); MR n.s. 11: 468–9 (Aug 1793); AF II: 2157.
IU x813.Im5e; ESTC t055731 (BI BL [vol. 1 only], Eu; NA ICU, MeB).

Notes. The introduction to Robert R. Hare's 1964 facsimile reprint of *The Emigrants* argues
that the novel is largely the work of Mary Wollstonecraft, although with substantial contributions by Imlay, and makes the same point about the authorship of Imlay's *Topographical
Description of the Western Territory of North America.* However, in the introduction to their
1998 Penguin edn. of *The Emigrants,* Amanda Gilroy and W. M. Verhoeven make it clear that
there is no evidence of any contribution by Wollstonecraft to either work.
Preface. Epistolary.
Post-dated; adv. as published SJC 4–6 Dec 1792 and LC 72: 538 (4–6 Dec 1792). Re-adv., with
quotation from MR, SJC 5–7 Sept 1793.
Further edn: Dublin, 1794 (Printed for C. Brown, 1 vol., 12mo), ESTC n003394.

CR: 'This work has two objects professedly in view, the one to recommend the government and manners of America, in preference to those of our own country—the other, to recommend divorces' (p. 155). 'There are here and there, in this work, strokes of local
description which are entertaining; but the style, we are sorry to observe, is intolerably
inflated, and at the same time very incorrect' (p. 156) '. . . for the faults of *orthography*, which
are likewise frequent in these Letters, we presume the *printer* is to be responsible, as we imagine the Americans do not push their love of independence so far as to reject the legislative
authority of Dr Johnson, though a Tory, in this department' (p. 158).

MR [William Enfield]: 'In a novel written by the intelligent and lively author of the topographical description of the western territory of America, the public will naturally look for
something more than a sentimental tale; and we can assure our readers that they will find in
these volumes many things which are not commonly to be perceived in writings of this class.
Not that the author is incapable of unfolding the tender passions, and of expressing its

enchanting emotions. He frequently pours forth high and almost idolatrous encomiums on the fair sex; and he describes the rise and progress of love with all the ardour of youthful sensibility:—but he comprehends within the plan of his work many other objects which will render it interesting to the philosopher as well as to the lover' (p. 468).

1793: 24   KNIGGE, [Adolf Franz Friedrich Ludwig von], Baron.
THE GERMAN GIL BLAS; OR, THE ADVENTURES OF PETER CLAUS.
TRANSLATED FROM THE GERMAN OF BARON KUIEGGE [*sic*]. IN
THREE VOLUMES.
> London: Printed for C. and G. Kearsley, Johnson's Head, (No. 46) Fleet-Street, 1793.
> I vii, 292p; II iv, 248p; III iv, 240p. 12mo. 9s sewed (MR, SDA, SJC).
> MR n.s. 10: 194–6 (Feb 1793); AF II: 2413.
> BL 838.d.25; EM 5448: 6; ESTC t092292 (BI BMu, C, O; NA CSmH, IU, ViU &c.).

Notes. Trans. of *Geschichte Peter Clausens* (Frankfort, 1783).
Prefatory advertisement (iii–iv) contains this comment on national novel-writing talents: 'The Germans seldom separate the useful from the agreeable; the imagination of their novel writers is of a cast peculiar to themselves, less extravagant than the Italians, yet not less fertile than that of their Gallic neighbours, though more gentle and subordinate to nature, averse to exaggeration, almost ever keeping within the bounds of probability' (p. iv).
Postdated; adv. as published SDA 1 Dec 1792 with reference to the 'very high character given of this Work in the foreign Reviews'. Adv. SJC 25–27 June 1793; 'The above work has been very highly spoken of by the English as well as Foreign Reviewers.'
Further edn: Dublin, 1793 (Printed by N. Kelly, for Messrs. P. Byrne, J. Moore, W. Jones, and J. Rice, 2 vols., 12mo), ESTC n007119. French trans. Paris, 1789 (*Le Gil Blas allemand*) (BN).

MR [William Enfield]: 'Perhaps it may be said that no fictitious tales are more pleasing than those which exhibit lively and varied pictures of human life and manners; and such tales, well executed, are as useful as they are amusing: for they enable the reader to contemplate the world, reflected as from a mirror, without the trouble and hazard of immediate intercourse. In this respect, the work now before us has considerable merit. Like the French Gil Blas, its hero passes through a rapid succession of adventures, and mixes with a great diversity of characters. . . . Our chief objection to the work is that almost all the characters, both in high and low life, are very deficient in moral merit' (pp. 194–195).

1793: 25   LE MAIRE, [Henri].
THE FRENCH GIL BLAS; OR, ADVENTURES OF HENRY LANSON. BY
M. LE MAIRE, OF NANCY. TRANSLATED FROM THE THIRD EDI-
TION IN FRENCH. IN FOUR VOLUMES.
> London: Printed for C. and G. Kearsley, Johnson's Head, Fleet-Street, 1793.
> I iv, 300p; II iv, 275p; III iv, 279p; IV iv, 306p. 12mo. 12s sewed (MR, SJC).
> CR n.s. 9: [323]–6 (Nov 1793); MR n.s. 12: 392–6 (Dec 1793); AF II: 2484.
> BL 636.d.20-23; EM 2741: 3; ESTC t114280 (BI O; NA CLU-S/C).

Notes. Trans. of *Le Gil-Blas françois ou aventures de Henry Lançon* (Paris, 1790).
2-pp. table of contents (iii–iv) in each vol. 1 p. advs. end vol. 3.
Adv. SDA 11 June 1793; adv. SJC 25–27 June 1793. Adv. SDA 18 Dec 1793 as *The Adventures*

of Henry Lanson, not improperly called The Gil Blas of France, From the Similitude (yet Originality) of his Adventures to the celebrated Gil Blas of Santillane.

CR: 'It is written in an easy manner, and is by no means destitute of amusement, though it is very far, indeed, from deserving to be ranked with the novel of Le Sage, with which the title seems, rather imprudently, to provoke a comparison' (p. [323]). 'We cannot... recommend it in point of morality; and, with regard to its merits in a literary view, it contains greater variety of scenes than of manners, and more of amusement than of interest' (p. 324).

MR rev. [Thomas Holcroft] opens: 'The title, *Gil Blas*, has lately been assumed in several instances, and, as it appears to us, for two reasons; the popularity of the original and legitimate Gil Blas; and the nature of the plan, which demands no kind of unity, but suffers the narrator to give either his own history, or the histories of as many other people as he shall please. M. Le Maire has amply profited by this licence; and his *Gil Blas*, whose name is *Lanson*, tells us much more of other people than of himself:—but the work has a still greater fault: its principal topic is love, or rather sensuality. The doctrine, which has done such infinite mischief, that love is omnipotent, is continually preached in this work; and licentiousness is justified by the consideration that it was irresistible' (pp. 392–3).

1793: 26   [LITTLEJOHN, P.].
HENRY, A NOVEL. IN TWO VOLUMES. BY THE AUTHOR OF THE CYPHER; OR, WORLD AS IT GOES.

London: Printed for William Lane, at the Minerva Press, Leadenhall-Street, 1793.
I 235p; II 268p. 12mo. 6s (CR), 6s sewed (SDA).
CR n.s. 9: 475–6 (Dec 1793); AF II: 1899.
BL C.192.a.186; ESTC t227105.

Notes. 1 p. adv. end vol. 1.
The Cipher 1791: 45.
Adv. SDA 31 July 1793; additional booksellers are E. Harlow, Pall-mall; Shepherd and Reynolds, and J. Kearby, Oxford-street; Simmonds and Parsons, Paternoster-row.

CR: 'In all our drudgery through the flimzy compositions from Leadenhall-street, we have scarcely met with any task more difficult, than the patient though fruitless search after something to commend in this novel. The author of it seems perfectly qualified for this kind of writing, from the happy talent he possesses, spreading a very scanty portion of ideas over a prodigious surface of paper' (p. 475).

1793: 27   [LOUVET DE COUVRAY, Jean-Baptiste].
THE LIFE AND ADVENTURES OF THE CHEVALIER DE FAUBLAS; INCLUDING A VARIETY OF ANECDOTES RELATIVE TO THE PRESENT KING OF POLAND. IN FOUR VOLUMES.

London: Printed for R. Faulder, New Bond-street; and E. Jeffery, Pall-Mall, 1793.
I vi, 361p; II 314p; III 320p; IV 367p. 12mo. 16s sewed (CR), 14s boards (MR), 14s sewed (SJC).
CR n.s. 12: 234–5 (Oct 1794); MR n.s. 12: 339 (Nov 1793); AF II: 2609.
BRG BC 843.69 LOU 1–4; ESTC n033827 (NA NNPM).

Notes. Trans. of *Une Année de la vie du chevalier de Faublas* (Paris, 1787).
Preface 1, v–vi.

Adv., 'Translated from the original French', SJC 11–13 July 1793; 1st bookseller is T. Evans, Paternoster-row.

Adv. OPA 8 May 1795; additional bookseller is H.D. Symonds, Paternoster-row.

Further edns: Dublin, 1796 (Printed for J. Milliken, 3 vols., 12mo) ESTC n025586; ESTC has 2 American edns. of an abridged translated selection from the same original, *Love and Patriotism or, The extraordinary adventures of M. Duportail*, Philadelphia, 1797, EM 1513: 30, ESTC w013657 and Boston, 1799, ESTC w013658; WC has 51 entries, most of them French, for pre-1851 versions of part or all of this work; NSTC lists edn. in 1811. Extracts from *The Life and Adventures of the Chevalier de Faublas*, 'The Adventures of the Baron de Lovzinski', published in *Lady's Magazine* and *Hibernian Magazine*, 1794–95, RM 64.

CR: 'On any other occasion than that of fulfilling our duty to the public, we should be ashamed to confess that we have turned over the leaves of this uncommonly licentious performance.... Acknowledging, as justice obliges us to do, the powers of this writer, it becomes us to mark his abuse of them with the most severe reprehension: nor shall we notice the book any farther than is necessary to warn the sober and the good, who, under certain restrictions, admit novels into their range of family reading, against permitting these volumes to contaminate the imaginations of young people with images which are not forgotten at pleasure' (p. 234).

MR [George Edward Griffiths]: 'We had hoped that the importation and naturalization of French details of foppery and immorality had nearly ceased; and we were sorry when the appearance of these volumes convinced us that the trade was not quite at an end. Among the numerous *evils*, however, which have been produced by the present commotions among the French, we trust that one *good* consequence will be the destruction of their attachment to the sort of life and the sort of reading, which, for so many years, has been productive of this worse than frivolous species of literature.'

1793: 28   MATHEWS, Mrs.
SIMPLE FACTS; OR, THE HISTORY OF AN ORPHAN. IN TWO VOLUMES. BY MRS. MATHEWS.

> London: Printed by S. Low, Great Portland Street for the author: And Sold by Mr Richardson, Royal Exchange; Hookham & Carpenter, Old and New Bond Street; and Messrs. Scatcherd & Whitaker, Ave-Maria Lane, 1793.
> I 213p; II 214p. 12mo. 6s boards (MR), 6s sewed (SJC).
> MR n.s. 12: 474 (Dec 1793); AF II: 2752.
> BL 12613.b.21; EM 279: 2; ESTC t074662.

Notes. Adv. SJC 22–24 Jan 1793; list of booksellers does not include Scatcherd & Whitaker.

MR [William Enfield]: 'As the orphan's distresses are particularly adapted to excite commiseration, they have always been a favourite subject of dramatic and narrative fiction. In the present novel, they are not exhibited with the bold design and lively colouring of superior genius, but with a degree of natural simplicity which is sufficient to entitle it to the character of an interesting performance.'

1793: 29   MILLIKIN, Anna.
CORFE CASTLE; OR, HISTORIC TRACTS. A NOVEL, IN TWO VOLUMES. BY ANNA MILLIKIN.

> Cork: Printed by James Haly, (King's Arms,) North Main-Street, 1793.

I xvi, 309p; II 307p. 12mo.
IU x823M599c; ESTC n032906.

Notes. List of subscribers 1, v–x; preface xi–xiv refers to 'that disapprobation with which female productions are generally received if unrecommended by a former specimen, or like this, unaided by interest' (p. xi); dedication to Lord Boyle signed Anna Millikin, 2 Apr 1793. In vol. 2 text of novel starts on p. 5.

1793: 30   [MOSER, Joseph].
LUCIFER AND MAMMON, AN HISTORICAL SKETCH OF THE LAST AND PRESENT CENTURY; WITH CHARACTERS, ANECDOTES, &C.
> London: Printed for J. Owen, No. 168, Piccadilly, and H. D. Symonds, Paternoster-Row, 1793.
> 296p. 12mo [BC has 8vo]. 3s (BC).
> BC 3: 444 (Apr 1794).
> PPL Of2.4942.D; ESTC n034010 (NA CtHT-W, DLC, InU-Li).

Notes. 3 pp. advs. end vol.
BC: 'The writer of this Sketch, a well-meaning, and in some respects, a diffident writer, should be told, that of all tedious and insupportable contrivances, unless managed with the most exquisite art, nothing is so killing as a long-continued allegory; and that the mode of conveying satire, by attributing bad actions to the agency of Demons, is too stale to be enlivened by any genius.'

1793: 31   PARSONS, [Eliza].
CASTLE OF WOLFENBACH; A GERMAN STORY. IN TWO VOLUMES. BY MRS. PARSONS, AUTHOR OF ERRORS OF EDUCATION, MISS MERE-DITH, WOMAN AS SHE SHOULD BE, AND INTRIGUES OF A MORNING.
> London: Printed for William Lane, at the Minerva Press, Leadenhall-Street and sold by E. Harlow, Pall-Mall, 1793.
> I 270p; II 258p. 12mo. 6s sewed (CR, SJC).
> CR n.s. 10: 49–52 (Jan 1794); AF II: 3231.
> O Vet.A5f.2690-1; EMf; ESTC t185360 (NA IU, ViU).

Notes. Errors of Education 1791: 55; *Miss Meredith* 1790: 58; *Woman As She Should Be* 1793: 33. *Intrigues of a Morning* (1792) is a play.
Adv. SJC 26–29 Oct 1793.
Further edns: London, 1794, ESTC n026976; London, 1824 (WC); London, 1835 (Summers, NSTC); London, 1839 (Summers); London, 1854 (WC).
CR: 'We do not pretend to give this novel as one of the first order, or even of the second; it has, however, sufficient interest to be read with pleasure. The terrible prevails, and the characters of the two heroes in crime, are *too* darkly tinted. The two stories, besides, are not sufficiently interwoven with one another. . . . There is no fine writing in these volumes; and now and then we meet with vulgarisms . . . but in point of moral tendency they are unexceptionable' (p. 50).

1793: 32   PARSONS, {Eliza}.
ELLEN AND JULIA. A NOVEL, IN TWO VOLUMES. BY MRS. PARSONS.

AUTHOR OF ERRORS OF EDUCATION, WOMAN AS SHE SHOULD BE, INTRIGUES OF A MORNING, AND CASTLE OF WOLFENBACH.

London: Printed for William Lane, at the Minerva Press, Leadenhall-Street; and sold by
E. Harlow, Bookseller to Her Majesty, Pall Mall, 1793.
I 287p; II 299p. 12mo. 6s sewed (MR, Min).
MR n.s. 14: 465 (Aug 1794).
BL 1608/1445; EM 8496: 3; ESTC t122374.

Notes. Dedication to Mrs Crespigny, Grove-House, Camberwell, signed Eliza Parsons,
London, 12 Nov 1793. 2-pp. preface. 1 p. advs. end vol. 1 and vol. 2.
Errors of Education 1791: 55; *Woman As She Should Be* 1793: 33; *Castle of Wolfenbach* 1793:
31. *Intrigues of a Morning* (1792) is a play.
Adv., 'now in the Press', SJC 24–26 Oct 1793.

MR [William Enfield]: '. . . we are of opinion this novel must depend for its success chiefly
on its moral merit. In the first volume, the story is diversified with many striking incidents,
but, through a great part of the second, the writer's invention appears to flag. The language,
though natural, is never wrought into elegance, and is sometimes negligent and even
ungrammatical.'

1793: 33   PARSONS, {Eliza}.
WOMAN AS SHE SHOULD BE; OR, MEMOIRS OF MRS. MENVILLE. A NOVEL. IN FOUR VOLUMES. BY MRS. PARSONS, AUTHOR OF ERRORS OF EDUCATION, MISS MEREDITH, AND INTRIGUES OF A MORNING.

London: Printed for William Lane, at the Minerva, Leadenhall-Street, and sold by E.
Harlow, Pall-Mall, 1793.
I 8, 274p; II 268p; III 236p; IV 223p. 12mo. 12s (CR), 12s sewed (SDA, SJC).
CR n.s. 9: 118 (Sept 1793).
BL 1607/2083; EM 4403: 1; ESTC t119025 (NA CLU-S/C, CtY, PU).

Notes. BL copy lacks sig. H10 of vol. 2. Dedication to H.R.H. the Duchess of Gloucester 5–8,
signed Eliza Parsons, London, 26 Feb 1793. Arabic numbering begins again with the first
page of the novel. 2 pp. advs. end vol. 1 and 1 p. at the end of vol. 4. Epistolary.
Parsons described the writing of this novel, during a six-month confinement to her room
with a broken leg: 'my leg on a pillow, splinters of bone continually working thro' which keep
me in extreme Tortures' (letter to Dr Dale, 17 Dec 1792, RLF 1: 21).
Errors of Education 1791: 55; *Miss Meredith* 1790: 58. *Intrigues of a Morning* (1792) is a
play.
Adv. SDA 13 Mar 1793; booksellers are Lane and Eliz. Hanton, Bookseller to Her Majesty,
Pall-Mall. Adv. SJC 26–29 Oct 1793.
Further edn: Dublin, 1793 (Printed by Messrs. P. Wogan and W. Jones, 2 vols., 12mo), EM
8177: 3, ESTC t137680.

CR: 'Mrs. Parsons has at least the merit, in this instance, of being the advocate of virtue,
and a writer of no inferior talents. The characters she has drawn have nothing new or even
striking in them, yet they are natural and consistent, and the events are generally interesting
without being extravagant.'

1793: 34   [PEACOCK, Lucy].
THE KNIGHT OF THE ROSE. AN ALLEGORICAL NARRATIVE; INCLUD-
ING HISTORIES, ADVENTURES, &C. DESIGNED FOR THE AMUSE-
MENT AND MORAL INSTRUCTION OF YOUTH. BY THE AUTHOR OF
THE ADVENTURES OF THE SIX PRINCESSES OF BABYLON, &C. AND
EDITOR OF THE JUVENILE MAGAZINE.

> London: Printed for, and Sold by Hookham and Carpenter, Bond-street; J. Marshall,
> Queen-street, Cheapside; S. Hazard, Bath; and by the Author, at the Juvenile Library,
> No. 259, Oxford-street, 1793.
> xix, 209p. 12mo. 3s (CR), 3s sewed (MR, SDA).
> CR n.s. 10: 120 (Jan 1794); MR n.s. 12: 339–40 (Nov 1793); AF II: 3275.
> BL 12611.f.13; CME 3-628-45102-7; EM 238: 6; ESTC t057360 (BI O; NA CaOHM,
> CLU-S/C; EA COR).

Notes. List of subscribers v–xix.
Adventures of the Six Princesses of Babylon 1785: 40.
Adv. SDA 1 July 1793.
Further edn: London, 1807 (WC, NSTC). German trans. Halle, 1794 (*Der Rosenritter, lehrre-
iches Buch für die Jugend*) (RS).

CR: 'To impress moral truths upon the heart by the assistance of the imagination has ever
been a favourite design with those who have devoted their labours to the instruction of
youth; but when the moral is trite, and the imagination languid, we fear the attempt will not
be attended with much success. It is extremely difficult to make allegory at once just and
entertaining; the novelty of this species of writing is worn off.'

MR [William Enfield]: 'To compare this allegory with the Fairy Queen would be trying it
too severely: but to those young readers for whose use it is designed, we may fairly promise,
from the perusal, much useful instruction, and some amusement' (p. 340).

1793: 35   [PILKINGTON, Miss].
ROSINA: A NOVEL. IN FIVE VOLUMES. BY THE AUTHOR OF DELIA,
AN INTERESTING TALE, IN FOUR VOLUMES.

> London: Printed for William Lane, at the Minerva, Leadenhall-Street, 1793.
> I 274p; II 288p; III 286p; IV 235p; V 230p. 12mo. 17s 6d (adv.).
> EurM 28: 323–4 (Nov 1795).
> C 7720.d.793–797; EM 163: 1; ESTC t066923 (BI BL, MRu; NA CSmH, DLC, ICN, IU,
> MH-H, ViU &c.).

Notes. For the distinction between Miss and Mary Pilkington, see FC.
2 pp. advs. end vol. 1, 2 pp. advs. end vol. 3, 1 p. advs. end vol. 4, and 2 pp. advs. end
vol. 5.
Delia 1790: 59.
Adv. end vol. 1 of *The Romance of the Cavern* (1793: 44).
Further edn: Dublin, 1793 (Printed for Messrs. P. Wogan, P. Byrne, J. Moore, W. Jones, and
J. Rice, 3 vols., 12mo), ESTC n012943.

EurM: 'The story, tho' simple, is highly interesting, and the incidents of it, which are
numerous, are very classically arranged; the language is correct and elegant throughout, and
in many parts not only beautiful but sublime.'

1793: 36   PORTER, Anna Maria.
ARTLESS TALES. BY ANNA MARIA PORTER. ORNAMENTED WITH A
FRONTISPIECE, DESIGNED BY HER BROTHER, R. K. PORTER.
> London: Printed, and sold for the Author, by L. Wayland, N° 2, Middle-Row, Holborn;
> T. Burnham, Bookseller, Northampton; and A. Clifton, Durham, 1793. [Vol. I].
> London: Printed For The Author, And Sold By Hookham And Carpenter, Bond Street,
> 1795. [Vol. II].
> I viii, 192p; II ii, 157p. 8vo. 3s (CR), 3s 6d sewed (MR) vol. 1; 3s 6d bound (CR), 3s sewed
> (MR) vol. 2.
> CR n.s. 9: 94–6 (Sept 1793), MR n.s. 12: 112–13 (Sept 1793), AF II: 3535 vol. 1; CR n.s.
> 15: 236 (Oct 1795), MR n.s. 18: 114 (Sept 1795), AF II: 3536 vol. 2.
> ViU PZ2.P67A 1793 [vol. 1], AWn PR 5725.O7.A7 [vol. 2]; ESTC n043004 [vol. 1] and
> t220387 [vol. 2] (BI AWn; NA InU [vol. 1]).

Notes. Vol. 1 dedication to the Earl of Bristol v–vi, signed Anna Maria Porter, Bedford-Street,
Covent-Garden, 16 Dec 1792; preface vii–viii. List of subscribers at end. Vol. 2 t.p. omits reference to frontispiece.

Vol. 2 preface (i–ii), curiously dated Dec 1793 [altered in ms. to 1794 in AWn copy] and
signed Anna Maria Porter, mentions the CR's complaint about the title of vol. 1 and says that
the author is now 16 and has learned a great deal since the publication of vol. 1.

Further edn: London, 1796, EM 8817: 10, ESTC t162111. German trans. Halle, 1795
(*Kunstlose Erzählungen*) (RS).

CR n.s. 9: 'With the author's leave, the epithet by which these Tales are characterised conveys no compliment; as Tales, to be good, require a very considerable degree of *art* in their
construction. It is, indeed, a great mistake to think that excellence in any way can be produced otherwise than by art, labour, and continued application' (p. 94). 'If this [a passage
quoted from one of the stories] was really written at the age of thirteen, it certainly shows an
uncommon brilliancy of fancy as well as very early cultivation' (p. 96).

MR n.s. 12 [Thomas Holcroft]: 'This small volume contains five tales; and the authoress
says that they were written at the age of thirteen. Deficient as they are, when compared with
the works of the mature mind, they are still extraordinary when considered as the effusions
of childhood; and we wish Miss Porter sedulously to exert those talents of which she has given
these early proofs' (pp. 112–13).

CR n.s. 15: '[The previous volume] gave us an idea of an early dawn of genius, which, we conceived, might with assiduous cultivation reward the care bestowed upon it. We are sorry this
care has *not* been bestowed. When, in the former publication, this young authoress sported her
fancy in fairy land, her excursions, if not very improving, could at least do her no great harm: but
the volume before us is filled with love adventures, and disgusts us with the most extravagant
language of a passion which at present she ought scarcely to be acquainted with, even by name.'

MR n.s. 18 [William Enfield]: 'This volume of artless tales ... bears marks of a ready invention; which are the more striking as the young author, who informs the public that she is now
sixteen, cannot be supposed to have written from actual experience and observation. ... The
impassioned style, in which these pieces are written, will probably render the volume more
acceptable to young ladies than to their governesses or parents.'

1793: 37   REEVE, Clara.
MEMOIRS OF SIR ROGER DE CLARENDON, THE NATURAL SON OF

EDWARD PRINCE OF WALES, COMMONLY CALLED THE BLACK
PRINCE; WITH ANECDOTES OF MANY OTHER EMINENT PERSONS OF
THE FOURTEENTH CENTURY. BY CLARA REEVE. IN THREE VOLUMES.

London: Printed for Hookham and Carpenter, Bond-Street, 1793.
I xxiii, 221p; II 249p; III 231p. 12mo. 9s sewed (CR, MR).
CR n.s. 10: 280–7 (Mar 1794); MR n.s. 14: 152–5 (June 1794); AF II: 3713.
BL 12613.f.14; EM 335: 6; ESTC t070080 (BI IPSr; NA CSmH, DLC, ViU &c.; EA GOT).

Notes. 3 pp. advs. end vol. 1; 8 pp. advs. end vol. 3.
Adv., 'On Tuesday, the 4th of June, will be published', SDA 31 May 1793; adv. 'In a few Days
will be published', SJC 1–4 June 1793; adv. as published SJC 4–6 June 1793.
Further edn: Dublin, 1794 (Printed by P. Wogan, 2 vols., 12mo), ESTC n021969. German
trans. Leipzig, 1795 (*Roger Clarendons Leben und Denkwürdigkeiten*) (EAG).
CR: '. . . the gleanings of historical anecdotes, which may be gathered from authors not
generally read, are seldom important or interesting; often we are presented with a mere list of
names. . . . The other inconvenience is, that those characters, on which the interest chiefly
falls, are, and in order to be new, must be, of the author's own creation.—Of the exhibition
of the *manners* of the times which, if well represented, would make a more pleasing part of
such a romance than a record of historical personages, there is not much, probably because
much was not to be found' (p. 281). '. . . though these volumes display much reading and
ingenuity, though the style is pure, and the sentiments (those excepted which tend to give a
false gloss to rank or antiquity) favourable to virtue, we must confess there is a want of interest which renders the general effect but feeble; and as to the end of historical information,
that . . . is destroyed by the omission of historical authorities' (p. 284).
MR [James Bannister]: '. . . she discovers a laudable zeal for the interests of virtue, and a
just abhorrence of vice. We are, however, sorry to observe that the subject and detail of her
history are tedious, that the manners are for the most part insipid, and that the characters are
generally uninteresting' (p. 153).

1793: 38   ROCHE, Regina Maria.
*THE MAID OF THE HAMLET. A TALE. BY REGINA MARIA ROCHE,
AUTHOR OF THE VICAR OF LANDSDOWN.

London: Printed for H. Long, corner of Sackville street, Piccadilly (SJC), 1793 (MR, BC,
    SJC).
2 vols. 12mo. 6s (CR), 6s sewed (MR, SJC).
CR n.s. 10: 472–3 (Apr 1794); MR n.s. 14: 465–6 (Aug 1794); AF II: 3852.
No copy located.

Notes. Dedication to the Duchess of Leinster (SJC).
Vicar of Lansdowne 1789: 64.
Adv. SJC 7–9 Jan 1794.
Further edns: London, 1800, ESTC t155067; Boston, 1801 (NUC); Dublin, 1802 (NUC,
NSTC); London, 1821 (NUC); London, 1833 (NUC). French trans. Paris, 1801 (*La Fille du
hameau*) (BN).
CR: 'If there are those who can find amusement in these two volumes, sufficient to beguile
the tædium of a rainy day, or the pain of a fit of the toothache, it is an amusement they may
be allowed to take without scruple, provided only they forget them again by the next day; for

as there is nothing in the story of the *Maid of the Hamlet*, which will contaminate the mind by passing through it, so neither is there any thing which can possibly improve it by being retained there.'

MR [William Enfield]: 'It affords little reason to suppose that the author's reading has extended far beyond the novelist's circulating library, and will contribute little toward augmenting the reader's acquaintance either with men or things. The tale is, however, amusing; the incidents are sufficiently romantic to keep up the reader's attention; and the sentiments and language, if not highly refined, are not unnatural. The performance, on the whole, is therefore above contempt.'

SHANDY, Mr, A SENTIMENTAL JOURNEY
See App. B: 12

1793: 39   SMITH, Charlotte.
THE OLD MANOR HOUSE. A NOVEL, IN FOUR VOLUMES. BY CHAR-
LOTTE SMITH.
London: Printed for J. Bell, no. 148, Oxford-Street, 1793.
I 280p; II 320p; III 353p; IV 363p. 12mo. 15s sewed (CR), 14s sewed (MR, SJC).
CR n.s. 8: 44–54 (May 1793); MR n.s. 11: 150–3 (June 1793); AF II: 4143.
BL 12614.bb.26; EM 289: 1; ESTC t071314 (BI C, O; NA CtY-BR, CSmH, DLC, IU, MH-H, NjP, TxU, ViU &c.).

Notes. Frontispiece. 1 p. advs. end vol. 4.
Adv., 'In the Press, and speedily will be published', SDA 12 Feb 1793; adv. 'On Wednesday the 27th, will be published', SJC 19–21 Feb 1793; adv. as published SDA 28 Feb 1793.
Further edns: London, 1793, ESTC t139257; Dublin, 1793 (Printed for Messrs. G. Burnet, P. Wogan, P. Byrne, H. Colbert, J. Moore [and 6 others in Dublin], 2 vols., 12mo), EM 4847: 4, ESTC t138787; London, 1810 (WC); London, 1822 (Summers); London, 1823 (Summers); NSTC lists edn. in 1810, 1820, 1822 and [1850?]. German trans. Leipzig, 1795 (*Das alte Schloss*) (RS). Facs: FCy.

CR describes the requisites of a good novel and measures Smith against them: '... we are forced to confess, that though we have found much to commend, we have also found much to disapprove' (p. 45). 'With regard to *character* in this novel, we find little that can be said to leave a clear and distinct image on the mind.... We are afraid we can say little of *plot*, for there seems to be none, but the *concealment of a will*, and still less of the *denouement*, which, in our opinion, is "most lame and impotent." ... She certainly possesses in no inferior degree the power to arrest and command attention, by a happy description of circumstances and objects awful, terrific, and sublime; and discovers such fertility of imagination, as often to multiply incident on incident, even when there appears no necessity for it. The pathetic, or the tender, we do not think is Mrs. Smith's forte; but the bold, the manly, the intrepid, and the dignified sentiments of the human breast are touched with no unskilful hand. The work is likewise, on the whole, written in an easy flowing style...' (pp. 52–3).
MR [William Enfield]: 'The main plot is diversified with many collateral occurrences, which all contribute to give unity to the whole. The narrative, if not in every particular guided by probability, is however too well filled up with incident to suffer the reader's attention to flag. The characters are drawn with strength and discrimination, and speak their own appropriate language.

This novel particularly contains many very successful imitations of the ordinary language of people in different classes of the inferior ranks, which may in some instances remind the reader of that great painter of manners, Henry Fielding' (pp. 150–1).

1793: 40   THOMSON, Rev. J[ames].
MAJOR PIPER; OR THE ADVENTURES OF A MUSICAL DRONE. A NOVEL. IN FIVE VOLUMES. BY THE REV. J. THOMSON.

London: Printed for G. G. J. and J. Robinson, Paternoster-Row, 1793.
I vii, 234p; II 266p; III 272p; IV 252p; V 219p. 12mo. 15s (CR), 15s sewed (MR, SJC).
CR n.s. 10: 472 (Apr 1794); MR n.s. 14: 465 (Aug 1794); AF II: 4461.
MnU WILS RAR 824T382 OM; ESTC n004436 (BI O).

Notes. 'To the Reader' 1, v–vii.
Adv. SJC 26–28 Nov 1793.
Further edn: Dublin, 1794 (Printed for Messrs. P. Wogan, P. Byrne, and W. Jones, 2 vols., 12mo), EM 6423: 2, ESTC t135341.

CR: '. . . we are obliged to wade through more absurdity than we ever remember to have encountered even in the pages of modern novels. Manners mistaken and misrepresented; conduct ridiculously absurd in characters laboured with the greatest care; adventures too improbable to amuse; and a vein of broad grotesque humour, of outré description, which Smollett introduced, and which his masterly hand could scarcely wield without exciting, at times, disgust. Under Mr. Thomson's management, it is intolerable.'

MR [Thomas Holcroft and Ralph Griffiths]: 'To analyze a work so vulgar, absurd, and in every respect contemptible, as is this meanest of the class of novels, would be a degradation of the noble art of criticism, for which we do not chuse to be answerable.'

1793: 41   {TODD, E.}.
D'ARCY. A NOVEL. IN ONE VOLUME. DEDICATED, BY PERMISSION, TO HIS ROYAL HIGHNESS THE DUKE OF YORK.

London: Printed for T. Dangerfield, Berkeley Square, 1793.
147p. 12mo.
NjP Ex 3934.92.328.11; ESTC n028437.

Notes. Dedication to H.R.H. the Duke of York, signed E. Todd.
Dublin edn. claims on title-page to be by Charlotte Smith and its dedication to H.R.H. Frederick, Duke of York is signed 'C. Smith' and refers to Sir Charles Asgill's having solicited and obtained for her the 'pleasing gratification' of dedicating the work to him.
Epistolary.
Further edns: Dublin, 1793 (Printed by Brett Smith, 1 vol., 12mo), ESTC t219583; Philadelphia, 1796, xESTC (WC).

1793: 42   [TOWERS, Joseph].
THE HISTORY OF PHILIP WALDEGRAVE. IN TWO VOLUMES.

London: Printed for T. Evans, No. 46, Paternoster-Row, 1793.
xvi, 247p; II xii, [203]p. 12mo. 6s boards (CR, MR).
CR n.s. 10: 330–1 (Mar 1794); MR n.s. 14: 113 (May 1794); AF II: 4509.
BL C.171.d.2; EMf; ESTC t208539 (NA CtY).

Notes. Last p. of vol. 2 misnumbered 20. Table of contents in each vol. 1 p. adv. end vol. 2.
Adv. SJC 14–17 Dec 1793.
Further edn: London, 1798, ESTC t167679.

CR: '. . . the history of Philip Waldegrave might easily be dispatched in half a dozen lines. . . . But the truth is, the ingenious author has made the story a mere vehicle for criticisms, biographical anecdotes, sentiments on life and manners, and anything else which may be supposed to have been stored in the common-place book, or in the recollection of a man of observation and general reading. The sentiments are such as become a man of liberality, virtue, and benevolence; and the characters are sketched from nature; but in neither the one nor the other do we meet with any thing new or uncommon; the subjects are very slightly connected, and the whole has more resemblance to an agreeable, but desultory conversation, than it has to any of the more elaborate and regular forms of composition.'

MR [William Enfield]: 'The present work differs much from the generality of novels; it does not abound in plot, intrigue, and surprising incidents; and, if its *simple story* incite the reader to pursue it, his attraction must centre in the conversations which are episodically introduced:—in these, the writer passes judgment on eminent characters, on literary productions, on painting, and on several other subjects; and little objection can be made to the propriety of his remarks, though they are too general to be instructive. Credit is, however, due to him for his departure from the general flippancy and *nothingness* of modern novel-writing. . . .'

1793: 43   [TRUSLER, John].
LIFE; OR, THE ADVENTURES OF WILLIAM RAMBLE, ESQ. WITH THREE FRONTISPIECES, DESIGNED BY IBBETSON, HIGHLY ENGRAVED, AND TWO NEW AND BEAUTIFUL SONGS, WITH THE MUSIC BY PLEYEL AND STERKEL. BY THE AUTHOR OF MODERN TIMES; OR, THE ADVENTURES OF GABRIEL OUTCAST. IN THREE VOLUMES.

London: Printed for Dr. Trusler, and sold at the Literary Press, N° 62, Wardour-Street,
    Soho, 1793.
I vi, 174p; II 215p; III 177p. 12mo. 10s 6d (CR), 10s 6d sewed (SDA, SJC).
CR n.s. 9: 118 (Sept 1793); AF II: 4547.
O 249.s.78-80; EM 2009: 3; ESTC t070718 (BI BL, E; NA MH-H).

Notes. Table of contents and errata 1, [iii]-vi. Frontispieces to all 3 vols. 1 p. adv. (for Trusler's *Modern Times*, 1785: 46) end vol. 1. In vols. 2 and 3 text of novel starts on p. 3. 3 pp. advs. (for Trusler's *Modern Times* and *Trusler's Monthly Communications*) end vol. 3.
BL copy has 2 folded leaves of music beginning vol. 1.
Adv., 'Embellished with Three beautiful engraved Frontispieces, designed by Ibbetson; And Two New very pleasing Airs, with the Music, by Pleyell and Sterkell' SDA 25 May 1793; adv. SJC 20–22 June 1793.

CR: 'From the sing-song and embellishments announced in the title of this work, we were led to entertain some suspicions as to its actual merit. And the fact is, that it ranks with the common herd of flimsy narratives. . . .'

1793: 44   [WALKER, George].
THE ROMANCE OF THE CAVERN; OR, THE HISTORY OF FITZHENRY AND JAMES. IN TWO VOLUMES.

London: Printed for William Lane, at the Minerva-Press, Leadenhall-Street, 1793.
I iv, 249p; II 242p. 6s (CR).
CR n.s. 10: 349 (Mar 1794).
Corvey; CME 3-628-45157-4; xESTC.

Notes. Preface i–iv. 3 pp. advs. end vol. 1; 2 pp. advs. end vol. 2. Vol. 2 t.p. lacks hyphen in 'Minerva Press'.
Adv., 'now in the Press', SJC 24–26 Oct 1793.
Blakey lists as 1792.

CR: 'This strange farrago is copied from various popular novels. The Romance of a Forest gave it the name; the Recess its heroes; and Ferdinand Count Fathom has supplied some of its most interesting events. Others are gleaned from different sources, which have left an impression on the mind, though not sufficiently deep to be traced to their origin. The whole is absurd and improbable: we had begun to mark the inconsistencies of the story; but they would have filled a volume: its own weight is sufficient to sink it. The events astonish without interesting: the heroes are sunk in despair, or raised to happiness, without the reader's feeling a pang or transport.'

[*The Romance of the Forest* 1791: 58; *The Recess* 1783: 15 and 1785: 37; *Ferdinand Count Fathom*, (1753), JR 193, AF I: 2592.]

1793: 45   [WEST, Jane].
THE ADVANTAGES OF EDUCATION, OR, THE HISTORY OF MARIA
WILLIAMS, A TALE FOR MISSES AND THEIR MAMMAS, BY PRUDEN-
TIA HOMESPUN, IN TWO VOLUMES.

London: Printed for William Lane, at the Minerva Press, Leadenhall-Street, 1793.
I 239p; II 236p. 12mo. 5s sewed (CR), 6s sewed (MR, SJC).
CR n.s. 9: 476 (Dec 1793); MR n.s. 16: 228–9 (Feb 1795); AF II: 4739.
BL Ch. 790/96; EM 6363: 6; ESTC t090520 (BI O; NA CaAEU, IU, MH-H &c.).

Notes. 2-pp. preface. 1 p. adv. end vol. 1.
Adv. SDA 31 July 1793; adv. SJC 24–26 Oct 1793.
Further edn: Dublin, 1799 (Printed by William Porter, and N. Kelly, 2 vols., 12mo), ESTC t208078; London, 1803 (WC, NSTC). French trans. n.p., n.d. (*Histoire de la Famille Glanville, ou les Effets de l'éducation*) (HWS). Facs: Fcy.

CR quotes the author's prefatory statement about her moral purpose and concludes: 'It is but justice to add, that her fancy has by no means misled her judgment in the execution of this task.'

MR [William Enfield]: 'Amid the multiplicity of fictitious tales which tend to excite romantic sentiments and false ideas of life, in young minds, it affords us pleasure to see this captivating species of writing sometimes employed, unequivocally and powerfully, for the purpose of effacing these false impressions, and substituting in their room the genuine dictates of good sense and prudence. This is the professed design of the present work; and we have seldom seen one better adapted to answer the end' (p. 228).

1794

ADOLPHUS DE BIRON
See THOMAS, Ann

1794: 1   ANON.
THE ADVENTURES OF HENRY FITZHERBERT, GENTLEMAN.

> London: Printed for Rawson and Co. Hull; and sold by Vernor and Hood, Birchin Lane, London, 1794.
> 199p. 12mo. 2s 6d sewed (SJC), 3s sewed (OPA).
> EngR 27: 83 (Jan 1796).
> BL 12612.de.16; EM 205: 1; ESTC t066883 (NA DFo).

Notes. Text of novel starts on p. 3.
Adv. SJC 24–26 Apr 1794; adv. OPA 1 Jan 1795.
    EngR: 'These are adventures neither worth relating nor writing. And there is a manner of relating adventures necessary to make even the most interesting be read with pleasure. Whether it be more owing to the nature of the adventures of Henry Fitzherbert, gentleman, or to his manner of relating them, it is difficult to determine; but we can say, for our part, they are not worth reading.'

ALF VON DEULMEN
See NAUBERT, Christiane Benedicte Eugenie

1794: 2   ANON.
ANGELINE; OR, SKETCHES FROM NATURE A NOVEL.

> London: Printed for Kerby, Lindsell, and King, Stafford Street, Old Bond Street, and Corner of Wimpole Street, Cavendish Square, 1794.
> I 215p; II 191p; III 183p. 12mo. 9s (CR).
> CR n.s. 12: 236–7 (Oct 1794).
> BL 12611.i.21; EM 197: 3; ESTC t057425 (BI MRu; NA CtY-BR, MH-H).

Notes. CR: 'This novel is particularly well calculated for a circulating-library; as the entertainment it affords will suit the generality of readers, and is unmixed with any sentiments which can corrupt the purity of the mind' (p. 237).

1794: 3   ANON.
ARGENTUM: OR, ADVENTURES OF A SHILLING.

> London: Printed for J. Nichols; and sold by J. Pridden, No. 100, Fleet-street, 1794.
> 167p. 8vo [MR has 12mo]. 2s 6d sewed (MR).
> MR n.s. 15: 228 (Oct 1794); AF II: 135.
> BL 12611.ee.8; EM 64: 9; ESTC t057427 (BI O; NA MH-H, NjP, PPL).

Notes. 1 p. adv. end vol.

MR [William Enfield]: 'By the help of a shilling which, naturally enough, passes from pocket to pocket, the reader is here introduced to the acquaintance of its owners, one after another:—but, as it is also very natural for a shilling to exchange masters in a pretty rapid succession, we are not permitted to remain with any one long enough to become acquainted with his character. Among the variety of portraits presented in this raree-show-book, some, however, are tolerably sketched, and the reader will find two or three little stories which may afford amusement for a few minutes.'

THE BROTHERS; A NOVEL
See App. A: 6

1794: 4 ANON.
CAROLINE DE MONTMORENCI: A TALE, FOUNDED IN FACTS. BY LA MARQUISE DE *****.

> London: Printed by G. Woodfall, for T. N. Longman, Paternoster-Row, 1794.
> 196p. 12mo [MR has 8vo]. 3s sewed (CR, MR).
> CR n.s. 11: 234 (June 1794); MR n.s. 15: 228 (Oct 1794); AF II: 610.
> BL 12613.gg.1; EM 202: 6; ESTC t108370 (NA ICN, MH-H).

Notes. 2 pp. advs. at end. 500 copies printed by Woodfall, 1794 (LA).
Epistolary. Adv. SJC 29–31 May 1794.
Adv. end vol. 3 of *Clara Duplessis* (1797: 50).

CR: 'This story, which is written in letters, consists rather of a series of detached episodes than of one uniform narrative. It may, as is said in the title-page, be really founded in fact; but we cannot say that it has any strong claim to interest the reader, in respect either of sentiment or information.'

MR [William Enfield]: 'A tender tale of disappointed love. . . . This short story is not destitute of affecting incidents, but does not display much originality of invention, nor any great degree of elegance of language.'

1794: 5 ANON.
CAROLINE MERTON, A NOVEL, FOUNDED ON FACTS; BY A LADY.

> London: Printed for the Author; and sold by W Richardson, Royal-Exchange; and all
>   other booksellers, 1794.
> I 184p; II v, 160p. 12mo. 5s sewed (CR), 6s sewed (MR), 6s boards (SJC).
> CR n.s. 12: 472–3 (Dec 1794); MR n.s. 16: 229–30 (Feb 1795); AF II: 611.
> CtY Im.C221.794; ESTC n043733 (NA ICU, NNU).

Notes. Prefatory address 'To the Reader', dated June 1794, bound beginning vol. 2 (in both CtY and ICU copies). Epistolary.
Adv., 'On Monday the 11th of August, will be published', SJC 31 July–2 Aug 1794.
German trans. Leipzig, 1795 (*Caroline Merton*) (RS).

CR: 'This novel, without claiming a very high rank among its numerous tribe, may be read with some pleasure and improvement. The cause of morality is supported upon proper principles, and characters are preserved with skill, and the story does no great violence to probability. *Founded on fact* is an assertion which we are seldom disposed to credit, and we would advise young writers especially, to drop it.'

MR [William Enfield]: 'Those who estimate a story by the quantity of love which it contains will be highly pleased with this novel. Perhaps a greater number of lovers have seldom been brought together within so narrow a compass; and their loves, too, so charmingly intertwined!' (p. 129).

CASTLE ZITTAW
See R., C.

1794: 6 ANON.
*THE CAVERN OF DEATH. A MORAL TALE.

> London: Printed for J. Bell, No. 148, Oxford-street, opposite New Bond-street (SJC), 1794 (SJC).
> 8vo. 116p. 2s 6d sewed (MR), 3s sewed (OPA).
> MR n.s. 14: 464–5 (Aug 1794); AF II: 650.
> No copy located.

Notes. Prefatory advertisement explains that the tale was originally serialized in the newspaper *True Briton.*
Adv. SJC 22–25 Feb 1794; adv., 'with a beautiful frontispiece', OPA 19 Feb 1795.
Further edns: London, 1794, EM 218: 5, ESTC t008502; Cork, 1795 (Printed by J. Connor, Circulating Library, 1 vol., 12mo) ESTC t162910; Dublin, 1795, EM 3457: 15, ESTC t061505; Philadelphia, 1795, ESTC w037348; Baltimore, 1795 (WC) xESTC; 1 post-1800 entry in WC. French trans. Paris, 1799 (*La Caverne de la Mort*) (Lévy).

> MR [George Edward Griffiths]: 'The story is told in correct and good language, and it is interesting and impressive; but we like not this mode of impression, which fills the mind of the juvenile reader with horrid ideas of supernatural agency, and makes him fancy, like Macbeth, that he sees bloody spectres flitting before his eyes, and ensanguined daggers streaming in the air.'

1794: 7 ANON.
COUNT RODERIC'S CASTLE: OR, GOTHIC TIMES, A TALE. IN TWO VOLUMES.

> London: Printed for William Lane, at the Minerva-Press, Leadenhall-Street, 1794.
> I 224p; II 246p. 8vo [MR has 12mo]. 7s sewed (CR), 6s sewed (MR, adv.).
> CR n.s. 13: 469 (Apr 1795); MR n.s. 16: 466–7 (Apr 1795); AF II: 878.
> BL 1607/3866; EM 2592: 1; ESTC t118881 (NA MnU).

Notes. 2 pp. advs. end vol. 2.
Adv., 'in the Press, and speedily will be published', MP 31 July 1794; still adv., 'In the Press and speedily will be published', SJC 2–4 Oct 1794; adv. as published MP 31 Oct 1794.
Adv. end vol. 2 of *The House of Tynian* (1795: 46): 'By the Author of the Carpenter's Daughter' (1791: 4).
Further edns: London, 1794, ESTC n002077; Baltimore, 1795, ESTC w037627; Philadelphia, 1795, ESTC w037628; London, 1846 (Summers, NSTC). German trans. Leipzig, 1796 (*Das Schloss des Grafen Roderich*) (EAG); French trans. Paris, 1807 (*Le château du comte Roderic*) (BLC).

> CR: 'Stories founded upon feudal institutions and usages, which, like the heathen mythology, are become now almost obsolete, require, to give them interest, no *common* energies of

fancy, or powers of description. The romance of Count Roderic's Castle, like the preceding [*The Duke of Clarence* 1795: 21], treats of battles and murders, woods and fortresses, heroes and heroines. But the incidents are *somewhat* better connected, the style less inflated, and the superstitious terrors, which are introduced, as usual, to heighten the effect, are accounted for....'

MR [William Enfield]: 'In works of fiction, fertility of invention is unquestionably the first excellence; and this excellence the author of this romantic tale now before us certainly possesses. The story at its first opening seizes irresistibly on the reader's fancy, and through the whole of the first volume rivets his attention to a crowded succession of incidents full of surprize and terror; and though, in the second volume, the mind is somewhat relieved from the uninterrupted suspense and agitation in which it has been kept, its interesting emotions are never suffered to flag; they are only turned into a different channel, in which curiosity and sympathy unite to afford him new pleasure.... this tale is conceived with originality, and elegantly written, and ... those readers who can find pleasure in things new, strange, and terrible, will be much gratified by a visit to Count Roderic's Castle.'

1794: 8 ANON.
*THE DUPE, A MODERN SKETCH.

London: Debrett (MR).
2 vols. 12mo. 5s (CR), 5s sewed (MR).
CR n.s. 10: 472 (Apr 1794); MR n.s. 14: 113–14 (May 1794); AF II: 1189.
No copy located.

Notes. BC gives date of 1793, format of 8vo and bookseller as 'Woodfall, &c.'

CR: 'Many good sort of men meet with an equal number of good sort of women; they marry, after some difficulties, and are, we suppose, very happy.—There is a fool also, who meets with artful and designing impostors: but this is less common; yet such adventures fill this flimzy performance.'

MR [William Enfield]: '... had the writer confined himself to his leading design, it is probable, from the comic strokes interspersed through the work, that he would have written two entertaining volumes:—but he has almost entirely destroyed the effect of the sketch, by grouping with the main figures many others, which have scarcely the most distant relation to them, and which are only brought in by pairs to fall in love with each other, and to fill up the picture.'

1794: 9 ANON.
EDWARD DE COURCY, AN ANCIENT FRAGMENT. IN TWO VOLUMES.

London: Printed for William Lane, at the Minerva Press, Leadenhall-Street, 1794.
I xii, 172p; II 192p. 8vo [MR has 12mo]. 6s sewed (MR).
MR n.s. 15: 466–7 (Dec 1794); AF II: 1216.
BL 12622.pp.9; CME 3-628-45067-5; EM 367: 5; ESTC t108636 (NA CaAEU; EA COR).

Notes. By same author as *Ranspach* (1797: 21).
'Editor's Preface' 1, v–xii. Verso of t.ps. of both vols have note: 'This tale includes a brief sketch of the civil and religious liberties of England in former times; and intended as a contrast to their flourishing condition at the end of the eighteenth century.'

Adv., 'in the Press, and speedily will be published', MP 31 July 1794; adv. as published MP 31 Oct 1794.

MR [William Enfield]: 'Notwithstanding the obvious objection which lies against this historical novel, in common with all productions of the same class, that its tendency is rather to confound than to illustrate history, we feel ourselves strongly impelled to recommend the present fictitious narrative to the attention of our readers. It represents, in a style considerably above that of the ordinary run of novels, the state of society in England, particularly with respect to civil and religious liberty, about the beginning of the fifteenth century, at the commencement of the civil war of the White and Red Roses; and the writer displays a liberal spirit, a well-cultivated understanding, and correct taste.'

1794: 10 ANON.
ELLEN RUSHFORD. A NOVEL. IN TWO VOLUMES.

> London: Printed for William Lane, at the Minerva Press Leadenhall-Street, 1794.
> I 198p; II 140p. 12mo. 6s sewed (CR, MP).
> CR n.s. 14: 225–6 (June 1795).
> BL 12612.bb.19; EM 130: 4; ESTC t064716.

Notes. Adv., 'in the Press, and speedily will be published', MP 31 July 1794; adv. as published MP 31 Oct 1794.

CR: 'In this novel there is no want of that, which we have too much reason to say, is a distinguishing characteristic of the productions from the "*Minerva* press," namely, the frivolous and the improbable. Such of our readers, therefore, as have no objection to novel reading on these conditions, may resort to Ellen Rushford for their afternoon's amusement.'

1794: 11 ANON.
THE EMIGRANTS: A GALLIC TALE. IN TWO VOLUMES.

> London: Printed for J. Bell, no. 148, Oxford-Street, 1794.
> I 202p; II 212p. 12mo. 6s sewed (CR, SJC).
> CR n.s. 12: 69–71 (Sept 1794); AF II: 1269.
> O 249.s.127,128; ESTC n065439 (NA CSmH).

Notes. 2 pp. advs. end vol. 1. Epistolary.

Adv., 'In the Press, and the 1st of March will be published', SJC 22–25 Feb 1794; adv. as published SJC 27–29 Mar 1790.

CR: 'This novel is carried on by letters, which are written with ease, and a degree of sprightliness; but the partiality of the writer is evident, in making all his patriot characters amiable, and all the aristocratic ones the reverse. . . . Exaggeration does no good to a cause' (p. 70).

EVENING RECREATIONS
See App. A: 7

1794: 12 ANON.
THE FAIR METHODIST; OR, SUCH THINGS ARE: IN THE COURSE OF A TOUR FROM LONDON TO CANTERBURY, AND DOVER; BATH AND BRISTOL HOT-WELLS. A SERIOUS NOVEL. FOUNDED IN TRUTH.

London: Printed for J. Bell, British Library, Strand, 1794.
I ix, 145p; II 306p. 8vo [CR has 12mo]. 6s (CR).
CR n.s. 12: 235–6 (Oct 1794).
BL 1156.i.14; EM 2901: 3, ESTC t123558 (BI BRw).

Notes. Dedication to Sir Rowland Hill 1, i–ix; unn. 3-pp. preface between dedication and text.
Pagination is almost continuous between the two volumes; vol. 1 ends with p. 145 and vol. 2
starts with p. 145.

CR: 'It is a simple tale, almost approaching to silliness, very plainly, and very dully related,
and conveys neither amusement nor instruction' (p. 235).

THE HAUNTED CASTLE, A NORMAN ROMANCE
See WALKER, George

THE HAUNTED PRIORY
See CULLEN, Stephen

HERMAN OF UNNA: A SERIES OF ADVENTURES
See NAUBERT, Christiane Benedicte Eugenie

IVEY CASTLE
See BROMLEY, Eliza Nugent

MADELINE; OR, THE CASTLE OF MONTGOMERY
See KELLY, Isabella

1794: 13   ANON.
THE MYSTIC COTTAGER OF CHAMOUNY: A NOVEL, IN TWO VOL-
UMES.

London: Printed for William Lane, at the Minerva-Press, Leadenhall-Street, 1794.
I 183p; II 170p. 12mo. 6s sewed (CR, MP).
CR n.s. 13: 229–30 (Feb 1795); AF II: 3026.
BL 12655.bb.38; EM 269: 9; ESTC t107264 (BI C; NA ViU).

Notes. By same author as *The Observant Pedestrian* (1795: 8) and *Montrose, or the Gothic Ruin*
(1799: 12).
4-pp. 'Address to the Public' signed 'The Authoress'. 1 p. advs. end vol. 1.
Adv. MP 21 Nov 1794; additional booksellers are Scatcherd and Co. Ave-Maria-Lane; Miller,
Old Bond street; Knight and Co. Booksellers to His Majesty, St James's-street.
Further edn: Dublin, 1795 (Printed for P. Byrne, H. Colbert and J. Potts, 1 vol., 12mo), EM
3558: 6, ESTC t055567; Philadelphia, 1795, ESTC w026851.

CR: 'It is not wholly destitute of merit, and we will so far encourage the benevolent
intention of the author, as to say that the reader's time will not be quite thrown away'
(p. 230).

THE NECROMANCER: OR THE TALE OF THE BLACK FOREST
See KAHLERT, Carl Friedrich

THE OFFSPRING OF RUSSELL
See SUMMERSETT, Henry

THE PARISIAN
See CHARLTON, Mary

THE PRINCE OF LEON
See HUGILL, Martha

SELIMA, OR THE VILLAGE TALE
See HOLFORD, Margaret

1794: 14   ANON.
THE TALES OF ELAM. IN TWO VOLUMES.
> London: Printed for William Lane, at the Minerva Press, Leadenhall-Street, 1794.
> I 124p; II 276p. 12mo. 6s sewed (CR, MR).
> CR n.s. 12: 358 (Nov 1794); MR n.s. 15: 354 (Nov 1794); AF II: 4339.
> NcU RBC PR3991.A1.T3 v.1, v.2; ESTC n046779.

Notes. Adv., 'in the Press, and speedily will be published', MP 31 July 1794; adv. as published MP 3 Sept 1794; additional booksellers are Knight and Co. Booksellers to his Majesty, St James's-street; Harlowe, Bookseller to the Queen, Pall-Mall; Millar, Bond-street; and Scatchard, Bookseller, Paternoster-Row.

CR: '. . . not worth a farthing.'

MR [William Enfield]: 'It may perhaps admit of debate whether the pleasure, which is taken in the extravagance and impossibility of Eastern fictions, be not the effect of childish taste, of the same kind with that which has given popularity to the stories of George and the Dragon, and Jack the Giant-killer; and whether they ought not therefore to be rejected with contempt by maturity of judgment. However this be, it seems very certain that, where imaginary beings are introduced merely to do what might as well be done by the ordinary powers of nature, they are entirely superfluous. This we apprehend to be very much the case with the machinery of these tales. . . . the stories must still be allowed a considerable share of merit, from the variety of incidents and character which they present, well suited to gratify the reader's curiosity, to impress his mind with pleasing images and sentiments, and to furnish him with useful lessons of moral wisdom.'

THE TWO COUSINS
See PINCHARD, Elizabeth

VICISSITUDES IN GENTEEL LIFE
See LEWIS, Alethea Brereton

THE VICTIM OF PASSION
See RAINSFORD, Mrs

THE VISIT FOR A WEEK
See PEACOCK, Lucy

1794: 15   ANON.
THE WEIRD SISTERS: A NOVEL, IN THREE VOLUMES.

> London: Printed for William Lane, at the Minerva Press, Leadenhall-Street, 1794.
> I 264p; II 240p; III 204p. 12mo. 9s sewed (CR, MR).
> CR n.s. 12: 358 (Nov 1794); MR n.s. 15: 466 (Dec 1794); AF II: 4728.
> BL 1507/1424; EM 2728: 4; ESTC t129455.

Notes. By same author as Waldeck Abbey (1795: 10) and A Butler's Diary (1792: 4).
Adv., 'in the Press, and speedily will be published', MP 31 July 1794; adv. as published MP 4
Oct 1794; additional booksellers are Scatchard, Ave-Maria-Lane; Miller, Old Bond street;
Knight and Co. Booksellers to His Majesty, St James's-street. Adv. SJC 2–4 Oct 1794.
Re-adv., with quotation from BC, SJC 5–7 Feb 1795.
Adv. end vol. 2 of The House of Tynian (1795: 46).

CR: 'The story, in its beginning, is agreeably romantic, and conducted through the subsequent stages without much variety of incident; but the progression is by steps consistent with
probability; and the three sisters are led, by their respective lovers, to the altar of Hymen at
the same time. We cannot, however, avoid remarking, that the French sentences which occur
in this work, are generally printed incorrectly.'

MR [William Enfield]: 'Their tale is not generally unnatural; unless it be unnatural for
innocent damsels, brought up in a cottage, to be the dupes of an intriguing governess; or for
young men of gallantry to be captivated by their charms, and to purchase their favour by
encountering dangers for their rescue.... On the whole, we cannot place this novel very high
in the scale of merit. The language is extremely inaccurate.'

1794: 16   BENNETT, [Anna Maria].
ELLEN, COUNTESS OF CASTLE HOWEL, A NOVEL, IN FOUR VOL-
UMES. BY MRS. BENNETT.

> London: Printed for William Lane, at the Minerva Press, Leadenhall-Street, 1794.
> I 241p; II 240p; III 223p; IV 234p. 12mo. 14s (CR), 12s sewed (MR, Min).
> CR n.s. 15: 118–19 (Sept 1795); MR n.s. 14: 74–7 (May 1794).
> BL 12614.h.12; EM 370: 1; ESTC t073510 (BI O; NA CtY, CSmH, DLC, MH-H, NjP,
>   PU, ViU &c.).

Notes. 1 p. advs. end vol. 4.
Adv., 'In a few Days will be published', SJC 13–15 Feb 1794.
Further edns: Dublin, 1794 (Printed by P. Wogan, 2 vols., 12mo), ESTC t202652; Dublin,
1794, ESTC t153940; London, 1805 (WC, NSTC). French trans. Paris, 1822 (Hélène, comtesse
de Castle-Howel) (BN).

CR: the novel contains '... greater discrimination of character, variety, and interest, than
is usually met with in works of a similar nature' (p. 118).

MR: '... we have been much entertained with the first three volumes of the present production, as they abound in many of the excellencies which we have enumerated:—but as the time
is come for us to grasp the wand of the censor more forcibly than we have hitherto attempted
on similar occasions, we select this performance for the express purpose of pointing out a
growing error in modern novels; viz. the giving too much weight to the Passion of Love' (p. 75).

1794: 17   [BROMLEY, Eliza Nugent].
IVEY CASTLE, A NOVEL; CONTAINING INTERESTING MEMOIRS OF

TWO LADIES, LATE NUNS IN A FRENCH ABOLISHED CONVENT.
WRITTEN BY THE AUTHOR OF LAURA AND AUGUSTUS, &C. IN
TWO VOLUMES.

London: Printed for J. Owen, No. 168, Piccadilly, 1794.
I 247p; II 208p. 12mo. 6s sewed (CR, MR).
CR n.s. 12: 472 (Dec 1794); MR n.s. 15: 353 (Nov 1794); AF II: 4805.
Corvey; CME 3-628-45079-9; xESTC.

Notes. Epistolary.
Laura and Augustus 1784: 13.

CR: 'An insipid mediocrity so generally prevails throughout this novel, that it becomes
unnecessary to say any thing of the improbability of the fable, or the vulgarity of the style. It
would not be difficult to construct a machine for making such novels as *Ivey Castle.*'

MR [William Enfield]: 'What has been satirically said of some women may be truly said of
many novels, that they have no character. Their incidents are so trite, and their language is so
hackneyed, that to undertake to delineate them by any discriminating features were a hopeless task. This is the case with respect to Ivey Castle; in which Cupid, as usual, plays at cross-
purposes, till, tired with teazing and fretting his votaries, he at last kindly condescends to
make them happy. The tale is on the whole amusing, and in its general tendency we observe
nothing improper....'

1794: 18   [CHARLTON, Mary].
THE PARISIAN; OR, GENUINE ANECDOTES OF DISTINGUISHED
AND NOBLE CHARACTERS. IN TWO VOLUMES.

London: Printed for William Lane, at the Minerva Press, Leadenhall-Street, 1794.
I 231p; II 216p. 12mo. 6s sewed (CR, Min), 6s (MR).
CR n.s. 13: 116 (Jan 1795); MR n.s. 16: 466 (Apr 1795); AF II: 670.
BL 12611.bb.15; EM 3411: 7; ESTC t033004.

Notes. Dedication (unn.) 'To My Readers'.
Adv. MP 30 Oct 1794.
Adv., 'in the Press, and speedily will be published', MP 31 July 1794; as *Laure, or the
Parisian.*
Adv. end vol. 1 of *The Mystic Cottager of Chamouny* (1794: 13), as *Laura; or, the Parisian.*

CR: 'The *genuine* anecdotes upon which this novel is founded, are certain *fictions* respecting a part of the family of the late wretched duke of Orleans, a man who surely required not
the blackening of imagination. Madame Genlis, we know not why, is made to partake of the
duke's infamy, while she is represented as pursuing a conduct too vulgarly absurd for a
woman of her sense and talents. The story, in other respects, however, is not ill told; and the
modern manners of certain fashionable inhabitants of St George's and St James's parishes,
are held up to proper ridicule.'

MR [William Enfield]: '... we find little, either in the fable, sentiments, or language, to
entitle it to any high degree of commendation. Its chief merit consists in the lively exhibition
of some of the frivolities of high life. Several of the characters are strongly marked with the
negligent gaiety of fashionable manners. The story, considered as an entire plot, produces
little effect: but some of the incidents are not unamusing, and the piece, all together, may
afford a tolerable *lounge.*'

1794: 19   [CONTANT] D'ORVILLE, [André-Guillaume].
PAULINE, OR THE VICTIM OF THE HEART. FROM THE FRENCH OF
DORVILLE. IN TWO VOLUMES.

> London: Printed for William Lane, at the Minerva Press, Leadenhall-Street, 1794.
> I xv, 263p; II 224p. 12mo. 6s sewed (CR).
> CR n.s. 13: 115–16 (Jan 1795).
> Corvey; CME 3-628-45065-9; ESTC t200848 (NA CtY).

Notes. Trans. of Le mariage du siècle ou lettres de madame la comtesse de Castelli à madame la baronne de Fréville ('En France', 1766).
1 p. adv. end vol. 1. Epistolary.

CR: 'The translator of this novel, in delineating some of the characters, has deviated, but with judgment, from the authority of the original. The Dramatis Personæ, if we may be allowed to call them by that name, are painted, in a few instances, with peculiar energy of expression. Partly founded, it is said, in facts, and partly fictitious, the whole is well calculated to show the dangerous consequences which flow from permitting ourselves to be fascinated by the specious exterior, the light attraction, and the frivolous accomplishment; the objects intended to be displayed.'

1794: 20   [CULLEN, Stephen].
THE HAUNTED PRIORY: OR, THE FORTUNES OF THE HOUSE OF
RAYO. A ROMANCE FOUNDED PARTLY ON HISTORICAL FACTS.

> London: Printed for J. Bell, no. 148, Oxford-Street, opposite Bond-Street, 1794.
> 256p. 8vo. 4s (CR), 4s sewed (SJC).
> CR n.s. 11: 468 (Aug 1794); AF II: 950.
> MH-H *EC75.C8978.794h; EM 3058: 8; ESTC n017266 (NA CSmH, CtY, PU, ViU &c.).

Notes. Adv., 'In the Press, and the 1st of March will be published, In One Volume, Crown Octavo, printed the same Size as the Castle of Otranto', SJC 22–25 Feb 1794; adv. as published SJC 27–29 Mar 1794.
Further edns: Dublin, 1794 (Printed for William Jones, 1 vol., 12mo), EM 368: 6, ESTC t071311; New York, 1794, ESTC w038848; New York, 1794, ESTC w012587; London, 1796, EM 3001: 9, ESTC n007128; Philadelphia, 1850 (WC).

CR: '... the reader ... may be disposed to require a little more probability than he will meet with in this tale, which is frigid, though romantic, and does not make amends by the graces of fiction for quitting the plain and useful path of history and fact.'

1794: 21   DAVIES, J{ohn}.
ADOLESCENCE; OR, JUVENILE PROSPERITY AND COTTAGE
FRIENDSHIP. BY J. DAVIES.

> London: Printed for the Author; And sold by Dilly, Poultry; Newbery, St Paul's Church-
>   Yard; Mathews, Strand; Jordan, Fleet-Street; and Trapp, Paternoster-Row, 1794.
> xvi, 149p. 12mo.
> NjP Extran 3708.23.311; ESTC n049996.

Notes. Dedication 'To the Governors and Subscribers / To the Philanthropic Society, and Supports of Sunday Schools', signed 'John Davies', iii–viii; preface ix–xvi.

D'ORVILLE
See CONTANT D'ORVILLE, André Guillaume

1794: 22   DUTTON, Thomas.
THE HERMIT OF THE ALPS; OR, THE FATAL PROGRESS OF ERROR, A PATHETIC NARRATIVE, FOUNDED UPON FACT, TO WHICH IS ADDED CONSCIOUS BENEVOLENCE, A TALE OF OTHER TIMES. BY THOMAS DUTTON, ESQ.

> London: Printed by and for J. Roach, Woburn Street, New Drury Theatre Royal, 1794
> 84p. 12mo.
> MnU WILS RAR MnU 824D954 OH; ESTC n001057 (EA ZWTU).

Notes. Frontispiece. Text begins on p. 3. 'The Hermit of the Alps' pp. 3–39; 'Conscious Benevolence' pp. 40–55; 'The Victim of Sensibility' pp. 56–84.

FLAMMENBERG, Lawrence
See KAHLERT, Carl Friedrich

1794: 23   GODWIN, William.
THINGS AS THEY ARE; OR, THE ADVENTURES OF CALEB WILLIAMS. BY WILLIAM GODWIN. IN THREE VOLUMES.

> London: Printed for B. Crosby, Stationers-Court, Ludgate-Street, 1794.
> I 293p; II 285p; III 304p. 12mo. 10s 6d sewed (CR, MR).
> CR n.s. 11: 290–6 (July 1794); MR n.s. 15: 145–9 (Oct 1794); AF II: 1649.
> C 7720.d.750–752; EM 4154: 1; ESTC t094133 (BI BL, O; NA CtY-BR, CSmH, ICN, IU, MH-H, NjP, TxU, ViU &c.).

Notes. Adv. LC 75: 511 (27–28 May 1794).
Further edns: Dublin, 1795 (Printed for John Rice, 2 vols., 12mo), EM 3762: 3, ESTC t120583; Philadelphia, 1795, ESTC w028047; London, 1796, EM 3703: 2, ESTC t073517; London, 1797, ESTC t126499; Philadelphia, 1802 (WC); WC has 15 further entries between 1800 and 1850; NSTC lists edns. in 1816, 1818, 1831 and 1832. French trans. Geneva, 1795 (*Caleb Williams, ou les Choses comme elles sont*) (Lévy); German trans. Riga, 1795 (*Caleb Williams, ein philosophischer Roman*) (RS).

CR: 'The moral is excellent, but the necessity of *religious* principle, without which we are persuaded no real virtue can exist in the human heart, is not so strongly enforced, as the nature of the story would admit. The characters are extremely well drawn; and the pictures of modern manners are in most instances but too faithfully delineated. The political reflections, which however are not very numerous, might in general have been spared; and in a future edition, which we doubt not so very interesting and entertaining a book must soon come to, we would recommend to the author to expunge a considerable part of them at least.

It is but justice to add, that this work ranks greatly above the whole mass of publications which bear the name of novels, if perhaps we except the productions of Fielding, Smollet [*sic*], and Burney. In the construction and conduct of the narrative, it is even, in our opinion, superior to them' (p. 290).

MR [William Enfield]: 'Between fiction and philosophy there seems to be no natural alliance:—yet philosophers, in order to obtain for their dogmata a more ready reception, have often judged it expedient to introduce them to the world in the captivating dress of fable.... In writing the Adventures of Caleb Williams, this philosopher had doubtless some higher object in view; and it is not difficult to perceive that this object has been to give an easy passport, and general circulation, to some of his favourite opinions' (pp. 145–6). 'With due allowance for systematical eccentricity, (the reader will pardon the paradoxical expression,) this performance, interesting but not gratifying to the feelings and the passions, and written in a style of laboured dignity rather than of easy familiarity, is singularly entitled to be characterized as a work in which the powers of genius and philosophy are strongly united' (p. 149).

1794: 24   GOSLING, Jane.
ASHDALE VILLAGE: A MORAL WORK OF FANCY. BY JANE GOSLING.

> Printed for the Author; And sold by G. G. J. and J. Robinson Paternoster-Row, London; by W. Ward, J. Cales, J. Northall, E. Ridgard, T. Pierson, and J. Smith, Booksellers, Sheffield. And by Mrs. Gosling, in Norfolk-Street, Sheffield, n.d. [ESTC: 1794?].
> I xvii, 242p; II 256p. 8vo [MR has 12mo]. 7s sewed (CR), 6s sewed (MR).
> CR n.s. 12: 358–9 (Nov 1794); MR n.s. 15: 109 (Sept 1794); AF II: 1683.
> ICN Case Y155.G69; ESTC n031045.

Notes. CR: 'The amiable diffidence expressed by Mrs. Gosling, justly gives her a particular claim to such an indulgence; and we should think ourselves deficient, on our part, did we not pay the tribute of approbation to her laudable efforts, as a novelist.'

MR [William Enfield]: 'If it should be thought that she is somewhat deficient in that original invention and that artificial arrangement of materials, by means of which professed artists in this way entice and fix the attention of their readers; or in that ease, perspicuity, and propriety of language, which distinguish well-educated persons in the higher classes of life, whence most of the characters in this novel are taken; she has at least the merit of representing instructive incidents, and of communicating good sentiments, moral, prudential, and religious. The story has been left unfinished: but the kind encouragement of the public would probably induce the author to complete her plan.'

1794: 25   GUNNING, [Elizabeth].
LORD FITZHENRY: A NOVEL. BY MISS GUNNING. IN THREE VOLUMES.

> London: Printed for J. Bell, No. 148, Oxford-Street, 1794.
> I 258p; II 259p; III 275p. 12mo. 10s 6d sewed (CR).
> CR n.s. 12: 473 (Dec 1794); AF II: 1756.
> Corvey; CME 3-628-45044-6; ESTC t171772 (BI MRu; NA CtY, IU).

Notes. Epistolary.
Further edn: Dublin, 1794 (Printed for Messrs. P. Byrne, W. Jones, J. Moore, J. Halpen, and G. Folingsby [imprint to vol. 2 reads 'Printed by William Porter, for P. Wogan' and 5 others], 2 vols., 12mo), ESTC n018914.

CR: 'Through the whole narrative, Miss Gunning's vivacity appears with particular advantage; and she has conducted the story with such ingenious address, that, after a series of obstacles, the happy votaries all come forward in exulting *trio*, to the altar of Hymen.'

1794: 26   GUNNING, [Elizabeth].
THE PACKET: A NOVEL. BY MISS GUNNING.

> London: Printed for J. Bell, no. 148, Oxford-Street, 1794.
> I 260p; II 252p; III 254p; IV 274p. 12mo. 12s sewed (CR).
> CR n.s. 11: 178–81 (June 1794); AF II: 1759.
> C 7720.d.575-576; EM 254: 2; ESTC t074660 (BI BL; NA CaOHM, IU, NjP &c.).

Notes. Further edn: Dublin, 1794 (Printed by Thomas Burnside, for Messrs. P. Wogan, P. Byrne, J. Moore, W. Jones, J. Rice, and H. Colbert, 2 vols., 12mo), EM 4847: 3, ESTC t120689.

CR: 'The language though not elegant, nor every where free from colloquial inaccuracies, is easy; the tale is pathetic, and the catastrophe strongly interests the feelings. The story is, indeed, told in too diffuse a manner, and mixed up with much alloy, which diminishes its value; but in the more interesting situations we think there is much merit, nor is it a small part of that merit that none but virtuous feelings are called forth throughout the whole work' (p. 178).

HARLEY, Mrs
See HUGILL, Martha

1794: 27   HELME, Elizabeth.
DUNCAN AND PEGGY: A SCOTTISH TALE. BY ELIZABETH HELME, AUTHOR OF LOUISA; OR, THE COTTAGE ON THE MOOR: &C. &C. &C. IN TWO VOLUMES.

> London: Printed for J. Bell, no. 148, Oxford-Street, 1794.
> I 295p; II 323p. 12mo. 7s sewed (CR), 6s sewed (LC).
> CR n.s. 14: 113 (May 1795).
> BL 012635.df.5; CME 3-628-45058-6; EM 498: 1; ESTC t108187 (BI E; NA CtY, CSmH, MH-H, ViU; EA COR).

Notes: Louisa; or, the Cottage on the Moor 1787: 38.
Adv. SJC 27–29 Mar 1794. Adv. LC 75: 318 (1–3 Apr 1794).

CR: 'An artless tale, written with simplicity, which may prove an agreeable amusement as a relaxation from graver studies.'

1794: 28   HELME, William.
*HENRY STUKELEY; OR THE EFFECTS OF DISSIPATION. BY WILLIAM HELME.

> London: Dangerfield, 1794 (MR).
> 3 vols. 12mo. 9s sewed (CR, MR).
> CR n.s. 11: 467 (Aug 1794); MR n.s. 16: 230 (Feb 1795).
> No copy located.

Notes. CR: '. . . the author has made ample use of the privileges of fiction, by abundance of recognitions and wonderful turns of fortune; by means of which, not only the hero of the piece, but every one connected with him, is made superlatively happy at the end of the third volume.—Every one who was lost is found; every one who was ruined is reinstated in the favours of fortune, to the infinite satisfaction of the good-natured reader; and nobody is left unhappy but two or three hardened villains, whom one is glad to see punished.—With regard to the execution, there is certainly nothing of fine writing in it, neither is it so deficient as many works of this class, which it has been our fortune to peruse.'

MR [William Enfield]: 'This novel is presented to the public as "a plain unvarnished tale;" and such, in truth, it is. Henry Stukeley belongs to the inferior class of heroes. His boyish frolics, his juvenile amours, and his subsequent adventures by sea and land, are little adapted, either in the incidents themselves, or in the manner in which they are related, to afford pleasure to readers of cultivated taste.'

1794: 29   HOLCROFT, Thomas.
THE ADVENTURES OF HUGH TREVOR. BY THOMAS HOLCROFT.
London: Printed for Shepperson and Reynolds, no. 137, Oxford-Street, 1794.
I vii, 250p; II 208p; III 249p. 12mo. 10s 6d sewed (MR, CR).
CR n.s. 13: 139–43 (Feb 1795); MR n.s. 15: 149–53 (Oct 1794); AF II: 1997.
BL 12612.de.17; EM 206: 4; ESTC t066947 (BI WIS; NA CaAEU, CtY-BR, PU &c.).
Notes. Vols. 4, 5 and 6 1797: 45.
Adv. SJC 31 May–3 June 1794.
Further edns: London, 1794, EM 1497: 1, ESTC n014865; Dublin, 1795–98 (Printed for H. Colbert, 4 vols., 12mo), ESTC n029516; London, 1801 (WC, NSTC). German trans. Leipzig, 1795 (*Hugo Trevor, sein Leben und seine Schicksale*) (EAG); French trans. Paris, 1798 (*Les Aventures de Hugues Trevor ou le Gilblas anglais* (BGR).

CR: 'Novels preach as well as sermons; some occasionally, and in subservience to the adventures; of others, the adventures are subservient to the design of introducing or exploding certain principles, or exposing the errors of all received practices and opinions; of this latter kind is Hugh Trevor. The sentiments of its author are well known, and those of a certain set of authors, who have the zeal of apostles, if not their faith, and who are indefatigable in assailing, sometimes with argument and sometimes with satire, the strong holds of systems and establishments. Wild and enthusiastic as any of those which they mean to destroy, are the theories which they are solicitous to promulgate, but we will not, as some would, add *dangerous*, because to truth there can be no danger from discussion, nor to what is useful from the most scrutinizing exposure' (p. 139).

MR [William Enfield]: '. . . we readily admit that a novel is a proper vehicle for the communication of moral truth. Its suitableness for this purpose, however, arises not so much from the opportunity which it affords of interweaving moral sentiment or speculative discussion with narrative, as from the field which it furnishes for the exhibition of characters, in which the reader may contemplate, as in a mirror, men as they are, or as they ought to be. Perhaps we have few writers, among our present race of wits, more capable of delineating men as they are than Mr. Holcroft. He appears to have conversed much with the world, and to have been a diligent and shrewd observer of manners. He possesses, also, a happy freedom and boldness of pencil, which enable him to draw his portraits, if not actually from the life, yet with all the effect of living manners . . . ' (p. 149). MR concludes: '. . . a performance which displays great abilities and very peculiar tenets' (p. 153).

1794: 30   [HOLFORD, Margaret, the elder].
SELIMA, OR THE VILLAGE TALE, A NOVEL, IN A SERIES OF LETTERS, BY THE AUTHORESS OF FANNY. IN SIX VOLUMES.

London: Printed and sold for the Authoress, by T. Hookham, New Bond-Street; and P. Broster, Chester, n.d. [ESTC: 1794].

I 326p; II 285p; III 279p; IV 267p; V 252p; VI 203p. 12mo. 10s sewed (CR), 18s boards (MR), 18s sewed (SDA).

MR n.s. 14: 112 (May 1794); AF II: 2034.

BL 1152.h.4; EMf; ESTC t084487.

Notes. Epistolary. Novel ends on p. 186 of vol. 6, followed by 'An Elegy on the Death of Louis the Sixteenth.'

Fanny 1785: 35.

Post-dated; adv. as published SJC 2–3 Nov 1793. Adv., 'On Tuesday the 5th of November will be published', SDA 1 Nov 1793; adv. as published SDA 9 Nov 1793.

MR [William Enfield]: 'The story is not barren of incident; and, toward the catastrophe, it becomes interesting: but it is not, throughout, contrived and arranged with that art which is requisite to excite and preserve an eager curiosity. A secondary tale is interwoven which hangs as a dead weight on the principal narrative. . . . The characters, both in high and low life, though not unnatural, have little prominence of feature and boldness of expression. No great variety either of sentiment or of reflection is introduced; and the language, though easy, never rises into elegance.'

1794: 31   [HUGILL, Martha].
THE PRINCE OF LEON. A SPANISH ROMANCE. IN TWO VOLUMES. BY MRS. HARLEY, AUTHOR OF JULIANA ORMESTON, &C.

London: Printed for J. Barker, Russell Court, Drury Lane, 1794.

I vi, 259p; II 276p. 12mo.

MH-H *EC75.H8727.794p; EM 1285: 11. ESTC n011483 (NA PU).

Notes. Preface 1, v–vi. 5 pp. advs. end vol. 1. Text of novel starts on p. 7 in vol. 1 and p. 5 in vol. 2.

Juliana Ormeston 1793: 22.

1794: 32   HUTTON, George.
AMANTUS AND ELMIRA: OR, INGRATITUDE. EXEMPLIFIED IN THE CHARACTER OF INGRATUS. BY GEORGE HUTTON.

London: Printed for B. Crosby, No. 4, Stationers Court, Ludgate Street, 1794.

xii, 174p. 12mo. 3s (CR, adv.), 3s sewed (MR).

CR n.s. 12: 237 (Oct 1794); MR n.s. 15: 353 (Nov 1794); AF II: 2142.

BRU ENC; xESTC.

Notes. Preface v–viii, signed 'G. H.'; table of contents ix–xii. Drop-head title: 'Ingratitude: A Moral Tale'. 6 pp. advs. end vol.

Adv. end vol. 2 of *Arville Castle* (1795: 1).

CR: 'As the first production of a young writer, this novel is entitled to indulgence, and the goodness of his intention is every where apparent. . . . Amantus and Elvira [*sic*] will not be read with indifference by those who think it fair, or natural, to draw a character uniformly vicious, at all times and seasons, and in which no trait, even the smallest, of goodness can be discerned.'

MR [William Enfield]: 'Nothing can be urged against the design of this publication . . . but, with all the candour which we wish to exercise toward the first productions of a young writer, we cannot justly commend the execution. . . . we are unable to discover, either in the incidents of the piece, or in the manner in which they are related, many traces of that rising genius which would promise, on farther maturity of judgment, productions more acceptable to the public. The story abounds with absurdities, and the style is incorrect.'

1794: 33   JEPHSON, Robert.
THE CONFESSIONS OF JAMES BAPTISTE COUTEAU, CITIZEN OF FRANCE. WRITTEN BY HIMSELF: AND TRANSLATED FROM THE ORIGINAL FRENCH, BY ROBERT JEPHSON, ESQ. ILLUSTRATED WITH NINE ENGRAVINGS. IN TWO VOLUMES.
> London: Printed for J. Debrett, Piccadilly, 1794.
> I 257p; II 232p. 12mo. 8s boards (AR).
> AR 18: 504–5 (App [Apr/May 1794]).
> C 7720.d.841,842; EM 9: 5; ESTC 129718 (BI BL, Dt; NA CtY, DLC, NjP &c.).

Notes. ESTC: In fact by Jephson.
Frontispiece vol. 1 and illustrations in both vols. 1: 6-pp. preface; 6-pp. table of contents. 2: 4-pp. table of contents.
Adv., 'Speedily will be published, Printed on a Wove Paper . . . And illustrated by Eight Characteristick Engravings', SJC 12–14 Dec 1793.
AR reviews under 'Novels'.
Further edn: Dublin, 1794 (Printed by Zachariah Jackson, 2 vols., 12mo), ESTC n026911.

> AR: ' . . . in truth, this story seems throughout a mere fiction, written for the unnecessary purpose of loading the french nation with new reproach, for the enormities practised among them since the commencement of the revolution. Their dreadful story, without exaggeration, makes humanity shudder. Why, then, attempt to load it with details which credulity herself cannot swallow? Why call in the aid of imagination to blacken a picture, already not to be viewed without horrour!' (p. 504).

1794: 34   [KAHLERT, Carl Friedrich]; [TEUTHOLD, Peter (trans.)].
THE NECROMANCER: OR THE TALE OF THE BLACK FOREST: FOUNDED ON FACTS. TRANSLATED FROM THE GERMAN OF LAWRENCE FLAMMENBERG, BY PETER TEUTHOLD. IN TWO VOLUMES.
> London: Printed for William Lane, at the Minerva-Press Leadenhall-Street, 1794.
> I 227p; II iii, 248p; 12mo. 6s sewed (CR, MR).
> CR n.s. 11: 469 (Aug 1794); MR n.s. 16: 465–6 (Apr 1795); AF II: 4395.
> ICN Y952.K118; EM 3941: 4; ESTC t014934 (BI BL; NA CLU-S/C, ICN, ViU &c.).

Notes. Trans. of Der Geisterbanner (Breslau, 1792).
"Lawrence Flammenberg" is a pseudonym (ESTC).
In ICN copy translator's preface is bound in vol. 2 (in BL copy it is in the expected place).
Adv., 'In the Press', SJC 3–5 Apr 1794.
Further edn: Dublin, 1795 (Printed by Brett Smith, 2 vols., 12mo), ESTC n041767. Serialised in different trans. in several magazines, 1793–1806, RM 239, 944, 949.

> CR: 'We are assured that the strange events related in these volumes, are founded on facts,

the authenticity of which can be warranted by the translator, who has lived many years not far from the principal place of action. Exclusive of the entertainment arising from this narrative, it has in view an additional purpose, of greater importance to the public. It exposes the arts which have been practised in a particular part of Germany, for carrying on a series of nocturnal depredations in the neighbourhood, and infusing into the credulous multitude a firm belief in the existence of sorcery.'

MR [William Taylor]: 'In the mind of man there is a predisposition to credulity, which too often renders the very means adopted as a remedy, a proximate cause of new disease' (p. 465).' The extraordinary events, which occupy the first volume, are, in the second, not very dexterously, unravelled. . . . Of the style of this novel, we have only to observe that it is not improperly adapted to a work which, we doubt not, will eagerly be pursued by those who are ever on the watch for something new and strange' (p. 456).

1794: 35   [KELLY, Isabella].
MADELINE; OR, THE CASTLE OF MONTGOMERY, A NOVEL. IN THREE VOLUMES.
> London: Printed for William Lane, at the Minerva-Press, Leadenhall-Street, 1794.
> I 224p; II 275p; III 246p. 12mo. 9s sewed (CR, MP, adv.).
> CR n.s. 12: 472 (Dec 1794).
> MH-H *EC8.H3585.794m; EM 1005: 9; ESTC n003931 (BI MRu; NA CaAEU, CtY, ViU).

Notes. 1 p. advs. end vol. 2; 2 pp. advs. end vol. 3.
Adv. MP 31 July 1794.
Adv. end vol. 1 of *Eva* (1799: 53).
Further edn: London, 1795, ESTC t118930.

> CR: 'This novel is rendered interesting, more by variety of subject, than either by the nature, or relative transition, of the incidents which it contains. Madeline is not so much the real, as the nominal heroine of the narrative. The moral, however, is of the highest importance to the attainment of tranquillity and happiness; and, on this account, the production is entitled to a decent rank in the circulating libraries.'

KRAMER, Professor
See NAUBERT, Christiane Benedicte Eugenie, 1794: 41

1794: 36   [LEWIS, Alethea].
VICISSITUDES IN GENTEEL LIFE. IN FOUR VOLUMES.
> Stafford: Printed by Arthur Morgan. And sold by T. Longman, Paternoster-Row, London, 1794.
> I xi, 312p; II 303p; III 308p; IV 280p. 12mo. 12s sewed (CR, SJC).
> CR n.s. 13: 229 (Feb 1795); AF II: 2542.
> CtY Im.L585.794; ESTC n063121.

Notes. List of subscribers 1, v–xi. Epistolary. Not by Frances Jacson.
Adv. SJC 5–7 Aug 1794. Adv. LC 76: 117 (31 July–2 Aug 1794).

> CR: 'The vicissitudes in human life afford a copious subject for the narrative either of the novellist or biographer, at the same time that they contain the most instructive lessons of moderation, fortitude, and virtue. The writer of the present novel seems to have projected it

618   1794

with these views. The various fortune of the personages exemplifies appositely the design; while the sentiments, no less than the incidents, concur in exhibiting the several characters to the reader's observations. In different parts of the work, the editor has not been sufficiently attentive to correct typographical errors; but they are, in general, of little importance to the sense; and the variety of vicissitudes is calculated to render the perusal, if not highly interesting, at least so in a degree to preserve always the attention from languor.'

1794: 37   LIOMIN, [Louis-Augustin].
THE SHEPHERDESS OF ARANVILLE: A ROMANCE. TRANSLATED FROM THE FRENCH OF M. LIOMIN.

> London: Printed by J. Adlard, No. 39, Duke-street, West-Smithfield: and sold by Owen, No. 168, and Marlow, No. 169, Piccadilly; and Parsons, No. 21, Paternoster-Row, 1794.
> 175p. 12mo. 3s sewed (CR).
> CR n.s. 13: 468 (Apr 1795).
> PU Singer-Mend PQ3889.L5.B413.1794; ESTC n064441.

Notes. Trans. of *La bergère d'Aranville* (Neuchâtel, 1792).
Further edns: NSTC lists edns. in 1808 and 1826.

CR: 'In some of the glass shops in town, our readers may have observed a lack-lustre piece of French manufacture, whose clumsy workmanship forms a striking contrast to the elegance and brilliancy of the brittle ware which surrounds it; and which stands there to convince the world of the superiority of the British artist. Upon the same patriotic principle do we suppose the Shepherdess of Aranville to have been translated into English. And it must be confessed, that if this was the intention of the translator, it has been amply fulfilled; for though the stuff produced by our English manufacturers of novels is sometimes poor enough, it is seldom so very flimsy and despicable as is this nonsense of French extraction.'

1794: 38   MATHEWS, Mrs.
PERPLEXITIES; OR, THE FORTUNATE ELOPEMENT. BY MRS. MATHEWS, AUTHOR OF SIMPLE FACTS. IN THREE VOLUMES.

> London: Printed by Sampson Low, Berwick Street, for J. Bell, No. 148, Oxford Street, 1794.
> I 214p; II 214p; III 174p. 12mo. 10s 6d sewed (CR).
> CR n.s. 12: 473 (Dec 1794).
> CLU-S/C PR 4986 M52p; ESTC n020112 (NA NcD).

Notes. 2 pp. advs. end vol. 3.
Simple Facts 1793: 28.

CR: 'The present narrative is conducted in a natural progression, without any aid from the interposition of extraordinary incident. The characters are delineated with perspicuity, if not with precision. . . .'

1794: 39   MOSER, Joseph.
TURKISH TALES: IN TWO VOLUMES. BY JOSEPH MOSER.

> London: Printed for William Lane, at the Minerva-Press, Leadenhall-Street, 1794.
> I iv, 200p; II 200p. 8vo [MR has 12mo]. 6s (CR), 6s sewed (MR, MP).

CR n.s. 12: 237 (Oct 1794); MR n.s. 15: 226 (Oct 1794); AF II: 2987.

MH-H EC75.M853; CME 3-628-51114-3; EM 4253: 8; ESTC n014226 (NA CaAEU, CtY; EA COR).

Notes. Preface i–iv.

Adv. MP 31 July 1794.

Extracts from *Turkish Tales* published in *Lady's Magazine* and *Hibernian Magazine*, 1794–95, RM 957.

CR: 'Thus far we can say in favour of these Tales, that they are neither ill written nor unamusing. The author, indeed, has the modesty only to contend, that like simples in medicine, they can "do no harm."'

MR [William Enfield]: 'We have often been surprized at the degree of admiration and praise which has been bestowed on those laboured productions, in which northern industry has attempted in vain to supply the place of eastern fire; and we have smiled to see with how much pains many writers have loaded their pages with pompous language, and have aggrandized their fictions with supernatural machinery, in order to produce a mass of absurdity under the title of an eastern tale. We are therefore disposed to applaud the good sense of the author of these volumes, in venturing to write Turkish tales without copying the bloated style of former writers of this class, or invoking the aid of giants, dwarfs, genii, dæmons, and other supernatural agents. In doing this, he may perhaps, according to the common idea, have rendered his work less eastern: but he has at the same time made it the more natural; or, at least, more consonant to the judgment and feelings of an European reader; and, by these means, he has also avoided many painful efforts to swell himself up, like the frog in the fable, to an imaginary standard of excellence.'

1794: 40   [NAUBERT, Christiane Benedicte Eugenie]; BOOTH, Miss A. E. (*trans.*).

ALF VON DEULMEN; OR, THE HISTORY OF THE EMPEROR PHILIP, AND HIS DAUGHTERS. TRANSLATED FROM THE GERMAN BY MISS A. E. BOOTH. IN TWO VOLUMES.

London: Printed for J. Bell, No 148, Oxford Street, opposite Bond-Street, 1794.

I xx, 300p; II 305p. 8vo. 12s (BC), 12s boards (OPA).

BC 6: 189–90 (Aug 1795); AF II: 412.

BL 12554.m.5; EM 138: 5; ESTC t099894 (BI AWn, C; NA C-S, CaOHM, CLU-S/C &c.).

Notes. Trans. of *Alf von Dülmen* (Frankfurt, 1791).

'A Prefatory Account of the Secret Tribunal and Free Judges of Westphalia' 1, v–xx.

Adv., 'elegantly printed by Bulmer', OPA 16 Feb 1795.

BC: 'This is a tragedy, and a very deep one, in the form of a history, and a series of letters. . . . The date of the first of these letters, which is 1198, affords ample room to the author for mixing (according to a fashion which has lately prevailed) the fictions of fancy with the truths of history. A good use, however, is here made of this liberty.'

1794: 41   [NAUBERT, Christiane Benedicte Eugenie].

HERMAN OF UNNA: A SERIES OF ADVENTURES OF THE FIFTEENTH CENTURY, IN WHICH THE PROCEEDINGS OF THE SECRET TRIBUNAL, UNDER THE EMPERORS WINCESLAUS AND SIGISMOND,

ARE DELINEATED. IN THREE VOLUMES. WRITTEN IN GERMAN BY
PROFESSOR KRAMER.

> London: Printed for G. G. J. and J. Robinson, Pater-noster-Row, 1794.
> I xv, 280p; II 291p; III 268p. 12mo. 9s sewed (CR, LC).
> CR n.s. 14: 68–79 (May 1795); AF II: 3035.
> ICN Case Y1565.C85; EMf; ESTC n017436 (BI C, O; NA CtY, CSt, ViU &c.).

Notes. Trans. of *Hermann von Unna, eine Geschichte aus den Zeiten der Vehmegerichte* (Leipzig, 1788).

Kramer is Christiane Benedicte Eugenie Naubert. Originally published anonymously in 1788.
Adv. LC 75: 95 (25–28 Jan 1794).

Further edns: London, 1794, EM 174: 4; ESTC t099901; Dublin, 1794 (Printed by William Porter, for P. Wogan, P. Byrne, J. Moore, and W. Jones, 2 vols., 12mo), EM 3841: 1, ESTC t130115; London, 1796, EM 3829: 1, ESTC t144038. French trans. Metz, 1791 (*Herman d'Unna, ou Aventures arrivées au commencement du xve siècle*) (BN).

CR: 'For this singular and interesting novel we are indebted to the pen of professor Kramer, the author of many literary productions' (p. 68). 'The peculiar interest of this work, no doubt, rests on the account, so novel and so striking, of the secret tribunal; but perhaps the author has availed himself of it too much, and introduced it rather too often.... As to the translation, we believe it to be faithful; and the style is easy, but has no peculiar pretensions to elegance' (p. 79).

1794: 42   PARSONS, [Eliza].
LUCY: A NOVEL, IN THREE VOLUMES. BY MRS. PARSONS.

> London: Printed for William Lane, at the Minerva Press, Leadenhall-Street, 1794.
> I 281p; II 288p; III 263p. 12mo. 10s 6d sewed (CR), 6s sewed (MR), 9s sewed (MP, Min).
> CR n.s. 11: 234–5 (June 1794); MR n.s. 15: 227–8 (Oct 1794); AF II: 3236.
> BL 12612.ff.16; EM 242: 5; ESTC t067332 (NA CSmH, CtY, NNU).

Notes. 1 p. advs. end vol. 1 and 1 p. advs. end vol. 3.
Adv. MP 31 July 1794.

CR: 'The incidents in this novel are, in general, of a romantic nature; but conducted with great plausibility. The characters are well supported; the sentiments highly favourable to virtue; and it abounds with situations extremely interesting to the tenderest feelings of the heart' (p. 235).

MR [William Enfield]: 'Without possessing, in any high degree, those excellencies which distinguish the first class of novels, this tale will command attention by the mere power of incident and business. The scenery and characters, in the beginning of the story, are romantic and interesting.... The rest of the story, in which the heroine is introduced into the world, and passes through a variety of trials, though less original, is amusing.'

1794: 43   [PEACOCK, Lucy].
THE VISIT FOR A WEEK; OR, HINTS ON THE IMPROVEMENT OF
TIME. CONTAINING ORIGINAL TALES, ANECDOTES FROM NAT-
URAL AND MODERN HISTORY, &C. DESIGNED FOR THE AMUSE-
MENT OF YOUTH. BY THE AUTHOR OF THE SIX PRINCESSES OF
BABYLON, JUVENILE MAGAZINE, AND KNIGHT OF THE ROSE.

London: Printed for Hookham and Carpenter, Bond-Street; and for the author, at the
Juvenile Library, No. 259, Oxford-Street, 1794.

330p. 12mo. 3s 6d boards (MR).

MR n.s. 15: 356–7 (Nov 1794).

C 7720.d.607; EM 2069: 6; ESTC t137589 (BI BL, E; NA CaOHM, CaOTP, CLU-S/C).

Notes. 4-pp. advs. end vol.

Adventures of the Six Princesses of Babylon 1785: 40; *Knight of the Rose* 1793: 34.

Further edns: London, 1795, EM 3874: 3, ESTC t137594; London, 1796, EM 3602: 19, ESTC
t118238; Philadelphia, 1796, ESTC w028545; Philadelphia, 1801 (WC); London, 1806 (WC);
WC has 6 further entries for 1800 to 1850; NSTC lists edns. in [1804], 1806, 1812, 1813, 1818
and 1823. German trans. Leipzig, 1798–99 (*Besuch von einer Woche*) (Price); French trans.
London, 1817 (*Visite d'une semaine*) (HWS).

MR [William Enfield]: 'It is a presage in favour of the next generation, that the present
times furnish such a variety of books for the use of young persons, which so happily unite
amusement with instruction, that they can scarcely fail to entice them into the love of knowledge and virtue. The volume before us is entitled to some distinction in this class.'

1794: 44   PEARSON, S[usanna].
THE MEDALLION. BY S. PEARSON. DEDICATED (BY PERMISSION)
TO HIS ROYAL HIGHNESS THE PRINCE OF WALES. IN THREE VOL-
UMES.

London: Printed for G. G. and J. Robinson, Pater-Noster-Row, 1794.

I 8, 229p; II 236p; III 211p. 12mo. 9s sewed (CR, MR).

CR n.s. 12: 99–102 (Sept 1794); MR n.s. 15: 227 (Oct 1794); AF II: 3288.

CLU-S/C PR 5165.P335m; ESTC n021894 (NA InU-Li, TxHR).

Notes. Robinson paid 25 gns. on 3 Jan 1794 to S. Pearson for *The Medallion* (RA); Bentley
records Pearson's name as Sarah, but the Robinson receipt is signed only with 'S' and all
other sources give her name as Susanna.

Dedication to H.R.H. the Prince of Wales, signed S. Pearson, 1, 3–5; address 'To the
Reviewers' 7–8.

Adv., 'New Novel. Next Week will be published', LC 75: 271 (18–20 Mar 1794).

CR: 'We may observe, respecting this production, without meaning any disparagement,
that it is not such a medallion as will gratify a Virtuoso, intent on the collection of ancient
medals; but it may figure with *eclat* in a circulating library, and be thought not unworthy the
protection to which it has aspired, especially when considered as the work of a female writer'
(p. 102).

MR [William Enfield]: 'Any thing animate or inanimate, that can be supposed to change
masters or to shift places, whether it be a parrot or a devil, a guinea, a medallion, or a post-
chaise, may in the hands of an ingenious writer be made the convenient vehicle of humour or
satire. Such an imaginary adventurer may serve as a string to bind together a number of
detached stories, or characters, and may give to a work, which would otherwise be perfectly
miscellaneous, an appearance of unity. In a novel, however, the characters and incidents of
which are connected by the thread of the narrative, such a contrivance is not only superfluous but becomes an incumbrance. The Medallion in the present production answers no purpose which might not, with a small degree of contrivance, have been much better effected
without it. Independently of this unnecessary fiction, the work has sufficient unity of plan;

and the principal characters which appear, at the opening, are continued on the stage until the catastrophe. . . . the volumes are on the whole lively and amusing: their chief merit consists in the humorous exhibition of comic characters, and in the introduction of some interesting episodical stories. . . .'

1794: 45   [PINCHARD, Elizabeth].
THE TWO COUSINS, A MORAL STORY, FOR THE USE OF YOUNG PERSONS. IN WHICH IS EXEMPLIFIED THE NECESSITY OF MODERATION AND JUSTICE TO THE ATTAINMENT OF HAPPINESS. BY THE AUTHOR OF THE BLIND CHILD AND DRAMATIC DIALOGUES.
London: Printed for E. Newbery, at the corner of St. Paul's Church-yard, 1794.
vii, 144p. 12mo. 2s (LP).
BL N.2207(1); EM 2071: 4; ESTC t132928 (BI O, BMp, LVu; NA CaOTP, CSmH, MH-H &c.).
Notes. Address to the Public v–vii.
The Blind Child 1791: 56.
Adv. LP 20–23 Mar 1795.
Further edns: Boston, 1796, ESTC w028406; London, 1798, EM 1494: 28, ESTC n014137; New York, 1799, ESTC w025008. German trans. Leipzig, 1795 (*Die beiden Muhmen, oder man kann ohne Mässigkeit nicht glücklich seyn*) (EAG).

1794: 46   R., C.
CASTLE ZITTAW: A GERMAN TALE. BY C. R. IN THREE VOLUMES.
London: Printed for William Lane, at the Minerva Press, Leadenhall-Street, 1794.
I 244p; II 246p; III 234p. 12mo. 9s sewed (CR, SJC).
CR n.s. 14: 113–14 (May 1795).
NNS; xESTC.
Notes. 2 pp. advs. end vol. 2.
Adv., 'in the Press, and speedily will be published . . . *Castle of Zittaw*', MP 31 July 1794; still adv., 'In the Press and speedily will be published . . . *Castle of Zettan*', SJC 2–4 Oct 1794; adv. as published MP 28 Oct 1794.

1794: 47   RADCLIFFE, Ann.
THE MYSTERIES OF UDOLPHO, A ROMANCE; INTERSPERSED WITH SOME PIECES OF POETRY. BY ANN RADCLIFFE, AUTHOR OF THE ROMANCE OF THE FOREST, ETC. IN FOUR VOLUMES.
London: Printed for G. G. J. and J. Robinson, Paternoster-Row, 1794.
I 428p; II 478p; III 463p; IV 428p. 12mo. £1 boards (CR, MR).
CR n.s. 11: 361–72 (Aug 1794); MR n.s. 15: 278–83 (Nov 1794); AF II: 3673.
C Rom.76.91-; ESTC t062063 (BI BL, D, O &c.; NA CtY-Walpole, CtY-BR, CSmH, DLC, IU, NjP, NN, TxU, ViU &c.; EA QU, SU, ZAP).
Notes: Romance of the Forest 1791: 58.
Scott reports that 'the booksellers felt themselves authorized in offering what was then considered an unprecedented sum' of £500 to Radcliffe for *The Mysteries of Udolpho* (p. vi).

Adv., 'In a few Days will be published, In Four very large Volumes', LC 75: 391 (22–24 Apr 1794); adv. as published SJC and LC 8–10 May 1794.

Further edns: London, 1794, EM 8429: 1, ESTC t119307; Dublin, 1794 (Printed by Hillary and Barlow, for Messrs. P. Wogan, W. Jones, and H. Colbert, 3 vols., 12mo), EM 2813: 5, ESTC t114421; London, 1795, EM 8508: 1, ESTC t154761; Dublin, 1795, EM 8833: 3, ESTC t118667; Boston, 1795, EM 3938: 1, ESTC w006558; 3 further entries in ESTC; WC has 23 entries between 1800 and 1850; NSTC lists edns. in 1823 and 1828. Extracts from *The Mysteries of Udolpho* published in *European Magazine* and *Hibernian Magazine*, 1794, RM 932. German trans. Riga and Leipzig 1795–96 (*Udolpho's Geheimnisse*) (EAG); French trans. Paris, 1797 (*Les Mystères d'Udolphe*) (Lévy); Italian trans. Livorno, 1816/17 (Rogers).

CR: 'The same powers of description are displayed, the same predilection is discovered for the wonderful and the gloomy—the same mysterious terrors are continually exciting in the mind the idea of a supernatural appearance, keeping us, as it were, upon the very edge and confines of the world of spirits, and yet are ingeniously explained by familiar causes; curiosity is kept upon the stretch from page to page, and from volume to volume, and the secret, which the reader thinks himself on the point of penetrating, flies like a phantom before him, and eludes his eagerness till the very last moment of a protracted expectation' (p. 361). 'The Mysteries of Udolpho are indeed relieved by much elegant description and picturesque scenery; but in the descriptions there is too much of sameness. . . . Curiosity is raised oftener than it is gratified; or rather, it is raised so high that no adequate gratification can be given it. . . . The manners do not sufficiently correspond with the æra the author has chosen . . .' (p. 362).

MR [William Enfield]: 'The works of this ingenious writer not only possess, in common with many other productions of the same class, the agreeable qualities of correctness of sentiment and elegance of style, but are also distinguished by a rich vein of invention, which supplies an endless variety of incidents to fill the imagination of the reader; by an admirable ingenuity of contrivance to awaken his curiosity, and to bind him in the chains of suspence; and by a vigour of conception and a delicacy of feeling which are capable of producing the strongest sympathetic emotions, whether of pity or of terror. Both these passions are excited in the present romance, but chiefly the latter; and we admire the enchanting power with which the author at her pleasure seizes and detains them' (p. 279). 'Without introducing into her narrative any thing really supernatural, Mrs. Radcliffe has contrived to produce as powerful an effect as if the invisible world had been obedient to her magic spell; and the reader experiences in perfection the strange luxury of artificial terror, without being obliged for a moment to hoodwink his reason, or to yield to the weakness of superstitious credulity' (p. 280).

1794: 48 [RAINSFORD, Mrs].
THE VICTIM OF PASSION; OR, MEMOIRS OF THE CONTE DE SAINT JULIEN. IN THREE VOLUMES.

London: Printed for Hookham and Carpenter, Bond Street, 1794.
I 215p; II 203p; III 189p. 12mo. 10s 6d sewed (CR), 9s sewed (SJC).
CR n.s. 13: 116–17 (Jan 1795).
IU x823.V664; xESTC.

Notes. Adv. SJC 27–29 May 1794.
Further edns: London, 1794, ESTC t221258; Dublin, 1795 (Printed by Brett Smith, for

Messrs. P. Wogan, P. Byrne, J. Halpen, J. Rice, W. Jones, and G. Folingsby, 1 vol., 12mo), ESTC n063204; London, 1799, xESTC (Corvey), CME 3-628-45149-3.

CR: 'The conte, properly *comte*, de St. Julien is so much obscured by surrounding objects, that it is with difficulty we discover his fortune in the progress of the narrative. The attention, however, is generally kept awake by the different agitations of some congenial and deeply affected *inamorato*; whose joint effusions supply the place of incidents, in extending the production to its present length.'

1794: 49   ROBINSON, [John].
SYDNEY ST. AUBYN. IN A SERIES OF LETTERS, BY MR. ROBINSON, AUTHOR OF LOVE FRAGMENTS, &C.

> London: Printed for R. Hindmarsh, Printer to His Royal Highness The Prince of Wales, for I. Herbert, No. 6, Pall-Mall, 1794.
> I xii, 227p; II xxiv, 240p. 12mo. 6s (CR), 7s sewed (MR).
> CR n.s. 11: 468 (Aug 1794); MR n.s. 16: 229 (Feb 1795); AF II: 3818.
> MH-H *EC75.R5638.794s; EM 4253: 3; ESTC n021555 (BI O).

Notes. Vol. 1 1-p. prefatory advertisement, dedication to Miss —— vii–viii; table of contents ix–xii. Vol. 2 table of contents v–vii; introduction to the second volume ix–xxiv. Epistolary. *Love Fragments* 1782: 19.

CR: 'These Letters may be considered as so many episodical productions, generally connected, in some degree, with two principal characters, the termination of whose history appears to be the object of the whole. The Letters are more remarkable for an appearance of interest, in the different correspondents, than any high degree of sympathy excited in the reader by the progress of the narrative. They are written, however, with vivacity, and, in general, with correctness of expression.'

MR [William Enfield]: 'The story of this novel has the merit of being uncommon, without being unnatural. The author, without roving into the boundless regions of romance, finds means to amuse his readers with a domestic tale, in which the principal characters are placed in situations which have perhaps seldom occurred in real life, but which may easily be conceived to occur, and suffer extreme disappointment and distress merely through indiscretion, without any heinous criminality.... The tale is, on the whole, interesting; and it is told in a style which, if not to be admired for extraordinary elegance, is suitable to the subject, easy and simple.'

1794: 50   ROBINSON, M{aria} E{lizabeth}.
THE SHRINE OF BERTHA: A NOVEL, IN A SERIES OF LETTERS. IN TWO VOLUMES. BY MISS M. E. ROBINSON.

> London: Printed for the Author, by W. Lane, at the Minerva-Press, Leadenhall-Street; sold by Scatchard, Paternoster-Row; Miller, Old Bond-Street; Knight and Triphook, Booksellers to his Majesty, St James's-Street, 1794.
> I 232p; II 232p. 12mo. 6s sewed (CR, MR).
> CR n.s. 11: 468 (Aug 1794); MR n.s. 15: 108–9 (Sept 1794); AF II: 3843.
> BL 12622.pp.8; EM 471: 15; ESTC t094338 (NA CtY).

Notes. Dedication to the author's mother, signed Maria Elizabeth Robinson. Epistolary.
Adv. SJC 3–5 Apr 1794.
Further edn: London, 1796, EM 4373: 13, ESTC t057364.

CR: 'Other literary productions are valuable in different degrees, according to the proportion of truth or of utility which they contain; but *Novels*, as their sole purpose is entertainment, must either be the most amusing, or the most insipid of publications. We cannot say that the two volumes before us belong to the *former* class.'

MR [Christopher Lake Moody]: 'Miss M. Robinson . . . has the merit of having imagined an interesting tale, which includes the usual incidents of this species of composition, without being spun out to an immoderate length. Passionate love mutually conceived at first sight between a beautiful young couple, and ending, after some difficulties and embarrassments, in the vulgar catastrophe of a marriage, is the sum and substance of the *Shrine of Bertha*: but the letters are short and, on the whole, well-written; the business does not lag . . .' (p. 108).

1794: 51 ROBINSON, M{ary}.
THE WIDOW, OR A PICTURE OF MODERN TIMES. A NOVEL, IN A SERIES OF LETTERS, IN TWO VOLUMES. BY MRS. M. ROBINSON, AUTHOR OF POEMS, AINSI VA LE MONDE, VANCENZA, MODERN MANNERS, &C. &C. London: Printed for Hookham and Carpenter, Bond Street, 1794.

> I 182p; II 187p. 8vo [MR has 12mo]. 6s boards (CR, MR).
> CR n.s. 12: 102 (Sept 1794); MR n.s. 14: 38–40 (May 1794); AF II: 3842.
> C 5727.e.79.1/1; EM 3054: 16; ESTC n024959 (BI O; NA MH-H, ViU).

Notes. Dedication to 'that Public, and those Liberal Critics, who have so highly distinguished my Former Productions . . .', signed Mary Robinson. End vol. 1 1-p. adv. for other works by the same author and 4-pp. adv. for Hookham's library (or 'Literary Assembly'). Epistolary. 1,500 copies printed by order of the author, H&C.
Vancenza 1792: 50.
Further edn: Dublin, 1794 (Printed for Messrs. P. Wogan, P. Byrne, W. Jones, and J. Halpen, 1 vol., 12mo), ESTC t119377. French trans. n.p., n.d. (*La Veuve anglaise*) (HWS); German trans. Leipzig, 1795 (*Die Wittwe*) (RS).

CR: 'This is one of the most insipid novels which, in the course of our labours, we have had occasion to peruse. The characters are fashionably vicious without any fashionable brilliancy to compensate for depravity. O! for a warning voice to prevent those, at least, in whom age has not yet destroyed the capabilities of improvement, from dreaming away their hours in turning over publications like these, while the interesting walks of history, and the fair fields of fancy, and the rich mines of science, solicit their notice, and offer their treasures to their persevering investigation!'

MR [William Enfield]: 'In the present novel . . . she has succeeded better than in her former prose productions, in attempting to throw off the pomp of poetical diction, and to reduce her style to the tone of polite epistolary correspondence:—but the principal merit of these volumes is their exhibiting a *picture of modern times*, in which the features of fashionable folly and depravity are drawn with a skilful hand, and with such strokes of deformity as are well adapted to excite contempt and indignation. The incidents are well contrived and arranged; the characters are agreeably diversified and strongly marked; and the sentiments, throughout, are such as ought to leave a due impression on the mind of the reader in favour of virtue' (p. 38).

ROCHE, Regina Maria, THE MAID OF THE HAMLET
See 1793: 38

1794: 52   SMITH, Charlotte.
THE BANISHED MAN. A NOVEL. BY CHARLOTTE SMITH. IN FOUR VOLUMES.

> London: Printed for T. Cadell, jun. and W. Davies, (successors to Mr. Cadell) in the Strand, 1794.
> I xi, 233p; II xii, 236p; III 224p; IV 340p. 12mo. 14s sewed (CR), 14s boards (MR).
> CR n.s. 13: 275–8 (Mar 1795); MR n.s. 16: 133–5 (Feb 1795); AF II: 4130.
> C 7720.d.245; EM 2009: 1; ESTC t070700 (BI BL, MRu, O; NA CSmH, CtY, IU, MH-H, PU, ViU &c.).

Notes. Preface 1, v–xi concerns Smith's personal circumstances. Defends herself against a reviewer's comment that she writes too much about this subject. Vol. 2: 'Avis au Lecteur' iii–xii concerns the possibilities of fiction and is, for the most part, a dialogue between the author and a friend.

Adv., 'In a few Days will be published', LC 76: 100 (26–29 July 1794).

Further edns: Dublin, 1794 (Printed by Z. Jackson, for Messrs. P. Wogan, P. Byrne, W. M'Kenzie, W. Jones [and 4 others; printer's name omitted from vol. 2 imprint], 2 vols., 12mo), ESTC n000078; London, 1795, ESTC n000079. German trans. Hamburg, 1795 (*Der Verbannte*) (RS).

CR: 'The ends proposed by Mrs. Smith in this publication seem to have been, first, to furnish her bookseller with a certain number of volumes; next, to reinstate herself in the opinion of those who have been offended by the turn of her politics in a former publication, and to do away all suspicion of her having embraced the wrong side of the question; and, lastly, to give vent to her feelings, and claim the sympathy of the public for the distresses and perplexities of her private concerns. The first motive is natural; the second may be prudent; but the third we cannot but consider as equally unwise and unjustifiable' (p. 275). '. . . though, as a whole, we cannot think it equal to what Mrs. Smith is capable of, there are many sketches which afford a degree of entertainment' (p. 276).

MR [William Enfield]: 'Towards a writer to whom the public has been so often and so much indebted for amusement as to Mrs. Charlotte Smith, considerable indulgence is due . . .' (p. 133). 'In some parts of the story, the reader's sympathy is strongly excited: in others, he is amused with a glowing and even comic representation of characters; and the work throughout discovers a ready invention and a correct taste' (p. 134).

1794: 53   SMITH, Charlotte.
THE WANDERINGS OF WARWICK. BY CHARLOTTE SMITH.

> London: Printed for J. Bell, No. 148, Oxford-Street, 1794.
> 288p. 12mo. 4s sewed (CR), 4s (MR).
> CR n.s. 11: 84–9 (May 1794); MR n.s. 14: 113 (May 1794); AF II: 4147.
> C S727.d.79.93; CME 3-628-45181-7; EM 92: 6; ESTC t057370 (BI BL, E, O; NA CtY, CSmH, MH-H, NjP, PU, ViU &c.; EA COR).

Notes. Further edn: Dublin, 1794 (Printed for P. Wogan, P. Byrne, J. Moore, W. Jones, W. Porter, H. Colbert, and J. Rice, 1 vol., 12mo), ESTC n035557. German trans. Leipzig, 1794 (*Warwick's Reisen*) (EAG). Facs: BWN.

CR: 'The productions of Mrs. Charlotte Smith, though marked with pretty different degrees of comparative merit, are all stamped with knowledge of the world and fertility of invention; they all shew considerable powers of description, and a vein of poetical fancy, and are all entitled to rank far above the common run of these kind of publications.

The present story is built upon the ground-work of her last novel, *The Old Manor House* [1793: 39], and is a kind of episodiacal [*sic*] story of one of the dependent characters, so that the author has not the trouble of introducing her hero to us as a new acquaintance. We are not sure whether this is perfectly judicious; it rather tends to take off the interest, by taking off the gloss and novelty of the story; and, perhaps, implies more recollection of the preceding piece, than an author has a full right to expect with regard to a fictitious story, which has been now published some time.'

MR [William Enfield]: '... the story is not only interesting but instructive.... In the course of the story Mrs Smith has not neglected to introduce, after her usual manner, such miscellaneous reflections on interesting topics, and such accounts of real characters, as every intelligent reader will think a sufficient compensation for a short interruption of the fictitious narrative.'

1794: 54 [SUMMERSETT, Henry].
THE OFFSPRING OF RUSSELL. A NOVEL. IN TWO VOLUMES.
London: Printed for William Lane, at the Minerva-Press Leadenhall-Street, 1794.
I 179p; II 198p. 12mo. 6s sewed (CR, MR).
CR n.s. 14: 226 (June 1795); MR n.s. 16: 229 (Feb 1795); AF II: 4299.
MH-H *EC75.Su646.794o; EM 1499: 3; ESTC n010557 (BI C).
Notes. 2 pp. advs. end vol. 2.
Adv., 'in the Press, and speedily will be published', MP 31 July 1794; adv. as published MP 31 Oct 1794.
CR: 'From the title of this work we expected an historical novel; but our expectation was not answered. The Offspring of Russell is a female, the story romantic, and the style affected.'
MR [William Enfield]: 'The character of this novel may be expressed in one word; it is romantic.... The sentiments are frequently extravagant; the passions are expressed with a degree of vehemence beyond nature; and the style, where it rises above familiarity, is rather bloated than elegant. Nevertheless, the general effect is interesting; and the reader, who peruses the story with a disposition to be amused, will not lose his labour.'

1794: 55 {THOMAS, Ann}.
ADOLPHUS DE BIRON. A NOVEL. FOUNDED ON THE FRENCH REVOLUTION. IN TWO VOLUMES.
Plymouth: Printed by P. Nettleton, for the Authoress, at Millbrook; of whom they may be had; and of Messrs. Nettleton, Wills, and Barnikel, in Plymouth; Mr Huss, Stonehouse; Messrs. Hoxland, Fraser, and Heydon, Dock; and of Mr Woolmer, Exeter, n.d. [ESTC: 1795?].
I 252p; II 195p. 12mo. 6s sewed (CR).
CR n.s. 12: 472 (Dec 1794).
MH-H *EC75.T3612.795a; EM 4249: 13; ESTC n032457 (NA PU).
Notes. Dedication to Lady Eliot, signed Ann Thomas, and 3-pp. preface (unn.). 12-pp. list of subscribers end vol. 2. Epistolary.
CR: 'The subject relates chiefly to the distresses of individuals, in consequence of the anarchy in France; the revolutionary government is deplored by the suffering parties, in terms of the warmest sympathy, intermixed with just indignation. This novel, though connected with affairs of national concern, is copiously blended with the intercourse and reciprocal cares of

private life; while to render the catastrophe conformable to common practice, the history concludes with a marriage.'

TOUCHIT, Timothy, **LA SOURICIERE**
See App. B: 13

1794: 56   [WALKER, George].
THE HAUNTED CASTLE, A NORMAN ROMANCE. IN TWO VOL-UMES.

> London: Printed at the Minerva-Press, for William Lane, Leadenhall-Street, 1794.
> I viii, 156p; II 148p. 8vo [CR has 12mo]. 6s (CR), 5s sewed (SJC).
> CR n.s. 13: 229 (Feb 1795).
> O Vet.A5f.618–619; ESTC n017268 (NA ViU).

Notes. Adv. SJC 3–5 Apr 1794.

CR: 'We are very sorry to find, by the preface to this novel, that *gain* is the author's chief motive for writing, not because we think that motive is an improper one, but because we are convinced the end cannot be answered by such publications as the Haunted Castle. That the author, however, may be more successful in his next attempt, as he possesses some powers of invention, we would recommend to his serious consideration, the difference betwixt raising expectation and gratifying it. It might also be worth his while to consider that divine justice may be vindicated without the introduction of hobgoblins, and that it is not necessary to write two volumes to verify the good old adage, "murder will out."'

1795

THE ABBEY OF SAINT ASAPH
See KELLY, Isabella

1795: 1   ANON.
ARVILLE CASTLE. AN HISTORICAL ROMANCE.

> London: Printed for B. Crosby, No. 4, Stationers Court, Ludgate Street; and T. White, at his Circulating Library, No. 22, Down's Street, Piccadilly, 1795.
> I 211p; II 189p. 12mo. 6s sewed (MR, CR).
> CR n.s. 16: 115 (Jan 1796); MR n.s. 19: 88 (Jan 1796); AF II: 149.
> BL N.1892; EM 2012: 2; ESTC t071901.

Notes. 3 pp. advs. end vol. 2.
Adv. SJC 3–5 Dec 1795.
Another 1795 edn. appears identical apart from the imprint (Printed for T. White, at his Circulating Library, No. 22, Downs's Street, Piccadilly; and B. Crosby, No. 4, Stationers Court, Ludgate Street) ESTC n004296 (I 211p; II 189p. 12mo).

CR: 'To those who can be amused by a wild, romantic story, violating, without scruple, all the laws of nature and probability,—about forests and banditti,—murders and apparitions,—wandering damsels, and faithful lovers,—the Castle of Arville may afford a delectable and perfectly harmless entertainment.'

MR [Arthur Aikin]: 'If false grammar, the grossest mistakes in chronology, prating ghosts, and the union of utter impossibilities, constitute the perfection of historical romance; this before us has the most unequivocal claim to the public notice.'

1795: 2   ANON.
AUGUSTA DENBEIGH; A NOVEL. IN THREE VOLUMES.

London: Printed for William Lane, at the Minerva Press, Leadenhall-Street, 1795.
I 199p; II 179p; III 166p. 12mo. 10s 6d (CR), 9s sewed (MP).
CR n.s. 15: 119 (Sept 1795).
MH-H *EC75.A100.795a4; EM 1003: 5; ESTC n005288.

Notes. 1 p. adv. end vol. 1 and vol. 2; 2 pp. advs. end vol. 3.
Adv., 'In the Press, and speedily will be published', MP 21 Nov 1794; adv. as published MP 12 Mar 1795.
Further edn: Dublin, 1795 (Printed by Brett Smith, for Messrs. P. Wogan, P. Byrne, J. Rice, W. Jones, and G. Folingsby, 1 vol., 12mo), EM 2511: 16; ESTC n015926.

CR: 'Trite as all this undoubtedly is,—in justice to the author, we must observe, that some of the scenes in high life are painted with a considerable degree of dramatic spirit; some of the follies and caprices of fashion happily displayed; and that, throughout the whole, there is nothing to be found inimical to morals, or offensive to delicacy.'

1795: 3   ANON.
*AUSTENBURN CASTLE. IN TWO VOLUMES. BY AN UNPATRONIZED FEMALE.

London: Printed for William Lane (adv.), 1796 (CR).
2 vols. 12mo. 6s sewed (adv., CR).
CR n.s. 16: 222 (Feb 1796); AF II: 176.
No copy located.

Notes. Adv. MP 12 Dec 1795.
Adv. end vol. 3 of Abbey of Clugny (1796: 65).
Further edn: Dublin, 1796 (Printed by Thomas Burnside, for Messrs. P. Wogan, P. Byrne, J. Rice, J. Boyce, and W. Porter, 2 vols., 12mo), EM 8172: 5, ESTC t142296. Vol. 2 printed by John Barlow (ESTC).

CR: 'Since Mrs Radcliffe's justly admired and successful romances, the press has teemed with stories of haunted castles and visionary terrors; the incidents of which are so little diversified, that criticism is at a loss to vary its remarks. The present work will not be found devoid of entertainment by those who have a taste for such compositions.—But we could wish the writers, who mingle history with fiction, would pay a little more regard to truth. Why Godfrey of Bouillon, the pious and virtuous hero of the crusades, should be held up as a monster of atrocity, by the fair author of Austenburn Castle, is a question that we are unable to solve.'

THE CASTLE OF OLLADA
See LATHOM, Francis

CICELY; OR, THE ROSE OF RABY
See MUSGRAVE, Agnes

1795: 4   ANON.
THE CYPRIOTS; OR, A MINIATURE OF EUROPE IN THE MIDDLE OF THE FIFTEENTH CENTURY. BY THE AUTHOR OF THE MINSTREL. IN TWO VOLUMES.

> London: Printed by S. Low, Berwick Street, for J. Bell, No. 148, Oxford Street, opposite New Bond-Street, 1795.
> I 290p; II 286p. 12mo. 7s boards (CR), 7s sewed (OPA).
> CR n.s. 14: 226 (June 1795); AF II: 244.
> MH-H *EC75.a.100.795c3; EM 1002: 19; ESTC n005452 (NA ICN).

Notes. Authorship assigned to James Beattie by ESTC, NUC etc. because of his poem *The Minstrel* but it seems much more likely that *The Cypriots* is by the anonymous author of the novel *The Minstrel* (1793: 10), also set in the fifteenth century.
1 p. advs. end vol. 2.
Adv. OPA 2 Mar 1795.

   CR: 'The historical events, though but little interspersed with fiction, are connected by a story of a romantic nature, but not altogether unsuitable to the period in which the incidents are supposed to have taken place. Our young readers may find, in the perusal of this work, some information blended with entertainment.'

THE DEMOCRAT
See PYE, Henry James

1795: 5   ANON.
THE DIAMOND RING; OR, SUCCESSFUL ARTIFICES OF THREE LONDON WIVES.

> London: Printed for D. Brewman, at his Warehouse for Dr. Walker's Jesuits Drops and all other Patent Medicines, No. 45, Old Bailey, 1795.
> 75p. 12mo. 1s (t.p.).
> BL 1262.df.9; EM 164: 5; ESTC t066890.

Notes. Frontispiece; 1 p. advs. end vol.

THE DUKE OF CLARENCE
See FOSTER, E. M., Mrs

ELISA POWELL, OR TRIALS OF SENSIBILITY
See DAVIES, Edward

1795: 6   ANON.
THE ENCHANTER; OR WONDERFUL STORY TELLER: IN WHICH IS CONTAINED A SERIES OF ADVENTURES, CURIOUS, SURPRISING, AND UNCOMMON; CALCULATED TO AMUSE, INSTRUCT, AND IMPROVE YOUNGER MINDS.

London: Printed for William Lane, at the Minerva-Press, Leadenhall-Street, 1795.
127p. 12mo.
CaAEU PR1281 E56 1795; ESTC n006978 (NA CLU-S/C).

Notes. Contains five stories. 1 p. advs. end vol.

THE EVENING WALK; A SENTIMENTAL TALE
See RICKMAN, Thomas Clio

THE FATE OF SEDLEY
See SUMMERSETT, Henry

THE FUGITIVE, AN ARTLESS TALE
See BURTON, Mrs

HENRY
See CUMBERLAND, Richard

JEMIMA. A NOVEL
See HUGHES, Anne

MEMOIRS OF MADAME DE BARNEVELDT
See DU CASTRE D'AUVIGNY, Jean

MEMOIRS OF PLANETES
See NORTHMORE, William

1795: 7   ANON.
MONTFORD CASTLE; OR THE KNIGHT OF THE WHITE ROSE. AN HISTORICAL ROMANCE OF THE ELEVENTH CENTURY. IN TWO VOLUMES.

London: Printed for B. Crosby, No. 4, Stationers' Court, Ludgate Street, n.d. [1795].
I iv, 307p; II 299p. 12mo. 7s sewed (MR, CR).
CR n.s. 16: 115 (Jan 1796); MR n.s. 19: 88 (Jan 1796); AF II: 2922.
BL 1490.s.11; EM 2294: 4; ESTC t077099 (BI C; NA PU).

Notes. Dedication to H.R.H. the Princess of Wales dated 4 May 1795.
Adv. MP 5 June 1795; additional bookseller is J. Lee, New street, Covent-Garden. Adv. OPA 9 June 1795.
Adv. end vol. 2 of *Arville Castle* (1795: 1).
German trans. Berlin, 1796 (*Das Schloss Montford*) (RS).
CR: 'A tale of chivalry, when the knights were all valiant, and the damsels fair.—There is little novelty in the incidents of this romance, or force in the sentiments. The style is neither elegant, nor particularly defective. The story is intended to exemplify the mischiefs of ecclesiastical domination.'
MR [Arthur Aikin]: 'This performance is neither of the first nor of the lowest rank: we have seen many of the kind superior to it, and many its inferiors. It inculcates no maxims

hostile to good morals; its sins against strict grammatical propriety are very rare, and probably are rather slips of the pen than deliberate mistakes: but, if its defects be few, its beauties are so likewise. . . . It will, indeed, interest the feelings, and keep alive the passions, of those who are fond of castles, knights, tournaments, caverns, banditti; and all the chivalrous accompaniments of tales of this nature.'

MYSTERIES ELUCIDATED, A NOVEL
See MACKENZIE, Anna Maria

NETLEY ABBEY: A GOTHIC STORY
See WARNER, Richard

1795: 8   ANON.
THE OBSERVANT PEDESTRIAN; OR, TRAITS OF THE HEART: IN A SOLITARY TOUR FROM CAERNARVON TO LONDON IN TWO VOLUMES, BY THE AUTHOR OF THE MYSTIC COTTAGER.

> London: Printed for William Lane, Minerva-Press, Leadenhall-Street, 1795.
> I 196p; II 234p. 12mo. 6s (CR), 6s sewed (OPA).
> CR n.s. 15: 341–2 (Nov 1795); AF II: 3097.
> BL 1480.aa.1; CME 3–628–45128–0; EM 2204: 8; ESTC t097496 (NA CaAEU, CtY; EA COR).

Notes: The Mystic Cottager of Chamouny 1794: 13. Also by same author: *Montrose, or the Gothic Ruin* (1799: 12).
4-pp. preface (unn.).
WC has *Farther Excursions of the Observant Pedestrian* (London, 1801); NSTC has *Observant Pedestrian Mounted* (1815).
Adv., 'In the Press and speedily will be published', MP 13 Dec 1794; adv. 'in a few days will be published', OPA 14 May 1795.

> CR: 'The humane and benevolent dispositions which are displayed in, and designed to be promoted by, these little volumes, disarm us of our critical severity. But we would admonish the writer to trust less, in future, to "the inspirations of the heart," and to attend more, if not to *elegance*, to propriety and correctness of composition. . . . The incidents of this tour are, perhaps, in themselves too simple to be sufficiently interesting: in a work of fancy we are entitled to expect greater varieties and bolder flights:—neither are the sentiments, nor the language, appropriate to the incidents' (p. 341).

PHANTOMS OF THE CLOISTER; OR, THE MYSTERIOUS MANUSCRIPT
See H., I.

PLAIN SENSE, A NOVEL
See JACSON, Frances

ROBERT AND ADELA
See THOMSON, Anna

SECRESY; OR, THE RUIN ON THE ROCK
See FENWICK, Eliza

THE SORCERER: A TALE
See WÄCHTER, Georg Philip Ludwig Leonhard

1795: 9   ANON.
SUCH FOLLIES ARE: A NOVEL. IN TWO VOLUMES.

> London: Printed for William Lane, at the Minerva Press, Leadenhall-Street, 1795.
> I 197p; II 262p. 8vo. 6s (BC), 6s sewed (LC).
> BC 6: 189 (Sept 1795).
> BL 12611.aaa.9; CME 3-628-45183-3; EM 162: 5; ESTC t108473 (EA COR).

Notes. 1 p. advs. end vol 1; 2 pp. advs. end vol. 2. Epistolary.
Adv., 'in the Press, and speedily will be published', MP 31 July 1794; adv. as published MP 31 Oct 1794.
Adv. LC 77: 149 (10–12 Feb 1795).

> BC: 'Mr Seaforth, his wife, and eldest son, are represented as aristocrats, and no less foolish and wicked than our neighbours, of the distracted republic one-and-indivisible, would wish all such persons to be thought. Mr Hanbury is a merchant, retiring from business with a splendid fortune, most honourably acquired. Of course, he and his family are contrasted with the Seaforths. The story is not worth detailing any further. . . .'

SUSANNA; OR, TRAITS OF A MODERN MISS
See BULLOCK, Mrs

THE TRADITIONS, A LEGENDARY TALE
See SHERWOOD, Mary Martha

THE UNFORTUNATE ATTACHMENT
See BACULARD D'ARNAUD, François-Thomas Marie de

THE VICTIM OF MAGICAL DELUSION
See TSCHINK, Cajetan

1795: 10   ANON.
WALDECK ABBEY. A NOVEL. IN TWO VOLUMES. BY THE AUTHOR OF THE WEIRD SISTERS, BUTLER'S DIARY, &C.

> London: Printed for William Lane, at the Minerva Press, Leadenhall-Street, 1795.
> I 213p; II 198p. 12mo. 6s (CR), 6s sewed (MP).
> CR n.s. 15: 236 (Oct 1795).
> BL C.108.ppp.12; EM 5163: 3; ESTC t122539.

Notes. Frontispiece in vol. 1. 3 pp. advs. end vol. 1 and 2 pp. advs. end vol. 2.
The Weird Sisters 1794: 15; A Butler's Diary 1792: 4.
Adv. MP 31 Aug 1795; additional Booksellers are Miller, Bond-Street; and Knight and Triphook, Booksellers to His Majesty, St James's-Street.

CR: 'It is to be wished that these fair novelists would attend a little more to the rendering of their works correct as well as *harmless*: and, that they would avoid corrupting the language, with a solicitude similar to that which they so laudably manifest for the morals of their readers. While they soar above all rules of common sense and common grammar, their ideas are involved in a confusion of words, resembling a wilderness of flowering weeds, which it would be impossible to separate or disentangle.'

1795: 11   [BACULARD D'ARNAUD, François-Thomas Marie de].
*THE UNFORTUNATE ATTACHMENT; OR, MEMOIRS OF MR. AND MRS. DE LA BEDOYERE. A TRUE HISTORY, WRITTEN IN THE YEAR 1746. TRANSLATED FROM THE FRENCH, BY A LADY.
> Bath: Printed and sold by S. Hazard; sold also by Vernor and Hood, Birchin-Lane, London (OPA), 1795 (CR).
> 2 vols. 12mo. 6s sewed (CR, OPA).
> CR n.s. 13: 346 (Mar 1795).
> No copy located.

Notes. Trans. of *Les Époux malheureux, ou histoire de Monsieur et Madame de la Bédoyère*, first pub. in 1745 or 1746, and as augmented in a revised Paris edn. of 1783. Attributed to Baculard d'Arnaud in an edn. of 1758.
Adv., 'For the benefit of a French Ecclesiastic', OPA 1 Jan 1795.
   CR: 'A pathetic tale, translated from the French. . . . We should have felt more sympathy for Mr. Bedoyere's sorrows, had they been sustained with more dignity. Circumstances, in themselves affecting, simply related, have a stronger hold upon the affections, than the endless repetition of exclamatory periods and over-wrought sentiment. Novel-writers, in general, seem not aware, that though sensibility adds grace and interest to virtue, it may degenerate into weakness. Magnanimity and fortitude are becoming in both sexes, and are expected, more especially, from that which is complimented with being the strongest. The education of men is rather calculated to make them struggle with, and conceal their sensations (yet this may be carried to affectation), than indulge, like Mr Bedoyere, in unavailing lamentations, weeping, wailing, and swooning.'

1795: 12   BIRD, John.
THE CASTLE OF HARDAYNE, A ROMANCE. IN TWO VOLUMES. BY JOHN BIRD.
> Liverpool: Printed by J. M'Creery, And sold by Messrs. C. and G. Kearsley, Fleet-Street, London, 1795.
> I 232p; II 224p. 12mo. 6s (CR), 6s sewed (MR).
> CR n.s. 15 (Sept 1795): 119–20; MR n.s. 19: 351 (Mar 1796); AF II: 357.
> BL 1153.l.12; EM 3417: 11; ESTC t143266 (NA MH-H).

Notes. Text of novel starts on p. 5 in both vols.
Further edn: Boston, New York, Buffalo and Baltimore, 1846 (*The Banditti of the Castle of Hardayne*).
   CR: 'The Castle of Hardayne displays no inconsiderable powers of invention and description, and will not fail to amuse those who are not hackneyed in this species of composition.'
   MR [Arthur Aikin]: 'To those who are fond of ruined castles, of mysteries, and of banditti,

these volumes will afford considerable pleasure. The language is spirited and luxuriant, the descriptions in general are good, and the incidents, some few excepted, are highly interesting; they now and then, it is true, verge on the extreme of possibility, but in a romance such things are partly allowable.'

1795: 13   BOLAS, Thomas.
THE ENGLISH MERCHANT: OR THE FATAL EFFECTS OF SPECULATION IN THE FUNDS: A NOVEL. BY THOMAS BOLAS. IN TWO VOLUMES.

> London: Printed for William Lane, at the Minerva-Press, Leadenhall-Street, 1795.
> I 260p; II 286p. 12mo. 6s (BC), 6s sewed (MP, SJC).
> BC 8: 671–2 (Dec 1796).
> PU Singer-Mend.PR.4149.B9.E6.1795; ESTC n047801.

Notes. Dedication 'with all due deference and respect, to that very respectable body of men, The Merchants and Traders of the British Empire' signed Thomas Bolas, East-Lane, Walworth; followed by a Latin verse 'The Author's Address to the Reader'. 2 pp. advs. end each vol. Epistolary.
Adv. MP 5 June 1795; additional Booksellers are Scatchard, Ave Maria lane; Miller, Old Bond-Street; Hodgson, Wimpole-Street; and Knight and Co. Booksellers to His Majesty in St James's-Street.
Adv. SJC 14–16 July 1795.
  BC: 'What the avocation of Mr. Bolas has been, we know not; but it evidently has not been that of a literary man.'

1795: 14   BREWER, George.
THE MOTTO: OR HISTORY OF BILL WOODCOCK. IN TWO VOLUMES. BY GEORGE BREWER.

> London: Printed for G. Sael, no. 192, Strand, 1795.
> I ix, 216p; II 248p. 12mo. 6s sewed (CR, MR).
> CR n.s. 14: 355–6 (July 1795); MR n.s. 18: 111 (Sept 1795); AF II: 464.
> BL 12612.c.11; EM 168: 5; ESTC t066386 (NA CSmH, IU).

Notes. Introduction iii–ix. 4 pp. advs. end vol. 2.
Adv. OPA 14 May 1795.
  CR: '. . . while he confines himself to the kitchen no one can dispute the propriety of his descriptions. The remainder of the story has indeed nothing to recommend it. It is too absurd for plain uncultivated sense, and too vulgar for the misses' (p. 355).
  MR [William Enfield]: 'Authors commonly adapt their productions to the understandings and tastes of the higher classes of readers, and forget that there are numerous inferior classes, which have as much occasion for instruction, and as much right to be amused, as their betters. The present writer has avoided this error, and has very condescendingly provided a tale, the incidents, sentiments, and language of which are happily suited to the comprehension of those readers who know nothing of the learning of the schools, and the manners of high life.'

1795: 15   [BULLOCK, Mrs].
SUSANNA; OR, TRAITS OF A MODERN MISS; A NOVEL. IN FOUR VOLUMES.

London: Printed for William Lane, at the Minerva-Press, Leadenhall-Street, 1795.
I 240p; II 250p; III 246p; IV 251p. 12mo. 12s sewed (CR, MP).
CR n.s. 14: 113 (May 1795); AF II: 526.
Corvey; CME 3-628-45199-X; ESTC t200840 (NA IU, ViU).

Notes. Frontispiece vol. 1. 2 pp. advs. end vol. 2; 2 pp. advs. end vols. 3 and 4.
Adv., 'In the Press, and speedily will be Published', MP 28 Oct 1794; adv. 'on the 1st of January, will be published', MP 21 Nov 1794; adv. as published MP 27 Dec 1794.
Adv. end vol. 2 of *The Castle of Ollada* (1795: 28).

CR: 'The writer of Traits of a Modern Miss seems to have had in view Mrs Lennox's celebrated Female Quixote: but the characters of Susanna and Mrs Lennox's Arabella are by no means equally interesting: the mistakes of the latter are the errors of genius—and superior minds will ultimately correct themselves. But the weak, versatile Susanna is characterised as a ridiculous compound of affectation and vanity: her frailties have not even the excuse of sensibility, nor her follies the charm of vivacity. Those who love ridicule may be entertained with this work, which is written with humour.—It may also be read with advantage by any modern miss, who may be exposed, by habits of indolence, an uncultivated mind, or negligent guardians, to the temptation of committing similar absurdities.'
[Charlotte Lennox, *The Female Quixote* 1752, JR 138, AF I: 1588].

1795: 16   [BURTON, Mrs].
THE FUGITIVE, AN ARTLESS TALE, IN A SERIES OF LETTERS. IN TWO VOLUMES.

London: Printed for W. Richardson, under the Royal Exchange, 1795.
I 197p; II 213p. 12mo. 7s sewed (CR), 5s sewed (LC), 6s sewed (SJC), 6s boards (GEP).
CR n.s. 16: 473 (Apr 1796).
InU-Li PR 3991.A1.F958; ESTC n018497.

Notes. Adv. for the same author's *Laura, or the Orphan* (1797: 30), GEP 15–17 Mar 1798, has 'By Mrs Burton, Author of the Fugitive, an Artless Tale'.
Epistolary.
Adv. SJC 28–30 Apr 1795; adv. LC 77: 499 (23–26 May 1795).
French trans. Paris, 1803 (*La fugitive de la forêt*) (HWS).

CR: 'The Fugitives are French emigrants,—their dangers and escapes, though containing nothing very new or striking, are not uninteresting. The story is little tinctured with politics, and wholly free from party spirit. . . . many may be entertained with it, no one will be offended.'

1795: 17   [CUMBERLAND, Richard].
HENRY; IN FOUR VOLUMES. BY THE AUTHOR OF ARUNDEL.

London: Printed for Charles Dilly, in the Poultry, 1795.
I vii, 316p; II iv, 328p; III v, 311p; IV v, 304p. 12mo. 12s sewed (CR, MR).
CR n.s. 13: 444–53 (Apr 1795); MR n.s. 17: 133–8 (June 1795); AF II: 966.
BL 838.b.20,21; EM 2386: 1; ESTC t115224 (BI C, O; NA CtY-BR, CSmH, IU, MH-H).

Notes. Advertisement to the Reader 1, iii–iv, signed 'The Author'; table of contents v–vii.
Table of contents in vols. 2, 3 and 4.
Arundel 1789: 37.

Adv., 'On the 30th of January will be published. . . . Containing Twelve Books, with a prefatory Chapter to each', LC 77: 37 (8–10 Jan 1795); adv. as published LC 77: 159 (12–14 Feb 1795). 3rd edn. adv. GEP 29–31 Mar 1798.

Further edns: London, 1795, ESTC n007198; Dublin, 1795 (Printed for P. Wogan, P. Byrne, W. Jones, H. Colbert, J. Milliken [and 3 others], 2 vols., 12mo), EM 2816: 2, ESTC t129419; London, 1798, EM 6879: 1, ESTC t130659; Philadelphia, 1802 (WC); London, 1824 (WC); 1 further post-1800 edn. in WC; NSTC lists edns. in 1824 and 1825. German trans. Bremen, 1796–97 (*Heinrich. Eine Geschichte*) (EAG); French trans. Paris, 1799 (*Henry*) (BGR); Dutch trans. Amsterdam, 1800 (*Henry: in vier deelen*) (WC).

CR: 'In the novel before us he has professedly taken Fielding for his model; he imitates him in several scenes from low life, as well as in his introductory chapters; and he has taken occasion to introduce a sarcastic fling at his more sentimental rival, Richardson' (p. 444). 'Upon the whole, it would be unjust not to allow that this novel is enriched with humour, variety, and character, though in many parts tedious; and that the story of Lady Crowbery excites interest: but in point of morals we are obliged to pronounce it very blameable' (p. 449).

MR [Thomas Holcroft]: 'We are well convinced that the author is really a lover of mankind, and has a sincere desire of promoting good morality, but it is somewhat astonishing to us that he should have so mistaken the means . . .' (p. 135). 'Appropriate language, in which each character speaks not only in the tone of the passion that he feels, but in the idiom that is characteristic of his habits, manners, and rank in life, is one of the most captivating charms of good writing. To this, we think, Mr C. has not been sufficiently attentive' (p. 136).' . . . while perusing his work, we have frequently both laughed and shed tears; and . . . as we cannot afford time to point out all its defects, we have still much less the means of noticing all its merits. On the former we dwell most, invidious as it may appear, because, in order that any fault should be corrected, it must necessarily be specified: while, with respect to the latter, a general but sincere acknowlegement may afford the author sufficient encouragement to attempt more unalloyed excellence' (p. 138).

D'AUVIGNY, Jean du Castre
See DU CASTRE D'AUVIGNY, Jean

1795: 18   [DAVIES, Edward].
ELISA POWELL, OR TRIALS OF SENSIBILITY: A SERIES OF ORIGINAL LETTERS COLLECTED BY A WELSH CURATE. IN TWO VOLUMES.

London: Printed for G. G. and J. Robinson, Pater Noster-Row, 1795.
I 299p; II 300p. 12mo. 7s boards (MR), 7s sewed (SJC), 6s sewed (LC).
MR n.s. 18: 228 (Oct 1795); AF II: 1003.
MH-H *EC8.D2868.795e; EM 3517: 15; ESTC (NA CtY-BR).

Notes. Robinson paid 20 gns. on 10 Jan 1795 to Edward Davies of Chipping Sodbury, Gloucestershire, for *Eliza Powell* (RA).
Epistolary.
Adv. SJC 28–30 Apr 1795; adv. LC 78: 7 (30 June–2 July 1795).
Further edn: Dublin, 1795 (Printed for Messrs. Wogan, Byrne and Rice, 1 vol., 12mo), ESTC t178744.

MR [William Enfield]: 'As a pathetic tale, this is a performance of considerable merit. The situation and incidents are uncommonly interesting, and are well contrived to leave on the mind of the reader a strong impression of the folly of concealment, and the fatal consequence of yielding the reins to passion.'

1795: 19   [DU CASTRE D'AUVIGNY, Jean]; GUNNING, [Elizabeth] *(trans.)*.
MEMOIRS OF MADAME DE BARNEVELDT. TRANSLATED FROM
THE FRENCH BY MISS GUNNING. IN TWO VOLUMES.

> London: Printed by and for S. Low, Berwick Street, Soho; and E. Booker, New Bond-
> Street, 1795.
> I 353p; II 325p. 8vo. 12s boards (CR, MR).
> CR n.s. 15: 480 (Dec 1795); MR n.s. 18: 345–6 (Nov 1795); AF II: 1757.
> BL 12510.e.16; EM 60: 11; ESTC t093334 (BI O).

Notes. Trans. of *Mémoires de Madame de Barneveldt* (Paris, 1732).
2 pp. advs. end vol. 2.
Adv. LC 78: 328 (1–3 Oct 1795).
Further edns: London, 1796, ESTC t160487; London, 1796, ESTC t093333; Dublin, 1796
(Printed by P. Wogan, P. Byrne, J. Moore, W. Jones, J. Rice, and H. Colbert, 2 vols., 12mo),
ESTC n052558.
CR: 'To repay the trouble of wading through the tedious narrative of unnatural and
improbable events which fill these two octavo volumes, we now and then stumble upon a
lively thought, a lucky caricature, or a judicious remark. . . .'
MR [Arthur Aikin]: '. . . it may reasonably be expected that no book should be translated,
which does not possess considerable intrinsic merit; yet it has happened that the depravity of
public taste, or the defective judgments of individuals, has considerably augmented our
native stock of indifferent performances, by importation of foreign works which seldom
prove to be valuable acquisitions, even to the circulating libraries' (p. 345).

1795: 20   [FENWICK, Eliza].
SECRESY; OR, THE RUIN ON THE ROCK. IN THREE VOLUMES. BY A
WOMAN.

> London: Printed for the Author, And Sold by William Lane, Leadenhall-Street; Knight
> and Co. Booksellers to His Majesty, St. James's-Street; Miller, Old Bond-Street;
> Hodgson, Wimpole-Street; E. Harlow, Bookseller to the Queen, Pall-Mall; And
> Scatchard, Paternoster-Row, n.d. [1795].
> I iv, 228p; II 216p; III 295p. 12mo. 9s sewed (CR, MR).
> CR n.s. 14: 349–51 (July 1795); MR n.s. 18: 110 (Sept 1795); AF II: 1423.
> Corvey; CME 3-628-45172-8; ESTC n036602 (NA ViU).

Notes. Dedication to 'Eliza B—' vol. 1, iii–iv. Epistolary.
Adv. MP 9 Apr 1795 and OPA 18 Apr 1795.
Another 1795 London edn. (Printed for G. Kearsley, No. 46, Fleet Street. 12mo. I iv, 228p;
II 216p; III 295p.) ESTC t139121, BL Cup.403.i.10.
Facs: FCy.
CR: 'In the course of our critical labours we are so frequently satiated by extravagant fic-
tion that the romantic title of this work rather repelled than stimulated curiosity: but the las-
situde with which we began to peruse it, ere we had proceeded far, gave place to a more
awakened attention' (p. 349). '. . . the incidents and situations . . . are novel,—the language
animated and forcible;—the characters, sentiments, and reflections, bespeak a more

philosophic attention to the phenomena of the human mind than is generally either sought for, or discovered, in this lighter species of literary composition' (p. 351).

MR [William Enfield]: 'The story is in some parts extravagantly improbable: but the characters are drawn with great strength; the passions are naturally and forcibly expressed; and, in fine, the production deserves a place of some distinction in the list of interesting novels.'

1795: 21   [FOSTER, E. M., Mrs].
THE DUKE OF CLARENCE. AN HISTORICAL NOVEL. IN FOUR VOL-
UMES. BY E. M. F.

> London: Printed for William Lane, at the Minerva-Press, Leadenhall-Street, 1795.
> I 251p; II 303p; III 230p; IV 244p. 12mo. 12s boards (CR), 12s sewed (MR, LC, adv.).
> CR n.s. 13: 468–9 (Apr 1795); MR n.s. 17: 108 (May 1795); AF II: 1489.
> BL 012618.df.1; EM 326: 3; ESTC t115064 (NA CaAEU, IU, PU &c.).

Notes. 1 p. advs. end vols. 1 and 2; 2 pp. advs. end vol. 3.
Adv., 'In the Press', MP 31 Oct 1794; adv. 'Next Week will be published', LC 77: 64 (15–17 Jan 1795). Re-adv. SJC 17–19 Feb 1795; 'This is an interesting Story established on an eventful Part of the History of England, and will be found not only to contain Amusement, but will record on the Mind a variety of Circumstances appertaining to Affairs of this Country.'
Adv. end vol. 2 of *The Castle of Ollada* (1795: 28).
Further edns: Dublin, 1795 (Printed by W. Folds, for Messrs. P. Wogan, P. Byrne, J. Halpin, and W. Jones, 2 vols., 12mo), ESTC n007242; London, 1818 (Summers); NSTC lists edn. in 1831.

CR: 'This is truly a romantic story. . . . Those who can be entertained by surprising coinci-dences, in which the laws of nature and probability are violated without scruple, may beguile a vacant hour, without any hazard to their morals by the perusal of this novel; the tendency of which is perfectly pure, and strict *poetical justice* is administered to every heroic personage. The work, upon the whole, displays some powers of invention; but we would advise the writer to cultivate, in future, a more correct tale.'

MR [William Enfield]: 'It requires more reading than commonly falls to the share of our novel writers, to give to an historical tale the characteristic features of the age in which it is placed. . . . the story is marked with few of the peculiar traits of antient English manners and customs, and has few references to the real history of the times; it has therefore but a slender title to the character of an *historical* novel. It has, however, some claim to commendation as an interesting love-tale, in which a variety of passions, highly excited by a quick succession of uncommon incidents, are strongly expressed; and which, through a tolerably well connected narrative, occupies the reader's curiosity, and exercises his sympathy. The principal charac-ters are well conceived and delineated; and the language, though not particularly elegant, will seldom offend the reader by any gross violations of accuracy. The piece, however, is not with-out its defects.'

1795: 22   GOOCH, E[lizabeth] S[arah] Villa-Real.
THE CONTRAST: A NOVEL. IN TWO VOLUMES. BY E. S. VILLA-REAL
GOOCH.

> London: Printed for the Author, and sold by C. and G. Kearsley, Fleet Street, 1795.
> I 209p; II 219p. 12mo. 6s sewed (CR, SJC).

CR n.s. 13: 345–6 (Mar 1795); AF II: 1668.

MH-H *EC75.G5904.794c; EM 996: 52; ESTC n002014 (NA CtY).

Notes. 1 p. adv. facing t.p.; 3 pp. advs. end vol. 1; 1 p. advs. end vol. 2.

Post-dated; adv. as published SJC 11–13 Dec 1794.

Further edns: Dublin, 1795 (Printed for P. Wogan, P. Byrne, J. Rice, and G. Folingsby, 1 vol., 12mo), EM 8822: 03, ESTC t119378; Wilmington, DE, 1796, ESTC w037596; Wilmington, Delaware, 1796, ESTC w037595.

CR: 'An apology for fashionable frailties (to make use of no harsher term) is not likely to have the most favourable effects on the morals or happiness of the rising generation. The present state of society is sufficiently corrupt, and stands in need of antidotes rather than emollients. . . . Happily there is not sufficient energy or interest in the style of this novel, to render it particularly seductive.'

1795: 23   GROSSE, [Karl Friedrich August].
THE DAGGER. TRANSLATED FROM THE GERMAN OF GROSSE.

London: Printed for Vernor and Hood, Birchin-Lane, 1795.

183p. 12mo. 2s 6d sewed (CR), 3s sewed (MR).

CR n.s. 16: 116 (Jan 1796); MR n.s. 19: 207 (Feb 1796); AF II: 1747.

PU Singer-Mend.PT22181.G614D63; ESTC n006889 (NA ViU).

Notes. Trans. of *Der Dolch* (Berlin, 1794–5).

5 pp. advs. end vol.

CR: 'There is originality in the incidents of this little work,—the sentiments are impassioned,—the style glowing,—and, from the *denouement*, some useful truths may be extracted.'

MR [William Taylor]: 'This interesting and pathetic tale is translated from the German of Grosse. . . . A lively method of narration, and a dramatic discrimination of character, may be ranked among the merits of an author. The completeness of the fable, and its well-timed catastrophe, in the English impression, are merits of the translator; who has judiciously omitted some hacknied episodical adventures.'

1795: 24   {H., I.}.
PHANTOMS OF THE CLOISTER; OR, THE MYSTERIOUS MANU-
SCRIPT. A NOVEL. IN THREE VOLUMES.

London: Printed for William Lane, At the Minerva Press, Leadenhall-Street, 1795.

I 208p; II 227p; III 226p. 12mo. 9s (BC), 6s sewed (LC), 10s 6d (OPA).

BC 6: 544 (Nov 1795).

ViU *PZ2.P484 1795; ESTC n020210.

Notes. Dedication to Eliza and Maria, signed I. H. Prefatory address 'To the Reader'. 1 p. advs. end vol. 2.

Adv., 'In the Press, and speedily will be published', SJC 28–31 Mar 1795; adv., 'will be published . . . In the beginning of May', SJC 28–30 Apr 1795. Adv., 'In a few Days will be published, ornamented with an elegant Frontispiece', OPA 2 May 1795. Adv., 'embellished with an engraved frontispiece', LC 78: 3 (30 June–2 July 1795).

BC: 'Ghosts, goblins, and chimeras dire; of which, after all, the moral is good, for vice is punished and virtue rewarded.'

1795: 25 [?HUGHES, Anne].
JEMIMA. A NOVEL. IN TWO VOLUMES. BY THE AUTHOR OF ZORI-ADA, OR VILLAGE ANNALS, &C.

London: Printed for William Lane, at the Minerva-Press, Leadenhall-Street, 1795.
I 236p; II 223p. 12mo. 6s sewed (CR).
CR n.s. 15: 479–80 (Dec 1795); AF II: 2101.
MH-H *EC75.H8742.795j; EM 998: 9; ESTC n001028.

Notes. In a letter of 18 Oct 1804 (RLF 2: 74) Phebe Gibbes claimed authorship of *Zoriada* (1786: 24).
4 pp. advs. end vol. 2.
Adv., 'In the Press, and speedily will be published', SJC 28–31 Mar 1795.
   CR: 'An artless and amusing tale, which, if it exhibits no superior powers of invention, displays great benevolence of sentiment. The writer neither aims at elaborate description, nor romantic adventure, but, with unaffected simplicity, entertains the more from making no extraordinary pretension. An amiable family picture is delineated; and the several characters, without having any claim to originality, are not ill supported.'

1795: 26 [JACSON, Frances].
PLAIN SENSE, A NOVEL, IN THREE VOLUMES.

London: Printed at the Minerva-Press, for William Lane, Leadenhall-Street, 1795.
I 232p; II 235p; III 281p. 8vo. 9s (EngR), 9s sewed (SJC, adv.).
EngR 27: 483 (May 1796); AF II: 2235.
PU PR.3541.L355.P55.1795; ESTC n020256 (NA CtY, NjP, ViU &c.).

Notes. ESTC gives author as Alethea Lewis. On authorship see Joan Percy's article on Jacson in the *British Library Journal* 23: 1 (Spring 1997) pp. 81–97.
1 p. advs. end vol. 2; 3 pp. advs. end vol. 3.
Adv. SJC 27 Feb-1 Mar 1796; additional Booksellers are Hodgson, Wimpole-Street; Kirby, Oxford-Street; Miller, Old Bond-Street; and Knight and Co., Booksellers to his Majesty.
Adv. end vol. 3 of *The Abbey of Clugny* (1796: 65).
Further edns: London, 1796, EM 2266: 9, ESTC t060911; Dublin, 1796 (Printed by Brett Smith, for Charles Brown, 2 vols., 12mo), EM 2599: 4, ESTC t120534; London, 1799, CME 3-628-48474-X, EM 7029: 5, ESTC t066915; Philadelphia, 1799, ESTC w027651.
   EngR: 'We recommend this as a novel much above the general class of that kind of writing.'

1795: 27 [KELLY, Isabella].
THE ABBEY OF SAINT ASAPH. A NOVEL. IN THREE VOLUMES. BY THE AUTHOR OF MADELINE, OR THE CASTLE OF MONTGOMERY.

London: Printed for William Lane, at the Minerva-Press, Leadenhall-Street, 1795.
I 174p; II 238p; III 196p. 12mo. 9s sewed (CR, MR).
CR n.s. 14: 349 (July 1795); MR n.s. 18: 229 (Oct 1795); AF II: 2352.
BL 1607/1994; EM 3109: 11; ESTC t118930 (BI MRu; NA MH-H).

Notes. Frontispiece vol. 1. 2 pp. advs. end vols. 1 and 2.
Madeline 1794: 35.

Adv., 'In the Press, and speedily will be published', MP 21 Nov 1794; adv. as published MP 30 Mar 1795.

Adv., 'embellished with an elegant Frontispiece of an interesting Scene', SJC 28–31 Mar 1795. Re-adv., 'Ornamented with a Frontispiece of an interesting Scene of Elinor and Jennet', SJC 31 Mar–2 Apr 1795; additional Booksellers are Scatcherd, Paternoster-Row; Miller, Bond-Street; Hodgson, Wimpole-Street; and Knight and Co. Booksellers to His Majesty in St James's-Street.

Adv. end vol. 1 of *Eva* (1799: 54).

Facs: GN III.

CR: 'In humble imitation of the well-known novels of Mrs. Radcliffe, the Abbey of St Asaph is duly equipped with all the appurtenances of ruined towers, falling battlements, moats, draw-bridges, Gothic porches, tombs, vaults, and apparitions.'

MR [William Enfield]: '[The two hackneyed tales] are interwoven with a sufficient variety of subordinate incidents to render the whole tolerably amusing; and some good moral reflections are interspersed. Had the author been contented with relating the rise, progress, obstruction, and completion of these tender attachments, we should have pronounced the novel on the whole a pleasing performance: but he has thought it necessary, in compliance with the present rage for the terrible, to conduct the reader into a horrid cavern. . . . The gross improbability and ludicrous absurdity of this part of the work are sufficient to annihilate the small portion of merit, which might otherwise have been ascribed to this performance.'

1795: 28   [LATHOM, Francis].
THE CASTLE OF OLLADA. A ROMANCE. IN TWO VOLUMES.

London: Printed for William Lane, at the Minerva-Press, Leadenhall-Street, 1795.
I 220p; II 231p. 12mo. 6s bound (CR), 6s sewed (MR, SJC).
CR n.s. 14: 352 (July 1795); MR n.s. 18: 229–30 (Oct 1795).
CaAEU PR 4878.L17.C35 1795; ESTC n028691 (NA ICU [missing]).

Notes. In vol. 1 pp. 211–12 misbound after 213–14, and 215–16 misbound after 217–18; in vol. 2 pp. 223–4 misbound after p. 210. 1 p. advs. end vol. 2.

Adv., 'In the Press, and speedily will be published', SJC 28–31 Mar 1795; adv. as published SJC 4–7 Apr 1795.

Adv., as *Castle of Ollada, a Wonderful Tale*, LC 78: 3 (30 June–2 July 1795).

Further edn: London, 1831 (Corvey), CME 3-628-47954-1.

CR: 'Another haunted castle! Surely the misses themselves must be tired of so many stories of ghosts, and murders,—though to the misses the ghosts of this novel present perhaps the most harmless part of the dramatis personæ.'

MR [William Enfield]: 'This performance is very properly entitled a Romance. The writer appears to have a fancy plentifully stored, from former romances, with images of love and terror, and a memory not ill furnished with the terms and phrases which belong to the school of fiction. . . . Had the writer confined himself to his love-tale, and opened it more at large by a fuller display of scenery, sentiment, and character, the performance would have been more complete: but in order to gratify the fashionable taste, he has introduced a story of a castle supposed to be haunted by ghosts, but at length discovered to be inhabited by a set of coiners; which will, we apprehend, afford the reader little amusement. . . . notwithstanding the defects of this performance, we discern in it promising marks of ingenuity.'

1795: 29 {MACKENZIE, Anna Maria}.
MYSTERIES ELUCIDATED, A NOVEL. IN THREE VOLUMES. BY THE
AUTHOR OF DANISH MASSACRE, MONMOUTH, &C.

London: Printed for William Lane, at the Minerva Press, Leadenhall-Street, 1795.
I xvi, iv, 152p; II 194p; III 208p. 12mo. 9s sewed (CR, MR), 6s sewed (LC).
CR n.s. 16: 359 (Mar 1796); MR n.s. 18: 227–8 (Oct 1795); AF II: 2659.
BL C.108.ppp.11; EMf; ESTC t130706 (BI O; NA NcU).

Notes. Frontispiece vol. 1. Prefatory address 'To the Readers of Modern Romance', signed
Anna Maria Mackenzie, 1, i–xvi; dedication to H.R.H. Caroline, Princess of Wales i–iv.
2 pp. advs. end vol. 2.
Danish Massacre 1791: 47; *Monmouth* 1790: 55.
Adv., 'In the Press, and speedily will be published', SJC 28–31 Mar 1795; adv., 'In a few Days
will be published', SJC 28–30 Apr 1795.
Adv. LC 78: 3 (30 June-2 July 1795).

CR: 'Her story is founded on the civil dissensions in the time of Edward the Second, his
tragical death (which is depicted with pathos), and the fall of Mortimer, intermixed with a
variety of fictitious incidents.—Invention is displayed, and curiosity interested. Mrs
Mackenzie is wonderfully loyal and refined,—kings are objects of her idolatry,—and female
delicacy and gentleness are delineated in the true spirit of ancient times. . . . The style of the
work is throughout incorrect, consequently often obscure.'

MR [William Enfield]: 'This publication belongs to the class of *historical novels*; a species
of writing against which we have repeatedly stated objections that appear to us unsurmount-
able, arising from its tendency to lodge in the memory of the young reader a confused mass
of facts and fictions. . . . The cruel fate of the wretched Edward at Berkley Castle is pathetically
described: the characters of Mortimer and Isabella are introduced in a manner very consistent with historical truth; and the story is diversified by pleasing description, and told in
correct language.'

1795: 30 MEEK[E], [Mary].
COUNT ST. BLANCARD, OR, THE PREJUDICED JUDGE, A NOVEL. IN
THREE VOLUMES. BY MRS. MEEK [*sic*].

London: Printed for William Lane, at the Minerva Press, Leadenhall-Street, 1795.
I 211p; II 228p; III 210p. 12mo. 12s (CR), 9s sewed (MR, adv. *Agnes*), 10s 6d (adv.
    Abbey).
CR n.s. 15: 342 (Nov 1795); MR n.s. 18: 228–9 (Oct 1795); AF II: 2807.
BL Cup.403.i.6; ESTC t139125 (NA ViU).

Notes. Frontispiece vol. 1. 1 p. advs. end vol. 1. Epistolary.
Adv., 'In a few days will be published', MP 24 July 1795.
Adv. end vol. 2 of *Abbey of Clugny* (1796: 65); adv. end vol. 1 of *Agnes and Leonora* (1799: 85).
Facs: GN III.

CR: 'This novel, we are informed in the concluding page, is a translation from the French.
The story turns upon the prejudices of high birth,—prejudices which in France no longer
exist. . . . The Count St Blancard is, in other respects, an entertaining and well-connected
story, and may agreeably beguile a leisure hour.'

MR [Charles Burney the younger]: 'This work is avowedly a translation from the French.

It is probably the labour of some industrious emigrée; as the French idiom predominates, and some errors of the press are discoverable. The story is well chosen, and is divested of the immorality, party, and levity, which are too frequently found in the lighter productions of French writers.—To those who seek amusement in tracing the former manners of France, we may recommend this little work. It may divert a solitary hour, without endangering youth or disgusting age.'

1795: 31   [MILLIKIN, Anna].
EVA, AN OLD IRISH STORY. BY THE AUTHORESS OF CORFE CASTLE.
Cork: Printed by J. Connor, at the Circulating Library, Castle Street, 1795.
235p. 12mo.
BL 1607/5358; EM 8324: 7; ESTC t119330 (BI D).

Notes. 2-pp. list of subscribers (unn.) preceded by prefatory advertisement:
'Many of the Subscribers to Eva residing at a distance from this City, rendered it so difficult to collect their names, that it is feared some have been omitted; the Authoress however hopes, that it will not be attributed to any inattention on her part: and avails herself of this opportunity, to offer her most grateful acknowledgments to those friends, who have so kindly exerted themselves in her favour, as to enable her to produce the following List, without having recourse to the public Prints.'
1 p. advs. end vol.
Corfe Castle 1793: 29.

MITCHELL, Margaret, TALES OF INSTRUCTION AND AMUSEMENT
See App. A: 8

1795: 32   [MUSGRAVE, Agnes].
CICELY; OR, THE ROSE OF RABY. AN HISTORIC NOVEL, IN FOUR VOLUMES.
London: Printed for William Lane, at the Minerva Press, Leadenhall-Street, 1795.
I xvi, 232p; II 234p; III 245p; IV 190p. 12mo. 12s boards Lane (CR).
CR n.s. 17: 113–14 (1796); AF II: 3017.
BL Cup.403.i.7; EM 7205: 6; ESTC t131303 (BI O; NA CtY, NjP, TxHR &c.).

Notes. Introduction i–xvi. Pagination continuous Roman-Arabic; text of novel starts on p. 17. 2 pp. advs. end vol. 2; 3 pp. advs. end vol. 3. Each vol. is a single letter by Cicely.
Adv., 'In the press, and speedily will be published . . . *Cecilia of Raby*', MP 13 Dec 1794; adv. as published MP 12 Nov 1795.
Further edns: London, 1796, ESTC n005141; Cork, 1805 (Printed by J. Connor, 2 vols. in 1, no format) (WC); London, 1816 (CaAEU); London, 1830 (Summers); London, 1831 (WC). German trans. Leipzig, 1820 (*Cäcilie, oder die Rose von Raby*) (RS).
CR: 'It has been frequently and justly observed, that the mixture of truth which renders an historical novel interesting, makes it also deceptive. . . . We do not mean to be the apologist of falsehood: but the title of Novel or Romance, though affixed to the term Historical, ought in reality to deceive no one. . . . the present work displays powers of invention, and agreeably amuses by the variety of its incidents, which are founded on the civil wars between the contending houses of York and Lancaster, the white and red roses.'

1795: 33   [NORTHMORE, William].
MEMOIRS OF PLANETES, OR A SKETCH OF THE LAWS AND MANNERS OF MAKAR. BY PHILELEUTHERUS DEVONIENSIS.

> London: Printed by Vaughan Griffiths, Strand; and sold by J. Johnson, St. Paul's Church Yard; and J. Owen, Piccadilly, 1795.
> viii, 143p. 8vo. 3s 6d boards (MR).
> MR n.s. 18: 22–4 (Sept 1795).
> BL 12613.gg.17; EM 187: 3; ESTC t108459 (BI Dt; NA CSmH, PU &c.).

Notes. Address to the reader v–viii, 'Dated amid the vice of London, March 16 1795'.

MR [William Taylor]: 'Plato set the example of describing an imaginary commonwealth, in order to explain his idea of what a people may become, if the rulers shall philosophize, or philosophers rule.... [The author] is ... too learned and philosophical for a novelist; and, in order to instruct, he continually forgets to entertain' (p. 22). 'The style of this volume is throughout simple and pure; and the typography is very neat' (p. 24).

1795: 34   PARKER, Mary Elizabeth.
ORWELL MANOR. A NOVEL, BY MARY ELIZABETH PARKER, IN THREE VOLUMES.

> London: Printed for the Author, at the Minerva Press, Leadenhall-Street, 1795.
> I 12, 260p; II 198p; III 240p. 12mo. 9s sewed (MR, LC), 10s 6d (OPA).
> MR n.s. 18: 111 (Sept 1795); AF II: 3220.
> BL C.175.l.17; EMf; ESTC t127123 (NA CtY, ViU).

Notes. List of subscribers 1, 1–12; text of novel starts on new p. 1. 4 pp. advs. end vol. 1; 2 pp. advs. end vol. 2.

Adv., 'In the Press, and speedily will be published', SJC 28–31 Mar 1795; adv., 'In a few Days will be published', SJC 28–30 Apr 1795. Adv., 'By Mrs Parker of Lewes, The Subscribers to this Work are most respectfully informed, it is now at Press in great forwardness', MP 1 Apr 1795.

Adv., 'Next Week will be published', OPA 2 May 1795; additional booksellers are Scatcherd, Ave Maria-lane; Hodgson, Wimpole-street; Miller, Old Bond-street; Knight and Co. Booksellers to his Majesty, St James's-street. Adv. LC 78: 3 (30 June 2 July 1795).

Further edn: Dublin, 1795 (Printed for P. Wogan, P. Byrne, W. Jones, and J. Rice, 1 vol., 12mo), EM 3522: 7, ESTC n033436.

MR [William Enfield]: 'This novel is introduced to the public under the patronage of a handsome list of subscribers, and we bring it before our readers as a performance not wholly unworthy of such an introduction. It relates a complete tale of love, of which the incidents are well arranged to produce an interesting effect: it exhibits a considerable number of characters, such as may be easily conceived to have been copied from real life; and the sentiments which it ascribes to them are natural, and often strongly impassioned. The principal faults are in the style, which is negligent, and often grammatically inaccurate.'

1795: 35   PARSONS, [Eliza].
THE VOLUNTARY EXILE, IN FIVE VOLUMES. BY MRS. PARSONS, AUTHOR OF LUCY, &C. &C.

> London: Printed for William Lane, at the Minerva Press, Leadenhall-Street, 1795.

I 226p; II 242p; III 248p; IV 244p; V 292p. 12mo. 15s sewed (CR, MR, adv.).
CR n.s. 14: 352–3 (July 1795); MR n.s. 17: 463 (Aug 1795); AF II: 3240.
BL 12612.ff.17; EM 243: 1; ESTC t067331 (BI MRu; NA CSmH, CtY, MH-H).

Notes. Frontispiece vol. 1.

Lucy 1794: 42.

Adv. SJC 17–20 Jan 1795; adv. is headed 'This Day were published' but continues: 'The Subscribers are respectfully informed this Novel is in great forwardness, and will speedily be published. Ornamented with an engraved Frontispiece, describing one of the most interesting Scenes.'

Adv., 'In a few days will be published', LC 77: 149 (10–12 Feb 1795); adv., 'ready for delivery to Subscribers, and the Trade', OPA 24 Feb 1795; adv. as published OPA 27 Feb 1795.

Adv. end vol. 2 of *The Castle of Ollada* (1795: 28).

Further edn: Dublin, 1795 (Printed for P. Wogan, P. Byrne, Wm. Jones, John Rice, and H. Fitzpatrick, 2 vols., 12mo), ESTC t179408.

CR: 'The Voluntary Exile is written in an unaffected sensible style: the incidents, in the first volume particularly, are probable, interesting, and affecting, and interspersed with a variety of excellent and judicious observations. . . . the merit . . . consists rather in its general good sense and tendency, than in any particularly brilliant or striking passages. It abounds too much in episode, by which the interest of the principal story is weakened,—which story, with the episodes, turns too invariably on the subject of love. . . . Neither is the present work entirely exempt from another error common to novelists;—horror is crowded upon horror till our sympathy becomes exhausted, and we read of faintings, death, and madness, with perfect apathy.'

MR [William Enfield]: 'This novel, though by no means to be ranked in the first class of fictitious tales, has too much merit to be wholly overlooked, or to be consigned to oblivion by indiscriminate censure. The narrative, it is true, if examined by the rules of criticism, appears very faulty. Far from gratifying the reader with the perception of unity of design, it confounds his recollection by a multiplicity of distinct and unconnected stories. . . . Notwithstanding this and other defects in the structure of the piece, the tales themselves are natural exhibitions of such occurrences as may be easily conceived to pass in real life, and are very well adapted to impress on the reader maxims of prudence and morality. . . . Her men and women are such as are commonly found in the world; and she makes them speak such a language, and express such sentiments, as are familiar to every one who converses with mankind.'

PORTER, Anna Maria, **ARTLESS TALES**
See 1793: 36

1795: 36   [PYE, Henry James].
THE DEMOCRAT: INTERSPERSED WITH ANECDOTES OF WELL KNOWN CHARACTERS. IN TWO VOLUMES.

London: Printed for William Lane, at the Minerva-Press, Leadenhall-Street, 1795.
I iv, 170p; II 188p. 8vo [MR and LC have 12mo]. 6s sewed (MR, LC), 9s sewed (adv.).
MR n.s. 19: 207–8 (Feb 1796); AF II: 3655.
O Mar.536; ESTC n001901 (NA CtY, CSmH, IU, ViU).

Notes. Table of contents i–iv. 2 pp. advs. end vol. 1.

Adv. LC 78: 52 (14–16 July 1795); additional booksellers are Hodgson, Wimpole-street; Scatchard, Ave Maria-lane; Miller, Old Bond-street; Knight and Co. Booksellers to his Majesty, St James's-street.

Adv. end vol. 4 of *Disobedience* (1797: 48).

Further edns: New York, 1795 (WC), xESTC; London, 1796, ESTC t107716. German trans. Berlin and Leipzig, 1796 (*Der Demokrat*) (EAG).

MR [Bryan Edwards]: 'What he calls *anecdotes of well-known characters* appears to be nothing more than the petty, local, and temporary scandal of a country town; and perhaps it may not unreasonably be suspected that the book was written solely to gratify a passion for illiberal invective against persons who are not properly before the public' (p. 207).

1795: 37 [RICKMAN, Thomas Clio].
THE EVENING WALK; A SENTIMENTAL TALE. INTERSPERSED WITH POETIC SCRAPS. BY A YOUTH OF SEVENTEEN.

> London: Printed for J. Walker, No. 44, Paternoster Row, and Thomas Clio Rickman,
> No. 7, Upper Mary-le-Bone Street, 1795.
> iv, 185p. 12mo. 3s (EngR), 3s sewed (SJC).
> EngR 26: 72 (July 1795); AF II: 3784.

BL 12613.cc.15; EM 201: 5; ESTC t070088 (NA CaOHM, CaQMM, CSmH).

Notes. Prefatory advertisement i–iv.

Adv. SJC 16–19 May 1795.

EngR: 'This tale . . . displays not a small degree of both alertness of mind and delicacy of sentiment; and although it wants that regularity, propriety, and chasteness, which are formed only by a good education and maturity of judgment, it does honour to so young an author as a youth of seventeen.'

1795: 38 ROBINSON, [John].
AUDLEY FORTESCUE; OR THE VICTIMS OF FRAILTY. A NOVEL. IN TWO VOLUMES. BY MR. ROBINSON.

> London: Printed for William Lane, at the Minerva Press, Leadenhall-Street, 1795.
> I 230p; II 189p. 12mo. 6s boards (CR), 7s sewed (adv.), 6s sewed (MP).
> CR n.s. 16: 115–16 (Jan 1796); AF II: 3816.

PU PR.3669.R185.A9.1795; ESTC n030564 (NA CtY).

Notes. Adv., 'In the Press', MP 31 Oct 1794; adv., 'In the Press, and speedily will be published', SJC 28–31 Mar 1795; adv. as published MP 20 Oct 1795.

Adv. end vol. 2 of *The Abbey of Clugny* (1796: 65).

Further edn: Dublin, 1796 (Printed for P. Wogan, P. Byrne, J. Rice, J. Moore, W. Jones, 1 vol., 12mo), EM 7722: 3, ESTC t120726.

CR: 'That human beings are frail, is by no means a modern discovery: but we do not perceive the utility of these descriptions, which are more calculated to mislead than benefit' (p. 115).

SAINT PIERRE, Jacques-Henri-Bernardin de; WILLIAMS, Helen Maria (trans.), PAUL AND VIRGINIA
See 1788: 71

1795: 39   SCHILLER, [Johann Christoph Friedrich]; [BOILEAU, Daniel (*trans.*)].
**THE GHOST-SEER; OR, APPARITIONIST. AN INTERESTING FRAG-
MENT, FOUND AMONG THE PAPERS OF COUNT O*****. FROM THE
GERMAN OF SCHILLER.**

>   London: Printed for Vernor and Hood, Birchin-Lane; Binns, Leeds; and Rawson,
>   Hull, 1795.
>   242p. 8vo [MR has 12mo]. 3s (MR), 3s sewed (OPA).
>   MR n.s. 18: 346–7 (Nov 1795); AF II: 394.
>   BL 635.a.15; EM 88: 7; ESTC t100179 (BI C, O, Ota).

Notes. Trans. of *Der Geisterseher. Eine Geschichte aus den Memoiren des Grafen O*** first published in *Thalia* 4–8 (1787–89) and first published separately Leipzig, 1789.
Adv. OPA 16 Feb 1795.
Further edns: New York, 1796, ESTC w012400; NSTC lists edns. of different trans. in 1831
and 1835.

   MR [William Taylor]: 'The Ghost-Seer is a novel of great originality. It has pointed out a
new source of the TERRIBLE,—the pursuit of an influence over the invisible world,—and
has given birth to imitations nearly as contemptible as they are multifarious.... The translation is ... with respect to language, well executed; and the work is interesting.'

1795: 40   [SHERWOOD, Mary Martha].
**THE TRADITIONS, A LEGENDARY TALE. IN TWO VOLUMES. WRIT-
TEN BY A YOUNG LADY.**

>   London: Printed for William Lane, Minerva, Leadenhall-Street, 1795.
>   I xxviii, 210p; II 234p. 12mo. 7s (CR), 7s sewed (MR, LC).
>   CR n.s. 14: 353–5 (July 1795); MR n.s. 18: 229 (Oct 1795); AF II: 4075.
>   BL 1488.aa.32; EMf; ESTC t062636 (BI O; NA DLC, IU, MH-H, NjP, PU).

Notes. 1 p. advs. end vol. 2. Dedication to Mr and Mrs St Quentin. List of subscribers
v–xxviii.
Adv., 'In a few Days will be published', SJC 28–30 May 1795; LC 78: 3 (30 June–2 July 1795);
additional booksellers are Miller, Bond-street; Hodgson, Wimpole-street; and Knight and
Co Booksellers to his Majesty, St James's-street.
Further edn: London, 1796, ESTC n013790.

   CR: 'The interest is well kept up; the sentiments are of a superior cast to the general run of
the novels of the day; and the moral deserves particular commendation.
   The faults are such as a maturer judgment will naturally lead the author to correct and
avoid. And should she again be tempted to weave the web of fancy, she will find advantage in
taking her materials from common life' (p. 353).
   MR [William Enfield]: 'The piece is of the romantic cast, and is more adapted to raise
astonishment and terror than to excite pity. The language is correct, and the story is of good
moral tendency. The principal fault of the work is that it gives too much encouragement to
superstition, by connecting events with preceding predictions, and by visionary appearances, for which the reader is not enabled to account from natural causes.'

1795: 41   SMITH, Charlotte.
MONTALBERT. A NOVEL. BY CHARLOTTE SMITH. IN THREE VOLUMES.

London: Printed by S. Low, Berwick Street, Soho; for E. Booker, No. 56, New Bond Street, 1795.

I 259p; II 257p; III 326p. 12mo. 12s sewed (CR), 12s (MR), 12s boards (OPA), 12s sewed or 15s neatly bound (SJC).

CR n.s. 20: 469 (Aug 1797); MR n.s. 19: 87–8 (Jan 1796); AF II: 4142.

BL 012635.df.4; CME 3-628-45178-7; EM 216: 2; ESTC t098239 (BI C, O; NA CtY-BR, CSmH, DLC, MH-H, NjP, PU, ViU &c.; EA COR).

Notes. Adv. OPA 9 June 1795; adv. SJC 20–23 June 1795.
Further edns: Dublin, 1795 (Printed for P. Wogan, P. Byrne, W. Jones, J. Rice, J. Moore [and 4 others in Dublin], 2 vols., 12mo), ESTC n004187; Philadelphia, 1795, ESTC w004352; Philadelphia, 1800, ESTC w026252. German trans. Erlangen 1798 (*Montalbert*) (EAG); French trans. Paris, 1800 (*Montalbert et Rosalie*) (BGR).

CR: 'It is not inferior, in our opinion, to any of Mrs Smith's productions; the scenes are natural, the characters strongly drawn, and the language, with a few exceptions, pure and flowing. The incidents are numerous, but skilfully united in one great design; and the cause of innocence and virtue is upheld with dignity and force.'

MR [Arthur Aikin]: 'The public have so often borne witness to the superior abilities of Mrs Smith as a novel writer, that there is now little left for us to say, more than merely announcing the work before us, and adding that it does not by any means disgrace its parentage.' Rev. congratulates Smith on having controlled her tendency, shared with some other novelists, to excessive description of scenery (p. 87).

1795: 42   [SUMMERSETT, Henry].
THE FATE OF SEDLEY: A NOVEL, BY THE AUTHOR OF THE OFF-SPRING OF RUSSELL. IN TWO VOLUMES.

London: Printed for William Lane, Minerva Press, Leadenhall-Street, 1795.

226p. 8vo. 6s sewed (CR), 7s sewed (adv.), 6s (SJC).

CR n.s. 16: 222 (Feb 1796); AF II: 4297.

PU PR.3991.A7.O33.1795; ESTC n008056.

Notes. Epistolary. 2 pp. advs. end vol. 1.
The Offspring of Russell 1794: 54.
Adv., 'In the Press, and speedily will be published', SJC 28–31 Mar 1795; adv. as published SJC 4–7 Apr 1795.
Adv. end vol. 2 of *The Abbey of Clugny* (1796: 65).

CR: 'We must not presume to give an opinion of this work, the author of which declares, that from such fastidious pedantic egots, as the critics, liberality of sentiment is not to be expected.'

BC 8: 'Another novel ending in suicide: here, however, it is palliated, by being the act of declared insanity. We cannot delight in these dismal delineations ...' (p. 179).

1795: 43   [THOMSON, Anna].
ROBERT AND ADELA: OR, THE RIGHTS OF WOMEN BEST MAIN-TAINED BY THE SENTIMENTS OF NATURE. IN THREE VOLUMES.

London: Printed for G. G. and J. Robinson, Pater-Noster-Row, 1795.

I 263p; II 288p; III 281p. 12mo. 10s 6d boards (CR), 9s 6d boards (MR), 9s sewed (SJC, OPA).

CR n.s. 16: 471–2 (Apr 1796); MR n.s. 18: 227 (Oct 1795); AF II: 3803.

MRu 823.69 R540; CME 3-628-45167-1; EM 3360: 12; ESTC n013038 (NA CtY, IU, PU &c.; EA COR).

Notes: Emily Dundorne (1799: 93) is 'By Mrs Thomson, Author Of Robert And Adela De Montfort'. For more information about author's name, see note to *Labyrinths of Life* 1791: 70.

Epistolary. Drop-head title in each volume is 'Robert and Adela de Montfort'.

Adv. SJC 16–18 June 1795 and OPA 22 June 1795.

Further edn: Dublin, 1795 (Printed for P. Byrne, P. Wogan, W. Jones, and G. Folingsby, 2 vols., 12mo), EM 1471: 38, ESTC n013039.

CR: 'The French revolution has not only afforded an ample field for the historian, the politician, and the moralist, but has supplied abundance of matter to the novel-weavers of the present times.—Robert and Adela are two French emigrants, whose adventures are indeed of a very extraordinary nature' (p. 471).

MR [William Enfield]: 'The design of this novel is to counteract the influence of the doctrine, which has lately been maintained with so much ingenuity, concerning the rights of women.... The [heroine's] character is throughout well supported, and the lesson suggested in the title is strongly enforced. This is, however, by no means the whole business of the novel. Other very natural and interesting tales of love are related, and many lively descriptions and pertinent reflections are interspersed.... The story is ingeniously constructed, but the style is not, on the whole, correct.'

1795: 44   TSCHINK, Cajetan; WILL, P[eter] (*trans.*)].
THE VICTIM OF MAGICAL DELUSION; OR, THE MYSTERY OF THE REVOLUTION OF P——L: A MAGICO-POLITICAL TALE. FOUNDED ON HISTORICAL FACTS, AND TRANSLATED FROM THE GERMAN OF CAJETAN TSCHINK. BY P. WILL.

London: Printed for G. G. and J. Robinson, Pater-Noster-Row, 1795.
I vii, 252p; II 284p; III 329, xip. 12mo. 9s (CR), 10s 6d sewed (MR, LC).
CR n.s. 15: 63–74 (Sept 1795); MR n.s. 17: 462–3 (Aug 1795); AF II: 4810.
BL 12613.e.17; EM 292: 4; ESTC t070083 (BI E, O; NA CSmH, MH-H, ViU &c.).

Notes. Trans. of *Geschichte eines Geistersehers* (Vienna, 178*).
Robinsons paid P. Will £40, 25 May 1795, for translating *The Victim of Magical Delusion* (RA).
Translator's preface 1, i–vii. Translator's 'Address to his Thinking Readers' end vol. 3, i–xi.
Adv., 'This Week will be published', SJC 9–12 May 1795. Adv., 'Next Week will be published', LC 77: 499 (23–26 May 1795); still adv., 'Next Week will be published', LC 78: 22 (4–7 July 1795); adv. as published SJC 16–18 June 1795 and LC 78: 116 (1–4 Aug 1795).
Further edn: Dublin, 1795 (Printed by Brett Smith. For Messrs. P. Wogan, P. Byrne, W. Jones, and G. Folingsby, 2 vols., 12mo), ESTC t177078.

CR: 'This novel is of a construction as singular as its object is foreign to the common purposes of this species of writing. Instead of the vicissitudes of courtship, aided by the usual concomitants of jealousy, disappointment, hairbreadth escapes, and parental severity, we have here a bold attack upon popular superstition, and the belief in magical operations, or those disguised appearances which ignorance induces many to think supernatural' (pp. 63–4).

MR [William Taylor]: 'This novel, like the Necromancer [1794: 34], is one of those numberless imitations to which the Ghost-seer of the celebrated Schiller [1795: 39] has given rise in Germany. The author, like most copyists, seizes rather the peculiarities than the beauties of his model; and, by overleaping too freely the fences of probability, he loses that impression of reality which is so favourable to vivid interest.'

1795: 45   [WÄCHTER, Georg Philip Ludwig Leonhard]; [HUISH, Robert? (*trans.*)].
THE SORCERER: A TALE. FROM THE GERMAN OF VEIT WEBER.

> London: Printed for J. Johnson, in St Paul's Church-Yard, 1795.
> 210p. 8vo. 3s 6d boards (CR), 2s 6d (MR).
> CR n.s. 17: 113 (May 1796); MR n.s. 21: 458–60 (Dec 1796); AF II: 4647.
> C XIX.8.25; EM 2583: 6; ESTC t100455 (BI BL; NA CSmH, PU, ViU &c.; EA SU).

Notes. Trans. of *Die Teufelsbeschwörung* first published in vol. 4 of Veit Weber, *Sagen der Vorzeit* (Berlin, 1787–98). ESTC: Trans. attributed to Robert Huish.

CR: 'The author of the Sorcerer displays no common talents. However phlegmatic a people the Germans may have been accounted, it is certain they excel in the impassioned style of writing. . . . The catastrophe of the present work harrows up the soul with emotions too shockingly vivid to be gratifying; they exceed in a great degree all the limits of pleasure which critics point out as the sources of the satisfaction we receive from the perusal of works of this nature,—and we shut the book with a sensation of horror bordering on disgust.'

MR [Samuel Rose]: 'The terrific is principally attempted in all these narratives, and the scene of event is mostly laid in the age of feudal anarchy. Doctrines of the modern philosophy have tinctured the author's mind; and he seldom misses an opportunity of attacking the superstitions of popery, and the tyranny of hereditary institutions. The style is of that kind which the French term the *convulsionary*. It is all effort, all hyperbole: it breaks a butterfly upon a wheel: it sends for the steeds of Juno to take a morning ride: every sentence dispatches the imagination to the very boundaries of the universe. This fatigues; yet the author has great force of fancy, much originality in the invention of his fable, and steadily attends to that unity of end and that climax of interest which are so perpetually neglected in English works of art.'

1795: 46   WALKER, George.
THE HOUSE OF TYNIAN. A NOVEL. IN FOUR VOLUMES. BY GEORGE WALKER.

> London: Printed for William Lane, at the Minerva Press, Leadenhall-Street, 1795.
> I 215p; II iv, 199p; II 248p; IV 213p. 12mo [CR has 8vo]. 12s boards (CR), 12s sewed (MP).
> CR n.s. 15: 342–4 (Nov 1795); AF II: 4662.
> C S727.d.79.42–45; ESTC n017040 (BI BL; NA CoFS).

Notes. Preface is bound at the beginning of vol. 2. 1 p. adv. end vols. 1 and 2; 3 pp. advs. end vol. 4.

Adv., 'In the Press, and speedily will be published', SJC 28–31 Mar 1795; adv. as published MP 8 Oct 1795.

Further edns: Dublin, 1796 (Printed for P. Wogan, P. Byrne, W. Jones, and J. Rice, 1 vol., 12mo), ESTC n017084; Dublin, 1796, EM 4156: 1, ESTC t118775.

CR: 'The press daily teems with so many insipid publications of this nature, that we are happy in being able to give our testimony in favour of a work, which, if it does not belong to the highest class of novels, is yet removed at an equal distance from the common rank. The author displays some discrimination and knowledge of the human heart, in the delineation of character,—a humane and liberal manner of thinking in the occasional reflections,—and much ingenuity in disentangling the lovers from the delicate embarrassments in which he had involved them' (p. 342).

1795: 47   [WARNER, Richard].
NETLEY ABBEY: A GOTHIC STORY. IN TWO VOLUMES.
> Southampton: Printed for the Author, by T. Skelton. And sold by C. Law, Ave Mary
> Lane, London, 1795.
> I 205p; II 191p. 12mo.
> BL C.123.f.18; CME 3-628-45127-2; EM 4233: 6; ESTC t124770 (NA ICU, NNU; EA
> COR).

Notes. Further edns: London (Lane), 1795, EM 1012: 16, ESTC n004242 [a reissue of the Southampton edn. with cancel title-pages]; Philadelphia, 1796, ESTC w024309; Baltimore, 1796 (WC), xESTC. German trans. Berlin and Leipzig, 1796 (*Kloster Netley*) (Price); French trans. Paris, 1801 (*L'Abbaye de Netley, histoire du Moyen Age*) (Lévy). Facs: GN II.

Lane edn. adv., 'In a few Days will be published', OPA 18 Apr 1795. Still adv., 'in a few days will be published', OPA 14 May 1795. Then adv., with heading 'A CAUTION TO BOOK-SELLERS', OPA 26 May 1795; 'As a Copy is in Circulation, with a Country Printer's Name in the Title, the Publick are cautioned to order LANE's EDITION, with an engraved elegant Frontispiece of two Characters, and a View of Netley Abbey'. In footnotes to the two next advs. (for *Secresy* and *Mysteries Elucidated*, 1795: 20 and 29) *Netley Abbey* is still being announced as 'In a few days will be published'.

WEBER, Veit
See WÄCHTER, Georg Philip Ludwig Leonhard

1795: 48   WILKINS, Charles (*trans.*).
THE STORY OF DOOSHWANTA AND SAKOONTALĀ. EXTRACTED FROM THE MAHĀBHĀRATA, A POEM IN THE SANSKREET LAN-GUAGE, TRANSLATED BY CHARLES WILKINS, ESQR. ORIGINALLY PUBLISHED IN THE ORIENTAL REPERTORY VOL. II. BY A. DALRYM-PLE. 1794.
> London: Printed for F. Wingrave, Successor to Mr. Nourse, in the Strand, 1795.
> xii, 115p. 12mo. 3s 6d sewed (CR), 3s sewed (MR).
> CR n.s. 17: 431–5 (Aug 1796); MR n.s. 21: 256–9 (Nov 1796); AF II: 4800.
> O Douce M 611; EM 2140: 24; ESTC n023416 (BI Ct; NA MH-H &c.).

Notes. Introduction i–xii signed A. Dalrymple and dated 1 Dec 1794. Story ends on p. 82; notes follow.
Originally published in the *Oriental Repertory* vol. 2 (1794). 44-pp. folio version printed by George Bigg also published in London in 1795, EM 5159: 2, ESTC t076184.

CR: 'In the episode before us are many beautiful specimens of poetical imagery, and much that will be found peculiarly pleasing to the admirers of elegant simplicity' (p. 432).

MR [Alexander Geddes] offers little more than plot summary.

1795: 49 [WILLIAMS, John (ed.?)].
THE CURATE OF ELMWOOD. A TALE. EDITED BY ANTHONY PASQUIN, ESQ.

London: Printed for Martin and Bain, Fleet-Street, 1795.

143p. 8vo [RT has 12mo]. 2s 6d (RT).

RT 6: 352–5 (Sept 15–30 1795).

BL N.2064(1); EM 2069: 3; ESTC t073513.

Notes. ESTC says that Williams (pseud.: Anthony Pasquin) is real author; however, he was 12 years old when the first magazine version appeared.

First issued as a short chapbook, *The History of Julia, or, the Adventures of a Curate's Daughter.* Some edns. have the author statement 'by Mr McMillan' (ESTC). Earlier short versions published in 4 magazines, 1773–85, and reprinted in 1809, RM 732.

Text of novel starts on p. 5.

Further edns: London, 1797, EM 2447: 10, ESTC t099915; London, 1798, ESTC t076264; London, 1799, ESTC n052577; London, 1799, ESTC t186934; 2 further entries in ESTC; London, 1805 (WC).

Most later edns. are entitled *The Village Curate, and his Daughter Julia* and *Julia; or the Adventures of the Daughter of a Village Curate.*

1795: 50 YEARSLEY, Ann.
THE ROYAL CAPTIVES: A FRAGMENT OF SECRET HISTORY. COPIED FROM AN OLD MANUSCRIPT, BY ANN YEARSLEY.

London: Printed for G. G. and J. Robinson, Pater-noster-Row, 1795.

I iv, 248p; II 254p; III 299p; IV 312p. 12mo. 12s sewed (MR) 4 vols; 6s sewed (CR, SJC) vols. 1–2; 6s sewed (SJC) vols. 3–4.

CR n.s. 13: 191–7 (Feb 1795) and n.s. 14: 391–8 (Aug 1795); MR n.s. 16: 112–14 (Jan 1795) and n.s. 19: 452–3 (Apr 1796); AF II: 4964, 4965.

ICN Y155.Y3; EM 233: 2; ESTC t057814 (BI BL, E, O &c.; NA CtY, CSmH, IU, PU &c.).

Notes. Preface 1, i–iv.

Summers reports that G. Robinson told Joseph Cottle that he paid £200 for this book.

Vols. 1–2 adv. SJC 20–23 Dec 1794; vols. 3–4 adv. SJC 28–30 Apr 1795.

Further edns: Dublin, 1795 (Printed by J. Stockdale, for P. Wogan, P. Byrne, J. Moore, J. Milliken, and G. Folingsby, 2 vols., 8vo), ESTC t118739; Philadelphia, 1795, ESTC w022017; Philadelphia, 1795, ESTC w022016; Philadelphia, 1796, ESTC w023301. Serialised as 'The History of an Unfortunate Royal Captive', *Weekly Entertainer*, 1795, RM 554. Facs: FCy.

CR n.s. 13: 'She appears to have studied the history of the age in which her personages are supposed to have lived, as well as of the real characters introduced; the costume is generally well preserved, and there is nothing improbable in her characters, acting as she has made them act, if we suppose them placed in the same situations' (p. 192). 'Having said so much in favour of this novel, we may be allowed to object to the style, which is often too poetical, and often laboured to a degree of stiffness. The incidents also, though not more improbable than are usually met with in novels, do not so easily pass one into the other as to exclude the idea of the marvellous. But the principal recommendation is, that the interest is kept up; and curiosity, however powerfully awakened, is not disappointed' (p. 197).

CR n.s. 14: 'The present volumes, we are happy to find, are no less a proof of her willingness to profit by advice, than of her ability to complete the undertaking in a manner gratifying to the expectation raised' (p. 392).

MR 16 [Thomas Holcroft]: 'The almost continued inflation of the style, and the writer's frequent power of expression; the crude and disjointed manner in which she has planned and pursued her story, with the occasional force discovered in the incidents, in the characters which are delineated, and in the bold philosophy at which Mrs Y. aims; are equally conspicuous. . . . The incidents are generally improbable; not because events more strange and incredible have not happened, but because, in the writer's haste to produce great effects, she has neglected the minutiæ which are necessary for that purpose' (p. 113). 'Those who buy books will much more frequently buy worse than better; and those who love to encourage an enterprizing and, however abashed and subdued, no vulgar spirit, will not think their money ill bestowed' (p. 114).

1796

ADELA NORTHINGTON, A NOVEL
See BURKE, Anne

1796: 1   ANON.
THE ADVENTURES OF A PIN, SUPPOSED TO BE RELATED BY HIMSELF, HERSELF, OR ITSELF.

London: Printed for J. Lee, New Street, Covent Garden, n.d. [1796].
ii, 187p. 12mo. 3s sewed (CR).
CR n.s. 18: 343 (Nov 1796); AF II: 26.
O Hope 8° 19; ESTC n004826 (NA CtY, ICN, MnU).

Notes. Preface i–ii. 5 pp. advs. end vol.
ESTC date: 1790?
Adv., 'Shortly will be published', end vol. 2 of *Arville Castle* (1795: 1).
Further edn: London, 1803 (Summers).

CR: 'We hope the writer of these Adventures is in earnest in the last paragraph of his Preface. The best fate which we can wish to his performance, and the fate which most probably awaits it, is (in his own language) "a gentle dip in the waters of oblivion."'

1796: 2   ANON.
AGATHA; OR, A NARRATIVE OF RECENT EVENTS. A NOVEL, IN THREE VOLUMES.

London: Printed for the Author, And sold by C. Dilly, Poultry; Hookham & Carpenter, Bond Street, & Allen & West, Paternoster-Row, 1796.

I 303p; II 272p; III 220p. 12mo. 12s boards (CR, MR).
CR n.s. 18: 110 (Sept 1796); MR n.s. 20: 231 (June 1796); AF II: 42.
BL 12614.dd.8; EM 418: 7; ESTC t072449 (BI O; NA CSmH, MH-H, NjP, PU &c.).

Notes. Engraved t.ps. containing a different illustration in each volume. 2 pp. advs. end vol. 3.

Adv., 'In the Press, and will be published about the end of this Month', SJC 15–17 Mar 1796; 'Each Volume will be embellished with an engraved Title, ornamented with an Historical Vignette, designed by T. Stothard, R.A. and engraved by B. Grainger. A few Copies, intended for the Libraries of the Curious, having been taken off on superfine Vellum Paper with Proofs of the Vignettes; the Publick are requested, in order to prevent Disappointment, to be early in their Application. The Price in Boards of the Superiour Edition will be 15s.—Impressions on common Paper 12s. in Boards.' Adv. as published SJC 7–9 June 1796.

Adv., 'Embellished with Vignettes, designed by Stothard, and engraved by B. Granger', GEP 27–30 Jan 1798; adv. also announces that 'a few Copies upon Vellum Paper, hot-pressed, with Proofs of the Vignettes may be had, Price 15s. in Boards' and that 'The above Work having been translated, in France, notwithstanding its counter-revolutionary Principles, and published at Paris, some Copies of the Translation are expected over; Orders for which, transmitted to Mr Allen, will be duly attended to on their arrival.'
Still adv. as 'This Day was published' GEP 25–27 July 1799.

French trans. Paris, 1797 (*Agatha; ou, la religieuse anglaise*) (BGR); German trans. Berlin, 1799 (*Agatha, oder Erzählung kürzlich vorgefallener Begebenheiten*) (EAG).

CR: 'This novel seems to have been written merely with a design to exhibit the French revolution in the most disgusting point of view; for the story is tedious and improbable, and the characters insipid or out of nature.'

MR [Arthur Aikin]: 'When a novelist assumes the grave and important character of an historian, it is incumbent on him to adduce his proofs and to cite his authorities, that no doubt may remain on the mind of the reader concerning his veracity.'

ALBERT DE NORDENSHILD
See CRAMER, Karl Gottlob

ANTOINETTE, A NOVEL
See PLUMPTRE, Anne

1796: 3   ANON.
AUGUSTA FITZHERBERT; OR, ANECDOTES OF REAL CHARACTERS. IN A SERIES OF LETTERS. BY THE AUTHOR OF THE CASTLE OF MOWBRAY, ST. BERNARD'S PRIORY, &C. IN TWO VOLUMES.
London: Printed for B. Crosby, no. 4, Stationers-Court, Ludgate-Street, 1796.
I 235p; II 213p. 12mo. 6s sewed (CR).
CR n.s. 18: 474 (Dec 1796); AF II: 173.
O 249.s.577, 578; xESTC.

Notes. The author of *The Castle of Mowbray* (1788: 60), *St. Bernard's Priory* (1786: 25), etc. is Martha Hugill, but in her preface to her *Isidora of Gallicia* (1797: 47) she explicitly denies authorship of *Augusta Fitzherbert* and says that the t.p. declaration was a marketing idea of Crosby's.

Epistolary.

Adv., 'In the Press, and speedily will be published', OPA 9 Mar 1796.

CR: 'The unfortunate are frequently advised to look below them; and it may be some comfort to the author of the Castle of Mowbray, St. Bernard's Priory, &c. to be informed, that we have been obliged to read worse novels than even Augusta Fitzherbert, or Anecdotes of *real* Characters.'

AUSTENBURN CASTLE

See 1795: 3

1796: 4 ANON.
BERKELEY HALL: OR, THE PUPIL OF EXPERIENCE. A NOVEL. IN THREE VOLUMES.

London: Printed for J. Tindal, Great Portland Street, Oxford Street, 1796.

I 324p; II 402p; III 411p. 12mo. 10s 6d boards (CR), 10s 6d sewed (MR, OPA).

CR n.s. 19: 112–13 (Jan 1797); MR n.s. 22: 92–3 (Jan 1797); AF II: 312.

MH-H *EC75.A100.796; EM 1496: 24; ESTC n015614 (NA MnU).

Notes. Adv. OPA 18 Mar 1796.

CR: 'The design of the present work is to ridicule (under the form of a novel) political innovation. The story or novel part of the work has little interest; the characters are generally *outré*, and many of the events very improbable. Some humourous experiments and adventures are related. . . . Upon the whole, this performance displays some invention, and would have afforded more entertainment, had it been compressed into a narrower compass, by abridging some conversations and reasonings, which, in their present state, the generality of readers will be inclined to pass over, and by omitting many anecdotes and recitals, which are common and uninteresting, and wholly unconnected with the principal narrative. Unity of plan is as essential to a good novel, as to an epic poem.'

MR: 'The scene of this work is laid in America; and the time is a short period before the late revolution in that country. The author has freely given the reins to his fancy, and in consequence, has produced many absurdities and incongruities: but it is an entertaining performance, and by no means the common production of a hackney novel-writer. Metaphysics and polemical discussions frequently occur: more reading, and more learning, than are usual in this line of composition, are displayed; and some interesting delineations are given of the manners and customs of the American Indians.'

CAMILLA: OR, A PICTURE OF YOUTH
See BURNEY, Frances

CLARENTINE. A NOVEL
See BURNEY, Sarah Harriet

CONSEQUENCES: OR, ADVENTURES AT RRAXALL CASTLE
See SURR, Thomas Skinner

EDWARD
See MOORE, John

1796: 5   ANON.
ELOISE DE MONTBLANC. A NOVEL. IN FOUR VOLUMES.

> London: Printed for William Lane, at the Minerva Press, Leadenhall-Street, 1796.
> I 247p; II 264p; III 173p; IV 164p. 12mo. 12s sewed (CR, Min).
> CR n.s. 23: 233 (June 1798); AF II: 1262.
> O Vet.A5f.2630-2633; CME 3-628-45038-1; ESTC n008632 (NA CtY, OU, PU; EA COR).

Notes. ESTC: sometimes attributed to Lady Mary C—r.
2-pp. preface (in which the author describes herself as a 'female Pen of Seventeen' whose first literary attempt this is) dated 4 June 1796. 1 p. advs. end vol. 1 and 3 pp. advs. end vol. 3.
Adv., 'In the Press, and speedily will be published', SJC 5–7 Apr 1796; still adv. 'speedily will be published', SJC 4–7 June 1796.

CR: 'We wish . . . that the lady had not thought it necessary to write *four* volumes. There is no *law* in favour of that number; and the business of this novel might have been dispatched in two volumes with more advantage to the author, and less weariness on the part of her readers.'

1796: 6   ANON.
ELVIRA; OR, THE WORLD AS IT GOES. A NOVEL. DEDICATED TO MRS. SAWBRIDGE. BY THE AUTHOR OF SEMPRONIA. IN TWO VOLUMES.

> London: Printed for J. Bell, no. 148, Oxford-Street, opposite Bond Street, 1796.
> I viii, 189p; II 189p. 12mo. 6s sewed (CR).
> CR n.s. 16: 471 (Apr 1796); AF II: 1267.
> MH-H *EC75.A100.796e; EM 1011: 5; ESTC n008615 (NA CSmH).

Notes. Dedication 1, v–viii. 1 p. advs. end vol. 2.
Post-dated; reviewed RT 30 Nov-15 Dec 1795.
Sempronia 1790: 26.

CR: 'A strange farrago of incongruities.—Sometimes the author speaks in the third person, and sometimes in the first, making herself a party with the personages of the drama. The story is unconnected and improbable, without having either incident or sentiment sufficient to render it interesting. Many of the characters in which originality is attempted, are absurd, inconsistent, and ill supported.'

1796: 7   ANON.
*THE EMPRESS MATILDA, A NOVEL, IN A SERIES OF LETTERS; IN TWO VOLUMES. BY A LADY.

> London: Printed and sold by T. Wilkins, Aldermanbury; and C. Law, Ave-Maria-lane (SJC), 1796 (SJC).
> 8vo. 6s (BC), 6s sewed (SJC).
> BC 9: 434 (Apr 1797).
> No copy located.

Notes. Dedication to H.R.H. the Duchess of York (SJC). Epistolary.
Adv. SJC 2–5 July 1796.

BC: 'One of the most humble performances that ever came from the hands of any gentleman, or any lady.'

1796: 8 ANON.
*FATALITY: A NOVEL, IN THREE VOLUMES.

> London: Printed by and for Sampson Lowe [sic], Berwick-street, Soho; and sold by
> C. Law, Ave-Maria-lane; and Booker, Bond-street (OPA), 1796 (BC).
> 3 vols. (OPA). 12mo. 9s (BC).
> BC 9: 434 (Apr 1797).
> No copy located.

Notes. Perhaps a trans. of *La fatalité, roman poétique* by Jean-Baptiste-Christophe Grainville (a re-working of *Ismène et Tarsus*, 1785) pub. Paris, 1791.
Adv. OPA 9 Apr 1796.

BC: 'We congratulate the public on this writer's incapacity for working much mischief. His dullness is a sufficient antidote to his mischievousness. To inflame the passions of young people, by impure narrations, put into the mouth of the heroine herself, appears to be the chief aim of this despicable story; which is proved, by many symptoms in the style, to have been borrowed from some modern *French* teacher of morality.'

1796: 9 ANON.
THE FEMALE GAMESTER; OR, THE PUPIL OF FASHION. A NOVEL. IN TWO VOLUMES.

> London: Printed for the Author; and sold by Vernor and Hood, Birchin-Lane, 1796.
> I 217p; II 247p. 12mo. 6s sewed (CR).
> CR n.s. 19: 111–12 (Jan 1797); AF II: 1409.
> O Jessel.e.502; EMf; ESTC t191084 (NA ICN).

Notes. Dedication to E. P. Salamon, Esquire, of Finchley, signed 'The Author', London, 28 Mar 1796. 2-pp. prefatory advertisement. Epistolary.
Adv., 'By a Lady', OPA 18 Apr 1796.

CR: 'This novel, if it does not rank among the highest class, has spirit and interest. . . . The style of our author is sometimes lively and forcible, but frequently careless. . . . upon the whole, this production has merit, and can scarcely fail to arrest the attention, and interest the affections of the reader.'

A GOSSIP'S STORY, AND A LEGENDARY TALE
See WEST, Jane

HANNAH HEWIT; OR, THE FEMALE CRUSOE
See DIBDIN, Charles

HERMSPRONG; OR, MAN AS HE IS NOT
See BAGE, Robert

THE HISTORY OF NED EVANS
See HERVEY, Elizabeth

JULIA DE SAINT PIERRE
See CRAIK, Helen

1796: 10   ANON.

THE LAUGHABLE ADVENTURES OF CHARLES AND LISETTE; OR, THE BEARDS. TO WHICH IS ADDED, THE STROLLING STUDENT.

London: Printed for the Translator: and sold by Vernor and Hood, Birchin-Lane; and all other Booksellers, 1796.

190p. 12mo. 2s 6d sewed (CR, MR).

CR n.s. 17: 239 (June 1796); MR n.s. 20: 232 (June 1796); AF II: 2471.

BL 12510.ee.26; EMf; ESTC t071216.

Notes. An expanded version of *Les Capucins sans barbe, histoire napolitaine arrivée en 1761* (ESTC; BGR).

Text of novel starts on p. 3.

CR: 'The humour of this work consists in gross ribaldry and licentious description.'

1796: 11   ANON.

*THE LAUNCH. A NOVEL. WRITTEN BY A LADY.

London: Printed for the Author, and sold by W. Lubbock, at his Circulating Library, No. 23, Rathbone (OPA), 1796 (OPA).

2 vols. 12mo. 7s sewed (CR, OPA).

CR n.s. 16: 472 (Apr 1796).

No copy located.

Notes. Adv. OPA 18 Mar 1796.

CR: 'This novel soars so sublimely above all the rules of common orthography, common grammar, and common sense,—the characters are so *super-celestial,*—and the language so far removed from that which custom has sanctioned in the daily intercourses of life,—that, should any of our fair novel-readers be endowed with sufficient patience to labour through the work, they must have recourse to Johnson's Dictionary, to discover the sense of nineteen out of twenty of the words. . . .'

1796: 12   ANON.

*LAURA; OR, THE VICISSITUDES OF FORTUNE.

London: Printed for H. Lowndes, No. 77, Fleet-street (SJC), 1796 (SJC).

2 vols. 12mo. 6s sewed (SJC).

No copy located.

Notes. Adv. SJC 2–5 July 1796.

1796: 13   ANON.

LOVE'S PILGRIMAGE; A STORY FOUNDED ON FACTS. COMPILED FROM THE JOURNAL OF A DECEASED FRIEND. IN THREE VOLUMES.

London: Printed for T. N. Longman, Paternoster-Row, 1796.

I xii, 218p; II 199p; III 191p. 12mo. 9s sewed (CR, MR), 9s boards (SJC, adv.).

CR n.s. 17: 112–13 (May 1796); MR n.s. 20: 346 (July 1796); AF II: 2616.

BL 1154.g.14; EM 2450: 7; ESTC t078888 (BI O; NA PPL).

Notes. Preface v–xii.

LA: 750 copies printed by Strahan; what seems to read 'Miss Reeves' given as the recipient of the unspecified copyright payment. She might therefore be the author—no other instance of an intermediary appears in the LA H4 novel entries—but the absence of costings also suggests unusual circumstances.

Adv. SJC 25–27 Feb 1796. Adv. end vol. 3 of *Clara Duplessis* (1797: 50).

Further edns: Philadelphia, 1799, ESTC w011401; Philadelphia, 1799, ESTC w023287.

CR: 'This is a curious story.... There is too little of sentiment in this work, and too much of local description, to render it very interesting; nor are these descriptions enlivened by imagery, or distinguished by taste. As a work of fancy, it wants the enthusiastic glow of passion, or the shifting scene of incident, which, allowing scope for genius and invention, gives the spirit to fiction, and which is requisite to fix attention.'

MR [Arthur Aikin]: 'An improbable story, of which the main incident is utterly repugnant to every idea of delicacy and honour.'

1796: 14   ANON.

THE MAGNANIMOUS AMAZON; OR, ADVENTURES OF THERESIA, BARONNESS VAN HOOG, WITH ANECDOTES OF OTHER ECCENTRIC PERSONS.

London: Printed for Vernor and Hood, Birchin-Lane, Cornhill, 1796.

x, 348p. 12mo. 3s 6d sewed (CR, MR), 2 vols. 5s sewed (SJC).

CR n.s. 17: 238–9 (June 1796); MR n.s. 20: 232 (June 1796); AF II: 2689.

BL 12611.f.8; EM 124: 1; ESTC t057450 (NA CtY-BR, MH-H, NN, PU).

Notes. Preface v–x; text of novel starts on p. 13.

Adv. SJC 17–19 Mar 1796.

CR: 'A novel, said to be translated from the Dutch, and which is presented to us as a favourable specimen of Dutch literature.

The editor has either been unfortunate in his selection, or the phlegmatic republicans are better calculated for commercial speculation than to excurse in the regions of fancy.

The work consists of a number of adventures, unconnected and episodical,—many of them extravagant, all uninteresting, and few probable.'

MR: 'The novel is a translation from the Dutch, and is the groundwork on which a recent publication, entitled "The Memoirs of Mad. Barnevelt," [1795: 19] has been formed. The story is clumsy, and, in our opinion, should have been suffered to remain in its native Boeotian atmosphere.'

THE MANSION HOUSE: A NOVEL
See BREWER, James Norris

MARIA; OR, THE VICARAGE
See STABBACK, Thomas

MATILDA AND ELIZABETH: A NOVEL
See PURBECK, Elizabeth and Jane

1796: 15   ANON.
MEMOIRS OF THE ANCIENT HOUSE OF CLARENDON. A NOVEL. IN THREE VOLUMES.

London: Printed for William Lane, at the Minerva-Press, Leadenhall-Street, 1796.
I 204p; II 291p; III 232p. 12mo. 9s sewed (CR, Min).
CR n.s. 20: 471 (Aug 1797).
BL 12611.aaa.2; CME 3-628-45109-4; EM 162: 3; ESTC t054973 (NA PU; EA COR).

Notes. Handwritten note end vol. 2 in BL copy: 'A deucedly long winded story'.
Adv., 'In the Press, and speedily will be published', SJC 5–7 Apr 1796.
Adv. end vol. 2 of *Court Intrigue* (1799: 44).

CR: 'The scene of the novel before us is laid in England; the story is interesting, and delineates, with pleasing vivacity, the military and domestic manners of the feudal times. . . . The various characters it exhibits are naturally drawn; and the sentiments and language evince the author to possess the talent of pathetic and elegant composition.'

1796: 16   ANON.
MEMOIRS OF THE MARQUIS DE VILLEBON, IN A SERIES OF LETTERS. A NOVEL FOUNDED ON FACTS; IN TWO VOLUMES.

Salisbury: Printed by J. Easton: for T. Cadell, jun. and W. Davies (successors to Mr Cadell) in the Strand; and G. and T. Wilkie, Pater-noster-Row, London, 1796.
I 215p; II 196p. 12mo. 6s sewed (MR, LC).
MR n.s. 22: 91 (Jan 1797); AF II: 2831.
BL C.108.s.3; EM 4790: 1; ESTC t135333.

Notes. Epistolary.
Adv. LC 81: 359 (13–15 Apr 1797).

MR [Arthur Aikin]: 'The epistolary style is of all others the most difficult to sustain with spirit and propriety. As each person has a peculiar character of thought, and manner of expressing himself, it is necessary for an author to command a sufficient variety of style, suited to the different actors whom he employs. In these memoirs, this important object is totally overlooked; and, as far as character of style is concerned, any letter might with equal propriety be attributed to any one of the *dramatis personæ.* The plot is deficient in incident and interest. The language is not wholly free from offences against grammatical accuracy. . . .'

MODERN NOVEL WRITING, OR THE ELEGANT ENTHUSIAST
See BECKFORD, William

THE MONK: A ROMANCE
See LEWIS, Matthew Gregory

MONTGOMERY; OR, SCENES IN WALES
See PLUMPTRE, Annabella

THE MYSTIC CASTLE
See SINGER, Mr

THE NEAPOLITAN; OR, THE TEST OF INTEGRITY
See MACKENZIE, Anna Maria

THE PAVILION. A NOVEL
See DE CRESPIGNY, Mary Champion

PRINCESS COQUED∪UF AND PRINCE BONBON
See DU BOCAGE, Michel-Joseph, seigneur de Bléville

1796: 17   ANON.
ROACH ABBEY: A TALE. IN TWO VOLUMES.

>London: Printed for Vernor and Hood, Birchin-Lane, by R. Ferguson and Co. Liver-
>pool; And sold by them and by Rawson and Co. Hull, n.d. [ESTC: 1794?].
>I 151p; II 150p. 8vo. 4s sewed (OPA, adv.).
>BL RB.23.a.11131; ESTC t227056.

Notes. Text of novel starts on p. 5.
Adv. OPA 8 Apr 1796; 3 vols.
Adv. end vol. 2 of J. C. Schulz's *Maurice* (1796: 79).

1796: 18   ANON.
THE SIAMESE TALES: BEING A COLLECTION OF STORIES TOLD TO
THE SON OF THE MANDARIN SAM-SIB, FOR THE PURPOSE OF
ENGAGING HIS MIND IN THE LOVE OF TRUTH AND VIRTUE. WITH
AN HISTORICAL ACCOUNT OF THE KINGDOM OF SIAM. TO
WHICH IS ADDED THE PRINCIPAL MAXIMS OF THE TALAPOINS.
TRANSLATED FROM THE SIAMESE.

>London: Printed for Vernor and Hood, Birchin Lane, Cornhill; and Champante and
>Whitrow, Jewry-Street, Aldgate, 1796.
>ii, 196p. 12mo. 2s (CR), 2s 6d bound (SJC).
>CR n.s. 23: 115 (May 1798); AF II: 4087.
>BL 12703.b.1; EM 269: 12; ESTC t112304 (BI C, E, O; NA CaAEU, CSmH, ICN, MH-H;
>EA TaLn).

Notes. In entry for Baltimore edn. ESTC notes attribution to George Brewer.
Frontispiece. Table of contents. Introduction pp. [i]–ii. Historical account of the kingdom of
Siam 1–16.
Adv., 'A Companion to the Arabian Night's Entertainments', SJC 9–11 June 1796.
Further edn: Baltimore, 1797, ESTC w022280.

> CR: 'They are sufficiently interesting to attract the attention of youth; and, although they
>possess none of the splendid imagery of the Arabian tales, their morality is such as cannot be
>presented in too many shapes.'

THE SPRITE OF THE NUNNERY
See TRAPP, Joseph

TRAVELS BEFORE THE FLOOD
See KLINGER, Friedrich Maximilian von

THE WANDERER OF THE ALPS
See SINGER, Mr

1796: 19   ANON.
WOODLAND COTTAGE. A NOVEL. IN TWO VOLUMES.
London: Printed for Hookham and Carpenter, Old Bond Street, 1796.
I xx, 229p; II 228p. 12mo. 7s sewed (CR).
CR n.s. 18: 341 (Nov 1796); AF II: 4925.
BL 12612.ccc.2; EM 231: 1; ESTC t066920 (NA CtY-BR, CSmH, IU, MH-H, PU &c.;
    EA ZAP).

Notes. Dedication to Lady Elizabeth Drummond iii–v. List of subscribers ix–xx. Text of novel
starts on p. 5 in vol. 1.
Adv. SJC 11–14 June 1796 with no price.
Further edn: London, 1799 (Corvey).
   CR: 'More rectitude of principle, than powers of imagination, is displayed in her production; but if it is not entitled to high praise, neither is it deserving of censure; young persons
may find from the perusal of it amusement and benefit.'

1796: 20   ARNOLD, S[amuel James].
THE CREOLE; OR, THE HAUNTED ISLAND. IN THREE VOLUMES. BY
S. ARNOLD, JUNIOR.
London: Printed by C. Whittingham; for C. Law, Stationers' Court; Hookham, Bond
    Street; and Bell, Oxford Road, 1796.
I xxiv, 160p; II viii, 196p; III viii, 208p. 12mo. 10s 6d (CR), 10s 6d sewed (MR), half a
    guinea (OPA).
CR n.s. 19: 225–7 (Feb 1797); MR n.s. 21: 207–8 (Oct 1796); AF II: 142.
BL 12612.bb.2; EM 219: 4; ESTC t064719 (BI O; NA CLU-S/C).

Notes. Vol. 1 Preface v–xv; list of subscribers xvii–xx; table of contents xxi–xxiv. Vols. 2 and
3 table of contents v–viii.
Adv. OPA 20 Sept 1796.
   CR: 'To write a good novel (perhaps one of the most arduous and delicate of literary
labours) requires a knowledge of the human mind, its propensities and passions,—an extensive acquaintance with, or an accurate observation on, men and manners,—penetration to
discern, acuteness to catch, sensibility to feel, judgment to discriminate, taste to select, and
imagination to paint, not merely the varieties, but the most interesting features, of the
human character.' This author does not meet this high standard, but he is not advised to give
up the pen, 'but, before he resumes it, seriously to consider the hints which we have, with a
friendly intention, suggested' (p. 226).
   MR [James Burney]: 'It appears to be the principal intention of this novel, to shew how
much more we ought to place a reliance on the knowlege of morality and religion than on
ignorance, for the preservation of innocence, or for advancing the interests of virtue. Mr
Arnold has adopted the fashionable practice of introducing pieces of poetry in his narrative,
some of which possess considerable merit.'

1796: 21   [BAGE, Robert].
HERMSPRONG; OR, MAN AS HE IS NOT. A NOVEL. IN THREE VOL-
UMES. BY THE AUTHOR OF MAN AS HE IS.

> London: Printed for William Lane, at the Minerva-Press, Leadenhall-Street, 1796.
> I 244p; II 242p; III 268p. 12mo. 9s boards (CR), 9s sewed (MR, MP).
> CR n.s. 23: 234 (June 1798); MR n.s. 21: 21–4 (Sept 1796); AF II: 191.
> MH-H *EC75.B1465.796h; EMf; ESTC n017626 (BI BL, C, D, O; NA CtY-BR, CSmH,
> IU, NjP, PU &c.).

Notes. 4 pp. Advs. end vol. 1; 2 pp. advs. end vol. 2.
Man as He Is 1792: 29.
Adv., 'In a few Days will be Published', MP 5 Dec 1795; adv. as published MP 25 Dec 1795.
Further edns: Dublin, 1796 (Printed by Brett Smith, for P. Wogan, P. Byrne, J. Moore, and J.
Rice, 2 vols., 12mo), EM 63: 6, ESTC t057334; London, 1799, EM 4340: 1, ESTC t130284;
Philadelphia, 1803 (WC); London, 1809 (WC); London, 1810 (WC); WC has 1 further entry
between 1800 and 1850. German trans. Liegnitz and Leipzig, 1799 (*Hermsprung; oder Adel-
stolz und Menschenwerth*) (EAG). Facs: N.

> CR: 'This novel must be distinguished from the common sort. The author displays an
> intimate acquaintance with human nature, and delineates it with the pen of a master.'
> MR [William Taylor]: 'We feel . . . disposed to ascribe a higher rank of excellence to this
> than the former novel: it wanders less from its main purpose; there are equal beauties of
> detail; and the elevated soul of Hermsprong is a prominent and fine delineation of the
> accomplished, firm, frank, and generous man, worthy to be impressed as a model for imita-
> tion' (p. 21). 'We hope for frequent entertainment from the pen of this amusing, instructive,
> and singular genius' (p. 24).

1796: 22   [BECKFORD, William].
MODERN NOVEL WRITING, OR THE ELEGANT ENTHUSIAST; AND
INTERESTING EMOTIONS OF ARABELLA BLOOMVILLE. A RHAP-
SODICAL ROMANCE. INTERSPERSED WITH POETRY. IN TWO VOL-
UMES. BY THE RIGHT HON. LADY HARRIET MARLOW.

> London: Printed for G. G. and J. Robinson, 1796.
> I ii, 243p; II 232p. 12mo. 7s boards (CR, MR).
> CR n.s. 18: 472–4 (Dec 1796); MR n.s. 20: 477 (Aug 1796); AF II: 260.
> BL 12614.bb.15; EM 288: 5; ESTC t063184 (BI O; NA CtY-BR, MH-H, NjP &c.).

Notes. Dedication 'To her Grace the Duchess of ———' 1, i–ii. Vol. II ends with 'An Humble
Address to the Doers of that excellent and Impartial Review, called The British Critic'
(pp. 217–32).
German trans. Weissenfels, 1798 (*Miss Arabella Bloomville, ein rhapsodistischer Roman*)
(RS). Facs: FCy.

> CR: 'To the friends of mirth and satire, this production will afford a delectable entertain-
> ment. In flights of wild and digressive humour, Tristram Shandy, compared with the present
> performance, is a regular and methodical work. Our author seems, by his rambling, uncon-
> nected style, to intend a satire on the obscure, desultory, incorrect manner of the inferior
> modern novelists: neither do those of a higher class entirely escape the shafts of his ridicule:
> a variety of quotations, both in poetry and prose, many of them from writers of celebrity, are
> introduced, in circumstances so ludicrous, and attended with combinations so whimsical, as

to render them, in their new situations, truly laughable. . . . Under an apparently light and sportive manner, some strokes of keen and ingenious satire are levelled, not merely at authors and books, but at men and measures.'

MR [Arthur Aikin] calls it '. . . this truly comic, diverting, and satiric performance; the design of which is to burlesque the ordinary run of our circulating-library novels.'

BC 9 (Jan 1797): 'This is a very humorous and successful, though sometimes overcharged, attack upon modern novel-writing, which certainly gives too frequent occasion for the exercise of such weapons as the author here uses. There is a great deal of good food for laughter in these volumes, in which we have heartily joined, though we ourselves are occasionally the subject of the writer's humour.' BC notes that the book has been attributed to Mr Merry.

BONHOTE, Elizabeth, BUNGAY CASTLE: A NOVEL
See 1797: 27

1796: 23   [BREWER, James Norris].
THE MANSION HOUSE: A NOVEL. IN TWO VOLUMES. WRITTEN BY
A YOUNG GENTLEMAN.
> London: Printed for William Lane, at the Minerva-Press, Leadenhall-Street, 1796.
> I viii, 181p; II 175p. 12mo. 6s (BC), 6s sewed (Min).
> BC 8: 672 (Dec 1796); AF II: 465.
> Corvey; CME 3-628-45113-2; EM 8820: 10; ESTC t172631 (BI MRu).

Notes. Prefatory advertisement vol. 1, v–vi. 1 p. adv end vol. 1; 2 pp. advs. beginning vol. 2.
Adv., 'Preparing for the Press . . . *Emma; or, the Mansion House*', SJC 5–7 Apr 1796.

BC: 'An advertisement to these volumes informs the reader that they were written by a young gentleman, for his amusement, and that he knows them to be full of imperfections. So they are, but they are perfectly harmless.'

1796: 24   [BURKE, Anne].
ADELA NORTHINGTON, A NOVEL. IN THREE VOLUMES.
> London: Printed for W. Cawthorne, British Library, Strand, 1796.
> I 254p; II 194p; III 266p. 12mo. 10s 6d sewed (CR, MR); 10s 6d boards or 12s bound
> (LC).
> CR n.s. 17: 351 (July 1796); MR n.s. 19: 454 (Apr 1796); AF II: 539.
> BL N.2321; CME 3-628-45000-4; EM 2071: 2; ESTC t074657 (NA CLU-S/C. MH-H;
> EA COR).

Notes. Adv. LC 79: 179 (20–23 Feb 1796); 'Written by Mrs. Burke'.

CR: 'Credit is due to the writer of this work for good intention:—but a style so careless and incorrect, incidents so unconnected, and characters so heterogeneous, we have seldom seen. In the events towards the catastrophe, which are equally improbable and impracticable, the author evidently designs to surprise the reader, and is not unsuccessful. No sufficient motives are assigned for the violent measures pursued by the personages so unexpectedly introduced: the whole transaction is not merely a violation of all the laws of probability, and such as could not have taken place in this country, but has no connecting link to unite it with the preceding circumstances of the story. It is not enough for a novelist to heap together a mass of surprising adventures and uncommon characters, without attending to the unities of time, person, place and circumstance.'

MR [Arthur Aikin]: 'We find little in this work on which the most candid criticism can dwell with pleasure; it is replete with incident, and yet fails to excite attention,—for the actions are improbable, the characters out of nature, and the events in general disgusting; while the tale of misery is repeated so often as at length to be read with indifference, or to excite emotions of a very painful nature.'

1796: 25   BURKE, [Anne].
THE SORROWS OF EDITH: OR, THE HERMITAGE OF THE CLIFFS: A DESCRIPTIVE TALE, FOUNDED ON FACTS. IN TWO VOLUMES. BY MRS. BURKE, AUTHOR OF ELA, OR DELUSIONS OF THE HEART, &C.
> London: Printed for B. Crosby, No. 4, Stationer's Court, Ludgate-Street, 1796.
> I iv, 209p; II 194p. 12mo. 6s sewed (CR, MR).
> CR n.s. 17: 239 (June 1796); MR n.s. 21: 460–1 (Dec 1796); AF II: 543.
> ViU RB PZ2.B87S 1796; ESTC n037165.

Notes. Dedication to H.R.H. the Duchess of York. 7 pp. advs. end vol. 1 and 5 pp. advs. end vol. 2.
Ela 1787: 32.
Adv., 'In the Press, and speedily will be published', OPA 9 Mar 1796.
   CR: 'Though the story of this novel is very confused, we yet allow it to possess considerable merit. The incidents are various and interesting, the sentiments in general just and benevolent, and the style is easy and correct.'
   MR [William Enfield]: 'This novel is characterised in the title by an improper epithet. It should not have been called a *descriptive*, but a *pathetic* tale. The writer deals little in descriptions either of scenes of nature, human characters, or romantic pictures: but she relates a tale, which, without splendid scenery, philosophical sentiments, or even an highly embellished style, will interest the heart of the reader.'

1796: 26   [BURNEY, Frances].
CAMILLA: OR, A PICTURE OF YOUTH. BY THE AUTHOR OF EVELINA AND CECILIA. IN FIVE VOLUMES.
> London: Printed for T. Payne, at the Mews-Gate; and T. Cadell Jun and W. Davies (Successors to Mr Cadell) in the Strand, 1796.
> I xlviii, 390p; II 432p; III 468p; IV 432p; V 556p. 12mo. £1 1s sewed (CR, MR).
> CR n.s. 18: 26–40 (Sept 1796); MR n.s. 21: 156–63 (Oct 1796); AF II: 547.
> BL 1206.b.17-21; CME 3-628-45029-2; EMf; ESTC t144705 (BI D, E, O &c.; NA CtY-BR, CSmH, DLC, ICN, IU, MH-H, NjP, NN, PU, TxU, ViU &c.; EA COR, SU, WIW).

Notes: Evelina 1778: 10; *Cecilia* 1782: 15. 4,000 copies printed July 1796 (Strahan 17 f. 92).
Burney wrote on 19 June 1795 that the idea of publishing by subscription was 'in many— MANY ways unpleasant & unpalatable to us both' but the profits from *Camilla* were intended as 'a little portion' for her son and the '*so* enormous' costs of printing made subscription the only way of publishing for themselves (Burney, *Journals*, 124–125). Burney's correspondence for July 1795 shows a great deal of discussion of the financial aspects of this publication; she reports being told that the booksellers (Lowndes and Payne) made very large profits from *Evelina* and *Cecilia* (Burney, *Journals*, 140).

MP 16 July 1795 and SJC 28–30 July 1795: 'Proposals for Printing by Subscription, a New Work . . . by the Authour of Evelina and Cecilia. To be delivered on or before the 1st Day of July 1796. The Subscription will be One Guinea; to be paid at the time of Subscribing. Subscriptions will be received by T. Payne, at the Mews Gate; J. Edwards, Pall-Mall; J. Robson, Bond-street; Cadell and Davies, in the Strand; and Robinsons, Paternoster-Row.' Re-adv. with its title SJC 11–13 Feb 1796.

Adv. as published SJC 16–19 July 1796; 'The Subscribers are requested to apply for their Copies to the respective Booksellers, to whom they paid their Subscriptions. Those who subscribed to the Ladies who kept Books, may receive their Copies on application to the Publishers.'

Extracts published LC 80: 249 and 257 (10–13 and 13–15 Sept 1796).

Further edns: Dublin, 1796 (Printed by William Porter, for G. Burnet, R. Cross, P. Wogan, P. Byrne [and 26 others in Dublin], 3 vols., 12mo), EM 280: 1, ESTC t107618; Cork, 1796, ESTC t187670; Boston, 1797, ESTC w019993; New York, 1797, ESTC w030199; New York, 1797, ESTC w030123; ESTC has further entry; WC has 3 entries between 1800 and 1850; NSTC lists edns in 1802 and 1840. French trans. Paris, 1797 (*Camilla, ou la Peinture de la jeunesse*) (BN); German trans. Berlin and Stettin, 1798 (*Kamilla oder ein Gemälde der Jugend*) (EAG).

CR begins with general argument that the best novels 'require powers of invention and fancy not inferior to those which are necessary to the construction of an epic poem'; long, favourable review is mostly quotations.

MR [William Enfield]: 'In the present work, Mrs D'Arblay . . . with equal judgment and modesty, pursues the track in which she has already acquired so much deserved reputation; without suffering herself to be diverted from her native bent by an affectation of excelling in different kinds of writing, and without catching the infection of that taste for the marvellous and the terrible, which, since the appearance of her former productions, has, with some writers, become the fashion of the day. We have not perused the story of Camilla without seeing reason to admire its general structure, nor without feeling ourselves interested in the occurrences and catastrophe. Our chief pleasure, however, has arisen from the highly animated scenes of life and manners which have passed before us, and from the accurate and lively portraits of various characters, which the writer has drawn, if not from individual originals, at least from that great general exemplar, the world' (pp. 156–7).

1796: 27   [BURNEY, Sarah Harriet].
CLARENTINE. A NOVEL. IN THREE VOLUMES.

London: Printed for G. G. and J. Robinson, Paternoster-row, 1796.
I 304; II 296; III 274. 12mo. 10s 6d boards (MR), 10s 6d sewed (SJC).
CR n.s. 23: 471–2 (Aug 1798); MR n.s. 21: 452–6 (Dec 1796); AF II: 550.
BL 12613.g.5; CME 3-628-45020-9; EM 334: 7; ESTC t070068 (BI O; NA CSmH, ICN, MH-H, NjP, TxU &c.; EA COR).

Notes. Adv., 'Next Week will be published', SJC 21–23 June 1796.

Further edns: Dublin, 1797 (Printed by P. Wogan, 2 vols., 12mo), ESTC t162210; London, 1816 (WC, NSTC); Philadelphia, 1818 (WC); Philadelphia, n.d. [?1800 1899] (WC); NSTC lists edn in 1815. French trans. Paris, 1819 (*Clarentine*) (BN, NSTC).

CR: 'In its construction, a perfect regularity of plan is preserved; the events rise in a series, exhibiting the education, early virtues, taste and sensibility, and the more mature sentiments, independent spirit and chastened affection of Caroline. The dialogue is easy, often humorous, and pleasingly descriptive of modern manners and follies. . . . This work, in our opinion, is greatly superior to novels of the ordinary stamp; and it discovers talents from which much may be expected in this department of literature.'

MR [George Edward Griffiths]: 'The work before us does not abound with any striking delineation of character, artful contexture of fable, nor peculiar illustration of any moral or religious truth: but the language is easy, spirited, and flowing; the heroine is strictly virtuous; the conduct of the principal persons in the history is, on the whole, unexceptionable; and the tale is throughout interesting.'

1796: 28   CAMBON, J. J.
CLEMENTINA BEDFORD. A NOVEL. IN LETTERS AND NARRATIVE. BY J. J. CAMBON.

> London: Printed for H. D. Symonds, no. 21, Paternoster-Row, [1796].
> xii, 258p. 12mo. 3s (half-title, CR), 3s sewed (MR).
> CR n.s. 17: 239 (June 1796); MR n.s. 20: 346 (July 1796); AF II: 586.
> MH-H *NC7.C1425.796c; EM 1001: 11; ESTC n002247 (BI O; NA CtY).

Notes. Dutch sources do not support the attribution of this work to Maria Gertruida de Cambon.
Date is actually printed as MDCCLCVI. Preface v–xii. Epistolary.
Adv. OPA 18 Apr 1796.

CR: 'A tame, uninteresting story, little calculated either to touch the heart or captivate the fancy.'

MR: 'The chief recommendation of this novel is that it is short; yet we do not think that those who have read it once will feel much inclination to re-peruse it.'

1796: 29   COLE, William.
THE CONTRADICTION. BY THE REV. WILLIAM COLE.

> London: Printed for T. Cadell, Jun. and W. Davies, (successors to Mr Cadell), Strand, 1796.
> xx, 11, 248p. 12mo. 5s boards (MR, SJC).
> MR n.s. 22: 220–1 (Feb 1797); AF II: 747.
> BL N.1738; EM 1925: 6; ESTC t071895 (BI C; NA CtY-BR, ICN, IU, MH-H, NjP).

Notes. Preface 'To the Reader in General' i–ix; preface 'To the Particular Reader' xi–xx; list of subscribers 1–11; Arabic numbering restarts with 1st p. of novel.
Adv. SJC 24–27 June 1797.

MR: 'The reverend author of the work before us writes like a worthy man, but he is very deficient in his attempts to emulate the style of the unrivalled STERNE. The comic Muse is scared by this gentleman's black coat; and therefore we would advise him to confine his future attentions to her graver sister, Urania' (p. 221).

1796: 30   COURTNEY, Mrs.
ISABINDA OF BELLEFIELD. A SENTIMENTAL NOVEL IN A SERIES OF LETTERS. BY MRS. COURTNEY.

> London: Printed for S. Bagster, N°. 81, Strand, 1796.
> I vi, 300p; II 279p; III 266p. 12mo. 10s 6d sewed (CR, SJC).

CR n.s. 18: 110–11 (Sept 1796); AF II: 893.
Corvey; CME 3-628-45022-5; ESTC t212848.

Notes. Dedication 'to the Public' vol. 1, v–vi. Epistolary.

Adv., 'Handsomely printed on woven paper', SJC 2–4 June 1796.

Further edn: Dublin, [1795?] (Printed for P. Wogan, J. Moore, J. Milliken, W. McKenzie, and J. Rice, 2 vols., 12mo), EM 4250: 6, ESTC n033464.

CR: 'The gentle writer of this *sentimental* tale is so willing to avail herself of all the privileges of her *sex*, and so humbly throws herself upon our clemency, that we feel ourselves utterly disarmed of our critical acumen. Her production is made up of the usual incidents and sentiments which compose the *generality* of this species of publication (we always mean to except a distinguished and superior class).'

1796: 31   [CRAIK, Helen].
JULIA DE SAINT PIERRE. A NOVEL. IN THREE VOLUMES.

London: Printed for William Lane. At the Minerva-Press, Leadenhall-Street, 1796.
I iv, 270p; II 336p; III 399p. 12mo. 10s 6d sewed (OPA, Min).
CtY-BR In.C853.796J; xESTC.

Notes. Frontispiece vol. 1. Dedication to Mrs. —— 1, i–iv, signed 'The Author', Nov 1796. 2 pp. advs. end vol. 1, 1 p. advs. end vol. 3.

Adv., 'In the Press, and speedily will be published', SJC 5–7 Apr 1796; adv. OPA 26 Nov 1796.

1796: 32   [CRAMER, Karl Gottlob].
ALBERT DE NORDENSHILD: OR, THE MODERN ALCIBIADES. A NOVEL, TRANSLATED FROM THE GERMAN. IN TWO VOLUMES.

London: Printed for G. G. and J. Robinson, Paternoster Row, 1796.
I 347p; II 311p. 12mo. 7s boards (CR), 7s half bound (MR), 7s sewed (SJC).
CR n.s. 17: 194–8 (June 1796); MR n.s. 20: 346 (July 1796); AF II: 927.
BL 12557.bbb.8; EM 174: 5; ESTC t129711 (BI Ota; NA ViU).

Notes. Trans. of *Hermann von Nordenschild*, parts 4 and 5 of *Der deutsche Alcibiades* (Weissenfels and Leipzig, 1790–92).

Adv., 'Next Saturday will be published', SJC 20–23 Feb 1796.

CR: 'The novel before us is certainly an object of literary curiosity, as affording a picture of the manners in the interior parts of Germany, and probably rather of the last age than the present. A national character, more remote from all that we see in this country, can scarcely be conceived; and many passages will appear in the highest degree tinctured with romance, which, we doubt not, are fair delineations of nature in the scene which the author has undertaken to depict.

Independent however of this circumstance, the novel before us partakes of the genius of the German literary productions—the story is wild, fanciful, and in some measure improbable; but it is highly interesting, and must be entertaining to all classes of readers.'

MR: 'This novel is interesting, and contains some marks of genius: but the fable is preposterous, and the translation is indifferent.'

1796: 33   CREECH, Mrs.
MARY; OR, THE USES OF ADVERSITY. A NOVEL IN 2 VOLUMES. BY MRS. CREECH.

Cork: Printed by J. Connor, At the Circulating Library, Castle-Street, 1796.

I xvi, 195p; II 191p. 12mo.

D I 6551 Cork 1796; ESTC t171970.

Notes. Vol. 1 Preface v–vii; list of subscribers ix–xvi. Epistolary.

1796: 34 CULLEN, Stephen.

THE CASTLE OF INCHVALLY: A TALE—ALAS! TOO TRUE. BY STEPHEN CULLEN, AUTHOR OF THE HAUNTED PRIORY, ETC. ETC. IN THREE VOLUMES.

London: Printed for J. Bell, No. 148, Oxford-Street, opposite Bond-Street, 1796.

I 294p; II 332p; III 307p. 12mo. 10s 6d sewed (CR), 10s 6d (OPA).

CR n.s. 20: 118 (May 1797); AF II: 949.

ICN Case Y155.C885; CME 3–628–45023–3; EM 5160: 6; ESTC t120483 (BI BL, O; NA CaAEU, MH-H, RPB-JH; EA COR).

Notes: The Haunted Priory 1794: 20.

Adv. OPA 19 Nov 1796; additional booksellers are G. G. and J. Robinson, Paternoster-Row; and C. Law, Ave Maria-lane.

Further edns: Hackney, 1820 (WC, NSTC); London, 1846 (Summers).

CR: 'The success of several deservedly popular novels and romances has occasioned the reading public to be pestered with innumerable tales of distressed lovers, enchanted castles, &c. &c. When we consider the very high price of that valuable article *paper*, we are sorry to be under the necessity of pronouncing that this story, *in three volumes*, has nothing in its circumstances, characters, sentiments, or style, that renders it worthy of critical notice.'

1796: 35 [DE CRESPIGNY, Mary Champion].

THE PAVILION. A NOVEL. IN FOUR VOLUMES.

London: Printed for William Lane, at the Minerva Press, Leadenhall-Street, 1796.

I viii, 288p; II 298p; III 255p; IV 212p. 12mo. 14s sewed (CR, MR), 14s sewed and fine paper 18s (SJC).

CR n.s. 17: 476 (Aug 1796); MR n.s. 20: 345 (July 1796); AF II: 1019.

BL N.2729; EM 7104: 1; ESTC t095847 (NA CSmH, CtY, IU, MH-H, NjP, PU, ViU &c.).

Notes. Dedication to Sir Henry Martin, Bart. (called 'Preface' in running head) v–viii, signed 'The Author'.

Adv., 'In the Press, and speedily will be published', SJC 5–7 Apr 1796; adv. as published SJC 12–14 May 1796.

Adv. end vol. 2 of *Court Intrigue* (1799: 44).

CR: 'A composition of the usual ingredients which go to make up a modern novel (we would always be understood to except a certain class)—the incidents trite, and the sentiment feeble, neither distinguished by originality, nor embellished by genius. The manners of high-life are depictured [*sic*] without the polish which, in the estimation of the superficial, supplies the place of more valuable qualities—while of those of the commercial world, a representation is given equally illiberal and unjust.'

MR [Arthur Aikin]: 'So numerous are the novels which have been published of late years, that it requires no common abilities to invent one at present, in which either the plot or many of the incidents should not bear a striking resemblance to those that are to be found in others, already published. This is the case with the volumes before us. To the merit of originality they can lay small claim: but the moral is good; and they are by no means deficient in exciting a considerable degree of interest.'

1796: 36   [DIBDIN, Charles].

HANNAH HEWIT; OR, THE FEMALE CRUSOE. BEING THE HISTORY OF A WOMAN OF UNCOMMON MENTAL, AND PERSONAL ACCOMPLISHMENTS; WHO, AFTER A VARIETY OF EXTRAORDINARY AND INTERESTING ADVENTURES IN ALMOST EVERY STATION OF LIFE, FROM SPLENDID PROSPERITY TO ABJECT ADVERSITY, WAS CAST AWAY IN THE GROSVENOR EAST-INDIAMAN: AND BECAME FOR THREE YEARS THE SOLE INHABITANT OF AN ISLAND, IN THE SOUTH SEAS. SUPPOSED TO BE WRITTEN BY HERSELF.

> London: Printed for C. Dibdin, at his Music Warehouse, no. 411, Strand, n.d. [1796].
> I xviii, 220p; II 271p; III 275p. 8vo. 12s (CR), 10s 6d sewed or 15s elegantly bound (OPA).
> CR n.s. 23: 114 (May 1798); AF II: 1070.
> C 7720.d.1723–1725; CME 3–628–45050–0; EM 2473: 2; ESTC t107055 (BI BL, E; NA CtY, CSmH, DLC, ICN, MH-H &c.; EA COR, ZWTU).

Notes. ESTC gives date as 1792.
Preface 1, i–xviii.
Adv., 'Mr. Dibdin's Novel . . . The First Week in May will be published', OPA 14 Apr 1796.

CR: 'This is a professed imitation of the Robinson Crusoe of De-Foe; but it does not exhibit one spark of the genius displayed in that celebrated novel. It affords little amusement, and excites little interest. The adventures are grossly improbable, the dialogue vulgar, and the sentiments trite.'

1796: 37   [DU BOCAGE, Michel-Joseph, seigneur de Bléville].

PRINCESS COQUEDÆUF AND PRINCE BONBON, A HISTORY AS ANCIENT AS IT IS AUTHENTIC. TRANSLATED FROM THE NEUSTRIAN TONGUE INTO FRENCH BY M. DEGBACOBUB, AND FROM FRENCH INTO ENGLISH BY R. C. F.R.S. A.S.S. ACAD. PAR. VIND. PETROB. HOLM. LUGD. GOT. COMPL. EBUR. DUBL. ABERD. MEDIOL. PATAV. BURD. FLOR. SION. ROTHOM. GRUBST. SOCIUS PASTOR ARCADE, &C. &C. &C.

> London: Printed for P. Elmsly, in the Strand, 1796.
> vii, 164p. 8vo. 3s 6d boards (CR).
> CR n.s. 21: 87–90 (Sept 1797); AF II: 3606.
> BL 1509/1290; EM 2910: 2; ESTC t081120 (NA ViU).

Notes. Trans. of *La princesse Coque d' œuf et le Prince Bonbon* (La Haye, 1745).
ESTC: Variously attributed to Mlle—de Lubert and to M. J. Dubocage de Bléville.
Historical and Chronological Preface iii–vii.

CR: 'This is a ludicrous story, after the manner of Rabelais, the satire of which, if any is intended, is not very obvious' (p. 87). 'This whimsical production, we think, may prove no bad companion for the gout, though far too eccentric for serious criticism' (p. 90).

1796: 38　　[DUCRAY-DUMINIL, François-Guillaume]; [PEACOCK, Lucy (*trans.*)].
AMBROSE AND ELEANOR; OR, THE ADVENTURES OF TWO CHIL-
DREN DESERTED ON AN UNINHABITED ISLAND. TRANSLATED
FROM THE FRENCH. WITH ALTERATIONS, ADAPTING IT TO THE
PERUSAL OF YOUTH, FOR WHOSE AMUSEMENT AND INSTRUC-
TION IT IS DESIGNED. BY THE AUTHOR OF THE ADVENTURES OF
THE SIX PRINCESSES OF BABYLON; JUVENILE MAGAZINE; VISIT
FOR A WEEK, &C.

> London: Printed for R. and L. Peacock, At the Juvenile Library; and sold by Messrs.
> Hookham and J. Carpenter, Bond-Street, 1796.
> vi, 212p. 12mo. 3s (CR), 3s sewed (MR).
> CR n.s. 17: 350–1 (July 1796); MR n.s. 20: 346 (July 1796); AF II: 3274.
> BL Ch.790/98; EM 7251: 2; ESTC t096711 (BI C; NA CtY-BR, CLU-S/C, FU).

Notes. Free and abridged trans. of *Lolotte et Fanfan ou les aventures de deux enfans abandon-
nés dans une isle déserte* (Charle's-Town [sic] and Paris, 1788).
Frontispiece. Prefatory advertisement v–vi.
Adventures of the Six Princesses 1785: 40; *Visit for a Week* 1794: 43.
Further edns: London, 1797, ESTC t162327; Philadelphia, 1799, ESTC w015326; Baltimore,
1798 (WC); Baltimore, 1799, ESTC w015325; London, 1807 (WC); WC has 3 further entries
between 1800 and 1850; NSTC lists edns in 18—, 1807 and 1820.
　　CR: '. . . the story is a most improbable fiction; the incidents are by no means new, and the
concluding events show little ingenuity and less judgment. Some of the scenes however are
well arranged, and the descriptive parts are animated and impressive' (p. 351).
　　MR: 'While we have Robinson Crusoe in our language, it is little worth while to translate,
from another tongue, so inferior a production as these adventures.'

1796: 39　　FISHER, J[oshua] B[ridges].
UNDER THE PATRONAGE OF HER GRACE THE DUCHESS OF RUT-
LAND: THE HERMITAGE, A NOVEL, BY J. B. FISHER.

> [London?]: Printed for the Author, 1796.
> I xxii, 167p; II 190p. 12mo.
> ICU PR4699.F72H4 1796; ESTC n051256.

Notes. T.ps. are engraved. Prefatory advertisement 1, iii, preface v–x, dedication xii–xiv, list
of subscribers xv–xix. In vol. 2 text begins on p. 5.

1796: 40　　FITZ-JOHN, Matilda [pseud?].
JOAN!!! A NOVEL. BY MATILDA FITZ-JOHN. IN FOUR VOLUMES.

> London: Printed for Hookham and Carpenter, Old Bond Street, 1796.
> I 268p; II 280p; III 298p; IV 345p. 12mo. 14s sewed (CR, MR).
> CR n.s. 18: 236 (Oct 1796); MR n.s. 21: 460 (Dec 1796); AF II: 1448.
> BL 12613.e.5; CME 3–628–45045–4; EM 292: 3; ESTC t070072 (NA IU, MH-H, PU,
> ViU &c.; EA COR).

Notes. Dedication 'To the Memory of a Departed Friend.'

Copyright bought by Hookham for 60 gns.; 750 copies printed, with 509 sold at a loss of £9.19.2, H&C G/22.

Adv. SJC 11–14 June 1796.

CR: 'This novel has a great deal of plot and intricacy, and displays some invention and ingenuity; but it is difficult sufficiently to connect and render probable a variety of complicated incidents.... The language and conversations in many parts of the work are vulgar; yet, upon the whole, it has some merit and interest, carrying the reader forward by its shifting scenes, and is well calculated to beguile a languid or a vacant hour.'

MR [William Enfield]: 'The mystical meaning of the triple mark of interjection, annexed to the name in the title of this novel, we cannot decypher. We find nothing very *wonderful* either in the character or the story of this Joan.... On the whole, this performance has too many faults to rank highly among novels; yet, to readers not fastidiously nice in this kind of entertainment, it may be amusing.'

1796: 41   GENLIS, [Caroline-Stéphanie-Félicité Ducrest de Mézières, comtesse de]; BERESFORD, [James] (*trans.*).
THE KNIGHTS OF THE SWAN; OR, THE COURT OF CHARLEMAGNE: A HISTORICAL AND MORAL TALE: TO SERVE AS A CONTINUATION TO THE TALES OF THE CASTLE; AND OF WHICH ALL THE INCIDENTS THAT BEAR ANALOGY TO THE FRENCH REVOLUTION ARE TAKEN FROM HISTORY. TRANSLATED FROM THE FRENCH OF MADAME DE GENLIS, AUTHOR OF THE THEATRE OF EDUCATION, ADELAIDE & THEODORE, &C. BY THE REV. MR. BERESFORD.

>London: Printed for J. Johnson, St. Paul's Church-Yard, 1796.
>I xviii, 258p; II 288p; III 250p. 12mo. 9s boards (MR, SJC).
>MR n.s. 22: 93 (Jan 1797); AF II: 306.
>BL 636.d.24; EM 3915: 3; ESTC t144835 (BI C, O; NA MH-H, ViU, &c.).

Notes. Trans. of *Les Chevaliers du cygne* (Paris, 1795).
1: 1-p. Epistle Dedicatory to ****, 12-pp. Preface, 2-pp. table of contents bound at end; 2: 2-pp. table of contents; 3: 2-pp. table of contents (front) and 2-pp. Address to the Public (back). Notes and translation of the French and Italian mottoes end each vol.
Adv., 'In a few Days will be published', SJC 12–14 July 1796; Johnson also has the French original on sale; adv. as published SJC 11–13 Aug 1796.
Adelaide and Theodore 1783: 9.
Further edns: Edinburgh, 1796, ESTC n004658; Dublin, 1797 (Printed for P. Wogan, P. Byrne, H. Colbert, J. Milliken, J. Chambers [and 6 others in Dublin], 2 vols., 12mo), EM 3251: 5, ESTC n033289; London, 1799 [abridgement, *The Age of Chivalry*], EM 7062: 1; ESTC t144663.

MR [William Taylor] refers to review of original in MR n.s. 19: 551 and continues: 'We have only to repeat that, in this romance of chivalry, the incidents are amusingly varied, and the moral is generally unexceptionable: but the spirit of event is often modern, the manners of the age are imperfectly preserved, and the painting is frequently too indelicate and luxuriant for the sober taste of this country.'

GESZNER, A. H.
See MELTZER, Adolph Heinrich

1796: 42   GOMERSALL, A[nn].
THE DISAPPOINTED HEIR: OR, MEMOIRS OF THE ORMOND FAM-
ILY. A NOVEL. IN TWO VOLUMES. BY A. GOMERSALL, AUTHOR OF
ELEONORA, CITIZEN, &C.

> Exeter: Printed and Published by J. M'Kenzie and Son, Booksellers, Stationers, etc.
> High-Street; Also, by W. Richardson, Bookseller, Cornhill; And by Hookham and
> Carpenter, Bond-Street, London, 1796.
> I 240p; II 244p. 12mo. 7s sewed (MR, SJC).
> MR n.s. 22: 220 (Feb 1797); AF II: 1664.
> Corvey; CME 3–628–45074–8; EM 1112: 9; ESTC n006749 (NA MH-H).

Notes. On author's name see note to 1789: 42.
1-p. prefatory advertisement vol. 1.
Eleonora 1789: 42; The Citizen 1790: 43.
Adv. SJC 17–19 Nov 1796; 'By Mrs. A. Gomersall, of Exeter'; additional bookseller is Mr
Rowe, Great Marlborough-street, Carnaby Market.

MR: 'This work will rank with those novels which one neither laments to have read nor to
have missed reading; which may be taken up with innocence and laid down without impatience; and which neither convulses the reader by ludicrous images, nor renders him melancholy by pathetic scenes, nor terrifies him by horrid incidents. It, however, inculcates and
enforces moral maxims, and is not deficient in interest.'

1796: 43   GOOCH, [Elizabeth Sarah Villa-Real].
THE WANDERINGS OF THE IMAGINATION. BY MRS. GOOCH. IN
TWO VOLUMES.

> London: Printed for B. Crosby, No. 4, Stationers-Court, Ludgate-Street, 1796.
> I x, 143p; II 148p. 8vo. 6s sewed (CR, SJC).
> CR n.s. 16: 220–1 (Feb 1796); AF II: 1670.
> BL 12612.aaa.32; EM 332: 3; ESTC t064752 (NA NcU).

Notes. Preface 1, iii–x.
Possibly post-dated; adv., 'On Monday next, Dec. 14, will be published, Neatly printed', SJC
10–12 Dec 1795. Reviewed RT Dec 15–31 1795.

CR: 'The first volume contains an affecting story, which, if founded on facts, affords a
shocking instance of human depravity, or rather, of the corrupt state of society. The general
tendency of the work is to inculcate humane and benevolent sentiments. . . . In the second
volume, the writer's imagination wanders into the regions of fiction, and gives birth to an
amusing little Spanish tale.'

1796: 44   GROSSE, [Karl Friedrich August]; TRAPP, Joseph (trans.).
THE GENIUS: OR, THE MYSTERIOUS ADVENTURES OF DON CARLOS
DE GRANDEZ. BY THE MARQUIS VON GROSSE. TRANSLATED FROM
THE GERMAN, BY JOSEPH TRAPP, TRANSLATOR OF STOEVER'S
LIFE OF LINNÆUS, PICTURE OF ITALY, &C. &C. IN TWO VOLUMES.

London: Printed for Allen and West, Nº 15, Paternoster-Row, n.d. [MR, Bodl.: 1796].
I 228p; II 216p. 12mo. 6s sewed (CR), 9s sewed (MR).
CR n.s. 18: 342 (Nov 1796); MR n.s. 22: 93 (Jan 1797); AF II: 4516.
O 249.s.257; xESTC.

Notes. Trans. of *Der Genius* (Halle, 1790–94), itself apparently a derivative of *Memoiren des Marquis von G***s* (Berlin, 1787–98). The narrative (but not the specific text) is therefore close to 45 below.

CR: 'In imitation of some of his more successful countrymen, who have harrowed up our imaginations with tales of magic and mysterious horror, the present writer has introduced a sufficient number of ghostly stories and marvellous adventures—in the recital of which, he has not more grossly violated the laws of nature and probability, than those of composition. The principal part of the story consists in a wretched imitation of the account of the secret tribunal, in the popular novel of Herman of Unna [1794: 41]. Events equally ridiculous, unconnected, and uninteresting, are jumbled together, without method or meaning, resembling the wild ravings of a maniac. The whole production seems an abortive conception, miserably executed, and as ill translated.'

MR [William Taylor]: 'Scenes of supernatural horror, ill connected, in frightful succession agitate the reader: but they furnish some situations not unworthy of selection by future writers, who possess a less disorderly imagination.'

1796: 45   GROSSE, [Karl Friedrich August]; WILL, P[eter] (*trans.*).
HORRID MYSTERIES. A STORY. FROM THE GERMAN OF THE MARQUIS OF GROSSE. BY P. WILL. IN FOUR VOLUMES.

London: Printed for William Lane, at the Minerva-Press, Leadenhall-Street, 1796.
I xii, 264p; II 296p; III 232p; IV 252p. 12mo. 12s sewed (CR), 14s sewed (SJC, Min).
CR n.s. 21: 473 (Dec 1797).
Corvey; CME 3-628-45056-X; ESTC t166402 (BI Ota; NA CtY-BR).

Notes. Although the same story as the brief *Der Genius* (Halle, 1790–94—see 44 above), it is apparently a trans. of the much fuller *Memoiren des Marquis von G***s* (Berlin, 1787–98). 'The Translator's Preface' i–xii.

Adv., 'In the Press, and speedily will be published', SJC 5–7 Apr 1796; adv. as published SJC 23–26 July 1796; additional booksellers are Miller, Old Bond-Street; and C. Law, Ave-Maria-Lane.
CR points out close similarities to *The Victim of Magical Delusion* (1795: 44).

1796: 46   GULLIVER, Lemuel, jun. [pseud.].
MODERN GULLIVER'S TRAVELS. LILLIPUT: BEING A NEW JOURNEY TO THAT CELEBRATED ISLAND. CONTAINING A FAITHFUL ACCOUNT OF THE MANNERS, CHARACTERS, CUSTOMS, RELIGION, LAWS, POLITICS, REVENUE, TAXES, LEARNING, GENERAL PROGRESS IN ARTS AND SCIENCES, DRESS, AMUSEMENTS, AND GALLANTRY OF THOSE FAMOUS LITTLE PEOPLE. FROM THE YEAR 1702 (WHEN THEY WERE FIRST DISCOVERED AND VISITED BY CAPTAIN LEMUEL GULLIVER, THE FATHER OF THE COMPILER OF THIS WORK), TO THE PRESENT ÆRA, 1796. BY LEMUEL GULLIVER, JUN.

London: Printed for T. Chapman, Fleet Street, 1796.

viii, 226p. 12mo. 3s boards (MR).

MR n.s. 21: 117 (Sept 1796).

BL 12611.ccc.15; EM 165: 1; ESTC t057331 (BI MRu; NA CtY, CSmH, DLC, ICN, IU, NjP &c.).

Notes. ESTC: sometimes attributed to H. Whitmore. Erroneously attributed to Elizabeth Graham.

Dedication to the Duke of Bedford iii–iv; table of contents v–viii.

MR [William Enfield]: 'A medley of extravagance and absurdity, destitute of every character which might entitle it to be considered as a sequel to Swift's Voyage to Lilliput.'

1796: 47   GUNNING, [Elizabeth].

THE FORESTERS. A NOVEL. ALTERED FROM THE FRENCH BY MISS GUNNING. IN FOUR VOLUMES.

London: Printed by and for Sampson Low, Berwick Street, Soho; and sold by C. Law, Ave-Maria Lane; and William Jackson, no. 198, Oxford Street, 1796.

I 190p; II 190p; III 189p; IV 186p. 12mo. 12s (EngR).

EngR 27: 274–7 (Mar 1796); AF II: 1754.

BL C.175.a.18; CME 3-628-45041-1; EM 4827: 7; ESTC t127121 (BI TAU; NA CLU-S/C, MH-H, NNU; EA COR).

Notes. In fact an original work, not an alteration (ESTC).

1 p. advs. end vol. 4.

Further edn: Dublin, 1796 (Printed by William Porter, for P. Wogan, P. Byrne, J. Milliken, W. Porter, J. Rice [and 5 others in Dublin], 2 vols., 12mo), EM 5067: 1, ESTC t118911.

EngR: 'This excellent novel . . . is far above the common style of compositions of this kind, as, together with much amusement, it conveys a good moral lesson throughout the whole, and exposes, to the young and unexperienced, the danger and difficulties attendant on vows rashly made. The style is easy, such as might justly be expected from the pen of our fair and accomplished author.

The great merit of this work consists in curiosity raised, and well kept alive, until the general *denouement* or catastrophe of the whole' (pp. 274–5).

1796: 48   GUNNING, [Susannah].

*DELVES, A WELCH TALE. BY MRS. GUNNING.

London: Sold by Allen and West, no. 15, Paternoster-Row (SJC), 1796 (SJC).

2 vols. 12mo. 10s sewed (CR), 9s sewed (SJC Apr), 6s (SJC June).

CR n.s. 18: 236 (Oct 1796); AF II: 1761.

No copy located.

Notes. Adv., 'speedily will be published', SJC 7–9 Apr 1796; adv. as published SJC 7–9 June 1796.

Further edns: London, 1796, EM 137: 8; ESTC t067330; London, 1796, ESTC t126814.

CR: 'We have been much entertained with this Welch Tale; it is told with humour and simplicity, and with some strokes of nature and pathos. Delves, and his dog Trimbush, fasten themselves on the reader's affections; we pursue them with interest and pleasure through their frolicks and peregrinations. The scenes and conversations are characteristic; the plot is simple, the style unaffected, and the *dénûment* happy and satisfactory. It is a production more particularly calculated to amuse young persons by its pleasantry and *naïveté*.'

1796: 49   HAMILTON, Eliza[beth].
TRANSLATION OF THE LETTERS OF A HINDOO RAJAH; WRITTEN PREVIOUS TO, AND DURING THE PERIOD OF HIS RESIDENCE IN ENGLAND. TO WHICH IS PREFIXED A PRELIMINARY DISSERTATION ON THE HISTORY, RELIGION, AND MANNERS, OF THE HINDOOS. IN TWO VOLUMES. BY ELIZA HAMILTON.

> London: Printed for G. G. J. and J. Robinson, No. 25, Paternoster Row, 1796.
> I lx, 272p; II 343p. 8vo. 10s boards (MR, SJC).
> CR n.s. 17: 241–9 (July 1796); MR n.s. 21: 176–81 (Oct 1796); AF II: 1790.
> BL 12621.p.3; EM 327: 4; ESTC t056854 (BI E, O, MRu; NA CSmH, ICN, TxU &c.; EA NUN).

Notes. Dedication to Warren Hastings. Preliminary dissertation 1, i–lx about the history and customs of the Hindoos, followed by a 4-pp. glossary (unn.). Epistolary.
Adv., 'Next Week will be published', SJC 21–23 June 1796.
Further edns: Dublin, 1797 (Printed for H. Colbert, 2 vols., 12mo), EM 5167: 4, ESTC t055907; London, 1801 (WC); London, 1811 (BLC); Boston, 1819 (WC).
CR: 'In the course of the work we find a regular narrative, enlivened with many interesting and well drawn characters. The whole is founded on the supposed fact of a young Indian of rank forming an intimacy with an accomplished Englishman, whose representation of the state of his own country produces in the Rajah an insatiable curiosity to visit a country which his romantic imagination had pictured as the wonder of the universe. . . . Through the whole, miss Hamilton displays a considerable knowledge of modern life, with very strong powers of ridicule and irony, and no inconsiderable acquaintance with the manners and literature of the East' (pp. 241–2).
  MR [Alexander Hamilton]: 'It is . . . scarcely necessary to inform our readers that this is a work of fiction and fancy, designed to place before the view of the English reader a picture of the prevalent manners and customs of his country, in the novel colours of a supposed Hindoo painter' (pp. 176–7). 'Although this publication is well supported throughout, and affords much entertainment, and many just and pointed remarks respecting the present state of our own country, we must acknowlege our opinion that the portion of the work which is evidently most laboured is the least deserving of commendation; and that Miss H. is less happy in her descriptions of Hindoo manners, than in her delineations of scenes at home, where she is better acquainted' (p. 179).

1796: 50   HAYS, Mary.
MEMOIRS OF EMMA COURTNEY. BY MARY HAYS. IN TWO VOLUMES.

> London: Printed for G. G. J. and J. Robinson, Pater-Noster-Row, 1796.
> I 11, 184p; II 220p. 12mo. 6s sewed (CR), 6s boards (MR).
> CR n.s. 19: 109–11 (Jan 1797); MR n.s. 22: 443–9 (Apr 1797); AF II: 1862.
> BL 12612.bbb.12; EM 131: 2; ESTC t114712 (NA CaAEU).

Notes. Preface 1, 5–11; Arabic numbering restarts with 1st p. of novel.
Adv., 'This Month will be published', SJC 19–22 Nov 1796.

Further edn: New York, 1802 (WC). French trans. Paris, 1799 (*La Chapelle d'Ayton ou Emma Courtney*) (BGR). Facs: FCy.

CR: 'The early part of this history is pleasing: in the subsequent periods, the principles and the characters must be examined with candour. . . . we do not hold up Emma Courtney as a character for general imitation, any more than, we presume, the authoress herself would. . . . Strong sensibilities require more than ordinary management: the passions, the source of personal enjoyment and of public utility, may easily become our own tormentors, and the spring of injustice to others.'

MR [William Taylor]: 'These memoirs rise above the class of vulgar novels, which aspire only to divert the unoccupied mind. . . . The fair writer aims at the solution of a moral problem which is eminently important . . .' (p. 443). 'We refrain from minute criticisms on plot, incident, or character, in a work which is marked by such uncommon features as those which characterise the present volumes' (p. 449).

1796: 51   HELME, Elizabeth.
THE FARMER OF INGLEWOOD FOREST, A NOVEL. IN FOUR VOL-
UMES. BY ELIZABETH HELME.

> London: Printed for William Lane, at the Minerva-Press, Leadenhall-Street, 1796.
> I iii, 230p; II 235p; III 225p; IV 230p. 12mo. 14s sewed (CR, Min).
> CR n.s. 19: 227 (Feb 1797); AF II: 1887.
> Corvey; CME 3-628-45059-4; ESTC n004957 (NA CtY-BR, PU, IU, ViU &c.).

Notes. Frontispiece vol. 1. Dedication to Mrs Hastings i–iii signed E. Helme. 1 p. advs. end vol. 2; 3 pp. advs. end vol. 3; 2 pp. advs. end vol. 4.
Adv., 'In the Press, and speedily will be published', SJC 5–7 Apr 1796.
Further edns: London, 1800 (WC); Cork, 1801 (Printed by J. Connor, 2 vols.) (Loeber). London, 1841 (WC); London, 1850 (WC); WC has 10 entries between 1800 and 1850, including 2 of *The History of Emma*, taken from *The Farmer of Inglewood Forest*; NSTC lists edns. in 18—, 1801, 1822, 1833, 1841 and [1850?]. French trans. Paris, 1818 (*Le fermier de la forêt d'Inglewood*) (BN).

CR: 'The incidents on which this story is founded are improbable; but that is no objection with the generality of those readers, for whose entertainment these productions are intended; and it may be read by any person without a fear of exciting evil passions, or inculcating any pernicious principles whatever.'

1796: 52   [HERVEY, Elizabeth].
THE HISTORY OF NED EVANS. IN FOUR VOLUMES.

> London: Printed for G. G. J. and J. Robinson, 1796.
> I 282p; II 231p; III 215p; IV 231p. 12mo. 14s boards (CR), 14s sewed (MR, GEP).
> CR n.s. 18: 341 (Nov 1796); MR n.s. 21: 207 (Oct 1796); AF II: 1927.
> O 249.r.33-36; ESTC n033078 (NA CtY, NjP).

Notes. Adv. GEP 29–31 Mar 1798.
Attribution to Jane West by Bodl. and BGR..
Further edns: Dublin, 1796 (Printed by John Rice; and sold by H. and P. Rice, Philadelphia, 2 vols., 12mo), EM 4337: 3, ESTC t130957; London, 1797, ESTC t070090; Dublin, 1797, ESTC n003633. French trans. Paris, 1800 (*Histoire de Ned Evans*) (BGR).

CR: 'The character and adventures of Ned Evans bear occasionally too close a resemblance to Fielding's inimitable Tom Jones; and Molly Price is a faint copy from Moll Seagrim. These volumes, however, are valuable for the sentiments of piety which they contain; the descriptions and incidents sometimes rise above mediocrity, and no-where offend against delicacy or good morals'

MR [Arthur Aikin]: 'Though not the production of a first rate writer, and exhibiting various marks of imitation, this novel has afforded us considerable pleasure in the perusal. . . . The sentiments are uniformly pure and laudable; and, indeed, the work is distinguished by the religious air pervading it.'

1796: 53   HEY, Richard.
EDINGTON: A NOVEL. BY RICHARD HEY, ESQ. IN TWO VOLUMES.

> London: Printed for Vernor and Hood, Birchin Lane, Cornhill, 1796.
> I 218p; II 231p. 12mo. 6s sewed (CR, MR).
> CR n.s. 16: 360 (Mar 1796); MR n.s. 19: 351 (Mar 1796); AF II: 1933.
> C 7720.d.1372; EM 232: 2; ESTC t066935 (BI BL; NA CtY-BR, MH-H, NjP, PU &c.).

Notes. Adv. SJC 17–19 Mar 1796.

CR: 'This novel contains a simple, domestic, rural tale,—a tale that does credit to the humane feelings, benevolent affections, and unaffected good sense of the author. We feel particular pleasure in recommending it to our young readers. There are some scenes in the second volume, which, without being highly wrought up, touch the heart, and, while moving, can scarcely fail to mend it.'

MR [Arthur Aikin]: 'We found much difficulty in labouring through about half of the first volume of this work: but, as we proceeded, we observed a very apparent improvement, and from the whole derived no small satisfaction.'

1796: 54   HOWELL, [Ann].
ANZOLETTA ZADOSKI. A NOVEL. IN TWO VOLUMES. BY MRS. HOWELL, AUTHOR OF GEORGINA, &C. &C.

> London: Printed for William Lane, at the Minerva-Press, Leadenhall-Street, 1796.
> I 189p; II 214p. 8vo. 6s sewed (CR, OPA).
> CR n.s. 21: 356 (Nov 1797); AF II: 2082.
> MH-H *EC75.H8394 796a; EM 998: 7; ESTC n003837 (BI O; NA CtY, ViU).

Notes. 1 p. advs. pp. end vol. 1.
Georgina 1796: 55.
Adv. OPA 26 Nov 1796.
Adv., 'Preparing for the Press', SJC 5–7 Apr 1796.
French trans. Paris, 1799 (*Anzoletta Zadoski*) (BGR); German trans. Erfurt, 1804 (*Anzoletta, die schöne Unbekannte*) (Price).

CR: 'There is little in this novel to distinguish it from the common run of such publications. The author appears to have studied brevity as one quality in a work of entertainment; and her characters [*sic*] are so feebly sketched, and her incidents so rapid and confused, that the affections are seldom engaged, and the attention, where it does happen to be kept up, ends in disappointment. The moral tendency, however, is to be commended. . . .'

1796: 55   HOWELL, [Ann].
GEORGINA, A NOVEL. IN TWO VOLUMES. BY MRS. HOWELL.

London: Printed for William Lane, at the Minerva Press, Leadenhall-Street, 1796.
I 200p; II 267p. 8vo. 7s sewed (CR), 6s sewed (CR, Min, Min).
CR n.s. 16: 472–3 (Apr 1796).
ICN Y155.H83; CME 3-628-45069-1; ESTC n018370 (NA CtHT-W; EA COR).

Notes. Frontispiece. 1 p. advs. end vol. 2.
Adv., *Georgina; or, Advantages of Grand Connexions*, SJC 4–7 June 1796.
French trans. Geneva and Paris, 1788 (*Georgina, histoire véritable*) (BN); German trans.
Tübingen, 1790/92 (*Georgina; eine wahre Geschichte*) (RS).

CR: 'This novel is, perhaps, best described by negatives. It is not ill written,—it neither offends decency, good manners, nor good morals. . . . In fine, those who are not too fastidious,—who love to be amused, while the mind is passive,—who require neither bold images, strong emotions, brilliant thoughts, nor original conceptions,—may find, in the perusal of Georgina, an agreeable entertainment to beguile the passing hour.'

1796: 56   ILIFF, Edward Henry.
ANGELO, A NOVEL, FOUNDED ON MELANCHOLY FACTS. WRITTEN BY EDWARD HENRY ILIFF, (LATE OF THE THEATRE ROYAL, HAY-MARKET.) IN TWO VOLUMES.

London: Printed by M. Allen, and sold by Allen and West, No. 15, Paternoster-Row, 1796.
I iv, 158p; II 164p. 12mo. 5s sewed (CR, MR).
CR n.s. 17: 351–2 (July 1796); MR n.s. 20: 232 (June 1796); AF II: 2151.
BL RB.23.a.7369; ESTC t223491.

Notes. Dedication to John King iii–iv. 1 p. advs. end vol. 1.
Adv., 'speedily will be published', SJC 7–9 Apr 1796; adv. as published SJC 7–9 June 1796.

CR: 'For the morality of this novel we cannot say much. . . . The style is upon the whole light and easy, though rather too much interlarded with words not in common use. There are some philosophical observations in this work that do the author credit. . . .'
MR: 'The puny offspring of affectation and morbid sensibility.'

1796: 57   INCHBALD, [Elizabeth].
NATURE AND ART. IN TWO VOLUMES. BY MRS. INCHBALD.

London: Printed for G. G. and J. Robinson, Paternoster Row, 1796.
I 192p; II 203p. 8vo. 7s boards (CR, MR), 7s sewed (SJC).
CR n.s. 16: 325–30 (Mar 1796); MR n.s. 19: 453 (Apr 1796); AF II: 2173.
C S727.d.79.4-5; BL Microfilm PB Mic 35946; EMf; ESTC t114292 (BI BL, O, WIS; NA CtY-BR, CSmH, IU, NjP, ViU &c.).

Notes. Robinson paid £150 for *Nature and Art* on 11 Jan 1796 (Boaden 2: 3). In 1800 Inchbald was paid £600 by 'her bookseller' (Boaden 2: 35–36) which Tompkins presumes to be Robinson for *Nature and Art* and *A Simple Story* (1791: 41), although Inchbald had dealings with other booksellers who published her plays. In 1810 Inchbald again sold the copyright to the two novels, to Longman (Boaden, vol. 2, p. 164).
Adv., 'Next Week will be published', SJC 13–16 Feb 1796; adv. as published SJC 16–18 Feb 1796.
Further edns: Dublin, 1796 (Printed by William Porter, for P. Wogan, P. Byrne, J. Milliken,

J. Rice [and 4 others in Dublin], 1 vol., 12mo), EM 7651: 17, ESTC t020767; London, 1797, ESTC t064756; London, 1810 and London, 1824 [with Frances Brooke's *History of Lady Julia Mandeville*] (WC); London, 1820 (WC); WC has 5 further entries between 1800 and 1850; NSTC lists edn. in 1810. Extracts from *Nature and Art* published in *Moral and Political Magazine*, 1796, RM 943. French trans. Paris, 1797 (*La Nature et l'Art par mistriss Inchbald*) (BGR); German trans. Leipzig, 1797 (*Natur und Kunst oder Der Karakter des Menschen gründet sich auf der Erziehung*) (RS). Facs: RWN (of 1797 2nd edn.).

CR: 'The talents of Mrs. Inchbald, as a novelist and dramatic writer, are too well known to the world to require any encomium in addition to those they have already received.... in literature it may be laid down as an axiom, that where a large portion of applause and success attends a writer, there must be something either of the useful or the pleasing to attract public attention' (p. 325). 'The pathos is touched by Mrs. Inchbald with a masterly hand; nor is her skill inferior in delicate and pointed sarcasm' (p. 326).

MR [Arthur Aikin]: 'This work will do much credit to the talents of the fair writer: the incidents are highly interesting; the language, if not splendid and highly polished, is at least pure and easy; the sentiments are just; and the satire is keen and pointed without descending to personality. We might deviate from this general praise, in criticizing some improbabilities, some impossibilities, and some improprieties: but we must not dilate.'

1796: 58   KELLY, [Isabella].
THE RUINS OF AVONDALE PRIORY. A NOVEL, IN THREE VOLUMES, BY MRS. KELLY, AUTHOR OF MADELINE, ABBEY ST. ASAPH, &C.

London: Printed for William Lane, at the Minerva-Press, Leadenhall-Street, 1796.
I 216p; II 242p; III 206p. 12mo. 9s (BC), 9s sewed (adv., Min).
BC 10: 434 (Oct 1797); AF II: 2356.
BL 12611.bb.12; EM 3876: 6; ESTC t122130 (EA COR).

Notes. T.p. to vol. 1 of BL copy missing. 2 pp. advs. end vol. 2.
Madeline 1794: 35; *Abbey of Saint Asaph* 1795: 27.
Adv., 'In the Press, and speedily will be published', SJC 5–7 Apr 1796; adv. as published SJC 23–26 July 1796.
Adv. end vol. 1 of *Eva* (1799: 54).
Further edns: West Smithfield, 1824 (Summers); London, 1846 (Summers).

BC: 'The novel before us, is entitled to no mean place among the better productions of this description. The characters which enter into its narrative are rendered interesting, by the events in which they are involved, and the unaffected language in which they are represented.'

1796: 59   [KLINGER, Friedrich Maximilian von]; [TRAPP, Joseph (*trans.*)].
TRAVELS BEFORE THE FLOOD. AN INTERESTING ORIENTAL RECORD OF MEN AND MANNERS IN THE ANTEDILUVIAN WORLD, INTERPRETED IN FOURTEEN EVENING CONVERSATIONS BETWEEN THE CALIPH OF BAGDAD & HIS COURT. TRANSLATED FROM THE ARABIC.

London: Printed for G. G. J. and J. Robinson, 1796.
I v, 238p; II 217p. 8vo. 7s boards (AR).

AR 24: 520–3 (Nov 1796); AF II: 2412.

C Q-20-73-; EM 330: 4; ESTC t064911 (BI BL; NA InU-Li, LU, MH-H).

Notes. Trans. of *Reisen vor der Sündfluth* (Riga, 1795).

Robinson paid 15 gns. on 28 Mar 1796 to Jos: Trapp for the copyright to the manuscript of *Travels Before the Flood* (RA).

Engraved t.p.

Further edn: Carlisle, PA, 1797, ESTC w027101.

AR: 'Whether the surest and best road to the temple of truth lie through the enchanted ground of fiction, may admit of much dispute. . . . the tendency of the tale is rather to produce an indolent and selfish dissatisfaction with the world in it's present state, than to excite benevolent wishes and exertions for it's improvement' (p. 520).

1796: 60   LANSDELL, Sarah.

MANFREDI, BARON ST. OSMUND. AN OLD ENGLISH ROMANCE. IN TWO VOLUMES. BY SARAH LANSDELL, TENTERDEN.

London: Printed for William Lane, at the Minerva-Press, Leadenhall-Street, 1796.

I viii, 186p; II 144p. 8vo [CR has 12mo]. 6s sewed (CR, SJC).

CR n.s. 20: 353 (July 1797); AF II: 2462.

O 256.f.2337–8; CME 3-628-45081-0; ESTC t219585 (EA COR).

Notes. Introduction v–viii.

Author's name obliterated on both t.ps. in Bodleian copy and handwritten on fly-leaf of vol. 2. Handwritten note, dated 6 October 1809, on leaf before half-title to vol. 1 reads: 'No other apology can be offered for this puerile work than that it was written at the early age of eighteen ['seventeen' has been crossed out] at a time when the authoress had not one literary friend or the advantage of access to books and lived remote from the world amidst the rude inhabitants of a country hamlet. It was written also, almost by stealth compleated in 12 days and copied only once; a gentleman (with whom the authoress had then no acquaintance) correcting partially for her grammatical inaccuracies.'

2 pp. advs. end vol. 1. Last item on 2nd p. of advs. is John Palmer's *Mysteries of the Black Tower* [*The Mystery of the Black Tower*, 1796: 70]; a handwritten annotation reads 'From this, the authoress has been accused of borrowing her Incidents'.

Adv. SJC 5–7 June 1798.

CR: '. . . criticism must do its duty by pronouncing that the romance of Manfredi has little interest of sentiment or incident, and that the characters of the "baron St. Osmund" and "lady Egwinor" are palpably copied from Shakspeare's Macbeth.'

1796: 61   LARA, Catherine.

*DURVAL AND ADELAIDE. BY CATHERINE LARA.

London: Ridgway (MR).

12mo. 3s 6d sewed (CR, MR).

CR n.s. 18: 474–5 (Dec 1796); MR n.s. 19: 454 (Apr 1796); AF II: 2463.

No copy located.

Notes. CR: 'French sentiment (at least, those high-wrought notions of fantastic honour and loyalty, which were inculcated under the old feudal system of government) is too fanatical and too artificial for plain English common sense' (p. 475).

MR [Arthur Aikin] says that the comments on *Louis de Boncoeur* [1796: 62] 'will apply, with little variation, to the present piece: which is not, however, translated with the same care.'

1796: 62   LARA, Catherine.
LOUIS DE BONCOEUR. A DOMESTICK TALE. BY CATHARINE LARA. IN TWO VOLUMES.

> London: Printed for James Ridgway, York Street, St. James's Square; and William Moore, No. 8, Leadenhall-Street, 1796.
> I viii, 171p; II 214p. 12mo. 7s sewed (CR, MR).
> CR n.s. 18: 474 (Dec 1796); MR n.s. 19: 453–4 (Apr 1796); AF II: 2464.
> BL 1607/1874; EM 2722: 8; ESTC t119368.

Notes. Preface v–viii. Epistolary.

CR: 'The language of genuine sensibility and affection is very distinct from this extravagance, which may produce affectation or provoke disgust, but will never touch the heart.'

MR [Arthur Aikin]: 'This tale, as we are informed in the preface, is translated from the French, with alterations and additions. The characters and manners, being French, may appear extravagant to merely English readers: but even they will, on the whole, be considerably pleased with this performance; for it is superior to our common novels, both in its composition and tendency. The translation also possesses considerable merit.'

1796: 63   LEWIS, M[atthew] G[regory].
THE MONK: A ROMANCE. IN THREE VOLUMES. BY M. G. LEWIS, ESQ. M.P.

> London: Printed for J. Bell, Oxford-street, 1796.
> I 232p; II 287p; III v, 315p. 12mo. 9s sewed (CR), 10s 6d (MR), 10s 6d sewed (SJC).
> CR n.s. 19: 194–200 (Feb 1797); MR n.s. 23: 451 (Aug 1797); AF II: 2551.
> ICN Case 3A.1579; EM 6424: 3; ESTC t132693 (BI BL, O; NA GEU, IU, OCIW; EA ZWTU).

Notes. Newberry copy has preface and other preliminaries bound in vol. 3.

Adv. SJC 17–19 Mar 1796; additional booksellers are E. Booker, New Bond-street; and C. Law, No. 14, Ave Maria-Lane.

Further edns: London, 1796, ESTC t146748; London, 1796 [i.e. 1798?], ESTC n061396; Waterford, '1796' [?post 1818] (Printed for J. Saunders, 3 vols., 12mo), ESTC t169350; Dublin, 1796 (Printed by Brett Smith, for P. Wogan, P. Byrne, W. Jones, and G. Folingsby, 2 vols., 12mo), ESTC n001357; London, 1797, ESTC t108214; ESTC has 9 further entries for versions published in London, Boston, Waterford, and Dublin from 1795 to 1800 (edns. are problematic—one, RCN n061396 held by Harvard, for example, 'utilizes variously the sheets of the first, second, and third editions at random, with titlepages for the second issue of the first edition'). The official 1st edn. was published 12 Mar 1796, but at least 2 copies exist in private hands (not in ESTC) with 1795 on the t.p. (see Howard Anderson, 'The Manuscript of M. G. Lewis's *The Monk*: Some Preliminary Notes,' *P.B.S.A.* 62: 3 [1968], 427–34). WC has 15 entries 1800–1850, including 2 further French trans. Summers has 7 pages concerning numerous edns.; NSTC lists edns. in 1801/2, 1802, 1805, 1807, 1808, 1818, [1820?] and [1840?]. French trans. Paris, 1797 (*Le Moine*) (Lévy); German trans. Leipzig, 1797 (*Der Mönch*) (Price).

CR: '. . . cheaply as we estimate romances in general, we acknowledge, in the work before us, the offspring of no common genius' (p. 194). 'Not without reluctance then, but in full conviction that we are performing a duty, we declare it to be our opinion, that the Monk is a romance, which if a parent saw in the hands of a son or daughter, he might reasonably turn pale' (p. 197).

MR: 'A vein of obscenity . . . pervades and deforms the whole organization of this novel, which must ever blast, in a moral view, the *fair* fame that, in point of ability, it would have gained for the author; and which renders the work totally unfit for general circulation' (p. 451).

1796: 64   [MACKENZIE, Anna Maria].
THE NEAPOLITAN; OR, THE TEST OF INTEGRITY. A NOVEL. IN THREE VOLUMES. BY ELLEN OF EXETER.

> London: Printed for William Lane, at the Minerva Press, Leadenhall-Street, 1796.
> I iii, 213p; II 211p; III 288p. 12mo. 10s 6d sewed (CR, MR).
> CR n.s. 21: 229–30 (Oct 1797); MR n.s. 22: 221 (Feb 1797); AF II: 2660.
> ViU *PZ2.M322N 1796; ESTC n048808.

Notes. 1 p. advs. end vol. 2. Dedication to Richard Cumberland, Esq., signed Ellen of Exeter. French trans. Paris, 1798 (*La Famille Napolitaine par mistriss Ellen d'Exeter*) (BGR).

CR: 'There is nothing that harasses a poor reviewer's temper, or wearies his attention more, than a novel without a plan, and a set of characters that seem to be brought together without any general interest or design that might serve to connect the incidents which happen to them, and give the whole something like the form of a composition. Other readers may throw down the book as soon as they feel disgust or languor: but we must still go on with jaded attention, and at last are obliged to perform a duty disagreeable to ourselves, and painful to others' (p. 229).

MR: 'The tale here recorded might have been interesting, if condensed into a much smaller compass: but it drags heavily, with tedious minuteness, through seven hundred pages.'

1796: 65   MEEKE, [Mary].
THE ABBEY OF CLUGNY. A NOVEL. BY MRS. MEEKE, AUTHOR OF COUNT ST. BLANCARD. IN THREE VOLUMES.

> London: Printed for William Lane, at the Minerva-Press, Leadenhall-Street, 1796.
> I 218p; II 223p; III 199p. 12mo. 9s sewed (CR, MR).
> CR n.s. 16: 473 (Apr 1796); MR n.s. 19: 453 (Apr 1796); AF II: 2806.
> BL C.122.e.30; EMf; ESTC t153077 (NA CSmH, PU).

Notes. MR and Blakey date as 1795. 1 p. advs. end vol. 2.
Count St. Blancard 1795: 30.
Adv. SJC 27 Feb-1 Mar 1796.

CR: 'The Abbey of Clugny, without having any claim to originality, is superior to the common class of novels.—The incidents are well connected and interesting,—the style, if not elegant, is unaffected,—many of the observations are sensible and judicious. The story is not broken in upon by tiresome and impertinent episodes, so common with inferior novelists, always tending to weaken, if not destroy, the effect of the principal action.'

MR [Charles Burney, the younger]: 'This work is certainly far superior to its predecessor mentioned in the title: but the inaccuracies of the printer are too numerous not to demand loud reprehension. . . . The story of this novel is told with ease and vivacity. Ghosts are in the fashion; and, as we were entertained by the spectre which haunts this sacred retirement, we cannot blame the fair writer for following the mode.'

1796: 66   [MELTZER, Adolph Heinrich].
LAURA; OR THE INFLUENCE OF A KISS. BY A. H. GESZNER. TRANS-LATED FROM THE GERMAN.

>London: Printed for Vernor and Hood, Birchin Lane, Cornhill, 1796.
>181p. 8vo. [CR and MR have 12mo]. 3s 6d sewed (CR, MR).
>CR n.s. 22: 357 (Mar 1798); MR n.s. 22: 92 (Jan 1797); AF II: 2817.
>NNU Fales Foreign; ESTC n054269.

Notes. Trans. of *Laura; oder, Der Kuss in seinen Wirkungen* (Berlin, 1792).
A. H. Geszner is Adolph Heinrich Meltzer (ESTC).
Engraved t.p. Illustrations. Dedication to Laura (3–6), signed Adlo Henrich Geszner; text of novel begins on p. 7. Primarily epistolary.
CR: 'We cannot applaud either the design or the execution of this work. The prints annexed to it are contemptible; but they are as good as the work deserves.'
MR: 'This novel might have been suffered to escape translation; its incidents are founded on manners which are not English, and should never be suffered to become so. There is no occasion for men to bid each other welcome and farewell with a kiss: nor to familiarize women with such unbashful intercourse of the sexes.'

1796: 67   [MOORE, John].
EDWARD. VARIOUS VIEWS OF HUMAN NATURE, TAKEN FROM LIFE AND MANNERS, CHIEFLY IN ENGLAND. BY THE AUTHOR OF ZELUCO. IN TWO VOLUMES.

>London: Printed for A. Strahan, and T. Cadell jun. and W. Davies (Successors to Mr. Cadell) in the Strand, 1796.
>I 519p; II 596p. 8vo. 16s boards (CR, MR).
>CR n.s. 19: 15–21 (Jan 1797); MR n.s. 21: 399–403 (Dec 1796); AF II: 2934.
>BL 635.f.22,23; CME 3-628-45134-5; EM 2356: 2; ESTC t114000 (BI C, E, O &c.; NA CtY-BR, CSmH, ICN, MH-H, NjP, PU, TxU, ViU; EA COR, P, TaLN).

Notes. 3 pp. advs. end vol. 2.
Zeluco 1789: 54.
Adv., 'On Saturday next will be published', OPA 3 Oct 1796; adv. as published OPA 8 Oct 1796.
Further edns: Dublin, 1797 (Printed for P. Wogan . . ., 2 vols., no format) (WC); Mount-Pleasant, NY, 1798, ESTC w031810; London, 1816 (WC); London, 1827 (WC); NSTC lists edns. in 1824 and 1827. Extract from *Edward*, 'The Excellent Wife', published in 4 magazines, 1796–97, RM 377. French trans. Paris, 1797 (*Edouard, ou l'enfant trouvé*) (BGR); German trans. Leipzig, 1797 (*Eduard Ebeling, ein treues Gemälde der Natur*) (EAG).
CR: 'Edward will be found to have little claim to notice upon the common ground of these productions, an interest created by the hero of the story; for the thread of adventure by which he is connected with the other characters of the piece, is slight; and in general the incidents are such as barely keep up its title to the name of a regular novel: but it has great merit as a

series of conversation-pieces, exhibiting sketches of real life and manners. In this way of writing Dr Moore excels; and his knowledge of characters, shrewdness of remark, and strokes of genuine humour, are calculated to afford much instruction and entertainment' (p. 15).

MR [John Gillies]: 'The scenes . . . which he has hitherto exhibited, were chiefly copied from the manners of other countries: but the present work is of British manufacture, and almost entirely confined to the illustration of our domestic usages and national customs' (p. 399). 'The entertainment given by Edward can be enjoyed with reflection; and a second reading of the volumes will point out discriminations of character, and strokes of humour, which on the first perusal, perhaps, escaped observation' (p. 403).

1796: 68   MOSER, Joseph.
THE HERMIT OF CAUCASUS, AN ORIENTAL ROMANCE. IN TWO VOLUMES. BY JOSEPH MOSER, AUTHOR OF TURKISH TALES, &C. &C.

> London: Printed for William Lane, at the Minerva-Press, Leadenhall-Street, 1796.
> I xii, 252p; II 249p. 12mo. 6s sewed (MR, SJC).
> CR n.s. 25: 233 (Feb 1799); MR n.s. 22: 467–8 (Apr 1797); AF II: 2982.
> BL C.171.d.1; EMf; ESTC t208530.

Notes. Preface i–xii. 3 pp. advs. end vol. 2.
Turkish Tales 1794: 39.
Adv., In a few Days will be published, SJC 5–7 Apr 1796.
Adv. end vol. 2 of *Court Intrigue* (1799: 44).

MR [William Taylor]: 'Dr. Hawkesworth and other writers of Oriental tales have accustomed us to expect, in such productions, that the muse of composition should exchange the tight robe of European elegance for the flowing embroidery of Asiatic luxury. . . . Our increased knowlege of the manners and opinions of the East renders us acutely sensible to every violation of *costume* in incident or idea. . . . In the history of the Calif Vathek [1786: 15], it would require the learning of a German professor to detect an incongruity. These incongruities, however, we find in the present volumes. . . . His style is polished; his morality is respectable; his whole manner is entertaining and pleasing: but his fancy is timid. . . .'

1796: 69   PALMER, John.
THE HAUNTED CAVERN: A CALEDONIAN TALE. BY JOHN PALMER, JUN.

> London: Printed for B. Crosby, No. 4, Stationers Court, Ludgate Street, 1796.
> ii, 248p. 12mo. 3s sewed (CR, MR).
> CR n.s. 15: 480 (Dec 1795); MR n.s. 19: 88 (Jan 1796); AF II: 3202.
> BL N.2049(1); EM 2014: 3; ESTC t073528 (BI E; NA CU-Riv).

Notes. Dedication to Miss Farren.
Post-dated; adv. as published SJC 3–5 Dec 1795.
Adv. end vol. 2 of *Arville Castle* (1795: 1).
Further edns: Dublin, 1796 (Printed for P. Wogan, P. Byrne, J. Boyce, W. Jones, J. Rice, and G. Folingsby, 12mo) ESTC t212601; Baltimore, 1796, ESTC w012670; Bennington, VT, 1796, ESTC w011522; New York, 1797 (WC), xESTC. French trans. n.p., n.d. (*La caverne habitée*) (HWS); German trans. Leipzig and Münster, 1799 (*Eldred und Jenny, oder die Geisterhöhle*) (RS).

CR: 'In truth we are almost weary of Gothic castles, mouldering turrets, and "cloud inveloped battlements"—The tale of shrieking spectres, and bloody murders, has been repeated till it palls upon the sense. . . . The little interest which this Caledonian story might have had (in which, however, we perceive not a vestige of originality) is destroyed, by its being split into innumerable episodes.'

MR [Arthur Aikin]: 'This little piece is not remarkable either for the incidents or the purity of the language,—we mean with respect to *grammatical idiom*; and in novel writing, like poetry, to fall short of excellence is to fail in the only object worth attempting: mediocrity is attainable by most, but it is only the rare combination of fancy with judgment and general information, that can save a work of pure fiction from neglect.'

1796: 70 PALMER, John.
THE MYSTERY OF THE BLACK TOWER, A ROMANCE, BY JOHN PALMER, JUN. AUTHOR OF THE HAUNTED CAVERN.

London: Printed for the Author, by William Lane, at the Minerva-Press, Leadenhall-Street, 1796.

I xvi, 202p; II 193p. 12mo. 7s (BC), 7s sewed (SJC, adv.), 6s sewed (Min).
BC 10: 435 (Oct 1797).
MH-H *EC75.P1824.796m; EM 1498: 26; ESTC n010998 (NA CtY-BR, PPL).

Notes. Dedication to Mrs. Vernon 1, v–vii; 8-pp. list of subscribers ix–xvi.
The Haunted Cavern 1796: 69.
Adv., 'Preparing for the Press . . . *Enchantment of the Black Rock*', SJC 5–7 Apr 1796; adv. as published SJC 8–10 Sept 1796; additional booksellers are Miller, Old Bond-Street; and C. Law, Ave-Maria-Lane.
Adv. end vol. 1 of *The Legacy* (1798: 20).
French trans. Paris, 1799 (*Les Mystères de la tour noire*) (BGR).
BC: 'It appears essential to romance, that the scenes it describes, should either be remote from the times in which we live, or the people with whom we converse. The first of these rules has been obeyed by Mr Palmer; and he has thrown his scenery back into the reign of Edward the Third, an æra of chivalry and warlike enterprise, perfectly favourable to his design. His conception of the subject is, in other respects, sufficiently just: and by the introduction of a facetious Welch Squire, he has enlivened the solemnity of his graver scenes, with occasional flashes of humour. The romance is certainly executed with ability; and discovers such talents for the species of composition, as may be said to merit the protection of the public.'

1796: 71 PARSONS, [Eliza].
THE MYSTERIOUS WARNING, A GERMAN TALE. IN FOUR VOLUMES. BY MRS. PARSONS. AUTHOR OF VOLUNTARY EXILE, &C.

London: Printed for William Lane, at the Minerva Press, Leadenhall-Street, 1796.

I 4, 2, 280p; II 250p; III 291p; IV 266p. 12mo. 12s (CR), 12s sewed (SJC, adv.).
CR n.s. 16: 474 (Apr 1796); AF II: 3237.
BL 1153.f.32; EM 2382: 3; ESTC t141205 (NA ICN, IU, MH-H, ViU).

Notes. Frontispiece. Dedication to H.R.H. the Princess of Wales 1, 1–4, signed Eliza Parsons, Leicester-Square, No. 22, 15 Nov 1795; A Card 1–2. 1 p. advs. end vol. 3.
The Voluntary Exile 1795: 35.

Adv., 'On Monday next will be published, With an elegant Engraving', SJC 17–19 Nov 1795; title simply *Mysterious Warnings; By Mrs. Parsons*; additional booksellers are Hodgson, Wimpole-street; Miller, Old Bond-street; and Knight and Co. Booksellers to his Majesty, St James's-street.

Adv. end vol. 3 of *The Abbey of Clugny* (1796: 65).

CR: 'We have before had occasion to observe, that the novels of Mrs. Parsons would be more interesting, if her plans had more unity: when the principal narrative is frequently broken in upon by different stories, however entertaining in themselves, attention flags, the mind experiences a kind of disappointment, loses the connection, proceeds languidly, and is not easily reanimated.'

1796: 72   PARSONS, [Eliza].
WOMEN AS THEY ARE. A NOVEL, IN FOUR VOLUMES, BY MRS. PARSONS, AUTHOR OF MYSTERIOUS WARNINGS, &C.

> London: Printed for William Lane, at the Minerva- Press, Leadenhall-Street, 1796.
> I viii, 252p; II 264p; III 256p; IV 284p. 12mo. 12s sewed (CR), 14s sewed or 16s fine paper (OPA).
> CR n.s. 21: 472 (Dec 1797); AF II: 3242.
> BL Cup.403.y.11; CME 3-628-45143-4; EM 6467: 3; ESTC t140067 (NA CtY-BR, MH-H, PU, ViU; EA COR).

Notes. Frontispiece to vol. 1. Dedication to Mrs. Anson, of Shuckborough-Manor, Staffordshire. Epistolary.

The Mysterious Warning 1796: 71.

Adv. OPA 11 Nov 1796.

CR: 'Although there are many instructive lessons presented in this novel, we fear there is less amusement than our young readers will expect. As a composition, the story is rather deficient in interest; the events, however various, being of the common kind, and ending in a manner which cannot fail to be anticipated.'

1796: 73   [PLUMPTRE, Annabella].
MONTGOMERY; OR, SCENES IN WALES. IN TWO VOLUMES.

> London: Printed for William Lane, at the Minerva, Leadenhall-Street, 1796.
> I 260p; II 325p. 12mo. 7s sewed (CR, OPA).
> CR n.s. 19: 111 (Jan 1797).
> MH-H *EC8.P7371.796m; EM 1278: 3; ESTC n012293 (NA ViU).

Notes. Adv. OPA 26 Nov 1796.

Adv. end vol. 3 of *Disobedience* (1797: 48).

CR: '. . . though the novel begins very abruptly, it proceeds very agreeably. The style, though not flowery or elegant, is in the main neat and correct; the sentiments are important; the moral is good. The advocate for the female sex will approve it; the benevolent mind will discover traces of a good heart; and youth of neither sex will be betrayed into scenes of wantonness and paths of folly: the story itself is natural, and not uninteresting: the errors of a mistaken, rather than a neglected education, are illustrated, and the unhappy consequences of people suffering themselves to become creatures of morbid feelings, the dupes of their imagination, and the victims of superstition.'

1796: 74   [PLUMPTRE, Anne].
ANTOINETTE, A NOVEL, IN TWO VOLUMES.

> London: Printed for William Lane, at the Minerva-Press, Leadenhall-Street, 1796.
> I 234p; II 252p. 12mo. 6s sewed (CR), 9s sewed (MP).
> CR n.s. 16: 221–2 (Feb 1796); AF II: 3410.
> Corvey; CME 3-628-45002-0; ESTC n031027 (BI C; NA CaAEU, PU).

Notes. Adv. MP 24 Dec 1795.
Further edn: Philadelphia, 1800, ESTC w011650.

> CR: 'It has not the least reference to the affairs of France; and for this reason, we could have wished it had appeared under another name: the present is apt to mislead readers. . . . The morality is unexceptionably pure; the principles are liberal; the reader is led on gradually to events interesting and striking; the language is in the main neat and correct, and the issue of the history fortunate and agreeable. On the whole this novel has considerable merit; and we think the writer might display her powers of description a little more freely' (p. 221).

1796: 75   [PURBECK, Elizabeth and Jane].
MATILDA AND ELIZABETH: A NOVEL. BY THE AUTHORS OF HONO-
RIA SOMERVILLE, RAINSFORD PARK, THE BENEVOLENT QUIXOTE,
&C. &C. IN FOUR VOLUMES.

> London: Printed by and for Sampson Low, Berwick Street, Soho; and sold by C. Law,
>   Ave-Maria Lane, and Booker, Bond Street, 1796.
> I 223p; II 198p; III 196p; IV 197p. 12mo. 12s sewed (CR), 12s (SJC, OPA).
> CR n.s. 18: 342 (Nov 1796); AF II: 3642.
> PU PR.5193.P87.M3.1796; CME 3-628-45117-5; ESTC n034945 (NA CtY; EA COR).

Notes. 3 pp. advs. end vol. 4. Epistolary.
Honoria Sommerville 1789: 60; *Raynsford Park* 1790: 60; *William Thornborough, the Benevolent Quixote* 1791: 57.
Adv., 'In a few Days will be published', SJC 9–12 Apr 1796; adv., 'On Saturday, April 16, will be published', OPA 9 Apr 1796.
Further edn: Dublin, 1796 (Printed for P. Wogan, P. Byrne, J. Moore, and H. Colbert, 2 vols., 12mo), ESTC n052560. German trans. Leipzig, 1799 (*Matilde und Elisabeth*) (EAG).

> CR: 'There is nothing in this novel to distinguish it from the generality of publications of a similar nature. . . . To those who seek only to beguile the passing hour, who read only for amusement, and do not discriminate too nicely, the present production may afford a perfectly innocent entertainment. . . .'

1796: 76   ROBINSON, Mary.
ANGELINA; A NOVEL, IN THREE VOLUMES. BY MRS. MARY ROBIN-
SON, AUTHOR OF POEMS, VANCENZA, THE WIDOW, &C. &C. &C. &C.

> London: Printed for the Author, and sold by Hookham and Carpenter, no. 147, New
>   Bond Street, 1796.
> I 310p; II 309p; III 411p. 12mo. 13s 6d boards (CR, MR).
> CR n.s. 16: 397–400 (Apr 1796); MR n.s. 19: 350–1 (Mar 1796); AF II: 3822.
> C S727.d.79, 80; EM 327: 3; ESTC t094331 (BI BL; NA CtY-BR, IU, PU, ViU &c.).

Notes. 1 p. advs. end vol. 1 and 2 pp. advs. end vol. 2. 750 copies printed, and their rapid sale induced a 2nd edn. which proved slow to move, H&C. Epistolary.

Vancenza 1792: 50; *The Widow* 1794: 50.

Adv., 'In a few days will be published, in THREE LARGE VOLUMES . . . interspersed with several pieces of poetry', MP 29 Dec 1795.

Adv. OPA 1 Jan 1796.

Further edn: Dublin, 1796 (Printed by N. Kelly, for P. Wogan, P. Byrne, J. Moore, W. Jones, and J. Rice, 2 vols., 12mo), ESTC n030267; London, 1813 (Summers). French trans. n.p., n.d. (*Angelina*) (HWS); German trans. Erlangen, 1799–1800 (*Angelina*) (EAG).

CR: 'Were we permitted to consider this novel as a burlesque upon the extremes of romantic absurdity, we should certainly pronounce it a work of considerable merit. We have seldom seen the nonsensical jargon of mock sentiment, and overstrained hyperbole, more happily exposed to ridicule' (p. 397).

MR [Arthur Aikin]: 'Interesting as these volumes are, we should be negligent of our duty to the public, were we to bestow on them unqualified approbation. . . . with all its faults we are little inclined to condemn; for we are persuaded that it cannot but excite a lively interest in those who read it. . . .'

1796: 77   ROBINSON, Mary.
HUBERT DE SEVRAC, A ROMANCE, OF THE EIGHTEENTH CENTURY; BY MARY ROBINSON, AUTHOR OF POEMS, ANGELINA, THE SICILIAN LOVER, THE WIDOW, &C. &C. &C. IN THREE VOLUMES.

London: Printed for the Author, by Hookham and Carpenter, Old-Bond-Street, 1796. I 322p; II 307p; III 319p. 12mo. 12s sewed (CR, MR), 10s 6d boards (OPA).
CR n.s. 23: 472 (Aug 1798); MR n.s. 22: 91 (Jan 1797); AF II: 3826.
BL 12614.eee.17; CME 3-628-45170-1; EM 293: 2; ESTC t072170 (NA MH-H, PU, ViU; EA COR).

Notes. Text of novel starts on p. 5 in vols. 1 and 2. 1 p. advs. end vol. 1.

Angelina 1796: 76; *The Widow* 1794: 50. *The Sicilian Lover* (1796) is a play.

Adv. OPA 26 Nov 1796.

Further edn: Dublin, 1797 (Printed by B. Smith, C. Browne, and H. Colbert, 2 vols., 12mo), ESTC n033543. French trans. Paris, 1797 (*Hubert de Sévrac, ou histoire d'un émigré*) (BGR); German trans. Halle, 1797–98 (*Hubert von Sevrac*) (Price).

CR: 'It is an imitation of Mrs Radcliffe's romances, but without any resemblance that may not be attained by a common pen.'

MR [Arthur Aikin]: 'This work possesses many of the beauties, and some of the faults, which characterise that species of modern novels called *Romances*. The mysterious, the horrible, the pathetic, and the melancholy, are the leading features of this kind of writing.'

1796: 78   ROCHE, Regina Maria.
THE CHILDREN OF THE ABBEY, A TALE. IN FOUR VOLUMES. BY REGINA MARIA ROCHE.

London: Printed for William Lane, at the Minerva-Press, Leadenhall-Street, 1796. I iii, 324p; II 343p; III 284p; IV 306p. 12mo. 16s (BC), 14s sewed (SJC).
BC 11: 77 (Jan 1798).
C S727.d.79.17–20; EM 6155: 1; ESTC t119309 (BI BL; NA ViU).

Notes. Frontispiece in vol. 1; dedication to Major General Sir Adam Williamson i–iii. 1 p. advs. end vol. 2.

Adv., 'In the Press, and speedily will be published', SJC 5–7 Apr 1796; adv. as published SJC 4–7 June 1796; additional booksellers are Miller, Old Bond-Street; and C. Law, Ave-Maria-Lane.

Further edns: Philadelphia, 1796 (WC); London, 1797, ESTC t108515; London, 1798, ESTC n027797; Cork, 1798 (Printed by J. Haly, M. Harris, and J. Connor, 2 vols., 12mo), ESTC t165215; London, 1800, ESTC n027798; ESTC has 1 further entry; WC has 15 entries 1800–1850; Summers has 14 edns. 1800–1850; NSTC lists edns. in 1809, 1816, [182–], 1822, 1822/28, 1825, 1826, 1827, 1828, 1834, 1839, 1839/40, [1840?], 1843, [1850?]. French trans. Paris, 1797 (*Les enfans de l'abbaye*) (BGR); German trans. Brunswick, 1803 (*Die Erben*) (EAG).

BC: 'This is a very entertaining and well-written production, and one which we can safely recommend to our female readers, with the single exception, that the character of Adela, though very well drawn, is somewhat too romantic. Yet, by many readers, this will, perhaps, be thought the very essence of its merit, and the best part of our commendation.'

SAINT PIERRE, Jacques-Henri-Bernardin de, **PAUL AND VIRGINIA**
See 1788: 71

1796: 79　SCHULZ, [Joachim Christoph Friedrich].
MAURICE, A GERMAN TALE. BY MR. SCHULTZ [*sic*]. TRANSLATED FROM THE FRENCH.

> London: Printed for Vernor and Hood, Birchin Lane, 1796.
> I 227p; II 193p. 12mo. 6s sewed (CR, MR).
> CR n.s. 22: 238 (Feb 1798); MR n.s. 22: 92 (Jan 1797); AF II: 3975.
> BL 837.b.13; EM 2446: 2; ESTC t100453.

Notes. Trans. of *Moritz; ein kleiner Roman* (Dessau and Leipzig, 1785).
1 p. adv. end vol. 1 and 3 pp. advs. end vol. 2.
French trans. Lausanne and Paris, 1789 (*Maurice*) (BGR), itself a trans. of *Moritz.*

CR: 'To enlarge on its properties might perhaps gratify those who have an interest in the propagation of immorality, by exciting the curiosity of readers of a certain taste.'

MR [Arthur Aikin]: 'This work possesses many of the beauties, and some of the faults, which characterise that species of modern novels called *Romances*. The mysterious, the horrible, the pathetic, and the melancholy, are the leading features of this kind of writing.': 'Extravagance, and excessive passions, together with a power of rivetting the reader's attention, are the usual characteristics of German plays and novels; nor is the work before us an exception to the general observation.'

1796: 80　[SINGER, Mr].
THE MYSTIC CASTLE; OR, ORPHAN HEIR. A ROMANCE. BY THE AUTHOR OF THE WANDERER OF THE ALPS. IN TWO VOLUMES.

> London: Printed for William Lane, at the Minerva-Press, Leadenhall-Street, 1796.
> I 240p; II 256p. 8vo [ESTC has 12mo], 6s sewed (Min).
> MH-H *EC75.Si641.796m; CME 3-628-45124-8; EM 1495: 54; ESTC n012415 (EA COR).

Notes. Adv., 'Preparing for the Press', SJC 5–7 Apr 1796.
The Wanderer of the Alps 1796: 81.
French trans. Paris, 1798 (*Le Château Mystérieux, ou l'Heretier Orphelin*) (Lévy).

1796: 81   [SINGER, Mr].
THE WANDERER OF THE ALPS: OR, ALPHONSO. A ROMANCE. IN
TWO VOLUMES.

> London: Printed for William Lane, at the Minerva-Press, Leadenhall-Street, 1796.
> I 296p; II 267p. 12mo. 7s sewed (CR, Min).
> CR n.s. 20: 352–3 (July 1797); AF II: 4106.
> NjP 3600.001.955; ESTC n025018 (NA MH-H).

Notes. Advs. end vol. 2.
Adv., 'Preparing for the Press', SJC 5–7 Apr 1796.
    CR: 'In the story which occupies these two volumes, there is very little originality or merit
to apologise for a feeble and bombastic style. . . . it is only in the truly chivalrous character of
"Osmond" that the author suspends our disgust at the hackneyed and borrowed machinery
of *haunted castles, skeletons, banditti,* &c.' (p. 353).

1796: 82   SMITH, Charlotte.
MARCHMONT: A NOVEL. BY CHARLOTTE SMITH. IN FOUR VOLUMES.

> London: Printed by and for Sampson Low, Berwick Street, Soho, 1796.
> I xvi, 309p; II 256p; III 268p; IV 442p. 12mo. 16s sewed (MR), 16s (SJC), 16s or £1 extra
>   large and fine paper (OPA).
> CR n.s. 19: 256–60 (Mar 1797); MR n.s. 22: 468 (Apr 1797); AF II: 4140.
> BL 12614.b.32; CME 3-628-45177–9; EM 228: 4; ESTC t070720 (BI C, O; NA CtY,
>   CSmH, DLC, ICN, IU, MH-H, NjP, PU, ViU &c.; EA COR).

Notes. Preface 1, v–xvi. 2 pp. advs. end vol. 4.
Adv., 'On Monday next will be published, in Four Volumes', OPA 24 Oct 1796; 'Fifty copies
are printed on an extra large and fine Paper, hot-pressed, price 1l. which will be ready for
delivery on Saturday'.
Adv. SJC 3–5 Nov 1796.
Further edns: Dublin, 1797 (Printed by William Folds, for P. Wogan, P. Byrne, J. Exshaw, W.
Porter, J. Moore [and 6 others in Dublin], 4 vols., 12mo), ESTC n004432; London, 1803
(Summers). German trans. Leipzig, 1797 (*Marchmont, ein Roman*) (EAG).
    CR: 'In pourtraying the peculiar and distinguishing features of individual character, few
authors have been more successful. . . . We are prepared by the Preface (in which the author
introduces the story of her own misfortunes) to expect the appearance of the attorney to
whose agency she attributes much of the calamity she has experienced. Mrs. Smith would
have done well to have considered that to draw the character of the enemy by whom we consider ourselves injured, requires a degree of coolness and of candour, that falls to the lot of
few' (p. 236). 'In describing the scenes of nature, Mrs. Smith has not in this work fallen short
of her usual excellence' (p. 257).
    MR [Arthur Aikin]: 'If the iniquities committed by means of our system of laws occupy a
large part, and perhaps encroach too much on the conclusion of the story, the author's personal circumstances and misfortunes may well form a sufficient apology; while they give rise

to scenes and situations much more interesting than the vaulted galleries and castle-dungeons of some modern romances, by chilling the heart with the dreadful conviction that, even in this land of comparative freedom, similar acts of cruelty and injustice not only *may be* but actually *are* perpetrated.'

1796: 83   [STABBACK, Thomas].
MARIA; OR, THE VICARAGE. A NOVEL. IN TWO VOLUMES.

London: Printed for Hookham and Carpenter, Bond-Street, 1796.
I v, 247p; II 262p. 12mo. 6s sewed (CR).
CR n.s. 18: 475 (Dec 1796); AF II: 2713.
BL 12613.e.11; EM 202: 3; ESTC t070096 (NA MH-H).

Notes. Attributed to Rev. Thomas Stabback (ESTC, Summers).
Preface iii–v. 1 p. adv. for Hookham's library end vol. 1; 2 pp. advs. for Hookham and Carpenter's publications end vol. 2.

CR: 'These little volumes appear to have been the production of a young, amiable, uncorrupted mind; and we give the writer credit for laudable intention. . . . The style would have been better had it been less laboured; *measured prose* disgusts the ear by its mellifluous, monotonous uniformity: and descriptions of inanimate nature (in which this novel abounds), unconnected with passion or sentiment, must always be tiresome and uninteresting.—Nevertheless, this performance is not ill calculated to please young readers. . . .'

1796: 84   [SURR, Thomas Skinner].
CONSEQUENCES: OR, ADVENTURES AT RRAXALL CASTLE, A NOVEL. IN TWO VOLUMES. BY A GENTLEMAN.

London: Printed for T. Boosey, Old Broad Street, near the Royal Exchange, 1796.
I ii, 219p; II 216p. 12mo. 6s (CR, MR).
CR n.s. 18: 110 (Sept 1796); MR n.s. 20: 231–2 (June 1796); AF II: 4306.
MH-H EC8.Su786; EM 1492: 4; ESTC n015056 (BI C, O).

Notes. Prefatory advertisement, London, May 1796, 1, i–ii. Epistolary.
Adv. SJC 7–9 Dec 1797.
Further edn: Dublin, 1812 (as *Modern Adventures in Fashionable Life*) (CtY-BR). German trans. Coburg and Leipzig, 1799 (*Die Folgen, oder Begebenheiten in dem Schlosse Raxall*) (Price).

CR: 'The tale he relates is short and simple, and, if it displays no superior powers of invention, or bold flights of imagination, manifests good sense and just reflection, and is not ill calculated to exemplify the obvious and important moral which it enforces—the *consequences* that result from a vicious example, and the neglect of a virtuous education.'

MR [Arthur Aikin]: 'The object of this novel, namely, to shew the important consequences of a good or bad education, is truly commendable; and the story by which they are exemplified is far from contemptible. The writer does not indeed aspire to the highest rank, but we conceive that there are many more below than superior to him.'

1796: 85   THOMSON, A[lexander] (*trans.*).
THE GERMAN MISCELLANY; CONSISTING OF DRAMAS, DIALOGUES, TALES, AND NOVELS. TRANSLATED FROM THAT LANGUAGE, BY A.

THOMSON, AUTHOR OF A POEM ON WHIST; THE PARADISE OF TASTE, &C.

> Perth: Printed for R. Morison Junior, For R. Morison & Son, Perth; H. Mitchel, Edinburgh; and Vernor & Hood, Birchin-Lane, London, 1796.
>
> 282p. 12mo. 3s boards (CR, MR).
>
> CR n.s. 20: 357–9 (July 1797); MR n.s. 22: 359 (Mar 1797); AF II: 4452.
>
> O 249s.83; EM 2722: 1; ESTC t097592 (BI C, E, Ota; NA CaOHM, CSmH, CtY-BR &c.).

Notes. 1-p. (unn.) 'Advertisement by the Translator', Deanstone, 1 Nov 1796.

CR: 'He has . . . presented the public with a very interesting volume. The pieces which he has selected, are such as none can read without amusement, few without receiving instruction,—and that instruction of no mean importance' (p. 358).

MR [William Taylor]: '. . . the mine of German works of popular entertainment will afford to the English adventurer much employment, before its better ore will be exhausted. The present is . . . a well-chosen entertaining volume.'

1796: 86   [?TRAPP, Joseph (*trans.*)].
THE SPRITE OF THE NUNNERY; A TALE, FROM THE SPANISH. BY THE AUTHOR OF THE LIFE OF LINNÆUS, &C. IN TWO VOLUMES.

> London: Printed for S. Hall, No. 376, Oxford Street, and J. Barker, at the Dramatic Repository, Russell Court, Drury Lane, 1796.
>
> I 175p; II 156p. 12mo.
>
> BL 12490.c.26; EM 85: 7; ESTC t130919 (EA COR).

Notes. Joseph Trapp trans. *The Life of Linnaeus* (London, 1794) by Dietrich Heinrich Stoever. Text of novel starts on p. 9 in vol. 1 and p. 5 in vol. 2. 1′ pp. advs. end vol. 1, beginning with lower half p. 175.

1796: 87   [WÄCHTER, Georg Philip Ludwig Leonhard].
THE BLACK VALLEY; A TALE, FROM THE GERMAN OF VEIT WEBER, AUTHOR OF THE SORCERER.

> London: Printed for J. Johnson, in St. Paul's Church-Yard, 1796.
>
> 152p. 12mo [MR and CR have 8vo]. 2s 6d sewed (CR), 2s 6d (MR).
>
> CR n.s. 19: 227 (Feb 1797); MR n.s. 21: 458–60 (Dec 1796); AF II: 4646.
>
> MiEM PT 2551.W6B5513 1796; ESTC n032200.

Notes. Trans. of *Das heilige Kleeblatt* (1788), published as vol. 2 of *Sagen der Vorzeit* 7 vols. (Berlin, 1787–1798).

Vet Weber is Georg Philip Leonhard Wächter (ESTC).

Text of novel starts on p. 3.

MiEM copy has bookplate of Lane's Circulating Library.

CR: 'A tale sufficiently interesting, and the work of no "weak master." The author's intention seems to be, *to slay the slain,* by ridiculing superstition, and holding up friars to contempt and abhorrence.'

MR reviews together with the author's *The Sorcerer,* for comment see 1795: 45.

1796: 88   WALKER, George.
THEODORE CYPHON; OR, THE BENEVOLENT JEW: A NOVEL. IN

THREE VOLUMES. BY GEORGE WALKER, AUTHOR OF THE HOUSE OF TYNIAN, &C.

London: Printed for B. Crosby, No. 4, Stationers Court, Ludgate Street, 1796.
I viii, 255p; II 237p; III 224p. 12mo. 9s sewed (CR, MR).
CR n.s. 17: 238 (June 1796); MR n.s. 20: 476–7 (Aug 1796); AF II: 4663.
ViU *PZ2.W34T 1796; ESTC n046961 (BI C [vol. 1 only]; NA MiU PU).

Notes. Preface. 3 pp. advs. end vol. 2.
The House of Tynian 1795: 46.
Adv., 'In the Press, and speedily will be published', OPA 9 Mar 1796.
Further edns: Dublin, 1796 (Printed for John Rice, 2 vols., 12mo), EM 4022: 3, ESTC t119508; NSTC lists edns. in 1803 and 1823. German trans. Hildburghausen, 1797–98 (Theodor Cyphon) (Price); French trans. Paris, 1800 (Théodore Cyphon, ou le Juif bienfaisant) (BGR).

CR: 'This very tragical novel is well written; and the characters are forcibly delineated, though several of them are rather overcharged.... The work ... is well calculated to show the undue power of rank and wealth to oppress and to destroy the poor, and will afford the reader much entertainment, particularly if he be fond of gloomy scenes, and can derive pleasure from tales of murder, violation, parental tyranny, and public execution.'

MR [Arthur Aikin]: 'Of late ... it has been discovered that a novel is a very effectual and interesting vehicle for truths and speculations of the utmost importance, in moral and political philosophy; and men of very superior abilities have employed their time and talents in cultivating this species of writing.... With regard to the work before us, we acknowlege that we experienced considerable pleasure from its perusal. It possesses the art of strongly interesting the feelings, by delineating the tragical effects of power under the influence of passion.'

RT 8 (Apr 1796): 'It is a Political Novel, without one single word of Politics ...' (p. 217).

WEBER, Veit
See WÄCHTER, Georg Philip Ludwig Leonhard

1796: 89   [WEST, Jane].

A GOSSIP'S STORY, AND A LEGENDARY TALE. IN TWO VOLUMES. BY THE AUTHOR OF ADVANTAGES OF EDUCATION.

London: Printed for T. Longman, Pater-Noster-Row, 1796.
I xi, 226p; II vi, 225p. 12mo. 7s sewed (CR), 6s sewed (MR), 7s boards (SJC, adv.).
CR n.s. 21: 228–9 (Oct 1797); MR n.s. 22: 92 (Jan 1797); AF II: 4741.
C 7720.d.922; EM 2506: 16; ESTC n001431 (BI BL, MRu; NA CSmH, CaAEU, CLU-S/C &c.).

Notes. 1: 1-p. dedication, 4-pp. introduction (iii–viii), 3-pp. table of contents (ix–xi); 2: table of contents iii–vi.
Advantages of Education 1793: 45.
Adv. SJC 20–22 Oct 1796.
Adv. end vol. 3 of Clara Duplessis (1797: 50).
Further edns: London, 1797, EM 175: 4; ESTC t057330; London, 1798, ESTC t154439; London, 1799, ESTC n007342; Dublin, 1799 (Printed by William Porter, 1 vol., 12mo) ESTC n007344; NSTC lists edn. in 1804. German trans. Leipzig, 1798 (Eine Klatschgeschichte) (Price).

CR: 'This novel may be recommended as an antidote to the pernicious maxims inculcated in most of the modern tales of *sentiment*; and while it deserves the highest commendations for its utility, it is scarcely less valuable for the entertainment it affords' (p. 228). '. . . the Gossip's Story is one of the very few books of the kind, which every reader will wish had been longer' (p. 229).

MR [Arthur Aikin]: 'The *Legendary Tale*, having very little connexion with the chief subject of these volumes, might as well have been omitted. . . . We can, however, recommend the *Story* as uniting to a great degree of interest the rarer qualities of good sense and an accurate knowlege of mankind. . . . Amusement is combined with utility, and fiction is enlisted in the cause of virtue and practical philosophy.'

1796: 90   WIELAND, C[hristoph] M[artin]; [TOOKE, William (*trans.*)].
PRIVATE HISTORY OF PEREGRINUS PROTEUS, THE PHILOSOPHER. BY C. M. WIELAND. TRANSLATED FROM THE GERMAN. IN TWO VOLUMES.

> London: Printed for J. Johnson, in St. Paul's Churchyard, 1796.
> I 298p; II 382p. 12mo. 7s boards (CR), 7s 6d sewed (MR).
> CR n.s. 23: 472–3 (Aug 1798); MR n.s. 22: 349–50 (Mar 1797); AF II: 4496.
> BL 1206.e.6; EM 2612: 3; ESTC t099054 (BI MRu; NA DLC, IU, ViU).

Notes. Trans. of *Geheime Geschichte des Philosophen Peregrinus Proteus* (Leipzig, 1791).

CR: 'In this work he derides Christianity; but the attempt to depreciate it will not, we think, be successful, as he admits the beneficence of its precepts while he disbelieves its divine authority. Some of the love-scenes are drawn with so luxuriant a pencil, that it would be improper to recommend these volumes to the attention of the young. A few trite moral sentiments, exalted by the charms of language, are a poor compensation for the mischiefs that follow a direct incitement of the voluptuous passions.'

MR [William Taylor]: 'In our xviiith vol. p. 523, we observed in general of the writings of this author, that they are accused of inculcating a hopeless epicurism, and are justly reprehensible for the frequent introduction of scenery licentiously voluptuous. To the latter charge, especially, the novel before us is certainly obnoxious' (pp. 349–50).

1796: 91   WIELAND, [Christoph Martin].
SELECT FAIRY TALES, FROM THE GERMAN OF WIELAND. BY THE TRANSLATOR OF THE SORCERER, AND THE BLACK VALLEY OF WEBER. IN TWO VOLUMES.

> London: Printed for J. Johnson, No. 72, St. Paul's Church-Yard, 1796.
> I 236p; II 303p. 12mo. 7s boards (CR, MR).
> CR n.s. 22: 357 (Mar 1798); MR n.s. 25: 213–14 (Feb 1798); AF II: 4795.
> CLU-S/C PT2568.A13 1796; ESTC n021721 (NA FU; EA ZAP). WC also has PSt & RPB.

Notes. CR: 'The fictions display little genius; and some of the descriptions are criminally licentious. . . . We do not see the propriety of calling these pieces *Fairy* Tales, as we only observe one fairy in the whole of them.'

MR [William Taylor]: 'We have some doubts whether the fairy tales, of which these volumes contain elegant translations, may confidently be ascribed to Wieland. They bear, however, a considerable resemblance to the mode of fiction which characterizes this writer, who every where delights to loiter over descriptions of beautiful and voluptuous scenery; and is as sure to introduce the graceful dances of beautiful and wanton nymphs between his incidents as the manager of the opera. Be this as it may, the stories are fanciful and amusing, and deserved translation.'

1797

1797: 1   ANON.
ABSTRACT. A CHARACTER FROM LIFE. IN TWO VOLUMES.

London: Printed for William Lane, at the Minerva-Press, Leadenhall-Street, 1797.
I 243p; II iv, 236p. 8vo [MR has 12mo]. 6s sewed (CR, MR).
CR n.s. 19: 227 (Feb 1797); MR n.s. 22: 91–2 (Jan 1797); AF II: 6.
PU Singer-Mend.PR.3991.A1.A27.1797; ESTC n029155.

Notes. Vol.1 begins with an Abstract addressed to 'Courteous Reader' pp. 1–18; vol. 2 begins with 'Advice to the Reader' i–iv. Epistolary.
Post-dated; adv., 'Shortly will be published', OPA 11 Nov 1796; adv. as published OPA 19 Dec 1796.
Adv. SJC 3–5 Jan 1797.

CR: 'This novel can do no harm; and as the illustrious medical philosopher, Dr John Brown (Elem. of Med. Vol. II. p. 178) recommends, in cases of mania and pervigilium, that the patient should have stupid books read to him, it may even do much good.'

MR [Arthur Aikin]: 'The plan and execution of this work do not discover talents that are in any respect superior to those of the generality of novel-writers. The great object of the author is to combat certain opinions with regard to marriage, that have lately become fashionable among many of our modern speculatists. As far as these opinions are erroneous and mischievous, so far the present writer deserves praise for his intentions: we wish that we could say as much for his *literary* merit.'

1797: 2   ANON.
ADELINE DE COURCY. IN TWO VOLUMES.

London: Printed for T. Cadell, Jun. and W. Davies, in the Strand, 1797.
I 190p; II 179p. 12mo. 6s sewed (CR, MR).
CR n.s. 22: 238 (Feb 1798); MR n.s. 26: 107 (May 1798); AF II: 20.
ICN Y155.A24; EM 1590: 2; ESTC n015179 (NA MH-H, TxHR).

Notes. ICN copy has bound in following t.p. the 3-pp. dedication from Elizabeth Isabella Spence's *Helen Sinclair* (1799: 87).
Adv. SJC 9–11 Nov 1797; adv. GEP 30 Jan–1 Feb 1798.

CR: 'The story is of the common cast. . . . The moral, however, is good; and Adeline de Courcy may employ a few vacant hours with some advantage, although it does not entitle the authoress to a high rank as a novelist.'

MR [James Bannister]: 'The story of this novel is romantic. . . . The character of Zodisky is not such as we often observe in life; but the example of his honour, generosity, and disinterested love, is not only pleasing to the reader's imagination, but may have a good effect on his heart. . . . These volumes appear to be the production of a female pen.'

ALLEGORICAL MINIATURES FOR THE STUDY OF YOUTH
See App. A: 9

1797: 3   ANON.
ANASTATIA: OR, THE MEMOIRS OF THE CHEVALIER LAROUX. INTERSPERSED WITH A VARIETY OF ANECDOTES FROM REAL LIFE. IN TWO VOLUMES. BY A LADY.

> Dublin: Printed by John Chambers, 5, Abbey-Street, 1797.
> I viii, 238p; II 231p. 12mo.
> D 82369a3; ESTC n030938 (BI Dt; NA InU-Li, IU).

Notes. Vol. 1 Address to the Public i–ii; 6-pp. list of subscribers iii–2. In both vols. text of novel starts on p. 3.

AZEMIA: A DESCRIPTIVE AND SENTIMENTAL NOVEL
See BECKFORD, William

1797: 4   ANON.
THE CASTLE OF BURKTHOLME. A NOVEL. IN THREE VOLUMES.

> London: Sold by T. N. Longman, Pater-Noster-Row, 1797.
> I 304p; II 283p; III 262p. 12mo [BC has 8vo]. 12s sewed (MV), 12s boards (SJC).
> BC 12: 542 (Nov 1798); AF II: 637.
> IU x823.C2793; ESTC n043970.

Notes. Epistolary.
Adv. SJC 13–15 June 1797.

BC: 'The incidents and characters which enter into the story, and the descriptions interspersed, where occasion suggests, are natural and pleasing. The general conduct of the novel is sufficiently artful to interest; and the volumes may, we think, be read without offence to good taste, or injury to virtue.'

MV 2 (1797), pp. 464–5: 'We have never read, from an unknown pen, a novel so truly excellent as the one now before us; it abounds in strokes of nature, feeling, and originality. It carries the reader through a chain of incidents, at once interesting and probable; and though, perhaps, there are more personages introduced than are strictly required for the conduct of the plot; their characters are all so varied, and so accurately depicted; so uniformly sustained, that it is impossible to dwell for more than a moment upon this fault.'

1797: 5   ANON.
CHARLES DACRES: OR, THE VOLUNTARY EXILE. AN HISTORICAL NOVEL, FOUNDED ON FACTS. IN TWO VOLUMES.

> Edinburgh: Printed by John Moir, Paterson's Court, 1797.
> I xiii, 126p; II 112p. 12mo.
> BL 12654.ee.42; EM 193: 6; ESTC t067800.

Notes. Part of the imprint has been deleted in ink in both volumes (ESTC).
1-p. description of contents ([v]); 1-p. dramatis personae ([vii]) headed 'A General View of
The Characters contained in this Work'; prefatory address 'To the Reader' vii–xiii. Pagination continuous Roman-Arabic; text of novel starts on p. 15 of vol. 1. In vol. 2 text of novel
starts on p. 3. Novel ends on p. 109 of vol. 2; pp. 111–12 have a list of subscribers.

THE CHURCH OF ST. SIFFRID
See HERVEY, Elizabeth

CLARA DUPLESSIS, AND CLAIRANT
See LAFONTAINE, August Heinrich Julius

THE COUNT DE SANTERRE: A ROMANCE
See SELDEN, Catharine

COUNT DONAMAR: OR, ERRORS OF SENSIBILITY
See BOUTERWEK, Friedrich

THE COUSINS OF SCHIRAS
See SENAC DE MEILHAN, Gabriel

1797: 6   ANON.
DAYS OF CHIVALRY. A ROMANCE.

> London: Printed at the Minerva-Press, Leadenhall-Street; and sold by Hodgson,
> Wimpole-Street, and Miller, Old Bond-Street, 1797.
> I viii, 173p; II 174p. 8vo [CR has 12mo]. 6s sewed (CR, Min).
> CR n.s. 23: 473 (Aug 1798); AF II: 1018.
> BL Cup.403.y.13; EM 8225: 2; ESTC t140099 (NA CLU-S/C).

Notes. Frontispiece. Preface i–viii.
Adv. end vol. 2 of *Court Intrigue* (1799: 44).
　CR: 'This production of a female pen, humbly termed by the authoress an "unoffending
trifle," contains a pleasing variety of incidents, not ill related or unhappily combined.'

DISOBEDIENCE. A NOVEL
See JACSON, Frances

EDMUND OF THE FOREST
See MUSGRAVE, Agnes

ELIZABETH. A NOVEL
See CARVER, Mrs

THE ENGLISH NUN. A NOVEL
See SELDEN, Catharine

1797: 7   ANON.
THE FORCE OF EXAMPLE; OR, THE HISTORY OF HENRY AND CARO-LINE: WRITTEN FOR THE INSTRUCTION AND AMUSEMENT OF YOUNG PERSONS.

> London: Printed for E. Newbery, corner of St. Paul's Church-Yard, 1797.
> 159p. 12mo [MR has small 8vo]. 2s bound (MR).
> CR n.s. 27: 228 (Oct 1799); MR n.s. 28: 333 (Mar 1799); AF II: 1478.
> BL 1210.l.16; EM 2733: 2; ESTC t117681 (BI AWn, O; NA CaOHM, CaOTP, CLU-S/C &c.).

Notes. Attributed to Mrs Pilkington in Roscoe, J139.
6 pp. advs. end vol.

CR: 'This tale indicates no great ability in the writer; but it may amuse young readers without injuring their morals.'

MR [Jabez Hirons]: 'Some imperfections might be pointed out in this little volume, but its general character is that of important instruction and utility.... This book may entertain and improve the young, as well as those who are not generally included in this description; and it merits their attention.'

FRAGMENTS: IN THE MANNER OF STERNE
See BRANDON, Isaac

1797: 8   ANON.
THE GOVERNESS, OR COURTLAND ABBEY. A NOVEL.

> Bath: Printed By S. Hazard; And Sold by Vernor and Hood, Birchin Lane, London, and all other Booksellers, 1797.
> I xii, 310p; II 309p; III 287p; IV 249p. 12mo. 12s sewed (MR).
> MR n.s. 25: 213 (Feb 1798); AF II: 1684.
> IU x823.G747.V4; ESTC n065851.

Notes. List of subscribers.

MR [George Edward Griffiths]: 'An advertisement to this work informs us that "it was written in an hour of melancholy," and that the friends of the writer persuaded her that, "in her unfortunate situation, the attempt was every way laudable." In circumstances of adversity, all innocent endeavours at extrication are, indeed, praiseworthy; and the morality of the present novel is commendable. We wish that we could say much more in recommendation of the performance.'

GRASVILLE ABBEY: A ROMANCE
See MOORE, George

1797: 9   ANON.
THE HEIR OF MONTAGUE. A NOVEL. IN THREE VOLUMES.

> London: Printed at the Minerva-Press, for William Lane, Leadenhall-Street, 1797/98.
> I (1798) 300p; II (1798) 267p; III (1797) 346p. 12mo. 10s 6d boards (CR), 10s 6d sewed (adv., Min).

CR n.s. 24: 471 (Dec 1798).

BL 12613.g.10; EM 244: 1; ESTC t070912 (NA CaAEU, MH-H).

Notes. Frontispiece to vol. 1. 1 p. advs. end vol. 2 and 2 pp. advs. end vol. 3. Adv. end vol. 2 of *Court Intrigue* (1799: 44).

CR: 'Although the characters in this novel are copies, and the incidents are of the common kind, it may be considered as usefully tending to expose the errors of youthful indiscretion and vulgar prejudices. Much of this, as of most modern novels, is thrown into the form of dialogue, probably from a supposition that it is easy to write that way; but this, we are sorry to add, has been seldom justified by the specimens which have fallen in our way.'

1797: 10 ANON.
HENRY SOMERVILLE, A TALE, BY THE AUTHOR OF HARTLEBOURN CASTLE. IN TWO VOLUMES.

London: Printed for J. Bell, no. 148, Oxford-Street, 1797.

I 194p; II 244p. 12mo. 6s boards (CR).

CR n.s. 20: 471–2 (Aug 1797); AF II: 1902.

BL 12611.aaa.27; EM 63: 3; ESTC t108867 (BI O; NA CaOTV).

Notes. Hartlebourn Castle 1793: 5.

Further edns: Dublin, 1798 (Printed by Brett Smith, for Charles Browne, 1 vol., 12mo), ESTC n007243; Dublin, 1798, ESTC t208030.

CR: 'This production is interesting as a story, and discovers traits of philosophical discrimination, not frequently to be found in the effusions of novel-writers' (p. 471).

1797: 11 ANON.
THE HISTORY OF JULIA & CECILIA DE VALMONT. WRITTEN BY A YOUNG LADY, LATELY DECEASED. IN TWO VOLUMES.

Cork: Printed by J. Connor, at the Circulating-Library, Castle-Street, 1797.

I xx, 238p; II 464p. 8vo.

CSmH 356488; ESTC t167609 (BI D [vol. 1 only]).

Notes. Formerly attributed to Sophia Briscoe.

According to the preface (1, v–vii), the author, aged 16, now 'lies mouldering in the dust'. The author's age and the comment in the preface (by 'a close and tender relative') that her modesty would not have permitted publication if she had lived make it unlikely that this author is Sophia Briscoe, author of *Miss Melmoth* (1771: 38) and *The Fine Lady* (1772: 31). List of subscribers 1, ix–xx. In vol. 1 p. 39 misnumbered 38 and p. 229 misnumbered 22.

THE HISTORY OF SIR GEORGE WARRINGTON
See PURBECK, Elizabeth and Jane

THE HORRORS OF OAKENDALE ABBEY
See CARVER, Mrs

1797: 12 ANON.
THE HOUSE OF MARLEY. A NOVEL. IN TWO VOLUMES.

London: Printed for William Lane, at the Minerva-Press, Leadenhall-Street, 1797.

I 256p; II 296p. 12mo. 7s sewed (Min).

MH-H *EC75.A100.797h; CME 3-628-45062-4; EM 998: 5; ESTC n003775 (EA COR).

Notes. Frontispiece to vol. 1.

1797: 13   ANON.
THE INQUISITION.

London: Printed for Vernor and Hood, Birchin-Lane, By Merritt and Wright, Liverpool: And sold by them and by Rawson and Co. Hull, n.d. [ESTC: 1797].

I 265p; II 223p. 8vo [CR has 12mo]. 6s sewed (CR, MR).

CR n.s. 21: 232–5 (Oct 1797); MR n.s. 23: 211 (June 1797); AF II: 2194.

BL RB.23.a.9961; EMf; ESTC n016951 (NA CLU-S/C, PU).

Notes. CR: 'This novel is superior to many; and the author's intention is certainly very commendable' (p. 232).

MR [Arthur Aikin]: 'To those who make a general practice of novel reading, we may recommend these volumes, for they might easily have worse of the kind. Those, however, who occasionally peruse works of fiction as a recreation from severer studies, will be but little satisfied with this. The merely fictitious part is not destitute of fancy: but to just and accurate discrimination of character, and to all the higher qualities of the novel, the work before us has very small pretensions.'

INTERESTING TALES
See SHOWES, Mrs

THE IRISH HEIRESS, A NOVEL
See PATRICK, Mrs F. C.

1797: 14   ANON.
THE KNIGHTS; OR SKETCHES OF THE HEROIC AGE. A ROMANCE. IN THREE VOLUMES.

London: Printed for David Ogilvy and Son, no. 315, Holborn, 1797.

I xxiv, 214p; II 231p; III 212p. 12mo. 12s 6d sewed (CR), 9s sewed (MR).

CR n.s. 22: 237 (Feb 1798); MR n.s. 25: 453–6 (1798); AF II: 2427.

O 249.s.603-605; xESTC.

Notes. T.ps. to vols. 2 and 3 omit 'In three volumes'. Preface 1, v–xxiv, signed 'The Author', 13 Nov 1797 concerns the 'alliance of history with fiction' (p. xxii) and explains the reasons for 'laying the scene of a fictitious story in the twelfth century' (p. v).
MR gives date of 1798.

CR: 'This romance is not ill written; nor is it deficient in interest.'

MR [William Taylor]: 'Not many romances of knighthood have as yet diversified the literature of circulating libraries; and it is with some claim to novelty that an author may lay his scenes in the age of chivalry, and adhere to the customs of feudal manners. This is the case in the volumes before us; the adventures of the *Knights* are indeed wholly fictitious, and not even attached to regular history by the introduction of some celebrated chieftain: but they adhere with meritorious fidelity to that consistency, or poetic probability, which the supposititious events demand' (p. 453).

1797: 15   ANON.
*THE LOTTERY, OR MIDSUMMER RECESS; INTENDED FOR THE INFORMATION AND AMUSEMENT OF YOUNG PERSONS OF BOTH SEXES. THE SECOND EDITION.

> No copy of 1st edn. located, nor reviews. This edn: Uttoxeter: Printed and sold by R. Richards; sold also by W. Richardson, London, 1797.
> iv, 224p. 12mo.
> BL 1507/465; EM 3919: 15; ESTC t128867.

Notes. The possibility remains that in 'this puffing age' this was in fact the 'first' edn. or at least a second issue of that edn.

1797: 16   ANON.
MILISTINA: OR, THE DOUBLE INTEREST. A NOVEL. IN TWO VOL- UMES. DEDICATED TO THE MARCHIONESS TOWNSEND.

> London: Printed and sold by Sampson Low, Berwick Street, Soho, and C. Law, Ave-Maria Lane, 1797.
> I vi, 216p; II 205p. 12mo. 1s 6d [*sic*](BC), 6s (adv., ME).
> BC 12: 426 (Oct 1798); AF II: 2864.
> O Vet.A5f.183; EM 1008: 11; ESTC n003970 (NA CtY, MH-H).

Notes. Adv. LC 81: 569 (13–15 June 1797).
Adv. end vol. 2 of *Emily Dundorne* (1799: 93).

   BC: 'As a composition, this is by no means ill written, but it is entitled to no considerable praise for its invention or contrivances.'

THE MYSTERIOUS WIFE. A NOVEL
See MEEKE, Mary

1797: 17   ANON.
ORIENTAL FABLES, ANECDOTES, AND TALES. TRANSLATED FROM THE FRENCH.

> London: Printed for T. Cadell, Jun. and W. Davies, Successors to Mr. Cadell in the Strand, 1797.
> 176p. 8vo [MR has 12mo]. 2s 6d (MR).
> MR n.s. 24: 104–5 (Sept 1797).
> C X.29.7/1; ESTC t181669 (NA CLU-S/C, ICU).

Notes. Open with 3-pp. list of contents (unn.): 14 Fables, 12 Oriental Anecdotes and 4 Ori- ental Tales. Fables range in length from 1′ to 10 pp, the Anecdotes from 2 to 3 pp. and the Tales from 15 to 16 pp.

   MR [Alexander Hamilton]: 'These pleasing stories are written with all that vivacity which the French know so well how to infuse into compositions of this nature; they are very short, very moral, and frequently very witty.... The translation is in general executed with ease and elegance.'

1797: 18   ANON.
THE ORPHAN OF BOLLENBACH; OR, POLYCARP THE ADVENTURER. A ROMANCE. FROM THE GERMAN.

London: Printed by R. Noble, Shire-Lane, Temple-Bar; For T. Boosey, No. 4, Old
   Broad-Street, Near the Royal Exchange, 1797.
vii, 188p. 12mo. 2s 6d (ME 1798).
Corvey; CME 3–628–45036–5; xESTC

Notes. Introduction pp. v–vii.

PARENTAL DUPLICITY; OR THE POWER OF ARTIFICE
See M., P. S.

1797: 19   ANON.
PERCY, OR THE FRIENDS, A NOVEL.

Salisbury: Printed and sold by J. Easton; sold also by G. and T. Wilkie, No. 57,
   Paternoster-Row, London, 1797.
I 214p; II 110p. 12mo. 5s boards (CR, LC).
CR n.s. 20: 354 (July 1797).
BL 012612.df.13; EM 5770: 5; ESTC t067641 (NA MH-H, NjP).

Notes. Dedication to the Countess of Oxford.
Adv. LC 81: 359 (13–15 Apr 1797); additional bookseller is J. Bell, No. 148, Oxford-street.

   CR: 'The author need not have deprecated the severity of criticism, which we believe few
would take the trouble to exercise on a production so much below the most insipid of its
kind.'

1797: 20   ANON.
THE POSTHUMOUS DAUGHTER: A NOVEL. IN TWO VOLUMES.

London: Printed and published by G. Cawthorn, British Library, 132, Strand, 1797.
I xxviii, 249 p; II xvi, 320p. 12mo. 7s (ME 1798).
BL 12654.f.9; EM 485: 3; ESTC t107267 (NA IU, MH-H, PU &c.).

Notes. Dedication to 'the most beautiful and most amiable Woman in the Kingdom' iii–xi,
signed 'The Compiler' and dated Nov. 1797. Detailed list of the contents of every letter 1,
xiii–xxviii and 2, i–xvi. In vol. 2 text of novel starts on p. 3. 1 p. advs. end vol. 1. Epistolary.

1797: 21   ANON.
RANSPACH, OR MYSTERIES OF A CASTLE; A NOVEL, IN TWO VOL-
UMES. BY THE AUTHOR OF EDWARD DE COURCY, &C.

Uttoxeter: Printed by R. Richards, and sold by W. Richardson, London, 1797.
I 210p; II 196p. 12mo. 7s sewed (CR, GEP).
CR n.s. 22: 238–9 (Feb 1798).
BL 12614.bbb.12; EM 229: 3; ESTC t071391.

Notes: Edward de Courcy 1794: 9.
Adv. GEP 29–31 Mar 1798.

   CR: 'The class of readers among whom this book will circulate, will probably not object to
confusion of costume, inaccuracy of diction, or incoherence of narrative, as it treats of a hero
and heroine endowed with the usual virtues, whose loves meet with the usual obstacles, and
the ordinary conclusion.'

ROSE CECIL
See C—, Lady Mary

THE SHROVE-TIDE CHILD; OR, THE SON OF A MONK
See PIGAULT-LEBRUN, Charles-Antoine

1797: 22   ANON.
THE SUBMISSIONS OF DEPENDENCE, A NOVEL. INTERSPERSED
WITH POETRY.

> London: Printed for Messrs. Hookham and Carpenter, No. 14, Old Bond Street, 1797.
> 276p. 12mo. 3s sewed (CR), 3s 6d sewed (MR).
> CR n.s. 20: 353–4 (July 1797); MR n.s. 24: 341–2 (Nov 1797); AF II: 4292.
> MH-H EC75.A100.797s; xESTC (BI O).

Notes. 1-p. prefatory advertisement. Epistolary.
Prefatory adv. says that the 'reader will find the epistolary style dropt in several places, and narrative adopted', although adv. claims that these passages were originally part of letters.

CR: 'This work is rather a collection of scraps and fragments than a regular story. The characters are feebly sketched, and the outlines are common. . . . The poetical pieces are above mediocrity; and the general story, though hastily and negligently told, will add somewhat to instruction, if not to amusement.'

MR: 'This work we have perused with patience, (as in duty bound,) but we cannot commend it with integrity. The language is marked by great inequalities. Description and sentiment are sometimes well expressed; but the writer very often deviates into vulgarity, provincialisms, and other imperfections. The conduct of the story is all absurdity; and the characters that are introduced are chiefly fools or profligates, with whose nonsense or villainy the reader of taste is perpetually disgusted.'

1797: 23   ANON.
ULRIC AND ILVINA: THE SCANDINAVIAN TALE. IN TWO VOLUMES.

> London: Printed for Allen and West, No. 15, Paternoster Row, 1797.
> I iv, 110p; II 154p. 12mo. 4s sewed (CR).
> CR n.s. 21: 230–2 (Oct 1797); AF II: 4574.
> BL N.1854(1); EM 2010: 3; ESTC t071904 (BI O).

Notes. Verse preface 1, i–iv, claiming that the work is by a young woman of eighteen.

CR: 'The tale itself is one of those romances which are filled with horrors,—that are calculated to frighten without interesting,—and that make the reader feel disgust instead of pity' (p. 231). 'We wish the author success in her literary career; though we fear she will be disappointed, if she expects much from her Scandinavian Tale. We do not forget, however, that she is young, and that there is time for improvement' (p. 232).

VAURIEN: OR, SKETCHES OF THE TIMES
See DISRAELI, Isaac

THE VILLAGE CURATE, AND HIS DAUGHTER JULIA
See 1795: 49

WALSH COLVILLE
See PORTER, Anna Maria

1797: 24 BAHRDT, C[arl] F[riedrich].
ALL'S WELL THAT ENDS WELL; OR, ALVARO AND XIMENES. A
SPANISH TALE. TRANSLATED FROM THE GERMAN OF DR. C. F.
BAHRDT. IN TWO VOLUMES.
> London: Printed for B. Crosby, No. 4, Stationer's-Court, Ludgate Street, 1797.
> I ii, 224p; II 199p. 12mo. 6s sewed (MR).
> MR n.s. 23: 451–2 (Aug 1797); AF II: 199.
> PU Singer-Mend.PT.1815.B5.A813.1797; ESTC n029845 (NA MH-H).

Notes. Trans. of *Alvaro und Ximenes* (Halle, 1790).
'Advertisement' i–ii, London 1 Feb 1797.
French trans. Paris, 1800 (*Alvaro et Ximenès ou les coups de l'amour et de la fortune*) (BGR).
   MR [William Taylor]: 'The whole narrative, though improbable, is amusing; and the
translation is fully worthy of the somewhat inelegant original' (p. 452).

1797: 25 [BECKFORD, William].
AZEMIA: A DESCRIPTIVE AND SENTIMENTAL NOVEL. INTER-
SPERSED WITH PIECES OF POETRY. BY JACQUETTA AGNETA MAR-
IANA JENKS, OF BELLEGROVE PRIORY IN WALES. DEDICATED TO
THE RIGHT HONORABLE LADY HARRIET MARLOW. TO WHICH
ARE ADDED, CRITICISMS ANTICIPATED. IN TWO VOLUMES.
> London: Printed by and for Sampson Low, no. 7, Berwick Street, Soho, 1797.
> I xii, 254p; II 253p. 12mo. 7s sewed (CR, MR), 7s (LC).
> CR n.s. 20: 470 (Aug 1797); MR n.s. 24: 338 (Nov 1797); AF II: 259.
> O 12 Theta 1170-1171; EMf; ESTC n005285 (NA CLU-S/C, CtY-BR, MBAt).

Notes. Dedication to the Right Honourable Lady Harriet Marlow (Beckford's own nom-de-
plume in *Modern Novel Writing* [1796: 23]), signed J. A. M. Jenks, Belle Grove Priory, 1 Mar
1797, v–viii; 'Exordium Extraordinary' ix–xii. 1 p. advs. end vol. 1. The novel ends on p. 231
of vol. 2; the last section (pp. 233–53) is addressed 'To the Reviewers of all the Reviews; all the
Magazines; and all the Newspapers' and, as its running head, 'Criticisms Anticipated', suggests, provides criticism to save the reviewers' trouble. T.p. to vol. 1 in O copy is badly
defaced.
Adv., 'In a few Days will be published', LC 81: 569 (13–5 June 1797; adv. as published LC 82:
84 (22–25 July 1797).
Further edn: London, 1798, EM 4538: 2, ESTC t062059. French trans. Paris, 1808 (*Arnold et
la belle musulmane*) (DBI). Facs: FCy.
   CR: 'This performance is written upon the plan of *Modern Novel Writing* [1796: 22], but is
far inferior in point of execution; and we think the author might have employed his talents in
some other mode of satire on the same subject, rather than in servile imitation of a work so
recent. He is not devoid of humour; and the absurdity of the greater part of modern novels is
capable of being represented in various and ridiculous lights.' CR again identifies author as
Robert Merry.
   MR: '*Azemia* . . . is an entertaining compound of good taste and good writing,—just satire

and whimsical fancy;—adjuncts which, under the direction of GENIUS, (as in the case before us,) whatever be the singularities or defects of the composition, can never fail of producing a work that will prove acceptable to many readers. . . .'

1797: 26 BENNETT, [Anna Maria].
THE BEGGAR GIRL AND HER BENEFACTORS. IN SEVEN VOLUMES. BY MRS. BENNETT, AUTHOR OF WELCH HEIRESS, JUVENILE INDISCRETIONS, AGNES DE-COURCI, AND ELLEN COUNTESS OF CASTLE HOWELL.

> London: Printed for William Lane, at the Minerva-Press, Leadenhall-Street, 1797.
> I vii, 271p; II 316p; III [271]p; IV 357p; V 306p; VI [339]p; VII 414p. 12mo. £1 11s 6d sewed (CR), £1 11s 6d sewed or £ 1 18s 6d on fine paper (SJC).
> CR n.s. 22: 356–7 (Mar 1798); AF II: 297.
> BL 12612.e.9; CME 3-628-45013-6; EM 210: 1; ESTC t067328 (BI C, O; NA CtY-BR, CSmH, ICN, IU, MH-H, NjP, PU, ViU &c.; EA COR).

Notes. Last p. of vol. 3 [271] misnumbered 270; last p. of vol. 6 [339] misnumbered 338. Dedication to H.R.H the Duchess of York 1, i–vii. 1 p. advs. end vol. 5.

Anna; or, Memoirs of a Welch Heiress 1785: 22; *Juvenile Indiscretions* 1786: 16; *Agnes De-Courci* 1789: 31; *Ellen, Countess of Castle Howel* 1794: 16.

Adv., 'Will positively be published on Monday Next', SJC 6–8 July 1797; 'And on Saturday Copies will be delivered to the Trade.—As such only will be delivered, which are subscribed for, the Booksellers are requested to send in their Names. Persons resident in the Country, will be pleased to be early in their Orders to their Correspondents in London.'

Further edns: Dublin, 1797 (Printed by P. Wogan, 3 vols., 12mo), ESTC t120865; Dublin, 1798, ESTC t137327; London, 1799, ESTC t120251; Philadelphia, 1801 (WC); London, 1813 (WC). French trans. Paris, 1798 (*Rosa, ou la Fille mendiante et ses bienfaiteurs*) (BN); German trans. Leipzig, 1798–1801 (*Das Bettlermädchen und ihre Wohlthäter*) (EAG).

CR: 'Whenever quantity shall become the criterion of merit, we shall perhaps be able to estimate the value of this work more agreeably to the author's wishes than at present. . . . we are apprehensive that readers of novels are not always gifted with the requisite patience to peruse seven volumes in order to discover what might have been much better told in three. There are scenes of tenderness, delineations of character, and some attempts at humour, which will not fail to please: but upon the whole, the story is eked out with a strange excess of digression, and with many superfluous characters' (p. 356).

BIRCH, John Brereton (*trans.*)
See SENAC DE MEILHAN, Gabriel

1797: 27 BONHOTE, {Eliz}[abeth].
BUNGAY CASTLE: A NOVEL. BY MRS. BONHOTE. AUTHOR OF THE PARENTAL MONITOR, &C. IN TWO VOLUMES.

> London: Printed for William Lane, at the Minerva-Press, Leadenhall-Street, 1796 [1797].
> I xix, 283p; II 288p. 12mo [BC has 8vo]. 7s (BC), 7s sewed (SJC, adv.).
> CR 21: 234–5 (Oct 1797); AF II: 400.

BL 12612.aaa.28; CME 3-628-45017-9; EM 332: 2; ESTC t064725 (NA CtY, IU, ViU &c.; EA COR).

Notes. Dedication (to Charles, Duke of Norfolk) signed Eliz. Bonhote, Bungay 1797. Introduction vii–xix. 1 p. advs. end vol. 1.

Adv., 'Shortly will be published', OPA 7 Dec 1796. Adv. SJC 16–18 May 1797.

Adv. end vol. 2 of *Disobedience* (1797: 48).

1797: 28   [BOUTERWEK, Friedrich].
COUNT DONAMAR: OR, ERRORS OF SENSIBILITY: A SERIES OF LET-
TERS, WRITTEN IN THE TIME OF THE SEVEN YEARS WAR, TRANS-
LATED FROM THE GERMAN. IN THREE VOLUMES.

> London: Printed for J. Johnson, N° 72, St. Paul's Church Yard, 1797.
> I 312p; II 320p; III 320p. 12mo. 10s 6d boards (CR), 10s 6d sewed (MR, SJC).
> CR n.s. 21: 471 (Dec 1797); MR n.s. 27: 94 (Sept 1798); AF II: 428.
> ViU *PZ2.C682 1797; ESTC n028060 (NA CSmH).

Notes. Trans. of *Graf Donamar* (Frankfurt and Leipzig, 1792–93).

Epistolary.

Adv., 'In a few Days will be published', SJC 17–20 June 1797.

French trans. Paris, 1798 (*Le comte de Donamar*) (BGR).

CR: 'That this is a work of genius, is indisputable. The story is original, the events combined with singular felicity, and the characters preserved with a critical attention to nature. The language abounds in splendid imagery, striking turns of sentiment, and a glow of passion, not unworthy of the greatest of poets. But, while we do this justice to the author's talents, we must regret that they have been misapplied, and that the general tendency of the work is not favourable to virtue.'

MR [James Bannister]: 'This work contains all the bloated magnificence of diction, extravagance of imagination, and wild eccentricity of adventure, by which many of the German novels are distinguished; and we fear, also, that its tendency is unfavourable to the cause of religion and virtue.'

1797: 29   [BRANDON, Isaac].
FRAGMENTS: IN THE MANNER OF STERNE.

> London: Printed for the Author: and sold by Debrett, Piccadilly; and Murray & High-
> ley, Fleet Street, 1797.
> 139p. 8vo. 6s boards (CR, MR).
> CR n.s. 23: 353–6 (July 1798); MR n.s. 24: 271–4 (Nov 1797); AF II: 457.
> BL N.2064(2); EM 2069: 4; ESTC t040145 (BI C; NA CSmH, ICN, MH-H, NjP, TxU
> &c.).

Notes. Illustrations.

Further edns: London, 1798, EM 6665: 24, ESTC t040146; Regensburg, 1800, ESTC n031691; Leipzig, 1800, ESTC n003313. Extracts from *Fragments*, 'Anna, a Fragment', published in 6 magazines between 1797 and 1815, RM 109. French trans. Paris, 1800 (*Fragmens à la manière de Sterne*) (BGR); German trans. Leipzig, 1800 (*Fragmente in Sternes Manier*) (RS).

CR: 'Among the many attempts in imitation of Sterne, these fragments have as great a resemblance to the original as any that we have yet seen' (p. 353).

MR [Ralph Griffiths]: 'The benevolent sentimentality, the exquisite pathos, the happy abruptness of transition, and the peculiar felicity of expression, which gave to the *whimsical romances* of Sterne such a pleasing air of originality, are in a great measure caught by his present imitator, who, to the best of our recollection, after the lapse of so many years, approaches nearer to his prototype than any of that admired writer's former copyists' (p. 271).

BRISCOE, Sophia
See 1797: 11

1797: 30   BURTON, Mrs
LAURA, OR THE ORPHAN. A NOVEL, IN TWO VOLUMES. BY MRS. BURTON, AUTHOR OF THE FUGITIVE, AN ARTLESS TALE.

> London: Printed for W. J. and J. Richardson, Royal Exchange, 1797.
> I viii, 278p; II vi, 302p. 12mo. 6s sewed (CR), 7s boards (SJC).
> CR n.s. 23: 234 (June 1798); AF II: 561.
> CtY-BR Im B953.797L; ESTC n063460.

Notes. Table of contents 1, v–viii, followed by 5-pp. list of subscribers. Table of contents 2, v–vi. 2 pp. advs. end vol. 1.
The Fugitive, an Artless Tale 1795: 16.
Adv. SJC 13–15 Mar 1798.
French trans. Paris, 1799 (*Laure, ou la grotte du père Philippe*) (BGR).
> CR: 'A rapid succession of improbabilities.'

1797: 31   [C—, Lady Mary].
ROSE CECIL. A NOVEL. IN THREE VOLUMES.

> London: Printed for William Lane, at the Minerva-Press, Leadenhall-Street, 1797.
> I 295p; II 343p; III 348p. 12mo. 10s 6d (CR).
> CR n.s. 25: 234 (1799); AF II: 3872.
> BL N.2356; CME 3-628-45163-9; EMf; ESTC t144408 (NA CLU-S/C, CtY, MH-H, NjP &c.; EA COR).

Notes. Blakey: 'Attributed by a Minerva Library Catalogue of 1814 to Lady Mary C—' (p. 182).
On the page following the t.p. are quoted the critic-defying 1st 8 lines of Pope's *Essay on Criticism*.
> CR: '"When an old bachelor marries a young woman," says Sir Peter Teazle, "what is he to expect?"—Precisely what he will find in these volumes—that she will love a young man better, and break her husband's heart as soon as possible. Such is the morality of this novel; and we therefore enter our protest against it.'

1797: 32   [CARVER, Mrs].
ELIZABETH. A NOVEL. IN THREE VOLUMES.

> London: Printed for William Lane, at the Minerva-Press, Leadenhall-Street, 1797.
> I ii, 192p; II 208p; III 192p. 8vo. 9s sewed (SJC, Min).
> Corvey; CME 3-628-45052-7; EM 1102: 8; ESTC n006214 (NA MH-H, CSdS, PU).

Notes. Blakey: 'Attributed to Mrs Carver in a Minerva Library Catalogue of 1814' (p. 181).
Adv., 'Preparing for the Press', SJC 5–7 Apr 1796; adv. SJC 5–7 June 1798.

1797: 33 [CARVER, Mrs].
THE HORRORS OF OAKENDALE ABBEY. BY THE AUTHOR OF ELIZA-BETH.

London: Printed for William Lane, at the Minerva-Press, Leadenhall-Street, 1797.
172p. 8vo. 4s 6d sewed (Min).
PU Singer-Mend. PR4452.C58.H6.1797; ESTC n001861.

Notes. Blakey: 'Attributed to Mrs. Carver in a Minerva Library catalogue of 1814' (p. 181).
Elizabeth 1797: 32.
Further edns: New York, 1799, ESTC w012785; Frankford, PA, 1812 (WC).

1797: 34 CHARLTON, Mary.
ANDRONICA, OR THE FUGITIVE BRIDE, A NOVEL, IN TWO VOL-UMES. BY MARY CHARLTON.

London: Printed for William Lane, at the Minerva-Press, Leadenhall-Street, 1797.
I 239p; II 271p. 12mo. 6s sewed (CR, adv.), 7s sewed (Min).
CR n.s. 21: 117 (Sept 1797); AF II: 669.
Corvey; CME 3-628-45011-X; ESTC t200844.

Notes. Frontispiece. 1 p. advs. end vol. 1.
Adv. end vol. 2 of *Court Intrigue* (1799: 44).
French trans. Paris, 1799 (*Andronica, ou l'épouse fugitive*) (BN).

CR: 'The incidents of this novel are pretendedly derived from a part of the early history of England, Greece, and France, but without even such an adherence to fact as to entitle it to the name of a historical romance. It approaches, however, nearer to the construction of the old romance, than almost any of those which are now called by that name. The events, without being indebted to supernatural aid, are sufficiently surprising to catch the attention of the reader; and the language is neat and appropriate, without falling into unnatural and extravagant expression. Many of the situations are affecting, and the moral tendency unexceptionable.'

1797: 35 DIDEROT, [Denis].
JAMES THE FATALIST AND HIS MASTER. TRANSLATED FROM THE FRENCH OF DIDEROT. IN THREE VOLUMES.

London: Printed for G. G. and J. Robinson, Pater-Noster-Row, 1797.
I xxiii, 283p; II 286p; III 248p. 8vo [MR has 12mo]. 10s 6d boards (CR), 12s sewed (MR).
CR n.s. 20: 433–45 (Aug 1797); MR n.s. 23: 350 (July 1797); AF II: 1094.
BL 012550.h.10; EM 65: 1; ESTC t138418 (BI O; NA DLC, IU, MH-H, PU &c.).

Notes. Trans. of *Jacques le fataliste et son maître* (Paris, 1796).
'To the Memory of Diderot' i–xxiii; pagination continuous Roman-Arabic.
Adv., with *The Nun* [1797: 36], 'Next Week will be published', SJC 31 Jan–2 Feb 1797; 'These

Posthumous Works of the celebrated Diderot, were presented to the National Institute of France, by Prince Henry of Prussia, and have excited the greatest interest upon the Continent.' Extracts from different trans. published in *Belle Assemblée* and *Monthly Panorama*, 1810, RM 1058.

CR: '. . . it is easy to see that in the present *jeu d'esprit* he has had Tristram Shandy in view. There is also somewhat of the spirit of Voltaire's romances discernible in this; but, after all, the body of the work seems to be made up of anecdotes which were current in the polite circles at Paris; and we suspect that under feigned names some actual facts are narrated. In this view the publication will afford entertainment, and probably satisfaction, to many readers, as exhibiting a very lively picture of that general corruption of principle, and horrid dissoluteness of conduct, which pervaded all the higher classes of society under the old despotism of France' (pp. 433–4).

MR [William Taylor] mentions previous reviews in n.s. 13, pp. 518–19 [rev. of Dutch trans.] and n.s. 21, pp. 578–9 [of French original] and adds brief comments: '. . . the translation is executed with great vivacity and propriety, and is far superior to most of those handicraft compositions, in which foreign wares are usually retailed to a British public. This work is, on many accounts, an excellent *study* for those who write books of fancy.'

1797: 36   DIDEROT, [Denis].
THE NUN. BY DIDEROT. TRANSLATED FROM THE FRENCH.
> London: Printed for G. G. and J. Robinson, Paternoster-Row, 1797.
> I 263p; II 246p. 8vo [MR has 12mo]. 8s boards (CR, MR).
> CR n.s. 19: 420–4 (Apr 1797); MR n.s. 23: 348–50 (July 1797); AF II: 1096.
> BL N.2208; EM 2071: 1; ESTC t073512 (NA CtY-BR, ViU; EA COR).

Notes. Trans. of *La Religieuse* (Paris, 1797).
Adv., with *James the Fatalist* [1797: 35], 'Next Week will be published', SJC 31 Jan–2 Feb 1797; 'These Posthumous Works of the celebrated Diderot, were presented to the National Institute of France, by Prince Henry of Prussia, and have excited the greatest interest upon the Continent.'
Further edns: Dublin, 1797 (Printed by Brett Smith, 1 vol., 12mo), EM 5: 6, ESTC t138419.

CR: 'The publication of this work in France may probably be seasonable, since, as the spirit of fanaticism is certainly not quite extinct, it will serve to reconcile the minds of some readers to the abolition of the religious orders, who might still have regarded it as a kind of sacrilege; and as we are convinced that no ordinance or institution can be more hostile to true religion, or more inconsistent with justice and liberty, than the various forms of monkery, we cannot but approve the object of the publication. We wish the second volume had been written less in the spirit of a Frenchman, and that more regard had been paid by the author to the delicacy of his readers' (pp. 423–4).

MR [William Taylor]: 'This original and impressive novel will probably have a great effect in rendering it disreputable for catholic parents to immure their children in convents' (p. 350).

1797: 37   [D'ISRAELI, Isaac].
VAURIEN: OR, SKETCHES OF THE TIMES: EXHIBITING VIEWS OF THE PHILOSOPHIES, RELIGIONS, POLITICS, LITERATURE, AND MANNERS OF THE AGE. IN TWO VOLUMES.

London: Printed for T. Cadell, junior, and W. Davies, (Successors to Mr. Cadell) in the
  Strand; and J. Murray and S. Highley, No. 32, Fleet-Street, 1797.
I xxiii, 300p; II 323p. 12mo. 8s sewed (CR, SJC).
CR 21: 293–300 (Nov 1797); AF II: 1106.
C 7720.d.1043-; EM 633: 9; ESTC t077691 (BI BL, E, O &c.; NA CSmH, ICN, MH-H,
  PU &c.).

Notes. Table of contents 1, iii–iv; preface v–xix; prefatory advertisement xx–xxiii.
In vol. 2 leaf P1 is misplaced so that pp. 313–14 come between p. 322 and p. 323.
Adv. SJC 16–18 Feb 1797.

  CR: 'There is no regular story that serves to bind the whole together. . . . We remark, however, with pleasure, that we have received much amusement and some instruction from the
perusal of these volumes. The author, in his sketches, shows that he has observed men and
manners with much critical acumen. His style is lively, sportive, and often sarcastically
severe. Some of the characters are drawn with a masterly hand; and his observations on the
wild notions of modern philosophers not only appear to us, for the most part, extremely just,
but are given with pointed neatness and effect' (p. 293).

1797: 38   DOUGLAS, James.
THE HISTORY OF JULIA D'HAUMONT: OR THE EVENTFUL CON-
NECTION OF THE HOUSE OF MONTMELIAN WITH THAT OF
D'HAUMONT. BY THE REV. JAMES DOUGLAS, OF CHIDDINGFORD,
SUSSEX.

London: Printed and sold by G. Cawthorn, British Library, 132, Strand, 1797.
I 203p; II 192p. 12mo.
BL 12613.aaa.9; EM 160: 5; ESTC t065080 (NA CLU-S/C).
Notes. In vol. 2 text of novel starts on p. 5.

1797: 39   FOX, [Joseph].
SANTA-MARIA; OR, THE MYSTERIOUS PREGNANCY. A ROMANCE.
IN THREE VOLUMES. BY I. FOX.

London: Printed for G. Kearsley, No. 46, Fleet-Street, 1797.
I xvi, 264p; II 231p; III 307p. 12mo. 10s 6d sewed (MR, GEP), Half a guinea (SJC).
CR n.s. 22: 113 (Jan 1798); MR n.s. 23: 210–11 (June 1797); AF II: 1497.
BL 12611.f.20; CME 3-628-45073-X; EM 166: 3; ESTC t057806 (BI O; NA CLU-S/C,
  CtY-BR, ViU &c.; EA COR).

Notes. Dedicatory epistle to the Duke of Marlborough iii–vi; prefatory epistle (to the reader)
vii–xvi.
Adv. SJC 18–20 Apr 1797; adv. GEP 6–9 Apr 1799.
2 French trans. Paris, 1800 (*Santa Maria, ou la Grossesse Mystérieuse* and *Agathina ou la
Grossesse*) (BGR).

  CR: 'Our modern romance-writers appear to be extremely desirous of ascertaining how
far it is possible to carry extravagance and absurdity; and the experiment of this author,
though not absolutely decisive, approaches as nearly to decision as most of the attempts
which we have witnessed.'
  MR [Arthur Aikin]: 'A very poor and evident imitation of the style and character of

Mrs Radcliffe's romances. Here are wonders that excite no surprise; horrors which are destitute of interest; and a pompous phraseology that only betrays the barrenness of the sentiments' (pp. 210–11).

GABRIELLI
See MEEKE, Mary

1797: 40 [?GONZALEZ, Esteban].
THE HISTORY OF VANILLO GONZALES, SURNAMED THE MERRY BACHELOR. IN TWO VOLUMES. FROM THE FRENCH OF ALAIN-RENÉ LE SAGE, AUTHOR OF THE CELEBRATED NOVELS OF "GIL BLAS", AND "THE DEVIL ON CRUTCHES."

London: Printed for G. G. J. and J. Robinson, Pater-Noster-Row, 1797.
I 354p; II 383p. 12mo. 9s boards (CR), 9s sewed (MR), 7s sewed, 8s bound (GEP), 8s sewed (SJC).
CR n.s. 22: 302–6 (Mar 1798); MR n.s. 24: 103 (Sept 1797); AF II: 2487.
C Rom.2.S2; EM 2607: 5; ESTC t120779 (BI BL, O; NA CLU, NjP, TxU &c.).

Notes. Trans. of Alain-René Le Sage's *Histoire d'Estanville Gonzalez, surnommé le garçon de bonne humeur* (Paris, 1734), itself a French translation of *Vida y hechos de Estebanillo Gonzalez* (Amberes, 1646) by Esteban González but which is also sometimes attributed to Luis Vélez de Guevara (ESTC).
7-pp. preface (unn.).
Gil Blas 1st trans. into English 1716; *Le Diable Boiteux: or the Devil upon Two Sticks* 1st trans. 1708.
Adv., 'Next Week will be published', SJC 15–17 June 1797; adv. GEP 29–31 Mar 1798 and SJC 27–29 Mar 1798.
Extracts from *The History of Vanillo Gonzales* published in *Lady's Magazine*, 1797–98, RM 1172.
CR: '... in Vanillo we are disgusted with low caricature, and with a patchwork of incidents, to which the title of "a history" is scarcely applicable. We discover this, indeed, without advancing beyond a few pages of the first volume . . .' (p. 303). 'Who is there that is not reminded of something better by the perusal of these preposterous adventures? Yet we are far from denying that there are parts of the work which have an undoubted claim to originality; and that pedantry, avarice, and empiricism, as the translator insists, are very successfully ridiculed in the characters of the licentiate Salablanca, the old knight, Dr Arriscador, and his coadjutor Potoschi' (p. 306).
MR [William Taylor]: 'In the general turn of character and business, this novel very strongly resembles Gil Blas; and it too frequently throws the interest on the side of roguery, fraud, and debauch, to be very favourable to morality: but it is full of incident, and of entertaining adventures, and seems to be not ill translated.'

1797: 41 GUNNING, [Elizabeth].
THE ORPHANS OF SNOWDON. A NOVEL. BY MISS GUNNING. IN THREE VOLUMES.

London: Printed for H. Lowndes, No. 77, Fleet Street, 1797.
I 240p; II 239p; III 241p. 12mo. 10s 6d boards (CR), 10s 6d sewed (SJC).

CR n.s. 21: 473–4 (Dec 1797).

BL C.124.g.11; EM 4790: 6; ESTC t124617 (NA KyU).

Notes. Frontispiece vol. 1. 2 pp. advs. end vol. 3.

Adv., 'In the Press, and speedily will be published', SJC 9–11 Mar 1797; adv. as published, 'Embellished with an elegant Frontispiece', SJC 20–22 June 1797.

   CR: 'The incidents of this tale are not remarkable for novelty, for variety, or for the interest which they excite. The story, jejune in itself, is not much improved by the mode of recital: affectation and frivolity alternately prevail; and, though some *traits* of nature and *pathos* are observable, the volumes contain little that can please or instruct' (p. 474).

1797: 42   GUNNING, [Susannah].
LOVE AT FIRST SIGHT. A NOVEL. FROM THE FRENCH. WITH ALTER-ATIONS AND ADDITIONS. BY MRS. GUNNING. IN FIVE VOLUMES.

   London: Printed for H. Lowndes, Fleet-Street, 1797.
   I 224p; II 243p; III 206p; IV 212p; V 211p.12mo. 15s boards (CR), 15s sewed (SJC).
   CR n.s. 21: 42–7 (Sept 1797); AF II: 1763.
   Corvey; CME 3-628-45043-8; EMf; ESTC t117983 (BI BL; NA DLC, MH-H).

Notes. 1 p. advs. end vol. 5. Epistolary.

Adv., 'In the Press, and speedily will be published', SJC 9–11 Feb 1797; adv. as published SJC 9–11 Mar 1797.

   CR complains at length that '. . . the good sense of our fair country-women should be perverted, their natural sensibility polluted, and their taste corrupted, by the trash that issues from the press in the form of novels, tales, and romances' (p. 43) but acknowledges that Gunning's novel has some good points: 'some just descriptions of French manners before the revolution, some sketches of characters, which we think natural and nicely discriminated, and a few delineations of passion that are interesting and not common' (p. 43).

1797: 43   HARE, M.
THE BASTILE, OR, MANLY SENSIBILITY. A NOVEL, IN TWO VOLUMES. BY M. HARE.

   Cork: Printed by James Haly, 1797.
   I viii, 247p; II 245p. 12mo.
   MH-H 18491.3.60; ESTC n043555.

Notes. Dedication to Countess dé Civrac 1, v–vi, signed M. Hare; preface vii–viii, indicating that subscribers had been collected but so few that a list was unwarranted.

1797: 44   [HERVEY, Elizabeth].
THE CHURCH OF ST. SIFFRID. IN FOUR VOLUMES.

   London: Printed for G. G. and J. Robinson, Paternoster-Row, 1797.
   I 267p; II 245p; III 260p; IV 351p. 12mo. 14s boards (MR), 14s sewed (CR, SJC, GEP).
   CR n.s. 21: 116–17 (Sept 1797); MR n.s. 24: 202–3 (Oct 1797); AF II: 1926.
   BL C.123.fff.19; CME 3-628-45019-5; EM 5842: 1; ESTC t124771 (NA CSmH, IU, PU, ViU &c.; EA COR).

Notes. Adv., 'Next Week will be published', SJC 15–17 June 1797.

Adv. GEP 29–31 Mar 1798.
Further edn: Dublin, 1798 (Printed for William Porter, and Nicholas Kelly, 2 vols., 12mo), EM 8933: 4, ESTC t118816. French trans. Paris, 1800 (*L'Eglise de Saint-Siffrid*) (BGR); German trans. Leipzig, 1801–02 (*Die heilige Sanct-Siegfriedskirche*) (RS).

CR: 'This novel is certainly superior to the majority of flimsy publications of similar description, which grace the shelves of our circulating libraries. The style is natural and flowing. The characters are in general well drawn, though none of them are remarkable for originality. Some exceptions may be taken to the plot, which is rather too complicated. . . . the author has certainly succeeded in exciting a good deal of interest, which, however, would have been still more considerable, had the work been compressed into a narrower compass.'

MR [William Smyth]: 'This performance is well written; the plot sufficiently abounds in incident; the story is told with perspicuity and consistency; and the moral sentiments are useful and unexceptionable. . . . The characters are well discriminated and strongly contrasted. . . . We must observe, however, that there is not much novelty of situation nor of character in this tale; and we think that Ethelreda's imprisonment in the Castle of St Siffrid, though in her case voluntary, reminds us too closely of the Mysteries of Udolpho [1794: 47]; while Carloville bears too strong a resemblance to Montano: yet, on the whole, we have been both entertained and interested in the perusal of this novel.'

1797: 45   HOLCROFT, Thomas.
THE ADVENTURES OF HUGH TREVOR. BY THOMAS HOLCROFT.

> [Vols. 4, 5, 6] London: Printed for G. G. and J. Robinson, Pater-Noster-Row; and Shepperson and Reynolds, no. 137, Oxford-Street, 1797.
>
> IV 214p; V 216p; VI 204p. 12mo. 10s 6d boards (CR), 10s 6d sewed (MR, SJC).
>
> CR n.s. 21: 189–95 (Oct 1797); MR n.s. 23: 281–7 (July 1797); AF II: 1997.
>
> C 5727.d.79.48-50; EM 206: 4; ESTC t066947 (BI BL; NA CaAEU, CSmH, CtY-BR, MH-H &c.; EA TaLn).

Notes. Vols. 1–3 1794: 29.
Adv., 'On Thursday, the 25th Instant, will be published . . . The Three concluding Volumes', SJC 13–16 May 1797.
Further edns: Dublin, 1795–98 (Printed for H. Colbert, 4 vols., 12mo), ESTC n029516; London, 1801 (WC). French trans. Paris, 1798 (*Les Aventures de Hugues Trévor*) (BGR).
According to CR, these volumes have 'the same beauties and the same faults' as the earlier volumes (p. 189).

MR [William Enfield]: 'The general characters of the performance are still so much the same, that we may properly refer our readers to our account of the first three volumes . . .' (p. 281). '. . . we find in these volumes less variety of interesting occurrences than in the former, yet we would not be understood to insinuate that the author's inventive powers have deserted him: the reader will meet with several incidents, in the course of the narrative, which will forcibly strike his imagination, and tenderly touch his feelings' (p. 283).

1797: 46   HOWELL, [Ann].
THE SPOILED CHILD. A NOVEL, BY MRS. HOWELL, AUTHOR OF GEORGINA, ANZOLETTA ZADOSKI, &C.

> London: Printed for William Lane, at the Minerva Press, Leadenhall-Street, 1797.
>
> I 208p; II 195p. 12mo. 7s (CR), 6s sewed (adv., Min).

CR n.s. 25: 233 (Feb 1799); AF II: 2087.

CaAEU PR 4809.H194.S76 1797; ESTC n046287.

Notes. In vol. 2 p. 69 misnumbered 9.

Georgina 1796: 55; *Anzoletta Zadoski* 1796: 54.

Adv., 'Speedily will be published', SJC 27–29 Apr 1797.

Adv. end vol. 2 of *Court Intrigue* (1799: 44).

CR: 'The injurious tendency of a blind parental fondness, and the fatal consequences of dissipation, are well displayed in this novel: the story is interesting, and the language in which it is conveyed preserves a respectable mediocrity: of the characters it cannot be said that they are drawn with nice discrimination; but we may allow that they faithfully represent many originals, which are to be found in the circles of real life.'

1797: 47　HUGILL, [Martha].

ISIDORA OF GALLICIA: A NOVEL. IN TWO VOLUMES. BY MRS. HUGILL, AUTHOR OF COUNTESS OF HENNIBON, JULIA ORME-STON, THE PRINCE OF LEON, &C. &C.

London: Printed for Lee and Hurst, Paternoster Row, 1797/98.

I viii, 207p; II 196p. 12mo. 6s sewed (CR), 6s (adv.).

CR n.s. 22: 478 (Apr 1798); AF II: 2109.

ViU *PZ2.H37Is 1797; ESTC n016836 (NA CtY-BR).

Notes. Preface v–viii, unsigned but with address: No. 36, Mary-le-bone-street, Golden-square. 4-pp. list of subscribers.

Countess of Hennebon 1789: 47; *Julia Ormeston* 1793: 22; *The Prince of Leon* 1794: 31.

Adv. end vol. 2 of *Emily Dundorne* (1799: 93).

French trans. Paris, 1798 (*Le Château de Gallice*) (BGR); German trans. Erfurt, 1799 (*Albertine von Gallicien*) (RS).

CR: 'The first volume of this novel pleased us. The story does not exceed the bounds of probability, and yet keeps the attention alive; but, when we came to the perusal of the second, we were not inclined to continue our commendation. Subterranean passages, damp vaults, murders, and a variety of horrors, form the greater part of its contents. The incidents also are so confused, and the story so complicated, that it is difficult to trace the plot, or unravel the perplexity.... However, though we cannot give the present work the highest praise, we are willing to allow it some merit.'

1797: 48　[JACSON, Frances].

DISOBEDIENCE. A NOVEL. IN FOUR VOLUMES. BY THE AUTHOR OF PLAIN SENSE.

London: Printed for William Lane, at the Minerva-Press, Leadenhall-Street, 1797.

I 266p; II 220p; III 247p; IV 266p. 12mo. 14s sewed (CR, SJC).

CR n.s. 25: 232–3 (1799); AF II: 2234.

BL 1607/2084; CME 3-628-45031-4; EM 6647: 7; ESTC t105955 (BI MRu; NA CSmH, CtY, ICN, IU, MH–H, NjP, ViU &c.; EA COR, ZAP).

Notes. ESTC gives author as Alethea Lewis. On authorship see Joan Percy's article on Jacson in the *British Library Journal* vol. 23: 1 (Spring 1997) pp. 81–97.

2 pp. advs. end vol. 1 and 1 p. advs. end vol. 3 (ICN copy also has 4 pp. advs. end vol. 2).

Plain Sense 1795: 26.
Adv. SJC 27–29 Apr 1797.
Adv. end vol. 2 of *Court Intrigue* (1799: 44).

CR: 'The curiosity of the reader of novels will naturally expect considerable gratification from any production by the author of "Plain Sense." In the perusal of these volumes, that curiosity will not be disappointed; but we think it will not be so fully gratified as in the former instance. The story is not equally interesting; and it is in some places rendered tedious by the political allusions and rhapsodical declamations in favour of emigration to America.'

JENKS, Jacquetta Agneta Mariana
See BECKFORD, William

1797: 49   KELLY, Isabella.
JOSCELINA: OR, THE REWARDS OF BENEVOLENCE. A NOVEL. DEDICATED, BY PERMISSION, TO HER ROYAL HIGHNESS THE DUCHESS OF YORK. BY ISABELLA KELLY, AUTHOR OF MADELINE ABBEY, ST. ASAPH, &C. &C. IN TWO VOLUMES.

London: Printed for the Author; And Sold by T. N. Longman, Paternoster-Row, 1797.
I vii, 207p; II 198p. 12mo. 6s sewed (CR), 7s sewed (MR, adv.), 7s boards (SJC).
CR n.s. 21: 116 (Sept 1797); MR n.s. 24: 339–41 (Nov 1797); AF II: 2354.
Corvey; CME 3-628-45097-7; ESTC n018419 (BI O; NA InU-Li, ViU).

Notes. 3-pp. dedication to H.R.H. the Duchess of York. 2 pp. advs. end vol. 2.
Madeline 1794: 35; *The Abbey of St Asaph* 1795: 27.
Adv. SJC 3–6 June 1797. 750 copies printed May 1797 (Strahan 17 f. 97).
Adv. end vol. 1 of *Eva* (1799: 54).
Further edn: London, 1798, ESTC t225844 [ESTC notes probability that this Lane edn. was a reissue of the 1797 Longman edn. with cancel title-pages]. French trans. Hamburg and Brunswick, 1799, ESTC t149769.

CR: 'This novel is not ill adapted to the taste of those whose imaginations are familiarised to scenes of horror.'

MR [James Bannister]: 'The performance before us, which is styled a novel, contains many of those wild and extravagant incidents that are peculiar to romance. The story is improbable, and affords little of that instruction which novels ought to convey to the young and inexperienced, for the regulation of their conduct in life.—The writer appears not to have given herself much concern about the preservation of the truth and consistency of her characters' (p. 339). 'The language of the work, though impassioned, and sometimes rising above the style of ordinary novels, is incorrect' (p. 341).

1797: 50   [LAFONTAINE, August Heinrich Julius]; [WOODBRIDGE, Mr (*trans.*)].
CLARA DUPLESSIS, AND CLAIRANT: THE HISTORY OF A FAMILY OF FRENCH EMIGRANTS. TRANSLATED FROM THE GERMAN. IN THREE VOLUMES.

London: Printed for T. N. Longman, Paternoster-row, 1797.
I 268p; II 279p; III 277p. 12mo. 10s 6d sewed (CR), 10s 6d boards (MR, SJC).

CR n.s. 21: 355–6 (Nov 1797); MR n.s. 27: 94 (Sept 1798); AF II: 2441.

C 7746.d.75-; EMf; ESTC t166559 (BI BL; NA CLU-S/C, ViU).

Notes. Trans. of *Klara du Plessis und Klairant* (Berlin, 1794), possibly via the French, despite the title. French trans. Paris, 1797 (*Claire Duplessis et Clairant*) (BGR).

6 pp. advs. end vol. 3. 750 copies printed by Strahan, July 1797 (Strahan 17 f. 97); Woodbridge paid £21 (20 gns.) for 'translating' and 9s. spent on the 'copy to print from' (LA). Not wholly epistolary, but much of the text consists of letters.

Adv. SJC 6–8 June 1797; adv. quotes from MR's comments on German original. Adv. end vol. 3 of *A Tale of the Times* (1799: 95).

CR: 'This novel is said to have acquired great fame on the continent, and not undeservedly, merely considered as a work of a rich and luxuriant imagination. Measured, however, by the more solid standard of English thought, it will probably have fewer admirers' (p. 355).

MR [William Taylor] refers to review of original in n.s. 24 p. 565: '. . . of which these three volumes contain a flowing and sufficiently correct translation, but made apparently through the medium of the French version. The story preserves its nature and its interest.'

1797: 51   LEE, Harriet and Sophia.
CANTERBURY TALES FOR THE YEAR 1797. BY HARRIET LEE.
CANTERBURY TALES. VOLUME THE SECOND. BY SOPHIA LEE.
CANTERBURY TALES. VOLUME THE THIRD. BY SOPHIA AND HAR-
RIET LEE.

London: Printed for G. G. and J. Robinson, Paternoster-Row, 1797 [vol. 1].

London: Printed for G. G. J. and J. Robinson, Paternoster-Row, 1798 [vol. 2].

London: Printed for G. G. and J. Robinson, Paternoster-Row, 1799 [vol. 3].

I xxiii, 396p; II 564p; III 522p. 8vo. vol. 1 6s boards (CR, MR); vol. 2 7s boards (CR, MR); vol. 3 7s boards (CR, MR).

Vol. 1 CR n.s. 22: 170–3 (Feb 1798), MR n.s. 25: 469–70 (Apr 1798), AF II: 2491; vol. 2 CR n.s. 23: 204–9 (June 1798), MR n.s. 27: 416–19 (Dec 1798), AF II: 2500; vol. 3 CR n.s. 26: 186–93 (June 1799), MR n.s. 30: 236–7 (Oct 1799), AF II: 2506.

C S727.c.79.18–20; CME 3–628–48017–5; EM 6124: 4; ESTC t142428 (BI BL, O, TAU; NA CSmH, CtY, MH-H, NjP, PU, TxU, ViU &c.; EA GOT, COR [vol. 1 only], ZAU [vol. 1 only], TaLN [vol. 2 only]).

Notes. Vol. 1 introduction (iii–xxiii) sets the scene, like a much-shortened version of Chaucer's General Prologue. This vol. contains the Traveller's Tale, the Poet's Tale, the Frenchman's Tale, and the Old Woman's Tale. Vol. 2 contains the Young Lady's Tale. Vol. 3 contains the Officer's Tale and the Clergyman's Tale.

Vol. 4 1801: 42; vol. 5 1805: 49.

Vol. 2 adv., 'In the Press, And on Saturday, the 28th instant, will be published', GEP 24–26 Apr 1798.

Vol. 3 adv., 'This Month will be published', MP 3 May 1799; adv. as published MP 4 June 1799.

Further edns: London, 1799–1800, EM 5355: 1, ESTC t142587; London, 1803–05 (WC); London, 1826 (WC); London, 1832 (WC); WC has 2 further entries between 1800 and 1850; NSTC lists edns. in 1801, 1804, 1799/1805, 1831, 1832, 1833, 1837, and 1842. Extract from vol. 3 of *The Canterbury Tales*, 'The Denouement', published in 5 magazines, 1799, RM 300. German trans. Leipzig, 1798–99 (*Erzählungen aus Canterbury*) (Price).

CR n.s. 22: 'We are happy to announce a work, which, while it possesses the quickness of narration, and the vivacity of dialogue, is not disgraced by the profligate principles of what the French writer [Marmontel], or rather his English translator, has thought proper to call his *moral* tales' (p. 171). 'We expect the second volume with impatience, as we have seldom been able to notice any work with more unqualified approbation' (p. 173).

MR n.s. 25 [William Smyth]: 'We have perused with pleasure the tales of this lively and ingenious writer, and we recommend them to our young readers as both instructive and entertaining' (p. 469).

CR n.s. 23: 'We have pointed out the faults of this tale with some minuteness, because any production of miss Lee merits attention. We cannot think the present performance equal to her Recess; but it is certainly the offspring of genius' (p. 209).

MR n.s. 27 [James Bannister]: 'The story of the two Emilys, occupying the whole of this volume, abounds with a great variety of incidents, and with many striking and affecting scenes, and is not without a considerable mixture of that distress and horror which are congenial to the present fashionable taste. The texture of the fable, however, is wild and romantic; little attention is paid to probability; and although manners are well described, and many observations are interspersed which seem to evince a knowlege of the human heart, yet we cannot compliment Miss S. Lee on the truth and consistency of her characters' (p. 416).

CR n.s. 26: '[The *Canterbury Tales*] have amused and interested us; and we are only dissatisfied that they are limited to three volumes' (p. 193).

MR n.s. 30 [John Ferriar]: 'We have been greatly interested and gratified by the perusal of this additional volume, which is fully equal in merit to the former part of the work.'

1797: 52   LEE, {Margaret}.
CLARA LENNOX; OR, THE DISTRESSED WIDOW. A NOVEL. FOUNDED ON FACTS. INTERSPERSED WITH AN HISTORICAL DESCRIPTION OF THE ISLE OF MAN. BY MRS. LEE. DEDICATED, BY PERMISSION, TO H.R.H. THE DUCHESS OF YORK. IN TWO VOLUMES.

> London: Printed for the Authoress, by J. Adlard, no. 39, Duke-Street, West Smithfield;
>   And Sold by J. Parsons, no. 21, Paternoster-Row, 1797.
> I xii, 199p; II [228]p. 12mo. 6s sewed (CR), 7s (ME 1798).
> CR n.s. 23: 114–15 (May 1798); AF II: 2497.
> C 7720.d.174; EM 1925: 7; ESTC t072361 (BI BL; NA PU, TxHR).

Notes. List of subscribers [v]–[vi]; Dedication to H.R.H. the Duchess of York vii–viii, signed Margaret Lee; preface ix–xii, signed M. Lee. Last page of vol. 2 is misnumbered 218. Epistolary.
Further edn: London, 1797, ESTC n027119. French trans. Paris, 1798 (*Clara Lennox, ou la veuve infortunée*) (BGR).

> CR: '. . . it may be read with some advantage as well as with pleasure. But it contains none of those striking delineations of conduct or passion which show an intimate knowledge of the human mind; and the language is often vulgar and ungrammatical' (p. 115).

1797: 53   LEIGH, Sir Samuel Egerton.
MUNSTER ABBEY, A ROMANCE: INTERSPERSED WITH REFLECTIONS ON VIRTUE AND MORALITY: WRITTEN BY SIR SAMUEL EGERTON LEIGH: IN THREE VOLUMES.

Edinburgh: Printed by John Moir, Paterson's Court: for W. Creech, Cross, and S. Cheyne, George Street: for Hookham & Carpenter, New Bond Street, Vernor & Hood, Birchin Lane, London, 1797.

I xlvi, 195p; II 200p; III 195p. 12mo. 10s 6d sewed (CR).

CR n.s. 22: 237–8 (Feb 1798).

BL 12613.d.11; CME 3-628-45095-0; EM 202: 1; ESTC (BI O; NA CSmH, ICN, MH-H, PU &c.; EA COR).

Notes. Prefatory advertisement by the author's widow iii–iv. Dedication to the Duchess of Marlborough signed with the author's full name v–vi; preface vii–xii; list of subscribers xiii–xlvi. Text of novel starts on p. 25 in vol. 1 and p. 3 in vols. 2 and 3.

French trans. Paris, 1797 (*L'Abbaye de Munster*) (BGR).

CR: 'The fable of this piece is uninteresting, the language incorrect and inelegant; and, by endeavouring to put sentiment into the mouths of his characters on the most trifling occasions, the author often renders his work ridiculous' (p. 237).

LEPRINCE DE BEAUMONT, Jeanne-Marie; NEWMAN, S[arah] (trans.), **LETTERS OF MADAME DU MONTIER**. 1st trans. as *The History of a Young Lady of Distinction* (London, 1754), JR 245, AF I: 743.

LE SAGE, Alain René, **THE HISTORY OF VANILLO GONZALES**
See GONZALEZ, Esteban

1797: 54   M., P. S.
PARENTAL DUPLICITY; OR THE POWER OF ARTIFICE. A NOVEL IN THREE VOLUMES. BY P. S. M.

London: Printed for G. Kearsley, No. 46, Fleet-Street, 1797.

I 268p; II 257p; III 256p. 12mo. 10s 6d sewed (CR, MR).

CR n.s. 21: 472 (Dec 1797); MR n.s. 26: 106 (May 1798); AF II: 3213.

Corvey; CME 3-628-45139-6; xESTC.

Notes. 2 pp. advs. end vol. 2 and ½ p. adv. on p. 256 of vol. 3.

Adv. GEP 8–10 Feb 1798.

CR: '. . . this fable is not new. It is managed, however, with much skill, and produces a very lively interest in the fate of all the parties. The characters are drawn with consistency; and the incidents, though leading to a conclusion which the reader will foresee, are recounted in a manner which keeps up the attention throughout the whole.'

MR [James Bannister]: '. . . it is but justice to the author to observe that his characters, though not always delineated with the greatest strength or propriety, are such as may be found in fashionable life. . . . We think it a defect in the novel, that after all [Fitzallen's] nefarious deeds, justice does not overtake him. In other respects, the moral tendency of the work is unexceptionable; and it may afford amusement and some degree of instruction.'

1797: 55   MARSHALL, Edmund.
EDMUND AND ELEONORA: OR MEMOIRS OF THE HOUSE OF SUMMERFIELD & GRETTON. A NOVEL, IN TWO VOLUMES. BY THE REV. EDMUND MARSHALL, A.M.

London: Printed for John Stockdale, London; by W. Epps, Margate, 1797.
I viii, 365p; II ii, 375p. 8vo. 10s 6d boards (CR, MR).
CR n.s. 20: 117–18 (May 1797); MR n.s. 22: 349 (Mar 1797); AF II: 2723.
BL N.2377; EM 2472: 4; ESTC t090308 (NA CtY, ICN, NjP &c.).

Notes. Dedication in both vols. to 'the Independent Freeholders of the County of Kent' signed 'The Author' and dated from Charing, Kent, 1797. Introduction v–viii. Text of novel starts on p. 3 of vol. 2. 1–p. 'Postscript' is p. [376] of vol. 2.
Adv., 'In a few Days will be published', SJC 24–26 Jan 1797; adv. as published SJC 11–14 Feb 1797.
French trans. Paris, 1797 (*Edmond et Eléonora*) (BN).

CR: 'As a novel, these memoirs are perhaps *unique*: for they exhibit none of those dramatic vicissitudes, in which the principal characters in similar productions are generally made to play their parts;—on the contrary, with scarcely a single exception, every body is *so good*, and every circumstance turns out *so happily*, that the feelings and mind of the reader are not subjected to a single pang, or to a moment of suspense through the whole two volumes!—The work, however, is respectable in point of style, and for the precepts of moral and religious duty it uniformly inculcates' (p. 117).

MR [George Edward Griffiths]: These memoirs 'are characterized by the circumstance of their origin, for they appear to be the production of an amiable and benevolent clergyman, unacquainted with the artifices of a practised novel-writer, and little versed in the machinery of incident and the developement of plot.'

1797: 56 [MEEKE, Mary].
THE MYSTERIOUS WIFE. A NOVEL, IN FOUR VOLUMES. BY GABRIELLI.

London: Printed for William Lane, at the Minerva-Press, Leadenhall-Street, 1797.
I ii, 299p; II 280p; III 267p; IV 299p. 12mo. 12s sewed (CR), 14s sewed (Min).
CR n.s. 23: 232–3 (June 1798); AF II: 2809.
BL 12654.cc.42; CME 3-628-45085-3; EM 485: 1; ESTC t107119 (NA CaAEU, CtY, NjP; EA COR).

Notes. Dedication to Mrs. Arthur Young.
CR: 'They are written in a very entertaining manner; and although there are symptoms of a desire of prolonging the anxieties of the husband, merely to eke out four volumes, yet we question whether many of the ordinary readers of novels will complain of the length' (p. 233).

1797: 57 MEEKE, [Mary].
PALMIRA AND ERMANCE. A NOVEL. IN THREE VOLUMES. BY MRS. MEEKE, AUTHOR OF COUNT ST. BLANCARD.

London: Printed for William Lane, at the Minerva-Press, Leadenhall-Street, 1797.
I 248p; II 248p; III 255p. 12mo. 10s 6d sewed (CR, SJC).
CR n.s. 24: 236–7 (Oct 1798).
BL C.175.m.36; CME 3-628-45129-9; EMf; ESTC t127125 (EA COR).

Notes. Adv. SJC 19–21 Sept 1797; additional booksellers are Miller, Old Bond-street; Lloyd, Harley-street; Hodgson's, Wimpole-street; and Scatchard, Ave-Maria-lane.
Count St. Blancard 1795: 30.
German trans. Gotha, 1803 (*Palmira; eine englische Geschichte*) (RS).

CR: 'Innocent entertainment, without any fixed purpose of the moral kind, appears to be the object of this novel. The characters, principally those of France under the old government, are drawn with spirit. The dialogue is lively; and the incidents of the first and second volumes are interesting. . . . In the third volume, the story is unnecessarily spun out; but, upon the whole, this is one of the most amusing of the second-rate novels.'

1797: 58   [MOORE, George].
GRASVILLE ABBEY: A ROMANCE. IN THREE VOLUMES.

London: Printed for G. G. and J. Robinson, Pater Noster Row, 1797.
I 259p; II 262p; III 271p. 12mo. 10s 6d boards (MR), 10s 6d sewed (CR, SJC).
CR n.s. 21: 115–16 (Sept 1797); MR n.s. 25: 453 (Apr 1798); AF II: 2931.
ICN Rare PR 3605 M34G7; CME 3-628-45051-9; ESTC n047440 (EA COR, TALn [vol. 1 only]).

Notes. Originally published in the *Lady's Magazine* (preface refers to this); published there in 47 parts between 1793 and 1797 and published in part in *Sentimental and Masonic Magazine* 1793–97, RM 478.
2nd edn. adv. SJC 2–5 Sept 1797; 'First printed in the Lady's Magazine,and re-printed at the request of many Subscribers to that Work'; 2nd edn. adv. GEP 8–10 Nov 1798.
Further edns: Dublin, 1798 (Printed for P. Wogan, P. Byrne, G. Burnet, H. Colbert, and J. Rice, 2 vols., 12mo), ESTC n002356; Cork, 1798, ESTC n030851; Salem, Mass., 1799, ESTC w020412; London, 1832 (Summers). French trans. Paris, 1798 (*L'Abbaye de Grasville*) (Lévy); German trans. Prague, 1799 (*Die Abtey von Grasville*) (EAG). Facs: GNII.
CR: 'Grasville Abbey is by no means the most contemptible of the romances which have lately fallen in our way; and perhaps it will be thought much superior to many of them. The story is uninterrupted by digressions, and the interest it creates is powerful. The situations, likewise, have the merit of being new and striking. Excepting that there is an abbey furnished with caverns, ghosts, and dead bodies, here is no servile imitation of former works of this kind; and, allowance being made for a foundation of the mysterious sort, probability will not appear to be very grossly violated.'
MR [William Smyth]: 'The conduct of this story displays considerable talents for narration, and is rendered respectable by its general tenor and tendency to discourage immorality. . . . As the author of Grasville Abbey appears to be possessed of talents, we cannot excuse the palpable imitation of "the Romance of the Forest," [1791: 58] and "the Mysteries of Udolpho," [1794: 47] which so often occur in these volumes.'

1797: 59   MOSER, Joseph.
MORAL TALES: CONSISTING OF THE RECONCILIATION, A SKETCH OF THE BELVOIR FAMILY, A FAIRY TALE IN THE MODERN STILE. CLEMENTIA AND MALITIA, A FAIRY TALE IN THE ANCIENT STILE. CHARLES AND MARIA, A NOVEL, FOUNDED ON FACT. THE BEST HEART IN THE WORLD, A NOVEL, THE OFFSPRING OF FANCY. BY JOSEPH MOSER, ESQ. AUTHOR OF THE TURKISH TALES, AND HERMIT OF CAUCASUS, &C. &C. IN TWO VOLUMES.

London: Printed for F. and C. Rivington, No. 62, St. Paul's Church-Yard; and J. Hatchard, no. 173, Piccadilly, 1797.

I vi, 237p; II 274p. 12mo. 7s boards (CR), 7s sewed (MR, SJC).

CR n.s. 23: 115 (May 1798); MR n.s. 25: 346–7 (Mar 1798); AF II: 2984.

BL 838.b.34; EM 2389: 1; ESTC t083803 (BI D; NA CtY-BR).

Notes. Preface 1, iii–vi. Pagination continuous Roman-Arabic. Contents vol. 1: 'The Reconciliation, a Fairy Tale' pp. 9–237. Contents vol. 2: 'Clementia and Malitia, a Fairy Tale in the Ancient Stile' pp. 3–47; 'Charles and Maria, or the Unfortunate Attachment; a Novel founded on Fact' pp. 51–230; 'The Best Heart in the World, a Novel, the Offspring of Fancy' pp. 233–74. 2 pp. advs. end vol. 2.

Adv., 'To-morrow will be published', SJC 19–21 Dec 1797.

Turkish Tales 1794: 39; *Hermit of Caucasus* 1796: 68.

CR: 'In the modern fairy tale, the introduction of the fairy is useless. Mr. Moser mentions "fays, fairies, and elves," as different species of airy beings. This is strange ignorance for one who makes use of their agency.'

MR [Arthur Aikin]: 'These pieces are of various merit. The first two are unquestionably the best, but they may all be read with interest, and they all uniformly tend to promote the cause of good morality.'

1797: 60   [MUSGRAVE, Agnes].
EDMUND OF THE FOREST. AN HISTORICAL NOVEL. IN FOUR VOLUMES. BY THE AUTHOR OF CICELY, OR THE ROSE OF RABY.

London: Printed for William Lane, at the Minerva-Press, Leadenhall-Street, 1797.

I 252p; II 269p; III 288p; IV iv, 288p. 12mo. 14s sewed (CR, SJC).

CR n.s. 21: 354–5 (Nov 1797); AF II: 3018.

BL C.192.a.106; CME 3-628-45122-1; ESTC n009105 (NA ViU; EA COR).

Notes. In BL copy the last leaf of vol. 2 (following 1 p. adv.) is a duplicate of pp. 67–8 and appears to be conjoined with pp. 265–6. In this copy the introduction is bound at the beginning of vol. 4, although it is marked 'vol. I'.

Cicely; or the Rose of Raby 1795: 32.

Adv. SJC 7–9 Mar 1797; additional booksellers are Miller, Old Bond-street; C. Law, Ave-Maria-lane; and Messrs. Hodgson's, Wimpole-street.

Adv. end vol. 2 of *Court Intrigue* (1799: 44).

French trans. Paris, 1799 (*Edmond de la forêt*) (BGR).

CR: 'Horrors are multiplied on horrors, new characters on new characters, until the reader is bewildered in a maze, from which the assistance even of the author is unable to extricate him.'

1797: 61   PARSONS, {Eliz}[a].
THE GIRL OF THE MOUNTAINS. A NOVEL, IN FOUR VOLUMES, BY MRS. PARSONS, AUTHOR OF WOMEN AS THEY ARE, &C.

London: Printed for William Lane, at the Minerva-Press, Leadenhall-Street, 1797.

I 279p; II 282p; III 288p; IV 273p. 12mo. 14s sewed (SJC, Min).

BL Cup.403.i.4; CME 3-628-45145-0; EM 6464: 4 and 6465: 1; ESTC t139127 (NA MiDW, ViU; EA COR).

Notes. Dedication to H.R.H. Princess Sophia Matilda of Gloucester, signed Eliz. Parsons. 2 pp. advs. end vol. 2 and 3 pp. at end of vol. 4.

Women As They Are 1796: 72.

Adv., 'Speedily will be published', SJC 27–29 Apr 1797; adv. as published SJC 16–18 May 1797.

Further edns: Dublin, 1798 (P. Byrne, 2 vols., 12mo), ESTC n017943; Philadelphia, 1801 (WC).

1797: 62   PARSONS, [Eliza].
AN OLD FRIEND WITH A NEW FACE. A NOVEL. IN THREE VOL-UMES. BY MRS. PARSONS.

> London: Printed for T. N. Longman, Paternoster-Row, 1797.
> I 240p; II 249p; III 258p. 12mo. 10s 6d (BC), 10s 6d boards (SJC, adv.).
> BC 11: 562 (May 1798).
> BL Cup.403.y.20; CME 3-628-45130-2; EM 6424: 6; ESTC t140068 (NA CaAEU, CtY-BR, CLU-S/C &c.; EA COR).

Notes. Dedication to Lady Howard, signed 'The Author'.

750 copies printed by Woodfall, June 1797; Parsons sold copyright sold for £60 and 20 copies (LA).

Adv. SJC 27–29 June 1797.

Adv. end vol. 3 of *Clara Duplessis* (1797: 50).

BC: 'Mrs Parsons has justly obtained some degree of reputation as a writer of novels, and the present is entitled to considerable praise. We must, nevertheless, observe as the critic did to Sir Fretful Plagiary, there is *a falling off* in the last volume.'

1797: 63   [PATRICK, Mrs F. C.].
THE IRISH HEIRESS, A NOVEL, IN THREE VOLUMES.

> London: Printed for William Lane, at the Minerva-Press, Leadenhall-Street, 1797.
> I 196p; II 213p; III 185p. 12mo. 10s 6d sewed (CR), 9s sewed (Min).
> CR n.s. 25: 119 (Jan 1799); AF II: 3254.
> BL Cup.403.y.12; CME 3-628-45094-2; EM 8352: 7; ESTC t130394 (NA CaAEU, CtY-BR, PU; EA COR).

Notes. Frontispiece to vol. 1. 1 p. adv. end vol. 2 and 1 p. advs. end vol. 3.

CR: 'While the Irish heiress remained in her own country, the narrative bore many marks of reality. It was a plain tale, in which the writer and heroine appeared to be one and the same; but her departure for France destroyed the illusion, and we afterwards find the grossest fictions blended with real events. . . . There are certainly parts of this novel which claim approbation: but the misfortune of the writer seems to have been, the adjustment of a plan, which he (or perhaps she) had not skill or patience to execute.'

1797: 64   [PIGAULT-LEBRUN, Charles-Antoine].
THE SHROVE-TIDE CHILD; OR, THE SON OF A MONK. A NOVEL. TRANSLATED FROM THE FRENCH. IN TWO VOLUMES.

> London: Printed by Baylis, Greville-Street; and sold by Lee and Hurst, Paternoster-row; Miller, Old Bond-street; Bell, Oxford-street, 1797.
> I ii, 282p; II ii, 318p. 8vo. 8s sewed (CR), 7s (GEP).
> CR n.s. 22: 478 (Apr 1798).
> BL 12611.bbb.10; EM 169: 3; ESTC t108514.

Notes. Trans. of *L'Enfant du carnaval* (Rome, 1796) (BGR).

2-pp. preface (unn.); table of contents in each volume.

Adv. GEP 12–14 Dec 1799.

CR: 'This novel abounds with the frivolity and indecency for which French works of fiction are remarkable.'

1797: 65   PILKINGTON, M[ary].
EDWARD BARNARD; OR, MERIT EXALTED; CONTAINING THE HISTORY OF THE EDGERTON FAMILY. BY M. S. PILKINGTON.

London: Printed for E. Newbery, at the corner of St. Paul's Church-Yard, 1797.

167p. 12mo. 2s 6d (GM).

GM 68: 879 (Oct 1798); AF II: 3344.

C S727.d.79.63; EM 2014: 5; ESTC t073529 (BI BL, O; NA CSmH, CtY, NjP &c.).

Notes. Frontispiece. Text of novel starts on p. 3.

French trans. Paris, 1812 (*Édouard Bernard, ou Histoire de la famille Egerton*) (BN).

1797: 66   PILKINGTON, [Mary].
OBEDIENCE REWARDED, AND PREJUDICE CONQUERED; OR, THE HISTORY OF MORTIMER LASCELLS. WRITTEN FOR THE INSTRUCTION AND AMUSEMENT OF YOUNG PEOPLE. BY MRS. PILKINGTON.

London: Printed for Vernor & Hood, No. 31, Poultry; and E. Newbery, Corner of St. Paul's Church-Yard, 1797.

206p. 12mo. 2s 6d (CR), 2s 6d boards (MR), 3s bound (GEP).

CR n.s. 22: 349 (Mar 1798); MR n.s. 26: 91 (May 1798); AF II: 3352.

BL Ch.790/236; EM 4486: 9; ESTC t135981 (BI MRu, O; NA CLU-S/C, FU, NNPM; EA SSL).

Notes. Frontispiece. 6 pp. advs. at end.

Adv. GEP 6–8 Nov 1798.

French trans. Paris, 1800 (*Mortimer Lascells*) (BGR).

CR: 'This work deserves commendation, as it inculcates the duty of obedience to parents, and promotes filial affection. It is also likely to be of some service in teaching young persons to conquer the absurd prejudices and antipathies which they too often acquire in the nursery' (p. 349).

MR [Jabez Hirons]: 'The history of Mortimer is but short, as the reader may expect when he is informed that it is not extended beyond his fifteenth year; but his family scenes and connections, his compliance as to the course of life proposed for him, the affection and wisdom of his mother, with other circumstances and incidents, are likely to interest the young reader, and at the same time convey principles and sentiments that may be useful in any station.'

1797: 67   [PORTER, Anna Maria].
WALSH COLVILLE: OR, A YOUNG MAN'S FIRST ENTRANCE INTO LIFE. A NOVEL.

London: Printed for Lee and Hurst, Paternoster Row, and T. C. Jones, Rathbone Place, 1797.

218p. 8vo. 4s boards (CR).

CR n.s. 21: 474–5 (Dec 1797); AF II: 4367.

BL 1463.g.4; EMf; ESTC t220171.

Notes. Further edn: London, 1833 (WC). Facs: FCy.

CR: 'The story of this novel exposes in lively colours the dangerous dissipation, of which the higher ranks of the army have (we fear too justly) been accused.'

1797: 68 PRATT, [Samuel Jackson].

FAMILY SECRETS, LITERARY AND DOMESTIC. BY MR. PRATT. IN FIVE VOLUMES.

London: Printed for T. N. Longman, Paternoster-Row, 1797.

I ii, 461p; II xi, 405p; III viii, 411p; IV xi, 396p; V viii, 679p. 12mo. £1 5s (CR), £1 5s boards (MR, SJC).

CR n.s. 20: 398–401 (Aug 1797); MR n.s. 23: 56–60 (May 1797); AF II: 3569.

BL 012613.f.14; CME 3-628-45138-8; EM 188: 1; ESTC t085829 (BI C, MRu; NA CtY, CSmH, ICN, IU, MH-H, ViU &c.; EA COR).

Notes. Each volume dedicated to a different recipient: vol. 1 'To the Reviewers of Literature' i–ii; vol. 2 to Mrs. Cockburn of Madras iii–vi; vol. 3 to the Rev. Mr. Potter, Prebendary of Norwich iii–iv; vol. 4 to Doctor O'Leary v–vi; vol. 5 to John Fonblanque v–viii. Table of contents in each volume (unn. in vols. 1 and 5).

Printed concurrently by 4 printers, Feb 1797: vols. 1 & 5 by Baldwin, vol. 2 by Hamilton, vol. 3 by Strahan, vol. 4 by Bye and Law; 1,000 copies printed by Strahan Feb 1797 (Strahan 17 f. 97); Pratt sold 'copyright of first edition' for £225 (LA).

Adv., 'This Month will be published', SJC 21–24 Jan 1797; adv. as published SJC 9–11 Feb 1797.

Adv. end vol. 3 of *Clara Duplessis* (1797: 50).

Further edns: London, 1798, ESTC t066927; Cork, 1800 (Printed by J. Connor), ESTC n018425. French trans. Paris, 1800 (*Les Secrets de famille*) (BGR).

CR: 'The sentiments of this novel are in the high strain of heroic love; some comic characters, and particularly Partington, a sea captain, is introduced; but his is by no means a natural one: and upon the whole, though there is as much love and delicate distress as may perhaps induce a profest novel reader to get through the five volumes, it is in vain we look for the powers which embellished, with so much interesting pathos, the simple story of Emma Corbett [1780: 23]' (p. 399).

MR [William Smyth]: 'Under an inauspicious title, Mr Pratt has introduced to a numerous set of readers a novel that has the merit of being at once tender, pathetic, and full of love; and which may be a more uncommon circumstance, of love mixed with the greatest discretion:—a novel which, however, will offend by its prolixity, its violations of probability, and its unchastized style' (p. 56).

1797: 69 [PURBECK, Elizabeth and Jane].

THE HISTORY OF SIR GEORGE WARRINGTON; OR THE POLITICAL QUIXOTE. BY THE AUTHOR OF THE FEMALE QUIXOTE. IN THREE VOLUMES.

London: Printed for J. Bell, Oxford-Street, 1797.

I 207p; II 219p; III 184p. 12mo. 10s 6d sewed (CR).

CR n.s. 23: 112–14 (May 1798); AF II: 3640.

O 12 Theta 1624-1626; EM 8744: 1; ESTC t204341 (NA CSmH, CtY-BR).

Notes. Not by Charlotte Lennox, author of *The Female Quixote* (1752, JR 138–141, AF I: 1588). *Female Quixote* seems to be an error for *Benevolent Quixote,* the subtitle of the Purbecks' *William Thornborough* (1791: 57).

Further edn: London, 1797, ESTC n033282.

CR: 'In these volumes we do not find any thing that can deprave the understanding, or corrupt the heart; and it is proper to add, that there are some happy delineations of character, and just remarks on the manners and principles of the present age' (p. 113).

1797: 70   RADCLIFFE, Ann.
THE ITALIAN, OR THE CONFESSIONAL OF THE BLACK PENITENTS. A ROMANCE. BY ANN RADCLIFFE, AUTHOR OF THE MYSTERIES OF UDOLPHO, &C. &C. IN THREE VOLUMES.

London: Printed for T. Cadell Jun. and W. Davies (Successors to Mr Cadell) in the Strand, 1797.

12mo. I xii, 336p; II 360p; III 444p. 15s sewed (MR, SJC).

CR n.s. 23: 166–9 (June 1798); MR n.s. 22: 282–4 (Mar 1797); AF II: 3672.

C S727.d.79.11-13; EM 2472: 3; ESTC t062064 (BI BL, MRu; NA CtY-BR, CSmH, IU, MH-H, PU, ViU).

Notes: The Mysteries of Udolpho 1794: 47. 2,000 copies printed Dec 1796 (Strahan 17 f. 84). Scott reports that the booksellers purchased *The Italian* for £800 (viii).

Post-dated; adv., 'On Saturday the 10th of December, will be published', SJC 29 Nov–1 Dec 1796; adv. as published OPA 12 Dec 1796 and SJC 13–15 Dec 1796.

2nd edn. 'corrected' adv. LC 81: 358 (13–15 Apr 1797).

Further edns: Dublin, 1797 (Printed for P. Wogan [etc.], 2 vols., no format) (WC); London, 1797, ESTC t114428; Mount-Pleasant, NY, 1797, ESTC w038535; Philadelphia, 1797, ESTC w012880; London, 1805 (WC); WC has 7 further entries between 1800 and 1850; NSTC lists edns. in 1824, 1826, 1828, 1833 and 1840. 2 French trans. Paris, 1797 (*L'Italien, ou le confessionnal des pénitens noirs* and *Eléonore de Rosalba, ou le Confessionnal des Pénitents Noirs*) (BGR, Lévy); German trans. Königsberg, 1797–99 (*Die Italienerin, oder DerBeichtstuhl der schwarzen Büssenden*) (EAG); Italian trans. Milan, n.d. (Rogers); Spanish trans. Barcelona, 1836 (Rogers).

CR: '. . . it was probable that, as [the modern romance's] constitution (if we may so speak) was maintained only by the passion of terror, and that excited by trick, and as it was not conversant in incidents and characters of a natural complexion, it would degenerate into repetition, and would disappoint curiosity. . . . The Mysteries of Udolpho [1794: 47] fell short of the Romance of the Forest [1791: 58], by the tedious protraction of events, and by a redundancy of description: the Italian falls short of the Mysteries of Udolpho, by reminding us of the same characters and the same scenes; and, although the descriptive part is less prolix, the author has had recourse to it in various instances, in which it has no natural connexion with the story. There are, however, some scenes that powerfully seize the imagination, and interest the passions' (p. 166).

MR [Arthur Aikin] makes a distinction between the 'most excellent, but at the same time the most difficult, species of novel-writing [which] consists in the accurate and interesting representation of such manners and characters as society presents' and the 'modern

Romance; in which high descriptions, extravagant characters, and extraordinary and scarcely possible occurrences combine to rivet the attention, and to excite emotions more thrilling than even the best selected and best described natural scene'; Radcliffe occupies 'a very distinguished rank' in the second group (pp. 282–3).

1797: 71   ROBINSON, Mary.
WALSINGHAM; OR, THE PUPIL OF NATURE. A DOMESTIC STORY. BY MARY ROBINSON, AUTHOR OF ANGELINA—HUBERT DE SEVRAC— THE WIDOW—VANCENZA, &C. &C. &C. IN FOUR VOLUMES.

London: Printed for T. Longman, Pater-Noster-Row, 1797.
I 335p; II 333p; III 338p; IV 401p. 12mo. 16s boards (MR), 16s sewed (GEP).
CR n.s. 22: 553–8 (App [Apr/May 1798]); MR n.s. 26: 441–4 (Aug 1798); AF II: 3841.
BL Cup.406.h.23; EM 6425: 12; ESTC t137692 (BI AWn, LEu; NA CtY-BR, DLC, IU, MH-H, NjP, ViU; EA TaLn).

Notes. 1,000 copies printed by Strahan, Nov 1797 (Strahan 17 f. 98); Robinson sold copyright for £150 (LA). Epistolary.
Angelina 1796: 76; Hubert de Sevrac 1796: 77; The Widow 1794: 50; Vancenza 1792: 50.
Adv., 'In a few Days will be published', SJC 16–18 Nov 1797; adv. GEP 6–9 Jan 1798.
Further edns: Dublin, 1798 (Printed by B. Smith, for P. Wogan, C. Brown, H. Colbert, W. Porter, and J. Rice, 2 vols., 12mo), ESTC t181020. 2 French trans. Paris, 1798 (D'Harcourt, ou l'héritier supposé and, fuller trans., Walsingham, ou l'enfant des montagnes) (HWS); German trans. Berlin and Stettin, 1799 (Walsingham oder Das Naturkind) (RS). Facs: FCy, BWN.
CR: 'The language is easy, and not inelegant; but it does not possess that energy which brings to our recollection the idea of "thoughts that breathe, and words that burn." The incidents are, for the most part, new and interesting. Walsingham, however, ranks not so high in our opinion as some other works of Mrs. Robinson. The general plan is without any moral tendency' (p. 556–7).
MR [Thomas Wallace]: 'Although this is a long story, we have read the greater part of it with a degree of interest which we do not generally feel in the perusal of novels. In the first volume particularly, our curiosity was very agreeably arrested by the instructive manner in which Walsingham relates his story; the language is generally correct, and sometimes elegant; and the sentiments, though not in every instance perhaps above exception, are yet calculated to excite a spirit of thought and inquiry concerning subjects on which it behoves man to think and determine. We confess, however, that in the second volume the genius of the writer seems to have been exerted with much less effect; the thread and spirit of the narrative are broken; and curiosity is baffled by long recitals of uninteresting conversations, by forced attempts to introduce living characters and local allusions, and by the pains taken to bring reviewers into contempt and abhorrence!
In the remaining volumes, we were alternately prompted to proceed in our perusal by the occurrence of attracting situations, and to throw aside the work with disgust at the improbability and inconsistency of the incidents; but we persevered with fortitude to the end; when lo! the improbabilities and inconsistencies which had shocked us, and which, we apprehend, will shock many readers who have less perseverance than reviewers must have, resolved themselves into one great and gigantic WONDER:—a touch of romance on which a novelist seldom ventures. Sir Sidney Aubrey ... turns out to be a YOUNG LADY ... and she at length becomes the wife of Walsingham!' (pp. 441–2).'

SANDERS, Charlotte, **THE LITTLE FAMILY**
See App. A: 10

1797: 72   [SELDEN, Catharine].
**THE COUNT DE SANTERRE: A ROMANCE. BY A LADY. IN TWO VOL-
UMES.**

> Bath: Printed by R. Crutwell; and sold by C. Dilly, Poultry, London, 1797.
> I 310p; II 294p. 12mo. 7s (CR), 7s sewed (MR, SJC).
> CR n.s. 21: 354 (Nov 1797); MR n.s. 24: 199–202 (Oct 1797); AF II: 4002.
> MH-H *EC75.A100.797c; EM 1007: 29; ESTC n004710 (NA CSmH).

Notes. In vol. 2 text of novel starts on p. 3.
Adv., 'On Thursday, June 1, was published', SJC 3–6 June 1797.

CR: 'The writer possesses considerable descriptive powers in scenes of nature, and a taste for picturesque beauties, which may be employed to much better purpose than to ornament a romance abounding in such gross improbabilities as the present. The usual furniture of modern romances,—old castles,—long galleries,—deep vaults,—sullen echoes,—flitting lights,—murders and revivals, are jumbled here in a confusion which forms a greater mystery than any the authoress pretends to unravel. We cannot expect that novel-writers will have any pity for reviewers: but, for their own sakes, we could wish that they would cease to build castles in the air, and return to *terra firma*, to common life, and common sense.'

MR [James Bannister]: 'Of all compositions, none seems to baffle the powers of criticism so much as romance; for the authors of the works which bear that name fancy that they may indulge their imaginations without controul, violate probability with impunity, and present to the reader characters which never did and never can exist. The fair writer of the work before us appears to have made use of this licence in its fullest extent: for we have no true delineation of character; and the events, so far from being probable, are scarcely within the verge of possibility; yet the fancy is captivated by some incidents of an unexpected and extraordinary nature, and above all by those gloomy and horrid scenes, on which the authoress exerts all her powers of description . . .' (p. 199).

1797: 73   [SELDEN, Catharine].
THE ENGLISH NUN. A NOVEL.

> London: Printed for William Lane, at the Minerva-Press, Leadenhall-Street, 1797.
> 215p. 8vo. 4s 6d (BC), 4s 6d sewed (SJC, Min).
> BC 11: 316 (Mar 1798).
> MH-H *EC8.Se482.797e; CME 3-628-45040-3; EM 1010: 4; ESTC n002258 (NA PU,
>   ViU; EA COR).

Notes. 2-pp. prefatory advertisement.
Adv. SJC 5–7 June 1798.
Adv. end vol. 2 of *Court Intrigue* (1799: 44).
Further edn: New York, 1806 (WC).

BC: 'A very unexceptionable, interesting, and affecting tale, related in a good style, and calculated at once to excite the most tender feelings, and, by the example of the principal personages, to animate the fortitude of those who may be placed in situations of similar difficulty and trial.'

1797: 74   [SENAC DE MEILHAN, Gabriel]; BIRCH, John Brereton (*trans.*).
THE COUSINS OF SCHIRAS. IN TWO VOLUMES. TRANSLATED FROM
THE FRENCH BY JOHN BRERETON BIRCH, ESQ.

> London: Printed for William Lane, at the Minerva-Press, Leadenhall-Street, 1797.
> I 219p; II 200p. 8vo [CR has 12mo]. 6s sewed (CR, SJC).
> CR n.s. 20: 469–70 (Aug 1797); AF II: 351.
> BL 12512.aa.27; EM 7: 9; ESTC t094715 (NA CtY, DLC, MH-H).

Notes. Trans. of *Les deux cousins, histoire véritable* (Paris, 1790) (BGR).
Adv., 'Preparing for the Press', SJC 5–7 Apr. 1796. Post-dated; adv. as published SJC 17–20
Dec 1796.
   CR: 'The tale, ... on the whole, is sprightly, agreeable, and moral.'

1797: 75   [SHOWES, Mrs].
INTERESTING TALES. SELECTED AND TRANSLATED FROM THE
GERMAN.

> London: Printed for William Lane, at the Minerva-Press, Leadenhall-Street, 1797.
> 239p. 12mo. 3s (CR), 3s 6d sewed (Min).
> CR n.s. 23: 115 (May 1798); AF II: 4084.
> MH-H *EC75.Sh825.797i; EM 2136: 15; ESTC n008324 (NA ViU).

Notes. Blakey: 'Attributed by a Minerva Catalogue of 1814 to Mrs Showes' (p. 182).
Pagination errors throughout.
   CR: 'We have some doubts whether these tales were translated from the German; but we
are clearly of opinion that they were not worth the trouble of translation.'

1797: 76   STYLES, John.
*MIRANDA: A NOVEL, IN A SERIES OF LETTERS. BY JOHN STYLES,
WRITTEN IN HIS FIFTEENTH YEAR.

> London: Mitchell, 1797 (CR).
> 12mo. 3s boards (CR).
> CR n.s. 20: 118 (May 1797); AF II: 4291.
> No copy located.

Notes. CR: 'Among his subscribers ... are some who ought to have given him more friendly
advice than to publish what, in a few years, he will heartily wish had been suppressed.'

1797: 77   SUMMERSETT, Henry.
PROBABLE INCIDENTS: OR, SCENES IN LIFE, A NOVEL, BY HENRY
SUMMERSETT. IN TWO VOLUMES.

> London: Printed for William Lane, at the Minerva-Press, Leadenhall-Street, 1797.
> I 199p; II 208p. 8vo [CR has 12mo.] 6s sewed (CR, Min).
> CR n.s. 22: 357–8 (Mar 1798); AF II: 4300.
> BL 1489.cc.85; CME 3-628-45197-3; EM 2265: 3; ESTC t060940 (NA MH-H; EA COR).

Notes. CR: 'There is nothing very improbable in these *Incidents*, if we take our notions of
probability from the greater part of modern novels. Where the author, however, endeavours
most to interest his readers, he approaches a little to the marvellous; and we cannot

compliment him on the general execution of the work. It frequently reminded us of the incidents in Roderic Random; and the remembrance was far from being favourable to the imitator.'

1797: 78   WALKER, George.
CINTHELIA; OR, A WOMAN OF TEN THOUSAND. IN FOUR VOL-
UMES. BY GEORGE WALKER, AUTHOR OF THEODORE CYPHON,
&C. &C.

> London: Printed for B. Crosby, Stationers'-Court, Ludgate-Street, 1797.
> I vii, 218p; II 258p; III 259p; IV 274p. 12mo. 14s sewed (MR, CR).
> CR n.s. 23: 352–3 (July 1798); MR n.s. 26: 106–7 (May 1798); AF II: 4660.
> BL 838.b.22,23; CME 3-628-45204-X; EM 2386: 2; ESTC t097411 (NA NjP; EA
> COR).

Notes. Preface 1, v–vii.
Theodore Cyphon 1796: 88.
Adv. SJC 7–9 Dec 1797; adv. GEP 12–14 Dec 1799.
French trans. Paris, 1798 (*Cinthelia, ou une sur dix-mille*) (BGR).

CR: 'We meet with pleasing and interesting passages in this novel; and some knowledge of the world is manifested by the writer; but various parts of the performance are frivolous, and it is degraded by the general inaccuracy of the diction' (p. 353).

MR [James Bannister]: 'In this novel, we meet with that lofty strain of high-flown senti-ment, and that affected refinement of manners, which shine with tinsel glare in many of our modern publications. No false principle of morality is inculcated; and the example of Cinthelia may not be without its use. . . . The incidents are not beyond what might be sup-posed to happen in real life; but they are for the most part of a melancholy and unpleasing nature. . . . Some of the scenes may be censured as indelicate; and we can say little in favour of the language, which is frequently vulgar.'

1797: 79   WOODWARD, G[eorge] M[outard].
*AN OLIO OF GOOD BREEDING: WITH SKETCHES ILLUSTRATIVE
OF THE MODERN GRACES: BY G. M. WOODWARD.

> London: Clarke, 1797 (MM).
> 4to. 12s boards (MM).
> MM 4: 42–43 (1797).
> No copy located.

Notes. Further edn: NSTC lists edn. in 1801.

AMMORVIN AND ZALLIDA. A NOVEL
See CHARLTON, Mary

1798: 1 ANON.
THE ANIMATED SKELETON. IN TWO VOLUMES.

London: Printed at the Minerva-Press, for William Lane, Leadenhall-Street, 1798.
I xi, 152p; II 176p. IV p. 8vo. 6s sewed (SJC), 7s (GEP).
MH-H 17438.47.15; CME 3-628-45001-2; EM 1282: 1; ESTC n014790 (NA ICN; EA COR).

Notes. Preface v–xi. Drop-head title 'Count Richard; or, the Animated Skeleton.'
Adv. SJC 5–7 June 1798; adv. GEP 23–26 Feb 1799.
French trans. Paris, 1799 (*Le Château d'Albert, ou le squelette ambulant*) (BGR).

ARTHUR FITZ-ALBINI, A NOVEL
See BRYDGES, Sir Samuel Egerton

CALAF: A PERSIAN TALE
See HOLFORD, Margaret

1798: 2 ANON.
CAROLINE. IN THREE VOLUMES. BY A LADY.

London: Printed for Hookham and Carpenter, no. 14, Old Bond-Street, 1798.
I 189p; II 202p; III 202p. 12mo. 7s 6d sewed (CR), 10s 6d sewed (MR).
CR n.s. 22: 478 (Apr 1798); MR n.s. 27: 453 (Dec 1798); AF II: 609.
BL 12613.f.12; EM 241: 2; ESTC t080589 (BI MRu; NA CtY-Walpole, CSmH, IU, MH-H).

Notes. Title on 1st p. of each volume is 'History of Caroline'. Epistolary.

CR: 'We have scarcely ever read any thing so improbable and uninteresting as the contents of these pages, even in this age of absurdity, when milliners and staymakers scatter their ridiculous inventions, under the title of a novel. As every woman is now "a lady," we need not examine our author's pretensions to this title; but, from the occasional vulgarity of her language and descriptions, they cannot be very high.'

MR [Arthur Aikin]: 'Elegance, vivacity, or accurate delineation of manners, can hardly be expected in the general overflowing mass of the novels of the times; and the volumes before us are certainly not entitled to rank among the capital works of this branch of literature. Freedom from vulgarisms, from gross improbabilities, from licentious descriptions, and from tedious narrations, may be mentioned in favour of this production; and to how few of the novels of the day can even this negative praise be justly given?'

THE CASTLE OF BEESTON
See BROSTER, John

THE CASTLE OF SAINT DONATS
See LUCAS, Rev. Charles

THE CASTLE ON THE ROCK
See KENDALL, A.

CONFESSIONS OF A BEAUTY
See CROFFTS, Mrs

DELORAINE. A DOMESTIC TALE
See MARTIN, Mrs

DERWENT PRIORY; OR, MEMOIRS OF AN ORPHAN
See KENDALL, A.

THE ENAMOURED SPIRIT. A NOVEL
See 1791: 32, ALVAREZ; OR, IRRESISTIBLE SEDUCTION

1798: 3 ANON.
GERALDINA, A NOVEL, FOUNDED ON A RECENT EVENT. IN TWO VOLUMES.

London: Printed for G. G. and J. Robinson, Paternoster-Row, 1798.
I 275p; II 300p. 12mo. 7s boards (CR, MR), 7s sewed (GEP).
CR n.s. 23: 234 (June 1798); MR n.s. 26: 457–8 (Aug 1798); AF II: 1597.
Corvey; CME 3-628-45063-2; ESTC n007149 (NA PU).

Notes. Possibly by Anna Thomson; t.p. to her *Pride of Ancestry* (1804: 66) lists *Geraldine* as a previous work.
Epistolary.
Adv. GEP 29–31 Mar 1798.
French trans. Paris, 1799 (*Géraldina, nouvelle, tirée d'une histoire récente*) (HWS); German trans. Berlin, 1799 (*Geraldina, eine wahre Geschichte*) (EAG).

CR: 'We are sorry that any person could be so destitute of delicacy, as to make the event to which the title alludes the subject of a novel. There must have been an equal want of genius; or the author would not have produced a piece which has so little merit.'

MR [Thomas Wallace]: 'This work is written in the *epistolary* manner, so favourable to the amplification of those frothy and insipid ideas (if ideas they can be called) which constitute the bulk of this kind of composition. The reader, therefore, will have to encounter the labour of extracting the plot and incident from the raw material; and he must read the same story related by each person in the drama, with the addition of a large portion of sentiment, advice, and opinion, corresponding with those respective personages. This done, he will be rewarded with *three elopements* and a *suicide*' (p. 457).

1798: 4 ANON.
GODFREY DE HASTINGS. A ROMANCE. IN THREE VOLUMES.

London: Printed at the Minerva-Press, for William Lane, Leadenhall-Street, 1798.
I 318p; II 258p; III 191p. 12mo. 10s 6d sewed (CR), 12s (GEP).

CR n.s. 28: 235 (Feb 1800).

PU PR 3991.A1.G62.1798; CME 3–628–45072–1; ESTC n016972 (NA CtY; EA COR).

Notes. Adv. GEP 23–26 Feb 1799.

CR: 'This romance exhibits a picture of the days of chivalry, and of the manners of the English during the reign of the third Edward. A tedious sameness is too prevalent in the volumes, though it must be allowed that some parts are pleasing and even interesting. The language is affected rather than elegant, and pompous rather than precise or correct. . . .'

1798: 5 ANON.
GOMEZ AND ELEONORA: TRANSLATED FROM A SPANISH MANU-SCRIPT.

London: Printed for James Wallis, No. 46, Pater-Noster-Row, 1798.

I v, 248p; II 256p. 12mo. 7s (CR).

CR n.s. 25: 358 (Mar 1799); AF II: 1667.

BL 1607/1881; EM 2298: 3; ESTC t119046 (BI O; NA CaAEU, MnU, MH–H).

Notes. Preface i–v. Pagination continuous Roman-Arabic; text of novel starts on p. 7 of vol. 1. In vol. 2 text of novel starts on p. 5. 4 pp. advs. end vol. 2.

CR: 'We are informed in the preface, that this "narrative was communicated to the translator in manuscript, with permission to make what use of it he should think proper;" and he thought *proper* to publish it "with all its imperfections on its head," with all its indecent scenes, and immoral sentiments—with even a story of *incest,* related in terms which seem almost to imply approbation.'

1798: 6 ANON.
HE WOULD BE A PEER. AN ENGLISH STORY. IN TWO VOLUMES.

London: Printed by Baylis, Greville-Street. Sold by Lee and Hurst, Paternoster-row; Bell, Oxford-street; Millar, Old Bond-street; and Wright, Piccadilly, opposite Old Bond-street, 1798.

I 216p; II 199p. 12mo. 5s sewed (CR).

CR n.s. 24: 237 (Oct 1798).

RPB PR 3991.A1.H43; xESTC.

Notes. CR: 'This is very far from being a good novel; but the absurdity of the story renders it diverting.'

THE HEIR OF MONTAGUE. A NOVEL
See 1797: 9

1798: 7 ANON.
HENRY DE BEAUVAIS. A NOVEL. IN TWO VOLUMES.

London: Printed at the Minerva-Press, for William Lane, Leadenhall-Street, 1798.

I 208p; II 190p. 12mo. 7s sewed (CR), 7s (GEP).

CR n.s. 25: 118–19 (Jan 1799).

Corvey; CME 3-628-45141-8; ESTC n055239 (NA CaAEU).

Notes. 2 pp. advs. end vol. 2.

Adv. GEP 23–26 Feb 1799.

Further edn: Dublin, 1800 (Printed for J. Rice, 2 vols., 12mo), ESTC t223107.

CR: 'The author of this novel has not gone into remote periods for the adventures of his hero and heroine. The French revolution in 1789 supplies him with an opportunity of mangling the events of that year to his purpose; Henry de Beauvais having been rescued from the Bastile on the 14th of July, where he had been confined *twelve days!*'

1798: 8 ANON.
HENRY WILLOUGHBY. A NOVEL. IN TWO VOLUMES.

London: Printed for G. Kearsley, Fleet-Street, 1798.

I ii, 300p; II 287p. 12mo. 7s sewed (CR), 7s boards (MR), 7s sewed (SJC).

CR n.s. 23: 472 (Aug 1798); MR n.s. 27: 233 (Oct 1798); AF II: 1903.

MH-H *EC75.A100.798h; EM 1005: 10; ESTC n003788 (NA CtY-BR).

Notes. Preface (1, i–ii) concerns the fact that the young author 'has spent the most valuable part of his past life, in a profession eminently hostile to the pursuits of literature, and the cultivation of the understanding', i.e. at sea.

Adv. SJC 26–29 May 1798.

Further edn: Dublin, 1799 (Printed for J. Rice, 2 vols., 12mo) ESTC n007202.

CR: 'In this novel there appears to be a mixture of truth and fiction; and, though its composition is irregular (for the story is left incomplete), so many probable adventures are related in it, and so many just remarks on life and manners are interspersed, that we cannot but recommend it as superior, in point of utility, to those productions of the kind, where the main purpose is the perplexity of courtship terminating in a fortunate union. The author has introduced some well known characters, delineated in Smollet's manner, and not without a considerable portion of his spirit and force.'

MR [Christopher Lake Moody]: 'He must have painted from imagination, and not from experience; his characters are unnatural; they never did nor could exist; and his system, which he gradually developes, in regard to the renovation of society, is as impracticable as his representation of the present state of it is incorrect.'

1798: 9 ANON.
HUMAN VICISSITUDES; OR, TRAVELS INTO UNEXPLORED REGIONS. IN TWO VOLUMES.

London: Printed for G. G. J. and J. Robinson, Pater-Noster-Row, 1798.

I vi, 252p; II vi, 262p. 12mo. 6s sewed (MR, GEP).

MR n.s. 29: 90 (May 1799).

MH-H *EC75.A100.798h3; EM 1013: 34; ESTC n003787 (NA NjP).

Notes. 2 pp. advs. end vol. 2.

Adv., 'Tuesday next will be published', GEP 20–22 Nov 1798.

MR [Alexander Hamilton]: 'We may venture to predict that these regions will not often be explored twice by the same traveller. To contrast the moral and political state of England with those of an imaginary people, of innocent manners and acute understandings, seems to have been the design of the writer: but the pen of Gulliver has long been missing; and certainly the author of this jejune performance has not found it.'

1798: 10   ANON.
THE INVASION; OR, WHAT MIGHT HAVE BEEN. A NOVEL. IN TWO VOLUMES.

> London: Printed for H. D. Symonds, no. 20, Paternoster-Row, 1798.
> I viii, 298p; II iv, 306p. 12mo. 7s (CR), 7s sewed (SJC).
> CR n.s. 25: 358 (Mar 1799); AF II: 2201.
> BL 12611.bb.11; CME 3-628-45141-8; EM 125: 1; ESTC t096729 (NA CSmH, PU; EA COR).

Notes. Verse dedication 'To an Eminent Artist' 1, [iii]; detailed table of contents in each vol. lists the writer and recipient of each letter 1, v–viii and 2, iii–iv. 6 pp. advs. end vol. 2. Epistolary.
Adv. SJC 24–27 Nov 1798.

CR: 'Scarcely any allusions are made to the invaders; and, with the title of a political novel, this has only the common interest of a hackneyed story, full of trite sentiments and tedious repetitions.'

JAQUELINA OF HAINAULT
See FOSTER, E. M.

THE KNIGHTS; OR SKETCHES OF THE HEROIC AGE
See 1797: 14

THE LEGACY. A NOVEL
See CARVER, Mrs

1798: 11   ANON.
THE LIBERTINES: A NOVEL. IN TWO VOLUMES.

> Cambridge: Printed by W. Watson; for G. G. and J. Robinson, Pater Noster Row, London, 1798.
> I 201p; II 217p. 12mo. 6s boards (CR), 6s sewed (MR).
> CR n.s. 25: 472 (Apr 1799); MR n.s. 29: 91 (May 1799); AF II: 2560.
> BL 12612.bbb.16; CME 3-628-45115-9; EM 168: 4; ESTC t066376 (BI O; EA COR).

Notes. 4-pp. preface (unn.) concerning the Inquisition.
Further edn: Cork, 1800 (as *The Libertines; or, Monkish Mysteries*; Printed by John Connor, 1 vol., 12mo), EM 1007: 23, ESTC n002907. German trans. Berlin, 1800 (*Die Wildfänge*) (RS).

CR: 'The author informs us that he first conceived the plan or rather the subject of this novel from reading the accounts of the Spanish and Portuguese inquisitions.... From some of the incidents related in those accounts, a fable has been constructed, which strongly interests the mind, and has a powerful tendency to promote an attachment to the milder system of ecclesiastic discipline which has distinguished our church since the reformation. The author seems apprehensive that an analogy may be discovered in different scenes and passages to the romance of the Monk [1796: 63]; but the resemblance is not striking; and, in point of entertainment, this novel is equal, while it is far superior, in moral tendency, to that popular work.'

MR [William Smyth]: 'The purport of these volumes is to expose the vices and enormities committed in the intercourse between male and female convents.... The work is full of convent intrigues and diabolical anecdotes of inquisitorial tyranny:—but, regarding novels chiefly as books of amusement, we cannot recommend the present volumes to our readers, as the story does not appear to be conducted by a writer who is possessed of powers sufficient to render gloomy stories agreeable to the imagination, or to seize on it forcibly by the magic of the pen. The plot is intricate; and the poetry interspersed is too flimsy to relieve the irksomeness of the general plan.'

LINDOR; OR, EARLY ENGAGEMENTS
See SELDEN, Catharine

LLEWELLIN: A TALE
See O'KEEFFE, Adelaide

MELBOURNE. A NOVEL
See MARTIN, Mrs

THE MIDNIGHT BELL, A GERMAN STORY
See LATHOM, Francis

1798: 12   ANON.
MORAL AMUSEMENTS; OR, A SELECTION OF TALES, HISTORIES, AND INTERESTING ANECDOTES; INTENDED TO AMUSE AND INSTRUCT YOUNG MINDS.

> Bath: Printed by S. Hazard, for Vernor and Hood, no. 31, Poultry, and E. Newbery, St. Paul's Church-Yard, 1798.
> iv, 175p. 18mo [CR and MR have 12mo]. 1s 6d (MR), 1s 6d 'Vellum Back' (GEP).
> CR n.s. 25: 351 (Mar 1799); MR n.s. 27: 330 (Nov 1798); AF II: 2942.
> BL 12835.a.34; EM 4374: 5; ESTC (NA OOxM).

Notes. Frontispiece. 1 p. advs. end vol.
Adv. GEP 6–8 Nov 1798.
Further edns: London, 1798, ESTC n035135; London, 1799, t073661.
    CR: 'These tales are chiefly oriental. They are not ill selected, and may serve the combined purposes of utility and entertainment.'
    MR [Jabez Hirons]: 'So many are the selections of this kind which have presented themselves to the public, that it can hardly be supposed that, in one form or another, and in different works, we should not have met with these which are here collected.... Their tendency ... certainly recommends them to notice; besides which, the tales are interesting, and can hardly fail of exciting young minds to proper reflections.'

MORE GHOSTS!
See PATRICK, Mrs F. C.

1798: 13   ANON.
[MORT CASTLE] DEDICATED BY PERMISSION TO HER ROYAL

HIGHNESS THE DUCHESS OF YORK, MORT CASTLE. A GOTHIC STORY.

[London]: Sold by J. Wallis, 16 Ivy Lane, n.d. [ESTC: 1798].
248p. 8vo. 3s 6d (ME).
MH-H *EC75.A100.798m2; EM 1107: 5; ESTC n010226 (BI BL).

Notes. Engraved t.p. with illustration. Dedication to H.R.H. the 'Dutchess of York' 1–4; list of subscribers [5]–8. Pagination continuous; text of novel starts on p. 9.

THE NEW MONK, A ROMANCE
See S., R.

PHEDORA; OR, THE FOREST OF MINSKI
See CHARLTON, Mary

POSTHUMOUS WORKS OF THE AUTHOR OF A VINDICATION OF THE RIGHTS OF WOMAN
See WOLLSTONECRAFT, Mary

THE ROCK; OR, ALFRED AND ANNA
See BARNBY, Mrs

THE SICILIAN. A NOVEL
See MEEKE, Mary

1798: 14   ANON.
THE SORROWS OF MATILDA, A NOVEL IN TWO VOLUMES: THE JUVENILE ATTEMPT OF A YOUNG LADY.

London: Printed for Lee, and Hurst, No. 32, Paternoster-Row, 1798.
I 8, 168p; II 168p. 12mo. 6s sewed (CR, GEP).
CR n.s. 25: 118 (Jan 1799); AF II: 4187.
BL C.171.a.2; EM 4787: 4; ESTC t127122.

Notes. Dedication to H.R.H. the Duchess of York 5–8; Arabic numbering starts again with first page of novel. In vol. 2 text of novel starts on p. 5.
Adv. GEP 12–15 May 1798.

CR: 'We would not censure too harshly what we believe to be a first offence. We only hope that it may be the last.'

STATIRA: OR, THE MOTHER
See SHOWES, Mrs

THE STEP-MOTHER: A DOMESTIC TALE
See WELLS, Helena

THE STRANGER; OR, LLEWELLYN FAMILY
See EVANS, Robert

THE SUBTERRANEAN CAVERN
See PILKINGTON, Miss

TALES OF THE COTTAGE
See PILKINGTON, Mary

TALES OF THE HERMITAGE
See PILKINGTON, Mary

THEOPHA; OR, MEMOIRS OF A GREEK SLAVE
See ELLIA, Felix

THE TOWER; OR THE ROMANCE OF RUTHYNE
See LANSDELL, Sarah

A WELSH STORY
See BARKER, Mary

1798: 15 {BARKER, Mary}.
A WELSH STORY. IN THREE VOLUMES.

>London: Printed for Hookham and Carpenter, Old Bond Street, 1798.
>I xii, 284p; II 268p; III 234p. 12mo. 10s 6d (ME).
>BL 12613.f.6; EM 241: 1; ESTC t088381 (BI O; NA CtY, CLU-S/C, PU).

Notes. Dedication to H.R.H. the Duchess of York iii–iv, signed Mary Barker. List of subscribers v–xii. 6 pp. advs. end vol. 3. 750 copies printed at a cost of about £120 and a loss to the author of some £48 (HA).

1798: 16 [BARNBY, Mrs].
THE ROCK; OR, ALFRED AND ANNA. A SCOTTISH TALE, IN TWO VOLUMES. BY A YOUNG LADY, HER FIRST LITERARY ATTEMPT.

>London: Printed for the Author, and sold by Lee and Hurst, Paternoster Row; Harding, Pall Mall; No. 52, Newman Street; and No. 21, Sommers' Place East, Sommers' Town, 1798.
>I x, 161p; II 158p. 12mo. 7s sewed (CR).
>CR n.s. 23: 114 (May 1798); AF II: 223.
>BL N.1893; EM 2011: 2; ESTC t071892.

Notes. Imprint information on t.p. to vol. 2 is as above but with the addition of 'No. 6, Great Newport Street' at the end. List of subscribers 1, vi–x. Epistolary.
Further edns: London, 1799, ESTC t218020; Maidstone, 1801 (Summers).
   CR: 'This tale is crowded with adventures; the language is frequently inaccurate; and the ideas are sometimes confused.'

1798: 17 BELLAMY, Thomas.
SADASKI; OR, THE WANDERING PENITENT. BY THOMAS BEL-LAMY. AUTHOR OF MISCELLANIES IN PROSE AND VERSE, &C. &C. &C. IN TWO VOLUMES.

London: Printed for G. Sael, Strand: and sold by H. D. Symonds, Paternoster-Row; W. Earle, Frith-Street; and by the author, King–Street, Covent-Garden, 1798.
I 176p; II 144p. 8vo [MR and CR have 12mo]. 6s sewed (CR), 7s sewed (MR, adv.).
CR n.s. 24: 114–15 (Sept 1798); MR n.s. 26: 459 (Aug 1798); AF II: 275.
BL 12614.aa.5; EM 188: 2; ESTC t070724 (BI O; NA CtY-BR).

Notes. In vol. 2 text of novel starts on p. 5.
Adv. end *Lessons from Life* (1799: 22).

CR: 'Mr Bellamy is not deficient in invention; and he possesses some descriptive powers; but he employs those talents too extravagantly in this tale, the general moral of which is not very clear, although useful lessons may be deduced from parts.'

MR [Thomas Wallace]: 'In this *romance*, the reader will find a considerable share of *enchantment* that will not *enchant* him. The style is designed to imitate the eastern manner, but it is only the turgid verbosity of that manner which the writer has been able to copy. The plot and incidents are all of the most marvellous nature, and deserve praise only for aiming to illustrate that virtue and vice respectively tend to produce happiness and misery. Even in a moral view, however, the author fails; for the virtues of his hero are preserved only by supernatural interposition, and are ultimately rewarded only by supernatural means.'

1798: 18   [BROSTER, John].
THE CASTLE OF BEESTON, OR, RANDOLPH, EARL OF CHESTER. AN HISTORICAL ROMANCE.

London: Printed for R. Faulder, New Bond-Street, 1798.
I 176p; II 182p. 8vo [MR has 12mo].
MR n.s. 29: 90 (May 1799); AF II: 494.
MH-H *EC8.B7945.798c; CME 3-628-45007-1; EM 1290: 20; ESTC n015053 (NA IU; EA COR).

Notes. MR [William Smyth]: 'An attempt to mix historical facts with the inventions of fancy generally proves unsuccessful, for two classes of readers are probably disappointed:—the lovers of romance deem such stories not sufficiently amusing; and the adherents to historical accuracy accuse the motley writer of inconsistency and falsehood.—In the volumes before us, the plot exhibits little ingenuity; the observations and sentiments manifest no unusual sagacity; and the diction is frequently rendered tumid by affectation, and obscure by grammatical inaccuracies.'

1798: 19   [BRYDGES, Sir Samuel Egerton].
ARTHUR FITZ-ALBINI, A NOVEL. IN TWO VOLUMES.

London: Printed for J. White, Fleet-Street, 1798.
I 307p; II 260p. 12mo. 7s sewed (CR, MR).
CR n.s. 26: 355–7 (July 1799); MR n.s. 27: 318–21 (Nov 1798); AF II: 517.
C 7720.d.268; EM 332: 4; ESTC t064722 (BI BL, O; NA CaAEU, CSmH, MH-H &c.).

Notes. Adv. SJC 18–20 Oct 1798. 2nd edn. adv. MP 14 May 1799; 'For an account of this spirited and well written Novel see the British Critic January 1799; the Anti-Jacobin Review, December 1798, and January 1799; and the Monthly Review, November 1798.'
Further edns: London, 1799, ESTC t086924; NSTC lists edn. in 1810.

CR: 'There is a want of interest in this story; but we must allow that it is the production of no common talents. Its tendency seems to be to support that pride of birth, which the preponderance of the commercial interest, and the growth of the new philosophy, are alike destroying' (p. 355).

MR [William Taylor]: 'The chief object of this well-written novel seems to be to plead the cause of birth against fortune. It represents loftiness of sentiment, and disinterestedness of character, as exclusively allotted to the high-born; and as sources of perpetual mortification and disappointment to the possessor. Both of these representations, as universal axioms, we think, are contradictory to experience: but the general morality of the work is unexceptionable' (p. 318). 'These volumes certainly merit perusal, and are evidently the production of no common writer' (p. 321).

1798: 20   [CARVER, Mrs].
THE LEGACY. A NOVEL. IN TWO VOLUMES.

> London: Printed at the Minerva-Press, for William Lane, Leadenhall-Street, 1798/99.
> I 210p; II 246p. 12mo. 6s sewed (CR), 6s (LC).
> CR n.s. 28: 236 (Feb 1800); AF II: 629.
> Corvey; CME 3-628-45107-8; ESTC t200847 (BI O; NA CaAEU, CtY-BR, ICU).

Notes. Blakey: Attributed to Mrs Carver by a Minerva Library Catalogue of 1814.
Frontispiece vol. 1. Vol. 2 dated 1799. 2 pp. advs. end each vol.
Adv. LC 85: 278 (19–21 Mar 1799).

CR: 'Those readers who are fond of tales of sanguinary horror, who wish to have spectres conjured up before them, and to dive into the mysteries of castles and abbeys, will not be highly entertained with a performance unsuitable to their taste. Nor will those who derive pleasure from well-described scenes of common life reap much gratification from the perusal of the Legacy, as it is a work of little merit, though it may beguile some hours which might otherwise prove tedious.'

CAZOTTE, Jacques, THE ENAMOURED SPIRIT
See 1791: 32, ALVAREZ; OR, IRRESISTIBLE SEDUCTION

1798: 21   [CHARLTON, Mary].
AMMORVIN AND ZALLIDA. A NOVEL. IN TWO VOLUMES.

> London: Rinted [*sic*] for William Lane, at the Minerva-Press, Leadenhall-Street, 1798.
> I 249p; II missing. 12mo. 6s sewed (CR), 7s sewed (Min).
> CR n.s. 22: 357 (Mar 1798); AF II: 668.
> ViU [vol. 1 only] *PR3291.A1A5; ESTC n042513.

Notes. 3 pp. advs. end vol. 1.
French trans. Paris (ie Leipzig), 1798 (*Ammorvin et Zallida, roman chinois*) (Price); German trans. Stettin, 1832 (*Zallida, die chinesische Kaiserbraut, oder Politik und Liebe*) (RS).

CR: 'The complaint of sameness, urged against modern novels, is considerably obviated by the author of this piece, who has selected for his hero a no less personage than an emperor of China; but what is gained by this adventurous step does not contribute greatly to the amusement of the reader. The incidents and hair-breadth 'scapes are as marvellous and extravagant as if the scene had been laid in any part of Europe; and we confess we have not found ourselves deeply interested in the fate of the love-sick emperor, who rambles from place to place amidst the greatest dangers, and at length obtains the mistress of his soul by the accustomed wonderful interposition of the author's ingenuity.'

1798: 22   CHARLTON, Mary.
PHEDORA; OR, THE FOREST OF MINSKI. A NOVEL. IN FOUR VOLUMES. BY MARY CHARLTON.

> London: Printed at the Minerva-Press, for William Lane, Leadenhall-Street, 1798.
> I 303p; II 351p; III 405p; IV 400p. 12mo [ESTC has 8vo]. 18s (ME), 18s sewed (Min).
> BL N.2737; CME 3-628-45014-4; EM 6881: 10; ESTC t073780 (NA CaAEU, MnU, MH-H &c.; EA COR).

Notes. Frontispiece to vol. 1. 1 p. adv. end vols. 2 and 3. Vol. 4 of BL copy has been trimmed so that it is an inch smaller in height.
French trans. Paris, 1799 (*Phedora, ou la Forêt de Minski*) (Lévy).

CLARIS DE FLORIAN, Jean Pierre, *Estelle*
See FLORIAN, Jean Pierre Claris de (1791: 36)

1798: 23   CLARK, Emily.
IANTHÉ, OR THE FLOWER OF CAERNARVON, A NOVEL, IN TWO VOLUMES. DEDICATED, BY PERMISSION, TO HIS ROYAL HIGHNESS THE PRINCE OF WALES. BY EMILY CLARK, GRAND-DAUGHTER OF THE LATE COLONEL FREDERIC, SON OF THEODORE, KING OF CORSICA.

> London: Printed for the Author; and sold by Hookham and Carpenter, Old Bond Street, 1798.
> I viii, 256p; II 273p. 12mo. 6s sewed (CR), 8s boards (MR).
> CR n.s. 24: 237 (Oct 1798); MR n.s. 26: 458–9 (Aug 1798); AF II: 711.
> BL 12614.f.11 (imperf.); CME 3-628-45021-7; EM 2210: 4; ESTC t061496 (NA MH-H; EA COR).

Notes. Introduction 1, v–viii, followed by 11-pp. list of subscribers (unn.). Pp. 9–16 of vol. 1 missing in BL copy.
The author received £43.1s in subscriptions and a further net profit of £1 from 229 copies sold by Hookham, H&C G/137, 126.
French trans. Paris, 1801 (*Janthé, ou la Rose du Mont-Snodon et les cinq rivaux*) (HWS).

CR: 'The performance of a descendant of this unfortunate family has claims upon the public benevolence, which it should never be the business of criticism to counteract. Among the multitude of novels that swarm from the press, those which are inferior to Ianthé are more numerous than those which surpass it.'

MR [Thomas Wallace]: 'We cannot think of scrutinizing too narrowly a performance written with such a view, and under such circumstances; and we therefore deem it enough to state that, though it cannot be placed in the first rank of English novels, neither does it deserve the lowest place among publications of that class' (p. 459).

1798: 24   [CROFFTS, Mrs].
CONFESSIONS OF A BEAUTY. IN TWO VOLUMES. FROM THE FRENCH.

London: Printed at the Minerva-Press, for William Lane, Leadenhall-Street, 1798.
I 284p; II 266p. 12mo. 7s (CR, GEP).
CR n.s. 25: 358 (1799); AF II: 831.
CtY-BR In.C874.798; xESTC.

Notes. Blakey: Attributed to Mrs Croffts by a Minerva Library Catalogue of 1814.
Adv. GEP 23–26 Feb 1799.

CR: 'If this novel had remained in its original language, the interests of morality would have suffered less than they now do from its extended circulation.'

1798: 25 [ELLIA, Felix].
THEOPHA; OR, MEMOIRS OF A GREEK SLAVE; AS RELATED BY HER LOVER, ENVOY FROM THE COURT OF FRANCE TO THE SUBLIME PORTE.

London: Printed by S. Low, Berwick-Street, Soho, 1798.
I 257p; II 252p. 12mo. 6s (NLR), 6s sewed (adv.).
NLR 1 (Apr 1799): 408; AF II: 4407.
MH-H *EC75.A100.798t2; EM 1475: 28; ESTC n014289 (NA CaAEU).

Notes. Adv., 'In the Press, And will be published Nov. 1' with no price given, GEP 25–27 Oct 1798. Adv., 'altered from the French by Felix Ellia Esq. Author of the Norman Banditti' [1799: 34], GEP 28 Feb-2 Mar 1799.
Adv. end vol. 2 of *Emily Dundorne* (1799: 93).

1798: 26 [EVANS, Robert].
THE STRANGER; OR, LLEWELLYN FAMILY. A CAMBRIAN TALE. IN TWO VOLUMES.

London: Printed at the Minerva-Press, for William Lane, Leadenhall-Street, 1798.
I 314p; II 283p. 12mo. 7s sewed (CR), 8s (GEP), 7s (LC).
CR n.s. 27: 474 (Dec 1799).
CFu WG.30(1798); xESTC.

Notes: The Dream (1801: 26) says on t.p. that it is by Robert Evans, A.M., author of *The Stranger.*
2 pp. advs. end vol. 1; 1 p. advs. end vol. 2.
Adv. GEP 23–26 Feb 1799; adv. LC 85: 278 (19–21 Mar 1799).
German trans. Berlin, 1799 (*Der Fremde oder die Familie Llewellyn*) (EAG); French trans. Paris, 1802 (*L'Etranger, ou la Famille Llewellyn*) (BGR).

CR: 'This novel exhibits some correct features of real life, and is recommended by the moral of rewarding the perseverance and the energies of virtue and genius.'

1798: 27 [FOSTER, E. M., Mrs].
JAQUELINA OF HAINAULT: AN HISTORICAL NOVEL, IN THREE VOLUMES, BY THE AUTHOR OF "THE DUKE OF CLARENCE."

London: Printed for J. Bell, no. 148, Oxford-Street, 1798.
I 206p; II 143p; III 182p. 12mo. 9s boards (CR), 9s sewed (MP).
CR n.s. 26: 116–17 (May 1799); AF II: 1490.
BL 12611.e.21; EM 62: 6; ESTC t057341 (NA CaOLU).

Notes. 2 pp. advs. end vol. 1 and 2 pp. advs. end vol. 3.

The Duke of Clarence 1795: 21.

Adv. MP 2 Feb 1799; 'by Mrs Foster'.

Further edns: Dublin, [1794?] (P. Wogan, J. Moore, W. Porter, B. Dornin, G. Folingsby, and T. Codd, 1 vol., 12mo) ESTC n052555; London, 1800, ESTC t212788.

CR: 'This piece does not rise above the generality of historical novels: yet the perusal of such a work is better than idleness, and we wish that circulating libraries contained no worse productions than Jacquelina of Hainault' (p. 116).

GRIFFIN, Elizabeth, **THE FRIENDS**

See App. A: 11

1798: 28   HANWAY, Mary Ann.

ELLINOR; OR, THE WORLD AS IT IS. A NOVEL. IN FOUR VOLUMES. BY MARY ANN HANWAY.

London: Printed at the Minerva-Press, for William Lane, Leadenhall-Street, 1798.

I viii, 321p; II 345p; III 342p; IV 383p. 12mo. 18s boards (CR, MR), £1 (adv.).

CR n.s. 23: 114 (May 1798); MR n.s. 26: 221 (Jun 1798); AF II: 1802.

BL 012611.h.38; EM 127: 4; ESTC t064753 (NA IU, MH-H, PU &c.).

Notes. Preface i–viii.

Adv. SJC 27–29 Mar 1798.

Adv. end vol. 1 of *Agnes and Leonora* (1799: 85).

Further edn: London, 1799, ESTC n000744. Facs: FCy.

CR: 'The story is interesting; and the sentiments are unexceptionable. We sometimes meet with an unpleasant pertness in the style; but it would be well if circulating libraries contained no worse books than Ellinor.'

MR [William Smyth]: 'While our neighbours on the Continent disgrace brilliant talents by displaying in their tales, &c. incidents intended to inflame the passions, to pervert the imagination, or to depreciate the solid value of religious and moral principles, it is with pleasure that we peruse the tales and novels of our own country; which, for the most part, are advocates for sobriety and virtue. Conscious of such commendable designs, we love not to press with too much severity rules of criticism, on any defect of execution. On this account, we are sorry to say that, in the voluminous work before us, the narrative seems rather prolix, that the language is sometimes too florid and incorrect, and that there is a want of sufficient novelty in the plan and the characters.'

1798: 29   HOLDER, [Henry Evans].

THE SECLUDED MAN; OR, THE HISTORY OF MR. OLIVER. IN TWO VOLUMES. BY THE REV. MR. HOLDER, (CANTILENA CAPTIVITATIS.).

London: Printed at the Minerva-Press, for William Lane, Leadenhall-Street, 1798.

I 240p; II 207p. 12mo. 6s sewed (CR), 8s (GEP).

CR n.s. 25: 473 (Apr 1799).

Corvey; CME 3-628-45061-6; xESTC; BI O; WC shows InU.

Notes. Adv. GEP 23–26 Feb 1799.

CR: 'We are sorry to see the name of a clergyman, and, we believe, a philologist, in the title-page of so dull a novel as the present. We do not mean to say that we have not perused *worse* performances, and such as were likely to produce more injury than merely a waste of time: the latter consequence, however, is sufficient to make us regret that the Secluded Man has not remained in a state of *seclusion* from the public.'

1798: 30   HOLFORD, Margaret, the younger].
CALAF: A PERSIAN TALE. IN TWO VOLUMES.

> London: Printed for Hookham and Carpenter, Old Bond Street, 1798.
> I vi, 227p; II 229p. 12mo. 7s sewed (CR, MR).
> CR n.s. 25: 118 (Jan 1799); MR n.s. 27: 453–4 (Dec 1798); AF II: 2029.
> C 7720.d.1289-1290; ESTC t187692 (BI O).

Notes. Prefatory address to the reader (iii–vi) is signed 'A Friend of the Author' and says that the author is seventeen. 1 p. advs. end vol. 2. 500 copies printed at a cost of about £53 and a loss to the author of some £20 (HA).
Further edn: London, 1800, ESTC n003187.

   CR: 'This fictitious narrative, we are informed in the preface, comes from the pen of a young lady of seventeen. From that age it would be unreasonable to expect much; yet there is a promise of improvement, which we would wish to encourage. The tale is not uninteresting; and the *manners* of the East are preserved with care. The *language*, however, is not always that of oriental *nature*.'

   MR [Arthur Aikin and Ralph Griffiths]: 'What may be reasonably expected from the generality of young ladies at this age, we have here found:—we throw aside the pen of criticism; recollecting, as we do, (with not over-fond remembrance,) that we too *have been young* writers.'

HUGILL, Martha, **ISIDORA OF GALLICIA**
See 1797: 47

1798: 31   HUNTER, Maria.
ELLA; OR, HE'S ALWAYS IN THE WAY. IN TWO VOLUMES. BY MARIA HUNTER, AUTHORESS OF FITZROY.

> London: Printed at the Minerva-Press, for William Lane, Leadenhall-Street, 1798.
> I viii, 200p; II 208p. 12mo. 7s boards (CR), 7s (GEP).
> CR n.s. 24: 470 (Dec 1798).
> Corvey; CME 3-628-45066-7; ESTC n065935 (NA CtY-BR).

Notes. Preface i–viii. 2 pp. advs. end vol. 2.
Fitzroy 1792: 40.
Adv. GEP 23–26 Feb 1799.

   CR: 'The plan of this novel has little regularity. It seems to have been intended only as a vehicle for the introduction of characters from what the authoress calls *nature*. Some of these, as well as the incidents, are delineated with the pen of a caricaturist; and, with the exception of a few just though trite reflections on education and seduction, the moral tendency of the work is not very obvious.'

1798: 32   [KENDALL, A., Mrs].
THE CASTLE ON THE ROCK: OR, MEMOIRS OF THE ELDERLAND FAMILY. BY THE AUTHOR OF DERWENT PRIORY.

London: Printed for H. D. Symonds, Paternoster-Row, 1798.
I 219p; II 304p; III 405p. 12mo. 10s 6d boards (MR, GEP).
MR n.s. 25: 453 (Apr 1798); AF II: 2367.
CaAEU PR 4839.K23.C34 1798; ESTC n026974 (NA CaOTU).

Notes. 2-pp. preface. In vol. 1 p. 28 misnumbered 48.
Derwent Priory 1798: 33.
Adv., 'In a few days will be published', GEP 6–9 Jan 1798.
Adv. end vol. 2 of *Derwent Priory* (1798: 33).
Further edns: Dublin, 1799 (Printed by John Rice, 2 vols., 12mo) ESTC n026975; London, 1845, NSTC 2C10992. French trans. Paris, 1798 (*Eliza, ou Mémoires de la Famille Elderland*) (BGR); German trans. Berlin and Stettin, 1799 (*Die Abtei Derwent*) (WC).

MR [William Smyth]: 'These volumes will afford amusement by the variety of characters pourtrayed in them, and by a sufficient diversity of incidents. . . . Though written with no great powers of invention, and distinguished by no uncommon elegance nor vigour of style, this novel forcibly retains throughout the attention of the reader of sensibility. . . .'

1798: 33   [KENDALL, A., Mrs].
DERWENT PRIORY; OR, MEMOIRS OF AN ORPHAN. IN A SERIES OF LETTERS. FIRST PUBLISHED PERIODICALLY; NOW REPUBLISHED, WITH ADDITIONS. BY THE AUTHOR OF "THE CASTLE ON THE ROCK." IN TWO VOLUMES.

London: Printed for H. D. Symonds, Paternoster-Row, 1798.
I viii, 228p; II 276p. 8vo [MR has 12mo]. 7s sewed (MR).
MR n.s. 26: 457 (Aug 1798); AF II: 2368.
BL C.187.a.17; CME 3-628-45032-2; EM 6291: 1; ESTC t119017 (NA MH-H; EA COR).

Notes. Prior publication in 22 parts in *Lady's Magazine* Jan 1796–Sept 1797, RM 304; RM also reports publication in 22 parts in 2 additional magazines.
Introduction v–viii. 4 pp. advs. end vol. 2. Epistolary.
Castle on the Rock 1798: 32.
Adv., 'in the Press and speedily will be published', SJC 3–6 Feb 1798.
Further edns: Cork, 1799 (Printed by J. Connor, J. Haly, and M. Harris, 1 vol., 8vo), EM 2509: 1, ESTC n006205; NSTC lists edn. in 1845. French trans. Paris, 1798 (*Le Prieuré de Derwent*) (HWS); German trans. Berlin and Stettin, 1799 (*Die Abtey Derwent*) (EAG).

MR [Thomas Wallace]: 'Whether it be that lords are, in modern times, become so numerous as to bear a very considerable proportion to the mass of the community, or that there is something in a title which annexes a sort of adventitious dignity to the trite sentiments that abound in novels, we know not: but it is certain that in all the minor works of this description, the actors are seldom below "the degree of nobility". . . . In the present composition, there is no deviation from this established practice. . . .'

1798: 34   KING, Sophia.
WALDORF; OR, THE DANGERS OF PHILOSOPHY. A PHILOSOPHICAL TALE. BY SOPHIA KING, AUTHOR OF "THE TRIFLES FROM HELICON."

London: Printed for G. G. and J. Robinson, Paternoster-Row, 1798.
I 220p; II 218p. 12mo. 6s sewed (CR, MR).
CR n.s. 24: 112–14 (Sept 1798); MR n.s. 26: 221–2 (June 1798); AF II: 2406.
BL 12612.bbb.14; EM 133: 5; ESTC t064755 (NA MH-H).

Notes: Trifles of Helicon (1798) by Charlotte and Sophia King is a collection of verse.
Adv., 'In the Press, And in a few Days will be published', GEP 24–26 Apr 1798.
French trans. n.p., 1798 (*Waldorf ou les dangers de la philosophie*) (BGR). Facs: FCy.

CR: 'There are various errors in this work; but the radical defect is, that its philosophy, by which the writer means atheism, is not represented as false. . . . The style is sometimes affected; but it is frequently nervous; and, faulty as the work is, it discovers powers that may rise to excellence' (p. 114).

MR [William Smyth]: 'This novel attempts a more arduous and a more important office, than to correct the follies of the day by a display of ludicrous characters and events; or to delight the imagination by scenes of pathos, or to appal it by gigantic fictions of horror. Miss King styles her performance *a philosophical tale*. She advances, with virtue and religion on her side, to combat the modern vindicators of atheism and libertinism. . . . Though we give due merit to the writer for her good design, we think that she has undertaken too weighty a task.'

1798: 35   KOTZEBUE, [August Friedrich Ferdinand von].
*THE HISTORY OF MY FATHER: OR HOW IT HAPPENED THAT I WAS BORN. A ROMANCE. IN 12 CHAPTERS.TRANSLATED FROM THE GERMAN OF KOTZEBUE.

London: Treppass (MR).
12mo. 3s 6d boards (MR).
CR n.s. 23: 233–4 (June 1798); MR n.s. 30: 94 (Sept 1799); AF II: 2434.
No copy located.

Notes. Trans. of *Die Geschichte meines Vaters* (Leipzig, 1788).
CR refers to rev. of French version in App. to n.s. 19 [Apr/May 1797].

MR [Robert Woodhouse]: 'This tale, though not written like the Candide of Voltaire to ridicule any particular system, has a faint resemblance to that work in the cast of its sentiments, in its style, and in the abrupt manner with which we are led from one event to another. Like Voltaire, too, the author lets fly his shafts against religion; shafts which either miss their object or rebound from it, for they are neither aimed with skill, nor pointed by wit. . . . We cannot deny that the present work affords some entertainment, though it possesses not exquisite humour and refined pleasantry. Some part of the wit (if wit it really be) is lost on us, either from the obscurity of the allusions, or through the fault of the translator.'

1798: 36   KOTZEBUE, August [Friedrich Ferdinand] von; THOMPSON, Benjamin (trans.).
ILDEGERTE, QUEEN OF NORWAY. IN TWO VOLUMES. FROM THE GERMAN OF AUGUSTUS VON KOTZEBUE. BY BENJAMIN THOMPSON, JUN. TRANSLATOR OF THE STRANGER, AS PERFORMED AT THE THEATRE ROYAL, DRURY-LANE.

London: Printed at the Minerva-Press, for William Lane, Leadenhall-Street, 1798.

I 168, 9p; II 160p. 12mo. 6s sewed (CR), 7s sewed (MR), 7s (GEP).

CR n.s. 26: 477 (Dec 1799); MR n.s. 29: 334 (July 1799); AF II: 4430.

BL 1206.e 10, 11; EM 2380: 1; ESTC t135696 (BI O; NA CLU-S/C, MiU, MnU &c.).

Notes. Trans. of *Ildegerte, Königin von Norwegen* (Reval/Leipzig, 1788).

ESTC corrects publication date to 1799 on the basis of the review dates, but the MR gives 1798 as the publication date.

Notes at end of vol. 1 separately paginated but notes at end of vol. 2 on pp. 159–60.

Adv. GEP 23–26 Feb 1799.

Further edn: Philadelphia, 1800, ESTC w030595.

An earlier novel, also called *Ildegerte, Queen of Norway* (1721, ESTC t055136) was a trans. of *Histoire d' Ildegerte* by Eustache Le Noble.

CR: 'The dramatic celebrity of Kotzebue will doubtless recommend this piece to the notice of the English reader: it is a romance illustrative of the chivalrous bravery of the northern nations, and interspersed with the doctrines of the runic mythology. Of the incidents no more can be said than that they would form a *showy* pantomime for one of our winter theatres: there are, however, many sentiments which breathe the candour of genius and of virtue, and which are conveyed with due eloquence in the language of the translator, who has proved himself capable of doing justice to the effusions of his author.'

MR [William Taylor]: 'This prose epopæa may bear comparison with several of the heroic romances of Ossian. It is indeed not narrated with equal loftiness, nor with equal taste; and many modernisms occur . . . which disturb the illusion, and unpleasantly recall the imagination from other times to our own:—but the story has great interest; the style has a poetical glow, and a rhapsodical rapidity; the touches of deep pathos and sublime sentiment are many; and the interspersed allusions to Gothic mythology are classically selected.'

1798: 37   LAFONTAINE, August [Heinrich Julius].
SAINT JULIEN; OR, MEMOIRS OF A FATHER. BY AUGUSTUS LA FONTAINE. TRANSLATED FROM THE GERMAN.

London: Printed for J. Bell, no. 148, Oxford-Street, 1798.

279p. 12mo. 6s boards (CR), 4s sewed (MP).

CR n.s. 26: 236 (June 1799); AF II: 2443.

BL 1154.k.15; EMf; ESTC t101310 (BI O; NA CLU-S/C, IU, NSyU).

Notes. Trans. of *Familie Saint Julien*, vol. 3 of *Familiengeschichten* (11 vols. Berlin, 1797–1804). 4 pp. advs. end vol.

Adv. GEP 25–27 Oct 1798: 'The Novel of St Julien, from a German Original, is translating from the French Copy, under the Inspection of Mrs Charlotte Smith, and will be ready for Publication in December.' Adv., 'In one large Volume', MP 21 Feb 1799; 'This beautiful work is part of the History of Families; the remainder will be published in a few days.' [See also *The Family of Halden* 1799: 61].

Further edn: London, 1799, EM 2527: 6, ESTC t101309. French trans. Paris, 1798 (*Saint-Julien, ou mémoire d'un père de famille*) (BGR).

1799 London edn. adv., 'copiously and accurately Translated', 'enriched with a prefatory Address and Historical and Explanatory Notes', and published by William Lane, GEP 2–5 Feb 1799. This rival translation is said to be greatly superior to 'any other copy which may be obtruded on [the public's] judgment': 'The translator has closely followed the German Original; the story is copiously and accurately told, without any abbreviation or mutilation;

its language improved, where the idiom of the German required, and made soft to the English ear. The Book has been printed in that marked style of superiority which has ever distinguished works committed to the care of the Minerva Press.'

CR: 'This is a tale of some interest founded on the domestic calamities produced by the French revolution. The Shandean traits of character in the beginning of the story would better have been omitted, as they are neither preserved nor remembered as the story proceeds.'

CR refers to review of original: n.s. 25, 236.

1798: 38   LAMB, Charles.

A TALE OF ROSAMUND GRAY AND OLD BLIND MARGARET. BY CHARLES LAMB.

London: Printed for Lee and Hurst, no. 32, Pater-Noster-Row, 1798.
134p. 8vo [MR has 12mo]. 2s 6d (CR), 2s 6d sewed (MR), 2s 6d boards (MP).
CR n.s. 25: 472–3 (Apr 1799); MR n.s. 32: 447 (Aug 1800); AF II: 2450.
BL C.59.b.8; EMf; ESTC t126492 (BI O, WIS; NA CSmH, ICN, TxU, ViU &c.).

Notes. Dedication to Marmaduke Thompson. Text of novel starts on p. 5.
Adv. MP 5 Jan 1799; additional bookseller is Pearson in Birmingham.
Further edns: Birmingham, 1798 (WC); London, 1836 (WC). German trans. Berlin, 1801 (*Rosamunde Gray und die alte blinde Margarethe*) (EAG).

CR: 'This little tale reminded us strongly of Mackenzie's style; and the imitation, we think, equals the original. The story is perhaps too simple: but it is so related as to invite a frequent perusal; and it abounds with passages which the reader will wish to remember, and which he will be the better for remembering' (p. 472).

MR: Thomas Wallace]: 'In the perusal of this pathetic and interesting story, the reader, who has a mind capable of enjoying rational and moral sentiment, will find much gratification. Mr Lamb has here proved himself skilful in touching the nicest feelings of the heart, and in affording great pleasure to the imagination, by exhibiting events and situations which, in the hands of a writer less conversant with the springs and energies of the *moral sense*, would have made a very "*sorry figure*."'

1798: 39   {LANSDELL, Sarah}.

THE TOWER; OR THE ROMANCE OF RUTHYNE. IN THREE VOLUMES. BY THE AUTHORESS OF MANFREDI.

London: Printed for the Authoress, by Harry Smith; and sold by Hookham and Carpenter, Bond-Street, 1798.
I iii, 141p; II 168p; III 163p. 8vo. 10s 6d (ME).
MH-H *EC75.L291; EM 1497: 4; ESTC n013718 (BI E; NA MH-H, ViU).

Notes. Dedication to Mrs Marriott 1, i–iii, signed Sarah Lansdell. Pagination Roman-Arabic is continuous; text of novel begins on p. 5.
Manfredi 1796: 60.
1797 proposals for publishing by subscription ESTC t141825.

1798: 40   [LATHOM, Francis].

THE MIDNIGHT BELL, A GERMAN STORY, FOUNDED ON INCIDENTS IN REAL LIFE. IN THREE VOLUMES.

London: Printed for H. D. Symonds, No. 20, Paternoster-Row, 1798.

I 209p; II 233p; III 246p. 12mo. 10s 6d sewed (CR, MR).

CR n.s. 23: 472 (Aug 1798); MR n.s. 26: 340 (July 1798); AF II: 2469.

C S727.d.79.14–16; CME 3-628-45116-7; EMf; ESTC t173059 (BI BL; NA CaAEU, IU, NjP &c.; EA COR).

Notes. ESTC: Sometimes wrongly attributed to George Walker.

Adv., 'speedily will be published', GEP 15–17 Mar 1798; adv. as published GEP 26–28 Apr 1798.

Further edns: Dublin, 1798 (N. Kelly, 2 vols., 12mo), ESTC t202830; Cork, 1798, ESTC t173060; Philadelphia, 1799, ESTC w026024; NSTC lists edn. in 1825. French trans. Paris, 1798 (*La Cloche de minuit*) (BGR); German trans. Erfurt, 1800 (*Die Mitternachtsglocke*) (RS).

CR: 'As this novel has no prefatory address, we know not whether it is a translation from the German, or an original work; but we are inclined to think that the latter description is more applicable to it. The serious incidents are founded on the passion of jealousy; the concomitant circumstances of ghosts, murders, midnight bells, &c. are introduced with the usual mysterious apparatus; and the story will not be the less relished because not very probable. The authors of works on this plan seem not to care how absurd and contradictory the story may be in its progress, provided they can make all plain and evident at the conclusion; but, indeed, they do not always attend even to this point.'

MR [William Taylor]: 'The novel belongs to the school of terror; midnight bells, dismal dungeons, lonely tapers, banditti, murders, thunder-storms, all but supernatural horrors, conspire to agitate the reader. Much curiosity is excited; and, although its gratification be protracted by supernumerary episodes, it is eventually not disappointed.'

1798: 41   LISTER [pseud.].

VERONICA; OR, THE MYSTERIOUS STRANGER. A NOVEL. IN TWO VOLUMES. BY LISTER.

London: Printed at the Minerva-Press, for William Lane, Leadenhall-Street, 1798.

I 212p; II 225p. 12mo. 7s (GEP), 6s sewed (LC).

NLR 1: 405 (Apr 1799).

BL 12613.d.20; CME 3-628-45104-3; EM 292: 2; ESTC t070075 (NA CSmH, CtY-BR, InU-Li; EA COR).

Notes. Adv. GEP 23–26 Feb 1799; adv. LC 85: 278 (19–21 Mar 1799).

1798: 42   LLOYD, Charles.

EDMUND OLIVER. BY CHARLES LLOYD. IN TWO VOLUMES.

Bristol: Printed by Bulgin and Rosser, for Joseph Cottle, and sold in London by Messrs. Lee and Hurst, Paternoster-Row, 1798.

I xii, 252p; II 294p. 12mo. 8s boards (CR).

CR n.s. 23: 302–306 (July 1798); AF II: 2579.

C S727.d.79.53-54; EM 4372: 1; ESTC t147282 (BI BL, O; NA CLU-S/C, CSmH, NNPM; EA TaLn).

Notes. Epistolary.

German trans. Erfurt, 1799–1800 (*Edmund Olliver, Seitenstück zu Rousseaus Heloise*) (EAG).

CR: 'We cannot conclude without strongly recommending this performance, as it possesses the irresistible eloquence of Werter, or the Nouvelle Héloïse, and contains no principle from which the most rigid moralist or the most devout Christian can justly dissent' (p. 306).

1798: 43 LOUVET [DE COUVRAY, Jean-Baptiste].
EMILY DE VARMONT; OR DIVORCE DICTATED BY NECESSITY; TO WHICH ARE ADDED THE AMOURS OF FATHER SÉVIN. FROM THE FRENCH OF LOUVET, LATE PRESIDENT OF THE NATIONAL CONVENTION OF FRANCE, AUTHOR OF FAUBLAS, &C. IN THREE VOLUMES.
>   London: Printed for G. Kearsley, no. 46, Fleet-Street, 1798.
>   I 207p; II 215p; III 259p. 12mo. 10s 6d sewed (CR, MR).
>   CR n.s. 22: 235–7 (Feb 1798); MR n.s. 26: 327–30 (July 1798); AF II: 2608.
>   BL 12511.aa.33; EM 57: 3; ESTC t113664 (BI O; NA IU, PU, ViU).

Notes. Trans. of Émile de Varmont, ou le divorce nécessaire et les amours du curé Sevin (Paris, 1791) (BGR).
Epistolary.
The Life and Adventures of the Chevalier De Faublas 1793: 27.
Adv. GEP 15–17 Feb 1798; 'Of the following interesting Novel, it may be proper to observe, that it had considerable influence in producing two memorable Decrees of the National Convention, the one authorising Divorces, the other allowing Priests to marry'.
>   CR: '. . . we perceive with pleasure, that several gross indelicacies in the French have been either wholly suppressed in the translation, or so far softened and disguised, as to be no longer capable of exciting a blush on the cheek of British modesty' (p. 235).
>   MR [William Taylor]: 'The tendency of the Novel before us is to render prominent the evils of ill-suited marriages, and to countenance the wish for facility of divorce. Its morality, therefore, is exceptionable; and its success would be a symptom of the declension of manners. In Paris, indeed, where the energy and licentiousness of barbaric times have superseded the polish and effeminacy of excessive refinement, this novel appears in its place, and may expect popularity; but in London, we trust, the author of the adventures of the Chevalier de Faublas is never to become a favourite instructor. . . . The story is grossly improbable' (p. 328).

1798: 44 [LUCAS, Rev. Charles].
THE CASTLE OF SAINT DONATS; OR, THE HISTORY OF JACK SMITH. IN THREE VOLUMES.
>   London: Printed at the Minerva-Press, for William Lane, Leadenhall-Street, 1798.
>   I xliv, 170p; II 280p; III 232p. 12mo. 10s 6d sewed (CR, MR), 12s (GEP).
>   CR n.s. 26: 357 (July 1799); MR n.s. 29: 89–90 (May 1799); AF II: 2621.
>   MH-H *EC8.L9623.798c; CME 3-628-45009-8; EM 1494: 13; ESTC n014986 (NA ViU; EA COR).

Notes. Introduction (signed C. L.) 1, iii–xliv; 2-pp. preface (unn.).
Adv. GEP 23–26 Feb 1799.
Further edns: Baltimore, 1800 (WC); Baltimore, 1801 (WC). French trans. 1803 (Le Château de Saint-Donats, ou Histoire du fils d'un Emigré échappé aux massacres en France) (Lévy).

CR: 'From a sprightly introduction to these volumes, it should seem that the writer is not unacquainted with the vicissitudes of the literary world. The story of the novel possesses a degree of interest beyond many productions of the kind; and some of the characters are drawn with an agreeable vivacity.'

MR [William Smyth]: 'The author of this novel is a person of talents and observation: but the hero of his tale is a rake; who, in time, and before the spirits of youth have wholly subsided, is reformed, and married to a fair, rich, and virtuous woman, whom his altered conduct entitles him to espouse. We do not greatly approve such examples. . . . The characters in this work, though not new, are distinctly pourtrayed. . . . In short, novel-readers will not be disappointed if they look for entertainment in these volumes.'

1798: 45   MACKENZIE, Anna Maria.
DUSSELDORF; OR, THE FRATRICIDE. A ROMANCE. IN THREE VOLUMES. BY ANNA MARIA MACKENZIE.

> London: Printed at the Minerva-Press, for William Lane, Leadenhall-Street, 1798.
> I 238p; II 237p; III 216p. 12mo. 10s 6d sewed (CR, SJC), 12s (GEP).
> CR n.s. 24: 236 (Oct 1798); AF II: 2656.
> ViU *PZ2.M322Du 1798; CME 3-628-45114-0; ESTC n006426 (NA MnU; EA COR).

Notes. Illustrations.
Adv. SJC 5–7 June 1798; adv. GEP 23–26 Feb 1799.
Further edn: Dublin, 1798 (Printed for the Proprietors, 3 vols., 12mo), ESTC n006427.
French trans. Paris, 1798 (*Le Fratricide, ou les mystères du Château de Dusseldorf*) (BGR).

CR: 'With regard to the incidents of this romance, the writer imitates those of Mrs. Radcliffe; but she is far from being equal to that lady in this branch of composition. It seems to be agreed that those who write on the horrific plan must employ the same instruments—cruel German counts, each with two wives—old castles—private doors—sliding pannels—banditti—assassins—ghosts, &c.

We have often had occasion to censure the absurd and incorrect language of novels in general; and from such censure this romance is not exempt.'

1798: 46   [MARTIN, Mrs].
DELORAINE. A DOMESTIC TALE. IN TWO VOLUMES.

> London: Printed at the Minerva-Press, for William Lane, Leadenhall-Street, 1798.
> I 308p; II 300p. 12mo. 7s sewed (CR).
> CR n.s. 24: 356 (Nov 1798).
> PU Singer-Mend.PR.4984.M13.O4.1798; CME 3-628-45027-6; ESTC n006271 (NA TxHR; EA COR).

Notes. Blakey: Attributed to Mrs Martin by a Minerva Library Catalogue of 1814.
Preface signed 'Helen of Herefordshire'.

CR: 'It never rises above mediocrity; the incidents are of the common kind; the characters are imperfectly and feebly sketched; and those from which we expected most, are left unfinished.'

1798: 47   [MARTIN, Mrs].
MELBOURNE. A NOVEL. IN THREE VOLUMES. BY THE AUTHOR OF DELORAINE.

London: Printed at the Minerva-Press, for William Lane, Leadenhall-Street, 1798.
I 227p; II 300p; III 310p. 12mo. 10s 6d sewed (CR, SJC), 12s (GEP).
CR n.s. 27: 115 (Sept 1799); AF II: 2725.
BL 1608/4205; CME 3-628-45108-6; EM 2257: 1; ESTC t121179 (NA MH-H; EA COR).

Notes. Blakey: Attributed to Mrs Martin by a Minerva Library Catalogue of 1814.
2 pp. advs. end vol. 3.
Deloraine 1798: 46.
Adv. SJC 14–17 July 1798; adv. GEP 23–26 Feb 1799.
Adv. end vol. 2 of *Court Intrigue* (1799: 44).
CR: 'Upon the whole, if an interesting story, a moral tendency, and much useful delineation of character and manners, can recommend a novel, Melbourne deserves the applause of criticism.'

1798: 48   [MEEKE, Mary].
THE SICILIAN. A NOVEL. IN FOUR VOLUMES. BY THE AUTHOR OF THE MYSTERIOUS WIFE.

London: Printed at the Minerva-Press, for William Lane, Leadenhall-Street, 1798.
I 351p; II 344p; III 218p; IV 237p. 12mo. 12s (CR).
CR n.s. 25: 234 (Feb 1799); AF II: 2811.
BL Cup.403.i.9; EM 6814: 1; ESTC t139666 (BI MRu; NA CaAEU).

Notes. 2 pp. advs. end vol. 3; 3 pp. advs. end vol. 4.
The Mysterious Wife 1797: 56.
CR: 'The author of this production discovers some ability in detailing the incidents, and draws some of his characters in natural and lively colours; but he wearies the reader by prolonging the work after the *denouement* has taken place, when no expectation remains to be gratified. The fourth volume is altogether useless.'

1798: 49   MUSGRAVE, Agnes.
THE SOLEMN INJUNCTION. A NOVEL. IN FOUR VOLUMES. BY AGNES MUSGRAVE, AUTHOR OF CICELY OF RABY, &C.

London: Printed at the Minerva-Press, for William Lane, Leadenhall-Street, 1798.
I 294p; II 286p; III 304p; IV 342p. 12mo. £1 (GEP), 14s sewed (Min).
CR n.s. 25: 358 (Mar 1799).
BL 1153.e.21; CME 3-628-45123-X; EM 3918: 1; ESTC t147587 (BI LEu; NA ViU; EA COR).

Notes. Frontispiece to vol. 4. 2 pp. advs. end vol. 1.
Cicely; or, the Rose of Raby 1795: 32.
Adv. GEP 23–26 Feb 1799.
CR: 'Not quite so dull as many *solemn* things of the same kind, nor sufficiently interesting to any beside the *persevering* readers, by whose appetite for fictitious narratives our circulating libraries are supported.'

1798: 50   NICOLAI, [Christoph] Friedrich; DUTTON, Thomas (*trans.*).
THE LIFE AND OPINIONS OF SEBALDUS NOTHANKER. TRANSLATED

FROM THE GERMAN OF FRIEDRICH NICOLAI, BY THOMAS DUTTON, A.M.

London: Printed by C. Lowndes, and sold by H. D. Symonds, no. 20, Paternoster-Row, 1798.

I xviii, 356p; II 395p; III 289p. 12mo. 5s sewed (CR), 9s sewed (MR).

CR n.s. 19: 479–80 (Apr 1797); MR n.s. 22: 248–53 (Mar 1797) [vol. 1], MR n.s. 26: 583–6 (App [Aug/Sept 1798]) [vols. 2 & 3]; AF II: 1191.

C 7746.d.83; EM 2379: 11; ESTC t099061 (BI BL, Ota; NA CU-A, MdBJ, MH-H &c.).

Notes. Trans. of *Das Leben und die Meinungen des Herrn Magister Sebaldus Nothanker* (Berlin and Stettin, 1773–76).

Dedication to the Marquis of Lansdowne; author's preface. Text in vol. 3 begins on p. 3.

CR gives date of 1796.

MR n.s. 22 [William Taylor]: 'Of the works of Nicolai, none has so reasonable a prospect of longevity as the history of Sebaldus Nothanker. Nearly thirty years have elapsed since it was undertaken;—since the literature which it satirizes, and the manners which it describes, were prevailingly those of protestant Germany:— but the stupendous improvement, which so short an interval has effected, occasions the people of that region to cherish with exultation an honest memorial of their antient rusticity' (p. 248).

MR n.s. 26 [Ralph Griffiths]: 'Our readers will, no doubt, deem it sufficient that we have announced to them the continuation and conclusion of M. Nicolai's lively and humorous satire on bigotry, superstition, and intolerance' (p. 583). 'We do not join with those who deem M. Nicolai an enemy to Religion: the *pernicious engraftments on that sacred stock* are the proper objects of his satire' (p. 586).

1798: 51   [?O'KEEFFE, Adelaide].

LLEWELLIN: A TALE. IN THREE VOLUMES. HUMBLY DEDICATED IN POETICAL ADDRESS TO HER ROYAL HIGHNESS THE PRINCESS CHARLOTTE AUGUSTA OF WALES.

London: Printed and published by G. Cawthorn, British Library, No. 132, Strand Sold also by Messrs Richardson, Royal-Exchange; and J. Wright, Piccadilly, 1798/99.

I (1799) ix, 334p; II (1798) 423p; III (1799) 426p. 10s 6d (NLR), 0s 6d boards (MP).

NLR 1: 507 (May 1799).

BL 12613.f.13; CME 3-628-45105-1; EM 217: 3; ESTC t070092 (BI E, O; NA CaOHM, CLU-S/C; EA COR).

Notes. Author attribution: FC. WC attributes to Grace Buchanan Stevens.

Verse dedication (dated Sept. 1796) to H.R.H. Princess Charlotte Augusta of Wales v–ix.

Adv. MP 19 July 1799; 'It comprehends all the various historical incidents of that period, heightened and connected by the aid of fiction. . . . On the whole, it is a picture of the human heart, and gleaning of the Sciences, embellished with the fanciful charms that a vivid imagination can bestow.'

1798: 52   PARSONS, [Eliza].

ANECDOTES OF TWO WELL-KNOWN FAMILIES. WRITTEN BY A DESCENDANT; AND DEDICATED TO THE FIRST FEMALE PEN IN

ENGLAND. PREPARED FOR THE PRESS BY MRS. PARSONS, AUTHOR OF "AN OLD FRIEND WITH A NEW FACE," &C. &C. IN THREE VOLUMES.

> London: Printed for T. N. Longman, Paternoster-Row, 1798.
> I viii, 282p; II 299p; III 277p. 12mo. 10s 6d sewed (CR), 10s boards (MR, GEP), 10s 6d boards (SJC, adv.).
> CR n.s. 23: 353 (July 1798); MR n.s. 27: 332–3 (Nov 1798); AF II: 3230.
> BL 1607/3785; EM 2417: 2; ESTC t119670 (BI BL; NA CtY-BR, ICN, MH-H, ViU).

Notes. Preface by the Compiler 1, v; Preface by the Editor vii–viii.
An Old Friend with a New Face 1797: 62.
Adv. SJC 1–3 Mar 1798; adv. GEP 3–6 Mar 1798.
Adv. end vol. 3 of *A Tale of the Times* (1799: 95).

CR: 'The outline of this story is said to have been sent to the editor by an unknown friend. Whether this statement is true or false, is of little consequence to the public. The story itself is interesting; but the interest becomes weaker after the first volume.'

MR [James Bannister]: 'Though this novel does not exhibit those highly-wrought scenes of distress of which writers of fictitious history are generally fond, it is sufficiently impassioned to affect the heart and to engage the attention.... The laudable tendency of this work is to inspire a love of virtue.'

1798: 53   [PATRICK, Mrs F. C.].
MORE GHOSTS! IN THREE VOLUMES. BY THE WIFE OF AN OFFICER, AUTHOR OF THE IRISH HEIRESS.

> London: Printed at the Minerva-Press, for William Lane, Leadenhall-Street, 1798.
> I xiii, 238p; II 240p; III 264p. 12mo. 10s 6d sewed (CR), 12s (GEP).
> CR n.s. 24: 236 (Oct 1798); AF II: 3256.
> MH-H *EC75.P2753.798m; CME 3-628-45132-9; EM 1489: 24; ESTC n010225 (EA COR).

Notes. Prefatory address 1, i–xiii (signed 'An Officer's Widow'). Pagination continuous Roman-Arabic; text of novel starts on p. 15 in vol. 1.
The Irish Heiress 1797: 63.
Adv. GEP 23–26 Feb 1799.

CR: '*More Ghosts* would have been superfluous in the present state of novel-writing, had not the author of this work conjured up *her* ghosts with a view of dissipating the horrors, lately excited in the tender breasts of many a boarding-school miss, by the more artful and terrific dealers in the article. The ghosts in this piece are rather cunning than terrible; and they add considerably to our entertainment. The characters are more analogous to those of real life, than the faultless monsters which are indebted to imagination only for a temporary existence; and their adventures lead, by easy and natural means, to many just reflections on the errors of education and the irregularity of the passions.'

1798: 54   PHILLIPS, Mrs Lucius [or Phebe GIBBES?].
HEAVEN'S BEST GIFT. A NOVEL. IN FOUR VOLUMES. BY MRS. LUCIUS PHILLIPS, A NEAR RELATION TO MAJOR GENERAL PHILLIPS.

London: Printed for the Author, and Sold by W. Miller, New Bond-Street; and Lloyd,
Harley-Street, n.d. [1798].
I 209p; II 211p; III 228p; IV 240p. 12mo. 14s boards (CR), 14s sewed (SJC, Min).
CR n.s. 24: 114 (Sept 1798); AF II: 3328.
Corvey; CME 3-628-45155-8; xESTC.

Notes. In a letter of 18 Oct 1804 (RLF 2: 74) Phebe Gibbes claimed authorship of this novel.
4-pp. list of subscribers vol. 1.
Adv. SJC 5–7 June 1798.

CR: 'The story is absurd and inconsistent, even with all the latitude that writers of fiction
may claim; and the characters are made up of the worst *traits* that are scattered over many
novels.'

1798: 55 [PILKINGTON, Miss].

THE SUBTERRANEAN CAVERN; OR, MEMOIRS OF ANTOINETTE DE
MONTFLORANCE. IN FOUR VOLUMES. BY THE AUTHOR OF DELIA
AND ROSINA.

London: Printed at the Minerva-Press, for William Lane, Leadenhall-Street, 1798.
I 228p; II 251p; III 252p; IV 303p. 12mo. 14s sewed (CR), 16s (GEP).
CR n.s. 27: 474 (Dec 1799).
Corvey; CME 3-628-45182-5; ESTC n024522 (NA CtY-BR, PU, ViU).

Notes. For authorship see note in FC.
1 p. adv. end vol. 2; 1 p. adv. end vol. 4. Epistolary.
Delia 1790: 59; *Rosina* 1793: 35.
Adv. GEP 23–26 Feb 1799.

CR: 'The incidents of this novel are interesting, and display the early characteristics of the
French revolution in very critical and lively attitudes.
The characters display traits of genius. . . . we consider the Subterranean Cavern as a novel
much superior to the common class of similar productions. The style is, perhaps, too uniformly florid; but it sometimes rises into genuine eloquence.'

1798: 56 [PILKINGTON, Mary].

TALES OF THE COTTAGE; OR STORIES, MORAL AND AMUSING FOR
YOUNG PERSONS. WRITTEN ON THE PLAN OF THAT CELEBRATED
WORK, LES VEILLÉES DU CHATEAU, BY MADAME LA COMPTESSE
DE GENLIS.

London: Printed for Vernor and Hood, in the Poultry; and sold by E. Newbery, Corner
of St Paul's Church-Yard, 1798.
viii, 218p. 12mo. 2s (MR), 2s 'Bound, Vellum Back' (GEP).
MR n.s. 27: 330 (Nov 1798); AF II: 3354.
BL 12830.e.108; EM 4374: 6; ESTC t073674 (NA CLU-S/C, NjP).

Notes. Preface v–vi; table of contents vii–viii. Illustrations. 2 pp. advs. end vol.
Adv. GEP 6–8 Nov 1798.
Further edns: Dublin, 1799 (Printed for T. Jackson, 1 vol., 12mo), ESTC t210843; London,
1799, ESTC t135978; London, 1800, ESTC t135977; NSTC lists edns. in 1803, 1807 and 1816.
French trans. Londres [Paris], 1799 (*Contes de la chaumière*) (BGR).

MR [Jabez Hirons]: 'A collection of interesting stories . . . which may safely be recommended to the attentive perusal of those for whom it is particularly designed, as calculated to please, inform, and improve.'

1798: 57   [PILKINGTON, Mary].
TALES OF THE HERMITAGE: WRITTEN FOR THE INSTRUCTION AND AMUSEMENT OF THE RISING GENERATION.

London: Printed for Vernor and Hood, Poultry; and sold by E. Newbery, the Corner of St. Paul's Church-yard, 1798.
228p. 12mo. 2s (CR, MR), 2s 'Vellum Back' (GEP).
CR n.s. 25: 110 (Jan 1799); MR n.s. 27: 466–7 (Dec 1798); AF II: 3355.
BL Ch.790/8; ESTC t097220 (BI LVu, O; NA CtY-Walpole, MiDW).

Notes. Frontispiece. 2 pp. advs. end vol.
Adv. GEP 6–8 Nov 1798.
Further edns: Philadelphia, 1800 (WC); London, 1807 (WC); London, 1811 (WC); NSTC lists edns. in 1800, 1805, 1809 and 1815.
CR: 'Some of these tales are superior to the others in style and interest. The whole may impress important duties upon young minds.'
MR [Jabez Hirons]: 'The tales are all adapted to instruct and improve the mind, as well as to engage the attention' (p. 467).

1798: 58   PLUMPTRE, Anne.
THE RECTOR'S SON, IN THREE VOLUMES, BY ANNE PLUMPTRE, AUTHOR OF ANTOINETTE.

London: Printed for Lee and Hurst, No. 32, Pater-Noster-Row, 1798.
I 298p; II 275p; III 283p. 12mo. 10s 6d sewed (CR, MR).
CR n.s. 23: 114 (May 1798); MR n.s. 26: 107–8 (May 1798); AF II: 3418.
BL 1489.cc.66; CME 3-628-45153-1; EM 2265: 1; ESTC t060972 (BI C, MRu; EA COR).

Notes. 4 pp. advs. end vol. 3.
Antoinette 1796: 74.
Adv. GEP 15–17 Mar 1798.
German trans. Berlin, 1799 (Des Pfarrers Sohn) (EAG); French trans. n.p., n.d. (Le Fils du curé) (HWS).
CR: 'Those readers who do not regard the probability of a story may derive pleasure from this work. Though we do not consider it as having any great merit, it is not altogether contemptible.'
MR [William Smyth]: 'Though this novel be written with too little attention to the "lucidus ordo" which brings various events to the mind with pleasure, and all the force of impression, yet it affords many lessons from which youthful readers may gather instructions. . . . Some part of the narration appears to us to be romantic; and some of the circumstances are improbable.'

1798: 59   PORTER, Anna Maria.
OCTAVIA. BY ANNA MARIA PORTER. IN THREE VOLUMES.

London: Printed for T. N. Longman, No. 39, Paternoster-Row, 1798.
I iv, 249p; II 239p; III 228p. 12mo. 10s 6d boards (CR, MR).
CR n.s. 24: 471–2 (Dec 1798); MR n.s. 28: 346 (Mar 1799); AF II: 3537.
Corvey; CME 3-628-45136-1; xESTC.

Notes. 2-pp. dedication to Mrs. Crespigny signed Anna Maria Porter, London, 11 Oct 1798.
2 pp. advs. end vol. 1. 500 copies printed Oct 1798 (Strahan 17 f. 98).
Adv. GEP 27–30 Oct 1798.
Adv. end vol. 3 of *A Tale of the Times* (1799: 95).
Further edns: London, 1804 (Summers); London, 1833 (WC). French trans. Paris, 1801
(*Octavia*) (BN).

CR: 'Miss Porter may with care become respectable as a poetess; but we would advise her
to relinquish the task of writing novels' (p. 472).

MR [George Edward Griffiths]: 'The incidents and personages of this work are trite and
trifling, and the cant language of fashion is repeated till it fatigues: but some of the characters
are well delineated, the dialogue is often sprightly, and the tendency of the whole is the promotion of virtue.'

1798: 60   PRATT, [Samuel Jackson].
PITY'S GIFT: A COLLECTION OF INTERESTING TALES, TO EXCITE
THE COMPASSION OF YOUTH FOR THE ANIMAL CREATION.
ORNAMENTED WITH VIGNETTES. FROM THE WRITINGS OF MR.
PRATT. SELECTED BY A LADY.

London: Printed for T. N. Longman, Paternoster-Row; and E. Newbery, St. Paul's
Church-Yard, 1798.
viii, 147p. 12mo. 2s (CR), 2s boards (MR, GEP).
CR n.s. 26: 358–9 (July 1799); MR n.s. 27: 329 (Nov 1798); AF II: 3583.
BL 8435.a.26; EM 526: 23; ESTC t085824 (BI O; NA CaOHM, CaOTP, CLU-S/C &c.).

Notes. 'A Lady' is possibly Laetitia Pilkington (ESTC).
Introduction v–viii. Illustrations. 1 p. advs. end vol.
Adv., 'Embellished with 14 fine Wood Engravings', GEP 7–9 June 1798.
Further edns: London, 1798, EM 8713: 4, ESTC t085823; Philadelphia 1801, 1807 and 1808
(WC); New York, 1804 (WC); NSTC lists edns. in 1801, 1807, 1810 and 1816.

CR: 'The writings of Mr. Pratt are so well known to the public, that it would be unnecessary to examine critically the contents of this little volume. The selection is not injudicious;
and it may repress the too common propensity of children to harass and torment helpless
animals' (p. 358).

MR [Jabez Hirons]: 'As *Pity's cause* ought always to be pleaded, we cannot but approve the
exertions of this lady who presents these selections to youth, in favour of the *animal creation*.
They are fifteen in number, and the greater part are drawn from the "Gleanings" of Mr. Pratt.
The stories, whatever minute defects they may have, will interest the attention of youth, and
are calculated for their improvement.'

1798: 61   ROCHE, Regina Maria.
CLERMONT. A TALE. IN FOUR VOLUMES. BY REGINA MARIA
ROCHE, AUTHOR OF THE CHILDREN OF THE ABBEY, &C. &C.

London: Printed at the Minerva-Press, for William Lane, Leadenhall-Street, 1798.

I 247p; II 218p; III 255p; IV 339p. 12mo. 14s sewed (CR, SJC), 16s (GEP).

CR n.s. 24: 356 (Nov 1798).

BL 1152.h.1; CME 3-628-45156-6; EM 6873: 6; ESTC t144530 (NA CtY-BR, InU-Li, ViU &c.; EA COR).

Notes: Children of the Abbey 1796: 78.

Adv. SJC 27–29 Mar 1798 and GEP 23–26 Feb 1799.

Further edns: Dublin, 1799 (Printed by William Porter, for P. Wogan, H. Colbert, W. Porter, and N. Kelly, 2 vols., 12mo), ESTC n003015; Philadelphia, 1802 (WC); NSTC lists edn. in 1836. French trans. Paris, 1798 (*Clermont*) (Lévy). Facs: NN.

CR: 'This tale reminds us, without any great pleasure, of Mrs. Radcliffe's romances. In Clermont mystery is heaped upon mystery, and murder upon murder, with little art, and great improbability. This writer, indeed, claims murders as her *forte*; for, not content with such as are connected with the story, she details three instances at considerable length as episodes. We have also the usual apparatus of dungeons, long galleries, clanking chains and ghosts, and a profusion of picturesque description which, though it displays some merit, serves only to interrupt the narrative.'

1798: 62   S., R.

THE NEW MONK, A ROMANCE, IN THREE VOLUMES. BY R. S. ESQ.

London: Printed at the Minerva-Press, for William Lane, Leadenhall-Street, 1798.

I vii, 162p; II 192p; III 194p. 12mo. 10s 6d sewed (CR, SJC), 12s (GEP).

CR n.s. 24: 356–7 (Nov 1798); AF II: 3049.

O 250.q.279; CME 3-628-45125-6; EMf; ESTC t188164 (BI BL; NA CLU-S/C, CtY-BR, ViU; EA COR).

Notes. Summers suggests Richard Sickelmore as possible author.

Preface (1, i–vii) explains the author's reasons for ridiculing *The Monk* (1796: 63).

Adv. SJC 5–7 June 1798; adv. GEP 23–26 Feb 1799.

CR: 'The Monk of Mr. Lewis has been assailed in various ways, and, in our opinion, never without justice. The present is a burlesque parody on the whole work, the monk being here a methodist preacher, and his first temptation a leg of pork, &c. There is considerable humour in some parts, and particularly in the poetical imitations; but the undertaking, upon the whole, was too great for the author's stock of wit. Vulgarity and indecency are frequently observable; and the description of the new monk's death is disgusting. The author's purpose would have been more successfully answered by a selection of certain passages. The *whole* of the Monk cannot be injured by ridicule.'

1798: 63   [SELDEN, Catharine].

LINDOR; OR, EARLY ENGAGEMENTS. A NOVEL. IN TWO VOLUMES. BY THE AUTHOR OF THE ENGLISH NUN, AND COUNT DE SAN-TERRE.

Reading: Printed Sold by Snare and Co. Sold also by W. Treppess, No. 31, St Martin's-Le-Grand, London, 1798.

I 232p; II 161p. 12mo. 7s boards (CR).

CR n.s. 26: 477 (Aug 1797); AF II: 4004.

CaAEU PR 5349.S416.L74 1798; ESTC n063612.

Notes. In vol. 2 p.[41] misnumbered.

English Nun 1797: 73; *Count de Santerre* 1797: 72.

CR: 'This is a convenient *summer* novel, as it will not fatigue the reader by the complexity of its plot, or by the profundity of its sentiments.'

1798: 64   [SHOWES, Mrs].

STATIRA: OR, THE MOTHER. A NOVEL. BY THE AUTHOR OF INTER-ESTING TALES.

London: Printed at the Minerva-Press, for William Lane Leadenhall-Street, 1798.
200p. 8vo [CR and MR have 12mo]. 3s (CR), 3s 6d (MR), 4s (GEP).
CR n.s. 25: 473 (Apr 1799); MR n.s. 27: 233 (Oct 1798); AF II: 4086.
BL N.2518; EM 7133: 3; ESTC t074446 (NA ViU).

Notes. Blakey: Attributed to Mrs. Showes by a Minerva Library Catalogue of 1814.

Interesting Tales 1797: 75.

Adv. GEP 23–26 Feb 1799.

CR: 'This volume contains two novelettes, nearly of the same length, founded on the passion of jealousy. That which is entitled Statira is the more interesting and instructive; the other is extravagant and feeble. They seem to have been translated from the German.

MR [Alexander Hamilton]: 'This volume may communicate little interest to the reader, but will convey no injury to his morals. The design is to exhibit the fatal effects of jealousy, as exemplified in two tragical but improbable stories.'

1798: 65   SICKLEMORE, R[ichard].

EDGAR; OR, THE PHANTOM OF THE CASTLE. A NOVEL. IN TWO VOLUMES. BY R. SICKLEMORE.

London: Printed at the Minerva-Press, for William Lane, Leadenhall-Street, 1798.
I 4, 160p; II 159p. 8vo [CR has 12mo]. 7s (CR), 6s (LC), 6s sewed (adv., Min).
CR n.s. 23: 473 (Aug 1798); AF II: 4093.
Corvey; CME 3-628-45190-6; xESTC.

Notes. List of subscribers (pp. 1–2) is misplaced and follows preface (pp. 3–4). 1 p. advs. end vol. 2.

Adv. LC 85: 278 (19–21 Mar 1799). Adv. end vol. 2 of *Court Intrigue* (1799: 44).

French trans. Paris, 1799 (*Edgar, ou le Pouvoir du Remords*) (Lévy).

CR: 'Although we cannot assign a very high rank to this production, we do not think it contemptible; and it will afford some entertainment to the *amateurs* of horror. It was written for a benevolent and useful purpose; and its moral is, that the efforts of an honest mind, though poor and unprotected, will ultimately rise superior to the deep-laid machinations of vice, though armed with wealth and power.'

1798: 66   SLEATH, [Eleanor].

THE ORPHAN OF THE RHINE. A ROMANCE, IN FOUR VOLUMES. BY MRS. SLEATH.

London: Printed at the Minerva-Press, for William Lane, Leadenhall-Street, 1798.
I ii, 248p; II 239p; III 255p; IV 292p. 12mo. 14s boards (CR), 16s (GEP).

CR n.s. 27: 356 (Nov 1799).

CtY-BR In Sl22 798P; xESTC; WC has ViU.

Notes. Frontispiece vol. 1. In CtY-BR copy vol. 1 has t.p. to vol. 4, and vol. 2 pp. 227–30 are missing (replaced by photocopy). Prefatory advertisement 1, i–ii.

Adv. GEP 23–26 Feb 1799.

Facs: NN.

CR: 'The creative genius and the descriptive powers of Mrs. Radcliffe have given considerable popularity to the modern romance; and, even as critics, we have perused the productions of that authoress with no small degree of interest and gratification. If, however, we have sinned in suffering ourselves to be seduced by the blandishments of elegant fiction, we endure a penance adequately severe in the review of such vapid and servile imitations as the Orphan of the Rhine, and other recent romances.'

1798: 67 SMITH, Charlotte.
THE YOUNG PHILOSOPHER: A NOVEL. IN FOUR VOLUMES. BY CHARLOTTE SMITH.

London: Printed for T. Cadell, jun. and W. Davies, in the Strand, 1798.

12mo. I viii, 274p; II 278p; III 284p; IV 400p. 16s boards (CR), 16s sewed (MR, GEP).

CR n.s. 24: 77–84 (Sept 1798); MR n.s. 28: 346–7 (Mar 1799); AF II: 4149.

CtY Im.Sm53 798; CME 3-628-45180-9; EM 2017: 7; ESTC t071900 (BI BL, C, O; NA CSmH, MH-H, NjP, PU, ViU; EA COR).

Notes. Adv. GEP 16–19 June 1798.

Further edn: Dublin, 1798 (Printed for P. Wogan, H. Colbert, W. Porter, J. Moore, H. Fitzpatrick, J. Rice, and N. Kelly, 2 vols., 12mo), EM 8833: 4, ESTC t165738. French trans. Paris, 1799 (*Le jeune philosophe*) (RS). Facs: FCy.

CR: 'Her stories do not agitate like the mysterious horrors of Mrs. Radcliffe; they do not divert like the lively caricatures of Mrs. D'Arblay; but, more true to nature than either, they awaken that gentle and increasing interest which excites our feelings to the point of pleasure, not beyond it' (p. 77).

MR: [Samuel Rose and Thomas Wallace] [Rose:] 'We have received so much pleasure from all Mrs. Smith's productions in this line of composition, that we feel certain of entertainment when we hear of a new performance from her pen.—Though we have not been altogether disappointed in the present instance, our pleasure has not been so great as on some former occasions; for we think that the interest of this work is by no means equal to some of her earlier pieces, and that the characters are not so well supported' (p. 346). [Wallace:] 'Though we do not deem this one of the best and most interesting of Mrs Smith's productions, we can recommend it to the attention of our readers, as it possesses many of her distinguished excellencies, and in various scenes shews an intimate acquaintance with life and the secret recesses of the human heart' (p. 347).

1798: 68 SPIESS, C[hristian] H[einrich]; [PLUMPTRE, Annabella (*trans.*)].
THE MOUNTAIN COTTAGER; OR, WONDER UPON WONDER. A TALE. FROM THE GERMAN OF C. H. SPIESS.

London: Printed at the Minerva-Press, for William Lane, Leadenhall-Street, 1798.

296p. 12mo. 3s 6d sewed (AR, adv.), 4s (GEP).

AR 28: 518 (Nov 1798); AF II: 4218.

BL 1608/1981; EM 4850: 2; ESTC t121005.

Notes. Trans. of *Mäusefallen und Heckelkrämer* (Prague, 1792). AR says that the translator was Anne Plumptre, Annabella's sister; an adv. for *The Mountain Cottager* at end vol. 2 of *Eva* (1799: 54) and end vol. 2 of *Veronica* (1798: 41) quotes the passage from AR on this point. However, the t.p. of Annabella Plumptre's 1799 trans. of August Wilhelm Iffland's play *The Foresters* says that the trans. is 'by Bell Plumptre, translator of the Mountain Cottager'.

Adv. GEP 23–26 Feb 1799.

Further edns: Cork, 1800 (Printed by John Connor, 1 vol., 8vo), ESTC t170277; Philadelphia, 1800, ESTC w026274.

AR: 'A pleasant and ingenious tale, lively, fanciful, and well written.'

1798: 69   SUMMERSETT, Henry.
ABERFORD, A NOVEL; OR WHAT YOU WILL. BY HENRY SUMMERSETT.

London: Printed for J. Hatchard, No. 173, Piccadilly; and Lee and Hurst, No. 32, Pater-Noster-Row, 1798.

xxiv, 170p. 12mo. 3s 6d (ME).

BL C.141.b.7; EM 4230: 11; ESTC t126826 (NA CLU-S/C, MH-H).

Notes. Dedication to Miss Keppel v–vi, signed 'The Author'. Verse preface vii–xiii. List of subscribers xv–xxii; table of contents xxiii–xxiv. Prose ends on p. 144; the remainder is set out as verse and headed 'Wanderings in May; an Unfinished Prosaic Composition, put into lines of nine, ten, and eleven syllables'.

1798: 70   SURR, T[homas] S[kinner].
GEORGE BARNWELL. A NOVEL. IN THREE VOLUMES. BY T. S. SURR, AUTHOR OF CONSEQUENCES, A NOVEL; AND CHRIST'S HOSPITAL, A POEM.

London: Printed for H. D. Symonds, no. 20, Paternoster Row, 1798.

I xii, 228p; II 243p; III 237p. 12mo. 10s 6d boards (CR, GEP).

CR n.s. 24: 472 (Dec 1798); AF II: 4307.

MH-H *EC8.Su786.798g; CME 3-628-45198-1; EM 1278: 7; ESTC n010000 (NA MnU, MiDW, NcU; EA COR).

Notes. Prefatory advertisement 1, v–viii; 'Prefatory Dialogue' in verse ix–xii; text of novel starts on p. 3. 2 pp. advs. end vol. 3.

Based on George Lillo's play *The London Merchant* (1731).

Consequences 1796: 84.

Adv., 'founded on the popular Tragedy of the same Name', GEP 10–13 Nov 1798.

Further edns: Dublin, 1798 (Printed for P. Wogan, H. Colbert, W. Porter, J. Moore, and N. Kelly, 2 vols., 12mo), EM 4049: 7, ESTC n010001; Dublin, 1799, ESTC n010002; Philadelphia, 1800, ESTC w039085; Boston, 1800, ESTC w012395; NSTC lists edns. [as *Barnwell*] in 1807, 1834 and 1857; Boston, 1826 (WC); Boston, 1828 (WC). Extract from *George Barnwell*, abridged by Sarah Wilkinson, published in *Tell-Tale*, 1804, RM 578. French trans. Paris, 1799 (*Barnwell, traduit de l'anglais*) (BGR).

CR: 'Mr Surr's novel does not display excellence of the first class; but in a circulating library it will be very respectable. . . . for the whole of its sentiments and tendency, no work can be more unexceptionable than the present.'

1798: 71   TOMLINS, Elizabeth Sophia.
ROSALIND DE TRACEY. A NOVEL, IN THREE VOLUMES. BY ELIZA-
BETH SOPHIA TOMLINS, AUTHOR OF THE VICTIM OF FANCY, &C. &C.
>London: Printed for Charles Dilly, 1798.
>I 262p; II 302p; III 360p. 12mo. 10s 6d boards (CR), 10s 6d sewed (MR, GEP).
>CR n.s. 25: 118 (Jan 1799); MR n.s. 27: 331–2 (Nov 1798); AF II: 4493.
>BL Cup.403.i.2; EMf; ESTC t135340.

Notes. Preface 1, iii–vi.
Victim of Fancy 1787: 51.
Adv., 'On the 30th of this Month will be published', GEP 21–23 June 1798; additional book-sellers are Hookham and Carpenter and Wright.
Further edn: Dublin, 1799 (Printed by Brett Smith, for G. Burnett, P. Wogan, C. Brown, J. Moore, G. Folingsby, 2 vols., 12mo), ESTC n013249.
 CR: 'This is a novel composed upon the most approved receipt—a dependent young lady, perfectly amiable and accomplished, but of unknown parentage—the man whom she does not like, obstinate; and the man whom she does like, jealous—persecutions, difficulties, dis-tresses—a discovery of the lady's parents—and a marriage—these are the ingredients; and we must allow that they are blended *secundum artem.*'
 MR [Thomas Wallace]: 'If the critical reader should not meet, in this work, with language so elegant, sentiments so refined and appropriate, and characters so boldly conceived and delineated, as in a few productions of the highest order in this class, he will yet find in it a tale not uninteresting, and a concatenation of probable incidents, connected with such displays of life and manners as will amuse the fancy without vitiating the heart' (p. 331).

1798: 72   VERRI, [Alessandro].
THE ROMAN NIGHTS; OR, DIALOGUES AT THE TOMBS OF THE
SCIPIOS. TRANSLATED FROM THE ITALIAN OF COUNT VERRI.
>London: Printed by W. and C. Spilsbury, Snow-hill, For P. Molini; And sold by Faulder, New-Bond-street; White and Son, Fleet-street; Becket, Pall-Mall; and Shepperson and Reynolds, No. 137, Oxford-street, 1798.
>334p. 12mo. 3s 6d (ME).
>CR n.s. 26: 236–7 (June 1799).
>C 7740.e.23; EM 1365: 2; ESTC t128779 (BI BL, O; NA CLU-S/C, MA, PPL &c.).

Notes. Trans. of *Le Notti Romane al sepolcro degli Scipioni* (Rome, 1792).
1-p. prefatory advertisement follows t.p.; 4-pp. table of contents; 1-p. errata list.
Further edns: NSTC lists edns. in 1825, 1825/26, 1832 and 1850. French trans. Paris, 1817 (*Les Nuits romaines*) (BN).
 CR: 'Those who wish to observe the bad side of every illustrious character, and who would habituate themselves to scepticism by seeing the facts of history questioned, should peruse the Roman Nights. They are written with animation, and do credit to the talents of count Verri; but this is one of those books that a reader peruses with little interest, and which leave him in an unpleasant state of mind.'

1798: 73   [WELLS, Helena].
THE STEP-MOTHER: A DOMESTIC TALE, FROM REAL LIFE. BY A LADY.
IN TWO VOLUMES.

> London: Printed for T. N. Longman, Paternoster-Row, 1798.
> I viii, 245p; II 246p. 12mo. 7s boards (CR, MR).
> CR n.s. 24: 237 (Oct 1798); MR n.s. 26: 459 (Aug 1798); AF II: 4732.
> ScU SpC 813S.W46s v.1/v.2; ESTC n036476.

Notes. Pencilled note in ScU copy 'Helena Wells later Mrs. Whitford of South Carolina (Charleston)'. 2nd edn. has signed preface.
Preface 1, v–viii. 500 copies printed May 1798 (Strahan 17 f. 98).
Adv. GEP 12–15 May 1798.
Further edn: London, 1799, EM 3528: 2, ESTC n033434.

CR: 'There is much merit in these volumes; but it is injudicious to give the history of two generations in the same work. Each volume now comprehends a distinct story.'

MR [Thomas Wallace]: 'This is *really* a domestic story, in which the incidents are natural, indeed, but at the same time not very interesting. "From real life" it may probably have been taken, for we meet nothing in it but what in common life is daily seen to happen. . . . if the reader be not gratified either by interesting incident or elegant language, he will not meet with any sentiment or anecdote which will endanger his virtue; nor with any of those false views of human life which tend to corrupt the heart, and to mislead the imagination.'

1798: 74   [WOLLSTONECRAFT, Mary].
POSTHUMOUS WORKS OF THE AUTHOR OF A VINDICATION OF
THE RIGHTS OF WOMAN. IN FOUR VOLUMES.
THE WRONGS OF WOMAN. [vols. I and II].

> London: Printed for J. Johnson, no. 72, St Paul's Church-Yard; and G. G. J. and J.
>   Robinson, Paternoster-Row, 1798.
> I 181p; II 196p. III 192p. IV 195p. 8vo. 14s boards (MR, SJC).
> CR n.s. 22: 414–19 (Apr 1798); MR n.s. 27: 325–7 (Nov 1798); AF II: 4919.
> BL 629.d.11; EM 5521: 9; ESTC t114184 (BI D, E, O; NA CSmH, ICN, MH-H, NjP).

Notes. Edited by William Godwin. Vols. 1 and 2 contain *The Wrongs of Woman.* Vol. 1 5-pp. preface (unn.) signed W. Godwin; 5-pp. 'Author's Preface' (unn.); half-title: 'The Wrongs of Woman, or Maria; a Fragment'.
Adv., 'In the press, and speedily will be published', SJC 23–26 Dec 1797; adv. also offers, 'In One Volume of the same size, price 3s.6d. in boards, With a portrait, engraved by Heath, from a picture by Opie, painted a few Weeks before her Death', Godwin's *Memoirs of the Authour of a Vindication of the Rights of Woman.*
French trans. Paris, 1798 (*Maria, ou le Malheur d'être femme*) (HWS); German trans. Leipzig, 1800 (*Maria oder das Unglück Weib zu seyn*) (EAG). Facs: FCy.

CR: 'In this [*The Wrongs of Woman*] we find a vigorous display of fancy, and often a richness of imagery in pourtraying the passions, and especially the distresses of certain situations, which convince us that Mrs. Godwin's particular *forte* was novel-writing—not, as commonly understood, a mere tissue of chit-chat, lovers' quarrels, and parents' cruelty, all ending in a splendid wedding and a great fortune—but a tale of interest and intellect, leading to important lessons of life, because built on the realities of life, and embellished only where embellishment is necessary to catch the attention and gratify taste.' (p. 417).

MR [Christopher Lake Moody]: 'Had Mrs. Wollstonecraft Godwin lived to finish her "Maria," the story might have been more satisfactory to her readers: but its moral effect or utility would not, we apprehend, have been at all increased' (p. 325). 'While . . . we would do ample justice to the abilities manifested in this fragment, we cannot admire its moral tendency' (p. 326).

1798: 75   YOUNG, M{ary} J{ulia}.
ROSE-MOUNT CASTLE; OR, FALSE REPORT. A NOVEL. IN THREE VOLUMES. BY M. J. YOUNG.

> London: Printed at the Minerva-Press, for William Lane, Leadenhall-Street, 1798.
> I 3, 259p; II 273p; III 278p. 12mo. 10s 6d boards (CR), 10s 6d sewed (Min).
> CR n.s. 24: 470 (Dec 1798).
> Corvey; CME 3-628-5219-8; ESTC n013327 (BI O; NA NNS).

Notes. Dedication to Mrs. Trant pp. 1–3, signed Mary Julia Young. 1 p. advs. end vol. 1; 1 p. advs. end vol. 2; 2 pp. advs. end vol. 3.

CR: 'We cannot recommend this work either for entertainment or instruction. It is almost destitute of fable or of any excitement to curiosity, if we except the introduction of a gang of Irish *defenders,* who rob and murder in a very *sentimental* style, and one of whom becomes afterwards a personage of high consequence in the groupe of lords and dukes, having relinquished his *youthful error.* Many characters are introduced, and coupled in love-matches, all which prove abundantly prosperous; but there are no traits in their history so interesting as to compensate their vapid and common-place conversation, which occupies the greater part of the work.'

1799

1799: 1   ANON.
*ADVENTURES OF THE PYRENEAN HERMITS. TRANSLATED FROM THE SPANISH.

> London: Hurst (CR).
> Small 8vo. 1s (CR, ME).
> CR n.s. 33: 113 (Sept 1801); AF II: 35.
> No copy located.

Notes. CR: 'The author does not inform us who is the original author of this tale, so that we cannot turn to see if it be a translation from the Spanish or not. This, however, will be but little sought after by those who are likely to read it.'

THE ARISTOCRAT, A NOVEL
See PYE, Henry James

1799: 2   ANON.

AUGUSTA; A NOVEL, IN THREE VOLUMES, FROM THE FRENCH, BY A LADY.

> London: Printed for the translator, and sold by Earle and Hemet, No. 47, Albermarle Street, Piccadilly, 1799.
> I 190p; II 206p; III 176p. 8vo. [CR has 12mo]. 10s 6d boards (CR), 10s 6d (adv.).
> CR n.s. 29: 472 (Aug 1800); AF II: 171.
> CaAEU PR 3991.A1.A92 1799; ESTC n046308.

Notes. Trans. of *Augusta; roman* (1798, rev. CR n.s. 23: 547–9 and MR n.s. 27: 331).
1-p. prefatory address (unn.) by the translator, signed L. H. In vol. 1 p. 97 misnumbered 98. 2 pp. advs. end vol. 2. Epistolary.
Adv. end *Misanthropy and Repentance* (1799: 49).

   CR: 'Some of the letters which compose this novel are amusing; others are sentimentally dull.'

AZALAIS AND AIMAR
See FABRE D'OLIVET, Antoine.

BATTLERIDGE: AN HISTORICAL TALE
See COOKE, Cassandra

1799: 3   ANON.

THE BUDGET, OR MORAL AND ENTERTAINING FRAGMENTS. REPRESENTING THE PUNISHMENT OF VICE, AND THE REWARD OF VIRTUE.

> London: Printed for E. Newbery, the corner of St. Paul's Church-Yard, by G. Woodfall, No. 22, Paternoster-Row, 1799.
> 175p. 12mo. 1s 6d (MM).
> MM 9: 89 (Feb 1800); AF II: 525.
> BL 012806.i.2; EM 4176: 5; ESTC t112751 (NA CLU-S/C, TxU).

Notes. ESTC notes that NUC attributes this to Mary Pilkington.
Frontispiece. 1-p. prefatory advertisement (unn.).
Further edn: Wilkesbarre, PA, 1801 (WC)
   MM: 'We applaud the motive which prompted to literary exertion; and we welcome endeavours which hereafter may lead to more distinguished success.'

CONFESSIONS OF A BEAUTY
See CROFFTS, Mrs (1798: 24)

COUNT DI NOVINI
See SANDS, James

COURT INTRIGUE: OR, THE VICTIM OF CONSTANCY
See GREEN, Sarah

1799: 4 ANON.
EASTERN ANECDOTES OF EXEMPLARY CHARACTERS; WITH
SKETCHES OF THE CHINESE HISTORY. IN ONE VOLUME. INSCRIBED
TO HER ROYAL HIGHNESS THE DUCHESS OF YORK. DESIGNED FOR
YOUTH.

> London: Printed by Sampson Low, no. 7, Berwick-Street, Soho: and sold by Hurst,
> Paternoster-Row; Messrs. Carpenter and Co. No. 14, Old Bond-Street; and Peacock,
> at the Juvenile Library, no. 259, Oxford-Street, 1799.
> xi, xvi, xxiii, 176p. 8vo [BC has 12mo]. 3s (BC).
> BC 14: 564 (Nov 1799); AF II: 1202.
> BL 10608.ee.36; EM 926: 3; ESTC t088341 (BI ABu, O; NA CLU-S/C, TxHR).

Notes. Dedication [v]; list of subscribers vii–xi; prefatory advertisement xiii–xvi; introduction i–xxiii. Text of novel starts on p. 25.

EMILIA AND ALPHONSO
See SOUZA-BOTELHO, Adélaïde-Marie-Émilie Filleul, marquise de Flahaut

1799: 5 ANON.
THE ENCHANTED MIRROR, A MOORISH ROMANCE.

> Salisbury: Printed and Sold by J. Easton. Sold also by E. Newbery, St Paul's Church-
> Yard, London, 1799.
> iv, 123p. 12mo. 1s 6d (NLR, GEP).
> NLR 1: 616 (June 1799).
> C 7720.d.1139; EM 2271: 12; ESTC t117216 (BI BL, O).

Notes. Verse address 'To Mary' iii–iv. 2-pp. table of contents. 1 p. advs. end vol.
Adv. GEP 12–14 Dec 1799.
Further edn: London, 1800, ESTC n006263.

NLR: 'As the title implies, we have enchantment employed in the story; we have knights and tournaments, saloons of mirrors, and cauldrons of renovation; but if fiction ever be allowable in aid of instruction, we think it has been not improperly nor ineffectually employed on the present occasion.'

THE FAIRY OF MISFORTUNE
See DUBOIS, Edward

1799: 6 ANON.
FALSE FRIENDSHIP; OR, NATURE IN MASQUERADE. A NOVEL.
FOUNDED IN TRUTH. CONSISTING OF LETTERS WHICH HAVE
ACTUALLY PASSED BETWEEN PERSONS IN FASHIONABLE LIFE,
UPON THE MOST AFFECTING SUBJECTS. IN TWO VOLUMES.

> London: Printed for W. Treppass, no. 31, St. Martin's-le-Grand, 1799.
> I 199p; II 224p. 12mo. 7s (ME).
> BL RB.23.a.6498; EMf; ESTC t223016.

Notes. A reissue with cancel t.ps.; original not yet identified (ESTC).

Text of novel starts on p. 11 in both vols. 1,000 copies printed by Strahan, Feb 1799 (LA). Epistolary.

FEDARETTA
See FOSTER, Mrs E. M.

1799: 7   ANON.
FILIAL INDISCRETIONS; OR, THE FEMALE CHEVALIER. IN THREE VOLUMES.

> Wakefield: Printed for the Author, by Elizabeth Waller, and Rowland Hurst: and sold by G. G. and J. Robinson, Paternoster-Row, London, 1799.
> I 236p; II 249p; III 190p. 12mo. 10s 6d sewed (MR).
> MR n.s. 33: 207–8 (Oct 1800); AF II: 1440.
> O Vet.A5f.1929-1931; EMf; ESTC t185414.

Notes. Epistolary.

MR [James Burney]: 'The work is written with considerable spirit: but some parts manifest a glow and licence of description, which will not be suitable to every class of readers.'

THE FORCE OF PREJUDICE, A MORAL TALE
See WILDMAN, Joseph

FREDERIC LATIMER
See LEMAISTRE, John Gustavus

1799: 8   ANON.
HAMLAIN; OR, THE HERMIT OF THE BEACH. A MORAL REVERIE. CALCULATED FOR THE INSTRUCTION AND AMUSEMENT OF YOUTH.

> London: Printed for E. Newbery, the corner of St. Paul's Church-Yard, by G. Woodfall, No. 22, Paternoster-Row, 1799
> 198p. 12mo.
> BL 1506/586; EM 6638: 14; ESTC t083114 (BI AWn; NA CaOTP, CtY, CtY-Walpole &c.; EA NUN).

Notes. Text of novel starts on p. 3.

THE HAPPY FAMILY AT EASON HOUSE
See SANDHAM, Elizabeth, App. A: 13

HARCOURT. A NOVEL
See MEEKE, Mary

HELEN SINCLAIR: A NOVEL
See SPENCE, Elizabeth Isabella

THE HISTORY OF JACK AND HIS ELEVEN BROTHERS
See App. A: 12

1799: 9   ANON.
IMMELINA. A NOVEL. IN THREE VOLUMES.

London: Printed at the Minerva-Press, for William Lane, Leadenhall-Street, 1799.
I 228p; II 204p; III 214p. 12mo. 9s sewed (CR, MP).
CR n.s. 27: 475 (Dec 1799); AF II: 2158.
CtY Im.Im6.779; CME 3-628-45091-8; ESTC n054081 (NA ICU; EA COR).

Notes. 2 pp. advs. end vol. 3.
Adv., 'In the Press', MP 2 Feb 1799; adv. as published MP 30 May 1799; additional booksellers are Miller, Bond street; Lloyd, Harley street; Hodgson, Wimpole-street; and
Scatchard, Ave Maria-lane.
  CR: 'The merit of this performance is not very great. The incidents are trite; the characters
are in no respect original; and the language is not correct. But the work will amuse and
interest many readers; and it will not injure the morals of any.'

1799: 10   ANON.
*INDISCRETION; A NOVEL. IN 2 VOLS.

London: Richardson (NLR).
2 vols. 6s. (NLR).
NLR 1: 407–8 (Apr 1799).
No copy located.

Notes. NLR: 'This novel is composed in an easy, unaffected style; but, like most others, dis-
closes much unnecessary distress. It developes, at the same time, some whimsical characters
which are not destitute of point and originality.'

THE JESUIT; OR, THE HISTORY OF ANTHONY BABINGTON, ESQ.
See PATRICK, Mrs F. C.

JOSEPHINE. A NOVEL
See TAYLOR, Miss

LESSONS FROM LIFE
See BELLAMY, Thomas

LETTERS WRITTEN FROM LAUSANNE
See CHARRIÈRE, Isabelle-Agnès-Élisabeth van Tuyll van Serooskerken van Zuylen

THE LITTLE EMIGRANT, A TALE
See PEACOCK, Lucy

MARGARITA. A NOVEL
See SHERWOOD, Mary Martha

1799: 11   ANON.
MEMOIRS OF THE DANBY FAMILY: DESIGNED CHIEFLY FOR THE

ENTERTAINMENT AND IMPROVEMENT OF YOUNG PERSONS. BY A LADY.

London: Printed for E. Newbery, Corner of St. Paul's Church-Yard, 1799.
xii, 258p. 12mo. 4s Newbery (NLR, LC).
NLR 1: 93 (Jan 1799).
C S727.d.79.81; EM 1872: 6; ESTC t095174 (BI BL; NA CaOTP, CLU-S/C, FU &c.).

Notes. Dedication (addressed to 'My dear Children') v–xii. Frontispiece. 6 pp. advs. at end.
Adv. LC 65: 39 (8–10 Jan 1799).

NLR: 'Sensible, moral and amusing; and well adapted to the end proposed in the title page.'

MISANTHROPY AND REPENTANCE
See HEMET, John

1799: 12   ANON.

MONTROSE, OR THE GOTHIC RUIN, A NOVEL. IN THREE VOLUMES. BY THE AUTHOR OF "THE MYSTIC COTTAGER," AND "OBSERVANT PEDESTRIAN."

London: Printed for R. Dutton, Birchin-Lane, Cornhill, 1799.
I 287p; II 255p; III 252p. 12mo. 10s 6d sewed (CR, GEP).
CR n.s. 27: 239 (Oct 1799); AF II: 2926.
ViU *PZ2.M657 1799; CME 3-628-45131-0;ESTC n035138 (NA CtY, IU; EA COR).

Notes. Advs. end vol. 2.
The Mystic Cottager 1794: 13; *The Observant Pedestrian* 1795: 8.
Adv. GEP 23–25 Apr 1799.

CR: 'It will be sufficient to observe, that this is a novel of the common stamp.'

1799: 13   ANON.

A NORTHUMBRIAN TALE. WRITTEN BY A LADY.

London: Printed by S. Hamilton, Falcon-Court, Fleet-Street; and Sold by J. Debrett,
Piccadilly, and L. B. Seeley, Ave-Maria-Lane, 1799.
vii, 301p. 12mo. 4s 6d boards (MR), 4s 6d (MP).
MR n.s. 33: 103 (Sept 1800); AF II: 3081.
BL 012611.e.43(1); CME 3-628-45137-X; EM 198: 7; ESTC t002755 (NA MH-H; EA COR).

Notes. Dedication to Miss Stevenson, Morton-Hall, Chiswick v–vii.
Adv. MP 21 Dec 1799.

MR [James Burney]: 'This is a tale of other times; and while the readers of novels continue to tolerate the dolorous adventures of luckless knights pent up in the dungeons of moated castles, their entertainment may be cheaply, and we doubt not will be plentifully furnished. The most predominating characteristic of this species of composition is, that formal soporific manners are substituted for imitations of nature.'

1799: 14   ANON.

THE ORPHAN HEIRESS OF SIR GREGORY. AN HISTORICAL FRAGMENT, OF THE LAST CENTURY.

London: Printed by and for Sampson Low, Berwick Street, Soho: and sold by C. Law, Ave Maria Lane; and E. Booker, New Bond Street, 1799.

234p. 12mo. 4s boards (CR), 4s sewed (MR, GEP).

CR n.s. 28: 475–7 (Apr 1800); MR n.s. 30: 94–5 (Sept 1799); AF II: 3181.

MH-H *EC75.A100.799o; EM 1274: 5; ESTC n010645 (BI O; NA CLU-S/C).

Notes. Dedication to Viscount Palmerston; prefatory advertisement by the 'editor' (unn.). Adv., 'will be published in the Course of the Month . . . neatly printed and hot-pressed' and no price given, GEP 28 Feb-2 Mar 1799; adv. as published GEP 28–30 Mar 1799.

CR: 'In this interesting little work we only object to the impropriety of affixing imaginary guilt on historical characters. The novel displays much feeling and much imagination' (p. 475).

MR [James Bannister and George Edward Griffiths]: '. . . free use is made of the agency of supernatural beings, ghosts, and awful warnings and omens: but it may be truly said that the tendency of the relation is conducive "to the interests of morality;" [quoted from the author's preface] that pious, virtuous and loyal sentiments are everywhere expressed and inculcated; and that the composition altogether displays considerable talents.'

A PIECE OF FAMILY BIOGRAPHY
See DUBOIS, Edward

REBECCA. A NOVEL
See FOSTER, E. M.

1799: 15 ANON.
THE REBEL: A TALE OF THE TIMES. IN TWO VOLUMES. BY A LADY.

Southampton: Printed by T. Skelton: and sold by B. Law, AveMary Lane, London, 1799.

I vi, 264p; II 287p. 12mo. 7s (ME),7s sewed (LC).

CLU-S/C PR3991.A1R16; ESTC n014245.

Notes. Introduction v–vi.

Adv. LC 85: 400 (23–25 Apr 1799).

Further edn: Dublin, 1801 (Printed by J. Stockdale for P. Wogan, W. Porter, J. Rice, J. Halpen, H. Colbert, B. Dornin, G. Folingsby, and J. Stockdale, 1 vol., no format) (WC, NSTC).

REGINALD, OR THE HOUSE OF MIRANDOLA
See MARTIN, Mrs

THE RESTLESS MATRON. A LEGENDARY TALE
See SHOWES, Mrs

THE RING, OR THE MERRY WIVES OF MADRID
See TÉLLEZ, Gabriel

ROSALIND. A NOVEL
See TAYLOR, Miss

ST. JULIAN
See 1798: 37

SIGEVART, A TALE
See MILLER, Johann Martin

SIGISMAR
See WHITFIELD, Henry

SKETCHES OF MODERN LIFE
See WILLIAMS, William Frederick

1799: 16   ANON.
THE SPIRIT OF THE ELBE: A ROMANCE. IN THREE VOLUMES.
> London: Printed for T. N. Longman and O. Rees, Paternoster-Row, 1799.
> I iv, 158p; II 200p; III 162p. 12mo. 9s boards (CR, MR).
> CR n.s. 26: 357–8 (July 1799); MR n.s. 30: 93 (Sept 1799); AF II: 4220.
> Corvey; CME 3-628-45194-9; ESTC n037354 (NA CaAEU).

Notes. Dedication to Miss Gunning iii–iv, signed 'The Author', London, Jan 1799. 6 pp. advs. end vol. 3. 750 copies printed by Strahan, Feb 1799 (LA).
Adv. GEP 28 Feb–2 Mar 1799.
Further edns: Dublin, 1800 (Printed by W. Porter, 2 vols., 12mo), ESTC t118946; Cork, 1800, ESTC t221161.

CR: 'To those who are fond of the marvellous, this romance will afford entertainment, though its fictions are not the most extravagant that we have observed in this species of composition. The author's discretion has not allowed him to introduce more than *one ghost*, the intrusion of which many readers will probably forget amidst the pleasure of contemplating some interesting traits of old German manners.'

MR [James Bannister]: 'That species of eloquence, which may be termed the false pathetic, pervades the whole work. The events are improbable, if not impossible; the spirits of the night are called to exercise their ghostly functions; and the characters are such as bear no similitude to any beings that we have ever known.'

THE STORY OF AL RAOUI (London, 1799) not included as it is principally a re-trans. of Nights 689–691 of the *Arabian Nights*.

SUZETTE'S DOWRY
See FIÉVÉE, Joseph

A TALE OF THE TIMES
See WEST, Jane

1799: 17   ANON.
THE VILLAGE ORPHAN; A TALE FOR YOUTH. TO WHICH IS ADDED,

THE BASKET-MAKER, AN ORIGINAL FRAGMENT. ORNAMENTED WITH VIGNETTES ON WOOD.

London: Printed by C. Whittingham, for Longman and Rees, Paternoster Row, n.d. [1799].

140p. 12mo. 2s 6d (t.p.), 2s 6d boards (CR, MR).

CR n.s. 31: 469 (Apr 1801); MR n.s. 30: 345 (Nov 1799); AF II: 4620.

BL RB.23.a.7149; ESTC n048767 (NA CaOTP, CaOHM, CLU-S/C &c.).

Notes. ESTC suggests publication date of 1797.

Small engraving on t.p. and at beginnings and ends of chapters. 1-p. prefatory advertisement.

Adv., 'Ornamented with Vignettes on Wood', SJC 14–16 May 1799 and GEP 23–25 May 1799.

Further edns: Philadelphia, 1800, ESTC w025047; NSTC lists edn. in 1802.

CR: 'This tale is prettily narrated; but we can by no means appreciate it as a tale for youth. It is better adapted for the class of novel readers who have attained their twenty-fifth year....'

MR [Jabez Hirons]: 'This is a romantic, but inoffensive tale: and certainly its tendency is, according to the professed design, to advance the interests of benevolence and rectitude.'

1799: 18 ANON.

WAREHAM PRIORY; OR, THE WILL: A NOVEL, FOUNDED ON FACTS. BY THE WIDOW OF AN OFFICER.

London: Printed by J. Aspin, Lombard-Street, Whitefriars; published by J. Barker, no. 19, Great Russell-Street, Covent-Garden, 1799

I xii, 161p; II 222p. 12mo.

BRu ENC; ESTC n066338 (NA CtY).

Notes. List of subscribers i–xii. Epistolary.

1799: 19 ANON.

WESTBROOK VILLAGE. A NOVEL. IN TWO VOLUMES.

London: Printed at the Minerva-Press, for William Lane, Leadenhall-Street, 1799.

I 298p; II 306p. 12mo. 7s sewed (CR, MP).

CR n.s. 28: 117 (Jan 1800); AF II: 4750.

Corvey; CME 3-628-45209-0; ESTC n035700 (NA CaAEU).

Notes. 2 pp. advs. end vol. 1; 6 pp. advs. end vol. 2.

Adv. MP 9 Nov 1799; additional booksellers are Miller, Bond-street; Hodgson, Wimpole-street; Lloyd, Harley-street; Kirby, Oxford-street; and Scatchard, Ave Maria-lane.

CR: 'This novel contains many features of real life, and many sentiments valuable for their correctness and importance in our intercourse with society.'

1799: 20 ANON.

THE WITCH, AND THE MAID OF HONOUR. IN TWO VOLUMES.

London: Printed for the author; and sold by T. N. Longman and O. Rees, Paternoster-Row, 1799.

I viii, 276p; II 216p. 12mo. 7s 6d boards (CR), 7s boards (SJC, GEP).

CR n.s. 28: 355 (Mar 1800); AF II: 4857.

BL 12612.e.12; CME 3-628-45220-1; EM 333: 2; ESTC t066919 (BI O; NA CtY-BR, ICN, MH-H; EA COR).

Notes. Dedication (p. [v]) 'To the Maids of Honour' signed 'The Old Woman' and dated 1 May, 1799. Preface vii–viii. Vol. 2 pp. 214–16 are 'The Author's Apology'.
500 copies printed by Strahan, May 1799 (LA; Strahan 17 f. 122).
Adv. 8–11 June 1799: 'By the Old Woman'. Adv. GEP 13–15 June 1799.

CR: 'A strange title is followed by a preface equally strange. . . . It relates to the times of queen Elizabeth and king James I. and the manners of those times are, in many instances, well preserved; but the novel is not very interesting.'

1799: 21A   BARTHÉLEMY, [Jean-Jacques].
CHARITE AND POLYDORUS, A ROMANCE. TRANSLATED FROM THE FRENCH OF THE ABBÉ BARTHELEMY, AUTHOR OF THE TRAVELS OF ANACHARSIS, WITH AN ABRIDGEMENT OF THE LIFE OF THE AUTHOR, BY THE LATE DUKE OF NIVERNOIS.
London: [Printed for Charles Dilly], 1799.
12mo. 2s (CR), 2s sewed (MR, GEP).
CR n.s. 27: 116 (Sept 1799); MR n.s. 29: 334 (July 1799); AF II: 229.
BL 838.a.42; EM 8500: 7; ESTC t081005.

Notes. Trans. of *Les Amours de Carite et de Polydore, roman traduit de grec* (Paris, 1760).
Adv. GEP 2–4 Apr 1799: 'This amusing little Romance, now presented to the Public, is from the pen of the celebrated Abbe Barthelemy, whose name must continually suggest the ideas of Learning and Genius, and sufficiently recommend every Work to which it is prefixed.'
Further edn: Dublin, 1799 (Printed by H. Colbert, 1 vol., 12mo), ESTC t081006.

CR: 'We cannot affirm that the translation is executed in an elegant or masterly manner; but it claims the merit of fidelity.'

MR [William Taylor] reviews both trans. together with virtually no comment, referring the reader to rev. of original in MR n.s. 27.

1799: 21B   BARTHÉLEMY, J[ean]-J[acques].
CARITE AND POLYDORUS. TO WHICH IS PREFIXED, A TREATISE ON MORALS. BY J. J. BARTHÉLEMY, AUTHOR OF THE TRAVELS OF ANACHARSIS. WITH THE LIFE OF THE AUTHOR.
London: Printed for Otridge and Son; R. Faulder; J. Walker; R. Lea; J. Cuthell, J. Nunn; Ogilvy and Son; Lackington, Allen and Co; and Vernor and Hood, 1799.
xiv, 213p. 12mo. 3s sewed (CR, MR).
CR n.s. 27: 239 (Oct 1799); MR n.s. 29: 334 (July 1799); AF II: 228.
BL 12512.ee.15; EM 12: 1; ESTC t081004 (BI O; NA CaOHM, CLU-S/C, CSmH).

Notes. Trans. of *Les Amours de Carite et de Polydore, roman traduit de grec* (Paris, 1760).
'Life of the Author' iii–xiv; 'A Treatise on Morals' 1–69; *Carite and Polydorus* starts on p. 73.
1 p. advs. end vol.
Adv., 'In a few days will be published' with title as *Charete and Polydorus, a Romance, translated from the French of the Abbe Barthelemy* and no price given, GEP 14–16 May 1799; publishers are Vernor and Hood, W. Otridge and Son, R. Faulder, R. Lea, J. Walker, J. Cuthell,

Lackington, Allen and Co., Ogilvy and Son, and J. Nunn. Adv. as published, 'Printed on a fine wove Paper', GEP 25–27 June 1799.

CR: 'The romance is better translated than the treatise; but both might be improved by an able translator.'

MR [William Taylor] reviews both trans. together with virtually no comment, referring the reader to rev. of original in MR n.s. 27.

1799: 22   [BELLAMY, Thomas].
LESSONS FROM LIFE; OR, HOME SCENES.

> London, Printed for G. Sael, no. 192, Strand, 1799.
> 172p. 12mo. 1s 6d (t.p., NLR).
> NLR 1: 93 (Jan 1799); AF II: 2526.
> CtY Im L566.799; ESTC n063465.

Notes. Frontispiece. Dedication to 'Parents and Guardians of Youth' signed T. B. p. [iii]; 1–p. address 'To the Reader' p. [iv]; index v–vii; Pagination continuous Roman-Arabic; text of novel starts on p. 9.

NLR: 'To produce a volume proper to be put in the hands of young persons requires a genius and invention of a different cast from that of novel or romance writing, in which species of composition this author appears to be a proficient.'

1799: 23   BIDLAKE, J[ohn].
EUGENIO; OR, THE PRECEPTS OF PRUDENTIUS. A MORAL TALE. BY J. BIDLAKE, A.B. &C. &C. CHAPLAIN TO HIS ROYAL HIGHNESS THE DUKE OF CLARENCE, AND MASTER OF THE GRAMMAR-SCHOOL, PLYMOUTH.

> London: Printed for T. Chapman, no. 151, Fleet-street, 1799.
> viii, 171p. 12mo. 2s 6d (CR), 2s 6d boards (MR).
> CR n.s. 27: 356–7 (Nov 1799); MR n.s. 30: 467 (Dec 1799); AF II: 341.
> CLU-S/C CBC PZ6.B474e.1799; ESTC n002458 (NA OU).

Notes. 4 pp. advs. beginning vol. Dedication to Lieut. General Grenville, Colonel of the 23d Regiment of Foot, or Royal Welsh Fuzileers [*sic*] v–vi; preface vii–viii.

CR: 'The production before us is not distinguished by variety of incident or character, but is valuable for the sound morality which it inculcates.'

MR [James Bannister]: '. . . this volume has a tendency to promote the cause of religion and virtue, and may convey much useful instruction to young readers.'

1799: 24   BITAUBÉ, [Paul-Jérémie].
THE BATAVIANS; OR, VIRTUE AND VALOUR CROWNED BY PER-SEVERANCE. FROM THE FRENCH OF C. BITAUBÉ, MEMBER OF THE NATIONAL INSTITUTE OF FRANCE, AND OF THE ROYAL ACADEMY OF SCIENCES AND BELLES-LETTRES OF PRUSSIA.

> London: Printed for G. G. and J. Robinson, Pater-Noster-Row, 1799.
> I xv, 284p; II 266p. 12mo. 7s sewed (MR), 7s boards (LC).
> MR n.s. 33: 208–9 (1800).
> MH-H KPD 174; xESTC.

Notes. Trans. of *Les Bataves* (Paris, 1797), itself a reworking of the author's *Guillaume, en dix chants* (Amsterdam, 1773) and *Guillaume de Nassau* (Paris, 1775).

Translator's advertisement [v]–viii, dated 1 Aug 1799; author's preface x–xv. T.p. to vol. 1 of MH-H copy torn, with loss of most of imprint.

Serialised as 'The Dutch Patriots of the Sixteenth Century', *Lady's Magazine*, 1811–15, RM 336.

Adv. LC 86: 379 (17–19 Oct 1799).

MR rev. of original in App n.s. 22: 511–13 [Apr/May 1797].

1799: 25   BREWER, J[ames] N[orris].

A WINTER'S TALE. IN FOUR VOLUMES. BY J. N. BREWER, AUTHOR OF THE MANSION HOUSE, &C.

> London: Printed at the Minerva Press, for William Lane, Leadenhall-Street, 1799.
> I viii, 293p; II 272p; III 255p; IV 279p. 12mo. 16s (ME), 16s sewed (MP).
> AJR 6: 53–5 (May 1800); AF II: 466.
> Corvey; CME 3-628-45005-5; ESTC t200839.

Notes. Frontispiece. 'To the Reader' v–viii, signed J. N. Brewer, 25 Oct 1799. 3 pp. advs. end vol. 1; 1 p. advs. end vol. 3; 1 p. advs. end vol. 4.

The Mansion House 1796: 23.

Adv. MP 5 Dec 1799; additional booksellers are Miller, Bond-street; Hodgson, Wimpole-street; Lloyd, Harley-street; Kirby, Oxford-street; and Scatchard, Ave Maria-lane.

1799: 26   CHAMBERS, Marianne.

HE DECEIVES HIMSELF. A DOMESTIC TALE, IN THREE VOLUMES. BY MARIANNE CHAMBERS, DAUGHTER OF THE LATE MR. CHARLES CHAMBERS, MANY YEARS IN THE SERVICE OF THE HON. EAST-INDIA COMPANY, AND UNFORTUNATELY LOST IN THE WINTERTON.

> London: Printed for C. Dilly in the Poultry, 1799.
> I xxiv, 287p; II 270p; III 234p. 12mo. 10s 6d (MR), 10s 6d sewed (GEP).
> MR n.s. 30: 97–8 (Sept 1799); AF II: 657.
> BL 12613.aaa.5; EM 160: 3; ESTC t055555 (NA IU, MH-H).

Notes. Dedication to Thomas Powell, of Bristol, the author's grandfather, v–ix. List of subscribers xi–xxiv.

Adv., 'On Tuesday the 30th instant, will be published', GEP 18–20 July 1799.

MR [James Burney]: 'It certainly requires some talents to write even a *mediocre* novel; and to such claims we cannot deny Miss Chambers's right, although she may perhaps *deceive herself.*'

1799: 27   CHARLTON, Mary.

ROSELLA, OR MODERN OCCURRENCES. A NOVEL. IN FOUR VOL-UMES. BY MARY CHARLTON, AUTHOR OF PHEDORA, &C.

> London: Printed at the Minerva-Press, for William Lane, Leadenhall-Street, 1799.
> I 308p; II 296p; III 302p; IV 307p. 12mo. 14s sewed (MP, adv.).
> NLR 2: 180 (Aug 1799).

BL Cup.403.y.4; CME 3-628-45015-2; EM 3874: 2; ESTC t140061 (BI C; MH-H, PU, ViU &c.; EA COR).

Notes. 4 pp. advs. end vol. 4.

Phedora 1798: 22.

Adv., 'Next week will be published', MP 10 June 1799; additional booksellers are Miller, Bond-street; Kirby, Oxford-street; Lloyd, Harley-street; and Scatchard, Ave Maria-lane.

Adv. end vol. 2 of *Azalais and Aimar* (1799: 36).

Further edn: Dublin, 1800 (Printed for P. Wogan, W. Porter, and W. Burns, 2 vols., 12mo), ESTC t169488.

NLR: 'The reader of this novel will not have to complain of a want of incidents: indeed, they are, we think, rather crowded. The *personae dramatis* are numerous, and some of them well sketched. Perhaps it will not much discredit the fair author, if we observe, that where, in our opinion, she has been least successful, has been in the *slip-slop* dialect, which, nevertheless, she seems to have been fond of putting into the mouths of her her inferior personages. The general merits of "Rosella" are much above mediocrity.'

1799: 28   [CHARRIÈRE, Isabelle-Agnès-Elisabeth van Tuyll van Serooskerken · van Zuylen].
LETTERS WRITTEN FROM LAUSANNE. TRANSLATED FROM THE FRENCH.

Bath: Printed by R. Cruttwell; and sold by C. Dilly, Poultry, London, 1799.

I 175p; II 220p. 12mo. 7s boards (CR), 5s sewed (MR).

CR n.s. 27: 238 (Oct 1799); MR n.s. 29: 88–9 (May 799); AF II: 672.

BL 12613.aaa.20; EM 160: 6; ESTC t074650 (BI E; NA PPL).

Notes. Trans. of *Lettres écrites de Lausanne* (Toulouse, 1785) and of *Caliste, ou la continuation des lettres écrites de Lausanne* (Geneva and Paris, 1787) (BGR).

Dedication to the Marchioness of S——. In vol. 2 text of novel starts on p. 5. Epistolary.

CR: 'This is a delightful work. Without the bustle and intrigue of common novels, it interests and deeply affects. The story of Calista is little connected with that of the first volume; but one more interesting or more beautifully related we never remember: he who can peruse it without emotion must be destitute of taste and feeling.'

MR [Alexander Hamilton]: 'Love and marriage, the usual themes of the novelist, occupy exclusively the pages of this narrative; and, worn as the subjects are, we have perused it with considerable interest;—yet we cannot wish it an extensive circulation amongst our fair countrywomen, whose stricter morals can derive little improvement from the example of their Gallic neighbours, either before or since the revolution.'

1799: 29   [COOKE, Cassandra].
BATTLERIDGE: AN HISTORICAL TALE, FOUNDED ON FACTS. IN TWO VOLUMES. BY A LADY OF QUALITY.

London: Printed and published by G. Cawthorn, British Library, No. 132, Strand; sold also by Messrs. Richardson, Royal-Exchange; W. West, Paternoster-Row; and J. Wright and J. Hatchard, Piccadilly, 1799.

I viii, 264p; II 254p. 12mo. 7s boards (CR), 7s (MP).

CR n.s. 27: 238 (Oct 1799); AF II: 852.

BL 12613.aa.11; EM 239: 9; ESTC t068560 (NA CLU-S/C, ICN, MH-H).

Notes. Preface i–viii. In vol. 2 text of novel starts on p. 5. 2 pp. advs. end vol. 1 (pp. 263–4).
Adv. MP 19 July 1799.

CR: 'The time assigned to the principal tale is the last century; and the manners of the Cromwellian period are in some instances well preserved: but the work is not very amusing; and, in point of composition, it is despicable.'

1799: 30   [CURTIES], T. J. Horsley.
ETHELWINA, OR THE HOUSE OF FITZ-AUBURNE. A ROMANCE OF FORMER TIMES. IN THREE VOLUMES. BY T. J. HORSLEY.

> London: Printed at the Minerva-Press, for William Lane, Leadenhall-Street, 1799.
> I iii, 235p; II 238p; III 271p. 12mo. 10s 6d (ME), 10s 6d sewed (MP).
> Corvey; CME 3-628-45070-5; ESTC n016969 (NA CtY).

Notes. In preface to his *Ancient Records* (1801: 19) the author explains that fear caused him to send *Ethelwina* 'into the world as an orphan' under only his Christian name of Horsley.
Preface i–iii. 4 pp. advs. end vol. 1; 2 pp. advs. end vol. 2, 1 p. end vol. 3.
Adv., 'In the Press', MP 2 Feb 1799; by Mr. Horsley. Adv. as published MP 16 May 1799; additional booksellers are Miller, Bond-street; Hodgson, Wimpole-street; Lloyd, Harley-street; Kirby, Oxford-street; and Scatchard, Ave Maria-lane.
French trans. Paris, 1802 (*Ethelwina*) (Lévy); German trans. Leipzig, 1803 (*Ethelwina oder das Fräulein von Westmoreland*) (EAG).

DIDEROT, Denis, **THE NATURAL SON**
See LOAISEL DE TREOGATE, Joseph-Marie (1789: 51)

1799: 31   D'ISRAELI, I[saac].
ROMANCES, BY I. D'ISRAELI.

> London: Printed for Cadell and Davies, Strand; Murray and Highley, Fleet-street; J.
>   Harding, St James's-street; and J. Wright, Piccadilly, 1799.
> xix, 314p. 8vo. 8s boards (CR, MR).
> CR n.s. 26: 52–9 (May 1799); MR n.s. 29: 121–8 (June 1799); AF II: 1105.
> C 7700.d.588; CME 3-628-51016-3; EM 64: 3; ESTC t057324 (BI BL, E, MRu; NA
>   CSmH, MH-H, PU, ViU &c.; EA COR, ZWTU).

Notes. 'A Poetical Essay on Romance and Romancers' i–xix. 2 pp. advs. end vol.
Adv., 'printed on Whatman's best wove Post, and embellished with a Frontispiece', GEP 3–5 Jan 1799.
Further edns: Philadelphia, 1803 (WC); New York, 1803 (WC); NSTC lists edns. in 1801, 1803 and 1807. German trans. of parts, Leipzig, 1802 (*Liebe und Demuth*) (RS), and Leipzig, 1802 (*Die Liebenden*) (Price).

CR: 'In a romance an English reader generally expects enchantment, or at least the appearance of enchantment—an old castle, though it is not absolutely necessary that it should belong to a giant—and a ghost, or a deception more incredible than the actual apparition would be. None of these ingredients, however, can be found in the romances of M. d'Israeli. Love is the theme of all' (p. 52).

MR [Alexander Hamilton]: 'The mind of Mr d'Israeli, naturally susceptible of vivid impressions, seems to have caught a richness of fancy from his intimacy with Oriental poetry; and his language, except in a few unfortunate sentences, is elegant' (p. 121).

1799: 32 [DUBOIS, Edward].
THE FAIRY OF MISFORTUNE; OR, THE LOVES OF OCTAR AND
ZULIMA. AN EASTERN TALE. TRANSLATED FROM THE FRENCH BY
THE AUTHOR OF A PIECE OF FAMILY BIOGRAPHY. THE ORIGINAL
OF THE ABOVE WORK IS SUPPOSED TO BE IN THE SANSCRIT IN
THE LIBRARY OF THE GREAT MOGUL.

> London: Printed for J. Bell, no. 148, Oxford-Street, opposite New Bond-Street, 1799.
> 193p. 12mo. 3s (CR, ME), 3s sewed (MP).
> CR n.s. 26: 357 (July 1799); AF II: 1157.
> BL 12512.d.1; EM 5895: 8; ESTC t129713 (NA ICU, NcU; EA ZAP).

Notes. ESTC assumes that this work is probably an original, not a translation.
1-p. prefatory advertisement says that the tale 'was first printed at the Hague, in the year 1754,
after a version made by an anonymous author in French, according to a translation in ARABIC,
which, agreeable to the information he gives us, *fell into his hands when he was at Dehli* [*sic*].'
3-pp. adv. end vol., with extensive review quotations, for Dubois' *Piece of Family
Biography* (1799: 33).
Adv., 'On Monday will be published', MP 22 June 1799.
  CR comments on the 'spirit and felicity' of the trans.

1799: 33 [DUBOIS, Edward].
A PIECE OF FAMILY BIOGRAPHY. IN THREE VOLUMES. DEDI-
CATED TO GEORGE COLMAN, ESQ.

> London: Printed for J. Bell, no. 148, Oxford-Street, opposite New Bond-Street, 1799.
> I xii, [228]p; II viii, 235p; III viii, 219p. 12mo. 10s 6d sewed (MR, MP).
> CR n.s. 25: 233–4 (Feb 1799); MR n.s. 30: 370–5 (Dec 1799); AF II: 1158.
> BL Cup.403.i.12; CME 3-628-45146-9; EM 7266: 1; ESTC t139118 (BI O; NA PU; EA
>   COR).

Notes. Final page of vol. 1 is misnumbered 287. Vol. 1: dedication to Colman iii–v; table of
contents vii–xii. Vols. 2 and 3: table of contents v–viii.
Adv., 'In the course of next week will be published . . . *Natural Curiosities; or, a Piece of Fam-
ily Biography; a Satirical Novel*', MP 29 Jan 1799; adv. as published, still as *Natural Curiosities*,
MP 13 Feb 1799.
Further edn: Dublin, 1802 (Printed by J. Stockdale; for P. Wogan, W. Porter, J. Rice, B.
Dornin and J. Stockdale, 1 vol., no format) (WC).
  MR [Robert Woodhouse]: 'His plot is simple, yet sufficient to create interest; his remarks
are just, without being too obvious; he always endeavours to please, and he not infrequently
instructs. In our commendation of his performance, however, we must make considerable
reserve and limitation. Undoubtedly he has some title to wit, but he weakens that title by his
constant endeavours to enforce it; . . . his reading or learning is too ostentatiously displayed;
many of the criticisms that affect wit and cleverness are only puerile and quaint; the language
is sometimes incorrect; and the construction of the sentences is often inelegant' (p. 371).

1799: 34 ELLIA, Felix.
NORMAN BANDITTI, OR THE FORTRESS OF COUTANCE. A TALE.
IN TWO VOLUMES. BY FELIX ELLIA.

London: Printed at the Minerva-Press, for William Lane, Leadenhall-Street, 1799.

I 256p; II 286p. 12mo. 7s sewed (CR, adv. *Court*), 8s (GEP, adv. *Ethelwina*), 8s sewed (adv. *Eva*).

CR n.s. 27: 474–5 (Dec 1799); AF II: 1251.

Corvey; CME 3-628-45039-X; ESTC t200846 (NA CaAEU, CtY-BR).

Notes. Adv. SJC 22–25 Dec 1798; adv. GEP 23–26 Feb 1799.

Adv. end vol. 1 of *Ethelwina* (1799: 30); adv. end vol. 1 of *Eva* (1799: 54); adv. end vol. 2 of *Court Intrigue* (1799: 44).

CR: 'A feeble and vapid exhibition of the machinery of our popular modern romances—a story without interest, principally turning on an incident (the confinement of a father by his son) borrowed from Schiller's Tragedy of the Robbers.'

1799: 35 [F., E.].

THE CASTLES OF MONTREUIL AND BARRE; OR THE HISTORIES OF THE MARQUIS LE BRUN AND THE BARON LA MARCHE, THE LATE INHABITANTS AND PROPRIETORS OF THE TWO CASTLES. A GOTHIC STORY.

London: Printed and Sold by S. Fisher, No. 10, St. John's Lane, Clerkenwell; also sold by T. Hurst, No. 32, Paternoster Row; and R. C. Staines, Chelmsford, 1799.

50p. 12mo. 6d (t.p.).

MnU WILS RAR 824C2794 I; EM 2136: 19; ESTC n014985 (NA CaOHM, MH-H; EA ZWTU).

Notes. Previously printed in the *Lady's Magazine*, by E. F. (as 'The Two Castles, a Romance') in 1797–98 in 11 parts and in the *Hibernian Magazine* in 1797–99, RM 1282.

Frontispiece. Text begins on p. 3.

Further edn: Liverpool, n.d. [ESTC: 1800?], ESTC t223121.

1799: 36 [FABRE D'OLIVET, Antoine].

AZALAIS AND AIMAR, A PROVENCAL HISTORY OF THE THIR-TEENTH CENTURY. FROM AN ANCIENT MANUSCRIPT. IN THREE VOLUMES.

London: Printed at the Minerva-Press, for William Lane, Leadenhall-Street, 1799.

I xii, 232p; II 203p; III 191p. 12mo. 10s 6d sewed (CR), 9s sewed (MP, adv.).

CR n.s. 27: 475 (Dec 1799); AF II: 179.

Corvey; CME 3-628-45004-7; ESTC t200841.

Notes. Trans. of *Azalais et le Gentil Aimar histoire provençale, traduite d'un ancien manuscrit provençal* (Paris, 1799). In French original 'Avertissement du traducteur' claims that the 'histoire provençale ... est tombé entre [ses] mains par un hasard'.

'Advertisement of the English Translator' i–iv; preface v–xii. 1 p. advs. end vol. 2; 1 p. end vol. 3.

Adv. MP 11 Nov 1799; additional booksellers are Miller, Bond-street; Lloyd, Harley-street; Hodgson, Wimpole-street; Kirby, Oxford-street; and Scatchard, Ave Maria-lane.

Adv. end vol. 2 of *Court Intrigue* (1799: 44).

CR: 'Those readers who are pleased with a recurrence to the days of chivalry, will reap entertainment from this romance. The manners and *costume* of those times are, in general, well preserved by the author; but the narrative is sometimes tedious and uninteresting.'

1799: 37   [FIÉVÉE, Joseph]; [HEMET, John (*trans.*)].
SUZETTE'S DOWRY; OR THE HISTORY OF MADAM DE SENNETERRE. RELATED BY HERSELF. TRANSLATED FROM THE FRENCH.

> London: Printed by J. Nichols, Earl's Court, Newport Street, for Earle and Hemet, No. 47, Albemarle Street, Piccadilly, 1799.
> 223p. 12mo.
> NLR 3: 82 (Jan 1800); AF II: 1437.
> BL 12510.c.10; EM 60: 2; ESTC t100398.

Notes. Trans. of *La Dot de Suzette* (Paris, 1798).
MM 9: 91 (Feb 1800) names Hemet as translator.
3 pp. advs. end vol.
Further edns. (as *Suzette's Marriage Portion*): NSTC lists edns. in 1803.
> NLR: 'A novel of *mediocre* merit very lamely translated. The idiom is French throughout.'

1799: 38   [FOSTER, Mrs E. M.].
*FEDARETTA, A NOVEL, BY A LADY; EMBELLISHED WITH A FRON-TISPIECE.

> London: Printed for Crosby and Letterman, No. 4, Stationer's-Court, Paternoster-row (GEP), 1799 (GEP).
> 2 vols. 6s (GEP).
> No copy located.

Notes: Light and Shade (1803: 30), attrib. to Mrs Foster, lists *Fedaretta* as by the same author.
Adv. GEP 12–14 Dec 1799.
French trans. Paris, 1803 (*Fedaretta*) (HWS).

1799: 39   [FOSTER, E. M., Mrs].
REBECCA. A NOVEL. IN TWO VOLUMES.

> London: Printed at the Minerva-Press, for William Lane, Leadenhall-Street, 1799.
> I 304p; II 308p. 12mo. 7s (NLR, ME).
> NLR 1: 507 (May 1799).
> Corvey; CME 3-628-45159-0; ESTC t212428.

Notes. 4 pp. advs. end vol. 2.
Blakey: the same author's *Judith* (1800: 34) attributed to Mrs Foster by a Minerva Catalogue of 1814.
Adv., 'In the Press', MP 15 Jan 1799; adv. as published MP 9 Mar 1799; additional booksellers are Miller, Bond-street; Lloyd, Harley-street; Hodgson, Wimpole-street; Lee, Blandford-street, Manchester-square; and Scatchard, Ave Maria-lane.

GENLIS, Caroline-Stéphanie-Félicité Ducrest de Mézières, comtesse de, **THE AGE OF CHIVALRY**
See **THE KNIGHTS OF THE SWAN** (1796: 41)

1799: 40   GENLIS, [Caroline-Stéphanie-Félicité Ducrest de Mézières, comtesse de]; [O'HINKLEY, Matthew (*trans.*)].
RASH VOWS, OR THE EFFECTS OF ENTHUSIASM. A NOVEL. TRANS-LATED FROM THE FRENCH OF MADAME DE GENLIS, AUTHOR OF THE THEATRE OF EDUCATION, ADELAIDE AND THEODORE, &C. &C. IN THREE VOLUMES.

>   London: Printed for T. N. Longman and O. Rees, Paternoster-Row, 1799.
>   I iv, 270p; II 258p; III 277p. 12mo. 10s 6d boards (CR, MR), 12s sewed (adv.).
>   CR n.s. 26: 117 (May 1799); MR n.s. 29: 467–8 (Aug 1799); AF II: 510.
>   BL 1152.i.16; EM 3567: 1; ESTC t143950 (BI C, O; NA CaAEU, CLU-S/C, CtY, ICN).

Notes. Trans. of *Les Voeux téméraires* (Hamburg, 1798).
Dedication to Lady Edward Fitzgerald, and Mrs. Henrietta Matthieson iii–iv. 6 pp. advs. end vol. 3.
Adelaide and Theodore 1783: 9.
750 copies printed by Strahan, Jan 1799; 28 copies paid for by L. L'Homme, French book-seller of New Bond St; £39.18s (38 gns.) paid to Matthew O'Hinkley for 'translating' (LA).
Adv., 'speedily will be published' with no price given, GEP Jan 15–17 1799; adv. as published MP 25 Jan 1799 and GEP 29–31 Jan 1799.
Adv. end vol. 3 of *A Tale of the Times* (1799: 95).
Further edn: Dublin, 1799 (Printed by J. Stockdale, for J. Rice, 2 vols., 12mo), ESTC n048258.
CR refers the reader to rev. of original, n.s. 24: 562–9.

  MR [James Bannister] finds 'less to praise than on some former occasions': 'We are less amused by variety of incident, less instructed by a judicious discrimination of character, and less improved by an elevated strain of morality: while the sentiments are more forced, more unnatural; and the manners are more artificial' (p. 467).

1799: 41   GENLIS, [Caroline-Stéphanie-Félicité Ducrest de Mézières, comtesse de].
THE YOUNG EXILES, OR, CORRESPONDENCE OF SOME JUVENILE EMIGRANTS. A WORK INTENDED FOR THE ENTERTAINMENT AND INSTRUCTION OF YOUTH. FROM THE FRENCH OF MADAME DE GENLIS.

>   London: Printed for J. Wright, opposite Bond-street, Piccadilly; and H. D. Symonds, Pater-noster Row, 1799.
>   I viii, 376p; II 354p; III 363p. 12mo. 12s boards (CR, MR), 10s 6d sewed (GEP).
>   CR n.s. 26: 480 (Aug 1799); MR n.s. 33: 101–2 (Sept 1800); AF II: 513.
>   BL 12511.aa.34; EM 3605: 4; ESTC t145023.

Notes. Trans. of *Les petits emigrés* (Paris, 1798).
Preface vol. 1, iii–vi; epistle dedicatory 'to My Grand-Children' vii–viii. 1 p. advs. end vol. 3.
Epistolary.
Adv., 'speedily will be published', GEP 6–9 Apr 1799; still adv. 'speedily will be published' LC 85: 443 (7–9 May 1799); adv. as published MP 31 May 1799.
Adv., 'Speedily will be published, *The Young Exiles; or, Correspondence between Emigrant Children* . . . for G. G. and J. Robinson', MP 5 Feb 1799.

Further edns: London, 1799, ESTC n047070; Dublin, 1799 (Printed for V. Dowling, and J. Stockdale, 2 vols., 8vo), ESTC n047071.

CR refers the reader to rev. of original, App n.s. 25: 509–15 [Apr/May 1799].

MR [Elizabeth Moody]: 'The letters before us, though addressed to young persons and written principally for their amusement and instruction, are by no means so frivolous as to preclude those of maturer years from a participation of the repast; for they are both moral and entertaining, and are interspersed with a variety of interesting anecdotes.'

1799: 42   GODWIN, William.
ST. LEON: A TALE OF THE SIXTEENTH CENTURY. BY WILLIAM GODWIN. IN FOUR VOLUMES.

> London: Printed for G. G. and J. Robinson, Paternoster-Row; R. Noble, Printer, Great Shire-Lane, 1799.
>
> I xii, 331p; II 331p; III 286p; IV 336p. 12mo. 16s sewed (CR, MR), 16s boards (LC).
>
> CR n.s. 28: 40–8 (Jan 1800); MR n.s. 33: 23–9 (Sept 1800); AF II: 1648.
>
> BL 12613.e.7; EM 276: 6; ESTC t094266 (BI E, MRu, O; NA CSmH, ICN, MH-H, PU, TxU, ViU &c.; EA SU, ZWTU).

Notes. Adv., 'Early in November will be published', LC 86: 407 (24–26 Oct 1799); title is given as *Travels of St. Leon. A Tale of the Sixteenth Century.*

Adv., 'Monday next, will be published', GEP 23–26 Nov 1799.

Further edns: London, 1800, EM 3664: 3, ESTC t120446; Dublin, 1800 (Printed for P. Wogan, G. Burnet, P. Byrne, W. Porter, W. Jones [and 5 others], 2 vols., 12mo), EM 3704: 1, ESTC t073518; Dublin, 1800, ESTC t160343; Dublin, 1800, ESTC n022980; NSTC lists edns. in 1801, 1816, 1831, 1831, 1835, 1839, 1840; WC has 9 entries between 1800 and 1850. French trans. Paris, 1800 (*Saint-Léon, Histoire de Seizième Siècle*) (BGR); German trans. Hamburg, 1800 (*Saint Leon*) (Price). Facs: GN I (1831 edn.).

CR: '. . . the composition is, in general, worthy of praise' (p. 48).

MR [Christopher Lake Moody]: 'Is it a mode of instruction which such a philosopher ought to select? Is truth obliged to invoke the aid of the wildest fictions; and will it be said that virtue and contentment are best taught in the school of romance?' (p. 24) 'If all Mr Godwin's writings were of this complexion, we should read them with more satisfaction, and bestow on them a more liberal praise . . .' (p. 29).

1799: 43   GOOCH, {Eliz}[abeth] {Sarah} Villa-Real.
FANCIED EVENTS: OR, THE SORROWS OF ELLEN. A NOVEL, IN TWO VOLUMES. BY MRS. VILLA-REAL GOOCH.

> London: Printed and published by Geo. Cawthorn, British Library, Strand: sold also by Messrs. Richardson, Royal-Exchange; W. West, Paternoster-Row; J. Hatchard and J. Wright, Piccadilly; and all other booksellers, 1799.
>
> I xii, 246p; II 210p. 12mo. 7s (NLR).
>
> NLR 2: 181 (Aug 1799); AF II: 1669.
>
> BL 1607/1387; CME 3-628-45075-6; EM 8567: 4; ESTC t118834 (NA CaAEU; EA COR).

Notes. Preface v–xii, signed Eliz. Sarah Villa-Real Gooch.

German trans. Liegnitz and Leipzig, 1800 (*Helenens Leiden*) (EAG).

NLR: 'The plaintive and affectionate sensibility of the author of the *"Wanderings of the Imagination,"* [1796: 43] appears to infinite advantage in the novel before us; nor should we forget, though her mind is often clouded with horrid and painful prospects, we are frequently charmed with lively and enchanting descriptions of scenes and situations in which the author seems to have tasted the cup of sweetness and content.'

1799: 44   [GREEN, Sarah].
COURT INTRIGUE, OR THE VICTIM OF CONSTANCY, AN HISTORICAL ROMANCE. IN TWO VOLUMES. BY THE AUTHOR OF MENTAL IMPROVEMENT.

> London: Printed at the Minerva-Press, for William Lane, Leadenhall-Street, 1799.
> I 215p; II 201p. 12mo. 7s sewed (CR, MP), 7s (ME).
> CR n.s. 28: 116 (Jan 1800); AF II: 880.
> CaAEU PR 4728 G264 C86 1799; ESTC n068073.

Notes. Running-title: 'Victim of Constancy'. 15 pp. advs. end vol. 2. Epistolary.
Adv. MP 19 Dec 1799.

CR: The incidents of this novel are supposed to commence during the civil wars of England, in the time of Charles I. . . . Though there are no licentious passages in this story, it is rather vulgarised by the introduction of *lord Rochester* and *Nell Gwynn*.'

GRIFFIN, Elizabeth, THE FRIENDS
See App. A: 11

1799: 45   GUNNING, [Elizabeth].
THE GIPSY COUNTESS: A NOVEL. IN FOUR VOLUMES. BY MISS GUNNING.

> London: Printed for T. N. Longman and O. Rees, Paternoster Row, 1799.
> I iii, 238p; II 239p; III 239p; IV 231p. 12mo. 14s boards (CR, MR).
> CR n.s. 27: 475 (Dec 1799); MR n.s. 32: 94 (May 1800); AF II: 1755.
> BL Cup.403.i.16; CME 3-628-45042-X; EM 6602: 1; ESTC t139665 (NA CaAEU, CaOLU, CtY &c.; EA COR).

Notes. Introduction i–iii; Pagination continuous Roman-Arabic; text of novel starts on p. 5 of vol. 1. Epistolary.
Adv., 'In a few Days will be published', SJC 18–21 May 1799; adv. LC 8–11 June and GEP 13–15 June 1799 with no price.
Further edn: Dublin, 1799 (Printed for G. Burnet, P. Wogan, H. Colbert, W. Porter, J. Moore, and 10 others, 2 vols., 12mo), ESTC n007207; London, 1799 (WC), xESTC.

CR: 'The past and the present are strangely blended in this novel.'
MR [James Burney]: 'The first two volumes of this novel contain too much dissertation and digression; and narratives, little connected, displace each other by turns, as if for the express purpose of preventing a continuation of interest.'

1799: 46   HAYS, Mary.
THE VICTIM OF PREJUDICE. IN TWO VOLUMES. BY MARY HAYS, AUTHOR OF THE MEMOIRS OF EMMA COURTNEY.

London: Printed for J. Johnson, St. Paul's Church-Yard, 1799.

I iii, 212p; II 232p. 12mo. 6s boards (CR, MR).

CR n.s. 26: 450–2 (Aug 1799); MR n.s. 31: 82 (Jan 1800); AF II: 1863.

PU Singer-Mend.PR.4769.H6.V5.1799; ESTC n048539.

Notes. 2-pp. 'Advertisement to the Reader'.

Memoirs of Emma Courtney 1796: 50.

German trans. Berlin, 1799 (*Das Opfer des Vorurtheils*) (EAG); French trans. Paris, 1800 (*La Victime du préjugé*) (BGR). Facs: RWN.

CR: 'It is the offspring of talents much above mediocrity; but we do not hesitate to pronounce that they are employed in a manner highly dangerous to the peace and welfare of society' (p. 450).

MR [Christopher Lake Moody]: 'Mary, the heroine of this little tale, is, to the credit of the author's pencil, a spirited and affecting sketch, but somewhat out of nature; and the principle which it is designed to inculcate by no means follows from the premises. By the novels which issue from this school, love, which is a transient passion, is to be complimented, in all cases, at the expence of the regulations and institutions of society; and a respect for virtue and decorum is to be classed in the list of vulgar prejudices. Love, which is generally our happiness, may and will sometimes be our misery.'

1799: 47   HELME, Elizabeth.
ALBERT; OR, THE WILDS OF STRATHNAVERN. IN FOUR VOLUMES. BY ELIZABETH HELME, AUTHOR OF LOUISA; OR, THE COTTAGE OF THE MOOR, &C. &C. &C.

London: Printed by and for Sampson Low, Berwick Street, Soho, 1799.

I 236p; II 240p; III 215p; IV 264p. 12mo. 14s boards (CR), 14s sewed (MR, LC).

CR n.s. 28: 477 (Apr 1800); MR n.s. 30: 95 (Sept 1799); AF II: 1882.

BL C.171.a.5; CME 3-628-45057-8; EM 8516: 4; ESTC t126712 (BI O; NA CtY, IU, MH-H, ViU &c.; EA COR).

Notes. 1 p. advs. end vol. 3.

Louisa; or, the Cottage on the Moor 1787: 38.

Adv. SJC 13–16 Apr 1799: 'Berwick-street, April 8. Sampson Low repectfully informs the Publick, that Mrs HELME's new Novel, entitled, ALBERT; or, The WILDS of STRATH-NARVON, in 4 vols. will be published the latter End of this Month.'

Adv. LC 85: 500 (23–25 May 1799).

Further edns: Dublin, 1800 (Printed for P. Wogan, and N. Kelly, 2 vols., 12mo), ESTC n029555; NSTC lists edn. in 1821; London, 1823 (Summers). French trans. Paris, 1800 (*Albert ou le désert de Strathnavern*) (BGR); Spanish trans. Paris, 1834 (*Alberto, o el Desierto de Strathnavern*) (BN).

CR: 'This novel contains little originality or strength of character; but it is amusing in its story, and respectable for the propriety of moral sentiment.'

MR: '. . . we fear that she must not flatter herself with any expectation of figuring among the foremost of our literary countrywomen.'

1799: 48   HEMET, John.
CONTRADICTIONS; OR, WHO COULD HAVE THOUGHT IT? A NOVEL, FROM THE FRENCH, IN TWO VOLUMES. BY JOHN HEMET.

London: Printed for Earle and Hemet, No. 47, Albemarle Street, Piccadilly, 1799.
I 224p; II 236p. 8vo [CR has 12mo]. 7s sewed (CR, adv.).
CR n.s. 28: 236 (Feb 1800); AF II: 1895.
BL 12510.aaa.19; CME 3-628-45055-1; EM 330: 3; ESTC t131382 (NA CaAEU, ICN; EA COR).

Notes. Adv. end vol. 2 of *Augusta* (1799: 2).

CR: 'A work which may amuse a reader in those idle moments when he is not disposed to exert either his feelings or his judgment.'

1799: 49 {HEMET, John (*trans.*)}.
MISANTHROPY AND REPENTANCE: A NOVEL, FROM THE GERMAN.

London: Printed for Earle and Hemet, no. 47, Albermarle Street, Piccadilly. Sold also by T. Hurst, no. 32 Paternoster-Row, 1799.
iv, 211p. 12mo.
MM 8: 97 (Aug 1799).
O 249.s. 283; xESTC.

Notes. Trans. of *Menschenhass und Reue.*
Frontispiece. Preface iii–iv, signed John Hemet, 47 Albermarle Street, Aug 1799, claims that this novel is the original from which August Friedrich William von Kotzebue took the plot of his play *The Stranger* or *Misanthropy and Repentance* (*Menschenhass und Reue*, Mainz and Berlin, 1789) but acknowledges that it seems 'rather surprising' that 'the *original* did not make its appearance until fifteen months after the *copy theatric* had given so much delight to the German, English and French audiences'. 4 pp. advs. end vol.
MM gives Bellamy as bookseller.
MM mentions the translator's claim that the drama of *The Stranger* is 'founded on this novel'.
French trans. 1799 (*Misantropie et Repentir*) (ME).

HORSLEY, T. J.
See CURTIES, T. J. Horsley

1799: 50 HUTCHINSON, {A. A.}.
EXHIBITIONS OF THE HEART; A NOVEL, IN FOUR VOLUMES. DEDICATED (BY PERMISSION) TO THE QUEEN. BY MISS HUTCHINSON.

London: Printed for the Author, and sold by G. Kearsley, Fleet-Street; T. Davison, Printer, Lombard-street, Fleet-street, 1799.
I xi, 280p; II 261p; III 312p; IV 342p. 12mo. 16s sewed (CR), £1 1s sewed (MR).
CR n.s. 29: 472 (Aug 1800); MR n.s. 32: 438 (Aug 1800); AF II: 2137.
BL 12614.h.10; EM 327: 1; ESTC t073533 (NA ICU, MH-H).

Notes. Dedication to the Queen, signed A. A. Hutchinson, Nov 1799, 1, iii–v; list of subscribers vii–xi.
Proposals for printing *Exhibitions of the Heart* ESTC n042454.
Further edn: London, 1800 (WC), xESTC.

CR: 'On the whole, these volumes deserve to be regarded as interesting; and Miss Hutchinson seems, on some occasions, to have intermixed her narrative with adventitious incidents from real life; at least she has given them in different places an air of reality.'

MR [James Burney]: 'Though we cannot recommend the novel as possessing much more merit than the every-day productions of the same kind, it may be read without injury to the good cause of virtue, or the interests of morality; and the remarks on early education, which the fair writer has taken occasion to introduce into her narrative, are just and useful.'

1799: 51   INĀYAT-ALLĀH; SCOTT, Jonathan (*trans.*).
BAHAR-DANUSH; OR, GARDEN OF KNOWLEDGE. AN ORIENTAL ROMANCE. TRANSLATED FROM THE PERSIC OF EINAIUT OOLLAH. BY JONATHAN SCOTT, OF THE EAST INDIA COMPANY'S SERVICE, PERSIAN SECRETARY TO THE LATE GOVERNOR GENERAL OF BENGAL, WARREN HASTINGS, ESQ. AND TRANSLATOR OF FERISHTA'S HISTORY OF DEKKAN, AND OF THE REIGNS OF THE LATER EMPERORS OF HINDOSTAN. IN THREE VOLUMES.

> Shrewsbury: Printed by J. and W. Eddowes: for T. Cadell, jun. and W. Davies, in the Strand, London, 1799.
> I xv, lxxv, 211p; II 328p; III 304p. 8vo. 15s boards (CR, MR).
> CR n.s. 28: 57–63 (Jan 1800); MR n.s. 32: 233–6 (July 1800); AF II: 3981.
> BL 88.b.25–27; CME 3-628-45162-0; EMf; ESTC t101920 (BI AWn, O, Oc; NA ICN, NjP, PU &c.; EA COR, GOT).

Notes. Translation of the *Bahār Dānish*, a collection of tales, principally satires on women.
Translator's preface i–xv; prefatory introduction xiii–xxxvii; author's preface xli–xlv; introduction by the author xlvii–lxxv. Dedication to William Ouseley dated 1 Sept 1799. According to the translator's preface, Alexander Dow's earlier trans., *Tales, Translated from the Persian of Inatulla of Delhi* (1768, I xvii, 275p, II 245p, 8vo; JR 1217, AF I: 673), translated only a third of the work and was 'widely distant from' the original (p. ii). ICN copy has pencil note on fly-leaf: 'This is the first complete English translation of these tales'.
Adv., 'In a few Days will be published' with no price, GEP 9–12 Nov 1799; adv. as published GEP 30 Nov–3 Dec 1799.
Further edn: NSTC lists edn. in 1809. German trans. Leipzig, 1802 (*Bahar Danush, oder der Garten der Erkenntniss*) (Price).
   CR: 'With a wish that captain Scott may give us, through some other channel, the complete translation of this story, we close our observations on a work which we admire' (p. 63).
   MR [Alexander Hamilton]: '... the invention of the author is less exercised in weaving the tissue of his stories, than in burying the stories themselves under a mass of metaphor; the incidents, indeed, occupied apparently but a small portion of his care, and for the most part exhibit little artifice...' (p. 233).

1799: 52   IRELAND, W[illiam] H[enry].
THE ABBESS, A ROMANCE. BY W. H. IRELAND, THE AVOWED AUTHOR OF THE SHAKESPEAR PAPERS, &C. &C. IN FOUR VOLUMES.

> London: Printed for Earle and Hemet, no. 47, Albemarle-Street, Piccadilly, 1799.
> I xxiii, 241p; II 239p; III 214p; IV 211p. 12mo. 14s boards (CR), 14s sewed (adv. *Augusta*), 16s sewed (adv. *Misanthropy*).

CR n.s. 28: 355–6 (Mar 1800); AF II: 2206.

BL Cup.404.b.6; EM 6464: 3; ESTC t130395 (NA CSmH, InU-Li, ViU &c.).

Notes. Dedication to John-Frank Newton i–iv, signed W. H. Ireland, London, May 1799. 'A Few Words by way of Preface' v–xiii; verse prologue xv–xxiii.

Adv. end vol. 2 of *Augusta* (1799: 2); adv. end *Misanthropy and Repentance* (1799: 49).

Further edns: Baltimore, 1801 (WC); Baltimore, 1802 (WC); London, 1834 (WC). French trans. Paris, 1814 (*L'Abbesse*) (BN); Spanish trans. Madrid, 1822 (*La Abadesa*) (BN). Facs. GNII.

   CR: 'It is neither better nor worse than such as are regularly produced at the Leadenhall-street manufactory.'

1799: 53   JONES, Harriet.
BELMONT LODGE. A NOVEL. IN TWO VOLUMES. BY HARRIET JONES, OF MAIDSTONE.

> London: Printed for the author at the Minerva-Press, and sold by William Lane, Leadenhall-Street, 1799.
>
> I 9, 312p; II 367p. 12mo. 9s (ME), 10s (SJC Apr), 10s 6d (SJC June).
>
> ICN Y155.J72; EM 2294: 2; ESTC t076287 (BI BL).

Notes. List of subscribers vol. 1, 1–9, followed by unn. 1-p. introduction concerning the author's having written at the age of 19, 'under the deepest depression of mind, in order to alleviate the sorrows of a suffering parent'.

Adv. SJC 25–27 Apr 1799: 'The Subscribers to this Work are respectfully informed, their Copies will be delivered in a few Days; and next Week it will be published in 2 vols. 12mo. price 10s. at the Minerva Press, and sold by iam Miller, Bond-street.'

Adv. SJC 4–6 June 1799; author's name given as Miss Mary Jones.

1799: 54   KELLY, Isabella.
EVA. A NOVEL. IN THREE VOLUMES. DEDICATED BY PERMISSION TO HER ROYAL HIGHNESS THE DUCHESS OF GLOUCESTER. BY ISABELLA KELLY, AUTHOR OF MADELINE, ABBEY OF ST. ASAPH, AVONDALE PRIORY &C. &C.

> London: Printed at the Minerva-Press, for William Lane, Leadenhall-Street, 1799.
>
> I 5, 242p; II 262p; III 281p. 12mo. 9s (NLR), 12s (MP), 10s 6d sewed (LC).
>
> NLR 2: 180 (Aug 1799).
>
> ViU Vault *PZ2.H43E 1799; CME 3-628-45089-6; ESTC n009489 (NA CtY-BR; EA COR).

Notes. Dedication to H.R.H. the Duchess of Gloucester. List of subscribers pp. 1–5 (this list appears at end of vol. 1 in CtY-BR copy). 2 pp. advs. end vol. 1, 2 pp. advs. end vol. 2; 2 pp. advs. end vol. 3.

Madeline 1794: 35; *Abbey of St Asaph* 1795: 27; *The Ruins of Avondale Priory* 1796: 58.

Adv., 'In the Press, and speedily will be published', MP 9 Mar 1799. Adv. LC 85: 516 (28–30 May 1799).

French trans. Paris, 1803 (*Eva*) (HWS, NSTC).

   NLR: 'In conformity with the ghost-loving taste of the times, we have here the walking spectre of the *murdered Agatha*, and all the concomitant horrors of such preternatural appearances. We do not, however, mean to depreciate this work below its merits, though the author has, perhaps, thought it necessary to sacrifice propriety to "solid pudding." The story is interesting, and told for the most part in better language than is commonly met with in works of this description.'

1799: 55   KER, Anne.
THE HEIRESS DI MONTALDE; OR, THE CASTLE OF BEZANTO: A NOVEL. IN TWO VOLUMES. BY MRS. ANNE KER. DEDICATED, BY PERMISSION, TO HER ROYAL HIGHNESS THE PRINCESS AUGUSTA SOPHIA.

> London: Printed for the Author; and sold by Earle and Hemet, Frith Street, Soho, 1799.
> I 232p; II 191p. 12mo. 7s sewed (adv.).
> NLR 2: 388–9 (Oct 1799).
> BL 838.b.26; CME 3-628-45100-0; EM 2385: 2; ESTC t116100 (NA CaAEU, CLU-S/C; EA COR).

Notes. Dedication to H.R.H. Princess Augusta Sophia, signed Anne Ker; 1-p. solicitation of subscriptions for the author's next work, *Adeline St Julian* (1800: 46); 2-pp. list of subscribers to this one.
Adv. end vol. 2 of *Augusta* (1799: 2).

   NLR: 'The Heiress de Montalde is a wretched imitation of Mrs Radcliffe's manner, but the black horror of the mysterious tale is not brightened by a single ray of that lady's genius. The plot is confused, the incidents contemptible, and the language destitute of all characteristic propriety.'

1799: 56   KING, Sophia.
CORDELIA, OR A ROMANCE OF REAL LIFE. IN TWO VOLUMES. BY SOPHIA KING, AUTHOR OF TRIFLES FROM HELICON; & WALDORF, OR DANGERS OF PHILOSOPHY.

> London: Printed at the Minerva-Press, for William Lane, Leadenhall-Street, 1799.
> I 212p; II 193p. 12mo. 6s sewed (CR, MP).
> CR n.s. 28: 235–6 (Feb 1800); AF II: 2404.
> Corvey; CME 3-628-45099-3; ESTC 027439 (NA CaAEU, ViU [vol. 1 only]).

Notes. 3 pp. advs. end vol. 2.
Waldorf 1798: 34.
Adv. MP 8 July 1799; additional booksellers are Miller, Bond-street; Lloyd, Harley-street; Hodgson, Wimpole-street; Kirby, Oxford-street;and Scatchard, Ave Maria-lane.
French trans. Paris, 1800 (*Cordelia, ou faiblesse excusable, histoire de la vie telle qu'elle est*) (BGR).

   CR: 'This is a gloomy tale, not very probable in its incidents, and not very interesting in its progress or attractive in its style.'

1799: 57   KNIGGE, Adolf [Franz Friedrich Ludwig von], Baron.
THE HISTORY OF THE AMTSRATH GUTMAN, WRITTEN BY HIMSELF. PUBLISHED BY ADOLPHUS BARON KNIGGE. TRANSLATED FROM THE GERMAN.

London: Printed for Vernor and Hood, Poultry, 1799.
xi, 312p. 12mo. 3s 6d sewed (MR, GEP).
MR n.s. 34: 321 (Mar 1801); AF II: 2414.
O Vet.A5e.4222; ESTC n017567 (NA ViU).

Notes. Trans. of Knigge's *Geschichte des Amtsraths Gutmann* (Hanover, 1794).
Preface of the Translator v–xi. Pagination continuous Roman-Arabic; text of novel starts on p. 13.
Adv. MP 17 Oct 1799 and GEP 19–22 Oct 1799.
Further edns: London, 1800 (Summers); London, 1801 (Summers); London, 1802 (Family Misfortunes; or *The History of Frederick Gutman, Amstrath of Mehlbach*) (OBgU). Dutch trans. Dordrecht, 1813 (*Geschiedenis van den Ambstraad Goedman*) (BN).

MR [Ollyett Woodhouse]: 'Though the style of this work is harsh and unpleasant, we have found some amusement in the perusal of it. The characters are well delineated, it contains some humorous passages, and on the whole it is more interesting and less objectionable than the generality of German novels.'

1799: 58 KOTZEBUE, A[ugust Friedrich Ferdinand] von.
THE CONSTANT LOVER; OR, WILLIAM AND JEANETTE: A TALE. FROM THE GERMAN OF A. VON KOTZEBUE. TO WHICH IS PRE-FIXED AN ACCOUNT OF THE LITERARY LIFE OF THE AUTHOR.

London: Printed for J. Bell, no. 148, Oxford-Street, 1799.
I xxvii, 288p; II iv, 302p. 12mo. 8s boards (CR, MP).
CR n.s. 26: 117 (May 1799); AF II: 2431.
BL 1152.a.3; EM 4963: 8; ESTC t135703 (NA CtY, MH-H).

Notes. Trans. of *Geprüfte Liebe*, published in vols. 4 and 6 of *Die Jüngsten Kinder meiner Laune* (Leipzig, 1793–97).
Vol. 1: contents v–vi; Dedication (signed 'Kotzebue' to 'My Friend Charles George Grau-mann, St Petersburgh' vii–ix; 'My Literary Life' written by Kotzebue xi–xxvii. Vol. 2: con-tents iii–iv.
Adv., 'In two large Volumes', MP 2 Feb 1799.
Further edns: Dublin, 1799 (Printed by William Porter, for P. Wogan, H. Colbert, W. Porter, J. Moore, and N. Kelly, 2 vols., 12mo), ESTC t204541; Boston, 1799, ESTC w030586; New York, 1799, ESTC w030585; New York, 1801 (WC).

CR: 'A book more completely amusing we have seldom perused.'

1799: 59 KOTZEBUE, August [Friedrich Ferdinand] von; THOMPSON, Benjamin (*trans.*).
THE ESCAPE. A NARRATIVE, FROM THE GERMAN OF AUGUSTUS VON KOTZEBUE. BY BENJAMIN THOMPSON, TRANSLATOR OF THE STRANGER, AS PERFORMED AT THE THEATRE-ROYAL, DRURY-LANE.

London: Printed for Vernor and Hood, no. 31, Poultry, 1799.
119p. 8vo. 2s 6d (CR, MP).
CR n.s. 28: 240 (Feb 1800); AF II: 4427.
BL RB.23.a.8709; ESTC n009285 (NA PPL, ViU).

Notes. Trans. of *Die Flucht*, published in vol. 3 of *Die Jüngsten Kinder meiner Laune* (6 vols. Leipzig, 1793–97).

Adv. MP 17 Oct 1799.

Further edn: London, 1804 (WC). WC also shows 3 American edns. as *The Adventures of Joseph Pignata.*

CR: 'If it be the narrative of a real escape from the Inquisition, Kotzebue, by not announcing it as such, has deprived the reader of the chief source of interest. If, as we suspect, it be a fictitious tale, there is little merit in copying from what is here called *Trenk's romance.*'

1799: 60   KOTZEBUE, August [Friedrich Ferdinand] von; WILL, P[eter] (*trans.*).

THE SUFFERINGS OF THE FAMILY OF ORTENBERG, A NOVEL. TRANSLATED FROM THE GERMAN OF AUGUST VON KOTZEBUE, BY P. WILL, MINISTER OF THE REFORMED CONGREGATION IN THE SAVOY. IN THREE VOLUMES.

> London: Printed for C. Geisweiler, 54, Pall Mall; G. G. and J. Robinson, and H. D. Symonds, Paternoster-Row; G. C. Keil, Magdeburg; B. G. Hoffman, Hamburg; and J. B. Beygang, Leipzig, 1799.
>
> I 210p; II 204p; III 218p. 12mo. 9s sewed (CR, MP).
>
> CR n.s. 30: 352–3 (Nov 1800); AF II: 4809.
>
> BL 012553.e.30; EM 5795: 6; ESTC t155383.

Notes. Trans. of *Die Leiden der Ortenbergischen Familie* (vol. 1 Petersburg, 1785; vol. 2 Leipzig, 1788).

Adv. MP 18 July 1799.

Further edns: Dublin, 1799 (G. Burnet, P. Wogan, W. Porter, W. Jones, J. Halpen [and 6 others in Dublin], 2 vols., 12mo), ESTC n026019; Dublin, 1799, ESTC t155382; Philadelphia, 1800, ESTC w030957; New York, 1800, ESTC w019241.

CR: 'This novel is not very regular in its plan or construction; but it claims the merit of sentiment and pathos, and, in various passages, *traits* of humour are discernible.'

1799: 61   LAFONTAINE, Augustus [Heinrich Julius].

THE FAMILY OF HALDEN: A NOVEL. BY AUGUSTUS LA FONTAINE. TRANSLATED FROM THE GERMAN.

> London: Printed for J. Bell, no. 148, Oxford-Street, 1799.
>
> I 285p; II 280p; III 274p; IV 274p. 12mo. 14s (AR, MP).
>
> AR n.s. 1: 600–1 (June 1799); AF II: 2442.
>
> BL 12547.ccc.13; EM 5616: 7; ESTC t099903 (BI C; NA IU, ViU).

Notes. Trans. of 'Familie von Halden' first published as vols. 1 and 2 of *Familiengeschichten* (6 vols. Berlin, 1797–1804).

1-p. prefatory advertisement vol. 1 concerns Lafontaine. Vol. 2 of BL copy lacks t.p.

Adv. MP 11 Mar 1799; 'These two novels [*Family of Halden* and *Saint Julien* {1798: 37}] form the whole of the original work, comprehended under the title of Histories of Families. The reputation of the author is so high on the Continent, that he is styled the German Fielding.'

French trans. Paris, 1803 (*La Famille de Halden*) (BN).

1799: 62   [LAFONTAINE, August Heinrich Julius]; WENNINGTON, William (*trans.*).

THE MAN OF NATURE OR NATURE AND LOVE FROM THE GERMAN OF MILTENBERG BY WILLIAM WENNINGTON. (AFTER THE EDITION BAUER 1797) WITH NOTES ILLUSTRATIVE COMPARATIVE BY THE TRANSLATOR.

> London: Printed for the Translator, Thavies Inn, Holborn, and for Joseph Gerold, in Vienna, 1799.
> xxix, 447p. 8vo. Fine Paper, 7s boards (MR), CR gives no price.
> CR n.s. 28: 117 (Jan 1800); MR n.s. 32: 143–6 (June 1800); AF II: 4736.
> C 7746.c.57; EM 5878: 6; ESTC t100448 (BI BL; NA CSmH).

Notes. Trans. of *Naturmensch* (Halle, 1792).
Engraved t.p. List of subscribers v–xv with 3 handwritten additions at end. 2 pp. advs. end vol.
Further edn: London, 1807 (WC). French trans. Paris, 1801 (*William Hillnet, ou la Nature et l'amour*) (BN).
CR: 'An improbable story, which did not deserve to be translated, told in the language of affectation.'
MR [John Ferriar]: 'We cannot discern the great superiority in point of invention and design, which the translator attributes to his original in this novel. The leading incidents are drawn from Dr. Johnson's Rasselas, and from a French novel intitled *The Man of Nature*, which was published about thirty years ago' (p. 143).
[*The Man of Nature* 1773: 35; *The Prince of Abissinia* {*Rasselas*}, 1759, JR 495, AF I: 1436.]

1799: 63   LAFONTAINE, August [Heinrich Julius]; WILL, P[eter] (*trans.*).
ROMULUS, A TALE OF ANCIENT TIMES, TRANSLATED FROM THE GERMAN OF AUGUSTUS LAFONTAINE, BY THE REV. P. WILL, MINISTER OF THE GERMAN CONGREGATION IN THE SAVOY.

> [London]: Printed for R. Phillips, 71, S^t. Paul's Church Yard, By T. Adlard, N° 39, Duke Street, Little Britain, and T. Gillet, Crown Court, Fleet Street, n.d. [1799].
> I 11, 322p; II 320p. 12mo. 8s boards (MR, LP), 8s boards or 8s 6d half bound for libraries (MP).
> MR n.s. 34: 321 (Mar 1801); AF II: 4808.
> BL C.171.bb.1; EMf; ESTC t200762 (NA CLU-S/C).

Notes. Trans. of vol. 2 of *Sagen aus dem Alterthume* (Berlin, 1799).
ESTC gives date as 1800. Adv., 'On Monday next will be published', MP 30 Sept 1799. Also adv. LP 20–22 Nov 1799.
Dedication to Miss Planta by the translator [1]; preface 3–11 offers the present title as a contrast to recent licentious German romances; Arabic page sequence begins again with the 1st page of the novel. 2 pp. advs. end vol. 1; 4 pp. advs. end vol. 2.
Further edns: Baltimore, 1814 as *A Tale of ancient Times, entitled Romulus* (WC); NSTC lists edn. in 18—. French trans. Paris, 1801 (*Romulus, roman historique*) (BN).
MR [Ollyett Woodhouse]: 'This interesting and amusing tale deserved a translator who was better versed in the English language than Mr Will necessarily could be.'
NLR 2: 'The best interests of piety and morality are promoted by the incidents which form this interesting novel...' (p. 389).

1799: 64   LATHOM, Francis.
MEN AND MANNERS. A NOVEL. IN FOUR VOLUMES. BY FRANCIS LATHOM, AUTHOR OF THE MIDNIGHT BELL, CASTLE OF OLLADA, &C.

>London: Printed for J. Wright, opposite Bond-street, Piccadilly; and H. D. Symonds, Pater-noster Row, 1799.
>
>I 334p; II 353p; III 271p; IV 343p. 12mo. 14s sewed (CR, MR), 14s boards (MP, GEP).
>
>CR n.s. 27: 114–15 (Sept 1799); MR n.s. 31: 136–41 (Feb 1800; AF II: 2468.
>
>C S727.d.79.55–58; CME 3-628-45096-9; EMf; ESTC n004047 (BI E; NA CaAEU, ICN, PU, ViU &c.; EA COR).

Notes. In UCLA copy imprint in vol. 4 is variant—'Printed by William Thorne, for J. Wright; and H. D. Symonds'—but Cambridge copy has same imprint in all 4 vols. 2 pp. advs. end vol. 2; 1 p. end vol. 4.

The Midnight Bell 1798: 40; *Castle of Ollada* 1795: 28.

Adv. MP 5 Apr 1799 and GEP 6–9 Apr 1799.

'A New Edition' adv. GEP 19–21 Dec 1799.

Further edns: Dublin, 1799 (Printed by William Porter, for Burnet, Gilbert, Wogan, Colbert, W. Porter [and 5 others], 4 vols., 12mo), EM 367: 4, ESTC t138326; London, 1799/1800, ESTC n004048. German trans. Berlin, 1799 (*Schilderung heutiger Menschen und heutiger Sitten*) (EAG).

CR: 'From the general insipidity of novels, we are disposed to speak with approbation of those which, though far from being entitled to the praise of excellence, exhibit some strength of character, and an interesting variety of incident. On this principle we are induced to give our favorable suffrage to the production before us, which, notwithstanding some glaring faults, is evidently the offspring of a pen accustomed to mark with precision the vicissitudes of real life' (p. 114).

MR [Elizabeth Moody]: 'We are sorry that we have not been more entertained with the whole of this novel: but we readily acknowlege that we have occasionally received pleasure from the comic powers of Mr. Lathom; and that we have met with scenes not unworthy of the drama, where the ridicule is well painted which results from pride, ostentation, and vanity, grafted on low birth, mean education, and defective intellects. Prolixity is the great fault of this author, and it is indeed too common an error' (p. 141).

1799: 65   [LEMAISTRE, John Gustavus].
FREDERIC LATIMER: OR, THE HISTORY OF A YOUNG MAN OF FASHION. IN THREE VOLUMES.

>London: Printed by Luke Hansard, No. 6, Great Turnstile, Lincoln's-Inn Fields, For T. Cadell, Jun. and W. Davies, in the Strand, 1799.
>
>I 169p; II 235p; III 187p. 8vo [MR has 12mo]. 10s 6d boards (CR), 10s 6d sewed (MR, MP).
>
>CR n.s. 29: 471 (Aug 1800); MR n.s. 32: 438 (Aug 1800); AF II: 2519.
>
>BL N.1805; CME 3-628-45054-3; EMf; ESTC t071898 (BI O, MRu; NA CSmH, NjP, PU &c.; EA COR).

Notes. 1-p. preface dated from London, 16 Nov 1799.

Adv., 'In a few Days will be published', MP 15 Nov 1799; adv. as published MP 22 Nov 1799.

Further edn: NSTC lists 1801 edn. French trans. Paris, 1801 (*Frédéric Latimer, ou histoire d'un jeune homme à la mode*) (HWS, WC).

CR: 'The follies and absurdities of fashion are well satirised by the author; and the work, which is said to be his first attempt, deserves sufficient encouragement from the public to induce him to renew his exertions.'

MR [Thomas Wallace]: 'In these volumes, the reader will find the vices and follies of the woman of fashion, the frauds of the gambler, the arts of the coquette, the levity and generosity of youth, and the dignity of worth and wisdom, described with considerable judgment, in the course of a story of which the plot is interesting, and, except one or two incidents towards the *denouement*, sufficiently natural.'

1799: 66   [MARTIN, Mrs].
REGINALD, OR THE HOUSE OF MIRANDOLA. A ROMANCE. IN THREE VOLUMES. BY THE AUTHOR OF MELBOURNE, &C.

> London: Printed at the Minerva-Press, for William Lane, Leadenhall-Street, 1799.
> I iii, 293p; II 291p; III 292p. 12mo. 12s (ME), 12s sewed (MP, adv.).
> NLR 3: 82 (Jan 1800); AF II: 2726.
> MH-H *EC75.A100.799r2; CME 3-628-45161-2; EM 1490: 50; ESTC n013075 (NA CtY; EA COR).

Notes. ESTC: Attributed to Mrs. Martin in a Minerva Library catalogue of 1814.
Preface (1, i–iii) concerns the difficulty of following in Mrs Radcliffe's footsteps. 3 pp. advs. end vol. 1; 1 p. advs. end vol. 2.
Melbourne 1798: 47.
Adv. MP 19 Dec 1799.
Adv. end vol. 1 of *Adelaide de Narbonne* (1800: 25).

> NLR: 'This is professedly an imitation of Mrs. Radcliffe's "Udolpho;" [1794: 47] and, in our opinion, not an unsuccessful one. The story is well told, and is calculated to promote the exercise of the moral virtues.'

1799: 67   MEEKE, [Mary].
ELLESMERE. A NOVEL. IN FOUR VOLUMES. BY MRS. MEEKE.

> London: Printed at the Minerva-Press, for William Lane, Leadenhall-Street, 1799.
> I 238p; II 260p; III 292p; IV 310p. 12mo. 14s (ME).
> BL 1152.c.6; CME 3-628-45126-4; EM 6332: 6; ESTC t147288 (NA MiU, NjP; EA COR, ZDP).

Notes. Adv., 'In the Press', MP 2 Feb 1799.

1799: 68   [MEEKE, Mary].
HARCOURT. A NOVEL. IN FOUR VOLUMES. BY THE AUTHOR OF THE MYSTERIOUS WIFE, &C.

> London: Printed at the Minerva-Press, for William Lane, Leadenhall-Street, 1799.
> I 356p; II 338p; III 288p; IV 352p. 12mo. 18s sewed (CR, MP), 16s sewed (adv.).
> CR n.s 29: 116 (May 1800); AF II: 2808.
> BL Cup.403.i.3; CME 3-628-45049-7; EM 6565: 6; ESTC t139697 (NA CaAEU, ViU; EA COR).

Notes. 2 pp. advs. end vol. 2.

The Mysterious Wife 1797: 56.

Adv. MP 5 Sept 1799; additional booksellers are Miller, Bond-street; Lloyd, Harley-street; Hodson [*sic*], Wimpole-street; Kerby, Oxford-street; and Scatchard, Ave Maria-lane.

Adv. end vol. 1 of *Anecdotes of the Altamont Family* (1800: 54).

1799: 69 [MILLER, Johann Martin]; L., H. (*trans.*).

SIGEVART, A TALE. TRANSLATED FROM THE GERMAN, BY H. L.

> Chelsea: Printed by D. Jacques; for G. Polidori, 1799.
>
> I 270p; II 225p. Small 12mo. 5s sewed (MR); inferior paper 5s, fine 7s sewed (verso of t.p.), CR gives no price.
>
> CR n.s. 27: 116 (Sept 1799); MR n.s. 34: 321 (Mar 1801); AF II: 2869.
>
> BL 12551.a.32; EM 3988: 2; ESTC t150346 (BI C; NA CaOLU, DLC).

Notes. Trans. of *Siegwart. Eine Klostergeschichte* (Leipzig, 1776).

French trans. Basle, 1783/85 (*Sigevart, dédié aux âmes sensibles*) (BGR).

CR: 'This tale seems to be the production of a school-boy: it is minute in circumstances, tedious in narration, uninteresting in story.'

MR [Ollyett Woodhouse]: 'We doubt whether this little work possesses sufficient interest to reward the generality of readers for their trouble in perusing it: yet it appears to be written by a person who possesses considerable powers of imagination, and is capable of discerning and delineating characters.'

MILTENBERG

See LAFONTAINE, Auguste Heinrich Julius (1799: 62)

1799: 70 PARSONS, [Eliza].

THE VALLEY OF ST. GOTHARD, A NOVEL. IN THREE VOLUMES. BY MRS. PARSONS, AUTHOR OF ANECDOTES OF TWO WELL-KNOWN FAMILIES, MYSTERIOUS WARNINGS, AN OLD FRIEND WITH A NEW FACE, &C. &C. &C.

> Brentford: Printed by P. Norbury; and sold by J. Wallis, No. 46, Pater-Noster-Row, 1799.
>
> I 262p; II 276p; III 252p. 12mo. 12s boards (CR), 12s sewed (MP).
>
> CR n.s. 26: 358 (July 1797); AF II: 3239.
>
> CtY-BR Im P254.799v; CME 3-628-45142-6; EM 4402: 2; ESTC t119026 (BI BL; NA ViU; EA COR).

Notes. Dedication to M. G. Lewis, author of *The Monk* (1796: 63), 'With the warmest admiration of splendid talents, and the highest respect for personal merit'.

Anecdotes of Two Well-known Families 1798: 52; *The Mysterious Warning* 1796: 71; *An Old Friend With a New Face* 1797: 62.

Adv., 'On Saturday next, June 1, will be published', MP 29 May 1799.

CR: 'This is neither better nor worse than her former productions: it will probably have many readers and many admirers.'

1799: 71 {PATRICK, Mrs F. C.}.

THE JESUIT: OR, THE HISTORY OF ANTHONY BABINGTON, ESQ.

AN HISTORICAL NOVEL, BY THE AUTHORESS OF 'MORE GHOSTS,'
'THE IRISH HEIRESS,' &C. IN THREE VOLUMES.

> Bath: Printed by R. Cruttwell, (for the authoress;) and sold by C. Dilly, Poultry, London,
> 1799.
>
> I xx, 213p; II 256p; III 336p. 12mo. 10s 6d boards (CR), 10s 6d sewed (MR, SJC, GEP).
> CR n.s. 27: 115 (Sept 1799); MR n.s. 30: 95–7 (Sept 1799); AF II: 3255.
> Corvey; CME 3-628-45088-8; ESTC n048921 (NA CaAEU, IU).

Notes. Dedication to Mrs. Johnstone, Pulteney-Street v–vi signed F. C. Patrick, Bath, Mar
1799; preface vii–xx signed 'The Editor', Mar 1799. Text of novel starts on p. 5 in vols. 2
and 3.

More Ghosts! 1798: 53; *Irish Heiress* 1797: 63.

Adv. 21–23 May 1799 and GEP 18–20 July 1799.

German trans. Berlin and Stettin, 1800 (*Der Jesuit, eine wahre Geschichte*) (EAG).

CR: 'Here we have a tale of more than common merit. Of those which, since the Ghost Seer
[1795: 39], have hinged upon supernatural illusions, this is perhaps the only one that does
not disgust by the impossibility of its incidents.'

MR [James Burney]: 'On the whole, this is no ordinary novel, either in plan or in the
degree of interest which it excites.'

1799: 72   [PEACOCK, Lucy].

THE LITTLE EMIGRANT, A TALE. INTERSPERSED WITH MORAL
ANECDOTES AND INSTRUCTIVE CONVERSATIONS. DESIGNED
FOR THE PERUSAL OF YOUTH. BY THE AUTHOR OF THE ADVEN-
TURES OF THE SIX PRINCESSES OF BABYLON, VISIT FOR A WEEK,
JUVENILE MAGAZINE, &C. &C.

> London: Printed by S. Low, Berwick Street, Soho; for the Author, at the Juvenile
> Library, N°. 259, Oxford Street; and sold by Messrs. Carpenter, Old Bond Street; C.
> Law, Ave-Maria Lane; and E. Newbery, the Corner of St Paul's Church-Yard, 1799.
> ii, 203p. 12mo. 3s bound (MR, GEP).
> MR n.s. 29: 464 (Aug 1799); AF II: 3276.
> BL 1210.m.17; EM 5791: 10; ESTC t118008 (BI O; NA CaOHM, CaOTP, CLU-S/C &c.).

Notes. Frontispiece. Prefatory advertisement i–ii. 1 p. advs. end vol.

The Adventures of the Six Princesses of Babylon 1785: 40; *Visit for a Week* 1794: 43.

Adv. GEP 16–19 Feb 1799.

Further edns: NSTC lists edns. in 1802 and 1820; London, 1826 (WC). French trans. Paris,
1826 (*La petite émigrée*) (BN).

MR [William Smyth]: 'The publication before us affords many useful lessons for youth;
and it is not without instructive passages in science.'

1799: 73   PILKINGTON, [Mary].

HENRY; OR THE FOUNDLING: TO WHICH ARE ADDED, THE PREJU-
DICED PARENT; OR, THE VIRTUOUS DAUGHTER. TALES, CALCU-
LATED TO IMPROVE THE MIND AND MORALS OF YOUTH. BY MRS.
PILKINGTON.

> London: Printed for Vernor & Hood, Poultry, 1799.

173p. 12mo. 1s 6d (CR), 1s 6d boards (MR), 1s 6d 'Vellum Back' (GEP).
CR n.s. 31: 227 (Feb 1801); MR n.s. 28: 332 (Mar 1799); AF II: 3347.
O Vet.A5f.422; EMf; ESTC n007757 (NA CLU-S/C, FU, KEmU &c.).

Notes. Frontispiece. Text of novel starts on p. 3. 4 pp. advs. end vol.
Adv., 'with an elegant Frontispiece', GEP 2–5 Feb 1799.
Further edn: Philadelphia, 1801 (WC).

MR [Jabez Hirons]: 'If readers, whether in more early or advanced life, will permit themselves, at the same time that they are amused or interested, to mark with care the lessons of virtue and truth which rising circumstances present, or the cautions and warnings which they suggest, there is little doubt of their receiving at least a present, and perhaps a lasting, benefit.'

1799: 74 PILKINGTON, [Mary].
*THE SPOILED CHILD; OR, INDULGENCE COUNTERACTED. BY MRS. PILKINGTON.

London: Vernor and Hood (MR).
12mo. 1s 6d (CR), 1s 6d Half bound (MR).
CR n.s. 31: 346 (Mar 1801); MR n.s. 31: 428 (Apr 1800); AF II: 3353.
No copy located.

Notes. CR: 'A very excellent story to show the pernicious effects of humouring children, intermixed with many other entertaining and moral anecdotes.'

MR [Jabez Hirons]: 'The short narrative is intermixed with incidents and tales, which engage the attention of the reader; though the style of some of them may possibly be rather too high.'

1799: 75 PROBY, W[illiam] C[harles].
THE MYSTERIOUS SEAL, A ROMANCE. IN THREE VOLUMES. BY W. C. PROBY.

London: Printed for R. H. Westley, Nº. 159, opposite the New Church, in the Strand, 1799.
I 241p; II 201p; III 190p. 12mo. 7s sewed (MR), 10s 6d sewed (CR), 10s 6d (GEP).
CR n.s. 26: 358 (July 1799); MR n.s. 30: 471 (Dec 1799); AF II: 3613.
BL C.171.a.9; CME 3-628-45144-2; EMf; ESTC t127126 (BI BMp, O; EA COR).

Notes. Adv., 'On Saturday will be published, in three handsome Volumes', GEP 25–27 Apr 1799; adv. gives author's full names.

CR: 'This seems to be the production of a very young man. The story has little novelty, and the execution displays little merit.'

MR [James Bannister]: '. . . it would not be easy to give an analysis of the fable, which is wild, strange, and intricate. It contains no delineation of either character or manners; and, although the author disdains to be confined by the restraints of good sense, propriety, consistency, or probability, we meet with little variety of incident; but we are supplied with an abundant store of dark plots, wicked contrivances, and scenes of horror, copied in part from "the Mysteries of Udolpho," [1794: 47] and yet more from "the Castle Spectre"' [a 1797 play by Matthew G. Lewis].

1799: 76 [PYE, Henry James].
THE ARISTOCRAT, A NOVEL. IN TWO VOLUMES. BY THE AUTHOR OF THE DEMOCRAT.

London: Printed by and for Sampson Low, Berwick Street, Soho: and sold by C. Law, Ave Maria Lane; and E. Booker, New Bond Street, 1799.

I 216p; II 194p. 12mo. 7s sewed (CR, MR), 7s (LC).

CR n.s. 26: 358 (July 1799); MR n.s. 29: 468–9 (Aug 1799); AF II: 3653.

BL 1607/1579; CME 3-628-45003-9; EM 4161: 6; ESTC n016002 (BI O; NA CaOHM, MH-H; EA COR).

Notes. 2 pp. advs. end vol. 2.

The Democrat 1795: 36.

Adv. LC 85: 211 (28 Feb–2 Mar 1799).

CR: The story does not 'contain any interest more than sufficient to excite the transient curiosity of the subscribers to circulating libraries.'

MR [William Smyth]: 'This is a pleasing production; and though the characters are not new, nor the incidents very striking, yet an uniform interest is preserved in the mind of the reader, by the ease and elegance of the composition, and by the unvaried purity of the sentiments.'

1799: 77   REEVE, Clara.

DESTINATION: OR, MEMOIRS OF A PRIVATE FAMILY. BY CLARA REEVE, AUTHOR OF "THE OLD ENGLISH BARON, &C." &C. IN THREE VOLUMES.

London: Printed for T. N. Longman and O. Rees, Paternoster-Row, 1799.

I 244p; II 218p; III 212p. 12mo. 10s 6d sewed (CR, MR), 10s 6d boards (MP).

CR n.s. 27: 115 (Sept 1799); MR n.s. 30: 97 (Sept 1799); AF II: 3711.

BL C.171.a.1; CME 3-628-45160-4; EMf; ESTC t127124 (BI IPSr; NA CtY-BR, MH-H, ViU &c.; EA COR).

Notes. 7 pp. advs. end vol. 3.

750 copies printed by Strahan, June 1799; Reeve sold copyright for £60 (LA).

The Champion of Virtue [*The Old English Baron*] 1777: 16.

Adv. MP 28 June 1799.

Further edn: Dublin, 1799–1800 (Printed by T. Burnside, for Burnet, Wogan, Porter, J. Moore, W. Jones [and 7 others], 2 vols., 12mo), ESTC n008591. Prospectus for London edn. ESTC t118125 (BL 1600/1199).

CR: 'The incidents, though neither affecting nor uncommon, are so likely to have happened, and the characters bear such a resemblance to many which we meet in the walks of life, that we perused the work with the pleasure of a calm unagitated curiosity.'

1799: 78   ROBINSON, Mary.

THE FALSE FRIEND: A DOMESTIC STORY. BY MARY ROBINSON, AUTHOR OF POEMS, WALSINGHAM, ANGELINA, HUBERT DE SEVRAC, &C. &C. IN FOUR VOLUMES.

London: Printed for T. N. Longman and O. Rees, Paternoster-Row, 1799.

I 336p; II 343p; III 336p; IV 367p. 12mo. 16s boards (CR), 16s sewed (MR, MP).

CR n.s. 26: 117 (May 1799); MR n.s. 30: 98 (Sept 1799); AF II: 3825.

BL 12632.s.29; EM 365: 3; ESTC t094332 (NA CaAEU, CtY-BR, PU &c.).

Notes. 4 pp. advs. end vol. 4. 1,000 copies printed by Strahan, Feb 1799 (Strahan 17 f. 122); Robinson sold copyright for £150 (LA). Epistolary.

Walsingham 1797: 71; *Angelina* 1796: 76; *Hubert de Sevrac* 1796: 77.

Adv. MP 16 Feb 1799 and GEP 23–26 Feb 1799.

Further edn: London, 1799, ESTC t094333. French trans. Paris, 1799 (*Le Faux ami*) (BGR); German trans. Rudolstadt, 1800–01 (*Der falsche Freund*) (EAG).

CR: 'Mrs. Robinson is one of those writers who possess more genius than judgement.'

MR [James Burney]: 'The story is of a melancholy cast, and composed of events not the most probable; yet it is interesting, and would have been so in a much greater degree, if the proprieties of character had been more observed.'

1799: 79 ROBINSON, [Mary].

THE NATURAL DAUGHTER. WITH PORTRAITS OF THE LEADEN-HEAD FAMILY. A NOVEL. BY MRS. ROBINSON, AUTHOR OF POEMS, WALSINGHAM, THE FALSE FRIEND, &C. &C. &C. IN TWO VOLUMES.

London: Printed for T. N. Longman and O. Rees, Paternoster-Row, 1799.

I 288p; II 286p. 12mo. 7s (CR), 7s boards (MR, GEP).

CR n.s. 28: 477 (Apr 1800); MR n.s. 32: 93–4 (May 1800); AF II: 3830.

BL 12654.a.16; CME 3-628-45171-X; EM 555: 2; ESTC t094335 (BI E; NA InU-Li, IU, NNU &c.; EA COR).

Notes. 2 pp. advs. end vol. 2. 1,000 copies printed; Robinson sold copyright for £60 (LA).

Walsingham 1797: 71; *The False Friend* 1799: 78.

Adv. GEP 27–29 Aug 1799.

Further edn: Dublin, 1799 (Printed by Brett Smith, for Wogan, Burnet, Porter, Moore, Jones [and 5 others], 2 vols., 12mo), ESTC n040615.

CR: 'From a perusal of the first pages of this novel we were led to expect a production superior to the general trash of the circulating library: We have, however, been completely disappointed; nor can the interspersion of a few pieces of elegant poetry, in these two volumes, protect them from the unqualified censure which the absurd improbability of the incidents related in them, and the plotless insipidity of the story, demand.'

MR [James Burney]: 'Fancy has been little restrained in the composition of this novel, and the satirical talent of the writer has not lain dormant. The story may be said to possess more of entertainment than of probability; a predominance which will readily find favour with the generality of readers, (and, critics as we are, we cannot in conscience much blame their taste,) than if it had been reversed' (p. 93).

1799: 80 ROWSON, [Susanna].

REUBEN AND RACHEL; OR, TALES OF OLD TIMES. A NOVEL. IN TWO VOLUMES. BY MRS. ROWSON, AUTHOR OF CHARLOTTE, MENTORIA, FILLE DE CHAMBRE, &C. &C.

London: Printed at the Minerva-Press, for William Lane, Leadenhall-Street, 1799.

I 281p; II 315p. 12mo. 7s sewed (CR).

CR n.s. 28: 116–17 (Jan 1800); AF II: 3884.

BL 12611.aaa.24; CME 3-628-45164-7; EM 169: 1; ESTC t139045 (EA COR).

Notes. Other edn: Boston, 1798, ESTC w021955.

Charlotte 1791: 60; *Mentoria* 1791: 61; *Fille de Chambre* 1792: 51.

Adv., 'Just published', MP 13 Sept 1799.

CR: 'This production is a strange medley of romance, history, and novel, in which the scenery is changed with the pantomimical rapidity of Voltaire's *Candide*. New characters and new narratives are frequently introduced; and we were in some measure surprised that a novelist of Mrs. Rowson's experience should have aukwardly thrown together, in two volumes, a number of stories sufficient (in the hands of a dexterous manufacturer) to have occupied nearly ten times the space on the shelves of a circulating library.'

1799: 81   SAINT-PIERRE, J[acques]-H[enri]-B[ernardin] de; KENDALL, E[dward] A[ugustus] (*trans.*).
AMASIS. FROM THE FRENCH OF J. H. B. DE SAINT PIERRE. BY E. A. KENDALL.

> London: Printed for Vernor and Hood, No. 31, Poultry, 1799.
> 162p. 8vo [MM and ME have 12mo]. 3s (ME).
> MM 8: 96 (Aug 1799).
> CLU-S/C PQ2065.A.7a.1799; ESTC n031287 (NA CaSSU, OU).

Notes. Extract from *L'Arcadie*, 1st pub. in 4th vol. of *Études de la nature* (Paris, 1788) (BGR; BN has only 1856 and 1888 edns.).
'Notes' pp. [129]–162. 2 pp. advs. end vol.
Further edns: Boston, 1795, ESTC w029692; Dublin, 1799 (Printed by William Folds, for Messrs. Burnet, P. Wogan, W. Porter, J. Moore, W. Jones [and 5 others], 12mo), EM 7240: 3, ESTC t185672.

MM: 'This is a sweet pastoral, in the manner of Gessner, in which there is much genuine simplicity, interspersed, indeed, with many classical allusions, calculated at the same time to inform and entertain the reader.'

SANDHAM, Elizabeth, THE HAPPY FAMILY AT EASON HOUSE
See App. A: 13

1799: 82   [SANDS, James].
COUNT DI NOVINI; OR, THE CONFEDERATE CARTHUSIANS. A NEAPOLITAN TALE. IN THREE VOLUMES.

> London: Printed for G. G. and J. Robinson, Paternoster-Row; R. Noble, Printer, Great Shire-Lane, 1799.
> I 254p; II 261p; III 261p. 12mo. 10s 6d sewed (CR, MR).
> CR n.s. 28: 236 (Feb 1800); MR n.s. 33: 209–10 (1800); AF II: 3943.
> C 7720.d.1556–1558; CME 3-628-45026-8; EMf; ESTC t165998 (BI BL; NA MH-H; EA COR).

Notes. Adv., 'Next week will be published', GEP 10–12 Dec 1799.
Further edn: Dublin, 1800 (Printed by J. Stockdale, for P. Wogan, P. Byrne, W. Porter, J. Rice, G. Folingsby, J. Stockdale, and W. Folds, 2 vols., 12mo), EM 2962: 10, ESTC t084069.

CR: 'A novel inartificial in story, rude in character, and coarse in dialogue.'
MR [James Burney]: 'On the whole, this work appears to be the hasty production of a pen which is capable of more finished productions.'

1799: 83 [SHERWOOD, Mary Martha].
MARGARITA. A NOVEL. IN FOUR VOLUMES. BY THE AUTHOR OF TRADITIONS.

London: Printed at the Minerva-Press, for William Lane, Leadenhall-Street, 1799.

I 353p; II 237p; III 226p; IV 277p. 12mo. 14s (AR, LC), 14s sewed (MP, adv.), 16s sewed (GEP).

AR n.s. 1: 415–16 (Apr 1799).

MH-H *EC8.Sh585.799m; CME 3-628-45112-4; EM 1010: 11; ESTC n003932 (NA IU; EA COR).

Notes. Frontispiece in vol. 1. 3 pp. advs. end vol. 1; 3 pp. advs. end vol. 2; 2 pp. advs. end vol. 3; 3 pp. advs. end vol. 4.

Traditions 1795: 40.

Sherwood was paid £40 for *Margarita* but the novel 'does not appear to have attracted much attention' (Darton 196).

Adv. MP 2 Feb 1799; additional booksellers are Miller, Bond-street; Lloyd, Harley-street; Kirby, Oxford-street; and Scatchard, Ave-Maria-lane. Also adv. GEP 23–26 Feb 1799.

Adv. end vol. 2 of *Court Intrigue* (1799: 44).

1799: 84 [SHOWES, Mrs].
THE RESTLESS MATRON. A LEGENDARY TALE. IN THREE VOLUMES.

London: Printed at the Minerva-Press, for William Lane, Leadenhall-Street, 1799.

I 232p; II 257p; III 244p. 12mo. 10s 6d sewed (CR, MP).

CR n.s. 27: 475–6 (Dec 1799); AF II: 4084.

BL C.171.a.7; CME 3-628-45165-5; EM 3710: 7; ESTC t127133 (NA CaAEU; EA COR).

Notes. 3 pp. advs. end vol. 2.

Adv. MP 5 Dec 1799; additional booksellers are Miller, Bond-street; Hodgson, Wimpole-street; Lloyd, Harley-street; Kirby, Oxford-street; and Scatchard, Ave Maria-lane.

CR: 'The *restless matron* is a spirit who wanders in a state of perturbation and anxiety till some curses connected with the family to which she belonged are removed. But we deem it unnecessary to give a sketch of an absurd, confused, and uninteresting tale, which will not repay the attention of the reader.'

1799: 85 SICKLEMORE, Richard.
AGNES AND LEONORA. A NOVEL. IN TWO VOLUMES. BY RICHARD SICKELMORE [*sic*], AUTHOR OF EDGAR, OR THE PHANTOM OF THE CASTLE, &C. &C.

London: Printed at the Minerva-Press, for William Lane, Leadenhall-Street, 1799.

I 194p; II 196p. 12mo. 6s sewed (LC).

NLR 1: 405–6 (Apr 1799).

CtY-BR Im.Si12.799A; ESTC n029533 (NA CaOTU, PBm; EA COR).

Notes. 2 pp. advs. end vol. 1.

Edgar 1798: 65.

Adv. LC 85: 205 (26–28 Feb 1799).

NLR: 'The scene is here placed in Spain. There are many improbabilities in this narrative, which are not compensated by a powerful interest.'

1799: 86   [SOUZA, Adélaïde-Marie-Émilie Filleul, marquise de Flahaut].
*EMILIA AND ALPHONSO, A NOVEL; BY THE AUTHORESS OF ADELA DE SENANGE; TRANSLATED FROM THE FRENCH.

> London: Printed for R. Dutton, No. 10, Birchin–lane, Cornhill (GEP).
> 2 vols. 12mo. 7s boards (CR), 7s sewed (GEP).
> CR n.s. 27: 238 (Oct 1799); AF II: 1270.
> No copy located.

Notes. Trans. of *Emilie et Alphonse ou danger de se*[sic] *livres à ses premières impressions* (Hamburg, 1799), rev. CR n.s. vol. 25, pp. 558–62.
Adèle de Sénange London, 1794, apparently not trans. into English.
Adv. GEP 18–20 June 1799.

> CR: 'The translation is miserably executed.'

1799: 87   {SPENCE, Elizabeth Isabella}.
HELEN SINCLAIR: A NOVEL. BY A LADY. IN TWO VOLUMES.

> London: Printed for T. Cadell, Jun. and W. Davies, in the Strand, 1799.
> I 211p; II 230p. 8vo [MR has 12mo]. 7s boards (CR), 7s sewed (MR, LC).
> CR n.s. 26: 477 (Aug 1799); MR n.s. 29: 89 (May 1799); AF II: 4210.
> E RB.s.1097; EM 1287: 2; ESTC n004688 (NA CSmH, CtY, MH-H).

Notes. 3-pp. dedication to Mrs. Fordyce, the author's aunt, signed 'Elizabeth Isabella Spence', London, Jan 1799.
Adv. LC 85: 20 (3–5 Jan 1799) and MP 8 Jan 1799.

> CR: 'Neither the characters nor the sentiments of this novel rise above mediocrity; but the story is interesting....'

> MR [James Bannister]: 'This work appears to be the effusion of a pure, virtuous, and benevolent mind;—the characters, though neither striking nor uncommon, are on the whole justly delineated; and, if the incidents do not surprise and astonish us, we observe fewer violations of probability than in the greater part of the novels which are poured out in such torrents from the press.'

1799: 88   SUMMERSETT, Henry.
MAD MAN OF THE MOUNTAIN. A TALE. IN TWO VOLUMES. BY HENRY SUMMERSETT, AUTHOR OF PROBABLE INCIDENTS, &C.

> London: Printed at the Minerva-Press, for William Lane, Leadenhall-Street, 1799.
> I 238p; II 207p. 12mo. 7s sewed (CR, MP).
> CR n.s. 29: 115 (1800); AF II: 4298.
> BL C.123.k.11; CME 3-628-45196-5; EM 3842: 1; ESTC t124785 (BI O; NA CaAEU, CtY-BR, CSmH; EA COR).

Notes. 1 p. advs. end vol. 2.
Probable Incidents 1797: 77.
Adv. MP 13 Sept 1799; additional booksellers are Miller, Bond-street; Hodgson, Wimpole-street; Lloyd, Harley-street; and Scatchard, Ave Maria-lane.
French trans. Paris, 1805 (*Le Fou de la Montagne*) (HWS).

1799: 89   [TAYLOR, Miss].
JOSEPHINE. A NOVEL. IN TWO VOLUMES. BY AN INCOGNITA.

London: Printed at the Minerva-Press, for William Lane, Leadenhall-Street, 1799.
I 252p; II 240p. 12mo. 7s (ME), 6s sewed (MP).
Corvey; CME 3-628-45101-9; xESTC.

Notes. Blakey: by the same author as *Rosalind* (1799: 90), attributed to Miss Taylor by a Minerva Library catalogue of 1814.
Adv., 'in the Press' and no price given, GEP 23–26 Feb 1799; adv. as published MP 9 Mar 1799; additional booksellers are Miller, Bond-street; Lloyd, Harley-street; Hodgson, Wimpole-street; Lee, Blandford-street, Manchester-square; and Scatchard, Ave Maria-lane.

1799: 90   [TAYLOR, Miss].
ROSALIND. A NOVEL. IN TWO VOLUMES. BY THE AUTHOR OF JOSEPHINE.

London: Printed at the Minerva-Press, for William Lane, Leadenhall-Street, 1799.
I 228p; II 248p. 12mo. 7s sewed (MP).
Corvey; CME 3-628-45158-2; ESTC n065922.

Notes. Blakey: attributed to Miss Taylor by a Minerva Library catalogue of 1814.
Adv. MP 19 Dec 1799.

1799: 91   [TÉLLEZ, Gabriel]; THOMPSON, Benjamin (*trans.*).
THE RING, OR THE MERRY WIVES OF MADRID: TRANSLATED BY BENJAMIN THOMPSON, TRANSLATOR OF THE STRANGER, AS PERFORMED AT THE THEATRE ROYAL, DRURY-LANE.

London: Printed for the Translator, And sold by Vernor and Hood in the Poultry; T. Hurst Paternoster-Row; C. Sutton, Nottingham; W. Rawson, Hull; and all other booksellers, 1799.
141p. 12mo. 2s 6d (t.p., CR, MR).
CR n.s. 27: 239 (Oct 1799); MR n.s. 30: 98 (Sept 1799); AF II: 4437.
MH-H *EC8.T3715.799t; EM 1492: 10; ESTC n013174 (NA NNS).

Notes. Freely translated and expanded from *Los tres maridos burlados* by Tirso da Molina, the pseudonym of Gabriel Téllez (ESTC).
Dedication (1 p. unn.) to Joseph Bilbie Esq., signed Benjamin Thompson, Nottingham, 1 July 1799.
Adv. MP 17 Oct 1799; *The Ring; or, the Merry Wives of Madrid; addressed to Cruel and Careless Husbands.*
CR: 'A story of three wives reclaiming their husbands from different faults, as improbable as the Arabian Nights Entertainments, and not so interesting.'
MR [James Burney]: 'A merry story; and "within the limits of becoming mirth:" translated with spirit.'

1799: 92   THOMAS, Francis Tracy.
MONK-WOOD PRIORY. BY FRANCIS TRACY THOMAS, CORNET IN THE EAST AND WEST LOTHIAN LIGHT DRAGOONS. IN TWO VOLUMES.

London: Printed by A. Strahan, Printers Street, for T. N. Longman and O. Rees, Pater-
noster-Row, 1799.

I iv, 226p; II 194p. 12mo. 7s sewed (CR), 7s boards (MR, LC).

CR n.s. 31: 236 (Feb 1801); MR n.s. 31: 82 (Jan 1800); AF II: 4420.

E Jac.V.6/2; CME 3-628-45216-3; ESTC t197414 (NA ICU; EA COR).

Notes. Dedication to Lady Charlotte Campbell 1, iii–iv. Epistolary until p. 141 of vol. 2 when
'the editor takes up his pen, in order to introduce the sequel of this story in narrative'. 5 pp.
advs. end vol. 2.

Adv. SJC 1–3 Oct 1799 and LC 86: 346 (8–10 Oct 1799).

CR: 'These letters may . . . afford the reader some cursory entertainment, though they have
not any particular claim to critical approbation.'

MR [James Burney]: 'This work is derived from the common Stock of ingredients, compounded with flowery sentiment. The principal character is an imitation of Lovelace: but *the
happy fate* provided for this gay libertine has, we believe, the merit of novelty.'

1799: 93   THOMSON, [Anna].
EMILY DUNDORNE; OR, THE EFFECTS OF EARLY IMPRESSIONS: A
NOVEL, IN THREE VOLUMES. BY MRS. THOMSON, AUTHOR OF
ROBERT AND ADELA DE MONTFORT, EXCESSIVE SENSIBILITY, FATAL
FOLLIES, THE LABYRINTHS OF LIFE, &C. &C.

London: Printed by and for Sampson Low, Berwick-street, Soho; and sold by C. Law,
Ave-Maria Lane, 1799.

I 199p; II 185p; III 192p. 12mo. 9s (NLR), 10s 6d (GEP).

NLR 1: 197 (Feb 1799).

O 249.s.20-22; xESTC.

Notes. For more information about author's name, see note to *Labyrinths of Life* 1791: 70.
3 pp. advs. end vol. 2.

Robert and Adela 1795: 43; *Excessive Sensibility* 1787: 50; *Fatal Follies* 1788: 75; *The Labyrinths
of Life* 1791: 70.

Adv., 'speedily will be published' but no price given, GEP 25–27 Oct 1798; adv. as published
GEP 28 Feb–2 Mar 1799.

NLR: 'This novel does not want for character, incident, nor interest; but seems to be incorrectly printed.'

1799: 94   WALKER, George.
THE VAGABOND, A NOVEL, IN TWO VOLUMES. BY GEORGE
WALKER, AUTHOR OF THEODORE CYPHON; CINTHELIA, OR, A
WOMAN OF TEN THOUSAND, &C. DEDICATED TO THE LORD
BISHOP OF LANDAFF.

London: Printed for G. Walker, no. 106, Great Portland Street, and Hurst, no. 32, Paternoster Row, 1799.

I xiv, 227p; II 266p. 12mo. 7s boards (CR).

CR n.s. 26: 237 (June 1799); AF II: 4665.

BL 12613.bb.24; EM 226: 2; ESTC n068568 (NA IU, PU, ViU &c.; EA COR).

Notes. Vol. 1, 2-pp. table of contents; dedication to 'the Right Reverend Father in God,

Watson, Lord Bishop of Landaff' v–vii, signed George Walker; preface ix–xiv. Vol. 2, 2-pp. table of contents.

Theodore Cyphon 1796: 88; *Cinthelia* 1797: 78.

Further edns: London, 1799, ESTC n047882; London, 1799, EM 4156: 2, ESTC t071312; Dublin, 1800 (Printed by D. Graisberry, for G. Burnet, P. Wogan, W. Porter, J. Moore, B. Dornin, J. Rice, and G. Folingsby, 1 vol., 12mo), ESTC n052557; Boston, 1800, ESTC w019919; Harrisonburg, VA, 1814 (WC). French trans. Paris, 1807, (*Le Vagabond, ou le Rencontre de deux philosophes républicains*) (BN).

CR: 'His story is highly improbable. To correct extravagance by extravagance, and absurdity by something as absurd, is not the mode which a wise man would follow. . . .'

1799: 95   [WEST, Jane].

A TALE OF THE TIMES. BY THE AUTHOR OF A GOSSIP'S STORY. DEDICATED BY PERMISSION TO MRS. CARTER. IN THREE VOLUMES.

> London: Printed for T. Longman and O. Rees, Paternoster-Row, 1799.
> I iv, 310p; II 312p; III 389p. 12mo. 12s (CR), 12s sewed (MR, MP).
> CR n.s. 25: 357 (Mar 1799); MR n.s. 29: 90–1 (May 1799); AF II: 4726.
> CtY Im.W520.799t; EM 138: 1; ESTC t064721 (BI C, O; NA CtY, DLC, IU, MH-H, NjP, TxU, ViU &c.; EA COR).

Notes. Prefatory advertisement iii–iv; 6 pp. advs. end vol. 3. Pages of the F gathering of vol. 1 are wildly out of order.

1,000 copies printed by Strahan, Jan 1799 (Strahan 17 f. 122); 'Author' paid £90 (LA).

A Gossip's Story 1796: 89.

Adv. MP 10 Jan 1799 and GEP Jan 15–17 1799; re–adv., with quotation from GM, MP 13 Mar 1799.

2nd edn. adv. GEP 23–25 May 1799.

Further edns: London, 1799, ESTC t060739; Dublin, 1799 (Printed by William Porter, 2 vols., 12mo), EM 5096: 7, ESTC t139495; NSTC lists edns. in 1801 and 1803. French trans. Paris 1800 (*Histoire du temps ou les mÉurs écossaises*). Facs: FCy.

CR: 'The authoress of this work is already distinguished in the circle of literature; and her reputation will doubtless be considerably increased by the propriety of sentiment, correct delineation of character, and nervous composition, which these volumes exhibit.'

MR [William Smyth]: 'This work is interesting, though too diffuse in its narration, and though it is rendered too prolix by the multiplicity of its reflections. . . . The language is uniformly correct; and the moral sentiments do honour to the writer's heart and understanding.'

1799: 96   [?WHITFIELD, Henry].

SIGISMAR. BY THE AUTHOR OF VILLEROY. IN THREE VOLUMES.

> London: Printed for R. Dutton, Birchin-Lane, Cornhill, 1799.
> I viii, 225p; II 206p; III 179p. 12mo [MM has 8vo]. 10s 6d (ME), 10s 6d sewed (MP).
> MM 8: 346–7 (Dec 1799); AF II: 4102.
> BL 12611.bbb.23; CME 3-628-45186-8; EM 64: 1; ESTC t108183 (NA CaAEU, NjP; EA COR).

Notes. ESTC: Sometimes attributed to Henry Whitfield.

Prefatory advertisement v–viii. 2 pp. advs. end vols. 1 and 2. Epistolary.

Villeroy 1790: 73.
Adv. MP 26 Nov 1799.
French trans. Paris, 1803 (*Sigismar*) (BGR).

MM: 'If this be not a novel of the first order, in point of composition, it possesses sufficient interest to engage the serious attention of the reader; and it has evidently been the aim of the author, throughout, to improve the morals, as well as to amuse the fancy. We should hope, however, that there are few females of so depraved a cast as one of the principal characters here pourtrayed. . . .'

1799: 97   {WILDMAN, Joseph}.
THE FORCE OF PREJUDICE, A MORAL TALE, IN TWO VOLUMES.

    London: Printed (by J. Barfield, Wardour-Street,) for the author, And to be had of him,
       No. 18, West-Street, Soho, 1799.
    I xxxiv, 252p; II 308p. 12mo. 7s boards (CR), MR has no price.
    CR n.s. 30: 231 (Oct 1800); MR n.s. 32: 438–9 (Aug 1800); AF II: 4798.
    BL 12614.f.12; EM 218: 8; ESTC t073507 (BI BMu, C, O; NA CLU-S/C, MH-H).

Notes. 2 pp. advs. beginning vol. 1, preceding t.p. Dedication to Lady Howard, signed Joseph Wildman, 19 Dec 1799. List of subscribers i–xxiv; preface xxv–xxxiv signed by the author, 12 Aug 1799; advertisement to the reader (unn.) 19 Dec 1799. 2 pp. advs. end vol. 2.
'Prospectus' promising delivery of the books in 2–3 weeks is dated 1 Mar 1800, ESTC t223402.
Further edn: London, 1800, EM 6647: 8, ESTC t128973.

    CR: 'Many of the readers of this novel may be inclined to dispute the applicability of the term *moral*, as a designation of the tale. They will not perhaps allow that a tale is strictly *moral*, which seems to give encouragement to illicit love, by holding out a seduced female as worthy of general respect and esteem.'

    MR [James Burney]: 'In the attempt to combat prejudice, the writer has designed to shew that, without offence to morality or decency, and without injury to human happiness, a female who has erred, who has repented of her errors, and who strictly perseveres in her recovered rectitude, may be again admitted to the full benefits of civilized society.'

1799: 98   [WILLIAMS, William Frederick].
SKETCHES OF MODERN LIFE; OR, MAN AS HE OUGHT NOT TO BE. A NOVEL. IN TWO VOLUMES.

    London: Printed for W. Miller, Old Bond Street, 1799.
    I 267p; II 242p. 12mo. 7s (CR), 7s sewed (MR, GEP).
    CR n.s. 25: 357–8 (Mar 1799); MR n.s. 30: 95 (Sept 1799); AF II: 4845.
    BL 12611.bbb.24; CME 3-628-45200-7; EM 169: 5; ESTC t108471 (NA MH-H; EA
      COR, GOT).

Notes. Author attribution from t.p. to *Fitzmaurice* (1800: 78); attribution not in ESTC.
1-p. prefatory advertisement (unn.).
Adv. GEP 26–29 Oct 1799; adv. includes quotation from MR.

    CR: 'Upon the whole, this production is superior to many of our modern novels.'

    MR [James Bannister]: 'The moral tendency of this novel is entitled to praise; for it exhibits, in a striking manner, the dreadful effects of gaming, duelling, coquetry, and illicit love. . . . Many objections might be made to the texture of the story; probability and consistency are frequently violated, and the catastrophe is perhaps too shocking.'

1799: 99   YOUNG, Mary Julia.
THE EAST INDIAN, OR CLIFFORD PRIORY. A NOVEL, IN FOUR VOL-
UMES. BY MARY JULIA YOUNG, AUTHOR OF ROSE-MOUNT CASTLE,
POEMS, &C.

> London: Printed for Earle and Hemet, No. 47, Albemarle-Street, Piccadilly, by John
> Nichols, Red-Lion-Passage, Fleet-Street. Sold also by T. Hurst, No. 32, Paternoster
> Row, 1799.
> I iii, 304p; II 292p; III 277p; IV 278p. 12mo. 16s (ME).
> BL 1607/2082; CME 3-628-45214-7; EM 4403: 2; ESTC t118949 (BI MRu; NA IEN,
> MH-H, NNS; EA COR).

Notes. Dedication to the Countess of Derby p. iii, signed 'The Author'.
Rose-Mount Castle 1798: 75.
Further edn: Dublin, 1800 (Printed for N. Kelly, and D. Graisberry, 2 vols., 12mo) ESTC
n001223.

APPENDIX A

'Novels' for children

A: 1   1783   [DAY, Thomas].
THE HISTORY OF SANDFORD AND MERTON, A WORK INTENDED FOR THE USE OF CHILDREN.

> London: Printed for J. Stockdale, Opposite Burlington-House, Piccadilly, 1783.
> vii, 215p. 12mo [CR and MR have 8vo]. 3s (CR, MR).
> CR 57: 235–6 (Mar 1784); MR 70: 126–30 (Feb 1784); AF II: 1014.
> InU-Li PR 3398.D3.H67; ESTC t070591 (BI BL [missing], Lsm; NA CLU-S/C, MH-H, &c.; EA ZWTU).

Notes. Preface [iii]–vii.

Vols 2 and 3 1786 and 1789 (App. A: 3 and 5).

Further edns: London, 1786–91, ESTC t070595; London, 1787, ESTC n017808; Dublin, 1787 (Printed by P. Byrne), ESTC t070592; Belfast, 1787 (Printed by Daniel Blow), ESTC n017832; Philadelphia, 1788, ESTC w012718; 32 further entries in ESTC; WC has 118 entries for the period 1800–1850. WC has 5 French trans. (Paris 1786/87,1803, 1805 and 1822 and Geneva, 1796); German trans. Brunswick, 1788 (*Geschichte Sandford's und Merton's für Kinder erzählt*) (EAG).

CR: 'Rousseau's sentiments, without his visionary refinements; his insight into human nature, without his scepticism, in many places seem to have influenced the author; and, if our advice is of any consequence, we would not only recommend this part of the work to the attention of the public, but the continuation of it to his own' (p. 235).

MR [William Enfield]: 'The history of Sandford and Merton bears evident marks of being the production of a writer who thinks and judges for himself, and whose pen is guided by a system of philosophy which allows no indulgence to fashionable follies. His great object seems to be, to inspire youth with a hardy spirit, both of passive and active virtue, and to lead them to form such habits of industry and fortitude, as shall produce a manly independence of character and a mind superior to the enticements of luxurious indulgence' (pp. 126–7).

A: 2   1783   [KILNER, Mary Ann].
WILLIAM SEDLEY; OR, THE EVIL DAY DEFERRED.

> London: Printed and sold by John Marshall and Co No 4, Aldermary Church-Yard in Bow-Lane, n.d. [ESTC: 1783?].
> viii, 211p. 12mo. 2s 6d (CR, MR).
> CR 56: 480 (Dec 1783); MR 70: 158 (Feb 1784); AF II: 2400.
> BL N.1648; EM 7353: 2; ESTC t070704 (BI C; NA CaOTP, CLU-S/C).

Notes. Frontispiece dated October 1st 1783. 2 pp. advs. for children's books end vol. Dedication to Master —— v–viii; pagination continuous Roman-Arabic; text of novel starts on p. 9.

Further edn: London, 1816 (WC).

CR: '. . . well calculated for the moral improvement of young children.'

MR [William Enfield]: has '. . . the merit of condescending to the understandings of children, and affording them amusement and instruction, without falling into the common fault of those who write for masters and misses, that of being absurd and nonsensical, in order to make themselves entertaining.'

A: 3   1786   [DAY, Thomas].

THE HISTORY OF SANDFORD AND MERTON, A WORK INTENDED FOR THE USE OF CHILDREN. VOL II.

London: Printed for John Stockdale, opposite Burlington-House, Piccadilly, 1786.
306p. 12mo. 3s (CR), 3s 6d bound (MR, LEP).
CR 61: 470 (June 1786); MR 75: 361–4 (1786); &c.
O Vet.A5f.108; ESTC t070591 (BI Lsm; NA CtY-BR, ICN, MH-H, &c.; EA ZWTU).

Notes. Vol. 2 1783 (A: 1); vol. 3 1789 (A: 5).
Frontispiece. 2½ pp. advs. end vol., beginning on p. 306.
Adv., 'in the Press, and speedily will be published, Embellished with a beautiful Frontispiece, representing a Bull-Baiting', LEP 31 Jan–2 Feb 1786; adv. as published LEP 15–18 Apr 1786.
Further edns: London, 1786–91, ESTC t070595; Dublin, 1787 (Printed by P. Byrne, 2 vols., 12mo), EM 5317: 2, ESTC t070592; Belfast, 1787 (Printed by Daniel Blow), ESTC n017832; Philadelphia, 1788, ESTC w012718; Philadelphia, 1793, ESTC w012617; 32 further entries in ESTC for one or more of the 3 vols.

CR prefers the first part: 'The glowing hand, which sketched in the picture with so much spirit, seems fatigued; and, unless it is again re-animated, we shall be contented with announcing only the subsequent volumes.'

MR: 'The sensible and ingenious Author (Mr Day) possesses in great perfection the happy art of conveying useful information, just and manly sentiments, and important precepts, in the form of dialogue and story' (p. 361).

A: 4   1788   [DAY, Thomas].

THE HISTORY OF LITTLE JACK. BY THE AUTHOR OF SANDFORD AND MERTON. EMBELLISHED WITH TWENTY-TWO BEAUTIFUL CUTS.

London: Printed for John Stockdale, opposite Burlington-House, Piccadilly, 1788.
112p. 12mo. 1s (CR), 1s bound (MR).
CR 66: 583 (App [Dec 1788/Jan 1789]); MR 79: 174 (Aug 1788); AF II: 1013.
CLU-S/C CBC D33hi 1788 c.2; ESTC n007590 (BI C [lacks t.p.]).

Notes. Illustrations. 4 pp. advs. end vol.
According to Price, first pub. 1783 and German trans. same year but all other sources (biographies of Day and ESTC) agree that Little Jack first pub. 1788 in Stockdale's *Children's Miscellany.*
Sandford and Merton App. A: 1, 3 and 5.
Further edns: London, 1788, ESTC n007601; Dublin, 1789 (Printed by William Porter, 1 vol., 16mo), ESTC n033042; Dublin, 1795, ESTC t167640; Boston, 1795, ESTC w025151; Philadelphia, c.1795, ESTC w013248; 4 further entries in ESTC; German trans. Leipzig, 1793 (*Der kleine Jack, eine Volksgeschichte*) (EAG); French trans. Paris, 1803 (*Histoire du petit Jacques*) (BN); WC has 27 entries between 1800 and 1850 (some with title *The Forsaken Infant, or, Entertaining History of Little Jack*).

MR [George Edward Griffiths]: 'This instructive little history. . . is embellished with twenty-two neat wooden cuts.'

A: 5   1789   [DAY, Thomas].
THE HISTORY OF SANDFORD AND MERTON, A WORK INTENDED FOR THE USE OF CHILDREN. VOL III.

> London: Printed for John Stockdale, opposite Burlington House, Piccadilly, 1789.
> 308p. 12mo. 3s (CR), 3s sewed (MR).
> CR 68: 328–329 (Oct 1789); MR n.s. 4: 84 (Jan 1791); AF II: 1016.
> O Vet.A5f.109; ESTC t070591 (BI BMu, Lsm, O &c.; NA CtY-BR, ICN, IU, MH-H, PU, TxU &c.; EA ZWTU).

Notes. Vol. 1 1783 (A: 1); vol. 2 1786 (A: 3).

4 pp. advs. end vol.

Adv., 'In the Press, and speedily will be published, with a beautiful Frontispiece, designed by Stothard, and engraved by Medland', DWR 20 July 1789.

Further edns: London, 1786–91, ESTC t070595; Belfast, 1791 (Printed by Wm. Magee, 1 vol., 18mo), ESTC t191097; London, 1791, ESTC n007769; Philadelphia, 1793, ESTC w012617; London, 1798, ESTC n007481; 32 further entries in ESTC for one or more of the 3 vols.

CR: 'In the second we thought the author's spirit seemed to fail; but the conclusion deserves our commendation. It is conducted with spirit, with judgment, and propriety. The tales, interspersed, are interesting and instructive. The scene is judiciously varied, and much information respecting the manners of different nations, and the customs of different countries, occur in this volume.'

MR [William Enfield]: 'This third volume of a justly admired work does equal credit, in all respects, to its late ingenious author, with the two former. The story of the little heroes is not, indeed, much advanced in this volume: but the young reader's attention is agreeably arrested by a variety of tales at once highly amusing and instructive.'

A: 6   1794   ANON.
THE BROTHERS; A NOVEL, FOR CHILDREN. ADDRESSED TO EVERY GOOD MOTHER, AND HUMBLY DEDICATED TO THE QUEEN.

> Henley: Printed and sold by G. Norton; sold also by Hookham and Carpenter, New Bond-street; Owen, Piccadilly; Laking, Curzon-street, May Fair; Champante and Whitrow, Jury-street and Cheyne, Sweeting's Alley, Cornhill, London, 1794.
> vi, 188p. 8vo.
> BC 4: 426 (Oct 1794).
> BL 1489.ff.56; EM 2210: 5; ESTC t060909 (NA CaOTU, CLU-S/C).

Notes. WC attributes to Eliza Andrews.

Dedication to the Queen. 'Address to Parents' v–vi. Pagination continuous Roman-Arabic; text of novel starts on p. 7.

Another version also published in London in 1794 has the same page count but a slightly different imprint: 'Henley: Printed and sold by G. Norton; sold also by Champante and Whitrow; and C. and T. Cheyne', ESTC n015732.

Further edn: Henley, 1795, ESTC t112305.

BC: 'This little novel is written for the very useful purpose of recommending the strictest care in education, and of illustrating, in the contrasted characters of two brothers, the good consequences of that care, and the opposite evils of neglect. The language is pure and good, and the story sufficiently interesting to support the attention of children, not too young.'

A: 7   1794   ANON.
EVENING RECREATIONS: A COLLECTION OF ORIGINAL STORIES, FOR THE AMUSEMENT OF HER YOUNG FRIENDS. BY A LADY.

London: Printed for J. Deighton, No. 325, Holborn, 1794.
viii, 220p. 8vo [MR has 12mo]. 2s 6d (CR), 2s 6d sewed (MR, SJC).
CR n.s. 10: 355–6 (Mar 1794); MR n.s. 15: 234–5 (Oct 1794); AF II: 133.
BL Ch.790/113; ESTC t118184 (BI REu; NA CLU-S/C).

Notes. Further edns: London, 1797, EM 6086: 17, ESTC t077111; New York, 1802 (WC); Keene, NH, 1809 (WC).
Adv. SJC 21–23 Jan 1794; 'An Elegant Present for Young Ladies or Gentlemen.'
CR: 'In addition to the instruction and amusement which this little volume was meant to afford to the younger set of readers, it will furnish them with a very useful and improving exercise, which did not perhaps occur to the author. We recommend it to any boy or girl who has made a tolerable progress in the spelling book and English grammar, to take every morning a page of the Evening Recreations, and read it carefully, till he or she has found out and corrected all the faults of orthography, and inaccuracies of construction, some of which occur in every leaf. . . . '
MR [Jabez Hirons]: 'This collection of tales has certainly on the whole a tendency to engage the attention and contribute to the improvement of young minds: but we are sorry to add that the unknown authoress has allowed herself to compose, and to publish, with a degree of haste which has somewhat injured the performance' (p. 234).

A: 8   1795   MITCHELL, M[argaret].
TALES OF INSTRUCTION AND AMUSEMENT. WRITTEN FOR THE USE OF YOUNG PERSONS. BY MISS MITCHELL. IN TWO VOLUMES.

London: Printed for E. Newbery, Corner of St. Paul's Church Yard, 1795.
I viii, 215p; II 230p. 12mo. 6s boards, 6s bound (MR, OPA).
CR n.s. 14: 109–12 (May 1795); MR n.s. 17: 475–6 (Aug 1795); AF II: 2897.
O Vet.A5e.4063; EM 7399: 2; ESTC t103373 (BI BL, BUYs; NA CtY, CLU-S/C, IU &c.).

Notes. ESTC gives author's name as Mrs. Ives Hurry.
Dedication to Miss Harrison and Miss M. A. Harrison 1, iii–vi, signed M.M.; preface vii–viii, 5 Dec 1794, Copford Hall; 2-pp. table of contents (unn.). Frontispiece to each vol.
Adv., 'with a Frontispiece to each, neatly engraved', LP 20–23 Mar 1795.
Further edn: Dublin, 1795 (Printed for P. Wogan, P. Byrne, W. Jones, J. Rice, and J. Potts, jun., 1 vol., 12mo), ESTC t117969.
CR: 'The lessons of disinterested benevolence, fortitude, humility, and prudence, contained in these "Tales of Instruction,"—though, from their appropriate simplicity of diction, peculiarly well adapted to the tender minds of the young,—may be studied with advantage by those who have attained a more advanced period of life' (p. 109).
MR [William Enfield]: 'The method of conveying moral instruction by means of tales has been always found so acceptable, as well as beneficial, that it is not at all surprising that books of this sort should multiply without end; and when it is considered how powerful are the

charms of novelty, especially to young minds, variety of this kind will rather be regarded as a public benefit than a burthen' (p. 475).

A: 9   1797   ANON.
ALLEGORICAL MINIATURES FOR THE STUDY OF YOUTH. BY THE AUTHOR OF THE BROTHERS, A NOVEL FOR CHILDREN.

> London: Printed for G. Norton, Henley; And sold by Darton and Harvey, Gracechurch-Street; Champante and Whitrow, Jewry-Street, Aldgate; and C. and T. Cheyne, Sweeting's-Alley, Cornhill, n.d. [1797].
> x, 84pp. 12mo. 1s (BC).
> BC 11: 456 (Apr 1798); AF II: 62.
> PPL O Eng Alle; ESTC n015900 (NA FU).

Notes. ESTC date: 1800?; BC dates as 1797.
Dedication to Miss Rich, of Sunning.
The Brothers App. A: 6.

BC: 'The present little volume consists of tales, which are chiefly allegorical; but the veil is not so thick, as to prevent the young student from tracing out the useful moral beneath.'

A: 10   1797   SANDERS, Charlotte.
THE LITTLE FAMILY. WRITTEN FOR THE AMUSEMENT AND INSTRUC-TION OF YOUNG PERSONS. BY CHARLOTTE SANDERS.

> Bath: Printed by R. Cruttwell; and sold by C. Dilly, Poultry, London, 1797.
> I xv, 151p; II 160p. 12mo. 5s sewed (CR, MR).
> CR n.s. 22: 471 (Apr 1798); MR n.s. 26: 89 (May 1798); AF II: 3939.
> BL Ch.790/38; ESTC t100308 (NA CLU-S/C, FU).

Notes. Dedication to 'My Young Friends' v–vii; list of subscribers ix–xv. In vol. 2 text of novel starts on p. 5.
Adv. SJC 3–6 Nov 1798.
Further edns: Haverhill, MA, 1799, ESTC w013627; London, 1800, EM 6363: 3, ESTC t100307; London and York, 1808, NSTC S357.

CR: 'This work is a proper manual for children, being well calculated for their "amuse-ment and instruction." There are some parts of it, indeed, which are not so useful as they might have been rendered; but this negative censure is all that can justly be said against it.'

MR [Jabez Hirons and Ralph Griffiths]: 'We have been peculiarly pleased with the perusal of this compendium of moral amusement for young readers; especially with the author's particular attention to the culture of benevolence and compassion. . . . On the whole, what-ever slight imperfections a critic might discover in these little volumes, we may justly recom-mend them as having a tendency to inform and meliorate the understanding and the heart, while they serve, very agreeably, to amuse the imagination.'

A: 11   1798   GRIFFIN, Elizabeth.
THE FRIENDS; OR, THE CONTRAST BETWEEN VIRTUE AND VICE. A TALE. DESIGNED FOR THE IMPROVEMENT OF YOUTH. BY ELIZA-BETH GRIFFIN, AUTHOR OF THE SELECTOR, AND MORAL AMUSE-MENTS, &C. &C.

Orford: Printed by R. Slatter, for B. Crosby, near Stationers-Hall, Ludgate-Street, London, 1798.

vii, 170p. 12mo. 2s (CR).

CR n.s. 27: 228 (Oct 1799).

CLU-S/C CBC.G875f; ESTC n003319.

Notes. Frontispiece. Preface v–vii. 10 pp. advs. end vol.

Further edns: London, 1799, EM 274: 2, ESTC t073520; London, 1800, ESTC n018637.

CR: 'Mr Day's History of Sandford and Merton has anticipated, with greater ingenuity and effect, the subject of this little history, which however may be recommended as conveying useful lessons to the minds of tender youth.'

A: 12   1799   ANON.

*THE HISTORY OF JACK AND HIS ELEVEN BROTHERS: CONTAINING THEIR SEPARATION, TRAVELS, ADVENTURES, &C. INTENDED FOR THE USE OF LITTLE BROTHERS AND SISTERS.

West, 1799 (MR); West and Hughes, 1799 (CR).

12mo. 1s 6d boards (CR, MR).

CR n.s. 28: 469 (Apr 1800); MR n.s. 34: 102–3 (Jan 1801); AF II: 1961.

No copy located.

Notes. Further edn: Dublin, 1800 (Printed for G. Burnet, W. Porter, B. Dornin, P. Wogan, T. Burnside, J. Stockdale, G. Folingsby, N. Kelly, R. E. Mercier and Co. and P. Moore, 1 vol., 12mo), ESTC n017657.

MR [Jabez Hirons]: 'This is not an uninteresting, though but an imperfect performance: as the plan is too wide and extensive to be well executed in so short a compass.'

A: 13   1799   [SANDHAM, Elizabeth].

THE HAPPY FAMILY AT EASON HOUSE. EXHIBITED IN THE AMIABLE CONDUCT OF THE LITTLE NELSONS AND THEIR PARENTS. INTERSPERSED WITH SELECT PIECES OF POETRY.

London: Printed for T. Hurst, no. 32, Pater-noster-Row, 1799.

190p. 12mo. 2s (CR).

CR n.s. 31: 346 (Mar 1801); AF II: 3941.

BL Ch.790/75; EM 6421: 12; ESTC t133455 (NA CaOTP, CLU-S/C, FU).

Notes. ESTC notes that the book is advertised in the LC of 21–24 Dec 1799 as a publication of E. Newbery.

Frontispiece.

Further edns: London, 1822 (WC); London, 1824 (WC); Southampton, 1822, NSTC 2S4107.

Selected non-fiction associated with the novels

B: 1   1771   [BARBÉ-MARBOIS, François, Marquis de].
LETTERS FROM THE MARCHIONESS OF POMPADOUR: FROM
MDCCLIII TO MDCCLXII INCLUSIVE. IN TWO VOLUMES.
LETTERS OF THE MARCHIONESS OF POMPADOUR: FROM
MDCCXLVI TO MDCCLII INCLUSIVE. [3rd. vol.]

London: Sold by W. Owen, in Fleetstreet; and T. Cadell, in the Strand, 1771 [2 vols.].
London: Sold by T. Cadell, in the Strand, 1772 [3rd. vol.].
[1771 vols.]: I xii, 176p; II 151p. 8vo. 5s (CR), 5s sewed (MR), 5s sewed or 6s bound
(LC). [1772 vol.] 176p. 8vo [CR and MR have 12mo]. 2s 6d sewed (CR, MR).
[1771 vols.]: CR 32: 294–8 (Oct 1771); MR 46: 53–6 (Jan 1772). [1772 vol.]: CR 34:
296–300 (Oct 1772); MR 47: 244 (Sept 1772).
[1771 vols.]: BL 1085.h.9; EM 3911: 9; ESTC t146522 (BI Dt, E, O; NA CLU-S/C, KU-S,
MoU, &c.). [1772 vol.]: BL 1454.b.24; EM 3758: 1; ESTC t147368 (BI Dt, MRu; NA
CSmH, DLC, ICN, MH-H &c.).

Notes. Trans. of Lettres de Madame la Marquise de Pompadour. Not by Jeanne-Antoinette
Poisson, Marquise de Pompadour. ESTC: A fictitious collection, attributed to the Marquis
François de Barbé-Marbois.
[1771 vols.]: 13 pp. 'Contents' to both vols. end vol. 2. Epistolary. [1772 vol.]: 2-pp.
prefatory advertisement and 8-pp. table of contents (unn).
French and English versions of 1771 vols. adv. LC 30: 383 (7–19 Oct 1771). Extracts
published LC 30: 381, 385, 401 and 449 (17–19, 19–22 and 24–26 Oct and 7–9 Nov 1771).
3-vol. sets, both of the French and English versions, of the correspondence from 1746 to
1762, each priced at 7s 6d sewed or 9s bound 'in three Pocket Volumes', adv. SJC 2–4
Feb 1773.
Further edn: Dublin, n.d. [1771?] (Printed for J. Exshaw, H. Saunders, W. Sleater, D. Cham-
berlaine, J. Potts, J. Hoey, jun. and R. Moncrieffe, 2 vols. in 1, 12mo), EM 2813: 2, ESTC
t130529.
ESTC has 27 entries for Lettres de Madame le Marquise de Pompadour (Londres: chez
G. Owen; et T. Cadell) between 1771 and 1787.
CR 32: 'Whether genuine or spurious, [the letters] are written in an agreeable manner . . .'
(p. 295).
MR 46 [Ralph Griffiths] is suspicious of the authenticity of the letters.
CR 34 refers to rev. of the 2 previous volumes, 'the authenticity of which is certainly somewhat questionable' and says that the new ones 'partake of the same strain of vivacity with the
other letters attributed to the marchioness of Pompadour' (p. 296).
MR 47: 'Whatever literary merit the series of letters contained in the former publication
may possess, we think, with our Editor, that the present correspondence is by no means of
inferior worth. It abounds with sensible remarks, agreeable sallies of imagination, and

notable anecdotes; and may (so far as the Reader can consider it as genuine) contribute to give the public a very advantageous opinion of this celebrated Lady's mental abilities.'

B: 2   1771   [DUBOIS-FONTANELLE, Joseph-Gaspard]; GRIFFITH, [Elizabeth] (trans.).
THE SHIPWRECK AND ADVENTURES OF MONSIEUR PIERRE VIAUD, A NATIVE OF BOURDEAUX, AND CAPTAIN OF A SHIP. TRANSLATED FROM THE FRENCH, BY MRS. GRIFFITH.

> London: Printed for T. Davies, in Russel-Street, Covent-Garden, 1771.
> xii, 276p. 8vo. 4s sewed (LC).
> CR 31: 238–9 (Mar 1771); MR 44: 421–2 (May 1771).
> C 7508.c.4; EM 5: 3; ESTC t138378 (BI BL, D, O &c.; NA CSmH, DLC, ICN, MH-H, PU &c.).

Notes. Trans. of *Naufrage et aventures de Monsieur Pierre Viaud* (Bordeaux and Paris, 1768). ESTC gives name as Jean-Gaspard; BN as Joseph-Gaspard.
Frontispiece. French Editor's Preface v–viii; Translator's Preface ix-xii.

CR and MR review under 'Miscellaneous'. GM treats as factual work and gives extensive summary in Apr, May and June 1771 (vol. 41, pp. 173–7, 219–21 and 268–71). Does not appear to be fiction, but Mayo includes 4 versions 1771–1807 (RM 1140–1143).
Adv., 'In the Press, and will be published in a few Days', LC 29: 239 (7–9 Mar 1771).
Extracts published LC 29: 309 and 316 (28–30 Mar and 30 Mar–2 Apr 1771).
Further edns: Dublin, 1771 (Printed for James Williams, 1 vol., 12mo), EM 4853: 20, ESTC t119521; Dover, NH, 1799, ESTC w008165; London, 1800 (Grieder). German trans. Frankfurt, 1778 (*Der Schiffbruch, ein Mährchen in veir Acten*) (EAG).

B: 3   1775   [COMBE, William].
LETTERS FROM ELIZA TO YORICK.

> London: Printed for the Editor, 1775.
> xv, 67p. 8vo. 2s (CR, MR), 1s 6d (SJC).
> CR 39: 129–33 (Feb 1775); MR 52: 370–71 (Apr 1775).
> BL 1086.b.24(2); EM 1923: 10; ESTC t013275 (BI O; NA CLU, MH-H; EA ZWTU).

Notes. ESTC: Spurious letters, purporting to be sent by Eliza Draper to Laurence Sterne. Attributed to William Combe.
Cf. Sterne, *Letters from Yorick to Eliza* London: Printed for W. Johnston, 1773, xviii, 64p 8vo, ESTC t014743.
MR has Evans as bookseller; CR has Kearsley and Evans.
A variant in the same year, described by the ESTC as a reissue, 'Printed for the Editor, and entered in the Hall-book of the Company of Stationers, the 15th April, 1775', ESTC t038487.
Adv., 'On Monday next will be published', SJC 13–15 Apr 1775; adv. contains the note 'These Letters are entered in the Hall Book of the Company of Stationers.'
Further edn: Ludlow, 1799, ESTC t222480. Included in *Letters from Yorick to Eliza* (Altenburg, 1776) ESTC t014709 and *Letters written between Yorick and Eliza* (Vienna, 1795 and 1797) ESTC t014781 and t205570.
CR: 'The authenticity of these Letters is so well supported, that we cannot entertain the least doubt of their being the production of the author of Tristram Shandy' (p. 129).

MR: 'As to the Letters themselves, there is not a great deal in them; but they are Sterne's; and every thing from his pen will be precious in the eyes of his numerous admirers.'

B: 4   1778   [PHILLIPS, Peregrine].
A SENTIMENTAL DIARY, KEPT IN AN EXCURSION TO LITTLE HAMP-TON, NEAR ARUNDEL, AND TO BRIGHTHELMSTONE, IN SUSSEX.

> London: Printed for J. Ryall, in Union-Street, Westminster, and sold by W. Lee, Printer, in Lewes, and all the Booksellers and News-Carriers in Town and Country. n.d. [ESTC: 1778?].
> vii, 88p. 8vo. 2s (CR, MR).
> CR 46: 400 (Nov 1778); MR 59: 398 (Nov 1778).
> C 7474.d.143; EM 792: 6; ESTC t110103 (BI BL [imperf.], MRu; NA DLC, MB, MH-H).

Notes. Novel written in the form of a diary, diary extracts dated August/September 1778. Preface dated Oct 21 1778. Imitation of Sterne's *Sentimental Journey*. CR and MR review under 'Miscellaneous'.
See App. B: 6 for vol. 2.
'New Edition' adv., with quotations from MR and CR, GND 3 Dec 1778.

CR: 'The author of this Diary treads in the steps of the late celebrated Mr. Sterne, whose manner he has imitated with considerable address. We therefore doubt not of his affording amusement to those readers who take pleasure in productions of the light and fantastic kind.'

MR: 'Relates, with pleasantry, the incidents which attended an excursion (apparently a real one) to the places mentioned in the title; with observations, and moral reflections, some-what in the manner of Sterne: but Sterne had the rare merit of originality.'

B: 5   1780   [PHILLIPS, Peregrine].
A DIARY KEPT IN AN EXCURSION TO LITTLE HAMPTON, NEAR ARUNDEL, AND BRIGHTHELMSTON, IN SUSSEX, IN 1778; AND ALSO TO THE LATTER PLACE IN 1779. IN TWO VOLUMES.

> London: Printed for the Author; And sold by J. Bew, Pater-Noster-Row; and M. Dav-enhill, Cornhill, 1780.
> I viii, 100p; II vii, 127p. 8vo. 2s each vol. (half-titles), 2s sewed (MR) vol. 2.
> MR 63: 148 (Aug 1780).
> BL 291.b.21; EM 6867: 7; ESTC t161307 (BI C, CHIr, E; NA CaOHM).

Notes. ESTC: Vol. 1 is another edn. of Phillips' 1778 *Sentimental Diary* [App. B: 4 above].
'To the Reader' vol. 1, pp. v–viii, signed 'The Editor', London, 21 Oct 1778; 'To the Editor of the Diary published in 1778' vol. 2, pp. v–vii, signed 'The Author', London, Nov 1779. In vol. 2 pagination continuous Roman-Arabic; text starts on p. 9. 1 p. advs. end vol. 2.
Further edn. adv., 'In two neat Pocket Volumes, Price 4s. sewed in Marble Paper, Embellished with a beautiful View of Brighthelmston-Bay, the Clift, and Part of the Town, designed by Stothard, and engraved by Heath', SJC 5–7 Apr 1785.

MR complains about the author's 'very often, repeating old stories new vamped, and cracking such jokes as have probably afforded him more pleasure than he is able to convey to those who are to crack them over again' and continues: 'This disciple of Sterne's does not seem to be aware, that it would be as commendable to imitate the good English as the good humour of his master.'

B: 6 1781 ANON.

REVERIES OF THE HEART; DURING A TOUR THROUGH PART OF ENGLAND AND FRANCE: IN A SERIES OF LETTERS TO A FRIEND.

London: Printed for J. Johnson, No. 72, St. Paul's Church-Yard, 1781.

I 188p; II 192p. 8vo. 4s sewed (MR, CR).

CR 51: 351–4 (May 1781); MR 66: 238 (Mar 1782).

MH-H *EC75.St 455S H781r; EM 1484: 15; ESTC n012671 (BI C; NA MdBJ).

Notes. Epistolary.

CR: '[We] ... were greatly and disagreeably surprised to find, that this vehicle, in the shape and appearance of a novel, was only made use of, by a verbose and violent patriot, to convey to the world his political sentiments on the present state of our public affairs, a topic of late so universally hackneyed and worn out, as to become extremely disgustful' (p. 352). 'Though we do not think highly of this performance, we are notwithstanding of opinion that the writer is by no means destitute of parts and capacity, and seems possessed of sentiment and philanthropy' (p. 354).

MR [Samuel Badcock]: 'The title sufficiently expresses the design of the work; and the execution is such as merits at least indulgence, if not applause. A lively vein of Shandean hilarity runs through it, superior at least to some of the modern imitators of Sterne,—the bungling menders of his old and worn-out pen!'

B: 7 1781 [MACNALLY, Leonard].

SENTIMENTAL EXCURSIONS TO WINDSOR AND OTHER PLACES, WITH NOTES CRITICAL, ILLUSTRATIVE, AND EXPLANATORY, BY SEVERAL EMINENT PERSONS, MALE AND FEMALE. LIVING AND DEAD.

London: Printed for J. Walker, Pater-noster-Row, 1781.

249p. 12mo. 2s 6d sewed (CR), 2s 6d (MR).

CR 52: 398–400 (Nov 1781); MR 65: 389 (Nov 1781).

BL 12330.aa.22; EM 639: 13; ESTC t128528 (BI C, D; NA CtY, InU-Li, NjP).

Notes. Dedicated to Charles Macklin.

CR reviews under 'Miscellaneous'; MR reviews under 'Novels'.

Further edn: London, 1782, EM 7469: 16, ESTC t069515.

CR: 'Imitations of the inimitable Tristram are become so frequent as to render the perusal of them to the last degree tedious and disgusting: not a month passes wherein we are not pestered with sentimental journeys, adventures, &c. in the Shandean style and manner. Amongst these the author of Excursions to Windsor stands forth an avowed disciple of the Sternian school; and seems, by mere dint of extraordinary diligence and attention, to have imitated his master with some degree of success ...' (p. 398).

MR [Samuel Badcock] refers to 'the tiresome track of his excursions'.

B: 8 1783 [MACKENZIE, Anna Maria].

JOSEPH. IN FIVE BOOKS. BY A. M. COX.

London: Printed for the Author, by H.D. Steel, No. 51, Lothbury, near Coleman-Street, And sold by the following Booksellers: Mr. Dodsley, Pall-Mall; Mr. Flexney, Holborn; and Mr. Fielding, Pater-Noster-Row, 1783.

12, 230p. 8vo. 3s (CR, MR).

CR 56: 398–9 (Nov 1783); MR 70: 159 (Feb 1784); AF II: 915.

BL 1568/6367; ESTC t226510.

Notes. ESTC: A. M. Cox is Anna Maria Mackenzie.

A treatment of the biblical story.

1-p. prefatory advertisement (unn.). 12-pp. list of subscribers.

CR and MR review this under 'Miscellaneous'.

MR [William Enfield]: 'In truth the meretricious ornaments of redundant metaphors and prosaic rythmus [*sic*] are most injudiciously applied to a story, which, in its original form, is a perfect model of simplicity.'

B: 9   1788   ANON.
CONTINUATION OF YORICK'S SENTIMENTAL JOURNEY.

London: Printed for the Author, at the Literary-Press, No. 14, Red-Lion-Street, Clerkenwell; and sold by all Book-sellers, 1788.

132p. 12mo. 2s 6d sewed (MR), 2s 6d (MC).

CR 66: 584 (App [Dec 1788/Jan 1789]); MR 79: 468 (Nov 1788); AF II: 846.

BL 1080.i.54; EM 7613: 14; ESTC t012595 (NA InU-Li).

Notes. 1-p. prefatory advertisement.

Laurence Sterne's *Sentimental Journey* was published in 1768, JR 1234.

Adv. MC 21 Mar 1788.

MR: 'The Author is very happy in imitating the breaks and dashes, and scanty pages of the otherwise inimitable Sterne. In these respects he even excels his original: his breaks and dashes are much longer; and his pages are replete with nothing. Sterne had but one blank leaf in a volume; but this book (if you measure by meaning) is all blank, from the beginning to FINIS.'

B: 10   1788   ANON.
A TOUR, SENTIMENTAL AND DESCRIPTIVE, THROUGH THE UNITED PROVINCES, AUSTRIAN NETHERLANDS, AND FRANCE; INTERSPERSED WITH PARISIAN, AND OTHER ANECDOTES: WITH SOME OBSERVATIONS ON THE HOWARDIAN SYSTEM. TWO VOLUMES.

London: Printed for W. Lowndes, No. 77, Fleet-street, 1788.

I xi, 228p; II 176+p. 12mo. 5s sewed (MR, MC).

MR 79: 372–3 (Oct 1788).

BL 10270.aa.11; EM 863: 4; ESTC t062285 (NA MH-H, NN).

Notes. Dedication 'to My Printer' i–ii; address to the reader v–vi; 'The Prolegomena' vii–xi. Pages missing in vol. 2 after p. 176.

Adv. MC 27 Feb 1788.

MR classifies under 'Novel' but RG has crossed out this word and queried it in the margin.

MR [Andrew Becket]: 'To say that this Shandyan performance is destitute of merit, were to forfeit our pretensions to candour; to that impartiality, which the Public, by their continued favour, have consequently supposed us to possess; and yet to bestow on it a hearty and unconditional commendation, is wholly impossible. The writer is a man of abilities, and lively in an uncommon degree:—but of his liveliness we have reason to complain. Through-out the whole of his production there is too great an affectation of appearing witty. He deliv-ers, or at least attempts to deliver, almost every sentence with a point: and almost every character is dismissed with a joke. This, by being too frequently indulged, degenerates into pertness and insipidity.'

B: 11   1789   [HALL, William Henry].
THE DEATH OF CAIN, IN FIVE BOOKS; AFTER THE MANNER OF THE DEATH OF ABEL. BY A LADY.

> London: Printed for C. Stalker, Stationers'-Court, Ludgate-Street, 1789.
> xii, 147p. 12mo. 2s sewed (MR).
> CR 70: 102 (July 1790); MR n.s. 4: 230–1 (Feb 1791); AF II: 1781.
> BL 4412.h.2; ESTC t065122.

Notes. Prefatory advertisement iii–iv; preface v–viii; dedication to Viscountess Duncannon signed 'The Author' and dated 1 Dec, 1789 ix–xii. 13 pp. advs. end vol.
Further edns: Dublin, 1790 (Printed for H. Chamberlaine, R. Cross, P. Byrne, J. Boyce, J. Moore, J. Jones, Grueber and M'Allister, W. Jones, 1 vol., 12mo), (Bodl.) xESTC; London, 1797, EM 5371: 14; ESTC t079546; London, 1800, EM 6163: 1, ESTC t130113.

CR: 'The sufferings of Cain are truly exemplary, and his mental miseries are exhibited in so striking a manner as is sufficient to harrow up the feeling mind. . . . In this attempt to com-plete Gessner's imperfect design no disrespect is meant: she assures us, and we will not con-tradict what we do not understand, that "his conceptive scopes stand unrivalled as they measure unlimited."'
MR [William Enfield]: 'What presumption! for a writer without invention, without taste, to take up the pen of Gesner [*sic*]! . . . . For our part, we can find nothing in the production either epic, poetic, or truly prosaic; and we are of opinion, that a more unsuccessful imitation of a popular work was never attempted.'

B: 12   1793   SHANDY, Mr [pseud.].
A SENTIMENTAL JOURNEY. INTENDED AS A SEQUEL TO MR. STERNE'S. THROUGH ITALY, SWITZERLAND, AND FRANCE. IN TWO VOLUMES. BY MR. SHANDY.

> Southampton: Printed for T. Baker; and S. Crowder, Paternoster-Row, London, 1793.
> I vi, 167p; II 191p. 8vo [MR has 12mo]. 5s sewed (MR, SJC).
> MR n.s. 12: 475 (Dec 1793); AF II: 4049.
> C 7720.d.941-942; EM 2458: 5; ESTC t113817 (BI BL, O; NA NcU).

Notes. Preface 1, iii–vi. In vol. 1 pagination continuous Roman-Arabic; text begins on p. 7. In vol. 2 text begins on p. 3.
Laurence Sterne's *A Sentimental Journey* (1768), JR 1234, AF I: 2640.
Adv. SJC 16–18 Apr 1793; A Sentimental Journey. Intended as a Sequel to Mr Stern's [*sic*], through Italy, Switzerland and France. Ending at the Execution of the French Monarch, with an Harangue to the People, at Verdun, who were about the Tree of Liberty there.
German trans. Hamburg, 1794 (*Empfindsame Reisen durch Halien, die Schweiz und Frankreich. Ein Nachtrag zu den Yorickschen*) (EAG).

MR [Thomas Holcroft]: 'The author, in his preface, tells us that he is "a base born son of Yorick, but no more like his father than he to Hercules." This is literally a fair and true account.'

B: 13   1794   TOUCHIT, Timothy [pseud.].
LA SOURICIERE. THE MOUSE-TRAP. A FACETIOUS AND SENTI-MENTAL EXCURSION THROUGH PART OF AUSTRIAN FLANDERS AND FRANCE. BEING A DIVERTISEMENT FOR BOTH SEXES. BY TIMOTHY TOUCHIT, ESQ. IN TWO VOLUMES.

London: Printed for J. Parsons, Paternoster-Row, 1794.
I viii, 181p; II 153p. 12mo.
C Oates.525-526; ESTC t194002 (BI E).

Notes. Prefatory advertisement v–viii.

Index of Authors and Translators

Numbers in italic indicate that the name is not the primary one in an entry.

ADAIR, James Makittrick 1790: 36
ADAMS, John 1791: 28
ALEXANDER, Judith 1789: 30
ANDREWS, Dr 1787: 27
ANDREWS, Eliza, *see* **App. A**: *6*
ANOIS, COUNTESS D', *see* MURAT, Henriette Julie de
ARBUTHNOT, John, *see* 1785: *41*
ARCQ, Philippe-Auguste de Sainte-Foix, Chevalier d' 1775: 17
ARMSTRONG, John, *see* 1790: *42*
ARNAUD, *see* BACULARD D'ARNAUD, François-Thomas-Marie de
ARNOLD, Samuel James 1796: 20
ATKINS, Harriot Westrop 1788: 41
AULNOY, Marie-Catherine Le Jumel de Barneville, comtesse d', *see* MURAT, Henriette Julie de
AUSTIN, Mrs 1771: 36

BACON, James 1791: 29
BACON, Theophilus James 1784: 10
BACULARD D'ARNAUD, François-Thomas-Marie de 1772: 29, 1773: 24; 1786: 13, 14; 1795: 11; *see also* 1775: *31*; 1788: *67*
BAGE, Robert 1782: 12; 1784: 11; 1787: 28; 1788: 42; 1792: 29; 1796: 21
BAHRDT, Carl Friedrich 1797: 24
BALLIN, Rossetta 1790: 37
BANCROFT, Edward 1770: 22
BARBÉ-MARBOIS, François, marquis de **App. B**: 1
BARKER, Mary 1798: 15
BARNBY, Mrs 1798: 16
BARTHÉLEMY, Jean-Jacques 1799: 21A, 21B
BASTIDE, Jean-François de 1782: 13
BEAUMONT, Jeanne Marie le Prince de, *see* LEPRINCE DE BEAUMONT, Marie
BEAURIEU, Gaspard Guillard de, *see* GUILLARD DE BEAURIEU, Gaspard
BEATTIE, James, *see* 1795: *4*
BECKFORD, William 1786: 15; 1796: 22; 1797: 25; *see also* 1791: *53*
BÉCU, Jeanne, comtesse du Barry, *see* 1771: *54*
BEDDOES, Thomas (*trans.*) 1791: *53*
BELLAMY, Thomas 1798: 17; 1799: 22
BELLOY, Pierre-Laurent Buirette de, *see* 1790: *14*

BENNETT, Agnes Maria, *see* BENNETT, Anna Maria
BENNETT, Anna Maria 1785: 22; 1786: 16; 1789: 31; 1794: 16; 1797: 26; *see also* 1792: *49*
BENOIT, Françoise Albine 1791: 30
BENTHAM, Jeremy (*trans.*) 1774: *33B*
BERESFORD, [James] (*trans.*) 1796: *42*
BERKELEY, George Monck 1784: 12; 1787: 29; 1788: 43
BEUVIUS, Adam 1786: 17
BICKNELL, Alexander 1775: 18; 1776: 7, 8; 1779: 6; 1789: 32
BIDLAKE, John 1799: 23
BILDERBECK, Ludwig Benedict Franz, Freiherr von 1792: 30
BILLARDON DE SAUVIGNY, Edme-Louis 1786: 18
BIRCH, John Brereton (*trans.*) 1797: *74*
BIRD, John 1795: 12
BITAUBÉ, Paul-Jérémie 1799: 24
BLOWER, Elizabeth 1780: 12; 1782: 14; 1785: 23; 1788: 44
BOILEAU, Daniel (*trans.*) 1795: *39*
BOLAS, Thomas 1795: 13
BOLDERO, S. 1788: *33*
BONHOTE, Elizabeth 1772: 30; 1773: 25; 1776: 9; 1787: 30; 1789: 33; 1790: 38; 1797: 27
BOOTH, Miss A. E. (*trans.*) 1794: *40*
BOUGEANT, Guillaume-Hyacinthe 1789: 34
BOUTERWEK, Friedrich 1797: 28
BOUVERIE, Georgina 1787: 31
BOYS, Mrs S. 1785: 24
BRANDENBURGH-ANSPACH AND BAYREUTH, Elizabeth, Margravine of, *see* CRAVEN, Elizabeth
BRANDON, Isaac 1797: 29
BREWER, George 1791: 31; 1793: 15; 1795: 14; *see also* 1796: *18*
BREWER, James Norris 1796: 23; 1799: 25
BRIDGES, Thomas 1770: 23
BRISCOE, C. W. 1786: 19
BRISCOE, Sophia 1771: 37; 1772: 31; *see also* 1779: *8*; 1797: *11*
BRISSOT DE WARVILLE, Jacques-Pierre, *see* 1791: *40*
BROMLEY, Eliza Nugent 1784: 13; 1788: 45; 1794: 17

BROOKE, Frances 1777: 9; 1790: 39; *see also*
(*trans.*) 1770: *30*, 1774: *1*
BROOKE, Henry 1770: 24, 1774: 24
BROOKS, Indiana 1789: 35
BROSTER, John 1798: 18
BRYDGES, Sir Samuel Egerton 1792: 31;
1798: 19
BULLOCK, Mrs 1795: 15
BURKE, Anne 1785: 25; 1787: 32; 1788: 46;
1796: 24, 25
BURNE, James (*trans.*) 1773: *35*
BURNEY, Frances 1778: 10; 1782: 15; 1796: 26;
see also 1780: *3*; 1787: *31*
BURNEY, Sarah Harriet 1796: 27
BURTON, Mrs 1795: 16; 1797: 30

C—, Lady Mary 1797: 31
C., Mrs 1789: 36
CADMUS, the Milesian, *see* 1775: *17*
CAMBON, J. J. 1796: 28
CAMBON, Maria Geertruida de 1790: 40;
see also 1796: *28*
CAMPE, Joachim Heinrich 1788: 47
CARRA, Jean-Louis 1773: 26
CARTER, John 1773: 27
CARTWRIGHT, Mrs H 1779: 7; 1780: 13; 1785:
26, 27; 1786: 20; 1787: 33
CARVER, Mrs 1797: 32, 33; 1798: 20
CAVENDISH, Georgiana, Duchess of
Devonshire 1773: 28; 1779: 8
CAZOTTE, Jacques 1791: 32; 1792: 32
CHAMBERS, Marianne 1799: 26
CHARLTON, Mary 1794: 18; 1797: 34; 1798: 21,
22; 1799: 27
CHARRIÈRE, Isabelle-Agnès-Élisabeth van
Tuyll van Serooskerken van Zuylen, Mme de
1799: 28
CHATER, John 1773: 29
CHAVIS, Denis 1792: 32
CHÉRENSI, Benjamin Frère [pseud.?] 1791: 33
CHIARI, Abbé Pietro 1771: 38, 39
CHILCOT, Harriet, *see* MEZIERE, Harriet
CHODERLOS DE LACLOS, Pierre-Antoine-
François, *see* LACLOS, Pierre-Antoine-
François Choderlos de
CLARIS DE FLORIAN, Jean Pierre, *see*
FLORIAN, Jean Pierre Claris de
CLARK, Emily 1798: 23
CLARKE, Elizabeth [later COBBOLD]
1791: 34
CLARKE, Henry 1788: 48
COGAN, Thomas 1776: 10
COLE, William 1796: 29
COLLYER, Joseph (trans.) 1776: *13A*
COLTON, Henry 1771: 40
COMBE, William 1775: 19; 1781: 15, 16; 1784:
14; 1790: 41; App. B: 3

CONSTANT DE REBECQUE, Samuel de
1788: 49; *see also* 1785: *4*
CONTANT D'ORVILLE, André-Guillaume
1794: 19
COOKE, Cassandra 1799: 29
COOPER, Maria Susanna 1775: 20, 21
COURTNEY, Mrs 1796: 30
COX, A. M. *see* MACKENZIE, Anna Maria
CRADOCK, Joseph 1775: 22
CRAIK, Helen 1796: 31
CRAMER, Karl Gottlob 1796: 32
CRAVEN, Elizabeth, Margravine of Branden-
burgh-Anspach and Bayreuth 1779: 9
CRÉBILLON, Claude-Prosper Jolyot de
1770: 25
CREECH, Mrs 1796: 33
CROFFTS, Mrs 1798: 24
CROFT, Sir Herbert 1780: 14
CUBIERES-PALMEZEAUX, Michel 1788: 50
CULLEN, Stephen 1794: 20; 1796: 34
CUMBERLAND, Richard 1789: 37; 1795: 17
CURTIES, T. J. Horsley 1799: 30

DALRYMPLE, Frances Eleanor, *see* 1791: *57*
DALTON, Maria Regina, *see* ROCHE, Maria
Regina
DAUBENTON, Marguerite 1789: 38A, 38B
D'AUCOR, Claude Godard, *see* GODARD
D'AUCOR, Claude
D'AUVIGNY, Jean du Castre, *see* DU CASTRE
D'AUVIGNY, Jean
DAVIES, Edward 1795: 18
DAVIES, John 1794: 21
DAWE, Anne 1770: 26
DAY, Thomas **App. A:** 1, 3, 4, 5
DE CRESPIGNY, Mary Champion 1796: 35
DELACROIX, Jacques-Vincent 1773: 30
DENT, John 1785: 28
D'ERBIGNY, Henri Lambert, Marquis de
Thibouville, *see* THIBOUVILLE, Henri-
Lambert d'Erbigny de
DE VERE, Marquis [pseud.] 1770: 27
DE VERGY, *see* TREYSSAC DE VERGY Pierre
Henri
DEVONSHIRE, Duchess of, *see* CAVENDISH,
Georgiana, Duchess of Devonshire
DIBDIN, Charles 1793: 16; 1796: 36
DIDEROT, Denis 1797: 35, 36; *see also* 1789: *51*
DIGGES, Thomas Atwood 1775: 23
D'ISRAELI, Isaac 1797: 37; 1799: 31
DODD, Charles 1787: 34
DORAT, Claude-Joseph 1774: 25
D'ORVILLE, *see* CONTANT D'ORVILLE, André
Guillaume
DOUGLAS, James 1797: 38
DU BOCAGE, Michel-Joseph, seigneur de
Bléville 1796: 37

DU BOIS, Lady Dorothea 1770: 28
DUBOIS, Edward 1799: 32, 33
DUBOIS-FONTANELLE, Joseph-Gaspard
    1788: 51; **App. B:** 2; *see also* 1789: *39*
DU CASTRE D'AUVIGNY, Jean 1795: 19
DUCRAY-DUMINIL, François-Guillaume
    1796: 38
DUFF, William 1773: 31
DUTTON, Thomas 1794: 22; *see also (trans.)*
    1798: *50*

EDEN, Anna 1790: 42
EDWARDS, Miss 1780: 15
ELLEN of Exeter, *see* MACKENZIE, Anna
    Maria
ELLIA, Felix 1798: 25; 1799: 34
ELLIOTT, Miss 1780: 16; 1781: 17, 18; 1783: 7, 8
Eminent Lady, an 1793: 7
ÉPINAY, Louise-Florence-Pétronille Tardieu
    d'Esclavelle, dame de La Live, marquise d'
    1787: 35
ERSKINE, Lady Frances 1772: 32
ESPENSCHEID, Gertrude Elliott, *see* 1781: *18*
EUSTATHIUS MACREMBOLITES 1788: 52
EVANS, Robert 1798: 26

F., E. 1799: 35
FABRE D'OLIVET, Antoine 1799: 36
FALQUES, Marianne-Agnès, *see* FAUQUE DE
    LA CÉPÈDE, Marianne-Agnès Pillement
Farmer's Daughter in Gloucestershire, a
    1772: 27
FAUQUE DE LA CÉPÈDE, Marianne-Agnès
    Pillement, Mme Falques 1774: 26
FELL, Mrs 1792: 33
Female, a 1787: 15; 1796: *5*
FENWICK, Eliza 1795: 20
FERGUSS, Miss 1777: 10
FIÉVÉE, Joseph 1799: 37
FINGLASS, Esther 1789: 39
FISHER, Joshua Bridges 1796: 39
FITZ-JOHN, Matilda [pseud?] 1796: 40
FLAMMENBERG, Lawrence, *see* KAHLERT,
    Carl Friedrich
FLEMING, Francis 1770: 29
FLORIAN, Jean Pierre Claris de 1787: 36; 1791:
    35, 36; 1792: 34, 35
FOGERTY, Mrs 1773: 32, 33
FONTANIEU, Gaspar Moise Augustin de, *see*
    1789: *55*
FOSTER, E. M., Mrs 1795: 21; 1798: 27; 1799:
    38, 39
FOX, Joseph 1791: 37; 1793: 17; 1797: 39
FRAMÉRY, Nicolas-Étienne 1770: 30
FRANKLIN, William *(trans.)* 1793: 18
FRÈRE, Benjamin, *see* CHÉRENSI, Benjamin
    Frère

FROMAGET, Nicolas 1774: 27
FULLER, Anne 1786: 21, 22; 1789: 40

GABRIELLI, *see* MEEKE, Mary
GALES, Winifred Marshall, *see* 1787: *15*
GAYOT DE PITAVAL, François, *see* 1787: *49*
GENLIS, Caroline-Stéphanie-Félicité Ducrest de
    Mézières, comtesse de 1783: 9; 1785: 29;
    1796: 41; 1799: 40, 41; *see also* 1798: *56*
GERRANS, B. *(trans.)* 1792: *58*
GESZNER, A. H., *see* MELTZER, Adolph
    Heinrich
GIBBES, Phebe 1777: 11; 1778: 11; 1786: 23;
    1788: 53; 1789: 41; *see also* 1786: *24*; 1795: *25*;
    1798: *54*
GIFFARD, John, *see* GREEN, John Richards
GIFFORD, Arthur 1785: 30
GINNADRAKE, Timothy, *see* FLEMING,
    Francis
GODARD D'AUCOR, Claude 1783: 10
GODWIN, William 1784: 15, 16, 17; 1794: 23;
    1799: 42; *see also* 1798: *74*
GOETHE, Johann Wolfgang von 1779 : 10; *see*
    also 1788 : *80*
GOLDSMITH, Oliver 1780: 17; *see also* 1772: *24*
GOMERSALL, Ann 1789: 42; 1790: 43;
    1796: 42
GONZALEZ, Esteban 1797: 40
GOOCH, Elizabeth Sarah Villa-Real 1795: 22;
    1796: 43; 1799: 43
GOODRICKE, Henry *See* 1791: *65*
GOOSEQUILL, Benjamin, *see* ADAIR, James
    Makittrick
GORJY, Jean-Claude 1789: 43; 1790: 44, 45;
    1791: 38, 39
GOSLING, Jane 1794: 24
GOUPIL, Pierre Étienne Auguste, *see* 1791: *40*
GRAFIGNY, Françoise d'Issembourg d'Happon-
    court, Mme de 1774: 28
GRAHAM, Elizabeth, *see* 1796: *46*
GRAVES, Richard 1773: 34; 1779: 11; 1785: 31;
    1790: 46; *see also (trans.)* 1779: *10*
GREEN, John Richards *(trans.)* 1791: 40
GREEN, Sarah 1790: 47; 1799: 44
GRIFFIN, Elizabeth **App. A:** 11
GRIFFITH, Elizabeth 1771: 41; 1776: 11; 1780:
    17; *see also (trans.)* **App. B:** *2*; 1774: *25*
GRIFFITH, Elizabeth and Richard 1770: 31
GRIFFITH, Richard 1770: 32
GROSSE, Karl Friedrich August 1795: 23; 1796:
    44, 45
GUEVARA, Luis Vélez de, *see* GONZALEZ,
    Esteban
GUILLARD DE BEAURIEU, Gaspard 1773: 35
GULLIVER, Lemuel, jun. [pseud.] 1796: 46
GUNNING, Elizabeth 1794: 25, 26; 1796: 47;
    1797: 41; 1799: 45; *see also (trans.)* 1795: *19*

GUNNING, Susannah (née Minifie) 1792: 36; 1793: 19; 1796: 48; 1797: 42
GWYNN, Albinia 1785: 32, 33

H., I. 1795: 24
HADLEY, George, see 1793: 1
HALL, John (trans.) 1790: 40
HALL, William Henry 1792: 37; App. B: 11
HALLER, Albrecht von 1772: 33
HAMILTON, Anthony 1793: 20
HAMILTON, Elizabeth 1796: 49
HAMILTON, Lady Mary 1776: 12; 1777: 12; 1778: 12; 1782: 16
HANWAY, Mary Ann 1798: 28
HARE, M. 1797: 43
HARLEY, Mrs, see HUGILL, Martha
HARWOOD, Edward (trans.) 1776: 13B
HASWELL, Susanna, see ROWSON, Susanna
HAWEIS, Thomas 1783: 11, 12
HAWERS, Thomas, see HAWEIS, Thomas
HAWKE, Cassandra, Lady 1788: 54
HAYLEY, William 1789: 44
HAYS, Mary 1796: 50; 1799: 46
HAYWOOD, Eliza 1788: 55
HEATH, Henry Feron, Junior 1787: 37
HELME, Elizabeth 1787: 38; 1788: 56; 1794: 27; 1796: 51; 1799: 47; see also 1791: 39
HELME, William 1794: 28
HELVETIUS, Mr [pseud?] 1774: 29
HEMET, John 1799: 48, 49; see also 1799: 37
HENLEY, Samuel (trans.) 1786: 15
HERIOT, John 1787: 39; 1788: 57
HERON, Mary 1790: 48
HERON, [Robert] (trans.) 1792: 32, 34
HERVEY, Elizabeth 1788: 58; 1790: 49; 1796: 52; 1797: 44
HEY, Richard 1796: 53
HIGGS, Henry 1785: 34
HILDITCH, Ann, see HOWELL, Ann
HOFLAND, Barbara, see 1790: 52
HOLCROFT, Thomas 1780: 18; 1783: 13; 1792: 38; 1794: 29; 1797: 45; see also 1785: 29; 1786: 18, 34
HOLDER, Henry Evans 1798: 29
HOLFORD, Margaret, the elder 1785: 35; 1794: 30
HOLFORD, Margaret, the younger 1798: 30
HOLLOWAY, William 1792: 39
HOMESPUN, Prudentia, see WEST, Jane
HOOPER, William (trans.) 1772: 36
HOWELL, Ann 1787: 40; 1789: 45, 46; 1793: 21; 1796: 54, 55; 1797: 46
HUGHES, Anne 1786: 24; 1787: 41; 1788: 59; 1795: 25
HUGILL, Martha 1786: 25; 1788: 60; 1789: 47; 1793: 22; 1794: 31; 1797: 47; see also 1796: 3
HUISH, Robert (trans.) 1795: 45

HULL, Thomas, see 1771: 20
HUNTER, Anna Maria, see HUNTER, Maria
HUNTER, Maria 1792: 40; 1798: 31
HURRELL, Tamary Eliz, see 1790: 29
HUTCHINSON, A. A., Miss 1799: 50
HUTCHINSON, William 1772: 34; 1775: 24; 1792: 41
HUTTON, George 1794: 32

ILIFF, Edward Henry 1796: 56
IMLAY, Gilbert 1793: 23
'INĀYAT ALLĀH 1799: 51
INCHBALD, Elizabeth 1791: 41; 1796: 57; see also 1786: 5
IRELAND, William Henry 1799: 52

JACOBI, Johann Georg 1789: 48
JACSON, Frances 1795: 26; 1797: 48
JAMES, William 1786: 26
JEBB, Richard 1790: 71
JENKS, Jacquetta Agneta Mariana, see BECKFORD, William
JENNER, Charles 1770: 33
JEPHSON, Robert 1794: 33
JOHNSON, Mrs 1786: 27, 28; 1787: 42; 1789: 49; 1791: 42
JOHNSON, Mrs, author of Calista, see MACKENZIE, Anna Maria
JOHNSON, Theophilus 1783: 14
JOHNSTONE, Charles 1774: 30; 1775: 25; 1781: 19; 1786: 29
JONES, Harriet 1799: 53

KAHLERT, Carl Friedrich 1794: 34
KÂRIM, Muhammad, see 1793: 18
KEATE, George 1779: 12
KEIR, Elizabeth 1785: 36; 1787: 43
KEIR, Susanna Harvey, see 1785: 36
KELLY, Hugh 1771: 42
KELLY, Isabella 1794: 35; 1795: 27; 1796: 58; 1797: 49; 1799: 54
KENDALL, A. 1798: 32, 33
KENDALL, Edward Augustus (trans.) 1791: 64; 1799: 81
KER, Anne 1799: 55
KILNER, Dorothy, see 1781: 1
KILNER, Mary Ann App. A: 2
KING, Sophia 1798: 34; 1799: 56
KLINGER, Friedrich Maximilian von 1796: 59
KNIGGE, Adolf Franz Friedrich Ludwig von, Baron 1793: 24; 1799: 57
KNIGHT, Ellis Cornelia 1790: 50; 1792: 42
KOTZEBUE, August Friedrich Ferdinand von 1798: 35, 36; 1799: 58, 59, 60
KRAMER, Professor, see NAUBERT, Christiane Benedicte Eugenie

L., H. (*trans.*) 1799: *69*
L., W. 1790: 51
LACLOS, Pierre-Antoine-François Choderlos de 1784: 18
Lady, a 1770: 3, 9, 10, 17, 20; 1771: 6, 17, 22, 48; 1772: 5, 20; 1773: 3; 1774: 7, 11, *20*, 21, 22; 1775: 8, *17*; 1776: 4, 12; 1777: 7, 10, 12, 17; 1778: *3*, 4, 9, 11; 1779: 3; 1780: 4; 1781: 4, 7; 1782: *3*, 8, *10*; 1783: 2, 17; 1784: 1, 5, 8, 20; 1785: 3, 11, 13, 16, 19, 20, *30*, 32, 33, 35, 36; 1786: 9, 23; 1787: *2*, 6, *12*, *14*, 42, 51; 1788: 7, 13, 20, 25, 34, 35, 38; 1789: 5, 7, 18, 20, *25*, 46, 59; 1790: 22, 28, 34, *73*; 1791: 9, *13*, 18, 26, 27, 56; 1792: 3, *7*, 8, 17, 23; 1794: 5; 1795: *11*; 1796: 7, *9*, 11; 1797: 3, *72*; 1798: 2, *60*, 73; 1799: 2, 12, 13, 15, 87, *see also* Eminent Lady, Female, Lady of Distinction, Lady of Quality, Officer's Daughter, Old Woman, Unpatronized Female, Widow Lady, Widow of an Officer, Young Lady
Lady of Distinction, a 1788: 16; 1789: 12
Lady of Quality, a 1771: 15; 1799: 29
LAFONTAINE, August Heinrich Julius 1797: 50; 1798: 37; 1799: 61, 62, 63
LAMB, Charles 1798: 38
LANGHORNE, John 1771: 43
LANSDELL, Sarah 1796: 60; 1798: 39
LARA, Catherine 1796: 61, 62
LA ROCHE, Marie Sophie von 1776: 13A, 13B
LA ROCHE-GUILHEM, Anne de 1772: 35
LA SALLE, Adrien-Nicolas, marquis de 1790: 52
LATHOM, Francis 1795: 28; 1798: 40; 1799: 64
LATTER, Mary 1771: 44
LAVALLÉE, Joseph, marquis de Boisrobert 1788: 61; 1790: 53
LAWRENCE, Herbert 1771: 45
LEE, Harriet 1786: 30
LEE, Harriet and Sophia 1797: 51
LEE, Margaret 1797: 52
LEE, Sophia 1783: 15; 1785: 37; *see also* 1786: *14*
LEGRAND D'AUSSY, Pierre-Jean-Baptiste 1786: 31
LEIGH, Sir Samuel Egerton 1797: 53
LE MAIRE, Henri 1793: 25
LEMAISTRE, John Gustavus 1799: 65
LEMOINE, Henry 1786: 32
LE MOINE, L. H. (*trans.*) 1788: *51*
LENNOX, Charlotte 1790: 54; 1791: 43; *see also* 1797: *69*
LÉONARD, Nicolas-Germain 1788: 62
LE PILEUR D'APLIGNY 1779: 13
LEPRINCE DE BEAUMONT, Marie 1775: 26, 27
LE SAGE, Alain-René, *see* GONZALEZ, Esteban
LE SUIRE, Robert-Martin 1791: 44
LEWIS, Alethea 1794: 36
LEWIS, L. 1789: 50

LEWIS, Matthew Gregory 1796: 63
LIOMIN, Louis-Augustin 1794: 37
LISTER [pseud.] 1798: 41
LITTLEJOHN, P. 1791: 45; 1793: 26
LLOYD, Charles 1798: 42
LOAISEL DE TRÉOGATE, Joseph-Marie 1789: 51
LONG, Edward 1774: 31
LOUVET DE COUVRAY, Jean-Baptiste 1793: 27; 1798: 43
LUBERT, Mlle. de, *see* 1796: *37*
LUCAS, Rev. Charles 1798: 44
LUDGER, Conrad (*trans.*) 1789: *48*
LYONS, Lewis (*trans.*) 1787: *35*

M., E. 1780: 19
M., P. S. 1797: 54
MCDONALD, Andrew 1784: 19; 1791: 46
MACEUEN, Mr (*trans.*) 1772: *37*
MACKENZIE, Anna Maria 1783: 16; 1786: 33; 1788: 63; 1789: 52; 1790: 55; 1791: 47; 1792: 43; 1795: 29; 1796: 64; 1798: 45; App. B: 8
MACKENZIE, Henry 1771: 46, 1773: 36; 1777: 13; *see also* 1773: *31*, 1780: *7*
McMILLAN, Mr 1780: 17; *see also* 1795: *49*
MACNALLY, Leonard App. B: 7
MALTHUS, Daniel (*trans.*) 1779: *10*
MAN, Henry 1775: 28, 29; 1791: 48, 49
MANSEL, Henry 1782: 17
MANTE, Thomas 1781: 20; *see also* 1782: *21*
MARLEY, Daniel 1770: *8*
MARMONTEL, Jean-François 1792: 44
MARSHALL, Edmund 1797: 55
MARTEN, Thomas (*trans.*) 1771: 47
MARTIN, Mrs 1798: 46, 47; 1799: 66
MASTERMAN, Miss, *see* SKINN, Ann Emelinda
MATHEWS, Mrs 1793: 28; 1794: 38
MATHEWS, Eliza Kirkham 1785: 38; 1789: 53; 1790: 56; 1791: 50; 1792: 45
MEADES, Anna, *see* 1771: *20*
MEEKE, Mary 1795: 30; 1796: 65; 1797: 56, 57; 1798: 48; 1799: 67, 68
MELMOTH, Courtney, *see* PRATT, Samuel Jackson
MELTZER, Adolph Heinrich 1796: 66
MERCIER, Louis-Sébastien 1772: 36
MERRY, Robert, *see* 1796: *22*; 1797: *25*
MEZIERE, Harriet (née Chilcot) 1785: 39
MILES, E. 1791: 51
MILLER, Johann Martin 1799: 69
MILLIKIN, Anna 1793: 29; 1795: 31
MINIFIE, Margaret 1780: 20; 1783: 17
MITCHELL, Margaret (afterwards HURRY) App. A: 8
MOLINA, Tirso da, *see* TÉLLEZ, Gabriel
MONTOLIEU, Jeanne-Isabelle-Pauline Polier de

Bottens, dame de Croussaz, baronne de
  1786: 34
MOORE, George 1797: 58
MOORE, John 1789: 54; 1796: 67
MORE, Hannah, *see* 1789: *25*
MORGAN, Elizabeth (*trans.*) 1791: *36; see also*
  1787: *36*
MORRIS, Mrs R. P. 1784: 20; 1791: 52
MORVILLIERS, Nicolas Masson de, *see* 1785: *1*
MOSER, Joseph 1793: 30; 1794: 39; 1796: 68;
  1797: 59
MOUHY, Charles de Fieux, Chevalier de
  1789: 55
MULLER, Richard 1782: 18
MURAT, Henriette Julie de Castelnau, comtesse
  de 1778: 13
MURDOCH, John (*trans.*) 1773: 24; 1783: 18
MURPHY, Arthur, *see* 1772: *24*; 1789: 38A
MUSÄUS, Johann Karl August 1791: 53
MUSGRAVE, Agnes 1795: 32; 1797: 60;
  1798: 49
MYLIUS, August, *see* 1786: *38*

N, Sir Francis, *see* TREYSSAC DE VERGY, Pierre
  Henri
NĀRĀYANA BHATTA 1787: 44
NAUBERT, Christiane Benedicte Eugenie
  1789: 56; 1794: 40, 41
NICHOLS, Elizabeth Eyton 1771: 48
NICHOLSON, Mr 1787: 45, 46; 1788: 64;
  1789: 57
NICOLAI, Christoph Friedrich 1798: 50
NIXON, Capt. 1788: 65
NOGARET, François Félix, *see* TREYSSAC DE
  VERGY, Pierre Henri, AUTHENTIC MEM-
  OIRS
NORMAN, Elizabeth 1789: 58
NORTHMORE, William 1795: 33
NUGENT, Miss 1779: 14; *see also* 1782: *2*

O'CONNOR, E. 1789: 59; 1791: 54
OCTAVIA 1784: *9*
O'HINKLEY, Matthew (*trans.*) 1799: 40
O'KEEFFE, Adelaide 1798: 51
OPIE, Amelia Alderson 1790: 57

PALMER, Miss 1780: 21
PALMER, Charlotte 1792: 46, 47; *see also*
  1780: *21*
PALMER, John 1796: 69, 70
PARAGRAPH, Peter, *see* ADAIR, James
  Makittrick
PARKER, Mary Elizabeth 1795: 34
PARRY, Catherine 1784: 21
PARSONS, Eliza 1790: 58; 1791: 55; 1793: 31,
  32, 33; 1794: 42; 1795: 35; 1796: 71, 72; 1797:
  61, 62; 1798: 52; 1799: 70

PASTORELLA, Sylvania [pseud.] 1788: 66
PATRICK, Mrs F. C. 1797: 63; 1798: 53; 1799: 71
PEACOCK, Lucy 1785: 40; 1786: 35; 1793: 34;
  1794: 43; 1799: 72; *see also* 1796: *38*
PEARSON, Susanna 1794: 44
PENN, James 1779: 15
PENNYLESS, Peter, *see* WORSLEY, Robert
PERRIN, Pierre 1792: 48
PHILLIPS, Mrs Lucius 1798: 54
PHILLIPS, Peregrine **App. B:** 4, 5
PIDANSAT DE MAIROBERT, Mathieu-
  François 1779: 16
PIGAULT-LEBRUN, Charles-Antoine 1797: 64
PILKINGTON, Miss 1790: 59; 1793: 35;
  1798: 55
PILKINGTON, Laetitia, *see* 1798: *60*
PILKINGTON, Mary 1797: 65, 66; 1798: 56, 57;
  1799: 73, 74; *see also* 1797: *7*; 1799: *3*
PILPAY *See* 1787: *44*
PINCHARD, Elizabeth 1791: 56; 1794: 45
PLUMPTRE, Annabella 1796: 73, 1798: *68*
PLUMPTRE, Anne 1796: 74; 1798: 58; *see also*
  1798: *68*
POLESWORTH, Humphry (pseud) 1785: 41
POMPADOUR, Jeanne-Antoinette Poisson, Mme
  Le Normand d'Étioles, marquise de, *see*
  App. B: *1*
PORNEY, Mr (*trans.*) 1780: 22
PORTER, Anna Maria 1793: 36; 1797: 67;
  1798: 59
POTT, Joseph Holden 1786: 36
POTTER, A. M., *see* 1785: *43*
POTTER, John 1771: 49; 1784: 22; 1785: 42;
  1788: 67
POTTER, T. 1785: 43
POULIN, John (*trans.*) 1789: *56*
PRATT, Samuel Jackson 1775: 30; 1776: 14;
  1777: 14, 15; 1779: 17, 18; 1780: 23; 1797: 68;
  1798: 60; *see also* 1772: *24*; 1790: *31*
PROBY, William Charles 1799: 75
PURBECK, Elizabeth and Jane 1789: 60;
  1790: 60; 1791: 57; 1796: 75; 1797: 69
PYE, Henry James 1789: 61; 1795: 36; 1799: 76
PYE, Jael-Henrietta 1786: 37

R., C. 1794: 46
RADCLIFF, John 1790: *71*
RADCLIFFE, Ann 1789: 62; 1790: 61; 1791: 58;
  1794: 47; 1797: 70
RADCLIFFE, Mary Ann 1790: 62, 63
RAINSFORD, Mrs 1794: 48
RAITHBY, John 1792: 49
RASPE, Rudolph Erich 1786: 38
REBECQUE, Constant de, *see* 1785: *4*
REEVE, Clara 1777: 16; 1783: 19; 1788: 68;
  1791: 59; 1793: 37; 1799: 77; *see also* 1792: *14*
RENWICK, William 1771: 50; 1776: 15; 1788: 69

RÉTIF DE LA BRÉTONNE, Nicolas-Edme
   1770: 34, 1790: 64
RICCOBONI, Marie-Jeanne Laboras de
   Mézières 1772: 37; 1778: 14; 1784: 23
RICH, W. P. 1780: 24; see also 1791: 19
RICKMAN, Thomas Clio 1795: 37
ROBERTS, R. 1774: 28; 1775: 27
ROBINSON, John 1782: 19; 1794: 49; 1795: 38
ROBINSON, Maria Elizabeth 1794: 50
ROBINSON, Mary 1792: 50; 1794: 51; 1796: 76,
   77; 1797: 71; 1799: 78, 79
ROBINSON, Pollingrove 1789: 63
ROCHE, Regina Maria 1789: 64; 1793: 38; 1796:
   78; 1798: 61
ROGERS, A. 1777: 17
ROUSSEAU, Jean-Jacques 1783: 20; see also
   1781: 16; 1790: 15
ROWSON, Susanna 1786: 39; 1788: 70; 1789:
   65; 1791: 60, 61; 1792: 51; 1799: 80
RUDD, Margaret Caroline 1789: 66
RUSSELL, William 1771: 51
RUTLIDGE, Chevalier James 1787: 47; 1791: 62
RYVES, Elizabeth 1789: 67

S., R. 1798: 62
SABINA 1790: 65
SADI 1773: 37
SADLER, Robert 1791: 63
SAINT PIERRE, Jacques-Henri-Bernardin de
   1788: 71; 1791: 64; 1799: 81
SAINTE-FOIX, Philippe-Auguste de, Chevalier
   d'Arcq, see ARCQ, Philippe-Auguste de
   Sainte-Foix, Chevalier d'
SANDERS, Charlotte App. A: 10
SANDHAM, Elizabeth App. A: 13
SANDS, James 1799: 82
SAYER, Edward 1791: 65
SCHILLER, Johann Christoph Friedrich
   1795: 39
SCHULZ, Joachim Christoph Friedrich 1796: 79
SCOTT, Helenus 1782: 20; 1790: 66
SCOTT, Jonathan (trans.) 1799: 51
SCOTT, Sarah 1772: 38
SEALLY, Mr, see 1782: 11
SEALLY, John 1772: 39; 1776: 16
SELDEN, Catharine 1797: 72, 73; 1798: 63
SENAC DE MEILHAN, Gabriel 1797: 74
SEYMOUR, John 1788: 61
SHANDY, Mr [pseud.] App. B: 12
SHELDON, Ann 1787: 48
SHERWOOD, Mary Martha 1795: 40; 1799: 83
SHOWES, Mrs 1797: 75; 1798: 64; 1799: 84
SICKLEMORE, Richard 1798: 65; 1799: 85;
   see also 1798: 62
SIDDONS, Henry 1791: 66, 67
SIMES, Thomas 1770: 35
SINGER, Mr 1796: 80, 81

SKINN, Ann Emelinda 1771: 52
SLEATH, Eleanor 1798: 66
SMEDLEY, Menella Bute, see 1776: 4
SMITH, Charlotte 1787: 49; 1788: 72; 1789: 68;
   1791: 68; 1792: 52; 1793: 39; 1794: 52, 53;
   1795: 41; 1796: 82; 1798: 67; see also 1782: 11;
   1793: 41
SMOLLETT, Tobias 1771: 53
SMYTH, Maria 1783: 21
SOUZA, Adélaïde-Marie-Émilie Filleul,
   marquise de Flahaut 1799: 86
SPENCE, Elizabeth Isabella 1799: 87
SPENCER, Sarah Emma 1788: 73
SPIESS, Christian Heinrich 1798: 68
SQUIRREL, Harriett 1790: 67
STABBACK, Thomas 1796: 83
STEVENS, George Alexander 1788: 74
STEVENS, Grace Buchanan, see 1798: 51
STOCKDALE, Percival (trans.) 1778: 14
STREET, Miss 1790: 68; 1791: 69; 1792: 53, 54
STREET, Thomas George (trans.) 1792: 48
STYLES, John 1797: 76
SULIVAN, Stephen (trans.) 1773: 37
SUMMERSETT, Henry 1794: 54; 1795: 42;
   1797: 77; 1798: 69; 1799: 88; see also 1779: 4
SURR, Thomas Skinner 1796: 84; 1798: 70

TAYLOR, Miss (of Twickenham) 1779: 14;
   see also 1782: 2
TAYLOR, Miss 1799: 89, 90
TÉLLEZ, Gabriel 1799: 91
TENCIN, Claudine-Alexandrine Guérin,
   marquise de 1775: 31
TEUTHOLD, Peter (trans.) 1794: 34
THELWALL, John 1792: 55
THIBOUVILLE, Henri-Lambert d'Erbigny,
   marquis de 1770: 36
THISTLETHWAITE, James 1777: 18; 1778: 15
THOMAS, Ann 1794: 55
THOMAS, Francis Tracy 1799: 92
THOMPSON, Benjamin (trans.) 1798: 36;
   1799: 60, 91
THOMSON, Alexander (trans.) 1785: 44;
   1796: 85
THOMSON, Anna 1787: 50; 1788: 75; 1791: 70;
   1795: 43; 1799: 93
THOMSON, Harriet, see THOMSON, Anna
THOMSON, Rev. James 1790: 69; 1793: 40
THOMSON, William 1783: 22; 1789: 69; see also
   1788: 75
TIMBURY, Jane 1788: 76; 1789: 70; 1790: 70;
   1791: 71; see also 1770: 13
TODD, E. 1793: 41
TODD, Elizabeth 1788: 77
TOMLINS, Elizabeth Sophia 1785: 45; 1787: 51;
   1792: 56; 1798: 71
TONE, Theobald Wolfe 1790: 71

TOOKE, William (*trans.*) 1796: *90*
TOUCHIT, Timothy [pseud.] **App. B**: 13
TOWERS, Joseph 1793: 42
TRAPP, Joseph (*trans.*) 1796: *44, 59, 86*
TREYSSAC DE VERGY, Pierre Henri 1770: 37, 38, 39; 1771: 54, 55, 56; 1772: 40, 41
TRUSLER, John 1785: 46; 1793: 43
TSCHINK, Cajetan 1795: 44
TURNER, Daniel 1774: 32
TYPO, Dr 1780: *1*

USTICK, Anne, *see* 1787: *32*
USSIEUX, Louis d' 1782: 21

VAUCLUSE, Mademoiselle Fauques de, *see* FAUQUE DE LA CÉPÈDE, Marianne-Agnès Pillement
VAUGHAN, Thomas 1781: 21
VERRI, Alessandro 1798: 72
VISHNUSARMÁ 1787: 44
VOLTAIRE, François-Marie Arouet 1774: 33A, 33B; 1776: 17

W, C. 1774: 34
WÄCHTER, Georg Philip Ludwig Leonhard 1795: 45; 1796: 87
WALKER, George 1793: 44; 1794: 56; 1795: 46; 1796: 88; 1797: 78; 1799: 94; *see also* 1798: *40*
WALKER, Lady Mary, *see* HAMILTON, Lady Mary
WALL, Anne 1771: 57
WALWYN, B. 1783: 23; 1785: 47
WARNER, Richard 1795: 47
WARREN, William, *see* 1773: *18*
WARTON, Jane 1783: 24; 1784: 24
WARVILLE, Jacques-Pierre Brissot de 1791: *40*
WAY, Gregory Lewis 1778: 16
WEBER, Veit, *see* WÄCHTER, Georg Philip Ludwig Leonhard
WELLS, Helena 1798: 73
WENNINGTON, William (*trans.*) 1799: *63*
WEST, Jane 1793: 45; 1796: 89; 1799: 95; *see also* 1796: *52*

WHITE, James 1789: 71; 1790: 72; 1791: 72
WHITE, Joseph 1774: 35
WHITFIELD, Henry 1790: 73; 1799: 96
WHITMORE, H., *see* 1796: *46*
Widow Lady, a 1788: 12
Widow of an Officer, the 1787: *24*; 1799: 18
WIELAND, Christoph Martin 1771: 58; 1773: 38, 39; 1796: 90, 91; *see also* 1776: *13A, 13B*; 1786: *17*. For *Henrietta of Gerstenfeld*, *see* BEUVIUS, Adam
WILDMAN, Joseph 1799: 97
WILKINS, Charles (*trans.*) 1787: *44*; 1795: 48
WILL, Peter (*trans.*) 1795: *44*; 1796: *45*; 1799: *60, 63*
WILLIAMS, Helen Maria 1790: 74; *see also* 1771: *3*; 1788: *69*
WILLIAMS, John 1795: 49
WILLIAMS, William Frederick 1799: 98
WILMOT, Frederick 1771: 59
WILSON, Charles Henry 1792: 57
WINTERSTED, Mr (*trans.*) 1771: *58*
WOLLSTONECRAFT, Mary 1788: 78, 79; 1798: 74; *see also* 1790: *40*; 1793: *23*
WOODBRIDGE, Mr (*trans.*) 1797: 50
WOODWARD, George Moutard 1797: 79
WORSLEY, Robert 1770: 40
WRIGHT, George 1788: 80
WRIGHT, Thomas 1791: 73
WYNNE, John Huddlestone 1771: 60; 1786: 40

YEARSLEY, Ann 1795: 50
YEO, James 1782: 22
YOUNG, Arthur, *see* 1775: *9*
YOUNG, Mary Julia 1791: 74; 1798: 75; 1799: 99
Young Lady, a 1771: *23*; 1772: 9; 1773: 2; 1778: 1; 1780: 12; 1784: 6, 13; 1785: *7*, 38, 45; 1786: 22, 25; 1787: 3, 17, 18, 31; 1789: 65; 1790: 3; 1791: 15; 1792: 15, 37; 1795: *40*; 1798: 14, 16

ZIYA UL-DIN NARSHABI 1792: 58

Index of Titles

ABBESS, A ROMANCE 1799: 52
ABBEY OF CLUGNY 1796: 65
ABBEY OF SAINT ASAPH 1795: 27
ABERFORD, A NOVEL 1798: 69
ABSTRACT. A CHARACTER FROM LIFE
1797: 1
ADELA NORTHINGTON, A NOVEL 1796: 24
ADELAIDE AND THEODORE 1783: 9
ADELAIDE; OR, CONJUGAL AFFECTION
1785: 1
ADELINE DE COURCY 1797: 2
ADELINE; OR THE ORPHAN 1790: 1
ADOLESCENCE; OR, JUVENILE PROSPERITY
1794: 21
ADOLPHUS DE BIRON 1794: 55
ADOLPHUS; OR, THE UNNATURAL
BROTHER 1791: 1
ADVANTAGES OF DELIBERATION 1772: 1
ADVANTAGES OF EDUCATION 1793: 45
ADVENTURES OF A BANK-NOTE 1770: 23
ADVENTURES OF A CORK-SCREW 1775: 1
ADVENTURES OF A FOOTMAN see 1773: 18
ADVENTURES OF A HACKNEY COACH
1781: 1
ADVENTURES OF A JESUIT 1771: 1
ADVENTURES OF A PIN 1796: 1
ADVENTURES OF A RUPEE 1782: 20
ADVENTURES OF A SPECULIST 1788: 74
ADVENTURES OF A WATCH! 1788: 1
ADVENTURES OF ALONSO 1775: 23
ADVENTURES OF AN ACTOR 1782: 1
ADVENTURES OF ANTHONY VARNISH
1786: 29
ADVENTURES OF BOBBY LOUNGE 1791: 2
ADVENTURES OF CHRISTOPHER CURIOUS
1788: 2
ADVENTURES OF HENRY FITZHERBERT,
GENTLEMAN 1794: 1
ADVENTURES OF HUGH TREVOR 1794: 29,
1797: 45
ADVENTURES OF JOHN OF GAUNT
1790: 72
ADVENTURES OF JONATHAN CORNCOB
1787: 1
ADVENTURES OF KING RICHARD COEUR-
DE-LION 1791: 72
ADVENTURES OF LUCIFER IN LONDON
1786: 1
ADVENTURES OF MONSIEUR PROVENCE
1787: 47

ADVENTURES OF NUMA POMPILIUS
1787: 36
ADVENTURES OF THE PYRENEAN HER-
MITS 1799: 1
ADVENTURES OF THE SIX PRINCESSES
1785: 40
AEROSTATIC SPY 1785: 2
AFFECTED INDIFFERENCE 1771: 2
AFFECTING HISTORY OF TWO YOUNG
GENTLEWOMEN 1780: 1
AGATHA; OR, A NARRATIVE OF RECENT
EVENTS 1796: 2
AGE OF CHIVALRY (1799) see p. 673
AGITATION: OR, MEMOIRS OF GEORGE
WOODFORD 1788: 3
AGNES AND LEONORA 1799: 85
AGNES DE-COURCI, A DOMESTIC TALE
1789: 31
ALAN FITZ-OSBORNE 1786: 21
ALBERT DE NORDENSHILD 1796: 32
ALBERT; OR, THE WILDS OF STRATHNAV-
ERN 1799: 47
ALBERTINA. A NOVEL 1789: 1
ALBINA, A NOVEL 1786: 2
ALF VON DEULMEN 1794: 40
ALFRED AND CASSANDRA 1788: 4
ALLEGORICAL MINIATURES App. A: 9
ALL'S RIGHT AT LAST 1774: 1
ALL'S WELL THAT ENDS WELL 1797: 24
ALMERIA BELMORE 1789: 59
ALVAREZ; OR, IRRESISTIBLE SEDUCTION
1791: 32
ALWYN: OR THE GENTLEMAN COMEDIAN
1780: 18
AMANTUS AND ELMIRA 1794: 32
AMASIS. FROM THE FRENCH 1799: 81
AMBROSE AND ELEANOR 1796: 38
AMERICAN HUNTER 1788: 5
AMICABLE QUIXOTE 1788: 6
AMMORVIN AND ZALLIDA 1798: 21
AMOUROUS TALE OF THE CHASTE LOVES
OF PETER THE LONG 1786: 18
ANASTATIA: OR, THE MEMOIRS OF THE
CHEVALIER LAROUX 1797: 3
ANCHORET. A MORAL TALE 1773: 1
ANDRONICA, OR THE FUGITIVE BRIDE
1797: 34
ANECDOTES OF A CONVENT 1771: 3
ANECDOTES OF THE DELBOROUGH
FAMILY 1792: 36

ANECDOTES OF THE LIFE, ADVENTURES, AND VINDICATION, OF A MEDICAL CHARACTER 1790: 36
ANECDOTES OF TWO WELL-KNOWN FAMILIES 1798: 52
ANGELINA; A NOVEL 1796: 76
ANGELINE; OR, SKETCHES FROM NATURE 1794: 2
ANGELO, A NOVEL 1796: 56
ANIMATED SKELETON 1798: 1
ANNA: A SENTIMENTAL NOVEL 1782: 2
ANNA MELVIL 1792: 1
ANNA; OR, MEMOIRS OF A WELCH HEIRESS 1785: 22
ANNA ST. IVES: A NOVEL 1792: 38
ANTOINETTE, A NOVEL 1796: 74
ANZOLETTA ZADOSKI 1796: 54
APPARITION. A TALE 1788: 7
APPEARANCE IS AGAINST THEM 1786: 3
ARABIAN TALE, FROM AN UNPUBLISHED MANUSCRIPT 1786: 15
ARABIAN TALES 1792: 32
ARGAL; OR THE SILVER DEVIL 1793: 1
ARGENTUM: OR, ADVENTURES OF A SHILLING 1794: 3
ARGUS; THE HOUSE-DOG AT EADLIP 1789: 53
ARISTOCRAT, A NOVEL 1799: 76
ARLEY; OR, THE FAITHLESS WIFE 1790: 2
ARNOLD ZULIG, A SWISS STORY 1790: 56
ARPASIA; OR, THE WANDERER 1786: 4
ARTHUR FITZ-ALBINI, A NOVEL 1798: 19
ARTLESS TALES 1793: 36
ARULIA; OR, THE VICTIM OF SENSIBILITY 1790: 3
ARUNDEL 1789: 37
ARVILLE CASTLE 1795: 1
ASHDALE VILLAGE 1794: 24
ASHTON PRIORY 1792: 2
ASPASIA; OR, THE DANGERS OF VANITY 1791: 30
ASSIGNATION; A SENTIMENTAL NOVEL 1774: 2
AUDLEY FORTESCUE; OR THE VICTIMS OF FRAILTY 1795: 38
AUGUSTA; A NOVEL 1799: 2
AUGUSTA DENBEIGH; A NOVEL 1795: 2
AUGUSTA FITZHERBERT; OR, ANECDOTES OF REAL CHARACTERS 1796: 3
AUGUSTA; OR, THE DEPENDENT NIECE 1788: 8
AUGUSTA; OR, THE FEMALE TRAVELLERS 1787: 27
AUSTENBURN CASTLE 1795: 3
AUTHENTIC AND INTERESTING MEMOIRS OF MISS ANN SHELDON 1787: 48

AUTHENTIC MEMOIRS OF THE COUNTESS DE BARRÉ 1770: 54
AZALAIS AND AIMAR 1799: 36
AZEMIA: A DESCRIPTIVE AND SENTIMEN-TAL NOVEL 1797: 25

BAHAR-DANUSH; OR, GARDEN OF KNOWLEDGE 1799: 51
BANISHED MAN 1794: 52
BARHAM DOWNS 1784: 11
BARON MUNCHAUSEN'S NARRATIVE 1786: 38
BARON OF MANSTOW 1790: 4
BARONESS OF BEAUMONT 1792: 3
BASTARD OF NORMANDY 1793: 17
BASTARD; OR, THE HISTORY OF MR. GRE-VILLE 1784: 1
BASTILE: OR, HISTORY OF CHARLES TOWNLY 1789: 2
BASTILE, OR, MANLY SENSIBILITY 1797: 43
BATAVIANS 1799: 24
BATTLERIDGE: AN HISTORICAL TALE 1799: 29
BEATRICE, OR THE INCONSTANT 1788: 9
BEGGAR GIRL AND HER BENEFACTORS 1797: 26
BELINDA, OR, THE FAIR FUGITIVE 1789: 36
BELLE GROVE 1771: 4
BELLE PHILOSOPHE 1774: 3
BELLE WIDOWS 1789: 66
BELLEVILLE LODGE 1793: 2
BELMONT CASTLE 1790: 71
BELMONT GROVE 1785: 3
BELMONT LODGE 1799: 53
BENEDICTA 1791: 3
BENEVOLENT MAN 1775: 18
BERKELEY HALL 1796: 4
BETSY; OR, THE CAPRICES OF FORTUNE 1771: 5
BIRMINGHAM COUNTERFEIT 1772: 2
BLACK VALLEY; A TALE 1796: 87
BLANDFORD RACES 1782: 3
BLANSAY 1790: 44
BLENHEIM LODGE 1787: 2
BLIND CHILD 1791: 56
BRITISH KNIGHT ERRANT 1790: 5
BROTHER. A NOVEL 1771: 6
BROTHERS; A NOVEL App. A: 6
BUDGET, OR MORAL AND ENTERTAINING FRAGMENTS 1799: 3
BUNGAY CASTLE 1797: 27
BURTON-WOOD 1783: 16
BUTLER'S DIARY 1792: 4

CALAF: A PERSIAN TALE 1798: 30
CALEB WILLIAMS 1794: 23
CALISTA, A NOVEL 1789: 52

CAMILLA: OR, A PICTURE OF YOUTH
1796: 26
CAMILLA; OR, THE CORRESPONDENCE OF
A DECEASED FRIEND 1785: 4
CANTERBURY TALES 1797: 51
CAPRICIOUS FATHER 1775: 2
CAPTIVE; OR, THE HISTORY OF MR
CLIFFORD 1771: 7
CAPTIVES: OR, THE HISTORY OF CHARLES
ARLINGTON, ESQ; 1771: 8
CARITE AND POLYDORUS 1799: 21B
CAROLINE DE MONTMORENCI 1794: 4
CAROLINE. IN THREE VOLUMES 1798: 2
CAROLINE MERTON 1794: 5
CAROLINE OF LICHTFIELD; A NOVEL
1786: 34
CAROLINE; OR THE DIVERSITIES OF FOR-
TUNE 1787: 41
CAROLINE: OR, THE HISTORY OF MISS
SEDLEY 1787: 3
CAROLINE, THE HEROINE OF THE CAMP
1790: 6
CARPENTER'S DAUGHTER, OF DERHAM-
DOWN 1791: 4
CASKET; OR, DOUBLE DISCOVERY 1785: 34
CASTLE OF BEESTON 1798: 18
CASTLE OF BURKTHOLME 1797: 4
CASTLE OF HARDAYNE 1795: 12
CASTLE OF INCHVALLY 1796: 34
CASTLE OF MOWBRAY 1788: 60
CASTLE OF OLLADA 1795: 28
CASTLE OF SAINT DONATS 1798: 44
CASTLE OF ST VALLERY 1792: 5
CASTLE OF WOLFENBACH 1793: 31
CASTLE ON THE ROCK 1798: 32
CASTLE ZITTAW 1794: 46
CASTLES OF ATHLIN AND DUNBAYNE
1789: 62
CASTLES OF MONTREUIL AND BARRE
1799: 35
CATHARINE; OR, THE WOOD OF
LLEWELLYN 1788: 64
CAUTIOUS LOVER 1772: 3
CAVERN OF DEATH 1794: 6
CECILIA, OR MEMOIRS OF AN HEIRESS
1782: 15
CECILIA; OR, THE EASTERN LOVERS
1773: 26
CELESTINA 1791: 68
CHAMPION OF VIRTUE 1777: 16
CHARACTERS OF THE PRESENT MOST
CELEBRATED COURTEZANS 1780: 2
CHARITE AND POLYDORUS 1799: 21A
CHARLES ALTMAN 1790: 7
CHARLES AND CHARLOTTE 1777: 14
CHARLES AND TERESA 1774: 35
CHARLES DACRES 1797: 5

CHARLES HENLEY 1790: 47
CHARLES; OR, THE HISTORY OF A YOUNG
BARONET 1779: 1
CHARLOTTE. A TALE OF TRUTH 1791: 60
CHATEAU DE MYRELLE, OR LAURA 1791: 5
CHILD OF CHANCE 1786: 40
CHILD OF MISFORTUNE 1777: 18
CHILD OF NATURE 1774: 29
CHILD OF PROVIDENCE 1792: 6
CHILD OF WOE 1789: 58
CHILDREN OF THE ABBEY 1796: 78
CHURCH OF ST SIFFRID 1797: 44
CICELY; OR, THE ROSE OF RABY 1795: 32
CINTHELIA; OR, A WOMAN OF TEN
THOUSAND 1797: 78
CIPHER; OR, THE WORLD AS IT GOES
1791: 45
CITIZEN, A NOVEL 1790: 43
CLANDESTINE LOVERS 1788: 10
CLARA AND EMMELINE 1788: 56
CLARA DUPLESSIS, AND CLAIRANT 1797: 50
CLARA LENNOX; OR, THE DISTRESSED
WIDOW 1797: 52
CLARENTINE 1796: 27
CLEMENTINA BEDFORD 1796: 28
CLERIMONT, OR, MEMOIRS OF THE LIFE
AND ADVENTURES OF MR. B******
1786: 19
CLERMONT. A TALE 1798: 61
COALITION; OR FAMILY ANECDOTES
1785: 24
COLONEL ORMSBY 1781: 2
COLUMELLA; OR, THE DISTRESSED
ANCHORET 1779: 11
COMETILLA; OR VIEWS OF NATURE 1789: 63
CONFESSIONS OF A BEAUTY 1798: 24
CONFESSIONS OF A COQUET 1785: 5
CONFESSIONS OF JAMES BAPTISTE
COUTEAU 1794: 33
CONFIDENTIAL LETTERS OF ALBERT
1790: 42
CONFLICT. A SENTIMENTAL TALE 1790: 48
CONQUESTS OF THE HEART 1785: 45
CONSCIOUS DUPLICITY 1791: 6
CONSEQUENCES: OR, ADVENTURES AT
RRAXALL CASTLE 1796: 84
CONSTANCE: A NOVEL 1785: 38
CONSTANT LOVER; OR, WILLIAM AND
JEANETTE 1799: 58
CONSTANTIA; OR THE DISTRESSED
FRIEND 1770: 1
CONTEMPLATIVE MAN 1771: 45
CONTINUATION OF YORICK'S SENTIMEN-
TAL JOURNEY App. B: 9
CONTRADICTION 1796: 29
CONTRADICTIONS; OR, WHO COULD
HAVE THOUGHT IT? 1799: 48

CONTRAST: A NOVEL 1795: 22
CONTRAST; OR; HISTORY OF MISS WEL-
DON AND MISS MOSELY 1771: 9
CONTRAST: OR THE OPPOSITE CONSE-
QUENCES OF GOOD AND EVIL HABITS
1787: 4
CONVENT: OR, THE HISTORY OF SOPHIA
NELSON 1786: 22
CONVERSATIONS OF EMILY 1787: 35
COOMBE WOOD 1783: 17
COQUETILLA; OR, ENVY ITS OWN
SCOURGE 1771: 10
CORDELIA, OR A ROMANCE OF REAL LIFE
1799: 56
CORFE CASTLE 1793: 29
CORRESPONDENCE OF TWO LOVERS
1788: 62
CORRESPONDENTS, AN ORIGINAL NOVEL
1775: 3
COTTAGE OF FRIENDSHIP 1788: 66
COUNT DE HOENSDERN 1792: 45
COUNT DE POLAND 1780: 20
COUNT DE RETHEL 1779: 2
COUNT DE SANTERRE 1797: 72
COUNT DI NOVINI 1799: 82
COUNT DONAMAR 1797: 28
COUNT RODERIC'S CASTLE 1794: 7
COUNT ST. BLANCARD 1795: 30
COUNTESS OF HENNEBON 1789: 47
COURT INTRIGUE 1799: 44
COUSINS OF SCHIRAS 1797: 74
COXHEATH-CAMP 1779: 3
CREOLE; OR, THE HAUNTED ISLAND
1796: 20
CUCKOLDOM TRIUMPHANT 1771: 59
CURATE OF COVENTRY 1771: 49
CURATE OF ELMWOOD 1795: 49
CURSE OF SENTIMENT 1787: 34
CYANNA OF ATHENS 1792: 30
CYPRIOTS; OR, A MINIATURE OF EUROPE
1795: 4

DAGGER. TRANSLATED FROM THE GER-
MAN 1795: 23
DAMON AND DELIA 1784: 15
DANGER OF THE PASSIONS 1770: 36
DANGEROUS CONNECTIONS 1784: 18
DANGERS OF COQUETRY 1790: 57
DANISH MASSACRE, AN HISTORIC FACT
1791: 47
D'ARCY. A NOVEL 1793: 41
DARNLEY VALE; OR, EMELIA FITZROY
1789: 33
DAUGHTER: OR THE HISTORY OF MISS
EMILIA ROYSTON 1775: 20
DAYS OF CHIVALRY 1797: 6
DE MONTMORENCY 1790: 8

DEATH OF CAIN, IN FIVE BOOKS App. B: 11
DEATH'S A FRIEND 1788: 11
DELIA, A PATHETIC AND INTERESTING
TALE 1790: 59
DELICATE OBJECTION 1775: 4
DELICES DU SENTIMENT 1781: 3
DELINEATIONS OF THE HEART 1792: 49
DELORAINE. A DOMESTIC TALE 1798: 46
DELVES, A WELCH TALE 1796: 48
DEMOCRAT: INTERSPERSED WITH ANEC-
DOTES 1795: 36
DENIAL; OR, THE HAPPY RETREAT 1790: 69
DÉNOUEMENT: OR, HISTORY OF LADY
LOUISA WINGROVE 1781: 4
DERWENT PRIORY 1798: 33
DESMOND. A NOVEL 1792: 52
DESTINATION: OR, MEMOIRS OF A
PRIVATE FAMILY 1799: 77
DEVIL IN LOVE (1793) see 1791: 32
DEVIL UPON TWO STICKS IN ENGLAND
1790: 41
DIAMOND RING; OR, SUCCESSFUL ARTI-
FICES 1795: 5
DIARY KEPT IN AN EXCURSION App. B: 5
DINARBAS; A TALE 1790: 50
DISAPPOINTED HEIR: OR, MEMOIRS OF
THE ORMOND FAMILY 1796: 42
DISGUISE, A DRAMATIC NOVEL 1771: 11
DISINTERESTED LOVE; OR THE HISTORY
OF SIR CHARLES ROYSTON 1776: 1
DISINTERESTED LOVE; OR, THE MODERN
ROBIN GREY 1788: 12
DISINTERESTED MARRIAGE 1774: 4
DISINTERESTED NABOB 1787: 5
DISOBEDIENCE. A NOVEL 1797: 48
DISTRESSED DAUGHTER 1770: 2
DISTREST VIRTUE 1781: 5
DIVORCE. IN A SERIES OF LETTERS 1771: 12
DONCASTER RACES 1789: 32
DOUBLE DISAPPOINTMENT 1774: 5
DOUBLE SURPRISE: A NOVEL 1783: 1
DOUBTFUL MARRIAGE 1792: 41
DOVEDELL HALL 1792: 39
DUCHESS OF YORK 1791: 7
DUEL, OR NATURE WILL PREVAIL 1789: 3
DUKE OF CLARENCE 1795: 21
DUKE OF EXETER 1789: 4
DUNCAN AND PEGGY 1794: 27
DUPE, A MODERN SKETCH 1794: 8
DUPED GUARDIAN 1785: 26
DURVAL AND ADELAIDE 1796: 61
DUSSELDORF; OR, THE FRATRICIDE
1798: 45

EARL STRONGBOW 1789: 71
EAST INDIAN, OR CLIFFORD PRIORY
1799: 99

EASTERN ANECDOTES 1799: 4
EDAL VILLAGE 1781: 6
EDELFRIDA, A NOVEL 1792: 7
EDEN VALE 1784: 21
EDGAR; OR, THE PHANTOM OF THE
    CASTLE 1798: 65
EDINGTON: A NOVEL 1796: 53
EDMUND AND ELEONORA 1797: 55
EDMUND OF THE FOREST 1797: 60
EDMUND OLIVER 1798: 42
EDMUND; OR, THE CHILD OF THE CASTLE
    1790: 9
EDWARD. A NOVEL 1774: 6
EDWARD AND HARRIET, OR THE HAPPY
    RECOVERY 1788: 13
EDWARD AND SOPHIA 1787: 6
EDWARD BARNARD 1797: 65
EDWARD DE COURCY 1794: 9
EDWARD: OR, SORROWS FROM SEPAR-
    ATION 1791: 8
EDWARD. VARIOUS VIEWS OF HUMAN
    NATURE 1796: 67
EDWIN AND ANNA 1785: 6
EDWIN AND JULIA 1774: 7
EDWY; SON OF ETHELRED THE SECOND
    1791: 9
EFFECTS OF THE PASSIONS 1788: 51
EGG, OR THE MEMOIRS OF GREGORY
    GIDDY, ESQ 1772: 4
ELA: OR, THE DELUSIONS OF THE HEART
    1787: 32
ELEGANT TALES, HISTORIES, AND EPISTLES
    OF A MORAL TENDENCY 1791: 28
ELEONORA, A NOVEL, IN A SERIES OF
    LETTERS 1789: 42
ELEONORA: FROM THE SORROWS OF
    WERTER 1785: 25
ELFRIDA; OR, PATERNAL AMBITION
    1786: 23
ELISA POWELL, OR TRIALS OF SENSIBILITY
    1795: 18
ELIZA BEAUMONT AND HARRIET
    OSBORNE 1789: 35
ELIZA CLELAND, A NOVEL 1788: 14
ELIZABETH. A NOVEL 1797: 32
ELIZABETH PERCY; A NOVEL 1792: 8
ELLA; OR, HE'S ALWAYS IN THE WAY
    1798: 31
ELLEN AND JULIA 1793: 32
ELLEN, COUNTESS OF CASTLE HOWEL
    1794: 16
ELLEN RUSHFORD 1794: 10
ELLEN WOODLEY 1790: 38
ELLESMERE. A NOVEL 1799: 67
ELLINOR; OR, THE WORLD AS IT IS
    1798: 28
ELOISA DE CLAIRVILLE 1790: 10

ELOISE DE MONTBLANC 1796: 5
ELOPEMENT; OR PERFIDY PUNISHED
    1771: 40
ELVINA; A NOVEL 1792: 9
ELVIRA; OR, THE WORLD AS IT GOES
    1796: 6
EMBARRASSED ATTACHMENT 1791: 10
EMBARRASSED LOVERS 1775: 5
EMIGRANTS, OR THE HISTORY OF AN
    EXPATRIATED FAMILY 1793: 23
EMIGRANTS: A GALLIC TALE 1794: 11
EMILIA AND ALPHONSO 1799: 86
EMILIA DE ST AUBIGNE 1788: 46
EMILIUS AND SOPHIA; OR, THE
    SOLITARIES 1783: 20
EMILY: A NOVEL 1792: 10
EMILY BENSON 1791: 54
EMILY DE VARMONT 1798: 43
EMILY DUNDORNE 1799: 93
EMILY HERBERT 1786: 5
EMILY; OR, THE FATAL PROMISE 1792: 11
EMMA CORBETT 1780: 23
EMMA DORVILL 1789: 5
EMMA; OR, THE CHILD OF SORROW 1776: 2
EMMA: OR THE UNFORTUNATE ATTACH-
    MENT 1773: 28
EMMELINE, THE ORPHAN OF THE CASTLE
    1788: 72
EMPRESS MATILDA 1796: 7
ENAMOURED SPIRIT (1798) see 1791: 32
ENCHANTED MIRROR 1799: 5
ENCHANTER; OR WONDERFUL STORY
    TELLER 1795: 6
ENGLISH MERCHANT 1795: 13
ENGLISH NUN 1797: 73
ERMINA; OR, THE FAIR RECLUSE 1772: 5
ERRORS OF EDUCATION 1791: 55
ERRORS OF INNOCENCE 1786: 30
ERRORS OF NATURE 1783: 23
ERRORS OF SENSIBILITY 1793: 3
ESCAPE. A NARRATIVE 1799: 59
ESTELLE (1798) see 1791: 35
ETHELINDE, OR THE RECLUSE OF THE
    LAKE 1789: 68
ETHELWINA, OR THE HOUSE OF FITZ-
    AUBURNE 1799: 30
EUGENIA AND ADELAIDE 1791: 11
EUGENIO; OR, THE PRECEPTS OF PRUDEN-
    TIUS 1799: 23
EUGENIUS: OR, ANECDOTES OF THE
    GOLDEN VALE 1785: 31
EUPHEMIA 1790: 54
EVA. A NOVEL 1799: 54
EVA, AN OLD IRISH STORY 1795: 31
EVELINA, OR, A YOUNG LADY'S ENTRANCE
    INTO THE WORLD 1778: 10
EVENING RECREATIONS App. A: 7

EVENING WALK; A SENTIMENTAL TALE 1795: 37

EXAMPLE: OR THE HISTORY OF LUCY CLEVELAND 1778: 1

EXCESSIVE SENSIBILITY; OR, THE HISTORY OF LADY ST. LAURENCE 1787: 50

EXCURSION. IN TWO VOLUMES 1777: 9

EXCURSION OF OSMAN, THE SON OF ABDALLAH 1792: 12

EXHIBITIONS OF THE HEART 1799: 50

EXILES; OR, MEMOIRS OF THE COUNT DE CRONSTADT 1788: 68

EXPEDITION OF HUMPHRY CLINKER 1771: 53

EXPEDITION OF LITTLE PICKLE; OR, THE PRETTY PLOTTER 1792: 13

EXPLANATION; OR, AGREEABLE SURPRISE 1773: 2

EXTRACT FROM THE LIFE OF LIEUTENANT HENRY FOLEY 1782: 4

FAIR CAMBRIANS 1790: 11

FAIR HIBERNIAN 1789: 6

FAIR IMPOSTOR 1792: 14

FAIR METHODIST; OR, SUCH THINGS ARE 1794: 12

FAIR SYRIAN, A NOVEL 1787: 28

FAIRY OF MISFORTUNE 1799: 32

FAIRY RING, OR EMELINE 1783: 2

FAIRY TALES, SELECTED FROM THE BEST AUTHORS 1788: 15

FALSE FRIEND: A DOMESTIC STORY 1799: 78

FALSE FRIENDS. A NOVEL 1785: 7

FALSE FRIENDSHIP; OR, NATURE IN MASQUERADE 1799: 6

FALSE GRATITUDE: A NOVEL 1773: 3

FALSE STEP 1771: 13

FAMILY OF HALDEN 1799: 61

FAMILY PARTY 1791: 74

FAMILY PICTURE 1783: 13

FAMILY SECRETS 1797: 68

FAMILY SKETCHES 1789: 7

FANCIED EVENTS 1799: 43

FANNY: A NOVEL 1785: 35

FANNY; OR, THE DESERTED DAUGHTER 1792: 15

FANNY VERNON 1789: 8

FARMER OF INGLEWOOD FOREST 1796: 51

FASHIONABLE DAUGHTER 1774: 32

FASHIONABLE FOLLIES 1781: 21

FASHIONABLE FRIEND 1773: 25

FASHIONABLE INFIDELITY 1789: 9

FASHIONABLE LIFE 1781: 7

FATAL AFFECTION 1774: 8

FATAL COMPLIANCE 1771: 14

FATAL CONNEXION 1773: 32

FATAL EFFECTS OF DECEPTION 1773: 4

FATAL EFFECTS OF INCONSTANCY 1774: 25

FATAL FOLLIES 1788: 75

FATAL FRIENDSHIP 1770: 3

FATAL MARRIAGE 1785: 8

FATALITY 1796: 8

FATE OF SEDLEY 1795: 42

FATE OF VELINA DE GUIDOVA 1790: 62

FAULT WAS ALL HIS OWN 1771: 48

FAVOURITE TALES 1787: 7

FAVOURITE. A MORAL TALE 1771: 15

FAVOURITES OF FELICITY 1785: 42

FEATURES FROM LIFE 1788: 44

FEDARETTA 1799: 38

FEELINGS OF THE HEART 1772: 6

FEMALE FRAILTY 1772: 7

FEMALE FRIENDSHIP 1770: 4

FEMALE GAMESTER 1796: 9

FEMALE MONITOR 1781: 8

FEMALE SENSIBILITY (1783) see 1778: 6

FEMALE STABILITY 1780: 21

FEMALE WERTER 1792: 48

FILIAL INDISCRETIONS 1799: 7

FILLE DE CHAMBRE 1792: 51

FINE LADY A NOVEL 1772: 31

FITZROY; OR, IMPULSE OF THE MOMENT 1792: 40

FLIGHTS OF INFLATUS 1791: 48

FOLLIES OF ST. JAMES'S STREET 1789: 10

FOOL OF QUALITY. VOLUME V 1770: 24

FORCE OF EXAMPLE 1797: 7

FORCE OF LOVE 1785: 28

FORCE OF PREJUDICE 1799: 97

FORESTERS. A NOVEL 1796: 47

FORTESCUE; OR, THE SOLDIER'S REWARD 1789: 11

FORTUNATE BLUE-COAT BOY 1770: 5

FORTUNATE SISTERS 1782: 5

FORTUNE TELLER 1774: 9

FOSCARI, A VENETIAN TALE 1790: 12

FRAGMENT OF THE HISTORY OF THAT ILLUSTRIOUS PERSONAGE, JOHN BULL 1785: 41

FRAGMENTS: IN THE MANNER OF STERNE 1797: 29

FRAILTIES OF FASHION 1782: 6

FRANCIS, THE PHILANTHROPIST 1786: 27

FREAKS OF FORTUNE 1790: 13

FREDERIC AND LOUISA 1792: 16

FREDERIC LATIMER 1799: 65

FREDERIC: OR, THE FORTUNATE BEGGAR 1772: 8

FREDERIC, OR THE LIBERTINE 1788: 67

FREDERICA: OR THE MEMOIRS OF A YOUNG LADY 1792: 17

FREDERICA RISBERG 1793: 4

FREDERICK AND ALICIA 1791: 12

FRENCH ADVENTURER 1791: 44
FRENCH GIL BLAS 1793: 25
FRIEND OF VIRTUE 1789: 55
FRIENDS: OR, ORIGINAL LETTERS OF A
    PERSON DECEASED 1773: 5
FRIENDS; OR, THE CONTRAST BETWEEN
    VIRTUE AND VICE App. A: 11
FRIENDSHIP AND MATRIMONY 1782: 17
FRIENDSHIP IN A NUNNERY 1778: 11
FUGITIVE, AN ARTLESS TALE 1795: 16

GABRIELLE DE VERGY 1790: 14
GALATEA A PASTORAL ROMANCE 1791: 35
GAMESTERS: A NOVEL 1786: 33
GENERAL ELECTION 1775: 6
GENEROSITY 1792: 18
GENEROUS ATTACHMENT 1787: 8
GENEROUS BRITON (1792) see p. 558
GENEROUS HUSBAND 1771: 16
GENEROUS INCONSTANT 1771: 17
GENEROUS LOVER 1771: 38
GENEROUS SISTER 1779: 7
GENIUS: OR, THE MYSTERIOUS ADVEN-
    TURES 1796: 44
GENUINE AND ENTERTAINING MEMOIRS
    1787: 9
GENUINE ANECDOTES AND AMOROUS
    ADVENTURES OF SIR RICHARD EASY
    1782: 7
GENUINE DISTRESSES OF DAMON AND
    CELIA 1771: 50
GENUINE MEMOIRS OF MISS FAULKNER
    1770: 6
GENUINE MEMOIRS OF MISS HARRIET
    MELVIN 1772: 9
GEORGE BARNWELL 1798: 70
GEORGE BATEMAN 1782: 14
GEORGINA, A NOVEL 1796: 55
GEORGINA HARCOURT 1791: 13
GEORGINA: OR MEMOIRS OF THE
    BELLMOUR FAMILY 1787: 31
GERALDINA, A NOVEL 1798: 3
GERMAN GIL BLAS 1793: 24
GERMAN MISCELLANY 1796: 85
GERTRUDE; OR, THE ORPHAN OF
    LLANFRUIST 1791: 14
GHOST-SEER; OR, APPARITIONIST 1795: 39
GILHAM FARM 1781: 9
GIPSY COUNTESS 1799: 45
GIRL OF THE MOUNTAINS 1797: 61
GODFREY DE HASTINGS 1798: 4
GOMEZ AND ELEONORA 1798: 5
GONSALVO OF CORDOVA 1792: 34
GOSSIP'S STORY 1796: 89
GOVERNESS, OR COURTLAND ABBEY
    1797: 8
GRASVILLE ABBEY: A ROMANCE 1797: 58

GREENWOOD FARM 1778: 2

HADLEIGH GROVE 1773: 6
HALF-PAY OFFICER 1788: 57
HAMLAIN; OR, THE HERMIT OF THE
    BEACH 1799: 8
HANNAH HEWIT 1796: 36
HAPPY ART OF TEAZING 1787: 10
HAPPY FAMILY AT EASON HOUSE
    App. A: 13
HAPPY RELEASE 1787: 11
HARCOURT. A NOVEL 1799: 68
HARCOURT; A SENTIMENTAL NOVEL
    1780: 3
HARRIET AND SOPHIA 1789: 12
HARRIET: OR, THE INNOCENT ADULTRESS
    1771: 18
HARTLEBOURN CASTLE 1793: 5
HARTLY HOUSE, CALCUTTA 1789: 41
HAUNTED CASTLE, A NORMAN ROMANCE
    1794: 56
HAUNTED CAVERN: A CALEDONIAN TALE
    1796: 69
HAUNTED PRIORY 1794: 20
HE DECEIVES HIMSELF 1799: 26
HE IS FOUND AT LAST 1775: 7
HE WOULD BE A PEER 1798: 6
HEAVEN'S BEST GIFT 1798: 54
HEERFORT AND CLARA 1789: 56
HĔĔTŌPĂDĒS OF VĔĔSHNŌŌ-SĂRMĀ
    1787: 44
HEIR OF MONTAGUE 1797: 9
HEIRESS DI MONTALDE 1799: 55
HELEN SINCLAIR: A NOVEL 1799: 87
HELENA, A NOVEL 1788: 16
HELENA: OR, THE VICISSITUDES OF A
    MILITARY LIFE 1790: 66
HELOISE: OR, THE SIEGE OF RHODES
    1788: 43
HENRIETTA OF GERSTENFELD 1786: 17
HENRIETTA, COUNTESS OSENVOR 1770: 37
HENRY, A NOVEL 1793: 26
HENRY AND ISABELLA 1788: 59
HENRY . . . BY THE AUTHOR OF ARUNDEL
    1795: 17
HENRY DE BEAUVAIS 1798: 7
HENRY; OR THE FOUNDLING 1799: 73
HENRY SOMERVILLE 1797: 10
HENRY STUKELEY 1794: 28
HENRY WILLOUGHBY 1798: 8
HERMAN OF UNNA 1794: 41
HERMIONE, OR THE ORPHAN SISTERS
    1791: 43
HERMIT OF CAUCASUS 1796: 68
HERMIT OF SNOWDEN 1789: 67
HERMIT OF THE ALPS 1794: 22
HERMIT OF THE ROCK 1779: 13

HERMITAGE; A BRITISH STORY 1772: 34
HERMITAGE, A NOVEL 1796: 39
HERMSPRONG; OR, MAN AS HE IS NOT
    1796: 21
HISTORIC TALES 1788: 17
HISTORY OF AGATHON 1773: 38
HISTORY OF AMELIA HARCOURT 1777: 1
HISTORY OF ARSACES 1774: 30
HISTORY OF CAPTAIN AND MISS RIVERS
    1787: 12
HISTORY OF CHARLES FALKLAND, ESQ.
    1787: 13
HISTORY OF CHARLES MANDEVILLE
    1790: 39
HISTORY OF CHARLES WENTWORTH, ESQ.
    1770: 22
HISTORY OF CHRISTINA, PRINCESS OF
    SWABIA 1784: 23
HISTORY OF COUNT GLEICHEN 1786: 13
HISTORY OF ELIZA WARWICK 1778: 3
HISTORY OF FANNY MEADOWS 1775: 21
HISTORY OF FEMALE FAVOURITES 1772: 35
HISTORY OF GEORGINA NEVILLE 1791: 15
HISTORY OF HENRIETTA MORTIMER
    1787: 14
HISTORY OF JACK AND HIS ELEVEN
    BROTHERS App. A: 12
HISTORY OF JOHN JUNIPER, ESQ. 1781: 19
HISTORY OF JULIA & CECILIA DE VAL-
    MONT 1797: 11
HISTORY OF JULIA D'HAUMONT 1797: 38
HISTORY OF LADY ANNE NEVILLE 1776: 7
HISTORY OF LADY BARTON 1771: 41
HISTORY OF LADY BETTESWORTH
    1780: 19
HISTORY OF LADY CAROLINE RIVERS
    1788: 77
HISTORY OF LADY EMMA MELCOMBE
    1787: 15
HISTORY OF LADY SOPHIA STERNHEIM
    1776: 13A
HISTORY OF LEWIS DE MARCHMENT
    1780: 24
HISTORY OF LITTLE JACK App. A: 4
HISTORY OF LORD AIMWORTH 1773: 7
HISTORY OF LORD ASHBORN 1773: 8
HISTORY OF LORD BELFORD 1784: 2
HISTORY OF LORD STANTON 1774: 10
HISTORY OF MADEMOISELLE DE BELEAU
    (1775) *see* p. 230
HISTORY OF MAY-FLOWER 1793: 20
HISTORY OF MELINDA HARLEY 1777: 2
HISTORY OF MISS CAROLINA MANNERS
    1772: 10
HISTORY OF MISS DORINDA CATSBY
    1772: 11
HISTORY OF MISS GREVILLE 1787: 43

HISTORY OF MISS HARRIOT FAIRFAX
    1780: 4
HISTORY OF MISS HARRIOT MONTAGUE
    1770: 7
HISTORY OF MISS LEONORA MEADOWSON
    1788: 55
HISTORY OF MISS MARIA BARLOWE 1777: 3
HISTORY OF MISS MEREDITH 1790: 58
HISTORY OF MISS PAMELA HOWARD
    1773: 9
HISTORY OF MISS TEMPLE 1777: 17
HISTORY OF MR STANLY AND MISS
    TEMPLE 1773: 10
HISTORY OF MR. CECIL AND MISS GREY
    1771: 19
HISTORY OF MR. CHARLES FITZGERALD
    1770: 8
HISTORY OF MY FATHER 1798: 35
HISTORY OF NED EVANS 1796: 52
HISTORY OF PHILARIO AND CLEMENTINA
    1777: 4
HISTORY OF PHILIP WALDEGRAVE 1793: 42
HISTORY OF RHEDI 1773: 31
HISTORY OF SANDFORD AND MERTON
    App. A: 1, 3, 5
HISTORY OF SIDNEY AND VOLSAN 1772: 29
HISTORY OF SIR CHARLES BENTINCK,
    BART. 1788: 45
HISTORY OF SIR CHARLES DORMER 1770: 9
HISTORY OF SIR GEOFFRY RESTLESS
    1791: 49
HISTORY OF SIR GEORGE WARRINGTON
    1797: 69
HISTORY OF SIR HENRY CLARENDON
    1785: 9
HISTORY OF SIR WILLIAM HARRINGTON
    1771: 20
HISTORY OF THE AMTSRATH GUTMAN
    1799: 57
HISTORY OF THE CURATE OF CRAMEN
    1777: 5
HISTORY OF THE HON. MRS. ROSEMONT
    1781: 17
HISTORY OF THE HONOURABLE EDWARD
    MORTIMER 1785: 32
HISTORY OF THE MISS BALTIMORES
    1783: 3
HISTORY OF TOM RIGBY 1773: 29
HISTORY OF TOM WESTON 1791: 31
HISTORY OF VANILLO GONZALES 1797: 40
HONORIA SOMMERVILLE 1789: 60
HORRID MYSTERIES 1796: 45
HORRORS OF OAKENDALE ABBEY 1797: 33
HOUSE OF MARLEY 1797: 12
HOUSE OF TYNIAN 1795: 46
HOW SHE LOST HIM 1780: 5
HUBERT DE SEVRAC 1796: 77

HUMAN VICISSITUDES 1798: 9
HUMPHRY CLINKER 1771: 53
HUSBAND'S RESENTMENT 1776: 3

IANTHÉ, OR THE FLOWER OF
　CAERNARVON 1798: 23
IDEAL TRIFLES 1774: 11
ILDEGERTE, QUEEN OF NORWAY 1798: 36
ILL EFFECTS OF A RASH VOW 1789: 13
ILLICIT LOVE 1791: 52
ILLUSIONS OF SENTIMENT 1788: 18
IMMELINA. A NOVEL 1799: 9
IMOGEN; A PASTORAL ROMANCE 1784: 16
INCOGNITA: OR, EMILY VILLARS 1783: 4
INDEPENDENT. A NOVEL 1784: 19
INDIAN ADVENTURER 1780: 6
INDIAN COTTAGE 1791: 64
INDISCREET CONNECTION 1772: 12
INDISCREET MARRIAGE 1779: 14
INDISCRETION; A NOVEL 1799: 10
INNOCENT FUGITIVE 1789: 49
INNOCENT RIVALS 1786: 6
INQUISITION 1797: 13
INQUISITOR; OR, INVISIBLE RAMBLER
　1788: 70
INTEGRITY AND CONTENT 1792: 46
INTEGRITY, OR THE HISTORY OF SOPHIA
　FRANCOURT 1790: 52
INTERESTING MEMOIRS 1785: 36
INTERESTING SKETCH OF GENTEEL LIFE
　1782: 8
INTERESTING STORY OF EDWIN AND JULIA
　1788: 19
INTERESTING TALES 1797: 75
INVASION; OR, WHAT MIGHT HAVE BEEN
　1798: 10
INVOLUNTARY INCONSTANT 1772: 13
IPHIGENIA, A NOVEL 1791: 16
IRISH GUARDIAN 1775: 8
IRISH HEIRESS 1797: 63
IRISHMAN; OR THE FAVOURITE OF
　FORTUNE 1772: 14
ISABELLA: OR, THE REWARDS OF GOOD
　NATURE 1776: 8
ISABINDA OF BELLEFIELD 1796: 30
ISIDORA OF GALLICIA 1797: 47
ISMENE AND ISMENIAS 1788: 52
IT IS AND IT IS NOT A NOVEL 1792: 47
ITALIAN LETTERS 1784: 17
ITALIAN, OR THE CONFESSIONAL OF THE
　BLACK PENITENTS 1797: 70
IVEY CASTLE 1794: 17

JAMES THE FATALIST AND HIS MASTER
　1797: 35
JAMES WALLACE 1788: 42
JAQUELINA OF HAINAULT 1798: 27

JEALOUS MOTHER 1771: 21
JEMIMA. A NOVEL 1795: 25
JESSY; OR, THE BRIDAL DAY 1771: 22
JESUIT: OR, THE HISTORY OF ANTHONY
　BABINGTON 1799: 71
JOAN!!! A NOVEL 1796: 40
JOHN BUNCLE, JUNIOR, GENTLEMAN
　1776: 10
JOSCELINA: OR, THE REWARDS OF
　BENEVOLENCE 1797: 49
JOSEPH App. B: 8
JOSEPHINE. A NOVEL 1799: 89
JOURNEY TO LONDON 1774: 12
JULIA, A NOVEL 1790: 74
JULIA BENSON 1775: 9
JULIA DE GRAMONT 1788: 54
JULIA DE ROUBIGNÉ 1777: 13
JULIA DE SAINT PIERRE 1796: 31
JULIA STANLEY 1780: 7
JULIANA. A NOVEL 1786: 28
JULIANA ORMESTON 1793: 22
JULIET GRENVILLE 1774: 24
JULIET; OR THE COTTAGER 1788: 20
JULIUS; OR, THE NATURAL SON 1789: 51
JUVENILE INDISCRETIONS 1786: 16

KENTISH CURATE 1786: 32
KINSMAN OF MAHOMET 1774: 27
KNIGHT OF THE ROSE 1793: 34
KNIGHTS OF THE SWAN 1796: 41
KNIGHTS; OR SKETCHES OF THE HEROIC
　AGE 1797: 14

LABYRINTHS OF LIFE 1791: 70
LADY ALMIRA GRANTHAM 1792: 19
LADY JANE GREY 1791: 17
LADY'S TALE 1786: 7
LAKE OF WINDERMERE 1791: 69
LANE'S ANNUAL NOVELIST 1786: 8
LAUGHABLE ADVENTURES OF CHARLES
　AND LISETTE 1796: 10
LAUNCH. A NOVEL 1796: 11
LAURA; A NOVEL 1791: 46
LAURA AND AUGUSTUS 1784: 13
LAURA: OR LETTERS FROM SOME PERSONS
　IN SWITZERLAND 1788: 49
LAURA; OR, ORIGINAL LETTERS 1790: 15
LAURA; OR THE INFLUENCE OF A KISS
　1796: 66
LAURA, OR THE ORPHAN 1797: 30
LAURA; OR, THE VICISSITUDES OF FOR-
　TUNE 1796: 12
LAURA VALMONT 1791: 18
LAURENTIA. A NOVEL 1790: 65
LEARNING AT A LOSS 1778: 16
LEGACY. A NOVEL 1798: 20
LEON A SPARTAN STORY 1791: 66

LESSON FOR LOVERS 1783: 5
LESSONS FROM LIFE 1799: 22
LETTERS BETWEEN AN ENGLISH LADY
AND HER FRIEND AT PARIS 1770: 10
LETTERS BETWEEN AN ILLUSTRIOUS
PERSONAGE AND A LADY OF HONOUR
1785: 10
LETTERS BETWEEN CLARA AND ANTONIA
1780: 8
LETTERS BETWEEN TWO LOVERS, AND
THEIR FRIENDS 1781: 15
LETTERS FROM A FRENCH NOBLEMAN TO
MADEMOISELLE DE P— 1793: 6
LETTERS FROM CLARA 1771: 23
LETTERS FROM ELIZA TO YORICK App. B: 3
LETTERS FROM ELIZABETH SOPHIA DE
VALIERE 1772: 37
LETTERS FROM HENRIETTA TO MORVINA
1777: 6
LETTERS FROM LORD RIVERS TO SIR
CHARLES CARDIGAN 1778: 14
LETTERS FROM THE DUCHESS DE CRUI
AND OTHERS 1776: 12
LETTERS FROM THE MARCHIONESS OF
POMPADOUR App. B: 1
LETTERS MORAL AND ENTERTAINING
1780: 13
LETTERS OF AN ITALIAN NUN 1781: 16
LETTERS OF CHARLOTTE 1786: 26
LETTERS OF MADAME DU MONTIER (1797)
see p. 720
LETTERS OF MARIA 1790: 68
LETTERS OF THE MARCHIONESS OF
POMPADOUR App. B: 1
LETTERS TO AND FROM THE COUNTESS
DU BARRY 1779: 16
LETTERS TO ELEONORA 1771: 43
LETTERS TO HONORIA AND MARIANNE
1784: 24
LETTERS WRITTEN FROM LAUSANNE
1799: 28
LIBERAL AMERICAN 1785: 11
LIBERAL OPINIONS 1775: 30
LIBERTINE. A NOVEL 1791: 29
LIBERTINE HUSBAND RECLAIMED 1774: 13
LIBERTINES: A NOVEL 1798: 11
LIDORA; AN ANCIENT CHRONICLE 1791: 38
LIFE, ADVENTURES AND AMOURS OF
SIR R P 1770: 11
LIFE, ADVENTURES, AND HISTORY OF MISS
MORETON 1791: 19
LIFE AND ADVENTURES OF ANTHONY
LEGER, ESQ; 1789: 14
LIFE AND ADVENTURES OF THE
CHEVALIER DE FAUBLAS 1793: 27
LIFE AND ADVENTURES OF THE PRINCE OF
SALERMO 1770: 27

LIFE AND EXTRAORDINARY ADVENTURES,
THE PERILS AND CRITICAL ESCAPES OF
TIMOTHY GINNADRAKE 1770: 29
LIFE AND OPINIONS OF SEBALDUS
NOTHANKER 1798: 50
LIFE OF LAMENTHER 1771: 57
LIFE OF MISS CATLANE 1788: 21
LIFE OF MRS JUSTMAN 1782: 16
LIFE; OR, THE ADVENTURES OF WILLIAM
RAMBLE, ESQ. 1793: 43
LINDOR AND ADELAÏDE 1791: 65
LINDOR; OR, EARLY ENGAGEMENTS
1798: 63
LITERARY AMUSEMENTS; OR, EVENING
ENTERTAINER 1781: 10
LITTLE EMIGRANT 1799: 72
LITTLE FAMILY App. A: 10
LLEWELLIN: A TALE 1798: 51
LOCKET; OR, THE HISTORY OF
MR. SINGLETON 1774: 14
LORD FITZHENRY: A NOVEL 1794: 25
LORD WALFORD. A NOVEL 1789: 50
LORD WINWORTH 1787: 16
LOTTERY, OR MIDSUMMER RECESS
1797: 15
LOUIS AND NINA 1789: 43
LOUIS DE BONCOEUR 1796: 62
LOUISA. A NOVEL 1790: 49
LOUISA: A SENTIMENTAL NOVEL
1771: 24
LOUISA FORRESTER 1789: 15
LOUISA MATHEWS 1793: 7
LOUISA; OR, THE COTTAGE ON THE MOOR
1787: 38
LOUISA; OR, THE REWARD OF AN AFFEC-
TIONATE DAUGHTER 1790: 16
LOUISA WHARTON 1780: 9
LOVE AND MADNESS 1780: 14
LOVE AT FIRST SIGHT 1797: 42
LOVE AT FIRST SIGHT: OR THE HISTORY OF
MISS CAROLINE STANHOPE 1773: 11
LOVE FRAGMENTS 1782: 19
LOVE IN A COTTAGE 1785: 47
LOVE IN A NUNNERY 1772: 15
LOVERS: OR THE MEMOIRS OF LADY MARY
SC—— 1772: 40
LOVES OF CALISTO AND EMIRA; OR, THE
FATAL LEGACY 1776: 16
LOVES OF CAMARUPA AND CAMALATA
1793: 18
LOVE'S PILGRIMAGE 1796: 13
LOYOLA. A NOVEL 1784: 3
LUCIFER AND MAMMON 1793: 30
LUCILLA: OR THE PROGRESS OF VIRTUE
1770: 34
LUCINDA HARTLEY 1790: 17
LUCINDA OSBORN 1787: 17

LUCINDA; OR, THE SELF-DEVOTED
   DAUGHTER 1781: 20
LUCRETIA; OR, VIRTUE THE BEST DOWRY
   1790: 18
LUCY: A NOVEL 1794: 42
LUMLEY-HOUSE: A NOVEL 1787: 18

MAD MAN OF THE MOUNTAIN 1799: 88
MADELINE; OR, THE CASTLE OF MONT-
   GOMERY 1794: 35
MAGDALEN (1783) see p. 318
MAGNANIMOUS AMAZON 1796: 14
MAID OF KENT 1790: 19
MAID OF QUALITY 1770: 12
MAID OF THE FARM 1784: 10
MAID OF THE HAMLET 1794: 38
MAIDEN AUNT 1776: 4
MAJOR PIPER 1793: 40
MALE COQUET. A NOVEL 1788: 76
MALE-COQUETTE; OR, THE HISTORY OF
   THE HON. EDWARD ASTELL 1770: 13
MAMMUTH; OR, HUMAN NATURE
   DISPLAYED 1789: 69
MAN AS HE IS 1792: 29
MAN IN THE MOON 1783: 22
MAN OF BENEVOLENCE 1789: 16
MAN OF EXPERIENCE 1778: 15
MAN OF FAILING 1789: 17
MAN OF FEELING 1771: 46
MAN OF HONOUR 1771: 60
MAN OF NATURE 1773: 35
MAN OF NATURE OR NATURE AND LOVE
   1799: 62
MAN OF THE WORLD 1773: 36
MANFREDI, BARON ST. OSMUND 1796: 60
MANON LESCAUT (1786) see p. 387
MANSION HOUSE 1796: 23
MAPLE VALE 1791: 20
MARCHMONT: A NOVEL 1796: 82
MARCUS FLAMINIUS 1792: 42
MARGARITA. A NOVEL 1799: 83
MARIA: A NOVEL 1785: 23
MARIA CECILIA 1788: 61
MARIA HARCOURT 1788: 22
MARIA, OR THE GENEROUS RUSTIC
   1784: 12
MARIA; OR, THE OBSEQUIES OF AN
   UNFAITHFUL WIFE 1785: 12
MARIA; OR, THE VICARAGE 1796: 83
MARIAMNE: OR, IRISH ANECDOTES 1793: 8
MARRIAGE: OR, HISTORY OF FOUR WELL-
   KNOWN CHARACTERS 1771: 47
MARRIED LIBERTINE 1775: 10
MARRIED VICTIM 1772: 16
MARY, A FICTION 1788: 78
MARY DE-CLIFFORD 1792: 31
MARY; OR, THE USES OF ADVERSITY 1796: 33

MASQUED WEDDINGS 1781: 18
MASQUERADES; OR, WHAT YOU WILL
   1780: 10
MATILDA AND ELIZABETH 1796: 75
MATILDA FITZ-AUBIN, A SKETCH 1792: 20
MATILDA: OR, THE EFFORTS OF VIRTUE
   1785: 13
MAURICE, A GERMAN TALE 1796: 79
MAXIMS OF GALLANTRY 1793: 15
MEDALLION 1794: 44
MELASINA; OR THE FORCE OF PASSION
   1793: 9
MELBOURNE. A NOVEL 1798: 47
MELISSA AND MARCIA; OR THE SISTERS
   1788: 58
MELWIN DALE, A NOVEL 1786: 9
MEMOIRS AND ADVENTURES OF A FLEA
   1785: 14
MEMOIRS AND OPINIONS OF MR
   BLENFIELD 1790: 20
MEMOIRS OF A BARONESS 1792: 56
MEMOIRS OF A CLERGYMAN 1774: 15
MEMOIRS OF A DEMI-REP OF FASHION
   1775: 11
MEMOIRS OF A GENTLEMAN 1774: 34
MEMOIRS OF A PYTHAGOREAN 1785: 44
MEMOIRS OF A SCOTS HEIRESS 1791: 50
MEMOIRS OF AN AMERICAN 1773: 30
MEMOIRS OF AN HERMAPHRODITE
   1772: 41
MEMOIRS OF AN UNFORTUNATE LADY OF
   QUALITY 1774: 16
MEMOIRS OF ANTONINA, QUEEN OF ABO
   1791: 40
MEMOIRS OF COLONEL DIGBY AND MISS
   STANLEY 1773: 33
MEMOIRS OF EMMA COURTNEY 1796: 50
MEMOIRS OF FRANCIS DILLON, ESQ;
   1772: 17
MEMOIRS OF JULIA DE M***** 1791: 62
MEMOIRS OF LADY ELIZA AUDLEY (1779)
   see p. 277
MEMOIRS OF LADY WOODFORD 1771: 25
MEMOIRS OF MADAME DE BARNEVELDT
   1795: 19
MEMOIRS OF MAITRE JACQUES, OF SAVOY
   1775: 12, 1783: 6
MEMOIRS OF MARIA, A PERSIAN SLAVE
   1790: 21
MEMOIRS OF MARY 1793: 19
MEMOIRS OF MISS ARABELLA BOLTON
   1770: 14
MEMOIRS OF MISS SOPHY STERNHEIM
   1776: 13B
MEMOIRS OF MISS WILLIAMS 1771: 26
MEMOIRS OF MR. WILSON 1771: 27
MEMOIRS OF PLANETES 1795: 33

MEMOIRS OF SIR ROGER DE CLARENDON 1793: 37

MEMOIRS OF THE ANCIENT HOUSE OF CLARENDON 1796: 15

MEMOIRS OF THE CELEBRATED MISS ANN C—Y 1773: 12

MEMOIRS OF THE COUNT OF COMMINGE 1775: 31

MEMOIRS OF THE COUNTESS D'ANOIS 1778: 13

MEMOIRS OF THE DANBY FAMILY 1799: 11

MEMOIRS OF THE MANSTEIN FAMILY 1783: 11

MEMOIRS OF THE MARCHIONESS DE LOUVOI 1777: 12

MEMOIRS OF THE MARQUIS DE ST. FORLAIX 1770: 30

MEMOIRS OF THE MARQUIS DE VILLEBON 1796: 16

MEMOIRS OF THE MISS HOLMSBYS 1788: 73

MEMOIRS OF THE RIGHT HONOURABLE LORD VISCOUNT CHERINGTON 1782: 18

MEMOIRS OF THE YEAR TWO THOUSAND FIVE HUNDRED 1772: 36

MEMOIRS RELATING TO THE QUEEN OF BOHEMIA 1772: 32

MEN AND MANNERS 1799: 64

MENTAL TRIUMPH 1789: 18

MENTORIA; OR THE YOUNG LADY'S FRIEND 1791: 61

MERCENARY MARRIAGE 1773: 13

MIDNIGHT BELL 1798: 40

MILISTINA: OR, THE DOUBLE INTEREST 1797: 16

MINOR; OR HISTORY OF GEORGE O'NIAL, ESQ. 1788: 23

MINSTREL; OR, ANECDOTES OF DISTIN-GUISHED PERSONAGES 1793: 10

MIRANDA: A NOVEL 1797: 76

MISANTHROPY AND REPENTANCE 1799: 49

MISFORTUNES OF LOVE 1785: 15

MISOGUG: OR, WOMEN AS THEY ARE 1788: 50

MISPLACED CONFIDENCE 1776: 15

MISS MELMOTH 1771: 37

MISTAKES OF THE HEART 1771: 55

MODERN ANECDOTE OF THE ANCIENT FAMILY OF THE KINKVERVANKOTSDAR-SPRAKENGOTCHDERNS 1779: 9

MODERN ATALANTIS 1784: 4

MODERN COUPLE 1770: 15

MODERN FINE GENTLEMAN 1774: 17

MODERN GULLIVER'S TRAVELS 1796: 46

MODERN HERO IN THE KINGDOM OF CATHAI 1791: 33

MODERN HUSBAND 1789: 19

MODERN MINIATURE 1792: 21

MODERN NOVEL WRITING 1796: 22

MODERN SEDUCTION 1777: 11

MODERN TIMES 1785: 46

MONIMIA. A NOVEL 1791: 21

MONK: A ROMANCE 1796: 63

MONK-WOOD PRIORY 1799: 92

MONMOUTH; A TALE 1790: 55

MONTALBERT 1795: 41

MONTFORD CASTLE 1795: 7

MONTGOMERY; OR, SCENES IN WALES 1796: 73

MONTROSE, OR THE GOTHIC RUIN 1799: 12

MORAL AMUSEMENTS 1798: 12

MORAL TALES 1797: 59

MORAL TALES, AFTER THE EASTERN MANNER 1772: 39

MORAL TALES. TRANSLATED FROM THE FRENCH 1775: 26

MORE GHOSTS! 1798: 53

MORETON ABBEY 1785: 39

MORNING RAMBLE 1775: 13

MORT CASTLE 1798: 13

MORTIMORE CASTLE 1793: 21

MOTTO: OR HISTORY OF BILL WOODCOCK 1795: 14

MOUNT HENNETH 1782: 12

MOUNT PELHAM 1789: 45

MOUNTAIN COTTAGER 1798: 68

MR. BENTLEY, THE RURAL PHILOSOPHER 1775: 28

MUNSTER ABBEY 1797: 53

MUNSTER VILLAGE 1778: 12

MUTABILITY OF HUMAN LIFE 1777: 7

MUTUAL ATTACHMENT 1782: 13

MYRTLE: OR, EFFECTS OF LOVE 1784: 5

MYSTERIES ELUCIDATED 1795: 29

MYSTERIES OF UDOLPHO 1794: 47

MYSTERIOUS SEAL 1799: 75

MYSTERIOUS WARNING 1796: 71

MYSTERIOUS WIFE 1797: 56

MYSTERY OF THE BLACK TOWER 1796: 70

MYSTIC CASTLE 1796: 80

MYSTIC COTTAGER OF CHAMOUNY 1794: 13

NABOB. A NOVEL 1785: 16

NATURAL DAUGHTER 1799: 79

NATURAL SON (1799) see 1789: 51

NATURE, A NOVEL 1770: 39

NATURE AND ART 1796: 57

NEAPOLITAN; OR, THE TEST OF INTEGRITY 1796: 64

NECROMANCER: OR THE TALE OF THE BLACK FOREST 1794: 34

NEGRO EQUALLED BY FEW EUROPEANS
   1790: 53
NETLEY ABBEY 1795: 47
NEW AND COMPLETE COLLECTION OF
   INTERESTING ROMANCES 1780: 22
NEW ENTERTAINING NOVELLIST 1785: 17
NEW MODERN STORY-TELLER 1772: 18
NEW MONK, A ROMANCE 1798: 62
NEW MORAL TALES 1792: 44
NEW ROBINSON CRUSOE 1788: 47
NEW SYLPH, OR, GUARDIAN ANGEL
   1788: 24
NEW TALES 1792: 35
NEWS-PAPER WEDDING 1774: 18
NIECE; OR, THE HISTORY OF SUKEY
   THORNBY 1788: 53
NIGHT AND MOMENT 1770: 25
NOBLE ENTHUSIAST 1792: 22
NOBLE FAMILY 1771: 36
NOBLE LOVERS 1772: 19
NORMAN AND BERTHA 1790: 22
NORMAN BANDITTI 1799: 34
NORTHUMBRIAN TALE 1799: 13
NOVELLETTES MORAL AND SENTIMENTAL
   1785: 43
NOVELLETTES, SELECTED FOR THE USE OF
   YOUNG LADIES 1780: 17
NUN 1797: 36
NUN; OR, THE ADVENTURES OF THE
   MARCHIONESS OF BEAUVILLE 1771: 28
NUNNERY FOR COQUETTES 1771: 29

OBEDIENCE REWARDED 1797: 66
OBSERVANT PEDESTRIAN 1795: 8
OCTAVIA 1798: 59
OFFSPRING OF FANCY 1778: 4
OFFSPRING OF RUSSELL 1794: 54
OLD ENGLISH BARON 1777: 16
OLD FRIEND WITH A NEW FACE 1797: 62
OLD MAID 1771: 52
OLD MANOR HOUSE 1793: 39
OLIO OF GOOD BREEDING 1797: 79
OLIVIA; OR, DESERTED BRIDE 1787: 30
OMAR AND ZEMIRA 1782: 22
OMEN; OR, MEMOIRS OF SIR HENRY
   MELVILLE 1785: 30
ORIENTAL FABLES 1797: 17
ORIGINAL LOVE-LETTERS 1784: 14
ORIGINAL NOVELS, POEMS, AND ESSAYS
   1790: 67
ORIGINAL STORIES, FROM REAL LIFE
   1788: 79
ORIGINAL TALES, HISTORIES, ESSAYS AND
   TRANSLATIONS 1785: 18
ORLANDO AND LAVINIA 1792: 23
ORLANDO AND SERAPHINA 1787: 45
ORPHAN. A NOVEL 1783: 7

ORPHAN HEIRESS OF SIR GREGORY
   1799: 14
ORPHAN MARION 1790: 23
ORPHAN OF BOLLENBACH 1797: 18
ORPHAN OF THE RHINE 1798: 66
ORPHAN SISTERS 1793: 11
ORPHAN SWAINS 1774: 19
ORPHANS OF SNOWDON 1797: 41
ORWELL MANOR 1795: 34
OSWALD CASTLE 1788: 25
OTHO AND RUTHA 1780: 15
OXONIAN: OR, THE ADVENTURES OF
   MR G. EDMUNDS 1771: 30

PACKET: A NOVEL 1794: 26
PALACE OF ENCHANTMENT 1788: 26
PALACE OF SILENCE 1775: 17
PALINODE: OR, THE TRIUMPHS OF VIRTUE
   OVER LOVE 1771: 56
PALMIRA AND ERMANCE 1797: 57
PARENTAL DUPLICITY 1797: 54
PARISIAN; OR, GENUINE ANECDOTES
   1794: 18
PARSONAGE HOUSE 1780: 12
PARSON'S WIFE 1789: 20
PATHETIC HISTORY OF EGBERT AND
   LEONORA 1792: 37
PAUL AND MARY (1789) see p. 448
PAUL AND VIRGINIA (1795 and 1796) see p. 448
PAUL AND VIRGINIE 1788: 71
PAULINE, OR THE VICTIM OF THE HEART
   1794: 19
PAVILION. A NOVEL 1796: 35
PEACEFUL VILLA 1793: 12
PEASANT; OR, FEMALE PHILOSOPHER
   1792: 33
PEGGY AND PATTY 1783: 24
PENITENT FATHER 1793: 13
PENITENT PROSTITUTE 1788: 27
PERCY, OR THE FRIENDS 1797: 19
PERFIDIOUS GUARDIAN 1790: 24
PERJURED LOVER 1790: 25
PERPLEXITIES OF LOVE 1787: 19
PERPLEXITIES OF RICHES 1771: 31
PERPLEXITIES; OR, THE FORTUNATE
   ELOPEMENT 1794: 38
PERSIANA, THE NYMPH OF THE SEA 1791:
   22
PERUVIAN LETTERS 1774: 28
PHANTOMS OF THE CLOISTER 1795: 24
PHANTOMS: OR, THE ADVENTURES OF A
   GOLD-HEADED CANE 1783: 14
PHEDORA; OR, THE FOREST OF MINSKI
   1798: 22
PHILANTHROPIC RAMBLER 1790: 70
PHILARO AND ELEONORA 1792: 24
PHILOSOPHER IN BRISTOL 1775: 19

PHILOSOPHICAL QUIXOTE 1782: 9
PHOEBE; OR DISTRESSED INNOCENCE
   1788: 28
PICTURES OF LIFE 1790: 64
PICTURES OF THE HEART 1783: 18
PIECE OF FAMILY BIOGRAPHY 1799: 33
PILGRIM: OR, A PICTURE OF LIFE 1775: 25
PITY'S GIFT 1798: 60
PLACID MAN 1770: 33
PLAIN SENSE 1795: 26
PLATONIC GUARDIAN 1787: 42
PLATONIC MARRIAGE 1786: 20
PLEASING COMPANION 1788: 29
PLEASING VARIETY 1789: 21
PLEXIPPUS: OR, THE ASPIRING PLEBEIAN
   1790: 46
POLITE REPOSITORY 1791: 23
POPULAR TALES OF THE GERMANS
   1791: 53
PORTRAIT. A NOVEL 1783: 8
PORTRAIT OF LIFE 1770: 16
POSTHUMOUS DAUGHTER 1797: 20
POSTHUMOUS WORKS OF A LATE
   CELEBRATED GENIUS 1770: 32
POSTHUMOUS WORKS OF THE AUTHOR
   OF A VINDICATION 1798: 74
POWIS CASTLE 1788: 30
PRECIPITATE CHOICE 1772: 20
PREDESTINED WIFE 1789: 22
PREDICTION; OR, THE HISTORY OF MISS
   LUCY MAXWELL 1770: 17
PREPOSSESSION; OR, MEMOIRS OF COUNT
   TOULOUSSIN 1792: 25
PRINCE ARTHUR 1779: 6
PRINCE OF LEON 1794: 31
PRINCESS COQUEDOEUF AND PRINCE
   BONBON 1796: 37
PRIVATE HISTORY OF PEREGRINUS
   PROTEUS 1796: 90
PRO & CON 1771: 44
PROBABLE INCIDENTS 1797: 77
PROGRESS OF LOVE 1789: 23
PRUDENT ORPHAN 1774: 20
PRUDENTIAL LOVERS 1773: 14
PUPIL OF ADVERSITY 1788: 31
PUPIL OF NATURE (1771) see p. 170
PUPIL OF PLEASURE 1776: 14

QUAKER. A NOVEL 1785: 19

RADZIVIL. A ROMANCE 1790: 63
RAJAH KISNA 1786: 10
RAKE: OR, THE ADVENTURES OF TOM
   WILDMAN 1773: 15
RAMBLE OF PHILO 1788: 65
RAMBLES OF FANCY 1786: 35
RAMBLES OF MR FRANKLY 1772: 30, 1776: 9

RANSPACH, OR MYSTERIES OF A CASTLE
   1797: 21
RASH VOWS 1799: 40
RATTLE. A NOVEL 1787: 20
RAYNSFORD PARK 1790: 60
REASON TRIUMPHANT OVER FANCY
   1773: 39
REBECCA. A NOVEL 1799: 39
REBEL: A TALE OF THE TIMES 1799: 15
RECESS; OR, A TALE OF OTHER TIMES
   1783: 15, 1785: 37
RECLAIMED PROSTITUTE 1772: 21
RECLUSE. A FRAGMENT 1787: 37
RECLUSE OF THE APPENINES 1792: 53
RECLUSE: OR, HISTORY OF LADY
   GERTRUDE LESBY 1789: 39
RECTOR'S SON 1798: 58
REGINALD, OR THE HOUSE OF
   MIRANDOLA 1799: 66
RELAPSE, A NOVEL 1780: 16
RELAPSE: OR, MYRTLE-BANK 1789: 24
RENCONTRE: OR, TRANSITION OF A
   MOMENT 1785: 33
RESTLESS MATRON 1799: 84
RETALIATION; OR, THE HISTORY OF SIR
   EDWARD OSWALD 1787: 33
RETRIBUTION: A NOVEL 1788: 63
REUBEN AND RACHEL 1799: 80
REUBEN, OR, THE SUICIDE 1787: 21
REVERIES OF THE HEART App. B: 6
REVOLUTION. A NOVEL 1781: 11
RICH YOUNG COUNTRY 'SQUIRE
   1787: 22
RING: A NOVEL 1784: 6
RING, OR THE MERRY WIVES OF MADRID
   1799: 91
RIVAL BROTHERS 1784: 20
RIVAL FRIENDS 1776: 5
ROACH ABBEY 1796: 17
ROBERT AND ADELA 1795: 43
ROCK OF MODREC 1792: 55
ROCK; OR, ALFRED AND ANNA 1798: 16
ROMAN NIGHTS 1798: 72
ROMANCE OF REAL LIFE 1787: 49
ROMANCE OF THE CAVERN 1793: 44
ROMANCE OF THE FOREST 1791: 58
ROMANCES 1799: 31
ROMULUS, A TALE OF ANCIENT TIMES
   1799: 63
ROSA DE MONTMORIEN 1787: 40
ROSALIND DE TRACEY 1798: 71
ROSALIND. A NCVEL 1799: 90
ROSARA; OR, THE ADVENTURES OF AN
   ACTRESS 1771: 39
ROSE CECIL 1797: 31
ROSELLA, OR MODERN OCCURRENCES
   1799: 27

ROSE-MOUNT CASTLE; OR, FALSE REPORT 1798: 75
ROSENBERG: A LEGENDARY TALE 1789: 46
ROSINA: A NOVEL 1793: 35
ROYAL ADVENTURERS 1773: 16
ROYAL CAPTIVES 1795: 50
RUINS OF AVONDALE PRIORY 1796: 58

SADASKI; OR, THE WANDERING PENITENT 1798: 17
ST ALMA, A NOVEL 1791: 39
ST BERNARD'S PRIORY 1786: 25
SAINT JULIAN'S ABBEY 1788: 32
SAINT JULIEN; OR, MEMOIRS OF A FATHER 1798: 37
ST LEON 1799: 42
ST RUTHIN'S ABBEY 1784: 7
SALLIES OF GENIUS 1770: 18
SAMIANS; A TALE 1771: 32
SANTA-MARIA 1797: 39
SCHOOL CANDIDATES 1788: 48
SCHOOL FOR DAUGHTERS 1775: 14
SCHOOL FOR FATHERS 1788: 33
SCHOOL FOR HUSBANDS 1774: 21
SCHOOL FOR MAJESTY 1780: 11
SCHOOL FOR TUTORS 1788: 34
SCHOOL FOR WIDOWS 1791: 59
SCHOOL OF VIRTUE 1787: 23
SCOTCH PARENTS 1773: 27
SCOTCHMAN: OR, THE WORLD AS IT GOES 1770: 39
SECLUDED MAN 1798: 29
SECRESY; OR, THE RUIN ON THE ROCK 1795: 20
SEDUCTION, OR THE HISTORY OF LADY REVEL 1787: 24
SELECT COLLECTION OF ORIENTAL TALES 1776: 6
SELECT FABLES FROM GULISTAN 1773: 37
SELECT FAIRY TALES 1796: 91
SELF-DECEIVED: OR, THE HISTORY OF LORD BYRON 1773: 17
SELF-TORMENTOR, A NOVEL 1789: 25
SELIMA, OR THE VILLAGE TALE 1794: 30
SEMPRONIA 1790: 26
SENTIMENTAL CONNOISSEUR 1778: 5
SENTIMENTAL DECEIVER 1784: 8
SENTIMENTAL DIARY App. B: 4
SENTIMENTAL EXCURSIONS TO WINDSOR App. B: 7
SENTIMENTAL EXHIBITION 1774: 31
SENTIMENTAL JOURNEY App. B: 12
SENTIMENTAL LOVE ILLUSTRATED 1789: 48
SENTIMENTAL LUCUBRATIONS 1770: 40
SENTIMENTAL MEMOIRS 1785: 20
SENTIMENTAL SPY 1773: 18

SENTIMENTAL TALES 1771: 51
SENTIMENTAL TRAVELLER (1780?) see 1778: 8
SEQUEL TO THE PHILANTHROPIC RAMBLER 1791: 71
SERIES OF GENUINE LETTERS, BETWEEN HENRY AND FRANCES 1770: 31
SEYMOUR CASTLE 1789: 26
SHENSTONE-GREEN 1779: 17
SHEPHERDESS OF ARANVILLE 1794: 37
SHIPWRECK AND ADVENTURES OF MONSIEUR PIERRE VIAUD App. B: 2
SHRINE OF BERTHA 1794: 50
SHROVE-TIDE CHILD 1797: 64
SIAMESE TALES 1796: 18
SIBERIAN ANECDOTES 1783: 12
SICILIAN ROMANCE 1790: 61
SICILIAN. A NOVEL 1798: 48
SIDNEY CASTLE 1792: 26
SIEGE OF AUBIGNY 1782: 21
SIEGE OF BELGRADE 1791: 24
SIGEVART, A TALE 1799: 69
SIGISMAR 1799: 96
SIMPLE FACTS 1793: 28
SIMPLE STORY 1791: 41
SKETCH OF THE TIMES 1781: 12
SKETCHES FROM NATURE 1779: 12
SKETCHES FROM NATURE; OR, THE HISTORY OF HENRY AND EMMA 1778: 6
SKETCHES OF MODERN LIFE 1799: 98
SLAVE OF PASSION 1790: 27
SLAVERY: OR, THE TIMES 1792: 43
SOCRATES OUT OF HIS SENSES 1771: 58
SOLEMN INJUNCTION 1798: 49
SOLICITUDES OF ABSENCE 1788: 69
SOLITARY CASTLE 1789: 57
SOLYMAN AND FATIMA 1791: 73
SOMERSET; OR, THE DANGERS OF GREATNESS 1792: 27
SOMERVILLE BOWER 1791: 25
SON OF ETHELWOLF 1789: 40
SOPHIA; OR, THE EMBARRASSED WIFE 1788: 35
SORCERER: A TALE 1795: 45
SORROWS OF EDITH 1796: 25
SORROWS OF MATILDA 1798: 14
SORROWS OF THE HEART 1787: 39
SORROWS OF WERTER 1779: 10
SOURICIERE. THE MOUSE-TRAP App. B: 13
SPANISH MEMOIRS 1787: 29
SPECTRE 1789: 61
SPIRIT OF THE ELBE 1799: 16
SPIRITUAL QUIXOTE 1773: 34
SPOILED CHILD 1797: 46
SPOILED CHILD; OR, INDULGENCE COUNTERACTED 1799: 74
SPRITE OF THE NUNNERY 1796: 86

STATIRA: OR, THE MOTHER 1798: 64
STATUE ROOM 1790: 37
STELLA. A PASTORAL ROMANCE 1791: 36
STELLINS; OR, THE NEW WERTER 1793: 14
STEP-MOTHER: A DOMESTIC TALE 1798: 73
STORM; OR, THE HISTORY OF NANCY AND
  LUCY 1772: 22
STORY OF AL RAOUI (1799) *see* p. 772
STORY OF DOOSHWANTA AND SAKOON-
  TAL 1795: 48
STORY OF LADY JULIANA HARLEY 1776: 11
STORY OF THE METHODIST-LADY 1770: 19
STRANGER; OR, LLEWELLYN FAMILY
  1798: 26
SUBMISSIONS OF DEPENDENCE 1797: 22
SUBTERRANEAN CAVERN 1798: 55
SUCH FOLLIES ARE 1795: 9
SUFFERINGS OF THE FAMILY OF ORTEN-
  BERG 1799: 60
SURRY COTTAGE 1779: 15
SUSANNA; OR, TRAITS OF A MODERN MISS
  1795: 15
SUSPICIOUS LOVERS 1777: 8
SUTTON-ABBEY 1779: 4
SUZETTE'S DOWRY 1799: 37
SWORD; OR, FATHER BERTRAND'S HIS-
  TORY 1791: 34
SYDNEY AND EUGENIA 1790: 28
SYDNEY PLACE 1788: 36
SYDNEY ST. AUBYN 1794: 49
SYLPH; A NOVEL 1779: 8

TALE OF ROSAMUND GRAY 1798: 38
TALE OF THE TIMES 1799: 95
TALES: ENTERTAINING AND SYMPA-
  THETIC 1788: 37
TALES OF A PARROT 1792: 58
TALES OF AN EVENING 1792: 44
TALES OF ELAM 1794: 14
TALES OF IMAGINATION 1790: 29
TALES OF INSTRUCTION AND AMUSE-
  MENT App. A: 8
TALES OF THE CASTLE 1785: 29
TALES OF THE COTTAGE 1798: 56
TALES OF THE HERMITAGE 1798: 57
TALES OF THE TWELFTH AND THIR-
  TEENTH CENTURIES 1786: 31
TALES, ROMANCES, APOLOGUES,
  ANECDOTES, AND NOVELS 1786: 11
TALES. TRANSLATED FROM THE FRENCH
  1792: 44
TANCRED. A TALE OF ANCIENT TIMES
  1791: 37
TAUREAU BLANC 1774: 33A
TEARS OF SENSIBILITY 1773: 24
TENDER FATHER 1775: 15
TERENTIA; A NOVEL 1791: 42

TEST OF FILIAL DUTY 1772: 38
TEST OF HONOUR 1789: 65
THEMIDORE. A NOVEL 1783: 10
THEODORA 1770: 28
THEODORE, A DOMESTIC TALE 1792: 54
THEODORE CYPHON 1796: 88
THEODOSIUS AND ARABELLA 1786: 37
THEOPHA; OR, MEMOIRS OF A GREEK
  SLAVE 1798: 25
THINGS AS THEY ARE 1794: 23
THOUGHTLESS WARD 1777: 10
TOUR OF VALENTINE 1786: 36
TOUR, SENTIMENTAL AND DESCRIPTIVE
  App. B: 10
TOWER; OR THE ROMANCE OF RUTHYNE
  1798: 39
TRADITIONS, A LEGENDARY TALE 1795: 40
TRANSLATION OF THE LETTERS OF A
  HINDOO RAJAH 1796: 49
TRAVELS BEFORE THE FLOOD 1796: 59
TRAVELS FOR THE HEART 1777: 15
TRAVELS OF HILDEBRAND BOWMAN,
  ESQUIRE 1778: 7
TRIAL: OR THE HISTORY OF CHARLES
  HORTON ESQ. 1772: 23
TRIFLER: OR, A RAMBLE AMONG THE
  WILDS OF FANCY 1775: 29
TRINKET. A NOVEL 1774: 22
TRIP TO MELASGE 1778: 8
TRIP TO WEYMOUTH 1790: 30
TRIUMPH OF BENEVOLENCE 1772: 24
TRIUMPH OF FRIENDSHIP 1789: 70
TRIUMPH OF PRUDENCE OVER PASSION
  1781: 13
TRIUMPH OF TRUTH 1775: 27
TRIUMPHS OF CONSTANCY 1790: 31
TRIUMPHS OF FORTITUDE 1789: 27
TRUE NARRATIVE OF AN UNFORTUNATE
  ELOPEMENT 1770: 35
TURKISH TALES 1794: 39
TUTOR OF TRUTH 1779: 18
TUTOR; OR, THE HISTORY OF GEORGE
  WILSON 1771: 42
'TWAS RIGHT TO MARRY HIM 1774: 23
'TWAS WRONG TO MARRY HIM 1773: 19
TWIN SISTERS 1788: 38
TWO COUSINS 1794: 45
TWO MENTORS 1783: 19
TYRANNY OF LOVE 1789: 28

ULRIC AND ILVINA 1797: 23
UNDUTIFUL DAUGHTER 1771: 33
UNEQUAL ALLIANCE 1772: 25
UNFASHIONABLE WIFE 1772: 26
UNFORTUNATE ATTACHMENT 1795: 11
UNFORTUNATE CALEDONIAN IN
  ENGLAND 1781: 14

UNFORTUNATE LOVERS 1788: 80
UNFORTUNATE SENSIBILITY 1784: 9
UNFORTUNATE UNION 1778: 9
UNGUARDED MOMENT 1771: 34
UNHAPPY WIFE, A SERIES OF LETTERS 1770: 20
USONG. AN EASTERN NARRATIVE 1772: 33

VAGABOND, A NOVEL 1799: 94
VALE OF FELICITY 1791: 26
VALE OF GLENDOR 1785: 27
VALE OF IRVIN 1788: 41
VALENTINE. A NOVEL 1790: 32
VALLEY OF ST GOTHARD 1799: 70
VANCENZA; OR, THE DANGERS OF CREDULITY 1792: 50
VATHEK 1786: 15
VAURIEN: OR, SKETCHES OF THE TIMES 1797: 37
VERONICA; OR, THE MYSTERIOUS STRANGER 1798: 41
VICAR OF BRAY 1771: 35
VICAR OF LANSDOWNE 1789: 64
VICISSITUDES IN GENTEEL LIFE 1794: 36
VICISSITUDES OF FORTUNE 1773: 20
VICTIM OF A VOW 1790: 33
VICTIM OF DECEPTION 1788: 39
VICTIM OF FANCY 1787: 51
VICTIM OF MAGICAL DELUSION 1795: 44
VICTIM OF PASSION 1794: 48
VICTIM OF PREJUDICE 1799: 46
VICTORIA. A NOVEL 1786: 39
VICTORINA, A NOVEL 1790: 45
VILLAGE CURATE, AND HIS DAUGHTER JULIA, see 1795: 49
VILLAGE LOVERS 1792: 28
VILLAGE MEMOIRS 1775: 22
VILLAGE OF MARTINDALE 1787: 46
VILLAGE ORPHAN 1799: 17
VILLEROY; OR, THE FATAL MOMENT 1790: 73
VIOLET HILL 1791: 51
VIRTUE IN DISTRESS 1772: 27
VIRTUOUS VILLAGERS 1784: 22
VISIT FOR A WEEK 1794: 43
VIZIRS: OR, THE ENCHANTED LABYRINTH 1774: 26
VOLUNTARY EXILE 1795: 35
VOYAGES AND ADVENTURES OF THE CHEVALIER DUPONT 1772: 28

WAITING MAID 1775: 16
WALDECK ABBEY 1795: 10
WALDORF; OR, THE DANGERS OF PHILOS-OPHY 1798: 34
WALSH COLVILLE 1797: 67

WALSINGHAM; OR, THE PUPIL OF NATURE 1797: 71
WANDERER OF THE ALPS 1796: 81
WANDERING ISLANDER 1792: 57
WANDERINGS OF THE IMAGINATION 1796: 43
WANDERINGS OF WARWICK 1794: 53
WANLEY PENSON 1791: 63
WARBECK: A PATHETIC TALE 1786: 14
WAREHAM PRIORY 1799: 18
WAY TO LOSE HIM 1773: 21
WAY TO PLEASE HIM 1773: 22
WEDDING RING 1779: 5
WEEK AT A COTTAGE 1775: 24
WEIRD SISTERS 1794: 15
WELSH STORY 1798: 15
WEST INDIAN 1787: 25
WESTBROOK VILLAGE 1799: 19
WHIM; OR, THE MUTUAL IMPRESSION 1790: 34
WHITE BULL, AN ORIENTAL HISTORY 1774: 33B
WIDOW OF KENT 1788: 40
WIDOW, OR A PICTURE OF MODERN TIMES 1794: 51
WILLIAM AND CHARLES 1789: 29
WILLIAM OF NORMANDY 1787: 26
WILLIAM SEDLEY App. A: 2
WILLIAM THORNBOROUGH 1791: 57
WILLIAM WALLACE 1791: 67
WILMOT; OR THE PUPIL OF FOLLY 1782: 10
WINTER'S TALE 1799: 25
WITCH, AND THE MAID OF HONOUR 1799: 20
WOMAN AS SHE SHOULD BE 1793: 33
WOMAN OF LETTERS 1783: 21
WOMAN OF QUALITY 1786: 12
WOMEN AS THEY ARE 1796: 72
WONDERFUL TRAVELS OF PRINCE FAN-FEREDIN 1789: 34
WOODBURY: OR THE MEMOIRS OF WILLIAM MARCHMONT, ESQ. 1773: 23
WOODLAND COTTAGE 1796: 19
WOODLEY PARK 1791: 27
WREATH OF FRIENDSHIP 1790: 35
WRONGS OF WOMAN 1798: 74

YOUNG EXILES 1799: 41
YOUNG GRANDISON 1790: 40
YOUNG HOCUS 1790: 51
YOUNG JAMES 1776: 17
YOUNG LADY OF FORTUNE 1789: 30
YOUNG PHILOSOPHER: A NOVEL 1798: 67
YOUNG PHILOSOPHER, OR THE NATURAL SON 1782: 11

YOUNG WIDOW; OR, THE HISTORY OF
   CORNELIA SEDLEY 1789: 44
YOUNG WIDOW; OR, THE HISTORY OF MRS
   LEDWICH 1785: 21
YOUNGER BROTHER 1770: 21
YOUNGER BROTHER: A NOVEL 1793: 16

YOUNGER SISTER 1770: 26

ZELIA IN THE DESERT 1789: 38A
ZELIE IN THE DESERT 1789: 38B
ZELUCO 1789: 54
ZORIADA: OR, VILLAGE ANNALS 1786: 24

Index of Booksellers and Printers

All indexed names are alphabetically ordered under the town of publication. In many cases, full names are supplied rather than the shortened form in the imprint. Names without symbols were listed as booksellers ('printed for' or 'sold by' etc.); exceptions, including particular entry numbers, are indicated as follows:

†   Both printer and bookseller
(†)   Printer only

It is essential to note that imprint inclusions and descriptions, which largely determine this index, can be no certain indication of the bookselling and printing partnerships responsible for the particular novels listed. To note only two of many cautions, some partners, associates, and financial contributors were not included in the imprint, and many of those listed simply as booksellers were also the printers of the book at their own premises.

Where symbols precede the entry number they relate only to that particular item. Where the symbols are placed after the indexed name they relate to all following entries; further symbols against particular entry numbers indicate further exceptions (e.g. (†) showing that the bookseller was given only as the printer in this particular case). In a few lists of entry numbers for a printer (†), †† precedes an entry number where the printer was, in this specific case, simply listed as bookseller only.

(?†) indicates, usually in the case of Irish booksellers, that the imprint 'printed by' probably means 'printed for'.

* indicates printed for or by the author or 'proprietor' *but* this does not include many arrangements hidden from title-page wording.

Item numbers in italics refer to imprint information in the notes.

Names in italics are predecessor printers or booksellers, mentioned either in the imprint or as a significant reference in the notes.

Indexed names include all those listed in imprints and advertisements and notices recorded in the entries, but printers and bookseller of Irish *further editions* include (from the notes section of the entries) only names recorded by ESTC; where ESTC abbreviates the list of names with a reference such as 'and 6 others in Dublin' the omissions have not been added. Obvious misprints in ESTC of Irish booksellers' names have been corrected against the originals; in at least one case a false name is also suspected.[1]

BATH
Bally, W. 1770: *29
Bull, Lewis 1791: *32*; *see also* Hazard and Bull
Cruttwell, Richard (†) 1770: *29; 1771: *50;
    1785: *32*; 1787: 44; 1797: 72; 1799: 28, *71;
    App. A: 10
Frederick, William 1770: *29
Hazard
Hazard, Samuel 1775: (†)12; 1789: *†31;
    1792: (†)19; 1793: 34; 1795: †11; 1797: (†)8;
    1798: (†)12
Hazard and Bull 1791: 33
Leake, Henry 1770: *29
Marshall, John 1787: 44
Meyler, W. 1790: *32*
Mills 1791: *32*
Pratt and Clinch 1780: *20, 23
Taylor, William 1770: *29

Tennent, A. 1770: *29

BELFAST
Blow, Daniel (†) App. A: 1, 3
Magee, William (†) App. A: 5
BERWICK
Taylor, R. 1776: 6

BIRMINGHAM
Pearson 1798: *38*
Piercy, E.(†) 1791: 49
Swinney, Myles 1791: 48

BRENTFORD
Norbury, Philip (†) 1799: 70

BRIGHTON [BRIGHTHELMSTONE]
Bowen, Joseph 1782: 11

[1] We are extremely grateful to Mary Pollard, Marsh's Library, Dublin, for her advice here.

BRISTOL
Bulgin and Rosser (†) 1798: 42
Cottle, Joseph 1798: 42
Routh, George(†) (*) 1775: 19
Shiercliff, Edward 1789: *31

CAMBRIDGE
Watson, W. (†) 1798: 11

CARLISLE
Jollie, Francis 1792: 41

CHELMSFORD
Gray and Frost 1777: 16
Staines, R. C. 1799: 35

CHELSEA
Jacques, Dennett (†) 1799: 69
Polidori, G. 1799: 69

CHESTER
Broster, Peter 1794: *30

CHIPPENHAM
Forty, W. 1785: *12

COLCHESTER
Keymer, William † 1777: *16

CORK
Connor, John (†) 1794: 6; 1795: 31, 32; 1796: 32,
    51, 78; 1797: 11, 68; 1798: 11, 33, 68
Haly, James (†) 1790: 66; 1793: 29; 1796: 78;
    1797: 43; 1798: 33
Harris, Michael (†) 1796: 78; 1798: 33
Trant, James (†) 1788: *41

COVENTRY
Luckman, Thomas 1791: 48

DUBLIN
Archer, John 1788: 59, 60
Armitage, Thomas 1775: 27
Barlow, John (†) 1795: 3
Bates, Thomas Morton (†) 1791: 61
Beatty, John 1775: 21, 29; 1776: 13B; 1781: 10,
    18; 1782: 2, 10, 12, 18; 1783: 13, 15, 16, 17, 18;
    1784: 5; 1785: 33; 1786: 16
Bonham, George (†) 1781: 18; 1782: 11
Boyce, John 1795: 3; 1796: 69; App. B: 11
Bradley, Hulton 1770: 12
Brown[e], Charles 1786: 23; 1793: 23; 1795: 26;
    1796: (†)77; 1797: 10; 1797: 71; 1798: 71
Burnett [Burnet], George 1775: 29; 1780: 23;
    1781: 18; 1783: 11; 1784: 6, 13; 1785: 31, 37;
    1786: 30, 33; 1787: 38; 1788: 25; 1789: 31, 37;
    1792: 36; 1793: 39; 1796: 26; 1797: 58; 1798: 71;
    1799: 42, 45, 60, 64, 77, 79, 81, 94; App. A: 12

Burns, W. [?pseud] 1799: 27
Burnside, Thomas (†) 1792: 55; 1793: 2; 1794:
    26; 1795: 3; 1799: 77; App. A: ††12
Burton, Robert 1781: 10, 21; 1782: 2, 8, 10, 12,
    18; 1783: 13, 15, 16, 17, 18; 1784: 13, 18; 1785:
    21, 29; 1786: 20, 30, 33; 1787: 12, 49
Byrn, James 1777: (†)13, 18
Byrn, James and Richard (†) 1780: 3, 20; 1782: 8
Byrne, Patrick 1781: 1, 21; 1782: 15; 1783: 17, 18,
    24; 1784: 18; 1785: 31, 32, 35; 1786: 4, 20,
    (†)21, 23, 24, 33, (†)38; 1787: 2, 12, 15, 17, 28,
    32, 41, 42, (†)43, 49; 1788: 17, 22, 25, 33, (†)43,
    44, 46, 51, 59, 60, 63, 64, 67, 70, 71, 74; 1789: 6,
    7, 11, 31, 36, 37, 38A, 39, 40, 44, 55, 58, 60, 71;
    1790: 35, 39, 49, 50, 53, 54, 59, 71, 74; 1791: 7,
    26, 35, 41, 42, 47, 50, 53, 54, 58, 59, 66, 68, 73;
    1792: 17, 18, 20, 26, 29, 32, 34, 35, 36, 38, 41,
    43, 44, 45, 48, 49, 50, 52, 53, 55, 56; 1793: 2,
    (†)8, 19, 22, 24, 35, 39, 40; 1794: 13, 25, 26, 41,
    48, 51, 52, 53; 1795: 2, 3, 17, 18, (?†)19, 21, 22,
    34, 35, 38, 41, 43, 44, 46, 50; 1796: 21, 26, 41,
    47, 57, 63, 69, 75, 76, 82; 1797: 58, 61; 1799: 42,
    82; App. A: (†)1, (†)3, 8; App. B: 11
Cash, John 1778: 11; 1780: 17; 1783: 15; 1784:
    17, 18; 1785: 24, 32, 35; 1786: 2, 4, 5, 24, 33
Chamberlaine, Dillon (d. 1780) 1770: *(†) 1, 3,
    23,*(†)24, 30, 32, 33; 1771: 40, 45, 46; 1772: 24,
    30, 35, 38; 1773: 34, 36; 1774: 21; 1775: (†)20,
    26; 1776: 1, 2, 10, 17; 1777: 7, 17; 1778: 3; and
    with post-mortem designation, as printed by
    his widow, Hannah (see also below) 1786: 26;
    1787: 32; 1788: 33, 51; App. B: 1
Chamberlaine, Hannah 1786: *18; 1789: 55, 68;
    App. B: 11
Chamberlaine, Hannah, and Rice, John 1790:
    39, 74
Chambers, John 1796: 4; 1797: (†)3
Codd, Thomas 1798: 27
Colbert, Harriet 1787: 42; 1788: 38, 54; 1789:
    (†)26, 31, 38A, 40, 44, (†)67; 1790: 39, 54, 74;
    1791: 7, 28, 59; 1792: 52; 1793: 19, 39; 1794: 13,
    26, 29, 47, 53; 1795: 17, (?†)19; 1796: 41, 49,
    (†)75, (†)77; 1797: 45, 58, 71; 1798: 61, 67, 70;
    1799: 15, (†)21A, 45, 58, 64
Colbert, Stephen (d. 1786) 1773: †1, (†)28;
    1776: (†)5; 1778: (†)14; 1780: †5, *†11, †12,
    (†)16, (†)21; 1781: *(†)13; 1784: (†)11, 17;
    1786: 5, (†)14; and post-mortem as 'Messr(s)'
    1787: 2, 34; 1788: 23
Colles, William 1770: 22; 1771: 40, 45; 1775: 25,
    29; 1777: 15; 1779: 8; 1783: 19; 1785: 35;
    1786: 4, 20, 24, 26; 1787: 12, 34, 38, (†)47
Company of Booksellers [United Company of
    Booksellers] 1774: 30; 1775: 11, 20; 1777: 13;
    1779: 4, 16; 1780: 16; 1786: 18
Corcoran, Bartholomew 1776: 10, 11; 1777: 9;
    1778: 9, 10

Cross, Edward 1779: *13*; 1781: *10, 15, 21*; 1782: *10, 12*

Cross, Nicholas 1782: *8*

Cross, Richard 1776: *11*; 1777: *9, 17, 18*; 1778: *9, 10*; 1779: *12, 13*; 1780: *20*; 1781: *19*; 1782: *2, 18*; 1784: *14*; 1791: *50, 68*; 1792: *32*; 1796: *26*; **App. B**: *11*

Davis, James Moore (†) 1784: *17*; 1785: *46*; 1786: *4*

Dornin, Bernard 1787: *2, 27*; 1788: *25, 44, 46, 51*; 1789: *6, 11, 31, 37, 55*; 1790: *54*; 1798: *27*; 1799: *15, 33, 94*; **App. A**: *12*

Dowling, Vincent 1799: *41*

Draper, George 1790: *54*; 1791: *28, 31*; 1792: *48*

Ennis, Richard 1780: *10*

Ewing, Thomas 1775: *28*

Exshaw, John I (d. 1776) 1770: *30, 32, 33*; 1771: *20, 29, 53*; 1772: *35*; 1775: *3*; **App. B**: *1*

Exshaw, John II 1777: *(†)16*; 1781: *(†)2*; 1783: *17, 18*; 1784: *14, 19, 23*; 1785: *34, 37*; 1786: *(†)20, 30, 34*; 1787: *(†)5*; 1791: *(†)43*; 1796: *82*

Fitzpatrick, Hugh (†) 1791: *66*; 1795: *35*; 1798: *67*

Fitzsimons, Richard 1776: *12*; 1778: *3, 10*; 1779: *5*

Flin, Laurence Larkin 1775: *29*

Folds, William (†) 1795: *21*; 1796: *82*; 1799: *81, ††82*

Folingsby, George 1792: *41*; 1794: *25, 48*; 1795: *2, 22, 43, 44, 50*; 1796: *63, 69*; 1798: *27, 71*; 1799: *15, 82, 94*; **App. A**: *12*

Gilbert, William 1775: *29*; 1781: *19*; 1782: *2, 11*; 1783: *11, 12, 18, 19*; 1786: *2, 16, 24, 34*; 1787: *15, 28, 38, 41, 49*; 1788: *25, 64*; 1789: *34*; 1799: *64*

Graisberry, Daniel I (d. 1785) 1781: *(†)21*

Graisberry, Daniel II 1799: *(†)94, 99*

Graisberry, Mary (†) 1786: *2, 34*; 1787: *41*

Grierson, George (†) 1789: *2*

Grueber, Arthur 1789: *44*; 1790: *53, 54*; 1791: *4, 26, 31, 42, 47, 58, 61, 66, 72*; 1792: *17, 18, 36, 38, 44, 48, 49, 50, 55, 56*

Grueber, Arthur, and McAlister, Randal 1788: *61, 70*; 1789: *34, 38A, 40, 54*; 1790: *49, 50, 59, 72*; **App. B**: *11; see also* McAlister, Randal

Hallhead, William 1775: *29*

Halpen, John 1786: *23*; 1787: *2, 12, 17, 27, 28, 32, 42*; 1788: *22, 23, 25, 33, 44, 46, 51, 54, 60, 64, 67, 71, 74*; 1789: *6, 7, 36, 37, 39, 55, 60, 71*; 1791: *7, 28, 42, 59, 61, 66, 68*; 1792: *18, 36, 48, 56*; 1794: *25, 48, 51*; 1795: *21*; 1799: *15, 60*

Heery, Thomas 1786: **18*; 1787: *28*

Henshall, Thomas (†) 1781: *10*; 1783: *17*

Higl[e]y, Patrick 1778: *2*; 1779: *(†)16*; 1780: *16*; 1781: *18*; 1782: *†2*

Hillary, John, and Barlow, John (†) 1794: *47*

Hoey, James, jun. 1770: *(†)8, 12, 23*; 1771: *46*; 1772: *31, 35*; 1776: *1*; **App. B**: *1*

Hoey, Peter (†) 1772: *20*; 1773: *2*; 1778: *12*

Hunter, William *(†)* 1791: *42*

Husband, John Abbott [Abbot] 1770: *†15*; 1771: *45*; 1773: *25, 35, 36*; 1774: *35*; 1783: *(†)16*

Ingham, Charles 1770: *32*

Jackson, Christopher 1771: *2*; 1773: *(†)23, 31*; 1775: *7, 31*; 1776: *13B, 14*; 1779: *10, 18*; 1780: *3, 7*; 1781: *1, (†)7, 15*

Jackson, Thomas 1775: *19*; 1789: *62*; 1791: *55*; 1798: *56*

Jackson, Zachariah (†) 1788: *61*; 1789: *34*; 1790: *41, 72*; 1791: *72*; 1792: *3*; 1793: *1*; 1794: *33, 52*

Jenkin[s], Caleb 1772: *23, 24, 31, 37, 38*; 1773: *25, 34, 35, 36*; 1774: *35*; 1775: *25, 29*; 1780: *16*; 1781: *15*; 1784: *5, 18*; 1785: *21, 29, 33, 34, 45, 46*

Jones, John 1787: *17, 28, 32*; 1788: *44, 46, 54, 59, 60, 64, 70, 71, 78*; 1789: *6, 7, 31, 34, 36, 37, 40*; 1790: *49, 50, 54, (†)58, 59, 72*; 1791: *28, 47, 64, 73*; 1792: *38, 48, 50*; **App. B**: *11*

Jones, William 1788: *70*; 1789: *41*; 1790: *(†)40, 41, 49, 50, 53, 54, 59, 72*; 1791: *4, 26, 28, 31, 64*; 1792: *18, 20, 26, 34, 41, 43, 44, 45, 48, 53*; 1793: *2, 19, 22, 24, (†)33, 35, 40*; 1794: *20, 25, 26, 41, 47, 48, 51, 52, 53*; 1795: *2, 17, (?†)19, 21, 34, 35, 38, 41, 43, 44, 46*; 1796: *63, 69, 76*; 1799: *42, 60, 77, 79, 81*; **App. A**: *8*; **App. B**: *11*

Kelly, Nicholas 1793: *(†)24, (†)45*; 1796: *(†)76*; 1797: *44*; 1798: *40, 61, 67, 70*; 1799: *47, 58, 99*; **App. A**: *12*

Kidd, William (†) 1776: *10*

Leathley, Ann[e] 1771: *53*

Lewis, Christopher 1786: *23*; 1787: *12, 15, 17, 27, 28, 34*; 1788: *33, 67*; 1789: *37, 40*

Lodge, Charles 1775: *9*

Lynch, Elizabeth 1772: *30*

M'Allister, Randal 1791: *4, 7, 42, 61, 64, 73*; 1792: *18, 41, 44, 48; see also* Grueber and McAlister

Mackenzie, [William] 1783: *18*

McKenzie, William 1790: *35, 39, 54, 74*; 1791: *4, 28, 41, 42, 53, 58, 66*; 1792: *17, 32, 49, 52, 55*; 1794: *52*; 1796: *30*

Marchbank, Robert 1770: *†26*; 1784: *13, 17*; 1785: *24*; 1786: *33*

Mercier, Richard Edward **App. A**: *12*

Milliken, John 1793: *27*; 1795: *17, 50*; 1796: *30, 41, 47, 57*

Mills, Michael 1775: *22*; 1782: *12*

Mitchell, Ann (†) 1773: *29*

Mitchell, John 1772: *38*

Moncrieffe, Richard 1770: *10, 23*; 1771: *11, 46*; 1772: *23, 35*; 1773: *35, 36*; 1775: *25*; 1781: *18*; 1782: *12, 15*; 1783: *11, 19*; 1784: *5, 6, 13, 14, 18, 19, 23*; 1785: *21, 29, 33, 34, 37, 45, 46*; 1786: *2, 4, 16, 26, 30, 33, 34*; 1787: *38*; 1788: *33*; 1789: *37*; **App. B**: *1*

Moore, James 1785: *(†)23*; 1786: *23, 33*; 1787: *12, 15, 27, 28, 34, 49*; 1788: *22, 23, 25, 33, 44, 54, 59, 60, 67, 70, 71, 74*; 1789: *11, 31, 36, 37, 39, 40,*

58, 60, 71; 1790: *35, 49, 50, 54, 59, 61;* 1791: *4,
7, 26, 41, 47, 53, 59, 61, 66, 68, 73;* 1792: *17, 18,
20, 26, 32, 34, 35, 38, 43, 44, 48, 49, 50, 52, 53,
55, 56;* 1793: *2, 19, 22, 24, 35, 39;* 1794: *25, 26,
41, 53;* 1795: *(?†)19, 38, 41, 50;* 1796: *21, 30, 75,
76, 82;* 1798: *27, 67, 70, 71;* 1799: *45, 58, 77, 79,
81, 94;* **App. B:** *11*

Moore, Peter **App. A:** *12*

Parker, John 1782: *2, (†)18;* 1783: *17;* 1785: *31,
32, 35;* 1788: *(†)22, (†)54, 59, (†)63;* 1789: *58,
71;* 1790: *35;* 1791: *7, 64;* 1792: *38, 45*

Porter, James 1770: *4, 10, 12, 22, 23, 37, 40*

Porter, William 1784: *17;* 1786: *†5, (†)20;*
1787: *12, (†)32, (†)59;* 1789: *(†)6;* 1791: *(†)41,
(†)50, †53, (†)59;* 1792: *†35;* 1793: *(†)45;*
1794: *(†)25, (†)41, 53;* 1796: *(†)26,
†47, (†)57, 82, (†)89;* 1797: *44, 71;* 1798: *27,
†61, 67, 70;* 1799: *15, (†)16, 27, 33, 42, 45, †58,
60, †64, 77, 79, 81, 82, 94, (†)95;* **App. A:**
(†)4, 12

Potts, James 1770: *3, 22, 30, 32, 33;* 1771: *3, 46,
(†)52;* 1772: *23, 24, 30, 31, 35, 37, 38;* 1773: *25,
34, 35, 36;* 1775: *25;* 1776: *2, 10, 17;* 1777: *18;*
1779: *12;* 1783: *13, 17;* 1794: *13;* **App. A:** *8;*
App. B: *1*

Powell, Samuel 1770: *12*

Price, Samuel 1774: *21;* 1775: *26;* 1776: *1, 2, 11,
12;* 1777: *7, 9, 15, 17, 18;* 1778: *3, 9, 10;* 1779: *3,
5, 8, 12, 13;* 1780: *10, 16, 19, 20, 23;* 1781: *2, 10,
15, 18, 19, 21;* 1782: *2, 8, 10, 11, 12, 15, 20;*
1783: *11, 12, 16, 19;* 1784: *5, 6, 19, 23;* 1785: *24,
29, 33, 34, 45*

Rea, John (†) 1783: *18;* 1784: *14, 23;* 1785: *34;*
1786: *23;* 1787: *2, 12, 49;* 1790: *50*

Rhames, Robert (†) 1783: *13;* 1792: *32*

Rice, John 1790: *54;* 1791: *4, 7, (†)9, 28, 31, 64,
73;* 1792: *18, 20, 26, 34, 41, 43, 44, 45, 48, 53;*
1793: *2, 22, 24, 35;* 1794: *23, 26, 48, 53;* 1795: *2,
3, 18, (?†)19, 22, 34, 35, 38, 41, 46;* 1796: *21, 30,
47, (†)52, 57, 69, 76, 88;* 1797: *58, 71;* 1798: *7, 8,
(†)32, 67;* 1799: *15, 33, 40, 82, 94;* **App. A:** *8*

Saunders, Henry 1770: *3, 23, 30, 32, 33;* 1771: *20,
29, 53;* 1772: *23, 35;* **App. B:** *1*

Sheppard, Josiah 1774: *21;* 1776: *1, 17;* 1778: *3;*
1779: *12;* 1781: *2, 15, 19;* 1783: *11;* 1784: *18, 19;*
1789: *68*

Sleater, William I & II (elder d. 1789, but the
Sleaters are indistinguishable in many
imprints) 1770: *3, 22, 30, 32, 33;* 1771: *20, 45,
46;* 1772: *23, 24, 30, 35;* 1773: *34, 36;* 1775: *26;*
1776: *2, 11;* 1777: *7, 9;* 1778: *9;* 1780: *10, 16, 20,
23;* 1781: *2, 15;* 1782: *11, 12;* 1783: *15, 16, 17;*
1787: *(†)3;* 1791: *4, 50, 58;* **App. B:** *1*

Smith, Brett 1773: *(†)31;* 1781: *(†)15;* 1787:
(†)38; 1790: *(†)54, (†)61;* 1792: *29;* 1793: *(†)8,
(†)22, (†)41;* 1794: *(†)34, (†)48;* 1795: *(†)2,
(†)26, (†)44;* 1796: *(†)21, (†)63, (†)77;*

1797: *(†)10, (†)36, (†)71;* 1798: *(†)71;*
1799: *(†)79*

Smith, William [III] and William Jr [IV]
1771: *29*

Spotswood, William (†) 1771: *25;* 1782: *20*

Stewart and Co. 1772: *31*

Stockdale, John 1795: *(†)50;* 1799: *†15, †33,
(†)40, 41, †82;* **App. A:** *12*

Todd, Thomas 1770: *7*

United Company of Booksellers, *see* Company of
Booksellers

Vallance, James 1772: *29*

Walker, Thomas 1770: *4, 10, 12, 22, 23, 37;* 1771: *3,
33, 35, 40, 45;* 1772: *23, 24, 31, 37, 38;* 1773: *25,
34, 35, 36;* 1774: *(†)3, 35;* 1775: *29;* 1779: *3, 8,
13;* 1780: *23;* 1781: *10, 18, 21;* 1782: *2, 8, 10, 11,
12, 15, 18, 20;* 1783: *12, 13, 15, 16, 17, 18, 24;*
1784: *6, 13, 18, 19;* 1785: *21, 29, 34, 45, 46;*
1786: *26*

Watson, Samuel 1770: *12, 33;* 1776: *17;*
1785: *45*

Watson, William 1774: *21;* 1775: *26;* 1776: *2;*
1777: *7, 18;* 1780: *10, 20;* 1781: *2;* 1786: *20, 34;*
1787: *32;* 1788: *23;* 1789: *68*

Webb, Thomas 1782: *18;* 1783: *17*

White, Luke 1779: *9;* 1781: *21;* 1782: *2, 20;*
1783: *9, 12, 13, 18;* 1784: *5, 18;* 1785: *21, 22, 24,
32, 33, 46;* 1786: *2, 4, 5, 16, 20, 23, 24, 26, 27,
30, 33;* 1787: *32, 41, 49;* 1788: *23, 54, 58, 71;*
1789: *37, 38A, 40, 44, 68, 71*

White, Richard 1790: *29, 50, 53, 54, 56, 72;*
1791: *31, 42, 64, 73*

Whitestone, Henry 1783: *15;* 1785: *24;* 1786: *2,
16;* 1787: *12, 28, 34, 41, 49; see also* Whitestone,
William and Henry

Whitestone, William 1774: *21;* 1775: *1, 8, 26, 28;*
1776: *1, 10, 11, 17;* 1777: *7, 9, 15, 17, 18;*
1778: *3, 9, 10;* 1779: *3;* 1780: *20;* 1781: *2, 21;*
1782: *8, 10, 12, 20;* 1785: *31, 35;* 1787: *15, 17;*
see also Whitestone, William and Henry

Whitestone, William and Henry 1776: *12;*
1779: *5;* 1780: *16, 23;* 1781: *10;* 1782: *11;*
1783: *19;* 1784: *6*

Wilkinson, Thomas 1776: *12;* 1777: *15;* 1779: *3,
5;* 1781: *19*

Williams, James 1770: *3, 4, 10, 12, 22, 23, 32, 33,
37, 40;* 1771: *11, 35, 37, 45, 46;* 1772: *3, 23, 24,
26, 30, 31, 37, 38;* 1773: *9, 25, 34, 35, 36;*
1774: *24, 35;* 1775: *25;* 1776: *12;* 1777: *15;*
1779: *3, (†)4, 5, 8, 12, 13;* **App. B:** *2*

Wilson [Mary] (†) 1788: *16*

Wilson, Peter 1775: *22*

Wilson, Peter and William 1770: *12*

Wilson, William 1771: *35;* 1772: *36;* 1777: *17;*
1779: *8;* 1782: *15;* 1783: *12;* 1784: *14, 18, 23;*
1785: *31;* 1791: *41*

Wogan, Patrick 1787: *2, 27, 32, 38, 42;* 1788: *22,*

25, 44, 46, 51, 54, 59, 60, 63, 64, 67, 71, 74;
1789: *6, 7, 11, 31, 36, 37, 38A, 39, 40, 44, 55, 58,*
60, 68, 71; **1790:** *35, 39, 49, 54, 59, 74;* **1791:** *26,*
28, 31, 41, 47, 50, 53, 58, 59, 61, 68; **1792:** *17,*
20, 26, 29, 32, 34, 35, 36, 41, 43, 44, 45, 48, 49,
50, 52, 53, 55, 56; **1793:** *2, (†)8, 19, 22, (†)33,*
35, (†)37, 39, 40; **1794:** *(†)16, 25, 26, 41, 47, 48,*
51, 52, 53; **1795:** *2, 3, 17, 18, (?†)19, 21, 22, 34,*
35, 38, 41, 43, 44, 46, 50; **1796:** *21, 26, (†)27,*
30, 41, 47, 57, 63, 67, 69, 75, 76, 82; **1797:** *26,*
58, 70, 71; **1798:** *27, 61, 67, 70, 71;* **1799:** *15, 27,*
33, 42, 45, 47, 58, 60, 64, 77, 79, 81, 82, 94;
App. A: *8, 12*

DURHAM
Clifton, A. 1793: *36

EDINBURGH
Balfour, Elphingstone 1792: 32
Balfour, John 1785: 36
Bell, John 1776: 6
Bell & Bradfute 1792: 32
Cheyne, S. 1797: 53
Creech, William 1776: 6; 1777: 13; 1785: 36;
    1787: 36; 1797: 53
Cross 1797: 53
Dickson, James 1792: 32
Elliot, Charles 1776: 6; 1780: 15; 1784: 12, 19;
    1785: 18; 1787: 29; 1788: 43, 46, 50;
    1789: 28; 1791: 46; *see also* Elliot and Kay,
    London
Gordon, William 1776: 6
Guthrie, A. 1792: 34
Hill, P. 1792: 32
M'Cliesh, James 1777: 2
Mitchel, H. 1796: 85
Moir, John (†) 1797: 5, 53
Murray & Cochran (†) 1780: *15

EXETER
M'Kenzie, J. and Son † 1796: 42
Woolmer 1794: *55

GLASGOW
Booksellers, all 1785: 17

HALIFAX
Edwards, William and Son 1790: 43

HAMBURG
Hoffman, Benjamin Gottlob 1799: 60

HENLEY
Norton, G. **App. A:** †6, 9

HEREFORD
Parker, William Henry † 1791: 33

HULL
Rawson, W. 1799: *91
Rawson & Co. 1793: 1; 1794: 1; 1795: 39;
    1796: 17; 1797: 13

IPSWICH
Shave, John 1777: *16*

LEEDS
Binns, John 1782: 19; 1790: 43; 1791: 51; 1795: 39

LEIPZIG
Beygang, J. B. 1799: 60

LEWES
Lee, William **App. B:** 4

LIVERPOOL
Ferguson, R. and Co. 1796: †17
M'Creery, J. (†) 1795: 12
Merritt and Wright † 1797: 13
Schofield, T. (†) 1792: 12
Smith, A. (†) *1791: 34
Wosencroft, Charles (†) 1786: 19

LONDON
Abraham, John † 1789: 65
Adlard, James (†) 1794: 37; 1797: *52
Adlard, Thomas (†) 1799: 63
Alexander, L. (†) *1789: 30
Allen 1789: 12, 21; 1790: 17
Allen, George 1773: 16; 1787: 16; 1788: 13, 35;
    1789: 36
Allen, Michael (†) 1796: 56; *see also* Allen & West.
Allen [Michael] & West 1796: *2, 44, 48, 56;
    1797: 23; *see also* Lackington and Allen
Almon, John 1770: 32; 1771: 13, 34, 50; 1775: *17;*
    1776: *4*
Appleyard 1789: 48
Aspin, Jehosaphet Clements (†) 1799: 18
Axtell, Thomas 1785: 14; 1786: 24; 1787: 24, 25,
    26; 1788: 18; 1789: 8; 1792: 30
Bagster, Samuel 1796: 30
Bain, James, *see* Martin and Bain
Baldwin, Henry (†) 1783: 20
Baldwin, Robert 1771: 12, 15, 18, 35, 39, *58;*
    1773: *17;* 1774: *2, 4, 9, 12;* 1775: *6, 29;* 1779: 17;
    1780: *20, 23; 1781: 19; 1783: 17, 20; 1785: 9,
    42, 45; 1786: 20, 33; 1787: *31, 51; 1797: 68*
Baldwin, T. (†) 1780: 1
Barfield, John (†) 1799: *97
Barker, James 1785: 7; 1788: 3; 1789: 39;
    1791: †*36; 1792: 24; 1793: 22; 1794: 31;
    1796: 86; 1799: 18
Barr, James Smith (†) 1789: 3; 1790: 2, 8
Barr, W. (†) 1790: *2*
Bateman, Joseph P. 1789: 19; 1790: 36

Bathurst, Charles 1783: 9

Baylis (†) 1797: 64; 1798: 6

Becket 1798: 72

Becket, Thomas 1770: 22; 1774: 15, 29, 30;
1775: 3, 21; 1776: 9, 13B, 16; 1778; 14;
1783: 20; 1785: 42; 1786: *35

Becket, Thomas, and Peter Abraham De Hondt
1770: 10, 32, 40; 1771: 3, 43; 1772: 30, 37;
1773: 25

Beilby, W 1790: 6, 52; 1791: *52

Bell 1792: 37, *50

Bell, A. 1771: 26

Bell, John 1770: 4, 16; 1771: 20, 52; 1772: *34;
1773: 5, *14, 23; 1776: 8; 1793: 5, 9, 19, 39;
1794: 6, 11, 12, 20, 25, 26, 27, 38, 40, 53;
1795: 4; 1796: 6, 20, 34, 63; 1797: 10, 19, 64, 69;
1798: 6, 27, 37; 1799: 32, 33, 58, 61

Bell, T. 1775: 1

Bellamy, Thomas 1798: 17; 1799: 49

Bensley, Thomas (†) 1785: *40; 1786: *35;
1787: 38; 1788: 54, *56

Bent, William 1792: 49, 55

Bentl[e]y, Edward 1791: 40; and Co. 1791: 62

Bew, Jane 1792: 44

Bew, John 1771: 18, 35; 1774: 6, 9, 13, 21, 25, 33B;
1775: 6, 14, 17, 23, 30; 1776: 4, 14; 1777: 1, 6, 7;
1778: 3, 4, 11, *16; 1779: 1, 7, *9; 1780: 8, 10;
1781: 8, 12, 15, 16; 1782: 3; 1783: *18, 23;
1784: 14; 1785: *12, *24, 26, 39, *41, 42;
1786: *6, 31, *39; 1787: *8, 21, 28; 1788: 11, 65;
1789: 14, 19; 1790: 14, 24, 28; 1791: 30, 44, 64,
73; 1792: 11, 15, 44; App. B: *5

Bigg, George (†) 1771: 1, 25; 1795: 48

Bingley, William 1770: 6; 1780: 1

Bird, John 1790: 51

Blackador, Walter (†) 1788: 70

Bladon, Samuel 1771: 39; 1772: 2, 5, 8, †11, 19;
1773: *26, 27, 32; 1779: *15; 1788: *73;
1791: 25

Booker, E. [often listed as Thomas Booker in
trade directories] 1795: 19, 41; 1796: 8, 63, 75;
1799: 14, 76

Booker and Moore 1788: *19

Boosey, John 1773: 29; 1774: 11; 1778: 15

Boosey, Thomas 1796: 84; 1797: 18

Bowen, Joseph 1782: 11

Bowyer, William (†) 1770: 3, 30; 1773: 34

Boyter 1788: *21

Brewman, Draper 1789: (†)48; 1795: 5

Brough, J.† 1770: 11, 39

Brown, Samuel 1778: 8

Brown, William 1775: 14, 17

Buckland, James 1785: *40; 1786: *35;
1789: *16

Bye, Deodatus, and Law, Henry 1797: 68

Cadell, Thomas 1771: 41, 46; 1772: 3; 1773: 31,
35, 36, 38; 1774: 28; 1775: 25, 27; 1776: 6, 7, 11;

1777: 9, 13; 1778: 7; 1782: 15; 1783: 9, 15;
1784: 12, 19; 1785: 23, 37; 1786: 26, 36; 1787: 4,
*43, 49; 1788: 71; 1789: 68; 1790: 54, 74;
1791: 68; 1793: 18; App. B: 1; see also Strahan
and Cadell

Cadell, Thomas 1794: 52; 1796: 16, 26, 29, 67;
1797: 17, 37, 69

Cadell, Thomas, jun., and William Davies
1794: 52; 1796: 16, 26, 29, 67; 1797: 2, 17, 37,
70; 1798: 67; 1799: 31, 51, 65, 87

Carnan, Thomas 1772: *38; 1775: 25 (error for
Cadell)

Carpenter, James 1791: *15, 42, 50; see also
Hookham and Carpenter

Carpenter and Co. 1799: 4, *72

Carruthers† 1787: *43

Cass, William 1783: 23; 1784: 13, 22; 1785: 4, 26,
28, 42

Cattermoul, John 1783: 10

Cawthorn, George 1797: 20, 38; 1798: †51;
1799: †29, †43

Cawthorne, W. 1796: 24

Champante, William, and Benjamin Whitrow
1789: 66; 1792: 13; 1796: 18; App. A: 6, 9

Chapman, Thomas 1796: 46; 1799: 23

Chater, J. 1770: 12, 17; 1771: 8, 42

Chater, M. 1772: 23, 24

Chesham, Francis, engraver 1791: 72

Cheyne, Charles and Thomas App. A: 6, 9

Clarke 1797: 79

Collyer, Joseph (engraver) 1774: 25

Cooke, A. see Riley and Cooke

Cooke, J. 1770: 5

Cooke, J. P. (†) 1786: *39; 1788: 11

Cooke, W. 1771: 1, 48

Cooper, M. 1778: 5

Cornish, John Dixcey (†) 1771: 51

Couch and Laking 1791: 12

Crosby, Benjamin 1794: 23, 32; 1795: 1, 7;
1796: 3, 25, 43, 69, 88; 1797: 24, 78; App. A: 11

Crosby, Benjamin, and Letterman 1799: 38

Crowder, John (†) 1788: 6; 1790: 42, 72

Crowder, Stanley 1789: 1; App. B: 12

Culver, D. 1774: 27

Curll, Edmund 1772: 21

Cuthell, John 1799: 21B

Dangerfield, Thomas 1793: 41; 1794: 28

Darton, William 1788: *19

Darton, William, and Joseph Harvey App. A: 9

Davenhill, William 1775: 14, 17; 1776: 4;
1777: *17

Davenhill, Mary 1779: *9; App. B: *5

Davies, Thomas 1770: 23; 1771: 41, 58; 1772: 3;
1774: 6; 1775: 22; App. B: 2

Davis, Lockyer 1783: 13

Davison, Thomas (†) 1799: *50

Debrett, John 1785: *41; 1786: 10; 1788: *73;

1792: 3; 1793: *6; 1794: 8, 33; 1797: *29;
    1799: 13
DeHondt, Peter Abraham, see Becket and
    DeHondt
Deighton, John 1790: 48; App. A: 7
Dennis [or Denis], John 1792: 43, 49
Desbrow, Benjamin 1779: 5, 13
Dibdin, Charles 1793: *16; 1796: *36
Dilly, Charles 1783: 19; 1785: 32; 1787: 36;
    1789: 37; 1790: 50, 64; 1791: 11, 18; 1792: 42;
    1794: *21; 1795: 17; 1796: *2; 1797: 72;
    1798: 71; 1799: 21A, 26, 28, *71; App. A: 10
Dilly, Edward and Charles 1773: 24; 1776: *15;
    1777: 8; 1778: 12
Dix, J. 1775: 11
Dodsley, James 1770: 29, 30, 33; 1771: 11, 32, 50;
    1773: 34; 1775: 20; 1777: 5; 1779: 10, 11, 12, 14;
    1780: *20; 1781: 21; 1782: 14; 1783: *16, 24;
    1784: 24; 1785: 2 (erroneously R. Dodsley), 31;
    1789: 41, 71; 1790: 46; App. B: *8
Dodsley, Robert see Dodsley, James
Domville, William 1774: 32
Donaldson, John 1774: 34
Doughty, John 1770: 19
Downes, Joseph 1793: *6
Drury, Walter 1792: 11
Dutton, Robert 1799: 12, 86, 96
Earle, William 1798: 17
Earle and Hemet 1799: *2, 37, 48, 49, 52, *55, 99
Edwards, James 1796: 26
Egerton, Thomas & John 1786: 31; 1788: 11, 43;
    1789: 50; 1792: 5, 35
Elliot, Charles, and Thomas Kay 1787: 29;
    1788: 43, 46, 50; 1789: 28; 1791: 46; see also
    Elliot, Charles, Edinburgh
Elmsley, Peter 1787: *31; 1796: 37
Evans, James 1789: 50; 1790: 54; 1791: 33;
    see also Evans, Thomas and James
Evans, Thomas 1770: 36; 1771: 56, 57; 1772: *10,
    40; 1793: 9, 27, 42; App. B: *3; see also Evans,
    Thomas and James
Evans, Thomas and James 1789: 34; 1791: 72
Faulder, Robert 1787: *1; 1788: *19; 1791: *34,
    *71; 1793: 27; 1798: 18, 72; 1799: 21B
Fawcett, Edmund (†) 1785: 2
Fell, Isaac 1770: 14
Fielding, John 1781: 11; 1783: *16; 1786: 10;
    App. B: *8
Fielding and Walker 1776: 15; 1777: 3, *17;
    1778: 1; 1779: 3; 1780: 17, 18
Fisher, S. † 1799: 35
Flexney, William 1775: 25; 1777: *17; 1783: *16;
    1788: 34; App. B: *8
Forbes, T. 1788: 43; 1792: 25
Ford, Samuel † *1790: 34
Forster, Christopher 1788: *68; 1789: 38B
Fox, James 1789: 70

Fuller 1786: *22
Fuller, John 1772: 9, 27
Gardner, Henry 1777: 1; 1778: *16
Geary, Charles 1787: 17
Geisweiler, Constantine 1799: 60
Gillett, Thomas (†) 1799: 63
Goadby, Samuel 1782: 7
Goldney, Henry 1782: 22
Goldsmith, William 1772: 8, 14, 39; 1775: 9, 28
Granger, B., engraver 1796: 2
Griffin, William 1771: 50
Griffiths, Vaughan (†) 1795: 33
Hall, Francis 1771: 27
Hall, S. 1796: 86
Hamilton, Archibald 1791: 26; 1792: 8, 11;
    1793: 9, 23; 1797: 68
Hamilton, Samuel (†) 1799: 13
Hansard, Luke (†) 1799: 65
Hanton, Elizabeth 1793: 33 (probable error for
    Elizabeth Harlow, below)
Harding, John 1798: *16; 1799: 31
Harlow, Elizabeth 1793: 8, 26, 31, 32, 33;
    1794: 14; 1795: *20
Harrison and Co. 1791: 59
Hatchard, John 1797: 59; 1798: 69
Hatchard, John, and John Wright, see Wright
    and Hatchard
Hawes, Clarke & Collins 1775: 24
Hazard, S. (†) 1787: 5
Heath, James, engraver 1798: 74; App. B: 5
Hemet, see Earle and Hemet
Herbert, Isaac 1794: 49
Heydinger, Charles 1773: 38, 39
Highley, Samuel, see Murray and Highley
Hindmarsh, Robert (†) 1794: 49
Hixon and Griffiths (†) 1792: 46
Hodgson 1795: 13, *20, 26, 27, *34, 36, 40;
    1796: 71; 1797: 6, 57, 60; 1799: 9, 19, 25, 30, 36,
    39, 56, 68, 84, 88, 89
Hogg, Alexander 1780: *22
Holdsworth, W. 1770: 35
Hood, Thomas, see Vernor and Hood
Hookham, J. 1786: 20, *22
Hookham, Thomas 1772: 16, 17; 1773: 28;
    1774: 5; 1779: 2; 1781: 17, 18, 20; 1782: 2, 21;
    1783: 1, 3, 7, 8; 1784: 1, 15, 18; 1785: 8, 20, 32,
    38; 1786: 13, 31, *35, *39, 40; 1787: 12, 14;
    1788: 7, 11, *12, 25, 38, 45, 49, 61, 67; 1789: 5,
    9, 14, 19, *31, 49, 50, 53, 62; 1790: 14, 16, 19,
    24, 28, 34, 49, 56, *58, 61; 1791: 1, 5, 14, *15,
    *31, 42, 50, 59; 1792: 11; 1794: *30; 1796: 20
Hookham, Thomas, and James Carpenter
    1791: 58; 1792: 7, 14, 21, 44, 45, 46, 47, 49;
    1793: 10, *15, *17, *28, 34, *36, 37; 1794: *43,
    48, 51; 1796: *2, 19, *38, 40, 42, *76, *77, 83;
    1797: 22, *24, 53; 1798: 2, 15, *23, 30, *39, 71;
    App. A: 6

Hughes *see* West, William
Hughes and Walsh 1789: *16
Hurst, Thomas 1799: 1, 4, 35, 49, *91, 94, 99;
  App. A: 13; *see also* Lee and Hurst
Jackson, Humanitas, and James Kerby 1788: *19*
Jackson, William 1796: 47
James, M. 1780: 2
Jameson, R. 1787: 10
Jeffery, Edward 1793: 27
Johnson 1777: 5
Johnson, Edward 1771: 26
Johnson, Edward 1782: *1*
Johnson, Joseph 1773: 10; 1775: 8; 1776: 10;
  1782: 9, 18; 1786: 15, 23, 36; 1787: 4; 1788: 77,
  78; 1789: *64; 1790: 40; 1795: 33, 45; 1796: 41,
  87, 90, 91; 1797: 28; 1798: 74; 1799: 46;
  App. B: 6
Johnston, William 1770: 1, 24, 31; 1771: 53;
  App. B: *3*
Jones, Benjamin 1772: 13, 20, 28
Jones, T. 1771: 5, 14; 1772: 13, 20, 28; 1773: 4,
  11, 20; 1776: *13A
Jones, T. C. 1797: 67
Jones, Thomas 1786: 3, 5, *22*
Jordan, Jeremiah Samuel 1794: *21
Juvenile Library 1793: 34; 1794: *43; 1796: *38;
  1799: 4, *(†)72
Kay, Thomas, *see* Elliot and Kay
Kearsley, Catherine and George II 1791: 63;
  1793: 24, 25; 1795: 12, *22
Kearsley, George I 1770: 34; 1771: 24; 1775: *14,
  17*, 31; 1779: 16; 1780: 14; 1781: 1; 1784: 4;
  1785: *41; 1786: 31; 1787: 38, 47; 1788: 1, 5,
  *19, 44, 55; 1790: 60, 68; Kearsley, George II
  1791: 28; 1792: 49; 1795: *20*; 1797: 39, 54;
  1798: 8, 43; 1799: *50; **App. B:** *3; *see also*
  Kearsley, Catherine and George II
Keith, George 1777: *5*
Kemmish, William† 1791: 2
Kerby, Lindsell and King 1794: 2
Kerby, James 1789: 22; 1791: 19; 1793: *26*;
  1795: *26*; 1799: *19, 25, 27, 30, 36, 56, 68, 83, 84*
Kerby, John 1789: 66
Kiernan, C.(†) 1770: *28
King *see* Kerby, Lindsell and King
Kirkman and Oney 1788: 28
Knight and Co. 1794: *13, 14, 15*; 1795: *13, *20,
  26, 27, *34, 36, 40*; 1796: *71*
Knight, Francis, and J. Triphook 1794: *50,
  1795: *10*
Knox, John 1774: 32
Lackington, James 1793: 7
Lackington, Allen and Co. 1799: 21B
Laking, Francis **App. A:** 6
Lane, William 1775: 4, 5; 1777: 14; 1778: *6*;
  1780: 6; 1781: *13*; 1782: 10, 13; 1783: 2, 4, 14;
  1784: 5, 8, 16; 1785: 1, *2*, 3, 5, 11, 13, 15, 16, 19,

22, 33; 1786: 2, 4, 8, 9, 12, 14, 16, 17, 27, 28, 29,
  37; 1787: 2, 6, 18, 19, 23, 27, 30, 40, 41, 42, 45,
  46; 1788: 4, 9, 14, 15, 20, 23, 24, 26, 29, 30, 31,
  32, 36, 37, 39, 42, 57, 58, 60, 63, 64, 66; 1789: 2,
  4, 7, 10, 11, 13, 15, 17, 33, 43, 45, 46, 47, 52, 57;
  1790: 1, 3, 4, 5, 7, 9, 10, 11, 12, 15, 20, 26, 30,
  32, 35, 38, 39, 44, 45, 47, 55, 57, 59, 62, 63, 65,
  73; 1791: 3, 4, 6, 7, 16, 17, 21, 22, 23, *29*, 37, 38,
  39, 43, 45, 47, 55, 60, 61, 66, 69, 74; 1792: 1, *2*,
  4, 6, 9, 10, 16, 18, 20, 22, 26, 27, 28, 29, 33, 36,
  40, 51, 53, 54, *58; 1793: 2, 3, 4, 8, 11, 14, 21,
  26, 31, 32, 33, 35, 44, 45; 1794: 7, 9, 10, 13, 14,
  15, 16, 18, 19, 34, 35, 39, 42, 46, *†50, 54, 56;
  1795: 2, 3, 6, 8, 9, 10, 13, 15, *20, 21, 24, 25, 26,
  27, 28, 29, 30, 32, 35, 36, 38, 40, 42, 46, *47*;
  1796: 5, 15, 21, 23, 31, 35, 45, 51, 54, 55, 58, 60,
  64, 65, 68, *†70, 71, 72, 73, 74, 78, 80, 81;
  1797: 1, 9, 12, 26, 27, 31, 32, 33, 34, 46, 48, *49*,
  56, 60, 61, 63, 73, 74, 75, 77; 1798: 1, 4, 7, 20,
  21, 22, 24, 26, 28, 29, 31, 36, *37*, 41, 44, 45, 46,
  47, 48, 49, 53, 55, 61, 62, 64, 65, 66, 68, 75;
  1799: 9, 19, 25, 27, 30, 34, 36, 39, 44, *53, 54,
  56, 66, 67, 68, 80, 83, 84, 85, 88, 89, 90; *see also*
  Minerva Press
Law 1792: 2
Law, Bedwell 1777: *4; 1778: 8; 1782: 8; 1784: 3;
  1792: *58; 1799: 15; and Son 1792: 41
Law, Charles 1795: 47; 1796: 7, 8, 20, *34, 45,
  47, *63, *70, 75, *78*; 1797: 16, *60*; 1799: 14, *72,
  76, 93
Lea, Richard 1774: 20; 1799: 21B
Leacroft, Samuel 1771: 10; 1773: 39
Lee 1799: *39, 89*
Lee, J. 1795: *7*; 1796: 1
Lee and Hurst 1797: 47, 64, 67; 1798: 6, 14, *16,
  38, 42, 58, 69
Letterman, *see* Crosby and Letterman
Lewis 1782: 16
Lewis, J. 1775: 18
Lewis, Thomas 1773: 7, 8
Lindsell *see* Kerby, Lindsell and King
Lister, George 1773: *26; 1782: 6
Literary Press 1790: 33; 1791: 10; 1793: *43;
  App. B: *(†)9
Literary Society 1785: *46; 1789: *42, 67
Lloyd, Edmund 1797: *57*; 1798: *54; 1799: *9, 19,
  25, 27, 30, 36, 39, 56, 68, 83, 84, 88, 89*
Logographic Press (†) 1785: 10, 38, *46; 1786: 20;
  1789: 18, 20, *42, 67; 1790: 22, 31, 41
Long, Henry 1793: 38
Longman, Thomas II 1787: 4
Longman, Thomas Norton 1794: 4, 36; 1796: 13,
  89; 1797: 4, *49, 50, 62, 68, 71; 1798: 52, 59,
  60, 73
Longman, Thomas Norton, and Owen Rees
  1799: 16, 17, *20, 40, 45, 77, 78, 79, 92, 95
Low, Sampson 1793: *(†)28; 1794: (†)38;

1795: (†)4, †19, (†)41; 1796: †8, †47, †75, †82;
  1797: †16, †25; 1798: (†) 25; 1799: (†)4, †14,
  †47, (†)72, †76, †93
Lowndes, Charles 1791: 62; 1798: (†)50
Lowndes, Henry 1796: 12; 1797: 41, 42
Lowndes, Thomas 1770: 3, 18, 26, 34; 1771: 6, 24,
  29, 37, 44; 1772: 26, 31; 1773: 9, 18; 1774: 3, 17,
  22, 31; 1776: 2, 3; 1777: 10; 1778: 10; 1779: 8;
  1780: 16; 1781: 6; 1782: 12
Lowndes, Thomas and Son 1783: 12
Lowndes, William 1785: 30, 34; 1791: 49;
  App. B: 10
Lowndes, Thomas and William 1783: 11;
  1784: 3
Lubbock, W. 1796: *11
Macgowan, James 1780: 12, 13; 1781: 2, 3
Macklew, Edward 1781: 12
March 1771: 10
McQueen, Peter 1788: 43
Marlow 1794: 37
Marshall, John and Co.† 1787: 35; 1793: 34;
  App. A: 2
Martin, Richard, and James Bain 1795: 49
Mathews, James 1794: *21
Medland, Thomas, engraver App. A: *5*
Midwinter, D. 1778: 5
Miller, William 1791: 29, 59; 1794: *13, 14, 15,*
  *50; 1795: 10, 13, *20, 26, 27, *34, 36, 40, 45;*
  1796: *70, 71, 78; 1797: 6, 57, 60, 64; 1798: 6,*
  54; 1799: 9, 19, 25, 27, 30, 36, 39, 53, 56, 68,
  83, 84, 88, 89, 98
Millidge, Josiah 1783: *18
Minerva Press (†) 1790: 4, 9, 12, 45, 65; 1791: 3,
  4, 6, 7, 16, 17, 21, 22, 23, *29*, 37, 38, 39, 43, 45,
  47, 55, 60, 61, 66, 69, 74; 1792: 1, 4, 6, 9, 10, 16,
  18, 20, 22, 28, 29, 33, 36, 40, 51, 53, 54, *58;
  1793: 2, 3, 4, 8, 11, 14, 21, 26, 31, 32, 33, 35, 44,
  45; 1794: 7, 9, 10, 13, 14, 15, 16, 18, 19, 34, 35,
  39, 42, 46, *51, 54, 56; 1795: 2, 6, 8, 9, 10, 13,
  15, 21, 24, 25, 26, 27, 28, 29, 30, 32, *34, 35, 36,
  38, 40, 42, 46; 1796: 5, 15, 21, 23, 31, 35, 45, 51,
  54, 55, 58, 60, 64, 65, 68, *70, 71, 72, 73, 74, 78,
  80, 81; 1797: 1, 6, 9, 12, 26, 27, 31, 32, 33, 34,
  46, 48, 56, 57, 60, 61, 63, 73, 74, 75, 77; 1798: 1,
  4, 7, 20, 21, 22, 24, 26, 28, 29, 31, 36, 41, 44, 45,
  46, 47, 48, 49, 53, 55, 61, 62, 64, 65, 66, 68, 75;
  1799: 9, 19, 25, 27, 30, 34, 36, 39, 44, *53, 54,
  56, 66, 67, 68, 80, 83, 84, 85, 88, 89, 90
Mitchell 1797: 76
Mitchell, Philip 1786: 10
Molini, Peter 1798: 72
Moore, William 1796: 62
Morgan, John 1789: *16
Murdell, J. 1778: 5
Murdoch, J. 1770: 38
Murray, John 1774: 33A; 1776: 17; 1777: 18;
  1782: 20; 1783: 22; 1785: *46*; 1786: *22*;

1787: 39; 1788: 75; 1789: 63, *69*; 1790: 24, 28;
  1791: 14, 53; 1792: 11
Murray, John, and Samuel Highley 1797: *29,
  37; 1799: 31
Newbery, Elizabeth 1791: 56; 1794: *21, 45;
  1797: 7, 65, 66; 1798: 12, 56, 57, 60; 1799: 3, 5,
  8, 11, *72; App. A: 8, *12*
Newbery, Francis 1770: 20, *21; 1771: 49, 50;
  1772: *33; 1773: 1; 1779: 6; 1780: 21
Newton, R. 1778: 5
Nichols, John 1794: 3; 1799: (†)37, (†)99
Nicoll [or Nichol], William 1771: 17; 1790: *70
Noble, Francis 1770: 15; 1771: 2, 4, 9, 22, 25, 33,
  40, 60; 1772: 6, 7, 12, 22, 25; 1773: 2, 3, 13, 17,
  19, 21, 22, 30; 1774: 1. 2, 4, 8, 12, 23; 1775: 2, 7,
  10, 13; 1777: 11; 1778: 2, 6, 13; 1779: 5, 13;
  1780: 19; 1781: 5, 9, 10; 1782: 5, 17; 1783: 5, 21;
  1784: 2, 7; 1785: *21, 27; 1786: 7; 1787: 11, 13,
  20, 33; 1788: 10, 40, 53
Noble, John 1770: 15; 1771: 2, 4, 9, 22, 25, 33,
  40, 60; 1772: 6, 7, 12, 22, 25; 1773: 2, 3, 13, 17,
  19, 21, 22, 30; 1774: 1, 2, 4, 8, 12, 23; 1775: 2, 7,
  10, 13; 1777: 11; 1778: 2, 6, 13; *Noble, John*
  1779: 5, 13
Noble, Richard (†) 1797: 18; 1799: 42, 82
Nourse, John 1775: 26; 1787: 44
Nourse, John 1795: 48
Nunn, James 1793: *9*; 1799: 21B
Ogilvy, David, and Speare 1791: 51
Ogilvy, David and Son 1797: 14; 1799: 21B
Oney *see* Kirkman and Oney
Otridge, William and Son 1799: 21B
Oulton, W. 1792: 11
Owen, J. 1792: *13;* 1793: 30; 1794: 17, 37;
  1795: 33; App. A: 6
Owen, William 1775: 12; 1783: 6; App. B: 1
Parker, Charles 1772: 35; 1777: 1
Parsley, Robert 1789: 48
Parsons, John 1785: 6; 1786: 32; 1791: 2;
  1793: *15, 26;* 1794: 37; 1797: *52; App. B: 13
Payne, Thomas 1796: 26
Payne, Thomas and Son 1782: 15
Peacock, R. and Lucy 1796: *38; 1799: 4; *see also
  Juvenile Library*
Pearch, George 1770: 32; 1771: 36
Perfetti, A. 1785: 40; 1786: 35
Phillips, Richard 1799: 63
Pownall, B. 1783: 23
Pridden, Humphrey Gregory 1788: 65
Pridden, John 1785: *40; 1786: 35; 1794: 3
Raithby, John 1789: *16
Randall, R. 1788: 2
Rees, Owen, *see* Longman and Rees
Reynolds, *see* Shepperson and Reynolds
Richardson 1790: 27; 1799: 10
Richardson, William 1777: *18;* 1781: †8; 1785: 9,
  10, 35; 1786: 20; 1788: 16; 1789: 18, 20, 27, *42,

50, 67; 1790: 24, 28, 41; 1791: 1, 8, 14, 32;
  1792: 11; 1793: *28; 1794: *5; 1795: 16;
  1796: 42; 1797: 15, 21
Richardson, William and James (†) 1770: 32
Richardson, William, James, and John 1797: 30;
  1798: 51; 1799: 29, 43
Richardson, William, and Leonard Urquhart
  1770: *25, *31*; 1771: 19, 50; 1778: 9; 1779: 4, 18;
  1784: 3, 9
Richie and Sammells (†) 1788: *68*
Rickman, Thomas Clio 1795: 37
Ridgway, James 1787: 9; 1789: 51; 1792: 17, 57;
  1796: 61, 62
Ridley, John 1771: *58*; 1775: *14*; *17*; 1776: *4*;
  1779: *14*
Riley 1789: 48
Riley, George 1771: 1, 48, *54*; 1774: 26; 1775: 15;
  1779: 6
Riley, George, and A. Cooke 1770: 2
Rivington, Francis and Charles 1797: 59
Roach, J. † 1794: 22
Roberts, John, *see* Robinson and Roberts
Robins, J. 1775: *16
Robinson, George, and John Roberts 1770: 13,
  32; 1771: 21, 31; 1772: 1
Robinson, George 1772: 36; 1774: 24; 1775: 30;
  1776: 12, 14; 1777: 2, 12, 16; 1778: 12; 1782: 4,
  17; 1785: 29, 42
Robinson, George, George and John 1788: 61;
  1795: 18, 43, 44, 50; 1796: 22, 27, 32, *34*, 57;
  1797: 35, 36, 44, 45, 51, 58; 1798: 3, 11, 34;
  1799: *7, 24, *41*, 42, 60, 82
Robinson, George, George, John and James
  1785: 25, 44; 1786: 11, 18, 30, 31, 34; 1787: *1,
  4, 5, 7, 15, 32, 34, 50; 1788: 33, *56, 62, 69, 74;
  1789: 6, *22*, *31, 35, 40, 44, 56, 59, 60; 1790: 21,
  42, 53, 72; 1791: 1, 9, 14, 41, 57, 70, *71; 1792:
  3, 5, 32, 43, 48, 52, 56; 1793: 40; 1794: *24, 41,
  44, 47; 1796: *26*, 49, 50, 52, 59; 1797: 40;
  1798: 9, 74
Robinson and Evans 1779: *14*
Robson, James 1774: *7*; 1776: 12; 1777: 12;
  1778: 12; 1787: *31; 1792: *58; 1796: *26*
Roson, John 1770: 7, 9, 27, 37; 1771: *7, 28, 30,
  54, *59*; 1772: 8, 15, 17, 21, *40*, 41; 1773: 6, 7, 8,
  12, *24*; 1774: 20
Row, Walter 1796: *42*
Ryall, John App. B: 4
Sabine, Thomas † 1780: 9; 1790: 25
Sabine, Thomas and Sons(†) 1780: 4
Sael, George 1793: 12; 1795: 14; 1798: 17;
  1799: 22
Scatcherd and Co. 1794: *13*
Scatcherd, James 1794: *14, 15*, *50; 1795: *13, *20,
  27, *34, 36*; 1797: *57*; 1799: *9, 19, 25, 27, 30, 36,
  39, 56, 68, 83, 84, 88, 89*
Scatcherd, James, and J. Whitaker 1782: *1*;

1785: 6, 10; 1786: *10*; 1788: 27; 1789: *66*;
  1790: 43; 1791: 12; 1793: *28
Scott, G. † 1770: 38
Searle, John 1789: 48
Seeley, Leonard Benton 1799: 13
Setchell, Henry 1788: 59
Sewell, John 1776: *4*; 1786: 31; 1788: *73*;
  1790: 69
Shatwell, Peter 1771: 55
Shepherd, Thomas 1771: 28; 1773: 7, 8, 12
Shepperson and Reynolds 1785: 47; 1788: 43;
  1792: 38; 1793: *26*; 1794: 29; 1797: 45;
  1798: 72
Simmons, William 1793: *26*
Smith, Harry (†) 1798: *39
Smith, J. 1770: 20
Smith, M. 1786: *38
Smith, S. 1772: 4; 1788: 72
Snagg, Richard 1773: 6, 32, 33; 1774: 14, 16,
  18, 19
Southern, John 1790: *70; 1791: *71
Spilsbury, Thomas (†) 1787: *38*
Spilsbury, William and Charles(†) 1798: 72
Stalker, Charles 1787: 16; 1788: 13, 22, 28, 43, 59,
  79; 1789: *22*, 24, 29, *30, 32, 67, 70; 1790: 13;
  1791: 12, 48; 1792: 37; 1793: 13; App. B: 11
Steel, David 1771: 38
Steel, Henry Draper (†) 1783: *†16; 1786: 34;
  App. B: *8
Stewart, William 1793: 9
Stockdale, John 1783: *18; 1784: 6, 21, 23;
  1785: 10; 1787: 36; 1788: 47, *68; 1789: 61;
  1791: 65; 1797: 55; App. A: 1, 3, 4, 5
Strahan, Andrew (†) 1796: *13*, ††67; 1797: *50,
  68, 71*; 1799: *16, 20, 40, 77, 78, 92, 95*
Strahan, Andrew, and Thomas Cadell 1785: 36;
  1789: 54
Strahan, William 1773: 36; 1777: 13; 1778: 7
Stratford, William and James 1791: 12
Swift, William T. 1785: *12; 1786: *25; 1787: 20
Symonds, Henry Delahoy 1783: *23*; 1784: *20;
  1785: 2, *26*; 1786: 1, *6, *22*; 1789: 26, 58;
  1790: 33, 37; 1791: 1, 12, 13, 14, 24, *52;
  1792: 11, 13, 31; 1793: *27*, 30; 1796: 28;
  1798: 10, 17, 32, 33, 40, 50, 70; 1799: 41, 60, 64
Taylor and Co. † 1791: *40*
Thorn, T. 1771: 59
Thorne, William (†) 1799: *63*
Thorne, William, and Mary Harrison (†)
  1787: *38*
Tindall, James 1796: 4
Tomlinson, Lewis 1783: *16*
Trant, James P. (†) 1788: *41
Trapp, Henry 1785: (†)20; 1794: *21
Treppass, William 1798: 35, 63; 1799: 6
Treppess, W., *see* Treppass, W.
Triphook, J., *see* Knight and Triphook

Urquhart, Leonard, *see* Richardson and Urquhart

Vernor, Thomas 1770: 12, 17; 1771: 8, 42; 1772: 23, 24; 1773: 29; 1774: 10; 1776: 5; 1788: 8, *51; 1789: 23, 55; 1790: 18, 23; 1791: 20; 1792: 34; 1793: 1; 1774: 10

Vernor, Thomas, and Thomas Hood 1794: 1; 1795: 11, 23, 39; 1796: *9, *10, 14, 17, 18, 53, 66, 79, 85; 1797: 8, 13, 53, 66; 1798: 12, 56, 57; 1799: 21B, 57, 59, 73, 74, 81, *91

Wade, John 1781: 14

Walker, George 1799: 94

Walker, John 1795: 37; 1799: 21B; **App. B:** 7. *See also* Fielding and Walker

Wallis, James 1798: 5, 13; 1799: 70

Wallis, John 1777: 15, *17; 1782: 19; 1791: 51

Walsh, *see* Hughes and Walsh

Walter, John 1772: *33; 1773: *24; 1774: *6; 1775: 6, *14, 17*, 30; 1776: *4; 1777: 12; 1778: 12; 1779: *14;* 1785: 10, *46; 1786: (†)20; 1787: 28, *31; 1788: 6; 1789: 18, 20, *42, 67; 1790: 22, 29, 31, 41

Wayland, Levi (†) 1789: 23; 1790: 18; 1792: 23; 1793: *†36

West, *see* Allen & West

West, William 1799: 29, 43; and Hughes **App. A:** 12

Westley, Robert Hall 1799: 75

Whatman, James, papermaker 1799: *31*

Wheble, John 1771: 47

Wheeble, W. 1771: 16

Whiston, John 1771: 45

Whitaker, J. *see* Scatcherd and Whitaker

White, Benjamin and Son 1788: 54; 1798: 72

White, John 1798: 19

White, Thomas 1793: 13; 1795: 1

Whitrow, Benjamin, *see* Champante and Whitrow

Whittingham, Charles (†) 1796: 20; 1799: 17

Wilkie 1791: 27

Wilkie, George 1784: 3, 11; 1785: 32

Wilkie, John 1770: 33; 1771: 23, 51; 1773: 39; 1774: 7; 1776: 1; 1777: 8

Wilkie, George and Thomas 1787: 51; 1789: 25, 38A, 69; 1791: 67; 1793: 20; 1796: 16; 1797: 19

Wilkins, Thomas 1785: (†)*41; 1786: (†)*22; 1789: †14; 1790: (†)14, †24, †28; 1791: †1, †14; 1792: †11; 1796: †7

Williams, John 1772: 18; 1773: 15

Wilson, M. 1785: 10

Wingrave, Francis 1795: 48

Woodfall, George 1771: 56; 1787: (†)*38*; 1794: (†)4, *8*; 1797: (†)*62*; 1799: (†)3, (†)8

Woodgate, H. 1780: 1

Wright, John 1798: 6, 51, *71;* 1799: 31, 41, 64

Wright, John, and John Hatchard 1799: 29, 43

MAGDEBURG
Keil, G. C. 1799: 60

MARGATE
Epps, W.(†) 1797: 55

NEWCASTLE
Elliot, *see* Hall and Elliot
Fisher, Richard 1782: 4
Hall and Elliot (†) 1790: 48
Slack, Thomas 1770: 18

NORTHAMPTON
Burnham, T. 1793: *36
Dicey, Thomas and Co. 1789: (†)34

NORWICH
Payne, John (†) 1780: 24
Stephens, G. Alfred 1780: 24

NOTTINGHAM
Sutton, C. 1799: *91

ORFORD
Slatter, R. † **App. A:** 11

OXFORD
Cooke, J. 1792: 5
Prince and Cook 1791: 33
Rann, C. 1788: 43

PARIS
Cazin 1788: 52

PERTH
Morison, Robert and Son 1792: 34; 1796: 85
Morison, Robert jun. 1792: (†)34; 1796: 85

PHILADELPHIA
Dobson, Thomas 1785: 18
Rice, H. and P. 1796: *52*

PLYMOUTH
Hoxland, Fraser, and Heydon 1794: *55
Nettleton, P. (†) 1794: *55
Nettleton, Wills, and Barnikel 1794: *55

READING
Jones, T. 1779: *14*
Snare and Co.† 1798:63

SALISBURY
Collins, Benjamin 1771: 53
Easton, James 1796: (†)16; 1797: †19; 1799: †5

SHEFFIELD
Cales, J. 1794: *24

Gosling, Mrs 1794: *24
Northall, J. 1794: *24
Pierson, T. 1794: *24
Ridgard, E. 1794: *24
Smith, J. 1794: *24
Ward, William 1794: *24

SHREWSBURY
Eddowes, Joshua and William (†) 1799: 51
Sandford, P. 1787: 28; 1791: 48

SOUTH SHIELDS
Churnside, James (†) 1787: *37

SOUTHAMPTON
Baker, Thomas 1785: †39; App. B: 12
Linden, James & Cunningham (†) 1782: 8
Shelton & Mills 1782: 8
Skelton, T. (†) 1795: *47; 1799: 15

STAFFORD
Morgan, Arthur (†) 1794: 36

STONEHOUSE
Huss 1794: *55

STRATFORD
Walford 1791: 48

UTTOXETER
Richards, R. 1797: †15, (†)21

VIENNA
Gerold, Joseph 1799: *63

WAKEFIELD
Hurst, Rowland (†) 1799: *7
Waller, Elizabeth (†) 1799: *7

WARWICK
Sharp, John 1791: 48

WATERFORD
Saunders, J. 1796: 63

WEYMOUTH
Holloway, W. (†) 1792: 39
Love, J. 1792: 39
Powell, S. (†) 1792: 39

WORCESTER
Holl & Smart 1791: 48

YORK
Etherington, Christopher 1770: 4, 16; 1771: 20,
    52; 1772: *†34; 1773: 23; 1776: 8
Todd, John 1788: 43

Notes Index

Numbers in italic indicate that the name itself does not appear in the entry.

Aikin, Anna Laetitia and John 1792: 5
Aikin, Mr 1777: 17
Aikin, Arthur 1795: 1, 7, 12, 19, 41; 1796: 2, 13, 16, 22, 24, 35, 52, 53, 57, 61, 62, 69, 76, 77, 79, 82, 84, 88, 89; 1797: 1, 13, 39, 59, 70; 1798: 2, 30
Alfieri, V.A. 1771: 16
Amory, Thomas 1776: 10
Ancaster, Dowager Duchess of 1789: 10
Anderson, Howard 1796: 63
Andrews, James Petit 1789: 61
Anne, Queen 1771: 43
Anne, HRH 1787: 20
Anson, Mrs 1796: 72
Apuleius 1789: 69
Arenswald, Capt. Von 1788: 61
Aristotle 1782: 3
Asgill, Sir Charles 1793: 41
Ashby, Miss 1787: 12
Augusta Sophia, HRH Princess 1799: 55

Badcock, Samuel 1779: 9; 1780: 10, 13, 15, 21; 1781: 1, 5, 6, 8, 9, 10, 11, 12, 13, 14, 15, 16, 17, 18, 20, 21; 1782: 3, 4, 5, 6, 7, 8, 9, 11, 12, 14, 15, 16, 19, 20; 1783: 1, 2, 3, 4, 5, 7, 8, 11, 12, 14, 15, 16, 17, 18, 19, 20, 21, 23, 24; 1784: 1, 2, 4, 6, 7, 8, 9, 11, 12, 13, 14, 15, 16, 17, 18, 19, 20, 21, 23; 1785: 1, 2, 3, 4, 5, 6, 7, 11, 13, 14, 15, 16, 19, 20, 21, 23, 25, 26, 28, 30, 31, 32, 33, 34, 37, 38, 39, 40, 44; 1786: 9, 14, 26, 27, 30, 31, 33, 34;
App. B: 6, 7
Baker, Sir Richard 1787: 31
Bannister, James 1793: 37; 1797: 2, 28, 49, 51, 54, 72, 78; 1798: 52; 1799: 14, 16, 23, 40, 75, 87, 98
Baxter 1770: 23
Beauchamps, see Godard de Beauchamps
Becket, Andrew 1786: 1, 2, 3, 5, 17, 18, 20, 21, 22, 23, 24, 32, 35, 40; 1787: 2, 5, 6, 7, 8, 10, 12, 13, 14, 15, 16, 17, 18, 19, 20, 24, 26, 27, 28, 29, 30, 31, 32, 33, 34, 38, 39, 40, 41, 42, 45, 46, 47, 48, 50, 51; 1788: 1, 3, 7, 8, 10, 11, 12, 13, 14, 15, 16, 18, 23, 24, 25, 28, 30, 31, 33, 34, 35, 36, 38, 39, 42, 44, 45, 46, 49, 51, 53, 54, 56, 57, 58, 59, 60, 61, 62, 63, 65, 68, 70, 71, 72, 73, 74, 75, 76, 77; 1789: 5, 7, 9, 13, 14, 16, 18, 19, 22, 23, 25, 28, 31, 33, 37, 38A, 40, 43, 44, 45, 49, 50, 53, 57, 58, 59, 60, 62, 64, 65, 68, 70; App. B: 10
Beckford, William 1796: 68

Bedford, Dowager Duchess of 1792: 36
Bedford, Duke of 1796: 46
Belloy, Pierre Laurent Buyrette 1790: 14
Bennet, Mrs 1781: 8
Beresford, Hon. Mrs 1791: 29
Berry, Miss 1775: 3
Bertie, Lady Priscilla 1779: 13
Bewley, Mrs 1792: 3
Bewley, William 1778: 7; 1792: 3
Bīdpā'ī 1787: 44
Bilbie, Joseph 1799: 91
Biron, Marshal 1792: 56
Boccase [Boccacio] 1786: 31
Bossuet, Jacques-Bénigne, Bishop of Meaux 1786: 31
Bourgeois, Sir Francis 1793: 17
Boyle, Lord 1793: 29
Briscoe, Sophia 1779: 8
Bristol, Earl of 1793: 36
Brooke, F. 1773: 5
Brooke, Frances 1770: 17; 1773: 5; 1781: 9
Broughton, Lady 1791: 36
Brown, John 1797: 1
Buccleugh, Duchess of 1776: 6
Buckingham, Marchioness of 1787: 34; 1789: 64
Burke, Edmund 1791: 58
Burney, Charles, the younger 1785: 45, 47; 1786: 7; 1795: 30; 1796: 65
Burney, Edward Francesco 1791: 72
Burney, Frances 1782: 14; 1785: 38, 45; 1786: 4, 22; 1787: 18, 31, 41, 42; 1788: 25, 59, 63; 1789: 25, 33, 52; 1790: 49; 1791: 42, 43; 1792: 20; 1794: 23; 1798: 67
Burney, James 1796: 20; 1799: 7, 13, 26, 45, 50, 71, 78, 79, 82, 92, 97

Camden, Lady 1773: 28
Campbell, Lady Charlotte 1799: 92
Carbery, Lord 1788: 17
Carden, Mrs 1790: 71
Carey, Henry 1787: 13
Caroline, HRH Princess, see Wales
Cartwright, Edmund 1779: 4, 11, 15; 1780: 8; 1782: 10
Catley, Ann 1773: 12
Cavendish, Georgiana, Duchess of Devonshire 1775: 27, 30; 1785: 32; 1786: 25, 39; 1787: 16; 1791: 35

Cervantes, Miguel 1773: 29, 34, 39; 1791: 35
Charlotte, Queen 1786: 26; 1787: 23; 1790: 50;
  App. A: 6
Charlotte Augusta, HRH Princess, *see* Wales
Charlotte Augusta Matilda, Princess Royal
  1785: 22
Chaucer, Geoffrey 1797: 51
Chesterfield, Lord 1776: 14; 1793: 15
Christmas, Mrs 1774: 35
Civrac, Countess de 1797: 43
Clarence, HRH William, Duke of 1792: 13
Cleland, John 1774: 2, 3, 9, 10, 12, 18, 19, 21,
  22, 23
Cobbett, William 1791: 40
Cockburn, Mrs 1797: 68
Cockburne, Lady 1788: 70
Colman, George 1786: 29; 1799: 33
Colman, George, the elder 1775: 3; 1789: 58
Conolly, Lady Louisa 1780: 11
Cooper, Rev. Dr and Mrs 1789: 33
Corneille, Pierre 1786: 31
Cottle, Joseph 1795: 50
Coventry, Francis 1771: 45
Cowley, Hannah 1785: 26
Cracroft, Ann 1771: 43
Craven, Lady 1781: 1
Crébillon, Claude-Prosper Jolyot de 1788: 51
Crespigny, Mrs 1793: 32; 1798: 59
Cumberland, Anne, Duchess of 1772: 17;
  1775: 15; 1787: 21; 1789: 68
Cumberland, Richard 1796: 64
Curl, Edmund 1771: 30; 1772: 21

Dacre, Lady 1792: 14
Dalrymple, A. 1795: 48
Damer, Hon. Mrs Lionel 1788: 3
Dartmouth, Earl of 1775: 18
Day, Thomas App. A: 11
Defoe, Daniel 1788: 47; 1796: 36, *38*
Delacour, Dr 1780: 23
Delaval, Sir Francis Blake 1788: 69
Delaval, Sir John Hussey 1771: 50; 1788: 69
Derby, Countess of 1799: 99
Devonshire, Duchess of, *see* Cavendish,
  Georgiana
Diderot, Denis 1789: 51
Diogenes 1771: 58
Dodd, William 1783: 24
Donellan, Mary Anne 1770: 6
Douglas, Mrs 1792: 47
Douglas, Lady Jane 1774: 16
Dow, Alexander 1799: 51
Doyle, John 1792: 40
Draper, Eliza App. B: 3
Drummond, Lady Elizabeth 1796: 19
Dubois-Fontanelle, Jean-Gaspard 1789: 55
Duncannon, Viscountess 1790: 37; App. B: 11

Edwards, Bryan 1795: 36
Eliot, Lady 1794: 55
Eliot, Sir John 1785: 37
Enfield, William 1774: 7, 15, 17, 20; 1775: 2, 4, 5,
  7, 8, 9, 13, 15, 17, 20, 21, 23, 25, 26, 27, 28, 29,
  30, 31; 1776: 2, 3, 4, 5, 12, 13A, 13B, 14, 16;
  1777: 1, 2, 3, 4, 5, 6, 7, 10, 11, 12, 13, 14, 15, 16,
  17, 18; 1778: 1, 2, 3, 4, 6, 8, 9, 10, 11, 12, 13, 14,
  16; 1779: 1, 2, 3, 5, 6, 7, 8, 10, 13, 14, 16, 17, 18;
  1780: 6, 12, 16, 18, 19, 20, 23; 1781: 2, 3; 1782:
  2; 1783: 9; 1784: 5; 1785: 8, 9, 22, 24, 27, 29, 35,
  36, 42; 1786: 4, 6, 10, 11, 15, 16, 37; 1787: 4;
  1788: 37, 50, 66, 67; 1789: 15, 17, 21, 39, 41, 42,
  61; 1790: 16, 18, 19, 40, 42, 43, 48, 58, 61, 68;
  1791: 15, 53, 58, 63, 68, 73; 1792: 3, 15, 17, 21,
  36, 42, 43, 44, 46, 48, 49, 50, 52, 56, 57, 58;
  1793: 10, 12, 20, 23, 24, 28, 32, 34, 36, 38, 39,
  42, 45; 1794: 3, 4, 5, 7, 8, 9, 14, 15, 17, 18, 23,
  24, 28, 29, 30, 32, 39, 42, 43, 44, 47, 49, 51, 52,
  53, 54; 1795: 14, 18, 20, 21, 27, 28, 29, 34, 35,
  40, 43; 1796: 25, 26, 40, 46; 1797: 45; App. A: 1,
  2, 5, 8; App. B: 8, 11
Erskine, Thomas 1791: 67

Fairford, Viscountess 1787: 50
Farren, Eliza 1796: 70
Farrer, Rev. Mr 1787: 37
Faulkner, George 1770: 6
Ferriar, John 1797: 51; 1799: 62
Fielding, Henry 1771: 45; 1773: 29; 1774: 16;
  1775: *22*; 1777: 17; 1780: 20; 1782: 14, 15;
  1785: 46; 1787: *13*; 1788: 42, 65, 66; 1789: 2,
  17; 1791: 31; 1792: 49; 1793: 39; 1794: 23;
  1795: 17; 1796: 52; 1799: 61
Fitzgerald, Lady Edward 1799: 40
Fitzherbert, Mrs 1785: 10; 1789: 28
Fitzou, Baron 1784: 12
Florian, Jean Pierre Claris de 1786: 11
Fonblanque, John 1797: 68
Fontanelle *see* Dubois-Fontanelle, Jean-Gaspard
Foote, Samuel 1786: 1
Fordyce, Mrs 1799: 87
Fox, Charles James 1783: 22; 1792: 12
Frankland, Charles 1774: 4

Galland, M. 1792: 32; 1793: 18
Galloway, John, Earl of 1783: 18
Garrick, David 1777: 9
Gavin, Luke Anthony 1771: 1
Geddes, Alexander 1795: 48
George, Prince of Wales 1784: 1; 1785: 10;
  1789: 40; 1791: 32
Gessner, Salomon 1786: 17; 1799: 81; App. B: 11
Gillies, John 1789: 54, 69; 1796: 67
Gilroy, Amanda 1793: 23
Glasgow, Countess of 1787: 43
Gloucester, HRH Duchess of 1793: 33; 1799: 54

Gloucester, Princess Sophia Matilda of 1797: 61
Godard de Beauchamps, Pierre-François
   1788: 52
Goethe, Johann Wolfgang von 1785: 25;
   1786: *17*, 26; 1787: *51*; 1788: *61*, 79; 1790: *27*,
   42; 1792: 48; 1793: 14; 1798: *42*
Goldsmith, Oliver 1771: *45*; 1774: 16; 1778: 15
Goodrich, Mrs 1792: 46
Gordon, Mr 1770: 22
Gordon, Eleanor 1787: 15
Graham, Kenneth W. 1786: 15
Graumann, Charles George 1799: 58
Grenville, Lieut. General 1799: 23
Griffiths, George Edward 1787: 35; 1788: 47;
   1790: 33; 1791: 31, 41; 1793: 27; 1794: 6;
   1796: 27; 1797: 8, 55; 1798: 59; 1799: 14;
   App. A: 4
Griffiths, Ralph 1770: 40; 1773: 38; 1774: 24;
   1775: 22; 1779: 12; 1788: 69; 1790: 69; 1791:
   72; 1793: 40; 1797: 29; 1798: 30, 50; App. A: 10;
   App. B: 1
Grosvenor, Richard, Lord 1771: 12, 18
Guevara, Luis Vélez de 1797: 40
Gunning, Elizabeth 1799: 16
Gwynn, Eleanor 1799: 44

Hackman, James 1780: 14
Halifax, Earl of 1770: 6
Hamilton, Duchess of 1781: 8
Hamilton, Alexander 1796: 49; 1797: 17; 1798: 9,
   64; 1799: 28, 31, 51
Hanbury, Mr 1795: 9
Hare, Robert R. 1793: 23
Harrison, Miss App. A: 8
Harrison, Miss M. A. App. A: 8
Hartwell, Francis John 1787: 39
Hastings, Mrs 1785: 24; 1786: 28; 1788: 44;
   1796: 51
Hastings, Warren 1796: 49
Hawkesworth, John 1770: 32; 1775: 27; 1796: 68
Hayley, William 1787: 51
Hayward, Charles 1775: 19
Heathfield, Lord 1789: 11
Herbelot, Barthélemy d' 1774: 26
Heron, Robert 1792: 44
Hill, Sir Rowland 1794: 12
Hillsborough, Countess of 1791: 55
Hirons, Jabez 1784: 24; 1786: 36; 1788: 77;
   1797: 7, 66; 1798: 12, 56, 57, 60; 1799: 17, 73,
   74; App. A: 7, 10, 12
Holcroft, Thomas 1792: 5, 29, 32, 45; 1793: 1, 7,
   25, 36, 40; 1795: 17, 50; App. B: 12
Howard, Lady 1797: 62; 1799: 97
Howard, John 1787: 46
Howe, Hon. Lady 1779: 6
Howe, Hon. Miss 1788: 64
Hume, David 1787: 45; 1790: 72

Hunter, Colonel 1789: 31
Hurrell, Tamary Eliz. 1790: 29

Ibbetson, Julius Caesar 1793: 43
Iffland, August Wilhelm 1798: 68
Irving, Lady Eliz. 1790: 66
Irwin, Viscountess 1789: 42; 1790: 43

James, William 1789: 66
Jerningham, Edward 1775: 21
Johnson, Samuel, dancing master 1772: 34
Johnson, Samuel 1782: 15; 1790: 50; 1793: 23;
   1796: 11; 1799: 62
Johnstone, Mrs 1799: 71
Johnstone, Charles 1782: *20*; 1793: 1
Jones, Sir William 1793: 18
Jordan, Dora 1792: 13

Kauffman, Angelica 1780: 23
Kenrick, William 1790: 15
Keppel, Miss 1798: 69
Kindersley, Jemima 1787: 5
King, John 1796: 56
King, Thomas 1783: 14
Kingston, Duchess of 1776: 7
Kirke, Colonel 1787: 45
Klopstock, Friedrich Gottlieb 1786: 17
Kotzebue, August Friedrich William von
   1799: 49

La Fontaine, Jean de 1786: 31
Langhorne, John 1771: 32; 1773: 37; 1774: 11;
   1775: 12; 1776: 7, 8, 10, 15; 1777: 8; 1778: 15
Lansdowne, Marquis of 1798: 50
Lavater, John Gaspard 1787: 36
Lee, Sophia 1786: 21; 1787: 26; 1788: 60; 1793: *44*
Leeds, Duchess of 1791: 70
Leinster, Duchess of 1793: 38
Lennox, Charlotte 1770: 17; 1787: 51; 1795: 15
Le Noble, Eustache 1798: 36
Le Sage, Alain-René 1785: 46; 1786: 1; 1787: *47*;
   1788: 65; 1793: 1, 25; 1797: 40
Lewes, R. 1789: 39
Lewis, Matthew Gregory 1798: *11*, 62; 1799:
   70, 75
Ligonier, Edward 1771: 16
Ligonier, Penelope 1771: 16
Lillo, George 1798: 70
Lindsay, Lady Anne 1788: 62
Lonsdale, Roger 1786: 15
Lucian 1789: 69
Lutherbourgh, Mr de 1781: 21
Luttrell, Colonel 1770: 14
Lyttelton, Thomas Lord 1775: 3, 30

McDermott, Peter 1781: 8
Mackenzie, Henry 1789: *16*; 1798: 38

Macklin, Charles **App. B**: 7
Maclean, Capt. 1775: 18
Macpherson, Eleonora 1773: 27
Macpherson, James 1798: *36*
Mahon, Viscountess 1782: 14
Man, Henry 1791: 48
Marivaux, Pierre Carlet de Chamblain de
    1773: 29
Marlborough, Duchess of 1789: 36; 1797: 53
Marlborough, Duke of 1797: 39
'Marlow, Lady Harriet' 1797: 25
Marmontel, Jean-François 1770: 16; 1797: 51
Marriott, Mrs 1798: 39
Martin, Sir Henry 1796: 35
Mary, HRH Princess 1785: 40
Massey, Hon. Mrs 1791: 52
Matthieson, Henrietta 1799: 40
Maty, Paul Henry 1788: 62
Messerati, Comtesse Elizabeth 1776: 16
Metastasio, Pietro 1789: 38A
Middleton, Lady 1789: 15
Miller, Lady 1779: 18
Miller, Joe 1773: 8
Molière, Jean-Baptiste Poquelin de 1786: 31
Molina, Tirso da 1799: 91
Monchy, Chevalier de, *see* Fieux, Charles de,
    Chevalier de Mouhy
Monmouth, James, Duke of 1790: 55
Monson, Lady 1781: 15
Montague, Elizabeth 1770: 17; 1787: 31;
    1790: 35
Moody, Christopher Lake 1788: 43; 1790: 74;
    1791: 48; 1794: 50; 1798: 8, 74; 1799: 42, 46
Moody, Elizabeth 1790: 26, 69; 1799: 41, 64
Mothe, Marie Catherine, comtesse d'Aulnoy
    1788: 28
Mouhy, Charles de Fieux, Chevalier de 1772: 15

Newenham, Mrs 1786: 21
Newton, John-Frank 1799: 52
Nichols, John Gough 1771: 48
Noble, Eustache Le 1798: 36
Nolcken, Baron 1787: 36
Noorthouck, John 1770: 1,3, 7, 9, 16, 23, 27, 33,
    34; 1771: 12, 15, 35;1773: 6, 8, 11, 12, 17, 25;
    1774: 32, 34; 1775: 1, 6, 11, 19; 1776: 11; 1782:
    21; 1788: 5, 9, 17, 20, 21, 27, 32; 1789: 10, 32,
    51, 71; 1790: 21, 23, 33, 46, 47, 70, 72; 1791: 7,
    11, 18, 20, 24, 28, 31, 50, 56, 59, 62, 70, 72;
    1792: 13, 19, 35
Norfolk, Charles, Duke of 1797: 27
Northumberland, Duke of 1776: 15
Nugent, Walter 1779: 14

Ogle, Thomas 1788: 19; 1789: 6, 35, 56; 1790:
    54, 56
O'Leary, Dr 1797: 68

Opie, John 1798: 74
Ossian, *see* Macpherson, James
Ouseley, William 1799: 51
Oxford, Countess of 1797: 19

Paget, Lady Caroline 1790: 29
Palmer, John 1796: 60
Palmerston, Viscount 1799: 14
Peach, Mrs 1775: 3
Pearne, Thomas 1772: 34; 1773: 1, 3, 16, 19, 20,
    21, 22, 23, 29; 1788: 78; 1790: 50; 1791: 65
Percy, Countess of 1781: 8
Percy, Lady Algernon 1781: 8
Percy, Joan 1795: 26; 1797: 48
Perrot, Sir Richard 1770: 11
Phillips, Ambrose 1770: 13
Pilkington, Laetitia 1798: 60
Pilpay *see* Bīdpā'ī
Pitt, William 1785: 41
Planta, Miss 1799: 63
Pleyel, Ignaz Josef 1793: 43
Pombal, Marquês de 1775: 23
Pope, Alexander 1788: 62; 1789: 19; 1797: 31
Portarlington, Caroline, Countess of 1791: 35
Portland, Duchess of 1787: 46
Potter, Rev. Mr 1797: 68
Powell, Thomas 1799: 26
Prault, Louis Laurent 1774: 35
Prévost, Antoine François 1776: 7; 1788: 51
Priestley, Joseph 1779: 11
Proctor, Lady Beauchamp 1775: 20

Queensberry, Duke of 1792: 23

Rabelais, François 1779: 9; 1796: 37
Racine, Jean 1786: 31
Radcliffe, Ann 1793: *44*; 1795: 3, 27; 1796: 77;
    1797: 39, *44, 58*; 1798: 45, 61, 66, 67; 1799: 55,
    66, *75*
Rapin de Thoyras, Paul 1790: 72
Raspe, Rudolf Erich 1791: *44*
Rawdon, Lord 1791: 24; 1792: 57
Ray, Martha 1780: 14
Reeve, Clara 1791: 58; 1792: *5*
Reeves, Miss 1796: 13
Rich, Miss **App. A**: 9
Richardson, Samuel 1771: 20, 22, 33; 1772: 27;
    1773: *10*, 28; 1774: 3; 1777: 17; 1778: 10;
    1780: 20, *23*; 1782: 14, 15; 1784: 2; 1785: 11;
    1788: *22, 38*, 49, 66; 1789: 44; 1790: *21*;
    1791: 59; 1795: 17; 1799: *92*
Ridpai, *see* Bīdpā'ī
Robinet, Jean-Baptiste-René 1772: 14
Rochester, John Wilmot, Earl of 1799: 44
Roddam, Mrs 1782: 22
Rose, Samuel 1787: 43; 1788: 6; 1795: 45; 1798: 67
Ross, Charles 1788: 57

Rousseau, Jean-Jacques 1773: 28; 1780: *23*; 1786: 31; 1788: 49, 51; 1790: 15; 1791: 39; 1792: 30; 1798: *42*; **App. A:** 1

Rutland, Mary Isabella, Duchess of 1781: 1; 1788: 69; 1789: 39; 1791: 37

St George, Lady 1790: 21

St Quentin, Mr and Mrs 1795: 40

Salamon, E. P. 1796: 9

Salisbury, Marchioness of 1790: 58

Salisbury, Marquis of 1793: 16

Samwell, Mr 1770: 32

Schiller, Johann Christoph Friedrich von 1795: 44; 1799: 34, *72*

Seaforth, Mr 1795: 9

Shakespeare, William 1790: 74; 1791: *11, 33*; 1794: *6*; 1796: 60

Shelburne, Lady 1784: 21

Sheridan, Frances 1770: 17

Sheridan, Richard Brinsley 1780: 18; 1797: *31, 62*

Shipley, Mrs 1778: 14

Siddons, Sarah 1791: 67

Smedley, Menella Bute 1776: 4

Smith, Dr 1792: 23

Smith, Charlotte 1792: 20; 1798: 37

Smith, Sir John 1792: 39

Smith, Nathaniel 1787: 44

Smollett, Tobias George 1771: 45; 1774: 16; 1777: 17; 1787: *25*; 1789: 2, 14; 1791: *14, 31*, 45; 1793: 1, 40, *44*; 1794: 23; 1797: *77*; 1798: 8

Smyth, William 1797: 44, 51, 58, 68; 1798: 11, 18, 28, 32, 34, 44, 58; 1799: 72, 76, 95

Socrates 1771: 58

Spawforth, Capt. 1790: 22

Spencer, Lavinia, Countess 1787: 31

Spenser, Dowager Countess 1784: 13

Spenser, Edmund 1779: 6; 1785: 40; 1788: 62; 1793: *34*

Sterkel, Johann Franz Xaver 1793: 43

Sterne, Laurence 1770: 32; 1771: 45, 46, 51; 1772: 30; 1776: 10; 1777: 15; 1778: 15; 1779: *12*; 1781: 1, *6*; 1782: 4; 1784: *9*; 1785: *10*; 1787: 47; 1789: 17, 43; 1790: *20, 30*, 68; 1792: 57; 1796: *22*, 29; 1797: *29, 35*; 1798: *37*; **App. B:** 3, 4, 5, 6, 7, 9, *10*, 12

Stevenson, Miss 1799: 13

Stoever, Dietrich Heinrich 1796: 86

Stormont, Lord 1777: 15

Stothard, Thomas 1796: 2; **App. A:** 5; **App. B:** 5

Strathmore, Countess of 1788: 75

Stuart, Gilbert 1770: 21, 30, 36; 1771: 2, 3, 8, 10, 11, 16, 21, 22, 23, 26, 31, 34, 36, 42, 43, 44, 46, 47, 49, 53, 56, 59; 1772: 1, 3, 5, 6, 7, 8, 11, 12, 13, 16, 17, 19, 20, 23, 24, 25, 26, 31, 35, 37, 38; 1773: 2, 30

Swift, Jonathan 1777: *3*; 1778: *7*; 1786: *38*; 1789: 69; 1796: 46; 1798: *9*

Taylor, Anna 1790: 36

Taylor, William 1794: 34; 1795: 23, 33, 39, 44; 1796: 21, 41, 44, 50, 68, 85, 90, 91; 1797: 14, 24, 35, 36, 40, 50; 1798: 19, 36, 39, 43, 50; 1799: 21A, 21B

Thompson, Marmaduke 1798: 38

Tooke, William 1771: 48

Townsend, George Viscount 1772: 14

Trant, Mrs 1798: 75

Trapp, Joseph 1790: 53

Trenck, Baron 1799: 59

Treyssac de Vergy, Pierre Henri 1770: 20; 1772: 14; 1775: 11

Tryon, Mary 1772: 39

Tschinck, Cajetan 1796: *45*

Vance, John A. 1784: 24

Vergy, *see* Treyssac de Vergy, Pierre Henri

Verhoeven, W. M. 1793: 23

Vernon, Mrs 1796: 70

Villiers, George, 2nd Duke of Buckingham 1787: *14*; 1788: *28*

Voltaire, François-Marie Arouet 1786: 3, 31; 1798: 35; 1799: 80

Wales, HRH Caroline, Princess of 1795: 7, 29

Wales, HRH Charlotte Augusta, Princess of 1798: 51

Wallace, Thomas 1797: 71; 1798: 3, 17, 23, 33, 38, 67, 71, 73; 1799: 65

Walpole, Horace, 4th Earl of Orford 1775: 3; 1777: *16*; 1779: 9; 1788: 7, 60; 1791: *37*, 58; 1792: *5, 42*; 1794: *20*

Ward, Hon. Mrs 1785: 23; 1788: 43

Warren, Lady 1791: 15

Warton, Thomas 1788: 62

Watson, Bishop of Landaff 1799: 94

Westmorland, Countess of 1785: 3; 1791: 9

Wilkes, John 1770: 39; 1781: 19; 1784: 4

Wilkinson, Sarah 1798: 70

William Henry, HRH Prince 1786: 16

Williams, Edward 1770: 32

Williamson, Major General Sir Adam 1796: 78

Williams-Wynne, Lady 1786: 27

Wollstonecraft, Mary 1790: 40; 1793: 23

Woodfall, William 1772: 33; 1773: 5, 10, 13, 24, 34, 35, 36, 39

Woodhouse, Ollyett 1799: 57, 63, 69

Woodhouse, Robert 1798: 35; 1799: 33

Woodington, Rhoda 1777: 10

York, HRH Duchess of 1792: 17; 1796: 7, 25; 1797: 26, 49; 1798: 13, 14, 15

York, HRH Frederick Duke of 1793: 41

Yorke, Anna 1785: 36

Young, Mrs Arthur 1797: 57